THE
YOUNG ADULT
READER'S ADVISER™

❧

VOLUME 1

THE BEST IN
LITERATURE AND LANGUAGE ARTS,
MATHEMATICS AND COMPUTER SCIENCE

THE YOUNG ADULT READER'S ADVISER™

VOLUME 1

The Best in Literature and Language Arts, Mathematics and Computer Science

British Literature • Commonwealth Literature • American Literature • World Literature • Language • Human Communication • Mass Communication • Writing • General Mathematics • Algebra • Geometry • Calculus, Trigonometry, and Analysis • Probability and Statistics • Recreational Mathematics, Puzzles, and Games • History of Computers • Social Impact of Computers • Computer Literacy • Computer Systems and Hardware • Peripherals/Input-Output Devices • Operating Systems • Computer Languages • Software Applications • Computers in Education • Computers in Business • Computers in the Arts • Artificial Intelligence • Advanced Topics in Computer Science

VOLUME 2

The Best in Social Sciences and History, Science and Health

American Government/Civics • Anthropology • Economics • Geography • Psychology • Sociology • United States History • World History • General Science • Biology • Earth Science • Chemistry • Physics • Mental and Emotional Health • Growth and Development • Body Systems • Nutrition, Diet, and Weight Control • Exercise and Fitness • Personal Care • Drugs • Communicable Diseases • Noncommunicable Diseases • Physical Disabilities • Consumer Health • Personal Safety and First Aid • Community Health • The Environment and Health

REVIEWERS AND CONSULTANTS

Kay Alexander
Art Education Consultant
Los Altos, CA

Professor Patricia Burt
School of Library Service
Columbia University
New York, NY

Kate Clarke
Librarian
Sandia Preparatory School
Albuquerque, NM

Dr. Mounir A. Farah
Chairman, Department of Social
    Studies
Monroe Public Schools
Monroe, CT

Marilee Foglesong
YA Coordinator for Manhattan
    Libraries
Office of YA Services
New York, NY

Professor Ellen C. K. Johnson
Department of Social and
    Behavioral Sciences
College of DuPage
Glen Ellyn, IL

Dr. Margaret A. Laughlin
Department of Education
University of Wisconsin at Green
    Bay
Green Bay, WI

Rebecca Leavy
Director, Educational Resources
    Center
Western Kentucky University
Bowling Green, KY

Carolyn Markuson
Supervisor of Libraries and
    Instructional Materials
Brookline Public Schools
Brookline, MA

Philip Meyler
Computer Coordinator
Collegiate School
New York, NY

David E. O'Connor
Department of Social Studies
E. O. Smith High School
Storrs, CT

Allen Stockett
Chairman, Department of English
Dundalk High School
Baltimore, MD

Dr. David A. Thomas
Department of Mathematical
    Science
Montana State University
Bozeman, MT
*Journal of Computers in Mathematics
and Science Teaching*

Dr. Robert Wandberg
Director of Health Education
Minnesota Department of Education
St. Paul, MN

Dr. Richard H. Wilson
Coordinator for Secondary Social
    Studies
Montgomery County Public Schools
Montgomery County, MD

Professor Clarence Wolff
Department of Physics and
    Astronomy
Western Kentucky University
Bowling Green, KY

Dr. Warren Yasso
Chairman, Mathematics and Science
    Education
Teachers College
Columbia University
New York, NY

THE
YOUNG ADULT
READER'S ADVISER™

✢

VOLUME 1

THE BEST IN
LITERATURE AND LANGUAGE ARTS,
MATHEMATICS AND COMPUTER SCIENCE

GENERAL EDITOR

Myra Immell
Education Consultant

CONSULTING EDITOR

Marion Sader

CONTRIBUTORS

Dr. Ronald T. LaConte, *Western Kentucky University*
Dr. Betsy S. Barber, *Western Kentucky University*
Herbert Klitzner, *Computer Software Solutions*

R. R. Bowker
NEW PROVIDENCE, NEW JERSEY

Published by R. R. Bowker, a division of Reed Publishing (USA) Inc.
Copyright © 1992 by Reed Publishing (USA) Inc.
All rights reserved
Printed and bound in the United States of America

Library of Congress Cataloging-in-Publication Data
The Young adult reader's adviser / general editor, Myra Immell :
contributing editor, Marion Sader.
    p.   cm.
    Includes bibliographical references and indexes.
    Contents: v. 1. The best in literature and language arts,
mathematics and computer science — v. 2. The best in social
sciences and history, science and health.
    ISBN 0-8352-3068-6 (set). — ISBN 0-8352-3069-4 (vol. 1). — ISBN
0-8352-3070-8 (vol. 2)
    1. Bibliography—Best books—Young adult literature. 2. Young
adult literature—Bibliography. 3. Young adults—Books and reading.
I. Immell, Myra. II. Sader, Marion.
Z1037.Y674 1992
[PN1009.A1]
011.62—dc20
                        92–3232
                          CIP

Editorial Development, Design, and Production
by Book Builders Incorporated, New York, NY

ISBN 0-8352-3068-6

9 780835 230681

CONTENTS

For the convenience of the user, the contents of both volumes are listed beginning on this page.

VOLUME 1

Illustrations   xix
Chronology   xxi
Preface   xxxix
How to Use This Book   xli

PART ONE: LITERATURE AND LANGUAGE ARTS	1
LITERATURE	4
British Literature	4
The Early Years	4
The Renaissance	9
The Restoration and The Eighteenth Century	18
The Romantic Period	30
The Victorian Age	39
The Twentieth Century	63
Commonwealth Literature	134
American Literature	148
The Early Years	149
Romanticism and The American Renaissance	155
The Rise of Realism	166
The Twentieth Century	185
World Literature	309
Classical Greek Literature	310
Greek Mythology	317
Latin Literature	319

French Language and Literature 325
   The French Language 325
   French Literature 326
Italian Language and Literature 345
   The Italian Language 345
   Italian Literature 346
Spanish Language and Literature 352
   The Spanish Language 352
   Spanish Literature 353
German Language and Literature 360
   The German Language 360
   German Literature 362
Scandinavian Literature 373
Eastern European and Yiddish Literature 381
Russian Literature 388
Latin American and Caribbean Literature 397
African Literature 409
Middle Eastern Literature 418
Asian Literature 420
   The Literature of South Asia 421
   Chinese Literature 422
   Japanese Literature 424
   Southeast Asian and Korean Literature 425

LANGUAGE ARTS 428

Language 428
Processes: The History of Modern English 429
   American Dialects 431
   Etymology 432
   Jargon and Slang 433
All in the Family: English Around the World 434
Principles of English and Descriptive Linguistics 434
   Grammar and Usage 435
   Idioms 436
   Sociolinguistics 437
   Semantics 437
   Names and Their Origins 438
Vocabulary Development and Fun with Words 439
Commercial and Political Persuasion 440
A Closer Look: Language, Image, and Politics 442
Wordsmiths on Language: Reflections and Advice 443

Human Communication 444
Verbal Messages 445
Interviewing 447
Nonverbal Language 448
Oral Interpretation 449
Public Speaking 449
Storytelling 451
Voice and Diction 451

Mass Communication   **451**

Mass Media, Mass Culture   452
   Nature and Effects   454
   Coping   454
Magazines   455
News Media   457
   History and Overview   457
   Nature and Effects   457
   A Closer Look   458
Cartoons   459
   Special Topic: Editorial Cartoons   459
Radio   461
Television   464
   Overview and History   464
   Cultural and Social Impact   465
   A Closer Look   466
   Reacting to TV   467
Movies   468
   Overview and History   468
   Art   469
   Science   469
   Representative Directors and Specific Films   470
   Films from Literature   473
   Animation   474
   Types and Stereotypes   475

Writing   **476**

Principles and Process   477
Style, Usage, and Mechanics   478
   Editing   479
   Models of Writing   480
Writers on Writing: Reflections and Advice   481
   Collections   481
   Individual Writers on Writing   482
Audience and Purpose   483
   Academic Writing   483
   Advertising Copy   483
   Biographies   483
   Business Communications   483
   Children's Books   484
   College Applications   485
   Filmscripts   485
   Letters   487
   News Stories and Features   487
   Nonfiction   488
   Plays   489
   Poems   489
   Resumes   490
   Stories and Novels   490
   Technical Reports and Manuals   491

PART TWO: MATHEMATICS AND COMPUTER SCIENCE   493

MATHEMATICS   496

General References and Histories in Mathematics   496

General Mathematics   504

Algebra   505

Geometry   510

   Euclidean Geometry   513
   Coordinate Geometry   514
   Geometry in Design, Form, Nature, and the Visual Arts   515
   Non-Euclidean, Transformational, and Abstract Geometry   516
   Projective Geometry   519
   Solid Geometry and Space   519

Calculus, Trigonometry, and Analysis   522

   Calculus and Precalculus   523
   Trigonometry   524
   Analysis   524

Probability and Statistics   528

Recreational Mathematics, Puzzles, and Games   534

COMPUTER SCIENCE   537

General References in Computer Science   537

History of Computers   539

Social Impact of Computers   553

Computer Literacy   556

Computer Systems and Hardware   557

   Advanced Systems   559
   History of Personal Computers   559

Peripherals/Input-Output Devices   560

   Input Devices: Keyboards, Mouse Pointers, and Handwriting   560
   Output Devices: Printers   561

Operating Systems   561

Computer Languages   562

   Assembly Languages   564
   Basic   564
   C   564
   Cobol   565
   Logo   565
   Pascal   565
   Other Languages   565

Software Applications   **566**
  Games   567
  Home and Leisure   567
  The Military   568
  Sports and Health   568

Computers in Education   **569**
  Disabled Users   571

Computers in Business   **571**
  Business and Finance   572
  Database Management Systems   572
  Information Retrieval and On-line Services   573
  Spreadsheets   573
  Statistics and Data Analysis   574
  Utilities   574
  Word Processing and Desktop Publishing   575

Computers in the Arts   **576**
  Animation   577
  Art, Music, and Literature   577
  Graphics and Image Processing   578
  Sound and Voice Processing   579
  Multimedia Processing   579

Artificial Intelligence   **580**
  Human, Social, and Philosophical Issues   582
  Expert Systems: Specific Areas   583
  Robots and Robotics   584

Advanced Topics in Computer Science   **584**
  Algorithms   585
  Compilers   586
  Data Structures   586

Appendix
    List of Publishers   589

Indexes
    Profile Index   609
    Author Index   619
    Title Index   693

VOLUME 2

Illustrations   xx
Chronology   xxi
Preface   xxxix
How to Use This Book   xli

PART ONE: SOCIAL SCIENCES AND HISTORY   1

SOCIAL SCIENCES   4

American Government/Civics   4
General References   4
Surveys and Theories   7
Citizenship and Civil Liberties and Rights   12
Comparative Political Systems   15
The Constitution   16
Ethics in Politics   19
The Federal Executive Branch   21
The Federal Judicial System   26
The Federal Legislative System   32
Federalism and States' Rights   35
International Relations   36
Political Behavior, Political Parties, Public Interest Groups   39
State and Local Government   40

Anthropology   41
Surveys and References   42
Culture   43
Economy   47
Evolution   48
Language and Communication   50
Modern Societies and Ethnographies   50
Religion   52
Social Structure   52

Economics   55
Surveys and Theories of the Field   55
Business Cycles   57
Capitalism and Free Enterprise   57
Comparative Economic Systems   58
Consumerism   61
The Economy   62
Forms of Business Enterprises   63
Government and Economics   64
Income, Wealth, and Poverty   68
Labor and Work   69
Money, Banking, and Financial Markets   70
Public Finance and Policy   71
World Economy   71

Geography   **74**

Atlases and Gazetteers   75
Surveys   76
Climate and Weather   80
Environmental Issues   81
Landforms and Bodies of Water   82
Movement   84
Population Patterns   84
Regions: Africa   85
Regions: Asia   86
Regions: Europe   87
Regions: Latin America   88
Regions: The Middle East   89
Regions: North America   90
Regions: Oceania   91
Regions: The Soviet Union   91
Tools of the Geographer   92
Types of Geography   93
Urban Patterns   93

Psychology   **94**

General References   95
History, Surveys, and Methods   95
Attitudes, Beliefs, and Values   97
Behavior   98
Cognition   103
Emotions   103
Groups   104
Heredity and Environment   105
Human Development   106
Intelligence and Artificial Intelligence   110
Learning   112
Motivation   112
Perception and Sensation   113
Personality   114
Psychological Disorders   121
Psychological Testing   122
Stress   123

Sociology   **123**

General References   124
History, Surveys, and Methods   124
Age and Aging   129
Communications   129
Community   130
Conflict and Conflict Resolution   132
Crime   133
Culture   133
Ethnic Groups   135

Family, Marriage, Life-Course Events   136
Interaction and Groups   138
Organizations   140
Population   141
Religion   142
Social Change   144
Social Stratification   144
Socialization   146
Urban Life   147
Women   147
Work   148

HISTORY   **151**

United States History   **151**

Histories, References, and Surveys   152
Native Americans and Early Explorers   157
Spanish, French, and Other European Colonies   160
The English Colonies and Colonial Life   161
Protest, Rebellion, and Revolution   163
The United States Constitution   166
Beginning of the New Nation—Nationalism and Growth   168
The Age of Jackson   180
Reform and Expansion   184
The Arts from 1760 to 1875   187
A Divided Nation—The Coming of the Civil War   188
The Civil War   192
Reconstruction   198
Settling the Last Frontier   200
Populism and the Rise of Industry   203
Immigration, Urbanization, and Civil Rights   206
The Arts in the Age of Enterprise   213
The Progressive Era—Politics, Reform, Change, and
  Expansion   218
World War I   223
The Twenties   225
The Great Depression and The New Deal   228
World War II   234
Postwar Foreign and Domestic Policy   237
The Turbulent Sixties   241
The Nixon and Ford Years   252
The Carter Years   255
The Reagan and Bush Years   256
The Arts of the Twentieth Century   260

World History   **271**

Histories, References, and Surveys   272
Prehistory   277
The Ancient Middle East   279

Ancient India and China   281
Ancient Greece   284
Ancient Rome   290
Ancient Africa and the Americas   298
The Byzantine Empire and the Emergence of Islam   301
Medieval Europe   304
Medieval India, China, and Japan   309
The Renaissance and Reformation   310
Exploration and Expansion   320
The Scientific Revolution and The Enlightenment   326
The Age of Absolutism   326
Revolution and Change in England and America   327
The French Revolution and Napoleon   329
Restoration, Revolution, and Reform   332
The Arts in Eighteenth-Century Europe   333
The Industrial Revolution   339
Nationalism in Europe   340
The Arts in Nineteenth-Century Europe   346
Imperialism in Africa and Asia   363
Nation Building in Latin America   369
World War I and Its Aftermath   371
The Rise of Totalitarian States   374
World War II and Its Aftermath   382
The Cold War   387
Africa   393
Asia   398
Europe and the Soviet Union   404
Latin America   408
The Middle East   411
The Arts of the Twentieth Century   414

PART TWO: SCIENCE AND HEALTH   429

SCIENCE   431

General Science   431
    General References   431
    Problem Solving and the Scientific Method   434
    Measurement and Selected Tools of Science   435

Biology   436
    General References   437
    Cells—The Building Blocks of Life   437
    Energy for Life   438
    Nucleic Acids and the Genetic Code   439
    Classification of Organisms   441
    Viruses and Bacteria   443
    Protists   446

Fungi 446
Plants 447
Animals 448
Invertebrates 448
Vertebrates 449
The Human Body 450
Reproduction and Development 451
Genetics and Heredity 452
Genetic Engineering 455
The Evolution of Life 456
The Origin of Humans 460
The Origin of Life 461
Animal Behavior 461
Ecology and the Environment 465
Conservation of Natural Resources 467

Earth Science **468**
Astronomy 468
The Solar System 474
Deep Space Astronomy 478
Space Exploration 480
Meteorology 483
The Atmosphere 484
Weather and Climate 484
The Atmosphere and Solar Radiation 485
Atmospheric Pollution 486
Oceanography 486
Marine Biology 488
Ocean Resources and Conservation 488
Geology 488
Minerals and Rocks 492
Weathering, Erosion, and Deposition 492
Crustal Movements 493
Plate Tectonics and Continental Drift 494
History of Earth and Prehistoric Life Forms 495
Earth Resources and Conservation 495

Chemistry **497**
Matter 497
Structure of the Atom 500
Chemical Reactions 504
Chemical Bonds 505
The Periodic Table 506
Solutions and Colloids 507
Acids, Bases, and Salts 507
Rates of Reactions 508
Types of Study: Electrochemistry 508
Types of Study: Nuclear Chemistry 508
Types of Study: Organic Chemistry 510
Types of Study: Biochemistry 511

Physics   **511**
General References   512
Mechanics: Forces and Motion   512
Mechanics: Work, Energy, and Power   516
States of Matter   518
Electromagnetic Waves: Light and the Quantum Theory   518
Sound   521
Electricity and Magnetism   522
Nuclear Physics   528

HEALTH   **530**

General References   **530**

Mental and Emotional Health   **536**
Suicide   537
Death   537
Relationships: In and Out of the Family   538
Dysfunctional Families   539

Growth and Development   **540**
Childhood   540
Adolescence   542
Pregnancy and Parenthood   543
Aging   544

Body Systems   **544**

Nutrition, Diet, and Weight Control   **549**
Eating Disorders   550

Exercise and Fitness   **551**

Personal Care   **552**

Drugs   **553**
Drug Abuse   554
Alcohol Abuse   555
Smoking   556

Communicable Diseases   **557**
Sexually Transmitted Diseases   559
AIDS   559

Noncommunicable Diseases   **561**

Physical Disabilities   **563**
Transplants, Artificial Parts, and Heart Surgery   565

Consumer Health   **565**

Personal Safety and First Aid   **566**

Community Health   **567**

The Environment and Health   **570**

Appendix
      List of Publishers   573

Indexes
      Profile Index   593
      Author Index   603
      Title Index   677

ILLUSTRATIONS
VOLUME 1

Hamlet and the Ghost by Eugene Delacroix   xlviii

The Love Letter by Jean Honoré Fragonard   20

The Cat That Walked by Himself by Rudyard Kipling   54

An Afternoon Hunt   83

The Repast of the Lion by Henri Rousseau   111

Alice Springs by William Ricketts   135

The Midnight Ride of Paul Revere by Grant Wood   149

Snap the Whip by Winslow Homer   168

Christ's Entry into Jerusalem by Romare Bearden   191

Mining by Thomas Hart Benton   216

Persistence of Memory by Salvador Dali   246

House by the Railroad by Edward Hopper   277

Black-figured Lekythos with women working wool   309

The Discovery of the Chest by N. C. Wyeth   342

The Wyndam Sisters by John Singer Sargent   377

Wooden mask   410

Initial page of the Gospel of Matthew   428

Writing on stone   444

Walt Disney and Donald Duck   452

Cover from The Saturday Evening Post, Jan. 17, 1920   476

Path of Life 1 by M. C. Escher   492

Pattern of a woven carpet depicted in a miniature painting   510

Trafalgar Square by Piet Mondrian   539

Inscription from Saudia Arabia   567

ILLUSTRATIONS

VOLUME 2

Hémisphère Centrale by Gérard Walk and Pierre Schenk   xlviii

Varoom! by Roy Lichtenstein   38

Stock Exchange by K. Dehmann   62

Prince Henry the Navigator   84

Don Manuel Osorio by Francisco de Goya   107

The Psychoanalyst by William Sharp   120

Reine Lefebvre and Margot by Mary Cassatt   137

Capt. Samuel Chandler by Winthrop Chandler   151

John Quincy Adams by John Sully   172

Lincoln in Camp by W. R. Leigh   197

Grace Goodhue Coolidge by Howard Chandler Christy   227

Campbell's Soup Can by Andy Warhol   254

Astronomical Globe: Celestial Sphere on the Back of
Pegasus by Gerhardt Emmoser   272

The Death of Socrates after painting by David   286

Nobleman on horseback followed by knight by Albrecht
Dürer   313

The Third of May by Francisco de Goya   344

Self-Portrait by Vincent van Gogh   359

Address of Lenin to the Second All-Russian Congress of
Soviets   377

Tea Curing   402

Thomas A. Edison dictating his morning's correspondence
to his phonograph by C. A. Powell   428

Ivory-Billed Woodpeckers by John James Audubon   458

Men on treadmill device charge giant crossbow by
Leonardo da Vinci   491

The Anatomy Lecture of Dr. Nicolaes Tulp by Rembrandt
Harmensz van Rijn   530

Colonies of penicillium notatus   558

CHRONOLOGY

Volume 1   Literature and Language Arts
            Mathematics and Computer Science

Volume 2   Social Sciences and History
            Science and Health

All persons profiled in each of the eight sections of *The Young Adult Reader's Adviser* appear here chronologically according to their birth year. Within each section of the text, profiled persons are arranged alphabetically by surname. For an alphabetical listing of all profiled persons, see the Profile Index.

VOLUME 1   LITERATURE

Homer
    c.700 BC
Aesop
    c.620–c.560 BC
Aeschylus
    524–456 BC
Sophocles
    c.496–c.406 BC
Euripides
    c.485–c.406 BC
Aristophanes
    c.448–c.388 BC
Plautus, Titus Maccius
    c.250–184 BC
Terence
    c.190–159 BC
Virgil
    70–19 BC
Horace
    65–8 BC
Ovid
    43 BC–AD 17
Seneca, Lucius Annaeus
    c.5 BC–AD 65
Dante Alighieri
    1265–1321
Petrarch (Francesco
    Petrarca)
    1304–1374

Boccaccio, Giovanni
    1313–1375
Chaucer, Geoffrey
    c.1340–1400
The Pearl Poet
    c.1390
Malory, Sir Thomas
    c.1405–1471
More, Sir Thomas
    1478–1535
Wyatt, Sir Thomas
    1503–1542
Cervantes Saavedra,
    Miguel de
    1547–1616
Spenser, Edmund
    1552–1599
Sidney, Sir Philip
    1554–1586
Bacon, Sir Francis
    1561–1626
Lope de Vega Carpio, Félix
    1562–1635
Marlowe, Christopher
    1564–1593
Shakespeare, William
    1564–1616
Jonson, Ben
    1572–1637

Donne, John
1573–1631
Webster, John
c.1580–c.1634
Bradford, William
1590–1657
Herrick, Robert
1591–1674
Herbert, George
1593–1633
Calderón de la Barca, Pedro
1600–1681
Milton, John
1608–1674
Bradstreet, Anne
c.1612–1672
Marvell, Andrew
1621–1678
Molière
1622–1673
Vaughan, Henry
1622–1695
Bunyan, John
1628–1688
Dryden, John
1631–1700
Pepys, Samuel
1633–1703
Racine, Jean
1639–1699
Taylor, Edward
c.1642–1729
Defoe, Daniel
1661–1731
Swift, Jonathan
1667–1745
Congreve, William
1670–1729
Pope, Alexander
1688–1744
Richardson, Samuel
1689–1781
Voltaire
1694–1778
Edwards, Jonathan
1703–1758
Fielding, Henry
1707–1754
Johnson, Samuel
1709–1784
Gray, Thomas
1716–1761
Goldsmith, Oliver
1728–1774

Cowper, William
1731–1800
Crèvecoeur, Michel-Guillaume Jean
de
1735–1813
Boswell, James
1740–1795
Goethe, Johann Wolfgang von
1749–1832
Sheridan, Richard Brinsley
1751–1816
Wheatley, Phillis
c.1753–1784
Blake, William
1757–1827
Burns, Robert
1759–1796
Schiller, (Johann Christoph)
Friedrich von
1759–1805
Radcliffe, Anne
1764–1823
Wordsworth, William
1770–1850
Brown, Charles Brockden
1771–1810
Scott, Sir Walter
1771–1832
Coleridge, Samuel Taylor
1772–1834
Austen, Jane
1775–1817
Lamb, Charles
1775–1834
Irving, Washington
1783–1859
Stendhal
1783–1842
Byron, Lord, George Gordon
1788–1824
Marryat, Captain Frederick
1792–1848
Shelley, Percy Bysshe
1792–1822
Bryant, William Cullen
1794–1878
Keats, John
1795–1821
Shelley, Mary Wollstonecraft
1797–1851
Balzac, Honoré de
1799–1850
Pushkin, Aleksandr
1799–1837

Dumas, Alexandre (père)
1802–1870
Hugo, Victor Marie
1802–1885
Emerson, Ralph Waldo
1803–1882
Hawthorne, Nathaniel
1804–1864
Andersen, Hans Christian
1805–1875
Browning, Elizabeth Barrett
1806–1861
Longfellow, Henry Wadsworth
1807–1882
Whittier, John Greenleaf
1807–1892
Gogol, Nikolai
1809–1852
Holmes, Oliver Wendell
1809–1894
Poe, Edgar Allan
1809–1849
Tennyson, Lord, Alfred
1809–1892
Thackeray, William Makepeace
1811–1863
Browning, Robert
1812–1889
Dickens, Charles
1812–1870
Brontë, Charlotte
1816–1855
Brown, William Wells
c.1816–1884
Thoreau, Henry David
1817–1862
Brontë, Emily
1818–1848
Eliot, George
1819–1880
Lowell, James Russell
1819–1891
Melville, Herman
1819–1891
Whitman, Walt
1819–1892
Baudelaire, Charles
1821–1867
Dostoevsky, Fyodor
1821–1881
Flaubert, Gustave
1821–1880
Arnold, Matthew
1822–1888

Collins, Wilkie
1824–1889
Ibsen, Henrik
1828–1906
Rossetti, Dante Gabriel
1828–1882
Tolstoy, Leo
1828–1910
Verne, Jules
1828–1905
Dickinson, Emily
1830–1886
Rossetti, Christina
1830–1894
Alcott, Louisa May
1832–1888
Carroll, Lewis
1832–1898
Alger, Horatio, Jr.
1834–1899
Carducci, Giosue
1835–1907
Twain, Mark
1835–1910
Gilbert, Sir William Schwenk
1836–1911
Harte, Bret (Francis Brett)
1836–1902
Swinburne, Algernon Charles
1837–1909
Hardy, Thomas
1840–1928
Zola, Emile
1840–1902
Bierce, Ambrose Gwinnett
1842–1914?
Lanier, Sidney
1842–1881
James, Henry
1843–1916
Cable, George Washington
1844–1924
France, Anatole
1844–1924
Hopkins, Gerard Manley
1844–1889
Sienkiewicz, Henryk
1846–1916
Stoker, Bram (Abraham)
1847–1912
Jewett, Sarah Orne
1849–1909
Strindberg, August
1849–1912

Maupassant, Guy de
1850–1893

Stevenson, Robert Louis
1850–1894

Chopin, Kate
1851–1904

Wilde, Oscar
1854–1900

Baum, L. (Lyman) Frank
1856–1919

Haggard, Sir Henry Rider
1856–1925

Shaw, George Bernard
1856–1950

Conrad, Joseph
1857–1924

Chesnutt, Charles W. (Waddell)
1858–1932

Aleichem, Sholem
1859–1916

Doyle, Sir Arthur Conan
1859–1930

Hamsun, Knut
1859–1952

Housman, A. E. (Alfred Edward)
1859–1936

Barrie, J. M. (Sir James Matthew)
1860–1937

Chekhov, Anton
1860–1904

Henry, O. (William Sydney Porter)
1862–1910

Wharton, Edith
1862–1937

Jacobs, W. W. (William Wymark)
1863–1943

Unamuno y Jugo, Miguel de
1864–1936

Kipling, Rudyard
1865–1936

Yeats, William Butler
1865–1939

Wells, H. G. (Herbert George)
1866–1946

Darío, Rubén
1867–1916

Galsworthy, John
1867–1933

Pirandello, Luigi
1867–1936

Gide, André
1869–1951

Leacock, Stephen
1869–1944

Masters, Edgar Lee
1869–1950

Robinson, Edwin Arlington
1869–1935

Bunin, Ivan
1870–1953

Norris, Frank (Benjamin Franklin
Norris, Jr.)
1870–1902

Saki
1870–1916

Crane, Stephen
1871–1900

Dreiser, Theodore
1871–1945

Johnson, James Weldon
1871–1938

Synge, John Millington
1871–1909

Dunbar, Paul Laurence
1872–1906

Cather, Willa
1873–1947

Chesterton, G. K. (Gilbert Keith)
1874–1936

Frost, Robert
1874–1963

Glasgow, Ellen
1874–1945

Lowell, Amy
1874–1925

Maugham, W. (William)
Somerset
1874–1965

Montgomery, L. M. (Lucy Maud)
1874–1942

Service, Robert W. (William)
1874–1958

Burroughs, Edgar Rice
1875–1950

Mann, Thomas
1875–1955

Rilke, Rainer Maria
1875–1926

Anderson, Sherwood
1876–1941

London, Jack
1876–1916

Rølvaag, Ole Edvart
1876–1931

Hesse, Hermann
1877–1962

Sandburg, Carl
1878–1967

Sinclair, Upton
1878–1968
Forster, E. M. (Edward Morgan)
1879–1970
Lindsay, Norman
1879–1969
Christie, Dame Agatha
1880–1976
O'Casey, Sean
1880–1964
Colum, Padraic
1881–1972
Wodehouse, P. G. (Pelham
Grenville)
1881–1975
Joyce, James
1882–1941
Undset, Sigrid
1882–1949
Woolf, Virginia
1882–1941
Kafka, Franz
1883–1924
Williams, William Carlos
1883–1963
Dinesen, Isak
1885–1962
Lawrence, D. H. (David
Herbert)
1885–1930
Lewis, Sinclair
1885–1951
Sassoon, Siegfried
1886–1967
Brooke, Rupert
1887–1915
Ferber, Edna
1887–1968
Jeffers, (John) Robinson
1887–1962
Moore, Marianne
1887–1972
Cary, Joyce
1888–1957
Chandler, Raymond
1888–1959
Eliot, T. S. (Thomas Stearns)
1888–1965
Mansfield, Katherine
1888–1923
O'Neill, Eugene
1888–1953
McKay, Claude
1889–1948

Mistral, Gabriela (Lucila Godoy de
Alcayaga)
1889–1957
Capek, Karel
1890–1938
Pasternak, Boris
1890–1960
Porter, Katherine Ann
1890–1980
Lagervist, Pär
1891–1974
Andric, Ivo
1892–1975
Buck, Pearl
1892–1973
MacLeish, Archibald
1892–1982
Millay, Edna St. Vincent
1892–1950
Tolkien, J. R. R. (John Ronald
Reuel)
1892–1973
Owen, Wilfred
1893–1918
Parker, Dorothy
1893–1967
Sayers, Dorothy L. (Leigh)
1893–1957
Cummings, E. E. (Edward Estlin)
1894–1962
Hammett, Dashiell
1894–1961
Huxley, Aldous
1894–1963
Priestley, J. B. (John Boynton)
1894–1984
Thurber, James
1894–1961
Graves, Robert
1895–1985
Cronin, A. J. (Archibald Joseph)
1896–1981
Fitzgerald, F. (Francis) Scott (Key)
1896–1940
Faulkner, William
1897–1962
Mitchinson, Naomi
1897–
Wilder, Thornton
1897–1975
Benét, Stephen Vincent
1898–1943
Brecht, Bertolt
1898–1956

Lewis, C. S. (Clive Staples)
1898–1963
Borges, Jorge Luis
1899–1986
Bowen, Elizabeth
1899–1973
Coward, Sir Noel
1899–1973
Forester, C. S. (Cecil Scott)
1899–1966
García Lorca, Federico
1899–1936
Hemingway, Ernest
1899–1961
Shute, Nevil
1899–1960
Hilton, James
1900–1954
O'Faolain, Sean
1900–
Wolfe, Thomas
1900–1938
Brown, Sterling
1901–1989
Hughes, Langston
1902–1967
Steinbeck, John
1902–1968
Waugh, Evelyn
1902–1966
Callaghan, Morley
1903–
Cullen, Countee
1903–1946
Hurston, Zora Neale
1903–1960
O'Connor, Frank
1903–1966
O'Dell, Scott
1903–1990
Orwell, George
1903–1950
Paton, Alan
1903–1988
Carpentier, Alejo
1904–1980
Greene, Graham
1904–1991
Isherwood, Christopher
1904–1986
Neruda, Pablo
1904–1973
Singer, Isaac Bashevis
1904–1991

West, Nathanael
1904–1940
Hellman, Lillian
1905–1984
Sartre, Jean-Paul
1905–1980
Warren, Robert Penn
1905–1989
Armour, Richard
1906–
Beckett, Samuel
1906–1989
Odets, Clifford
1906–1963
Senghor, Leopold Sedar
1906–
White, T. H. (Terence Hanbury)
1906–1964
Auden, W. H. (Wystan Hugh)
1907–1973
Du Maurier, Daphne
1907–1989
Fry, Christopher
1907–
Godden, (Margaret) Rumer
1907–
Heinlein, Robert
1907–1988
MacNeice, Louis
1907–1963
Michener, James
c.1907–
Moravia, Alberto
1907–1990
Fleming, Ian
1908–1964
L'Amour, Louis
1908–1988
Wright, Richard
1908–1960
Welty, Eudora
1909–
Anouilh, Jean
1910–1987
Golding, William
1911–
Milosz, Czeslaw
1911–
Williams, Tennessee
1911–1983
Boulle, Pierre
1912–
Cheever, John
1912–1982

Durrell, Lawrence
1912–1990
White, Patrick
1912–
Camus, Albert
1913–1960
Davies, Robertson
1913–
Hayden, Robert
1913–
Ellison, Ralph
1914–
Fast, Howard
1914–
Jarrell, Randall
1914–1965
Malamud, Bernard
1914–1986
Paz, Octavio
1914–
Thomas, Dylan
1914–1953
Bellow, Saul
1915–
Miller, Arthur
1915–
Walker, Margaret
1915–
Dahl, Roald
1916–1990
Herriot, James
1916–
Weiss, Peter
1916–1982
Böll, Heinrich
1917–1985
Brooks, Gwendolyn
1917–
Burgess, Anthony (John
Anthony Burgess
Wilson)
1917–
Clarke, Arthur C. (Charles)
1917–
Lowell, Robert
1917–1977
Burnford, Sheila
1918–1984
Solzhenitsyn, Alexandr,
1918–
Spark, Muriel
1918–
Ferlinghetti, Lawrence
1919–

Jackson, Shirley
1919–1965
Lessing, Doris (May)
1919–
Murdoch, Dame Iris
1919–
Pohl, Frederik
1919–
Salinger, J. D. (Jerome David)
1919–
Asimov, Isaac
1920–
Bradbury, Ray
1920–
Childress, Alice
1920–
Herbert, Frank
1920–1986
James, P. D. (Phyllis Dorothy)
1920–
Scott, Paul
1920–1978
Harris, Wilson
1921–
Lem, Stanislaw
1921–
Mowat, Farley
1921–
Amis, Kingsley
1922–
Gallant, Mavis
1922–
Kerouac, Jack
1922–1969
Larkin, Philip
1922–1985
Vonnegut, Kurt, Jr.
1922–
Behan, Brendan
1923–1964
Dickey, James
1923–
Gordimer, Nadine
1923–
Alexander, Lloyd
1924–
Baldwin, James
1924–1987
Bolt, Robert
1924–
Frame, Janet
1924–
Laurence, Margaret
1924–

Uris, Leon
1924–
Cardenal, Father Ernesto
1925–
Cormier, Robert
1925–
Hentoff, Nat (Nathan Irving)
1925–
O'Connor, Flannery
1925–1964
Fowles, John
1926–
Ginsberg, Allen
1926–
Knowles, John
1926–
Lee, Harper (Nelle Harper Lee)
1926–
Shaffer, Peter
1926–
Grass, Günter
1927–
Kerr, M. E.
1927–
Simon, Neil
1927–
Albee, Edward
1928–
Angelou, Maya
1928–
García Márquez, Gabriel
1928–
Guy, Rosa
1928–
Laye, Camara
1928–1980
Sillitoe, Alan
1928–
Wiesel, Elie (Eliezer)
1928–
Fuentes, Carlos
1929–
Kundera, Milan
1929–
Le Guin, Ursula K.
1929–
Osborne, John
1929–
Potok, Chaim
1929–
Rich, Adrienne
1929–
Achebe, Chinua
1930–

Ballard, J. G. (James Graham)
1930–
Hansberry, Lorraine
1930–1965
Hughes, Ted (Edward
James)
1930–
Pinter, Harold
1930–
Barthelme, Donald
1931–1989
Goldman, William
1931–
Le Carré, John
1931–
Morrison, Toni
1931–
Munro, Alice
1931–
Richler, Mordecai
1931–
Beti, Mongo
1932–
Heller, Joseph
1932–
Naipaul, V. S. (Vidiadhar
Surajprasad)
1932–
Plath, Sylvia
1932–1963
Puig, Manuel
1932–1990
Updike, John
1932–
Gaines, Ernest J.
1933–
Weldon, Fay
1933–
Baraka, Amiri
1934–
Cohen, Leonard
1934–
Greene, Bette
1934–
Peck, Richard
1934–
Soyinka, Wole
1934–
Allen, Woody
1935–
Brautigan, Richard
1935–1984
Gilchrist, Ellen
1935–

Mohr, Nicholasa
1935–

Silverberg, Robert
1935–

Hamilton, Virginia
1936–

Zindel, Paul
1936–

Myers, Walter Dean
1937–

Stoppard, Tom
1937–

Walsh, Gillian Paton
1937–

Blume, Judy
1938–

Klein, Norma
1938–1989

Ngugi Wa Thiong'o
1938–

Atwood, Margaret
1939–

Bambara, Toni
Cade
1939–

Drabble, Margaret
1939–

Hanrahan, Barbara
1939–

Heaney, Seamus
1939–

Lester, Julius
1939–

Coetzee, J. M. (John
Michael)
1940–

Mason, Bobbie Ann
1940–

Tyler, Anne
1941–

Bridgers, Sue Ellen
1942–

Highwater, Jamake
1942–

Voight, Cynthia
1942–

Giovanni, Nikki
1943–

Shepard, Sam
1943–

Taylor, Mildred
1943–

Emecheta, Buchi
1944–

Walker, Alice
1944–

King, Stephen
1947–

Hinton, S. E. (Susan Eloise)
1950–

Adams, Douglas
1952–

VOLUME 1   LANGUAGE ARTS

Webster, Noah
1758–1843

Nast, Thomas
1840–1902

Rogers, Will (William Penn Adair)
1879–1935

Keller, Helen
1880–1968

Mencken, H. L. (Henry Louis)
1880–1956

Thomas, Lowell
1892–1981

Pearson, Drew (Andrew Russell)
1897–1969

Winchell, Walter (Walter Winchel)
1897–1972

White, E. B. (Elwyn Brooks)
1899–1985

Disney, Walt (Walter Elias)
1901–1966

Hayakawa, S. I. (Samuel Ichiye)
1906–

Huston, John
1906–1987

Murrow, Edward R.
1908–1965

McDavid, Raven I., Jr.
1911–

McLuhan, (Herbert) Marshall
1911–1980

Terkel, Studs (Louis)
1912–

Wallace, Mike (Myron Leon)
1918–

Newman, Edwin (Harold)
1919–

Allen, Steve (Stephen
  Valentine Patrick William)
  1921–
Jaffee, Al (Allan)
  1921–
Serling, Rod (Edward
  Rodman)
  1924–1975
Baker, Russell
  1925–
Buchwald, Art (Arthur)
  1925–
Malcolm X (Malcolm Little; El-Hajj
  Malik El-Shabazz)
  1925–1965
Bombeck, Erma
  1927–
Chomsky, Noam
  1928–
Safire, William
  1929–

Wolfe, Tom (Thomas
  Kennerly)
  1931–
Paterson, Katherine
  (Womeldorf)
  1932–
Rank, Hugh (Duke)
  1932–
Moyers, Bill
  1934–
Allen, Woody (Allen
  Stewart Konigsberg)
  1935–
Dillard, Annie
  1945–
Spielberg, Steven
  1947–
Trudeau, Gary
  1948–
Lee, Spike (Shelton Jackson)
  1957–

VOLUME 1 MATHEMATICS

Pythagoras
  c.580–c.500 BC
Euclid
  fl. c.300 BC
Archimedes
  c.287–212 BC
Apollonius of Perga
  fl. 247–205 BC
Diophantus
  c. AD 250
Descartes, René
  1596–1650
Fermat, Pierre de
  1601–1665
Pascal, Blaise
  1623–1662
Leibniz, Gottfried
  Wilhelm
  1646–1716
Bernoulli, Jakob
  1654–1705
Euler, Leonhard
  1707–1783
Gauss, Carl Friedrich
  1777–1855
Cauchy, Augustin
  Louis
  1789–1857

Lobachevsky, Nikolai Ivanovitch
  1793–1856
Galois, Evariste
  1811–1832
Boole, George
  1815–1864
Weierstrass, Karl
  1815–1897
Cantor, Georg
  1845–1918
Klein, Felix
  1849–1925
Poincaré, Henri
  1854–1912
Hilbert, David
  1862–1943
Russell, Bertrand
  1872–1970
Noether, Emmy
  1882–1935
Ramanujan, Srinivara
  1887–1920
Fuller, R. Buckminster (Richard)
  1895–1983
Gödel, Kurt
  1906–1978
Gardner, Martin
  1914–

VOLUME 1   COMPUTER SCIENCE

Babbage, Charles
1791–1871
Lovelace, Countess of, Ada Augusta
1815–1852
Hollerith, Herman
1860–1929
Von Neumann, John
1903–1957
Hopper, Grace Murray
1906–

Mauchly, John
1907–1980
Turing, Alan
1912–1954
Shannon, Claude
1916–
Gates, William
1955–
Jobs, Steven
1955–

VOLUME 2   SOCIAL SCIENCES

Machiavelli, Niccolò
1469–1527
Hobbes, Thomas
1588–1679
Locke, John
1632–1704
Montesquieu, Charles Louis de
Secondat, Baron de la Brède et de
1689–1755
Rousseau, Jean Jacques
1712–1778
Smith, Adam
1723–1790
Burke, Edmund
1729–1797
Bentham, Jeremy
1748–1832
Marshall, John
1755–1835
Malthus, Thomas Robert
1766–1834
Humboldt, Friedrich Heinrich
Alexander von
1769–1859
Ricardo, David
1772–1823
Stevens, Thaddeus
1792–1868
Comte, Auguste
1798–1857
Mill, John Stuart
1806–1873
Guyot, Arnold
1807–1884
Marx, Karl
1818–1883

Engels, Friedrich
1820–1895
Wundt, Wilhelm
1832–1920
Holmes, Oliver Wendell, Jr.
1841–1935
James, William
1842–1910
Marshall, Alfred
1842–1924
Pavlov, Ivan Petrovich
1849–1936
Freud, Sigmund
1856–1939
Binet, Alfred
1857–1911
Veblen, Thorstein
1857–1929
Boas, Franz
1858–1942
Durkheim, Emile
1858–1917
Mackinder, Halford John, Sir
1861–1947
Mead, George Herbert
1863–1931
Weber, Max
1864–1920
Bethune, Mary McLeod
1875–1955
Jung, Carl Gustav
1875–1961
Kroeber, Alfred Louis
1876–1960
Bowman, Isaiah
1878–1950

Watson, John B. (Broadus)
1878–1958
Radcliffe-Brown, A. R. (Alfred
Reginald)
1881–1955
Frankfurter, Felix
1882–1965
Perkins, Frances
1882–1965
Rayburn, Sam (Samuel Taliaferro)
1882–1961
Keynes, John Maynard
1883–1946
Malinowski, Bronislaw
1884–1942
Sapir, Edward
1884–1939
Horney, Karen
1885–1952
Benedict, Ruth
1887–1948
Dulles, John Foster
1888–1959
Sauer, Carl Ortwin
1889–1975
Lewin, Kurt
1890–1947
Warren, Earl
1891–1974
Lynd, Robert Staughton
1892–1970
Lynd, Helen Merrel
1894–1982
Piaget, Jean
1896–1980
Allport, Gordon W. (Willard)
1897–1967
Murdock, George Peter
1897–1985
Redfield, Robert
1897–1958
Myrdal, Gunnar
1898–1987
James, Preston E.
1899–1986
Dollard, John
1900–1980
Stouffer, Samuel A.
1900–1960
Mead, Margaret
1901–1978
Erikson, Erik H.
(Homburger)
1902–

Lasswell, Harold D.
1902–1978
Parsons, Talcott
1902–1979
Leakey, Louis S. B.
1903–1972
Lorenz, Konrad
1903–1989
Robinson, Joan
1903–1983
Skinner, B. F. (Burrhus Frederic)
1904–1990
Galbraith, John Kenneth
1908–
Lévi-Strauss, Claude
1908–
Riesman, David
1909–
Rusk, Dean (David)
1909–
Merton, Robert King
1910–
Friedman, Milton
1912–
Ullman, Edward
1912–1976
Leakey, Mary D.
1913–
Ward, Barbara (Lady Jackson)
1914–1981
Whyte, William Foote
1914–
Bell, Daniel
1919–
Arrow, Kenneth J.
1921–
Kissinger, Henry Alfred
1923–
Chisholm, Shirley Anita St. Hill
1924–
Harris, Marvin
1927–
Kohlberg, Lawrence
1927–1987
Coles, Robert
1929–
O'Connor, Sandra Day
1930–
Rivlin, Alice Mitchell
1931–
Jordan, Barbara Charline
1936–
Leakey, Richard E. F.
1944–

VOLUME 2 HISTORY

Lao-Tzu
 c.604–531 BC
Confucius
 c.551–479 BC
Herodotus
 c.484–425 BC
Thucydides
 c.460–400 BC
Aristotle
 384–322 BC
Cicero, Marcus Tullius
 106–43 BC
Caesar, Julius
 c.100–44 BC
Virgil
 70–19 BC
Horace
 65–8 BC
Livy
 59 BC–AD 17
Plutarch
 C. AD 46–c.125
Tacitus, Cornelius
 C. AD 56–c.117
Pliny the Younger
 C. AD 61–c.112
Suetonius
 C. AD 69–c.140
St. Augustine
 AD 354–430
Saint Bede, the
 Venerable
 AD 673–735
Averroës
 1126–1198
Maimonides, Moses
 1135–1204
St. Thomas Aquinas
 1225–1274
Polo, Marco
 c.1254–c.1324
Ibn Batuta
 c.1304–c.1378
Columbus, Christopher
 1451–1506
Leonardo da Vinci
 1452–1519
Vespucci, Amerigo
 1454–1512
Erasmus, Desiderius
 c.1466–1536

Dürer, Albrecht
 1471–1528
Michelangelo (Buonarroti)
 1475–1564
Luther, Martin
 1483–1546
Raphael (Raphaello Santi)
 c.1483–1520
Cortés, Hernán
 1485–1547
Cellini, Benvenuto
 1500–1571
Calvin, John
 1509–1564
Palestrina (Giovanni
 Pierluigi)
 c.1525–1594
Drake, Sir Francis
 c.1540–1596
Hakluyt, Richard
 c.1552–1616
Purcell, Henry
 c.1659–1695
Bach, Johann Sebastian
 1685–1750
Handel, George Frederick
 1685–1759
Franklin, Benjamin
 1706–1790
Paine, Thomas
 1713–1809
Reynolds, Sir Joshua
 1723–1792
Gainsborough, Thomas
 1727–1788
Cook, Captain James
 1728–1779
Burke, Sir Edmund
 1729–1797
Haydn, Franz Joseph
 1732–1809
Washington, George
 1732–1799
Adams, John
 1735–1826
Jefferson, Thomas
 1743–1826
Adams, Abigail
 1744–1818
Madison, James
 1751–1836

Hamilton, Alexander
1757–1804
Monroe, James
1758–1831
Robespierre, Maximilien
1758–1794
Adams, John Quincy
1767–1848
Jackson, Andrew
1767–1845
Bonaparte, Napoleon
1769–1821
Clark, William
1770–1838
Park, Mungo
1771–1806
Metternich, Prince Klemens von
1773–1859
Lewis, Meriwether
1774–1809
Turner, Joseph Mallord William
1775–1851
Constable, John
1776–1837
Clay, Henry
1777–1852
Calhoun, John Caldwell
1782–1850
Webster, Daniel
1782–1852
Audubon, John James
1785–1851
Houston, Samuel
1793–1863
Catlin, George
1796–1872
Mann, Horace
1796–1859
Berlioz, Hector
1803–1869
Disraeli, Benjamin
1804–1881
Garrison, William Lloyd
1805–1879
Garibaldi, Giuseppi
1807–1882
Lee, Robert Edward
1807–1870
Gladstone, William Ewart
1809–1898
Lincoln, Abraham
1809–1865
Chopin, Frédéric
1810–1849

Liszt, Franz
1811–1886
Livingstone, David
1813–1873
Verdi, Giuseppe
1813–1901
Wagner, Richard
1813–1883
Bismarck, Otto von
1815–1898
Douglass, Frederick
1817?–1895
Victoria, Queen of Great Britain
1819–1901
Barton, Clara Harlowe
1821–1912
Burton, Sir Richard Francis
1821–1890
Grant, Ulysses S. (Simpson)
1822–1885
Garfield, James Abram
1831–1881
Brahms, Johannes
1833–1897
Degas, Edgar
1834–1917
Carnegie, Andrew
1835–1919
Homer, Winslow
1836–1910
Adams, Henry
1838–1918
Muir, John
1838–1914
Cézanne, Paul
1839–1906
Custer, George Armstrong
1839–1876
Chief Joseph
1840?–1904
Rodin, Auguste
1840–1917
Tchaikovsky, Peter Ilyich
1840–1893
Cassat, Mary
1845–1926
Gauguin, Paul
1848–1903
Riis, Jacob August
1849–1914
Martí, José
1853–1895
Van Gogh, Vincent
1853–1890

Sousa, John Philip
1854–1932
La Follette, Robert Marion
1855–1925
Sullivan, Louis Henry
1856–1924
Washington, Booker T. (Tallaferro)
1856–1915
Wilson, Woodrow
1856–1924
Taft, William Howard
1857–1930
Roosevelt, Theodore
1858–1919
Dewey, John
1859–1952
Addams, Jane
1860–1935
Bryan, William Jennings
1860–1925
Mahler, Gustav
1860–1911
Debussy, Achille Claude
1862–1918
Lloyd George, David
1863–1945
Strauss, Richard
1864–1949
Wright, Frank Lloyd
1867–1959
Du Bois, W. E. B. (William Edward
Burghardt)
1868–1963
Gandhi, Mohandas
Karamchand
1869–1948
Lenin, Vladimir Ilyich
1870–1924
Coolidge, Calvin
1872–1933
Churchill, Winston S.
1874–1965
Hoover, Herbert Clark
1874–1964
Ravel, Maurice
1875–1937
Duncan, Isadora
1878–1927
Stalin, Joseph
1879–1953
Steichen, Edward
1879–1973
Trotsky, Leon
1879–1940

Marshall, George Catlett
1880–1959
Antin, Mary
1881–1949
Bartók, Béla
1881–1945
Picasso, Pablo (Pablo Ruiz y
Picasso)
1881–1973
Roosevelt, Franklin Delano
1882–1945
Stravinsky, Igor
1882–1971
Gropius, Walter
1883–1969
Roosevelt, Anna Eleanor
1884–1962
Truman, Harry S.
1884–1972
Ben-Gurion, David
1886–1973
Chagall, Marc
1887–1985
Le Corbusier
1887–1965
O'Keeffe, Georgia
1887–1986
Berlin, Irving
1888–1989
Lawrence, T. E. (Thomas Edward)
1888–1935
Hitler, Adolf
1889–1945
Nehru, Jawaharlal
1889–1964
de Gaulle, Charles
1890–1970
Eisenhower, Dwight David
1890–1969
Prokofiev, Sergei
1891–1953
Kenyatta, Jomo
c.1893–1978
Mao Zedong
1893–1976
Khrushchev, Nikita
1894–1971
Lange, Dorothea
1895–1965
Meir, Golda
1898–1978
Ellington, Edward Kennedy
(Duke)
1899–1974

Armstrong, Louis
1900–1971
Adams, Ansel
1902–1984
Kennan, George
1904–
Hammarskjold, Dag (Hjalmar Agne
Carl)
1905–1961
Brezhnev, Leonid
1906–1982
Shostakovich, Dmitri
1906–1975
Carson, Rachel Louise
1907–1964
Johnson, Lyndon Baines
1908–1973
Goldwater, Barry Morris
1909–
Nkrumah, Kwame
1909–1972
Humphrey, Hubert
Horatio
1911–1978
Reagan, Ronald Wilson
1911–
Britten, Benjamin
1913–1976
Ford, Gerald R.
(Rudolph)
1913–
Nixon, Richard Milhous
1913–
Heyerdahl, Thor
1914–
Gandhi, Indira
1917–1984

Kennedy, John Fitzgerald
1917–1963
Wyeth, Andrew
1917–
Bernstein, Leonard
1918–1990
Mandela, Nelson
1918–
Sadat, Anwar
1918–1981
Cunningham, Merce
1919–
Friedan, Betty
1921–
Nyerere, Julius
1921–
McGovern, George Stanley
1922–
Bush, George Herbert Walker
1924–
Carter, James Earl (Jimmy) Jr.
1924–
Kennedy, Robert Francis
1925–1968
Malcolm X (Malcolm Little; El-Hajj
Malik El-Shabazz)
1925–1965
Thatcher, Margaret
1925–
Castro, Fidel
1927–
King, Martin Luther, Jr.
1929–1968
Gorbachev, Mikhail Sergeyevich
1931–
Tutu, Desmond
1931–

VOLUME 2 SCIENCE

Aristotle
384–322 BC
Archimedes
c.287–212 BC
Copernicus, Nicolaus
1473–1543
Brahe, Tycho
1546–1601
Bacon, Francis
1561–1626
Galileo
1564–1642
Kepler, Johannes
1571–1630

Boyle, Robert
1627–1691
Newton, Isaac
1642–1727
Halley, Edmond
1656–1742
Franklin, Benjamin
1706–1790
Linnaeus, Carolus
1707–1778
Hutton, James
1726–1797
Herschel, William
1738–1822

Lavoisier, Antoine Laurent
1743–1794
Lamarck, Jean Baptiste de
Monet de
1744–1829
Dalton, John
1766–1844
Faraday, Michael
1791–1867
Henry, Joseph
1797–1878
Lyell, Charles
1797–1875
Darwin, Charles Robert
1809–1882
Mendel, Gregor Johann
1822–1884
Pasteur, Louis
1822–1895
Wallace, Alfred Russel
1823–1913
Maxwell, James Clerk
1831–1879
Mendeleev, Dimitri Ivanovich
1834–1907
Koch, Robert
1843–1910
Edison, Thomas Alva
1847–1931
Pavlov, Ivan Petrovich
1849–1936
Shaw, William Napier
1854–1945
Planck, Max Karl Ernst
Ludwig
1858–1947
Morgan, Thomas Hunt
1866–1945
Curie, Marie
1867–1934
Rutherford, Ernest
1871–1937
Einstein, Albert
1879–1955
Wegener, Alfred Lothar
1880–1930

Bohr, Niels Henrik David
1885–1962
Frisch, Karl von
1886–1982
Hubble, Edwin Powell
1889–1953
Muller, Hermann Joseph
1890–1967
Oparin, Alexander Ivanovich
1894–1980
Krebs, Hans Adolf
1900–1981
Pauli, Wolfgang
1900–1958
Fermi, Enrico
1901–1954
Pauling, Linus Carl
1901–
McClintock, Barbara
1902–
Lorenz, Konrad Zacharias
1903–1989
Carson, Rachel Louise
1907–1964
Tinbergen, Nikolaas
1907–1988
Cousteau, Jacques–Yves
1910–
von Braun, Wernher
1912–1977
Crick, Francis Harry Compton
1916–
Wilkins, Maurice Hugh Frederick
1916–
Asimov, Isaac
1920–
Watson, James Dewey
1928–
Goodall, Jane
1934–
Sagan, Carl
1934–
Gould, Stephen Jay
1941–
Johanson, Donald Carl
1943–

VOLUME 2   HEALTH

Hippocrates
c.460–377 BC
Galen
c. AD 129–200

Vesalius, Andreas
1514–1546
Harvey, William
1578–1657

Nightingale, Florence
  1820–1910
Barton, Clara Harlowe
  1821–1912
Osler, William
  1849–1919
Cushing, Harvey
  1869–1939
Schweitzer, Albert
  1875–1965

Fleming, Alexander
  1881–1955
White, Paul Dudley
  1886–1973
Rusk, Howard
  Archibald
  1901–
Spock, Benjamin
  McLane
  1903–

PREFACE

The notion of a reference work that, for younger readers, would serve a function similar to that of Bowker's classic *The Reader's Adviser* became the propelling force in the development of this book.

Considered by many as the ultimate booklover's book, *The Reader's Adviser* is intended to be, as its subtitle states, "A Layman's Guide to Literature." From scholarly examinations of the classics to in-depth looks at new authors, new works, and new disciplines, *The Reader's Adviser,* through 13 editions and for more than 70 years, has been providing broad-based yet detailed book information for the general adult reading public as well as for professional librarians and educators.

By 1988, when *The Reader's Adviser* had grown to a set of six hefty volumes (from the original 1921 pamphlet), it became quite clear that such a set had become too unwieldy, complex, and scholarly for use by most young adult readers. This was coupled with the fact that there were new directions being taken in school curricula (the addition of elective courses, advanced placement courses, modern fiction units, and computer science studies). Also, there began a new type of literature, the growing body of "young adult literature," a publishing category that was virtually nonexistent before the 1960s. Add to these new directions the changing makeup of the school population and various current social and political trends (emphases on the women's movement, the need for multicultural readings, and a growing insistence on non-Western studies), and one is readily able to see the need for a young reader's edition of *The Reader's Adviser.*

Like its parent, *The Young Adult Reader's Adviser* is partly a work of reference and partly a book for browsing; so, one can utilize it to locate specific information and one is also able to read it for pleasure. Each broad discipline, whether it be American literature or world history, geography or computer science, physics or psychology (or any other area), opens with a brief introduction followed by general reading lists (where necessary) and then by profiles (biographical sketches) of individuals noteworthy in each field and subfield. The 851 profiles are followed by lists of selected "books by" and "books about" the individual. The more than 17,000 bibliographic entries are designed so that the user will be able both to locate a book in a library and to know where it is available for purchase and at what price. It is our hope that the young adult users will be so enticed by such a variety of subjects and fascinating personalities that a lifetime reading habit will be established.

The Young Adult Reader's Adviser is Bowker's newest offering in a long tradition of providing valuable reference materials to the school, library, and home. This tradition, now 120 years old, includes such well-known works as *Children's Books in Print, Reference Books for Young Readers, A to Zoo, Books Kids Will Sit Still For,* and the volumes in the *Best Books* series. This title, joining the others in the children's and young adult line of products, makes a vital contribution to our commitment to develop new tools for students and professionals.

Many people were helpful in preparing this premier edition of *The Young Adult Reader's Adviser.* To Myra Immell, general editor of the project, goes credit and our thanks for successfully translating a concept into a book; her editorial and organizational skills are supreme. We are especially grateful also to Lauren Fedorko, who bravely answered our summons to devise a concept and to coordinate all tasks involved in editorial development and production; she has been, throughout the entire process, a most patient and gracious leader and problem solver. Jill Wood, book designer, has proved with these pages that a reference book can also look attractive and be user-friendly. Our thanks also to Diane Schadoff, who, as project coordinator, successfully kept the balls in the air and maintained quality control with the "cast of thousands" involved in production. At Bowker, Julia Raymunt and Roy Crego, editorial production managers, efficiently supervised and reviewed the many production stages of the manuscript; Debbi Dalton, art director, produced the lively and attractive covers; and Angela Szablewski, editorial assistant, cheerfully supported everyone along the way.

MARION SADER
Publisher, R. R. Bowker
January 1992

HOW TO USE THIS BOOK

The Young Adult Reader's Adviser is a two-volume reference tool that encompasses the major areas of study, or the core curriculum, targeted by school systems across the United States—literature, language arts, mathematics, computer science, social sciences, history, science, and health. Easy-to-read and informative, these volumes were developed and designed to achieve two major purposes: (1) to provide students, teachers, and librarians with biographical and other interesting and relevant information about selected individuals of merit in each of the subject areas currently included in the middle school, junior high school, or high school curricula; and (2) to alert students, teachers, and librarians to the great wealth of core and supplementary works they may personally consult or recommend to others gaining insight into a given discipline, individual, topic, or theme.

SCOPE AND SEQUENCE

The Young Adult Reader's Adviser consists of bibliographies arranged by subject matter or by author as well as profiles of hundreds of literary figures, scientists, mathematicians, social scientists, and other notable individuals, both past and present. Great care has been taken in the categorizing of this content to remain within established educational frameworks and to maintain the integrity of each area of study. In each section and subsection, bibliographies and profiles are categorized under topics or themes that correspond to those in the standard curricula as well as to the units and chapters found in most current textbooks. Thus, the wide range of subjects will be familiar to librarians, teachers, and students who wish to locate a particular topic or do research on an individual associated with a given discipline or unit of study in which the researcher is immediately involved.

Each area of study naturally possesses unique characteristics. One of these is vocabulary. For example, in biology, the reader will encounter the subsection "Protists." Like other discipline-specific terms, this one is not defined because it is a term commonly used in biology classes and in textbooks and will be familiar to teachers and students of biology, as well as librarians.

Another characteristic unique to a given discipline is the grade level or levels at which it is taught. In the social sciences, for example, geography may be taught at the middle school, junior high school, and the high school levels, while other disciplines tend to be offered at only one level. An example of the latter case is American government, which is generally taught in grade twelve. For disciplines taught only at the higher grade levels, the bibliographies by necessity reflect a higher concept and reading level.

Still another feature of each discipline is the manner or order in which material is presented during the course of study. For example, in most United States and world history courses, events generally are presented chronologi-

cally. Some topics and themes, however, overlap and are intentionally introduced and studied separately. It is not uncommon in a United States history
course, for example, to study Reconstruction separately from the settling of the
last frontier even though the events of each topic cover much of the same time
period. To maintain a parallelism with the existing curricula, as well as to help
ensure the comfort level of student users, subsection titles in the history sections of *The Young Adult Reader's Adviser* approximate those of current history
textbooks and courses of study.

As in the compilation of almost all reference books, *The Young Adult Reader's
Adviser* required selectivity—focusing on some topics, themes, and individuals
to the exclusion of others. As explained in greater detail in the introduction to
each of the volumes' parts and subsections, determinations generally were
made on the basis of: state curriculum guidelines and frameworks; current
middle school, junior high school, and high school courses of study; and input
by librarians and educators. The sections of the work devoted to history,
however, presented a particular dilemma to the editors—having to choose
among an overwhelming number of individuals, both past and present, who
merit inclusion. With the interests and concerns of their young adult audience
in mind, the editorial staff elected to profile primarily those individuals who
wrote and published books and whose works are still in print and available for
use. As a result of this focus, some highly recognizable figures—such as Marie
Antoinette, Elizabeth I, and Hirohito—are not profiled.

ORGANIZATION

In *The Young Adult Reader's Adviser,* information is divided among the four
major areas of study, with each volume housing two main sections, or Parts.
In Volume 1, Part One is devoted to Literature and Language Arts, while Part
Two focuses on Mathematics and Computer Science. In Volume 2, Part One
is dedicated to the Social Sciences and History, while Part Two encompasses
Science and Health.

For ease of use, each Part is divided further into sections and subsections
that parallel commonly accepted courses of study in American schools. Volume
1, Part One (Literature and Language Arts) consists of two primary sections:
(a) a literature section divided into subsections devoted to British literature,
Commonwealth literature, American literature, and world literature; and (b) a
language arts section consisting of subsections dedicated to language, human
communication, mass communication, and writing. Part Two (Mathematics
and Computer Science) also consists of two main sections: (a) a mathematics
section composed of subsections dealing with references and histories as well
as with general mathematics, algebra, geometry, calculus and precalculus, trigonometry, analysis, probability and statistics, and recreational math; and (b) a
computer science section divided into more than a dozen subsections, each of
which focuses on one aspect—software applications, for example—of computer science.

Volume 2, Part One (Social Sciences and History) is also divided into two
sections: (a) a social sciences section made up of subsections devoted to the
disciplines of American government, anthropology, economics, geography,
psychology, and sociology; and (b) a section dedicated to history that is divided
into two subsections—United States history and world history. Part Two (Science and Health) consists of: (a) a science section divided into subsections
covering the disciplines of general science, biology, earth science, chemistry,
and physics; and (b) a health section divided by topic into more than a dozen
subsections dealing with such diverse health-related subjects as body systems,
mental and emotional health, personal care, drugs, and physical disabilities.

Where appropriate, subsections are broken down still further to focus on specific topics, themes, or periods of time. For example, the reader interested in researching the life and works of the twentieth-century American author Ernest Hemingway would turn first to Volume 1, Part One (Literature and Language Arts); then, more specifically, to the Literature section within Part One; then to the subsection American Literature; and last to the section titled The Twentieth Century, under which Ernest Hemingway and other twentieth-century American authors are chronicled alphabetically.

The organization of each volume and each part is designed to move the reader from the general to the specific. Each part opens with a theme-related piece of art and an introduction that discusses briefly the organization of and the rationale for that part. Immediately following is a specific section with its various subsections. Each subsection opens with a brief introduction that provides a framework for the area of study, the period, or the genre. With the exception of the literature and the science sections, the introduction is followed by listings of surveys, histories, and other reference books. Immediately following the general listings are the divisions devoted to specific themes or topics, each with its own listings of bibliographic entries and biographical profiles.

THE PROFILES

Organized alphabetically by surname, each of the profiles contains biographical information about an individual or group of individuals. The great majority also contain information about the individual's or group's works, achievements, theories, contributions, and role in society at the time. Following each profile are bibliographies of books by and about the person or group. In the "Books By . . ." sections, books are listed alphabetically, with a few clearly marked exceptions—such as the chronological listing of titles within a series. These are intended to provide an overview of the titles and types of books written by a given individual. The "Books About . . ." sections, which are organized alphabetically according to the surname of the author or editor, are intended to suggest where to look for much more extensive information than that provided in a profile.

THE BIBLIOGRAPHIC ENTRIES

The bibliographic entries are designed to help the reader locate a book in the library and, in the case of the librarian, tell him or her if it is available for purchase and at what price. For each title, when applicable, this vital information is provided: the author; title; series title; editor, translator, or compiler; number of volumes; publisher; date of publication; price; and ISBN. Here, for example, is a typical entry.

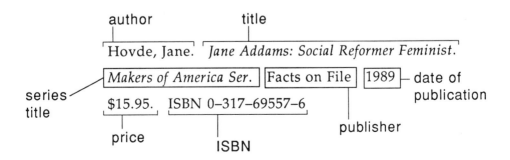

If a title consists of more than one volume and is listed with only one price and ISBN number, this is the price and ISBN number for the entire set. Although prices may change, they are listed primarily to alert the reader to the general price category into which a title falls and to assist the librarian in acquisition.

The titles of some books give an immediate and clear indication of their content or general topics. Others, however, do not. Therefore, to aid in selecting the most appropriate book, many of the bibliographic entries include brief, descriptive annotations. All of the entries in the "Books About . . ." sections, for example, are annotated with one-line descriptions. Also, all of the asterisked (*) or bulleted (■) entries in the "Books by . . ." sections are annotated. For instance, *The Autobiography of Miss Jane Pittman* is followed by this annotation: "Tale of black history in the South as seen through the eyes of a fictional 110-year-old black woman born a slave on a Louisiana plantation."

history of the United States since the Civil War. It is a testimony to Gaines's skill as a writer and storyteller that many people believe Jane Pittman was a real person. Indeed, the novel is frequently misshelved in the biography section of bookstores.

Of Gaines's other works, *Bloodline* (1976), a collection of five short stories, stands out for its powerful portrayals of young men in search of self-respect and dignity.

NOVELS BY GAINES

The Autobiography of Miss Jane Pittman (1971). Bantam 1982 $3.95. ISBN 0-553-26357-9
   Tale of black history in the South as seen through the eyes of a fictional 110-year-old black woman born a slave on a Louisiana plantation.
Catherine Cormier (1964). North Point 1981 $9.95. ISBN 0-86547-022-7
A Gathering of Old Men (1983). Random 1984 $4.95. ISBN 0-394-72591-3
In My Father's House (1978). Norton 1983 $6.70. ISBN 0-393-30124-9
Of Love and Dust (1967). Norton 1979 $8.95. ISBN 0-393-00914-9

SHORT STORY COLLECTION BY GAINES

Bloodline (1976). Norton 1976 $7.95. ISBN 0-393-00798-7 Five short stories that portray young men in search of dignity and depict adult life as viewed by children.

BOOK ABOUT GAINES

Stanford, Barbara Dodd, and Karmina Amin. *Black Literature for High School Students.* NCTE 1978. (o.p.) $6.00. ISBN 0-8141-0330-8 A resource book on teaching black

FEATURES

To provide additional information to librarians, teachers, and the younger readers in grades 6 through 8, the following features were made an integral part of *The Young Adult Reader's Adviser.*

(1) Book entries considered to be particularly appropriate for readers in grades 6 through 8 are marked with an asterisk (*) and are always annotated. (An example is the above annotation for *The Autobiography of Miss Jane Pittman.*)

(2) Entries that are marked with a square bullet (■) indicate a title that is appropriate only for very advanced high school students. These entries,

which are also annotated, tend to be found in bibliographies throughout the social sciences section—primarily anthropology, economics, psychology, and sociology. These disciplines are generally classified as one-semester elective courses in the high-school curriculum; in many instances they are offered only in grade 12. Occasionally, the bullet is used also with entries in the history section.

(3) For books written by profiled individuals, the date of the publication of the first edition, regardless of whether that edition is still in print, appears in parentheses after the title. Here is an example:

> *Jane Eyre* (1847). Bantam 1991 $2.50. ISBN 0-553-21140-4 The life and adventures of a young woman who comes to Thornfield Hall as a governess and falls in love with the Hall's mysterious owner, Mr. Rochester.

This book was originally published in 1847; this edition, currently in print, was published in 1991.

(4) Books that are no longer in print are clearly identified by the abbreviation *o.p.,* which appears in parentheses immediately following the publication date. (This out-of-print notice will save the reader time searching in publishers' catalogs and many bookstores for books that are difficult to locate and instead will send the reader to the library, which, fortunately, stocks many books that are no longer in print.)

CROSS-REFERENCES

Cross-references enable the reader to gain from the two volumes of *The Young Adult Reader's Adviser* the maximum amount of information relevant to the person or subject of interest. The reference *See* leads the reader to additional information on *another* person or subject relevant to the one being researched. The reference *See also* leads the reader to additional information on the *same* person or subject being researched.

Cross-references generally provide the name of the individual being referenced, the number of the volume in which the additional information appears, and the subsection name or names. For example, in reading the profile about the mathematician Fermat, the reader would see the statement that Fermat was also influenced by Diophantus. This statement is therefore followed by a cross-reference:

(*See* Diophantus, Vol. 1, Algebra.)

The reference tells the reader that in the Algebra section of Volume 1, he or she will find information about one of the people who influenced the life and thought of Fermat.

APPENDIX AND INDEXES

Each volume of *The Young Adult Reader's Adviser* includes a List of Publishers that lists alphabetically the abbreviations used for the publishers cited throughout the two volumes. Next to each abbreviation is the publisher's full name.

The three indexes appear last. They too appear in each of the two volumes. The first is the Profile Index, which includes, in alphabetical sequence, all authors who are profiled in the two volumes. The second index is the Author

Index, also in alphabetical sequence, which presents the authors of all books listed in the bibliographies of each volume. In addition, this listing includes editors, compilers, and translators. Finally, the alphabetical Title Index presents all books cited in the bibliographies of the two volumes.

The Young Adult Reader's Adviser is designed to provide a wealth of information with a minimum of confusion. As it is used in the library, classroom, or at home, for school reports or for browsing, we hope it will serve as a lively and informative guide to which a reader will turn again and again.

THE
YOUNG ADULT
READER'S ADVISER™

VOLUME 1

THE BEST IN
LITERATURE AND LANGUAGE ARTS,
MATHEMATICS AND COMPUTER SCIENCE

Hamlet and the Ghost
Lithograph by Eugene Delacroix (1843)

PART ONE

LITERATURE

AND

LANGUAGE ARTS

T he material in Part One has been assembled to provide students, teachers, librarians, and other interested readers with a selection of resources that offers information on topics and authors normally introduced in the English courses offered in upper middle school, in junior high school, and in senior high school. These listings of sources will be useful in a variety of ways. Readers can scan them when searching for a book on a particular subject or person. The profiles of the various authors and the listings of their major works will be of special help to readers gathering sources for a research report.

Teachers can develop or extend supplementary reading lists for units in literature or language arts by checking to see which works are suitable for their students and what is currently available. Teachers and librarians also will find this section useful for a quick review of a period, movement, or author, or for further developing a collection.

Of course, a reference book must be selective, focusing on some authors or topics to the exclusion of others. Some key writers or topics will inevitably be left out or treated more briefly than others. The problem of choosing what is to be included and what must be left out of a reference book is always a difficult one. Given the great wealth of books, it was an especially challenging task to make choices from all of British, American, and world literature, as well as from the various aspects of the language arts.

The books that are marked with an asterisk (*) are especially appropriate for younger readers, ages 12–14, in both reading level and content. Many of these books can be read with enjoyment and profit by older readers as well. Most of the remaining books listed are within the reading range of senior high school students, but a few are beyond the range of all but the most able readers. In cases where these challenging books have been included, they have been identified as especially difficult works in the author profiles. For example, the profile of the Irish author James Joyce notes that "His last two works, *Ulysses* and *Finnegan's Wake,* are extremely difficult to read, because of both their inventive use of language and their many layers of subtle meaning."

LITERATURE

To make the selections for the literature sections, the editors of *The Young Adult Reader's Adviser* began by studying the anthologies currently used in grades 6 through 12. The goal was to find out which authors continue to be read at these levels. Those authors that appeared in more than one major literature anthology were immediately included in *The Young Adult Reader's Adviser*. Other authors or topics were included according to their literary reputations, popularity, or importance.

The editors also consulted a number of bibliographies of recommended literature for young adults, such as the different editions of Bowker's *Juniorplots* and *Seniorplots*. Finally, they reviewed studies of the reading interests of students aged 12 to 18 to find out which authors were most popular with this age group. From all this data, the editors chose to include those authors that received the most favorable reviews, had the strongest reputations, or enjoyed the greatest popularity with young readers.

The question of organization also posed a good deal of thought. Literature anthologies in grades 6 through 10 are usually organized according to types (or genres) of literature (short stories, poems, etc.) or according to themes and topics. In grades 11 through 12, however, literature anthologies are most often organized chronologically as surveys of American or British literature. To accommodate both approaches, the American and British literature sections are arranged in chronological order according to the major periods of literary development, but the works of each author are listed according to type: novels, short stories, plays, poems, and nonfiction. In the world literature sections the authors are listed alphabetically by region and country. In addition, the writers from Australia, Canada, and New Zealand (known as Commonwealth writers) are clustered in a separate group labeled "Commonwealth Literature," which immediately follows the British literature section.

The profile of each author presents basic information about the author's life, education, career, and major works. The profiles are intended to give readers a general idea of what each author wrote and why and to help them select what they wish to read from an author's works, depending on their purpose. However, the profiles are by no means complete accounts of authors' lives or work.

For the most part, all the works by a given author that are currently in print are included. However, some authors, such as Agatha Christie, P. G. Wodehouse, or Louis L'Amour, have written so many books that space does not permit a comprehensive list. In these cases the works listed are a representative selection, reflecting the variety of the author's work. For example, in the case of Agatha Christie, at least one work featuring each of her detective heroes is included.

The works included in the Books About sections have been selected to give additional information about an author's life and work. In most cases the list has been limited to three books for each author. The serious student will find many more works about major authors listed in Bowker's annual editions of *Books in Print*. Brief descriptions of books that are out of print or especially important classic works have also been provided.

Whenever possible, the "books about" are readable, general discussions of an author's background, major ideas, and major works. On occasion, more specialized and narrowly focused books have also been included because they have something special to offer. At least one biography of each author has been included. Every effort has been made to list books that are currently in print and easily available from major publishers.

LANGUAGE ARTS

The term *language arts* as it is used here includes four major areas: *language* (the history and nature of the English language); *human communication* (the sending and receiving of interpersonal messages, both verbal and nonverbal); *mass communication* (the sending of information to large groups of people); and *writing* (the various kinds of written English). Although it is not possible here to treat these complex topics comprehensively, the subject breakdown does manage to include all the related areas of instruction covered in language arts and English courses in most American schools—both public and private.

Obviously, there is an enormous overlap among these areas; for example, writing is a medium of mass communication just as language is a form of human communication, and so forth. Students and teachers of Language Arts in search of a particular topic are encouraged to begin with the section that seems most applicable and then to skim through other sections to check for related materials.

✿✿ LITERATURE ✿✿

BRITISH LITERATURE

The section that encompasses British literature is organized both chronologically and alphabetically. There are six major categories that are arranged chronologically—The Early Years, The Renaissance, The Restoration and The Eighteenth Century, The Romantic Period, The Victorian Age, and The Twentieth Century. Within each of these literary time periods, writers are listed alphabetically, their last names appearing first. For each author, there is at least one list of books by that author; novels, poetry, plays, nonfiction, and collections are listed separately. Therefore, if readers are seeking out particular genres, or types of literature, they will readily find them.

In addition, there is a biographical sketch of each author. The sketch or profile not only provides information about major works and literary influences but usually offers interesting personal background. Further, the profile may refer the reader to related writers and their works, which also can be found in *The Young Adult Reader's Adviser.* Such connections between writers are usually necessary when doing research in a subject as broad as British literature.

Last, for most writers, there is a section with books about that writer. Among other types of publications, the section lists notable biographies for further reading and research. These books are limited to highly respected works. Wherever possible, very recent titles have also been included; however, in the case of the most contemporary writers—for example, a young adult author—no "book about" existed at the time of this compilation.

A major responsibility of the British literature section is to supplement standard listings of the most established writers with the works of newer or neglected writers, including of course literature by women. To the best of their ability, in a limited space, the editors, in their selection of both major and lesser known writers, have tried to represent the new developments in literary criticism, the altering interests of young adult readers, and the changes in cultural and intellectual concerns.

THE EARLY YEARS

Early English literature is generally defined as the work produced during the Middle Ages, the period that stretched from the end of the seventh century to the beginning of the fifteenth. In fact, this was actually two historical periods that embraced two different languages and literatures. In history the first period, up to the year 1066, is known as the Anglo-Saxon period, after the tribes of Angles and Saxons who settled in Britain around 450 AD. In literature this time is known as the Old English period, after the language spoken by the Anglo-Saxons.

The second period is known as the later Middle Ages. It dates from the year 1066, when the Norman French invaded Britain and conquered the Anglo-

Saxons. This historical change produced a change in language: the Old English of the Anglo-Saxons slowly fused with the French of the conquerors to produce a new Middle English language and literature by the end of the twelfth century.

Although the Anglo-Saxons dominated Britain for 600 years, they left very little written literature, primarily because theirs was an oral tradition. Their poetry was sung by bards, called "scops," who passed their literature orally from one generation to the next.

Then, in the seventh century, St. Augustine reintroduced Christianity to Britain. This religious change gave new importance to written records and laws, so that the ancient poems were finally written down by poets who had recently converted to Christianity. These writers tended to modify the old tales and traditions, making them more Christian and less pagan. Nevertheless, a poem like *Beowulf*, written by a Christian in the early part of the eighth century, still rests on ancient Anglo-Saxon values and beliefs. Such qualities as valor, loyalty, courage, and a willingness to accept what fate dictates characterize the heroes of these epics. They are serious and gloomy poems, the songs of warriors seeking immortality through their deeds in a dangerous and often unjust world.

Middle English literature, on the other hand, is concerned less with heroes than with daily human experience. Chaucer's Canterbury pilgrims, for example, are ordinary people, drawn from all walks of life, who display all the vices and weaknesses—as well as all the virtues and strengths—that characterize human beings. Likewise, the knights in Thomas Malory's retelling of the King Arthur legends are capable of sin and error as well as heroic feats. Consequently, the language of this literature is more direct than that of the early epics, and in Chaucer especially, it often echoes the speech of ordinary people.

The Normans also introduced feudalism and chivalry into England, which brought further changes to storytelling. Gloomy Anglo-Saxon tales gave way to French-influenced "romances." These stories of knights in armor slaying dragons and rescuing fair maidens continue to influence today's fantasy novels—and such games as "Dungeons and Dragons"! Of those medieval romances that have survived, *Sir Gawain and the Green Knight* and Thomas Malory's *Le Morte D'Arthur* are major contributions to the body of English literature.

The Middle English period also saw the rise of the popular ballad, the narrative poetry of the common people. Originally composed to be sung and danced to, folk poems such as "Lord Randal" and "Get up and Bar the Door" were passed on orally from generation to generation. Finally, they were collected and printed in the eighteenth century, when they became an acknowledged part of English literature.

BEOWULF *c.* 750 AD

This is the earliest known poem in English. It was written in Old English in a verse form that depends on strong accents and repeated sounds, as opposed to the rhymed verse of later English poetry.

Beowulf celebrates the almost superhuman feats of the hero Beowulf, who slays monsters and fights battles in medieval Denmark and Sweden. Although the poem displays the basic values and beliefs of the pagan Anglo-Saxons, it also shows strong elements of Christianity, which has led scholars to believe that the author must have been a Christian.

The one surviving manuscript of *Beowulf* was written by two scribes about the year 1000. However, references in the poem itself clearly identify it as having been composed earlier, and scholars believe that the original work had only one author.

EDITIONS OF BEOWULF

Alexander, Michael (tr). *Beowulf.* Penguin 1973 $2.25. ISBN 0-14-044268-5
*Nye, Robert (tr). *Beowulf.* Dell 1982 $2.50. ISBN 0-440-90560-5 Lively retelling suitable for young readers.
*Sutcliffe, Rosemary (tr). *Beowulf.* Peter Smith 1984 $14.75. ISBN 0-8446-6165-1 Young readers' version by a famous novelist.

BOOKS ABOUT BEOWULF

Chambers, Raymond W. (ed). *Beowulf: An Introduction.* Cambridge Univ Pr 1959. (o.p.) Introduction to *Beowulf* with a discussion of the stories of Offa and Finn.
*Gardner, John. *Grendel.* Random 1987 $5.95. ISBN 679-72311-0 The Beowulf legend retold from the monster's point of view.

CHAUCER, GEOFFREY   *c.* 1340–1400

Geoffrey Chaucer was the son of a London wine merchant. He had a long and varied career, serving as a page to Elizabeth, Countess of Ulster; a soldier in Edward III's army in France; a diplomat; and a government official in various offices. Chaucer was a gentleman of some stature in his society, important enough so that in 1359, when he was captured by the French during the Hundred Years' War, King Edward himself contributed to Chaucer's ransom. In 1372 Chaucer was sent as a trade ambassador to Italy, where he was strongly influenced by the writings of the Italian poets Dante, Petrarch, and Boccaccio.

Chaucer has made two great contributions to English literature. His poems themselves are masterpieces that have grown in stature over time. Furthermore, his decision to write in the Middle English vernacular, the speech of ordinary people, rather than in the Latin or French normally used by the poets of his day, paved the way for all the English writers who followed him. For very good reason, then, Chaucer is known as the father of English poetry.

Chaucer's *The Canterbury Tales* (1387–1400) is one of the world's major collections of narrative poetry (with some prose intermixed). Many of the tales are borrowed from Boccaccio's *Decameron.* (*See* Boccaccio, Vol. 1, World Literature: Italian Language and Literature.) The 24 tales are supposedly told by pilgrims who are journeying from London to the shrine of St. Thomas à Becket in Canterbury.

Although Chaucer never completed the entire cycle, what he did complete is generally regarded as one of the greatest works in the English language. Ironically, the enormous stature of *The Canterbury Tales* overshadows Chaucer's other works. *Troylus and Criseyde* (1385?) in particular ranks as one of the greatest love poems in English.

POETRY BY CHAUCER

The Canterbury Tales. Neville Coghill (ed). Penguin 1951 $2.95. ISBN 0-14-044022-4 Excellent modern English edition for young readers grade 9 and up.
The Canterbury Tales. Barbara Cohen (ed). Lothrop 1988 $17.95. ISBN 0-688-06201-6 Illustrated shortened version for young readers grade 5 and up.
The Canterbury Tales. A. Kent Hieatt and Constance Hieatt (eds). Bantam 1982 $2.95. ISBN 0-553-21082-3 Easy-to-read version suitable for grades 9–12.
The Portable Chaucer. Theodore Morrison (ed). Penguin 1977 $8.95. ISBN 0-14-015081-1 Contains selections from Chaucer's other poetry as well as selections from *The Canterbury Tales.*
Troylus and Criseyde. Neville Coghill (ed). Penguin 1971 $4.95. ISBN 0-14-044239-1

BOOKS ABOUT CHAUCER

Aers, David. *Chaucer: An Introduction.* Humanities 1986 $25.00. ISBN 0-391-03420-0 Brief introduction to Chaucer's writing, including the poet's exploration of society, religion, marriage, and sexual relations.

Howard, Donald R. *Chaucer: His Life, His Works, His World.* Fawcett 1989 $12.95. ISBN 0-449-90341-9 Biography of Chaucer that deals with Chaucer's life and literary work, and with the fourteenth century.

Payne, Robert O. *Geoffrey Chaucer.* G. K. Hall 1986 $16.95. ISBN 0-8057-6908-0 General study with solid biography and emphasis on *The Canterbury Tales.*

Schoek, Richard, and Jerome Taylor. *Chaucer Criticism: The Canterbury Tales.* Univ of Notre Dame Pr 1960 $6.95. ISBN 0-268-00036-0 An anthology of 18 varied critical approaches to *The Canterbury Tales.*

Stone, Brian. *Chaucer.* Penguin 1989 $5.95. ISBN 0-14-077185-9 Relates biography to works and gives details of the Italian influence.

Wetherbee, Winthrop. *Chaucer: The Canterbury Tales.* Cambridge Univ Pr 1989. ISBN 0-521-31159-4 Introduction to *The Canterbury Tales,* with chapters on "Gentles," "Churls," "Women," the "art and problems of tale-telling," and the reception of the work.

MALORY, SIR THOMAS   *c.* 1405–1471

Sir Thomas Malory is presumed to have been a knight from an old Warwickshire family. In about 1433 he inherited his father's estates; later in his life he spent some 20 years in jail accused of various crimes, including treason, burglary, and rape. He probably did not commit these crimes, however, because the age in which he lived (the time of the Wars of the Roses) was a turbulent one, and supporters of the party out of power were frequently jailed on false charges. Nevertheless, he was almost certainly in prison when he wrote his famous collection of tales about King Arthur, *Le Morte D'Arthur,* published in 1485 by William Caxton, the first English printer.

Malory's work is the most complete rendition of the story of Arthur. Malory's vigorous and musical language has captured the imaginations of each succeeding generation of readers.

BOOKS BY MALORY

**The Acts of King Arthur and His Noble Knights.* John Steinbeck (ed). Del Rey 1986 $4.95. ISBN 345-34512-6 *Le Morte D'Arthur* retold by one of America's greatest novelists.

King Arthur and His Knights. Eugene Vinaver (ed). Oxford Univ Pr 1975 $8.95. ISBN 0-19-601905-9

Le Morte D'Arthur. Crown 1988 $8.98. ISBN 0-517-02060-2

BOOKS ABOUT MALORY

Hicks, Edward. *Sir Thomas Malory: His Turbulent Career.* Hippocrene 1986 $16.50. ISBN 0-374-93885 Still useful and detailed biography.

Vinaver, Eugene. *Malory.* Folkcroft 1977. (o.p.) $27.50. Covers both biography and source study.

THE PEARL POET   *c.* 1390

The Old English poem *The Pearl* is a strong expression of sorrow, depicting the poet's mystical vision at the grave of a baby girl, possibly the poet's daughter. It is one of four anonymous poems, all written in the same handwriting and in the same difficult West Midland dialect, collected in an illustrated manuscript that was not discovered until the late nineteenth century. The other three poems are *Purity, Patience,* and *Sir Gawain and the Green Knight.* The resemblances among the four poems have persuaded some scholars that they are all the work of a single person, commonly called the Pearl Poet, but the issue remains hotly disputed. What is not disputed, however, is that *Gawain* is the gem of medieval poetic romances, unrivaled for its clarity, imagery, and energy.

POETRY BY THE PEARL POET

Pearl Poems: An Omnibus Edition. William Vantuono (ed). Garland 1984 $75.00. ISBN 0-8240-5450-4

Pearl Poems: An Omnibus Edition. Vol. 2 *Patience and Sir Gawain and the Green Knight.* William Vantuono (ed). Garland 1984 $80.00. ISBN 0-8240-5451-2

Pearl: A New Verse Translation. Marie Boroff (ed). Norton 1977 $3.95. ISBN 0-393-09144-9

Sir Gawain and the Green Knight. J. A. Burrow (ed). Penguin 1987 $5.95. ISBN 0-14-042295-1

Sir Gawain and the Green Knight. J. R. R. Tolkien (tr). Ballantine 1980 $3.50. ISBN 345-27760-0

BOOKS ABOUT THE PEARL POET

Blanch, Robert J. *Sir Gawain and the Green Knight: A Reference Guide.* Whitston 1984 $22.50. ISBN 0-87875-244-7 Annotated bibliography covering 1824–1978.

Moorman, Charles. *The Pearl Poet.* Sylvia E. Bowman (ed). Irvington 1968 $17.95. ISBN 0-8290-1722-4 Comprehensive study of all the poems with emphasis on *Sir Gawain and the Green Knight.*

Spearing, A. C. *The Gawain-Poet.* Cambridge Univ Pr 1976 $14.95. ISBN 0-521-29069-4 A critical analysis of the characters of Sir Gawain, the Green Knight, Pearl, Patience, and Purity.

POPULAR BALLADS

England's popular ballads are anonymous narrative songs that were originally preserved by oral repetition and only later written down. They were probably composed over a period of some 500 years, from 1200 to 1700. However, very few were printed before the eighteenth century, when Bishop Thomas Percy discovered a seventeenth-century manuscript containing a number of ballads. Percy's publication of the poems stimulated the interest of other writers, notably Sir Walter Scott, who then began to search Britain for more examples. Ballads are typically simple in form, spare in language, and dramatically tragic in mood, although some are humorous or ironic.

Two of the most famous of these ballads are "Barbara Allen" and "Lord Randal," both of which tell of lovelorn men dying at the hands of the cruel women they love.

COLLECTIONS OF BALLADS

English and Scottish Popular Ballads (1904). George L. Kittredge and C. H. Sargent (eds). 2 vols. Longwood 1978 $75.00. ISBN 0-89341-476-X

The Faber Book of Ballads. Matthew Hodgart (ed). Faber & Faber 1971 $5.95. ISBN 0-571-09688

The Viking Book of Folk Ballads of the English Speaking World. Albert B. Friedman (ed). Penguin 1982 $6.95. ISBN 0-14-006112-6

BOOKS ABOUT POPULAR BALLADS

Graves, Robert. *The English Ballad.* Haskell (repr of 1927 ed) $34.95. ISBN 0-8383-1284-5 Critical survey of ballads, with a long introduction to the ballad as a form, followed by 34 annotated ballads.

Henderson, Thomas F. *The Ballad in Literature.* Haskell 1969 repr of 1912 ed $75.00. ISBN 0-8383-0664-0 Traces development of both the popular and literary ballad.

Hodgart, Matthew. *The Ballads.* Norton 1966 $4.95. ISBN 0-393-00354-X Complete discussion of the poetry, music, folklore, and early and late history of the ballads, with chapters on ballads as literature and ballad scholarship.

THE RENAISSANCE

The flowering of humanistic thought and artistic expression in late medieval Europe was known as the Renaissance. This era began in Italy in the late fourteenth century but did not reach England for about 100 years. The Renaissance was brought to the British Isles by returning travelers excited by the Italian experience.

Although literary and artistic movements seldom have points of fixed beginning or end, the English Renaissance is commonly dated from 1485, when Henry VII became the first Tudor king. Its ending is usually considered to be 1660, when the crowning of Charles II ended England's short period without a monarch.

The coronation of Henry VII ended the Wars of the Roses, which had torn England apart for 100 years. The resulting sense of political stability was a necessary condition for the cultural rebirth that followed. Poets, playwrights, and scholars poured forth an abundance of new works, and experimented with new forms and new ideas. Poets such as Thomas Wyatt, Philip Sidney, Edmund Spenser, and William Shakespeare were inspired by Petrarch (*see* Petrarch, Vol. 1, World Literature: Italian Language and Literature) to compose some of the most beautiful love sonnets ever written. Renaissance poets also began to write in other forms never before seen in English, such as epigrams (brief, witty turns of phrase), pastorals (celebrations of country life), and epitaphs (brief poems to commemorate a death). These poets were especially skillful at setting words to music, and many of their lyrics survive as songs to this day.

It was in the field of drama, however, that the English Renaissance produced its greatest works. During the reign of Queen Elizabeth I (1558–1603), English drama developed rapidly. Although beginning with pale imitations of old Greek and Roman tragedies and crude comedies full of slapstick and horseplay, Renaissance drama soon became a highly refined art form in which playwrights like Shakespeare crafted brilliant plays that captivate audiences to this day. From 1590 until the Puritan Parliament closed all theaters in 1642, English playwrights produced a steady stream of plays that have become classics of English literature.

BACON, SIR FRANCIS   1561–1626

Sir Francis Bacon was educated at Cambridge University, studied law, and was elected to Parliament in 1584. Learned, widely experienced, ambitious, perhaps reckless, Bacon rose to become Lord Chancellor in the reign of James I. His political career ended in 1621 when he was imprisoned for taking bribes. Upon release from prison, Bacon was banished to his country estate, where he spent the rest of his life producing works of philosophy and literature.

Bacon is sometimes called the father of modern science because of his strong belief in observation and experimentation. He was the first English writer to use the word "essay" to describe his commentary, which includes 58 essays on literary topics.

WORKS BY BACON

The Essays. John Pitcher (ed). Penguin 1986 $6.95. ISBN 0-14-043216-7
Francis Bacon: A Selection of His Works. Sidney Warhaft (ed). Odyssey Pr 1965 $13.24.
   ISBN 0-672-63011-7

BOOK ABOUT BACON

Anderson, Fulton H. *Francis Bacon: His Career and His Thought.* Greenwood 1978 $85.00.
   ISBN 0-313-20108-0 Traces Bacon's rise to Lord Chancellor and shows development of his philosophy.

DONNE, JOHN   1573–1631

John Donne was born in London and educated at Oxford University and
Cambridge University. His early career was ruined by his secret marriage to the
17-year-old niece of his powerful employer, who disapproved of the union. He
eventually became a priest and rose to become Dean of St. Paul's Cathedral.
In his own time, he was far more famous as a preacher than as a poet, and, for
generations after his death, his poetry was considered eccentric and clumsy.
Donne was rediscovered early in the twentieth century and became the single
greatest influence on English poetry between the two world wars.

   Donne's early poetry (1590–1601) consists largely of sensual love lyrics
and satires on society. After his marriage, his poetry became increasingly serious and religious, particularly after 1615 when he entered the Church. Donne's
earnest and vigorous mind, expressed in flashing wit and startling metaphors,
continues to attract modern readers.

POETRY BY DONNE

The Complete English Poems of John Donne. A. J. Smith (ed). Penguin 1977 $8.95. ISBN
   0-14-042209-9

PROSE BY DONNE

The Complete Poetry and Selected Prose of John Donne. Charles M. Coffin (ed). Modern Lib 1952
   $8.95. ISBN 0-394-60440-7

BOOKS ABOUT DONNE

Bald, R. C. *John Donne: A Life.* Oxford Univ Pr 1986 $29.95. ISBN 0-19-812870-3
   Comprehensive biography with detailed attention to sources of the poems.
Clements, Arthur L. *John Donne's Poetry: An Annotated Text with Critical Essays.* Norton 1966
   $7.95. ISBN 0-393-09642-4 Very thorough and useful annotations of the major
   poems and valuable collection of essays.

HERBERT, GEORGE   1593–1633

One of the most important of the Renaissance poets, George Herbert led a brief
life that was unusually pure, pious, and intensely devoted to his office as an
Anglican priest. The 129 sacred poems in his collection known as *The Temple*
(1633) are a spiritual autobiography of extraordinary intensity. Herbert was
fond of traditional poetic forms, simple diction, and the rhythms of actual
speech, but the quiet intensity and deep reflection of his poems make them
both original and moving.

POETRY BY HERBERT

The English Poems of George Herbert. C. A. Patrides (ed). Biblio Dist 1981 $5.00. ISBN 0-460-11040-3

BOOKS ABOUT HERBERT

Charles, Amy M. *A Life of George Herbert.* Cornell Univ Pr 1977 $29.95. ISBN 0-8014-1014-2 Authoritative biography that focuses on Herbert's career and his relationships with family and acquaintances.

Chute, Marchette. *Two Gentle Men: The Lives of George Herbert and Robert Herrick.* Dutton 1959. (o.p.) $6.95. A biographical study of Herbert set against the background of his age.

Stewart, Stanley. *George Herbert.* G. K. Hall 1986 $21.95. ISBN 0-8057-6921-8 Comprehensive study of Herbert's life and works.

HERRICK, ROBERT 1591–1674

Robert Herrick is one of the Cavalier poets and the most gifted of the "tribe of Ben," the small band of poets influenced by Ben Jonson. Herrick is considered one of the greatest English songwriters. He published only one volume of verse, an astonishing collection of 1,200 poems known as the *Hesperides and Noble Numbers* (1648). Although Herrick was an Anglican priest, many of his poems deal with sensual pleasures, stressing the need to *carpe diem*—to seize the day—since youth and joy pass so quickly. Herrick's verse is intensely musical and reflects classical and Anglican ceremony, English folklore, and timeless myth. He is best known for his short poem, "To Virgins, To Make Much of Time," which begins "Gather ye rosebuds while ye may," encouraging young people to enjoy themselves while they still can.

POETRY BY HERRICK

The Complete Poetry of Robert Herrick. J. Max Patrick (ed). Norton 1968. (o.p.) $2.95.
Selected Poems. David Jesson-Dibley (ed). Carcanet 1980 $7.50. ISBN 0-85635-320-5

BOOK ABOUT HERRICK

Chute, Marchette. *Two Gentle Men: The Lives of George Herbert and Robert Herrick.* Dutton 1959. (o.p.) $6.95. Biographical novel about Herrick that effectively captures the flavor of his time.

JONSON, BEN 1572–1637

Ben Jonson is one of the great figures of English literature. His reputation, however, has suffered a severe and undeserved decline in the twentieth century. For generations after his death, he was regarded as almost the equal of Shakespeare as a playwright, as well as a poet of towering achievement. One of the first great all-around men of letters, Jonson tried many different types of work: actor and playwright, poet and critic, scholar and soldier. In his later years, he was the acknowledged arbiter of literary taste in London.

Jonson was a great comic dramatist and a poet of wide range and variety who composed lyrics, sonnets, satires, and odes. His poems in turn influenced the taste and style of younger poets of his time, especially the group who came to be known as the tribe of Ben.

POETRY BY JONSON

Ben Jonson: The Complete Poems. George Parfitt (ed). Penguin 1988 $10.95. ISBN 0-14-042227-3

PLAYS BY JONSON

Ben Jonson's Plays and Masques. Robert M. Adams (ed). Norton 1975 $9.95. ISBN 0-393-09035-3

BOOKS ABOUT JONSON

McLean, Hugh. *Ben Jonson and the Cavalier Poets.* Norton 1975 $11.95. ISBN 0-393-04387-8 Collection of poems by Jonson and the poets he inspired, plus critical essays.

Riggs, David. *Ben Jonson: A Life.* Harvard Univ Pr 1989 $35.00. ISBN 0-674-06625-1 Biographical study that also examines the literary profession in early modern England.

MARLOWE, CHRISTOPHER 1564–1593

Christopher Marlowe was born in the same year as Shakespeare. (*See* Shakespeare, Vol. 1, British Literature: The Renaissance.) At the time of his early death in 1593, his achievement towered over Shakespeare's.

The details of Marlowe's short life are very murky. Scholars believe that, while still a student at Cambridge, he began to engage in secret activities for the government. His death, in a tavern brawl at the age of 29, is shrouded in mystery.

It is known that Marlowe burst onto the Elizabethan theatrical scene in 1587 with the production of his two-part play, *Tamburlaine*. There he introduced the first of his "villain-heroes," unscrupulous central characters who fascinate the audience with their defiance and ambition. All of Marlowe's seven plays have central characters who test limits or strive against a humdrum and conventional world. Marlowe was the first dramatist to write in blank verse, the iambic pentameter line—a ten-syllable line in which the second, fourth, sixth, eighth, and tenth syllables are stressed—that became the model for Shakespeare and others.

POETRY BY MARLOWE

Complete Plays and Poems. J. B. Steanie (ed). Penguin 1969 $6.95. ISBN 0-14-043037-7

PLAYS BY MARLOWE

Complete Plays. E. D. Pendry and J. C. Maxwell (eds). Biblio Dist 1983 $7.50. ISBN 0-460-11383-6

BOOKS ABOUT MARLOWE

Bloom, Harold (ed). *Christopher Marlowe.* Chelsea 1986 $24.50. ISBN 0-87754-666-5 Solid collection of critical essays with modern perspective.

Leech, Clifford. *Christopher Marlowe: Poet for the Stage.* AMS 1986 $39.50. ISBN 0-404-62281-X View of Marlowe's work as a whole, demonstrating his moral neutrality, his successful use of comedy, and the stageworthy nature of his plays.

Pinciss, Gerald. *Christopher Marlowe.* Ungar 1975 $16.95. ISBN 0-8044-2694-5 A discussion of Marlowe and the Elizabethan theater, with an analysis of each of Marlowe's plays.

MARVELL, ANDREW   1621–1678

Andrew Marvell was both a Puritan and a sympathizer with the monarchy. A partisan of Charles I, he became tutor to Oliver Cromwell's ward, a friend of John Milton (*see* Milton, Vol. 1, British Literature: The Renaissance) and an official in Cromwell's government. He was later a member of the Restoration parliament, surviving remarkably well in the shifting political climate of his age.

Marvell's poetry is marked by a fascination with both the charm and the raw power of nature. His best known poem, "To His Coy Mistress," cleverly plays with the theme of *carpe diem*—seizing the day—before death or old age makes pleasure impossible. Marvell's verse combines wit, satire, deep thought, playfulness, and complexity in a way that is well suited to modern taste.

POETRY BY MARVELL

The Complete Poems. Elizabeth S. Donno (ed). Penguin 1977 $6.95. ISBN 0-14-042213-7

BOOKS ABOUT MARVELL

Craze, Dan S. *The Life and Lyrics of Andrew Marvell.* Barnes 1979. (o.p.) $28.00. An outline of Marvell's life, a new chronological order for the lyrics, and clear commentaries on the poems.

Donno, Elizabeth S. *Andrew Marvell: The Critical Heritage.* Routledge 1978 $65.00. ISBN 0-7100-8791-8 A chronological survey summarizing various critical appraisals of Marvell, with the reactions to his work by his contemporaries and later writers.

MILTON, JOHN   1608–1674

John Milton was born in London, where he lived most of his life. He attended Cambridge University in order to study for the ministry, but while he was there, he decided to be a poet instead. Milton's tremendous poetic gift showed itself early: in the two companion poems written in 1633, *L'Allegro* (the mirthful man) and *Il Penseroso* (the pensive man); in *Comus, A Masque,* a play that was acted in 1634; and in *Lycidas* (1637), a poem mourning the death of a college friend.

Milton turned away from poetry for a time to devote himself to the cause of the Parliamentary party in its struggle to take power from the king. From 1640 to 1660, he actively supported the Puritan cause (although he was hardly a devout Puritan), serving as Oliver Cromwell's Latin Secretary from 1649 to 1660. His greatest prose works, most arguing for "the establishment of real liberty," were written during this period.

After the defeat of Cromwell and the restoration of the monarchy, Milton returned to writing poetry and to his interest in religion. In 1667 he published *Paradise Lost,* a long epic poem, dealing with the Genesis account of the fall of humankind in the Garden of Eden. This poem, surely one of the world's greatest epics, is Milton's attempt "to justify the ways of God to man." It was followed in 1671 by *Paradise Regained,* Milton's story of Jesus and his temptation.

Milton's eyesight had been gradually failing for many years, and by 1652, the year his wife died, he was virtually blind. For the remaining 22 years of his life he was dependent on his three daughters to read him the books he so dearly loved, and to help him write. His youngest daughter took down from dictation all of *Paradise Lost.* The unhappiness of his final years as a blind invalid whose political party had been defeated echoes in his last great poem, *Samson Agonistes* (Samson the Wrestler) (1671), which is based on the biblical account of Samson's blindness and his deception at the hands of Delilah.

POETRY BY MILTON

The Complete Poetry of John Milton. John T. Showcross (ed). Doubleday 1971 $10.95. ISBN 0-385-02351-0

PROSE BY MILTON

John Milton: Complete Poems and Major Prose. Merritt Y. Hughs (ed). Odyssey Pr 1957 $26.56. ISBN 0-672-63178-4
The Portable Milton. Douglas Bush (ed). Penguin 1976 $7.95. ISBN 0-14-015044-7

BOOKS ABOUT MILTON

Miller, David M. *John Milton: Poetry.* G. K. Hall 1978 $15.95. ISBN 0-8057-6724-X
   Analysis and commentary on all major works as well as some minor ones.
Nicolson, Marjorie. *John Milton: A Reader's Guide to His Poetry.* Hippocrene 1971 $27.50.
   ISBN 0-374-96106-9 Biographical study with analyses of the major poems, the
   minor poems, the masques, and the sonnets.
Thorpe, James. *John Milton: The Inner Life.* Huntington Lib 1983 $25.95. ISBN 0-87328-
   079-2 Biographical study focusing on a psychological analysis of Milton.

MORE, SIR THOMAS   1478–1535

The son of a judge, Thomas More attended Oxford and then studied law at
Lincoln's Inn in London, where he became a barrister in 1501. More was a
deeply religious youth and while studying the law, he even lived at a monastery and considered becoming a priest. Instead, More entered Parliament in
1504, where he soon won the favor of King Henry VIII.

More rose rapidly in the world of government and politics to become
Speaker of the Commons and eventually Lord Chancellor in 1529. His fall was
even more rapid. He refused to support Henry VIII in his struggles with the
Pope, and was consequently tried for treason and executed in 1535. His death
was viewed as martyrdom by Catholics, and he was eventually made a saint
in 1935.

More's major contribution to English literature is the book *Utopia,* a description of an ideal religious society where all work hard and share equally
in what they produce and where the common sharing of pain and suffering,
as well as wealth, eliminates evil. The title of the book has since passed into
general use to describe any ideal society.

PROSE BY MORE

The History of King Richard III and Selections from the English and Latin Poems. Yale Univ Pr 1976
   $8.95. ISBN 0-300-01925-4
Utopia and Other Essential Writings. James Greene (ed). NAL 1984 $5.95. ISBN 0-452-
   00920-0

BOOKS ABOUT MORE

Bolt, Robert. *A Man for All Seasons.* Random 1966 $2.95. ISBN 0-394-70321-9 Play
   about More as a "hero of selfhood."
Kenny, Anthony. *Thomas More.* Oxford Univ Pr 1983 $5.95. ISBN 0-19-287573-6
   Study of the principal ideas of *Utopia* with an interpretation of its message, a
   biography, and a portrait of the Catholic values More defended.
Marius, Richard. *Thomas More: A Biography.* Random 1985 $12.95. ISBN 0-394-74146-3
   Biographical study that focuses on More as a man rather than a saint, drawing
   on More's own writing and the time period in which he lived.

SHAKESPEARE, WILLIAM 1564–1616

Although there are many myths and mysteries surrounding William Shakespeare, actually a great deal is known about his life. He was born in Stratford-on-Avon, son of a prosperous merchant and local politician who had the wealth to send him to the excellent Stratford Grammar School.

At 18 Shakespeare married Anne Hathaway, the 27-year-old daughter of a local farmer, and they had their first daughter six months later. He probably developed an interest in the theater by watching plays performed by traveling players in Stratford. Some time before 1592, he left his family to take up residence in London, where he began acting and writing plays and poetry.

By 1594 Shakespeare had become a member and part owner of an acting company called the Lord Chamberlain's Men, and he soon became the company's principal playwright. His plays enjoyed both great popularity and high critical acclaim. Before retiring to Stratford in 1610, he wrote more than three dozen plays (that we are sure of) and more than 150 poems. He was celebrated by Ben Jonson, one of the leading playwrights of the day, as a writer who would be "not for an age, but for all time," a prediction that has proved to be true.

Today, Shakespeare towers over all other English writers and has few rivals in any language. His genius and creativity continue to astound scholars, and his plays continue to delight audiences. Many have served as the basis for operas, ballets, musical compositions, and films.

While Jonson and other writers labored over their plays, Shakespeare seems to have had the ability to turn out work of exceptionally high caliber at an amazing speed. At the height of his career, he wrote an average of two plays a year as well as dozens of poems, songs, and possibly even verses for tombstones and heraldic shields, all while he continued to act in the plays performed by the Lord Chamberlain's Men. This staggering output is even more impressive when one considers its variety. Except for the English history plays, he never wrote the same kind of play twice. He seems to have had a good deal of fun in trying his hand at every kind of play.

There is a huge amount of Shakespeare scholarship. Every year dozens of studies are added to the hundreds that already exist. The works that are listed below are merely a small sample of the total. They have been selected because they are especially appropriate for young readers coming to Shakespeare for the first time.

PLAYS BY SHAKESPEARE

Complete Oxford Shakespeare. Stanley Wells (ed). 3 vols. Oxford Univ Pr 1988 $65.00. ISBN 0-19-812872-6
Complete Works. W. J. Craig (ed). Oxford Univ Pr 1943 $29.95. ISBN 0-19-254174-9

POETRY BY SHAKESPEARE

*Shakespeare's Sonnets. Louis B. Wright and Virginia La Mar (eds). Washington Square Pr 1967 $3.95. ISBN 0-671-6134-2 Folger Library edition suitable for grades 9 and up.
The Sonnets and Narrative Poems: The Complete Non-Dramatic Poetry. William Burto (ed). NAL 1986 $4.95. ISBN 0-451-52039-4

BOOKS ABOUT SHAKESPEARE

*Barnet, Sylvan. *A Short Guide to Shakespeare.* Harcourt 1974 $4.95. ISBN 0-15-681800-0 An easy-to-read introduction to reading and understanding Shakespeare's plays.

*Charney, Maurice. *How to Read Shakespeare: A New Guide to the Plays.* McGraw 1972 $6.95. ISBN 0-07-010659-2 Provides helpful background as well as reading techniques.

*Chute, Marchette. *Shakespeare of London.* Dutton 1957 $8.95. ISBN 0-525-48245-8 Fictionalized biography, accurate in detail.

Evans, Gareth L., and Barbara L. Evans. *The Shakespeare Companion.* Scribner's 1978. (o.p.) $5.95. Study that presents all aspects of Shakespeare—his life, his contemporaries, his time, his plays, his birthplace.

*Fair, Martha Harris. *Shakespeare's Plays for Young People.* Harris Acad $10.00. ISBN 0-911181-01-6 Very easy reading, suitable for grades 2–9.

Goddard, Harold C. *The Meaning of Shakespeare.* 2 vols. Univ of Chicago Pr 1960. Vol. 1 $13.95. ISBN 0-226-30041-2. Vol. 2 $11.95. ISBN 0-226-30042-0 Complete analysis of all of Shakespeare's plays.

*Lamb, Charles, and Mary Lamb. *Shakespeare.* Jean L. Scorso (ed). Unicorn Pub 1989 $14.95. ISBN 0-88101-094-4 New version of the classic rendering for young readers.

*Levi, Peter. *The Life and Times of William Shakespeare.* H. Holt 1989 $29.95. ISBN 0-8050-1199-4 Readable but scholarly biography that answers some questions surrounding Shakespeare's life.

*Mulherin, Jennifer. *Shakespeare for Everyone.* 6 vols. Silver 1988 $65.76. ISBN 0-382-09812-9 Good useful overview for grades 5–12; analyzes themes, characters, and plots.

*Papp, Joseph, and Elizabeth Kirkland. *Shakespeare Alive!* Bantam 1988 $4.50. ISBN 0-553-27081-8 Readable, entertaining look at Shakespeare's times as they relate to problems of staging his plays; from the director of the renowned New York Public Theater.

SIDNEY, SIR PHILIP   1554–1586

Sir Philip Sidney is perhaps the supreme example of the ideal Elizabethan gentleman, embodying the traits of soldier, scholar, and courtier that Elizabethans so admired. Born into a noble family, Sidney traveled widely in France, Germany, and Italy. He served Queen Elizabeth I as courtier and ambassador before his death in battle in the Low Countries, a brave death that added to his glamour.

Sidney's writings in prose and poetry were not intended for publication but rather for private circulation among his friends. His *A Defense of Poesie* (1595) is one of the great critical works in English and brilliantly epitomizes the Renaissance ideal in literature—to instruct as well as to delight. Sidney's sonnets have had a lasting influence on all love poetry.

POETRY BY SIDNEY

Poems of Philip Sidney. William Ringler (ed). Oxford Univ Pr 1962 $74.00. ISBN 0-19-811834-1

PROSE BY SIDNEY

An Apology for Poetry. Forrest Robinson (ed). Macmillan 1970 $5.99. ISBN 0-672-60254-7

Arcadia. Maurice Evans (ed). Penguin 1977 $7.95. ISBN 0-14-043111-X

BOOKS ABOUT SIDNEY

Kalstone, David. *Sidney's Poetry.* Norton 1970 $1.85. ISBN 0-393-00516-X Critical study of the poetry of Arcadia and Stella.

Kay, Dennis (ed). *Sir Philip Sidney: An Anthology of Modern Criticism.* Oxford Univ Pr 1988 $72.00. ISBN 0-19-811204-1 Substantial collection representing the full range of modern criticism.

SPENSER, EDMUND 1552–1599

Edmund Spenser was known as the poet's poet—a term coined by critic Charles Lamb two centuries after Spenser's death. The poet was born in London, where he attended school before going to Cambridge University in 1569. About 1579 he came to know Sir Philip Sidney (*see* Sidney, Vol. 1, British Literature: The Renaissance), to whom he dedicated his first significant work, *The Shepheardes Calendar* (1580).

Spenser hoped for advancement at the court of Queen Elizabeth I, but in 1580 he took a minor government position in Ireland, where he spent most of the rest of his life. In 1594 he married Elizabeth Boyle. The sonnet sequence, *Amoretti* (1595), reflects their romance, and his great marriage hymn, *Epithalamion* (1595), celebrates their wedding. Several years earlier, in 1590, at the urging of Sir Walter Raleigh whom he had met in Ireland, Spenser published the first three books of his greatest work, *The Faerie Queene.* In this poem Spenser uses the form of the epic romances of the late Middle Ages, but he gives his tales of knights and their adventures a deep allegorical meaning. He intended the work to consist of 12 books, but published only three more, in 1596. Spenser had a particularly strong influence on the Romantic poets, especially Keats and Wordsworth. (*See* Keats *and* Wordsworth, Vol. 1, British Literature: The Romantic Period.)

POETRY BY SPENSER

Edmund Spenser's Poetry. Hugh MacLean (ed). Norton 1982. $14.95. ISBN 0-393-95138-3

BOOKS ABOUT SPENSER

Bloom, Harold. *Edmund Spenser.* Chelsea 1986 $29.50. ISBN 0-87754-672-X Succinct biography followed by a thorough collection of personal comments by contemporaries of Spenser, plus critical essays on his work ranging from 1593 to 1902.

Heale, Elizabeth. *The Faerie Queene: A Reader's Guide.* Cambridge Univ Pr 1987 $10.95. ISBN 0-521-31679-0 Critical analysis of each book of *The Faerie Queene.*

Judson, A. C. *Notes on the Life of Edmund Spenser.* Kraus 1978 repr of 1943 ed $15.00. ISBN 0-527-46940-8 Clear narrative that draws on available data to present the most probable version of Spenser's life.

VAUGHAN, HENRY 1622–1695

Henry Vaughan was born in Wales and studied at Oxford University with his twin brother, Thomas. After fighting as a Royalist soldier during the English Civil War, he returned to Wales where he served as a physician for the last 20 years of his life. Together with his brother, he practiced alchemy—a primitive version of chemistry—and dabbled in magic, looking for hidden connections between the natural and the spiritual worlds. These interests are revealed in his religious poetry, *Silex Scintillans* (1650; second part, 1655), in which he writes about nature as an image of God.

POETRY BY VAUGHAN

The Complete Poems of Henry Vaughan. French Fogle (ed). Norton 1969 $8.95. ISBN 0-393-00438-4

BOOK ABOUT VAUGHAN

Simmonds, James D. *Masques of God: Forms and Theme in the Poetry of Henry Vaughan.* Univ of Pittsburgh Pr 1972 $29.95. ISBN 0-8229-3236-9 Major critical analysis of Vaughan's work with appendixes answering questions pertaining to his biography.

WEBSTER, JOHN   *c. 1580–c. 1634*

Very little is known about John Webster's life. He seems to have participated in many dramatic collaborations, but his undisputed work consists of only three plays: *The White Devil* (1612), *The Duchess of Malfi* (1614), and *The Devil's Law Case* (1623). His two great tragedies, *The White Devil* and *The Duchess of Malfi,* are darkly poetic and brooding. The central characters in both try unsuccessfully to fashion a meaningful life in a world that seems to be falling apart. Webster employs a full range of violent and sensational effects to render a physical sense of horror, especially in *The Duchess of Malfi.*

PLAYS BY WEBSTER

Webster: Three Plays. D. C. Gunby (ed). Penguin 1973 $6.95. ISBN 0-14-043081-4

BOOK ABOUT WEBSTER

Bradbrook, Muriel C. *John Webster.* Columbia Univ Pr 1980 $27.00. ISBN 0-231-05162-4 Biographical and critical study of Webster, focusing on both his personal and his literary life.

WYATT, SIR THOMAS   1503–1542

Sir Thomas Wyatt served King Henry VIII as a diplomat and as an ambassador to Spain and to the French Emperor Charles V. His poetry reflects the influence of French and Italian literature, particularly the work of the Italian poet Petrarch. (*See* Petrarch, Vol. 1, World Literature: Italian Language and Literature.) Wyatt introduced the Italian sonnet into English verse, translating and paraphrasing Petrarch's originals and using rhyme schemes borrowed from other Italian poets. As the sonnet was to become one of the chief English poetic forms, Wyatt's influence was quite significant. None of Wyatt's poetry, which includes epigrams, satires, devotional works and lyrics, as well as sonnets, was published during his lifetime. However, he had a powerful influence on later poets.

POETRY BY WYATT

Sir Thomas Wyatt: The Complete Poems. R. A. Rebholz (ed). Yale Univ Pr 1981 $11.95. ISBN 0-300-12688-9

BOOK ABOUT WYATT

Mason, H. A. (ed). *Sir Thomas Wyatt: A Literary Portrait.* Assoc Univ Pr 1986 $32.50. ISBN 0-8453-4512-5 Useful collection with valuable insight into sources of the sonnets.

THE RESTORATION AND THE EIGHTEENTH CENTURY

The year 1660 saw the end of 20 years of bitter civil war and the restoration of the monarchy in England. Consequently, England entered a new era that has come to be known by many names—the Neoclassical Period, the Enlightenment, the Augustan Age, the Age of Reason. None of these is totally accurate. The period they attempt to describe is a long and complex age that defies easy definition or a simple label. This is especially true of the literature of the age.

Therefore, for convenience, scholars usually divide these 140 years into three literary periods, each of which has its own central ideas and forms of expression, as well as its own major writers.

The first of these periods is commonly called the Restoration, or sometimes the Age of Dryden after its chief writer. Like the Elizabethan Age, it was a time dominated by playwrights and poets. When the monarchy was restored, one of the first acts of the new king, Charles II, was to reopen the theaters that had been closed since 1642. The stages were soon filled with the witty comedies of such gifted writers as William Congreve and John Dryden. These plays were called comedies of manners because they reflect the habits and way of life of the upper classes, particularly the clever war of words between men and women engaged in the battle of the sexes.

This period also saw renewed interest in classical Greece and Rome, which gave the name "Neoclassical" to the period. From this interest came so-called Augustan poetry, verse that depended on the clever use of words and surface style rather than deep emotion. Augustan poetry characteristically sprang from the head, not the heart, and was almost always composed in such Greek or Roman forms as odes or elegies.

By the early eighteenth century, as the extravagance, loose morals, and social snobbery of the upper classes grew more extreme, the literature began to change. Rather than merely depicting the way of life of the wealthy, writers began to attack it, mainly through the use of satire. Alexander Pope and Jonathan Swift, the two major writers of the period, each wrote biting attacks on the manners, morals, and even specific people of the time.

At the same time, criticism of society began to appear in a new form—in publications such as *The Tatler* and *The Spectator,* early versions of modern news magazines. Writers such as Joseph Addison and Richard Steele wrote critical essays for these journals, commenting directly on the ways of their society.

By the middle of the century, both Pope and Swift were dead, and English literature had begun to take yet another turn. Up to this point, poets and playwrights had dominated English literature. Now prose writers began to become more important. The leading figure of the age was essayist Samuel Johnson. The critical essay, now published in new magazines and gazettes, became even more popular. Novels also began to gain popularity. Earlier in the century, in 1719, Daniel Defoe had published *Robinson Crusoe,* generally considered to be the first English novel. By the middle of the century, Samuel Richardson, Henry Fielding, and Laurence Sterne had each made contributions to this new field of literature.

At the same time, Richard Sheridan and Oliver Goldsmith brought new plays to the stage. While similar in form to the old comedies of manners, these new works paid more attention to the feelings and emotions of the characters.

Poetry also saw new developments. Poets like William Cowper, Thomas Gray, and William Collins wrote verse that looked outward to nature for inspiration and inward to their souls for truth.

AUSTEN, JANE   1775–1817

Jane Austen's life is striking for the contrast between the great works she wrote in secret and the outward appearance of being quite dull and ordinary. Austen was born in the small English town of Steventon in Hampshire, and educated at home by her clergyman father. She was deeply devoted to her family. For a short time, the Austens lived in the resort city of Bath, but when her father died, they returned to Steventon, where Austen lived until her death at the age of 41.

The Love Letter.   Detail of oil painting by Jean Honoré Fragonard (1770s).
Courtesy of The Metropolitan Museum of Art, The Jules Bache Collection, 1949.
(49.7.49)

Austen was drawn to literature early. At age 15 she began writing novels
that satirized both the writers and the manners of the 1790s. Her sharp sense
of humor and keen eye for the ridiculous in human behavior give her works
lasting appeal. She is at her best in such books as *Pride and Prejudice* (1813),
Mansfield Park (1814), and *Emma* (1816), in which she examines and often ridicules the behavior of small groups of middle-class characters. Austen relies
heavily on conversations among her characters to reveal their personalities, and
at times her novels read almost like plays. Several of them have, in fact, been
made into films.

NOVELS BY AUSTEN

*The Complete Novels of Jane Austen (includes *Sense and Sensibility, Pride and Prejudice, Mansfield
Park, Emma, Northanger Abbey,* and *Persuasion*). Penguin 1983. ISBN 0-14-009002-9
Six novels focusing on young people and their relationships in love and marriage,
with a heroine in *Northanger Abbey* whose imagination runs wild because she has
read too many horror stories.

BOOKS ABOUT AUSTEN

Cecil, David. *A Portrait of Jane Austen.* Hill & Wang 1979 $9.95. ISBN 0-8090-1392-4
Biographical study of Austen, with good illustrations.
Halperin, John. *The Life of Jane Austen.* Johns Hopkins Univ Pr 1984 $12.95. ISBN
0-8018-3410-4 In-depth biography of Austen, focusing on her family and including a discussion of each of her completed novels.
Honan, Park. *Jane Austen: Her Life.* Fawcett 1988 $11.95. ISBN 449-90319-2 A biogra-
phy, using new and unpublished sources, with attention paid to each of the
novels.

BUNYAN, JOHN   1628–1688

John Bunyan is something of a misfit among the polished and sophisticated writers of the Restoration. The son of a humble mender of pots, he had little education before learning his father's trade. He was, however, an intensely religious man, who served in Oliver Cromwell's army. Even after the monarchy was restored, he continued to preach Baptist doctrine, for which he was twice imprisoned.

During his second imprisonment in 1675, Bunyan wrote *The Pilgrim's Progress* (1678). This is a long tale of the struggle of the individual against the forces of evil. It is an allegory in which specific characters and events represent universal traits and circumstances. The book was an immediate success, and eventually became the most widely read of books in English aside from the Bible. Its appeal was greatest to the lower classes who saw in the struggles of Bunyan's hero, Christian, reflections of their own struggles in life. American pioneers setting out to face the hardships of the wilderness often took with them only two books, the Bible and *The Pilgrim's Progress.* Readers of Louisa May Alcott's *Little Women* (1868) will remember the significance of *The Pilgrim's Progress* to the characters in that book. (*See* Alcott, Vol. 1, American Literature: The Rise of Realism.)

BOOKS BY BUNYAN

The Pilgrim's Progress (1678). Oxford Univ Pr 1984 $2.95. ISBN 0-19-281607-1
**The Pilgrim's Progress in Today's English.* Moody 1964 $6.95. ISBN 0-8024-6520-X A version that reads like an adventure story.

BOOKS ABOUT BUNYAN

*Dangler, Sandy. *John Bunyan: The Writer of Pilgrim's Progress.* Moody 1986 $3.95. Aimed at very young readers (grades 4–6), but useful even for those slightly older.
Froude, James A. *Bunyan.* John Morley (ed). AMS (repr of 1888 ed) $12.50. ISBN 0-404-51711-0 Comprehensive general study of life and works.
Sharrock, Roger. *John Bunyan.* Greenwood 1984 $35.00. ISBN 0-313-24528-2 Critical analysis of all Bunyan's major works, demonstrating how they are influenced by his religious experience and how they should be seen in light of biographical and historical information.

CONGREVE, WILLIAM   1670–1729

William Congreve was born into a well-to-do family in Yorkshire, England, and educated at Trinity College in Dublin, Ireland. Although he studied for the law, he never practiced it, deciding to write instead. After publishing a moderately successful novel, he turned to the theater, where he became famous as a writer of witty and elegant comedies. His plays *The Old Bachelor* (1693), *The Double Dealer* (1693), and *Love for Love* (1695) all proved to be extremely popular.

By the turn of the century, however, comedies of this sort had fallen out of fashion with critics and the public. Congreve's last play, *The Way of the World* (1700), was received poorly, and he virtually retired from the theater. Ironically, *The Way of the World* is performed today to highly appreciative audiences.

PLAYS BY CONGREVE

The Comedies of William Congreve (includes *The Way of the World, The Old Bachelor, The Double Dealer,* and *Love for Love*). Eric S. Rump (ed). Penguin 1986 $6.95. ISBN 0-14-043231-0

BOOKS ABOUT CONGREVE

Hodges, J. C. *William Congreve: The Man.* Kraus (repr of 1941 ed) $20.00. ISBN 0-527-41330-5 Illustrated biography, including genealogical tables.

Lindsay, Alexander, and Howard Erskine-Hall. *Congreve: The Critical Heritage.* Routledge 1989 $112.00. ISBN 0-415-02535 Extensive well-chosen collection of critical commentary.

COWPER, WILLIAM   1731–1800

William Cowper (pronounced "Cooper") was the son of a Hertfordshire clergyman. An unhappy child, he became an adult given to long fits of depression growing largely out of his fears of damnation. Throughout his life he drifted in and out of mental illness, drawing support from a large circle of close friends who continually helped bring him back to health.

Despite these problems Cowper managed to write a great deal of verse, most of it of high quality. The blank verse in which he wrote mirrored the natural rhythm of English speech. Cowper was much admired by young poets like William Wordsworth and Samuel Taylor Coleridge, giving him a powerful influence on the Romantic Movement. (*See* Coleridge *and* Wordsworth, Vol. 1, British Literature: The Romantic Period.)

POETRY BY COWPER

The Poetical Works of William Cowper. H. S. Milford (ed). AMS (repr of 1934 ed) $42.50. ISBN 0-404-14525-6

BOOKS ABOUT COWPER

King, James. *William Cowper: A Biography.* Duke Univ Pr 1986 $35.00. ISBN 0-8223-0513-5 Definitive biography, emphasizing Cowper's inner strengths and ambitions; makes use of important new information on his relationships with women, his literary career, and his final years.

Quinlan, Maurice. *William Cowper: A Critical Life.* Greenwood (repr of 1953 ed) $35.00. ISBN 0-8371-3425-0 Biographical study with comments on each poem.

DEFOE, DANIEL   1661–1731

Daniel Defoe was born in the year the monarchy was restored to England, and in many ways his life mirrors the dramatically changing times of the Restoration. The son of a butcher, he did not have the benefit of good social connections or a university education. He began his adult life in business, traveling widely and trying his hand at a number of ventures. He began writing in 1697 with an essay on economics, but he did not become a serious writer until his business failed. He turned first to journalism, and in 1704 began a newspaper called *The Review,* which continued to be published until 1713. In 1719, at the age of 59, he began writing a new kind of fiction, long prose narratives, which are generally considered to be the first novels in English. The first of these, *Robinson Crusoe* (1719), related the adventures of a shipwrecked sailor. It was an immediate success and other books quickly followed. The best of these is probably *Moll Flanders* (1722), the story of an unfortunate woman who gets in trouble with the law. Defoe is also known for *A Journal of the Plague Year,* a vivid, detailed fictionalized account of the plague that killed one-quarter of London's population in the early seventeenth century.

Defoe's long experience in journalism and business enabled him to bring to his fiction a keen eye for detail and a knowledge of the workings of the everyday world, giving his works a lasting vividness. This journalistic, realistic, detailed style also became influential for later writers of novels.

NOVELS BY DEFOE

A Journal of the Plague Year (1722). Anthony Burgess (ed). Penguin 1966 $4.95. ISBN 0-14-043015-8

Moll Flanders (1722). Bantam 1989 $2.95. ISBN 0-553-21328-8 Story of a woman's life of crime in the early eighteenth century.

Robinson Crusoe (1719). Bantam 1982 $1.95. ISBN 0-553-21105-6 The classic story of a shipwrecked sailor and his survival on a desert island.

BOOKS ABOUT DEFOE

Bell, Ian A. *Defoe's Fiction.* Barnes 1985 $28.00. ISBN 0-389-20550-1 Study of fiction, considering the relationship between Defoe's work as a whole and the genre of the novel.

Bloom, Harold (ed). *Daniel Defoe.* Chelsea 1987 $24.50. ISBN 1-55546-284-7 Collection of critical essays with modern perspective and analysis.

Richetti, John J. *Daniel Defoe.* G. K. Hall 1987 $17.95. ISBN 0-8057-6955-2 Thorough and comprehensive general study of life and works.

DRYDEN, JOHN   1631–1700

Born into a wealthy Puritan family, John Dryden received an excellent education at Westminster School and Cambridge University. After a brief period in government, he turned his attention almost entirely to writing.

Dryden was one of the first English writers to make his living strictly by writing, but this meant he had to cater to popular taste. His long career was astonishingly varied, and he turned his exceptional talents to almost all the literary forms.

Dryden dominated the entire Restoration period as poet, playwright, and all-round man of letters. He was the third poet laureate of England, but was dismissed in 1688 when he refused to take the oath of allegiance to the king. (A poet laureate is the officially honored poet of a monarch or another governmental ruler.)

In his old age Dryden was virtually a literary "dictator" in England, with an immense influence on eighteenth-century poetry. His verse form and his brilliant satires became models for other poets, but they could rarely equal his standard. Dryden was also a master of "occasional" poetry—verse written for a specific person or special occasion. Like most poets of his time, Dryden saw poetry as a way to express ideas rather than emotions, which makes his poetry seem cool and impersonal to some modern readers.

Dryden also wrote numerous plays that helped make him one of the leading figures of the Restoration theater. Today, however, he is admired more for his influence on other writers than for his own works.

POETRY BY DRYDEN

Dryden: Poems. Penguin 1985 $5.95. ISBN 0-14-05503-6

PLAYS BY DRYDEN

All for Love (1677). Nicholas J. Andrew (ed). Norton 1976 $4.95. ISBN 0-393-90006-1

Dramatic Works. Montague Summers (ed). 6 vols. Gordian 1968 $250.00. ISBN 0-87752-030-5

Marriage a la Mode (1672). Mark S. Auburn (ed). Univ of Nebraska Pr $4.95. ISBN 0-8032-6556-5

BOOKS ABOUT DRYDEN

Bloom, Harold (ed). *John Dryden.* Chelsea 1987 $24.50. ISBN 55546-277-4 Collection of critical essays with a wide range of modern perspectives.

Hollis, C. *Dryden.* Haskell 1974 $49.95. ISBN 0-8303-1753-7 Unusually comprehensive general study with commentary on both life and works.

Kinsley, James, and Helen Kinsley (eds). *Dryden: The Critical Heritage.* Routledge 1975 $65.00. ISBN 0-7100-6977-4 Representative collection of critical comments on Dryden, ranging from 1663 to 1810.

Walker, Keith. *Dryden.* Oxford Univ Pr 1987 $14.95. ISBN 0-19-281402-8 Collection of Dryden's poetry, with notes.

FIELDING, HENRY   1707–1754

Henry Fielding was born into an aristocratic family in Somerset and educated at the prestigious prep school Eton before leaving for London to study law. However, he quickly turned to writing plays, at which he was immediately successful. From 1728 to 1737, he turned out 25 new plays.

Then new censorship laws prevented Fielding from producing the political satires for which he was famous and so he had to leave the theater. Without a job or much money, he turned to law, journalism, and politics, all of which brought him into close contact with people from all walks of English life.

Fielding's varied background served him well when he started writing prose fiction in 1741. His first book, *Shamela* (1741), was a parody of Samuel Richardson's popular novel, *Pamela* (1740), and shows Fielding's gift for comic writing. The following year he published *Joseph Andrews* (1742), an even funnier novel recounting the adventures of a virtuous young man in a corrupt society. Fielding's masterpiece, *Tom Jones* (1749), has had a lasting influence on English literature, for in this book Fielding introduced the idea of unity to the novel. For the first time, a writer had tied together all the events and characters of a novel around one central theme. Later novelists imitated this quality. They were also influenced by Fielding's knowledge of English society, which makes *Tom Jones* a portrait of eighteenth-century England as well as the story of one young man. Both Tom's story and his society's nature were successfully transferred to the screen in the 1962 film, *Tom Jones.*

Fielding died at the age of 47. Before his work, the novel was looked down on as an inferior form. Fielding proved that the novel was capable of the highest achievements of art.

NOVELS BY FIELDING

*Joseph Andrews (1742) and *Shamela* (1741). Martin C. Battestein (ed). Houghton 1961 $8.36. ISBN 0-395-05150-9 Joseph Andrews and his sister Shamela each have their own comic novel in which they fight to keep their virtue in the wicked England of 1740.

* Tom Jones (1749). Modern Lib 1985 $10.95. ISBN 0-394-60519-5 Adventures of a young man and the amusing characters he meets as he seeks fame and fortune in eighteenth-century England.

BOOKS ABOUT FIELDING

Dircks, Richard T. *Henry Fielding.* G. K. Hall 1983 $14.50. ISBN 0-8057-6768-1 Critical study of Fielding's life, his comedies, his fiction, and his mature novels, especially *Tom Jones* and *Amelia.*

Varey, Simon. *Henry Fielding.* Cambridge Univ Pr 1986 $12.95. ISBN 0-521-27876-6 Concise study introducing the major work of Fielding; includes a discussion of Fielding the dramatist as well as the great comic novelist.

GOLDSMITH, OLIVER 1728–1774

Oliver Goldsmith was born into a family of Protestant clergymen and spent his early years in a number of grammar schools. He was a poor student and generally unpopular with his peers. After an equally unhappy time at Trinity College, Dublin, he tried a succession of failed ventures before taking to the road, working his way through Europe as a street performer who sang songs and played the flute. He returned to England in 1756 and, after another series of odd jobs, began eking out a living as a journalist.

Goldsmith's fortunes finally took a turn for the better in 1766 with the publication of his novel *The Vicar of Wakefield.* This novel is a fairy-tale-like account of the ups and downs of a rural family, featuring such plot turns as one daughter's kidnaping and another's being tricked into a false wedding ceremony. He then turned his attention to drama, creating *The Good Natured Man* (1768) and *She Stoops to Conquer* (1773). *She Stoops* is one of his best-known works, a spirited war of words between men and women as a high-born woman is mistaken for a servant by a man who falls in love with her. He went on to produce a variety of notable poems and essays, but he never managed to create a stable life for himself. As his friend Samuel Johnson (*see* Johnson and Boswell, Vol. 1, British Literature: The Restoration and The Eighteenth Century) once said of him, "No man was more foolish when he had not a pen in his hand, or more wise when he had."

NOVEL BY GOLDSMITH

The Vicar of Wakefield (1766). Penguin 1982 $2.50. ISBN 0-14-643159-4

PLAY BY GOLDSMITH

She Stoops to Conquer (1773). Vincent F. Hopper and Gerald B. Lahey (eds). Barron 1958 $4.95. ISBN 0-8120-0158-3

BOOKS ABOUT GOLDSMITH

Bloom, Harold (ed). *Oliver Goldsmith.* Chelsea 1987 $19.95. ISBN 1-55546-281-2 A succinct biography followed by a thorough collection of personal comments by his contemporaries, plus critical essays on Goldsmith ending with G. K. Chesterton's essay of 1902.
Danziger, Marlies. *Oliver Goldsmith and Richard Brinsley Sheridan.* Ungar 1978 $16.95. ISBN 0-8044-2129-3 General study of each writer with good background on eighteenth-century theater.
Gwynn, Stephen. *Oliver Goldsmith.* Haskell 1974 $49.95. ISBN 0-8389-1843-6 Biography with a focus on Goldsmith's poetry and drama.

GRAY, THOMAS 1716–1761

Thomas Gray was a shy, almost reclusive person. After an education at the prep school Eton and at Cambridge University, he traveled in Europe for two years. Then he returned to Cambridge, where he settled into a life of scholarship and writing.

Gray wrote little poetry, but what he did write is of such high quality that he is sometimes considered the most important poet of the mid-eighteenth century. His "Elegy Written in a Country Churchyard" (1751) has long been one of the most popular poems in English. It probably has more quotable lines than any other English poem. The "Elegy" shows the poet contemplating the graves of people who never had the chance to live truly full lives, as he muses about these lost opportunities.

Gray was much admired by the poets who followed him, especially William Wordsworth. He is frequently identified as a forerunner of the Romantic Period.

POETRY BY GRAY

Selected Poems. John Heath Stubbs (ed). Carcanet 1981 $7.50. ISBN 0-85635-317-5

BOOK ABOUT GRAY

Golden, Morris. *Thomas Gray.* G. K. Hall 1988 $19.95. ISBN 0-8059-6961-7 Outline of Gray's career, poetic style, and times, with separate chapters analysing each of Gray's poems.

JOHNSON, SAMUEL   1709–1784 AND BOSWELL, JAMES   1740–1795

Samuel Johnson and James Boswell create their own category—the greatest of literary biographers and, very possibly, the greatest of subjects. Boswell's biography of Johnson, one of the longest in the English language, became the standard for all the literary biographies that followed it.

Johnson was born into a family of limited means, so he managed to study for only a year at Oxford University. Later he was able to earn only a poor living, first from teaching, then from writing. Yet, while he never achieved great wealth, his essays, books, poems, and translations won him enormous respect among English writers and the literary public. He is especially well known for compiling the first major dictionary of the English language, known as *The Dictionary of the English Language.*

In 1763 Johnson met Boswell, a young Scot who had arrived in London only three years before. Almost immediately, Boswell began to record the conversations, opinions, and comings and goings of his new and famous friend. As Johnson rose to become the single most prominent man in English letters, Boswell wove these details, along with his own observations on Johnson's personality, into *The Life of Samuel Johnson, LL.D.* (1791). The biography reveals Johnson's intelligence, wit, and learning along with Boswell's skill as an observer and writer.

WORKS BY JOHNSON

Johnson: Selected Writings. R. T. Davies (ed). Penguin 1982 $7.95. ISBN 0-14-043033-4
Selected Essays from the Rambler, Adventurer and Idler. W. J. Bate (ed). Yale Univ Pr 1968 $12.95. ISBN 0-300-00016-2

BOOKS ABOUT JOHNSON

Boswell, James. *The Life of Samuel Johnson* (1791). Frank Brady (ed). Signet 1981 $3.95. ISBN 395-452-00752-6 Biography by a contemporary, re-creating conversations with Johnson and emphasizing his later years.
Engell, James. *Johnson and His Age.* Harvard Univ Pr 1984 $8.95. ISBN 0-674-48076-7 Collection of essays on Johnson and his contemporaries, focusing on his life and thought; on critical studies of his work; and on poets, politicians, and artists of the period.

BOOKS BY BOSWELL

Journal of a Tour to the Hebrides with Samuel Johnson (1785). Lawrence F. Powell (ed). Biblio Dist 1979 $14.95. ISBN 0-460-00387-9
The Life of Samuel Johnson (1791). Frank Brady (ed). Signet 1981 $3.95. ISBN 0-452-00752-6

BOOK ABOUT BOSWELL

Lewis, Dominic B. *James Boswell: A Short Life.* Greenwood 1980 $35.00. ISBN 0-313-22232-0 Vivid and lively biography that brings Boswell to life.

PEPYS, SAMUEL   1633–1703

Samuel Pepys (pronounced "peeps") served 28 years in the Admiralty after the Restoration and was twice Secretary of the Admiralty (similar to the U.S. Secretary of the Navy). He was the foremost authority on naval matters in his time. Although Pepys was not a man of letters, he has won fame for his candid and entertaining diary. The journal covers only nine years, 1660–1669, and was never written to be published. In fact, it was written in a code Pepys invented that was not deciphered until years after his death. Yet when Pepys's diary was first published in 1825, it established Pepys as an important writer. Pepys's diary, later published as *The Diary of Samuel Pepys,* is one of the best records available of English life after the Restoration. Two of its most memorable sections are Pepys' accounts of the Great Plague of London and the Great Fire of London.

WORKS BY PEPYS

A Pepys Anthology. Robert Latham and Linnet Latham (eds). Univ of California Pr 1987 $18.95. ISBN 0-520-06354-6

BOOKS ABOUT PEPYS

Barber, Richard. *Samuel Pepys, Esq.* Univ of California Pr 1970 $18.95. ISBN 0-520-01763-3 Portraits of Pepys and his contemporaries with commentary from a biographical exhibition by the National Portrait Gallery, covering the years of the *Diary* itself.
Bradford, G. *Samuel Pepys.* Haskell 1974 $52.94. ISBN 0-8383-2061-9 Well-documented biography that supplements and expands the *Diaries.*

POPE, ALEXANDER   1688–1744

Because he was born a Roman Catholic at a time when members of this religion were being oppressed in England, Alexander Pope attended no prestigious preparatory schools or universities. He was educated at home, studied hard, and began writing poetry at an early age. A childhood illness left him small and sickly for the rest of his life.

Pope wrote his verse *Essay on Criticism* (1711) at the early age of 21. This poem, together with *Windsor Forest* (1713) and *The Rape of the Lock* (1714) made him famous. *The Rape of the Lock* is a brilliant work, widely regarded as one of the greatest satiric poems in English. It deals with the loss of a lock of hair by a lady of fashion to a dashing suitor. Pope treats this trifling scene with all the pomp and seriousness of an ancient heroic epic, and the result is a brilliant, preposterous, and biting social satire. He also wrote other long poems satirizing aspects of English life and translations of the *Iliad* and the *Odyssey.*

POETRY BY POPE

Collected Poems. Bonamy Dobree (ed). Biblio Dist 1975 $5.95. ISBN 0-460-00760-2
Pope: Poetry and Prose. Penguin 1985 $4.95. ISBN 0-14-058508-7

BOOKS ABOUT POPE

Bloom, Harold. *Alexander Pope.* Chelsea 1986 $19.95. ISBN 0-87754-680-0 Succinct biography followed by a thorough collection of personal comments by contemporaries and critical essays on Pope ranging from 1717 to 1902.

Gooneratne, Yasmine. *Alexander Pope.* Cambridge Univ Pr 1976 $9.95. ISBN 0-521-29051-1 Critical study of Pope's poetry with the aim of showing its continuing relevance.

Mack, Maynard. *Alexander Pope: A Life.* Norton 1988 $14.70. ISBN 0-393-30529-5 Complete biographical study focusing on the man, his times, and analyses of his work.

RADCLIFFE, ANNE   1764–1823

Born Anne Ward, the daughter of a London merchant, this key writer married William Radcliffe, a publisher and editor, in 1786. Anne Radcliffe had always been fond of writing and with her husband's encouragement turned to literature as a hobby. The literary form she chose was the Gothic novel, so called because it was frequently set in a medieval castle. These tales hinged on suspense and mystery, almost always involving the supernatural. Gothic novels featured secret passages, strange noises in the night, and sudden appearances and disappearances, which terrified and delighted readers. Although Anne Radcliffe did not invent the Gothic novel, she refined it and gave it enormous popularity.

NOVELS BY RADCLIFFE

The Italian (1797). Frederick Gerber (ed). Oxford Univ Pr 1981 $6.95. ISBN 0-19-281572-5 Story of a man who tortures others because he himself is tormented.

The Mysteries of Udolpho (1794). Bonamy Dobree (ed). Oxford Univ Pr 1980 $6.95. ISBN 0-19-281502-4 Beautiful young Emily is carried off by her aunt to the sinister castle of Udolpho where strange and ghostly events commonly occur.

BOOK ABOUT RADCLIFFE

Murray, Gene. *Anne Radcliffe.* Twayne. (o.p.) A summary of the Gothic novel before Radcliffe, as well as a critical study of Radcliffe's work.

RICHARDSON, SAMUEL   1689–1781

Born the son of a carpenter, Samuel Richardson was too poor to receive a formal education and was apprenticed to a printer at the age of 17. As an apprentice, he wrote love letters for servant girls, studied at night to improve himself, and married the boss's daughter. Eventually he acquired his own print shop, became a successful printer, and wrote several undistinguished books of nonfiction.

Then, at age 50, Richardson made his first attempt at fiction with the novel *Pamela* (1740). The book was an immediate popular success and led directly to his masterpiece, *Clarissa* (1747–1748). Richardson's novels are intended to serve as moral guides—to show the rewards of virtue and the penalties of sin. But his skill in developing full, believable, and psychologically complex characters makes his novels much more than simple moral tales. Because his novels are so long (*Clarissa* runs to more than 1 million words and is the longest novel in English) and their plots so complicated, they can be difficult to follow. As a result, they are not as popular with modern readers as they deserve to be.

NOVELS BY RICHARDSON

Clarissa (1748). George Sherburn (ed). Houghton 1962 $8.36. ISBN 0-395-05164-9 A young girl is kidnapped by the man who loves her—with tragic results.

Pamela (1740). Peter Sabor (ed). Penguin 1981 $5.95. ISBN 0-14-043140-3 A young servant girl fights off the lustful advances of her master, and her virtue is eventually rewarded.

BOOKS ABOUT RICHARDSON

Bloom, Harold (ed). *Samuel Richardson.* Chelsea 1987 $19.95. ISBN 1-55546-286-3 Succinct biography followed by a thorough collection of personal comments by his contemporaries, as well as critical essays on Richardson ranging from 1748 to 1900.

Harris, Jocelyn. *Samuel Richardson.* Cambridge Univ Pr 1987 $12.95. ISBN 0-512-31542-5 Concise introduction to Richardson, with a close reading of *Pamela, Clarissa,* and *Sir Charles Grandison,* with a discussion of central themes of each.

SHERIDAN, RICHARD BRINSLEY   1751–1816

Richard Brinsley Sheridan was born into a theatrical family in Dublin. His father, a theater manager, and his mother, a playwright and novelist, intended their son to study law. However, at school young Richard fell in love with Elizabeth Linley, a young singer, and eventually fought two duels for her honor. After their marriage he quickly turned to writing plays, and his first, *The Rivals* (1775), became a popular success. In this play Sheridan introduces his most famous character, Mrs. Malaprop, whose consistent misuse of words ("He was as headstrong as an allegory [alligator] on the banks of the Nile.") continues to delight audiences today. From Mrs. Malaprop comes the term *malapropism* to denote a misuse of words. Sheridan went on to write many popular plays before being elected to Parliament in 1780 and devoting the rest of his life to politics. His most famous, and probably best, play is *The School for Scandal* (1777), a comedy of manners mocking the shallowness and hypocrisy of upper-class society.

PLAYS BY SHERIDAN

The Rivals (1775). J. Lavin (ed). Norton 1980 $6.95. ISBN 0-393-90044-4 Young lovers in the resort city of Bath encounter obstacles and entanglements as the dashing Captain Jack Absolute pursues the lovely Lydia Languish.

The School for Scandal and Other Plays (1777). Eric S. Rump (ed). Penguin 1989 $6.95. ISBN 0-14-043240-X In *The School for Scandal* three London dandies pursue the same lovely lady with hilarious results.

BOOKS ABOUT SHERIDAN

Auburn, Mark S. *Sheridan's Comedies: The Contexts and Achievements.* Univ of Nebraska Pr 1974 $19.50. ISBN 0-8032-0914-2 Critical analysis of the comedies that draws on literary, historical, and theater contexts, establishing Sheridan as a practical playwright concerned with writing financially successful plays.

Darlington, William. *Sheridan.* Haskell 1974 $39.95. ISBN 0-8383-1926-2 General study of life and works; part of *Studies in Drama* series.

SWIFT, JONATHAN   1667–1745

Jonathan Swift was born in Dublin, Ireland, to English parents. His father died seven months before Swift was born. Although raised by an uncle in Ireland and educated at Kilkenny School and Trinity College in Dublin, Swift yearned to live in England. This wish was granted in 1689 when he became secretary to another relative, Sir William Temple, and settled in Temple's house in Surrey. Disappointed with his slow advancement, Swift took a Master's degree at Oxford University and entered the church. He was assigned to a small parish in Ireland and eventually rose to become Dean of St. Patrick's Cathedral in Dublin in 1713.

Throughout his clerical career Swift was busy writing poetry, pamphlets, and essays, most of which attacked various aspects of English society and politics. For a time he served as chief propagandist for the Tory (conservative) government. His chief literary talent lay in the writing of satire, and he is generally regarded as the major satirist of his age and one of the greatest in all of English literature. One of his best-known works is *A Modest Proposal,* in which he ironically suggests that Irish poverty be solved by selling Irish infants for food.

Swift's most famous work, and the only piece of writing for which he was ever paid, is *Gulliver's Travels* (1726). The book's hero, Gulliver, represents ordinary, decent people. He travels to a variety of strange lands, where he encounters all the weakness, vice, and corruption that Swift saw in his own society. Ironically, this bitter look at some of the most dehumanizing aspects of civilization has become something of a children's classic because of the fantastic, fairy-tale quality of Gulliver's travels.

PROSE BY SWIFT

Gulliver's Travels (1726). Penguin 1983 $2.25. ISBN 0-14-006507-5 Gulliver's adventures in strange lands among strange peoples, including tiny creatures, giants, and intelligent horses.
Gulliver's Travels and Other Writings. Bantam 1984 $2.95. ISBN 0-553-21232-X
Journal to Stella (1768) Academy Chi Pubs 1986 $6.95. ISBN 0-86299-111-0
The Portable Swift. Carl Van Doren (ed). Penguin 1977 $8.95. ISBN 0-14-015037-4
A Tale of a Tub (1704). Angus Ross and David Woodley (eds). Oxford Univ Pr 1986 $3.95. ISBN 0-19-281689-6

POETRY BY SWIFT

Poetical Works. Herbert Davis (ed). Oxford Univ Pr 1967 $37.50. ISBN 0-19-254161-7

BOOKS ABOUT SWIFT

Hunting, Robert. *Jonathan Swift.* G. K. Hall 1967 $16.95. ISBN 0-8057-1520-7 Concise introduction to Swift's best poetry and prose arranged in loose chronological order; contains a selected bibliography.
Tuveson, Ernest (ed). *Swift: A Collection of Critical Essays.* Prentice 1964. (o.p.) $12.95. Reliable collection of solid critical essays by highly respected scholars; contains a chronology and selected bibliography.

THE ROMANTIC PERIOD

The Romantic Period in British literature is generally considered to begin in 1798, when two young poets—William Wordsworth and Samuel Coleridge—published a volume of poetry called *The Lyrical Ballads.* Scholars generally end the period in 1832, when laws passed by Parliament signaled the beginning of a new era in British history. The Romantic Period is a brief, but intense period, filled with turbulence and radical change. Some of the greatest literature of the English-speaking world was produced during this period, and the ideas born in this age continue to live today.

Of course, the Romantic ideas did not spring to life suddenly in 1798, nor did they die with the passage of the Reform Bill in 1832. These ideas had been building throughout the eighteenth century. In fact, several of the authors generally identified as "Romantics" were publishing works as early as the 1770s. Their ideas influenced the American Revolution in 1776 and the French Revolution in 1789, and early versions of these ideas can be found in the poetry of Thomas Gray and William Cowper.

Romantic ideas grew out of the changes in the social and political climate of the Western world toward the end of the eighteenth century. The single word that best describes the nature of this change is "revolution"—revolution against governments, against social restrictions, against economic systems, and, in literature, against the forms and conventions of the 1700s.

The new writers rejected the Neoclassical concept of literature that "instructs and delights," and they rejected the old idea that the form of literature is more important than the content. They believed instead that literature, particularly poetry, should be the outpouring of personal emotions, the expression of the individual soul. Romantics believed that writing should be free and spontaneous rather than confined within rigid and predictable forms. Poetry, they said, should spring from the heart, not the mind, as if it were spoken freely and easily directly to the reader.

Romantic writers viewed nature not as the insignificant backdrop to the affairs of humans but as a powerful force of which humanity is merely a part. These writers saw themselves in nature and nature in themselves, so that a natural object or event such as a storm could represent human emotion, or a person could be described through comparisons with an animal.

Romantic writers also rejected the idea of literature expressing only the noble or the grand. Instead they chose to draw their subjects and their images from ordinary life. Instead of writing of kings and queens, they wrote of field hands and sailors.

Finally, Romantic writers looked for beauty in the supernatural and the strange. They turned to the worlds of folklore, dreams, and superstition for stories and images.

Six poets dominated this age. Three of them—William Wordsworth, Samuel Taylor Coleridge, and William Blake began the era, and three others—John Keats, Percy Bysshe Shelley, and George Gordon, Lord Byron—ended it. They were hardly alone, however. Sir Walter Scott brought Romanticism to the novel; Charles Lamb and Thomas De Quincey translated it into essays, and Robert Burns transformed the folk ballads of his native Scotland into a new kind of poetry. The enduring fame and popularity of these writers shows the power of the new literature that sprang from their pens.

BLAKE, WILLIAM   1757–1827

The son of a successful London man of business, William Blake received no formal education, but was schooled at home, primarily by his mother. He read widely, acquired a good knowledge of the classics, and learned four languages. At the age of 14, he was apprenticed to an engraver. Although he learned printing as well, eventually he made a living by engraving and through his art.

Blake was a visionary whose social criticism was far ahead of its day. In both his thought and his poetry, he resembled the later Romantics, although he lived in the eighteenth century. Therefore, his poetry was hardly noticed in his own day and was only fully appreciated by those who came after him. Since his death, the short poems collected in *The Songs of Innocence* (1789) and

The Songs of Experience (1794) have come to be recognized as among the finest in the English language.

Blake also developed a complex and mystical religious mythology. He imagined a kind of natural Christianity in which human beings were free to develop—and to love one another—without artificial restraints. Blake's genius has been fully appreciated only in this century, and an enormous body of commentary on his works has developed.

POETRY BY BLAKE

Selected Poetry. W. H. Stevenson (ed). Penguin 1989 $4.95. ISBN 0-14-05896-6
Songs of Experience (1794). Dover 1971 $3.50. ISBN 0-486-22764-1
Songs of Innocence (1789). Dover 1984 $3.50. ISBN 0-486-34636-1

NONFICTION BY BLAKE

Complete Writings of William Blake. Geoffrey Keynes (ed). Oxford Univ Pr 1966 $13.95. ISBN 0-19-281050-2
William Blake. Michael Mason (ed). Oxford Univ Pr 1988 $45.00. ISBN 0-19-254196-X
William Blake. Peter Porter (ed). Crown 1986 $6.95. ISBN 0-517-562291-X

BOOK ABOUT BLAKE

Frye, Northrup. *Fearful Symmetry: A Study of William Blake.* Princeton Univ Pr 1947 $14.95. ISBN 0-691-01291-1 Extended critical essay—and Frye's first book—placing Blake in a literary context.

BURNS, ROBERT   1759–1796

Robert Burns was the son of a poor farmer. Although he received a modest education at home, he was largely self-taught. His first book, *Poems, Chiefly in the Scottish Dialect* (1786), raised him from obscurity to great though short-lived fame. He struggled for the rest of his life against poverty, hard drinking, a quick temper, and a passionate nature. He died at the age of 37 from rheumatic fever and the effects of heavy drinking.

Burns is the greatest of Scotland's poets and was for generations one of the most popular of all poets in the English language. Songs like "Auld Lang Syne," and "A Red, Red Rose" are loved everywhere, and poems like "Tam O'Shanter" and "To a Mouse" are universal favorites. Although Burns died before the end of the eighteenth century, his love of the life and speech of ordinary people, especially farmers, and his devotion to individual liberty, mark him as a Romantic born before his time.

POETRY BY BURNS

Poems and Songs. James Kinsley (ed). Oxford Univ Pr 1969 $13.95. ISBN 0-19-281114-2

BOOK ABOUT BURNS

Lindsay, Maurice. *Robert Burns: The Man, His Works, the Legend.* State Mutual 1988 $35.00. ISBN 0-7091-7598-1 Popular study of Burns and his work, with bibliographic footnotes.

BYRON, LORD, GEORGE GORDON   1788–1824

The life of George Gordon, Lord Byron, was so notorious that it is almost impossible to disentangle fact from legend. His mother, Catherine Gordon, was descended from King James I of Scotland. His father, Captain "Mad Jack"

Byron, was a spendthrift who squandered his wife's money as well as his own and eventually had to flee to France to avoid his creditors. The captain died when Byron was only three years old, and the boy was raised in Scotland by his mother and her family. At age 10 he unexpectedly inherited his uncle's title and estate and became the sixth Baron Byron of Rochdale. He was given the finest education but gained a reputation for wildness at Cambridge University. Incredibly handsome and dashing, he soon became known as a notorious womanizer.

Byron's poetry was no less sensational than his life. His poetic gifts were enormous, and he worked brilliantly in all poetic forms, from highly intellectual satires in the eighteenth-century tradition to swashbuckling narratives of high adventure. He was just 24 when he published *Childe Harold's Pilgrimage* (1812), a long narrative poem about exotic travels. Here was the first appearance of the "Byronic hero"—a powerful, mysterious figure, haunted by some nameless and unspeakable crime. The poem was an immediate success, and overnight Byron became the most sought-after figure in London society. He was a true celebrity in the modern sense of the word—famous for being famous. During the next three years, his escapades and amorous adventures were the talk of London, but involvement in a scandalous divorce caused him to leave England and never return.

On the continent Byron traveled widely, became friendly with the writers Percy and Mary Shelley (*see* M. Shelley *and* P. Shelley, Vol. 1, British Literature: The Romantic Period), and deepened his art. He worked on his masterpiece, *Don Juan* (pronounced "Joo-an") (1819–1824) but never completed it. Even the unfinished work, however, is now regarded as one of the great comic and satirical masterpieces of English poetry.

In a fitting ending to the life he led, Byron died "romantically," fighting in a war for Greek independence. It is said that on hearing the news of his death, women all over England wept openly, and the entire nation went into mourning.

POETRY BY BYRON

Byron: Poems. Penguin 1985 $6.95. ISBN 0-14-058507-0
Complete Poetical Works. James J. McGann (ed). 3 vols. Oxford Univ Pr 1981. Vol. 1 $64.00. ISBN 0-19-812763-4. Vol. 2 $64.00. ISBN 0-19-812764-2. Vol. 3 $64.00. ISBN 0-19-812765-0
Don Juan (1819–1824). Leslie Marchand (ed). Penguin 1988 $8.95. ISBN 0-14-042216-1

BOOKS ABOUT BYRON

Bloom, Harold (ed). *George Gordon, Lord Byron.* Chelsea 1986 $19.95. ISBN 0-87754-683-5 Collection of modern critical views of Byron's work.
Marchand, Leslie. *Byron: A Portrait.* Univ of Chicago Pr 1979 $7.95. ISBN 0-226-50536-0 One-volume condensation of Marchand's standard three-volume biography of Byron.

COLERIDGE, SAMUEL TAYLOR   1772–1834

Samuel Taylor Coleridge was the son of a vicar of a small village in Devon. Destined to follow in his father's footsteps, in 1791 he entered Cambridge University to study for the ministry. But he was drawn quickly to reformist and radical ideas and found life at university confining. He left in 1794 and never completed his degree. The following year, at the urging of his friend Robert Southey, he married Sara Fricker, a union that was to cause him great unhappiness in later years.

Coleridge wrote almost all of his great poems in just 14 months, soon after he and the poet William Wordsworth (*see* Wordsworth, Vol. 1, British Literature: The Romantic Period) became neighbors. These two young writers encouraged and inspired each other, and Coleridge wrote with a burst of enthusiasm that he was never to achieve again. *The Rime of the Ancient Mariner* (1798), "Kubla Khan" (1797), and the first part of "Christabel" (1798) were part of the production of this miraculous year, as were the best of the "Conversation Poems." It was also in 1798 that Coleridge and Wordsworth anonymously published *Lyrical Ballads,* which modern critics now cite as the beginning of the Romantic Age.

Four years later Coleridge was in deep despair. His "Dejection: An Ode" (1802) was a kind of heartbroken farewell to poetry. Opium addiction, a desperately unhappy private life, and severe psychological problems had combined to destroy the man's confidence and his capacity to work effectively. Coleridge never again wrote poetry of the high caliber of his 1797–98 works.

After 1816, Coleridge went to live with Dr. James Gilman, a physician who helped him fight his opium addiction. He continued to write, but worked almost entirely on literary criticism and social commentary. Although he produced important works in both these areas, it is for his unquestionably great poetry that Coleridge is best remembered.

POETRY BY COLERIDGE

Poems and Prose. Penguin 1985 $6.95. ISBN 0-14-058507-9
Poems of Samuel Taylor Coleridge. E. H. Coleridge (ed). Oxford Univ Pr 1912 $13.95. ISBN 0-19-281051-0
The Portable Coleridge. Ivor A. Richards (ed). Penguin 1977 $8.95. ISBN 0-14-015048-X

BOOKS ABOUT COLERIDGE

Bate, W. Jackson. *Coleridge.* Harvard Univ Pr 1987 $11.95. ISBN 0-674-13680-2 Biography that includes bibliographical footnotes.
Bloom, Harold (ed). *Samuel Taylor Coleridge.* Chelsea 1986 $24.50. ISBN 0-87754-684-3 Collection of modern criticism and interpretations.
Holmes, Richard. *Coleridge.* Oxford Univ Pr 1982 $4.95. ISBN 0-19-287591-4 Provides a unified portrait of Coleridge in which each work is given its place and a thematic treatment of Coleridge's writing.

KEATS, JOHN 1795–1821

The critic Douglas Bush has said that if one poet could be brought back to life to complete his career, the almost universal choice would be John Keats, who died at age 25 and is now regarded as one of the three or four supreme masters of English verse. Orphaned early, Keats trained for a medical career but gave it up to write poetry. His early work shows exceptional promise but is somewhat clumsy and unsure. His letters, on the other hand, are written casually but brilliantly, and show how constantly and diligently he worked to improve his skill.

In his tragically brief career, cut short by tuberculosis, Keats constantly experimented, often with dazzling success and always with steady progress. The unfinished poem *The Fall of Hyperion* (1820) is vastly superior to his earlier *Endymion* (1818) written just two years before. "Isabella" (1819) is a fine narrative poem, but "The Eve of St. Agnes" (1820), written a year later, is matchless. In every case Keats seems to have learned rapidly and well and to have improved on his earlier efforts.

Keats's supreme achievement lies in his development of the ode. In just a few months, he wrote "Ode on a Grecian Urn" (1820), "Ode to a Nightingale" (1820), "On Melancholy" (1820), and the marvelous "To Autumn" (1820). These poems, which approach perfection in their careful use of imagery and diction, have served as models for countless other poets.

Keats is the only Romantic poet whose reputation has steadily grown through all the changes in critical fashion. Once thought of as merely a poet of beautiful images but no serious thought, Keats is now appreciated for his powerful mind, sure grasp of poetic principles, and endless search for new forms and techniques.

POETRY BY KEATS

The Complete Poems. John Barnard (ed). Penguin 1977 $7.95. ISBN 0-14-042210-2

BOOKS ABOUT KEATS

Bate, W. Johnson. *John Keats.* Harvard Univ Pr 1979 $14.95. ISBN 0-674-47825-8 A life and critical analysis of Keats's poetry.
Bloom, Harold (ed). *John Keats.* Chelsea 1985 $24.50. ISBN 0-87754-608-8 A collection of modern critical views of Keats's work.

LAMB, CHARLES   1775–1834

Charles Lamb was born in London where his father was a clerk to a lawyer. He was educated at the same London school as Samuel Coleridge (*see* Coleridge, Vol. 1, British Literature: The Romantic Period), and the two became lifelong friends. Lamb served most of his life as a clerk for firms in London, so that his writing was only a sideline until his retirement in 1825. When his *Essays of Elia* (1823), the work for which he is best remembered, was published, he had already published some minor verse, a sentimental novel, an Elizabethan tragedy, extensive commentaries on Shakespeare's plays, two distinguished critical essays, and several books for children.

Lamb spent most of his life caring for his periodically insane sister, Mary, who had murdered their mother in a crazed rage. With Mary he published the well-known *Tales* from Shakespeare (1807), a retelling of the plays for young people. Aside from his essays, Lamb's major contribution to English literature was the friendship and support he gave to Coleridge and other writers of the Romantic Period.

POETRY BY LAMB

Lamb's Poetry for Children (1903). Ayer (repr of 1903 ed) $17.00. ISBN 0-8369-6113-7 Delightful collection of poems for younger people.

NONFICTION BY LAMB

Elia and The Last Essays of Elia (1823). Jonathan Bate (ed). Oxford Univ Pr 1987. ISBN 0-19-081764-7
The Portable Charles Lamb. John M. Brown (ed). Penguin 1980 $7.95 ISBN 0-14-015043-9
Tales from Shakespeare (1807). (coauthored with Mary Lamb) Penguin 1988 $2.25. ISBN 0-14-035088-8 Retelling of the plots of Shakespeare's plays.

BOOKS ABOUT LAMB

Barnett, George L. *Charles Lamb.* Irvington 1976 $17.95. ISBN 0-8057-6668-5 Biography tracing Lamb's life and works, with special focus on his essays and criticism.

Blunden, Edmund. *Charles Lamb and His Contemporaries.* Shoe String 1967 $26.00. ISBN 0-208-00461-0 Brief biography noting early influences and the development of Lamb's essay persona, Elia; originally delivered as lectures at Trinity College, Cambridge.

SCOTT, SIR WALTER   1771–1832

The son of an Edinburgh lawyer, Walter Scott was educated at the University of Edinburgh and in 1792 became a lawyer himself. Although he retained ties to the legal profession all his life, his primary interest was literature.

Scott began his literary career as a poet, composing long tales in verse that were enormously popular. *The Lay of the Last Minstrel* (1805), *Marmion* (1808), and *The Lady of the Lake* (1810) made him the most popular poet of his day. Sixty-five hundred copies of *The Lay of the Last Minstrel* were sold in the first three years after publication, a record for poetry sales at the time.

Scott's later romances in verse were not quite as popular, partly because of the works of the poet, Byron, who had begun to publish his own more passionate verse, which appealed greatly to the public.

Scott then abandoned poetry for the novel. In 1814 he published a historical novel, *Waverly,* the first of a series that have come to be known as the Waverly novels. He wrote 23 novels during the next 13 years. The Waverly novels range in setting from the year 1090 to 1700. In this magnificent series, Scott covered virtually every period in English history up to his own day. The most famous of these novels is *Ivanhoe,* the story of a young knight's adventures in love and war. The Waverly novels have historical backgrounds but are always based on fictitious central characters.

Novels by Scott

*The Bride of Lammermoor (1819). Biblio Dist 1979 $6.95. ISBN 0-460-01129-4 Story of the lovers Ravenswood and Lucy who are torn apart by a family feud.
*The Heart of Midlothian (1818). Biblio Dist 1980 $5.95. ISBN 0-460-01134-0 Effie Dean is accused of murdering her own child, but her sister Jeanie sets out to prove her innocence.
*Ivanhoe (1820). Bantam 1988 $3.50. ISBN 0-553-21326-1 Story of the struggles between the Norman conquerors and the native Saxons in twelfth-century England, told through the love story of Ivanhoe and Rowena.
*Kenilworth (1821). Airmont 1968 $2.25. ISBN 0-8049-0193-7 The events that led to the mysterious death of Amy Robsart in 1560.
*Quentin Durward (1823). Airmont 1969 $2.50. ISBN 0-8049-0312-5 Story of a young Scot of the 1400s caught up in the intrigues of King Louis XI of France.
*Waverly (1814). Penguin 1981 $5.95. ISBN 0-14-04307-2 Edward Waverly, a soldier, is torn between his loyalty to England and his love of Scotland.

Poetry by Scott

Complete Poetical Works. Houghton 1980 $8.95. ISBN 0-395-07493-2

Books about Scott

Lauber, John. *Sir Walter Scott.* G. K. Hall 1989 $19.95. ISBN 0-8057-6964-1 Includes a brief biographical sketch and chapters on Scott's poetry, critical essays, and novels.
Milgate, Jane. *Walter Scott: The Making of the Novelist.* Univ of Toronto Pr 1984 $14.95. ISBN 0-8020-6692-5 Criticism and interpretation with a bibliography.

SHELLEY, MARY WOLLSTONECRAFT   1797–1851

Mary Shelley was the daughter of William Godwin, the English philosopher and writer, and Mary Wollstonecraft, author of the *Vindication of the Rights of Women* (1792). At age 16 she fell in love with the poet Percy Shelley. (*See* P. Shelley, Vol. 1, British Literature: The Romantic Period.) In 1814 she ran off with him to the Continent. Two years later, after the death of his first wife, she married him.

Mary Shelley is best known for her novel of horror, *Frankenstein* (1818), which she wrote when Lord Byron (*see* Byron, Vol. 1, British Literature: The Romantic Period) proposed that he and each of his companions write a tale of the supernatural. *Frankenstein* was an immediate sensation, and none of her later work matches its power and style.

After Percy Shelley's death, Mary Shelley edited his writings and wrote biographies, articles, and fiction of her own to support herself and her son. Her use of a creation myth and her discussion of science in *Frankenstein*, along with her prominence as a struggling female writer, have made her of special interest to modern readers.

NOVELS BY SHELLEY

Falkner: A Novel. AMS (repr of 1837 ed) $44.50. ISBN 0-404-62110-4
The Fortunes of Perkin Warbeck: A Romance. AMS $84.50. ISBN 0-404-62114-7
*Frankenstein (1818). Maurice Hindle (ed). Penguin 1986 $2.25. ISBN 0-14-043237-X
    Story of a doctor who creates life and must live with the consequences.

SHORT STORY COLLECTIONS BY SHELLEY

Collected Tales and Stories. Charles E. Robinson (ed). Books Demand $105.50. ISBN 0-317-30463-1

BOOKS ABOUT SHELLEY

Mellor, Anne K. *Mary Shelley: Her life, Her Fiction, Her Monsters.* Routledge 1988 $14.95. ISBN 0-415-90147-2 Examines the entire range of Mary Shelley's life and writing, taking her out of the shadow of her famous husband and acknowledging the originality of *Frankenstein.*
Spark, Muriel. *Mary Shelley.* NAL 1988 $8.95. ISBN 0-452-00951-0 Commentary by the famous novelist on Mary Shelley's life and works; a revision of 1951 edition.
Sunstein, Emily W. *Mary Shelley: Romance and Reality.* Little 1989 $24.95. ISBN 0-316-82246-9 Biography of the creator of *Frankenstein*; for advanced readers.

SHELLEY, PERCY BYSSHE   1792–1822

The son of Sussex aristocrats, Percy Bysshe Shelley was by far the most radical of the English Romantic poets. For most of his adult life, he called for the complete overthrow of the existing order, especially that of organized religion.

Shelley was expelled from Oxford University because he refused to retract his atheistic beliefs. He soon quarreled with his wealthy father and was banished from home as well. He married impulsively and then abandoned his wife, running off to Italy with 16-year-old Mary Wollstonecraft Godwin, herself the daughter of radical parents (*see* M. Shelley, Vol. 1, British Literature: The Romantic Period). In Italy Shelley and the English poet Lord Byron (*see* Byron, Vol. 1, British Literature: The Romantic Period) became close friends and shared many adventures that made them the objects of endless, notorious rumor.

Shelley's generosity and kindness were praised by almost everyone who knew him. Extremely generous toward others and frugal with himself, he strove tirelessly for the betterment of humanity. For example, *Prometheus Unbound* (1820), a lyrical drama in four acts, calls for a rebirth of society through love and the elimination of all oppression. *Adonais* (pronounced A-doh-nay-iss) (1821), written to honor the memory of the poet John Keats, is one of the supreme elegies in English. *The Triumph of Life* (1822) has been hailed by the American-born poet and critic T. S. Eliot as the nearest approach in English to the Italian poet Dante's *Divine Comedy.*

Shelley's lyrics are marvelously varied and rich in sound and rhythm. "Like a star of Heaven / In the broad daylight / Thou art unseen—but yet I hear thy shrill delight," he wrote in "To a Skylark." This ecstatic praise of nature contrasts sharply with the harsh rhythms of his political critique in the sonnet "England in 1819": "An old, mad, blind, despised, and dying King; / Princes, the dregs of their dull race, who flow / Through public scorn—mud from a muddy spring. . . ." William Wordsworth regarded Shelley as the best poet then living.

Shelley's life was cut short at the age of 30, when he drowned in a boating accident in Italy. Like Keats (*see* Keats, Vol. 1, British Literature: The Romantic Period), his early death has left future generations frustrated at the thought of what he might have produced if he had lived longer. The extent to which his lines are quoted and his poems anthologized gives testimony to his enduring popularity.

POETRY BY SHELLEY

Poems. Penguin 1985 $4.95. ISBN 0-14-058504-4

NONFICTION BY SHELLEY

Political Writings. Harlan Davidson 1970 $1.95. ISBN 0-88295-089-4
Selected Essays on Atheism. Ayer $13.00. ISBN 0-405-03794-5

BOOKS ABOUT SHELLEY

Allott, Miriam (ed). *Essays on Shelley.* Barnes 1982 $28.50. ISBN 0-389-20127-8 Analysis of Shelley's thought, work, and reputation.
Pirie, David. *Shelley.* Taylor & Francis 1988 $13.00. ISBN 0-335-15082-9 Critical studies of Shelley's work that attempt to define his particular approach to Romanticism and to illustrate his influence on the movement.
Reiman, Donald H. *Percy Bysshe Shelley.* G. K. Hall 1970 $13.50. ISBN 0-8057-1488-X General introduction; "Twayne series" overview integrating Shelley's life and work.

WORDSWORTH, WILLIAM 1770–1850

Born in the Lake District of northern England, William Wordsworth was orphaned early, had an undistinguished career at Cambridge University, spent a year in France during the French Revolution, and returned to England a penniless radical. For five years he and his sister Dorothy lived very frugally in rural England, where they met Samuel Taylor Coleridge. (*See* Coleridge, Vol. 1, British Literature: The Romantic Period.)

Wordsworth and Coleridge formed a close friendship and decided to collaborate on a collection of a new kind of poetry. Called *The Lyrical Ballads* (1798), the volume opened with Coleridge's *The Rime of the Ancient Mariner* and ended with Wordsworth's *Tintern Abbey.* Between these two masterworks are at least a dozen other great poems. *Lyrical Ballads* is often said to mark the beginning of the English Romantic movement. In the second edition of the work, published in 1800, Wordsworth wrote a preface that still stands as the best description of the philosophy of the Romantic poets. In the preface he called for natural diction in poetry, subject matter dealing with ordinary men and women, and a return to emotions and the imagination. Literary critics, however, violently attacked the preface and the poems.

Before he was 30, Wordsworth had begun the supreme work of his life, *The Prelude* (1850), a long autobiographical work on "The Growth of the Poet's Mind," a theme never attempted before in poetry. Although finished in 1805, *The Prelude* was never published in Wordsworth's lifetime. Between 1797 and 1807, Wordsworth produced a steady stream of other magnificent poems, but little of his work from the last 40 years of his life is very remarkable.

After *Lyrical Ballads* Wordsworth turned for themes to his own life, his spiritual development, and his growth as a poet. More than any other poet of his time, he dealt with the mysterious bond between nature and humanity, and to this day is regarded as the most "nature-oriented" of the Romantics. His best-known works include "Lines Written on Westminster Bridge," a meditation on the futility of war, and "I Wandered Lonely as a Cloud," in which the poet describes the joy of seeing a field of daffodils.

POETRY BY WORDSWORTH

The Poems. 2 vols. Penguin 1989. Vol. 1 $12.95. ISBN 0-14-04211-0. Vol. 2 $12.95. ISBN 0-14-04212-9
Poems. W. E. Williams (ed). Penguin 1985 $4.95. ISBN 0-14-058506-0

BOOKS ABOUT WORDSWORTH

Durrant, Geoffrey H. *William Wordsworth.* Cambridge Univ Pr 1969 $10.95. ISBN 0-521-09584-0 Detailed critical studies of Wordsworth's major poems, focusing on the works themselves rather than biographical or historical background.
Noyes, Russell. *William Wordsworth.* G. K. Hall 1972 $15.95. ISBN 0-8057-1580-0 General introduction to Wordsworth's life and work.

THE VICTORIAN AGE

The Victorian Age is commonly dated by the reign of Queen Victoria. When Victoria was crowned Queen of Britain in 1837, London had about 2 million inhabitants; when she died in 1901, the city had a population of 6.5 million. That kind of growth was typical of her reign, the period of the greatest economic and political expansion in English history. At home the Industrial Revolution, which had begun at the end of the eighteenth century, swept the entire country. New factories, new roads, even entire new towns, seemed to appear overnight. Abroad, the British Empire, begun during the reign of Elizabeth I, grew equally swiftly, providing both the raw materials and the markets for Britain's new industries.

This new expansion brought prosperity and the feeling that anything was possible. The idea of progress, of the human race moving steadily ahead to a brighter future, had a strong hold on British society. In part this optimism was the result of a new faith in the power of science to solve human problems. Inventions like the telegraph, steam-powered looms and printing presses, faster railroad trains, and steam tractors and combines gave people the sense that science was unlocking the secrets of nature and was about to provide a good life for everyone.

Yet beneath this optimistic faith in progress and prosperity lay the reality of young children working overly long hours in dangerous factories, farmers driven from their land with no place to go, air and water pollution so bad that at times Parliament had to adjourn because of the stench from the Thames River, and women who had virtually no legal or political rights. Although most Britons were aware of these problems, many dismissed them as mere "growing pains," temporary conditions that would be cured by time and prosperity. Others were more deeply concerned and demanded new laws to strengthen the rights of workers, farmers, women, and children. By the end of Victoria's reign, life for the lower classes had improved considerably. Women had gained many new legal rights protecting their persons and property and were on their way to gaining the right to vote. Children were no longer working in unsafe factories. Nevertheless, serious problems still remained.

The idea of progress also affected the literature of the period. Unlike the early Romantics, the Victorians saw no need for radically reforming literature. Progress meant development, refinement, and improvement, not revolutionary change. Therefore, the Victorians continued to use the same basic literary forms and styles as the Romantics, seeking only to perfect them rather than change them.

The idea of progress also implied moral change for the better, and many Victorian writers sought to use literature to improve humanity. In their poems, stories, and novels, they explored human nature, exposed its weaknesses, and demonstrated how people could become better human beings. If the purpose of literature had once been to "delight and instruct," the emphasis in much of Victorian literature shifted from delight to instruction.

This does not mean that Victorian literature was dull. The novels of Charles Dickens and Thomas Hardy, for example, are often serious and dark, but they also provide wonderful reading. Likewise, the stories of Sir Arthur Conan Doyle, Rudyard Kipling, and Lewis Carroll still provide readers with endless delight. The poetry of Elizabeth Barrett Browning, Robert Browning, Alfred, Lord Tennyson, Matthew Arnold, and Rudyard Kipling continues to please readers to this day. The lessons Victorian writers tried to teach were frequently contained in powerful, absorbing literature—literature intended to raise questions and prod the reader to think. Many of these questions, about greed, about the corrupting influence of power, about the justness of poverty in a wealthy society, are still being asked.

ARNOLD, MATTHEW   1822–1888

Matthew Arnold was the son of Thomas Arnold, the headmaster who made Rugby (a private school for boys) into one of the best schools of its day. Matthew Arnold attended Rugby before moving on to Oxford University, where he was an unexceptional student except for winning a major prize for poetry. After completing his studies, he taught at Oxford briefly before becoming private secretary to an influential aristocrat. In 1851 he was appointed an inspector of schools, a position he held for the rest of his life. He published his first volume of poems, *The Strayed Reveller and Other Poems* in 1849 and went on to publish five more volumes before giving up poetry in 1867. In 1858, just as his poetic career was drawing to a close, he became Professor of Poetry at Oxford.

Arnold's work as inspector of schools brought him into close contact with the poverty and other social problems of Victorian England, which greatly influenced his thinking and writing. By 1860 he had turned almost entirely to writing literary criticism and essays on social problems, especially those involving education. He became known as one of the leading thinkers of his time and one of the most outspoken champions of social change.

Arnold's poetry has an air of melancholy, almost of quiet despair and shows little of the optimism or joy found in other Victorian poets. He seems at times to be almost overwhelmed by the problems of his time and frustrated by his powerlessness to do anything about them. He often seems to be a man trapped in a time with which he is out of tune. Yet his lyrics have a haunting quality that makes them difficult to forget and that keeps them popular with modern readers. "Dover Beach" (1867) has proved to be especially enduring in its claim that love is the only certainty in an uncertain world.

POETRY BY ARNOLD

Poems of Matthew Arnold. Kenneth Allott (ed). Longman 1979 $19.95. ISBN 0-882-48679-3

NONFICTION BY ARNOLD

Poetry and Criticism of Matthew Arnold. A. D. Culler (ed). Houghton 1961 $8.36. ISBN 0-395-05152-5
Selected Prose. P. J. Keating (ed). Penguin 1983 $7.95. ISBN 0-14-043058-X

BOOKS ABOUT ARNOLD

Honan, Park. *Matthew Arnold: A Life.* Harvard Univ Pr 1983 $12.50. ISBN 0-674-55465-5 The definitive biography; presents Arnold's development as an influential social thinker, literary critic, and poet.
Trilling, Lionel. *Matthew Arnold.* Harcourt 1979 $6.95. ISBN 0-15-657734-8 Focuses on development of Arnold's thought in relation to his times.

BRONTE, CHARLOTTE 1816–1855

Charlotte Brontë was the daughter of an eccentric clergyman who was curate of a small congregation in the isolated moorlands of Yorkshire. Her mother died when Brontë was only five, and she and her brother Branwell and sisters Anne and Emily (*see* E. Brontë, Vol. 1, British Literature: The Victorian Age) were raised by a stern aunt and their cold and busy father. The children drew closely together and relied on one another for comfort and companionship. While they attended nearby schools, they got most of their education from their father's books. They were also possessed of vivid imaginations and spent long hours writing stories and creating imaginary characters and worlds.

In 1824 Brontë and her two sisters were sent to a school for daughters of the clergy. They were generally unhappy there and returned home after only a year. They continued to share stories, write, and wander the lonely moors, a landscape which became a powerful influence in their lives. In 1835 Brontë tried teaching school, but gave it up after a few years to become a governess (a private tutor). Both experiences figured strongly in her later fiction. In 1842 she went to Belgium to learn how to run a private school. While there she became attached to her professor, a married man.

Brontë's first novel, *The Professor* (1857), was based on her experiences in Belgium. Rejected by several publishers, it was not printed until after her death. Her second novel, *Jane Eyre,* based in part on her experience as a governess, was published in 1847 and became an instant success. Brontë went on to write *Shirley* (1849), a novel about industrial strife, and *Villette* (1853), her masterpiece, about a shy schoolteacher's search for identity and love. These novels also drew on incidents from her own life and, like *Jane Eyre,* present a bleak view of the fate of a sensitive woman in a hostile society. This was a theme not previously treated in English fiction and, coupled with her insights into the psychology of loneliness and insecurity, contribute to Brontë's enduring popularity.

NOVELS BY BRONTE

Jane Eyre (1847). Bantam 1983 $1.95. ISBN 0-553-21140-4 The life and adventures of a young woman who comes to Thornfield Hall as a governess and falls in love with the Hall's mysterious owner, Mr. Rochester.

Shirley (1849). Margaret Smith and Herbert Rosengarten (eds). Oxford Univ Pr 1987 $4.95. ISBN 0-19-281562-8

Villette (1853). Mark Lilly (ed). Penguin 1980. $5.95. ISBN 0-14-043118-7

BOOKS ABOUT BRONTE

Berg, Maggie. *Jane Eyre: Portrait of a Life*. Twayne 1987 $18.95. ISBN 0-8057-7955-8 Emphasizes the autobiographical aspects of the novel.

Blom, Margaret. *Charlotte Brontë*. Twayne 1977 $16.95. ISBN 0-8057-6673-1 A critical study of the life and works of Brontë; suitable for young adults.

Fraser, Rebecca. *The Brontës: Charlotte Brontë and Her Family*. Fawcett 1990 $12.95. ISBN 449-90465-2 Feminist perspective that includes detailed sketches of Brontë's husband and publisher based on the discovery of previously unknown documents.

Gaskell, Elizabeth. *The Life of Charlotte Brontë*. Biblio Dist 1982 $4.95. ISBN 0-460-01318-1 Biography that gives a personal perspective—the author knew Charlotte Brontë personally—but that lacks reference to much material discovered later. First published in 1857.

BRONTE, EMILY   1818–1848

Emily Brontë, the sister of Charlotte (*see* C. Brontë, Vol. 1, British Literature: The Victorian Age), shared the same isolated childhood on the Yorkshire moors. Emily, however, seems to have been much more affected by the eerie desolation of the moors than was Charlotte. Her one novel, *Wuthering Heights* (1847), draws much of its power from its setting in that desolate landscape. Emily's work is also marked by a passionate intensity that is sometimes overpowering. According to English poet and critic Matthew Arnold, "for passion, vehemence, and grief she had no equal since Byron." This passion is evident in the poetry she contributed to the collection *(Poems by Currer, Ellis and Acton Bell)* published by the Brontë sisters in 1846 under male pseudonyms in response to the prejudices of the time. Her passion reaches full force, however, in her novel, *Wuthering Heights.*

Brontë's novel defies easy classification. It is certainly a story of love, but just as certainly it is not a "love story." It is a psychological novel, but is so filled with hints of the supernatural and mystical that the reader is unsure of how much control the characters have over their own actions. It may seem to be a study of right and wrong, but is actually a study of good and evil. Above all, it is a novel of power and fierce intensity that has gripped readers for more than 100 years.

BOOKS BY BRONTE

Complete Poems of Emily J. Brontë. C. W. Hatfield (ed). Columbia Univ Pr $27.50. ISBN 0-231-01222-5

Wuthering Heights (1847). Richard Dunn (ed). Norton 1989 $6.95. ISBN 0-393-95760-8 Story of a strange love affair between two brooding people who seem bent on hurting each other.

Books about Bronte

Benvenuto, Richard. *Emily Brontë.* G. K. Hall 1982 $12.50. ISBN 0-8057-7436-X Focuses on Brontë's independent spirit and surveys the various readings of *Wuthering Heights.*

Frank, Katharine. *A Chainless Soul: A Life of Emily Brontë.* Houghton 1990 $21.95. ISBN 0-395-42508-5 Attempts to demythologize the sentimental version of the Brontë family's story by focusing on Emily's eating disorder—anorexia—and the references to food in her work.

Gerin, Winifred. *Emily Brontë.* Oxford Univ Pr 1971 $9.95. ISBN 0-19-281251-3 Separates the facts about Brontë from the inferences and focuses on her development as a person.

*Pollard, Arthur. *The Landscape of the Brontës.* Dutton 1988 $22.95. ISBN 0-525-24637-1 A richly illustrated book that recreates the lives and the countryside.

BROWNING, ELIZABETH BARRETT 1806–1861

Elizabeth Barrett was born near Durham, England, the daughter of a successful father and the eldest of 12 children. She received a good education at home and showed promise as a writer while still young. As a young girl, she was taken seriously ill, and only partially recovered. When she was 30, her family moved to London, where she continued to write and eventually published *The Seraphim and Other Poems* in 1838. Hindered by poor health and grief over the sudden deaths of two brothers, she produced little more until the publication of *Poems* in 1844, a volume that received high praise and made her famous. It also prompted a letter from one of her admirers, Robert Browning (*see* R. Browning, Vol. 1, British Literature: The Victorian Age), with whom she began a correspondence that eventually led to their elopement in 1846.

Because of her father's strong objection to the marriage, the couple lived in Italy, where Barrett Browning completed an additional volume of *Poems* (1850). This work contained her most famous verses, "Sonnets from the Portuguese," love poems she wrote to Browning during their courtship. In 1856, Barrett Browning published *Aurora Leigh* (1856), her most ambitious work. *Aurora Leigh* is a long narrative poem describing the development of a poet's mind and the growth of a woman's art while touching on most of the serious problems of Victorian society. It was widely praised and made Elizabeth Barrett Browning one of the foremost poets of her day.

Barrett Browning has been known primarily as a composer of love sonnets, but with the recent interest in women writers, the rest of her work is again receiving attention.

Poetry by Browning

Poetical Works. Houghton 1974 $24.95. ISBN 0-395-18012-0
Sonnets from the Portuguese and Other Love Poems. Doubleday 1954 $10.95. ISBN 0-385-01463-5

Books about Browning

*Beiser, Rudolph. *The Barretts of Wimpole Street.* Little 1930 $14.95. ISBN 0-316-09223 Story of the Barrett family in London and Elizabeth and Robert Browning's courtship.

Forster, Margaret. *Elizabeth Barrett Browning.* Doubleday 1989 $19.95. ISBN 0-385-24959-4 Exceptional biography by noted novelist; winner of the Royal Society of Literature award.

*Forster, Margaret. *Lady's Maid.* Doubleday 1989 $21.95. ISBN 0-385-41792-6 Novel about the relationship between Elizabeth Barrett Browning and her lady's maid.

Woolf, Virginia. *Flush: A Biography.* Harcourt 1986 $4.95. ISBN 0-15-631952-7 The life of Elizabeth Barrett as seen through the eyes of her dog, Flush.

BROWNING, ROBERT   1812–1889

The son of a scholarly bank clerk, Robert Browning did not receive much formal education. He did, however, read widely in his father's extensive library at home, where he continued to live until his marriage to the poet Elizabeth Barrett (*see* E. Browning, Vol. 1, British Literature: The Victorian Age) in 1846. Because of her family's strong objection to the marriage, the couple moved to Italy, where they both continued to write and publish poetry. Throughout this period, Elizabeth was the better known of the pair, and it was not until after her death in 1861 when Robert returned to England that he began to achieve recognition for his work.

Browning began to write poetry early and published his first poem, *Pauline,* in 1833. He constantly experimented with new poetic forms and subject matter and, as a result, developed a reputation for being "obscure" and difficult to read, a charge that continues to be directed against him to this day. He has also been criticized for taking a neutral, almost unconcerned stance toward the social problems that so absorbed other Victorian writers.

Unlike most poets of his day, Browning did not write his poems as if they were direct statements from the poet to the reader. Instead he adopted a form known as the dramatic monologue in which a character speaks the lines as if acting in a play. Thus Browning created not only some of the most powerful poetry of the Victorian age, but also some of its most memorable characters, such as the Duke in "My Last Duchess," who drives his wife to her death. In his best poems of this type, Browning presents the reader with a convincing explanation of character and action without directly describing either—*how* the Duke causes the death, for example, is left chillingly ambiguous. Likewise, he avoided "poetic" language and lush images, choosing instead direct and sometimes even blunt expression. As a result, his poems have a strength and vigor not normally associated with nineteenth-century verse.

POETRY BY ROBERT BROWNING

The Poems. 2 vols. Penguin 1989. Vol. 1 $14.95. ISBN 0-14-042259-5. Vol. 2 $14.95. ISBN 0-14-042260-9

BOOKS ABOUT BROWNING

Bloom, Harold, and Adrienne Munich. *Robert Browning: A Collection of Critical Essays.* Prentice 1979 $7.95. ISBN 0-13-781476-3 Essays focusing on Browning's individual works, poetics, and thought.

Pearsall, Robert B. *Robert Browning.* G. K. Hall 1974 $17.95. ISBN 0-8057-1065-5 Places Browning's works in the context of his life.

CARROLL, LEWIS (PSEUDONYM OF REV. CHARLES LUTWIDGE DODGSON)   1832–1898

Born the son of a clergyman, Lewis Carroll was educated at Rugby and Oxford University, where he studied mathematics and where he eventually obtained a teaching position. In 1861 he was ordained as a priest in the Church of England. However, his extreme shyness and a lifelong problem with stuttering prevented him from doing much lecturing or preaching. He continued his study of mathematics and published works on geometry, algebra, and mathematical logic. As an adult he had the reputation of being eccentric and withdrawn.

In his diary of July 4, 1862, Carroll described "an expedition up the river to Godstowe with the three Lidells," the daughters of the dean of Christ's Church College, "on which occasion I told them the fairy tale of 'Alice's Adventures Underground,' which I undertook to write out for Alice." Thus began the history of one of the most famous children's stories ever written— one that changed the nature of children's literature forever by establishing that a story could be enjoyable for its own sake and not necessarily teach anything. Carroll followed *Alice's Adventures in Wonderland* (1865) with *Through the Looking Glass* (1872), both of which are almost always published together as a single book. He then went on to produce some of the best nonsense verse in the English language, including *The Hunting of the Snark* (1876).

Carroll's talent for mathematical puzzles, his marvelous ear for the sounds of words, his sense of the absurd, and his ability to see the world through a child's eyes have made his books favorites with generations of children. In recent years, however, he has been taken more seriously as a literary artist, and critics have discovered deeper symbolic and psychological meaning in his works.

NOVELS AND POETRY BY CARROLL

*Complete Works. Vintage 1976 $9.95. ISBN 394-71661-2 Contains *Alice in Wonderland, Through the Looking Glass, The Hunting of the Snark, Sylvie and Bruno, A Tangled Tale, Phantasmagoria,* as well as Carroll's verses, stories, games, puzzles, problems, and acrostics.

BOOKS ABOUT CARROLL

Clark, Beverly L. *Lewis Carroll.* Starmont 1989 $17.95. ISBN 0-8095-5000-8 Reader's guide emphasizing fantasy qualities of Carroll's work.

Kelly, Richard. *Lewis Carroll.* Twayne 1990 $18.95. ISBN 0-8057-6988-9 Critical survey of Carroll's writings, with concentration on Alice books.

COLLINS, WILKIE   1824–1889

Wilkie Collins was the son of a famous landscape painter. Although he showed an early desire to write, his father objected, so Collins studied law instead. Nevertheless, by the time he was 24, he had determined to give his full attention to writing. This ambition was encouraged by Charles Dickens (*see* Dickens, Vol. 1, British Literature: The Victorian Age), with whom he maintained a lifelong friendship and with whom he coauthored some minor works.

Collins tried his hand at a variety of literary forms, including plays and historical novels, but it was not until the publication of *The Woman in White* (1860), the first of his mystery novels, that he gained real fame. He followed this novel with three others: *No Name* (1862), *Armadale* (1866), and his best work, *The Moonstone* (1868). *The Moonstone* is generally regarded as the first detective novel in English and clearly shows Collins to be a master of both plot and suspense. The novelist's job, according to Collins, is to "make 'em laugh, make 'em cry, make 'em wait," all of which he did extremely well.

NOVELS BY COLLINS

*The Moonstone (1868). Biblio Dist 1977 $4.95. ISBN 0-460-01979-1 The unraveling of the mystery of the theft of a fabulous diamond, known as the moonstone.

*The Woman in White (1860). Julian Symons (ed). Penguin 1975 $3.95. ISBN 0-14-043096-2 The trials of Walter Hartright as he tries to discover the secret of the mysterious woman in white.

BOOK ABOUT COLLINS

Sayers, Dorothy L. *Wilkie Collins: A Critical and Biographical Study.* E. R. Gregory (ed). Friends Univ of Toledo 1977 $12.50. ISBN 0-918160-4 Study by noted mystery writer emphasizing Collins' influence on the mystery novel.

DICKENS, CHARLES   1812–1870

Charles Dickens's father, a clerk in the Navy pay office, was a pleasant, easygoing man who was almost constantly in debt. He was eventually sent to debtor's prison where he lived with Charles and his mother for a short time. Eventually the family slipped into complete poverty and young Dickens, at the age of 12, was sent to work in a factory, a humiliation he never forgot. Upon his father's release from prison, Dickens returned to school briefly, but left at age 15 to become a clerk in a law office, where he learned shorthand. Three years later he became a reporter for a London newspaper, and soon he was selling short articles and sketches to magazines. These sketches were published in 1836 in a volume called *Sketches by Boz.* They were a success, and Dickens's literary career had begun.

Dickens followed *Sketches by Boz* with the even more popular *The Pickwick Papers* (1836–1837), which like all of his novels was first published in serial form in magazines. Because he usually began publication of a new novel before he had finished writing it, he was always under pressure to complete the next installment. The pressure of having to meet deadlines seemed only to spur him to greater effort, however, and over the next several years, he produced a series of important and popular novels including *Oliver Twist* (1837–1839), *Nicholas Nickleby* (1838–1839) (the story of young Nicholas Nickleby, a fatherless youth, and his miserly uncle), *The Old Curiosity Shop* (1840–41), *Barnaby Rudge* (1841) (a historical romance set in the late eighteenth century, showing the effect of the anti-Catholic Gordon riots on a humble family and a pair of young lovers), *A Christmas Carol* (1843), and *Dombey and Son* (1846–1848) (the story of the merchant Dombey, his efforts to bring his unwilling son into his business, and his mistreatment of his faithful daughter).

Dickens made two trips to America for reading and lecture tours, in 1842 and 1867. He was extremely critical of the United States, writing both the novel *Martin Chuzzlewit* (1843–1844) as well as several articles criticizing Americans. *Martin Chuzzlewit* is the story of the selfish young architect Martin Chuzzlewit and the difficulties he encounters when he goes to seek his fortune in America: rude, tobacco-chewing Americans, a land swindle out West, and a climate that brings on fever.

In the books of this period, Dickens's flair for comic writing is evident. These books use comic techniques, such as satire and caricature, to comment on significant themes. The last novel of this type was *David Copperfield* (1850), Dickens's own "favorite child," in which he draws most heavily on his own childhood and youth for material.

After *David Copperfield*, Dickens's novels become increasingly serious and more pessimistic. Where he once had seen the possibility for society to improve itself, he now saw society as oppressing and crushing human beings. While he never lost his belief in the power of special people to rise above their circumstances and lead rich, full lives, he increasingly came to feel that for the masses there was little hope.

Perhaps ironically, Dickens's gloom produced some of his best writing. *Bleak House* concerns the failure of the British courts to produce justice, and contains brilliant descriptions of the dark, foggy streets of London. *Hard Times* tells the story of labor struggles in industrial England, featuring Dickens's striking images of a town that itself is like a factory, devouring all who live there and forcing them to become as similar as manufactured products. *Little Dorrit* takes up the British debtors' prisons, where bankrupt men used to be held with their families, portraying the difficulties of life for the children who grew up there.

Dickens's final work was left unfinished at his death. *The Mystery of Edwin Drood* tells the story of a young engineer who is reported missing, apparently killed. Literary critics argue over who committed the murder—and even over whether Drood actually was killed or whether he sailed for India—but Dickens left no notes and the mystery remains unsolved.

Dickens's contribution to English literature is immense. Not only did he leave the world a marvelous collection of stories and characters, but he also left a picture of Victorian society which, right or wrong, lives to this day.

NOVELS BY DICKENS

Barnaby Rudge (1841). G. W. Spence (ed). Penguin 1974 $5.95. ISBN 0-14-043090-3
Bleak House (1852–53). Bantam 1985 $4.95. ISBN 0-553-21223-0
*A Christmas Carol (1843). Bantam 1986 $1.95. ISBN 0-553-21244-3 The past, present, and future come together to help miser Ebeneezer Scrooge discover the true meaning of Christmas.
*David Copperfield (1849–50). Bantam 1981 $3.50. ISBN 0-553-21189-7 Story of a young boy's growth to manhood and the people he meets along the way.
Dombey and Son (1846–48). Penguin 1970 $5.95. ISBN 0-14-043048-2
*Great Expectations (1861). Bantam 1982 $3.95. ISBN 0-553-21265-6 The story of Pip, a poor young boy whose whole life changes when he receives a fortune from a mysterious donor.
Hard Times (1854). Bantam 1981 $2.25. ISBN 0-553-21016-5
Little Dorrit (1855–57). Penguin 1968 $5.95. ISBN 0-14-043025-3
Martin Chuzzlewit (1843–44). Penguin 1968 $6.95. ISBN 0-14-043031-8
The Mystery of Edwin Drood (1870). A. Cox (ed). Penguin 1986 $3.95. ISBN 0-14-009258-X
Nicholas Nickleby (1838–39). Bantam 1981 $4.95. ISBN 0-553-21265-6
*The Old Curiosity Shop (1840–41). Penguin 1972 $5.95. ISBN 0-14-043075-X The trials of Little Nell and her grandfather, who are hounded by the evil Daniel Quilp.
*Oliver Twist (1839). Bantam 1982 $2.50. ISBN 0-553-21102-1 The young orphan Oliver falls in with criminals that keep him from his kindly benefactor.
*The Pickwick Papers (1836–37). Bantam 1983 $4.95. ISBN 0-553-21123-4 The humorous adventures of Samuel Pickwick, his servant Sam Weller, and the other gentlemen of the Pickwick Club.
*A Tale of Two Cities (1859). Bantam 1989 $2.50. ISBN 0-553-21176-5 Story of the French Revolution and three young people caught up in its turmoil.

SHORT STORIES BY DICKENS

*Selected Short Fiction. Deborah A. Thomas (ed). Penguin 1976 $4.95. ISBN 0-14-043103-9 Tales of the supernatural and sketches of London life in the 1840s.

BOOKS ABOUT DICKENS

Bloom, Harold (ed). *Charles Dickens.* Chelsea 1987 $29.50. ISBN 0-87754-690-8 Collection of modern critical essays on Dickens.
*Goodman, Nancy. *Charles Dickens: Master Storyteller.* Kipling 1988 $7.95. ISBN 0-943718-34-1 Biography for young readers focusing on Dickens's sentimentality, humor, and social realism.
*Hornback, Bert G. *Great Expectations: A Novel of Friendship.* Twayne 1987 $17.95. ISBN 0-8057-7956-6 A critical analysis of this novel.
*Marcus, Steven. *Dickens: From Pickwick to Dombey.* Norton 1987 $6.95. ISBN 0-393-30286-5 A guide to the seven novels written during Dickens's early period.
Miller, J. Hillis. *Charles Dickens: The World of His Novels.* Harvard Univ Pr 1959 $22.50. ISBN 0-674-11000-5 Study of Dickens's novels from a social and cultural perspective.

DOYLE, SIR ARTHUR CONAN 1859–1930

Educated to be a physician at the University of Edinburgh, Arthur Conan Doyle decided in 1887 to add to his small income by doing some writing. That year he published a detective story called *A Study in Scarlet* (1887) and introduced to the world Sherlock Holmes, perhaps the most famous fictional character ever invented.

Conan Doyle went on to write other adventure novels before beginning in 1891 to regularly contribute Sherlock Holmes stories to the *Strand Magazine*. These extremely popular stories were eventually collected in *The Adventures of Sherlock Holmes* (1892) and *The Memoirs of Sherlock Holmes* (1894). In December of 1893, feeling that he was becoming trapped as a writer by his own creation, Conan Doyle attempted to kill off Holmes in one of his stories by having him plunge off a cliff together with his arch-enemy, Professor Moriarty. The reading public was outraged, and Conan Doyle was forced by popular demand to bring back his character. A new series of stories appeared in the *Strand* and were collected in 1905 in *The Return of Sherlock Holmes*.

Despite the enormous popularity of the Holmes adventures, Conan Doyle always resented being identified primarily as the writer who created Sherlock Holmes, believing that his other fiction was also worthy of recognition. However, little of his other work remains in print, while Holmes thrives on both the printed page as well as on film and television.

NOVELS AND STORIES BY DOYLE

*The Annotated Sherlock Holmes: The Four Novels and the Fifty-six Short Stories Complete. William S. Baring-Gould (ed). Crown 1986 $55.00. ISBN 0-517-56455-6 Contains all 56 stories and all four novels, with many terms and references clearly annotated and explained.

*Sherlock Holmes: The Complete Novels and Stories 2 vols. Bantam 1988. Vol. 1 $4.95. ISBN 0-553-21241-9. Vol. 2 $4.95. ISBN 0-553-21242-7 Contains all 56 stories and all four novels: *A Study in Scarlet* (1887), *The Sign of the Four* (1890), *The Hound of the Baskervilles* (1902), and *His Last Bow* (1917).

BOOKS ABOUT DOYLE

Carr, John D. *The Life of Sir Arthur Conan Doyle.* Carroll & Graf 1987 $8.95. ISBN 0-88184-372-5 Careful biography with the feel of a novel, based on Conan Doyle's own voluminous writings.

Cox, Don R. *Arthur Conan Doyle.* Ungar 1985 $16.50. ISBN 0-8044-2146-3 Detailed general study of Doyle's life and works.

Hardwick, Michael. *The Complete Guide to Sherlock Holmes.* St. Martin's 1987 $16.95. ISBN 0-312-00580-6 The life and times of Doyle's most famous character.

Jaffe, Jacquiline A. *Arthur Conan Doyle.* G. K. Hall 1987 $15.95. ISBN 0-8057-6954-4 General introduction to the life and work of Doyle with emphasis on the work.

Symons, Julian. *Conan Doyle: Portrait of an Artist.* Mysterious 1987 $9.95. ISBN 0-89296-926-1 A biography that points out similarities between Doyle and Holmes, his creation.

ELIOT, GEORGE (PSEUDONYM OF MARY ANN, OR MARIAN, EVANS) 1819–1880

George Eliot was born Mary Ann Evans on a Warwickshire farm in England, where she spent almost all of her early life. She received a modest local education and was particularly influenced by one of her teachers, an extremely religious woman whom the novelist would later use as a model for various characters.

Eliot read extensively, and was particularly drawn to the Romantic poets and German literature. In 1849, after the death of her father, she went to

London and became assistant editor of the *Westminster Review,* a radical magazine. She soon began publishing sketches of country life in London magazines.

At about this time Eliot began her lifelong relationship with George Henry Lewes. A married man, Lewes could not marry Eliot, but they lived together until Lewes's death.

Eliot's sketches were well received, and soon after she followed with her first novel, *Adam Bede* (1859). She took the pen name "George Eliot" because she believed the public would take a male author more seriously.

Like all of Eliot's best work, *Adam Bede* draws its characters and themes from English country life. Eliot knew country people well and had a keen ear for their speech. She used her detailed knowledge of rural life to make her stories believable.

Eliot's second novel, *The Mill on the Floss* (1860), is based in large part on her own life and her relationship with her brother. In it she begins to explore male-female relations and the way people's personalities determine their relationships with others. She returns to this theme in *Silas Marner* (1861), in which she examines the changes brought about in the life and personality of a miser through the love of a little girl.

In 1863, Eliot published *Romola.* Set against the political intrigue of Florence, Italy, of the 1490s, the book chronicles the spiritual journey of a passionate young woman.

Eliot's greatest achievement is almost certainly *Middlemarch* (1871). Here she paints her most detailed picture of English country life, and explores most deeply the frustrations of an intelligent woman with no outlet for her aspirations. This novel is now regarded as one of the major works of the Victorian era and one of the greatest works of fiction in English.

Eliot's last work was *Daniel Deronda.* In that work, Daniel, the adopted son of an aristocratic Englishman, gradually becomes interested in Jewish culture and then discovers his own Jewish heritage. He eventually goes to live in Palestine.

Because of the way in which she explored character and extended the range of subject matter to include simple country life, Eliot is now considered to be a major figure in the development of the novel.

NOVELS BY ELIOT

Adam Bede (1859). Penguin 1980 $4.95. ISBN 0-14-016188-0

Daniel Deronda (1876). Graham Handley (ed). Oxford Univ Pr 1988 $5.95. ISBN 0-19-281787-6

Felix Holt, the Radical (1866). Fred C. Thompson (ed). Oxford Univ Pr 1988 $5.95. ISBN 0-19-281781-7

**Middlemarch: A Study of Provincial Life* (1871). David Carroll (ed). Oxford Univ Pr 1988 $4.95. ISBN 0-19-281760-4 Story of the lives of seven people in rural England and how they affect each other, focusing on the intelligent Dorothea's unhappy marriage to a pompous older man.

* *The Mill on the Floss* (1860). Bantam 1987 $3.95. ISBN 0-553-21319-9 Story of a brother and sister torn apart by society's different treatment of men and women.

Romola (1863). Andrew Sanders (ed). Penguin 1980 $5.95. ISBN 0-14-043139-X

*Silas Marner (1861). Bantam 1981 $1.95. ISBN 0-553-21229-X Story of the miser Silas Marner, whose life is changed forever when he finds a baby girl on his doorstep.

BOOKS ABOUT ELIOT

Haight, Gordon S. *George Eliot.* Penguin 1985 $10.95. ISBN 0-14-058025-5 Definitive biography of Eliot based on Haight's work as editor of her letters; provides factual and detailed account of Eliot's life.

Lashi, Marghanita. *George Eliot.* Thames Hudson 1987 $9.95. ISBN 0-500-26023-0 Fully illustrated biography that links Eliot's life and her works.

GILBERT, SIR WILLIAM SCHWENK 1836–1911

Born, raised, and educated in London, W. S. Gilbert had little success in his first career as a lawyer, and he began to write humorous verse for magazines. These poems were collected and published as *The Bab Ballads* (1869), and they brought Gilbert his first popularity as an author. Gilbert then turned to the theater and began to write short, comic pieces, many of which mocked serious opera.

Gilbert's first full-length comedy in verse, *The Palace of Truth* (1870), was a well received production and led him to write other plays of this type, all of which were highly praised and popular. His real fame, however, came after he joined forces in 1871 with composer Arthur Sullivan, with whom he wrote comic operas. This partnership, though sometimes uncomfortable and often strained, lasted 25 years. During this time the two men produced 13 "Savoy" operas (so called because most were staged by Richard D'Oyly Carte at the Savoy Theater).

In the over 100 years that have passed since the two composers first began staging these operas, the names Gilbert and Sullivan have become inseparable, and their operas have continued to be extremely popular. Today's audiences appreciate the operettas' wit and charm, though they may not realize the extent to which Gilbert was satirizing the social customs, government policies, and prominent figures of his time.

Plays by Gilbert

The Complete Plays of Gilbert and Sullivan. Norton 1976 $12.95. ISBN 0-393-00828-2

Books about Gilbert

Dark, Sidney, and Rowland Grey. *W. S. Gilbert: His Life and Letters.* Ayer (repr of 1923 ed) $20.00. ISBN 0-405-08430-7 Entertaining biography that includes extracts from Gilbert's writings, reproductions of his sketches, and critical evaluation of his work.

Pearson, Hesketh. *Gilbert and Sullivan.* Amereon (repr of 1935 ed) $17.95. ISBN 0-89190-868-4 Anecdotal biography that deals with the personalities of Gilbert and Sullivan rather than their works and explores the rift that broke up their partnership.

HAGGARD, SIR HENRY RIDER 1856–1925

Henry Haggard was born in Norfolk, England, the son of a lawyer. Considered stupid by his father, he was sent to less well-known schools than his supposedly brighter brothers. In 1875 Haggard went to South Africa as secretary to the Governor of the province of Natal. He spent a total of six years there, becoming very familiar with African life and customs.

In 1881 Haggard returned to England to study law. He also began to write novels based on his African experiences. His first book, *King Solomon's Mines* (1885), was such a success that he abandoned the law and began to write full-time.

Along with the Scots poet and novelist Robert Lewis Stevenson, Haggard was one of the most widely read romance novelists of his time. He was fascinated by Africa's Zulu culture and wrote three novels set among the Zulu people. His books remain popular to this day and have formed the basis for several Hollywood movies and, recently, television programs. However, modern critics take issue with Haggard's view of Africa as "less civilized" than Europe, and of his traditional ideas about male and female roles. Despite these prejudices, Haggard's fiction has gained more praise from critics in recent years.

NOVELS BY HAGGARD

Allan Quartermain (1887). Amereon (repr of 1887 ed) $16.95. ISBN 0-89190-712-2 Adventure in the land of Zu-Vendis ruled by two beautiful queens.

Ayesha: The Return of She (1905). Dover 1978 $4.95. ISBN 0-486-23649-8 The sequel to *She;* further episodes in the life of the queen known as She Who Must Be Obeyed.

Child of Storm (1913). Amereon (repr of 1913 ed) $20.95. ISBN 0-89190-707-6 Adventures and struggles of a Zulu child.

King Solomon's Mines (1885). Oxford Univ Pr $2.25. ISBN 0-19-282204-7 Adventures of three men searching for the treasure of King Solomon's mines in the lost land of the Kukuanas.

Montezuma's Daughter (1893). Amereon 1976 $19.95. ISBN 0-89190-704-1 The sufferings of the Indians after the conquest of Mexico by Hernando Cortés.

Nada the Lily (1892). Dover 1979 $5.95. ISBN 0-87877-119-0 Umslopgaas, the Zulu chief, is involved in a series of exciting adventures.

She (1887). Airmont $1.95. ISBN 0-8049-0146-5 Adventures of Leo Vincey, whose quest for revenge leads him to the tombs of Kor, ruled by the mysterious queen known as She Who Must Be Obeyed.

BOOKS ABOUT HAGGARD

Higgins, D. S. *Rider Haggard: A Biography.* Scarborough Hse 1983 $21.95. ISBN 0-8128-2860-7 An illustrated biographical study, including a list of all of Haggard's works and their publication dates.

Katz, Wendy R. *Rider Haggard and the Fiction of Empire.* Cambridge Univ Pr 1988 $29.95. ISBN 0-521-33425-4 A study examining the literary and political implications of empire in Haggard's writing.

HARDY, THOMAS   1840–1928

Thomas Hardy, the son of a stonemason, was born in Dorset in the West Country of England. He was educated at local schools, but never attended a university. However, at the urging of his mother, he continued to read widely and thereby to educate himself.

At age 16 Hardy was apprenticed to an architect, going on in 1862 to join a firm of architects in London, where he remained for five years before returning to Dorset to practice law.

While working in London, Hardy had begun to write. His first novel was rejected by the publishers, and he destroyed it. His second try was successful. Titled *Desperate Remedies,* it was a complicated story of mystery, intrigue, and murder, and was published in 1871. In his third novel, *Under the Greenwood Tree* (1872), Hardy found the setting and themes with which he was most comfortable—the life and people of "Wessex" (his fictional name for Dorset) caught in a changing world.

In 1873, Hardy published *A Pair of Blue Eyes,* a study of class conflict drawing on his background in architecture. This novel features a memorable portrait of its heroine, Elfride, a fictional portrait of Hardy's fiancée.

Hardy's earlier work is pleasant and cheerful, but his later novels look at the darker side of rural English life. He shows his characters caught between the old country ways and the new "scientific" and efficient society that was growing around them. He portrays his characters as being trapped both by the natural cycles of weather and seasons and by rigid social codes of behavior.

Thus Hardy's heroes and heroines are almost always pushed to a tragic end by forces over which they have no control. He published several novels of this type, the most famous being *The Return of the Native* (1878), *The Mayor of Casterbridge* (1886), *Tess of the D'Urbervilles* (1891), and *Jude the Obscure* (1896).

When *Jude the Obscure* was greeted with a storm of criticism for its alleged "indecency," Hardy decided to give up writing novels. He devoted the rest of his life to writing poetry, much of which draws heavily on the folk songs and ballads he knew so well, reflecting his lifelong love of music. Many people feel Hardy is a better poet than he is a novelist. His poems are dark, pessimistic, and surprisingly modern.

NOVELS BY HARDY

Desperate Remedies (1871). St. Martin's 1977 $3.95. ISBN 0-312-19494-3
Far from the Madding Crowd (1874). Robert C. Shweck (ed). Norton 1988 $8.95. ISBN 0-393-95408-0 Story of impulsive Bathsheba Everdene and the three men in her life.
Jude the Obscure (1896). Bantam 1985 $3.50. ISBN 0-553-21191-9 The talented and ambitious Jude Frawley hoped for much from life but received little.
The Mayor of Casterbridge (1886). Richard Adams (ed). Longman 1988 $4.25. ISBN 0-582-33171-4 Tragic story of a man who sells his wife and child.
A Pair of Blue Eyes (1873). Alan Manford (ed). Oxford Univ Pr 1985 $4.95. ISBN 0-19-281684-5
The Return of the Native (1878). Bantam 1982 $2.50. ISBN 0-553-21269-9 Story of Clym Yeobright's return from Paris to his native town and his love for the ambitious and flighty Eustacia Vye.
Tess of the D'Urbervilles (1891). Longman 1988 $5.95. ISBN 0-582-019978-8 Tragic story of Tess, who is rejected by the man she loves and pursued by one she fears.
Under the Greenwood Tree (1872). David Wright (ed). Penguin 1978 $3.95. ISBN 0-14-043123-3 Life in rural Wessex through the story of Fanny Day and the three men who love her.
The Woodlanders (1887). Dale Kramer (ed). Oxford Univ Pr 1985 $4.95. ISBN 0-19-281600-4 Grace Melbury who is trapped in a marriage arranged by her wealthy father.

SHORT STORY COLLECTIONS BY HARDY

The Distracted Preacher and Other Tales. Penguin 1980 $5.95. ISBN 0-14-043124-1
Thomas Hardy: Selected Stories. St. Martin's 1980 $3.95. ISBN 0-312-71119-0
Wessex Tales (1883). St. Martin's 1978 $3.95. ISBN 0-312-86276-8

POETRY BY HARDY

Complete Poems. James Gibson (ed). Macmillan 1982 $14.95. ISBN 0-02-069600-0

BOOKS ABOUT HARDY

Butler, L. J. *Thomas Hardy.* Cambridge Univ Pr 1978 $11.95. ISBN 0-512-29271-9 Introduction to Hardy that focuses on his major novels and includes chapters on minor fiction and poetry.
Howe, Irving. *Thomas Hardy.* Alexia Dorszybski (ed). Macmillan 1985 $6.95. ISBN 0-02-052010-7 Critical analysis of Hardy's major works, early and lesser novels, lyric poems, and verse trilogy; discussion of Hardy scholarship in preface.
Millgate, Michael. *Thomas Hardy: A Biography.* Oxford Univ Pr 1985 $13.95. ISBN 0-19-281472-9 Definitive biography that draws extensively on diaries, notebooks, letters, local records, and contemporary newspapers to explore Hardy as man and artist.

HOPKINS, GERARD MANLEY   1844–1889

Gerard Manley Hopkins was born into a prosperous middle-class family. In 1863 he entered Oxford University, where he excelled as a student of the classics. While at Oxford he converted to Catholicism and decided to enter the priesthood. He was ordained a Jesuit priest in 1877. After serving in a number of small parishes, he was named Professor of Classics at University College, Dublin, where he remained until his early death from typhoid fever at the age of 44.

Hopkins was drawn to poetry early and had won a poetry prize while still at school. When he decided to enter the priesthood, he destroyed all the poems he had written at Oxford, believing that his duties in the church would not allow him time to write. Nevertheless, he continued to compose verse for himself and a few friends, although he never published any of it while he lived. Thirty years after his death, his friend Robert Bridges collected and published Hopkins's small but powerful body of poems.

Today Hopkins is recognized as an exceptionally gifted poet whose new ideas about the rhythm, meter, and language of poetry were far ahead of his time. Much of his poetry is religious, showing God to be both a universal presence and a part of everyday life. "Pied Beauty," for example, praises God for creating "dappled things," while in "The Windhover" the poet looks at a hawk and thinks of Christ.

Hopkins's poems are sometimes difficult to read because of their unusual use of language and their many layers of meaning. Despite these difficulties, however, Hopkins' popularity has grown over the years as more and more readers come to appreciate the artistry and technical beauty of his complex work.

POETRY BY HOPKINS

Poems of Gerard Manley Hopkins. W. H. Gardner and N. H. Mackenzie (eds). Oxford Univ Pr 1967 $10.95. ISBN 0-19-281094-4

BOOKS ABOUT HOPKINS

Kenyon Critics. *Gerard Manley Hopkins.* New Directions 1973 $2.45. ISBN 0-812-0479-0 Collection of eight essays reprinted from *The Kenyon Review;* includes a biographical sketch and studies of the poet's verse, symbolism and imagery, religious nature, and Victorian heritage.

Mackenzie, Norman H. *A Reader's Guide to Gerard Manley Hopkins.* Cornell Univ Pr 1981 $13.95. ISBN 0-8014-9221-1 Handy reference that provides authoritative interpretations of Hopkins' poetry and background on his life; includes cross references to other critical works and extended bibliography.

HOUSMAN, A. E. (ALFRED EDWARD)   1859–1936

A. E. Housman was a classical scholar who, while at Oxford University, was considered an exceptionally brilliant student. He did not do well on his final examinations, however, and was forced to accept work as a clerk in the patent office rather than the teaching position he wanted. He continued his classical scholarship while working in London, and ten years later his publications in various scholarly journals earned him a professorship at London University. He went on to take a similar post at Cambridge University.

Housman did not write a great deal of poetry. His most important work, *A Shropshire Lad* (1896), was followed by another small volume called *Last Poems*

(1922). Some remaining poetry was collected and published after his death as *More Poems* (1936).

Housman's fame rests almost entirely on *A Shropshire Lad,* in which he captures the late Victorian feeling of an era coming to an end. The poems are set in the English countryside where the pessimism and sadness of the young men who live there are often contrasted with the natural beauty that surrounds them. Unlike earlier Victorians, Housman saw little hope for the human race, and his poems are filled with a sense of intense frustration and wistfulness. This made his work very popular during and after World War I among readers who felt a sense of loss at the passing of the Victorian Age.

POETRY BY HOUSMAN

Collected Poems. Buccaneer 1983 $18.95. ISBN 0-941533-61-1
A Shropshire Lad (1896). Branden $2.95. ISBN 0-8283-1455-1

BOOKS ABOUT HOUSMAN

Ricks, Christopher. *A. E. Housman: A Collection of Critical Essays.* Prentice 1968 $1.95. ISBN 0-13-395905-8 Collection of essays by 14 noted critics and poets that analyze the value of Housman's poetry and discuss his romanticism and classical influences.

KIPLING, RUDYARD   1865–1936

Rudyard Kipling was born in Bombay, India, where his father was an art teacher and, later, the curator of a museum. When Kipling was six, he was sent back to England for schooling, and his unhappy years there formed the basis for some of his later fiction. At age 17 Kipling returned to India and took a job

The Cat That Walked by Himself.
Illustration by Rudyard Kipling (1902) from *Just So Stories.*

as a journalist on a magazine in Lahore. This experience sharpened his powers of observation, bringing him into close contact with people in all walks of Indian life and providing material for his fiction. He contributed stories and poems to the magazine and quickly became a popular writer, in England and India, so that when he returned to Britain in 1889, he was already well known. The following year he published *The Light That Failed,* a bitter autobiographical novel based on his five years as a boarder in England, separated from his parents in India.

In 1892 Kipling married an American woman and moved to Vermont for 4 years, an experience that caused him to develop some anti-American feelings, even though it was while he was in the United States that he wrote *The Jungle Book* (1894–1895), one of his best-known children's works.

By the time Kipling returned to England, he had become both the most famous poet and the most popular fiction writer in the country. In 1907 he became the first English writer to be awarded the Nobel Prize for literature.

While Kipling's poetry was, and is, extremely popular, his strength as a writer lies in the short story. His detailed sketches of life in India, his tales of soldiers in and out of battle, and his children's stories are all powerful, fascinating works. His reputation as an artist has suffered in recent years because of his strong support for the British Empire and condescending portrayal of Indians and other residents of the British colonies of his time. He has also been accused, with some justification, of being antifeminist, anti-American, and anti-German. Despite his political views and prejudices, however, Kipling has provided a vivid picture of the India of his time, leaving us with a great deal of memorable work.

NOVELS BY KIPLING

The Best Short Stories of Rudyard Kipling. Jeffrey Meyers (ed). Signet 1989 $4.50. ISBN 0-451-52140-4 Stories from all periods of Kipling's life.

Captains Courageous (1897). Bantam 1985 $1.95. ISBN 0-553-21190-0 Washed overboard from a ship, a spoiled boy becomes a man working on the boat that saved him.

SHORT STORY COLLECTIONS BY KIPLING

The Jungle Book (1894–95). Daniel Karlin (ed). Penguin 1989 $2.95. ISBN 0-14-043282-5 Story of Mowgli, a boy raised in the wild among the animals.

Just So Stories (1902). Peter Levi (ed). Penguin 1987 $2.95. ISBN 0-14-043302-3 Amusing tales of animals and how they got to be the way they are; for young children.

Kim (1901). Edward Said (ed). Penguin 1987 $2.95. ISBN 0-14-043281-7 The story of Kim, the orphaned son of an Irish soldier, who is raised by Hindus.

The Light That Failed (1890). John Lyon (ed). Penguin 1988 $5.95. ISBN 0-14-043283-3

Plain Tales from the Hills (1888). H. R. Woudhuysen (ed). Penguin 1987 $5.95. ISBN 0-14-043287-6 Tales that recreate the sights and smells of India.

Wee Willie Winkie (1888). Hugh Haughton (ed). Penguin 1988 $5.95. ISBN 0-14-043303-1 Fourteen stories from Kipling's last year in India.

POETRY BY KIPLING

Complete Poems. Doubleday 1989 $12.95. ISBN 0-451-52144-7

BOOKS ABOUT KIPLING

Green, Roger. *Kipling: The Critical Heritage.* Routledge 1971 $33.75. ISBN 0-7100-6978-2 Examination of Kipling's critical reputation during his lifetime, with reprints of essays and reviews from from 1886–1936.

Mallett, Philip. *Kipling Considered.* St. Martin's 1989 $35.00. ISBN 0-312-26157-8 Collection of essays by nine scholars; includes analysis of Kipling's language and use of names, interpretations of his works, and discussion of his values.

MARRYAT, CAPTAIN FREDERICK   1792–1848

A master of the sea tale, Frederick Marryat wrote novels that deal with life in the Royal Navy, in which he himself had served. Although Marryat's stories were written for children, they were read by old and young alike. *Masterman Ready* (1841) was once as popular with young male readers as Daniel Defoe's *Robinson Crusoe. Peter Simple* (1834) closely follows Marryat's own life; *Mr. Midshipman Easy* (1836) is the most humorous of the tales. Marryat's novels are all intended to teach a lesson, but the lessons never get in the way of the story or become so obvious that they bore the reader.

Marryat himself led an adventurous life, winning medals for bravery while in the navy and becoming a commander by the age of 23. He was able to use this background to give a sense of excitement and realism to his stories.

Novels by Marryat

*Jacob Faithful (1834). House Fire Pr 1989 $12.00. ISBN 0-929491-01-7 The story of a sailor who does his duty despite fearful obstacles.
*Mr. Midshipman Easy (1836). Biblio Dist 1970 $2.50. ISBN 0-460-01082-4 Tale of a young man who comes of age at sea, with sometimes hilarious results.
*Peter Simple (1834). Biblio Dist 1970 $14.95. ISBN 0-460-00232-5 Adventures at sea with the British Navy.
*The Phantom Ship (1839). AMS (repr of 1839 ed) $44.50. ISBN 0-404-6206-4 An eerie tale of mystery and suspense at sea.

ROSSETTI, CHRISTINA   1830–1894

Christina Rossetti, the youngest child of an exiled Italian patriot, was educated at home by her mother and showed a talent for poetry at an early age. Her first verses, *To My Mother, on the Anniversary of Her Birth* (1842), were published when she was only 12. As a child she suffered poor health and spent much of her time at home. Home, however, was a gathering place for many Italian exiles who met there to discuss art, politics, and other issues of the day, providing the young Rossetti with a lively atmosphere in which to grow. Rossetti was extremely religious and because of her beliefs refused two offers of marriage from men she admired.

For many years Christina Rossetti was known primarily as the sister of her more famous brother, Dante (*see* D. Rossetti, Vol. 1, British Literature: The Victorian Age), but in recent years her work has been recognized for its own worth. Her best-known poem is *Goblin Market* (1862), a long narrative poem dealing with the problem of temptation. She went on to publish *The Prince's Progress and Other Poems* (1866), *A Pageant and Other Poems* (1881), and *Verses* (1893). *A Pageant* contains the sonnet sequence "Monna Innominata," which has been compared to the "Sonnets from the Portuguese" of Elizabeth Barrett Browning. (*See* E. Browning, Vol. 1, British Literature: The Victorian Age.)

Rossetti's poetry draws deeply on her own emotions and experiences and is marked by color, strong images, and clarity. It frequently shows a longing for death and a sense of sorrow at being denied joy and fulfillment.

Poetry by Rossetti

Goblin Market (1862). Dover 1983 $2.50. ISBN 0-486-24516-0
Selected Poems. C. H. Sisson (ed). Carcanet 1985 $7.50. ISBN 0-85635-533-X

BOOKS ABOUT ROSSETTI

Birkhead, Edith. *Christina Rossetti and Her Poetry.* AMS (repr of 1930 ed) $7.25. ISBN 0-404-52503-2 Biographical and critical study; uses biographical material to introduce and explain poetry.

Harrison, Anthony. *Christina Rossetti in Context.* Univ of North Carolina Pr 1988 $12.95. ISBN 0-8087-4211-7 Close examination of Rossetti's poems in relation to their intellectual, artistic, and ideological contexts.

ROSSETTI, DANTE GABRIEL   1828–1882

Like his sister Christina (*see* C. Rossetti, Vol. 1, British Literature: The Victorian Age), Dante Gabriel Rossetti was educated at home. Unlike her, however, he was flamboyant and radical. Early in life he rejected his father's political ideals and economic beliefs, choosing instead to look to the past for his inspiration. He hated the emphasis on science that was so strong in Victorian society and longed for what he believed to be a simpler and gentler past.

A gifted painter, Rossetti first showed his rebellious nature in the world of art. With some friends he founded a movement called the Pre-Raphaelite Brotherhood, a group that wanted to return painting to the style of fourteenth- and fifteenth-century Italy, before the artist Raphael. Rossetti's group believed that those pre-Raphael painters were greater than those who came after Raphael. In addition to wanting more emphasis on the moral aspects of art, these rebels also believed in greater detail, more realism, and, above all, complete freedom of expression. They began to publish a magazine, *The Germ,* in which they expressed their ideas and in which Rossetti published some of his own poetry and that of his sister.

Like his painting, Rossetti's poetry relies on rich detail, especially imagery, and looks for its themes to mythology and the past. Rossetti wrote frequently of women and love, in terms that were considered bold at the time, prompting one critic to label Rossetti's group the "Fleshy School" of poetry.

POETRY BY ROSSETTI

Poems. Oswald Doughty (ed). Biblio Dist (repr of 1961 ed). (o.p.) $8.95.
The Sonnets by Dante Gabriel Rossetti. Found Class Repr 1986 $117.50. ISBN 0-89901-294-9

BOOKS ABOUT ROSSETTI

Angeli, Helen R. *Dante Gabriel Rossetti.* Ayer 1949 $22.50. ISBN 0-405-08206-1 Study of Rossetti in relation to his family and the men and women who knew him.

Johnston, Robert D. (ed). *Dante Gabriel Rossetti.* Twayne 1969. (o.p.) $11.95. Analysis of Rossetti's poetry and art that traces the theme of love to show the effect of his early thought on his mature work; minor emphasis on biography; contains a chronology and selected bibliography.

STEVENSON, ROBERT LOUIS   1850–1894

Robert Louis Stevenson was born in Edinburgh, the son of a prosperous engineer. As a youth he developed a lung disease that was to plague him the rest of his life. In 1867 he entered Edinburgh University to study engineering, but found he had no liking for the profession. He changed to law, becoming licensed in 1875.

While at Edinburgh, Stevenson contributed pieces to the university magazine and decided to become a writer. After he began work as a lawyer, he moved to France for his health. There he traveled a great deal and wrote two books based on his experiences, *An Inland Voyage* (1878) and *Travels with a Donkey in the Cevennes* (1879). During this period he also published essays in periodicals.

In 1879 Stevenson went to the United States in pursuit of an American woman he had met in France. Eventually, in 1883, he married her. He later wrote two travel books on his American experiences.

His new wife had a young son by a previous marriage, and Stevenson composed an adventure story for the boy. Originally titled *The Sea Cook,* it eventually became *Treasure Island* (1883) and launched Stevenson's career as a writer of adventure, romance, and mystery novels. Stevenson also wrote poetry: his *A Child's Garden of Verses* (1885) has become a classic of children's literature.

Once again seeking a climate more suited to his health, Stevenson settled in Samoa, where he continued to write until his death in 1894.

Long considered merely a writer of adventure tales and children's stories, Stevenson is now recognized as a writer of genuine literary merit. He is seen as a complex figure whose works deal with the question of good and evil, especially the notion that all people possess the capacity for both. He explored this theme most fully in the classic *Dr. Jekyll and Mr. Hyde* (1886).

NOVELS BY STEVENSON

*The Black Arrow (1888). Airmont 1964 $1.95. ISBN 0-8049-0020-5 In fifteenth-century England a band of outlaws called The Brotherhood of the Black Arrow fights against tyranny.

*Dr. Jekyll and Mr. Hyde (1886). Signet 1987 $2.25. ISBN 0-451-52138-2 Through his experiments, a scientist releases his own evil nature.

*Kidnapped (1886). Bantam 1982 $2.25. ISBN 0-553-21249-4 In the Scots uprising of 1775, young David Balfour is kidnapped and has to fight for his life and his honor.

*The Master of Ballantrae (1889). Airmont 1964 $1.95. ISBN 0-8049-0047-7 A lifelong feud between two brothers extends from Scotland to America.

*Treasure Island (1883). Emma Letley (ed). Oxford Univ Pr 1982 $2.25. ISBN 0-19-281681-0 Jim Hawkins discovers a treasure map, and the adventure begins.

SHORT STORY COLLECTIONS BY STEVENSON

*The Body Snatcher and Other Stories. Jeffrey Meyers (ed). Signet 1988 $2.50. ISBN 0-451-52153-6 Masterful tales of mystery and suspense.

*Weir of Hermiston and Other Stories. Penguin 1980 $4.95. ISBN 0-14-043138-1 Archie Weir is banished to Hermiston by his father, the notorious "hanging judge."

POETRY BY STEVENSON

*A Child's Garden of Verses (1885). Crown 1986 $6.98. ISBN 0-517-48924-4 Poems about the joys of childhood that will delight readers of all ages.

BOOKS ABOUT STEVENSON

Cooper, Lettice. *Robert Louis Stevenson.* Brown 1948 $4.95. ISBN 0-317-39777-X Brief biography which is also a critical study of Stevenson's writings.

Saposnik, Irving S. *Robert Louis Stevenson.* G. K. Hall 1974 $14.95. ISBN 0-8057-1517-7 Introduction to Stevenson's works; includes a biographical sketch and a discussion of literary forms, from essay to novel.

STOKER, BRAM (ABRAHAM) 1847–1912

Bram Stoker was born in Dublin, the son of a civil servant. Although a semi-invalid as a child, he went on to gain a reputation as a fine athlete at Trinity College, where he also excelled in mathematics and philosophy.

Stoker worked as a civil servant and a journalist before becoming the personal secretary of the famous actor Henry Irving. He also wrote 15 works of fiction, only one of which is very memorable—*Dracula* (1897). This work, involving hypnotism, magic, the supernatural, and other elements of gothic fiction, went on to sell over one million copies and is still selling strongly today. So well known has his fictional character become that today it is possible to visit the castle of Count Dracula in the Transylvanian region of Romania, a country that Stoker never visited. Several film versions of the story, both serious and comic, have made Stoker's work a part of modern mythology. His novel *The Lair of the White Worm* (1911) has also been made into a film. It and the novel *The Lady of the Shroud* are, like *Dracula,* fantastic tales of horror.

NOVELS BY STOKER

Dracula (1897). Signet 1986 $2.95. ISBN 0-451-52337-7 Classic tale of adventures of
the the vampire count Dracula.
The Lady of the Shroud (1909). Amereon (repr of 1909 ed) $15.95. ISBN 0-88411-134-2

BOOK ABOUT STOKER

Carter, Margaret. *Dracula: The Vampire and the Critics.* UMI 1988 $39.95. ISBN 0-8357-
1849-1 Anthology of critical essays with overview of changing evaluation of
Stoker's work; includes valuable bibliography of studies of Stoker's work.

SWINBURNE, ALGERNON CHARLES 1837–1909

Algernon Charles Swinburne, the son of an admiral, was educated in France and at Eton and Oxford University. He left the latter in 1858, one step ahead of expulsion. Seven years later, he published his first volume of poems, *Atalanta in Calydon,* and followed it in 1866 with *Poems and Ballads.* These works outraged some critics and delighted others, making Swinburne the most notorious poet in Europe. His reputation was due in part to his private life, which was openly defiant of the moral standards of the time. Swinburne was a rebel against almost all the conventions of his time, and his rebelliousness shows in both his poetic technique and his subject matter. His verse is most notable for its unusual patterns of sound and swinging rhythms, which move the reader quickly from line to line.

Swinburne led a wild personal life, drinking heavily and engaging in outrageous social behavior. His style of living took a toll on both his health and his work, and his later poems declined in vitality. He was forced to spend the last 30 years of his life in the care of a friend.

POETRY BY SWINBURNE

Poems and Ballads and Atalanta in Calydon. Morse Peckham (ed). Macmillan 1970 $10.95.
ISBN 0-672-51119-3
Selected Poems. L. M. Findley (ed). Carcanet 1987 $8.50. ISBN 0-85635-728-6

BOOKS ABOUT SWINBURNE

Chew, Samuel C. *Swinburne.* Shoe String 1966 repr of 1929 ed $29.00. ISBN 0-208-00557-9 Critical biography emphasizing Swinburne's poetry.

Thomas, Donald. *Swinburne: The Poet of His World.* Oxford Univ Pr 1979 $22.95. ISBN 0-19-520136-1 Biography that provides a brief overview of the "darker sides" of Swinburne's life.

TENNYSON, LORD, ALFRED   1809–1892

Alfred Tennyson was one of eight children of a poor Lincolnshire, England, clergyman. He was educated first at home by his father and then at Cambridge University, where he distinguished himself by graduating with honors.

Tennyson was drawn to poetry early and by the age of 14, upon hearing of the death of the English poet Lord Byron, he knew that he too must be a poet. He published his first poems, along with those of his brother, in *Poems by Two Brothers* (1827) the same year he entered Cambridge.

Tennyson had to withdraw from the university in 1831 when his father died, leaving the family in poor financial shape. He then entered a period known as The Ten Years' Silence during which, for a variety of personal and health reasons, he published nothing. When he emerged from this period, however, he unleashed a flood of remarkable poetry that made him the most popular poet in Britain and resulted in his being named Poet Laureate in 1850.

If there were a contest for the title "greatest Victorian poet," Tennyson would easily win the prize. He had an almost uncanny ear for the sound and rhythm of the English language and once claimed he knew the metrical value of every word in English except "scissors." His poetry shows his skill at using classical myth and legend to create a melancholy, wistful mood while commenting on important social and moral issues of his day.

Tennyson is sometimes criticized for being an "establishment" poet, someone who speaks for those in authority and advocates keeping things as they are. There is unquestionably an element of this sort in his work, and he was certainly deeply committed to the Victorian idea of progress. However, Tennyson was also aware of the contradictions in his society and raised disturbing questions about the injustices he saw.

POETRY BY TENNYSON

The Idylls of the King (1859). Airmont 1968 $2.75. ISBN 0-8049-0180-5 The legends of King Arthur and the Knights of the Round Table told in verse.

The Poetical Works of Tennyson. Houghton 1974 $25.00. ISBN 0-395-18014-7

BOOKS ABOUT TENNYSON

Jump, John D. *Tennyson.* Routledge 1967 $65.00. ISBN 0-7100-2941-1 Collection of 35 essays, chapters, and extracts from commentary by Tennyson's contemporaries from 1831 to 1891.

Pinion, Frank B. *A Tennyson Companion: Life and Works.* St. Martin's 1984 $29.95. ISBN 0-312-79107-0 Broadly chronological survey of Tennyson's works, emphasizing later poetry; includes biographical introduction and selection of illustrations.

Staines, David. *Tennyson's Camelot: The Idylls of the King and Its Medieval Sources.* Humanities 1982 $22.95. ISBN 0-88920-115-3 Study of *Idylls* that follows the chronology of the poem's composition and analyzes Tennyson's approach to his sources.

THACKERAY, WILLIAM MAKEPEACE   1811–1863

William Makepeace Thackeray was born in Calcutta, India, the only son of a prosperous officer in the East India Company. He was sent to school in England at age six and was generally unhappy. In 1828 he entered Cambridge University, where he spent more time playing cards than studying, and left in 1830 without graduating.

Thackeray studied law briefly and then drifted into journalism. His life took an unexpected turn in 1833 when he lost most of his inheritance in a bank failure and was forced to make his own living. He turned first to painting, studying art in London and Paris, but soon returned to writing for magazines. He contributed a steady flow of humorous sketches and satirical articles to a number of periodicals and built a reputation as one of the leading satirists of the day.

Thackeray used his gift for satire to produce "rogue" novels, stories of clever, but disreputable, central characters who, like modern con artists, make their way in society by taking advantage of the hypocrisy and insincerity of seemingly respectable people. His masterwork of this period is *Vanity Fair* (1847–48), in which the wily heroine, Becky Sharp, uses all her guile and cleverness to make her way in the world. The book was instantly popular and brought Thackeray fame and fortune. He went on to write several more successful novels. By 1860, however, he seems to have run out of ideas, and his last works are mere imitations of earlier ones.

Today Thackeray's reputation rests on *Vanity Fair, The History of Henry Esmond* (1852), and to some extent on *The Virginians* (1857–59), a sequel to *Henry Esmond.* Stanley Kubrick made a film of his novel *The Memoirs of Barry Lyndon* (1844). Although Thackeray is considered a major figure in Victorian literature, he never took writing novels seriously enough to rise to the rank of Charles Dickens or George Eliot. (*See* Dickens *and* Eliot, Vol. 1, British Literature: The Victorian Age.)

NOVELS BY THACKERAY

* The History of Henry Esmond (1852). Penguin 1970 $6.95. ISBN 0-14-043049-0 The life of Henry Esmond, from his youth through his adventures as a soldier to his move to America.

* The History of Pendennis (1848–50). Penguin 1972 $5.95. ISBN 0-14-043076-8 The life and loves of Arthur Pendennis as he grows to become a writer in Victorian England.

* The Memoirs of Barry Lyndon (1844). Andrew Sanders (ed). Oxford Univ Pr 1984 $7.95. ISBN 0-19-281667-5 Story of the life of a rogue, liar, swindler, cheat, and adventurer, told in his own words.

* Vanity Fair (1847–48). John Sutherland (ed). Oxford Univ Pr $4.95. ISBN 0-19-681642-X Story of Becky Sharp, clever and ambitious, and her friend Amelia, trusting and innocent.

BOOKS ABOUT THACKERAY

Bloom, Harold (ed). *William Makepeace Thackeray.* Chelsea 1987 $27.50. ISBN 1-55546-288-X Selection of contemporary critical essays by 13 scholars and critics, with introductory essay by editor, bibliography, notes on contributors, and chronology of Thackeray's life.

Ferris, Ina. *William Makepeace Thackeray.* G. K. Hall 1983 $14.50. ISBN 0-8057-6851-3 Study that explores grounds for Thackeray's relative obscurity; includes chronology of Thackeray's life.

WILDE, OSCAR 1854–1900

Oscar Wilde was born in Dublin, the son of a famous physician father and a literary mother. He was a brilliant student at school, earning honors in classical literature at Trinity College and then going on to Oxford University where he won a major poetry prize. While at Oxford, Wilde joined the Aesthetic Movement, a group of young intellectuals who believed that art was the most important thing in life and that it should be judged only on its beauty, not on its morality. Wilde became the champion of the movement and adopted the motto "Art for art's sake." In his personal life Wilde expressed his belief by dressing outlandishly and openly challenging social conventions, particularly through his homosexual relationships. Because of his brilliant wit and skill as a conversationalist, he was constantly sought after by London society.

Wilde's literary career was far ranging. He began by writing poetry, essays, book reviews, fairy tales, and children's stories. In 1891 he published *The Picture of Dorian Gray,* a novel that was to bring him yet more fame and more criticism. It was attacked as being "immoral" and "deprived" because it seemed to suggest that one could do whatever one wished in the name of art.

In the same year, Wilde turned his famous wit to the theater. He began writing the plays for which he is best known—*Lady Windemere's Fan* (1892), *A Woman of No Importance* (1893), *The Ideal Husband* (1894), and his masterpiece, *The Importance of Being Earnest* (1895). The plays are full of fresh, witty lines that are still quoted today.

In 1895, at the height of Wilde's career, the Marquess of Queensbury accused him of corrupting the Marquess's son, with whom Wilde had been having an affair. Wilde sued the Marquess for libel and lost. He was then charged with immoral practices, convicted, and sentenced to prison for two years. Three years after his release he died in France, a broken man. His last work was a long poem about prison life, "The Ballad of Reading Gaol." It has been said of Wilde that his greatest play was his life and that he himself was its most ardent spectator.

NOVEL BY WILDE

*The Picture of Dorian Gray (1891). Peter Ackroyd (ed). Penguin 1986 $2.95. ISBN 0-14-043187-X Story of a young man who never seems to grow older—and the terrible reason why.

SHORT STORY COLLECTION BY WILDE

*The Happy Prince and Other Stories. Penguin 1985 $2.25. ISBN 0-14-035050-0 Fables mostly for young children, but enjoyable for all ages.

PLAYS BY WILDE

The Importance of Being Earnest and Other Plays. Penguin 1986 $2.95. ISBN 0-14-048209-1 Contains *Salome, A Woman of No Importance, An Ideal Husband,* and *Lady Windemere's Fan.*

COLLECTIONS OF WILDE WORKS

The Complete Works of Oscar Wilde. Harper 1989 $12.95. ISBN 0-06-096393-X
The Wit and Humor of Oscar Wilde. Alvin Redman (ed). Dover 1959 $4.50. ISBN 0-486-20602-5

BOOKS ABOUT WILDE

Ellman, Richard. *Oscar Wilde.* Random 1988 $11.95. ISBN 0-394-75984-2 Sympathetic retelling of Wilde's story replete with unfamiliar facts and anecdotes.

Raby, Peter. *Oscar Wilde.* Cambridge Univ Pr 1988 $12.95. ISBN 0-521-27826-0 Introductory critical study of Wilde's works from his early poems to his plays with emphasis on his contribution to modern drama.

THE TWENTIETH CENTURY

Two massive and brutally destructive world wars divide the twentieth century into three distinct periods, each of which is also characterized by major changes in British literature.

As the twentieth century opened, Britain was at a new height of power and wealth. Its colonial empire stretched around the globe; its banks controlled world finances; its factories busily turned out more goods than ever before; its government was solid and stable; and its people were content and looking forward to endless peace and prosperity. The literature of this period was basically an extension of Victorian writing—patriotic, proud, optimistic, even a bit smug. While a few writers like James Joyce and D. H. Lawrence were experimenting with new forms and themes, their work was virtually lost in a sea of more traditional writing and had little impact on public taste. Ironically, these experimenters are studied and admired today, while more popular writers are all but forgotten.

This secure, stable world came to an abrupt end with the outbreak of war in 1914. In a rush of patriotism, young British men volunteered to fight by the thousands, expecting that British power would produce a quick and easy victory. But the war dragged on and casualties mounted. The nation, and especially young people, became increasingly disillusioned by what they came to believe was senseless slaughter. The World War I battle casualties were enormous—more than 900,000 British lives lost. Virtually an entire generation of young men was destroyed.

When the war ended in 1918, the British were bitter and cynical, and this attitude was clearly reflected in the literature of this second period. People wished to be free of the old romantic illusions that had led to the war and welcomed a new realism in literature.

Literary experiments widened. T. S. Eliot's *The Waste Land* (1922) used a radically new poetic form to express the popular theme of Europe as a vast and desolate land waiting to be reborn.

These so-called "years between the wars" were also marked by economic failures and widespread unemployment. This plus the Russian Revolution of 1917 caused many writers and thinkers to look toward the new communist society of the Soviet Union as a model for change.

Throughout this second period the emphasis was on experimentation and change as writers everywhere looked for new ideas and new forms of expression. Poets like Eliot and W. H. Auden; novelists such as Joseph Conrad, James Joyce, and D. H. Lawrence; and playwrights like George Bernard Shaw and Sean O'Casey changed completely the old ideas of what literature should be—and literature would never again be the same.

Once again, in 1939, Britain was drawn into a world war. This time, however, the nation had more warning and a much more realistic sense of what lay ahead. Again, the war was brutal, costing the British enormous losses of life and causing immense suffering. At the end of World War II, however, Britain emerged with a genuine sense of having won. In the words of British Prime Minister Winston Churchill, the war in many ways had been "Their finest Hour."

The end of the war brought new political alignments. Although the Soviet Union had been an ally in World War II, now it was the enemy in a new "cold war." This period also brought the end of the British Empire. Therefore, British writers turned again and again to the issue of Britain's place in the new world order, as well as to the individual's place in British society. Playwright John Osborne and other so called Angry Young Men of the 1940s and 1950s criticized the British system of rigid social class distinctions. Novelists like Paul Scott questioned the old imperial values, while mystery writers like John Le Carré examined Britain's adaptation to cold war politics.

Today, as the twentieth century draws to a close, political and economic conditions continue to change. And British writers continue to ask in their novels, plays, and poems, "Where are we going, and why?"

ADAMS, DOUGLAS   1952–

Douglas Adams was born and educated in Cambridge, England, receiving a B.A. with honors from Cambridge University. After graduation he went to work for the British Broadcasting Corporation as a radio scriptwriter and producer. He edited scripts for the popular science fiction television series *Doctor Who*, but became best known for his scripts for the radio and television series, *Hitchhiker's Guide to the Galaxy*. This series was so popular that Adams was asked to turn it into a book. Rather than merely transferring the scripts to novel form, he decided "to see if I could do it properly." The result was a thoroughly engaging novel that became popular in its own right, *The Hitchhiker's Guide to the Galaxy* (1979). He followed with *The Restaurant at the End of the Universe* (1980), and then went on to write two more novels in the same series, *Life, the Universe and Everything* (1982) and *So Long and Thanks for All the Fish* (1985). He recently launched a new series based on the adventures of Dirk Gently, private detective.

Called by one reviewer the "Monty Python of outer space," Adams has a flair for satire that masquerades as silliness. Behind all the laughter lurks a feeling that something is basically wrong and that society is somehow out of tune.

NOVELS BY ADAMS

Dirk Gently's Holistic Detective Agency (1988). Pocket 1989 $4.95. ISBN 0-671-92231-9 Adventures of Dirk Gently, who solves crimes with a little help from extraterrestrial friends.

The Hitchhiker's Guide to the Galaxy (1979). Pocket 1990 $4.95. ISBN 0-671-70159-2 Adventures of Arthur Dent and his alien friend Ford Prefect.

Life, the Universe and Everything (1982). Pocket 1985 $3.95. ISBN 0-671-60107-5 What happens when Arthur Dent and his alien friend Ford Prefect go to an end-of-the-world party.

The Long Dark Tea Time of the Soul (1989). Pocket 1990 $4.95. ISBN 0-671-69404-9 Dirk Gently investigates a lawyer and an advertiser who possess the soul of the god Odin.

The Restaurant at the End of the Universe (1980). Pocket 1982 $4.50. ISBN 0-671-66494-8 A journey to the low-rent neighborhood of the Cosmos.

So Long and Thanks for all the Fish (1985). Pocket 1985 $3.95. ISBN 0-671-52580-8 Arthur Dent, the alien Ford Prefect and the voivoid gang try to discover why all the dolphins disappeared.

PLAYS BY ADAMS

The Original Hitchhiker's Radio Scripts (1984). Crown 1985 $9.95. ISBN 0-517-55950-1

AMIS, KINGSLEY 1922–

Kingsley Amis was born into a Baptist family in southeast London. In 1947 he received his degree in English language and literature from St. John's College, Oxford. He has written poems, stories, and criticism for various periodicals. Until 1961 he lectured in English, first at University College, Swansea, then at Cambridge, until he retired in 1963 to devote himself full-time to his writing. Amis is one of the best known of the group of writers known as The Angry Young Men, so called because of their attacks on traditional British society in the 1940s and 1950s.

Amis's first novel, *Lucky Jim* (1954), is still considered to be his best. It is an entertaining satire of a young scholar at an English university. When the book won the Somerset Maugham Award in 1955, Amis's reputation was made. Since then, he has produced a steady stream of novels, most of which are comic and satirical.

Amis's targets are most often the hypocrisy and pretense of modern British society. His range is wide, however, and he has produced detective stories, spy stories, and science fiction as well as works dealing with the supernatural. A long-time fan of the fictional spy-adventurer James Bond, Amis has attempted to produce Bond books in the manner of Bond's creator, British author Ian Fleming. (*See* Fleming, Vol. 1, British Literature: The Twentieth Century.) *Colonel Sun* (1968), his first Bond adventure, written under the pseudonym Robert Markham, outraged the critics but seems to have delighted the public. One of his more recent novels, *The Old Devils* (1986), was awarded the prestigious Booker Prize. In addition to nonfiction books on the subjects of science fiction and James Bond, Amis has written both a study and a biography of Rudyard Kipling. (*See* Kipling, Vol. 1, British Literature: The Victorian Age.)

NOVELS BY AMIS

The Alteration (1976). Carroll & Graf 1988 $3.95. ISBN 0-88184-432-2
Difficulties with Girls (1988). Summit Bks 1989 $18.95. ISBN 0-671-67582-6
The Green Man (1969). Academy Chi Pubs 1986 $4.95. ISBN 0-89738-220-2
Jake's Thing (1978). Penguin 1980 $5.95. ISBN 0-14-005096-5
*Lucky Jim (1954). Penguin 1976 $4.95. ISBN 0-14-001648-1 Satire of a young teacher's discovery that education fails to open the door to the upper class.
The Old Devils: A Novel (1986). Harper 1988 $7.95. ISBN 0-06-097146-0
One Fat Englishman (1963). Summit Bks 1989 $8.95. ISBN 0-671-67119-7
Stanley and the Women (1984). Harper 1988 $6.95. ISBN 0-06-097145-2

NONFICTION BY AMIS

New Maps of Hell (1960). Ayer (repr 1975 ed) $18.95. ISBN 0-405-06321-0
Rudyard Kipling (1986). Thames Hudson 1986 $9.95. ISBN 0-500-26019-2

BOOKS ABOUT AMIS

Bradford, Richard. *Kingsley Amis.* Routledge 1989 $9.95. ISBN 0-304-49309-7 A critical study focusing on the satirical aspect of Amis's novels.
Gardner, Philip. *Kingsley Amis.* Twayne 1981. (o.p.) $11.95. ISBN 0-8057-6809-2 Critical study of the main themes in Amis's novels, poetry, and other works; includes a brief biography, chronology, and selected bibliography of writings by and about him.

AUDEN, W. H. (WYSTAN HUGH) 1907–1973

The most important poet of the "between the wars" generation is certainly W. H. Auden. The son of a doctor and a nurse, Auden was born in York, England and attended a series of private schools. He also enrolled in Oxford University, where he intended to study science, but changed to English literature. The force of his personality and the brilliance of his intellect established Auden as an important figure even during his student days. After graduation he quickly gained recognition as the foremost poet in a brilliant circle that included such English writers as C. Day Lewis, Stephen Spender, and Louis MacNeice. (*See* MacNeice, Vol. 1, British Literature: The Twentieth Century.) Auden was active in leftist, or radical, politics during the 1930s, and visited Spain and China, where there were active left-wing revolutionary movements. He had a lifelong passion for travel and in 1938 immigrated to the United States, where in 1946 he became a naturalized citizen. In 1956 he returned to England, where he served as Professor of Poetry at Oxford until 1961. Auden's many honors include the Pulitzer Prize, the Bollingen Prize, and the National Book Award.

Auden was a prolific poet and produced works in a wide variety of forms including long and short poems, verse drama, light and occasional verse, songs, opera libretti, and verse letters. His career encompasses significant changes in theme and style. He began by writing traditional verse, somewhat in the style of the English poet William Wordsworth (*see* Wordsworth, Vol. 1, British Literature: The Romantic Period), but later admired T. S. Eliot (*see* Eliot, Vol. 1, British Literature: The Twentieth Century), whose approach he found more in tune with the modern world. During the 1930s, his work became more political and was especially influenced by socialist writings and new psychological theories. By the end of World War II, Auden's poetry had become both more religious and more pessimistic as he came to believe that "poetry makes nothing happen."

POETRY BY AUDEN

Collected Poems. Random 1976 $34.50. ISBN 0-394-40895-0

BOOKS ABOUT AUDEN

Bloom, Harold (ed). *W. H. Auden.* Chelsea 1986 $24.50. ISBN 0-87754-640-1 Brief biography, followed by an excellent selection of personal remembrances and critical essays by such noted authors and critics as Auden's friend, Christopher Isherwood ("Notes on the Early Poetry"), John Hollander ("Auden at Sixty"), and John R. Boly ("The Orators: Portrait of the Auden of the Thirties."
Carpenter, Humphrey. *W. H. Auden: A Biography.* Houghton 1982 $10.95. ISBN 0-395-32439-X Definitive biography, using access to private and previously unpublished material, with focus on critical periods throughout Auden's life.
Smith, Stan. *W. H. Auden.* Basil Blackwell 1985 $9.95. ISBN 0-631-13515-4 Critical analysis showing the themes of doubleness, multiplicity, and division in Auden's work.

BALLARD, J. G. (JAMES GRAHAM) 1930–

J. G. Ballard was born in Shanghai, China. Imprisoned by the Japanese during World War II, he used this experience as the basis for his most successful novel, *Empire of the Sun* (1984), which was later made into a movie by Steven Spielberg.

Ballard began as a writer of science fiction, concentrating on the theme of how people adapt physically and psychologically to environments that are dramatically changed by natural catastrophes. The most famous of these novels are *The Drowned World* (1962), *The Drought* (1965), and *The Crystal World* (1966).

Ballard's more recent novels are dreamlike accounts of contemporary life, closer to fantasy than science fiction. In these novels he is primarily concerned with exploring the links between the external world of things and people and the internal world of feelings and ideas. As his stories unfold, it is sometimes hard to distinguish one world from the other.

NOVELS BY BALLARD

Concrete Island (1975). Random 1985 $3.95. ISBN 0-394-74107-2
Crash (1973). Random 1985 $3.95. ISBN 0-394-74109-9
The Crystal World (1966). Farrar 1988 $7.95. ISBN 0-374-52096-8 Story of a man who finds a lovely African city of jewels and crystal and then learns its terrible secret.
*The Day of Creation (1987). Macmillan 1989 $7.95. ISBN 0-02-041514-1 A scientist in Africa accidentally releases the flow of a new river, with surprising consequences.
*The Drowned World (1962). Carroll & Graf 1962 $3.95. ISBN 0-88184-324-5 The polar icecaps have begun to melt and the world will soon be flooded.
*Empire of the Sun (1984). Pocket 1987 $4.50. ISBN 0-671-68477-2 Story of a young British boy on his own in war-torn Shanghai.
High Rise (1977). Carroll & Graf 1988 $3.50. ISBN 0-88184-400-4
The Unlimited Dream Company (1979). Washington Square Pr 1985 $4.50. ISBN 0-671-60537-2

SHORT STORY COLLECTIONS BY BALLARD

Best Short Stories of J. G. Ballard. Pocket 1985 $3.95. ISBN 0-671-61451-7
The Terminal Beach (1964). Carroll & Graf 1987 $3.50. ISBN 0-88184-370-9
Vermilion Sands (1983). Carroll & Graf 1988 $3.50. ISBN 0-88184-422-5

BARRIE, J. M. (SIR JAMES MATTHEW) 1860–1937

James M. Barrie was born in Scotland, the son of a weaver. He completed all his education in Scotland, graduating from Edinburgh University in 1883. He worked as a journalist in Nottingham and London from 1883 to 1890. During that time he wrote numerous stories of Scots life that were collected and published in 1888.

In 1891 Barrie published his first novel, *The Little Minister,* which was a huge success. He then turned to the theater and wrote a number of successful plays including *Quality Street* (1902) and *The Admirable Crichton* (1902). The play for which he is best known and remembered, *Peter Pan,* was first staged in 1904.

While Barrie's plays are charming, funny, well crafted, and technically excellent, they are sometimes faulted by critics for being too sentimental. *Peter Pan* continues to be a favorite with modern audiences, but few of Barrie's other plays are staged today.

NOVEL BY BARRIE

The Little Minister (1891). Airmont 1968 $.75. ISBN 0-8049-0187-2

PLAY BY BARRIE

*Peter Pan (1904). Penguin 1986 $2.25. ISBN 0-14-035066-7 Classic story of the boy who refused to grow up.

BOOK ABOUT BARRIE

Mackail, Denis G. *Barrie: The Story of J. M. B.* Ayer (repr of 1941 ed) $34.00. ISBN 0-8369-6734-8 A complete, extremely detailed, and well-researched biography of Barrie.

BEHAN, BRENDAN   1923–1964

Brendan Behan was a child of the Dublin slums who joined the Irish Republican Army (IRA) at the early age of 14. The IRA was a group dedicated to driving the English out of Ireland, which England had conquered and colonized five centuries before. Two years later Behan was arrested for carrying explosives and sentenced to reform school as a terrorist. Upon his release he resumed his activities with the IRA and was again arrested and sent to prison. While in prison, he began to write—mostly short stories of life in lower-class Dublin.

In 1947, Behan was released again. He started writing seriously, and in 1954 his first play, *The Quare Fellow,* was produced in Dublin. The play, a grim comedy about a prisoner's last hours before being hanged, was moved to London in 1956 and made Behan famous.

Behan's success in the theater was accompanied by an almost total collapse of self-discipline. His drinking bouts and brawls became regular features of the tabloid newspapers. Although his second play, *The Hostage* (1959), enjoyed even greater success, Behan continued his heavy drinking. In 1964 alcohol and diabetes led to his early death.

Behan's autobiography, *Borstal Boy* (1958), describes his years in reform school. The book reveals both his creative power and his instinct for self-destruction.

PLAYS BY BEHAN

The Complete Plays (includes *The Quare Fellow, The Hostage,* and *Richard's Cork Leg*). Grove 1990 $9.95. ISBN 0-8021-3070-4

NONFICTION BY BEHAN

Borstal Boy (1958). Godine 1982 $10.95. ISBN 0-87923-415-6

BOOK ABOUT BEHAN

Mikhail, E. H. *Brendan Behan: Interviews and Recollections.* 2 vols. Barnes 1982. Vol. 1 $28.50. ISBN 0-389-20221-5. Vol. 2 $28.50. ISBN 0-389-20222-3 A collection of more than 100 interviews and brief memoirs by Behan's family, friends, contemporaries, and critics.

BOLT, ROBERT   1924–

Robert Bolt was born in Manchester, where he attended Manchester Grammar School and Manchester University. At college, he studied history, an interest that was to heavily influence his later plays.

Robert Bolt was teaching school when his play *Flowering Cherry* (1957) was staged in London. Its success persuaded him to devote himself entirely to the theater. *The Tiger and the Horse,* a drama of moral conflicts set in an Oxford college, appeared three years later.

Bolt's most famous, and perhaps best play, *A Man for All Seasons* (1960), dramatizes the conflict between Sir Thomas More and King Henry VIII. The play won the New York Drama Critics award for 1962, and the film version, for which Bolt wrote the screenplay, received several Oscars.

Bolt continues to write for films, having produced highly acclaimed screenplays for *Lawrence of Arabia, Doctor Zhivago,* and *Ryan's Daughter.* In his later plays he continues his interest in period settings and historical characters. *Vivat! Vivat! Regina* (1970) deals with the struggle between Elizabeth I and Mary, Queen of Scots, and *State of Revolution* (1977) revolves around Lenin, Trotsky, and the Russian Revolution.

PLAY BY BOLT

A Man for All Seasons (1960). Random 1966 $2.95. ISBN 0-394-70321-9

BOWEN, ELIZABETH 1899–1973

Elizabeth Bowen was born in Dublin and spent her early years in County Cork at her family's estate, Bowen's Court, which she later inherited. She was educated at Downe House School in Kent, England, and then traveled extensively in France and Italy until 1923, when she married and returned to London. She began her career by writing short stories and published her first volume *Encounters* in 1923. In 1926 she published another collection, *Ann Lee's.*

Bowen's first novel, *The Hotel,* appeared the following year. From then on until her death she produced a steady stream of fiction. *The House in Paris* (1935), one of her finest novels, draws on her experience of falling in love with a much younger man while married to a loving husband. Her most acclaimed work, *The Heat of the Day* (1949), is considered a classic story of love in wartime London; it too had autobiographical roots, this time in her relationship with Canadian diplomat Charles Ritchie.

Bowen is considered one of the most distinguished authors of the twentieth century. She was deeply concerned with the art and craft of writing and expressed her views in *Why Do I Write?* (1948). Her novels portray complex relationships among characters, most of whom are women. She frequently deals with "the death of the heart" of a sensitive girl or young woman, so that her stories are less concerned with comment on life and society and more on personal relationships and the emotions and feelings of her characters. In her much-anthologized "The Demon Lover," for example, a woman is haunted by the return of an arrogant fiancé who had been reported missing in action in World War I; now the happily married and much older woman fears this threat to her happiness—which may be coming from a ghost. In her work she constantly sought to achieve, as she put it, "the non-poetic statement of a poetic truth."

NOVELS BY BOWEN

The Death of the Heart (1938). Penguin 1989 $6.95. ISBN 0-14-008543-2
Eva Trout (1969). Penguin 1987 $6.95. ISBN 0-14-008542-4
Friends and Relations (1931). Penguin 1987 $5.95. ISBN 0-14-000398-3
The Heat of the Day (1949). Penguin 1988 $6.95. ISBN 0-14-001844-1
The Hotel (1927). Penguin 1988 $5.95. ISBN 0-14-000449-1
The House in Paris (1935). Penguin 1987 $6.95. ISBN 0-14-000535-8
The Last September (1929). Penguin 1987 $1985 $5.95. ISBN 0-14-000372-X
The Little Girls (1953). Penguin 1985 $6.95. ISBN 0-14-005785-4
To the North (1932). Penguin 1987 $6.95. ISBN 0-14-000534-X
A World of Love (1955). Penguin 1988 $5.95. ISBN 0-14-008541-6

SHORT STORY COLLECTION BY BOWEN

Collected Stories. Random 1982 $8.95. ISBN 0-394-75296-1

BOOKS ABOUT BOWEN

Coles, Robert. *Irony in the Mind's Life.* New Directions 1978 $4.95. ISBN 0-8112-0689-0
   Philosophical discussion on Bowen's treatment of youth in *The Death of the Heart.*
Glendenning, Victoria. *Elizabeth Bowen.* Avon 1986 $3.50. ISBN 0-380-44354-6 Richly
   detailed, illustrated biography exploring Bowen's contradictions and complexities.
Kenney, Edwin J. *Elizabeth Bowen.* Bucknell Univ Pr 1975 $1.95. ISBN 0-8387-7978-6
   Definition of Bowen's peculiarly Anglo-Irish literary sensibility that traces how
   she develops the themes of insecurity, isolation, and the loss of identity in her
   major novels.

BROOKE, RUPERT   1887–1915

Brooke is the best known of the poets who took a patriotic, somewhat idealized, view of World War I. He was born in Rugby, where his father was
headmaster of a house (dormitory) at the elite Rugby School. Blond, athletic,
and intelligent, Brooke was everyone's idea of the ideal youth. Some even
called him "the handsomest man in England."

Brooke went from Rugby School to King's College, Cambridge, where he
gained a reputation as an intellectual and an athlete. After graduation he
traveled in Germany and then returned to Cambridge to accept a fellowship.

Brooke had begun writing poetry in his earlier years at Cambridge and
continued to write on his return. By 1915 he had published several poems in
periodicals.

When war broke out in 1914, Brooke enlisted in the Royal Navy, but died
of blood poisoning on his way to the combat area in the Aegean. Perhaps
ironically, he is best remembered for his war poetry, which idealizes both
combat and patriotic feelings. This poetry stands in sharp contrast to that of
other young poets, such as Wilfred Owen (see Owen, Vol. 1, British Literature:
The Twentieth Century), whose works attack the senselessness of war.
Brooke's poetry has been criticized by some as being sentimentally patriotic,
but others find the criticism unfair since Brooke never had the opportunity to
experience combat or see war in its full horror.

POETRY BY BROOKE

The Complete Poems of Rupert Brooke. AMS (repr of 1942 ed) $17.50. ISBN 0-404-14647-3

BOOKS ABOUT BROOKE

De La Mare, W. *Rupert Brooke and the Intellectual Imagination.* Haskell 1972 repr of 1914 ed
   $29.95. ISBN 0-8383-1515-1 Long, chatty essay about Brooke, combining critical
   insight and personal observation.
Hassall, Christopher. *Rupert Brooke: A Biography.* Faber & Faber 1972 $5.95. ISBN 0-571-
   10196-8 Detailed, illustrated biography that also discusses Brooke's poetry.

BURGESS, ANTHONY (JOHN ANTHONY BURGESS WILSON)   1917–

John Anthony Burgess Wilson (he later shortened his name) was born in
Manchester, England, and was educated at Xaverian College and Manchester
University, where he studied linguistics and literature. After serving in World

War II, Burgess became a teacher. In 1949 he wrote his first novel, *A Vision of Battlements*, because, as he put it, he was "empty of music but itching to create." Later Burgess became a British colonial officer in Southeast Asia. While there he wrote the trilogy now entitled *The Long Day Wanes* (1956–59). During the 1960s he produced a flood of fiction—15 different works—including his famous *A Clockwork Orange* (1962), which was later made into a highly successful film.

Burgess's novels are characterized by sharp social satire and startling verbal invention and playfulness. A *New York Times* critic describes Burgess's work in this way: ". . . he attacks unreason with satire so swift we hardly know we've been hit before we're pronounced morally dead." His satiric ability is at its best in the *Enderby* books, novels about an antisocial poet confined to the bathroom of a small apartment and then thrown suddenly into the world again.

NOVELS BY BURGESS

A Clockwork Orange (1962). Ballantine 1988 $3.95. ISBN 0-345-00789-1
The Clockwork Testament (1976). McGraw 1984 $5.95. ISBN 0-07-008972-8
The Doctor Is Sick (1960). Norton 1979 $3.95. ISBN 0-393-00959-9
Enderby (1963). Norton 1968 $5.95. ISBN 0-393-08444-2
Enderby Outside (1968). McGraw 1984 $5.95. ISBN 0-07-008971-X
Enderby's Dark Lady (1984). McGraw 1986 $4.95. ISBN 0-07-008976-0
The Eve of St. Venus (1964). Norton 1979 $1.95. ISBN 0-393-00915-7
Honey for the Bears (1963). Norton 1978 $5.95. ISBN 0-393-00905-X
Nothing like the Sun (1964). Norton 1975 $6.95. ISBN 0-393-00795-2
The Wanting Seed (1962). Norton 1976 $7.95. ISBN 0-393-00808-8

BOOKS ABOUT BURGESS

Aggeler, Geoffrey. *Anthony Burgess.* G. K. Hall 1986 $35.00. ISBN 0-8161-8757-6 Collection of articles and essays on Burgess's novels written by a variety of critics.
Bloom, Harold. *Anthony Burgess.* Chelsea 1987 $19.95. ISBN 0-87754-676-2 Brief biography followed by an excellent selection of personal remarks and recollections about Burgess, reviews of his novels, and critical essays.
Coale, Samuel. *Anthony Burgess.* Ungar 1981 $16.95. ISBN 0-8044-2124-2 Biographical, analytical, and critical study presenting Burgess as a Catholic exile.

CARY, JOYCE 1888–1957

Poet, amateur painter, political scientist, and novelist, Joyce Cary was born in Ireland into an old English family. Despite the many hardships in his childhood, he always associated Ireland with "my dearest memories." His autobiographical novels, *Castle Corner* (1938) and *A House of Children* (1941), reflect Cary's youthful life in Ireland.

Cary studied art for several years but gave it up to enter Oxford University, where he first studied history but later changed to law. By the time he left Oxford, he had resolved to become a writer. Meanwhile, he was eager for adventure and went off to the Balkan War of 1912–13.

Later, in Africa, Cary served with the Nigerian colonial service, and during World War I he accompanied the West African Frontier Force on campaigns in the Cameroons. After he nearly died of a head wound, Cary left the military and returned to government service until 1920. Then, having had some success in selling his short stories, he settled in Oxford and devoted himself entirely to writing. But it was more than 10 years before Cary published his first novel, and more than 20 before he attained financial security.

Aissa Saved (1932) was the first of many books that established Cary's reputation as a novelist of great vigor, imagination, and technical skill. Some of his early novels, of which *Mr. Johnson* (1939) is the most powerful, are based on his experiences in Nigeria and deal with the confrontation between African culture and British colonial authority. Cary's best-known works, however, are those in which he explores the world of art—*Herself Surprised* (1941), *To Be a Pilgrim* (1942), and his masterpiece, *The Horse's Mouth* (1944), which became a film starring Alec Guinness. Cary also wrote a series of novels about political life in Britain.

Cary's particular genius is his ability to create exceptionally unusual, lively, and interesting characters, each of whom tells his or her own story with remarkable intensity, eliciting enormous sympathy and reader involvement.

NOVELS BY CARY

Except the Lord (1953). New Directions 1985 $7.95. ISBN 0-8112-0965-2
Herself Surprised (1941). Riverrun 1980 $6.95. ISBN 0-7145-0270-7
The Horse's Mouth (1944). Harper 1965 $4.95. ISBN 0-06-080046-1 The story of Gulley Jimson, an eccentric artist whose genius is exceeded only by his outrageous behavior.
A House of Children (1941). New Directions 1986 $8.95. ISBN 0-8112-1008-1
Mister Johnson (1939). New Directions 1989 $9.95. ISBN 0-8112-1030-8
Not Honor More (1955). New Directions 1986 $8.95. ISBN 0-8112-0966-0
Prisoner of Grace (1952). New Directions 1985 $7.95. ISBN 0-8112-0964-4
To Be a Pilgrim (1942). Amereon $20.95. ISBN 0-88411-314-6

BOOKS ABOUT CARY

O'Connor, William V. *Joyce Cary.* Columbia Univ Pr 1966 $3.00. ISBN 0-231-02680-3 Long essay showing both the traditional and modernist aspects of Cary's novels.
Roby, Kinley E. *Joyce Cary.* G. K. Hall 1984 $18.95. ISBN 0-8057-6863-7 Short analysis of Cary's life and novels.

CHESTERTON, G. K. (GILBERT KEITH)   1874–1936

G. K. Chesterton was born in London into a middle-class family of which he wrote ironically, "I regret that I have no gloomy and savage father to offer to the public gaze as the true cause of all my tragic heritage; no pale-faced and partially poisoned mother whose suicidal instincts have cursed me with the temptations of the artistic temperament."

Chesterton was educated at University College, London, and the Slade School of Art. He began his career as an editor in a publishing house, but soon turned to journalism. After writing for several magazines, he founded his own paper in 1911, and kept his journalistic ties for the rest of his life.

Chesterton's literary output was enormous: novels, stories, plays, poetry, essays, biographies, critical studies, and reviews. He is best remembered, however, for his stories of Father Brown, the detective priest, a character he invented before his conversion to Catholicism in 1922.

NOVEL BY CHESTERTON

The Man Who Was Thursday (1908). Carroll & Graf 1986 $3.50. ISBN 0-88184-225-7

SHORT STORY COLLECTIONS BY CHESTERTON

The Complete Father Brown. Penguin 1987 $9.95. ISBN 0-14-009766-X Collected stories of Father Brown, the famous detective-priest.
Thirteen Detectives. Penguin 1987 $5.95. ISBN 0-14-011435-X The solutions to a variety of mysteries by 13 detectives, one of them Father Brown.

POETRY BY CHESTERTON

Collected Nonsense and Light Verse. Dodd 1987 $14.95. ISBN 0-396-09022-2 Assortment of amusing poetry for all occasions.

BOOKS ABOUT CHESTERTON

Barker, Dudley. *G. K. Chesterton.* Scarborough Hse 1975 $5.95. ISBN 0-8128-1804-0 An illustrated biography covering the complete life.

Dale, Alzina Stone. *The Outline of Sanity: A Biography of G. K. Chesterton.* Eerdmans 1982 $18.95. ISBN 0-8028-3550-3 An up-to-date biography of Chesterton, focusing on the times in which he lived: features a useful bibliography.

CHRISTIE, DAME AGATHA   1880–1976

Born in Devonshire, England, the daughter of an American father and an English mother, Agatha Christie was educated at home and later studied singing in Paris. Her childhood and youth were typically middle-class and, according to her, uneventful. She was married in 1914 and divorced in 1928, two years after a much-publicized, mysterious disappearance, which she never fully explained. Christie later married an archaeologist and traveled with him to Syria and Iraq, which became the settings for some of her novels.

Christie is unquestionably the most famous detective novelist of the twentieth century, having produced more than 80 books, many of which were made into films and television series. She personally adapted some of her stories for the stage; *The Mousetrap* (1952) and *Witness for the Prosecution* (1953) were the most successful. *The Mousetrap,* the longest continuously running play in theater history, is still being performed in London.

Christie's stories follow the standard formula of the British detective story, which emphasizes intricate plots over character or setting. However, eccentric detectives, particularly Inspector Hercule Poirot and Miss Jane Marple, are engaging characters, even though they are predictable and not fully developed. Christie's novels are widely read all over the world, and her stories and characters appear on television screens regularly.

NOVELS BY CHRISTIE

The ABC Murders (1936). Pocket 1985 $3.50. ISBN 0-671-60063-X The killer is working through the alphabet and Hercule Poirot has very little time left to stop the murders.

Curtain (1975). Pocket 1987 $3.95. ISBN 0-671-54717-8 The last case of Hercule Poirot—one of the Belgian detective's toughest.

Death on the Nile (1937). Bantam 1983 $3.50. ISBN 0-553-36138-X Murder strikes while Poirot is on holiday in Egypt.

Murder at the Vicarage (1930) Berkley 1984 $3.50. ISBN 0-425-09453-7 The first case solved by Miss Marple, a gentle, kind, and shrewd observer of people.

The Murder of Roger Ackroyd (1926). Pocket 1983 $3.50. ISBN 0-671-49856-8 One of Hercule Poirot's most baffling cases.

Murder on the Orient Express (1934). Pocket 1985 $3.50. ISBN 0-671-52368-6 On a train bound for Istanbul, Poirot looks for a killer that he would rather not find.

The Mysterious Affair at Styles (1920). Bantam 1983 $3.50. ISBN 0-553-26587-3 Agatha Christie's first novel, and Hercule Poirot's first case.

The Secret Adversary (1922). Bantam 1983 $3.50. ISBN 0-553-26477-X Tommy and Tuppence Beresford decide to open a detective agency, with some comic results.

The Secret of Chimneys (1925). Berkley 1984 $2.95. ISBN 0-425-06802-1 Superintendent Battle of Scotland Yard joins the ranks of Christie's detectives; his first novel.

Sleeping Murder (1976). Bantam 1983 $3.50. ISBN 0-553-25678-5 The last case of the crafty and wily Miss Marple.

Ten Little Indians (1939). Pocket 1983 $3.95. ISBN 0-671-55222-8 With each murder another Indian figurine disappears; will the murderer be discovered before they are all gone?

SHORT STORY COLLECTIONS BY CHRISTIE

Double Sin and Other Stories (1961). Berkley 1987 $2.95. ISBN 0-425-06781-5 Some of Christie's best short early works.

The Golden Ball and Other Stories (1971). Bantam 1987 $9.95. ISBN 0-553-35065-X Collection of Christie's later stories.

Miss Marple: The Complete Short Stories. Berkley 1986 $7.95. ISBN 0-425-09486-3 Everybody's favorite inquisitive female detective solves more mysteries.

PLAYS BY CHRISTIE

The Mousetrap and Other Plays (includes *Witness for the Prosecution, Ten Little Indians, Verdict, Appointment with Death, The Hollow, Towards Zero,* and *Go Back for Murder*). Bantam 1986 $4.95. ISBN 0-553-25902-4 Some of Christie's most intriguing tales of murder, mayhem, and mystery in dramatic form.

NONFICTION BY CHRISTIE

Agatha Christie: An Autobiography. Harper 1985 $7.95. ISBN 0-06-097030-8 An honest self-portrait of the mystery story writer.

BOOKS ABOUT CHRISTIE

Gill, Gillian. *Agatha Christie: The Woman and Her Mysteries.* Free Pr 1990 $22.50. ISBN 0-02-911702-X The story of the secretive woman who is one of the world's most popular writers.

Morgan, Janet. *Agatha Christie: A Biography.* Harper 1986 $7.95. ISBN 0-06-09030-8 Illustrated biography covering the complete life of Christie and examining her writing in a biographical context.

Sanders, Dennis, and Len Lovallo. *An Agatha Christie Companion: The Complete Guide to Agatha Christie's Life and Work.* Delacorte 1984 $19.95. ISBN 0-385-29285-6 Brief description of each of Christie's mystery novels, short stories, plays, and films, including a list of titles categorized by genre.

CLARKE, ARTHUR C. (CHARLES)   1917–

Arthur C. Clarke was born in Minehead, Somerset, and attended Huish's Grammar School in Taunton. His career as a science writer and space pioneer began soon after he completed school and took a job in the audit department of the British government. As a hobby, he wrote several articles for the *Journal of the British Interplanetary Society.* Then, after serving in the Royal Air Force in World War II, Clarke used his wartime experience as the basis for a 1945 article in *Wireless World* suggesting that communications satellites in stationary orbit would be a worthwhile goal of the space program.

At about this time Clarke entered King's College, London, where he studied physics and mathematics; he graduated in 1949. For two years he wrote scientific articles for *Physics Abstracts,* but gave up the job to become a free-lance writer, science reporter, and underwater explorer. His early books on space and rocketry played a major role in building public support for the space program. Since 1956 he has lived in Sri Lanka.

Clarke's science fiction is notable for its technological accuracy and has been a source of information as well as entertainment for the general reading public. His most famous work, *2001: A Space Odyssey* (1968), later made into a film, shows Clarke's philosophical and visionary side.

Novels by Clarke

Childhood's End (1963). Ballantine 1987 $3.50. ISBN 0-345-34795-1 Novel of the next stage in the evolution of humanity.

The City in the Stars (1956). Signet 1957 $3.50. ISBN 0-451-14822-3 A human venture into outer space produces both surprises and new knowledge.

The Deep Range (1957). Signet 1981 $3.50. ISBN 0-451-14753-7 Fights with giant squid 12,000 feet beneath the sea.

The Fountains of Paradise (1979). Ballantine 1987 $3.95. ISBN 0-345-34794-3 In the second century King Kalidasa had a dream that another man tries to fulfill 2,000 years later.

Imperial Earth (1976). Ballantine 1976 $3.95. ISBN 0-345-35250-5 Saga of a cloned human who returns to Earth for the 500th anniversary of the United States.

Rama II (1989). (coauthored with Gentry Lee) Bantam 1989 $18.95. ISBN 0-553-05714-6 In the year 2196 another Raman spacecraft is approaching our solar system.

Rendezvous with Rama (1973). Ballantine 1988 $3.50. ISBN 0-345-35056-1 Winner of the Hugo and Nebula awards. A mission investigates a strange celestial body that appears in the outer reaches of the solar system.

The Sands of Mars (1951). Signet 1980 $2.50. ISBN 0-451-12312-3

2001: A Space Odyssey (1968). Signet $3.95. ISBN 0-451-15580-7 Discovery of a strange object sends a space team beyond Jupiter.

2010: Odyssey Two (1982). Ballantine $4.95. ISBN 0-345-30306-7 A sequel to *2001: A Space Odyssey,* this story has twists of its own.

2061: Odyssey Three (1988). Ballantine 1988 $4.95. ISBN 0-345-35879-1 Clarke's view of civilization developing into something worthy of the name.

Short Story Collections by Clarke

Expedition to Earth (1953). Ballantine 1975 $2.95. ISBN 0-345-32824-8 Eleven of the very best of Clarke's early stories.

The Nine Billion Names of God (1967). Signet 1987 $3.50. ISBN 0-451-14755-3 Stories of the unusual and bizarre from a master of science fiction; title story concerns a computer that threatens to end the world by fulfilling an old Tibetan prophecy about the nine million names of god.

Reach for Tomorrow (1956). Ballantine 1975 $3.50. ISBN 0-345-35376-5 Stories of futures that might be—and should be.

Report on Planet Three and Other Speculations (1972). Berkley 1985 $3.50. ISBN 0-425-07592-3

Tales of Ten Worlds (1962). Signet 1987 $3.50. ISBN 0-451-14978-5 Adventures throughout the solar system and beyond.

Wind from the Sun: Stories of the Space Age (1972). Signet 1973 $1.95. ISBN 0-451-11475-2

Books about Clarke

Fairley, John, and Simon Welfare. *Arthur C. Clarke's World of Strange Powers.* Putnam 1985 $19.95. ISBN 0-399-13066-7 Partly humorous, illustrated study of strange and unexplainable phenomena and how they appear in Clarke's work.

Olander, Joseph D., and Martin Harry Greenberg. *Arthur C. Clarke.* Taplinger 1977. (o.p.) $23.50. ISBN 0-8008-0401-5 An anthology of essays that develop alternative perspectives on Clarke's science fiction; contains a biographical note.

COLUM, PADRAIC 1881–1972

Born in an Irish workhouse (public institution for the poor) where his father was first a teacher and then a master, Padraic Colum received his education at a state school and later became a clerk for the Irish railway. Always interested in writing, he published some poems in *The United Irishman,* a periodical edited by Arthur Griffith, a strong supporter of Irish nationalism. Griffith encouraged Colum's first play, *The Saxon Shillin'* (unpublished), an anti-British work that led to Colum's involvement with the new Irish National Theatre Society.

Colum became a founder of the Abbey Theatre in Dublin and wrote several plays for the new theater: *Broken Soil* (1903), *The Land* (1905), and *Thomas Muskerry* (1910). In 1912 he married Mary Maguire, a teacher and writer, and two years later they immigrated to the United States, where he continued to write poetry in New York and Connecticut.

Colum felt that his Catholic and peasant roots gave him a closer tie to the Irish people than did the Protestant, Anglo-Irish background of many of his fellow Irish writers. His poetry usually deals with common people and rural landscapes in a straightforward, direct fashion. His lifelong interest in folklore is also evident in his poetry.

POETRY BY COLUM

Collected Poems (1953). Devin-Adair 1981 $15.00. ISBN 0-8159-5203-1

PLAYS BY COLUM

Selected Plays of Padraic Colum. Syracuse Univ Pr 1986 $18.00. ISBN 0-8156-2386-0

BOOK ABOUT COLUM

Sternlicht, Sanford. *Padraic Colum.* G. K. Hall 1985 $20.95. ISBN 0-8093-0412-0 An appreciation and critical study of Colum's life and work.

CONRAD, JOSEPH 1857–1924

Born Josef Konrad Korzeniowski in Poland, Joseph Conrad was the son of a Polish patriot and intellectual who was exiled to Russia because of his political beliefs. Young Conrad was tutored by his father until his death when Joseph was 11. His mother having died earlier, Conrad was sent to live with an uncle and complete his schooling. At 15 he decided to go to sea and left Poland for the French port of Marseilles, where he became a sailor on a merchant ship. Conrad sailed for 20 years on French and British ships, learning both languages and working his way up to master mariner.

While at sea Conrad began writing to improve his English and to pass the time between voyages. He drew his subjects almost entirely from his own sea experiences and those of his shipmates. When an illness contracted in Africa forced him to leave the sea, Conrad returned to London where he sought a publisher for his first book. Much to his surprise, he found one, and *Almayer's Folly* appeared in 1895. He followed this immediately with *The Outcast of the Islands* (1896), and his literary career had begun. Over the next several years Conrad produced a series of outstanding novels and novellas (short novels), many of which are considered modern literary landmarks. His work is generally acknowledged to have exerted a strong influence on the development of the modern novel. Although his views on Africa reflect the biases and limits of his time, his writing style and concerns are still hugely admired.

While Conrad's works are often tales of adventure, they are also serious studies of the human mind. He deals frequently with the hopelessness of human dreams. Like much of the modern fiction that was to follow, his books explore isolation, loneliness, and alienation. His heroes are often failures who suffer the painful awareness of dreams unrealized and opportunities lost.

NOVELS BY CONRAD

Almayer's Folly (1895). Penguin 1976 $4.95. ISBN 0-14-000036-4

*Heart of Darkness (1902) and *The Secret Sharer.* (1912). Bantam 1982 $1.95. ISBN 0-553-21214-1 Two of Conrad's most penetrating glimpses into the workings of the human mind—and soul.

*Lord Jim (1900). Penguin 1986 $1.95. ISBN 0-14-043169-1 Story of a young sailor whose one act of cowardice haunts him throughout his adventures in Malaysia.

The Nigger of the Narcissus (1897). Penguin 1988 $3.95. ISBN 0-14-043170-5
Nostromo (1904). Bantam 1989 $3.95. ISBN 0-553-21359-8
The Outcast of the Islands (1896). Penguin 1976 $3.95. ISBN 0-14-004054-4
The Secret Agent (1907). Penguin 1985 $2.50. ISBN 0-14-043228-0
Under Western Eyes (1911). Signet 1987 $3.50. ISBN 0-451-52114-5
Victory (1915). Doubleday 1971 $6.95. ISBN 0-385-09314-4
Youth (1902). Penguin 1976 $3.95. ISBN 0-14-004055-2

SHORT STORY COLLECTIONS BY CONRAD

Great Short Works. Harper. (o.p.) $5.95. ISBN 0-06-083039-5
Sea Stories. Carroll & Graf 1985 $8.95. ISBN 0-88184-177-3
Tales of Unrest. Penguin 1977 $3.95. ISBN 0-14-003885-X

BOOKS ABOUT CONRAD

Adelman, Gary. *Heart of Darkness: Search for the Unconscious.* Twayne 1987 $17.95. ISBN 0-8057-7953-1 A guide to the characters, structure, and themes in Conrad's masterpiece.
Bloom, Harold (ed). *Joseph Conrad.* Chelsea 1966 $24.50. ISBN 0-87754-642-8 A brief biography, followed by personal comments by Conrad's contemporaries and general critical reviews of his novels.
Gillon, Adam. *Joseph Conrad.* G. K. Hall 1982 $16.95. ISBN 0-8057-6820-3 A critical study of the novels, including biographical information, by the president of the Joseph Conrad Society.
Ryf, Robert. *Joseph Conrad.* Columbia Univ Pr 1970 $5.00 ISBN 0-231-03264-1 A long essay examining Conrad's vision of human experience.

COWARD, SIR NOEL   1899–1973

Born in Teddington, England, Noel Coward was educated both privately and attended a school for young actors. He made his stage debut at age 12 and appeared in *Peter Pan* when he was 14. A juvenile prodigy, Coward was by turns actor, director, composer, lyricist, writer, and playwright, with nearly 60 theater pieces to his credit by the time he died. Although he specialized in light comedy, he worked in many forms—patriotic spectacle, revue, musical, farce, even serious problem plays. *Hay Fever* (1925), *Private Lives* (1930), and *Blithe Spirit* (1941) have proved the most durable of his comedies, although in recent years some of his other plays, long out of print, have been revived. Many of his plays have been made into films.

Coward's work usually concerns well-educated and well-to-do or artistic Britishers with complicated romantic entanglement. Most of his plays focus on the comic efforts of these characters as they try to disentangle their love lives.

In 1964, when *Hay Fever* was placed in the repertory of Britain's newly organized National Theater, Coward expressed his gratitude by responding, "Bless you for admitting that I'm a classic." While at the time his statement seemed just another example of his famous droll humor, with every passing year, it is more like a prophecy.

NOVEL BY COWARD

Pomp and Circumstance (1960). Dutton 1982 $5.95. ISBN 0-525-48019-6

SHORT STORY COLLECTION BY COWARD

Collected Stories. Dutton 1986 $11.95. ISBN 0-525-48210-5

POETRY BY COWARD

Collected Verse. Graham Payne (ed). Routledge 1985 $18.95. ISBN 0-413-55140-7
Lyrics of Noel Coward. Overlook Pr 1983 $10.95. ISBN 0-87951-187-7

PLAYS BY COWARD

Three Plays (includes *Blithe Spirit, Hay Fever,* and *Private Lives*). Grove 1979 $7.95. ISBN 0-394-17535-2

NONFICTION BY COWARD

*Future Indefinite: An Autobiography (1954). Da Capo 1980 $9.95. ISBN 0-306-80126-4 After succeeding in his career, the witty playwright and actor Noel Coward remembers his difficult later years.
*Present Indicative: An Autobiography (1937). Da Capo 1980 $9.95. ISBN 0-306-80112-4 More sparkling wit from Coward in the form of his childhood memories.

BOOKS ABOUT COWARD

Gray, Frances. *Noel Coward.* St. Martin's 1987 $19.95. ISBN 0-312-00444-3 Complete look at how Noel Coward wrote plays and short stories.
Levin, Milton (ed). *Noel Coward.* G. K. Hall 1989 $17.95. ISBN 0-8057-7978-1 Critical looks at the major works of Noel Coward.

CRONIN, A. J. (ARCHIBALD JOSEPH)   1896–1981

A. J. Cronin was born in Scotland into a comfortable middle-class family. However, on the death of his father, the family was left with very little, and Cronin's early life was a constant struggle for survival.

Cronin was an excellent student at Dumbarton Academy and Glasgow University, graduating as a physician in 1919. He began practicing medicine in South Wales and London, and his experiences there with the medical problems of poor workers and miners figure heavily in his later fiction. He published his first novel, *Hatter's Castle,* in 1931. It was so successful that he gave up medicine to write full time. In his fiction, he draws heavily on his Scottish childhood and on his experiences with miners in Wales.

Although Cronin's novels have received only lukewarm reviews from critics, they have been enormously popular with the reading public. He has over 22 publishers around the world, and his books have sold many millions of copies. Nine of his novels have been made into films, and his characters have served as the basis for television series.

NOVELS BY CRONIN

Beyond This Place (1953). Little 1984 $6.95. ISBN 0-316-16192-6
*The Citadel (1937). Little 1983 $6.95. ISBN 0-316-16183-7 Story of a young doctor's struggle to bring medical care to a mining community.
The Green Years (1945). Little 1984 $6.95. ISBN 0-316-16193-4
*The Keys of the Kingdom (1942). Little 1984 $6.95. ISBN 0-316-16184-5 Story of a young Scots missionary in prerevolutionary China.
Shannon's Way (1950). Little 1984 $6.95. ISBN 0-316-16185-3
A Song of Sixpence (1964). Amereon $16.95. ISBN 0-89190-218-X
Three Loves (1932). David and Charles 1932 $22.95. ISBN 0-575-00069-4

BOOK ABOUT CRONIN

Salwak, Dale. *A. J. Cronin.* G. K. Hall 1985 $17.95. ISBN 0-8057-6884-X Recently released look at A. J. Cronin's work habits and creative processes.

DAHL, ROALD   1916–1990

Roald (pronounced "Roo-aal") Dahl was born in Llandaff, South Wales. He had a relatively uneventful childhood and was educated at Repton School. During World War II he served as a fighter pilot and for a time was stationed in Washington, D.C. Prompted by an interviewer, he turned an account of one of his war experiences into a short story that was accepted by the *Saturday Evening Post.* Thus, quite by accident, he was launched into a writing career. In all he published 12 wartime stories in the *Saturday Evening Post,* which were eventually collected in *Over to You* (1946).

Dahl's stories are often described as horror tales or fantasies, but neither description does them justice. He has the ability to treat the horrible and ghastly with a light touch, sometimes even a humorous one. His tales never become merely shocking or gruesome. His purpose is not to shock but to entertain, and much of the entertainment comes from the unusual twists in his plots, rather than from grizzly details.

Dahl has also become famous as a writer of children's stories. In some circles, these works have caused great controversy. Critics have charged that Dahl's work is anti-Semitic and denigrates women. Nevertheless, his work continues to be read: *Charlie and the Chocolate Factory* (1964) was made into a successful movie, and his books of rhymes for children continue to be very popular.

NOVEL BY DAHL

My Uncle Oswald (1979). Knopf 1980 $10.00. ISBN 0-394-51001-9

SHORT STORY COLLECTIONS BY DAHL

The Best of Roald Dahl. Random 1978 $9.95. ISBN 0-394-72549-2 Spine-chilling collection of some of Dahl's best tales.
  Kiss, Kiss (1959). Knopf 1959 $19.95. ISBN 0-394-43202-9
Over to You (1946). Penguin 1975 $4.95. ISBN 0-14-003574-5 Ten stories of flyers and flying.
Roald Dahl's Book of Ghost Stories. Farrar 1984 $5.95. ISBN 0-374-51868-8 Eerie collection from the master of the macabre.
Roald Dahl's Tales of the Unexpected (1979). Random 1979 $2.95. ISBN 0-394-74881-5 Stories by a master storyteller, many of which were made into a television series of the same name.

NONFICTION BY DAHL

Boy: Tales of Childhood. Penguin 1987 $6.95. ISBN 0-14-008917-9 Dahl's personal reminiscences from his youth.
Going Solo. Penguin 1987 $6.95. ISBN 0-14-010306-6 Dahl's adventures during World War II.

DRABBLE, MARGARET   1939–

Margaret Drabble was born in Sheffield, England, and educated at The Mount School in York and at Cambridge University. After graduation she worked for a while as an actress and then married Clive Swift, an actor, whom she later divorced.

Drabble's novels are frequently concerned with the struggle of an individual against the restrictions of conventional society. A number of her plots reflect situations in her own life. *A Summer Bird-Cage* (1963) tells of two sisters: one, very bright, has recently graduated from Oxford; the other, very pretty, is about to marry. *The Garrick Year* (1964) is based on her experiences in the theater world. The heroine of *The Needle's Eye* (1972) is a divorced woman with three children who becomes involved with a lawyer and is faced with a number of moral issues.

Drabble herself has three children, and the central problem in a number of her books is one that is often voiced by modern women: the divided loyalties of a mother who seeks more than the traditional joys of family life. Her novels stress the social and moral issues of modern life that confront her characters. In 1991, Drabble married the eminent British biographer Michael Holroyd.

NOVELS BY DRABBLE

The Garrick Year (1964). Plume 1984 $8.95. ISBN 0-452-26282-8
The Ice Age (1977). Plume 1985 $7.95. ISBN 0-452-26046-9
Jerusalem the Golden (1967). Plume 1987 $8.95. ISBN 0-452-25935-5
Middle Ground (1980). Ivy 1989 $4.95. ISBN 0-8041-0362-3
The Millstone (1965). Plume 1984 $6.95. ISBN 0-452-25967-2
A Natural Curiosity (1988). Penguin 1990 $8.95. ISBN 0-1401-2228-1
The Needle's Eye (1972). Ivy 1989 $4.95. ISBN 0-8041-0364-X
The Radiant Way (1987). Ivy 1989 $4.95. ISBN 0-8041-0365-X
Realms of Gold (1975). Ivy 1989 $4.95. ISBN 0-8041-0363-1
A Summer Bird-Cage (1963). Plume 1985 $6.95. ISBN 0-452-25761-1
The Waterfall (1969). Plume 1986 $8.95. ISBN 0-452-26192-9

BOOKS ABOUT DRABBLE

Sadler, Lynn V. *Margaret Drabble.* G. K. Hall 1986 $6.95. ISBN 0-8057-6926-9 Good general introduction to Margaret Drabble's life.
Storel, Nora. *Margaret Drabble: Symbolic Moralist.* Borgo 1989 $17.95. ISBN 0-8095-5201-9 Study of the moral thrust of Drabble's novels.

DU MAURIER, DAPHNE 1907–1989

Born in London, the daughter of an actor, Gerald Du Maurier, and granddaughter of the novelist, George Du Maurier, Daphne Du Maurier was educated in Paris. Of her early life, she wrote, "The Du Maurier family, like every other family in England, lived without fear of the future, happy in the security they believed to be enduring." In 1932 she married Lieutenant-General Sir Frederick Browning and moved to Cornwall, where she has lived most of her life.

Du Maurier began writing short stories of mystery and suspense for magazines in 1925, a collection of which appeared as *The Apple Tree* in 1952. Her first novel, *The Loving Tree,* was published in 1931. She followed with two more novels that enjoyed moderate success. Then, in 1936, she published *Jamaica Inn,* the first of the mystery-suspense romances that were to make her famous. Her most successful novel, *Rebecca,* appeared in 1938.

Du Maurier's tightly woven, highly suspenseful plots and her strong characters make her stories perfect for adaptation to film or television. Among her many novels that were made into successful films are *Jamaica Inn, Rebecca, Frenchman's Creek* (1941), *Hungry Hill* (1943), *My Cousin Rachel* (1952), and *The Scapegoat* (1957). Her short story "The Birds" (1953) was brought to the screen by director Alfred Hitchcock in a treatment that has become a classic horror-suspense film.

NOVELS BY DU MAURIER

Frenchman's Creek (1941). Bentley 1971 $16.00. ISBN 0-8376-0412-5
Hungry Hill (1943). Avon 1976 $3.95. ISBN 0-380-00044-X
Jamaica Inn (1936). Avon 1977 $3.95. ISBN 0-380-00072-5
The King's General (1946). Avon 1978 $3.50. ISBN 0-380-00210-8
The Loving Spirit (1931). Bentley 1971 $16.00. ISBN 0-8376-0415-X
Mary Anne (1954). Dell 1987 $3.95. ISBN 0-440-15208-9
*My Cousin Rachel (1952). Bentley 1971 $16.00. ISBN 0-8376-0413-3 Naive young man falls in love with his mysterious cousin.

The Parasites (1950). Bentley 1971 $16.00. ISBN 0-8376-0410-9
Rebecca (1938). Avon 1978 $3.50. ISBN 0-380-00917 Story of a new bride who becomes obsessed by the mysterious death of her husband's first wife.
The Scapegoat (1957). Carroll & Graf 1988 $4.50. ISBN 0-88184-409-8 Story of a man who is tricked into assuming another man's identity.

SHORT STORY COLLECTION BY DU MAURIER

Echoes from the Macabre (1977). Amereon $20.95. ISBN 0-88411-543-7

DURRELL, LAWRENCE   1912–1990

Lawrence Durrell was born in India, where his father was a British engineer. He had his early schooling there and then completed his education in England. His life was as rich and varied as his writings. Along with numerous odd jobs, he taught at the English Institute in Athens and at a Greek high school on Cyprus; edited a witty radical magazine in Paris; founded and edited several European poetry magazines; worked in public relations in Egypt and Yugoslavia; and directed the British cultural teaching centers in Athens and Argentina. Finally, the popular success of *The Alexandria Quartet* (1957–60) allowed him to live solely by writing.

The subject of much controversy, *The Alexandria Quartet* is Durrell's major achievement. It is a complex series of four novels in which different characters serve as narrators; and in which letters, journals, and other forms of writing are used to tell the story. These novels center not only on themes such as the nature of love and the purpose of art, but also focus on the setting of Alexandria and the changing culture it represents. At a deeper level, the novels are concerned with notions of time and reality, probing the reality of experience and the meaning of past and present. Durrell explores some of these same issues in his later series of novels, *The Avignon Quintet,* in which he once again uses different narrators and a variety of story-telling devices.

In addition to his novels, Durrell published several books of poetry. His poems are most often inspired by the Mediterranean Sea and the lands around it. Because of their involved and complicated sentence structure and their many references to classical myths and legends, these poems can be difficult to read.

NOVELS BY DURRELL

The Alexandria Quartet (1957–1960) (includes *Justine* [1957], *Balthazar* [1958], *Mountolive* [1958], *Clea* [1960]). Dutton 1964 $24.95. ISBN 0-525-48242-3
Constance. Penguin 1982 $5.95. ISBN 0-670-23909-7
The Dark Labyrinth (1947). Penguin 1978 $4.95. ISBN 0-14-005025-6
Livia: or, Buried Alive (1979). Penguin 1984 $6.95. ISBN 0-14-007101-6
Monsieur (1974). Penguin 1984 $6.95. ISBN 0-14-007102-4
Numquam (1970). Penguin 1979 $5.95. ISBN 0-14-005189-9
Pope Joan (1954). Overlook Pr 1984 $8.95. ISBN 0-87951-964-9
Quinx: Or the Ripper's Tale (1984). Penguin 1986 $5.95. ISBN 0-14-008059-7
Sebastian, or the Ruling Passions (1983). Penguin 1985 $6.95. ISBN 0-14-007705-7
Tunc (1968). Penguin 1979 $5.95. ISBN 0-14-005184-8

POETRY BY DURRELL

Collected Poems (1960). Penguin 1980 $22.95. ISBN 0-670-22792-7
The Ikons and Other Poems (1966). Black Swan Bks 1981 $15.00. ISBN 0-933806-01-9
Vega and Other Poems (1973). Overlook Pr 1974 $14.95. ISBN 0-87951-009-9

ELIOT, T. S. (THOMAS STEARNS)   1888–1965

T. S. Eliot was both a poet and a critic and during the 50 years following World War I was perhaps the most influential person in the English-speaking literary world. Born in St. Louis, Missouri, he traced his ancestry to Andrew Eliot, who emigrated from England to Massachusetts in the mid-1600s. He was educated at private schools in St. Louis and Massachusetts and then at Harvard University, where he also did graduate work. He studied abroad in France, Germany and, finally, at Oxford University in England. With the outbreak of World War I, he settled in London and in 1915 married Vivian Haigh-Wood. After his marriage, Eliot taught school for a while, then went to work in the foreign department of a large London bank. He continued to work in a bank even while writing successful—but unprofitable—poetry.

Eliot's marriage was unhappy and he eventually separated from Haigh-Wood in 1932, although the two were never divorced. In 1947 Haigh-Wood died in an institution where she had been confined for mental illness. In 1957, Eliot married his assistant, Valerie Fletcher, with whom he was happy.

Eliot had begun writing poetry while at Harvard, even then experimenting with new forms and subjects. His first major poem, "The Love Song of J. Alfred Prufrock," was published in 1915 and immediately established Eliot as a new poetic voice. His work was marked by fresh rhythms, unexpected images, and a dry, ironic humor. In 1917 he published his first volume of poetry, *Prufrock and Other Observations,* and followed this with two more collections, *Poems* (1919) and *Ara Vos Prec* (1920). *The Waste Land,* Eliot's masterpiece, was published in 1922. At first the poem created considerable controversy because of its unusual poetic techniques and pessimistic outlook, but in a short time it came to be viewed as a standard against which modern poetry should be measured.

In 1927 Eliot joined the Church of England and became a British citizen. From that point on, his work became more religious in subject and tone. In his poems *Ash Wednesday* (1930) and the *Four Quartets* (1935-42), he displays hope for man's salvation. His essays and criticism also became more conservative. In his later years, he concentrated on writing plays in verse; *Murder in the Cathedral* (1935), based on the story of Thomas à Becket, the man who challenged King Henry II and lost his life for it; and *The Cocktail Party* (1950) were the most successful. Even though he no longer commands the unquestioning respect given him up through the 1950s, Eliot continues to be a powerful and influential figure in English literature.

POETRY BY ELIOT

Collected Poetry. Harcourt 1963 $14.95. ISBN 0-15-118978-1
*Old Possum's Book of Practical Cats (1939). Harcourt 1968 $3.95. ISBN 0-15-668570-1
    Delightful comic verse on a variety of feline types; the basis for the musical *Cats.*

PLAYS BY ELIOT

The Cocktail Party (1950). Harcourt 1964 $4.95. ISBN 0-15-618289-0
The Confidential Clerk (1954). Harcourt 1964 $6.95. ISBN 0-15-622015-6
The Family Reunion (1939). Harcourt 1964 $6.95. ISBN 0-15-630157-1
Murder in the Cathedral (1935). Harcourt 1964 $3.95. ISBN 0-15-663277-2

BOOKS ABOUT ELIOT

Bloom, Harold (ed). *T. S. Eliot.* Chelsea 1985 $19.95. ISBN 0-87754-601-0 Life of T. S. Eliot focusing on Eliot's relationship to his literary forebears.
*Hastings, Michael. *Tom and Viv* (1984). Penguin 1985 $4.95. ISBN 0-14-007594-1
    Fictional biography that became a play about the life of "Tom" Eliot and his first wife, Viv.

Headings, Philip R. *T. S. Eliot.* G. K. Hall 1985 $7.95. ISBN 0-8057-7357-6 Life of T. S. Eliot, as well as a sampling of various critical responses to his work.
Williamson, George. *A Reader's Guide to T.S. Eliot.* Hippocrene 1990 $20.00. ISBN 0-88254-887-5 A poet's look at the life of T. S. Eliot; excellent critiques of Eliot's writing as well as a close look at his life and personality.

FLEMING, IAN   1908–1964

Born in London, the son of a rich banker and member of Parliament, Ian Fleming was educated at Eton College and briefly attended Sandhurst, the Royal Military College. In an effort to obtain a position in the Foreign Service, he studied languages in Germany and Switzerland for four years. He did not pass the Foreign Service examination, however, and took a job as a journalist instead. For four years he was Moscow correspondent for Reuters, the large British news service. According to Fleming, "It was at Reuters that I learned to write fast and, above all, to be accurate, because in Reuters if you weren't accurate you were fired, and that was the end of that." He worked briefly as a banker in a London firm and then in 1939 returned to Moscow as a correspondent for the London *Times.* When World War II began, Fleming became a member of Naval Intelligence, where he served throughout the war.

Fleming's international reputation is almost exclusively based on his spy novels built around the character James Bond, Agent 007. With their accuracy of detail, exotic and glamorous settings, emphasis on wealth and power, and use of violence, these books established a new model for the popular adventure novel. Their enormous popularity, and that of the movies into which they were made, proved that this mix of ingredients was a formula for success, one that has been imitated by writers of spy stories ever since.

An Afternoon Hunt.   Etching by an unknown artist (Nineteenth Century).

NOVELS BY FLEMING

Casino Royale (1955). Berkley 1985 $3.95. ISBN 0-441-09400-7
The Diamond Smugglers (1957). Amereon $2.95. ISBN 0-394-81948-9
Diamonds Are Forever (1956). Berkley 1986 $3.95. ISBN 0-441-14716-X
Dr. No (1958). Berkley 1985 $3.95. ISBN 0-441-15702-2
From Russia with Love (1957). Berkley 1986 $3.50. ISBN 1-55773-157-8
Goldfinger (1959). Berkley 1985 $3.95. ISBN 0-441-29806-0
Live and Let Die (1955). Berkley 1986 $3.50. ISBN 0-441-48510-3
The Man with the Golden Gun (1965). Signet 1988 $3.95. ISBN 0-451-11878-2
On Her Majesty's Secret Service (1963). Signet 1987 $3.50. ISBN 0-451-13707-8
The Spy Who Loved Me (1962). Berkley 1986 $3.50 ISBN 0-441-77870-4
Thunderball (1961). Berkley 1985 $3.95. ISBN 0-441-80863-8
You Only Live Twice (1964). Signet 1987 $2.95. ISBN 0-451-13708-6

SHORT STORY COLLECTIONS BY FLEMING

For Your Eyes Only (1960). Berkley 1985 $3.95. ISBN 0-441-24575-7
Octopussy (1966). Signet $2.50. ISBN 0-451-11878-2

BOOKS ABOUT FLEMING

Gardner, John. *Ian Fleming's James Bond: The Illustrated Sherlock Holmes Treasury.* Crown 1987
    $9.98. ISBN 0-517-64293-X Special "classics edition" featuring illustrations of the
    best of Ian Fleming's James Bond character.
Rosenberg, Bruce, and Ann H. Stewart. *Ian Fleming.* G. K. Hall 1969 $17.95. ISBN
    0-8057-6977-3 Fictional biography of the character James Bond.

FORESTER, C. S. (CECIL SCOTT)   1899–1966

C. S. Forester was born in Cairo and educated in England at Dulwich College
and Guy's Hospital. There he studied medicine before deciding to become a
writer. From the beginning Forester showed a preference for history, especially
military history. Two early books were biographies of Napoleon and his empress, Josephine. His first successful novel *Payment Deferred* (1926) is set during
World War I and deals with his favorite theme, individual courage in time of
war.

By the mid-1930s Forester had published several more stories of war and
heroism and had established his reputation as a historical novelist. In 1935 he
published *The African Queen,* which was made into an Oscar-winning film in
1952. From 1932 to 1939 Forester spent considerable time in Hollywood writing
screenplays. In 1936 and 1937 he also served as a war correspondent covering
the Spanish Civil War.

At about this time, Forester invented his most famous character, Horatio
Hornblower, a valiant British sailor of the late eighteenth and early nineteenth
centuries. In the first Hornblower novel, *Beat to Quarters* (1937), the hero is
already a respected captain in the British navy. However, in a series of 10 other
novels written over a period of 25 years, Forester recounts Hornblower's entire
naval career. These novels were brought to the screen in the 1951 film *Captain
Horatio Hornblower* with Gregory Peck in the title role. Several other of Forester's
novels were made into successful films as well.

NOVELS BY FORESTER

*The African Queen (1935). Little 1984 $8.95. ISBN 0-316-28910-8 Story of two people
    making an adventurous boat trip up an African river—as they fall in love.
*"The Horatio Hornblower Series." Collection of novels that tells the story of one
    man's exciting naval career as he rises from midshipman to admiral and peer of

the realm. The individual novels are listed below in approximately the order of Hornblower's career.

Mr. Midshipman Hornblower (1950). Little 1984 $7.95. ISBN 0-316-28912-4
Lieutenant Hornblower (1952). Little 1952 $16.95. ISBN 0-316-28907-8
Hornblower and the Atropos (1953). Little 1985 $7.95. ISBN 0-316-28929-9
Beat to Quarters (1937). Little 1985 $7.95. ISBN 0-316-28932-9
A Ship of the Line (1938). Little 1985 $7.95. ISBN 0-316-28936-1
Flying Colors (1939). Little 1989 $7.95. ISBN 0-316-28939-6
Commodore Hornblower (1945). Little 1945 $16.95. ISBN 0-316-28894-2
Lord Hornblower (1952). Little 1989 $7.95. ISBN 0-316-28901-9
Admiral Hornblower in the West Indies (1958). Little 1958 $17.95. ISBN 0-316-28901-9
Hornblower and the Hotspur (1962). Little 1985 $7.95. ISBN 0-316-28915-9
*The Last Nine Days of the Bismarck (1959). Little 1959. (o.p.) $14.95. ISBN 0-316-28905-1
Story of the sinking of Germany's most feared World War II battleship.

FORSTER, E. M. (EDWARD MORGAN) 1879–1970

E. M. Forster was born in London and educated at a fashionable London private school, where he developed an intense dislike for what he considered the snobbish attitudes of privileged schools. He went on to study at Cambridge University, where he was much happier and where he participated actively in the school's intellectual life.

After graduation Forster traveled to Italy and Greece and later spent a short time as a tutor to the children of a German noble family. In 1905 he returned to England for the publication of his first novel, *Where Angels Fear to Tread.* He continued to teach and write in England, publishing *The Longest Journey* in 1907 and *A Room with a View* in 1908, both of which received only lukewarm receptions. (*Room with a View* was later made into a film.) His fourth novel, however, *Howard's End* (1910), was widely praised and established his reputation as a first-rate author. This brilliant book tells the story of the witty, principled, and ambitious Schlegel sisters. Their search for romance and a meaningful existence becomes a vehicle for exploring how England is to be governed and who shall determine its future.

In 1912 Forster made the first of his two trips to India, where he came to despise the way the British treated the Indian People, and started a novel on this theme. When war broke out, Forster served with the Red Cross in Egypt until 1919.

In 1921 Forster became secretary to The Maharajah of Dewas Senior and returned with his employer to India, where he resumed work on the novel he had begun earlier. *A Passage to India* was published in 1924 and is generally recognized as Forster's finest work and one of the best novels of the twentieth century. It was made into a play in 1960 and a film in 1984.

Forster's great gift as a novelist was to bring his wit, vision, and skillful use of language to bear on complex social issues. His basic concern is the restrictions of "civilized" social behavior on "natural" human feelings. In particular, he attacks the British social system, especially its structure of social classes, as creating artificial limits on the full development of human emotions.

NOVELS BY FORSTER

Howard's End (1910). Bantam 1985 $3.95. ISBN 0-553-21208-7
The Longest Journey (1907). Random 1962 $4.95. ISBN 0-394-70040-6
A Passage to India (1924). Harcourt 1965 $5.95. ISBN 0-15-671142-7
A Room with a View (1908). Bantam 1988 $3.95. ISBN 0-553-21323-7
Where Angels Fear to Tread (1905). Random 1958 $3.95. ISBN 0-394-70061-9

SHORT STORY COLLECTIONS BY FORSTER

The Celestial Omnibus and Other Stories (1911). Random 1976 $3.95. ISBN 0-394-72176-4
Collected Tales. Knopf 1947 $14.95. ISBN 0-394-41978-2
The Eternal Moment and Other Stories (1928). Harcourt 1970 $4.95. ISBN 0-15-629125-8

BOOKS ABOUT FORSTER

Bloom, Harold (ed). *E. M. Forster.* Chelsea 1986 $24.50. ISBN 0-87754-643-6 Life of
    Forster as seen by one of the major critics writing on this period.
Trilling, Lionel. *E. M. Forster.* New Directions 1964 $5.95. ISBN 0-8112-0210-0 The
    stories behind many of the essays written by Forster.

FOWLES, JOHN 1926–

John Fowles studied at Oxford, joined the Royal Marines, and then became a
teacher before turning to writing. His first novel, *The Collector* (1963), was so
successful that after its publication he was able to devote all his time to fiction.
The Collector is about a lower-class young man whose lottery winnings enable
him to act out his fantasy of kidnapping a pretty young girl whom he has been
admiring from afar. Fowles returns to the theme of the enslavement of one
human being by another in his later novels.

Fowles's best-known work is *The French Lieutenant's Woman* (1969), which
became especially well known when an award-winning movie was made from
it. The novel portrays a betrayed woman who lived 100 years ago; Fowles uses
a modern narrator whose ironic commentary brings twentieth-century social
ideas into the work, creating a dual perspective of then and now.

In his essays Fowles describes the purpose of fiction as the pursuit of
artistic excellence. His goal in his novels, he says, is not only to tell a good story
but to craft the most technically perfect piece of fiction that he possibly can.

NOVELS BY FOWLES

The Collector (1963). Dell 1981 $4.50. ISBN 0-440-31335-X
Daniel Martin (1977). Signet 1978 $4.50. ISBN 0-451-12210-0
The French Lieutenant's Woman (1969). Signet 1981 $3.95. ISBN 0-451-13598-9
A Maggot (1985). Signet 1986 $4.50. ISBN 0-451-14476-7
The Magus (1966). Dell 1985 $5.95. ISBN 0-440-35162-6

SHORT STORY COLLECTION BY FOWLES

The Ebony Tower (1974). Signet 1975 $4.50. ISBN 0-451-15691-9

BOOKS ABOUT FOWLES

Conradi, Peter J. *John Fowles.* Routledge 1982 $5.95. ISBN 0-416-32250-6 A short
    history of the adventurous life led by John Fowles.
Olshen, Barry, and Toni A. Olshen. *John Fowles.* Ungar 1978 $16.95. ISBN 0-8044-
    2665-1 One in a series of reference guides, with plot summaries of each of John
    Fowles's works.

FRY, CHRISTOPHER 1907–

Success came to Christopher Fry after 38 years of living close to poverty. Fry
was born in Bristol, where his father, a poor architect, turned to doing missionary work in the city slums. In 1940, after alternating between teaching and

acting, Fry became director of the excellent Oxford Playhouse. When World War II broke out, he served in the Non-Combatant Corps because his Quaker religion would not allow him to bear arms.

Fry came to wide public attention after the war when his play *A Phoenix Too Frequent* (1946) was produced in London. The play tells the story of a widow who accepts a new lover while mourning beside her late husband's grave. It received high critical praise and proved very popular even though it was staged in a small, out-of-the-way theater.

Three years later, British actor-director John Gielgud's production of *The Lady's Not for Burning* (1948) brought Fry national success. The play was moved to New York, where it won the Drama Critics Circle Award for 1950. Fry later described this play as the "spring" piece in a cycle of four plays, each of which represented a season. It was followed by the autumn play, *Venus Observed* (1950), the winter piece, *The Dark Is Light Enough* (1954), and finally the summer play, *A Yard of Sun* (1970).

Because Fry's plays are written in verse, he has never achieved enormous popularity, although he does have a devoted following. His plays tend to be dynamic and lively, full of flamboyant and powerful language. His themes and stories are frequently drawn from the Bible, ancient history, or myth. Fry explains that he writes in verse because "poetry is the language in which man explores his own amazement."

PLAYS BY FRY

The Dark Is Light Enough (1954). Oxford Univ Pr 1954 $9.95. ISBN 0-19-500155-9
The Lady's Not for Burning (1948). Oxford Univ Pr 1977 $6.95. ISBN 0-19-519916-2
Selected Plays Oxford Univ Pr 1985 $11.95. ISBN 0-19-281873-2
Venus Observed (1950). Oxford Univ Pr 1950 $9.95. ISBN 0-19-500395-0
A Yard of Sun (1970). Oxford Univ Pr 1970 $9.95. ISBN 0-19-501245-3

BOOK ABOUT FRY

Roy, Emil. *Christopher Fry.* Southern Illinois Univ Pr 1968 $6.95. ISBN 0-8093-0315-9
A look at the poetry found within the drama of Christopher Fry.

GALSWORTHY, JOHN   1867–1933

John Galsworthy was born in Surrey, England, and educated at Harrow and Oxford University. He trained for the law and practiced briefly before deciding to write. Throughout his life he wrote plays and novels alternately.

Galsworthy's career as a dramatist began in 1906 with the production of *The Silver Box,* a play that portrayed two families, one rich and one poor. He was to use this same plot device later with great success in other plays and in his novels.

Galsworthy's masterwork is *The Forsyte Saga,* a series of six separate novels and two shorter, linking stories. He published the first novel in the series, *A Man of Property,* in 1906 and the last, *Swan Song,* in 1928. These stories detail the lives of different individuals and generations in the Forsyte family, a clan that Galsworthy uses to represent the wealthy British upper middle class of the early 1800s.

Galsworthy's work is generally noted for its emphasis on social and moral issues. Polish-born British author Joseph Conrad (*see* Conrad, Vol. 1, British Literature: The Twentieth Century) called Galsworthy a "humanitarian novelist" because of his attacks on social injustice. His novels were, in fact, influential in producing some social reforms in Britain, particularly in prisons.

In his later years, Galsworthy was given many honors, including honorary degrees from Oxford, Cambridge, and several other universities. After World War I he was offered a knighthood, which he refused. He did, however, accept the Order of Merit in 1929, and in 1932 he was awarded the Nobel Prize for literature.

NOVELS BY GALSWORTHY

The Forsyte Saga (1922). (Part of the series) Scribner's repr of 1933 ed $15.95. ISBN 0-684-17653-X
A Modern Comedy (1929). Macmillan 1987 $50.00. ISBN 0-02-542370-3

PLAYS BY GALSWORTHY

Ten Best Plays of John Galsworthy. Longwood 1976 $40.50. ISBN 0-7156-0797-9

BOOKS ABOUT GALSWORTHY

Dupré, Catherine. *John Galsworthy: A Biography.* Coward 1976. (o.p.) ISBN 698-10715-2 A good, general biography of Galsworthy for the student coming to his life and work for the first time; includes photographs, a list of Galsworthy's works, and a bibliography.

Gindin, James. *John Galsworthy's Life and Art: An Alien's Fortress.* Univ of Michigan Pr 1987 $29.95. ISBN 0-472-10075-0 A more scholarly biography and critical study whose intention is to insist on Galsworthy's stature as a serious artist; makes use of interviews with Galsworthy's family and includes photographs.

GODDEN, (MARGARET) RUMER 1907–

Rumer Godden was born in Sussex, England, and brought up in India. She came back to England at age 11 to be educated, and then returned to India. During the 1930s she operated a children's dancing school in Calcutta. During most of her later years, she has resided in England and Scotland.

Although known primarily as an author of children's books, Godden has written several novels for adults, six of which have been adapted for motion pictures or television. Among these are *Black Narcissus* (1939), for which she wrote the screenplay; *The Greengage Summer* (1958); and *In This House of Brede* (1969). While her books cover a wide range of settings and plots, three themes seem to dominate her work: the clash of different cultures, the innocence and vulnerability of children, and religion (two of her novels are set in a convent). It is the contrast of cultures, however, to which she most often returns. Godden's years in India have made her very sensitive to the way human beings from different cultural backgrounds respond differently to the same situation.

NOVELS BY GODDEN

An Episode of Sparrows (1955). Penguin 1989 $4.95. ISBN 0-14-034024-6 An unlikely combination of four very different characters is thrown together in postwar London.

The Greengage Summer (1958). Penguin 1986 $3.95. ISBN 0-14-031982-4 Two sisters discover that nothing is quite what it seems.

The Peacock Spring (1978). Penguin 1986 $3.95. ISBN 0-14-032005-9 A young girl's adjustment to a new life in India.

Thursday's Children (1983). Dell 1987 $3.25. ISBN 0-440-98790-3 Competition between a boy and his sister in ballet.

NONFICTION BY GODDEN

A House with Four Rooms (1989). Morrow 1989 $18.95. ISBN 0-688-08629-2
A Time to Dance, No Time to Weep: A Memoir (1987). Morrow 1987 $16.95. ISBN 0-688-07421-9

BOOK ABOUT GODDEN

Simpson, Hassell A. *Rumer Godden.* Twayne 1973. (o.p.) $5.50. A good general discussion of Godden's works as illuminated by events in her life; includes a brief biography, a chronology, and a bibliography.

GOLDING, WILLIAM 1911–

William Golding was born in Cornwall, England, and educated at Oxford University, where he began studying science before changing to literature and classics. After graduating he worked in the theater as an actor, writer, and producer. He then taught school for a while before serving with the Royal Navy in World War II.

Golding had published some poems before the war, but it was his first novel, *Lord of the Flies* (1954), that brought him public attention. At first the book sold slowly in the United States, but in the early 1960s it became popular on college campuses and developed into a bestseller. Golding describes its theme as "an attempt to trace the defects of human nature. The moral is that the shape of the society must depend on the ethical nature of the individual and not on any political system however logical or respectable."

Among Golding's other novels are *The Inheritors* (1955), about innocent Neanderthal Man's defeat and suppression by Homo Sapiens; *Pincher Martin* (1956), about a drowning man confronted by all the unanswered questions of his past life; and *The Spire* (1964), about the building of a great English cathedral. In *The Paper Men* (1984), Golding tells the story of a famous writer who cannot escape being hounded by an insistent American professor.

Almost all of Golding's writing is concerned with basic moral problems at the center of human existence. He looks closely at the good and evil instincts in humans and places his characters in situations where these instincts must conflict. Golding supplies no easy answers but raises disturbing and difficult questions.

Golding's work has been highly praised and honored in recent years. He won the Booker Prize, Britain's highest literary award, for *Rites of Passage* in 1980 and was awarded the Nobel Prize for literature in 1983.

NOVELS BY GOLDING

Close Quarters (1987). Farrar 1987 $16.95. ISBN 0-374-12510-4
Darkness Visible (1979). Farrar 1979 $14.95. ISBN 0-374-13502-9
Fire Down Below (1989). Farrar 1989 $17.95. ISBN 0-374-25381-1
Free Fall (1959). Harcourt 1962 $3.95. ISBN 0-15-633468-2
The Inheritors (1955). Washington Square Pr 1981 $3.95. ISBN 0-671-53139-5
*Lord of the Flies (1954). Putnam 1989 $3.95. ISBN 0-399-50148-7 Young boys' struggle for survival on a desert island.
The Paper Men (1984). Farrar 1984 $13.95. ISBN 0-374-22980-5
Pincher Martin (1956). Harcourt 1968 $4.95. ISBN 0-15-671833-2
The Pyramid (1967). Harcourt 1968 $3.95. ISBN 0-15-674703-0
Rites of Passage (1980). Farrar 1980 $14.95. ISBN 0-374-25086-3
The Spire (1964). Harcourt 1965 $6.95. ISBN 0-15-684741-8

Short Story Collection by Golding

The Scorpion God (1971). Harcourt 1984 $6.95. ISBN 0-15-679658-9

Play by Golding

The Brass Butterfly (1956). Faber & Faber 1969 $4.95. ISBN 0-571-09073-7

Books about Golding

Carey, John (ed). *William Golding: The Man and His Books.* Farrar 1987 $22.50. ISBN 0-374-29023-7 A friend of William Golding recalls the author's life.
Dick, Bernard F. *William Golding.* G. K. Hall 1987 $18.95. ISBN 0-8057-6925-0 A good general overview of Golding's life.
Gindin, James. *William Golding.* St. Martin's 1988 $19.95. ISBN 0-312-01617-4 Golding's public statements and other daily occurrences in his life.

GRAVES, ROBERT 1895–1985

Robert Graves was born in Wimbledon near London, the son of a famous Irish literary figure, A. P. Graves. He was educated at Charterhouse School, and served in France during World War I, where at one point he was severely wounded and falsely reported dead.

After the war, Graves completed his formal education at Oxford University. His tangled private life included two marriages and a period of 13 years in which he lived with poet Laura Riding. Graves spent most of his life in Majorca.

Graves's early poetry was dominated by his war experiences, and he developed a theory of poetry as the writer's expression of internal psychological conflicts. He also developed a highly individual style that drew heavily on classical literature and mythology. In addition, some of his early work borrows from nursery rhymes, ballads, and other simple poetic forms.

Graves had one of the most varied and productive careers in twentieth-century literature. Although devoted primarily to poetry, he produced a vast array of other works, including historical novels like *I, Claudius* (1934) (later a television series), plays, criticism, translations, and his sensitive and moving autobiography, *Goodbye to All That* (1929). In *The White Goddess* (1948) he proposed a theory of poetry which claimed that early human societies were organized and dominated by women and that the ancient Greeks and Hebrews had distorted and corrupted the values of these societies. True poetry, he believed, could only be achieved by those who recaptured these original female myths and ideas.

Novels by Graves

Claudius the God (1934). Random 1989 $9.95. ISBN 0-679-72573-3
Count Belisarius (1938). Farrar 1982 $12.95. ISBN 0-374-51739-8
Hercules, My Shipmate (1945). Farrar 1945 $9.95. ISBN 0-374-51677-4
Homer's Daughter (1955). Academy Chi Pubs 1987 $8.95. ISBN 0-89733-059-5
I, Claudius (1934). Random 1989 $8.95. ISBN 0-679-72477-X
King Jesus (1946). Farrar 1946 $10.95. ISBN 0-374-51664-2

Short Story Collection by Graves

Collected Short Stories. Penguin 1985 $6.95. ISBN 0-14-002881-1

NONFICTION BY GRAVES

Goodbye to All That. Doubleday 1957 $8.95. ISBN 0-385-09330-6 Autobiography that includes maps and drawings by Graves showing where he served during World War I; first published in 1929.
The Greek Myths. 2 vols. Penguin 1955. Vol. 1 $4.95. ISBN 0-14-020508-X. Vol. 2 $4.95. ISBN 0-14-020509-X

BOOKS ABOUT GRAVES

Bloom, Harold. *Robert Graves.* Chelsea 1987 $24.50. ISBN 0-87754-644-4 Collection of modern critical essays.
Snipes, Katherine. *Robert Graves.* Ungar 1979 $16.95. ISBN 0-8044-2825-5 General introduction to the life and works of Graves.

GREENE, GRAHAM   1904–1991

Graham Greene was the son of the headmaster at Berkhamsted School, which he attended before going on to Oxford University. After graduation he became a journalist, working first for the London *Times* and then for *The Spectator.* One of his assignments was to investigate and report on religious persecution in Mexico. During World War II he served in Africa in the British Foreign Office.

Greene names as the two great influences on his writing John Buchan, a master of the spy thriller, and the Catholic novelist François Mauriac. Greene's work clearly shows the tension produced by these two different influences. Some of his books, such as *The Confidential Agent* (1939) and *Our Man in Havana* (1958), are gripping spy stories, which he calls "entertainments," although they also deal with moral issues. Others are more obviously serious works dealing more directly with moral and religious questions. A convert to Catholicism in 1926, Greene is "primarily and passionately concerned with good and evil," with the place of God in a world of fallen mortals. His first truly Catholic novel was *Brighton Rock* (1938), in which he explored the concept of "the appalling strangeness of the mercy of God," a theme that was to recur in later novels such as *The Power and the Glory* (1940) and *The Heart of the Matter* (1948).

In addition to novels, Greene has written several plays and volumes of short stories. A number of his works have been made into films, and he himself is the author of several screenplays, including that for the Orson Welles film *The Third Man.* In 1952 Greene received the Catholic Literary Award.

NOVELS BY GREENE

Brighton Rock (1938). Penguin 1977 $3.95. ISBN 0-14-00442-4
The Comedians (1966). Penguin 1976 $4.95. ISBN 0-14-002766-1
The Confidential Agent (1939). Penguin 1981 $3.95. ISBN 0-14-001895-6
The Heart of the Matter (1948). Penguin 1978 $3.95. ISBN 0-14-001789-5
Our Man in Havana (1958). Penguin 1979 $4.95. ISBN 0-14-001790-9
The Power and the Glory (1940). Penguin 1977 $3.95. ISBN 0-14-001791-7
The Quiet American (1955). Penguin 1977 $4.95. ISBN 0-14-007192-2
Travels with My Aunt (1969). Penguin 1977 $4.95. ISBN 0-14-003221-5

SHORT STORY COLLECTION BY GREENE

Collected Stories. Penguin 1987 $7.95. ISBN 0-317-62620-5

BOOKS ABOUT GREENE

De Vitis, A. A. *Graham Greene.* G. K. Hall 1986 $7.95. ISBN 0-8057-6928-5 An examination of Greene's novels, including a complete listing of Greene's work and an excellent bibliography.

Hynes, Samuel (ed). *Graham Greene: A Collection of Critical Essays.* Prentice 1973. (o.p.) $4.90. ISBN 0-13-362251-7 A compilation of the best critical essays about Greene by highly respected scholars with an especially useful introduction by Hynes; contains a chronology and selected bibliography.

Kelly, Richard. *Graham Greene.* Ungar 1985 $16.95. ISBN 0-8044-2464-0 Careful analysis of Greene's life and works, covering his novels, "entertainments," short stories, and plays; includes a bibliography and index.

Sherry, Norman. *The Life of Graham Greene: Vol. 1: 1904–1939.* Penguin 1990 $15.95. ISBN 0-14-014450-1 A massive study, "going to the heart of Greene's darkly anguished worldview and the anxieties, guilts and demons that have driven him to create," according to *Publishers Weekly.*

HEANEY, SEAMUS   1939–

Often viewed as the leading poet of his generation, Seamus Heaney was born in County Derry in Northern Ireland. Educated entirely in Irish schools, he graduated from Queen's University, Belfast, with honors. He has held a variety of teaching jobs, including a post at Queen's University from 1966 to 1972.

In 1972 Heaney left turbulent, war-torn Belfast for a four-year stay in an Irish country cottage, where he produced the *Glanmore Sonnets* (1975) and other works. He and his family now live in Dublin, and he spends part of each year teaching at Harvard University in Cambridge, Massachusetts. A gifted critic as well as a poet, Heaney has also written a book of literary essays.

Heaney's first collection of poetry, *Death of a Naturalist* (1966), established his reputation, which has grown with each successive volume. He often writes of rural life in his native Ulster in an unsentimental and moving way. For example, his poem "Digging" establishes comparisons between rural hardship and the poet's own labor.

When Heaney turns to the past, he favors the Vikings rather than the Celtic heroes chosen by many Irish poets. He has also produced a powerful group of poems about the preservation of ancient tribal artifacts in Irish peat bogs, again making connections to his own role as a poet. Political themes relating to the troubles in Northern Ireland also appear in Heaney's work. He recently published a superb version of the story of one Irish hero who fascinates him, the medieval king Sweeney, in *Sweeney Astray* (1983).

POETRY BY HEANEY

Death of a Naturalist (1966). Faber & Faber 1985 $5.95. ISBN 0-571-09024-9
Door into the Dark (1969). Faber & Faber 1972 $4.95. ISBN 0-571-10126-7
Field Work (1979). Farrar 1979 $5.95. ISBN 0-374-51620-0
North (1975). Faber & Faber 1985 $5.95. ISBN 0-571-10813-X
Station Island (1984). Farrar 1985 $6.95. ISBN 0-374-51935-8
Sweeney Astray (1983). Farrar 1984 $7.95. ISBN 0-374-51894-7

BOOKS ABOUT HEANEY

Andrews, Elmer. *The Poetry of Seamus Heaney.* St. Martin's 1988 $35.00. ISBN 0-312-01597-6 A solid analysis of Heaney's subjects and style, book by book; features a useful bibliography.

Corcoran, Neil. *Seamus Heaney: A Faber Student Guide.* Faber & Faber 1986 $9.95. ISBN 0-571-13955-8 An in-depth study of Heaney's poetry with biographical information about the poet taken from interviews between Heaney and the author.

Morrison, Blake. *Seamus Heaney.* Routledge 1982 $7.95. ISBN 0-416-31900-9 Examination of Heaney's career and poetry in relation to Anglo-American and Irish traditions, as well as to the political climate of Northern Ireland.

HERRIOT, JAMES (PSEUDONYM OF JAMES ALFRED WIGHT) 1916–

James Herriot was born James Alfred Wight in northern England and studied veterinary medicine at Glasgow Veterinary College in Scotland. His writing has made him, beyond doubt, the most famous veterinarian in the world. Ironically, when Herriot began writing he had to assume a pen name because British laws prevent veterinarians from advertising, and a popular book might have been considered to be an advertisement.

Herriot's books recount his experiences as a veterinary surgeon in the Yorkshire countryside, beginning with his arrival fresh out of college and continuing into the years after World War II. The first book in the series, *All Creatures Great and Small* (1972), introduces the reader to Siegfried Farnham (also a pseudonym), the somewhat eccentric local veterinarian with whom Herriot works. The comic interplay between Siegfried and his younger brother Tristan lends a spirited light touch to these books.

Young Herriot's adventures—and misadventures—as he learns the ways of country veterinary medicine and the ways of the farmers he serves, make for lively and interesting reading. In a larger sense, however, the books are about the experiences of one man and one community. They describe and mourn the passing of the simple rural life of the past. Herriot has probably painted a far more romantic picture of life in the country than most farmers would recognize, yet his books still leave the reader with the sense that the life he describes really was better, and that its passing is a genuine loss.

NONFICTION BY HERRIOT

*All Creatures Great and Small (1972). Bantam 1977 $4.50. ISBN 0-553-25229-1 The problems and joys of a country veterinary surgeon.
*All Things Bright and Beautiful (1974). Bantam 1975 $4.50. ISBN 0-553-24851-0 Further adventures of a dedicated veterinarian in the Yorkshire dales of the 1930s.
*All Things Wise and Wonderful (1977). Bantam 1978 $4.50. ISBN 0-553-25446-4 Herriot leaves for service in the Royal Air Force during World War II.
*James Herriot's Dog Stories (1986). St. Martin's 1987 $4.95. ISBN 0-312-90143-7 Stories of some brave, eccentric, and lovable dogs.
James Herriot's Yorkshire (1981). Bantam 1982 $4.95. ISBN 0-553-25981
*The Lord God Made Them All (1981). Bantam 1981 $4.50. ISBN 0-553-24731-X Back from World War II, Herriot continues his veterinary practice and does some traveling.

HILTON, JAMES 1900–1954

James Hilton was born in Lancashire, England, but his family moved to London when he was a child. He was educated at Cambridge University, where he began contributing pieces to newspapers while still an undergraduate. After graduation, Hilton took a position as an instructor at Cambridge, where he wrote newspaper and magazine pieces—and novels.

Although Hilton published six novels during the 1920s, none of them received much attention. The turning point came in 1933, when he was asked by a magazine to submit a long short story for publication in the Christmas issue. The only catch was that it had to be ready in two weeks. Unable to come up with an idea, Hilton was about to abandon the project when he suddenly had an inspiration and in four days of furious writing turned out *Good-bye Mr. Chips* (1934), his most famous novel. Although *Lost Horizon* was published at about the same time, it did not create much of a stir. However, the runaway success of *Good-bye Mr. Chips,* particularly in the United States, brought with it renewed interest in Hilton's other works, and his career blossomed.

Hollywood decided to make a movie of *Lost Horizon,* and Hilton came to the United States to help with the script. He stayed on after the project was completed and became an American citizen in 1948. Although he continued to write novels, he devoted an increasing amount of his time to screenplays, becoming one of the most popular and highly paid scriptwriters in Hollywood. At his death, *Time* magazine wrote: ". . . Hilton served up a mellow blend of worldly wisdom and well-bred British morality that delighted the book clubs, Hollywood producers, and the general public, but alienated first-line critics."

NOVELS BY HILTON

Good-bye Mr. Chips (1934). Bantam 1969 $2.95. ISBN 0-553-25613-0 Traces the career of a British teacher.

Lost Horizon (1933). Pocket 1984 $3.95. ISBN 0-671-54148-X In the land of Shangri-La, life is eternally beautiful.

Random Harvest (1941). Carroll & Graf 1985 $4.50. ISBN 0-88184-125-0 The attempts of an amnesia victim to rediscover his life.

Was It Murder? (1931). Dover 1979 $4.95. ISBN 0-486-23774-5 Mystery and suspense in a private school.

We Are Not Alone (1937). Amereon (repr of 1937 ed) $13.95. ISBN 0-88411-843-6

HUGHES, TED (EDWARD JAMES)   1930–

Ted Hughes attended a grammar school in his native Yorkshire before spending two years as a ground mechanic in the Royal Air Force. He went on to Cambridge University, where he studied first literature and then anthropology, amassing some of the primitive lore that underlies his work. There he also met the American poet, Sylvia Plath (*see* Plath, Vol. 1, American Literature: The Twentieth Century), then a graduate student, whom he married in 1956. They lived in the United States until 1959, when they returned to England. Their marriage was troubled by Plath's recurring mental illness and the two were already separated when Plath committed suicide in 1963. Hughes remarried in 1970.

Hughes has worked as a rose gardener, a night security guard, and a reader for the Rank Organization, a large media and publishing business. In 1965, he became co-editor of the magazine *Modern Poetry in Translation.* Besides his poetry, Hughes has written children's verse, translations, and several plays. His long list of honors and prizes culminated in his appointment as Poet Laureate of Britain in 1984.

In both subject matter and technique, Hughes's poetry displays a violence that contrasts sharply with the work of most other contemporary British poets. His first book, *The Hawk in the Rain,* created a sensation upon its publication in 1957. Animals are a favorite subject of Hughes, particularly horses and birds of prey, and he has developed a character called Crow that appears in several volumes of his verse. His poetry aims to shock and disturb, often by showing instinctive forces overpowering rational, civilized behavior. Some of Hughes's animal poems are spoken from the point of view of the animal rather than from that of a human being.

POETRY BY HUGHES

Crow (1970). Harper 1981 $6.95. ISBN 0-06-090905-6
The Hawk in the Rain (1957). Faber & Faber 1968 $4.95. ISBN 0-571-08614-4
Lupercal (1960). Faber & Faber 1970 $4.95. ISBN 0-571-09246-2
Moortown (1979). Harper 1980 $12.45. ISBN 0-06-012016-9
New Selected Poems. Harper 1982 $10.95. ISBN 0-06-090925-0
Remains of Elmet (1979). Harper 1979 $17.00. ISBN 0-06-011953-5
River (1984). Harper 1984 $6.95. ISBN 0-06-091137-9
Under the North Star (1981). Penguin 1981 $16.95. ISBN 0-670-73942-1

BOOK ABOUT HUGHES

Sagar, Keith (ed). *The Achievement of Ted Hughes.* Univ of Georgia Pr 1983 $25.00. ISBN 0-8203-0650-9 A detailed critical account of Hughes's work as well as a comprehensive bibliography of writings by and about him.

HUXLEY, ALDOUS   1894–1963

Aldous Huxley was born into a distinguished family. His grandfather, T. H. Huxley, was a famous Victorian scientist and philosopher, and his elder brother, Julian, was a world-renowned biologist and science writer.

Huxley was educated at Eton College and Oxford University. After his graduation he became a journalist. He published several volumes of poetry, and then turned to fiction, publishing a series of witty and satirical novels.

While Huxley is always interesting and engages the reader's intelligence, he seldom touches the reader's emotions. His works are novels of ideas, and he uses both plot and character to define and analyze social issues.

Huxley became a very influential writer in the 1930s, as he described and satirized the free-living style of the "Roaring Twenties." His *Brave New World* (1932) was a sharply critical and ingenious look at a future dominated by technology. It continued to be an enormously popular book, especially in the United States, through the 1940s and 1950s. The passage of time has shown that in many respects Huxley's fears about the future were all too legitimate.

In 1937 Huxley moved to the United States and took up residence in California. His novel *After Many a Summer Dies the Swan* (1939) is set in Los Angeles and satirizes the Hollywood way of life. After settling in America, Huxley turned his attention away from social problems and became increasingly absorbed by mystical phenomena, especially the effects of mind-altering drugs.

Huxley received the Award of Merit Medal in 1959 from the American Academy of Arts and Letters. In 1962 he was elected a Companion of Literature by the British Royal Society of Literature, one of the highest literary awards in Britain.

NOVELS BY HUXLEY

*Brave New World (1932). Harper 1979 $4.95. ISBN 0-06-083-095-6 Classic look at a future dominated by technology.
*Brave New World Revisited (1958). Harper 1989 $4.95. ISBN 0-06-080983-3 A further look into the future.
Eyeless in Gaza (1936). Carroll & Graf 1989 $10.95. ISBN 0-88184-460-8
Island (1962). Harper 1989 $4.95. ISBN 0-06-080985-X
Point Counter Point (1928). Harper 1965 $4.95. ISBN 0-06-083048-4

BOOKS ABOUT HUXLEY

Bedford, Sybille. *Aldous Huxley.* Carroll & Graf 1985 $14.95. ISBN 0-88184-145-5 A massive biography based on Huxley's letters and the oral reminiscences of those who know him personally, including the author; contains a chronology and index.

Nance, Guinevera. *Aldous Huxley.* Continuum 1989 $18.95. ISBN 0-8044-2639-2 Biographical and critical examination of Huxley, focusing on his novels and how they are affected by his philosophical explorations.

Watts, Harold H. *Aldous Huxley.* G. K. Hall 1969 $15.95. ISBN 0-8057-1284-4 Survey of Huxley's early fiction, essays, and late writings; includes some biographical information.

ISHERWOOD, CHRISTOPHER 1904–1986

Christopher Isherwood was born in Cheshire, England, and educated at St. Edmund's School in Surrey, Repton College, and Cambridge University. At St. Edmunds he met British writer W. H. Auden (*see* Auden, Vol. 1, British Literature: The Twentieth Century) and the two became lifelong friends.

In 1928 and 1929, Isherwood was working as a private tutor in London. During this time he published his first novel, *All the Conspirators* (1928), a story dealing with an artist's attempt to break free from the restrictions of family. This early work shows Isherwood's fascination with movies, particularly with the idea of a camera capturing and recording scenes.

In his second novel, *The Memorial* (1932), Isherwood experimented with shifting the sequence of time in his story, much as filmmakers do when using flashbacks or dream episodes.

From 1930 to 1933, Isherwood lived in Berlin, where he made his living teaching English. This experience served as the basis for his best, and most famous, series of short novels, known collectively as *The Berlin Stories* (1946). Once again he writes as if he were a cinematographer shooting scenes for a film. So striking was this technique that in 1951 the playwright John Van Druten took Isherwood's Berlin stories and made them into a successful play called *I Am a Camera.* The play was subsequently made into the hit musical *Cabaret.*

In 1938 Isherwood and W. H. Auden made a tour of China and jointly wrote *Journey to a War* (1939). In late 1939 Isherwood and Auden immigrated to the United States and resided in California, where Isherwood began to write screenplays. During this time Isherwood also became close friends with Aldous Huxley. (*See* Huxley, Vol. 1, British Literature: The Twentieth Century.) He came to share Huxley's interest in the Vedas, ancient Hindu scriptures, and even translated some of these works into English.

FICTION BY ISHERWOOD

All the Conspirators (1928). New Directions 1979 $7.95. ISBN 0-8112-0725-0

The Berlin Stories (1946). New Directions 1954 $7.95. ISBN 0-8112-0070-1

The Memorial (1932). Farrar 1988 $8.95. ISBN 0-374-52067-4

BOOKS ABOUT ISHERWOOD

Summers, Claude J. *Christopher Isherwood.* Ungar 1980 $16.95. ISBN 0-8044-2846-8 An introduction to Isherwood's life and art, tracing his development and carefully examining his fiction.

Wilde, Alan (ed.) *Christopher Isherwood.* Twayne 1971. (o.p.) Sympathetic and thorough analysis of the man and his works, concentrating on the development of his ironic style over a 40-year period.

JACOBS, W. W. (WILLIAM WYMARK)   1863–1943

W. W. Jacobs was born in London, the son of a wharf manager. He grew up in and around the London docks and used this background extensively in his later fiction.

Jacobs entered the British Civil Service in 1893. At about the same time, he began publishing stories in magazines. He continued to hold his job as a clerk while he was writing and publishing, never quite trusting his literary talent to provide him a living. Finally, after publishing several volumes of short stories, he turned to writing full time.

Over the course of his career, Jacobs published over 20 collections of his stories, most of which deal with the dockworkers, stevedores, sailors, and other waterfront characters he knew so well. He also wrote a considerable number of tales of the supernatural and macabre, the best known of which is "The Monkey's Paw." Jacobs's stories are often filled with a dry and gentle humor that pokes fun at the peculiarities of his characters without ridiculing them.

SHORT STORY COLLECTIONS BY JACOBS

Cargoes: Famous Sea Stories (1896). Branden (repr of 1896 ed) $2.95. ISBN 0-8283-1430-6
The Monkey's Paw (1902). Troll 1982 $2.50. ISBN 0-89375-629-6
Night Watches (1914). David and Charles 1988 $13.50. ISBN 0-7126-0335-2

JAMES, P. D. (PHYLLIS DOROTHY)   1920–

P. D. James was born in Oxford, England, the daughter of a tax officer. She was educated at Cambridge Girl's High School. She worked for a short time as assistant stage manager at the Festival Theater in Cambridge before marrying Ernest C. B. White in 1941. During World War II James worked as a Red Cross nurse. When her husband returned from the war an invalid, she took a job as a hospital administrator in order to support her family. Following her husband's death in 1964, she entered the British Department of Home Affairs as a civil servant in the criminal department, from which she retired in 1979.

James began writing seriously in the late 1950s, and her first novel, *Cover Her Face* (1962), draws on her hospital experiences of that period. She went on to write nine more crime novels featuring Commander Adam Dalgleish, a professional Scotland Yard detective. She also created Cordelia Gray, a female private detective, who appears in two novels. In addition James has written other stories of crime and suspense.

While most mystery writers are content to present their readers with an interesting plot—a puzzle to be solved—James insists on presenting interesting, fully developed characters as well. For example, Dalgleish is a widower, still pained by his wife's death, and a published poet as well as a detective. Likewise, James's books delve much more deeply than most crime novels into the motives, emotions, and relationships of the characters. James presents a view of the world as a dangerous place, with evil always lurking just beneath the surface.

In 1967 James received the Crime Writers Association Prize. Her novels have been dramatized for television and are popular in the United States and Britain.

NOVELS BY JAMES

The Black Tower (1975). Warner Bks 1987 $3.95. ISBN 0-446-31435-8 The mysterious black tower holds the key to the mystery.

Cover Her Face (1962). Warner Bks 1982 $3.95. ISBN 0-446-34825-2 First of the Dalgleish mysteries, in which the inspector must discover which of her many enemies killed a sensuous and ambitious woman.

Death of an Expert Witness (1977). Warner Bks 1987 $8.95. ISBN 0-446-31472-2 A huge cast of characters gives Dalgleish a difficult problem.

Innocent Blood (1980). Warner Bks 1987 $4.95. ISBN 0-446-31177-4 The victim may not be as innocent as it first appears.

A Mind to Murder (1967). Warner Bks 1983 $3.95. ISBN 0-446-34828-7 Murder in a psychiatric clinic.

Shroud for a Nightingale (1971). Warner Bks 1987 $4.95. ISBN 0-446-31303-3 A training college for nurses becomes the scene of murder.

The Skull Beneath the Skin (1982). Warner Bks 1987 $4.95. ISBN 0-446-35372-8 Cordelia Gray joins Dalgleish on a tricky case.

A Taste for Death (1986). Warner Bks 1987 $4.95. ISBN 0-446-32352-7 Dalgleish struggles to find the motive as well as the killer.

Unnatural Causes (1967). Warner Bks 1987 $4.95. ISBN 0-446-31219-3 Death in a writer's colony by the sea.

An Unsuitable Job for a Woman (1972). Warner Bks 1987 $3.95. ISBN 0-446-34832-5 Private detective Cordelia Gray joins Dalgleish in solving mysteries.

BOOKS ABOUT JAMES

Gidez, Richard B. *P. D. James.* G. K. Hall 1986 $15.95. ISBN 0-8057-6924-2 A study of James's short fiction in the context of the tradition of the classic mystery.

Seibenheller, Norma. *P. D. James.* Ungar 1981 $16.95. ISBN 0-8044-2817-4 A critical and biographical study, including an examination of James's female characters, as well as information taken from conversations between James and the author.

JOYCE, JAMES　1882–1941

James Joyce was born in Dublin, Ireland, where he attended Belvedere College and University College, graduating in 1902. Soon after graduation he moved to Paris because of his frustration with life in Ireland. He returned to Dublin in 1903 for his mother's funeral and met Nora Barnacle there. The following year he and Nora left for the Continent, where they lived for the rest of their lives.

From 1905 to 1915, Joyce and Nora lived mainly in Trieste (then a part of the Austro-Hungarian Empire), where Joyce worked as a teacher of English. During this time he completed a collection of short stories, *Dubliners* (1914), and in 1909 and 1912 he made his last two visits to Ireland to make arrangements for its publication.

While living in Trieste, Joyce also completed his first novel, *A Portrait of the Artist as a Young Man* (1916). This work, which is largely autobiographical and details the struggles of its hero, Stephen Daedalus, as he grows to manhood and decides to become an artist, was first published in installments in the magazine *The Egoist* in 1914 and 1915.

With the outbreak of World War I, Joyce and his family moved to Zurich, Switzerland, where they remained throughout the war. Here Joyce worked steadily at the sequel to *Portrait of the Artist,* a novel that he eventually titled *Ulysses.* He attempted to publish the new novel in installments in an American magazine, *The Little Review,* where it appeared intermittently from April 1918 through December 1920. Because the novel was considered to be indecent, however, the magazine was forced to close down before the entire novel had appeared.

In 1920 Joyce moved again, this time to Paris, where *Ulysses* was finally published. It was several years, however, before the courts allowed it to be published in Britain or the United States.

Nevertheless, Joyce began work immediately on what was to be his last major work, a sprawling tale of an Irish saloon-keeper that is less a story than a brilliantly imaginative exercise in the use of the English language. For 17 years Joyce labored on this work, *Finnegan's Wake* (1939, serialized 1928–37). At the end of that time, he had produced what some critics call the greatest novel of the twentieth century and others term unreadable gibberish. Ironically, because *Finnegan* was so difficult to understand, it never provoked the charges of obscenity that plagued *Ulysses,* and publication was not interfered with.

Beyond question Joyce is one of the most influential writers of the twentieth century. While his total output amounts to only a few books, these works were powerful forces in shaping the ideas and styles of countless modern writers. His last two works, *Ulysses* and *Finnegan's Wake,* are difficult to read, both because of their inventive use of language and their many layers of subtle meaning.

NOVELS BY JOYCE

Finnegan's Wake (1939). Penguin 1982 $9.95. ISBN 0-14-006286-6
A Portrait of the Artist as a Young Man (1916). Penguin 1964 $3.95. ISBN 0-14-004221-0
Ulysses (1922). Random 1967 $15.95. ISBN 0-394-60486-5

SHORT STORY COLLECTION BY JOYCE

*Dubliners (1914). Penguin 1976 $4.95. ISBN 0-14-004222-9 Brilliant short stories about various characters living in Dublin; perhaps the most widely anthologized of which, "Araby," deals with a young boy's search for his own identity.

POETRY BY JOYCE

Collected Poems (1936). Penguin 1987 $6.95. ISBN 0-14-058593-1

PLAY BY JOYCE

Exiles (1918). Penguin 1977 $4.95. ISBN 0-14-048126-5

BOOKS ABOUT JOYCE

Benstock, Bernard. *James Joyce.* Ungar 1985 $7.95. ISBN 0-8044-6037-X An exploration of the style and narrative qualities of Joyce's major works, including his poetry, plays, and novels.
Ellman, Richard. *James Joyce.* Oxford Univ Pr 1982 $18.95. ISBN 0-19-503381-7 A literary biography, discussing Joyce's life as a father, husband, son, friend, and an artist.
Parrinder, Patrick. *James Joyce.* Cambridge Univ Pr 1984 $11.95. ISBN 0-521-28398-1 A study of Joyce's major works, including a discussion of his relationship with Ireland.

LARKIN, PHILIP   1922–1985

Born in Coventry, England, where his father served as city treasurer for 22 years, Philip Larkin was educated at King Henry VIII School in his native city and at Oxford University. Perhaps his most important friend at Oxford was

Kingsley Amis (*see* Amis, Vol. 1 British Literature: The Twentieth Century), who dedicated the novel *Lucky Jim* to him. Larkin reciprocated by dedicating his own collection *XX Poems* (1951) to Amis.

A librarian by profession, Larkin held various posts in British libraries after graduating from Oxford, and in 1955 became the librarian of Brynmor Jones Library at University of Hull. Besides his verse, Larkin wrote two novels in the 1940s, *Jill* (1946) and *A Girl in Winter* (1947). An enthusiastic jazz buff, he did feature stories on that subject for the newspaper *The Daily Telegraph* from 1961 to 1971.

Influenced at first by the poet W. B. Yeats (*see* Yeats, Vol. 1, British Literature: The Twentieth Century), Larkin soon became perhaps the finest poet of a new wave of English writers called the Movement, who avoided flowery language and sweeping themes in favor of restrained, rational poetry dealing with ordinary topics. Never a prolific poet, Larkin earned his high reputation through the quality rather than the quantity of his verse. Poems like "Church Going" or "The Whitsun Weddings" combine extraordinary skill with a subtle irony that makes major statements while seeming to describe ordinary events. Like the poet W. H. Auden (*see* Auden, Vol. 1, British Literature: The Twentieth Century), Larkin also excels in wryly comic verse.

NOVELS BY LARKIN

A Girl in Winter (1947). Overlook Pr 1985 $8.95. ISBN 0-87951-217-2
Jill (1946). Overlook Pr 1984 $7.95. ISBN 0-87951-961-4

POETRY BY LARKIN

High Windows (1974). Farrar 1974 $8.95. ISBN 0-374-51212-4
The North Ship (1945). Faber & Faber 1974 $4.95. ISBN 0-571-10503-3
The Whitsun Weddings (1964). Faber & Faber 1964 $4.95. ISBN 0-571-09710-3

BOOKS ABOUT LARKIN

Hassan, Salem K. *Philip Larkin and His Contemporaries: An Air of Authenticity.* St. Martin's 1988 $29.95. ISBN 0-312-01184-9 An examination of Larkin's style comparing Larkin to Thom Gunn, D. J. Enright, Kingsley Amis, and John Wain.
Salwak, Dale (ed). *Philip Larkin: The Man and His Work.* Univ of Iowa Pr 1988 $19.95. ISBN 0-87745-214-8 A collection of essays by 18 well-known writers and scholars, as well as excerpts from Larkin's letters and personal accounts of Larkin.

LAWRENCE, D. H. (DAVID HERBERT) 1885–1930

D. H. Lawrence was the son of a coal miner and a former schoolteacher. He was educated at Boys High School in his native Nottinghamshire. After leaving school, Lawrence worked as a clerk for a while before beginning a teacher training program at University College, Nottingham. In 1908 he began teaching at a boy's school in Croydon, a position he held primarily to support himself while writing.

In 1909 Lawrence had his first poems accepted for publication by a magazine. In the following year, his first novel, *The White Peacock* (1911), was accepted for publication. His second novel, *The Trespasser,* appeared in 1912, and the third and most important of his early works, *Sons and Lovers,* was published in 1913. In these three novels, especially in *Sons and Lovers,* Lawrence introduced the themes that would appear throughout his later fiction: human sexuality, the frustration of unfulfilled ambition, and the negative effects of industrialization on modern civilization.

In 1912 Lawrence ran off to Europe with Frieda von Richthofen, the wife of a professor at University College, Nottingham. They spent a year in Germany and Italy and were married in 1914 after von Richthofen's divorce. In the meantime Lawrence had published a book of verse, *Love Poems and Others* (1913), and had begun work on another novel, which eventually became two books, *The Rainbow* (1915) and *Women in Love* (1921). *The Rainbow* was banned as obscene almost immediately after publication, and *Women in Love* remained unpublished for several years because publishers were afraid to print it.

From childhood Lawrence had suffered problems with his lungs and spent much of his life seeking a healthy climate, living in Italy, Ceylon (Sri Lanka), Australia, New Mexico, and Mexico. He was, however, unable to cure the tuberculosis that finally killed him.

In his short career Lawrence produced novels, short stories, and poetry that have had a strong influence on modern English literature. His literary work was influential in its own right, but in addition the court cases arising from his frank treatment of sexual relations considerably widened the range of subject matter open to the modern novel.

Novels by Lawrence

Aaron's Rod (1922). Penguin 1976 $5.95. ISBN 0-14-000755-5
Four Short Novels (Love Among the Haystacks, The Ladybird, The Fox, The Captain's Doll). Penguin 1976 $4.95. ISBN 0-14-003726-8
Kangaroo (1923). Penguin 1980 $5.95. ISBN 0-14-000751-2
The Rainbow (1915). Penguin 1986 $5.95. ISBN 0-14-011980-9
Sons and Lovers (1913). Penguin 1982 $4.95. ISBN 0-14-043154-3
The Trespasser (1912). Penguin 1990 $6.95. ISBN 0-14-018210-1
The White Peacock (1911). Penguin 1990 $7.95. ISBN 0-14-018219-5
Women in Love (1921). Penguin 1982 $4.95. ISBN 0-14-043156-X

Short Story Collection by Lawrence

The Complete Short Stories. 3 vols. Penguin 1977. Vol. 1 $4.95. ISBN 0-14-004382-9. Vol. 2 $4.95. ISBN 0-14-004255-5. Vol. 3 $4.95. ISBN 0-14-004383-7

Poetry by Lawrence

The Complete Poems. Penguin 1977 $17.95. ISBN 0-14-042220-X

Plays by Lawrence

Three Plays (A Collier's Friday Night, The Daughter-in-Law, The Widowing of Mrs. Holroyd). Penguin 1982 $6.95. ISBN 0-14-000751-2

Books about Lawrence

Becker, George J. *D. H. Lawrence.* Ungar 1980 $6.95. ISBN 0-8044-6033-7 An introduction to Lawrence's work, including the major and lesser novels, novellas, and short stories.
Hosbaum, Phillip. *A Reader's Guide to D. H. Lawrence.* Thames Hudson 1981 $9.95. ISBN 0-500-15017-6 A study of Lawrence's poetry, novels, essays, travel books, criticism, and tales, focusing on psychological and structural elements and on the criticism of other Lawrence scholars.
Sagar, Keith. *A D. H. Lawrence Handbook.* Barnes 1982 $12.95. ISBN 0-389-20653-9 A reference book that includes chronological information, a thematic index, a travel calendar, a listing of films and sound recordings related to Lawrence, a selected bibliography, and a checklist of readings and of the major production of Lawrence's plays; also includes essays on the life and writings of the author, contributed by nine specialists on Lawrence.

LE CARRE, JOHN (PSEUDONYM OF DAVID JOHN MOORE CORNWELL) 1931–

John Le Carré was born David Cornwell in Dorset, England. He attended Sherborne School and the University of Berne, Switzerland. After a period of military service, some of which was with the British Secret Service, Le Carré entered Oxford University. He later taught for a short time at Eton College, the elite preparatory school, and then entered the British Foreign Service, where he remained for five years.

During this time, Le Carré began to write. Since, as a diplomat, he was forbidden to publish under his own name, he chose the pseudonym John Le Carré. In his first novel, *Call for the Dead* (1961), Le Carré introduced the character of George Smiley, a long-time veteran of the Secret Service, who became a recurring character in his later works. Smiley is an anti-hero, a man who, unlike Ian Fleming's dashing, adventurous James Bond, plods along at his job, not particularly liking what he is forced to do on many occasions. Through Smiley, Le Carré expresses his belief that the cold war was morally destructive for all who engaged in it. According to him, "There is no victory and no virtue in the Cold War, only a condition of human illness and a political misery." Le Carré also believes that the Western democracies "are in the process of doing things in defence of . . . society which may very well produce a society that is not worth defending."

Le Carré's novels have received high praise. Critics are divided on whether or not they are "high art," but agree that he is the best living writer of espionage novels, and probably the best ever. Le Carré's books have brought a new dimension of realism to this kind of story, revealing secret service agents as all too human. Tired, frightened, and prone to make blunders, Le Carré's agents are often the victims of dishonest bureaucrats and ambitious politicians. Le Carré's works have been made into countless films and television series in Britain and the United States.

NOVELS BY LE CARRE

Call for the Dead (1961). Bantam 1982 $3.95. ISBN 0-553-26623-3
The Honourable Schoolboy (1977). Bantam 1978 $4.95. ISBN 0-553-25197-X
The Little Drummer (1983). Bantam 1984 $4.95. ISBN 0-553-26757-4
The Looking Glass War (1965). Bantam 1984 $3.95. ISBN 0-553-23693-8
A Murder of Quality (1962). Bantam 1983 $3.95. ISBN 0-553-26443-5
The Naive and Sentimental Lover (1971). Bantam 1984 $4.50. ISBN 0-553-26821-X
A Perfect Spy (1986). Bantam 1987 $4.95. ISBN 0-553-26456-7
The Russia House (1989). Knopf 1982 $19.95. ISBN 0-394-57789-2
The Secret Pilgrim (1991). Knopf 1991 $21.95. ISBN 0-394-58842-8
A Small Town in Germany (1968). Dell 1970 $4.95. ISBN 0-440-18036-8
Smiley's People (1980). Bantam 1985 $4.95. ISBN 0-553-24687-7
The Spy Who Came in from the Cold (1963). Bantam 1984 $4.50. ISBN 0-553-26442-7
Tinker, Tailor, Soldier, Spy (1974). Bantam 1985 $4.95. ISBN 0-553-26778-7

BOOKS ABOUT LE CARRE

Lewis, Peter. *John Le Carré.* Ungar 1985 $16.95. ISBN 0-8044-2522-1 A study of the novels and their descriptions of espionage including quotations from interviews between Le Carré and the author.

Wolfe, Peter. *The Corridors of Deceit: The World of John Le Carré.* Bowling Green Univ Pr 1987 $15.95. ISBN 0-87972-382-3 Thorough study of Le Carré's novels, focusing on his treatment of espionage in the modern world.

LESSING, DORIS (MAY)   1919–

Doris Lessing was born in Persia (Iran) of English parents who later moved to Southern Rhodesia (now Zimbabwe) in Africa, where she grew up on a farm. In 1949, after a variety of jobs and two marriages, Lessing left Rhodesia and settled in England. Her first novel, *The Grass is Singing* (1950), is concerned with the psychological struggles of a white farmer's wife and her obsession with a black servant. This novel marks the beginning of Lessing's exploration of "inner space," the workings of the individual, private mind.

After completing *The Grass is Singing,* Lessing began a five-novel sequence in which she traced the story of Martha Quest, daughter of English settlers in "Zambesia" and politically active Communist (as Lessing once was). These five novels are collectively titled *The Children of Violence* (1952–1969). Besides exploring questions of racial tension, the novels also address Lessing's other major themes: the problems of the intelligent, liberated woman in a male-dominated society, and the clash between generations in which children emerge less ambitious than their parents.

With the completion of *Children of Violence* and another novel, *Briefing for a Descent into Hell* (1971), Lessing shifted her attention to "outer space" with five science fiction novels about the future. Her most recent work, however, has returned to the more realistic style of her earlier books.

In addition to her novels, Lessing has written several volumes of short stories, which some critics claim is her best work, as well as two autobiographical accounts of her arrival in England and her return visit to Africa.

NOVELS BY LESSING

Briefing for a Descent into Hell (1971). Random 1981 $3.95.
Documents Relating to the Sentimental Agents in the Volyen Empire (1983). Random 1984 $4.95. ISBN 0-394-72386-4
The Fifth Child (1988). Random 1989 $6.95. ISBN 0-679-72182-7
The Four-Gated City (1969). Plume $9.95. ISBN 0-452-25696-8
The Golden Notebook (1962). Bantam 1962 $5.95. ISBN 0553-26210-6
The Good Terrorist (1985). Random 1986 $5.95. ISBN 0-394-74629-5
The Grass Is Singing (1950). Plume 1976 $7.95. ISBN 0-452-25772-7
Landlocked (1965). Plume 1970 $3.95. ISBN 0-452-25138-9
The Making of the Representative for Planet Eight (1982). McKay 1988 $6.95. ISBN 0-679-72015-4
The Marriages Between Zones Three, Four and Five (1980). Random 1981 $7.95. ISBN 0-394-74978-2
Martha Quest (1952). Plume 1970 $6.95. ISBN 0-452-25968-1
Prisons We Choose to Live Inside (1987). Harper 1987 $6.95. ISBN 0-06-039077-8
A Proper Marriage (1954). Plume 1970 $7.95. ISBN 0-452-25789-1
Re: Colonized Planet 5—Shikasta (1979). Random 1981 $6.95. ISBN 0-394-74977-4
Ripple from the Storm (1958). Plume 1970 $6.95. ISBN 0-452-25632-1
The Sirian Experiments (1981). Random 1982 $7.95. ISBN 0-394-75195-7

SHORT STORY COLLECTIONS BY LESSING

The Habit of Loving (1957). Plume 1981 $8.95. ISBN 0-452-25704-2
Stories. Random 1980 $11.95. ISBN 0-394-74249-4

BOOKS ABOUT LESSING

Knapp, Mona. *Doris Lessing.* Ungar 1984 $16.95. ISBN 0-8044-2491-8 An introduction to Lessing's fiction and nonfiction, including an examination of her literary development from 1950 to 1983 and her ideas about feminism, mysticism, communism, and madness.

Pratt, Annis, and L. S. Dembo (eds). *Doris Lessing: Critical Studies.* Univ of Wisconsin Pr 1974. (o.p.) $4.90. ISBN 0-299-06564-2 An intriguing selection of essays that analyzes the author and her work; includes the transcript of an interview with Lessing and an especially handy checklist of works by and about Lessing.
Whittaker, Ruth. *Doris Lessing.* St. Martin's 1988 $24.95. ISBN 0-312-02057-0 A study of Lessing's life and work focusing on the major themes of her novels, including feminism, politics, colonialism, the nature of art, prophesy, madness, and dreams.

LEWIS, C. S. (CLIVE STAPLES)   1898–1963

C. S. Lewis was born in Belfast, Northern Ireland, the son of a lawyer. His mother died when he was 10, and he was sent to private schools, where he became fascinated with ancient myths and legends and continued the writing he had begun as a very young child. He was awarded a scholarship to Malvern College, but hated the school and withdrew soon after entering. He was tutored privately instead, and obtained a scholarship to Oxford University.

Lewis's studies were interrupted by World War I, and he served in the Infantry in 1917 and 1918. At the end of the war, he returned to Oxford, where he studied classics, philosophy, and English, graduating with honors in all areas. He taught at Oxford from 1925 to 1954, when he became a Professor of Medieval and Renaissance English at Cambridge University, a post he held until his death.

As a writer, Lewis's range was very wide. His first published book was an allegorical poem, *Dymer* (1926), written under the pen name Clive Hamilton. He went on to publish literary criticism, novels, and books on Christian doctrine. During World War II he became famous for a series of radio talks on Christianity, which were later collected and published as *Beyond Personality* (1944) and *Mere Christianity* (1952). His most famous works, however, are *The Screwtape Letters* (1942), a series of letters of instruction and encouragement from a shrewd old devil to his nephew Wormwood giving advice on how to tempt a human; and *The Chronicles of Narnia* (1950–56), a series of seven fantasy novels. Three additional works—*Out of the Silent Planet* (1938), *Perelandra* (1939), and *That Hideous Strength* (1945)—form a trilogy of philosophical science-fiction stories of life on other planets, ending in an earthly college community.

NOVELS BY LEWIS

*The Chronicles of Narnia (The Lion, the Witch and the Wardrobe; Prince Caspian; The Voyage of the Dawn Treader; The Silver Chair; The Horse and His Boy; The Magician's Nephew; The Last Battle) (1950–1956). Macmillan 1968 $19.95. ISBN 0-02-044280-7 Adventures of the noble lion Aslan as he fights the forces of evil to save the people of Narnia.
*Out of the Silent Planet (1938). Macmillan 1975 $3.95. ISBN 0-02-086950-9 Adventures of a Cambridge University professor who is kidnapped and taken to Mars.
*Perelandra (1939). Macmillan 1968 $3.95. ISBN 0-02-086950-9 Professor Ransom learns the secrets of living a moral life.
*That Hideous Strength (1945). Macmillan 1975 $3.95. ISBN 0-02-086920-7 The return of Ransom to Earth and his efforts to help humanity live more morally.

NONFICTION BY LEWIS

Mere Christianity (1952). Macmillan 1986 $5.95. ISBN 0-02-086940-1
The Screwtape Letters (1942). Macmillan 1982 $1.95. ISBN 0-02-086740-9

BOOK ABOUT LEWIS

Griffin, William. *Clive Staples Lewis: A Dramatic Life.* Harper 1986 $24.95. ISBN 0-06-250352-9 A detailed biography of Lewis with a description of his long struggle with religious faith.

MacNEICE, LOUIS   1907–1963

Born in Belfast and raised in Carrickfergus, Ireland, Louis MacNeice was the son of a minister who later became a bishop in the Church of Ireland. MacNeice never lost his sense of his Irish roots, even after his education in English schools and at Oxford University had made him ill-at-ease with the Puritan strain in his upbringing.

At Oxford, MacNeice became friends with the poets Stephen Spender and W. H. Auden (*see* Auden, Vol. 1, British Literature: The Twentieth Century), and they influenced his first volume of poems, *Blind Fireworks* (1929). After graduating from Oxford with honors, MacNeice accepted a lectureship in classics at Birmingham University and later taught at the University of London. He was never completely happy in academic life, so in 1941 he joined the British Broadcasting Corporation as a scriptwriter and producer, remaining there for the rest of his career. He also did a highly praised translation of the ancient Greek play *Agamemnon,* as well as a critical study of the poetry of William Butler Yeats. (*See* Yeats, Vol. 1, British Literature: The Twentieth Century.)

MacNeice described a poet as a person who is "able-bodied, fond of talking, a reader of the newspapers, capable of pity and laughter, appreciative of women, susceptible to physical impressions." He called for an "impure" poetry that would be more involved with life, more passionate and less detached, than the work of the poets who preceded him. MacNeice was deeply concerned with the social and political problems of the 1930s, but he expressed more doubts about Marxism as a solution than many of his contemporaries. He clearly saw the dangers posed by Adolf Hitler and fascism, but did not see much hope in looking to the Soviet Union for alternatives. His best verse brings wit and strong rhythms to bear on contemporary life and often recalls scenes of his youth.

Poetry by MacNeice

Selected Poems. Faber & Faber 1964 $5.95. ISBN 0-571-06089-7

Books about MacNeice

Longley, Edna. *Louis MacNeice: A Study.* Faber & Faber 1989 $9.95. ISBN 0-571-13748-2 Accessible overview of MacNeice's life and work; includes a bibliography and index.

Marsack, Robyn. *The Cave of Making: The Poetry of Louis MacNeice.* Oxford Univ Pr 1982 $15.95. ISBN 0-19-811732-9 Scholarly examination of MacNeice's poetry; includes a bibliography and index.

MAUGHAM, W. (WILLIAM) SOMERSET   1874–1965

Somerset Maugham was born in Paris, France, the son of a lawyer at the British Embassy. Orphaned at ten, he was sent to live with a clergyman uncle in England, where he completed his early education at King's School in Canterbury. Maugham studied philosophy for a year at Heidelberg University in Germany before beginning a study of medicine in London. Although he completed his medical training and received his license, he never practiced. In 1898, after a short period of travel, he settled in Paris.

Maugham's first novel, *Liza of Lambeth* (1897), drew on his personal knowledge of London to tell a story of life in the slums. In Paris he continued writing short stories and novels, and also began to write plays. With *Lady Frederick* (1907), he achieved his first success as a playwright. His success in the theater increased, but he gave up playwrighting in 1934. Throughout this period he continued to write fiction, producing several novels and volumes of short stories.

Maugham's first really successful novel was *Of Human Bondage* (1915), the story of a young medical student and artist who becomes involved in a love triangle with two women. Based extensively on Maugham's own experience, it was later made into a highly successful film, as were many of his novels.

While praised for his sharp powers of observation and his narrative skill, Maugham was never held in high regard by literary critics. However, he was extremely popular with the public in his lifetime, and his works continue to be widely read. Of his own work he once said, "I have never pretended to be anything but a storyteller. It has amused me to tell stories and I have told a great many."

NOVELS BY MAUGHAM

Cakes and Ale (1930). Penguin 1977 $4.95. ISBN 0-14-000651-6
The Moon and Sixpence (1919). Penguin 1977 $4.95. ISBN 0-14-000468-8
Of Human Bondage (1915). Penguin 1978 $5.95. ISBN 0-14-001861-1
The Razor's Edge (1945). Penguin 1978 $4.95. ISBN 0-14-001860-3

SHORT STORY COLLECTION BY MAUGHAM

Collected Short Stories. 4 vols. Penguin 1977. Vol. 1 $4.95. ISBN 0-14-00871-9. Vol. 2 $4.95. ISBN 0-14-001872-7. Vol. 3 $4.95. ISBN 0-14-001873-5. Vol. 4 $4.95. ISBN 0-14-001874-3

PLAYS BY MAUGHAM

Six Comedies. Ayer (repr of 1939 ed) $32.00. ISBN 0-405-07849-8

NONFICTION BY MAUGHAM

The Summing Up (1938). Penguin 1978 $4.95. ISBN 0-14-001852-2
A Writer's Notebook (1949). Penguin 1984 $5.95. ISBN 0-14-002644-4

BOOKS ABOUT MAUGHAM

Burt, Forrest D. *W. Somerset Maugham.* G. K. Hall 1985 $19.95. ISBN 0-8057-6885-8 A study of Maugham's work as illuminated by his life, including a one-chapter biography, a bibliography, and a chronology; a useful overview for the reader coming to Maugham for the first time.
Loss, Archie. *W. Somerset Maugham.* Ungar 1988 $19.95. ISBN 0-8044-2544-2 A study focusing on how Maugham influenced visual artists.
Morgan, Ted. *Maugham: A Biography.* Simon 1984 $12.70. ISBN 0-671-50581-5 A full biography with photos and indexes of Maugham's work by a noted biographer of poets, politicians, and royalty.

MITCHINSON, NAOMI 1897–

Naomi Mitchinson was born Naomi Haldane in Edinburgh, Scotland. Her father was a famous scientist, and her sister became a famous biologist. She was educated at Dragon School, Oxford, and at Oxford University, where she studied science. In 1916 she married Baron Gilbert Richard Mitchinson. She traveled extensively in many parts of the world and used her travel experiences and knowledge of other cultures in her novels and stories.

During her long career, Mitchinson has published over 70 books of different kinds; the historical novels and short stories written in the 1920s and 1930s are her best work. In her later years, Mitchinson turned to writing children's stories, with considerable success.

Mitchinson's strength lies in portraying a vivid, detailed, and realistic picture of life in other times. Her novels present not only the events of history but the feeling of the time as well. Of her work she wrote, "in historical fiction (or in writing about people of other cultures) . . . it is essential to get social and historical facts or probabilities as minutely correct as possible . . . and perhaps lead the reader to thinking about these facts, about what they have done to us (or we to them) and the situations in which we may yet be involved."

NOVELS BY MITCHINSON

The Blood of the Martyrs (1939). David and Charles 1989 $11.95. ISBN 0-86241-192-0
Travel Light (1952). Penguin 1987 $6.95. ISBN 0-14-016174-0

SHORT STORY COLLECTIONS BY MITCHINSON

Barbarian Stories (1929). Ayer (repr of 1933 ed) $14.50. ISBN 0-8369-3701-5
Delicate Fire (1933). Ayer (repr of 1933 ed) $20.00. ISBN 0-8369-3778-3
When the Bough Breaks and Other Stories (1924). Ayer (repr 1924 ed) $18.00. ISBN 0-8369-3929-9

MURDOCH, DAME IRIS   1919–

Iris Murdoch was born in Dublin, Ireland, of Anglo-Irish parents and was educated at Badminton School and Oxford University. After several government jobs, she returned to academic life, studying philosophy at Newnham College, Cambridge. In 1948 Murdoch became a Fellow and Tutor at St. Anne's College, Oxford. She has also taught at the Royal College of Art in London.

A professional philosopher, Murdoch began writing novels as a hobby, but quickly established herself as a genuine literary talent. Writer Elizabeth Bowen (*see* Bowen, Vol. 1, British Literature: The Twentieth Century) has said of Murdoch, "Everything she has written has been remarkable—stamped by the unmistakable authority of mind and vision."

Murdoch's first novel, *Under the Net* (1954), already showed "a deft touch, a delight in strange, intricate and puzzling plots, a wild intelligence and a defiance of the pigeonhole" *(Publishers Weekly)*. In *A Severed Head* (1961), she depicts a London society devoid of passion or conviction, a modern world of artificial rather than real emotions. Her subtle irony, her wit, her sense of the comic combine to make it an astonishing novel. Of *The Nice and the Good* (1968), which treats the many faces of love, critic Elizabeth Janeway said in the *New York Times,* "Sparkling, daring, great fun, the book sweeps up black magic, science fiction, thriller, and half-a-dozen kinds of novels into the wittiest sort of concoction. It is hard to imagine anyone not enjoying it." *The Sea, The Sea* (1978) was awarded the Booker Prize, Britain's highest literary honor.

NOVELS BY MURDOCH

An Accidental Man (1971). Penguin 1988 $7.95. ISBN 0-14-003611-3
The Bell (1958). Penguin 1987 $6.95. ISBN 0-14-001688-0
The Black Prince (1972). Penguin 1983 $7.95. ISBN 0-14-003934-1
The Book of the Brotherhood (1987). Penguin 1989 $8.95. ISBN 0-14-010470-4
Bruno's Dream (1969). Penguin 1976 $4.95. ISBN 0-14-003176-6
The Flight from the Enchanter (1955). Penguin 1987 $4.95. ISBN 0-14-001770-4

The Italian Girl (1964). Penguin 1979 $5.95. ISBN 0-14-002559-6
The Nice and the Good (1968). Penguin 1978 $6.95. ISBN 0-14-003034-4
The Red and the Green (1965). Penguin 1988 $6.95. ISBN 0-14-2756-4
The Sandcastle (1957). Penguin 1978 $6.95. ISBN 0-14-001474-8
The Sea, The Sea (1978). Penguin 1980 $7.95. ISBN 0-14-005199-6
The Unicorn (1963). Penguin 1987 $6.95. ISBN 0-14-002476-X

BOOKS ABOUT MURDOCH

Bloom, Harold (ed). *Iris Murdoch.* Chelsea 1986 $19.95. ISBN 0-87754-705-X Critical
  interpretations, anecdotes, essays, and lectures on Murdoch.
Rabinovitz, Rubin. *Iris Murdoch.* Columbia Univ Pr 1968 $5.00. ISBN 0-231-03000-2
  Part of the Columbia Essays on Modern Writers, this compact 48-page study
  provides a scholarly introduction to Murdoch's work; contains a selected bibliography.

O'CASEY, SEAN 1880–1964

Sean O'Casey was born into poverty in the slums of Dublin, Ireland. Because
of a childhood illness that affected his eyesight, he could not read properly
until he was 13. Denied much formal schooling, he read extensively once he
was able to, and so educated himself.

In his youth O'Casey worked mostly as a laborer: road builder, stevedore,
brickworker. He became actively involved in the Irish struggle to free the
country from British control, joining the Irish Citizen Army. However, because
he thought the independence movement was becoming anti-labor, he resigned
in 1914. His primary concern, then and later, was the welfare of the working
class.

After World War I and the Irish uprising of 1916, O'Casey turned to
writing plays, which he submitted to the Abbey Theater in Dublin, an organization devoted to promoting Irish playwrights and developing an Irish national theater. His first attempts were rejected, but in 1923 the Abbey staged
The Shadow of a Gunman, a play dealing with the guerilla war conducted by the
Irish Republican Army (IRA) before the signing of a peace treaty with Britain
in 1921. The Abbey also produced *Juno and the Paycock* (1925), a bitter comedy
describing the Irish Civil War and the unfulfilled hopes that followed the
settlement. O'Casey's last play at the Abbey, *The Plough and the Stars* (1926),
returned to the theme of the 1916 uprising, attacking both the Irish nationalists and the labor unions who argued with each other while the poor of
Dublin bore the pain of the conflict. The play set off a full-scale riot led by
those who felt O'Casey had defamed the cause of Irish independence. Feeling
rejected and disillusioned, O'Casey left Dublin for London and never lived in
Ireland again.

O'Casey's later plays became increasingly experimental and, although
they contributed new ideas and techniques to the development of drama, were
never as popular as his earlier more realistic works. Although he remained in
exile from Ireland, his work never lost its Irish settings or Irish themes, and the
six-volume autobiography that O'Casey produced is filled with his love of his
native land.

PLAYS BY O'CASEY

Seven Plays. St. Martin's 1985 $32.50. ISBN 0-312-71323-1
Three Plays: Juno and the Paycock; The Shadow of a Gunman; The Plough and the Stars. St. Martin's
  1968 $4.95. ISBN 0-312-80290-0

Nonfiction by O'Casey

Autobiographies One. Carroll & Graf 1984 $10.95. ISBN 0-88184-033-5 An autobiograph-
ical look at O'Casey's early life, including his work on his first plays and poems.
Autobiographies Two. Carroll & Graf 1984 $10.95. ISBN 0-88184-075-0 Second volume
of autobiography, concentrating on political change in Ireland.

Books about O'Casey

Bloom, Harold (ed). *Sean O'Casey.* Chelsea 1987 $19.95. ISBN 0-87754-647-9 Collected
social realist works of O'Casey edited by well-known writer of contemporary
criticism.
Da Rin, Doris. *Sean O'Casey.* Ungar 1977 $16.95. ISBN 0-8044-2136-6 Interpretations
of O'Casey's love of Irish themes.

O'CONNOR, FRANK (PSEUDONYM OF MICHAEL FRANCIS O'DONOVAN) 1903–1966

A master of the short story, Frank O'Connor was born Michael O'Donovan in
Cork City, Ireland, where he was also educated. The first part of his autobiography reveals that he took the name of his mother, whom he adored. O'Connor's
absorbing interest was the literary heritage of Ireland. He began writing in
Gaelic, the native Irish language. Although he later wrote in English, he translated many ancient Gaelic works into English and also wrote a highly praised
history of Irish literature.

Where O'Connor excelled, however, was the short story. Many of his early
stories were published in magazines, and beginning in the 1930s he published
collections regularly. His reputation and following increased steadily.

During the 1930s O'Connor was asked to write plays for the Abbey Theater, Ireland's national theater. These plays also proved to be successful. However, in 1958, in a dispute with the Abbey over censorship, he resigned as a
director of the theater and moved to the United States.

Not surprisingly, all of O'Connor's stories have an Irish background. Even
those tales whose source is elsewhere he rewrote with an Irish setting. His work
spans the entire range of the short story from the comic to the tragic.

Short Story Collections by O'Connor

Collected Stories of Frank O'Connor. Random 1982 $10.95. ISBN 0-394-71048-7
My Oedipus Complex (1963). Creative Ed 1986 $14.25. ISBN 0-88682-062-6

Plays by O'Connor

The Invincibles (1937). (coauthored with Hugh Hunt) Proscenium 1980 $2.95. ISBN
0-912262-67-2
Moses' Rock: A Play in Three Acts (1938). (coauthored with Hugh Hunt) Catholic Univ
Pr 1983 $6.95. ISBN 0-8132-0585-9

Books about O'Connor

Matthews, James. *Frank O'Connor.* Bucknell Univ Pr 1975 $1.95. ISBN 0-8387-7609-4
Bibliographic index to the life of O'Connor by Irish author and student of O'Connor; includes introduction on how different stages of O'Connor's life affected his
work.
Steinman, Michael. *Frank O'Connor at Work.* Syracuse Univ Pr 1989 $14.95. ISBN
0-8156-2475-1 Introductory volume on O'Connor's life, including stories of how
contemporaries shaped his writing.
Wohlgelernter, Maurice. *Frank O'Connor: An Introductory Study.* Columbia Univ Pr 1977
$29.50. ISBN 0-231-04194-2 Explains how to study O'Connor's work.

O'FAOLAIN, SEAN 1900–

Sean O'Faolain was born in Dublin, Ireland, and educated at the National University, Dublin. During the 1920s he was Director of Publicity for the Irish Republican Army (IRA), before going to Harvard University to complete his M.A.

O'Faolain taught briefly in the United States, then in 1933 returned to Ireland, where he held a teaching position in County Wicklow until he was able to support himself by writing.

O'Faolain's first book of short stories, *Midsummer Night's Madness,* was published in 1932. The following year he published his first novel, *A Nest of Simple Folk,* a story of Irish rebellion, which was widely praised. His writing concentrates on what he sees as the oppressiveness of Irish life, particularly the tyranny of the Irish Catholic Church.

The *Library Journal* has said of O'Faolain's love–hate feelings for Ireland, "There is an element in Irish fiction that someone has aptly described as malicious affection. O'Faolain has it to the greatest degree." About the writer, the *Journal* continues, "There is a melancholy strain along with the quiet chuckle, the nostalgic findings of a man who has lived and learned well. He is indeed a past master of the short story."

NOVELS BY O'FAOLAIN

Bird Alone (1936). Oxford Univ Pr 1986 $5.95. ISBN 0-19-281906-2
The Man Who Invented Sin (1948). Devin-Adair (repr of 1948 ed) $12.95. ISBN 0-8159-6212-6

SHORT STORIES BY O'FAOLAIN

Collected Short Stories of Sean O'Faolain. Little 1983 $29.95. ISBN 0-316-63294-5

BOOK ABOUT O'FAOLAIN

Bonaccorso, Richard. *Sean O'Faolain's Irish Vision.* SUNY 1987 $16.95. ISBN 0-88706-537-6 Critical interpretation of Irish literature and the vision of Ireland that infuses O'Faolain's work.

ORWELL, GEORGE (PSEUDONYM OF ERIC ARTHUR BLAIR) 1903–1950

George Orwell was born Eric Arthur Blair in Bengal, India, son of a British civil servant. He was sent to a private school in England, where he did well enough to earn a scholarship to Eton College, an elite preparatory school. After leaving school, Orwell joined the Imperial Police in Burma. During his five years in this job, he developed an intense hatred for British colonialism. He left the police force in disgust and returned to England penniless and with a desire to write.

For several years Orwell lived with virtually no income, part of the time as a tramp. He was later to record these years of poverty in *Down and Out in Paris and London* (1933). In 1930, however, he began to make a modest living from his writing, and soon began publishing articles and novels regularly. As Adolf Hitler rose to power in Germany, Orwell became increasingly alarmed at the prospect of war, and in the novel *Coming Up for Air* (1939) described his fears and political concerns.

After World War II, Orwell grew increasingly concerned about the loss of democracy and the rise and spread of rigidly controlled totalitarian states. His two most famous works grew out of this concern. *Animal Farm* (1945) reflects Orwell's anxiety about the rise of Communist totalitarianism in the Soviet

The Repast of the Lion.   Painting by Henri Rousseau (c. 1905).   Courtesy of The Metropolitan Museum of Art, Bequest of Sam A. Lewisohn, 1951. (51.112.5)

Union. Through the use of fable, Orwell shows how noble ideas can be swallowed up by the desire for power. In *1984* (1949), he takes this fear one step further and depicts a state so tightly controlled that individuals have no rights or freedoms and ordinary logic has become reversed ("War is Peace" and "Slavery is Freedom"). Orwell wrote *1984* in 1948 (although it was not published until the following year) so he devised the title for his chilling vision of the future by transposing the last two digits of the actual year, in an attempt to make that horrifying future seem imminent.

NOVELS BY ORWELL

*Animal Farm (1945). Plume 1983 $5.95. ISBN 0-452-262771-1 Story of farm animals who overthrow the farmer and take power for themselves.
Burmese Days (1936). Harcourt 1974 $5.95. ISBN 0-15-614850-1
The Clergyman's Daughter (1935). Harcourt 1969 $8.95. ISBN 0-15-618065-0
Coming Up for Air (1939). Harcourt 1969 $6.95. ISBN 0-15-619625-5
Keep the Aspidistra Flying (1936). Harcourt 1969 $6.95. ISBN 0-15-646899-9
*1984 (1949). Signet 1980 $3.95. ISBN 0-451-52123-4 The chilling story of one man's fight to free himself from the control of "Big Brother."

NONFICTION BY ORWELL

The Orwell Reader. Harcourt 1961 $7.95. ISBN 0-15-670176-6

BOOKS ABOUT ORWELL

Ferrell, Keith. *George Orwell: The Political Pen*. M. Evans 1985 $11.95. ISBN 0-87131-444-4 Description of Orwell's rebellious life.
Kalechofsky, Roberta. *George Orwell*. Ungar 1973 $16.95. ISBN 0-8044-24802-2 A readable introduction to Orwell that shows how his writing was influenced by his personal life, the people he knew, and the events of his time; contains a complete chronology and bibliography.

Myers, Jeffrey. *A Reader's Guide to George Orwell.* Littlefield 1977 $8.95. ISBN 0-8226-0339-X Indexed collection of Orwell's significant work and brief discussions on how Orwell started his projects.

Smith, David, and Michael Mosher. *George Orwell for Beginners.* Writers and Readers 1984 $4.95. ISBN 0-86316-066-2 A guide for students covering Orwell's politics and religious background.

OSBORNE, JOHN   1929–

John Osborne was born in London and educated at Belmont College in Devon, which he left at age 16 to become a writer for trade magazines. He soon turned to acting, however, and by 1955 was playing major roles in London theaters. Osborne also wrote plays. With his fourth, *Look Back in Anger* (1956), he established himself as a new voice in English drama, calling for a revolution in the English system of social classes. Osborne was soon the acknowledged leader of a new school of British playwrights known as The Angry Young Men.

Osborne's work portrayed the decline of the British Empire and the growing popular disillusionment with what he saw as an outmoded social system. Archie Rice, the central character in *The Entertainer* (1957), is a faded music-hall comedian whose son has been killed in Cyprus. Archie's present squalid life constrasts with the lost warmth and community of the music hall; his son's death represents the futility of Britain's overseas military ventures. In *Luther* (1961), Osborne presents an extended character study of the Protestant reformer Martin Luther. *Inadmissible Evidence* (1964) tells the story of Bill Maitland, a lawyer who is watching his whole life slip away.

While sometimes criticized for his merciless attacks on the British way of life, Osborne has also been credited with awakening a whole generation of playwrights to the need for carefully examining the world of which they are a part. While his plays have been faulted for being dominated by one "talky" character, they have also been praised for some of their experimental techniques.

In addition to writing for the theater, Osborne has written a number of screenplays and television scripts.

PLAYS BY OSBORNE

The Entertainer (1957). Penguin 1983 $5.95. ISBN 0-14-048178-8
Look Back in Anger (1956). Penguin 1982 $4.95. ISBN 0-14-048175-3
Luther (1961). Signet 1983 $3.95. ISBN 0-451-14474-0
A Patriot for Me (1966) and *A Sense of Detachment* (1972). Faber & Faber 1983 $7.95. ISBN 0-571-13041-0
Watch It Come Down (1975). Faber & Faber 1975 $5.95. ISBN 0-571-10854-7

BOOKS ABOUT OSBORNE

Ferrar, H. *John Osborne.* Columbia Univ Pr 1973 $5.00. ISBN 0-231-13361-3 A short history of Osborne's effect on modern writers.

Hinchliffe, Arnold P. *John Osborne.* G. K. Hall 1984 $19.95. ISBN 0-8057-6875-0 A "Twayne series" collection of critical essays about Osborne, including revisions of several older plays.

OWEN, WILFRED   1893–1918

Wilfred Owen was born in the village of Oswestry in Shropshire, England, the son of a very religious mother with whom he was quite close. His academic career was varied and largely unsuccessful. He attended several different schools, but never managed to do well enough to win a scholarship to a university. For a time, probably at the urging of his mother, he worked as a lay assistant to the vicar of Dunsden, teaching Bible classes and preparing to become a priest.

In 1913, Owen left for France, where he taught English until the outbreak of World War I. Then he enlisted in the army. He suffered injuries, several illnesses, and battle fatigue, and was sent back to England to recover. He returned to the front in 1918, and was awarded the Military Cross for gallantry in action. On November 4, 1918, one week before the war ended, he was killed by machine gun fire.

Owen began writing poetry when he was 10 or 11 years old and continued steadily for the rest of his short life. He wrote his best poems during his period of recuperation from his war injuries in 1917 and early 1918. In a draft preface to his poems, Owen wrote, "My subject is War, and the pity of War. The Poetry is in the pity."

Critics generally agree that Owen's small body of verse is powerful in its nightmarish descriptions of the horrors of battle and merciless in its attacks on old politicians who send young men to die. They rate it among the most moving antiwar statements made in modern literature.

POETRY BY OWEN

Collected Poems. New Directions 1964 $6.95. ISBN 0-8112-0132-5

BOOKS ABOUT OWEN

Breen, Jennifer (ed). *Wilfred Owen.* Routledge 1988 $12.95. ISBN 0-415-00733-X Selected works of Owen's poetry and prose, and a short introduction on Owen's life.

Stallworthy, James. *Wilfred Owen.* Oxford Univ Pr 1978 $4.95. ISBN 0-19-281215-7 Tables, maps and other graphics on Owen's life and places of residence.

PINTER, HAROLD   1930–

Harold Pinter was born in London's poor East End. After attending the Royal Academy of Dramatic Arts, he worked as an actor under the name of David Baron. While acting, he began writing plays.

Pinter's early works did not find much success, as both audiences and critics were baffled by his unusual use of everyday conversation. His third play, *The Birthday Party* (1958), closed after only a few performances when it was first staged. It was later successful in a televised presentation and was restaged in 1964 after Pinter had built his reputation with other plays. Today's more sophisticated audiences now find Pinter's work intriguing and exciting as it exposes the hidden pain and dark comedy lurking beneath the surface of everyday life.

Pinter's early plays are certainly difficult. Not only are his plots unusual, featuring absurd, unlikely events, but the dialogue and settings further contribute to an atmosphere of uncertainty that keeps the audience unsure of exactly what is happening. Violent acts seem to occur for no apparent reason, yet somehow they also seem to fit. The audience feels that there must be reason behind the action, but the reason is hard to explain.

Pinter has been called the inventor of a new kind of comedy, "the comedy of menace": his characters seem always to be in fear of something they cannot quite identify, while carrying on conversations that are witty, even cheerful. This brilliant mix of comedy and fear has influenced a generation of British and American playwrights.

Another source of difficulty is Pinter's constant experimentation. He changes technique and structure with virtually every play, making it almost impossible to define exactly what he is doing.

In addition to his plays for the stage, Pinter has written a considerable number of screenplays. Although they are more conventional and easier to understand than his theater work, they too are extraordinary mixtures of comedy, menace, intrigue, mystery, and pain.

PLAYS BY PINTER

Betrayal (1979). Grove 1988 $8.95. ISBN 0-8021-3080-1
The Birthday Party (1958). Grove 1989 $6.95. ISBN 0-394-17232-9
The Caretaker (1960). Grove 1988 $7.95. ISBN 0-394-17761-4
The French Lieutenant's Woman and Other Screenplays. Heineman 1985 $13.95. ISBN 0-413-48680-X
The Homecoming (1965). Grove 1989 $5.95. ISBN 0-394-17251-5
Old Times (1971). Grove 1988 $7.95. ISBN 0-394-17761-4
One for the Road (1983). Grove 1986 $8.95. ISBN 0-394-62363-0

BOOKS ABOUT PINTER

Bloom, Harold (ed). *Harold Pinter.* Chelsea 1987 $19.95. ISBN 0-87754-706-8 Several essays on Pinter's work by noted contemporaries, focusing on the subjects of lies, fidelity, and betrayal, edited and introduced by a major modern critic.
Hinchliffe, Arnold P. *Harold Pinter.* G. K. Hall 1981 $14.95. ISBN 0-8057-6784-3 A "Twayne series" collection of essays, on interpreting Pinter's plays and including revisions of later works.

PRIESTLEY, J. B. (JOHN BOYNTON)   1894–1984

J. B. Priestley was born in Bradford, in Yorkshire, England, where he completed his early education. After serving in the army in World War I, he attended Cambridge University. When Priestley graduated, he went to London and became a journalist.

Priestley's first literary success was the novel *The Good Companions* (1929), a lighthearted story of three people who form a singing group. He followed with *Angel Pavement* (1930), a tale of life in London. Priestley was primarily a novelist, but he also wrote plays. He was the dominant figure in the London theater throughout much of the 1930s.

Priestley's plays use everyday conversation to explore human emotion. His plays also include philosophical theories about time, and some political preaching. These works were very popular before World War II, but did not stand up well after the war. Today Priestley's plays are almost never performed, and no single play is currently in print. His novels and literary criticism have fared better, however, and both continue to be read and appreciated.

NOVELS BY PRIESTLEY

Angel Pavement (1930). Univ of Chicago Pr 1983 $8.95. ISBN 0-226-68210-2
The Good Companions (1929). Univ of Chicago Pr 1983 $9.95. ISBN 0-226-68223-4

SHORT STORY COLLECTION BY PRIESTLEY

The Other Place and Other Stories of the Same Sort (1953). Ayer (repr of 1953 ed) $18.00. ISBN 0-8369-3993-X

BOOKS ABOUT PRIESTLEY

Atkins, John. *J. B. Priestley.* Riverrun 1983 $12.95. ISBN 0-7145-3950-3 Priestley's life story from his childhood through his early adulthood.

Klein, Holger. *J. B. Priestley's Plays.* St. Martin's 1988 $35.00. ISBN 0-312-01599-2 The plays of Priestley with a biographical introduction.

SAKI (PSEUDONYM OF HECTOR HUGO MUNRO)   1870–1916

H. H. Munro—pen name "Saki"—was born in Burma, the son of an officer in the colonial police. As a young boy he was sent back to England for schooling and was raised by two aunts. After completing his education in England, he returned to Burma and joined the colonial police. Later he was sent back to England because of illness. Saki became a journalist who submitted articles to magazines and served as a foreign correspondent for London newspapers. He then began writing short stories and published his first collection, *Reginald,* in 1904.

When England entered World War I, Saki enlisted as a private, refusing a commission. He was killed in battle in 1916.

In his short life Saki wrote a sizable body of short stories as well as 2 novels. Only his stories have endured. His wit, sense of irony, and ability to poke fun at the English upper classes without seeming to do so have endeared him to generations of readers. Modern readers particularly enjoy his stories of the strange and supernatural, which, despite their subject matter, retain Saki's light touch.

"The Open Window" is one of Saki's most widely anthologized works. It concerns a young woman whose wild tales wreak hilarious havoc on all around her. "The Schwartz-Metterklume Method" is another wildly funny story about a woman who, mistaken for a governess, goes along with the mistake—and turns her employer's household upside down.

SHORT STORY COLLECTIONS BY SAKI

* *The Best of Saki.* Penguin 1977 $6.95. ISBN 0-14-004484-1 Great stories that range from humor to horror.

* *The Chronicles of Clovis* (1912). Penguin 1987 $4.95. ISBN 0-14-008355-3 Witty tales of the English upper class.

Complete Works of Saki. (1976) Dorset 1989 $19.95. ISBN 0-88029-259-8

BOOK ABOUT SAKI

Gillen, Charles H. *H. H. Munro (Saki).* Twayne 1969. (o.p.) A good overview of Saki's life and work, with a chronology and bibliography; focuses on illuminating the writer's work with references to his life, as well as on establishing Saki's diversity as a journalist, playwright, social portraitist, and writer of anti-militarist tracts, as well as his better-known roles as satirist and short-story writer.

SASSOON, SIEGFRIED   1886–1967

Born in Brenchley, England, Siegfried Sassoon was educated at Marlborough Grammar School and Cambridge University, which he left without obtaining a degree. In the years before World War I, he led the leisurely, somewhat intellectual, life of a wealthy young man of his generation, dividing his time between hunting and writing poetry.

With the beginning of the war, Sassoon enlisted and was commissioned and sent to France. He was wounded twice and received the Military Cross. Sassoon was shocked and disgusted by the horrors of war. His best poetry is about the monotony and agony of trench warfare. He was especially bitter about what he saw as the failure of the country's leaders to end the war quickly. Because of his outspoken protests while still in uniform, he expected to be court-martialed, but instead he was sent to a hospital to recover from "shell shock." There he met Wilfred Owen (*see* Owen, Vol. 1, British Literature: The Twentieth Century) who was also recuperating.

After the war Sassoon continued to write poetry and also became briefly involved in politics. In 1920 he edited and helped publish the poems of Wilfred Owen, who had not survived the war.

Sassoon's reputation rests largely on the small body of war poetry he wrote and on his autobiographical novel about his war experiences, *The Complete Memoirs of George Sherston* (1937). Both the poetry and the novel deliver a strong attack on the folly and horrors of warfare.

NOVELS BY SASSOON

The Complete Memoirs of George Sherston (1937). Faber & Faber 1937 $11.95. ISBN 0-571-09913-0
Memoirs of a Fox-Hunting Man (1928). Faber & Faber 1960 $6.95. ISBN 0-571-06454-X
Memoirs of an Infantry Officer (1930). Faber & Faber 1968 $6.95. ISBN 0-571-06410-X

POETRY BY SASSOON

Collected Poems 1908–1956. Faber & Faber 1986 $9.95. ISBN 0-571-17262-6
The War Poems of Siegfried Sassoon. Faber & Faber 1983 $6.95. ISBN 0-571-13010-0

NONFICTION BY SASSOON

The Old Century and Seven More Years (1938). Faber & Faber 1986 $11.95. ISBN 0-571-13960-4
Siegfried's Journey (1945). Faber & Faber 1986 $5.95. ISBN 0-571-11917-4
The Weald of Youth (1942). Faber & Faber 1986 $8.95. ISBN 0-571-13962-0

BOOK ABOUT SASSOON

Fussell, Paul (ed). *Siegfried Sassoon's Long Journey: Selections from the Sherston Memoirs.* Oxford Univ Pr 1983 $24.95. ISBN 0-19-503309-4 George Sherston's recollections of Sassoon during World War I, edited by a friend and critic.

SAYERS, DOROTHY L. (LEIGH)   1893–1957

Dorothy L. Sayers was born in Oxford, England, the daughter of a school headmaster. As a child she was tutored at home and read widely on her own. She was one of the first women to graduate from Oxford University, receiving both her Bachelor's and Master's degrees in 1920.

After graduation Sayers taught school for a short time, worked for a publishing firm, and took a job as an advertising copywriter. In her spare time she began to write mystery novels about an elegant British aristocrat, Lord Peter Wimsey, who solved crimes as a hobby.

The first Wimsey novel, *Whose Body?,* was published in 1923. By 1931 the Wimsey novels had become so popular that Sayers quit her advertising job to write full-time.

From the beginning, Sayers' novels showed a wit, intelligence, and style that set them apart from the ordinary detective story. Lord Peter is not only a detective, but also an interesting character who grows more complex with each novel. Unlike many modern fictional detectives to whom women flock, Lord Peter is rejected repeatedly by the one love of his life, and it is only by relentlessly pursuing her through several novels that he finally wins her.

Sayers has been credited with raising the detective story to a higher level and earning increased respectability for it. The Wimsey series was not only popular with the general public, but also highly praised by the critics. Several of the Wimsey novels have been made into movies as well as into a highly successful television series.

In addition to writing detective novels, Sayers also produced scholarly works. Trained in medieval languages, she completed a highly regarded translation of *The Divine Comedy,* a classic poem by the Italian poet Dante. (*See* Dante, Vol. 1, World Literature: Italian Language and Literature.) A devout Christian, she also wrote several religious books and plays.

NOVELS BY SAYERS

Busman's Honeymoon (1937). Harper 1986 $4.50. ISBN 0-06-080823-3 Lord Peter's honeymoon is interrupted by murder.

Clouds of Witness (1926). Harper 1987 $4.50. ISBN 0-06-080835-7 Murder reaches Lord Peter Wimsey in a more personal way when his brother and sister are prime suspects.

Gaudy Night (1935). Harper 1988 $4.50. ISBN 0-06-080907-8 Wimsey and his beloved Harriet Vane solve a mystery at Oxford University.

Have His Carcase (1932). Harper 1987 $4.50. ISBN 0-06-080909-4 Harriet Vane discovers a body on the beach and she and Lord Peter must solve the mystery.

Murder Must Advertise (1933). Harper 1986 $3.95. ISBN 0-06-080825-X Murder in an advertising agency.

The Nine Tailors (1934). Harcourt 1966 $4.95. ISBN 0-15-665899-2 The secret is in the ringing church bells.

Strong Poison (1930). Harper 1987 $4.50. ISBN 0-06-080908-6 Harriet Vane is accused of murder and Lord Peter must clear her.

Unnatural Death (1927). Harper 1987 $4.50. ISBN 0-06-080840-3 Lord Peter wrestles with his conscience.

The Unpleasantness at the Bellona Club (1928). Harper 1986 $4.50. ISBN 0-06-080828-4 Murder strikes at a quiet men's club.

SHORT STORY COLLECTIONS BY SAYERS

Hangman's Holiday (1933). Harper 1987 $4.50. ISBN 0-06-080837-3 A dozen stories, some with Wimsey.

In the Teeth of the Evidence (1939). Harper 1987 $4.50. ISBN 0-06-080838-1 Seventeen stories of murder and detection, some with Lord Peter.

Lord Peter: A Collection of All the Lord Peter Stories. Harper 1986 $8.95. ISBN 0-06-091380-0 All the Wimsey short stories in one volume.

Lord Peter Views the Body (1928). Harper 1986 $4.50. ISBN 0-06-080839-X Eleven Wimsey mysteries.

BOOKS ABOUT SAYERS

Hall, Trevor H. *Dorothy L. Sayers: Nine Literary Studies.* Shoe String 1980 $19.50. ISBN 0-208-01877-8 Illustrated guide to where Sayers did her writing; includes drawings and photos.

Hone, Ralph E. *Dorothy L. Sayers: A Literary Biography.* Kent Univ Pr 1981 $9.95. ISBN 0-87338-253-6 Essays on Sayers' life as a writer by a noted Sayers student.
Youngberg, Ruth T. *Dorothy L. Sayers: A Reference Guide.* G. K. Hall 1982 $32.00. ISBN 0-8161-8198-5 Indexed guide to Sayers' work, especially written for students.

SCOTT, PAUL   1920–1978

Born in London and educated in English preparatory schools, Paul Scott served in the British and Indian armies from 1940 to 1946. He also worked for a publishing house and acted as a literary agent before becoming a full-time writer.

Scott is best known for his novels about India during the last years of British rule. His major achievement is *The Raj Quartet* (1976), which was adapted into a major television miniseries, and its fine sequel, *Staying On* (1977), winner of the Booker Prize, Britain's highest literary honor. These works portray the breakdown of the colonial order in India and the stresses this caused for both British and the Indian people.

Scott uses history as a backdrop to show how individual lives are influenced by political events. Although his characters represent the clash of political and personal interests in a changing India, they never cease to be human beings who are interesting in their own right. They are people, not types.

Scott's fine eye for detail gives his books a feeling of realism and accuracy. He devotes considerable attention to his characters' occupations because, as he once said, he preferred "to write about people in relation to their work, which strikes me as a subject no less important than their private lives."

NOVELS BY SCOTT

The Bender (1963). Carroll & Graf 1986 $3.95. ISBN 0-88184-231-1
The Birds of Paradise (1962). Carroll & Graf 1986 $4.50. ISBN 0-88184-232-X
The Corrida at San Feliu (1964). Carroll & Graf 1986 $4.95. ISBN 0-88184-274-5
The Day of the Scorpion (1968). Avon 1979 $4.50. ISBN 0-380-40923-2
A Division of the Spoils (1975). Avon 1979 $4.50. ISBN 0-380-45054-2
The Jewel in the Crown (1966). Avon 1979 $4.50. ISBN 0-380-40410-9
The Love Pavillion (1960). Carroll & Graf 1987 $4.50. ISBN 0-88184-190-0
A Male Child (1956). Carroll & Graf 1987 $3.95. ISBN 0-88184-189-7
The Raj Quartet (includes *The Jewel in the Crown; The Day of the Scorpion; The Towers of Silence; A Division of the Spoils*) (1976). Morrow 1976 $27.50. ISBN 0-688-04212-0
Staying On (1977). Avon 1979 $3.50. ISBN 0-380-46045-9
The Towers of Silence (1971). Avon 1979 $4.50. ISBN 0-380-44198-5

SHAFFER, PETER   1926–

Born in Liverpool, Peter Shaffer spent three years working in coal mines before entering Cambridge University. After graduating he worked for a music publisher and for the New York Public Library before turning his talents to the theater.

Shaffer burst into public awareness at the very moment the new postwar British drama arrived on the London stage. The year 1958 saw several new young dramatists staging exciting new plays—including Shaffer's *Five Finger Exercise.* Considered the most promising British playwright, he followed this success with a double bill, *The Private Ear* and *The Public Eye* (1962), twin comedies that were very well received. *The Royal Hunt of the Sun* (1964), an imaginative evocation of the encounter between the Spanish conqueror Pizarro and the Inca priest-god Atahualpa, was highly praised and extremely successful in both London and New York. *Black Comedy* (1965) is a highly amusing farce that represented a sort of calm before the storm of his next two plays, *Equus* (1973) and *Amadeus* (1979). These two plays are psychological studies of highly civilized and repressed men, each forced to deal with powerful and dynamic figures with whom they cannot cope. Both plays were made into very successful films.

Shaffer has written screenplays and television scripts as well as stage plays, and has also published detective novels. His twin brother, Anthony, is also a playwright, most famous for the mystery *Sleuth*.

PLAYS BY SHAFFER

Amadeus (1979). Signet 1988 $3.95. ISBN 0-451-15894-6
Equus (1973). Penguin 1984 $3.95. ISBN 0-14-048185-0
Yonadab (1986). Harper 1988 $7.95. ISBN 0-06-03906-1

BOOK ABOUT SHAFFER

Plunka, Gene A. *Peter Shaffer: Roles, Rites, and Rituals in the Theater.* Fairleigh 1988 $34.50. ISBN 0-8386-3329-3 How Shaffer's work influenced the modern theater, by contemporary critic and scholar.

SHAW, GEORGE BERNARD   1856–1950

George Bernard Shaw was born in Dublin, Ireland, the child of Irish Protestant parents. His mother was a singing teacher and his sister Lucy was a musical-comedy actress.

Shaw was never fond of school and left it at age 15 to take a job with a real estate agent. Not finding office work to his liking, he followed his mother and sister to London. While there he read widely and educated himself.

Between 1879 and 1883, Shaw wrote five unsuccessful novels and some art and music criticism for magazines. He also became an active socialist and gained a reputation as a powerful political speaker.

Shaw had tried his hand at writing plays as early as 1885, but nothing of his was actually staged until 1892. Because these plays were considered too controversial to be approved for public performance, they were staged privately in theater clubs. Thus, by the time Shaw came to public attention in 1904, he had already written a sizeable number of plays.

From the outset Shaw had a reputation as something of a "bad boy" of the theater, writing plays that were considered bold and shocking. While some of his early plays drew good-sized audiences, he did not achieve real financial success until *Pygmalion* (1913). This comedy about a poor flower-seller who learns to pass for a duchess due to her clever speech teacher's lessons immediately caught the fancy of London theatergoers. It played to large audiences when it was first staged and has been revived regularly ever since. It was also the basis for the enormously popular 1955 musical comedy *My Fair Lady.*

While all of Shaw's plays can be called comedies, they have serious undertones as well. Shaw was acutely aware of social injustice and the plight of the poor. His own period of impoverishment in his early days in London left him with a lifelong sense that poverty is the most serious evil in the world. He also took several scathing looks at male-female relationships, calling for a recognition of women's equality.

Despite the outspoken positions expressed in his plays and his own attempt to appear brash and cantankerous, Shaw was actually a shy and sensitive person. He declined both knighthood and the Order of Merit when they were offered, and only reluctantly accepted the Nobel Prize for literature in 1925.

PLAYS BY SHAW

Androcles and the Lion (1913). Penguin 1963 $3.95. ISBN 0-14-048010-2 The meeting in ancient Rome of a Christian martyr and a friendly lion.

The Apple Cart (1929). Penguin 1956 $4.95. ISBN 0-14-048008-0

Arms and the Man (1894). Penguin 1950 $3.50. ISBN 0-14-048102-8 A woman is engaged to a dashing hero—but falls in love with an apparently ordinary man.

Back to Methuselah (1922). Penguin 1988 $5.95. ISBN 0-14-045014-9

Caesar and Cleopatra (1898). Penguin 1950 $3.95. ISBN 0-14-048100-1 Story of the aging Roman dictator and the young Egyptian queen.

Candida (1895). Penguin 1950 $4.95. ISBN 0-14-048103.

The Devil's Disciple (1901). Penguin 1950 $3.50. ISBN 0-14-048101-X

The Doctor's Dilemma (1906). Penguin 1950 $2.95. ISBN 0-14-048001-3

Heartbreak House (1920). Penguin 1965 $3.95. ISBN 0-14-048053-6

Major Barbara (1905). Penguin 1950 $2.95. ISBN 0-14-048007-2 Battle between a Salvation Army worker and a munitions manufacturer over the right way of life.

Man and Superman (1905). Penguin 1950 $2.95. ISBN 0-14-048006-4

Pygmalion (1913). Penguin 1950 $3.95. ISBN 0-14-048003-X Transformation of a poor girl into a polished lady.

St. Joan (with *Androcles and the Lion* and *Major Barbara*) (1923). Random $6.95. ISBN 0-394-60480-6 Joan of Arc must stand up for her beliefs.

BOOKS ABOUT SHAW

Evans, T. F. *Shaw: The Critical Heritage.* Routledge 1984 $15.00. ISBN 0-7102-0396-9 Critiques of Shaw's addresses, essays, and lectures.

Kaufman, R. J. (ed). *G. B. Shaw: A Collection of Critical Essays.* Prentice 1976. (o.p.) $4.90. A solid collection of essays by well-regarded scholars; contains an overview by the editor, a chronology, and selected bibliography.

McCabe, Joseph. *George Bernard Shaw.* Haskell 1974 $49.95. ISBN 0-8383-1749-9 Study of the works of Shaw by a respected contemporary of Shaw.

SILLITOE, ALAN 1928–

Alan Sillitoe grew up in the slums of the industrial city of Nottingham. He began to write while stationed in Malaya with the Royal Air Force. After the war he went to the island of Majorca, Spain, where he became a friend of Robert Graves (*see* Graves, Vol. 1, British Literature: The Twentieth Century), who encouraged him to write *Saturday Night and Sunday Morning* (1958). The novel concerns the life of Arthur Seaton, a young Nottingham factory worker who has rejected society's rules and lives only to please himself. Sillitoe's author fee for this book enabled him to afford a better diet, which he claims helped him recover from tuberculosis.

Saturday Night and Sunday Morning was made into an award-winning film in 1960. In 1960, Sillitoe's collection of short stories, *The Loneliness of the Long-Distance Runner* (1959), won the Hawthornden Prize, one of Britain's major awards. The title story was also made into a movie in 1962. The plot centers on a gifted and defiant reform-school boy who refuses to win a long-distance race which would bring honor to the school he rejects.

Sillitoe focuses on the "outsider," the person who deliberately chooses not to fit into society. His work both comments on the failures of society as a whole and tells a gripping tale of a single individual.

NOVELS BY SILLITOE

Out of the Whirlpool (1987). Harper 1988 $11.95. ISBN 0-06-015892-1
Saturday Night and Sunday Morning (1958). Knopf 1959 $16.54. ISBN 0-394-44377-2

SHORT STORY COLLECTION BY SILLITOE

The Loneliness of the Long-Distance Runner (1959). Signet 1986 $3.50. ISBN 0-451-16026-6

BOOK ABOUT SILLITOE

Hutchings, William. *Alan Sillitoe.* Starmont $9.95. ISBN 1-55782-060-2 Critical assessment of Sillitoe's work by a Sillitoe scholar.

SPARK, MURIEL   1918–

Muriel Spark was born Muriel Sarah Camberg in Edinburgh, Scotland, where she was educated at Gillespie's School for Girls. She lived for some years in central Africa, where she married S. O. Spark. Then, during World War II she returned to England, where she worked in the Political Intelligence Office of the Foreign Service.

Spark was editor of a poetry magazine from 1947 to 1949. She published her own volume of poems, *The Fanfarlo,* in 1952. She also wrote some literary criticism and biography before publishing her first novel, *The Comforters,* in 1957. The book was very favorably reviewed, and Spark's career as a novelist was launched.

Spark has been described as "our most chilling comic writer since Evelyn Waugh." (*See* Waugh, Vol. 1; British Literature: The Twentieth Century.) Her fiction is distinguished by its remarkable variety, wit, and craftsmanship. Spark's satire is sharp, but subtle, written in a polished style. Much of her writing is concerned with issues of catholicism and explores such topics as free will and the reasons why people act the way they do.

Spark became widely known in the United States when *The New Yorker* magazine devoted almost an entire issue to her novel *The Prime of Miss Jean Brodie* (1961), which was later made into a play and then an award-winning movie. Set in Edinburgh in the 1930s, the novel tells the story of Miss Brodie, a schoolteacher, her unorthodox approach to life, and its effect on a group of adolescent girls she has favored. The idol turns out to have feet of clay, and leaves a permanent—perhaps destructive—mark on the lives of all who knew her.

Spark's subsequent novels have all met with favorable reviews and enthusiastic public acceptance. She can aptly be called one of the foremost contemporary novelists.

NOVELS BY SPARK

The Abbess of Crewe (1974). Putnam 1984 $6.95. ISBN 0-399-50952-6
The Bachelors (1960). Putnam 1984 $6.95. ISBN 0-399-50929-1
The Ballad of Peckham Rye (1960). Putnam 1982 $5.95. ISBN 0-399-50650-0
The Comforters (1957). Putnam 1984 $6.95. ISBN 0-399-50931-3
The Driver's Seat (1970). Putnam 1984 $6.95. ISBN 0-399-50928-3
A Far Cry from Kennsington (1988). Houghton 1988 $17.95. ISBN 0-395-47694-1
The Girls of Slender Means (1963). Putnam 1982 $5.95. ISBN 0-399-50659-4
The Only Problem (1984). Putnam 1985 $7.95. ISBN 0-399-51126-1
* The Prime of Miss Jean Brodie (1961). Plume 1984 $6.95. ISBN 0-456-26179-1 Short novel about a schoolteacher and the way she influences some of her students.
Robinson (1958). Avon 1978 $1.25. ISBN 0-380-01388-6
Territorial Rights (1979). Putnam 1984 $6.95. ISBN 0-399-50930-5

SHORT STORY COLLECTION BY SPARK

Stories of Muriel Spark. Plume 1986 $7.95. ISBN 0-452-25880-4

BOOKS ABOUT SPARK

Bold, Alan. *Muriel Spark.* Routledge 1986 $17.95. ISBN 0-416-40360-3 An anthology of solid critical essays by well-known scholars; includes a biography.

Richmond, Velma. *Muriel Spark.* Ungar 1985 $16.95. ISBN 0-8044-2731-3 Insightful and lively study of all of Spark's novels; thoroughly up-to-date evaluation; includes a bibliography.

Walker, Dorothea. *Muriel Spark.* G. K. Hall 1988 $17.95. ISBN 0-8057-6960-9 Complete treatment of Spark and her work; contains a chronology, bibliography, and index.

STOPPARD, TOM   1937–

Tom Stoppard was born Tom Straussler in Zlin, Czechoslovakia, the son of a physician who moved to England in 1946. There young Stoppard completed his education and began a career as a journalist. He started writing plays in 1960 while still doing free-lance reporting for the Bristol *Evening World.*

Stoppard's first plays were radio and television scripts. He moved on to writing for the stage, but without much success. Then, in 1967, when the National Theater in London needed a last-minute substitute for a cancelled production of a Shakespearean play, it was decided to stage Stoppard's play, *Rosencrantz and Guildenstern Are Dead,* even though it had received poor reviews in its Edinburgh debut. From opening night the play—an ironic look at Shakespeare's *Hamlet* through the eyes of the two extremely minor characters of Rosencrantz and Guildenstern—was a smash hit and soon won universal acclaim. The following year in New York, it was chosen best play by the Drama Critics Circle, and Stoppard's reputation as a major playwright was established.

Stoppard's method has been to contrive explanations for highly unlikely encounters. He brings together in a play people who would probably never meet in real life and asks, "What would happen if they did meet?" Or he examines events, large and small, and finds unlikely explanations for them. His most recent plays have begun to deal with political questions and social issues. The political upheavals in Central Europe, especially in his native Czechoslovakia, have made him feel closer to the land of his ancestors, leading him to adapt older plays by European writers for the British stage.

PLAYS BY STOPPARD

The Dog It Was That Died (1982). Faber & Faber 1987 $7.95. ISBN 0-571-14739-9
Every Good Boy Deserves Favor and Professional Foul (1977). Grove 1987 $3.95. ISBN 0-8021-5154-8
Hapgood (1987). Faber & Faber 1988 $14.95. ISBN 0-57-15159-0
Jumpers (1972). Grove 1989 $7.95. ISBN 0-394-17866-1
Lord Malquist and Mr. Moon (1984). Faber & Faber 1985 $5.95. ISBN 0-571-11529-2
On the Razzle (1981). Faber & Faber 1983 $4.95. ISBN 0-571-11835-6
The Real Inspector Hound (1968). Grove 1970 $7.95. ISBN 0-394-17313-9
The Real Thing (1982). Faber & Faber 1983 $5.95. ISBN 0-571-12529-8
Rosencrantz and Guildenstern Are Dead (1967). Grove 1987 $6.95. ISBN 0-8021-3033-X
Rough Crossing (1983). Faber & Faber 1985 $5.95. ISBN 0-571-13595-1
Squaring the Circle (1985). Faber & Faber 1985 $5.95. ISBN 0-571-12538-7
Travesties (1974). Grove 1989 $4.95. ISBN 0-394-17884-X

BOOKS ABOUT STOPPARD

Corballis, Richard. *Stoppard: The Mystery and the Clockwork.* Routledge 1984 $10.95. ISBN 0-416-00981-6 An analysis of each of Stoppard's published works, designed to guide general readers through Stoppard's linguistic devices; contains the fullest available bibliography of works by and about Stoppard.

Harty, John III (ed). *Tom Stoppard: A Casebook.* Garland 1988 $55.00. ISBN 0-8240-9023-3 Valuable collection of essays with a wide variety of critical approaches to Stoppard's major works; designed for students and general readers as well as for scholars and teachers.

Rusinko, Susan. *Tom Stoppard.* G. K. Hall 1976 $6.95. ISBN 0-8057-6927-7 Traces the development of the Stoppard hero through essays on each of Stoppard's full-length stage dramas, novels, short and lesser plays, and radio and television dramas.

SYNGE, JOHN MILLINGTON   1871–1909

John Millington Synge was born into an Anglo-Irish family in Rathfarnham, near Dublin, Ireland. Because of poor health, he was educated at home by private tutors before entering Trinity College, Dublin. After graduating, Synge left for Europe to write poetry. If William Butler Yeats (*see* Yeats, Vol. 1, British Literature: The Twentieth Century) had not discovered him in Paris and persuaded him to return to Ireland to absorb its native traditions, the Irish theater might have lost one of its best playwrights.

When Synge returned to Ireland, he went to the west to be close to the rural roots of the country and its native Gaelic speakers. The result was two short plays: *In the Shadow of the Glen* (1903), in which a corpse comically returns to life and interrupts a widow's marriage plans, and *Riders to the Sea* (1904), about a mother's loss of her last son—one of the best one-act plays ever written. Synge's masterpiece, however, is *The Playboy of the Western World* (1907), in which a country lad becomes a hero when he boasts that he has murdered his father— and loses his popularity when it turns out that his father is still alive. The play touched off a riot when it was staged, partly because audience's resented Synge's satire of the hypocrisy and gullibility of Irish peasants, but mostly because one of the characters mentions the name of a woman's undergarment, a shocking word for the conservative Irish public. As a result, Synge's next play, *The Tinker's Wedding* (1909), was produced first in London. Synge, however, never saw the play performed; he was too ill with cancer, and died the following year.

PLAYS BY SYNGE

Complete Plays of John M. Synge (includes *The Playboy of the Western World; Riders to the Sea; In the Shadow of the Glen; Well of the Saints; The Tinker's Wedding; Dierdre of the Sorrows*). Random 1960 $4.95. ISBN 0-394-70178-X

BOOKS ABOUT SYNGE

Gerstenberger, Donna. *John Millington Synge.* Twayne 1990 $21.95. ISBN 0-805-76959-5 Careful analysis of Synge's life and works, covering his long prose pieces and each of the plays; includes a chronology, selected bibliography, and index.

Grene, Nicholas. *Synge: A Critical Study of the Plays.* Rowman 1975. (o.p.) The first full study to concentrate exclusively on Synge's plays; special emphasis on the relationship between Synge's work and its setting.

Skelton, Robin. *J. M. Synge.* Devin-Adair 1983 $3.95. ISBN 0-8159-6847-7 Highly respected biography of Synge's life; contains numerous pictures, illustrations, and maps, as well as a detailed chronology.

THOMAS, DYLAN   1914–1953

Dylan Thomas was born in Swansea, Wales, the son of a schoolteacher. He attended school locally, but declined university study in favor of becoming a professional writer. Thomas worked first in Swansea and then in London at a variety of literary jobs, including journalism and, eventually, writing film-scripts and radio plays.

In 1936 Thomas began a stormy marriage to writer-dancer Caitland Mac-Namara, a marriage that endured for the rest of his life. He fell into a pattern of working hard and drinking hard in London and then retreating to the Welsh countryside to recover.

In the early 1950s, Thomas made three celebrated poetry-reading tours of the United States, during which his outrageous behavior drew as much attention as his superb readings. Weakened by chronic alcoholism, he collapsed during his last tour and died in a New York City hospital.

The passage of time has not been good to Thomas. During his lifetime he was regarded as a major poet and the most important literary figure to come out of Wales. Today, however, his reputation has waned. While he retains a fairly wide popular readership, he is regarded by most critics as having been overrated. Some of his poems, however, like "Do Not Go Gentle into That Good Night" (about the death of his father) and "Fern Hill" (about the pleasures of youth), have stood the test of time and are likely to remain an essential part of our literary heritage, as is his memoir, "A Child's Christmas in Wales" (1945), and his verse drama, *Under Milk Wood* (1954).

Thomas's work explores the world of childhood and adolescence with sensitivity and sympathy. His poems celebrate the fullness of life. As he wrote in a note to his *Collected Poems* (1953), "These poems, with all their crudities, doubts, and confusion, are written for the love of Man and in praise of God, and I'd be a damn fool if they weren't."

Short Story Collections by Thomas

A Portrait of the Artist as a Young Dog (1940). New Directions 1956 $5.95. ISBN 0-8112-0207-0
Collected Stories. New Directions 1984 $10.95. ISBN 0-8112-0209-7

Poetry by Thomas

Collected Poems (1953). New Directions 1971 $7.95. ISBN 0-8112-0205-4

Play by Thomas

Under Milk Wood (1954). New Directions 1959 $4.95. ISBN 0-8112-0209-7

Nonfiction by Thomas

A Child's Christmas in Wales (1945). Godine 1980 $7.95. ISBN 0-87923-529-2 A touching memoir of family relations at holiday time.

Books about Thomas

Cox, Charles B. (ed). *Dylan Thomas: A Collection of Critical Essays.* Prentice 1966 $12.95. ISBN 0-13-919381-2 A compilation of the best critical essays by highly respected scholars with an especially useful introduction by Cox; contains a chronology and selected bibliography.
Tindall, William Y. *A Reader's Guide to Dylan Thomas.* Hippocrene 1973 $22.50. ISBN 0-374-979480-0 The clearest textual analysis available of Thomas's writing; contains precise and detailed analyses of his works; includes a bibliography and an index of poems and key names.

TOLKIEN, J. R. R. (JOHN RONALD REUEL)   1892–1973

J. R. R. Tolkien was born in South Africa, but when he was four his father died and the family moved to Birmingham, England. His mother died when he was 12, and he and his brother were raised by a Catholic priest.

After graduating from Oxford University, Tolkien served in the army in World War I, and then returned to Oxford for his master's degree. In 1923 he began teaching at the University of Leeds and five years later was appointed a professor at Oxford, where he remained until his death.

Tolkien was an expert on Old English language and literature and published many scholarly works in that field. It was his books for children, however, that brought him world fame.

In 1937 Tolkien published *The Hobbit,* a fantasy about gnomes, dragons, and a mythical land known as Middle-Earth, which existed before the era of humans beings. Then he wrote the story "Farmer Giles of Ham" (1949). Later he returned to the land of the Hobbits with *The Lord of the Rings* (1955), a much more complicated story told in three parts. A further book in this series, *The Silmarillion* (1977), was edited by Tolkien's son Christopher and published after the author's death.

While some readers have searched for hidden meanings in these stories, Tolkien himself maintained, "It is not about anything but itself." In the 1960s and 1970s the books became very popular and continue to have devoted readers today. Literary critics, however, show less enthusiasm. As critic Edmund Wilson put it, *The Hobbit* is "essentially a children's book . . . which has somehow got out of hand."

After Tolkien's death, his son assembled several volumes of fragments and tales taken from his father's notes and added his own comments about how his father wrote his books. He published these as *The Lays of Beleriand* (1984); *The Book of Lost Tales* (1984); *The Return of the Shadow* (1985); *The Treason of Isengard* (1985); *The Shaping of Middle-Earth* (1985); and *The Lost Road* (1987).

STORIES BY TOLKIEN

The Book of Lost Tales (1984). 2 vols. Houghton 1986. Vol. 1 $8.95. ISBN 0-395-40927-6. Vol. 2 $8.95. ISBN 0-395-42640-5

The Lays of Beleriand (1984). Houghton 1985 $16.95. ISBN 0-395-39429-5

The Lost Road and Other Writings (1987). Houghton 1987 $18.95. ISBN 0-395-45519-7

The Return of the Shadow (1985). Houghton 1989 $19.95. ISBN 0-395-49863-5

The Shaping of Middle-Earth (1985). Houghton 1986 $16.95. ISBN 0-395-42501-8

The Silmarillion (1977). Ballantine 1985 $3.95. ISBN 0-395-42501-8 Further adventures in Middle-Earth.

Smith of Wooten Major (1967) and *Farmer Giles of Ham* (1949). Ballantine 1986 $2.95. ISBN 0-345-33606-2 Two short tales; not part of the Middle-Earth stories.

Tolkien, Four Volumes (includes *The Hobbit,* 1937; *The Fellowship of the Ring,* 1954; *The Two Towers,* 1954; *The Return of the King,* 1955). Ballantine 1984 $19.80. ISBN 0-345-35711-6 The frightening and amusing adventures of Hobbit Bilbo Baggins, Gandalf, the wizard, and other mythical creatures.

The Treason of Isengard (1985). Houghton 1989 $19.95. ISBN 0-395-51562-9

Unfinished Tales (1980). Ballantine 1988 $5.95. ISBN 0-345-49863-5 Recently discovered tales of Middle-Earth.

POETRY BY TOLKIEN

The Adventures of Tom Bombadil (1962). Houghton 1978 $14.95. ISBN 0-395-26801-X Story of a "master of wood, water, and hill."

Oliphaunt. Contemporary Bks 1989 $3.95. ISBN 0-8072-4353-9 Fantastic tales suitable for very young children.

NONFICTION BY TOLKIEN

*The Shaping of Middle-Earth. Houghton 1986 $16.95. ISBN 0-395-42501-8 Background notes and information on Tolkien, edited by his son.

BOOKS ABOUT TOLKIEN

Carpenter, Humphrey. *Tolkien: The Authorized Biography*. Ballantine 1985 $3.50. ISBN 0-345-32729-2 Based on Tolkien's personal papers; a comprehensive guide to his life and literature.

Crabbe, Katharyn F. *J. R. R. Tolkien*. Ungar 1981 $18.95. ISBN 0-8044-2134-X Biography that stresses *The Hobbit* and the *The Lord of Rings* trilogy.

Foster, Robert. *The Complete Guide to Middle-Earth from The Hobbit to the Silmarillion*. Del Rey 1985 $3.95. ISBN 0-345-32436-6 Definitive concordance with detailed page references to all works.

Kocher, Paul. *Master of Middle-Earth: The Fiction of J. R. R. Tolkien*. Ballantine 1987 $2.95. ISBN 0-345-30636-8 Considers Tolkien's works as a whole, including short prose and verse narratives.

WALSH, GILLIAN PATON   1937–

Born Gillian Llewellyn in London, Jill Paton Walsh was educated at St. Michael's Convent and at Oxford University, from which she graduated with honors. She then taught English in London from 1959 to 1962. In 1961 she married Antony Paton Walsh.

Her first novel, *Farewell, Great King,* was published in 1972. Like several of her books, it had an historical setting. Walsh also frequently sets her stories during wartime, either modern or ancient. But the war she shows is never the setting for the gallant deeds of great heroes. Rather, it is a place full of genuine horrors and frightening perils that help to draw together her characters.

Walsh has also written moving novels dealing with the problems of growing up. *Goldengrove* (1972) and its sequel *Unleaving* (1976) are especially powerful works that follow a young girl's coming of age. According to critic Pamela Marsh, Walsh satisfies "all those adult readers who turn for their reading to the children's shelf and insist that they find good, well-plotted novels there."

NOVELS BY WALSH

*A Chance Child (1980). Avon 1980 $1.95. ISBN 0-380-48561-3 Creep emerges from a soggy cardboard box to begin time travel through the English Industrial Revolution.

*The Dolphin Crossing (1967). Dell 1990 $3.50. ISBN 0-440-40310-3 Story of two teenage boys who get involved in evacuating British soldiers from Dunkirk in World War II.

*The Emperor's Winding Sheet (1974). Farrar 1974 $13.95. ISBN 0-374-32160-4 Adventures of an English boy caught up in the last siege of Constantinople.

*Fireweed (1969). Farrar 1970 $14.95. ISBN 0-374-32310-0 Two English teenagers are thrown together during the bombing of London in World War II.

*Gaffer Samson's Luck (1985). G. K. Hall 1987 $11.95. ISBN 0-7451-0451-7 Tale of the friendship between a lonely teen and a crusty old man.

*Goldengrove (1972). Farrar 1985 $3.45. ISBN 0-374-42587-6 In a special Cornwall summer, Madge discovers who she really is.

*A Parcel of Patterns (1983). Farrar 1983 $10.95. ISBN 0-374-35750-1 Mall Percival remembers what the plague did to her village in 1660.

*Torch (1988). Farrar 1988 $12.95. ISBN 0-374-37684-0 In a future with no memory of the past, a group of Greek teenagers must save the last Olympic torch.

*Unleaving (1976). Farrar 1976 $11.95. ISBN 0-374-3842-2 Madge must fight both the sea and the turmoil within herself.

WAUGH, EVELYN 1902–1966

Born in Hampstead and educated at Oxford University, Evelyn Waugh came from a literary family. His elder brother, Alec, was a novelist, and his father, Arthur Waugh, was the influential head of a large publishing house. Even in his school days, Waugh showed signs of the profound belief in Catholicism and brilliant wit that were to mark his later years.

Waugh began publishing his novels in the late 1920s. He joined the Royal Marines at the beginning of World War II and was one of the first to volunteer for commando service. In 1944 he survived a plane crash in Yugoslavia and, while hiding in a cave, corrected the proofs of one of his novels.

Waugh's early novels, *Decline and Fall* (1927), *Vile Bodies* (1930), and *A Handful of Dust* (1934), established him as one of the funniest and most brilliant satirists the British had seen in years. He was particularly skillful at poking fun at the scramble for prominence among the upper classes and the struggle between the generations. He lived for a while in Hollywood, about which he wrote *The Loved One* (1948), a scathing attack on the United States's overly sentimental funeral practices. His greatest works, however, are *Brideshead Revisited* (1945), which has been made into a highly popular television miniseries, and the trilogy *Sword of Honor* (1965), composed of *Men at Arms* (1952), *Officers and Gentlemen* (1955), and *The End of the Battle* (1961).

NOVELS BY WAUGH

Black Mischief (1932). Little 1977 $7.95. ISBN 0-316-92609-4
Brideshead Revisited (1945). Little 1982 $7.95. ISBN 0-316-92634-5
Decline and Fall (1927). Little 1977 $7.95. ISBN 0-316-92607-8
The End of the Battle (1961). Little 1979 $7.95. ISBN 0-316-92620-5
A Handful of Dust (1934). Little 1977 $7.95. ISBN 0-316-92605-1
The Loved One (1948). Little 1977 $6.95. ISBN 0-316-92608-1
Men at Arms (1952). Little 1979 $7.95. ISBN 0-316-92628-0
Officers and Gentlemen (1955). Little 1979 $7.95. ISBN 0-316-92630-2
The Ordeal of Gilbert Pinfold (1957). Little 1979 $7.95. ISBN 0-316-92622-1
Put Out More Flags (1942). Little 1977 $7.95. ISBN 0-316-92612-4
Scoop (1938). Little 1977 $7.95. ISBN 0-316-92610-8
Vile Bodies (1930). Little 1977 $7.95. ISBN 0-316-92611-6

BOOKS ABOUT WAUGH

Crabbe, Katharyn. *Evelyn Waugh.* Ungar 1988 $16.95. ISBN 0-8044-2107-2 Thorough and sympathetic analysis of Waugh and his work; includes photographs, a chronology, and an index.

Donaldson, Frances. *Evelyn Waugh: Portrait of a Country Neighbor.* Weidenfeld 1967. (o.p.) An affectionate biography based on Waugh's personal papers, interviews with his son, and a long and close friendship; contains photographs of Waugh, his home, and his possessions.

Pryce-Jones, David (ed). *Evelyn Waugh and His World.* Little 1973. (o.p.) A collection of reminiscences, many by Waugh's close friends, that creates a guide to Waugh's life and works; includes photographs, letters, and illustrations.

WELDON, FAY 1933–

Fay Weldon was born in Worcester, England, where her father was a physician and her mother a writer. She was educated at the University of St. Andrews, from which she received her M.A. in 1954. Six years later, she married Ronald Weldon. Weldon worked as a propaganda writer for the British Foreign Office and then as an advertising copywriter for various firms in London before making writing a full-time career. Since the mid-1960s she has written novels, short stories, and radio and television plays.

The central subject of all Weldon's writing is the experience of women, especially their relationships with men. According to Weldon, "Women must ask themselves: What is it that will give me fulfillment? That's the serious question I'm attempting to answer." Despite her concern with women, Weldon has been criticized by some feminist groups for apparently presenting her fictional women with very limited options.

Weldon's style is marked by a careful attention to detail, vivid images, a sharp wit, and a wry sense of humor. Although most of her male characters are disagreeable, they are not the true villains of her novels. Her villains are, in fact, the traditional roles that men and women are supposed to play. Weldon looks at women in many different circumstances—at work, at home, at play, in politics, and especially in love—and shows not only how they are manipulated by men, but also how they allow themselves to be manipulated.

Recently, Weldon's novel *The Life and Loves of a She-Devil* (1983) has been made into a popular movie. It was formerly a successful television miniseries.

NOVELS BY WELDON

The Cloning of Joanna May (1990). Viking 1990 $18.95. ISBN 0-670-83090-9
Down Among the Women (1971). Academy Chi Pubs 1984 $7.95. ISBN 0-89733-116-8
The Fat Woman's Joke (1967). Academy Chi Pubs 1986 $6.95. ISBN 0-89733-236-9
Female Friends (1975). Academy Chi Pubs 1988 $7.95. ISBN 0-89733-290-3
The Heart of the Country (1988). Penguin 1988 $7.95. ISBN 0-14-010397-X
The Hearts and Lives of Men (1987). Dell 1989 $4.95. ISBN 0-440-20322-8
Leader of the Band (1988). Viking 1989 $18.95. ISBN 0-670-82440-2
The Lives and Loves of a She-Devil (1983). Ballantine 1985 $4.50. ISBN 0-345-32375-0
Remember Me (1976). Ballantine 1985 $3.50. ISBN 0-345-32976-6
The Rules of Life (1987). Harper 1988 $5.95. ISBN 0-06-091499-8
The Shrapnel Academy (1987). Penguin 1988 $6.95. ISBN 0-14-009746-5

SHORT STORY COLLECTION BY WELDON

Polaris and Other Stories (1985). Penguin 1989 $6.95. ISBN 0-14-009747-3

WELLS, H. G. (HERBERT GEORGE) 1866–1946

H. G. Wells was born in Bromley, England, the son of an unsuccessful merchant. After a limited education, he was apprenticed to a dry-goods merchant, but soon found he wanted something more out of life. He read widely and got a position as a student assistant in a secondary school, eventually winning a scholarship to the College of Science in South Kensington, where he studied biology under the British biologist and educator, Thomas Henry Huxley.

After graduating, Wells took several different teaching positions and began writing for magazines. When his stories began to sell, he left teaching to write full time.

Wells's first major novel, *The Time Machine* (1895), launched his career as a writer, and he began to produce a steady stream of science-fiction tales, short stories, realistic novels, and books of sociology, history, science, and biography, producing one or more books each year. Much of Wells's work is forward-looking, peering into the future to prophesy social and scientific developments, sometimes with amazing accuracy. Along with the French writer Jules Verne (*see* Verne, Vol. 1, World Literature: French Language and Literature), Wells is credited with popularizing science fiction, and such novels as *The Time Machine* and *The War of the Worlds* (1898) are still widely read.

Many of Wells's stories are based on his own experiences. *The History of Mr. Polly* (1910) draws on the life of Wells's father. *Kipps* (1905) uses Wells's experience as an apprentice, and *Love and Mr. Lewisham* (1900) draws on Wells's experiences as a teacher. Wells also wrote stories showing how the world could be a better place. One such story is *A Modern Utopia* (1905).

As a writer, Wells's range was exceptionally wide and his imagination extremely fertile. While time may have caught up with him (many of the things he predicted have already come to pass), he remains an interesting writer because of his ability to tell a lively tale.

NOVELS BY WELLS

*The First Men in the Moon (1901). Airmont $1.25. ISBN 0-8049-0078-7 The first earthlings reach the moon.
*The Food of the Gods (1904). Pendulum 1978 $2.95. ISBN 0-88301-314-2 A look into a strange and surprising future.
The History of Mr. Polly (1910). Houghton 1961 $7.16. ISBN 0-395-05149-5
*The Invisible Man (1897). Bantam 1988 $2.25. ISBN 0-553-21155-2 A man learns how to become invisible.
*The Island of Dr. Moreau (1896). Signet 1977 $2.50. ISBN 0-451-52191-9 A scientist develops strange new animals.
Kipps: The Story of a Simple Soul (1905). Oxford Univ Pr 1985 $6.95. ISBN 0-19-281477-X
Love and Mr. Lewisham (1900). Oxford Univ Pr 1983 $5.95. ISBN 0-19-281398-6
*The Time Machine (1895). Bantam 1988 $2.95. ISBN 0-553-21351-2 In the year 802,701 the world is divided between the peaceful Eloi and their Morlock enemies.
*The War of the Worlds (1898). Bantam 1988 $1.95. ISBN 0-553-21338-5 Earth is invaded by Martians.

SHORT STORY COLLECTION BY WELLS

Complete Short Stories St. Martin's 1988 $19.95. ISBN 0-312-15855-6

BOOKS ABOUT WELLS

Costa, Richard H. *H. G. Wells.* G. K. Hall 1985 $15.95. ISBN 0-8057-6887-4 Standard analysis and evaluation of Wells's life, work, and times; includes a chronology and index.
Draper, Michael. *H. G. Wells.* St. Martin's 1988 $24.95. ISBN 0-312-02090-2 A critical study emphasizing a close examination of important works; contains introductory biographical information and a bibliography.
*Martin, Christopher. *H. G. Wells*. Rourke 1989 $12.95. ISBN 0-86592-297-7 Wellwritten life of the well-known author who rose from poverty; suitable for younger teenagers.
Reed, John R. *The Natural History of H. G. Wells.* Ohio Univ Pr 1982 $29.95. ISBN 0-8214-0628-0 Traces the development of Wells's world view, concluding that it essentially remained constant over his life; contains pertinent quotes from Wells's work.

WHITE, T. H. (TERENCE HANBURY) 1906–1964

T. H. White was born in Bombay, India, where his father was a District Superintendent of Police. He moved to England when he was five years old and was educated at Cheltenham College and Cambridge University. After graduating from Cambridge, White taught school for six years before deciding to devote all of his time to writing.

White became fascinated with the story of King Arthur and the Knights of the Round Table and began his own fictional account of the tales. His first genuinely successful novel, *The Sword in the Stone* (1939), is a fantasy about young

Arthur's education. An offbeat, humorous retelling of the tale, it was highly popular and made White famous in both Britain and the United States.

White continued Arthur's story in three subsequent novels—*The Witch in the Wood* (1940), *The Ill-Made Knight* (1941), and *The Candle in the Wind* (1958). In 1958 the series was revised and bound together in a single volume, *The Once and Future King.* These stories served as the basis for the musical comedy *Camelot,* first produced on Broadway in 1960. A fifth novel in the series, *The Book of Merlyn,* was discovered among White's papers after he died and was published in 1977. Among the many readers captivated by White's stories was President John F. Kennedy (*see* J. Kennedy, Vol. 2, United States History: The Turbulent Sixties) who was particularly fond of the musical version of White's work. Kennedy's own administration became known to some as "Camelot," the name of King Arthur's court.

NOVELS BY WHITE

*The Book of Merlyn (1977). Univ of Texas Pr 1988 $8.95. ISBN 0-292-70769-X The conclusion to the story of King Arthur and Camelot, in which Merlyn demonstrates to Arthur how superior are peaceful animals to war-mongering humans.
*Mistress Masham's Repose (1946). Berkley 1984 $2.95. ISBN 0-425-07312-2 Story about the descendants of the Lilliputians of *Gulliver's Travels* and a girl who helps them.
* The Once and Future King (1958). Berkley 1983 $4.95. ISBN 0-425-09116-3 Story of King Arthur and his knights.
* The Sword in the Stone (1939). Dell 1978 $3.50. ISBN 0-440-98445-9 Tells of the education of young King Arthur, including time spent by Arthur as an animal learning from ants and falcons, and a visit with Robin Hood and Maid Marian.

BOOKS ABOUT WHITE

Crane, John K. *T. H. White.* Twayne 1974. (o.p.) $15.50. ISBN 0-805-71573-8 First full-length critical study of White's two dozen novels; contains numerous quotations from his hard-to-obtain works.
Warner, Sylvia Townsend. *T. H. White.* Jonathan Cape 1967. (o.p.) The brilliant biography that opened White scholarship in the late 1960s; contains especially useful materials from interviews and personal papers.

WODEHOUSE, P. G. (PELHAM GRENVILLE)   1881–1975

Although P. G. Wodehouse was born in England, his parents actually lived in Hong Kong, where his father was a civil servant. Wodehouse seldom saw his parents and spent most of his childhood in boarding schools or in the homes of various relatives during school vacations. After completing his education at Dulwich College, Wodehouse went to work as a clerk in a bank. Then, after three unsatisfying years, he left the bank and concentrated on his writing. Ironically, Wodehouse, often described as among the most British of British writers, lived most of his life outside of Britain, especially in the United States, of which he became a citizen in 1955.

Wodehouse began by writing stories for schoolboys, most of which appeared in the early 1900s in a popular boys' magazine called *The Captain.* His first novel for adults, *Love Among the Chickens,* appeared in 1906. Over the remaining 72 years of his life, he produced well over 100 novels and collections of short stories, as well as dozens of song lyrics, plays, and screenplays. Currently there are over 50 Wodehouse titles in print.

In his novels and stories, Wodehouse has created a cast of characters that has become legendary. Perhaps the most famous is Jeeves, the unflappable and resourceful butler of Bertie Wooster, the silly upper-class young Englishman. But Wodehouse also gave the world Psmith—who from childhood on delighted in making life difficult for those in authority—and the talkative but delightful Mr. Mulliner—who manages to turn everyday problems into hilarious tall tales.

Although critics have tended to dismiss Wodehouse as being "not serious," they, along with thousands of others, have laughed at his stories. Even Oxford University acknowledged Wodehouse's literary skill by making him an honorary Doctor of Literature in 1939. Wodehouse was knighted for his literary achievements in 1975.

In typically modest fashion, Wodehouse described his own career in this way: "Over the years I have built up a nice little conservative business and the pickings have been pretty good, but I realize that I am not one of the swells who have messages and significance and all that kind of thing . . . I know my place, and that place is down at the far end of the table among the scurvy knaves and scullions."

Because of the large number of Wodehouse books in print, the following lists present only a sample that will introduce the reader to the different Wodehouse characters and the different periods of his work.

NOVELS BY WODEHOUSE

The Code of the Woosters (1938). Random 1975 $3.95. ISBN 0-394-72028-8 Bertie Wooster finds himself in a tough spot, but Jeeves comes to the rescue.
The Mating Season (1949). Harper 1989 $7.95. ISBN 0-06-097248-3 The adventures and misadventures of young people in and out of love.
Psmith: Journalist (1912). Penguin 1981 $3.95. ISBN 0-14-003214-2 The hilarious story of Psmith's entry into the world of newspapers and reporting.

SHORT STORY COLLECTIONS BY WODEHOUSE

The Gold Bat and Other School Stories (1904). Penguin 1978 $6.95. ISBN 0-14-08080-5 Amusing stories of life in an English boarding school.
Most of P. G. Wodehouse. Fireside 1969 $12.95. ISBN 0-671-20349-5 A selection of stories that covers most of the Wodehouse cast of characters.
Mulliner Nights (1927). Random 1975 $4.95. ISBN 0-394-72027-X The ever-talkative Mr. Mulliner tells hilarious if unbelievable tales of his many relatives.
The Pothunters and Other Stories (1902–1910). Penguin 1986 $5.95. ISBN 0-14-008079-1 Some of the earliest Wodehouse tales of life in a boys' school, including "A Prefect's Uncle" and "Tales from St. Austin's."
The World of Jeeves. Harper 1989 $10.95. ISBN 0-06-097244-0 Collection of some of the best stories about Bertie Wooster and his butler Jeeves.
The World of Mr. Mulliner. Taplinger 1985 $11.95. ISBN 0-8008-8581-3 Stories about Mulliner in love, at work, and on the golf course.

BOOKS ABOUT WODEHOUSE

Hall, Robert A., Jr. *The Comic Style of P. G. Wodehouse.* Shoe String 1974 $20.00. ISBN 0-208-01409-8 The first thorough analysis of Wodehouse's style; demonstrates how he uses linguistic devices to create humor.
Jasen, David A. *P. G. Wodehouse: A Portrait of a Master.* Continuum 1981. (o.p.) Complete and comprehensive guide to Wodehouse's life by an author who knew him personally; contains extensive bibliographies.
Voorhees, Richard J. *P. G. Wodehouse.* Twayne 1966. (o.p.) $11.50. ISBN 0-805-71576-2 Useful overview of Wodehouse's life and work; includes a study of his short stories and novels, an analysis of his place in English literature, a chronology, and a selected bibliography.

WOOLF, VIRGINIA   1882–1941

One of the greatest writers of the twentieth century, Virginia Woolf was born Virginia Stephen, the daughter of critic, scholar, and essayist Sir Leslie Stephen. Raised in a large and unusually talented family, from early childhood she was surrounded by leading literary figures. When her father died in 1904, she moved with her sister Vanessa and two brothers to a section of London called Bloomsbury. Their house became the central meeting place for a collection of writers, artists, and intellectuals who became known as the Bloomsbury Group.

In 1912 she married Leonard Woolf, a writer and social reformer. Together they founded a publishing company called the Hogarth Press, which for years published the works of young writers whose daring and experimental books were not accepted by traditional publishing houses.

Woolf published her own first novel, *The Voyage Out,* in 1915, which began her brilliant and controversial career.

Woolf was a great experimenter: she tried constantly to push the novel in new directions and expand narrative frontiers. She abandoned the traditional form of narration by an outside observer. Instead she chose to write what her characters were thinking, putting their thoughts on paper seemingly as they thought them, a technique known as stream of consciousness. The novels *Mrs. Dalloway* (1925) and *To the Lighthouse* (1927) both use this technique, so that most of the action takes place within the characters and beneath the surface of events.

Woolf experiments further in *Orlando* (1928), the story of a person who begins life as a gentleman in the 1500s and ends it as a lady in the twentieth century. In *Flush* (1933), Woolf experiments with point of view, telling the story of the poet Elizabeth Barrett Browning (*see* E. Browning, Vol. 1, British Literature: The Victorian Period) through the eyes of her dog, Flush.

Throughout her life Woolf was plagued with mental problems. She experienced several breakdowns during which she hallucinated and heard voices. In 1941, fearing a major breakdown from which she might not recover, she committed suicide by drowning.

NOVELS BY WOOLF

Between the Acts (1941). Harcourt 1970 $5.95. ISBN 0-15-611870-X
Flush (1933). Harcourt 1976 $4.95. ISBN 0-15-631952-7
Jacob's Room (1922). Harcourt 1978 $6.95. ISBN 0-15-645742-3
Mrs. Dalloway (1925). Harcourt 1964 $5.95. ISBN 0-15-662863-5
Night and Day (1919). Harcourt 1973 $8.95. ISBN 0-15-665600-0
Orlando (1928). Harcourt 1973 $8.95. ISBN 0-15-670160-X
To the Lighthouse (1927). Harcourt 1964 $5.95. ISBN 0-15-690738-0
The Voyage Out (1915). Harcourt 1968 $7.95. ISBN 0-15-693625-9
The Waves (1931). Harcourt 1978 $5.95. ISBN 0-15-694960-1
The Years (1937). Harcourt 1969 $9.95. ISBN 0-15-699701-0

SHORT STORY COLLECTION BY WOOLF

Complete Shorter Fiction. Harcourt 1986 $16.95. ISBN 0-15-118983-8

NONFICTION BY WOOLF

A Writer's Diary. Leonard Woolf (ed). Harcourt 1969 $9.95 ISBN 0-15-698380-X

BOOKS ABOUT WOOLF

Beja, Morris. *Critical Essays on Virginia Woolf.* G. K. Hall 1985 $39.00. ISBN 0-8161-8753-3 A collection of outstanding critical essays by recognized authorities that provides a very useful summary to the different schools of Woolf criticism.

Bell, Quentin. *Virginia Woolf: A Biography.* Harcourt 1974 $9.95. ISBN 0-15-693580-5 Offers the fullest and most balanced account of Virginia Woolf's life; recognized as the standard biography, although recently criticized by feminists for its failure to appreciate the importance of the women in Woolf's life.

Bennett, Joan. *Virginia Woolf.* Cambridge Univ Pr 1975 $11.95. ISBN 0-521-09951-X A classic study, that traces the development of Woolf's creative process; includes an evaluation of Woolf's critical essays and her fiction.

YEATS, WILLIAM BUTLER   1865–1939

William Butler Yeats was born in Dublin, Ireland, the son of a famous lawyer and painter. When he was very young, his family moved to London, and during childhood he returned to Ireland only for summer vacations. In 1881, however, the family returned to Dublin, where Yeats, already determined to be a writer, began to study art.

Yeats developed a strong interest in mysticism and the supernatural, a fascination that was to last throughout his life. He also became active in the Irish Nationalist movement, in part because he fell in love with one of its leaders, the beautiful Maude Gonne. Although active in this movement, he was always more deeply involved in trying to revive a genuine Irish culture than he was in the struggle for political independence from Britain.

Yeats drew much of the inspiration for his early poetry from the area of Sligo in western Ireland, where he had visited relatives as a child. The natural beauties of the region inspired many of his poems. Throughout the 1890s he published several volumes of verse, much of it concerned with Irish myth and folklore.

Early in the twentieth century, Yeats's poetry began to change, moving from the somewhat romantic language of his earlier verse to a harder, more forceful style that dealt with politics rather than nature. His interest in the theater, begun years before, also began to deepen in this period, and he became an active leader of the Irish National Theater.

As Yeats grew older, his poetry changed again. It took on a more serious, pessimistic tone, as he began to feel more and more that the world was moving into a new—and less desirable—era.

Yeats scholars are always struck by the huge shifts in his style and interests that took place over his writing life. His famous poem "The Lake Isle of Innisfree" (1892) is a relatively traditional Romantic celebration of nature. *Cathleen ni Houlihan* (1902) is a play from Yeats's nationalist period, celebrating the appeal of the mystical Cathleen ni Houlihan, who appears both as an old woman and as a young queen, the spirit of Ireland who draws young men off to fight for the freedom of their country.

Later, in the bitter poem "The Second Coming" (1921), Yeats gives us a passionate tirade about the sad state of politics in the aftermath of World War I ("The best lack all conviction, while the worst/Are full of passionate intensity"). "Sailing to Byzantium" (1927) is an equally bitter and disappointed poem about a more personal topic—Yeats's descent into old age.

For years critics have debated whether Yeats or T. S. Eliot (*see* Eliot, Vol. 1, British Literature: The Twentieth Century), the American-born but naturalized British citizen, is the greatest English-speaking poet of the century. The debate is far from settled, although at the moment, Yeats seems to have the edge. Yeats was highly honored in his own lifetime, receiving the Nobel Prize for literature in 1923.

POETRY BY YEATS

The Poems of Yeats. Macmillan 1983 $24.95. ISBN 0-02-632940-9

PLAYS BY YEATS

Collected Plays. Macmillan 1953 $17.95. ISBN 0-02-632630-2

BOOKS ABOUT YEATS

Bloom, Harold. *Yeats.* Oxford Univ Pr 1972 $8.95. ISBN 0-19-501603-3 A solid analysis of Yeats's place within the English poetic tradition by an acknowledged expert in the field.

Unterrecker, John (ed). *Yeats: A Collection of Critical Essays.* Prentice 1963. (o.p.) A collection of highly respected essays on Yeats and his works from recognized scholars and critics; especially useful to the nonspecialist reader interested in both Yeats and his work.

COMMONWEALTH LITERATURE

The literature represented in this section is that of Australia, Canada, and New Zealand, countries that were once part of the British Commonwealth. Although today each is a separate nation, politically independent and culturally unique, their literature is often treated as a single body. In part this is because they share a common language—English—and a common heritage—British colonialism. But in addition, the writers of these countries focus on similar themes: the development from colonies to independent nations; the creation of their own identities, as separate cultures; and the tensions between native peoples and European settlers.

Many of the writers from these countries were educated in Britain or, in the case of some Canadians, in the United States. Thus they share an uncertainty about which literature is truly theirs. Should they imitate the dominant British or U.S. literature, or should they strive to create something new and unique to their own countries? Likewise, Quebec writers writing in French are torn between the Canadian experience and the French tradition. Many of the writers included here wrestled with these questions, and all arrived at different answers. Taken together, these writers represent a lively and dynamic new literature.

ATWOOD, MARGARET   1939– (CANADA)

Margaret Atwood was born in Ottawa, Canada, the daughter of a scientist. After growing up in northern Ontario and Quebec and attending the University of Toronto, she received a M.A. degree from Harvard University. A critic, editor, poet, and fiction writer with an international reputation, she has been

Alice Springs.   Sculpture by William Ricketts (Twentieth Century). Courtesy of SEF/Art Resource.

one of the most significant voices in Canadian literature since the publication of her first full-length book of poems, *The Circle Game* (1966). From the first, Atwood's poetry attracted attention with its originality and unusual form. For example, in *The Journals of Susanna Moodie* (1970) the "voice" of the poet is that of a somewhat proper Canadian colonial woman, creating a type of historical novel in poetry form. She also has made considerable use of native Indian mythology in her verse and has written on male-female relationships from a feminist viewpoint.

Toward the end of the 1960s, Atwood began to write fiction. Most of her novels feature a central female character who is forced by circumstance to examine her life and look closely at her own beliefs. In *Lady Oracle* (1976), for instance, the heroine stages her own fake death in order to find a new identity. In *Surfacing* (1972), a woman sets out to find her scientist father in the Quebec wilderness and discovers instead a new outlook on the relationship between humans and nature. *The Handmaid's Tale* (1985) is a chilling story of what the United States might be like if the religious Right came into political power, made into a successful movie. *Cat's Eye* tells the story of two women friends reunited after a long absence.

NOVELS BY ATWOOD

Bodily Harm (1981). Bantam 1983 $3.95. ISBN 0-553-23289-4
Cat's Eye (1989). Doubleday 1989 $18.95. ISBN 0-385-26007-3
The Edible Woman (1969). Warner Bks 1988 $4.95. ISBN 0-446-31498-6
The Handmaid's Tale (1985). Fawcett 1986 $4.95. ISBN 0-449-21260-2
Lady Oracle (1976). Fawcett 1987 $4.95. ISBN 0-449-21376-5
Surfacing (1972). Fawcett 1987 $4.50. ISBN 0-449-21375-7

SHORT STORY COLLECTION BY ATWOOD

Bluebeard's Egg and Other Stories (1984). Fawcett 1987 $4.95. ISBN 0-449-21417-6

POETRY BY ATWOOD

Journals of Susanna Moodie: Poems (1970). Oxford Univ Pr 1970 $7.95. ISBN 0-19-21376-5
Selected Poems. Houghton 1987 $9.95. ISBN 0-395-40422-3

BOOKS ABOUT ATWOOD

Rigney, Barbara H. *Margaret Atwood: A Critical Inquiry.* Barnes 1987 $7.95. ISBN 0-389-20743-8 A critical analysis focusing mostly on Atwood's novels through *The Handmaid's Tale;* one chapter also deals with the earlier poems.

Rosenberg, Jerome H. *Margaret Atwood.* G. K. Hall 1984 $5.95. ISBN 0-8057-6599-9 Another critical study emphasizing such earlier poems and novels as *Surfacing* and *The Edible Woman.*

BURNFORD, SHEILA   1918–1984 (CANADA)

Born Sheila Cochrane in Scotland, Burnford was educated privately in England, France, and Germany. In 1941 she married David Burnford, and from 1941 to 1942 she served in the Royal Naval Volunteer Aid Detachment. Following World War II she came to Canada, where she went on to write part time while raising a family.

While Burnford's essays and descriptions of the natural beauties of Canada have been popular, her fame as a writer rests primarily on her animal stories, *The Incredible Journey* (1961) and *Bel Ria* (1978). Since its first publication, *The Incredible Journey* has been a favorite with readers of all ages but especially with the young. In 1963 the book received the Canadian Book of the Year for Children Award. It has also been made into a successful movie by Walt Disney.

NOVELS BY BURNFORD

*Bel Ria (1978). Little 1978 $12.95. ISBN 0-316-11718-8 Story of a dog who changes the lives of each of its owners.

*The Incredible Journey (1961). Bantam 1977 $2.95. ISBN 0-553-26218-1 The adventures of a cat and two dogs who make a 250-mile journey across Canada to their home.

CALLAGHAN, MORLEY   1903– (CANADA)

Morley Callaghan was born and raised in Toronto, Canada, and was educated at St. Michaels College, University of Toronto, and Osgoode Hill Law School. While working as a reporter for the *Toronto Star,* he met the American writer Ernest Hemingway (*see* Hemingway, Vol. 1, American Literature: The Twentieth Century), who was working for the same paper and who encouraged Callaghan to publish his first novel, *Strange Fugitive* (1928). The following year Callaghan published his first collection of short stories, *Native Argosy,* stories of Canadian life acclaimed for their clean, economical prose in the style of Ernest Hemingway. In the same year, he traveled to Paris, where he again met Hemingway and became acquainted with James Joyce and F. Scott Fitzgerald. (*See* Joyce, Vol. 1, British Literature: The Twentieth Century *and* Fitzgerald, Vol. 1, American Literature, The Twentieth Century.)

Callaghan's short stories are considered his best work. They are written in a simple, direct, and easy-to-read style that shows his experience as a newspaper reporter.

Native Argosy (1929). Ayer (repr of 1929 ed.) $18.00. ISBN 0-8369-3292-7

COHEN, LEONARD   1934– (CANADA)

Leonard Cohen was born and raised in Montreal, Canada, and graduated from McGill University in 1955. He began graduate study at Columbia University, but dropped out to concentrate on his poetry and song-writing. He then returned to Montreal where he lived until 1963, the year he published his first novel, *The Favorite Game*.

After his novel came out, Cohen began a period of extensive travel, building a reputation as a singer and entertainer as well as a writer. Throughout the 1960s his songs and poems became extremely popular, especially with college students. His "Suzanne" was one of the most-recorded songs of the decade.

Today Cohen continues to be both songwriter and poet, with the result that his poetry is very difficult to classify. Much of it reflects a tension between the easy flow of song lyrics and the more formal structure of serious poetry as he works and reworks the themes of frustrated love and lonely, alienated individuals. As poet and lyricist, Cohen continues to enjoy wide popularity.

POETRY BY COHEN

Book of Mercy (1984). Random 1984 $9.45. ISBN 0-394-53949-4
Death of a Lady's Man (1978). Penguin 1979 $4.95. ISBN 0-14-042275-7

DAVIES, ROBERTSON   1913– (CANADA)

Playwright, journalist, actor, and novelist, Robertson Davies is one of Canada's best-known authors. Born in Thamesville, he grew up in Kingston, Ontario, where he later attended Queen's University. He then enrolled in Oxford University in England, where he was a member of a dramatic society. Upon graduating in 1938, he joined the Old Vic Theater Company, one of the most famous professional theater groups in Britain.

In 1940 Davies returned to Canada, where he became editor of the magazine *Saturday Night*. He was made Professor of English at the University of Toronto in 1960 and in 1963 became head of Massey College, a graduate school at the university.

Davies began his writing career in the 1950s with relatively light comic novels. Of these, his "Salterton" novels—*Tempest Tost* (1951), *Leaven of Malice* (1954), and *A Mixture of Frailties* (1958)—are the most important. Known as "satiric romances," they concern the petty, pretentious, and oppressive life in the small university town of Salterton, a fictional version of Davies' own Kingston. Likewise, *The Rebel Angels* (1982) is set in Ploughwright College, based on the real-life Massey College.

In the 1970s, Davies' writing took a more serious turn with the publication of the Deptford Trilogy: *Fifth Business* (1970), *The Manticore* (1972), and *World of Wonders* (1975). These novels look at the ways that deep-seated, ancient human beliefs influence civilized behavior. They are rooted in the theories of Swiss psychologist Carl Jung, who believed that certain basic *archetypes,* or myths, rule our behavior on a primitive level of which we may not be consciously aware.

NOVELS BY DAVIES

The Deptford Trilogy (1970–1975). Penguin 1985 $10.95. ISBN 0-14-006500-8
Fifth Business (1970). Penguin 1977 $4.95. ISBN 0-14-004387-X
Leaven of Malice (1954). Penguin 1980 $4.95. ISBN 0-14-005433-2
The Lyre of Orpheus (1989). Penguin 1989 $19.95. ISBN 0-670-82416-X
The Manticore (1972). Penguin 1977 $5.95. ISBN 0-14-004388-8
A Mixture of Frailties (1958). Penguin 1980 $4.95. ISBN 0-14-005432-4
The Rebel Angels (1982). Penguin 1983 $6.95. ISBN 0-14-006271-8
The Salterton Trilogy (1951–1958). Penguin 1986 $9.95. ISBN 0-14-008446-0
Tempest Tost (1951). Penguin 1980 $4.95. ISBN 0-14-005431-6
What's Bred in the Bone (1985). Penguin 1986 $7.95. ISBN 0-14-009711-2
World of Wonders (1975). Penguin 1977 $4.95. ISBN 0-14-004389-6

SHORT STORY COLLECTION BY DAVIES

High Spirits (1983). Penguin 1983 $6.95. ISBN 0-14-006505-9

NONFICTION BY DAVIES

One Half of Robertson Davies (1978). Penguin 1978 $6.95. ISBN 0-14-004967-3

BOOK ABOUT DAVIES

Peterman, Michael. *Robertson Davies*. G. K. Hall 1986 $19.95. ISBN 0-8057-0471-5 A critical study focusing on Davies as a dramatist and novelist; covers his novels through *The Rebel Angels*.

FRAME, JANET 1924– (NEW ZEALAND)

Janet Frame was born in Dunedin, New Zealand, and attended Dunedin Teachers' Training College and Otago University. After completing her education, she taught for a year and then became a nurse-companion in Dunedin. Frame was an unusual-looking woman from an uneducated family. This contributed to her being incorrectly diagnosed with mental problems, and for several years she was confined to psychiatric hospitals, an experience from which she draws material for her fiction. She has spent time away from New Zealand, primarily in England, but also in Europe and the United States.

Frame's first novel, *Owls Do Cry* (1957), deals with the break-up of a poor New Zealand family and is based on her own experiences growing up in a small New Zealand town. In her other works Frame frequently explores the boundary between sanity and insanity. She describes two kinds of insanity, that of the disturbed person and that of the disordered world. Her stories emphasize the importance of communication and reveal how language can help the individual achieve a more satisfying life. In *Intensive Care* (1970) and *Daughter Buffalo* (1972), she explores the human capacity to destroy.

Generally regarded as the leading New Zealand writer of her generation, Frame is held in high esteem by critics. Some, however, have faulted her for using her talent too narrowly, to express only her own sense of melancholy and despair.

NOVELS BY FRAME

The Carpathians (1988). Braziller 1988 $17.50. ISBN 0-8076-1205-7
Faces in the Water (1961). Braziller 1982 $5.95. ISBN 0-8076-0957-9
Living in the Maniototo (1979). Braziller 1979 $8.95. ISBN 0-8076-0926-9
Owls Do Cry (1957). Braziller 1982 $5.95. ISBN 0-8076-0956-0
Scented Gardens for the Blind (1963). Braziller 1980 $4.95. ISBN 0-8076-0986-2
A State of Siege (1966). Braziller 1981 $4.95. ISBN 0-8076-0986-2

POETRY BY FRAME

The Pocket Mirror (1967). Braziller 1967 $4.95. ISBN 0-8076-0408-9

NONFICTION BY FRAME

An Angel at My Table (1984). Braziller 1984 $12.95. ISBN 0-8076-1090-9 The second volume of Frame's autobiography, going through 1945, covering Frame's life as a writer.

The Envoy from Mirror City (1985). Braziller 1985 $14.95. ISBN 0-8076-1124-7 The third volume of Frame's autobiography, further exploring Frame's personal and writing life.

To the Is-Land (1982). Braziller 1982 $10.95. ISBN 0-8076-1042-9 The first volume of Frame's autobiography, set in New Zealand in the 1920s and 1930s, and covering her early experiences in mental hospitals.

GALLANT, MAVIS   1922– (CANADA)

Born in Montreal, Canada, as Mavis Young, Gallant moved frequently as an adolescent and young woman, attending 17 different schools in Canada and the United States. She married John Gallant, but divorced him in 1950, after working for the Canadian National Film Board and the *Montreal Standard.* Gallant then settled in Europe, mainly in Paris. She returned to Canada and in 1983–84 served as writer-in-residence at the University of Toronto.

Gallant's stories were clever, witty, and sophisticated from the first. They have appeared regularly in *The New Yorker* magazine. These tales, frequently dealing with the problems of living away from one's native country, are filled with sharp observations of human behavior and telling details of everyday living. Gallant is concerned with the sense of isolation and detachment that is so common in the modern world.

In 1981 Gallant was awarded the Order of Canada. She also received the Governor General's Award for her collection *Home Truths* (1981).

SHORT STORY COLLECTIONS BY GALLANT

From the Fifteenth District (1979). Random 1979 $8.95. ISBN 0-394-50719-3
Home Truths (1981). Dell 1987 $4.50. ISBN 0-440-33659-7
In Transit (1989). Random 1989 $17.95. ISBN 0-394-5757-5
The Other Paris (1955). Ayer (repr of 1955 ed) $18.00. ISBN 0-8369-3454-7
Overheard in a Balloon (1985). Norton 1988 $7.70. ISBN 0-393-30546-5
The Pegnitz Junction (1973). Graywolf 1984 $6.00. ISBN 0-915308-60-6

HANRAHAN, BARBARA   1939– (AUSTRALIA)

Born and raised in Adelaide, Barbara Hanrahan left Australia to live in London, where she studied art. Since 1964 she has had several exhibitions of her work in Europe and Australia, and a number of her paintings are displayed in the National Gallery of Australia.

In the 1970s Hanrahan turned to writing. Her autobiographical first novel, *The Scent of Eucalyptus* (1973), was favorably reviewed. The book is a rich and clear picture of an adolescent girl's mingling of fact and fantasy as she comes of age. Hanrahan's second novel, *Sea Green* (1974), is also based on Hanrahan's personal experiences. It tells the story of a young woman who leaves Australia for London.

Hanrahan's more recent novels have historical settings in the nineteenth and early twentieth centuries. In *The Frangipani Garden* (1980), she again draws on her own life to tell the story of a woman who must choose between being a popular but mediocre artist or an unrecognized artist who is true to her own beliefs. In *Annie Magdalene* (1985), she presents a seemingly ordinary woman who is really a large and heroic figure.

NOVELS BY HANRAHAN

The Albatross Muff (1977). Charles River $2.95. ISBN 0-7043-3827-0
Annie Magdalene (1985). Beaufort 1986 $13.95. ISBN 0-8253-0309-5
Dove: A Novel (1982). Univ of Queensland Pr 1989 $10.95. ISBN 0-7022-1890-1
The Frangipani Garden (1980). Univ of Queensland Pr 1981 $11.95. ISBN 0-7022-1563-5
The Peach Grove (1979). Univ of Queensland Pr 1980 $11.95. ISBN 7022-1459-0
Where the Queens All Strayed (1978). Univ of Queensland Pr 1984 $11.95. ISBN 0-7022-1305-5

LAURENCE, MARGARET   1924– (CANADA)

Margaret Laurence was born Jean Margaret Wymyss in Neepawa, Manitoba. Orphaned at an early age and brought up by relatives, in 1947 she graduated from United College in Winnipeg, Manitoba, and worked as a reporter. A year later she married engineer Jack Laurence. Although the couple lived in England, Somalia, and Ghana, Laurence never forgot her native Canadian prairie background. She has set her most famous novels in the fictional town of "Manawaka," which is very much like the town of her birth, Neepawa.

Laurence considers herself a religious writer who deals with social and moral issues. Her central characters see life as a quest, or search, for meaning. They are often people—mostly women—who are outsiders, cut off from society because they would not accept society's restrictions. In *The Diviners* (1974), she suggests that people can draw strength from their heritage, that the past may provide them with the power to develop visions that will in turn empower others.

NOVELS BY LAURENCE

The Diviners (1974). Bantam 1982 $4.95. ISBN 0-7704-2176-8
The Stone Angel (1964). Bantam 1981 $4.50. ISBN 0-7704-2177-6

LEACOCK, STEPHEN   1869–1944 (CANADA)

Stephen Leacock was born in Swanmore, England, but when he was six years old his parents moved to Canada and he "decided to go with them." He was one of 11 children of an unsuccessful farmer and an ambitious mother, a woman to whom Leacock no doubt owed his energy and drive.

Leacock was educated at Upper Canada College in Toronto, one of Canada's elite secondary schools. He returned to teach there while he obtained his degree in modern languages from the University of Toronto. He later received a Ph. D. degree in political economy from the University of Chicago, and then went to McGill University as Professor of Politics and Economics.

Leacock's first published works were scholarly books on Canadian history and economics, but he soon turned to what he did best—humor. Beginning with *Literary Lapses* in 1910, he produced an average of one humorous book a year for the rest of his life. Leacock was a master of taking an ordinary situation and drawing it out to absurd lengths. He also excelled in writing short sketches that read as if they should be spoken. He was, in fact, a popular lecturer and after-dinner speaker. Because of his humor and skill on the lecture platform, Leacock has frequently been compared to American humorist Mark Twain. (*See* Twain, Vol. 1, American Literature: The Rise of Realism.)

FICTION BY LEACOCK

Frenzied Fiction (1917). Ayer (repr of 1917 ed) $16.00. ISBN 0-8369-3594-2

Here Are My Lectures and Stories (1937). Ayer (repr of 1937 ed) $18.75. ISBN 0-518-10017-0

Laugh with Leacock. Dodd 1981 $5.95. ISBN 0-396-08024-3

Literary Lapses (1910). Ayer (repr of 1911 ed) $16.00. ISBN 0-8369-3561-6

Sunshine Sketches of a Little Town (1912). Ayer (repr of 1912 ed) $21.95. ISBN 0-8369-3595-0

Winsome Winnie and Other New Nonsense Novels (1920). Ayer (repr of 1920 ed) $13.00. ISBN 0-8369-3595-0

BOOK ABOUT LEACOCK

Lynch, Gerald. *Stephen Leacock: Humor and Humanity.* Univ of Toronto Pr 1988 $27.95. ISBN 0-7735-0652-7 A critical analysis of Leacock's works; discusses his humanist philosophy and relates it to his work.

LINDSAY, NORMAN   1879–1969 (AUSTRALIA)

Norman Lindsay was born in Creswick, Victoria, Australia, into a talented family that included five artists and three novelists in two generations. Around the age of 16, Lindsay left home for Melbourne, where he worked as an illustrator and cartoonist for several newspapers. When his cartoons of ragged "street kids" were criticized as being too unrealistic, he replied by publishing some stories of his childhood in Creswick, which he renamed "Redheap." These stories were later collected as *Saturdee* (1933), a work that has been called the Australian *Tom Sawyer.* Together with *Redheap* (1930) and *Halfway to Anywhere* (1947), it formed part of a trilogy that many consider Lindsay's most important fiction.

Lindsay had an unflattering view of human nature, which he saw as being "no better than it should be." This view, combined with his sharp wit and keen powers of observation, made his work controversial. Lindsay also made enemies because he made little effort to disguise the actual people and events he was describing in his fiction. The result was that *Redheap* was banned in Australia until 1959.

NOVEL BY LINDSAY

Saturdee (1933). AMS (repr of 1939 ed) $18.45. ISBN 0-404-14716-X

MANSFIELD, KATHERINE (PSEUDONYM OF KATHLEEN MANSFIELD BEAUCHAMP)   1888–1923 (NEW ZEALAND)

Katherine Mansfield was born in Wellington, New Zealand, the daughter of a wealthy businessman. She was educated in England at Queen's College, and upon her return to New Zealand in 1906, she began to write. After publishing a few short pieces in an Australian magazine, she left again for London in 1908. The following year, in an effort to declare her independence from her father, she made a hasty marriage, which lasted only a short time. Unhappy and disillusioned, she spent a year in Germany, where she wrote some bitter descriptions of German life that later appeared in *In a German Pension* (1911).

When Mansfield returned to England, she continued to write short stories for a number of magazines. In 1911 she met John Middleton Murray, a famous English critic and editor, who guided her career as a writer. They were married in 1918 after Mansfield's first husband divorced her. However, Mansfield soon discovered she had tuberculosis and, despite a move to the south of France, she died in 1923 at the young age of 35.

Mansfield's skill in crafting a short story was unmatched by any English writer of her time and by few since. Her clarity of detail and sharpness of observation set her apart from other writers. Mansfield was chiefly responsible for the rebirth of the short story that took place in England during and after her lifetime.

SHORT STORY COLLECTIONS BY MANSFIELD

Bliss and Other Short Stories (1919). Ayer (repr of 1919 ed) $21.00. ISBN 0-8369-4240-X

The Garden Party: Katherine Mansfield's New Zealand Stories (1920). New Amsterdam 1988 $35.00. ISBN 0-941533-38-7

* *The Short Stories of Katherine Mansfield.* Ecco 1983 $11.95. ISBN 0-88001-025-8 A collection of Mansfield's finest stories, including two of her most famous stories, "Bliss" and "The Garden Party."

**Stories.* Elizabeth Bowen (ed). Random 1956 $4.95. ISBN 0-394-70036-8 Mansfield at her best in stories that range in setting from London to New Zealand, collected by the major author Elizabeth Bowen.

POETRY BY MANSFIELD

The Poems of Katherine Mansfield (1923). Oxford Univ Pr 1989 $19.95. ISBN 0-19-558192-X

BOOKS ABOUT MANSFIELD

Kobler, J. F. *Katherine Mansfield: A Study of the Short Fiction.* G. K. Hall 1989 $18.95. ISBN 0-8057-8325-3 Original interpretations of some of Mansfield's most significant stories; provides a theoretical basis for understanding both her innovations in the use of telling detail to advance a narrative and the enduring relevance of her achievement.

Meyers, Jeffrey. *Katherine Mansfield: A Biography.* New Directions 1980 $10.50. ISBN 0-8112-0834-6 A major reinterpretation of available biographical material on Mansfield, based on interviews, research, and published and unpublished sources; focuses on Mansfield's life.

Nathan, Rhoda B. *Katherine Mansfield.* Ungar 1988 $16.95. ISBN 0-8044-2640-6 A biographical and critical assessment of Mansfield's work, concentrating on technique and analyzing Mansfield's themes, style, and influence; a good basic introduction to Mansfield's life and work.

MONTGOMERY, L. M. (LUCY MAUD)   1874–1942 (CANADA)

L. M. Montgomery was born and raised on Prince Edward Island in the Maritime Provinces of Canada. Upon completing her education, she taught school for several years while contributing articles and stories to magazines. After her marriage to Ewen Macdonald, a Presbyterian minister, she moved to Toronto. She began her most famous work, *Anne of Green Gables* (1908), as a contribution to a church newspaper. Once published, the novel proved so successful that Montgomery immediately wrote another, *Anne of Avonlea* (1909), and eventually, an entire series describing the life of the main character, Anne Shirley, as she grows from girl to young woman.

Montgomery then went on to create other characters around whom she could build new tales, including Jane of Lantern Hill and Pat of Silver Bush. Yet another series of tales, the "Emily" novels, closely follow the events in Montgomery's own life as they trace the adventures of Emily Starr from an orphaned childhood to a successful career as a writer.

Montgomery's novels were enormously successful when they were first published and have remained popular ever since. Although they are read by people of all ages, they appeal largely to young girls. Unfortunately Montgomery's later work, while readable and entertaining, failed to recapture the charm of the original *Anne of Green Gables.* However, a recent television miniseries based on the Anne books has also proved to be very popular.

NOVELS BY MONTGOMERY

Anne of Avonlea (1909). Signet 1987 $2.50. ISBN 0-451-52113-7 Sixteen-year-old Anne returns to Avonlea to teach in the village school.

Anne of Green Gables (1908). Signet 1987 $2.50. ISBN 0-451-52112-9 Anne, an 11-year-old orphan, tells how she wins the hearts of her foster parents.

Anne's House of Dreams (1917). Signet 1989 $2.95. ISBN 0-451-52319-9 Anne and her new husband embark on life together.

Anne of Ingleside (1918). Bantam 1981 $2.95. ISBN 0-553-21315-6 The childhood of Anne's children growing up on Prince Edward Island.

Anne of the Island (1915). Bantam 1976 $2.95. ISBN 0-553-21317-2 Anne goes off to college and finds new friends and romances.

Anne of Windy Poplars (1916). Bantam 1981 $2.95. ISBN 0-553-21328-0 Anne becomes a school teacher on Prince Edward Island.

The Blue Castle (1926). Bantam 1990 $2.95. ISBN 0-553-28051-1 Valancy Stirling, a dreamer, discovers that her life can be as exciting as the books she reads.

Emily Climbs (1925). Bantam 1990 $3.50. ISBN 0-553-26214-9 Emily goes to high school.

Emily of New Moon (1923). Bantam 1990 $3.50. ISBN 0-553-23370-X Emily, an 11-year-old orphan, goes to live with her two elderly aunts.

Emily's Quest (1927). Bantam 1983 $3.50. ISBN 0-553-26493-1 Emily combines a career as a writer with marriage.

The Golden Road (1913). Bantam 1990 $2.95. ISBN 0-553-21367-9 While spending the winter with the Kings, Sara Stanley helps the children start their own magazine.

Jane of Lantern Hill (1938). Bantam 1989 $2.95. ISBN 0-553-28049-X Jane Stuart's life changes when she discovers her father is still alive.

Kilmeny of the Orchard (1910). Bantam 1989 $2.95. ISBN 0-553-21377-6 A handsome young school teacher loves a shy, mute violinist.

Magic for Marigold (1930). Bantam 1989 $2.95. ISBN 0-553-28046-5 The Lesley family decides to name the new baby after the doctor who saved her life.

Mistress Pat (1935). Bantam 1989 $2.95. ISBN 0-553-28048-1 Pat must choose between a possibly lonely life at Silver Bush or leaving home for romance.

Pat of Silver Bush (1933). Bantam 1989 $2.95. ISBN 0-553-28047-3 Pat Gardner believes life at Silver Bush will go on the same forever—until the new baby arrives.

Rainbow Valley (1919). Bantam 1985 $3.50. ISBN 0-553-26921-6 The adventures of Anne's children and their friends.

Rilla of Ingleside (1921). Bantam 1985 $3.50. ISBN 0-553-26922-4 Anne's youngest child, Rilla, comes of age during World War I.

The Story Girl (1911). Bantam 1989 $2.95. ISBN 0-553-21366-0 Sara Stanley's fame as a story teller reaches far beyond her hometown.

A Tangled Web (1931). Bantam 1989 $3.50. ISBN 0-553-28050-3 Two families battle for possession of a family heirloom.

SHORT STORY COLLECTIONS BY MONTGOMERY

Chronicles of Avonlea (1909). Bantam 1988 $2.95. ISBN 0-553-21378-4 Twelve stories based on the unforgettable inhabitants of the town of Avonlea.

Further Chronicles of Avonlea (1912). Bantam 1988 $2.95. ISBN 0-553-21381-4 Fifteen more tales of the folk of Avonlea.

MOWAT, FARLEY 1921– (CANADA)

Farley Mowat was born in Belleville, Ontario, and raised in Saskatoon, Saskatchewan in Canada. He began study at the University of Toronto but left to serve in the military in World War II. After the war he spent two years in the Arctic and then returned to Toronto to complete his degree.

Mowat's first book, *People of the Deer* (1952), sets the tone for the rest of his writing career. In it Mowat describes how the Inuit (native) people of the Arctic have been mistreated by both missionaries and the government. When published, the book set off a heated controversy between those who agreed with Mowat's evaluation and those who said he exaggerated the Inuits' difficulties.

With almost every subsequent book, Mowat has provoked a new storm of controversy as he fights passionately to save the people and the environment of the Canadian North from what he sees as the insensitive policies of business and government. His popular work has made the public aware of the dangers threatening a very fragile part of Earth. Mowat's books have been translated into 23 languages and published in more than 40 countries. Environmentalists the world over regard him as a leading advocate of their cause.

FICTION BY MOWAT

Lost in the Barrens (1956). Bantam 1985 $3.50. ISBN 0-553-27529-9 Two teenage boys struggle to survive when they become lost in Canada's barren Arctic lands.

The Snow Walker (1975). Bantam 1977 $3.95. ISBN 0-770-42209-8 Collection of stories, fables, and essays describing the beauty and power of the Arctic region.

NONFICTION BY MOWAT

And No Birds Sang (1981). Bantam 1987 $3.95. ISBN 0-770-42237-3 Autobiographical account of Mowat's experiences in World War II, told with characteristic irony and humor.

The Boat Who Wouldn't Float (1968). Bantam 1981 $3.95. ISBN 0-553-27788-X Story of a leaky boat and the people who tried to sail it.

The Desperate People (1959). Bantam 1981 $3.95. ISBN 0-770-42323-X

The Dog Who Wouldn't Be (1957). Bantam 1981 $2.95. ISBN 0-553-27928-9 Story of Mutt, Mowat's boyhood dog.

Grey Seas Under (1958). Bantam 1990 $3.95. ISBN 0-770-42333-7

Never Cry Wolf (1963). Bantam 1984 $3.95. ISBN 0-553-27396-5 Informative and amusing portrait of the habits and character of wolves.

Ordeal By Ice (1960). Gibbs Smith 1989 $12.95. ISBN 0-07905-321-6

The People of the Deer (1952). Bantam 1981 $3.95. ISBN 0-770-42254-3

The Polar Passion (1967). Gibbs Smith 1989 $12.95. ISBN 0-87905-348-8

Sea of Slaughter (1986). Bantam 1986 $9.95. ISBN 0-553-34269-X

The Serpent's Coil (1961). Bantam 1982 $3.95. ISBN 0-770-42313-2

The Siberians (1970). Bantam 1990 $3.95. ISBN 0-553-24896-0 A fascinating account of Mowat's two trips to the Soviet Union and the environmental issues he encountered there.

A Whale for the Killing (1972). Bantam 1984 $3.95. ISBN 0-553-26752-3 True story of Mowat's attempt to save a whale trapped in a Newfoundland lagoon.

Woman in the Mists: The Story of Diane Fossey and the Mountain Gorillas of Africa (1986). Warner

Bks 1988 $10.95. ISBN 0-446-38720-7 The story of scientist Diane Fossey and her efforts to save the African gorilla population; became the successful film *Gorillas in the Mist.*

MUNRO, ALICE   1931– (CANADA)

Born Alice Laidlaw, Alice Munro grew up in Wingham, Ontario, and attended the University of Western Ontario in Canada. An avid writer from an early age, she is a particularly skillful and gifted author of short stories. Her first collection, *Dance of the Happy Shades* (1968), won a Governor General's Award. Her two novels, *Lives of Girls and Women* (1971) and *The Beggar Maid* (1978) are collections of episodes in the life of the central character, with each chapter reading as a separate story.

Munro's work is concerned with women's relationships, usually ordinary women or girls living in rural Ontario towns. She is especially interested in the tension between society's expectations and women's actual feelings. Munro is widely anthologized and highly regarded by U.S. and Canadian critics.

NOVELS BY MUNRO

The Beggar Maid (1978). Penguin 1984 $6.95. ISBN 0-14-006011-1
Lives of Girls and Women (1971). Plume 1983 $8.95. ISBN 0-452-26184-8

SHORT STORY COLLECTIONS BY MUNRO

Dance of the Happy Shades and Other Stories (1968). Penguin 1985 $6.95. ISBN 0-14-006681-1
The Moons of Jupiter (1982). Penguin 1984 $6.95. ISBN 0-14-006547-4
The Progress of Love (1987). Penguin 1987 $6.95. ISBN 0-14-009879-8
Something I've Been Meaning to Tell You (1974). Signet 1983 $2.95. ISBN 0-451-14343-4

BOOK ABOUT MUNRO

Blodgett, E. D. *Alice Munro.* G. K. Hall 1988 $19.95. ISBN 0-8057-8232-X A general introduction to Munro's life and works, focusing on Munro as a storyteller experimenting with what can and cannot be told.

RICHLER, MORDECAI   1931– (CANADA)

Born in Montreal, Canada, at the outset of the Depression, Mordecai Richler reflects in his best work his experiences growing up in the Jewish ghettos of Montreal around St. Urbain Street. Richler left Sir George Williams College without obtaining a degree in order to travel to Europe and begin a writing career. After a brief return to Canada, he left once again for England, where he has since spent most of his time.

Richler, who has developed a large and appreciative audience and received favorable critical attention, has been described as "the loser's advocate," an author who can arouse sympathy for unsympathetic characters. One of the most famous of his creations is Duddy Kravitz, hero of *The Apprenticeship of Duddy Kravitz* (1959). A hustler without a conscience, Duddy schemes his way out of the Jewish ghetto to become a landowner, whose greed ultimately costs him everything he really cares about. The success of this book led Richler to write other novels with similar themes. *Saint Urbain's Horseman* (1971) follows the exploits of Jake Hersch as he tries to bring together the Canadian and Jewish sides of his personality. *Joshua Then and Now* (1980) looks at Joshua Shapiro, who must face both past and present mistakes as he tries to confront his own moral responsibility for his actions.

NOVEL BY RICHLER

Joshua Then and Now (1980). Bantam 1985 $4.95. ISBN 0-7704-2035-4

NONFICTION BY RICHLER

Home Sweet Home: My Canadian Album (1984). Penguin 1985 $6.95. ISBN 0-14-007639-5

BOOKS ABOUT RICHLER

Davidson, Arnold E. *Mordecai Richler.* Ungar 1983 $16.95. ISBN 0-8044-2140-4 A critical analysis of Richler's work; each chapter is devoted to one of the novels, continuing through *Joshua Then and Now.*

Ramraj, Victor J. *Mordecai Richler.* G. K. Hall 1983 $21.95. ISBN 0-8057-6554-9 Another useful critical study of Richter's novels through *Joshua Then and Now,* considering them by locale, politics, and humor.

SERVICE, ROBERT W. (WILLIAM)   1874–1958 (CANADA)

Robert William Service was born in Preston, England, and raised in Scotland. He worked for the Commercial Bank of Scotland from 1889 until his departure for Canada in 1896. After traveling through western Canada, the United States, and Mexico, he resumed his banking career. In 1908 he was transferred to a bank in Dawson, in the Yukon Territory, a setting that became the source of most of his verse.

Although he did write some fiction, Service is almost exclusively associated with his colorful, humorous ballads about life on the northern frontier. Among the most famous of these are "The Cremation of Sam McGee" and "The Shooting of Dan McGrew." Service left Canada in 1912 to become a foreign correspondent, and this enormously popular poet of the frozen northland died in sunny, glamorous Monte Carlo on the French Riviera.

POETRY BY SERVICE

*The Best of Robert Service. Putnam $6.95. ISBN 0-399-55088-9 Contains all of Service's popular ballads, including "Dan McGrew" and "Sam McGee."

The Collected Verse of Robert Service. Putnam $17.95. ISBN 0-399-15015-3

Later Collected Verse. Putnam $17.95. ISBN 0-396-05214-2

More Collected Verse. Putnam $4.95. ISBN 0-396-06562-7

The Spell of the Yukon (1907). Putnam $8.95. ISBN 0-399-15011-0

SHUTE, NEVIL (PSEUDONYM OF NEVIL SHUTE NORWAY) 1899–1960 (AUSTRALIA)

Born in London, Nevil Shute earned an engineering degree at Oxford University and worked for several years as an aeronautical engineer before becoming managing director of an aircraft company. In 1938 he sold his interest in the company to become a full-time writer. In 1950 he immigrated with his family to a farm in Langwarin, in Victoria, Australia.

Shute was a prolific writer whose novels explore a wide range of themes and situations. He frequently called on his engineering background and scientific knowledge for details. *In the Wet* (1953) is a humorous look at the unlikely decision of the Queen of England to move from Britain to Australia. *On the Beach* (1957) is a grim prediction of the possible effects of a nuclear war. His hugely successful *A Town Like Alice* (1950) discloses the subtle appeal of a tiny town in Australia's isolated Northern Territory. Several of Shute's novels have been made into movies or television miniseries.

NOVELS BY SHUTE

The Breaking Wave (1955). Ballantine 1988 $3.50. ISBN 0-345-32173-1
The Chequer Board (1947). Ballantine 1988 $3.50. ISBN 0-345-00743-3
Most Secret (1945). Ballantine 1988 $3.95. ISBN 0-345-00709-3
*On the Beach (1957). Ballantine 1983 $3.95. ISBN 0-345-31148-5 In Australia the survivors of a nuclear war wait for the end of human life.
The Rainbow and the Rose (1958). Ballantine 1988 $2.95. ISBN 0-345-32251-7
A Town like Alice (1950). Ballantine 1987 $3.95. ISBN 0-345-35374-9

WHITE, PATRICK   1912– (AUSTRALIA)

Born in London of Australian parents, Patrick White has lived in both England and Australia. His heart and his genius, however, are Australian. Following schooling in England, which he describes as "a four-year prison sentence," White returned to Australia, where he worked as a hired hand on a sheep farm for two years. He then returned to England to complete his degree at Cambridge University in 1935. After graduating, White remained in London, working at his writing.

In 1939 White published his first novel, *The Happy Valley,* an ironic tale of life in an Australian mining town. His second novel, *The Living and the Dead* (1941), concerns a young man in England and Europe in the early days of the twentieth century. The "dead" in the title refers to people whose lives are restricted by their acceptance of the traditions of a dead past.

During World War II, White served in the Royal Air Force as an intelligence officer. After the war he returned to Australia and settled near Sydney.

White's writing has continued to explore Australian themes. In *The Tree of Man* (1955), White constructed a sprawling novel that covers Australian history from its earliest settlement by Europeans to modern times, exploring the roots of modern Australian society. In *Voss* (1957), he looks at an 1840 expedition into Australia's interior, showing how the vastness and harshness of the country can humble a proud man. *Riders in the Chariot* (1961) is an attack on the shallow values of modern suburban life that offended many Australian readers.

White is generally regarded as Australia's most important living writer. He is difficult to read, however, because of his extensive use of homoerotic symbolism, drawing on his experiences as a gay man, and because of his complicated method of telling a story through the uninterrupted flow of a character's thoughts. Nevertheless, his novels remain very popular, and in 1973 he was awarded the Nobel Prize for literature.

NOVELS BY WHITE

The Eye of the Storm (1973). Penguin 1988 $7.95. ISBN 0-14-003963-5
The Living and the Dead (1941). Penguin 1983 $6.95. ISBN 0-14-002623-1
Memoirs of Many in One (1986). Penguin 1988 $15.95. ISBN 0-670-81320-6
Riders in the Chariot (1961). Penguin 1985 $6.95. ISBN 0-14-002185-X
The Solid Mandala (1966). Penguin 1983 $6.95. ISBN 0-14-002975-3

The Tree of Man (1955). Penguin 1984 $6.95. ISBN 0-14-001657-0
The Twyborn Affair (1980). Penguin 1981 $6.95. ISBN 0-14-005544-4
The Vivesector (1970). Penguin 1986 $6.95. ISBN 0-14-003693-8
Voss (1957). Penguin 1984 $7.95. ISBN 0-14-001438-1

SHORT STORY COLLECTIONS BY WHITE

The Burnt Ones (1964). Penguin 1985 $6.95. ISBN 0-14-002776-9
The Cockatoos (1974). Penguin 1983 $6.95. ISBN 0-14-004463-9

NONFICTION BY WHITE

*Flaws in the Glass: A Self Portrait. Penguin 1983 $6.95. ISBN 0-14-006-293-9 Autobio-
graphical sketches of White's early childhood through his late sixties; set in
Australia, England, Africa, and Greece.

BOOKS ABOUT WHITE

Kiernan, Brian. *Patrick White.* St. Martin's 1980 $20.00. ISBN 0-312-59807-6 A full
account of White's artistic development and achievements from his early work
through *The Twyborn Affair;* useful and interesting.
Weigel, John A. *Patrick White.* G. K. Hall 1983 $18.95. ISBN 0-8057-6558-1 A brief
biography of White followed by a critical analysis of each of his novels and plays;
a good general introduction.

AMERICAN LITERATURE

The section embracing American literature is organized in a fashion that should
suit most readers. There are four major categories that are arranged chronologically—The Early Years, Romanticism and The American Renaissance, The Rise
of Realism, and The Twentieth Century. Within each of these literary time
periods, writers are listed alphabetically, their last names appearing first. For
each author, there is at least one list of books by that author; novels, poetry,
plays, nonfiction, and collections are listed separately. Therefore, if readers are
seeking out particular genres, or types of literature, they will readily find them.

In addition, there is a biographical profile of each author. The profile not
only provides information about major works and literary influences but usually offers interesting personal background. Further, the profile may refer the
reader to related writers and their works, which also can be found in *The Young
Adult Reader's Adviser.* Such connections between writers are usually necessary
when doing research in a subject as broad as American literature. ·

Last, for most writers, there is a Books About section that, among other
types of publications, lists notable biographies for further reading and research.
These books are limited to highly respected works. Wherever possible, very
recent titles have also been included; however, in the case of the most contemporary writers—for example, many young adult authors—no "book about"
existed at the time of this compilation.

A major responsibility of the American literature section is to supplement
standard listings of the most established writers with the works of newer or
neglected writers, including, of course, literature by American women and
literature by America's ethnic writers. To the best of their ability, in a limited
space, the editors, in their selection of both major and lesser known writers,
have tried to represent the diversity of American culture and history.

The Midnight Ride of Paul Revere. Painting by Grant Wood (1931).
© Estate of Grant Wood/VAGA, New York, 1991. The Metropolitan Museum of Art, Arthur H. Hearn Fund, 1950. Courtesy of Associated American Artists.

THE EARLY YEARS

Many thousands of years ago, Indians began to build civilizations in the Americas. They had their own rich tradition of stories, songs, poems, and histories. Unfortunately, theirs was primarily an oral tradition, and today there are few written records of these works. However, some Indian traditions continue to survive in both oral and written form, and many original Indian languages are still spoken.

In the late 1400s and 1500s European explorers and conquistadors came to the Americas, claimed land for their rulers, and took back precious metals and other riches. Along with them came missionaries, who tried to convert the Indians to Christianity. Although many of the adventurous Europeans kept journals and records and wrote letters, most of what they recorded survives more as historical documents than as literature.

The beginning of the tradition of American literature that people know today began with early colonists from England, settlers who came not to explore the new North American lands but to live there. British colonies in New England and Virginia saw the beginnings of both the United States and American literature.

At first the colonists were mainly concerned with staying alive in an untamed and alien environment. Then they turned to building their own societies. Later, as they sought independence from Britain, they concentrated on building a nation. Thus they devoted little time to the arts. What writing they did undertake was mostly practical, intended to record events, to inform, or to educate, rather than to entertain or amuse. Mostly diaries and journals, these works were not actually intended as literature. Nevertheless, they provide a rich record of the life and thought of the times.

Perhaps the best known of the early diarists is William Bradford, the governor of the Plymouth colony founded by English Puritans who came to the New World to escape religious persecution and build a new, pure society that conformed to their religious teachings. Bradford's records of the early days of the Plymouth settlement are a graphic description of the hardships the colonists endured, as well as their iron-willed faith that their God would sustain them. Bradford's diaries of later years show how the settlers became increasingly concerned with such worldly matters as selling furs, trading, and building houses. Thus, year by year, the diaries record how the colonists gradually moved away from the religious faith that had brought them to North America.

Another Puritan, Mary Rowlandson, wrote a detailed account of how she was held captive by Indians in 1676. Although her account is true, it is colored by the stereotypes and prejudices of the time about Indians. Its popularity in England, however, led a number of imitators to produce a mass of fictional "captivity" tales. Because these tales perpetuated the European prejudices of the time, they were often believed to be true and led to increased prejudice against Indians.

The Puritans considered poetry to be of little importance. They valued plain and direct speech, which would help people to keep to their strict religious teachings, and had little interest in forms they considered merely "decorative." Two Puritans, however, did produce exceptional poetry—Anne Bradstreet, who wrote poems to sing the praises of God, and Edward Taylor, a minister who composed a body of private religious poetry that he never expected anyone else to see. Because the Puritans valued humility and simplicity, Bradstreet and Taylor were reluctant to display their talents publicly. In fact, Taylor's poems were unknown until 1939, when they were discovered by accident.

By the beginning of the eighteenth century, the early European settlements in North America were solidly established colonies that had begun to grow and prosper. As colonists grew more concerned about their prosperity, church leaders grew more concerned about colonists' loss of faith. By the middle of the century, a movement known as the Great Awakening was begun by ministers and religious leaders trying to revive religious fervor in the colonies. One of the most powerful voices in this movement was that of the minister Jonathan Edwards, whose sermons moved people to scream and faint in his churches. These sermons were printed and widely read. Even today, they are notable for their power, intelligence, and elegant style.

In the second half of the eighteenth century, the primary concern of most educated, upper-class Americans was establishing and shaping a nation. Thus, most of the writing in this period was political and argumentative. Some American writers, however, did treat different themes. The poems of the slave Phillis Wheatley, for example, attracted attention in England as well as in America. She became the first African-American writer. Charles Brockden Brown's novels are another example. They were the first American fiction of any real importance, and his novel *Wieland* (1798) is still read today. A third such writer is the French immigrant Hector St. John de Crèvecoeur, who wrote a series of letters describing the American character in colorful detail. These early efforts were the source of many themes that were to continue in American literature—the role of black Americans and other ethnic groups in shaping American culture; the search for the true "American" story; and the exploration of the quintessentially "American" character.

BRADFORD, WILLIAM 1590–1657

William Bradford was born in the English village of Austerfield in Yorkshire. He began attending a Puritan church at the age of 12 and, shortly after turning 17, joined a congregation of Separatists, a wing of the Puritan movement that believed in "separating" themselves from evil influences. Bradford accompanied his congregation to Holland, and later played an important part in the group's decision to establish a colony in North America.

From the outset, Bradford was an important figure in the Plymouth colony. In 1621 he was elected governor, a post to which he was re-elected 30 times.

Between 1620 and 1647, Bradford wrote *Of Plymouth Plantation,* a history of the Pilgrims from the time they landed through their first 25 years as a colony. Because Bradford intended the history only to be read by members of his family, it was not published in its entirety until 1856. Throughout the eighteenth and nineteenth centuries, it served as the basis for historical research by other authors. It continues to be read for its fascinating account of such key incidents as the trip over on the *Mayflower,* the signing of the Mayflower Compact, and the election of the colony's first governor.

NONFICTION BY BRADFORD

Of Plymouth Plantation: Sixteen Twenty to Sixteen Forty Seven (1856). Samuel E. Morrison (ed). Knopf 1952 $22.00. ISBN 0-394-43895-7

BOOK ABOUT BRADFORD

Shepard, James. *Governor William Bradford and His Son Major William Bradford.* Higginson 1988 $23.00. ISBN 0-8328-0305-7 Accurate biography of two generations of Bradfords.

BRADSTREET, ANNE *c.* 1612–1672

Anne Bradstreet, born in England, was the daughter of Thomas Dudley, a prominent Puritan, who would later become the second governor of the Massachusetts Bay Colony. At age 16, she married Simon Bradstreet, and two years later she, her husband, and her father sailed to New England with the second wave of Puritan immigrants.

Life in the fledgling colony was harsh. Although Bradstreet suffered from frail health, she raised eight children and kept house while her husband rose to prominence in colonial politics. Furthermore, throughout her life, she devoted herself to writing poetry despite the pressure of her other duties.

Much of Bradstreet's work is historical, philosophical, or religious. Her religious poems, such as "Contemplations" and "The Flesh and the Spirit," are among her most memorable works. Contemporary critics, however, are most interested in the personal lyrics she addressed to her husband and her children, and these poems are the real foundation for her reputation.

Bradstreet's poetry was written for her own and her family's use. It was published only because her brother-in-law brought a collection of her poetry to England in 1650 and had it printed under the title *The Tenth Muse, Lately Sprung Up in America.* It was the first published book of poetry by a resident of North America and was widely read and admired in the English-speaking world.

POETRY BY BRADSTREET

The Works of Anne Bradstreet. Jeannie Hensley (ed). Harvard Univ Pr 1981 $10.95. ISBN 0-674-95999-X

BOOK ABOUT BRADSTREET

Piercy, Josephine K. *Anne Bradstreet.* New College & Univ Pr 1964 $5.95. ISBN 0-8084-0051-7 A good general introduction to Bradstreet's work, giving the beginning student an accurate sense of modern critical opinion about her.

BROWN, CHARLES BROCKDEN   1771–1810

Charles Brockden Brown was America's first important novelist, and the first in a long tradition of authors of psychological fiction; that is, fiction focusing on the inner thoughts of a single, tormented individual. Brown was born in Philadelphia in 1771, and after a brief career as a lawyer, turned to fiction. Between 1798 and 1801, he published six novels. *Wieland* (1798), his best-known work, was based on an actual murder case in New York. *Ormond* (1799) deals with an attempted seduction but is ultimately about conflicting values. *Arthur Mervyn* (1799) presents a realistic account of the yellow fever epidemic that occurred in Philadelphia in 1773. Three lesser-known novels, *Edgar Huntly* (1799), *Clara Howard* (1801), and *Jane Talbot* (1801), followed before Brown abandoned novel writing for a career in business and journalism.

Brown was influenced to become a socialist by the British social philosopher William Godwin, and sought in his novels to combine realistic observation with romantic ideals. His work is flawed by sentimentalism and an overemphasis on the horrific, but some of his novels continue to be read today for their literary as well as historical significance. Contemporary readers particularly enjoy *Wieland* for its intriguing study of a murder.

NOVEL BY BROWN

Wieland, or The Transformation (1798). Doubleday 1969 $5.95. ISBN 0-385-03100-9

BOOK ABOUT BROWN

Ringe, Donald A. *Charles Brockden Brown.* New College & Univ Pr 1966 $10.95. ISBN 0-8084-0071-1 A useful study and overview of Brown's work; part of the Twayne's U.S. Author series; gives beginning students a good general picture of the wide range of current critical opinion.

CREVECOEUR, MICHEL-GUILLAUME JEAN DE   1735–1813

Crèvecoeur, also known as Hector St. John de Crèvecoeur, was born in France in 1735. In 1754, he went to England, and a year later immigrated to Canada. There he fought in the Canadian militia in the French and Indian Wars. In 1759, Crèvecoeur began a 10-year career as a fur trader. Then, in 1769, he moved to New York, bought land in Orange County, married, and started life as a farmer.

Between 1769 and the beginning of the American Revolution, Crèvecoeur cleared his land and began to raise a family. This is the period when he most likely wrote the bulk of his *Letters from an American Farmer* (1782), for which he is known today.

When the Revolution came, Crèvecoeur, a Tory, supported the British, so he returned to France. He did not come back to America until 1783, when he returned as the French consul to New York, New Jersey, and Connecticut. He discovered that his home had been burned, his wife killed, and his children placed in the care of strangers as a result of an Indian raid. Crèvecoeur settled once again in New York with his children and performed his diplomatic duties until 1790, when he returned permanently to France.

Letters from an American Farmer was an immensely popular work in both the United States and France. It is still considered an insightful, if somewhat rosy, portrait of eighteenth-century American life.

NONFICTION BY CREVECOEUR

Letters from an American Farmer and Sketches of Eighteenth-Century America (1782). Penguin 1981 $5.95. ISBN 0-14-039006-5

BOOK ABOUT CREVECOEUR

Allen, Gay W., and Roger Asselineau. *Biography of Crèvecoeur: The Life of an American Farmer.* Penguin 1987 $19.95. ISBN 0-670-81345-1 Recent reliable biography.

EDWARDS, JONATHAN   1703–1758

Jonathan Edwards was born in Connecticut, the son of a Congregationalist minister and grandson of the Reverend Solomon Stoddard, a powerful local religious figure, known as the "Pope of the Connecticut Valley." At age 13, Edwards went to Yale University, where he studied theology. A few years after he graduated, in 1726, he joined his grandfather as a minister in Northampton, Massachusetts. When Stoddard died two years later, Edwards succeeded him as pastor.

Edwards is best known for the important part he played in the so-called Great Awakening, the revival of religious fervor in the 1730s and 1740s. His sermon "Sinners in the Hands of An Angry God" (1741) is one of the major works of that period—a sermon that portrayed Hell so graphically and convincingly that listeners cried out in anguish when it was delivered. Edwards's own experience of the Great Awakening is described in *A Faithful Narrative of the Surprising Work of God* (1737), as well as in some of his other works.

Edwards was very interested in science, which affected his views on religion and philosophy. He believed that God was actually present in the world, and that God's presence could be perceived through the senses. His "Personal Narrative" (1765) describes some of his experiences of perceiving God through profound encounters with nature. In this his thought anticipates that of the Transcendentalists, a famous group of American writers who focused on nature, including Ralph Waldo Emerson and Henry David Thoreau. (*See* Emerson *and* Thoreau, Vol. 1, American Literature: Romanticism and the American Renaissance.) Edwards's work may also be thought of as a bridge between the Puritans and the American Romantics.

In 1750 Edwards was dismissed from his position as a result of a disagreement over who should be considered members of the church. Edwards felt that members should have had a conversion experience—a direct experience of Christ. Most of his parishioners, however, favored the less stringent "Half-Way Covenant," which allowed church membership to almost anyone who wished to join. In 1751 Edwards began a ministry in the frontier town of Stockbridge, Massachusetts. There he remained until 1758, when he became president of the College of New Jersey (later Princeton University). He died later the same year, the result of an unsuccessful smallpox vaccination.

COLLECTION BY EDWARDS

Selected Writings of Jonathan Edwards. Harold P. Simonson (ed). Ungar 1970 $7.95. ISBN 0-8044-6132-5

BOOK ABOUT EDWARDS

Miller, Perry. *Jonathan Edwards.* Univ of Massachusetts Pr 1981 $10.00. ISBN 0-87023-328-9 The best single book on Edwards's work, placing the man in the context of his time, and written by the major American specialist in this period.

TAYLOR, EDWARD   *c.* 1642–1729

Edward Taylor was born in England. A staunch Puritan, he came to America in 1668 rather than sign an oath of loyalty to the Church of England. After graduating from Harvard University in 1671, he went to Westfield, Massachusetts, as a minister and physician and stayed there the rest of his life.

Although Taylor wrote poetry, he was secretive about it. Because he requested that none of his poetry be published, his work remained in manuscript and virtually unknown until 1939, when the critic and scholar Thomas H. Johnson discovered and published *The Poetical Works of Edward Taylor.*

Taylor wrote complex poetry about the nature of God and the universe, in the style of such seventeenth-century British poets as John Donne and George Herbert. (*See* Donne *and* Herbert, Vol. 1, British Literature: The Renaissance.) Unlike the British poets, his images, true to their New England origin, reflect the homely details of frontier life. Taylor's work is now considered by many critics to be the most important poetry written in colonial America.

POETRY BY TAYLOR

The Poetical Works of Edward Taylor (1939). Princeton Univ Pr 1944 $12.50. ISBN 0-691-01275-X

BOOK ABOUT TAYLOR

Grabo, Norman S. *Edward Taylor.* New College & Univ Pr 1961 $10.95. ISBN 0-8084-0117-3 A good general introduction to Taylor's work; part of Twayne's U.S. Author series, which gives readers an excellent picture of the range of contemporary critical opinion.

WHEATLEY, PHILLIS   *c.* 1753–1784

Phillis Wheatley, the first significant African-American writer, was a slave—and child prodigy. In 1761, Wheatley was brought to Boston, probably from present-day Senegal or Gambia. She became the property of John and Susannah Wheatley, who permitted her to learn to read and write and receive a good background in the classics and the Bible.

In 1770, Wheatley's poem on the death of the English evangelist George Whitefield won her widespread attention. She was taken to London, where she met many distinguished persons, among them the Lord Mayor of London, who recognized and assisted her poetic endeavors.

Despite Wheatley's fame, she continued to be held as a slave. Finally, after her owners died, Wheatley was freed. In 1778, she married John Peters, a free African American. Wheatley's final years were spent in great poverty, and when she died in 1784, she was buried in an unmarked grave.

Although Wheatley's poetry is relatively conventional in form, it is quite moving. Her best works focus on freedom, labor, and art.

POETRY BY WHEATLEY

Collected Works of Phillis Wheatley. Oxford Univ Pr 1989 $9.95. ISBN 0-19-505241-2

BOOKS ABOUT WHEATLEY

*Jensen, Marilyn. *Phillis Wheatley: Negro Slave of John Wheatley.* Lion 1987 $16.95. ISBN
   0-87460-326-9 A basic biography for grades 6–12.
Robinson, William H. *Phillis Wheatley and Her Writings.* Garland 1984 $61.00. ISBN
   0-8240-9346-1 A comprehensive introduction to Wheatley's life and poetry.

ROMANTICISM AND THE AMERICAN RENAISSANCE

At the beginning of the nineteenth century, most American writers still looked
to England for their models and inspiration. There they saw the beginnings of
a new movement in literature and the arts, a reaction against the emphasis on
logical thought that had dominated much of the eighteenth century. Writers
in this new movement were seeking truth and beauty in their hearts and souls,
and searching for meaning in nature and the supernatural. They turned away
from the pretense and hypocrisy of civilization, finding inspiration in the
seemingly uncorrupted innocence of nature. They also celebrated ordinary
people and the freedom of the individual. This was the Romantic movement.
(*See also* Vol. 1, British Literature: The Romantic Period.)

Many American writers were taken with these new ideas, which seemed
particularly appropriate for a new and vital nation founded on the idea of
individual freedom. But Americans did not merely copy their British counter-
parts. They took these European Romantic ideas and gave them a peculiarly
American form.

Instead of the relatively gentle English countryside, American writers
looked to the untamed wilderness of the American frontier. The people who
populated this frontier—pioneers, hunters, and American Indians—were seen
as models of unrestricted, natural, and somehow "pure" human beings. American Romantics thus developed the concepts of the "rugged individual" and the
"noble savage." These figures became a basic part of American literature.

Young Henry David Thoreau also turned to nature for his inspiration. He
built a small shack in the Massachusetts woods and wrote of his experiences,
urging those in the city to "simplify, simplify." At the same time, such writers
as Edgar Allan Poe and Nathaniel Hawthorne began to explore the realm of the
mysterious and supernatural.

As America approached the middle of the nineteenth century, another idea
began to be expressed more often and more forcefully. American writers
should stop looking to England for their models and develop instead a uniquely
American literature. Hand in hand with this concept went the assertion that
there were *already* American writers who were every bit as good as those in
England. In the stories and verse of Poe, the novels of Hawthorne, and the
poems of Ralph Waldo Emerson and Oliver Wendell Holmes, Americans found
literature of which they could be justifiably proud.

This feeling of an emerging new culture has become known as the American Renaissance, taking its name from the European Renaissance, the creative
explosion that took place in Europe 400 years earlier. Some of the imagination
and intellect that had been directed toward the founding of a new nation was
now being turned to the development of a national art.

In the early 1850s, three major American works were published: Nathaniel
Hawthorne's *The Scarlet Letter* (1850), Herman Melville's *Moby-Dick* (1851), and
Walt Whitman's *Leaves of Grass* (1855). The novels of Hawthorne and Melville
remain among the greatest works of fiction ever written in the United States,

and Whitman's volume of poems changed forever the way American poets would view their art. Ironically, another of America's greatest poets—Emily Dickinson—also wrote during this creative period, but she labored quietly and alone, sharing her work with only a few family members and friends. Yet the poems of this reclusive writer from Amherst, Massachusetts, are among the finest and most highly esteemed literary works of this period. In poetry and prose, American literature had come of age.

BRYANT, WILLIAM CULLEN   1794–1878

Like many Romantic poets, Bryant showed his talent at a very early age. He was born in the small town of Cummington, Massachusetts, and was educated by his father in the Greek and Roman classics. By the time he was 14, Bryant had published his first poem, "The Embargo." Before he was 20, he had written his most famous poem, "Thanatopsis," a meditation on death that explores his close affinity with nature and reveals his debt to such British "nature poets" as William Wordsworth. (*See* Wordsworth, Vol. 1, British Literature: The Romantic Period.)

Bryant went to Williams College for a year and then studied law, beginning his law practice in 1815. His lifelong passion, though, was literature. In 1821 he published his first collection of poems, and in 1825 he and his wife moved to New York City, where he became editor of a literary magazine, *The New York Review and Atheneum.* The magazine failed, but Bryant remained in New York, becoming a fixture on the literary scene. In 1829, he became editor-in-chief of the *Evening Post,* a position he held until his death, and where he became famous for his antislavery views.

Bryant's poetry is limited in scope and subject matter. He wrote sonorous verse inspired by the American landscape and was influenced by the British Romantics, especially Wordsworth, whom he admired greatly. Always solemn and stately, Bryant's verse seemed cold to poet James Russell Lowell (*see* Lowell, Vol. 1, American Literature: Romanticism and the American Renaissance), who spoke of Bryant's "iceolation." When he was nearly 80, Bryant translated Homer's *Iliad* and *Odyssey* into English blank verse.

POETRY BY BRYANT

Poetical Works of William Cullen Bryant. AMS 1969 $42.50. ISBN 0-404-01143-8

BOOKS ABOUT BRYANT

Bigelow, John. *William Cullen Bryant.* Chelsea 1980 repr of 1890 ed $5.95. ISBN 0-87754-160-4 A nineteenth-century general study of Bryant's life and works.
McLean, Albert F., Jr. *William Cullen Bryant.* New College & Univ Pr 1964 $10.95. ISBN 0-8084-0323-0 A good general introduction to Bryant's life and work.

EMERSON, RALPH WALDO   1803–1882

Ralph Waldo Emerson was the writer who most fully developed American Romantic thought. He was born in Boston, the son of a Unitarian minister, who died when Emerson was eight. His mother raised him and his four brothers by keeping a series of boarding houses. Emerson benefited greatly from his mother's hard work and educational goals. He attended Harvard College and Harvard Divinity School. While an undergraduate at Harvard, he began keeping journals, a custom he would follow for the rest of his life.

Emerson was ordained a Unitarian minister in 1826. For a time he was pastor of the Second Church of Boston, but in 1832 he resigned, no longer able in good conscience to perform his duties, since his religious beliefs had changed. After traveling in Europe, especially in England, Scotland, and Germany, he settled in Concord, Massachusetts, in 1834. There he began writing the essays and public addresses for which he became so famous.

Emerson's first book, *Nature,* appeared in 1836. This long essay set out the cornerstones of his philosophy—the importance of nature both in its own right and as a means of discovering the truth about the universe, the sanctity of the individual, and the importance of self-reliance. Emerson's poetry, which he began writing at the same time, explored these same ideas.

Emerson became increasingly popular as a lecturer, eventually speaking throughout the northeast and the Midwest. Meanwhile, his home in Concord became a center for the so-called Transcendentalists, a group of writers and philosophers who believed that humans could *transcend,* or get past, their human limits in order to perceive the presence of God in nature. The Transcendental Club, which met informally in Emerson's house, consisted of such thinkers as Bronson Alcott, Margaret Fuller, Jones Very, and others. Emerson was also close to Henry David Thoreau (*see* Thoreau, Vol. 1 American Literature: Romanticism and the American Renaissance), who, like Emerson, was fascinated by the roles and responsibilities of the individual.

In 1840, Emerson became one of the founders of *The Dial,* the influential periodical of Transcendental thought, which he edited from 1842 to 1844. His first series of *Essays* appeared in 1841. These essays, which included the famous "Self-Reliance," "The Over-Soul," and "Friendship," helped to expand his reputation, both in the United States and abroad.

In the 1850s and 1860s, Emerson was a tireless campaigner against slavery. By the time the Civil War had ended, however, his memory and mental capacities had begun to decline, and he produced very little in the last 15 years of his life.

Emerson's essays do not reveal a fully worked out philosophy. However, they do very effectively convey his ideas about the spiritual importance of the natural world as well as the supreme importance of the individual. It would be difficult to overestimate Emerson's influence on American thought. Philosopher Henry David Thoreau and poet Walt Whitman (*see* Whitman, Vol. 1, American Literature: The Rise of Realism) were his disciples and explored many of his ideas in their own work. Although novelists Nathaniel Hawthorne (*see* Hawthorne, Vol. 1, American Literature: The Rise of Realism) and Herman Melville (*see* Melville, Vol. 1, American Literature: Romanticism and the American Renaissance) did not share Emerson's optimism, his thought was extremely important to both of them. Emerson's work was also important to readers of all types, and his essays and lectures provided ordinary people with a philosophy that enriched their lives.

POEMS AND ESSAYS BY EMERSON

Essays and Lectures. Joel Porte (ed). Lib of America 1983 $27.50. ISBN 0-940450-15-1
Essays of Ralph Waldo Emerson. Robert E. Spiller (ed). Harvard Univ Pr 1987 $12.50. ISBN 0-674-26720-6
The Portable Emerson. Malcolm Cowley (ed). Penguin 1981 $7.95. ISBN 0-14-015094-3

BOOKS ABOUT EMERSON

Allen, Gay Wilson. *Waldo Emerson.* Viking 1981 $10.95. ISBN 0-14-006278-5 The best recent biography of Emerson.

Konvitz, Milton, and Stephen Whicher (eds). *Emerson: A Collection of Critical Essays.* Greenwood 1978 $29.75. ISBN 0-313-20469-1 A varied collection of views on Emerson's work and thought.

Porte, Joel. *Emerson: Prospect and Retrospect.* Harvard Univ Pr 1982 $6.95. ISBN 0-674-24917-8 A standard study of Emerson's thought and its influence on writers and readers.

HOLMES, OLIVER WENDELL   1809–1894

Oliver Wendell Holmes was a man with enough energy and talent for several careers. Born in Cambridge, Massachusetts, into an upper-class family, Holmes graduated from Harvard University in 1829. He became a physician and later a professor of anatomy, first at Dartmouth College and later at Harvard.

While Holmes was still a medical student, he published the popular poem "Old Ironsides" (1830), and two essays together called "The Autocrat of the Breakfast Table." Until the late 1850s, however, he remained an amateur writer, composing only occasional pieces for the delight of his friends and colleagues.

Then, in 1857, when the magazine *Atlantic Monthly* was founded, Holmes became a regular contributor of poems and essays, and his fame spread beyond the Boston community. *The Autocrat of the Breakfast Table* (1858) was the first of several collections of his monthly humorous essays. *The Professor at the Breakfast Table* (1860), *The Poet at the Breakfast Table* (1872), and *Over the Teacups* (1891) were all in the same humorous vein.

Holmes's poems quickly became well-known favorites, particularly "The Chambered Nautilus" and "The Deacon's Masterpiece." In addition, Holmes wrote three so-called medicated novels, *Elsie Venner* (1861), *The Guardian Angel* (1867), and *A Mortal Antipathy* (1885), all exploring psychological and genetic determinism. He retired from Harvard in 1882, but continued to write occasional poems and essays for the rest of his life. When Holmes died in 1894, he had become virtually an American institution.

POETRY BY HOLMES

The Poetical Works of Oliver Wendell Holmes. Eleanor M. Tilton (ed). Houghton 1975. (o.p.) $12.50. ISBN 0-395-18497-5

COLLECTION BY HOLMES

The Autocrat of the Breakfast Table (1858). Airmont 1968 $1.95. ISBN 0-8049-0159-7

BOOKS ABOUT HOLMES

Small, Miriam R. *Oliver Wendell Holmes.* G. K. Hall 1962. (o.p.) A survey of critical views on Holmes that also includes a chronology of his life and a selected bibliography.

Tilton, Eleanor M. *Amiable Autocrat: A Biography of Doctor Oliver Wendell Holmes.* Octagon 1976 repr of 1947 ed. (o.p.) $27.50. The standard biography, focusing on Holmes's life and work.

IRVING, WASHINGTON   1783–1859

Washington Irving is best remembered today as the author of humorous tales of New York rural life, especially "Rip Van Winkle" and "The Legend of Sleepy Hollow." He was a prolific author and one of the first American writers to receive international praise. Born in New York City into a large and wealthy family, Irving trained for the law but soon turned to writing. By the time he was 20, he was a regular contributor of travel sketches and satirical pieces to newspapers. His *History of New York* (1809) combined history with satire to become one of the first major satirical works in American literature.

In 1815 Irving went to England to work with his brother in an export business. The business failed, but Irving's writing provided him with a good living. He remained in Europe for the next 17 years, living mostly in England and France, and traveling extensively in Germany. In England, Irving's graceful style was much admired, and his best-known work, *The Sketch Book* (1820), contains his essays and stories from this period. In addition to praises of the English countryside, *The Sketch Book* includes "Rip Van Winkle" and "The Legend of Sleepy Hollow," both Americanized versions of European legends.

Irving returned to the United States in 1832, where he wrote several accounts of travel in the American West. In the late 1830s, he bought a house in the vicinity of Tarrytown, New York, and settled down for a short time. This domestic period ended in 1842, when he was appointed Minister to Spain and moved to Madrid for four years. Irving's stay in Spain inspired several books on Spanish history and geography, most notably *The Alhambra* (1832). Irving was as popular in Spain as he had been in England, and his work is still enjoyed there today.

When he returned to New York, Irving worked on a number of ambitious projects, including a five-volume biography of George Washington, which was completed in the last year of his life. However, he never regained the fame he experienced after the publication of *The Sketch Book.*

STORIES AND ESSAY BY IRVING

*The Legend of Sleepy Hollow and Other Selections from Washington Irving. Airmont 1964 $1.95. ISBN 0-8049-0050-7 Contains most of Irving's best stories.
Selected Works of Washington Irving. William Kelly (ed). McGraw 1983 $7.50. ISBN 0-07-554394-X

BOOKS ABOUT IRVING

Bowden, Mary W. *Washington Irving.* G. K. Hall 1981 $16.95. ISBN 0-8057-7341-2 A good general introduction to Irving's life and work.
Warner, Charles D. *Washington Irving. American Men and Women of Letters Ser.* Chelsea 1981 $4.95. ISBN 0-87754-153-1 A readable biography.

LANIER, SIDNEY   1842–1881

One of the foremost poets of the nineteenth-century South, Sidney Lanier was born and raised in Macon, Georgia. At age 14, he entered Oglethorpe University, where he studied poetry and music. Shortly after his graduation, the Civil War broke out, and Lanier volunteered for the Confederate Army. He served for nearly four years. The last month of his service was spent in a Union prison camp, where he contracted the tuberculosis that would eventually kill him.

After the war, Lanier, weakened by his illness, worked for a while in his father's law office, but his true interests were in poetry and music. Finally, he moved to Baltimore, where he became first flautist with the Peabody Orchestra. He became nationally known for his poems, published widely in magazines and later collected in book form in 1877, and in 1879 he became a lecturer in English at Johns Hopkins University.

Lanier tried to create the same effects of sound and rhythm in poetry as in music. In the most successful of his poems, such as "The Marshes of Glynn" and "The Song of the Chattahoochee," he achieved the musical effects he sought. This noted poet was also a poetry critic, as well as the author of critical essays on various novels.

POETRY BY LANIER

Selected Poems (1947). AMS (repr of 1947 ed) $21.50. ISBN 0-404-20150-2

BOOK ABOUT LANIER

Gabin, Jane S. *A Living Minstrelsy: The Poetry and Music of Sidney Lanier.* Mercer Univ Pr 1985 $15.95. ISBN 0-86554-155-8 A readable biography that gives equal weight to Lanier's musical and poetic careers.

LONGFELLOW, HENRY WADSWORTH   1807–1882

Henry Wadsworth Longfellow was the most famous American poet of his time, and is arguably the best-known American poet in history. At the peak of his popularity, *The Courtship of Miles Standish* (1858) sold 15,000 copies on its first day of publication. Late in his life, Longfellow was given a private audience with the British queen, Victoria, and his seventy-fifth birthday was the occasion for a national celebration.

Longfellow was born in Portland, Maine, and educated at Bowdoin College, in the same class as novelist Nathaniel Hawthorne. (*See* Hawthorne, Vol. 1, American Literature: Romanticism and the American Renaissance.) He showed such proficiency at languages that he was offered a professorship at Bowdoin on the condition that he spend some time in Europe. In 1829, after three years of traveling, Longfellow settled down at Bowdoin. In 1831 he married, but his wife died during a second trip to Europe four years later. In 1836 Longfellow began a long and distinguished tenure as a professor of romance languages at Harvard University.

Longfellow's first significant prose work, *Outre-Mer: A Pilgrimage Beyond the Sea* (1833–1835), was similar to writer Washington Irving's *The Sketch Book.* (*See* Irving, Vol. 1, American Literature: Romanticism and the American Renaissance.) His first volume of poetry, *Voices of the Night,* appeared in 1839. This was followed in 1841 by *Ballads and Other Poems,* which contained "The Village Blacksmith," "The Wreck of the Hesperus," "Paul Revere's Ride," and other much-loved works. For the next 20 years, Longfellow produced a great outpouring of popular poetry. The greatest of his works—*Evangeline* (1847), *Hiawatha* (1855), and *The Courtship of Miles Standish*—sold thousands of copies each and established his worldwide reputation.

In 1861 Longfellow's second wife was burned to death while using wax to seal locks of her children's hair into an album; Longfellow never really recovered from her death. He temporarily stopped writing poetry and began a translation of Dante's *Divine Comedy.* This work was finally published between 1865 and 1867, along with six original sonnets ("Divina Commedia") as commentary. In his later years, Longfellow did return to writing poetry but wrote nothing to match his earlier work.

Longfellow has been compared with Washington Irving, in that both brought European forms and style to American subjects. *Hiawatha,* for example, is written in the meter of the Finnish national epic, the *Kalevala,* and *Evangeline* uses classical Greek meters. Longfellow's enormous popularity, though, was probably due to his cheerfulness, his humanity, and the elegant simplicity of his verse. Several generations of children grew up memorizing his poetry.

Poetry by Longfellow

The Poetical Works of Longfellow. Houghton 1975 $25.00. ISBN 0-395-18487-8

Books about Longfellow

Arvin, Newton. *Longfellow: His Life and Work.* Greenwood 1977 $65.00. ISBN 0-8371-9505-5 According to *Library Journal,* "A good study but a poor biography."

Wagenknecht, Edward. *Henry Wadsworth Longfellow: His Poetry and Prose.* Ungar 1986 $16.95. ISBN 0-8044-2960-X A critical and biographical study that reviews virtually everything that Longfellow ever wrote.

Williams, Cecil B. *Henry Wadsworth Longfellow.* New College & Univ Pr 1964 $10.95. ISBN 0-8084-01556-6 An overview of Longfellow's life and works; part of Twayne's U.S. Author series.

LOWELL, JAMES RUSSELL 1819–1891

James Russell Lowell's reputation rests solidly on three books published in one year, 1848, when he was 29 years old. The three were *A Fable for Critics,* which contains satirical portraits in verse of Lowell's contemporaries; *The Bigelow Papers,* a satire on the Mexican-American War; and *The Vision of Sir Launfel,* an Arthurian tale. The latter was immensely popular in its time and was a classroom staple for many years.

Lowell was born in Cambridge, Massachusetts, and, with the exception of some years spent abroad, lived most of his life there. After graduating from Harvard University, he studied law for a while, but his major interests were literary and political. An ardent abolitionist, he devoted his literary skills to antislavery causes. In 1855 he succeeded Henry Wadsworth Longfellow (*see* Longfellow, Vol. 1, American Literature: Romanticism and the American Renaissance) as professor of romance languages at Harvard, and for the next 20 years wrote mostly literary criticism. He was the first editor of the *Atlantic Monthly,* serving from 1857 to 1861. Lowell was at various times a poet, a radical political writer, a conservative political writer, a satirist, an editor, a critic, a diplomat, and a teacher. He was successful in all of these efforts. In 1877 he was appointed Minister to Spain, and in 1880 Minister to England. He returned to Cambridge in 1885, where he lived quietly until his death.

Lowell is best known today for the witty comic portraits of *A Fable for Critics.*

Poetry by Lowell

The Poetical Works of Lowell. Houghton 1978 $15.00. ISBN 0-395-25726-3

Books about Lowell

McGlinchee, Claire. *James Russell Lowell.* New College & Univ Pr 1967 $10.95. ISBN 0-8084-0173-4 A general overview of Lowell's life and works, useful to those approaching Lowell for the first time.

Wagenknecht, Edward C. *James Russell Lowell: Portrait of a Many Sided Man.* Oxford Univ Pr 1971 $19.95. ISBN 0-19-501376-X A readable and useful biography especially helpful to the general student.

MELVILLE, HERMAN 1819–1891

Herman Melville was a descendant of prominent Dutch and English families long established in New York. He was born in New York City and grew up without much formal schooling, going to sea at age 20, after the financial failure and subsequent death of his father. His experiences sailing the South Seas on various ships formed the basis of his best fiction. His first two books, *Typee* (1846) and *Omoo* (1847)—partly romance and partly autobiographical travel books—were popular successes, particularly *Typee,* whose hero spends time among cannibals and has a romance with a South Sea maiden.

Melville's great epic, *Moby-Dick,* began as an adventure story, based on Melville's experiences aboard a whaling ship. But the novel was also shaped by Melville's conversations with his friend and neighbor in Pittsfield, Massachusetts, writer Nathaniel Hawthorne (*see* Hawthorne, Vol. 1, American Literature: Romanticism and the American Renaissance), as well as by Melville's own irrepressible imagination. Gradually, *Moby-Dick* became a work so different from previous novels that when it appeared in print readers and critics alike were puzzled.

The central figure in *Moby-Dick* is Moby-Dick himself, the great white whale whom all whalers fear. This whale becomes the obsession of Captain Ahab, a sea captain who has already lost one leg to the monster, and who dreams of achieving revenge.

Critics have attached many meanings to the symbol of Moby-Dick. They have speculated that the white whale represents the ultimate truth of human existence, the mystery of nature, or the evil of a forbidding universe. Ahab's obsession with vengeance has been seen as a study in human psychology as well as an exploration of philosophy, religion, and metaphysics (studies of the nature of the universe). Perhaps the greatest triumph of *Moby-Dick* is that it can be read on both levels: as a gripping adventure story and as a philosophical exploration.

Melville's next novel, *Pierre, or the Ambiguities* (1852), was considered even more puzzling than Moby-Dick, and his reputation never really recovered. He spent the rest of his life taking whatever jobs he could find (for years he worked as a customs inspector in New York) and borrowing money from relatives in order to write.

Critics today prize Melville's subsequent work highly, including the marvelous short pieces, "Bartleby the Scrivener" (1853) and "Benito Cerino" (1855). "Bartleby" is the story of a clerk who one day simply says "I prefer not to," whenever he is asked to do anything. Once again, the tale may be read on many levels: as the pathetic story of a sad and lonely man, as a study in the brutality of capitalism and the anonymous cruelty of America's cities, as a metaphysical exploration of human freedom.

Melville's Civil War poetry is rivaled only by Walt Whitman's *Drum Taps.* (*See* Whitman, Vol. 1, American Literature: The Rise of Realism.) His posthumously published *Billy Budd* (1924) is a brilliant novella that seems to settle some of the philosophical questions that had bothered Melville throughout his life.

Melville's reputation, however, rests most solidly on *Moby-Dick.* It is a difficult as well as a brilliant book, and critics have offered various interpretations of its complicated and ambiguous symbolism. All agree, however, that it is one of the greatest American novels ever written.

SHORT STORY COLLECTION BY MELVILLE

The Piazza Tales and Other Prose Pieces, 1839–1860. Northwestern Univ Pr 1985 $21.95. ISBN 0-8101-0551-9

NOVELS BY MELVILLE

*Billy Budd, Sailor (1924). Univ of Chicago Pr 1962 $5.95. ISBN 0-226-32132-0 The troubles of an innocent young man in a cruel world.

The Confidence Man: His Masquerade (1857). NAL 1964 $4.95. ISBN 0-452-00894-8
*Moby-Dick, or The White Whale (1851). Norton 1967 $9.95. ISBN 0-393-09670-X Story
of the exciting hunt for a great white whale.
*Omoo: A Narrative of Adventures in the South Seas (1847). Hendricks 1969 $18.00. ISBN
0-87532-013-9 The sequel to Melville's novel *Typee.*
Pierre, or The Ambiguities (1852). Northwestern Univ Pr 1972 $13.95. ISBN 0-8101-
0267-6
*Redburn: His First Voyage (1849). Northwestern Univ Pr 1972 $12.95. ISBN 0-8101-
0016-9 A portrait of life on a merchant ship in the North Atlantic.
*Typee: A Peep at Polynesian Life (1846). NAL 1964 $3.50. ISBN 0-451-51854-3 A novel
based on Melville's experiences on the island of Typee.
*White-Jacket, or The World in a Man-of-War (1850). Northwestern Univ Pr 1970 $12.95.
ISBN 0-8101-0258-7 Condemnation of the harsh life on a naval vessel.

BOOKS ABOUT MELVILLE

Franklin, H. Bruce. *The Wake of the Gods: Melville's Mythology.* Stanford Univ Pr 1963
$16.95. ISBN 0-8047-0137-7 A reinterpretation of Melville's major works,
demonstrating how mythology determines large parts of their structure and
meaning.
Hillway, Tyrus. *Herman Melville.* G. K. Hall 1979 $15.95. ISBN 0-8057-7256-1 A com-
prehensive introduction to Melville's life and work.
Howard, Leon. *Herman Melville: A Biography.* Univ of California Pr 1981 $11.95. ISBN
0-520-00575-9 Still the standard biography of Melville since its original publication in 1951.
Levin, Harry. *The Power of Blackness: Hawthorne, Poe, Melville.* Ohio Univ Pr 1980 $6.95.
ISBN 0-8214-0581-0 A study putting Melville in the context of other major
writers of his time.

POE, EDGAR ALLAN   1809–1849

Edgar Allan Poe's melodramatic life is as well known as his work. The son of
itinerant, alcoholic actors, Poe was born in Boston, Massachusetts. His father
died the year after he was born, and his mother died a year later in Richmond,
Virginia, where she had taken the family. From abject poverty, Poe was raised
to riches when he was taken in and informally adopted by John Allan, a
wealthy Richmond merchant. He was educated in England and in Richmond,
but his comfortable adolescence was marred by repeated quarrels with his
guardian. He spent a year at the University of Virginia, but was forced to leave
when Allan refused to honor his gambling debts.

In 1827, after a final violent argument with Allan, Poe began his own
wanderings, going first to Boston, where he published *Tamerlane* (1827) anonymously and then joined the army. In 1830, after a brief reconciliation with
Allan, he was admitted to the U.S. Military Academy at West Point. He agreed
to go there only to please Allan, however, and when their relations collapsed
again, he stopped going to classes and was expelled.

Poe then moved to Baltimore to stay with his aunt, Maria Poe Clemm, and
her young daughter, Virginia. There he wrote a number of stories, which he
began to publish in magazines and newspapers. His "MS Found in a Bottle"
(1833) won a literary contest, which led to a job with the *Southern Literary
Messenger* in Richmond. Poe moved to Richmond in 1835 with Mrs. Clemm and
13-year-old Virginia, whom he married after she turned 14 in 1836.

Poe had had occasional problems with drinking earlier in his life, but the
problem grew worse in Richmond. Although he wrote numerous reviews,
essays, and stories for the *Messenger* and helped increase its circulation substantially, in 1837 he was fired for drinking.

Poe spent the next 12 years in New York and Philadelphia, doing hack writing and working as an editor of various literary magazines. He was also drinking a great deal. In 1839, Poe became co-editor of *Burton's Gentleman's Magazine,* to which he contributed a number of stories, including "The Fall of the House of Usher." A collection of his macabre stories, *Tales of the Grotesque and Arabesque,* appeared in 1839. In 1841 he became literary editor of *Graham's Magazine,* and in that year invented the modern detective story with the publication of his tale, "The Murders in the Rue Morgue."

In 1844, Poe moved to New York and in 1845 published "The Raven," his famous poem of the supernatural. The work was immensely popular, and Poe became a significant figure in literary New York. He soon became the principal reviewer and later the owner of the *Broadway Journal,* a new literary review. As a reviewer, Poe was skilled at attacking others; his biting style made him popular with readers but gained him many enemies in the literary community. Poe also published his own stories in the *Broadway Journal,* including "The Pit and the Pendulum" and "The Premature Burial."

Although it appeared that Poe's fortunes were finally changing, the combination of fame and drinking proved disastrous. When his wife Virginia died in 1847, his condition deteriorated further. In June of 1849, he returned to Richmond, joined a temperance (antidrinking) society, and became engaged to a woman he had known when he was a child. In the fall of 1849, on the way to Philadelphia, he stopped off in Baltimore and disappeared. He was discovered some days later, drunk in a gutter. After four days in a hospital, he died.

As a poet and story writer, Poe was concerned chiefly with effect. In poetry, this meant such melancholy subjects as the loss of a beautiful woman and an emphasis on sound and rhythm, sometimes at the expense of meaning. Poe's stories also aim to achieve a single, powerful effect of horror. There is a good deal of disagreement over the quality of Poe's work, but he has had a huge influence, especially on French and British writers of the late nineteenth century. His enduring popularity is further testament to his literary skill, and he has continued to be read and enjoyed by generations of children and adults.

POETRY AND STORIES BY POE

Great Short Works of Edgar Allan Poe. Harper 1970 $5.95. ISBN 0-06-083093-X
The Portable Poe. Penguin 1977 $8.95. ISBN 0-14-015012-9
The Selected Poetry and Prose. McGraw 1951 $5.50. ISBN 0-07-553641-2

BOOKS ABOUT POE

Buranelli, Vincent. *Edgar Allan Poe.* G. K. Hall 1977 $15.95. ISBN 0-8057-7089-1 A general study of Poe's life and works; gives an excellent overview of the range of contemporary critical opinion.

Levin, Harry. *The Power of Blackness: Hawthorne, Poe, Melville.* Ohio Univ Pr 1980 $6.95. ISBN 0-8214-0581-0 A key study putting Poe in the context of other major writers of his time in their concern with blackness as a metaphor for evil.

Regan, Robert (ed). *Poe: A Collection of Critical Essays.* Prentice 1967 $15.95. ISBN 0-13-684936-9 A collection of essays that examines Poe's art and sensibility from a variety of critical perspectives; useful and interesting to the general reader.

THOREAU, HENRY DAVID   1817–1862

Henry David Thoreau described himself as "a mystic, a transcendentalist, and a natural philosopher to boot." He wrote essays about his ideas and emotions in the presence of nature. His wish to understand nature led him to Walden

Pond, near Concord, Massachusetts, where he lived from 1845 to 1847 in a cabin he built himself. His label of "transcendentalist" refers to a movement of writers and philosophers of the time, who believed they could *transcend,* or get past, human limits by perceiving God's presence in nature.

Thoreau was born in Concord, Massachusetts, and educated at Harvard University. After he graduated in 1837, he taught at a grammar school with his brother John for several years. After the school was closed in 1841, Thoreau began a life of apparent aimlessness but of great inner purpose. He lived in the Ralph Waldo Emerson (*see* Emerson, Vol. 1, American Literature: Romanticism and the American Renaissance) household for a while, acting as a general handyman while he studied philosophy. Then he began his two-year stay at Walden Pond. Throughout this period and for the rest of his life, Thoreau kept a journal (published in 14 volumes in 1906), which served as the source for his published writings.

Thoreau's first book, *A Week on the Concord and Merrimack Rivers* (1849), described a trip he and his brother had taken some years before. *Walden,* a record of his thoughts while living at Walden Pond, appeared in 1854. Several other books based on his travels, notably *The Maine Woods* (1864) and *Cape Cod* (1865), were published after his death.

Thoreau was an early proponent of nonviolent resistance. He was jailed briefly for refusing to pay a tax that supported the Mexican War. His essay "On Civil Disobedience" was acknowledged by Indian leader "Mahatma" Gandhi (*see* Gandhi, Vol. 2, World History: Imperialism in Africa and Asia), who read it in a South African jail, as the basis for his passive-resistance campaign to free India. The great American civil rights leader Martin Luther King, Jr., was also highly influenced by Thoreau's essay.

When Thoreau died in 1862, he was little known beyond a small circle of friends and admirers. Emerson lamented that "the country knows not yet, nor in the least part, how great a son it has lost." In this century, though, and especially in recent years, Thoreau has been recognized as perhaps the most original thinker of the transcendental group and one of the key figures of American Romantic literature.

NONFICTION BY THOREAU

Cape Cod (1865). Penguin 1987 $6.95. ISBN 0-14-017002-2
The Maine Woods (1864). Penguin 1988 $7.95. ISBN 0-14-017013-8
The Portable Thoreau. Penguin 1977 $8.95. ISBN 0-14-015031-5 Contains *Walden,* the essay "Civil Disobedience," and various other works, including selected poems.
Walden and Civil Disobedience. NAL 1973 $2.95. ISBN 0-14-039044-8

BOOKS ABOUT THOREAU

Krutch, Joseph Wood. *Henry David Thoreau.* Greenwood 1976 $22.50. ISBN 0-8371-6587-3. According to the *New Yorker* magazine, "A nearly perfect fusing of biography and critical study."
Richardson, Robert D. *Henry David Thoreau: A Life of the Mind.* Univ of California Pr 1986 $25.00. ISBN 0-520-05495-4 The best recent biography and critical study of Thoreau.

WHITTIER, JOHN GREENLEAF 1807–1892

John Greenleaf Whittier was a Poet and a Friend, or Quaker—member of a religion that does not believe in war. Thus he became known as the "man of peace and the poet militant." He said of himself that he "set a higher value on his name as appended to the Anti-Slavery Declaration in 1833 than on the title page of any book." His "Voices of Freedom," written to help end slavery, had a tremendous influence on the public.

Born in Massachusetts, Whittier's early career was closely allied with the abolitionist movement. For over 30 years, he wrote for a variety of abolitionist newspapers and worked actively for the antislavery cause. He was elected to the Massachusetts legislature in 1835 and was one of the founders of the Liberal Party. He also wrote poetry during this period. Most of it had political themes, but he also wrote New England nature poetry for which he would be later remembered.

After the Civil War ended slavery, Whittier focused more on lyric poetry. His greatest poem, *Snow-Bound: A Winter Idyll* (1866), depicts rural life on a family farm. He continues to be best known for his later poetry—"good Yankee rhymes," as he called them, characterized by simple sentiment and strong moral content.

POETRY BY WHITTIER

The Poetical Works of Whittier. Hyatt H. Waggoner (ed). Houghton 1975 $29.95. ISBN 0-395-21599-4

BOOK ABOUT WHITTIER

Leary, Lewis. *John Greenleaf Whittier.* New College & Univ Pr 1961 $5.95. ISBN 0-8084-0183-1 A good general study and critique of Whittier the man—as village poet, spokesman of freedom, and voice of New England—and of Whittier the poet—his use of words, his vision of beauty, and his concern with the past.

THE RISE OF REALISM

From 1861 to 1865, the United States was torn by civil war. This conflict brought suffering to virtually every family in the country and captured the attention of all of Europe. It was beyond question the most important event in the history of the nation so far. Yet the only literature to come out of the war, except for some poetry by Walt Whitman and Herman Melville, was either journalistic descriptions of battles or personal accounts of war experiences by amateur writers. The one great American novel based on the war, *The Red Badge of Courage* by Stephen Crane, was not published until 1895, and was written by a man who was not even born until after the war ended.

One reason writers seemingly ignored this momentous event was that the romantic concept of literature had no room for the horrible realities of such a war. The romantic novel was based on tales of daring exploits, brave deeds, and idealistic heroes. Somehow it did not fit the actual horrors of this bloody conflict.

In Europe, however, writers were experimenting with a new kind of novel, one that tried to describe life as it is rather than as it ought to be. These so-called realists were intent on recording the minute details of day-to-day living in an attempt to create genuine characters in authentic situations.

In the years after the Civil War, increasing numbers of American writers were drawn to this new realistic approach to literature. The romantic concept did not end, however. Throughout the remainder of the century, as the realistic movement grew, the romantic tradition remained strong, too. Frequently elements of both schools can be found in the same work.

One aspect of realism that was particularly important in American literature of this period was regionalism, or "local color." Writers such as Sarah Orne Jewett and Bret Harte looked closely at the speech and habits of the people around them and tried to capture them in writing. Likewise, Mark Twain's fiction portrayed the language and manners of people living along the Mississippi River, sometimes in stinging critiques of their shallowness and hypocrisy.

In their quest to present life as it really is, writers began to explore topics that had previously been considered "improper" subjects for fiction. Stephen Crane wrote *Maggie: A Girl of the Streets* (1893), which looks at the life of a girl who is physically abused by her drunken father and eventually driven to prostitution and suicide. Charles W. Chesnutt became the first important writer to look honestly at the interracial hostility of the post-Civil War South. In *The Awakening* (1899), Kate Chopin dealt candidly with female sexuality and the constraints of marriage.

Ambrose Bierce and Stephen Crane both looked back on the Civil War with horror and bitterness. Bierce, who had served in the war, wrote a number of violent and grisly stories of soldiers in combat, none of which even hints at heroism or glory. In *The Red Badge of Courage* and in his poetry, Crane portrayed war as both a testing ground for young men and a senseless machine for destroying them.

The growing interest in psychology and human behavior at the end of the nineteenth century prompted writers like Henry James and Edith Wharton to extend realism to the exploration of characters' minds. They concentrated on questions of human motivation, asking what makes people behave as they do, and so anticipated much of twentieth-century literature.

ALCOTT, LOUISA MAY   1832–1888

One of four daughters of transcendentalist Amos Bronson Alcott, Louisa May Alcott was born in Pennsylvania but grew up in Boston and Concord, Massachusetts. She was educated by her father, and had frequent contact with his literary friends, such as Ralph Waldo Emerson, Henry David Thoreau, and other members of the transcendentalist circle. (*See* Emerson *and* Thoreau, Vol. 1, American Literature: Romanticism and the American Renaissance.) The transcendentalists were a group of writers and philosophers who believed they could perceive evidence of God in nature, *transcending* or going beyond their human limitations. Her father's eccentric ideas and nonmaterialistic way of life often led to hard times for his family. As a result, Louisa May and her sisters worked at a variety of tasks from an early age in order to help economically provide for the family. Alcott's dream was to support the family by writing. To this end she wrote her first book at age 16, and published stories and sketches in the *Atlantic Monthly* and other periodicals. Her dream was finally achieved in 1868, when she published the novel *Little Women,* which was enormously popular and quickly became an American classic. *Little Men,* another charming children's novel, was published in 1871. Alcott was a prolific writer and wrote a great many other novels and stories, most of them for children, but none were as memorable as her "little" novels for which she is still honored today.

NOVELS BY ALCOTT

Behind A Mask: The Unknown Thrillers of Louisa May Alcott. Marion Stern (ed). Amereon $19.95. ISBN 0-88411-096-6 Eerie and blood-curdling tales of a mansion encircled by screaming peacocks and a female Dr. Jekyll and Mr. Hyde.

A Double Life: Newly Discovered Thrillers of Louisa May Alcott. Madeline Stern, *et al* (eds). Little 1988 $17.95. ISBN 0-316-03101-1 More scary stories and tales of horror.

Eight Cousins, or The Aunt Hill (1875). Penguin 1989 $2.95. ISBN 0-14-035112-4 The adventures and misadventures of Rose and her seven cousins.

Jo's Boys (1886). Signet 1987 $2.25. ISBN 0-451-52089-0 The story of Jo's sons 10 years after *Little Men.*

Little Men (1871). NAL 1986 $3.50. ISBN 0-451-52275-3 The little women are now grown up, and one of them runs a boys' school full of "little men."

Little Women (1868). NAL 1983 $3.95. ISBN 0-451-52341-5 Alcott's classic story of four girls growing up around the time of the Civil War.

BOOKS ABOUT ALCOTT

*Burke, Kathleen. *Louisa May Alcott.* Chelsea 1988 $16.95. ISBN 1-55546-637-0 A readable biography for grades 6–10; illustrated with historical prints.

*Greene, Carol. *Louisa May Alcott: Author, Nurse, Suffragette.* Childrens 1984 $15.85. ISBN 0-516-03208-9 A biography of Alcott written especially for young people.

ALGER, HORATIO, JR. 1834–1899

Horatio Alger's name has come to symbolize the rags to riches story. Born in Boston and raised in a strict Puritan household, Alger attended Harvard University and Harvard Divinity School. After spending some years in Europe, traveling and living a somewhat bohemian life, he returned to the United States, converted to Unitarianism, and was ordained a Unitarian minister in 1864.

Two years later, Alger moved to New York City to begin his literary career. He lived in the Newsboys Lodging House, which he later helped to support, and began the series of children's novels that would prove so tremendously popular. *Ragged Dick* was published in 1867, followed by over 100 other novels,

Snap the Whip. Painting by Winslow Homer (1872). Courtesy of The Metropolitan Museum of Art, Gift of Christian A. Zabriskie, 1950. (50.41)

including the famous *Luck and Pluck* (1869) and *Tattered Tom* (1871). The Alger formula was always the same: a poor but moral young man struggles against poverty and temptation but finally wins the gratitude of a wealthy benefactor, who rewards him with wealth and a good job.

Alger helped to define his time's worship of success, an attitude from which he himself benefited a great deal. Over 20 million copies of his books were published, and his rags-to-riches dream was shared by generations of Americans. Today few people read his works, but his name and his ideas have remained a part of the public consciousness.

NOVELS BY ALGER

Ragged Dick and Struggling Upward (1867, 1890). Penguin 1985 $4.95. ISBN 0-14-039033-2
 Two novels of young boys and their rise to success.
Tom, the Bootblack (1880). Amereon 1976 $17.95. ISBN 0-88411-812-6 Story of Tom's
 climb from shining shoes to riches.

SHORT STORY COLLECTION BY ALGER

*The Lost Tales of Horatio Alger. Acadia 1990 $21.95. ISBN 0-934745-11-0 The best of
 Alger's early tales featuring adventure, romance, and intrigue.

BOOK ABOUT ALGER

Hoyt, Edwin P. *Horatio's Boys: The Life and Works of Horatio Alger, Jr.* Scarborough 1974
 $8.95. ISBN 0-8128-6197-3

BIERCE, AMBROSE GWINNETT 1842–1914?

Ambrose Bierce was a brilliant, bitter, and cynical journalist. He is also the author of several collections of ironic epigrams and at least one powerful story, "An Occurrence at Owl Creek Bridge."

Bierce was born in Ohio, where he had an unhappy childhood. He served in the Union army during the Civil War. Following the war, he moved to San Francisco, where he worked as a columnist for the newspaper the *Examiner,* for which he wrote bitter satirical sketches.

Bierce wrote a number of horror stories, some poetry, and countless essays. He is best known, however, for *The Cynic's Word Book* (1906), retitled *The Devil's Dictionary* in 1911, a collection of such cynical definitions as "Marriage: the state or condition of a community consisting of a master, a mistress, and two slaves, making in all, two." Bierce's own marriage ended in divorce, and his life ended mysteriously. In 1913, he went to Mexico and vanished, presumably killed in the Mexican revolution.

BOOKS BY BIERCE

The Complete Short Stories of Ambrose Bierce. Ernest J. Hopkins (ed). Univ of Nebraska Pr
 1984 $10.95. ISBN 0-8032-6071-1
The Devil's Dictionary (The Cynic's Word Book) (1906). Dover $2.95. ISBN 0-486-20487-1
In the Most of Life (1896). Carol 1977 $2.95. ISBN 0-8065-0551-6

BOOK ABOUT BIERCE

Gaer, Joseph (ed). *Ambrose Gwinnett Bierce: A Bibliography and Biographical Data.* Burt Franklin 1935 $18.50. ISBN 0-8337-1253-5 A useful list of sources for the serious
 scholar of Bierce.

BROWN, WILLIAM WELLS *c.* 1816–1884

Born near Lexington, Kentucky, to a slaveholder father and a slave mother, William Wells Brown worked as a slave on the riverboats in St. Louis. At age 19, he leaped from a boat to freedom in Cincinnati. On his way to Canada, he was helped by Ohio Quaker Wells Brown, whose name the young fugitive took as his own. Over the course of his life, Brown was a handyman, steamboat steward, barber, banker, and doctor. He married Elizabeth Schooner, a Cleveland freewoman, with whom he had three daughters.

Having been denied formal education by his father, Brown taught himself and went on to become America's first black man of letters. In 1847, he published *The Narrative of William W. Brown, A Fugitive Slave,* which he followed in 1848 with a collection of song-poems, *The Antislavery Harp.* His vivid writing and antislavery lectures brought an invitation from French novelist Victor Hugo (*see* Hugo, Vol. 1, World Literature: French Language and Literature) to address the Paris Peace Congress of 1849. Brown was commissioned by the American Peace Society as their official delegate.

Brown stayed in Europe until 1854, where he studied medicine while continuing to write. In England he published the first novel by an African American, *Clotel: or, The President's Daughter* (1853), a fictional representation of one of Thomas Jefferson's slave children. He also published a travel book, *Three Years in Europe* (1852). Brown's other literary "firsts" included a play, *The Escape, or A Leap for Freedom* (1858); a history, *The Negro in the American Rebellion: His Heroism and Fidelity* (1867); and a memoir, *My Southern Home: The South and Its People* (1880). His literary accomplishments grew over the years, and this last book enjoyed a wide audience and considerable critical praise. In all, Brown published 11 major works, including two substantially revised editions of *Clotel* (1864, 1867).

NOVEL BY BROWN

Clotel: or, The President's Daughter (1853). Ayer (repr of 1953 ed) $21.00. ISBN 0-405-01853-3

NONFICTION BY BROWN

My Southern Home: The South and Its People (1880). Irvington 1989 $29.95. ISBN 0-83938-0177-7

The Negro in the American Rebellion: His Heroism and His Fidelity (1867). Carol 1971 $3.95. ISBN 0-8065-0238-X

The Rising Son (1873). Johnson Repr 1970 repr of 1873 ed $26.00. ISBN 0-384-059953-3

Sketches of Places and People Abroad (1855). Ayer 1977 $17.00. ISBN 0-8369-8705-5

BOOKS ABOUT BROWN

Farrison, William E. *William Wells Brown: Author and Reformer.* Univ of Chicago Pr 1969 $25.00. ISBN 0-226-23897-0 Excellent, well-documented biography of Brown concentrating on his rise as a novelist and how he used his reputation to win reforms for black people.

Heermance, J. Noel. *William Wells Brown and Clotel: A Portrait of the Artist in the First Negro Novel.* Shoe String 1969 $16.50. ISBN 0-208-00942-6 An examination of Brown that uses his first novel to illuminate his life.

Katz, William L. *Five Slave Narratives: A Compendium.* Ayer 1970 $20.00. ISBN 0-405-01823-1 Contains Brown's autobiography, *The Narrative of William W. Brown, a Fugitive Slave.*

CABLE, GEORGE WASHINGTON 1844–1924

George Washington Cable was born and raised in New Orleans. After serving in the Confederate army and working as a warehouse clerk, he started writing "local color" stories, which he published in New Orleans newspapers. His first collection, *Old Creole Days,* was published in 1879, and his most successful novel, *The Grandissimes,* was published a year later. (*Creole* refers to descendants of French or Spanish settlers in Louisiana.)

Cable was greatly attracted to certain aspects of Creole life, which he hoped to record before it disappeared. As time went on, though, he began to speak out against racial injustices in Louisiana and in the South in general, especially supporting prison reform and increased rights for African Americans. This brought a great deal of bitter criticism from fellow southerners and ultimately resulted in Cable moving north to Massachusetts. Cable continued to write until 1918, becoming a leader of the local color movement and preserving a part of American life in the South. However, his work is little read today.

Novel by Cable

The Grandissimes (1880). Penguin 1988 $5.95. ISBN 0-14-043322-8

Short Story Collections by Cable

Creoles and Cajuns: Stories of Old Louisiana. Arlin Turner (ed). Peter Smith 1959. (o.p.)
Old Creole Days (1879). Signet 1989 $3.95. ISBN 0-451-52349-0

Book about Cable

Butcher, Philip. *George W. Cable.* New College & Univ Pr 1962 $10.95. ISBN 0-8084-0143-2 Surveys Cable's life and work; gives a useful general overview for the beginning student.

CHESNUTT, CHARLES W. (WADDELL) 1858–1932

Charles W. Chesnutt was born in 1858 to free African Americans in Cleveland, Ohio. His parents had recently moved north from North Carolina to escape the repression of free African Americans that had increased in the years before the Civil War, as laws and customs increasingly restricted the rights of free black citizens. When the war ended, the family returned to North Carolina where Chesnutt resumed his education, which included the study of French, German, and Greek. Chesnutt began teaching at a very young age, and by the time he was 22, he was the head of a teacher training institute in Fayetteville, North Carolina. Becoming restless and feeling the urge to write, he moved, first to New York where he worked as a reporter, then back to Cleveland, where he would remain for the rest of his life.

Chesnutt first gained national attention in 1887 with the publication of one of his stories in the *Atlantic Monthly* magazine. For several more years, he continued to publish stories in major national magazines, but they did not appear in book form until 1899. He also gained fame for his novels, which dealt with black-white writer relations in the South.

Chesnutt was the first important black writer to present the conditions of slaves and the institution of slavery honestly. He was also the first to address the question of racial snobbery *among* African Americans, whose prejudice was based on skin tone and bloodlines. He was particularly interested in the problems and stresses confronting those who were virtually "white" in color while still considering themselves African American, since he himself was part of that group. His basic concern was with the injustice of the American caste system, which he saw as an obstacle to the moral development of all Americans.

Critics today find Chesnutt's work a fascinating exploration of the African-American experience, although by modern standards his style is somewhat sentimental.

NOVELS BY CHESNUTT

The Colonel's Dream (1905). Irvington (repr of 1905 ed) $16.00. ISBN 0-8398-0257-9
   Story of a white southern aristocrat who tries unsuccessfully to change the unfair systems of the South.
The House Behind the Cedars (1900). Univ of Georgia Pr 1988 $12.95. ISBN 0-8203-1021-2
   A tale of African Americans attempting to "pass" in Southern white society.
The Marrow of Tradition (1901). Univ of Michigan Pr 1969 $9.95. ISBN 0-472-06147-X
   The story of a black physician who hopes for interracial cooperation as he sets up a practice in the South.

SHORT STORY COLLECTIONS BY CHESNUTT

The Conjure Woman (1899). Univ of Michigan Pr 1969 $9.95. ISBN 0-472-06156-9 Tales of magic told by an old slave.
The Wife of His Youth (1899). Univ of Michigan Pr 1968 $9.95. ISBN 0-472-06134-8 Nine stories focusing on racial prejudice.

BOOK ABOUT CHESNUTT

Heermance, Noel. *Charles W. Chesnutt: America's First Great Black Novelist.* Shoe String 1974 $25.00. ISBN 0-208-01380-6 A comprehensive study of Chesnutt's life and work.

CHOPIN, KATE   1851–1904

Kate Chopin was born Katherine O'Flaherty in St. Louis, Missouri. Her father was an Irish immigrant and a successful businessman, and her mother was of French-Creole background and prominent in St. Louis society. Chopin was educated in Catholic schools in St. Louis. When she was still a young child, her father was killed in a railroad accident and, as a result, she grew very close to her mother. At this time, she also began to read widely.

Shortly after graduating from school, she met and married Oscar Chopin, son of a French-Creole plantation owner in Louisiana. The couple moved to New Orleans, where Chopin took on the role of a socially active housewife. After the death of her husband in 1883, she returned to St. Louis and began to write.

Chopin's stories are mostly "local color" pieces set among the Creoles and Cajuns of Louisiana. Her first novel, *At Fault* (1890), explores the stresses and tensions within a marriage. Chopin expanded this theme in her most famous novel, *The Awakening* (1899), which deals with a married woman who discovers the need for her own identity, and as a result, abandons her marriage and family to pursue her art. The book provoked an outcry from critics, who considered it immoral, and it was banned in Chopin's hometown of St. Louis. Angered and hurt by this reception, she never wrote again.

Today, Chopin is regarded as among the most important women in nineteenth-century American fiction and a significant figure in American feminist literature.

NOVEL AND STORIES BY CHOPIN

*The Awakening and Selected Stories. Bantam 1985 $3.95. ISBN 0-553-21330-X A novel of a woman's search for fulfillment and stories of the Louisiana bayou.

BOOKS ABOUT CHOPIN

Ewell, Barbara C. *Kate Chopin.* Ungar 1986 $16.95. ISBN 0-8044-2190-0 A useful general study of Chopin's life and works.

Skaggs, Peggy. *Kate Chopin.* G. K. Hall 1985 $16.95. ISBN 0-8057-7439-4 Another good general introduction to Chopin's life and works.

Toth, Emily. *Kate Chopin.* Morrow 1990 $27.95. ISBN 0-688-09707-3 Well-researched biography that succeeds in placing Chopin's life in its familial, cultural, and professional backgrounds.

CRANE, STEPHEN 1871–1900

Although he died of tuberculosis before he was 30 years old, Stephen Crane managed to combine an outstanding literary career with an adventurous life. He was born in New Jersey into a large and devout Catholic family. He attended Syracuse University for a year before beginning a career as a journalist in New York City.

No publisher would accept Crane's first book, *Maggie: A Girl of the Streets,* so he published it himself in 1893. So few copies were bought that it is now one of the most valued of rare books.

His second novel, *The Red Badge of Courage* (1895), was a different matter. It was well received by both readers and critics, and as a result Crane's career began in earnest. He had never seen war, but his portrait of young Civil War soldier Henry Fleming under fire rang so true that newspaper syndicates hired him to cover real wars. Thus Crane lived the life of a wandering journalist for virtually the rest of his life.

In late 1896, Crane was covering a gun-running expedition to Cuba when his ship, *The Commodore,* sank. He turned his ordeal in the lifeboat into a story, which portrayed a group of men in similarly harsh circumstances. "The Open Boat" became his most successful story.

While Crane was in Florida at this time, he met Cora Howarth Taylor, with whom he lived for the rest of his brief life.

In the summer of 1897, Crane went to England, where he became friends with such other writers as Henry James (*see* James, Vol. 1, American Literature: The Rise of Realism) and Joseph Conrad (*see* Conrad, Vol. 1, British Literature: The Twentieth Century). He covered the Greco-Turkish War and the Spanish-American War, but his health was poor and his financial situation increasingly desperate. Months before his death, he wrote *The Whilomville Stories* and published his second book of poetry, *War Is Kind.* His poems—brief, ironic, reflecting on the nature of the universe—were totally unlike the work of his contemporaries and have only recently been fully appreciated.

POETRY AND PROSE COLLECTION BY CRANE

Prose and Poetry. J. C. Levenson (ed). Lib of America 1984 $27.50. ISBN 0-940450-17-8

NOVELS BY CRANE

Maggie: A Girl of the Streets (1893). Bantam 1986 $3.50. ISBN 0-553-21355-5

The Red Badge of Courage and Other Writings (1895). Richard Chase (ed). Houghton 1960 $8.95. ISBN 0-395-05143-6

BOOKS ABOUT CRANE

Bassan, M. (ed). *Stephen Crane: A Collection of Critical Essays.* Prentice 1967 $12.95. ISBN 0-13-188888-9 Good representative collection of views on Crane's work.

Berryman, John. *Stephen Crane: A Critical Biography* (1950). Farrar 1982 $9.25. ISBN 0-374-51732-0 Good critical biography of Crane with a strong psychological slant.

Hoffman, Daniel G. *Poetry of Stephen Crane.* Columbia Univ Pr 1957 $15.00. ISBN 0-231-08662-8 The best available study of Crane's poetry.

DICKINSON, EMILY   1830–1886

One of the greatest American poets, Emily Elizabeth Dickinson was born in Amherst, Massachusetts, on December 10, 1830, and died 56 years later in the same house in which she was born. She seldom traveled, leaving her state only once in her life time, and her village only a few times. She was educated at Amherst Academy and Mount Holyoke Female Seminary, but most of her education came from her own reading of the Bible, Shakespeare, and contemporary British authors. Although in her youth Dickinson was a sociable, outgoing person, she withdrew from society later in her life, spending most of her time reading, writing, and gardening.

Critics have speculated a great deal on the reasons for Dickinson's withdrawal. Some believe she was in love with a man she could never marry, Charles Wadsworth, the married pastor of Arch Street Presbyterian Church in Philadelphia. In 1861, Wadsworth was assigned to San Francisco, and his leaving seems to have caused a crisis for Dickinson. Whether her feelings for Wadsworth were romantic or platonic, he had clearly been very important to her as someone who could understand her difficult, philosophical poetry and who could support her writing ambitions. Dickinson withdrew from the world outside her family about the time that Wadsworth left.

Other critics have seen Dickinson's withdrawal less as a reaction to a man or a love affair than as a woman's attempt to recreate herself as a serious, ambitious writer at a time when such a role was almost unknown for women. These critics point to Dickinson's persistent metaphor of herself as Jacob wrestling with the angel for a new identity. They suggest that Dickinson's seclusion was a way of avoiding traditional female roles—wife, mother, helper, "good neighbor"—so that she would be free the explore her genius and push herself to the outermost limits of her abilities as a poet. To these critics, Dickinson's secluded life was happy and rich, allowing her the freedom to realize her enormous potential.

Dickinson was an enormously prolific author. Her poems are short, but her output was immense—a total of 1,775 poems. Of these, only seven were published in her lifetime. The first collection of her verse appeared in 1890, but early editions of her poetry tended to smooth out their intentionally difficult style, emphasizing sentimental attitudes and hiding her dark wit. Nevertheless, she was recognized as a poet of top rank. Finally, in 1955, her complete poems were made available, and her genius became fully apparent.

For a while, it seems that Dickinson hoped for some kind of public recognition of her art. Around the time that Wadsworth was getting ready to move, she began a correspondence with Thomas Wentworth Higginson, editor of the prestigious *Atlantic Monthly* magazine and as such, supporter of many young poets. Although Higginson was kind to Dickinson in their correspondence, he could not imagine an audience for her unconventional work. Dickinson, however, continued to pursue her unique style, despite the lack of any outside encouragement.

Dickinson's poems sometimes seem to be written in a mysterious code. They usually begin with a metaphor—an image that represents another idea—and go on to explore the comparison. For example, the poem beginning "I taste a liquor never brewed" elaborates the metaphor of drunkenness to suggest the poet's wonder at the mystery of life.

In rhythm and form, Dickinson's poems are irregular. Their natural rhythm is often interrupted by dashes. Dickinson wrote about nature, love, loneliness, and death, and her profound doubts about the nature of these concepts are apparent in many of her poems. In the words of critic Josephine Pollitt, Dickinson's work illustrates "her insurgent imagination, her unconventional use of rhyme, her audacious experimentation with form and assonance."

POETRY BY DICKINSON

The Complete Poems of Emily Dickinson. Thomas H. Johnson (ed). Little 1960 $11.95. ISBN 0-316-18413-6

Final Harvest: Emily Dickinson's Poems. Thomas H. Johnson (ed). Little 1962 $9.95. ISBN 0-316-18415-2

BOOKS ABOUT DICKINSON

Anderson, Charles R. *Emily Dickinson's Poetry: Stairway of Surprise.* Greenwood 1982 $47.50. ISBN 0-313-23733-6 A comprehensive study of Dickinson's poetry, penetrating and discriminating; with 25 major poems selected for line-by-line analysis.

Ferlazzo, Paul J. *Emily Dickinson.* G. K. Hall 1988 $15.95. ISBN 0-8075-7180-8 A good introduction to Dickinson's life and poetry.

Johnson, Thomas H. *Emily Dickinson: An Interpretive Biography.* Atheneum 1967 $9.95. ISBN 0-689-70113-6 Reliable, scholarly, and fascinating biography by Dickinson's major editor.

*Olsen, Victoria. *Emily Dickinson.* Chelsea 1990 $17.95. ISBN 1-55546-649-4 An illustrated biography of Dickinson; well-suited to younger readers.

DUNBAR, PAUL LAURENCE   1872–1906

Paul Laurence Dunbar was born in Dayton, Ohio, the son of former slaves. After high school, where he was president of the literary society and class poet, he worked as an elevator operator and wrote poetry in his spare time.

In 1893, Dunbar published his first book of poetry, *Oak and Ivy,* which was a critical success. In 1896, his volume *Lyrics of Lowly Life* was published with a foreword by the age's major critic, William Dean Howells, who said that Dunbar was the first poet to "feel the Negro [sic] life aesthetically and express it lyrically."

For the next 10 years, Dunbar made his living as a literary individual, writing books—four novels in addition to his poetry—and giving lectures and public readings. Although best known for his dialect poems, he also wrote poems in a more formal style. His aim, he wrote, was to "be able to interpret my own people through song and story. . . ." He died in 1906 of tuberculosis.

POETRY BY DUNBAR

*Complete Poems. Dodd 1980 $5.95. ISBN 0-396-07895-8 Dunbar's poems of African-American life, including his four major volumes: *Lyrics of Lowly Life, Lyrics of the Hearthside, Lyrics of Sunshine,* and *Shadow.*

BOOKS ABOUT DUNBAR

*Gentry, Tony. *Paul Laurence Dunbar.* Chelsea 1988 $16.95. ISBN 1-55546-583-8 An informative chronicle of Dunbar's life and works and a good introduction for students grade 6 and up.

Lawson, V. *Paul Laurence Dunbar Critically Examined.* Gordon Pr 1941 $59.95. ISBN
  0-8490-0808-5 Interesting, scholarly review of Dunbar's works.
*McKissack, Patricia. *Paul Laurence Dunbar: A Poet to Remember.* Childrens 1984 $15.93.
  ISBN 0-516-03209-7 Good introduction to Dunbar and his work at a reading level
  of grades 6–12.

HARTE, BRET (FRANCIS BRETT)   1836–1902

Bret Harte, who became famous for his "local color" stories of California, was
born and raised in Albany, New York, the son of a schoolteacher who died
when Harte was nine. Harte first went to California in 1854, and lived in
Oakland with his mother and stepfather. When he was 21, he set off on his
own, traveling through northern California and working at a variety of jobs,
including panning for gold and riding shotgun for the Wells Fargo stagecoach
company.

In 1860 in San Francisco, Harte began working as a printer for a newspaper, the *Golden Era,* to which he was soon contributing stories. In 1868, he
became the editor of the *Overland Monthly,* the magazine in which he published his most memorable stories, including "The Luck of Roaring Camp"
and "The Outcasts of Poker Flat" (1869). In 1871, at the peak of his fame,
Harte left San Francisco for the East Coast, where he was offered $10,000 by
the publisher of the *Atlantic Monthly* for 12 sketches. Unfortunately, he was
unable to write anything approaching the quality of his earlier work, and his
reputation began to decline.

Harte spent the last years of his life abroad, first as U.S. Consul in Prussia
(a region of Germany) and Scotland, and later in England as a writer for British
magazines. Although he wrote prolifically during this period, he never rose
above pale imitations of his earlier work. His lack of popularity in the United
States reflected that fact.

At their best, Harte's stories caught the flavor of California life during its
most exciting period. However, unlike Mark Twain (*see* Twain, Vol. 1, American Literature: The Rise of Realism), with whom he is often compared, Harte
seldom wrote more than simple "local color" sketches.

SHORT STORY COLLECTION BY HARTE

The Outcasts of Poker Flat and Other Stories. Signet 1961 $4.95. ISBN 0-451-52346-6

BOOK ABOUT HARTE

Duckett, Margaret. *Mark Twain and Bret Harte.* Univ of Oklahoma Pr 1964. (o.p.) A
  useful study of Twain and Harte, two men whose careers are often compared.

HAWTHORNE, NATHANIEL   1804–1864

Nathaniel Hawthorne was born on July 4, 1804, in Salem, Massachusetts, into
an old Puritan family. One of his ancestors had been a judge in the Salem witch
trials, a fact that haunted Hawthorne in later life. Hawthorne was educated at
Bowdoin College. One of his classmates there, Franklin Pierce, later became
President of the United States—and Hawthorne's lifelong friend. Also in this
class was poet Henry Wadsworth Longfellow. (*See* Longfellow, Vol. 1, American Literature: Romanticism and the American Renaissance.)

Hawthorne never wanted to be anything but a writer. For 12 years after
graduating from college, he stayed at home, reading and writing. During this

period, he wrote some of his finest tales, as well as the historical novel *Fanshawe* (1828). Despite his efforts, Hawthorne had little success. Most of his publications were anonymous ones in magazines and holiday annuals.

However, in 1837, with the publication of *Twice-Told Tales,* his fortunes changed. *Twice-Told Tales* included such early stories as "The Maypole at Marymount" and "The Minister's Black Veil." The book was widely reviewed, and Hawthorne's reputation was made.

A year later, Hawthorne became engaged to Sophia Peabody, whom he married in 1842. They settled in Concord, Massachusetts, in a house called the Old Manse. In 1846, Hawthorne published *Mosses from an Old Manse,* another collection of tales. In the same year, he was appointed Surveyor of the Custom House in the Port of Salem, a political appointment that left him time to write. His satirical portrait of Custom House life can be found in "The Custom House" preface to *The Scarlet Letter* (1850). This novel, his first and greatest, won widespread acclaim in the United States and abroad. In a sense this masterpiece represented the culmination of themes Hawthorne had explored in his earlier tales—secret sin, guilt, and the effect of isolation on individuals. In 1851, Hawthorne published another historical romance, *The House of the Seven Gables.*

In 1853, Franklin Pierce became President, and he appointed his old friend Hawthorne American Consul to Liverpool, England. Hawthorne and his family, which now included a son and two daughters, lived in England until Pierce left office in 1857. Hawthorne spent the next two years in Italy, which became the setting for *The Marble Faun* (1860).

After his return to Massachusetts in 1860, Hawthorne's energies and abilities declined. He contributed only short pieces to the *Atlantic Monthly.* Although he worked on a number of full-length projects, he completed none of them before his death in 1864.

Hawthorne's work is one of the cornerstones of American literature. His novels are in the form of romances, partly realistic and partly symbolic tales, or *allegories.* This enabled him to explore areas of experience that neither pure realism or pure allegory could convey. His dark view of human nature was a major influence on novelist Herman Melville (*see* Melville, Vol. 1, American Literature: Romanticism and the American Renaissance), and the depth of his psychological probing influenced writers as diverse as Henry James (*see* James, Vol. 1, American Literature: The Rise of Realism) and William Faulkner. (*See* Faulkner, Vol. 1, American Literature: The Twentieth Century.)

NOVELS BY HAWTHORNE

The Blithedale Romance (1852). NAL 1981 $3.50. ISBN 0-451-52027-0

*The House of the Seven Gables (1851). Bantam 1981 $2.50. ISBN 0-553-21270-2 The effects of the curse of a man robbed of his property on the family of the man who cheated him.

The Marble Faun (1860). NAL 1990 $3.95. ISBN 0-452-00903-0.

*The Scarlet Letter (1850). Harry Levin (ed). Houghton 1960 $7.50. ISBN 0-395-05142-8 Classic romance of Puritan New England, portraying adulteress Hester Prynne's fall and subsequent redemption; tangled relationship with lover Arthur Dimmesdale and husband Roger Chillingsworth ends in Arthur's death.

SHORT STORY COLLECTIONS BY HAWTHORNE

Nathaniel Hawthorne's Tales. James McIntosh (ed). Norton 1987 $8.95. ISBN 0-393-95426-9

Selected Tales and Sketches. Penguin 1987 $5.95. ISBN 0-14-039057-X

*A Wonder Book for Girls and Boys (1852). Sharon 1981 $3.95. ISBN 0-89531-058-9 A retelling of classical myths for young readers, written when Hawthorne was in the Berkshires.

BOOKS ABOUT HAWTHORNE

Levin, Harry. *The Power of Blackness: Hawthorne, Poe, Melville.* Ohio Univ Pr 1980 $6.95. ISBN 0-8214-0581-0 Key study of Hawthorne, Edgar Allan Poe, and Herman Melville.

Mellow, James R. *Nathaniel Hawthorne in His Times.* Houghton 1982 $10.95. ISBN 0-395-32135-2 The best general biography of Hawthorne available.

HENRY, O. (WILLIAM SYDNEY PORTER)   1862–1910

An immensely prolific author, O. Henry at his peak was publishing a story a week, and writing even more. The typical O. Henry story is an expanded anecdote, ending in a sudden humorous or ironic turn of events. Although he wrote many stories set in Latin America and the Southwest, he is best known for his glimpses of the common folk of New York City, as in his famous story "The Gift of the Magi."

William Sydney Porter was born in North Carolina, where he received little schooling. In 1882 he moved to Texas, where he worked at a number of jobs including writing humorous stories for newspapers. In 1896, while working as a bank teller, he was indicted for embezzlement. He fled to South America but later returned and served three years in prison. Ironically, it was in prison that his writing matured, and upon his release he moved to New York City and began to make his living with his writing.

O. Henry's first book, *Cabbages and Kings,* was published in 1904. Between then and his death in 1910, he wrote literally hundreds of stories, among them such perennial favorites as "The Ransom of Red Chief," "The Last Leaf," and "The Furnished Room." His simple characters and twisting plots were beloved by millions of readers, and his formula has been followed by many popular writers since.

SHORT STORY COLLECTIONS BY O. HENRY

*The Best Short Stories of O. Henry. Random 1977 $9.95. ISBN 394-60423-7 Contains the most famous tales, including "The Cop and the Anthem" and "The Last Leaf."

*The Gift of the Magi. Ideals 1989 $2.95. ISBN 0-8249-8388-2 Perhaps the most famous O. Henry story, about a husband and wife's surprise Christmas gifts.

BOOKS ABOUT O. HENRY

Current-Garcia, Eugene. *O. Henry.* G. K. Hall 1972 $14.95. ISBN 0-8057-0368-3. An introduction to O. Henry's life and works.

Langford, Gerald. *Alias O. Henry: A Biography of William Sydney Porter.* Greenwood 1983 $45.00. ISBN 0-313-23964-9 A readable, comprehensive biography of O. Henry.

JAMES, HENRY   1843–1916

Henry James was the most prominent of a number of nineteenth-century American writers who chose to live in Europe. In much of his best fiction, James's subject is the contrast between the simplicity—some times the simple-mindedness—and naturalness—sometimes the vulgarity—of Americans, and the sophistication, refinement, and decadence of Europeans. James's style is detached and complex, as he records extremely fine psychological perceptions.

Henry James, Jr., was born into a wealthy New York family. His father lectured and wrote on religious and philosophical subjects. His brother, William James, became one of America's most important philosophers and psychologists. Taught by private tutors, Henry James received a cosmopolitan education, traveling often in Europe. He attended Harvard Law School, but was always more interested in literature than law. By the early 1860s, he was contributing to a number of literary periodicals, especially the *Atlantic Monthly,* whose editor, William Dean Howells, gave him great encouragement. After leaving Harvard, James lived in Cambridge, Massachusetts, when he was not traveling in Europe. In 1876 he decided to settle permanently in England.

Some of James's early work, such as the novel *Washington Square* (1881), is set in America. However, most of the best novels and stories, such as *The American* (1877) and *Daisy Miller* (1879), place an American in Europe to contrast the two cultures. For example, *The Portrait of a Lady* (1881), James's first real masterpiece, portrays a young American woman in a wealthy, sophisticated, and decadent European environment.

In James's middle period, roughly from 1881 to 1900, he wrote fewer novels and more stories and plays. He had a great ambition to be a playwright, but his style was not suited to the theater, since he focused so much on the psychological nuances of his characters. Between 1890 and 1895, he wrote seven plays, none of which was successful. Following the booing of his play *Guy Domville* (1895) on its opening night, James finally and reluctantly gave up his theatrical ambitions.

James's last three novels are *The Wings of the Dove* (1902), the story of a dying woman determined to live a lifetime in her last few months; *The Ambassadors* (1903), the tale of two Americans and their romantic complications in Europe; and *The Golden Bowl* (1904) the story of how European characters manipulate and betray a young American woman. These are especially demanding works. While in subject they are similar to his earlier novels, dealing with the contrast between American and European perceptions, in style they are extremely refined, complex in syntax, and rich in imagery and symbol. In 1916, angered at America's reluctance to enter World War I, James became a naturalized British citizen. The following year he died.

James's style has often been criticized for being too complicated and too wordy. Nevertheless, while critics today may disagree over individual works, virtually all consider him to be one of the greatest novelists in the English language.

NOVELS BY JAMES

The Ambassadors (1903). Norton 1964 $9.95. ISBN 0-393-09613-0
The American (1877). Norton 1978 $10.95. ISBN 0-393-09091-4
The Bostonians (1886). McGraw 1964 $5.50. ISBN 0-07-553642-0
*Daisy Miller (1878). Penguin 1987 $2.50. ISBN 0-14-043262-0 A young American woman loses her innocence in sophisticated Europe.
The Golden Bowl (1904). Penguin 1985 $3.95. ISBN 0-14-043235-3
The Portrait of a Lady (1881). Norton 1975 $12.95. ISBN 0-393-09259-3
The Princess Casamassima (1886). Penguin 1977 $6.95. ISBN 0-14-043254-X
*Turn of the Screw (1898). Airmont 1967 $1.75. ISBN 0-8049-0155-4 A governess cares for two mysterious children whom she begins to suspect are possessed by evil spirits.
*Washington Square (1881). Buccaneer $17.95. ISBN 0-89966-532-2 Story of a wealthy but plain young woman and a fortune-hunting young man.
The Wings of the Dove (1902). Norton 1978 $9.95. ISBN 0-393-09088-4

SHORT STORY COLLECTIONS BY JAMES

The Portable Henry James. Penguin 1977 $9.95. ISBN 0-14-015055-2
Tales of Henry James. Christof Weglin (ed). Norton 1984 $11.95. ISBN 0-393-95359-9

BOOKS ABOUT JAMES

Beach, Joseph W. *Method of Henry James.* Saifer 1954 $6.00. ISBN 0-87556-020-2 One of the best studies of James's development as an artist.

Edel, Leon. *Henry James: A Life.* Harper 1987 $12.95. ISBN 0-06-091432-7 A scholarly and comprehensive biography; the definitive work; this volume is a shortened version of the massive multivolume work by James's eminent and indefatigable biographer.

JEWETT, SARAH ORNE   1849–1909

Sarah Orne Jewett was one of the most important "local color" writers of the late nineteenth century. She was born in South Berwick, Maine, daughter of a doctor and descendant of distinguished New Englanders. The area of South Berwick is the locale for much of her fiction, and many of her characters were evidently drawn from her observation of her father's rural patients.

Jewett was influenced by Harriet Beecher Stowe's New England novels, and she tried to achieve the same effects in her own novels and stories. Her best work is *Deephaven* (1877), a series of sketches set in a fictionalized South Berwick; *A Country Doctor* (1884), about a woman who gives up romance to become a country doctor; *A White Heron* (1886), a collection of short stories; and *The Country of the Pointed Firs* (1896), another series of Maine sketches. Her work had a special influence on author Willa Cather. (*See* Cather, Vol. 1, American Literature: The Twentieth Century.)

STORIES AND NOVELS BY JEWETT

The Country of the Pointed Firs (1896). Norton 1982 $7.70. ISBN 0-393-00048-6
Deephaven and Other Stories (1877). Richard Cary (ed). New College & Univ Pr 1966 $9.95. ISBN 0-8084-0100-9

BOOKS ABOUT JEWETT

Cary, Richard. *Sarah Orne Jewett.* New College & Univ Pr 1962 $8.95. ISBN 0-8084-0272-2 A good general introduction to Jewett's life and work; part of Twayne's U.S. Author series.

Matthiessen, Francis Otto. *Sarah Orne Jewett.* Peter Smith 1965 repr of 1929 ed $11.25. ISBN 0-8446-1305-3 Still the best in-depth study of Jewett's work.

NORRIS, FRANK (BENJAMIN FRANKLIN NORRIS, JR.)   1870–1902

Frank Norris, one of the pioneers of American realism, is known for his vivid portraits of life at the beginning of the twentieth century. Born in Chicago, Norris moved to San Francisco with his well-to-do family when he was 14. He attended the University of California and Harvard University before becoming a war correspondent in South Africa and Cuba. His early works were popular romantic and historical stories. His novel *McTeague* (1899), however, was written under the influence of French writer Emile Zola (*see* Zola, Vol. 1, World Literature: French Language and Literature), and helped bring Zola's style of *naturalism*—extremely detailed, realistic portraits of social problems—to America. *McTeague,* set in a seedy section of the San Francisco Bay area, may well be Norris's masterpiece.

Norris's work *The Octopus* (1901) was the first of a projected trilogy of novels called *Epic of the Wheat. The Octopus* deals with the raising of wheat in California and the struggle between ranchers and railroad executives. *The Pit*

(1903), the next novel in the series, is about speculation on the Chicago wheat exchange (a kind of stock market). Norris never completed the series because he died suddenly after an operation for appendicitis.

Like Stephen Crane (*see* Crane, Vol. 1, American Literature: The Rise of Realism), a writer with whom Norris is frequently compared, Norris died too young to fulfill his considerable promise, but he continues to be read and admired today.

NOVELS BY NORRIS

McTeague (1899). NAL 1964 $3.95. ISBN 0-451-52281-8
The Octopus (1901). NAL 1964 $3.50. ISBN 0-451-51711-3

BOOK ABOUT NORRIS

French, Warren. *Frank Norris.* New College & Univ Pr 1962 $10.95. ISBN 0-8084-0134-3 A good general study of Norris's life and work; gives the beginning student a sense of the range of modern critical opinion of Norris.

TWAIN, MARK (PSEUDONYM OF SAMUEL LANGHORNE CLEMENS) 1835–1910

Samuel Clemens—steamboat pilot, prospector, and newspaper reporter—adopted the pen name "Mark Twain" when he began his career as a literary humorist. The pen name—a river pilot's term meaning "two fathoms deep" or "safe water"—appears to have freed Clemens to develop the humorous, deadpan manner that became his trademark.

During his lifetime, Twain wrote a great deal. Much of his writing was turned out quickly to make money. Even his least significant writing, however, contains flashes of wit and reveals his marvelous command of colloquial American English. His best work is his "Mississippi writing"—*Life on the Mississippi* (1883) and *The Adventures of Huckleberry Finn* (1884). In the latter novel Twain was able to integrate his talent for comic invention with his satirical cast of mind and sense of moral outrage. Novelist Ernest Hemingway declared *The Adventures of Huckleberry Finn* the greatest American novel and the source of all modern American fiction. Certainly it influenced Hemingway's own work and that of writers as diverse as Saul Bellow and J. D. Salinger. (*See* Bellow, Hemingway, *and* Salinger, Vol. 1, American Literature: The Twentieth Century.)

Twain was born in Florida, Missouri, and grew up in Hannibal, a small Southern town very similar to the one in which he places his heroes Tom Sawyer and Huckleberry Finn.

Twain was a printer for a time, and then became a steamboat pilot, a profession he regarded with great respect all his life. He traveled in the West, writing humorous sketches for newspapers. In 1865, he wrote the short story "The Celebrated Jumping Frog of Calaveras County," which was very well received. He then began a career as a humorous travel writer and lecturer, publishing *The Innocents Abroad* in 1869, *Roughing It* in 1872, and, co-authored with Charles Dudley Warner, *Gilded Age* in 1873. His best-known works, however, are the novels that came out of his childhood in Hannibal: *The Adventures of Tom Sawyer* (1876) and *The Adventures of Huckleberry Finn* (1884).

Critic and editor of the *Atlantic Monthly* William Dean Howells, a friend of Twain's, encouraged him to write for that periodical. Howells later wrote an affectionate memoir, *My Mark Twain,* in which he called Twain "the Lincoln of our literature." In 1894, a publishing house that Twain had invested in went bankrupt and Twain lost a great deal of money. This was but one of several fortunes he was to lose as a result of his poor business sense and propensity for unrealistic money-making schemes. His personal life was further blighted by the various deaths from illness of an infant son and two grown daughters and the long illness and eventual death of his wife. These experiences of success, failure, and sorrow may account for the contrasting extremes of humor and bitterness in Twain's writing. Toward the close of his life, the bitterness predominated, and Twain turned to writing satirical diatribes against God and humanity—so much so that his surviving daughter, Clara, refused to allow these works to be published in her lifetime.

NOVELS BY TWAIN

The Adventures of Huckleberry Finn (1884). Bantam 1981 $1.75. ISBN 0-553-21079-5 The sequel to *Tom Sawyer,* in which Huck and the slave Jim float down the Mississippi in an attempt to reach freedom.

The Adventures of Tom Sawyer (1876). Bantam 1981 $1.75. ISBN 0-553-21128-5 Story of the imaginative Tom Sawyer, his brother Sid, and their friends, based on Twain's childhood in Hannibal, Missouri.

A Connecticut Yankee in King Arthur's Court (1889). Bantam 1981 $1.95. ISBN 0-553-21143-9 Time travel lands a Connecticut engineer in Camelot.

Gilded Age: A Tale of Today (1873). (coauthored with Charles Dudley Warner) NAL 1985 $4.95. ISBN 0-452-00779-8

The Prince and the Pauper (1882). NAL 1964 $2.25. ISBN 0-451-52193-5 Story of what happens when Prince Edward and a pauper boy, identical in appearance, exchange identities.

Pudd'nhead Wilson (1894). Bantam 1984 $1.95. ISBN 0-553-211587-7 Lawyer Wilson uses fingerprints to solve a case of murder and mistaken identity.

SHORT STORY COLLECTION BY TWAIN

The Complete Short Stories. Bantam 1984 $4.50. ISBN 0-553-21195-1

NONFICTION BY TWAIN

The Autobiography of Mark Twain. Charles Neider (ed). Harper 1990 $8.95. ISBN 0-06-09025-4 A well-edited version of the mass of material left by Twain to serve as his autobiography.

Life on the Mississippi (1883). Bantam 1981 $1.95. ISBN 0-553-21142-0

Roughing It (1872). NAL $3.95. ISBN 0-451-52223-0

BOOKS ABOUT TWAIN

Duckett, Margaret. *Mark Twain and Bret Harte.* Univ of Oklahoma Pr 1964. (o.p.) A useful study of Twain and Harte, two men whose careers are often compared.

Kaplan, Justin. *Mr. Clemens and Mark Twain.* Simon 1983 $10.95. ISBN 0-671-20707-5 The best recent biography.

*Meltzer, Milton. *Mark Twain: A Writer's Life.* Watts 1985 $12.90. ISBN 0-531-10072-3 Fine portrait of the writer, using many quotations from Twain's writings.

Smith, Henry Nash. *Mark Twain: The Development of a Writer.* Harvard Univ Pr 1962 $16.00. ISBN 0-674-54875-2 A standard study of Twain's work.

WHARTON, EDITH   1862–1937

A good friend of novelist Henry James (*see* James, Vol. 1, American Literature: The Rise of Realism) and a woman who moved in wealthy and fashionable circles throughout her life in the Berkshires, Newport, Rhode Island, and Europe, Edith Wharton was well qualified to work within the tradition of social realism. She wrote novels of manners (fiction portraying the daily social life of the upper class), but her attitude was generally critical of the society she wrote about. Her psychological insight, irony, and satiric touches make her fiction well worth reading today.

Born Edith Newbold Jones in New York City, Wharton grew up in a privileged environment provided by her well-to-do parents. She was privately educated in New York and Europe, and began to write at a very young age. When she was 23, she married a wealthy Bostonian, Edward Wharton. In 1907, the couple moved to France, where Wharton spent most of the rest of her life. Her marriage was not a happy one, and they divorced in 1913.

Wharton's second novel, *The House of Mirth* (1905), became a best-seller and established her reputation. Its heroine, Lily Bart, is perhaps the best portrait of "the American girl" after Henry James's Daisy Miller (*see* James, Vol. 1, American Literature: The Rise of Realism), and the novel is still widely read. In *Ethan Frome* (1911), Wharton temporarily abandoned her New York society setting to portray a stark domestic tragedy in a small town in Massachusetts. *The Age of Innocence* (1920), set once again in New York, won a Pulitzer Prize. After that, Wharton's work was less successful. In *A Backward Glance* (1934), she provided many charming reminiscences of her friendships with Henry James and his contemporaries.

NOVELS BY WHARTON

* *The Age of Innocence* (1920). Scribner's 1983 $8.95. ISBN 0-684-71925-8 Conflict between convention and the hope for happiness in the life of a wealthy New York lawyer.
The Custom of the Country (1910). Scribner's 1985 $11.95. ISBN 0-684-71926-6
* *Ethan Frome* (1910). Scribner's 1987 $5.95. ISBN 0-684-18906-2 The tragic tale of farmer Ethan Frome, his wife Zenobia, and Mattie Silver, the woman he comes to love.
* *The House of Mirth* (1905). NAL 1964 $3.95. ISBN 0-451-52362-8 Lily Bart's ambitious attempts to find a suitable husband in old New York.

SHORT STORY COLLECTION BY WHARTON

Roman Fever and Other Stories. Scribner's 1978 $9.95. ISBN 0-684-71931-2

BOOKS ABOUT WHARTON

*Leach, William. *Edith Wharton.* Chelsea 1987 $16.95. ISBN 1-55546-682-6 A readable overview of Wharton's life and accomplishments for readers in grades 7–12.
Lewis, R. W. B. *Edith Wharton: A Biography.* Fromm Intl 1985 $12.95. ISBN 0-88064-020-0 A masterful biography of Wharton, which should remain the definitive study of Wharton's life.
McDowell, Margaret B. *Edith Wharton.* G. K. Hall 1976 $17.95. ISBN 0-8057-7164-6 A good general study of Wharton's life and works.

WHITMAN, WALT   1819–1892

Walt Whitman was born on Long Island and raised in Brooklyn, New York, the son of a carpenter. He left school when he was 11 years old to take a variety of jobs. By the time he was 15, Whitman was living on his own in New York City, working as a printer and writing short pieces for newspapers. He spent a few years teaching, but most of his work was either in journalism or politics. Gradually, Whitman became a regular contributor to a variety of Democratic Party newspapers and reviews, and early in his career established a rather eccentric way of life, spending a great deal of time walking the streets, absorbing life and talking with laborers. Extremely fond of the opera, he used his press pass to spend many evenings in the theater.

In 1846 Whitman became editor of the Brooklyn *Eagle,* a leading Democratic newspaper. Two years later, he was fired for opposing the expansion of slavery into the West.

Whitman's career as a poet began in 1855, with the publication of the first edition of his poetry collection *Leaves of Grass.* The book was self-published (Whitman probably set some of the type himself), and despite his efforts to publicize it—including writing his own reviews—few people read it. One reader who did appreciate it was essayist Ralph Waldo Emerson (*see* Emerson, Vol. 1, American Literature: Romanticism and the American Renaissance), who wrote a letter greeting Whitman at "the beginning of a great career." Whitman's poetry was unlike any verse that had ever been seen. Written without rhyme, in long, loose lines, filled with poetic lists and exclamations taken from Whitman's reading of the Bible, Homer, and Asian poets, these poems were totally unlike conventional poetry. Their subject matter, too, was unusual—the celebration of a free-spirited individualist whose love for all things and people seemed at times disturbingly sensual. In 1860, with the publication of the third edition of *Leaves of Grass,* Whitman alienated conventional thinkers and writers even more. When he went to Boston to meet Emerson, poet Henry Wadsworth Longfellow, essayist Oliver Wendell Holmes, and poet James Russell Lowell, they all objected to the visit. (*See* Longfellow, Holmes, *and* Lowell, Vol. 1, American Literature: Romanticism and the American Renaissance.)

With the outbreak of the Civil War, Whitman's attentions turned almost exclusively to that conflict. Some of the greatest poetry of his career, including *Drum Taps* (1865) and his magnificent elegy for President Abraham Lincoln, "When Lilacs Last in the Dooryard Bloom'd" (1865), was written during this period. In 1862, his brother George was wounded in battle, and Whitman went to Washington to nurse him. He continued as a hospital volunteer throughout the war, nursing other wounded soldiers and acting as a benevolent father-figure and confidant. Parts of his memoir *Specimen Days* (1882) record this period.

After the war, Whitman stayed on in Washington, working as a government clerk and continuing to write. In 1873 he suffered a stroke and retired to Camden, New Jersey, where he lived as an invalid for the rest of his life. Ironically, his reputation began to grow during this period, as the public became more receptive to his poetic and personal eccentricities.

Whitman tried to capture the spirit of America in a new poetic form. His poetry is rough, colloquial, sweeping in its vistas—a poetic equivalent of the vast land and its varied peoples. Critic Louis Untermeyer has written, "In spite of Whitman's perplexing mannerisms, the poems justify their boundless contradictions. They shake themselves free from rant and bombastic audacities and rise into the clear air of major poetry. Such poetry is not large but self-assured; it knows, as Whitman asserted, the amplitude of time and laughs at dissolution. It contains continents; it unfolds the new heaven and new earth of the Western world." American poetry has never been the same since Whitman tore it away from its formal and thematic constraints, and he is considered by virtually all critics today to be one of the greatest poets the country has ever produced.

POETRY AND PROSE BY WHITMAN

Complete Poetry and Selected Prose. J. E. Miller, Jr. (ed). Houghton 1972 $8.36. ISBN 0-395-05132-0
Leaves of Grass (1855). NAL 1971 $2.95. ISBN 0-451-51702-4
The Portable Whitman. Mark Van Doren (ed). Viking 1974 $9.95. ISBN 0-14-015078-1

BOOKS ABOUT WHITMAN

Allen, Gay W. *The Solitary Singer: A Critical Biography of Walt Whitman.* Univ of Chicago Pr 1985 $15.95. ISBN 0-226-01435-5 A detailed and thorough critical study of Whitman's life and works by a highly respected scholar.
Zweig, Paul. *Walt Whitman: The Making of the Poet.* Basic 1984 $8.95. ISBN 0-317-20657-5 One of the most useful and interesting studies of the development of Whitman as a poet.

THE TWENTIETH CENTURY

As the twentieth century began, the United States was a very different nation from what it is today. Despite the industrial growth of the late nineteenth century, two out of every three Americans still made their living from the land. In many important ways, the nation was isolated from the rest of the world. Except for a few experimenters, U.S. art and literature remained tied to the forms and traditions of the past. All of this was changed dramatically by America's entry into World War I in 1917.

Suddenly, the need for workers in factories that produced war goods increased sharply. Huge numbers of rural people began to move to the cities. As American troops became involved in a "European war," U.S. isolation from international politics ended forever. By the war's end the United States had become a world power in both politics and commerce.

In the arts and literature, as well as in business and industry, Americans began taking a new leadership role, rather than trying to imitate the artists of Europe. Now, as Ralph Waldo Emerson and Walt Whitman had urged, American writers began to find their own voice. They turned their attention to their own culture and examined it with a fierce new intensity.

American writers in the 1920s and 1930s looked hard at their nation and found much wrong with it. Some writers were inspired by the socialist ideas coming from the Soviet Union or by the suffering of Americans during the Great Depression. Both American and Soviet experiences led many writers to criticize old traditions and beliefs. Writers from the South, such as William Faulkner, looked behind the myth of gallant gentlemen and gracious southern ladies to find hypocrisy and decay. Midwestern writers like Sinclair Lewis and Sherwood Anderson looked beneath the surface neighborliness of the American small town and found people leading empty and desperate lives. In New York, a new generation of African-American writers founded a movement called the Harlem Renaissance, which examined African-American life in a new way. On the West Coast, John Steinbeck and others looked at the plight of migrant farm workers, hungry in a land of plenty.

Throughout this period, writers also searched for new forms in which to express their new ideas. New poets calling themselves imagists stripped their verse of all "fancy" language, shaping it into new rhythms and forms. Ernest Hemingway and other fiction writers likewise stripped the language of the novel and short story down to its bare essentials.

At the same time, writers began to reject plots that followed a smooth line from beginning to middle to end. Literature became more disjointed and fragmentary. Writers who were influenced by the psychological theories of Sigmund Freud tried to convey the flow of characters' thoughts by means of a narrative technique called stream of consciousness.

All of this experimentation and change was slowed somewhat by America's entry into World War II in 1941, when more traditional and patriotic values became influential. Soon after the war's end, however, artists and writers again began to question the values of American society and to challenge traditional beliefs. From the late 1950s through the 1960s, the civil rights movement was fueled by the ideas of writers like James Baldwin and Lorraine Hansberry, who at the same time were shaping a new generation of writers. And as America prospered and grew powerful, writers such as John Updike, Edward Albee, Kurt Vonnegut, Jr., and Joyce Carol Oates raised disturbing questions about the nation's moral values.

In the last quarter of this century, U.S. writers have continued to serve as the country's conscience. Today's writers call attention to racial and sexual injustice, to the loss of individuality, to the dangers of technology and conformity, and to the threats to the environment from a society that has lost touch with nature.

ALBEE, EDWARD 1928–

Born in Washington, D.C., Edward Albee was the adopted son of millionaire parents who owned a chain of theaters. An indifferent, rebellious student, Albee attended various private schools and—briefly—Trinity College in Connecticut. At age 21, he left both home and school to live in New York City. For nearly 10 years, he worked at odd jobs, while writing poetry and attempting novels, but publishing nothing.

Just before his thirtieth birthday, during a two-week period, Albee wrote *The Zoo Story* (1959). In the next year, he followed this one-act play with four others: *The Sandbox, Fam and Yam, The American Dream,* and *The Death of Bessie Smith,* all of which were successful. Albee's reputation as a powerful dramatist was established.

Albee's one-act plays attacked what he sees as the shallowness and hypocrisy of American middle-class values. His next play, *Who's Afraid of Virginia Woolf?* (1962), was an intense exploration of a human relationship. The drama consists of a night-long argument between a college professor and his wife, during which they involve another couple in their vicious verbal assaults and cruel psychological games. *Tiny Alice* (1965) is the story of a woman who tricks a Roman Catholic lay brother into marriage and then murders him. *A Delicate Balance* (1967) is the story of a family suddenly "invaded" by another couple driven to leave their own home by a mysterious and nameless fear. According to Albee, the play is "about how as you get older the freedom of choices becomes less and less, and you are left only with the illusion of freedom of actions and you become a slave of compromise."

Albee won the Pulitzer Prize for *A Delicate Balance* in 1966, and again for his play *Seascape* (1975). He also won the New York Drama Critics Circle Award for *Who's Afraid of Virginia Woolf?* His use of surreal, absurd situations to show that life is meaningless and most relationships are empty and destructive have caused critics to place his work in the movement known as Theater of the Absurd.

PLAYS BY ALBEE

American Dream and Zoo Story (1960, 1958). NAL 1963 $3.95. ISBN 0-451-15380-4 Two plays about the emptiness and hypocrisy of modern American life.

The Lady from Dubuque: A Play in Two Acts (1980). Macmillan 1980 $9.95. ISBN 0-689-10925-3

The Plays Vol. 2 (includes *Tiny Alice; A Delicate Balance; Box; Quotes from Chairman Mao*). Macmillan 1982 $9.95. ISBN 0-689-70614-6

The Plays Vol. 3 (includes *Seascape; Counting the Ways; Listening; All Over*). Macmillan 1982 $9.95. ISBN 0-689-70615-4
*The Sandbox and The Death of Bessie Smith (1960). NAL 1988 $6.95. ISBN 0-452-26083-3
Two plays about social blindness and insensitivity.
Who's Afraid of Virginia Woolf? (1962). NAL 1983 $4.95. ISBN 0-451-15871-7

BOOKS ABOUT ALBEE

Amacher, Richard. *Edward Albee.* G. K. Hall 1982 $17.95. ISBN 0-8057-5349-5 A good general introduction to Albee's life and works.
Bloom, Harold (ed). *Edward Albee.* Chelsea 1987 $19.95. ISBN 0-87754-707-6 A collection of modern critical essays including a useful description of Albee's techniques.
Esselin, Martin. *The Theater of the Absurd.* Overlook Pr 1973 $35.00. ISBN 0-87951-005-6 Definitive work on absurdism showing Albee's place in the movement.

ALEXANDER, LLOYD   1924–

Lloyd Alexander was born in Philadelphia. He studied at West Chester State Teachers College briefly before enlisting in the army during World War II. He was sent to Paris as a member of an army intelligence team and while there married and completed his degree at the Sorbonne. He then returned to the United States to live in a Philadelphia suburb, where he still resides.

From childhood Alexander was fascinated by ancient tales of adventure, particularly the stories of King Arthur and other medieval legends. He decided early that he wanted to be a writer, and on the eve of his high school graduation, he announced that he had decided to be a poet. It was not until after the war, however, that he began to write seriously—not poetry, but novels.

Alexander's first works were grim and serious and not successful with readers. When he turned to lighter works based on his own experiences, he was successful. He then began writing books for young readers, publishing two biographies of little-known Jews who were key American patriots.

In 1963 Alexander published his first fantasy novel, *Time Cat,* about a cat who takes a boy into different periods in the past. Then, while researching material for a book on ancient Welsh legends, Alexander got the idea of creating his own mythology. The result was his invention of a land called Prydain which became the setting for five novels, known as the *Prydain Chronicles: The Book of Three* (1964), *The Black Cauldron* (1965), *The Castle of Llyr* (1966), *Taran Wanderer* (1967), and *The High King* (1968).

In 1981 Alexander began a new series, *The Westmark Trilogy.* Although these novels are set in an imaginary ancient kingdom, they are not fantasy tales but rather historical adventure stories.

Alexander's most recent works are three novels relating the adventures of Vesper Holly, a teenage girl who in the late 1870s travels to the land of Illyria on the Adriatic sea to engage in an archaeological investigation.

NOVELS BY ALEXANDER

*The Beggar Queen (1984). Dell 1985 $3.25. ISBN 0-440-90548-6 Third book in the *Westmark Trilogy;* Duke Marianstat plots to overthrow the new government of Westmark.
*The Black Cauldron (1965). Dell 1980 $3.25. ISBN 0-440-90649-0 Second book in the *Prydain Chronicles;* Prince Gwydion leads the quest to destroy the Black Cauldron.
*The Book of Three (1964). Dell 1978 $3.50. ISBN 0-440-90702-0 First book in the *Prydain Chronicles;* young Taran and the great warrior Gwydion fight to save Prydain.
*The Castle of Llyr (1966). Dell 1980 $3.25. ISBN 0-440-91125-7 Third book in the *Prydain Chronicles;* on the Isle of Mona, Princess Eilonwy is trained to be a proper princess.
*The Drackenburg Adventure (1988). Dutton 1988 $12.95. ISBN 0-525-44389-4 Third book

in the Vesper Holly series; Brinnie's wife is kidnapped and Vesper must live among Gypsies.

The El Dorado Adventure (1988). Dell 1988 $2.95. ISBN 0-440-20068-7 Second book in the Vesper Holly series; Vesper and Brinnie travel to the country of El Dorado in Central America.

The High King (1968). Dell 1980 $3.50. ISBN 0-440-93574-1 Fifth book in the *Prydain Chronicles;* Taran raises an army to march against Arawn.

The Illyrian Adventure (1987). Dell 1987 $2.75. ISBN 0-440-94018-4 First book in the Vesper Holly series; Vesper searches for legendary treasure in Illyria.

The Jedera Adventure (1989). Dutton 1989 $12.95. ISBN 0-525-44481-5 Fourth book in the Vesper Holly series; Vesper journeys to the North African country of Bel-Saaba to make good an ancient debt.

The Kestrel (1982). Dell 1983 $2.95. ISBN 0-440-94393-0 Second book in the *Westmark Trilogy;* Theo and his companions combine forces to defend the kingdom.

Taran Wanderer (1967). Dell 1980 $3.25. ISBN 0-440-98483-1 Fourth book in the *Prydain Chronicles;* Taran goes questing for his parentage in hopes it will prove noble.

Time Cat (1963) Dell 1985 $3.25. ISBN 0-440-48677-7 A magical cat takes a boy on historical adventures.

Westmark (1982). Dell 1982 $3.25. ISBN 0-440-99731-3 First book in the *Westmark Trilogy;* Theo embarks on an adventure in the kingdom of Westmark with a doctor, a dwarf, and an urchin girl.

BOOK ABOUT ALEXANDER

Gallo, Donald R. (ed). *Speaking for Ourselves.* NCTE 1990 $12.95. ISBN 0-8141-4625-2 A fascinating collection of autobiographical sketches of 87 young-adult authors, including Alexander; authors share stories of how they started to write and of significant events that influenced them; includes complete list of published works and dates.

ALLEN, WOODY 1935–

See also Allen, Vol. 1, Mass Communication: Movies.

Woody Allen was a stand-up comic before he was a published writer. He has created a persona—the insecure neurotic, perpetual worrier, and born loser—which dominates his plays, movies, and essays.

Allen was born Allen Konigsberg in Brooklyn, New York, where he hated the local schools he attended. At an early age, Allen turned to writing essays as a way to deal with his lack of friends and social life, and to distinguish himself at school. While he was still in high school, he began writing jokes for newspaper columnists and celebrities. After studying for a brief time at New York University and the City College of New York, he left without graduating and went to work as a staff writer for the National Broadcasting Company (NBC), where he wrote comedy material for a number of popular television shows. He also became popular himself as a night club and television comic. As both writer and performer, Allen developed a style of comedy based on the view that life is a concentration camp from which no one escapes alive.

Since the 1960s Allen has devoted most of his creative energy to films, in which he writes, directs, and acts. His work has received high critical acclaim. Although his films and plays are called comedies, they look at very serious human problems, especially problems of relationships, in a way that is both funny and disturbing. His film *Annie Hall* (1977), which won four Academy Awards, is a subtle portrait of the insecurities fostered by modern American life. The film *Crimes and Misdemeanors* (1989) explores questions of morality and justice. All of Allen's work focuses on New York City—its ethnic diversity, its artists and actors, its intellectuals and professionals.

Many of Allen's essays appeared originally in *The New Yorker* magazine and were later collected in book form. Like his films, these pieces manage to be both funny and serious.

PLAYS AND SCREENPLAYS BY ALLEN

The Floating Light Bulb (1982). Random 1982 $10.00. ISBN 0-394-52415-2 A comic play about an unusual family.

Hannah and Her Sisters (1985). Random 1986 $5.95. ISBN 0-394-74749-6 A filmscript about the complex relationships of three sisters and the men in their lives.

Play It Again, Sam (1969). Random 1969 $10.00. ISBN 0-394-40663-X A play about a young man dominated by fantasies of Humphrey Bogart.

Sleeper (1973). Random 1978 $7.95. ISBN 0-394-50021-2 A filmscript about a man who awakens to find himself in a frightening and hilarious future.

Three Films: Broadway Danny Rose, Zelig, The Purple Rose of Cairo (1980–87). Random 1987 $12.95. ISBN 0-394-75304-6 Screenplays for three Allen films about the comic trials of "losers."

STORIES AND ESSAYS BY ALLEN

Getting Even (1971). Random 1971 $2.95. ISBN 0-394-72640-5 A collection of humorous essays from the late 1960s looking at popular psychology, intellectual pretension, and other comic targets.

Side Effects (1980). Ballantine 1986 $3.95. ISBN 0-345-34335-2 A collection of humorous works, including the famous story, "The Kugelmass Episode," in which a professor is transported into a novel and falls in love with a character.

Without Feathers (1975). Ballantine 1983 $3.50. ISBN 0-345-33697-6 A collection of Allen's humorous essays from *The New Yorker,* looking satirically at religion, Jewish culture, and other serious topics.

BOOKS ABOUT ALLEN

Brode, Douglas. *Woody Allen: His Films and Career.* Citadel 1987 $14.95. ISBN 0-8065-1067-6 Traces Allen's growth and development as a filmmaker and discusses his films through 1986.

Pogel, Nancy. *Woody Allen.* G. K. Hall 1988 $12.95. ISBN 0-8057-9309-7 A study of the most significant aspects of Allen's films and of his development as a filmmaker.

ANDERSON, SHERWOOD   1876–1941

Sherwood Anderson was born in Canton, Ohio, the son of Scots-American parents. He left school at age 14 and then drifted from job to job, working as a laborer, soldier in the Spanish-American War, advertising copywriter, and journalist. In 1904, he married the first of his four wives, the daughter of a prosperous Ohio businessman. Two years later he became manager of a paint factory, a position he held until 1912, when he suddenly left his job and family and set out to become a writer. He moved to Chicago where he became acquainted with a number of promising writers, including Carl Sandburg and Theodore Dreiser who encouraged him to keep on writing. (*See* Dreiser *and* Sandburg, Vol. 1, American Literature: The Twentieth Century.)

Anderson's first novel, *Windy McPherson's Son* (1916), received a moderately favorable reception, but neither it nor his second novel, *Marching Men* (1917), attracted much public attention. It was his third work, *Winesburg, Ohio* (1919) that made Anderson's reputation. This collection of related short stories about life in the small Midwestern town of Winesburg, Ohio, marked him as one of the new writers, like Sinclair Lewis (*see* Lewis, Vol. 1, American Literature: The

Twentieth Century), who were in revolt against life in a small-town America. Anderson's collection chronicles the lives of what he called "grotesques"— people whose passions and quirks did not fit into the narrow confines of "respectable" behavior as defined by the town. The main character of the collection is George, an autobiographical figure, who as a young journalist observes the townspeople, comes of age, and ultimately leaves Winesburg.

Anderson's 1920 novel, *Poor White,* was an account of the impact of technological change on the people in a small Ohio town. It further enhanced his reputation as an observer of life in middle America.

Anderson's influence on writers who followed him, particularly Ernest Hemingway and William Faulkner (*see* Faulkner *and* Hemingway, Vol. 1, American Literature: The Twentieth Century), was powerful. His spare, minimalist style, candid treatment of sex, and bleak view of American life prompted Faulkner to write admiringly that Anderson "was the father of my generation of American writers and the tradition of American writing which our successors will carry on. He has never received his proper evaluation."

NOVEL BY ANDERSON

Dark Laughter (1925). Amereon $19.95. ISBN 0-88411-277-2

SHORT STORY COLLECTIONS BY ANDERSON

Death in the Woods and Other Stories (1933). Norton 1986 $7.70. ISBN 0-87140-140-1
The Portable Sherwood Anderson. Penguin 1977 $8.95. ISBN 0-14-015076-5
Winesburg, Ohio (1919). Penguin 1988 $3.95. ISBN 0-14-043304-X

BOOKS ABOUT ANDERSON

Rideout, Walter B. *Sherwood Anderson: A Collection of Critical Essays.* Prentice 1974 $2.45. ISBN 0-13-036533-5 A variety of essays, assembled by the leading Anderson scholar, that examine Anderson's novels, stories, and writing career with unusual insight and perception.
Taylor, Welford D. *Sherwood Anderson.* Ungar 1977 $16.95. ISBN 0-8044-2861-1 An introduction to Anderson's life and writing containing commentary on his major works, a one-chapter biography, a chronology, and a bibliography.
Townsend, Kim. *Sherwood Anderson.* Houghton 1987 $22.95. ISBN 0-395-36533-3 A comprehensive and authoritative account of Anderson's life with substantial attention to his major works and his interaction with other writers.

ANGELOU, MAYA   1928–

Maya Angelou was born Marguerite Johnson in St. Louis, Missouri, and raised by her paternal grandmother, Annie Henderson, in Stamps, Arkansas, a small, segregated southern town with a strong Ku Klux Klan presence. In the famous first volume of her autobiography, *I Know Why the Caged Bird Sings* (1970), Angelou describes her childhood, including her early love of reading, particularly the works of English playwright William Shakespeare, whom she says she believed to be black because of the richness of his speech.

After giving birth to a son, Angelou moved to San Francisco in order to be near her own mother. As a teenage mother, she worked at a variety of legal and illegal jobs—cook, waitress, dancer, and madam. She also became the first black person to work on the city's streetcars. This period of her life is described in the second volume of her autobiography, *Gather Together in My Name* (1974). Eventually, however, Angelou became a singer and actress, making a round-the-world tour with the opera *Porgy and Bess* in 1954 and 1955. She continued

Christ's Entry into Jerusalem. Watercolor by Romare Bearden (1945). Courtesy of The Schomburg Center for Research in Black Culture, Art & Artifacts Division, The New York Public Library, Astor, Lenox, and Tilden Foundations.

her theatrical career in a variety of New York plays, most notably the 1960 off-Broadway production of French playwright Jean Genet's *The Blacks.*

In 1961, Angelou went to Egypt, where she worked for two years as associate editor of the *Arab Observer,* an English-language weekly in Cairo. Then she taught and acted at the University of Ghana's School of Music and Drama. She resumed her journalism career from 1964 to 1966 as the feature editor of *African Review.*

Angelou returned permanently to the United States in 1966. Her first literary success came with publication of the first volume of her autobiography, which was nominated for a National Book Award in 1970. In 1972, her first poetry collection—*Just Give Me a Cool Drink of Water 'fore I Diiie* (1971)—was nominated for a Pulitzer Prize. In the same year, her screenplay, *Georgia, Georgia,* became the first original screenplay by a black woman to be made into a film.

Angelou is still winning acclaim as writer, director, teacher, and performer. In all her work, she urges her audience to explore their heritage, to accept themselves, and to view African-American culture and traditions as a rich source of strength for all.

NONFICTION BY ANGELOU

All God's Children Need Traveling Shoes (1986). Random 1987 $3.95. ISBN 0-394-75077-2
*Gather Together in My Name (1974). Bantam 1985 $3.95. ISBN 0-553-266066-9 Second
    volume of Angelou's autobiography; account of her early struggles as a teenage
    mother.
The Heart of a Woman (1981). Bantam 1984 $3.95. ISBN 0-553-24689-5
*I Know Why the Caged Bird Sings (1970). Bantam 1971 $3.95. ISBN 0-553-25615-7 First
    volume of Angelou's autobiography; moving account of growing up in a segre-
    gated Southern town.

Singin' and Swingin' and Gettin' Merry like Christmas (1976). Bantam 1985 $4.50. ISBN
0-553-25199-6 Third volume of Angelou's autobiography; tells of her round-the-
world tour as actress and singer and of her efforts to become a performer in the
United States.

POETRY BY ANGELOU

And Still I Rise (1978). Random 1978 $11.95. ISBN 0-394-50252-3

Just Give Me a Cool Drink of Water 'fore I Diiie (1971). Random 1971 $12.45. ISBN 0-394-
47142-3

Oh Pray My Wings Are Gonna Fit Me Well (1975). Random 1975 $11.95. ISBN 0-394-
49951-4

BOOKS ABOUT ANGELOU

Elliot, Jeffrey M. (ed). *Conversations with Maya Angelou.* Univ Pr of Mississippi 1989
$25.95. ISBN 0-87805-361-1 Angelou's thoughts on creativity, black heritage, and
forging one's own identity.

Evans, Mari (ed). *Black Women Writers, 1950 to 1980: A Critical Evaluation.* Doubleday 1984
$12.95. ISBN 0-385-17125-0 A comprehensive look at contemporary black
women writers, with separate chapters considering each one in view of the black
female literary tradition; includes chapter on Angelou.

ARMOUR, RICHARD   1906–

Richard Armour was born in San Pedro, California, and educated in local
schools. He received his B.A. from Pomona College and his M.A. and Ph.D.
from Harvard University. He served in the U.S. Army antiaircraft artillery
division during World War II, rising to the rank of colonel.

Armour has been a career academic, holding teaching positions at a variety
of colleges, including the University of Texas, the College of the Ozarks, and
Scripps College. Since 1966, he has been professor of English and dean of The
Claremont Graduate School in California.

Armour began his writing career in 1937 with the publication of two
humorous poems. He has since contributed over 6,000 pieces of light verse and
prose to more than 200 magazines in the United States and England. He has
also published over 60 books, including collections of poems and articles that
first appeared in magazines. His works have been translated into many languages, including German, French, Portugese, and Japanese.

Armour writes both humor and satire; the humor to "relax and entertain"
the reader, the satire to "point out a wrong." His books are most popular among
junior high school, high school, and college students. As he said in an interview, "My greatest usefulness, I suppose, is to bring lightness as well as
enlightenment into the classroom." One of his books, *It All Started with Stones and
Clubs* (1967), a satire on war, is recommended reading at the U.S. Military
Academy at West Point and was purchased by every U.S. Army library in the
world.

POETRY BY ARMOUR

Armoury of Light Verse (1962). Branden 1962 $2.50. ISBN 0-8283-1424-1 A delightful
collection of verse on diverse subjects ranging from aardvarks to motorists.

Punctured Poems: Famous First Lines and Infamous Second Lines (1966). Woodbridge 1982 $3.95.
ISBN 0-912800-55-0 First lines of famous poems with the second line rewritten,
Armour-style.

PROSE BY ARMOUR

Anyone for Insomnia? A Playful Look at Sleeplessness (1982). Woodbridge 1982 $4.95. ISBN
0-912800-69-0

The Classics Reclassified (1960). Bantam 1972 $5.95. ISBN 0-553-33005-3 Parodies of seven classics, including *Moby Dick* and *Silas Marner*.

Educated Guesses: Light-Serious Suggestions for Parents and Teachers (1983). Woodbridge 1983 $9.95. ISBN 0-88007-127-3

Going Like Sixty: A Lighthearted Look at the Later Years (1974). McGraw 1976 $5.95. ISBN 0-07-002292-5

Twisted Tales from Shakespeare (1957). McGraw 1957 $5.95. ISBN 0-07-002251-8 A zany look at Julius Caesar, Lady Macbeth, and other Shakespearean characters.

ASIMOV, ISAAC 1920–

See also Asimov, Vol. 2, General Science: General References.

Isaac Asimov was born in Russia and came to the United States as a very young child. He was an extremely bright youngster, receiving his bachelor's degree from Columbia University at the age of 19. His education was interrupted by World War II, but in 1948 he received a Ph.D. in biochemistry from Columbia. Soon after, he joined the faculty of Boston University.

Asimov began writing science fiction in his teens, and throughout his university career, he contributed stories regularly to magazines. In the late 1950s he turned to writing full-time. His literary output has been enormous—over 125 books and at least that many articles and stories. His fame as a writer rests both on his science fiction and on his articles and books, which explain complex scientific principles in easily understood language.

Asimov's best-known works are probably the Foundation series (1951–1953) and his robot stories. The Foundation series tells the story of the collapse of the great million-planet Galactic Empire and the struggle to bring order out of the chaos that results. Built around one man's dream of what a better universe could be like, the series was given a Hugo Award as the best science fiction series of all time.

The robot series, beginning with *I, Robot* (1950), examines the relationship between humans and their machines. It proposes an ethical system based on three "laws of robotics" to keep robots from turning on their masters. Asimov followed this book with three novels that further explore this issue. In his latest works, such as *Foundation's Edge* (1982) and *Robots and Empire* (1985), he has begun to draw together all his earlier themes into a unified vision of the future.

NOVELS BY ASIMOV

Currents of Space (1952). Del Rey 1985 $3.95. ISBN 0-345-33544-9 Third and last novel in the Galactic Empire series, describing the empire at the height of its glory.

The End of Eternity (1955). Del Rey 1986 $3.95. ISBN 0-345-33655-0 Story about how Eternity Inc., a business firm, tries to control human history.

Fantastic Voyage (1966). Bantam 1984 $3.50. ISBN 0-553-27151-2 Microscopic people journey through a man's body trying to save his life.

Fantastic Voyage II: Destination Brain (1987). Bantam 1988 $4.95. ISBN 0-553-27327-2 Microscopic Americans and Soviets try to get information from the brain of a scientist in a coma.

Foundation and Earth (1986). Ballantine 1987 $4.95. ISBN 0-345-33996-7 Fifth Foundation novel; a search for long-dead Earth leads Trevize and Pelorat to the robot Olivaw.

The Foundation Trilogy (includes *Foundation, Foundation and Empire, Second Foundation*) (1963). Ballantine 1986 $12.95. ISBN 0-345-34088-0 Three novels that tell the story of the collapse of the Galactic Empire and the struggle of Foundation to save civilization.

Foundation's Edge (1982). Ballantine 1987 $4.95. ISBN 0-345-34088-4 Sequel to the *Foundation Trilogy;* takes Golan Trevize into space to learn whether the Second Foundation exists.

The Gods Themselves (1972). Del Rey 1988 $3.95. ISBN 0-345-33778-6 An extraterrestrial solution to Earth's energy crisis.

Nemesis (1989). Doubleday 1989 $18.95. ISBN 0-385-24792-3 Seventh Foundation novel; a red dwarf star orbits dangerously close to Earth.

A Pebble in the Sky (1950). Del Rey 1983 $3.95. ISBN 0-345-33563-5 First novel in the Galactic Empire series; the title refers to Earth, a mere "pebble" of the huge empire.

Prelude to Foundation (1988). Bantam 1989 $4.95. ISBN 0-553-27839-8 Sixth Foundation novel, introducing Harry Seldom and psychohistory, his mathematical science.

The Robot Trilogy (includes *The Caves of Steel, The Naked Sun, The Robots of Dawn*) (1984). Ballantine 1988 $14.95. ISBN 0-345-33119-2 Elijah Bailey, interplanetary detective, investigates the crimes of humans and robots.

Robots and Empire (1985). Ballantine 1986 $4.50. ISBN 0-345-32894-9 Novel that ties together three series—Empire, Foundation, and Robot.

The Stars, like Dust (1951). Del Rey 1983 $3.95. ISBN 0-345-33563-5 Second novel in the Galactic Empire series, describing the growth and evolution of the Galactic Empire.

SHORT STORY COLLECTIONS BY ASIMOV

Azazel (1988). Bantam 1990 $3.95. ISBN 0-553-28339-1 A collection of 18 short tales of fantasy, including the title story about a demon who is two-centimeters-tall.

The Best Science Fiction of Isaac Asimov. Signet 1988 $3.95. ISBN 0-451-15196-8 Includes some of Asimov's early stories as well as later robot tales.

The Bicentennial Man and Other Stories. Ballantine 1985 $3.50. ISBN 0-345-32071-9 Twelve stories including the title novelette about Andrew, the artistic robot.

The Early Asimov. 2 vols. Ballantine 1986. Vol. 1 $3.95. ISBN 0-345-32590-7. Vol. 2 $3.95. ISBN 0-345-32589-3 A unique collection of stories written during what is now known as the Golden Age of Science Fiction.

I, Robot (1950). Ballantine 1984 $3.95. ISBN 0-345-33139-7 A collection of robot stories from the 1940s introducing the three laws of robotics.

Nightfall and Other Stories. Ballantine 1984 $3.95. ISBN 0-345-31091-8 Asimov's own collection of 20 of his most successful stories.

Nine Tomorrows (1959). Ballantine 1985 $3.50. ISBN 0-345-34604-1 Nine visions of life in the not too distant future.

BOOKS ABOUT ASIMOV

Fiedler, Jean, and Jim Mele. *Isaac Asimov.* Ungar 1982 $15.95. ISBN 0-8044-2203-6 A comprehensive general introduction to the life and works of Asimov.

Gunn, James. *Isaac Asimov: The Foundations of Science Fiction.* Oxford Univ Pr 1982 $7.95. ISBN 0-19-503060-5 A study of Asimov's influence on science fiction with many references to his works.

BALDWIN, JAMES   1924–1987

James Baldwin was born in Harlem in New York City, the stepson of a preacher. While attending New York's De Witt Clinton High School, he worked for three years as a teenage preacher in his stepfather's church. After graduation in 1942, Baldwin worked at a variety of jobs: waiter, handyman, porter, dishwasher, office boy, and elevator operator. He also continued the writing he had begun in high school and contributed book reviews and other short pieces to magazines.

In 1945 Baldwin met novelist Richard Wright and won a fellowship that enabled him to devote more time to his writing. In 1948 he won a second fellowship and left the United States for Europe, where he settled in Paris. While there he published his first novel, *Go Tell It on the Mountain* (1953), the story of a young man growing up in Harlem.

Baldwin lived in Paris until the late 1950s, when he returned to the United

States and was soon caught up in the emerging civil rights movement. In the 1960s he became increasingly active in the movement, using his skills as a writer to explain the condition of African Americans. For example, in *Another Country* (1962), which is also set in Harlem, Baldwin shows how a hostile society can create frustrations that eventually destroy an individual.

Throughout the next 25 years, Baldwin produced a number of novels, plays, and collections of essays that won him critical acclaim and wide popularity. His essays, in particular, have won him the reputation of being one of the most effective African-American voices of our time. *Notes of a Native Son* (1955), *Nobody Knows My Name* (1961), and *The Fire Next Time* (1963) are among the most powerful indictments of racial tyranny ever written. The critic Edmund Wilson described Baldwin as "not only one of the best black writers that we have ever had in this country, [but] one of the best writers that we have."

NOVELS BY BALDWIN

Another Country (1962). Dell 1985 $5.95. ISBN 0-440-30200-5
Giovanni's Room (1956). Dell 1985 $4.95. ISBN 0-440-32881-0
Go Tell It on the Mountain (1953). Dell 1985 $4.95. ISBN 0-440-33077-6
If Beale Street Could Talk (1974). Dell 1986 $4.95. ISBN 0-440-34060-8 Story about the love of a young couple and their feuding families in an environment of hate.
Just Above My Head (1979). Dell 1990 $5.95. ISBN 0-440-14777-8
Tell Me How Long the Train's Been Gone (1968). Dell 1986 $1.95. ISBN 0-440-38581-4

SHORT STORY COLLECTION BY BALDWIN

Going to Meet the Man (1965). Dell 1986 $4.95. ISBN 0-440-32931-0

PLAYS BY BALDWIN

The Amen Corner (1968). Dell 1990 $1.75. ISBN 0-440-35837-X
Blues for Mr. Charlie (1964). Dell 1964 $1.75. ISBN 0-440-30637-X

POETRY BY BALDWIN

Jimmy's Blues: Selected Poems (1986). St. Martin's 1986 $11.95. ISBN 0-440-44247-5

NONFICTION BY BALDWIN

The Fire Next Time (1963). Dell 1985 $4.95. ISBN 0-440-32542-0
The Price of the Ticket: Collected Nonfiction 1948–1985 (1986). St. Martin's 1986 $9.95. ISBN 0-312-64306-3 A collection of Baldwin's most noted essays including the famous *Notes of a Native Son.*
The Evidence of Things Not Seen (1985). Holt 1986 $4.95. ISBN 0-8050-0138-7 An extended essay on the conviction of Wayne Williams for the Atlanta child murders.

BOOKS ABOUT BALDWIN

*Rossett, Lisa. *James Baldwin.* Chelsea 1989 $17.95. ISBN 1-55546-572-2 Sets Baldwin's life and ideals in the context of the civil rights movement and identifies his conflicts with other writers and activists.
*Troupe, Quincy (ed). *James Baldwin: The Legacy.* Simon 1989 $12.95. ISBN 0-671-67651-2 Contains memorial tributes from Baldwin's family and friends along with several lengthy interviews with Baldwin.
*Weatherby, W. J. *James Baldwin: Artist on Fire.* Dell 1990 $5.95. ISBN 0-440-20573-5 Connects events in Baldwin's life with incidents in his stories and essays.

BAMBARA, TONI CADE   1939–

Toni Cade Bambara was born Toni Cade in New York City but legally changed her name in 1970. She received a B.A. from Queens College in New York in 1959. She also did advanced study at the University of Florence in Italy and at the Ecole de Mime Etienne Decroux in Paris before completing a master's degree at the City College of New York in 1964. An avid scholar, she has continued to study at various institutions.

Bambara's work experience has been similarly varied, ranging from recreation director in a hospital psychiatry department to television production consultant to university professor. At present she divides her time between writing, consulting, and teaching.

During the 1960s Bambara was very active in the civil rights movement. She became especially involved in the cultural and artistic life of urban communities, an involvement she continues to maintain. Through this work she has kept in close touch with the feelings, problems, and language of grass-roots African Americans, who are the inspiration for her fiction.

Bambara's first book, *Gorilla, My Love* (1972), is a collection of short stories that describe in haunting detail the lives of African Americans in both large urban communities and small southern towns. These stories, like all her fiction, reveal Bambara's remarkable ear for everyday speech. As critic Ann Tyler notes, "Everything these people say you feel ordinary, real-life people are saying right now on any street corner. It's only that the rest of us didn't realize that it was sheer poetry they were speaking."

NOVELS BY BAMBARA

If Blessing Comes (1987). Random 1987 $6.95. ISBN 0-394-75087-0
The Salt Eaters (1981). Random 1981 $5.95. ISBN 0-394-75050-0

SHORT STORY COLLECTIONS BY BAMBARA

*Gorilla, My Love (1972). Random 1981 $4.95. ISBN 0-394-75049-7 Fifteen stories of African-American life, filled with remarkably real and familiar characters.
* The Sea Birds Are Still Alive (1977). Random 1982 $6.95. ISBN 0-394-71176-9 Ten stories of love, politics, and community, full of unforgettable characters.

BOOKS ABOUT BAMBARA

Sternberg, Janet (ed). *The Writer on Her Work.* Norton 1981 $10.95. ISBN 0-393-00071-0 Includes Bambara's essay "What It Is I Think I'm Doing Anyhow."
Tate, Claudia (ed). *Black Women Writers at Work.* Continuum 1984 $9.95. ISBN 0-8264-0243-7 An interview with Bambara as well as biographical background and commentary on her work.

BARAKA, AMIRI 1934–

Born Everett LeRoi Jones in Newark, New Jersey, Baraka briefly attended Howard University, but he left before completing his degree, joining the U.S. Air Force, where he served until 1956. Then he returned to New Jersey where he began his career as a writer. He first became known as a playwright and poet under his given name of LeRoi Jones. He became increasingly active in the civil rights movement and became one of the best-known of the African American writers who protested racism in the 1960s. In 1965 he converted to the Islamic faith and took the name of Imamu Amiri Baraka, later dropping the name "Imamu."

In addition to writing and working in the theater, Baraka has taught at a number of colleges and universities, including The New School for Social Research, Columbia University, the State University of New York at Stony Brook, and Rutgers University. He has also directed the Black Arts Repertory Theater in Harlem.

Always a maverick, Baraka's literary career has been marked by controversy. He is committed to the idea of using his art, especially his theater, as a weapon against oppression. His original attacks against racism have given way in recent years to broader attacks on the capitalist system, which Baraka, a Marxist, believes oppresses white and black citizens alike.

Baraka's work also brings together revolutionary art and the African-American experience. He draws his themes, characters, and voice from the African-American culture. However, Baraka does not wish merely to portray African-American experience, but desires to make his art the basis for advocating revolutionary change.

PLAYS BY BARAKA

The Baptism and The Toilet, Two Plays (1967). Grove 1967 $3.95. ISBN 0-802-17253-1
Dutchman and The Slave, Two Plays (1964). Morrow 1964 $7.95. ISBN 0-688-21084-8
Sidnee Poet Heroical (1975). Reed 1979 $5.95. ISBN 0-918408-12-1

POETRY BY BARAKA

It's Nation Time (1970). Third World 1970 $1.50. ISBN 0-88378-008-9
Reggae or Not! (1982). Contact 1982 $3.00. ISBN 0-936556-04-8

NONFICTION BY BARAKA

Black Music (1968). Morrow 1971 $8.95. ISBN 0-688-24344-4
Blues People: Negro Music in White America (1963). Morrow 1963 $9.95. ISBN 0-688-18474-X
The Music: Reflections on Jazz and Blues (1987). Morrow 1987 $22.95. ISBN 0-688-04388-7
Raise Race Rays Raze: Essays Since 1965 (1971). University Place 1971 $12.50. ISBN 0-685-77057-5

BOOKS ABOUT BARAKA

Baraka, Amiri. *The Autobiography of LeRoi Jones/Amiri Baraka.* Freundlich 1984 $16.95. ISBN 0-88191-000-7 Details Baraka's artistic and political views as well as his personal life.
Harris, William. *The Poetry and Poetics of Amiri Baraka: The Jazz Aesthetic.* Univ of Missouri Pr 1985 $20.00. ISBN 0-8262-0483-X Shows the influence of jazz music on Baraka's poetic principles.
Hudson, Theodore. *From LeRoi Jones to Amiri Baraka: The Literary Works.* Duke Univ Pr 1973 $23.95. ISBN 0-8223-0296-9 Scholarly analysis and criticism of Baraka's early work.

BARTHELME, DONALD   1931–1989

Born in Philadelphia, Donald Barthelme grew up in Texas, served in the army, worked as museum director in Houston, and did editorial work before establishing himself as a fiction writer. His first book, *Come Back, Dr. Caligari* (1964), is a collection of short stories, a form in which Barthelme is particularly comfortable.

In 1967, Barthelme's novel, *Snow White,* was published in *The New Yorker* magazine. It took up almost an entire issue, an honor few books have ever received. The novel is an unusual retelling of the fairy tale in which Snow White shares an apartment with seven short businessmen who have grown rich by selling Asian baby foods. The evil stepmother is named Jane Villiers de l'Isle Adam, and the prince turns out to be a real frog.

This kind of highly imaginative, farfetched writing is typical of Barthelme. His stories are filled with references to other literature and authors, and he frequently makes use of real people as fictional characters in a startling way. Barthelme also likes to break down barriers of time. For example, in one of his stories, he uses a typical "cowboys and Indians" story line to portray guerilla warfare in a modern urban ghetto.

Because Barthelme has been heavily influenced by movies and television, his writing often has the feel of a Monty Python film, where nothing is quite as it should be. He has even included a questionaire in a story to ask the reader how the story should proceed.

NOVEL BY BARTHELME

The Dead Father (1975). Pocket 1978 $2.25. ISBN 0-671-82305-1

SHORT STORY COLLECTIONS BY BARTHELME

City Life (1970). Pocket 1978 $2.25. ISBN 0-671-82304-3
Come Back, Dr. Caligari (1964). Little 1971 $7.95. ISBN 0-316-08254-6
Forty Stories (1989). Penguin 1989 $7.95. ISBN 0-14-011245-6
Great Days (1979). Pocket 1980 $2.50. ISBN 0-671-83673-0
Overnight to Many Distant Cities (1983). Penguin 1985 $6.95. ISBN 0-14-007580-1
Sadness (1972). Pocket 1980 $2.95. ISBN 0-671-83204-2
Sixty Stories (1981). Dutton 1986 $10.95. ISBN 0-525-48328-4
Unspeakable Practices, Unnatural Acts (1968). Pocket 1978 $2.25. ISBN 0-671-82306-X

BOOK ABOUT BARTHELME

Gordon, Louis. *Donald Barthelme.* G. K. Hall 1982 $14.50. ISBN 0-8057-7347-9 General introduction to Barthelme's life and fiction with discussions of individual works.

BAUM, L. (LYMAN) FRANK   1856–1919

L. Frank Baum, the author of 14 books about the magical land of Oz, was at various times a journalist, a dramatist, and the editor of a trade magazine for store-window decorators. His first book, *Father Goose: His Book* (1899), was very popular, but nothing to match the success of the book that followed a year later, *The Wonderful Wizard of Oz* (1900). The story of the little girl Dorothy and her dog Toto whirled off from the dull Kansas plain to the colorful and exciting land of Oz has continued to move readers for generations, as has the extraordinarily popular 1939 film version of the book. *The Wonderful Wizard of Oz* was followed by 13 sequels, including *The Land of Oz* (1904), *Ozma of Oz* (1907), *The Road to Oz* (1909), and *The Lost Princess of Oz* (1917). Baum wrote more than 60 books for children, including a number of books expressly for girls, published under the pseudonym Edith Van Dyne.

NOVELS BY BAUM

*The Oz Series. Fourteen books that recount the adventures of Dorothy and her friends as they discover the many surprising secrets of the enchanting land of Oz and its neighboring magic lands. They are listed below in the order in which they were written.
The Wonderful Wizard of Oz (1900). Ballantine 1986 $2.95. ISBN 0-345-33590-2
The Land of Oz (1904). Ballantine 1985 $3.50. ISBN 0-345-33568-6
Ozma of Oz (1907). Ballantine 1986 $2.95. ISBN 0-345-33589-9
Dorothy and the Wizard in Oz (1908). Ballantine 1985 $2.95. ISBN 0-345-34168-6
The Road to Oz (1909). Ballantine 1984 $2.95. ISBN 0-345-33467-1
The Emerald City of Oz (1910). Ballantine 1985 $3.50. ISBN 0-345-33464-7
The Patchwork Girl of Oz (1913). Ballantine 1985 $3.50. ISBN 0-345-33290-3

Tik-Tok of Oz (1914). Ballantine 1980 $3.50. ISBN 0-345-33435-3
The Scarecrow of Oz (1915). Ballantine 1980 $3.50. ISBN 0-345-33396-9
Rinkitink in Oz (1916). Ballantine 1980 $2.95. ISBN 0-345-33317-9
The Lost Princess of Oz (1917). Ballantine 1980 $3.50. ISBN 0-345-33367-5
The Tin Woodman of Oz (1918). Ballantine 1985 $3.50. ISBN 0-345-33436-1
The Magic of Oz (1919). Ballantine 1981 $2.95. ISBN 0-345-33288-1
Glinda of Oz (1920). Ballantine 1981 $2.95. ISBN 0-345-33394-2

BELLOW, SAUL 1915–

The son of immigrant Russian parents, Saul Bellow was born Solomon Bellows in a small town in Quebec, Canada. His family moved to Chicago when he was nine. A graduate of Northwestern University, Bellow did graduate work in anthropology at the University of Wisconsin until he decided to devote himself to writing. He served in the Merchant Marine in World War II and worked for publishing companies in New York before returning to the Midwest and settling into an academic career. Since 1962 he has been a faculty member at the University of Chicago.

Even before Bellow won the Nobel Prize for literature in 1976, *Newsweek* magazine called him "the most honored American novelist of his age." By 1975 he had received several Guggenheim Fellowships, a Pulitzer Prize, and three National Book Awards.

Bellow is one of the few writers to enjoy high standing among both critics and the general public, partly because he exists so comfortably between extremes. Bellow is neither very liberal nor very conservative in his politics but always aware of changing social conditions and in tune with the prevailing moods in America.

The Adventures of Augie March (1953) is generally considered to be the novel that first brought Bellow his current fame. It is a long, involved story of a young man and his encounters with the people who have influenced his life. In this book Bellow began to develop the style that has come to characterize his work. This style combines the movement and energy of city street talk with the plain speech of the Midwest and the more formal language of an intellectual. *The Adventures of Augie March* brought Bellow not only his first National Book Award, but wide public acceptance as a writer.

In his later works Bellow has avoided falling into any predictable pattern. These novels vary from the African adventures of a Yankee millionaire in *Henderson the Rain King* (1959) to the autobiographical story in *Herzog* (1964) of Moses Herzog, a twice-divorced professor who writes letters to people, both dead and alive, in an attempt to make sense of his life of failure and frustration.

Although most of Bellow's central characters are Jewish, and he himself comes from a Jewish background, his scope goes beyond what is suggested by the label "Jewish writer." His novels speak not just of the Jewish experience but of the human experience in the modern world. He appeals to all those who recognize parallels to their own lives in his stories.

NOVELS BY BELLOW

The Adventures of Augie March (1953). Penguin 1984 $6.95. ISBN 0-14-007272-1
Dangling Man (1944). Penguin 1988 $6.95. ISBN 0-14-001862-X
The Dean's December (1982). Washington Square Pr 1983 $4.50. ISBN 0-671-60254-3

Henderson the Rain King (1959). Penguin 1984 $5.95. ISBN 0-14-007269-1
Herzog (1964). Penguin 1984 $6.95. ISBN 0-14-007270-5
Humboldt's Gift (1975). Penguin 1984 $7.95. ISBN 0-14-007271-3
Mr. Sammler's Planet (1970). Penguin 1984 $6.95. ISBN 0-14-007317-5
More Die of Heartbreak (1987). Dell 1988 $4.95. ISBN 0-440-20110-1
Seize the Day (1961). Penguin 1984 $4.95. ISBN 0-14-007285-3
A Thief (1989). Penguin 1989 $6.95. ISBN 0-14-011969-8
The Victim (1947). Penguin 1988 $6.95. ISBN 0-14-002493-X

Short Story Collections by Bellow

Him with His Foot in His Mouth and Other Stories (1984). Pocket 1985 $4.50. ISBN 0-671-55247-3
Mosby's Memoirs and Other Stories (1968). Penguin 1984 $5.95. ISBN 0-14-007318-3
The Portable Saul Bellow (1977). Penguin 1977 $9.95. ISBN 0-14-015079-X

Books about Bellow

Bloom, Harold (ed). *Saul Bellow.* Chelsea 1986 $24.50. ISBN 0-87754-622-3 A collection of modern critical essays representing different schools of criticism.
Dutton, Robert P. *Saul Bellow.* G. K. Hall 1982 $17.95. ISBN 0-8057-7353-3 An overview of Bellow's life and work with discussions of individual titles.

BENET, STEPHEN VINCENT   1898–1943

Stephen Vincent Benét was the son of an army officer and spent his childhood moving from base to base. From his father he learned a love of history, which was to influence his later writing.

Benét began writing seriously while at Yale University and published his first volume of poetry before he graduated in 1919. He continued his studies at Yale and at the Sorbonne in Paris, and, at the same time, kept on publishing.

The major focus of Benét's writing is the American experience. His work is focused on the question of what it means to be an American. In *John Brown's Body* (1928), his best-known poem and the winner of a Pulitzer Prize, he examines how the Civil War shaped the American character. In *Western Star* (1943), a long Pulitzer Prize-winning narrative poem left unfinished at his death, he looks at the migrations of Europeans to North America in the 1600s.

Unlike most writers of his time, Benét composed verse that is quite traditional in form, using standard meters and rhyme schemes. However, his inventiveness appears in his innovative treatment of his subject matter and in his choice of words.

Although Benét wrote novels, he is best remembered for his poetry and short stories. The story "The Devil and Daniel Webster" is his best-known piece of fiction.

Short Story Collections by Benet

**The Devil and Daniel Webster and Other Stories.* Pocket 1980 $1.75. ISBN 0-671-42889-6
    Contains the classic story of a lawyer who can out-argue the Devil.
The Last Circle (1946). Ayer (repr of 1946 ed) $20.00. ISBN 0-8369-4217-5
Thirteen O'Clock, Stories of Several Worlds (1937). Ayer (repr of 1937 ed) $24.50. ISBN 0-8369-3793-7

Poetry by Benet

**John Brown's Body* (1928). Buccaneer 1980 $23.95. ISBN 0-89966-405-9 A long poem about the events and fascinating characters that precipitated the outbreak of the Civil War.

BOOK ABOUT BENET

Fenton, Charles. *Stephen Vincent Benét: The Life and Times of an American Man of Letters.* Greenwood 1978 $37.50. ISBN 0-313-20200-1 Essentially a biography that emphasizes Benét's American spirit; some attention to his works.

BLUME, JUDY   1938–

Judy Blume is unquestionably one of today's most popular writers of young adult fiction. Born Judy Sussman in Elizabeth, New Jersey, she attended local schools and then went on to New York University, where she met John Blume, a lawyer. They were married in her junior year, and their first child was born one year after she graduated. After living the life of a suburban housewife for several years, she grew restless and decided to write. Her first book, *The One in the Middle Is the Green Kangaroo* (1969), was written for primary school children, but her second, *Iggie's House* (1970), was aimed at an older audience.

Most of Blume's books deal with the problems of growing up, especially those problems typically faced at ages 11, 12, and 13. She concentrates on the ordinary concerns of ordinary kids: popularity, physical appearance, and sexual curiosity. Because she deals directly with the question of sex, some of Blume's books have caused concern in some communities. *Forever* (1975), which concerns a young girl's first sexual experiences, has been particularly controversial.

Blume has also written novels for adults, similarly focusing on relationships and romance in their themes.

NOVELS BY BLUME

*Are You There God? It's Me, Margaret (1970). Dell 1972 $2.95. ISBN 0-440-90419-6 Margaret Simon tries to cope with everything from choosing a religion to wondering why her body will not mature.

*Blubber (1974). Dell 1978 $2.95. ISBN 0-440-90707-1 The story of an overweight fifth-grade girl who is taunted by her classmates.

*Deenie (1973). Dell 1974 $3.25. ISBN 0-440-93259-9 Pretty 13-year-old Deenie learns that she must wear a back brace.

*Forever (1975). Pocket 1984 $3.50. ISBN 0-671-53225-1 The story of a young girl's first sexual experiences and what they mean to her.

*It's Not the End of the World (1972). Dell 1986 $3.25. ISBN 0-440-94140-7 Young children face their parents' divorce.

*Starring Sally J. Freedman as Herself (1977). Dell 1986 $3.25. ISBN 0-440-98239-1 Sally's fantasy world is disturbed by Adolf Hitler.

*Superfudge (1980). Dell 1981 $3.25. ISBN 0-440-48433-2 Fudge is about to enter kindergarten while he worries about the new baby in the house.

*Tales of a Fourth Grade Nothing (1972). Dell 1986 $2.95. ISBN 0-440-48474-X The story of Peter and his mischievous baby brother, Fudge.

*Then Again, Maybe I Won't (1971). Dell 1976 $2.95. ISBN 0-440-98659-1 When a young boy's family suddenly becomes rich, he must adjust to a new life.

*Tiger Eyes (1981). Dell 1982 $3.25. ISBN 0-440-98469-6 A young girl's father is killed in a robbery of his store, and she and her mother must start a new life.

BOOKS ABOUT BLUME

Gallo, Donald R. (ed). *Speaking for Ourselves.* NCTE 1990 $12.95. ISBN 0-8141-4625-2 A fascinating collection of autobiographical sketches of 87 young-adult authors, including Blume; authors share stories of how they started to write and of significant events that influenced them; includes complete list of published works and dates.

*Lee, Betsy. *Judy Blume's Story.* Dillon 1981 $8.95. ISBN 0-87518-209-7 A biography of
   Blume that also discusses her writing career; suitable for young readers.
Weidt, Margaret N. *Presenting Judy Blume.* G. K. Hall 1986 $18.95. ISBN 0-8057-8208-7
   An introduction to the life and works of Judy Blume.

BRADBURY, RAY   1920–

Ray Bradbury was born in Waukegan, Illinois, but moved with his family to
Los Angeles when he was 13. He attended Los Angeles High School, where he
wrote and produced a mimeographed magazine called *Futuria Fantasia.* During
these years he also fell in love with Hollywood and the movies. After graduating from high school, he joined a theater group in Los Angeles but left after
a year. He worked at odd jobs to support himself while writing. He sold his
first story in 1941, and was able to earn his living through writing just a few
years later.

Bradbury gained wide critical and popular recognition in 1950 with the
publication of *The Martian Chronicles,* a collection of short stories loosely linked
by brief narrative passages. While the stories are set on Mars, they are not
science fiction in the usual sense. Rather they are "frontier" stories that show
the problems of two cultures colliding—in this case Earthlings and Martians,
just as the European settlers and American Indians confronted each other in the
Old West. These tales marked Bradbury as a writer of vision and sensitivity,
a reputation he has lived up to in his later work.

While he unquestionably does his best work in the short story, Bradbury
has also published two excellent novels, *Fahrenheit 451* (1953) and *Something
Wicked This Way Comes* (1962). He has also written plays and screenplays, including the highly acclaimed script for the movie version of *Moby Dick.*

Bradbury sees the human imagination as being the key to success in any
endeavor, and his stories often focus on the power of the imagination to make
miracles. Ironically, this creator of sophisticated spaceships and other technological wonders admitted in a recent interview not only to a fear of flying but
to a dread of driving. He does not own an automobile and will ride in one only
when absolutely necessary, since he considers cars unsafe for human use.

NOVELS BY BRADBURY

Fahrenheit 451 (1953). Ballantine 1987 $3.95. ISBN 0-345-34296-8 A story of a future
   in which reading is a crime and all books are burned.
Something Wicked This Way Comes (1962). Bantam 1983 $3.50. ISBN 0-553-25774-9 After
   the performance of a carnival show, some of the town's residents begin to change
   form.

SHORT STORY COLLECTIONS BY BRADBURY

Dandelion Wine (1957). Bantam 1983 $3.95. ISBN 0-553-27753-7 A 12-year-old boy
   discovers that his small town hides many strange stories.
I Sing the Body Electric (1969). Bantam 1976 $3.95. ISBN 0-553-26319-6 A collection of
   stories about the strange and mysterious world of the imagination; title comes
   from famous poem by American writer Walt Whitman.
The Illustrated Man (1951). Bantam 1969 $3.50. ISBN 0-553-25483-9 The story of a man
   who is covered with tattoos, each tattoo having its own story.
The October Country (1955). Ballantine 1989 $4.95. ISBN 0-345-25040-0 A collection of
   19 stories, including "The Dwarf" and "The Lake."
The Toynbee Convector (1988). Bantam 1989 $3.95. ISBN 0-553-27957-2 Twenty-three
   stories, most of which begin in familiar settings and then move into the realm of
   the imagination.

POETRY BY BRADBURY

When Elephants Last in the Dooryard Bloomed (1973). Knopf 1973 $8.95. ISBN 0-394-47931-9 The title comes from a famous poem by American writer Walt Whitman.

BOOKS ABOUT BRADBURY

Mogen, David. *Ray Bradbury*. G. K. Hall 1986 $17.95. ISBN 0-8057-7464-5 Traces the literary influences that shaped Bradbury as well as the evolution of his style and reputation.

Toupence, William F. *Ray Bradbury*. Borgo 1988 $17.95. ISBN 0-89370-958-1 A reader's guide to Bradbury's fiction.

BRAUTIGAN, RICHARD   1935–1984

Richard Brautigan was born in either Spokane or Tacoma, Washington—reference sources disagree. Because of his reluctance to talk about his personal history, many details of Brautigan's early life are uncertain. Even Brautigan's father did not know of his existence until after his son's death, since he separated from his son's mother without knowing about her pregnancy.

Brautigan was very much a writer of the 1960s. His poetry, most of it written between 1957 and 1969, expresses the disenchantment with U.S. life felt by many young Americans during those years. Brautigan's verse praises the value of personal relationships and intimacy and scorns the pursuit of wealth and material possessions. He carried these same themes into his novels, beginning with *In Watermelon Sugar* (1964). Brautigan's narrators take life as it comes, always with good humor, seemingly unaware of any evil or catastrophe they may encounter. In *Trout Fishing in America* (1967), Brautigan's most popular novel, the narrator is searching for a morning of good fishing. The book follows him as he travels all over America through forests and cities, parks and campgrounds, even to a laundry and finally to a junkyard that sells used trout streams by the foot. Through such whimsical devices, Brautigan brings into sharp focus all the evils and emptiness he sees in the American society.

Since he was a voice of the 1960s, Brautigan became a speaker without a listener when the decade passed. His career steadily declined and, despondent, he took his own life in 1984.

NOVELS BY BRAUTIGAN

The Abortion: An Historical Romance 1966 (1970). Pocket 1975 $2.25. ISBN 0-671-82797-9
Dreaming of Babylon (1972). Dell 1978 $4.95. ISBN 0-385-28221-4
The Hawkline Monster: A Gothic Western (1975). Pocket 1981 $2.95. ISBN 0-671-43786-0
In Watermelon Sugar (1964). Dell 1973 $1.75. ISBN 0-440-34026-0

SHORT STORY COLLECTION BY BRAUTIGAN

Revenge of the Lawn: Stories 1962–1970 (1971). Pocket 1980 $2.95. ISBN 0-671-41852-1

POETRY BY BRAUTIGAN

Loading Mercury with a Pitchfork (1975). Simon 1976 $7.95. ISBN 0-671-22263-5

BOOK ABOUT BRAUTIGAN

Boyer, Jay. *Richard Brautigan*. Boise State Univ Pr 1987 $2.95. ISBN 0-88430-078-1 A brief introduction to Brautigan's works.

BRIDGERS, SUE ELLEN   1942–

Sue Ellen Hunsucker was born into a farm family in Greenville, North Carolina. In 1963 she married an attorney, Ben Oshel Bridgers, and in 1976 she completed her bachelor's degree at Western Carolina University.

Bridgers began writing in the early 1970s and has contributed stories to a number of magazines, including *Ingenue, Redbook, Carolina Quarterly,* and *Mountain Living.* She published her first novel, *Home Before Dark,* in 1976 and went on to publish four others.

Bridgers's stories focus on family relationships and the stresses that threaten family unity. She examines families struggling to survive problems such as mental illness, divorce, and even attempted suicide. Although the power of love is important in her novels, it is not presented as an automatic cure for all problems. In Bridgers's world people have to work hard at preserving love.

Bridgers's books also show the influence of her own rural background. Her settings are small southern towns and her characters cling to the values of a rural way of life that is fast fading from the American scene. Her novels are tinged with a sense of regret at this passing.

Young people play a central role in Bridgers's stories. However, her rich portraits of troubled families and hard-won love have a strong appeal to readers of all ages.

NOVELS BY BRIDGERS

*All Together Now (1979). Bantam 1980 $2.75. ISBN 0-553-26845-7 A 12-year-old girl's summer in a rural southern town causes people around her to sort out their own emotions.

*Home Before Dark (1976). Bantam 1985 $2.50. ISBN 0-553-26432-X The 14-year-old daughter of a migrant farmer is determined to put down roots and have a home.

*Notes for Another Life (1981). Bantam 1988 $2.95. ISBN 0-553-27185-7 A father's permanent mental illness forces a young girl and her brother to begin a new life.

*Permanent Connections (1987). Harper 1988 $2.95. ISBN 0-06-447020-2 When a young boy with drug problems is sent to a southern farm, he falls in love with a sensitive young girl.

*Sara Will (1985). Harper 1986 $14.95. ISBN 0-317-63004-0 The arrival of a teenage unwed mother radically changes the life of a 50-year-old unmarried woman.

BOOKS ABOUT BRIDGERS

Gallo, Donald R. (ed). *Speaking for Ourselves.* NCTE 1990 $12.95. ISBN 0-8141-4625-2 A fascinating collection of autobiographical sketches of 87 young-adult authors, including Bridges; authors share stories of how they started to write and of significant events that influenced them; includes complete list of published works and dates.

Hipple, Ted. *Presenting Sue Ellen Bridgers.* G. K. Hall 1990 $18.95. ISBN 0-8057-8213-3 An excellent overview of Bridgers's fiction and life.

BROOKS, GWENDOLYN   1917–

Gwendolyn Brooks was born in Topeka, Kansas, but moved as a child to Chicago, where she grew up and has since spent most of her life. Brooks graduated from Wilson Junior College in 1936 and married Henry L. Blakeley three years later. At age 13 she published her first poem in a children's magazine and has been writing poetry steadily ever since.

After the publication of her first book of poetry, *A Street in Bronzeville* (1945), Brooks was chosen one of the 10 Women of the Year by *Mademoiselle* magazine. In 1946 she received an award for creative writing from the American Academy of Arts and Letters and a Guggenheim Fellowship. Her second book of poems, *Annie Allen* (1949), won the 1950 Pulitzer Prize.

Brooks is recognized for her great technical skill as a poet. Her imagery is especially powerful, and she can create a whole scene in just a few lines. She is also known for providing rich portraits of African Americans, drawing on both feelings and political issues important to that community. Because Brooks's early poems are technically complex, they can be difficult to read, and so they tend to appeal to a more educated audience. Her later poetry, after 1967, is more direct, geared to reaching a wider audience through its forceful imagery and language. Brooks herself became especially concerned at this time with reaching the widest possible audience of African Americans.

Although Brooks is known primarily as a poet, she has also written a sensitive and moving novel, *Maud Martha* (1953). In her autobiography, *Report from Part I* (1972), she reflects on the influences that shaped her as a poet and as a person.

POETRY BY BROOKS

Aloneness (1971). Broadside 1971 $5.00. ISBN 0-910296-55-3 Poems for young people
  about the African-American experience.
Annie Allen (1949). Greenwood 1972 $35.00. ISBN 0-8371-5561-4
Beckonings (1975). Broadside 1975 $5.00. ISBN 0-685-51286-X
Family Pictures (1970). Broadside 1970 $5.00. ISBN 0-685-24799-6
Selected Poems (1963). Harper 1963 $6.95. ISBN 0-06-090989-7

NONFICTION BY BROOKS

Report from Part I. Broadside 1972 $17.95. ISBN 0-910296-82-0 An autobiography de-
  scribing significant influences on Brooks's art and life.

BOOKS ABOUT BROOKS

Melhem, D. H. *Gwendolyn Brooks: Poetry and the Heroic Voice.* Univ Pr of Kentucky 1987
  $12.00. ISBN 0-8131-1605-8 A close reading of Brooks's poetry with emphasis on
  her themes.
Stanford, Barbara Dodds, and Karima Amin. *Black Literature for High School Students.*
  NCTE 1978. (o.p.) $4.95. ISBN 0-8141-0330-8 Contains a chapter on Brooks,
  including an interview.

BROWN, STERLING   1901–1989

Sterling Brown was born in Washington, D.C., the son of a religion professor at Howard University. He attended public schools in Washington and completed his undergraduate education at Williams College in Massachusetts, where he graduated with honors and was elected to the Phi Beta Kappa honor society. He continued his education at Harvard University, receiving his master's degree in 1923. After leaving Harvard, Brown took teaching positions at several colleges before finally becoming a professor of English at Howard University in 1929. He remained at Howard for 40 years, retiring in 1969.

Brown's influence on African American literature, particularly poetry, has been profound. In an interview in *Ebony* magazine, critic and scholar Darwin Turner said, "I discovered that all trails led, at some point, to Sterling Brown. His *Negro Caravan* was *the* anthology of Afro-American literature. His unpublished study of Afro-American theater was *the* major work in the field. His study of images of Afro-Americans in American literature was a pioneer work. His essays on folk literature and folklore were preeminent. He was not always the best critic . . . but Brown was and is the literary historian who wrote the Bible [sic] for the study of Afro-American literature." In all, Brown contributed over 600 scholarly articles on American literature, both black and white, to a wide variety of journals.

Brown's own poetry is marked by two important characteristics: his use of authentic African-American dialect and African-American folklore. He is a skilled narrative poet, and his best-known works, such as the Slim Greer poems, tell captivating and often amusing stories in fresh and lively rhythms. With the black consciousness movement of the late 1960s, interest in Brown's poetry began to increase, and this once-neglected writer has begun to take his rightful place in the forefront of American literature.

POETRY BY BROWN

The Collected Poems of Sterling A. Brown. Michael Harper (ed). Harper 1980 $15.95. ISBN 0-06-010517-8
*The Last Ride of Wild Bill and Eleven Narrative Poems. Broadside 1975 $3.00. ISBN 0-910296-02-2 Lively and entertaining tales in verse.
*Southern Road (1932). Beacon 1974 $3.45. ISBN 0-8070-6387-8 Verse portraits of memorable Southern characters.

NONFICTION BY BROWN

The Negro Caravan (1941). (coauthored with Arthur P. Davis and Ulysses Lee) Ayer 1978 repr of 1941 ed $52.95. ISBN 0-405-01852-5
The Negro in American Fiction and Negro Poetry and Drama (1937). Ayer 1972 repr of 1937 ed $15.00. ISBN 0-405-01851-7

BOOKS ABOUT BROWN

Gabbin, Joane V. *Sterling A. Brown: Building the Black Aesthetic Tradition.* Greenwood 1985 $36.95. ISBN 0-313-23720-4 A critical biography with a comprehensive bibliography.
Wagner, Jean. *Black Poets of the United States.* Kenneth Douglas (tr). Univ of Illinois Pr 1973 $12.50. ISBN 0-252-00341-1 Includes an unusually comprehensive chapter on Brown.

BUCK, PEARL 1892–1973

Pearl Buck was born Pearl Sydenstricker in Hillsboro, West Virginia, while her missionary parents were on a brief visit to the United States. While still an infant, she returned with them to China, where she grew up. She was tutored privately there and then sent back to the United States to complete her education at Randolph-Macon Woman's College in Virginia. After graduation, she returned to China, where she soon after married an American resident, John Buck. She taught English in Nanking from 1921 to 1931.

Buck published her first novel, *East Wind: West Wind,* in 1930. It was an immediate success and led directly to her second—and best—work, the novel *The Good Earth* (1931). Based on her own experiences and her firsthand knowledge of the lives of Chinese peasants, this story of a family of poor Chinese farmers seemed to U.S. audiences to capture the spirit and the details of Chinese life, although Asian critics later found it sentimental and condescending. The book became a best-seller almost immediately and won high critical praise in the West. The book was awarded the Pulitzer Prize in 1931. Buck followed with two more novels about the same family, *Sons* (1932) and *A House Divided* (1935). Although they were popular, these two did not receive the same lavish praise that had been heaped on *The Good Earth.*

When the Japanese invaded China in 1931, conditions there grew tense, and in 1934 Buck returned to the United States, where she lived for the rest of her life. She continued writing at a furious pace and in 1936 published biographies of her father and mother, *Fighting Angel* and *The Exile.* These books were highly praised and, along with *The Good Earth,* helped Buck to win the Nobel Prize in 1938. She was the first female American writer to be so honored.

Over the last 35 years of her life, Buck produced a huge quantity of fiction—novels, children's books, and short stories—but none measured up to her earlier work. Her popularity has not stood the test of time, and today only a handful of her books remain in print.

NOVELS BY BUCK

Come My Beloved (1953). Pocket 1975 $1.75. ISBN 0-671-80084-1
Death in the Castle (1965). Amereon (repr of 1965 ed) $15.95. ISBN 0-8488-0435-X
The Good Earth (1931). Pocket 1983 $2.95. ISBN 0-671-50086-4 The story of a Chinese peasant family's rise from poverty to wealth.
The Patriot (1939). Crowell 1963 $8.95. ISBN 0-381-98048-0

SHORT STORY COLLECTIONS BY BUCK

Secrets of the Heart (1976). Crowell 1965 $14.45. ISBN 0-381-98287-4
The Woman Who Was Changed and Other Stories (1979). Crowell 1979 $11.95. ISBN 0-690-01789-8

BOOKS ABOUT BUCK

Doyle, Paul A. *Pearl S. Buck.* G. K. Hall 1980 $16.95. ISBN 0-8057-7325-8 A comprehensive general study of Buck's life and works with an exceptionally useful list of additional resources.
*LaFarge, Ann. *Pearl Buck.* Chelsea 1988 $17.95. ISBN 1-55546-645-1 An introduction for younger readers to Buck's life and works; primarily biography.
*Schoen, Celin V. *Pearl Buck: Famed American Author of Oriental Stories.* D. Steve Rahmas (ed). SamHar 1972 $2.50. ISBN 0-87157-030-0 A brief introduction for young readers to Buck's life and works.

BURROUGHS, EDGAR RICE   1875–1950

Edgar Rice Burroughs was born in Chicago, the son of a successful businessman. He attended a number of different private preparatory schools, including Phillips Andover Academy in Massachusetts, before finally graduating from Michigan Military Academy. He then drifted from job to job, including gold miner, storekeeper, and cowboy. He even served briefly in the U.S. Cavalry until he was discharged for being underage.

At age 36, Burroughs began writing, convinced he could write better stories than those in the adventure magazines he was so fond of reading. The result was a steady stream of stories and novels that have become a basic part of American popular literature.

Burrough's best-known and most enduring creation is Tarzan, the English aristocrat who is raised by apes in an African jungle. Burroughs wrote 25 Tarzan tales, all but one of which are still in print. Since Tarzan first appeared on the screen in 1917, there have been 42 movies based on him. In addition to the Tarzan stories, Burroughs also wrote a sizeable body of science fiction, the most notable being his Mars series, which recounts the adventures of John Carter on the dying planet of Mars.

Besides his fantasy and adventure stories, Burroughs also wrote *The War Chief* (1927) and *Apache Devil* (1933), a pair of realistic historical novels based on the final years of the Apache wars from the 1870s to the mid-1880s. These books have been praised for their historical accuracy and their sensitive and honest portrayal of Apache life.

Because of the large number of Burroughs books in print, only a sampling from each series is given below. Additional titles can be found in *Books in Print.*

NOVEL SERIES BY BURROUGHS

*The Tarzan Series (These exciting tales of the ape-man's exploits are arranged in the order that Burroughs wrote them.)
  Tarzan of the Apes (1914). Ballantine 1984 $3.50. ISBN 0-345-31977-X
  The Return of Tarzan (1915). Ballantine 1984 $2.95. ISBN 0-345-31575-8
  The Beasts of Tarzan (1916). Ballantine 1984 $2.25. ISBN 0-345-32433-1
  The Son of Tarzan (1917). Ballantine 1975 $2.50. ISBN 0-345-33556-2
  Tarzan and the Jewels of Opar (1918). Ballantine 1984 $2.50. ISBN 0-345-32161-8
  Tarzan the Untamed (1920). Ballantine 1984 $3.50. ISBN 0-345-32391-2
*The Mars Series. John Carter's thrilling adventures on the dying planet of Mars.
  The Chessmen of Mars (1922). Ballantine 1979 $2.95. ISBN 0-345-35038-3
  A Fighting Man of Mars (1931). Ballantine 1986 $3.50. ISBN 0-345-32956-8
  Gods of Mars (1918). Ballantine 1984 $3.50. ISBN 0-345-32439-0
  A Princess of Mars (1917). Ballantine 1985 $2.95. ISBN 0-33138-9
  Warlord of Mars (1919). Ballantine 1985 $2.95. ISBN 0-345-32453-6

OTHER NOVELS BY BURROUGHS

Apache Devil (1933). Buccaneer 1976 repr of 1933 ed $16.20. ISBN 0-89966-043-6 Story of the Apache chief Geronimo.
The War Chief (1927). Buccaneer 1976 repr of 1927 ed $16.95. ISBN 0-89966-044-4 Story of the Apache wars after the death of the Apache chief Cochise.

BOOKS ABOUT BURROUGHS

Holtsmark, Erling B. *Edgar Rice Burroughs.* G. K. Hall 1986 $15.95. ISBN 0-8057-7459-9 An excellent introduction to Burrough's life and works.
Holtsmark, Erling B. *Tarzan and Tradition: Classical Myth in Popular Literature.* Greenwood 1981 $35.00. ISBN 0-313-22530-3 Links the Tarzan books to superhero mythology.
Lupoff, Richard A. *Barsoom: Edgar Rice Burroughs and the Martian Vision.* Mirage 1976 $7.50. ISBN 0-88358-116-7 A study of Burroughs's science-fiction tales.

CATHER, WILLA   1873–1947

Willa Cather was born in Virginia but her family moved to Red Cloud, Nebraska, when she was nine years old. In 1890, finding Red Cloud too restrictive and conservative, Cather moved to Lincoln and later enrolled in the University of Nebraska. After graduation she moved again, this time to Pittsburgh, and became a journalist, but a few years later Cather abandoned newspaper work and became a high school English teacher. In 1905, she joined the staff of a major New York magazine, where she began writing seriously.

Cather's reputation has grown steadily over the years, and she is now considered to be a major American writer. Her style is straightforward and simple, and her books usually concern ordinary people and their daily lives. Her work has proved lasting because of her skill at telling a story and creating memorable characters.

The most popular of Cather's novels is *My Antonia* (1918), admired not only for its warm portrayal of a remarkably human character but also for the subtlety and skill with which Cather tells her story. Cather's own favorite was *Death Comes for the Archbishop* (1927), her fictionalized account of the first bishop appointed to the New Mexico territory. *The Song of the Lark* (1915) is the most autobiographical of Cather's novels. This story of singer Thea Kronberg is really a disguised version of Cather's own rise to fame. In *The Professor's House* (1925), Cather tells the story of a burnt-out, middle-aged historian whose life is contrasted with that of a creative, young inventor who is killed in World War I.

In addition to her novels, Cather wrote a sizeable number of short stories, some of which, like "Paul's Case" and "Neighbor Rosicky," have become widely anthologized classics.

NOVELS BY CATHER

Alexander's Bridge (1912). Signet 1988 $4.95. ISBN 0-452-00875-1
Death Comes for the Archbishop (1927). Random 1971 $5.95. ISBN 0-394-71679-5
A Lost Lady (1923). Random 1972 $3.95. ISBN 0-394-71705-8
My Antonia (1918). McKay 1990 $7.50. ISBN 0-679-72618-7 Story of how a prairie farm wife finds fulfillment in motherhood.
My Mortal Enemy (1926). Random 1961 $4.95. ISBN 0-394-70200-X
O Pioneers (1913). Signet 1989 $3.50. ISBN 0-451-52285-0 Story of a young Nebraska farm girl and her struggle for happiness.
One of Ours (1922). Signet 1989 $5.95. ISBN 0-394-71252-8 Story of a boy from the western plains who joins the army and is killed in France in World War I.
Shadows on the Rock (1931). Random 1971 $6.95. ISBN 0-394-71680-9
The Song of the Lark (1915). Houghton 1953 $8.95. ISBN 395-34530-8

SHORT STORY COLLECTIONS BY CATHER

Early Novels and Stories of Willa Cather. Dodd 1983 $8.95. ISBN 0-396-08268-8
The Troll Garden (1905). Meridian 1984 $3.95. ISBN 0-452-00714-3 Cather's first collection; contains the famous story "Paul's Case."
Willa Cather's Collected Short Fiction. Univ of Nebraska Pr 1970 $29.95. ISBN 0-8032-0770-0

BOOKS ABOUT CATHER

Bloom, Harold (ed). *Willa Cather.* Chelsea 1986 $24.50. ISBN 0-87754-623-1 A collection of modern critical essays by a major scholar of twentieth-century literature.
Gerber, Philip L. *Willa Cather.* G. K. Hall 1975 $16.95. ISBN 0-8057-7155-7 A general study of Cather's life and works.
McFarland, Dorothy T. *Willa Cather.* Ungar 1972 $16.95. ISBN 0-8044-2610-4 An introduction to the life and works of Cather.
*Woodress, James. *Willa Cather: A Literary Life.* Univ of Nebraska Pr 1987 $14.95. ISBN 0-8032-9708-4 Discusses the author's life as it relates to the characters and plots of her novels and stories.

CHANDLER, RAYMOND   1888–1959

Raymond Chandler was born in Chicago but moved to England with his mother when he was eight years old. He attended English schools and graduated from Dulwich College, London. In 1907 he became a British citizen and served in the Royal Air Force in World War I.

After the war, Chandler settled in California and held a number of different jobs, mostly in the oil business. During the Depression years of the 1930s, he turned to writing and between 1933 and 1939 published more than 20 detective stories.

In 1939, Chandler published his first novel, *The Big Sleep,* in which he introduced his famous detective hero, Philip Marlowe. He went on to write several more Philip Marlowe novels, publishing the last of them, *Playback,* in 1958, the year before he died.

Chandler is considered one of the best American mystery writers of the twentieth century, challenged only by Dashiell Hammett. (*See* Hammett, Vol. 1, American Literature: The Twentieth Century.) Chandler's creation, Philip Marlowe, is not only tough, but also witty, honorable, and sensitive—an extremely moral character whose primary concern is to search for the truth, regardless of the consequences. Chandler also portrays the world of racketeers, crooked cops, and politicians with remarkable vividness.

Several of Chandler's novels have been made into movies and television plays, and he also wrote several original screenplays.

NOVELS BY CHANDLER

The Big Sleep (1939). Vintage 1988 $5.95. ISBN 0-394-75828-5
Farewell, My Lovely (1940). Vintage 1988 $5.95. ISBN 0-394-75827-7
The High Window (1942). Vintage 1988 $5.95. ISBN 0-394-75826-9
The Lady in the Lake (1943). Vintage 1989 $5.95. ISBN 0-394-75825-0
The Little Sister (1949). Vintage 1985 $5.95. ISBN 0-394-75767-X
The Long Goodbye (1954). Vintage 1988 $5.95. ISBN 0-394-75768-1
Playback (1958). Vintage 1987 $5.95. ISBN 0-394-75766-1

SHORT STORY COLLECTION BY CHANDLER

Trouble Is My Business (1950). Vintage 1988 $8.95. ISBN 0-394-75764-0

BOOKS ABOUT CHANDLER

Marling, William. *Raymond Chandler.* G. K. Hall 1986 $18.95. ISBN 0-8057-7472-6 A good general introduction to Chandler's life and fiction.
Skinner, Robert E. *The Hard Boiled Explicator: A Guide to the Study of Dashiell Hammett, Raymond Chandler, and Ross Macdonald.* Scarecrow 1985 $17.50. ISBN 0-8108-1749-7 A study of the "hard-boiled" detective novel that places Chandler in context with other authors of the genre.

CHEEVER, JOHN 1912–1982

John Cheever was born in Quincy, Massachusetts, and educated at Thayer Academy in the nearby town of Braintree. He chose to become a writer rather than attend college, and at age 17, Cheever moved to New York to begin his career. He published stories in a number of magazines with marginal success until, in 1935, he began to write for *The New Yorker* magazine, soon becoming a regular contributor. By the time of his death, *The New Yorker* had published more than 100 of his stories, which depict upper-middle class life in Manhattan and its Westchester County and Connecticut suburbs.

Cheever's works are usually comic and often deal with life in the wealthier American suburbs. His first novel, *The Wapshot Chronicle* (1957), which won the National Book Award, and its sequel, *The Wapshot Scandal* (1964), are generally positive stories of life in the New England towns Cheever remembered from his youth. *Bullet Park* (1969), however, is a darker and more sinister tale, centered around the attempt to burn a child on a church altar. *Falconer* (1977), written after Cheever's hospitalization for heavy drinking, explores the themes of regeneration and brothers. His final book, *Oh What a Paradise It Seems* (1982), is considered by some critics to be a summary of Cheever's major themes and a final statement of his views on the loves, ambitions, and disappointments of his well-to-do characters.

While his novels have won him a wide following, Cheever's short stories are generally considered to be his best work, particularly those he wrote for *The New Yorker*. These generally focus on the contrast between the serene and civilized veneer of upper-middle class life and the dark undercurrents of frustration, misery, and betrayal that mark the characters' secret lives. In the frequently anthologized "The Country Husband," for example, the suburban husband Francis Weed is inspired by a life-threatening experience to reexamine his banal life—until suburban conformity once more overtakes him. His 1978 work, *The Stories of John Cheever*, won him the Pulitzer Prize. A collection of 61 short stories, including "The Swimmer," "The Country Husband," and "The Enormous Radio," it was highly praised by critics. In the words of the critic for the *New York Times*, the work "revived singlehand publishers' and readers' interest in the American short story."

NOVELS BY CHEEVER

Bullet Park (1969). Ballantine 1987 $3.95. ISBN 0-345-35006-5
Falconer (1977). Ballantine 1985 $3.95. ISBN 0-345-33145-1
Oh What a Paradise It Seems (1982). Ballantine 1983 $2.95. ISBN 0-345-33832-4
The Wapshot Chronicle (1957). Harper 1989 $8.95. ISBN 0-06-091618-4
The Wapshot Scandal (1964). Harper 1989 $7.95. ISBN 0-06-091617-6

SHORT STORY COLLECTION BY CHEEVER

The Stories of John Cheever (1978). Ballantine 1985 $5.95. ISBN 0-345-33567-8

BOOKS ABOUT CHEEVER

Cheever, Susan. *Home Before Dark: A Biographical Memoir of John Cheever.* Houghton 1984 $15.95. ISBN 0-395-35297-5 A sensitive and revealing portrait of the man and the writer; written by Cheever's daughter and based on 30 volumes of intimate journals kept by Cheever.

Coale, Samuel. *John Cheever.* Ungar 1977 $16.95. ISBN 0-8044-2126-9 A general introduction to Cheever's life and works appropriate for college undergraduates and general readers; contains a bibliography and chronology as well as discussions of major works.

Waldeland, Lynne. *John Cheever.* G. K. Hall 1979 $15.95. ISBN 0-8057-7251-0 An introduction to Cheever's life and works with emphasis on his major themes, development as a writer, and literary reputation; contains a chronology and bibliography.

CHILDRESS, ALICE   1920–

Alice Childress was born in Charleston, South Carolina, but grew up in Harlem in New York City. After high school she became an actress and then a director with the American Negro Theatre in New York.

In the late 1940s, Childress began to write plays for the American Negro Theatre. *Florence* (1949) was her first, produced at the Harlem theater. In 1955, her play *Trouble in Mind* was produced outside of Harlem. It was highly praised and won an Obie Award (for Off-Broadway productions) in 1956.

Childress continued her work for the theater and wrote several plays for television and the stage over the next few years. She spent the years 1966 to 1968 at the Radcliffe College Institute for Independent Study.

In 1973, Childress published her first novel for young readers, *A Hero Ain't Nothin' but a Sandwich.* Because of its honest and open portrayal of black urban life, the book caused some controversy and was banned from a school library in Savannah, Georgia. Highly praised by critics, however, it was nominated for a 1974 National Book Award and was selected in the same year as a Notable Book by the American Library Association. In 1981, Childress's second book for young readers, *Rainbow Jordan* (1981), was named a Best Book for Young Adults by the American Library Association. Childress has also written fiction for adults.

Childress's experience in the theater is evident in her novels. Her dialogue is vivid and real, and her characters are complex, engaging, and dramatically dynamic people. Her portrayals of the black experience, especially relationships within the black family, are exceptionally sensitive and genuine.

NOVELS BY CHILDRESS

A Hero Ain't Nothin' but a Sandwich (1973). Avon 1977 $2.95. ISBN 0-380-00132-2 Story of Benjie—young, black, and well on his way to being hooked on heroin.
Rainbow Jordan (1981). Avon 1982 $2.95. ISBN 0-380-58974-5 Story of 14-year-old Rainbow, whose mother does not care for her and who is pressured to grow up too fast.
Those Other People (1989). Putnam 1989 $13.95. ISBN 0-399-21510-7

BOOK ABOUT CHILDRESS

Gallo, Donald R. (ed). *Speaking for Ourselves.* NCTE 1990 $12.95. ISBN 0-8141-4625-2 A fascinating collection of autobiographical sketches of 87 young-adult authors, including Childress; authors share stories of how they started to write and of significant events that influenced them; includes complete list of published works and dates.

CORMIER, ROBERT   1925–

Robert Cormier was born and raised in Leominster, Massachusetts, and was educated at local schools. After attending Massachusetts's Fitchburg State College for a year, he began a career as a journalist, working as a writer for a radio station before becoming a reporter and then an editor. He published his first novel, *Now and at the Hour,* in 1960, but he did not receive wide attention as a writer until the publication of *The Chocolate War* in 1974. With this novel Cormier gained a reputation as a major writer of young adult fiction, a reputation that has grown with each new novel.

Cormier's stories place young people in situations that leave them little room for compromise. They are faced with difficult choices and have to grapple with serious questions, such as abuse of power and conflict between individuals and institutions. Cormier's work has been criticized by some for presenting too harsh a picture of life to young readers, but most reviewers have praised his books highly. To his critics Cormier replies that he writes novels with young adults as characters but does not write for a young adult audience specifically. His work is enormously popular with young readers nevertheless, and he is generally regarded as one of the two or three best writers of contemporary fiction for young adults.

NOVELS BY CORMIER

Beyond the Chocolate War (1985). Dell 1986 $3.25. ISBN 0-440-90580-X A sequel to *The Chocolate War* in which Obie is forced to confront the unmasked face of evil.
The Bumblebee Flies Anyway (1984). Dell 1988 $3.25. ISBN 0-440-90871-X The story of Barry Snow, a voluntary patient in an institute for experimental medicine.

**The Chocolate War* (1974). Dell 1986 $3.25. ISBN 0-440-94459-7 The story of a young man's refusal to be bullied by his school's secret society.

*Fade (1988). Dell 1989 $4.50. ISBN 0-440-20487-9 The story of young Paul Moreaux, who discovers he has inherited the ability to "fade."

*I Am the Cheese (1977). Dell 1978 $3.25. ISBN 0-440-94060-5 "A horrifying tale of government corruption, espionage, and counterespionage told by an innocent young victim," according to the *School Library Journal.*

**Other Bells for Us to Ring* (1990). Delacorte 1990 $13.95. ISBN 0-385-30245-2 The story of young Darcy, who remains unsure about the power of love until she gets a message in the form of a miracle.

SHORT STORY COLLECTION BY CORMIER

*Eight Plus One (1980). Bantam 1985 $2.75. ISBN 0-553-26815-5 "A collection of stories which probe human relationships—young to old, black to white, child to child," according to the *Journal of Reading.*

BOOKS ABOUT CORMIER

*Campbell, Patricia. *Presenting Robert Cormier.* Dell 1990 $4.95. ISBN 0-440-20544-1 "The book succeeds both as a critical evaluation of Robert Cormier's work and as a presentation of the author as a human being," according to *Horn Book.*

Gallo, Donald R. (ed). *Speaking for Ourselves.* NCTE 1990 $12.95. ISBN 0-8141-4625-2 A fascinating collection of autobiographical sketches of 87 young-adult authors, including Cormier; authors share stories of how they started to write and of significant events that influenced them; includes complete list of published works and dates.

CULLEN, COUNTEE 1903–1946

Countee Cullen was born Countee Porter in New York City. After the death of his mother, he was adopted by the Reverend and Mrs. Frederick A. Cullen and took their name. Cullen attended De Witt Clinton High School, where he was an outstanding student and the winner of a citywide poetry contest. After graduating from high school, Cullen enrolled in New York University, where he again excelled as a student, earning a Phi Beta Kappa key upon graduation. He went on to complete a master's degree in English at Harvard University and then to become assistant editor of *Opportunity, a Journal of Negro Life,* a magazine published by the Urban League.

In 1928, Cullen won a Guggenheim Fellowship, which enabled him to study and write in France for two years. While in Europe, he became friends with a number of important British poets and writers. On his return to the United States, he settled in Harlem, where, except for occasional visits to Europe, he remained for the rest of his short life, teaching English and French in a junior high school.

Cullen is considered one of the central figures in the Harlem Renaissance, a burst of artistic and cultural activity by black writers and artists in the 1920s and 1930s. His only novel, *One Way to Heaven* (1931), is a comedy about life in Harlem.

Although Cullen's poetry strongly reflects his African-American heritage and deals with themes central to the black experience, he did not consider himself a "black poet." He wrote, "I wish any merit that may be in my work to flow from it solely as the expression of a poet—with no racial consideration to bolster it up."

NOVEL BY CULLEN

One Way to Heaven (1931). AMS (repr of 1931 ed) $19.00. ISBN 0-404-11383-4

POETRY BY CULLEN

Color (1925). Ayer 1970 repr of 1925 ed $14.00. ISBN 0-405-01919-X

BOOK ABOUT CULLEN

Suchard, Alan R. *Countee Cullen.* G. K. Hall 1984 $17.95. ISBN 0-8057-7411-4 A good general introduction to Cullen's life and art.

CUMMINGS, E. E. (EDWARD ESTLIN) 1894–1962

E. E. Cummings (often published as "e. e. cummings"; he never capitalized the initials of his name after he became famous) was born into an intellectual family in Cambridge, Massachusetts. His father was a Congregational minister who also taught English at Harvard University. Cummings studied at Harvard, where he earned his bachelor's degree in 1915 and his master's degree in 1916. He developed a fondness for poetry while an undergraduate and became friends with a number of Harvard students who later became writers or editors.

During World War I, Cummings served in a French ambulance corps, where he and one of his friends were considered "undesirable" because of their strange appearances (they wore mustaches) and outspoken disrespect for French authority. As a result, Cummings was imprisoned by the French. He used this jail experience as the basis for his instantly successful novel *The Enormous Room* (1922).

Cummings's lasting reputation, however, is based on his poetry. He was one of the most technically innovative American poets of this century—using nonstandard capitalization and punctuation; running together normally separate words and phrases; and breaking lines in unconventional places. Cummings's poetry championed the underdog or the "little guy" in the struggle against authority. In his poetry Cummings consistently attacked what he saw as a society mired in conformity, slogans, and hypocrisy. As he said in the preface to his *Collected Poems* (1938), this "nonworld" is filled with "mostpeople" playing "impotent nongames of wrongright or rightwrong."

Cummings is considered to be among America's most important modern poets, and is still widely read and anthologized.

POETRY BY CUMMINGS

Complete Poems (1968). Harcourt 1980 $17.95. ISBN 0-15-621062-2
One Hundred Selected Poems (1954). Grove 1988 $5.95. ISBN 0-8021-2072-0

BOOKS ABOUT CUMMINGS

Kidder, Rushworth M. *E. E. Cummings: An Introduction to the Poetry.* Columbia Univ Pr 1979 $23.50. ISBN 0-231-04044-X A scholarly examination of Cummings's poetry and techniques for the serious reader.
Marks, Barry A. *E. E. Cummings.* G. K. Hall 1965 $14.95. ISBN 0-8057-0176-1 A comprehensive general introduction to the life and works of Cummings for the beginning student, including a one-chapter biography, a chronology, a bibliography, and attention to all major works.

DICKEY, JAMES 1923–

James Dickey was born in Atlanta, Georgia, and attended Clemson University in South Carolina. He left the university after one year to become a pilot in the United States Air Force during World War II. After the war he resumed his education at Vanderbilt University in Tennessee, where he published his first poem during his senior year. After graduation Dickey held a variety of jobs, working in advertising and teaching at several colleges and universities.

Dickey's literary output is varied. Although he devotes most of his time to his poetry, he has also written a best-selling novel, *Deliverance* (1970), collections of essays, and the screenplay of his novel. His personal life has been flamboyant, and he is known for his hard drinking and love of motorcycles.

Dickey's poetry is notable for its unusual techniques as well as for its exploration of violence and the will to power. His poems are often set on the page as separated phrases, causing the reader to experience the poems as short bursts of words. A frequent theme in his prose and poetry is the underlying animal nature of human beings. Dickey sees the instinctual aspect of human nature as more genuine than the outer layer of civilized behavior.

NOVELS BY DICKEY

Alnilam (1987). Doubleday 1987 $19.95. ISBN 0-385-06549-3
Deliverance (1970). Dell 1986 $3.85. ISBN 0-440-31868-8

POETRY BY DICKEY

Bronwen the Traw, the Shape-Shifter (1985). Harcourt 1986 $13.95. ISBN 0-15-212580-9
Poems (1968). Wesleyan Univ Pr 1978 $12.95. ISBN 0-8195-6055-3

BOOKS ABOUT DICKEY

Bloom, Harold (ed). *James Dickey.* Chelsea 1987 $19.95. ISBN 1-55546-272-3 A collection of modern critical essays on Dickey's work by such noted writers as novelists Joyce Carol Oates and Robert Penn Warren and critic Richard Howard.
Calhoun, Richard J., and Robert W. Hill. *James Dickey.* G. K. Hall 1983 $17.95. ISBN 0-8057-7391-6 A chronicle of Dickey's flamboyant life and an introduction to his works.

DREISER, THEODORE   1871–1945

Theodore Dreiser was born in Terre Haute, Indiana, the twelfth of 13 children. His childhood was spent in poverty, or near poverty, and his family moved often. In spite of the constant relocations, Dreiser managed to attend school, and, with the financial aid of a sympathetic high school teacher, he was able to attend Indiana University. However, the need for an income forced him to leave college after one year and take a job as a reporter in Chicago. Over the next 10 years, Dreiser held a variety of newspaper jobs in Pittsburgh, St. Louis, and finally, New York.

He published his first novel, *Sister Carrie,* in 1900, but because the publisher's wife considered its language and subject matter too "strong," it was barely advertised and went almost unnoticed. Today it is regarded as one of Dreiser's best works. It is the story of Carrie, a young woman from the Midwest, who manages to rise to fame and fortune on the strength of her personality and ambition, through her acting talent, and via her relationships with various men. Much of the book's controversy came from the fact that it portrayed a young woman who engages in sexual relationships without suffering the poverty and social downfall that were supposed to be the "punishment" for such "sin."

Dreiser's reputation has generally risen over the years. His best book and first popular success, *An American Tragedy* (1925), is now considered a major American novel, and his other works are widely taught in college courses. Like

Mining. Mural by Thomas Hart Benton (1930–31). Courtesy of The Bettmann Archive.

Sister Carrie, An American Tragedy also tells the story of an ambitious young person from the Midwest. In this case, however, the novel's hero is a man who is brought to ruin because of a horrible action he commits—he murders a poor young woman whom he has gotten pregnant, but whom he wants to discard in favor of a wealthy young woman who represents luxury and social advancement. As Dreiser portrays him, the young man is a victim of an economic system that torments so many with their lack of privilege and power and tempts them to unspeakable acts.

Dreiser is also known for the Cowperwood trilogy—*The Financier* (1912), *The Titan* (1914), and the posthumously published *The Store* (1947). Collectively the three books paint the portrait of a brilliant and ruthless "financial buccaneer."

Dreiser's strength as a novelist rests on his ability to tell a powerful story. The raw force of his narratives pulls the reader through sometimes clumsy prose and inflated language, and his skill in detailed description gives his stories a sense of realism and vitality. His plots convey a sense of inevitable tragedy to which the reader is a witness.

Dreiser is associated with Naturalism, a writing style that also includes French novelist Emile Zola. (*See* Zola, Vol. 1, World Literature: French Language and Literature.) Naturalism seeks to portray all the social forces that shape the lives of the characters, usually conveying a sense of the inevitable doom that these forces must eventually bring about.

Despite this apparent pessimism, Dreiser had faith in socialism as a solution to what he saw as the economic injustices of American capitalism. His socialist views were reinforced by a trip to the newly socialist Soviet Union, and in fact, Dreiser is still widely read in that country. There, as here, he is seen as a powerful chronicler of the injustices and ambitions of his time.

NOVELS BY DREISER

An American Tragedy (1925). Signet 1978 $5.95. ISBN 0-451-52465-9
The Financier (1912). Meridian 1967 $4.95. ISBN 0-452-00825-5
The "Genius" (1915). Meridian 1981 $5.95. ISBN 0-452-00753-4
Jennie Gerhardt (1911). Penguin 1989 $5.95. ISBN 0-14-039075-8
Sister Carrie (1900). Penguin 1981 $4.95. ISBN 0-14-03900-2
The Titan (1914). Meridian 1965 $4.95. ISBN 0-452-00756-9

BOOKS ABOUT DREISER

Lingeman, Richard. *Theodore Dreiser, An American Journey 1908–1945.* Putnam 1990 $39.95. ISBN 0-399-13520-0 The impressive second volume of the definitive biography of Dreiser, focusing on the last troubled years of his life.
Lingeman, Richard. *Theodore Dreiser, At the Gates of the City 1871–1907.* Putnam 1986 $22.95. ISBN 0-399-13147-7 A massive biography of Dreiser's early years, focusing on Dreiser's journalist background and his ultimate success with *Sister Carrie.*
Lundquist, James. *Theodore Dreiser.* Ungar 1974 $16.95. ISBN 0-8044-2563-9 A general study of Dreiser's life and works, including a bibliography and chronology as well as in-depth discussions of each major novel.
Matthiessen, Francis Otto. *Theodore Dreiser.* Greenwood 1973 repr of 1951 ed $27.50. ISBN 0-8371-6550-4 A critical biography of Dreiser by one of the preeminent scholars of American literature.

ELLISON, RALPH   1914–

Ralph Ellison was born in Oklahoma City, where he also attended school. In 1933, he entered Tuskegee Institute on a scholarship and studied music. When he left Tuskegee, he headed for New York City to make his name as a trumpeter. In New York, Ellison met novelist Richard Wright (*see* Wright, Vol. 1, American Literature: The Twentieth Century), who urged him to try writing. As a result, Ellison took a job as a writer and researcher with the Federal Writers' Project in New York, a government-funded project to increase employment by hiring writers. There Ellison began to publish stories and reviews. In 1942, he became editor of the *Negro Quarterly,* and in 1945 began work on a novel, *The Invisible Man,* which was published in 1952.

The novel was an enormous success and established Ellison's reputation as an important writer. On the strength of it, he went on to teach at a number of colleges and universities. His long-awaited second novel has not yet appeared, although parts of it have been printed in magazines.

The Invisible Man is the story of a young man's journey through one illusion after another in a frustrating, darkly comic pursuit of the American dream. It is often called the most important black novel since World War II. Ellison, however, rejects the claim that it is primarily a statement about the condition of African Americans. He insists that it is a novel about the search for identity in the chaotic modern world. Although the novel uses the black experience as its context, Ellison says that is simply because he knows that experience, that he can use it to address more universal concerns.

So far, some eight excerpts of Ellison's second novel have appeared, in such scholarly journals as the *Quarterly Review* and the *Massachusetts Review.* This work-in-progress seems to be a history of the American South, from the Jazz Age through the Civil Rights Movement, told through the story of a jazz musician and the light-skinned African-American boy he befriends. The boy eventually passes for white and becomes a white supremacist senator, in what some critics have seen as a rejection of both his own identity and of the key role of African Americans in America's history and culture. Like the title character in *The Invisible Man,* this character also tries to cling to illusions about the extent of his freedom and power.

In addition to his fiction, Ellison has published two collections of essays, *Shadow and Act* (1964) and *Going to the Territory* (1986), which include autobiographical memoirs as well as Ellison's reflections on literature and politics.

NOVEL BY ELLISON

The Invisible Man (1952). Random 1989 $6.95. ISBN 0-679-72313-7

NONFICTION BY ELLISON

Going to the Territory (1986). Random 1986 $10.95. ISBN 0-394-75062-4
Shadow and Act (1964). Random 1964 $6.95. ISBN 0-394-71716-3

FAST, HOWARD 1914–

Howard Fast was born and educated in New York City and worked at a variety of jobs before becoming a writer. During the Depression of the 1930s, Fast gained a reputation as a spokesperson for the political left. Although he later repudiated many of his earlier beliefs, Fast has been absorbed with the drama of political and social revolution throughout his long career. Several of his novels—for example, *Citizen Tom Paine* (1943) and *The Proud and the Free* (1950)— are concerned directly with the American Revolution. Others, such as *Spartacus* (1951), deal with the struggles of the oppressed in the ancient world. Fast's works are not limited to these concerns, however; his many novels cover a wide range of themes and issues.

Fast's novels have received only moderate critical approval but have been widely read. Many have been made into films, and *The Immigrants* (1977) served as the basis for a television miniseries. Fast's association with the Communist party caused him to be the object of a congressional investigation during the 1950s, along with many other artists and writers. In 1957, however, he published *The Naked God,* in which he detailed his disillusionment with the American Communist party and its politics.

NOVELS BY FAST

*April Morning (1961). Bantam 1962 $3.95. ISBN 0-553-27322-1 The story of a young man's baptism by fire during the bloody Battle of Lexington during the American Revolution.
*Citizen Tom Paine (1943). Grove 1987 $10.95. ISBN 0-8021-3604-X A novel about Tom Paine, one of the most interesting and important leaders of the American Revolution.
The Immigrants (1977). Dell 1987 $4.50. ISBN 0-440-14175-3
The Immigrant's Daughter (1985). Dell 1987 $4.50. ISBN 0-440-13988-0
The Legacy (1981). Dell 1983 $4.50. ISBN 0-440-14720-4
Max (1982). Dell 1983 $4.50. ISBN 0-440-16106-1
The Outsider (1984). Dell 1987 $3.95. ISBN 0-440-16778-7
The Pledge (1988). Dell 1989 $4.50. ISBN 0-440-20470-4
*Spartacus (1951). Dell 1980 $4.50. ISBN 0-440-17649-2 A novel about the revolt of gladiator-slaves in ancient Rome.

FAULKNER, WILLIAM 1897–1962

William Faulkner was born in New Albany, Mississippi, into a prominent southern family. When he was five, the family moved to Oxford, Mississippi, which he called home for the rest of his life.

Faulkner dropped out of high school after two years and took a job in his grandfather's bank. When the United States entered World War I, he tried to enlist but was rejected because he was too short. He then joined the Royal Canadian Air Force, but the war ended before he completed his training. He returned to Oxford and began to write while attending the University of Mississippi as a special student. He was encouraged by American fiction writer Sherwood Anderson (*see* Anderson, Vol. 1, American Literature: The Twentieth Century) to write fiction and his first novel, *Soldiers' Pay*, was published in 1926.

Most of Faulkner's novels are set in the rural Mississippi locale he knew so well. They all feature compelling portraits of disintegrating southern aristocrats, poor whites, and even more impoverished African Americans. These stories are set in a place not found on any map—Yoknapatawpha County—and portray several generations of characters from different levels of southern society. Many of these characters appear in more than one book, giving Faulkner's novels the feel of a historical chronicle or dynastic saga.

The Sound and the Fury (1929), about the decline of a southern aristocratic family that is held together largely by their black servants, is generally considered to be Faulkner's first major novel. In *As I Lay Dying* (1930), he recounts the tragicomic struggles of a poor white family to transport their mother's body to her hometown for burial. In both novels the narrator changes often, demanding close attention from readers. A more traditionally written work, and an easier introduction to Faulkner, is *Light in August* (1932), his novel about interracial conflicts. Faulkner's short stories are generally easier to read than his novels and offer a good introduction to his themes.

Faulkner was awarded the Nobel Prize in 1950 "for his powerful and artistically independent contribution to the new American novel," but he also deserved to win that honor for his contribution to world literature. Faulkner's evocation of the American South in the period between the two world wars and his ability to incorporate philosophical observations on the human condition seamlessly into the story have made him an international giant.

NOVELS BY FAULKNER

Absalom, Absalom (1936). Random 1972 $3.95. ISBN 0-394-71780-5
As I Lay Dying (1930). Random 1964 $2.95. ISBN 0-394-70254-9
A Fable (1954). Random 1978 $5.95. ISBN 0-394-72413-5
The Hamlet (1940). Random 1956 $4.95. ISBN 0-394-70139-9
Intruder in the Dust (1948). Random 1972 $5.95. ISBN 0-394-71792-9
Light in August (1932). Random 1989 $8.50. ISBN 0-679-72523-7
The Sound and the Fury (1929). Random 1987 $5.95. ISBN 0-394-74774-7
* Three Famous Short Novels: Spotted Horses, Old Man, and The Bear. Random 1958 $4.95. ISBN 0-394-70149-6 *Spotted Horses:* hilarious account of a horse auction; *Old Man:* story of a convict adrift with a pregnant woman during a flood; *The Bear:* story of a boy coming to terms with the adult world.

SHORT STORY COLLECTIONS BY FAULKNER

* Collected Stories of William Faulkner. Random 1977 $14.95. ISBN 0-394-60456-3 Forty-two stories from Faulkner's earliest works through 1948.
* Go Down Moses and Other Stories (1942). Random 1973 $5.95. ISBN 0-394-71884-4 Interrelated stories about African Americans in the South.

BOOKS ABOUT FAULKNER

Brodhead, Richard (ed). *Faulkner: A Collection of Critical Essays.* Prentice 1983 $6.95. ISBN 0-13-308270-9 A well-chosen selection of essays by major critics, including Cleanth Brooks on good and evil in Faulkner, Irving Howe on Faulkner's treatment of black people, and Hugh Kenner on Faulkner and the avant-garde.

Brooks, Cleanth. *William Faulkner: The Yoknapatawpha Country.* Louisiana State Univ Pr 1990 $16.95. ISBN 0-8071-1601-7 An analysis of the stories and novels that take place in Faulkner's imaginary country.

Brown, Calvin. *A Glossary of Faulkner's South.* Yale Univ Pr 1976 $9.95. ISBN 0-300-02240-9 A useful guide to key terms and place names in Faulkner's novels.

Friedman, Alan W. *William Faulkner.* Ungar 1985 $16.95. ISBN 0-8044-2218-4 A useful general study of Faulkner's life and works.

Hoffman, Frederick J. *William Faulkner.* G. K. Hall 1985 $17.95. ISBN 0-8057-0244-X Another comprehensive and readable introduction to Faulkner's life and works.

FERBER, EDNA 1887–1968

Edna Ferber was born in Kalamazoo, Michigan, but soon after completing her education moved to Milwaukee, Wisconsin, and later to Chicago to work as a journalist. While her midwestern roots and newspaper experiences heavily influenced her early work, she quickly began to range widely over the American experience for her later themes.

Ferber won early recognition for her stories of pioneering businesswomen, collected in *Roast Beef Medium* (1913), *Personality Plus* (1914), and *Emma McChesney and Co.* (1915). However, her most popular and probably her best works are her sweeping historical and regional novels: *Show Boat* (1926), *Cimmaron* (1929), *Saratoga Trunk* (1941), *Giant* (1952), and *Ice Palace* (1958).

Ferber had an ardent love for America, its people, and its landscape, and this love is evident in all her works. She took as much delight in portraying the grandeur of a sprawling Texas ranch in *Giant* as she did in detailing a rough and rural community in *So Big* (for which she won the Pulitzer Prize in 1924). Ferber's novels were enormously popular, and several were made into movies. *Show Boat* was the inspiration for the famous musical comedy of the same name.

NOVELS BY FERBER

American Beauty (1931). Fawcett 1980 $1.95. ISBN 0-449-22817-7

Cimarron (1929). Amereon (repr of 1929 ed) $22.95. ISBN 0-88411-548-8 A story of pioneer life in the Oklahoma territory; suffers from a stereotyped portrayal of American Indians.

Gigolo (1922). Ayer (repr of 1922 ed) $18.00. ISBN 0-8369-4011-3

Ice Palace (1958). Fawcett 1980 $1.95. ISBN 0-449-24124-6 A novel of life and adventure in Alaska.

Saratoga Trunk (1941). Amereon (repr of 1941 ed) $17.95. ISBN 0-89190-323-2

Show Boat (1926). Fawcett 1979 $1.95. ISBN 0-449-23191-7 The story of a family of actors who perform aboard a riverboat on the Mississippi.

So Big (1924). Fawcett 1979 $1.95. ISBN 0-449-23476-2 The story of a widowed schoolteacher and her struggles to raise a family while running a farm.

STORY STORY COLLECTIONS BY FERBER

Emma McChesney and Co. (1915). Ayer (repr of 1915 ed) $16.00. ISBN 0-8369-4010-5

Personality Plus (1914). Ayer (repr of 1914 ed) $15.00. ISBN 0-8369-3813-5

Roast Beef Medium (1913). Ayer (repr of 1913 ed). $18.00. ISBN 0-8369-4012-1

FERLINGHETTI, LAWRENCE 1919–

Lawrence Ferlinghetti was born Lawrence Ferling in New York City (possibly Yonkers), New York. In 1954, he changed his name back to Ferlinghetti, the original Italian form. Ferlinghetti received a bachelor's degree from the University of North Carolina, a master's from Columbia University, and a doctorate from the Sorbonne, University of Paris. He served in the United States Navy during World War I and was a command officer during the Allied invasion of Normandy.

During the 1950s, Ferlinghetti became associated with the Beat movement, a group of young writers who believed that poetry should speak to the concerns of ordinary people in a language they can understand, and should rouse them from conformity into an intense appreciation of life. In order to provide an outlet for these writers, Ferlinghetti established City Lights Books, a publishing company in San Francisco, which printed the works of such controversial Beat poets as Allen Ginsburg (*See* Ginsberg, Vol. 1, American Literature, The Twentieth Century).

Ferlinghetti's poetry is intended to be performed aloud rather than read silently. His style combines lyric elements characteristic of traditional poetry with satire and public oratory. While this combination has disturbed some critics, it strikes a responsive chord in many listeners and readers. Perhaps his best-known poem, "Coney Island of the Mind," typifies Ferlinghetti's style in its vivid portrait of the confusion and disarray of modern life. In recent years the critics also seem to be gaining a new appreciation of Ferlinghetti.

In addition to poetry, Ferlinghetti has written two novels. *Her* (1960) is an autobiographical tale of a young man's search for identity, and *Love in the Days of Rage* (1988) is a love story recalling the 1968 student uprisings in Paris.

NOVELS BY FERLINGHETTI

Her (1960). New Directions 1960 $6.95. ISBN 0-8112-0042-6
Love in the Days of Rage (1988). Obelisk 1990 $6.95. ISBN 0-525-48541-4

POETRY BY FERLINGHETTI

Endless Life: Selected Poems (1981). New Directions 1981 $7.95. ISBN 0-8112-0797-8
The Secret Meaning of Things (1969). New Directions 1969 $1.00. ISBN 0-8112-0045-0
Tyrannus Nix? (1969). New Directions 1969 $1.95. ISBN 0-8112-0047-7

BOOK ABOUT FERLINGHETTI

Smith, Larry. *Lawrence Ferlinghetti: Poet at Large.* Southern Illinois Univ Pr 1983 $9.95. ISBN 0-8093-1102-X A study of Ferlinghetti's poetry in the social and political context of his time.

FITZGERALD, F. (FRANCIS) SCOTT (KEY) 1896–1940

F. Scott Fitzgerald, one of the best-known authors of the twentieth century, was born in St. Paul, Minnesota. He spent much of his childhood in upstate New York where his father worked as a sales agent, then attended private schools in St. Paul and New Jersey before enrolling at Princeton University in 1913. In 1917 he left the university before graduating to enter the army.

While stationed in Montgomery, Alabama, Fitzgerald fell in love with

Zelda Sayre, a beautiful and popular southern belle. Always sensitive about not being wealthy, Fitzgerald despaired of being able to support Zelda in her accustomed style. Partly out of this despair, he wrote *This Side of Paradise* (1920), an autobiographical portrait of a young man's courtship of an aristocratic beauty. This first of the lost-generation novels (novels written by young Americans who felt "lost" and confused after World War I) was a spectacular success, which enabled Scott and Zelda to marry soon after its publication. They then embarked on a well-publicized spree of glamorous high living. Somehow Fitzgerald managed to write his best novel, *The Great Gatsby* (1925), in spite of heavy drinking, debts, and partying. But the wild lifestyle of the Fitzgeralds took its inevitable toll: Scott suffered serious health problems while Zelda gradually lapsed into incurable mental illness, which, while not caused by her way of life, was certainly not helped by it.

The tormented yet romantic lives of Scott and Zelda have intrigued readers of several generations—so much so that the couple themselves have become semifictional characters whose lives have been dramatized in movies and television series and in novels by other writers. Many feminist critics see Zelda as representing the woman who goes mad because she is not allowed any outlets for her own creative ambitions.

Fitzgerald published his fourth novel, *Tender is the Night,* in 1934. The book is the story of an expatriate couple, much like the Fitzgeralds, who wander among the fashionable cities of Europe, living a frenzied shallow life of drinking and party-going. The novel is a brilliant indictment of that expatriate generation's spiritual bankruptcy. Although critically praised, it did not sell well. Increasingly desperate for money, Fitzgerald wrote commercially profitable short stories and eventually went to Hollywood to write screenplays. His health weakened by alcoholism and worry, he died of a heart attack at the age of 44.

Today, Fitzgerald is still honored for his vivid and poetic style and for his portraits of the "Jazz Age" of the 1920s and the stock market crash and subsequent Depression of 1929. Readers of Fitzgerald are so entranced by his evocative writing that they often feel they themselves have lived through the times he wrote about.

NOVELS BY FITZGERALD

The Beautiful and the Damned (1921). Macmillan 1988 $6.95. ISBN 0-02-019950-8
The Great Gatsby (1925). Scribner's 1981 $4.95. ISBN 0-064-51516-4 The story of mysterious Jay Gatsby who loves the rich girl Daisy and longs to be part of her world.
The Last Tycoon (1941). Macmillan 1988 $4.50. ISBN 0-02-019950-3
Tender Is the Night (1934). Macmillan 1962 $5.95. ISBN 0-02-019930-9
This Side of Paradise (1920). Macmillan 1948 $4.95. ISBN 0-02-019880-1

SHORT STORY COLLECTIONS BY FITZGERALD

Flappers and Philosophers (1921). Macmillan 1988 $4.95. ISBN 0-02-065290-9
The Pat Hobby Stories (1962). Macmillan 1988 $4.95. ISBN 0-02-019910-4 Humorous stories of a fading filmscript writer in Hollywood.
The Stories of F. Scott Fitzgerald. Macmillan 1984 $6.95. ISBN 0-02-019940-6

BOOKS ABOUT FITZGERALD

Eble, Kenneth. *F. Scott Fitzgerald.* G. K. Hall 1977 $16.95. ISBN 0-8057-7183-2 A broad examination of Fitzgerald's life and works, focusing on his major themes and development as a writer and including a chronology and bibliography.

Gallo, Rose A. *F. Scott Fitzgerald.* Ungar 1978 $16.95. ISBN 0-8044-2225-7 A general
    introduction to Fitzgerald's life and works, appropriate for general readers; with
    bibliography, chronology, and discussions of major works.
Milford, Nancy. *Zelda.* Harper 1983 $8.95. ISBN 0-06-091069-0 A fascinating look at
    Fitzgerald's wife, Zelda, that illuminates the couple's tormented relationship.

FROST, ROBERT   1874–1963

Although Robert Frost was descended from New Englanders, he was born and
raised in San Francisco. He returned to New England when his father died in
1884. Frost studied at Dartmouth College and Harvard University, but gave up
college to write while he taught school. In 1912, he went to England, where he
lived for three years. After his return to the United States, he began to win
acclaim as a poet. He also taught at various colleges and helped found the
Breadloaf School for writers in Middlebury, Vermont. Frost was married and
had several children.

Frost became, in a sense, America's national poet. Not only was he Vermont's poet laureate (the state's "official" poet), but he received a special
congressional medal during the Eisenhower administration and was invited to
read one of his poems at the inauguration of President John F. Kennedy in 1961.
Such official recognition was ironic since his first books of poetry had to be
published in England, because no American publisher would take them.

Frost's poems tend to be set in rural New England. Images of birch trees,
snowy woods, stone walls separating old farms, and the like abound in his
work.

Frost's poetry is deceptively easy. His simple vocabulary and straightforward sentences capture the clipped, terse speech of New Englanders. But
within the smooth flow of words and images lie powerful ideas and sharp
ironies. Some of his poems take the form of monologues, in which speakers
address the reader directly, such as "Stopping by Woods on a Snowy Evening,"
or dialogues, in which speakers converse with each other as in "Death of the
Hired Man." In either case the diction is simple and authentic, yet the reader
is always aware that something more is being said than the surface meaning
of the words themselves. That, in the final analysis, is Frost's great talent—to
draw deep meaning from the commonplace.

POETRY BY FROST

*Collected Poems (1935). Buccaneer 1983 $25.95. ISBN 0-89966-442-3 The Pulitzer Prize-
    winning collection of Frost's verse, selected by the poet himself.
*Poems by Robert Frost: A Boy's Will and *North of Boston* (1913, 1914). Signet 1990 $3.95. ISBN
    0-451-52413-6 Frost's first two books of poetry in their original form; they
    brought him recognition, first in England, later in America.
*The Poetry of Robert Frost. Holt 1979 $12.95. ISBN 0-8050-0501-3 A selection of Frost's
    most popular poems, spanning his entire career.

BOOKS ABOUT FROST

Barry, Elaine. *Robert Frost.* Ungar 1973 $16.95. ISBN 0-8044-2016-5 A general study of
    Frost's life and works, including a bibliography and chronology.
Gerber, Philip L. *Robert Frost.* G. K. Hall 1982 $16.95. ISBN 0-8057-7348-7 A good
    general introduction to Frost's life and poetry, with discussions of the major
    works, a one-chapter biography, a chronology, and a bibliography.
Thompson, Lawrence. *Robert Frost: A Biography.* H. Holt 1981 $25.00. ISBN 0-03-050921-1
    The official biography of Frost, well researched and heavily documented.

GAINES, ERNEST J. 1933–

Although Ernest Gaines was educated in California (at San Francisco State College and Stanford University) and currently lives in San Francisco, his fiction is dominated by images and characters drawn from rural Louisiana, where he was born and raised. In recounting the struggle of African Americans to, in his words, "escape the influence of the past" and "just . . . be men," Gaines has skillfully crafted a small but powerful body of modern American fiction.

Unquestionably the best-known, and probably the best, of Gaines's novels is *The Autobiography of Miss Jane Pittman* (1971), a fictional account of the long life of a black woman born a slave on a Louisiana plantation. Through the stories of the many fascinating people who touch Jane's life, Gaines presents not only a moving perspective on the struggles of African Americans but also a social history of the United States since the Civil War. It is a testimony to Gaines's skill as a writer and storyteller that many people believe Jane Pittman was a real person. Indeed, the novel is frequently misshelved in the biography section of bookstores.

Of Gaines's other works, *Bloodline* (1976), a collection of five short stories, stands out for its powerful portrayals of young men in search of self-respect and dignity.

NOVELS BY GAINES

The Autobiography of Miss Jane Pittman (1971). Bantam 1982 $3.95. ISBN 0-553-26357-9
   Tale of black history in the South as seen through the eyes of a fictional 110-year-old black woman born a slave on a Louisiana plantation.
Catherine Cormier (1964). North Point 1981 $9.95. ISBN 0-86547-022-7
A Gathering of Old Men (1983). Random 1984 $4.95. ISBN 0-394-72591-3
In My Father's House (1978). Norton 1983 $6.70. ISBN 0-393-30124-9
Of Love and Dust (1967). Norton 1979 $8.95. ISBN 0-393-00914-9

SHORT STORY COLLECTION BY GAINES

Bloodline (1976). Norton 1976 $7.95. ISBN 0-393-00798-7 Five short stories that portray young men in search of dignity and depict adult life as viewed by children.

BOOK ABOUT GAINES

Stanford, Barbara Dodd, and Karmina Amin. *Black Literature for High School Students.* NCTE 1978. (o.p.) $6.00. ISBN 0-8141-0330-8 A resource book on teaching black literature that includes profiles of African-American authors, annotated bibliographies, sample curriculums, and discussions of how to approach various types of literature in the classroom.

GILCHRIST, ELLEN 1935–

Ellen Gilchrist was born in Vicksburg, Mississippi. She received a B.A. degree from Milsaps College in 1967. Her literary career began with the publication of *In the Land of Dreamy Dreams* in 1981. Originally published by the University of Arkansas Press and given virtually no promotion, this collection of short stories was publicized almost entirely by word of mouth. Its sales grew so steadily, however, that it soon gained the attention of both reviewers and a major publisher, who later reissued it. The central characters in Gilchrist's stories are adolescents trying desperately to match their dreams and ambitions with the demands of the world in which they live. Gilchrist, however, is not a young-adult author. Her tales are powerful, sometimes brutally realistic, pictures of tragic events.

Gilchrist's first novel, *The Annunciation* (1983), received only mixed reviews. Her second collection of short stories, *Victory over Japan* (1984), was much better received and won the 1984 American Book Award for fiction. She has since published three more collections of stories and a second novel.

NOVELS BY GILCHRIST

The Anna Papers (1988). Little 1988 $16.95. ISBN 0-316-31316-5
The Annunciation (1983). Little 1985 $7.95. ISBN 0-316-31308-4

SHORT STORY COLLECTIONS BY GILCHRIST

Drunk with Love (1986). Little 1987 $7.95. ISBN 0-316-31314-9
I Can Not Get You Close Enough (1990). Little 1990 $17.95. ISBN 0-316-31313-0
In the Land of Dreamy Dreams (1981). Little 1985 $7.95. ISBN 0-316-31304-1
Light Can Be Both Wave and Particle (1989). Little 1990 $8.95. ISBN 0-316-31312-2
Victory over Japan (1984). Little 1985 $7.95. ISBN 0-316-31307-6

GINSBERG, ALLEN   1926–

Allen Ginsberg was born in Paterson, New Jersey, the son of poet and teacher Louis Ginsberg. In 1948, he received a B.A. degree from Columbia University.

Ginsberg began writing poetry while still in school and first gained wide public recognition in 1956 with the long poem *Howl*. *Howl* has had a stormy history. When it was first recited at poetry readings, audiences cheered wildly. It was published by Lawrence Ferlinghetti's City Lights Books and printed in England (*see* Ferlinghetti, Vol. 1, American Literature: The Twentieth Century). Before the printed copies could be distributed, however, they were seized by U.S. customs officials as obscene. After a famous court case in which the poem was found not to be obscene, the work sold rapidly and Ginsberg's reputation was assured. Regarded as the foremost poet of the Beat generation, (a group of rebellious writers who opposed conformity and sought intensity of experience) Ginsberg's work is concerned with many subjects of contemporary interest, including drugs, sexual confusion, the voluntary poverty of the artist and rebel, and rejection of society. He is a poet with a significant message, and his criticism of American society is part of a long tradition of American writers who have questioned their country's values.

POETRY BY GINSBERG

Collected Poems. Harper 1988 $15.95. ISBN 0-06-091494-7

BOOK ABOUT GINSBERG

Merril, Thomas F. *Allen Ginsberg.* G. K. Hall 1988 $19.95. ISBN 0-8057-7510-2 An overview of and introduction to Ginsberg's life and poetry.

GIOVANNI, NIKKI   1943–

Nikki Giovanni was born in Knoxville, Tennessee. In 1967, she graduated from Fisk University with a major in history. Her first poems, collected in *Black Feeling, Black Talk* (1968) and *Black Judgement* (1969), were fiery verses tracing her development from student to militant activist in the civil rights movement. These poems were widely read during civil rights demonstrations of the late 1960s.

In 1969, Giovanni took a position teaching English at Rutgers University in New Jersey while continuing to write poetry. She has also written books of poetry for children. In a poll of high school students conducted by the University of Iowa, her poetry was one of only two collections chosen by the students as books they would recommend to others.

POETRY BY GIOVANNI

Black Feeling, Black Talk, Black Judgement (1968, 1969). Morrow 1970 $5.95. ISBN 0-688-25294-X

Cotton Candy on a Rainy Day (1980). Morrow 1980 $6.95. ISBN 0-688-08365-X

*Ego Tripping and Other Poems for Young People (1973). Chicago Review 1974 $5.95. ISBN 0-88208-019-9 Beautifully illustrated collection of African-American poetry for young readers.

My House (1972). Morrow 1972 $5.95. ISBN 0-688-05021-2

Sacred Cows and Other Edibles (1989). Morrow 1989 $6.70. ISBN 0-688-08909-7

Those Who Ride the Night Winds (1984). Morrow 1984 $5.95. ISBN 0-688-02653-2

The Women and the Men (1979). Morrow 1979 $5.95. ISBN 0-688-07947-4

NONFICTION BY GIOVANNI

Gemini: An Extended Autobiographical Statement on My First Twenty-Five Years of Being a Black Poet. Penguin 1976 $4.95. ISBN 0-14-004264-4 A collection of autobiographical essays differing in style and subject.

A Poetic Equation: Conversations Between Nikki Giovanni and Margaret Walker. (coauthored with Margaret Walker) Howard Univ Pr 1974 $9.95. ISBN 0-88258-003-5 Transcripts of wide-ranging discussions among two major black writers of art, poetry, and the black aesthetic.

GLASGOW, ELLEN 1874–1945

Born in Richmond, Virginia, of a mother who traced her ancestry to the aristocratic Cavalier settlers of Tidewater Virginia and a father descended from the more humble Scots-Irish settlers of the Shenandoah Valley, Ellen Glasgow was a writer of divided background. This may help to explain her ability to combine romantic sensibility with tough-minded realism. She herself divided her novels into two main groups. Her so-called novels of character and comedies include five main works: *The Battle-Ground* (1902), *The Deliverance* (1904), *Virginia* (1913), *Barren Ground* (1925), and *They Stooped to Folly* (1929). The group she called "social history in the form of fiction" includes *The Voice of the People* (1900), *The Romance of a Plain Man* (1909), *The Miller of Old Church* (1911), *Life and Gabriella* (1916), *The Sheltered Life* (1932), and *Vein of Iron* (1935). Her final novel in the latter group, *In This Our Life* (1941), won the 1942 Pulitzer Prize.

Because of poor health, Glasgow was educated at home and spent her entire life in retirement there. Her novels tend to feature strong heroines battling difficult social circumstances. *Barren Ground* is the story of a country woman working in a store, trying to earn enough to buy back her father's farm. *Vein of Iron* tells of the daughter of a Scots-Irish minister who becomes a community leader in the uprisings and protests of the Depression in Virginia's Shenandoah Valley.

Glasgow is a figure of considerable importance in the literary history of America. This is partly due to her superb technical skill and high artistic standards and partly to the fact that she was the first southern woman writer to break through the traditional romantic conventions of the novel, showing the way for many southern writers who followed her.

NOVELS BY GLASGOW

Barren Ground (1925). Harcourt 1985 $10.95. ISBN 0-15-610685-X
In This Our Life (1941). Amereon 1981 $19.95. ISBN 0-89190-152-3
The Sheltered Life (1932). Amereon (repr of 1932 ed) $19.95. ISBN 0-88411-646-8
Vein of Iron (1935). Harcourt 1967 $7.95. ISBN 0-15-693476-0
Virginia (1913). Penguin 1989 $4.95. ISBN 0-14-039072-3
The Voice of the People (1900). Irvington 1989 $19.50. ISBN 0-8398-0662-0

BOOKS ABOUT GLASGOW

Rouse, Blair. *Ellen Glasgow.* Irvington 1962 $4.95. ISBN 0-8290-0010-0 A general intro-
duction to Glasgow's life and works highlighting her artistic skills and her ability
to evoke the rich life of Virginia.

Thieboux, Marcelle. *Ellen Glasgow.* Ungar 1982 $16.95. ISBN 0-8044-2872-7 A general
study and analysis of Glasgow's life and fiction, extremely useful to the general
reader, including a one-chapter biography, a chronology, a bibliography, and
discussions of all the major works.

GOLDMAN, WILLIAM 1931–

Unlike many authors who have held a variety of jobs while trying to establish
themselves as writers, William Goldman has, in his own words, always been
"only a writer." Born in Chicago, Goldman completed his undergraduate education at Oberlin College and went on to graduate study at Columbia University. His first novel, *Temple of Gold* (1957), was published the year after he
received his master's degree, and it brought him immediate critical and popular
success. Many of his stories deal sympathetically with the trials and problems
of young people. His style is light, almost flippant, somewhat in the manner
of writer J. D. Salinger (*see* Salinger, Vol. 1, American Literature: The Twentieth
Century), with whom he is frequently compared.

Goldman's novels are characterized by a lively and fast-paced prose, a
sharp wit, and a cast of thoroughly engrossing characters. Four of his works,
Soldier in the Rain (1960), *No Way to Treat a Lady* (1964), *Marathon Man* (1974), and
The Princess Bride (1973), have been made into movies. He is also the author of
the successful screenplay for the film *Butch Cassidy and the Sundance Kid.*

NOVELS BY GOLDMAN

Boys and Girls Together (1964). Warner Bks 1988 $5.95. ISBN 0-446-35754-5
Brothers (1987). Warner Bks 1988 $4.95. ISBN 0-446-34680-2
The Color of the Light (1984). Warner Bks 1985 $4.95. ISBN 0-446-32587-2
Control (1982). Dell 1983 $4.95. ISBN 0-440-11464-0
Heat (1985). Warner Bks 1988 $3.95. ISBN 0-446-30000-4
Marathon Man (1974). Dell 1988 $4.95. ISBN 0-440-15502-9
*The Princess Bride (1973). Ballantine 1987 $3.95. ISBN 0-345-34803-6 An action/adven-
ture novel about a beautiful princess who is kidnapped.
Tinsel (1979). Dell 1980 $4.95. ISBN 0-440-18735-4

GREENE, BETTE 1934–

An award-winning writer of novels for young adults, Bette Greene was born
in 1934 in Memphis, Tennessee. She recalls that, as a child during the years of
World War II, she was envied by her friends because, although candy and sugar
were rationed, her father owned a country store and could give her all the
candy she wanted. She, however, considered herself "the unluckiest, unhappi-

est girl in town because my religion (Judaism) was alien to my community." Greene was later to write about this experience in the autobiographical *Summer of My German Soldier* (1973).

From 1950 to 1952, while still a teenager, Greene worked as a reporter on the *Memphis Commercial Appeal.* The following year she went to work for the Memphis Bureau of the United Press. Also during 1952, Greene attended the University of Alabama, and from 1953 to 1954, she studied at Memphis State University. In 1955, she went to New York and studied at Columbia University until 1956.

Greene later returned to Memphis, where she worked as a public information officer for the American Red Cross. In 1959, she married Donald Sumner Greene, a physician, with whom she later had three children. With Greene she went to Boston, where she worked as a public information officer at Boston State Psychiatric Hospital for several years, as well as spending a year at Harvard University.

Greene's first published book was *Summer of My German Soldier,* which was nominated for a National Book Award and received several other awards in 1973. Her next novel, *Philip Hall likes me. I reckon maybe.* (1974), received the American Library Association's Notable Children's Book award and two awards from the *New York Times* in 1974, as well as being named a Newbery Honor Book in 1975.

Greene is also the author of the screenplay for *Summer of My German Soldier,* which was made into an award-winning television movie. She continues to live in Brookline, Massachusetts, a suburb of Boston.

NOVELS BY BETTE GREENE

Get on out of here, Philip Hall (1981). Dell 1984 $2.75. ISBN 0-440-43038-0 Sequel to *Philip Hall likes me. I reckon maybe;* more about the relationship between young Beth and her friend Philip.

Morning Is a Long Time Coming (1978). Bantam 1988 $2.95. ISBN 0-553-27354-X Sequel to *Summer of My German Soldier;* portrays that novel's heroine at 18 and her trip to Germany in pursuit of her obsession.

Philip Hall likes me. I reckon maybe (1974). Dell 1975 $2.95. ISBN 0-440-45755-6 Story of 11-year-old Beth and her school rivalry—and romance—with her classmate Philip.

Summer of My German Soldier (1973). Bantam 1984 $2.95. ISBN 0-553-27247-0 Autobiographical novel about a young Jewish girl growing up in a small southern town during World War II.

BOOK ABOUT GREENE

Gallo, Donald R. (ed). *Speaking for Ourselves.* NCTE 1990 $12.95. ISBN 0-8141-4625-2 Collection of 87 autobiographical sketches of authors of young-adult books, including one of Greene discussing her childhood and her interest in writing.

GUY, ROSA   1928–

Rosa Guy was born in Trinidad, West Indies. Although she came to the United States at age four, she continues to employ West Indian dialect in her fiction, a reflection of her deep interest in her birthplace and its people and their speech. This interest is especially evident in her first novel, *The Friends* (1973), in which the central character has, like Guy, moved from the West Indies to Harlem.

The Friends and its two sequels, *Ruby* (1976) and *Edith Jackson* (1978), comprise a trilogy that movingly probes the quest of young black women for a sense of self-respect and identity. Guy explores the same theme in a different context in her Imamu Jones novels: *The Disappearance* (1980), *New Guys Around the Block* (1983), and *And I Heard a Bird Sing* (1987). These novels are all engrossing mystery stories which also deal with Imamu's struggle for identity.

Although the characters in Guy's novels are frequently young people, the themes, characterization, and plot development are those of adult fiction. Guy also brings to her work a deep understanding of life on the streets of New York, enabling her novels to become profound explorations of the condition of American youth.

NOVELS BY GUY

And I Heard a Bird Sing (1987). Delacorte 1987 $3.25. ISBN 0-440-20152-7 Story of Imamu Jones, who must solve a mystery that threatens his new life.

The Disappearance (1980). Dell 1988 $3.25. ISBN 0-440-92064-7 Story about a Harlem kid who uses his street knowledge to find a missing child.

The Friends (1973). Bantam 1983 $2.95. ISBN 0-553-26519-9 Story about a 14-year-old girl who moves from the West Indies to Harlem and finds a new friend.

Mirror of Her Own (1981). Delacorte 1981 $8.95. ISBN 0-385-28636-8 A young girl must overcome jealousy of her older sister to find her own identity.

My Love, My Love, or the Peasant Girl (1985). Holt 1985 $12.95. ISBN 0-03-000507-8 Story of the tragic love between a peasant girl and a rich man of mixed ethnic background on a Caribbean island.

New Guys Around the Block (1983). Delacorte 1983 $2.95. ISBN 0-440-95888-1 Imamu Jones teams up with two neighborhood newcomers to discover the mystery of the phantom burglar.

The Ups and Downs of Carl Davis III (1989). Delacorte 1989 $13.95. ISBN 0-385-29247-6 Story of 12-year-old Carl, who is sent from New York City to live with his grandmother in South Carolina.

BOOKS ABOUT GUY

Gallo, Donald R. (ed). *Speaking for Ourselves.* NCTE 1990 $12.95. ISBN 0-8141-4625-2 A fascinating collection of autobiographical sketches of 87 young-adult authors, including Guy; authors share stories of how they started to write and of significant events that influenced them; includes complete list of published works and dates.

Norris, Jerrie. *Presenting Rosa Guy.* G. K. Hall 1988 $15.95. ISBN 0-8057-8207-9 A critical biography of the writer who recreates Harlem life in her books for young adults.

HAMILTON, VIRGINIA 1936–

Virginia Hamilton was born in Yellow Springs, Ohio, and studied at Antioch College, Ohio State University, and the New School for Social Research. She published her first novel, *Zeely,* in 1967 and, in the years since, has produced a wide variety of novels ranging from mysteries to science fiction.

Hamilton's stories do not fit neatly into established categories. Instead, they combine a curious blend of myth, folklore, dreams, and symbols with a commonplace reality. In *The Planet of Junior Brown* (1971), Hamilton writes of a 262-pound musical prodigy slowly allowing his dream world to become his reality. The title character of *M. C. Higgins, the Great* (1974) perches atop a 40-foot pole, lost in dreams, while a mountain of mining waste slides toward his home. Because many of Hamilton's novels feature an extended family, the characters' relationships are complex and there are numerous subplots.

Hamilton's skill as a writer is widely acknowledged. Alice Walker calls *Zeely* "a finely woven tale," and poet Nikki Giovanni describes *M. C. Higgins, the Great* as "a powerful story" in which Hamilton "creates characters with whom we can identify and for whom we care." (*See* Giovanni *and* Walker, Vol. 1, American Literature: The Twentieth Century.)

Novels by Hamilton

Anthony Burns: The Defeat and Triumph of a Fugitive Slave (1988). Knopf 1988 $11.95. ISBN 0-394-88185-0 Story of an escaped slave who faces trial in Virginia.

Arilla Sundown (1976). Greenwillow 1976 $12.88. ISBN 0-688-84058-2 Story of 12-year-old Arilla Adams and her search for identity in a mixed black and American-Indian family.

Dustland (1980). Avon 1985 $1.95. ISBN 0-380-56127-1 A young girl, her brothers, and their friends use special powers to visit a barren land in the future.

* The House of Dies Drear* (1968). Macmillan 1970 $3.95. ISBN 0-02-043520-7 A young boy and his family probe a strange old house for its secrets.

Junius Over Far (1985). Harper 1985 $12.89. ISBN 0-06-022195-X Fourteen-year-old Junius and his father go off to rescue his grandfather from pirates on a Caribbean island.

Justice and Her Brothers (1978). Avon 1985 $1.95. ISBN 0-380-56119-0 A young girl, her brothers, and their friends discover they have strange powers.

A Little Love (1984). Berkley 1985 $2.50. ISBN 0-425-08424-8 Story of a young girl's journey in search of her father.

M. C. Higgins, the Great (1974). Macmillan 1987 $3.95. ISBN 0-02-043490-1 A young boy's attempt to convince his family that a huge pile of mine waste is moving toward their house.

* The Mystery of Drear House: The Conclusion of the Dies Drear Chronicle* (1987). Macmillan 1988 $3.95. ISBN 0-02-043480-4 A family tries to decide what to do with the treasure they have discovered in an old house.

* The Planet of Junior Brown* (1971). Macmillan 1986 $3.95. ISBN 0-02-043540-1 A friend helps bring a troubled boy back from his dream world to reality.

Sweet Whisper, Brother Rush (1982). Avon 1990 $2.95. ISBN 0-380-65193-9 A 14-year-old girl meets a handsome stranger who helps her understand herself and her mother.

A White Romance (1987). Putnam 1987 $14.95. ISBN 0-399-21213-2 Story of a friendship between two runners, one black and one white.

Zeely (1967). Macmillan 1986 $3.95. ISBN 0-689-71110-7 Story of a young brother and sister whose lives are changed by a six-and-a-half-foot woman.

Short Story Collections by Hamilton

In the Beginning (1988). Harcourt 1988 $18.95. ISBN 0-15-238740-4 Twenty-five stories from cultures around the world, about the creation of the earth and the first human beings.

* The People Could Fly: American Black Folk Tales* (1985). Knopf 1985 $9.95. ISBN 0-394-84301-8 A collection of traditional African-American folktales beautifully retold.

Nonfiction by Hamilton

W. E. B. Du Bois: A Biography (1972). Harper 1972 $13.89. ISBN 0-690-87256-9 A readable account of the life of the great African-American leader; suitable for grades six and up.

Books about Hamilton

Gallo, Donald R. (ed). *Speaking for Ourselves.* NCTE 1990 $12.95. ISBN 0-8141-4625-2 A fascinating collection of autobiographical sketches of 87 young-adult authors, including Hamilton; authors share stories of how they started to write and of significant events that influenced them; includes complete list of published works and dates.

Stanford, Barbara Dodd, and Karmina Amin. *Black Literature for High School Students.* NCTE 1978. (o.p.) $6.00. ISBN 0-8141-0330-8 A resource book on teaching black literature that includes profiles of African-American authors, annotated bibliographies, sample curriculums, and discussions of how to approach various types of literature in the classroom.

HAMMETT, DASHIELL 1894–1961

One of the most important detective story writers in all of modern literature, Dashiell Hammett himself served as a private detective for the Pinkerton Agency in his youth in San Francisco. His experiences as a soldier in both world wars also contributed to the development of the tough, cool, and intelligent heroes who appear in his novels. His most famous characters of this type, Sam Spade and the Continental Op (short for *operative,* "detective"), continue to serve as prototypes for mystery writers. Hammett also created the Thin Man, an elegant and shrewd detective in a sophisticated setting.

Hammett is distinguished by his sharp, economical prose and his ability to capture in print an essential toughness characteristic of a type of American male. This brought him admiration from critics and intellectuals as well as from the reading public. Authors Sinclair Lewis, Robert Graves, and André Gide, along with other famous writers, were admirers of Hammett. (*See* Gide, Vol. 1, World Literature: French Language and Literature; Graves *and* Lewis, Vol. 1, American Literature: The Twentieth Century.) Many of Hammett's novels, including *The Maltese Falcon* (1930) and *The Thin Man* (1934), were made into movies that are today considered classics; Hammett himself wrote the screenplay for *The Maltese Falcon* and collaborated on one for *The Thin Man.* Hammett also wrote original screenplays of high quality, such as *The Glass Key.*

NOVELS BY HAMMETT

Dashiell Hammett: Five Complete Novels. Crown 1986 $9.98. ISBN 0-517-61835-4
* The Glass Key (1931). Vintage 1989 $4.95. ISBN 0-394-71773-4 A novel about justice, friendship, politics, and murder.
* The Maltese Falcon (1930). Vintage 1989 $4.95. ISBN 0-394-71772-4 The first Sam Spade novel, featuring a motley cast of characters and the famous "black bird."
The Novels of Dashiell Hammett. Knopf 1965 $29.50. ISBN 0-394-43860-4
* Red Harvest (1929). Vintage 1989 $3.95. ISBN 0-394-71828-3 Hammett's first novel, featuring the Continental Op outwitting a gang of murderers.
* The Thin Man (1934). Vintage 1989 $2.95. ISBN 0-394-71774-0 Introduces Nick Charles, retired detective, and his wealthy wife Nora, up to their ears in crime.

SHORT STORY COLLECTIONS BY HAMMETT

* The Big Knockover (1966). Vintage 1989 $4.95. ISBN 0-394-71829-X A collection of Hammett's early stories assembled by Lillian Hellman, his longtime companion.
* The Continental Operative (1945). Vintage 1989 $4.95. ISBN 0-394-72013-X Collected from stories that originally appeared in *Black Mask* magazine, featuring Hammett's most hard-boiled detective.

BOOKS ABOUT HAMMETT

Dooley, Dennis. *Dashiell Hammett.* Ungar 1984 $15.95. ISBN 0-8044-2141-2 A good general introduction to Hammett's life and works.
Hellman, Lillian. *Scoundrel Time.* Little 1976 $15.95. ISBN 0-316-35515-1 Hammett's longtime companion reflects on the time when the House Un-American Activities Committee was harassing them for their left-wing politics.
Skinner, Robert E. *The Hard Boiled Explicator: A Guide to the Study of Dashiell Hammett, Raymond Chandler, and Ross Macdonald.* Scarecrow 1985 $17.50. ISBN 0-8108-1749-7 A study of the "hard-boiled" detective novel, placing Hammett in context with other authors of the genre.

HANSBERRY, LORRAINE 1930–1965

Lorraine Hansberry was born in Chicago, the daughter of a wealthy real estate broker. She was educated at the University of Wisconsin and then moved to New York, where she worked as a salesperson, cashier, and assistant to an off-Broadway producer before trying her hand at writing plays.

With the production of *A Raisin in the Sun* in 1959, Hansberry became the first black woman to have a play produced on Broadway. The play was an immediate success, running for 530 consecutive performances and winning the New York Drama Critics Circle Award.

The title of Hansberry's play comes from a line from the poem "Harlem" by Langston Hughes. (*See* Hughes, Vol. 1, American Literature: The Twentieth Century.) "What happens to a dream deferred? Does it dry up like a raisin in the sun?" The play tells the story of a black family facing threats and harassment for moving into a white neighborhood, as Hansberry's own family had experienced when she was eight years old. As they discuss the move and its consequences, the family members also discuss the entire range of problems confronting African Americans.

Hansberry's second play, *The Sign in Sidney Brustein's Window* (1964), deals with the moral dilemmas of Jewish intellectuals in New York's Greenwich Village. Her promising career was cut short by her death from cancer at the age of 35.

Plays by Hansberry

Lorraine Hansberry: The Collected Last Plays (1983). Robert Nemiroff (ed). Plume 1983 $12.95. ISBN 0-452-26448-0 Three provocative and powerful dramas *(Les Blancs, The Drinking Gourd,* and *What Use Are Flowers?)* edited by Hansberry's husband, Robert Nemiroff.

A Raisin in the Sun and *The Sign in Sidney Brustein's Window* (1959, 1964). Plume 1990 $9.95. ISBN 0-452-26485-5 Expanded twenty-fifth anniversary edition of Hansberry's two full-length plays.

To Be Young, Gifted, and Black (1969). Signet 1970 $4.95. ISBN 0-451-15952-7 A unique drama woven by Hansberry's husband out of selections from her published and unpublished work.

Book about Hansberry

Cheney, Anne. *Lorraine Hansberry.* G. K. Hall 1984 $17.95. ISBN 0-80057-7365-7 A comprehensive overview of and introduction to Hansberry's life and work.

HAYDEN, ROBERT 1913–

Robert Hayden was born in Detroit, Michigan, where he attended Detroit City College (now Wayne State University) from 1932 to 1936. Although he withdrew before graduating, he returned to complete his work, receiving a B.A. in 1942. Two years later he received a master's degree from the University of Michigan.

Hayden has been a professor of English at the University of Michigan and has also taught at other colleges and universities. He published his first book of poetry, *Heart-Shape in the Dust,* in 1940. Since then he has written seven additional volumes.

Hayden's poems embrace various styles and themes. Many are written in

African-American "street talk," capturing the vitality of black urban life. Others are more personal statements of his own emotions. Still others deal with broader social problems and the black cultural experience. Hayden's style varies from simple and direct to highly elaborate and complex. His voice and his craft establish him as an important figure in contemporary poetry.

POETRY BY HAYDEN

Collected Poems. Liveright 1985 $6.70. ISBN 0-87140-138-X
Words in the Mourning Time (1970). October 1970 $7.95. ISBN 0-8079-0161-X

HEINLEIN, ROBERT   1907–1988

Born in Butler, Montana, Robert Heinlein entered the United States Naval Academy at age 18 and was graduated and commissioned in 1929. He began writing science fiction in 1939, after taking an early retirement from the Navy because of a physical disability received in the line of duty.

Heinlein has had a powerful influence on the entire field of science fiction. By skillfully incorporating technical details into the fabric of his stories, Heinlein managed, almost single-handedly, to raise science fiction to a new level of sophistication and credibility. His stories broke the tradition of science fiction as mere sensational adventure, offering instead technically believable and well-written speculations on possible futures. With the publication of *Rocket Ship Galileo* in 1947, Heinlein further advanced the genre by uniting science fiction and the adolescent novel.

Heinlein's ideas on space travel influenced scientists as well as general readers and culminated in his employment as a television commentator on early Apollo missions to the moon. His later novels have been faulted by some critics for being too concerned with contemporary social issues projected into the future. Heinlein's popularity, however, remains very strong, and his influence on virtually all modern science-fiction writers is universally acknowledged.

NOVELS BY HEINLEIN

*Between Planets (1951). Ballantine 1984 $3.95. ISBN 0-345-32099-9 Story of Don Harvey, son of a Venutian mother and Earthling father, caught in a war between two planets.

*Citizen of the Galaxy (1957). Ballantine 1987 $3.95. ISBN 0-345-34244-5 Story of Thorby, adopted son of a noble space captain, who becomes a captive in an interstellar prison.

*The Door into Summer (1957). Ballantine 1986 $3.95. ISBN 0-345-33012-9 Story of a successful inventor who is tricked into a 30-year sleep.

*Double Star (1956). Ballantine 1986 $3.95. ISBN 0-345-33013-7 Story of a down-and-out actor who is kidnapped and taken to Mars to impersonate an important politician.

*Farmer in the Sky (1950). Ballantine 1985 $3.50. ISBN 0-345-32438-2 Story of a family that settles on an uninhabited planet.

*Have Spacesuit Will Travel (1958). Ballantine 1977 $3.50. ISBN 0-345-32441-2 Story of a young boy kidnapped by a giant extraterrestrial being.

*Red Planet (1949). Ballantine 1981 $3.50. ISBN 0-345-34039-6 Story of the exploits of Earthlings on Mars.

*Rocket Ship Galileo (1947). Ballantine 1985 $2.95. ISBN 0-345-33660-7 Story of four amateur astronauts who unexpectedly land on the moon.

*Space Cadet (1948). Ballantine 1984 $3.50. ISBN 0-345-35311-0 Story of a group of extraordinary boys who train to protect the peace of the solar system.

The Star Beast (1954). Ballantine 1977 $3.95. ISBN 0-345-35059-6 Story of Lummox, an alien beast, brought to Earth and adopted as a family pet.

Stranger in a Strange Land (1961). Ace 1987 $4.95. ISBN 0-441-79034-8 Story of an extraordinary human from Mars who is manipulated by politicians hoping to use his superior powers.

Time for the Stars (1956). Ballantine 1987 $3.50. ISBN 0-345-35191-6 Story of identical telepathic twins whose powers are vital to the completion of Earth's most important project.

Tunnel in the Sky (1955). Ballantine 1987 $3.50. ISBN 0-345-35373-0 Story of a survival test that goes wrong, stranding a small group of men and women in a strange land.

BOOKS ABOUT HEINLEIN

Clareson, Thomas D. *Robert A. Heinlein.* Starmont 1990 $9.95. ISBN 1-55742-130-7 A general introduction to Heinlein's life and works, emphasizing his philosophical approach to science fiction.

Stover, Leon. *Robert A. Heinlein.* G. K. Hall 1986 $17.95. ISBN 0-8057-7509-9 A general study and overview of Heinlein's life and fiction for the general reader, with a one-chapter biography, a chronology, a bibliography, and discussions of all the major works.

Thorner, J. Lincoln. *A Guide to the Worlds of Robert A. Heinlein.* Borgo 1989 $19.95. ISBN 0-87055-431-X A reader's guide to Heinlein's most important novels, assuming prior knowledge of plots.

HELLER, JOSEPH   1932–

Like Yossarian, the hero of his first and most successful novel, *Catch 22* (1961), Brooklyn-born Joseph Heller was a bombardier during World War II. He graduated from New York University, received an M.A. from Columbia University, and attended Oxford University on a Fulbright scholarship. He wrote *Catch 22* while working at advertising jobs at various magazines and corporations. The book was enormously successful and continues to be widely read, having sold almost 4 million copies to date.

Heller used his experience in the world of business and publishing to write his second novel, *Something Happened* (1974), a gloomy yet wry and humorous story about the moral bankruptcy of middle-class American life in the years after World War II. In *Good as Gold* (1979), Heller began a study of what it means to be a Jew, an exploration of ethnic identity that he continued in *God Knows* (1984).

Heller's later work has not achieved anything like the significance of *Catch 22.* That book still continues to stir the imaginations of millions of readers, and the phrase "Catch 22"—a bureaucratic impossibility whereby two documents are each required in order to obtain either one—has become a lasting part of our language.

NOVELS BY HELLER

Catch 22 (1961). Dell 1989 $4.95. ISBN 0-440-11120-X A hilarious story of life in the U.S. Army Air Corps in World War II, seen through the eyes of a bombardier who thinks only of going home.

God Knows (1984). Dell 1989 $5.95. ISBN 0-440-20438-0

Good as Gold (1979). Pocket 1980 $2.95. ISBN 0-671-82388-4

Picture This (1988). Ballantine 1989 $4.95. ISBN 0-345-35886-4

Something Happened (1974). Dell 1988 $5.95. 0-440-20441-0

BOOKS ABOUT HELLER

Merrill, Robert. *Joseph Heller.* G. K. Hall 1987 $17.95. ISBN 0-8057-7492-0 A comprehensive overview of and introduction to Heller's life and fiction.

Seed, David. *The Fiction of Joseph Heller: Against the Grain.* St. Martin's 1989 $24.95. ISBN 0-312-02795-8 A thoughtful and useful analysis of Heller's works and themes.

HELLMAN, LILLIAN 1905–1984

Born in New Orleans, Louisiana, Lillian Hellman was educated at New York and Columbia universities and worked as a publisher's reader, book reviewer, and theater publicist. Then Dashiell Hammett (*see* Hammett, Vol. 1, American Literature: The Twentieth Century), her longtime companion, encouraged her to write plays. Her first successful play, *The Children's Hour* (1934), dramatized the destruction of two teachers at a girls' boarding school by the lies spread by a malicious child.

In subsequent plays Hellman focused on antilabor violence (*Days to Come,* 1936) and the threat of fascism (*Watch on the Rhine,* 1941; *The Searching Wind,* 1944). Her best plays, *The Little Foxes* (1939) and *Another Part of the Forest* (1946), brilliantly combine comedy and melodrama to expose the greed and cruelty that lead to the breakup of a southern family.

Hellman's other important plays include *The Autumn Garden* (1951), about people with unfulfilled lives, and *Toys in the Attic* (1960), about a young man's escape from his possessive sisters. Hellman won the 1941 New York Drama Critics Circle Award for *Watch on the Rhine* and the 1960 award for *Toys in the Attic.*

Hellman also gained notoriety during the late 1940s and early 1950s, a time of political repression when federal and state government agencies were investigating anyone believed to be a Communist or to have political ideas that were in any way close to communism. Hellman's left-wing views caused her to be called to testify before Congress. Although she was risking a jail sentence for contempt of Congress, Hellman refused to testify about anyone else's activities or beliefs, agreeing only to testify about her own. Hellman claimed that government investigation of citizens' political beliefs was an infringement of free speech. She later wrote about this difficult period in her memoir, *Scoundrel Time.*

PLAYS BY HELLMAN

The Collected Plays of Lillian Hellman. Little 1972 $25.00. ISBN 0-316-35519-4
Six Plays by Lillian Hellman: The Children's Hour, Days to Come, The Little Foxes, Watch on the Rhine, Another Part of the Forest, The Autumn Garden. Random 1979 $9.95. ISBN 0-394-74112-9

NONFICTION BY HELLMAN

Three: An Unfinished Woman, Pentimento, Scoundrel Time. Little 1980 $19.95. ISBN 0-316-35514-3 Hellman's three memoirs providing insight into her times as well as her life; *Pentimento* is the basis for the film *Julia; Scoundrel Time* is her account of political repression and her response to it in the late 1940s and early 1950s.

BOOKS ABOUT HELLMAN

Falk, Doris V. *Lillian Hellman.* Ungar 1978 $16.95. ISBN 0-8044-2194-3 A comprehensive overview and introduction to Hellman's plays and memoirs.
Lederer, Katherine. *Lillian Hellman.* G. K. Hall 1979 $15.95. ISBN 0-8057-7275-8 An excellent introduction to Hellman's life and works, with corrections of previous misreadings.
*Towns, Saundra. *Lillian Hellman.* Chelsea 1989 $17.95. ISBN 1-55546-657-5 A good introduction to Hellman's works, specifically written for young readers.

HEMINGWAY, ERNEST   1899–1961

Despite the considerable negative criticism he received in his lifetime, it now seems clear that Ernest Hemingway was one of the literary giants of the twentieth century. He was an international writer whose subject was the world from upper Michigan to "the green hills of Africa." More than any other writer of this century, he showed that it is possible for a writer to be both popular and good.

Hemingway was born in Oak Park, Illinois, a Chicago suburb, the son of a doctor who loved outdoor sports and instilled in his son a similar love for these traditionally masculine activities. Hemingway decided to ignore college in order to become a reporter with the *Kansas City Star.* In World War I he went to Italy as an ambulance driver and later joined the Italian infantry, where he was severely wounded.

Sometime around 1921, Hemingway settled in Paris, as did other young American writers at the time, and his first books were published there. Hemingway's first successful novel, *The Sun Also Rises* (1926), is made up almost entirely of the conversations of a group of lost generation artists and writers in Paris. (The lost generation writers were Americans who felt "lost" and confused after the destruction of World War I; their ranks included F. Scott Fitzgerald (*see* Fitzgerald, Vol. 1, American Literature: The Twentieth Century) and the poet Gertrude Stein.) Hemingway used World War I Italy as the background for the love story of an English nurse and an American soldier in his 1929 novel *A Farewell to Arms.*

In 1927, Hemingway returned to America. He left again in 1936 to participate in the Spanish Civil War. *For Whom the Bell Tolls* (1940), probably his greatest novel, was the result of his Spanish experiences, as was the 1938 play, *The Fifth Column,* a study of espionage in wartime Spain.

For his many and varied services in World War II, Hemingway was decorated with the Bronze Star. Early in 1954, while on assignment for *Look* magazine, he and his fourth wife had two narrow escapes when planes on which they were traveling crashed in Africa.

One of Hemingway's most widely read novels, *The Old Man and the Sea* (1952), was published at about this time. The book is the symbolic story of an old fisherman who has wanted to catch a huge, legendary tuna his whole life. When he finally does catch the fish, however, he is too weak to haul it into his boat. By the time he reaches shore, dragging his prize behind him in the water, the fish is no more than a carcass, having been eaten by various sea creatures. The book won the Pulitzer Prize in 1953.

Hemingway was awarded the Nobel Prize for literature in 1954 for his many contributions to the body of American literature. Seven years later, in declining health, he committed suicide. He had an enormous impact on a whole generation of writers who came after him, including both Americans and such Canadian writers as Morley Callaghan. (*See* Callaghan, Vol. 1, Commonwealth Literature.)

NOVELS BY HEMINGWAY

Across the River and into the Trees (1950). Scribner's 1985 $5.95. ISBN 0-648-18496-6
A Farewell to Arms (1929). Macmillan 1982 $4.95. ISBN 0-02-051900-1
For Whom the Bell Tolls (1940). Macmillan 1988 $5.95. ISBN 0-02-051850-1
**The Old Man and the Sea* (1952). Macmillan 1987 $3.95. ISBN 0-02-051910-9 Story of
   an elderly Cuban fisherman and the fulfillment of his lifelong dream.
The Sun Also Rises (1926). Macmillan 1987 $4.95. ISBN 0-02-051870-6
To Have and Have Not (1937). Macmillan 1988 $4.95. ISBN 0-02-051880-3
Winner Take Nothing (1933). Macmillan 1988 $5.95. ISBN 0-02-051820-X

Short Story Collections by Hemingway

The Nick Adams Stories (1972). Scribner's 1981 $8.95. ISBN 0-684-16940-1 Stories of the young Nick Adams's passage into manhood; includes "The killers," in which Nick, working in a diner, overhears two hired killers planning to murder an ex-boxer.

The Hemingway Reader. Scribner's 1953 $7.95. ISBN 0-684-71872-3

The Short Stories of Ernest Hemingway. Macmillan 1987 $7.95. ISBN 0-02-051860-9

The Snows of Kilimanjaro and Other Stories (1961). Scribner's 1982 $3.95. ISBN 0-684-17471-5

Nonfiction by Hemingway

The Green Hills of Africa (1935). Macmillan 1988 $5.95. ISBN 0-02-051930-3

Books about Hemingway

Baker, Carlos. *Ernest Hemingway: A Life Story.* Macmillan 1988 $12.95. ISBN 0-02-001690-5 A scholarly, thoroughly researched, well-documented, yet very readable, biography of Hemingway.

Brian, Denis. *The True Gen: An Intimate Portrait of Hemingway by Those Who Knew Him.* Delacorte 1989 $10.95. ISBN 0-385-29738-6 "A marvelous oral biography compiled from interviews with more than 100 people who knew Hemingway . . ." writes *Publishers Weekly.*

*Burgess, Anthony. *Ernest Hemingway and His World.* Macmillan 1978 $10.95. ISBN 0-684-18504-0 Pictorial biography of a controversial American writer; suitable for younger readers.

Hays, Peter L. *Ernest Hemingway.* Continuum 1990 $18.95. ISBN 0-8264-0467-7 A concise biography with a critical analysis of Hemingway's works.

Hemingway, Mary Walsh. *How It Was.* Knopf 1976 $16.95. ISBN 0-394-40109-3 An intimate yet evenhanded biography by Hemingway's fourth wife.

Shaw, Samuel. *Ernest Hemingway.* Ungar 1982 $16.95. ISBN 0-8044-2823-9 A comprehensive general introduction to Hemingway's life and works.

HENTOFF, NAT (NATHAN IRVING)   1925–

Born and educated in Boston, Massachusetts, Nat Hentoff fell in love with music, especially jazz, at young age. One of his first jobs was working at a local radio station. He went on to build a considerable reputation as a jazz critic before beginning to write fiction. Hentoff is currently a well-known journalist at the New York-based newspaper *The Village Voice,* where he writes frequently about civil liberties and other political issues.

Hentoff's musical background comes through clearly in his first novel, *Jazz Country* (1965), the story of the problems of a talented, white teenage musician trying to enter the predominantly black jazz scene. Aside from being a moving story of a personal struggle, *Jazz Country* is also an exploration of the world of jazz and a study of racial attitudes.

Hentoff's novels frequently focus on social issues and their impact on young people, from the Vietnam War (*I'm Really Dragged, but Nothing Gets Me Down,* 1967) to censorship (*The Day They Came to Arrest the Book,* 1982). His youthful characters are bright, witty, and dogged in their quest for understanding, but though his characters grow in self-knowledge, they are ultimately frustrated in their search for clear answers. The most frequent criticism of Hentoff's novels is that the story can get lost in the discussion of issues.

Novels by Hentoff

The Day They Came to Arrest the Book (1982). Dell 1983 $2.95. ISBN 0-440-91814-6 Story of a small but vocal group that tries to keep *The Adventures of Huckleberry Finn* from being taught in school.

Does This School Have Capital Punishment? (1981). Dell 1983 $2.95. ISBN 0-440-92070-1 Story of a young boy who needs the help of an aging jazz musician in order to beat a drug charge.

Jazz Country (1965). Dell 1986 $2.25. ISBN 0-440-94203-9 Story of a young white New Yorker who wants more than anything in the world to be a jazz musician.

This School Is Driving Me Crazy (1975). Dell 1978 $2.95. ISBN 0-440-98702-4 Story of a 12-year-old boy who attends the school where his father is principal.

BOOK ABOUT HENTOFF

Gallo, Donald R. (ed). *Speaking for Ourselves.* NCTE 1990 $12.95. ISBN 0-8141-4625-2 A fascinating collection of autobiographical sketches of 87 young-adult authors, including Hentoff; authors share stories of how they started to write and of significant events that influenced them; includes complete list of published works and dates.

HERBERT, FRANK 1920–1986

Frank Herbert was born in Tacoma, Washington. He held a variety of jobs before he turned to writing science fiction.

Although Herbert has written more than two dozen books, his fame rests largely on the six novels of the *Dune* series: *Dune, Dune Messiah, Children of Dune, God Emperor of Dune, Heretics of Dune,* and *Chapterhouse: Dune.* In these elaborately structured, highly detailed stories, Herbert has created a complex but believable world. There he pushes a variety of contemporary problems to their extremes, exploring "what might happen if . . ." In one sense, these are ecological novels, concerned with preserving the delicate natural balance of the fragile planet of Dune. In another sense, they are social novels in which Herbert explores what happens to a society that abandons its own better judgment and puts its faith in a powerful leader. The world of Dune was brought to the screen in a 1985 film.

NOVELS BY HERBERT

Chapterhouse: Dune (1985). Ace 1987 $4.95. ISBN 0-441-10276-0 Sixth book in the Dune series; years later, a sisterhood tries to manipulate the civilization on Arrakis.

Children of Dune (1976). Ace 1987 $4.95. ISBN 0-441-10402-9 Third book in the Dune series; the descendents of the old civilization try to cope with the changes begun decades before.

Dune (1965). Ace 1987 $4.95. ISBN 0-441-17266-0 A novel about the effort to save a barren, dying planet, where water is the most precious substance.

Dune Messiah (1970). Ace 1987 $4.95. ISBN 0-441-17269-5 Second book in the Dune series; the story of Paul Atreides, prophet and emperor, and his sacrifice to save the planet.

God Emperor of Dune (1981). Ace 1987 $4.50. ISBN 0-441-29467-7 Fourth book in the Dune series; story of Leto Atreides, Paul's son, who fights to gain an empire.

Heretics of Dune (1981). Berkeley 1984 $3.50. ISBN 0-425-08732-8 Fifth book in the Dune series; centuries after the death of Leto, a shaky alliance spells the end of Dune.

The Soul Catcher (1971). Berkeley 1984 $3.50. ISBN 0-425-09141-4 Story of a young American Indian who becomes the incarnation of the spirit of his ancestors in order to avenge a crime.

The White Plague (1983). Berkeley 1983 $4.50. ISBN 0-425-09050-7 The chilling account of a future plague that begins in Ireland and kills only women.

Worlds Beyond Dune: The Best of Frank Herbert (includes *The Jesus Incident* (1979), *Whipping Star* (1970), *Destination Void* (1966), *The Godmakers* (1971), and *The Dosadi Experiment* (1977). Berkeley 1987 $17.95. ISBN 0-425-09465-0 Five novels of space and adventure—*not* part of the Dune series.

Books about Herbert

Herbert, Brian (ed). *The Notebooks of Frank Herbert's Dune.* Putnam 1988 $9.95. ISBN 0-399-51466-X Contains much previously unpublished material on Dune.

Toupence, William F. *Frank Herbert.* G. K. Hall 1988 $17.95. ISBN 0-8057-7514-5 A good general introduction to Herbert's life and works.

HIGHWATER, JAMAKE   1942–

Jamake Highwater was born in Glacier County, Montana, of Blackfoot and Cherokee Indian ancestry. He received a B.A. and M.A. from the University of California at Berkeley, a Ph.D. from the University of Chicago, and he has taught at various universities in the United States and Canada.

An accomplished writer and poet, Highwater has written 15 books on American Indian life and culture. His book *Anpao* (1977) combines many aspects of Indian folklore in a single tale that captures the spirit of Native-American culture and history. The book won many honors, including a Newbery Honor Award and Best Book for Young Adults Award from the American Library Association.

Highwater has also published collections of Indian art and ritual music and dance. He recently completed the third novel in his Ghost Horse trilogy, which traces a family of Native Americans through three generations.

In his work Highwater tries to impart not only a strong sense of Indian heritage but also "a purely Indian concept of reality and identity." "To the Indian mentality," he notes, "dead people walk and things go backward and forward in time, and these are absolutely real and vivid ideas to my head." This mystical strain, combined with Highwater's storytelling skills, make his writing exceptionally moving and powerful.

Novels by Highwater

Anpao: An American Indian Odyssey (1977). Harper 1980 $8.95. ISBN 0-06-131986-4 An epic tale combining many different Indian tales and legends.

The Ceremony of Innocence (1985). Harper 1985 $11.25. ISBN 0-06-022302-2 Second book in the Ghost Horse trilogy; the story of Amana's suffering, marriage, and motherhood.

Eyes of Darkness (1983). Lothrop 1985 $13.00. ISBN 0-688-41993-3 Story of an American Indian doctor caught between two cultures.

I Hear the Morning Star (1986). Harper 1986 $12.89. ISBN 0-06-022356-1 Third book in the Ghost Horse trilogy; the story of Sitko, Amana's grandson, in boarding school and after he returns to his mother.

Legend Days (1984). Harper 1984 $12.89. ISBN 0-06-022304-9 First book in the "Ghost Horse" trilogy; Amana, a young Indian girl, has a mystical experience and gains the power of an Indian warrior.

The Sun, He Dies (1980). NAL 1984 $6.95. ISBN 0-452-00681-3 A novel about the end of the Aztec world.

HINTON, S. E. (SUSAN ELOISE)   1950–

S. E. Hinton began writing at age 16 while still a high school student in Tulsa, Oklahoma. She published her first novel, *The Outsiders* (1967), at age 17. Based on observations of her fellow high school students who belonged to gangs, the book was different from the usual novel being offered to young adults at that time. It took a while before *The Outsiders* was "discovered" by young readers as the publisher originally marketed it as adult fiction, but when young people eventually found it, it became a huge success with them. The novel established Hinton as a new voice in young adult fiction and brought her enough money to attend the University of Tulsa.

Hinton has since written several other novels dealing with the problems of youth. Her central characters are young males from lower-class homes, frustrated with the lives they lead. For them, growing up is both dangerous and confusing as they try to cope with the tension between what they must appear to be and what they really are. Hinton's strength as a novelist lies in developing her characters, giving them a full range of human emotions: there are no stereotypes in her novels. Three of her books, *The Outsiders* (1967), *Rumble Fish* (1975), and *Tex* (1979), have been made into movies.

NOVELS BY HINTON

*The Outsiders (1967). Dell 1989 $3.25. ISBN 0-440-96769-4 When his best friend kills a member of a rival gang, a teenage boy finds himself caught up in a web of violence.

*Rumble Fish (1975). Dell 1989 $3.25. ISBN 0-440-97534-4 Story about a boy who wants more than anything to be like his older brother.

*Taming the Star Runner (1988). Dell 1989 $3.25. ISBN 0-440-20479-8 Story of a 16-year-old boy who moves to a ranch, where the riding instructor tries to tame both him and a wild horse.

*Tex (1979). Dell 1989 $3.25. ISBN 0-440-97850-5 Story of two brothers who are reconciled when they learn the truth about their drifter father.

*That Was Then, This Is Now (1971). Dell 1989 $3.25. ISBN 0-440-98652-4 Story of two young men whose friendship ends when one discovers that the other pushes drugs.

BOOKS ABOUT HINTON

Daly, Jay. *Presenting S. E. Hinton.* Dell 1989 $3.95. ISBN 0-440-20482-8 A general introduction to Hinton's life and works, with a separate chapter devoted to each novel.

Gallo, Donald R. (ed). *Speaking for Ourselves.* NCTE 1990 $12.95. ISBN 0-8141-4625-2 A fascinating collection of autobiographical sketches of 87 young-adult authors, including Hinton; authors share stories of how they started to write and of significant events that influenced them; includes complete list of published works and dates.

HUGHES, LANGSTON   1902–1967

Born in Joplin, Missouri, Langston Hughes spent most of his boyhood on the move, living at various times in Buffalo, New York; Cleveland, Ohio; Lawrence, Kansas City, and Topeka, Kansas; Mexico City; Colorado Springs; Lincoln, Illinois (where he finished elementary school); and Cleveland again (where he graduated from high school). After high school, Hughes lived in many American cities, traveled to Africa while working on a ship, and spent some time in Paris.

In later years Hughes explored the various forms of literature, writing poetry, drama, opera librettos, song lyrics, novels, short stories, articles, and essays, as well as numerous radio and television scripts. By doing so many things so well, Hughes established himself as one of the leading American writers of the twentieth century.

The title of Hughes's first novel, *Not Without Laughter* (1930), provides insight into the nature of his work as a whole. Humor pervades his writing, albeit a humor born of bitterness and sorrow. Hughes's stories look honestly at the dark side of life for African Americans in the years before and immediately after World War II, but they always find a kernel of humor, love, or hope. Perhaps one of his titles sums up his stance even better—*Laughing to Keep from Crying* (1952).

Hughes is best known for his poetry, which incorporates the style of the blues and the rhythms of jazz. He is also famous for his stories of "Simple," a down-to-earth man who philosophizes and jokes about life, love, and racial issues.

NOVEL BY HUGHES

Not Without Laughter (1930). Macmillan 1986 $5.95. ISBN 0-02-052200-2

SHORT STORY COLLECTIONS BY HUGHES

**The Best of Simple* (1961). Hill & Wang 1961 $6.95. ISBN 0-374-52133-6 A collection of stories that comment on many aspects of American life, especially race relations.
Laughing to Keep from Crying (1952). Amereon (repr of 1952 ed) $18.95. ISBN 0-88411-060-5
**Simple's Uncle Sam* (1965). Amereon (repr of 1965 ed) $15.95. ISBN 0-88411-709-X Stories about American life and politics told by a bar-stool philosopher.
**Something in Common and Other Stories* (1963). Hill & Wang 1963 $7.95. ISBN 0-8090-0057-1 A wide range of Hughes's stories about life, love, politics, and race relations.
The Ways of White Folks (1934). Random 1971 $4.95. ISBN 0-394-71304-4

PLAYS BY HUGHES

Five Plays by Langston Hughes (1963). Indiana Univ Pr 1963 $8.95. ISBN 0-253-20121-7

POETRY BY HUGHES

The Dream Keeper (1932). Knopf 1962 $9.99. ISBN 0-394-91096-6
The Panther and the Lark (1967). Knopf 1967 $12.95. ISBN 0-394-40419-X
*Selected Poems (1959). Random 1974 $6.95. ISBN 0-394-71910-7 Hughes's personal selection of his best poems.

COLLECTION BY HUGHES

The Langston Hughes Reader. Braziller 1981 $17.50. ISBN 0-8076-0057-1

NONFICTION BY HUGHES

**The Big Sea: An Autobiography* (1940). Thunder's Mouth 1986 $11.95. ISBN 0-938410-33-4 An autobiography that covers Hughes's life up to age 27.

BOOKS ABOUT HUGHES

Bloom, Harold (ed). *Langston Hughes.* Chelsea 1990 $22.50. ISBN 1-55546-376-2 A collection of modern critical essays by such distinguished scholars as Hughes biographer Arnold Rampersad ("The Origin of Poetry in Langston Hughes"), Onwuchekwa Jeme ("Jazz, Jive, and Jam") and Irwin T. Turner, on Hughes as a playwright.
Emanuel, James A. *Langston Hughes.* G. K. Hall 1967 $14.95. ISBN 0-8057-0388-8 A good general introduction to the life and works of Hughes, including a bibliography, a chronology, a one-chapter biography, and extensive discussion of how Hughes's works relate to his life.
*Rummel, Jack. *Langston Hughes.* Chelsea 1989 $9.95. ISBN 0-7910-0201-2 A general overview of Hughes's life and work, especially useful for young readers.

HURSTON, ZORA NEALE   1903–1960

Zora Neale Hurston was born and raised in Eatonville, Florida, a small, rural community that was the first incorporated, all-black town in America. Hurston's experience of living in a town run by African Americans shaped her entire life.

Hurston studied anthropology at Barnard College and Columbia University and served for a time as assistant to writer Fannie Hurst. Her lifelong interest in African-American culture and folklore dominates her work. She was one of the most prominent writers of the Harlem Renaissance, a flourishing of African-American culture centered in New York's black community of Harlem in the 1920s. More than most writers in this movement, Hurston captures the essence of the African-American cultural heritage and incorporates it into works of high literary quality. Her ear for black speech is exceptional, and she has been highly praised for capturing on paper the rhythms and texture of rural black dialect. Her stories, however, go far beyond mere descriptions of black culture. According to critic Judith Wilson, "her fiction is one of celebration of a black cultural heritage whose complexity and originality refutes all efforts to enforce either a myth of inferiority or a lie of assimilation."

NOVEL BY HURSTON

Their Eyes Were Watching God (1937). Univ of Illinois Pr 1978 $6.95. ISBN 0-252-00686-0
  The story of Janie and her search for happiness as she grows from girl to woman in love.

SHORT STORY COLLECTIONS BY HURSTON

The Gilded Six-Bits (1933). Redpath 1986 $4.95. ISBN 1-55628-006-8 Life in the all-black community of Eatonville, Florida.
Spunk: The Selected Stories of Zora Neale Hurston. Turtle Island 1985 $9.95. ISBN 0-913666-3 A collection of stories about black life in the rural South.

NONFICTION BY HURSTON

I Love Myself When I Am Laughing and Then Again When I Am Looking Mean and Impressive: A Zora Neale Hurston Reader (1979). Alice Walker (ed). Feminist Pr 1979 $9.95. ISBN 0-912670-66-5

BOOKS ABOUT HURSTON

Hemenway, Robert E. *Zora Neale Hurston: A Literary Biography.* Univ of Illinois Pr 1977 $10.95. ISBN 0-252-00807-3 The definitive work on Hurston, relating her work and life to demonstrate her groundbreaking contribution to African-American culture.
*Witcover, Paul. *Zora Neale Hurston.* Chelsea 1991 $17.95. ISBN 0-7910-1129-1 Biography of this black folklorist, author, and anthropologist during the Harlem Renaissance.

JACKSON, SHIRLEY   1919–1965

Shirley Jackson was born in San Francisco and was educated at the University of Rochester and at Syracuse University, from which she received a B.A. degree in 1940. Soon after graduation she married Stanley Edgar Hyman, a well-known author and critic.

When Jackson's best-known story, "The Lottery," was published in *The New Yorker* magazine in 1948, it generated more mail than the magazine had ever before received on a single piece. Most of those who wrote objected strongly to Jackson's portrayal of the evil in human nature.

This theme, that humans are more evil than good, runs through much of Jackson's work. She depicts people as being little more than mindless robots, doing what other people expect of them and seldom thinking for themselves. In other Jackson stories, a mindless, indifferent society frequently destroys innocent victims. She also often uses mystical or eerie settings, and strong elements of horror appear in her stories.

These works, however, are only one side of Jackson's art. She also wrote lighter descriptions of family life, including most notably *Life Among the Savages* (1949), a hilarious account of her own efforts at raising a family.

In all her work, Jackson is a skilled, highly disciplined writer who is as conscious of form and structure as she is of telling a good tale. The spine-chilling effect of her horror stories are as much the result of carefully applied craft as they are of her vision of humanity's dark side.

NOVELS BY JACKSON

The Bird's Nest (1954). Amereon (repr of 1954 ed) $18.95. ISBN 0-317-27727-8 A suspense story about a woman with multiple personalities.

The Haunting of Hill House (1959). Penguin 1984 $6.95. ISBN 0-14-007108-3 Story of two women caught in a web of supernatural circumstances.

The Sundial (1958). Penguin 1986 $5.95. ISBN 0-14-008317-0 Story of a group of religious zealots awaiting the end of the world.

We Have Always Lived in the Castle (1962). Penguin 1986 $5.95. ISBN 0-14-007107-5 Story of a family's murder of a relative by arsenic and the effect on the remaining three family members.

SHORT STORY COLLECTION BY JACKSON

The Lottery (1949). Farrar 1949 $8.95. ISBN 0-374-51681-2 Contains the famous title story and other chilling tales.

NONFICTION BY JACKSON

Come Along with Me (1968). Amereon (repr of 1968 ed) $17.95. ISBN 0-89190-621-5

Life Among the Savages (1949). Academy Chi Pubs 1989 $8.95. ISBN 0-89733-342-X Hilarious account of Jackson's family life in Vermont.

Witchcraft in Salem Village (1956). Random 1963 $8.99. ISBN 0-394-90369-2 Very readable account of the events leading up to the famous Salem witch trials.

BOOK ABOUT JACKSON

Friedman, Lenemaja. *Shirley Jackson.* G. K. Hall 1975 $14.95. ISBN 0-8057-0402-7 A good general introduction to Jackson's life and works, including a bibliography, a chronology, a one-chapter biography, and extensive discussion of how Jackson's works relate to her life.

JARRELL, RANDALL   1914–1965

In 1961 Randall Jarrell's collection of poetry *The Woman at the Washington Zoo* (1960) won the National Book Award. It was said that "each poem . . . has [Jarrell's] usual expert technical skill in the use of rhyme, of assonance, meter and imagery."

Poet, critic, novelist, and teacher, Jarrell was born in Nashville, Tennessee. He graduated from Vanderbilt University, where he also received his M.A. He later taught at the University of Texas, Sarah Lawrence College, and the Women's College of the University of North Carolina. He won a Guggenheim

Fellowship in 1947 and was awarded a grant from the National Institute of Arts and Letters in 1951. From 1956 through 1958, Jarrell served as poetry consultant at the Library of Congress; later he became literary editor of *The Nation* and poetry editor of *Partisan Review* and the *Yale Review.*

Jarrell's poetry is marked by a plain, almost colloquial, style, in which he addresses issues drawn from contemporary life. One of his basic concerns is the impact of science and technology on the modern world, forces which Jarrell sees as primarily causing confusion and uncertainty. His poetry also deals with the effects of war, most notably in "The Death of the Ball Turret Gunner," one of his best-known poems.

POETRY BY JARRELL

Complete Poems (1969). Farrar 1969 $12.95. ISBN 0-374-51305-8
Lost World: Last Poems (1965). Macmillan 1985 $7.95. ISBN 0-02-069740-6
Selected Poems (1964). Macmillan 1964 $5.95. ISBN 0-689-70109-8

NONFICTION BY JARRELL

The Letters of Randall Jarrell. Houghton 1985 $29.95. ISBN 0-395-34405-0
Poetry and the Age (1953). Ecco 1980 $6.95. ISBN 0-912946-70-9

BOOK ABOUT JARRELL

Rosenthal, M. L. *Randall Jarrell.* Univ of Minnesota Pr 1972 $1.25. ISBN 0-8166-0646-3
Pamphlet providing a brief introduction to Jarrell's poetry focusing on his major themes and techniques.

JEFFERS, (JOHN) ROBINSON 1887–1962

Robinson Jeffers was born in Pittsburgh, the son of a theology teacher whose frequent changes of jobs often forced his family to move. Therefore the family moved frequently before finally settling in California. Jeffers completed an undergraduate degree at Occidental College, and then went on to medical school for a year before deciding instead to become a poet. An inheritance left him financially secure and able to devote himself fully to his writing. He settled on a wild, isolated cliff in Carmel, California, where he set down the tragic folktales of northern California.

Jeffers was a poet concerned with cruelty and horror. His dramatic narrative poems are filled with scenes of blood and lust, and his verse shows vigorous beauty and great originality. He had little use for either religion or "the American way of life," and looked skeptically at the modern world, especially at science. Though he was pessimistic about the fate of humanity, he was enthralled by the beauty and power of nature. In his view, the works and cares of the human race were insignificant compared to the grandeur and endurance of nature. Jeffers was also captivated by the classical and Biblical worlds, and many of his poems reflect this admiration. Jeffers won the 1954 Pulitzer Prize for *Hungerfield and Other Poems* (1954), and continues to enjoy critical acclaim.

POETRY BY JEFFERS

The Alpine Christ and Other Poems (1947). Cayucos 1974 $20.00. ISBN 0-9600372-4-1
Dear Judas (1929). New Directions 1970 $7.70. ISBN 0-87140-133-4
Flagons and Apples (1912). Cayucos 1970 $20.00. ISBN 0-9600372-1-7
Rock and Hawk: Shorter Poems (1984). Random 1987 $19.95. ISBN 0-394-55679-7
Selected Poems (1938). Random 1965 $4.95. ISBN 0-394-70295-6
The Woman at Point Sur (1927). Liveright 1987 $7.70. ISBN 0-87140-115-0

BOOK ABOUT JEFFERS

Carpenter, Frederic I. *Robinson Jeffers.* New College & Univ Pr 1962 $10.95. ISBN 0-8084-0269-2 A general study of Jeffers's life and work, including a chronology, bibliography, and one-chapter biography; most of the book focuses on the relationship between Jeffers's life and his major works.

JOHNSON, JAMES WELDON   1871–1938

James Weldon Johnson was born in Jacksonville, Florida, and educated at Atlanta University and Columbia University. He was the first African American admitted to the Florida Bar after the Civil War. While practicing law, he wrote popular songs and spirituals. One of these, "Lift Every Voice and Sing," has been called by some "the black national anthem."

From 1906 to 1913, Johnson served as U.S. Consul to Nicaragua and Venezuela. He later became Executive Secretary of the National Association for the Advancement of Colored People (NAACP). In 1930, Johnson began teaching literature at Fisk University in Nashville, Tennessee, a position he held until his death in an automobile accident in 1938.

Although he wrote both fiction and nonfiction, Johnson is best known now for his poetry. He was an important leader of the Harlem Renaissance (an artistic movement of black writers and artists in the 1920s), and his collection of poems from this period, *God's Trombones* (1927), is considered his best book of poetry. A central theme in Johnson's work is black pride; he consistently celebrated the accomplishments of African Americans. His novel, *The Autobiography of an Ex-Colored Man* (1912), is about a black man who "passes" as white. It is a penetrating look at the life of an American black man in the early days of this century, and was highly influential on the writers who came after Johnson.

NOVEL BY JOHNSON

The Autobiography of an Ex-Colored Man (1912). Hill & Wang 1960 $7.95. ISBN 0-8090-0032-6

POETRY BY JOHNSON

Fifty Years and Other Poems (1917). AMS (repr of 1917 ed) $15.00. ISBN 0-404-01822-3
St. Peter Relates an Incident: Selected Poems (1935). AMS (repr of 1935 ed) $14.50. ISBN 0-404-11371-0

NONFICTION BY JOHNSON

Along This Way: The Autobiography of James Weldon Johnson. Da Capo 1973 repr of 1933 ed $49.50. ISBN 0-306-70539-7 Covers Johnson's years as a U.S. Consul and his time with the National Association for the Advancement of Colored People.
Black Manhattan (1930). Ayer 1968 repr of 1930 ed $24.95. ISBN 0-405-01822-3
Negro Americans: What Now? (1934). AMS (repr of 1938 ed) $12.50. ISBN 0-404-00075-4

BOOKS ABOUT JOHNSON

Fleming, Robert S. *James Weldon Johnson.* G. K. Hall 1987 $19.95. ISBN 0-8057-7491-2 A good general introduction to Johnson's life and works, focusing on how Johnson's writing can be illuminated by a study of his life; includes a one-chapter biography, chronology, and bibliography.
*Tolbert-Rouchaleau, Jane. *James Weldon Johnson.* Chelsea 1989 $9.95. ISBN 0-7910-0211-X An introduction to and general overview of Johnson's life and works, especially suitable for young readers.

KEROUAC, JACK   1922–1969

Jack Kerouac (christened Jean Louis Lebris De Kerouac) was born in Lowell, Massachusetts, of French-Canadian extraction. He interrupted his education at Columbia University to serve in the Merchant Marine in World War II. He spent the postwar years roaming the United States and Mexico with other young men, many of whom would become writers. The group, of which Kerouac was the leader, became known as the Beat Generation, a term Kerouac himself coined in 1952. His definition appeared in the *American College Dictionary* as he wrote it: *"Beat Generation*—members of the generation that came of age after World War II who espouse mystical detachment and relaxation of social and sexual tensions, supposedly as a result of disillusionment stemming from the cold war."

Kerouac's first novel, *The Town and the City* (1950), is a rather conventional story of family disintegration, but he found his own unique voice in his next work, *On the Road* (1957). It was the first of his books to reflect his method of "spontaneous prose." Written in 20 days on a single 120-foot roll of teletype paper, it makes use of free association in a way that Kerouac likened to improvised jazz. He saw *On the Road*—his account of his free-wheeling travels through postwar America—and most of his subsequent works as installments in one vast autobiography. His poetry, too, is very much influenced by jazz and improvisational techniques.

NOVELS BY KEROUAC

Big Sur (1962). McGraw 1981 $6.95. ISBN 0-07-034206-7
Desolation Angels (1965). Putnam 1978 $8.95. ISBN 0-399-50385-4

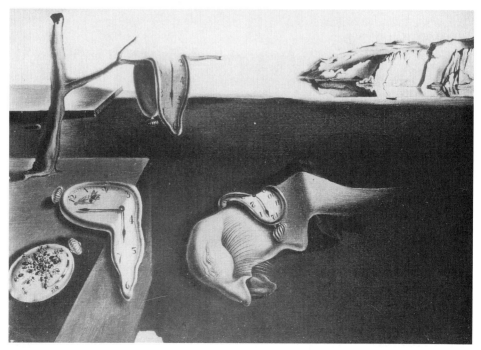

Persistence of Memory.   Painting by Salvador Dali (1931).   Courtesy of The Bettmann Archive.

The Dharma Bums (1958). Penguin 1971 $6.95. ISBN 0-14-004252-0
On the Road (1957). Penguin 1976 $5.95. ISBN 0-14-004259-8
The Subterraneans (1958). Grove 1989 $6.95. ISBN 0-8021-3186-7
Visions of Gerard (1963). McGraw 1976 $6.95. ISBN 0-07-034204-0

POETRY BY KEROUAC

Heaven and Other Poems (1977). Grey Fox 1977 $4.95. ISBN 0-912516-31-3
Scattered Poems (1971). City Lights 1971 $3.50. ISBN 0-87286-064-7

BOOKS ABOUT KEROUAC

Charters, Ann. *Kerouac: A Biography.* St. Martin's 1987 $10.95. ISBN 0-312-06617-9
Detailed, thoroughly researched biography of Kerouac heavily dependent on primary sources.

Hunt, Tina. *Kerouac's Crooked Road: Development of a Fiction.* Shoe String 1981 $27.50. ISBN 0-208-01871-9 An analysis of the various influences that shaped Kerouac's work.

KERR, M. E. (PSEUDONYM OF MARIJANE MEAKER)   1927–

M. E. Kerr was born in Auburn, New York. She attended a private preparatory school, Stuart Hall, in Staunton, Virginia, where she was suspended in her senior year for throwing darts at pictures of faculty members. Reinstated through the efforts of her family, she graduated and went on to the University of Missouri, where she studied English literature, completing her degree in 1949. Kerr then moved to New York City and took a job with a publisher, but left in less than a year to become a full-time writer.

Kerr has really had two writing careers. Under the names Ann Aldrich, Vin Packer, and M. J. Meaker, she has published more than 25 novels for adults. Most of these were written under the pseudonym Vin Packer and published between 1952 and 1969. In 1972, inspired by reading *The Pigman* (1968) by Paul Zindel (*see* Zindel, Vol. 1, American Literature: The Twentieth Century), she published her first novel for young adults, *Dinky Hooker Shoots Smack!* Each year since she has produced an average of one novel for younger readers.

Almost all of Kerr's juvenile fiction explores some aspect of love in the lives of teenagers. Typically, the characters in her books must come to grips with the sad fact that the people they love will often disappoint them. Yet the disappointment almost always brings new knowledge and a stronger sense of self-awareness, so that, although Kerr's stories lack a typical "happy ending," they are far from being depressing or pessimistic.

NOVELS BY KERR

Dinky Hooker Shoots Smack! (1972). Dell 1973 $2.95. ISBN 0-440-92030-2 Despite its title, not a story about drugs and addiction, but about a young girl whose parents are so busy with community activity that they have no time for her.

Fell (1987). Harper 1988 $2.95. ISBN 0-06-447031-8 Fast-talking 17-year-old John Fell enrolls in a prep school under another's name.

Gentlehands (1978). Bantam 1982 $2.75. ISBN 0-553-26677-2 Story of young Buddy, who learns that his grandfather is a notorious Nazi war criminal.

Him She Loves? (1984). Putnam 1984 $2.25. ISBN 0-448-47732-7 Seventeen-year-old Henry Schiller falls in love with the daughter of a television comic, who ridicules Henry in his act.

I Stay Near You (1985). Berkeley 1986 $2.50. ISBN 0-425-08870-7 Three related stories of three generations of the same family and their first loves.

If I Love You, Am I Trapped Forever? (1973). Dell 1974 $2.25. ISBN 0-440-94320-5 Story of Allen Bennett, a handsome athlete whose world begins to unravel during his senior year of high school.

Is That You, Miss Blue? (1975). Harper 1987 $2.95. ISBN 0-06-447033-4 Story of a
14-year-old girl's adjustment to life at a private school.
Love Is a Missing Person (1976). Harper 1987 $2.95. ISBN 0-06-447034-2 A girl spends
a confusing but instructive summer on eastern Long Island.
Night Kites (1986). Harper 1987 $2.75. ISBN 0-06-447035-0 Story of young Eric, who
tries to save his best friend from a bad romance while struggling with his own
romantic problems and with the knowledge that his older brother has AIDS.
The Son of Someone Famous (1974). NAL 1983 $2.50. ISBN 0-451-13722-1 Story of a young
teenager who wants to forget that he has a famous parent.
What I Really Think of You (1982). Harper 1982 $12.70. ISBN 0-06-023188-2 Story about
the children of Pentecostal preachers, one poor and the other a child of a rich
televangelist.

Nonfiction by Kerr

Me Me Me Me Me: Not a Novel. Signet 1984 $2.50. ISBN 0-451-13208-4 Kerr's autobiog-
raphy based on the diaries she wrote as a teenager.

Books about Kerr

Gallo, Donald R. (ed). *Speaking for Ourselves.* NCTE 1990 $12.95. ISBN 0-8141-4625-2
A fascinating collection of autobiographical sketches of 87 young-adult authors,
including Kerr; authors share stories of how they started to write and of significant events that influenced them; includes complete list of published works and
dates.
Nilsen, Alleen Pace. *Presenting M. E. Kerr.* Dell 1990 $3.95. ISBN 0-440-20540-9 A good
general introduction to Kerr's life and novels, including a very complete biography and a brief discussion of all her major books.

KING, STEPHEN 1947–

Born in Portland, Maine, the son of a sailor, Stephen King has become one of
the most popular writers of the twentieth century. After attending public
schools in Portland, King went on to the University of Maine, from which he
received a Bachelor of Science degree in 1970. In addition to teaching high
school English, King has worked as a janitor, in a laundry, and in a knitting
mill. He married Tabitha Spruce, a poet, in 1971, and has three children.

Writing under the name Richard Bachman as well as under his own name,
King has successfully produced over two dozen books in less than 20 years,
with total sales running above 10 million. Several of his novels and stories have
been made into highly popular films and television productions. His first novel,
Carrie (1974), introduced two elements that often appear in the work he has
done since: revenge and supernatural destructive power. In his stories, characters—human, animal, or mechanical—are often endowed with fearsome powers, which they use to destroy those who have previously wronged them.
King's tales range from macabre horror stories to science fiction and fantasy.

Despite King's enormous popularity, especially with young readers, he has
not always fared well with the critics. His fiction has been faulted for being
predictable and for dragging out scenes. Using a comparison to a baseball
pitcher, Richard R. Lingeman of *The New York Times* writes, "Mr. King is a
natural, but he lacks control; he simply rears back and lets fly with the fireball,
and lots of wild pitches result. That's a pity because his sheer rookie's energy
is engaging."

Because of the large number of King's books currently in print, the list below includes only about half those available. Other titles may be found in *Books in Print.*

NOVELS BY KING

*Carrie (1974). Signet 1975 $3.95. ISBN 0-451-15071-6 Story of a teenager shunned by her classmates, who discovers too late that she has a strange power.

*Christine (1983). Signet 1983 $4.95. ISBN 0-451-16044-4 An automobile is possessed by an evil spirit.

*Cujo (1981). Signet 1981 $4.95. ISBN 0-451-16135-1 Story of a rabid 200-pound St. Bernard that terrorizes two families.

* The Dark Half (1989). Penguin 1989 $21.95. ISBN 0-670-82982-X A successful writer must battle his pseudonym come to life.

* The Dark Tower: The Gunslinger (1984). NAL 1989 $5.95. ISBN 0-451-16052-5 First book in a fantasy series; in a stark and menacing land, a lone gunman stalks the man in black and battles the forces of evil.

* The Drawing of the Three (The Dark Tower II) (1989). Signet 1989 $5.95. ISBN 0-451-16352-4 Second book in the Dark Tower series; the gunslinger travels to a parallel world to choose three companions.

* The Eyes of the Dragon (1984). Signet 1987 $4.50. ISBN 0-451-15125-9 A medieval romance complete with wizards, princes, and demons.

*Firestarter (1980). Signet 1981 $4.50. ISBN 0-451-15031-7 A young girl with the power to start fires with her eyes battles the forces of evil.

*It (1986). Signet 1987 $5.95. ISBN 0-451-15927-6 Story of seven teenagers who battle alien evil in the sewers of a city.

*Misery (1987). Signet 1988 $4.95. ISBN 0-451-15355-3 A successful romance novelist is hounded by a psychotic fan.

*Pet Sematary (1983). Signet 1984 $4.95. ISBN 0-451-15775-3 Story of a typical all-American family that discovers a cemetery that can bring the dead back to life.

* The Shining (1977). Signet 1978 $4.95. ISBN 0-451-16091-6 A young boy must confront his psychotic father.

* The Stand (1978). Signet 1980 $5.95. ISBN 0-451-16095-9 Story of the world's last few survivors facing the deadly disease that wiped out the rest of humanity.

SHORT STORY COLLECTIONS BY KING

*Night Shift (1979). Signet 1987 $4.95. ISBN 0-451-16045-2 A chilling collection of 20 horror stories.

*Skeleton Crew (1985). Signet 1986 $4.95. ISBN 0-451-14293-4 A collection of stories that range from terror to eerie whimsy.

BOOKS ABOUT KING

Underwood, Tim, and Chuck Miller (eds). *Fear Itself: The Horror Fiction of Stephen King.* Signet 1985 $4.50. ISBN 0-451-15270-0 Thirteen essays dealing with such topics as King's popularity, the film adaptations of his novels, and his settings.

Underwood, Tim, and Chuck Miller (eds). *Kingdom of Fear: The World of Stephen King.* Signet 1987 $4.95. ISBN 0-451-16635-3 A collection of 17 essays by writers, critics, and filmmakers delving into King's life and works.

KLEIN, NORMA   1938–1989

Norma Klein was born in New York City, the daughter of a psychoanalyst. She began her higher education at Cornell University, but after one year transferred to Barnard College, from which she graduated with honors and membership in the Phi Beta Kappa honor society.

Klein began her literary career as a writer of short stories, publishing over

60 pieces between 1960 and 1970. She wrote her first novel, *Love and Other Euphemisms,* in 1970, but it was not published until two years later. In the meantime, the birth of her first child aroused Klein's interest in children's books, and in 1972 she published *Mom, the Wolf Man, and Me.* The book was highly praised by the critics and became immediately popular with young readers. It remains one of Klein's most widely read novels.

Klein's novels are frequently narrated by a young girl who is facing a personal problem, although later works are often narrated by teenage boys as well. The range of issues addressed in her books is wide, covering many of the most crucial, current concerns: divorce, gender discrimination, mental illness, Alzheimer's disease, physical handicaps, child pornography, and premarital sex, among others. In her novels Klein explores these problems openly and realistically, with no sugar coating or artificially happy endings. The result is fiction that speaks directly to young people's major concerns, a primary reason why Klein's books are so popular.

NOVELS BY KLEIN

Angel Face (1984). Fawcett 1984 $2.95. ISBN 0-449-70282-0 Story of 16-year-old Jason, whose mother becomes increasingly dependent on him after her husband leaves her.

Beginner's Love (1983). Fawcett 1984 $3.50. ISBN 0-449-70237-5 Frank, contemporary story about a young couple's first experience of love.

Bizou (1983). Fawcett 1987 $2.50. ISBN 0-449-70252-9 Story of the 13-year-old daughter of a black fashion model and a white journalist, who discovers some surprising things about her family.

Breaking Up (1980). Avon 1981 $2.50. ISBN 0-380-55830-0 A 15-year-old girl has to cope with her overprotective father, her gay mother, and her insensitive stepmother.

The Cheerleader (1985). Fawcett 1986 $2.95. ISBN 0-449-70190-5 Two 14-year-old boys become cheerleaders for the girls' softball team at school.

Family Secrets (1986). Fawcett 1987 $3.50. ISBN 0-449-70195 Story of Peter and Leslie who fall in love only to learn that her mother and his father plan to marry, making Peter and Leslie stepbrother and stepsister.

Going Backwards (1986). Scholastic 1987 $2.50. ISBN 0-590-40329-X Story of a family's reaction when Alzheimer's disease destroys the personality of a loved one.

Mom, the Wolf Man and Me (1972). Avon 1976 $2.50. ISBN 0-380-00791-6 Story of an 11-year-old girl who wants her mother to remain single.

My Life as a Body (1987). Fawcett 1988 $3.50. ISBN 0-449-70265-0 Augie, a senior at a private school, becomes attached to a brain-damaged student she is tutoring.

No More Saturday Nights (1988). Fawcett 1989 $3.50. ISBN 0-449-70304-5 Tim Weber, an unmarried father, goes to court to gain custody of his baby.

Older Men (1987). Fawcett 1988 $2.95. ISBN 0-449-70261-8 Story of a 16-year-old who must reexamine her life after her mother is hospitalized for mental illness.

Snapshots (1984). Fawcett 1986 $2.50. ISBN 0-449-70223-5 Story of 13-year-old Sean, who innocently photographs his friend's little sister and finds himself in the middle of a child pornography investigation.

BOOKS ABOUT KLEIN

Gallo, Donald R. (ed). *Speaking for Ourselves.* NCTE 1990 $12.95. ISBN 0-8141-4625-2 A fascinating collection of autobiographical sketches of 87 young-adult authors, including Klein; authors share stories of how they started to write and of significant events that influenced them; includes complete list of published works and dates.

Phy, Allene Stuart. *Presenting Norma Klein.* G. K. Hall 1988 $15.95. ISBN 0-8057-8205-2 Very readable general introduction to Klein's life and novels, including a chronology, a one-chapter biography, and extensive discussion of how Klein's life and works relate.

KNOWLES, JOHN   1926–

John Knowles was born in Fairmont, West Virginia, and educated at Phillips Exeter Academy in Hew Hampshire and Yale University in Connecticut. After graduating from Yale in 1949, Knowles went to work as a reporter for the Hartford, Connecticut, newspaper, the *Courant,* a position he held until 1952 when he left to become a free-lance writer. In 1956, Knowles became associate editor of *Holiday* magazine. He stayed there until 1960 when he became a full-time writer.

Knowles's first novel, *A Separate Peace* (1960), was highly acclaimed both in the United States and abroad and has been one of the most popular novels of the mid-twentieth century. Part of the literature curriculum in high schools all across America, the novel depicts life in a private boys' school in the early days of World War II. It was also made into a successful movie in 1972.

Knowles's later works have received neither the critical praise nor the popularity of *A Separate Peace. Peace Breaks Out* (1981) returns to Devon, the boys' school of *A Separate Peace,* in the days immediately following World War II. In the later work, however, the central character is a teacher rather than a student, and the novel lacks both the power and the sensitivity of the earlier work. Knowles's most recent work, *A Stolen Past* (1983), received mixed reviews and sold poorly. At this point it seems safe to say that Knowles's reputation at present rests largely on *A Separate Peace.*

NOVELS BY KNOWLES

*Peace Breaks Out (1981). Bantam 1982 $3.95. ISBN 0-553-25516-9 Pete Hallam, a former Devon student returns to his old school after the second world war to teach American history and becomes involved in a controversy sparked by a Nazi-loving student.
*A Separate Peace (1960). Bantam 1984 $3.50. ISBN 0-553-28041-4 Tells the story of the young men at a private school in the early days of World War II and how one of them discovers his capacity for evil.
A Stolen Past (1983). Ballantine 1984 $3.50. ISBN 0-345-31590-1

L'AMOUR, LOUIS   1908–1988

Louis L'Amour's life is almost as varied and exciting as his fiction. Born Louis LaMoore (he later changed the spelling) in Jamestown, North Dakota, to a father who was a veterinarian and seller of farm machinery, L'Amour stayed in school until he was 15, when his family left North Dakota. Instead of going with them, however, he struck out on his own. By the time he was 17, he had worked as a circus roustabout, lumberjack, miner, and ranch hand. He then went to sea as a merchant sailor, traveling to Shanghai, Singapore, Hong Kong, and Yokohama, among other places. One story has it that while in the Orient, he heard that there was $50,000 on board a sunken ship and, getting there before anyone else, he claimed the money. At age 19, the story goes, he took the money to Europe, where he lived until he had spent it all. Back in the United States, he took to the road again, getting whatever jobs he could, including one as a professional boxer. His record as a boxer was 54 wins and 5 losses.

In the late 1930s, L'Amour settled in Oklahoma City, where he decided to try writing for a living. After gathering 200 rejection slips, he finally began to sell stories to magazines. His new career was interrupted, however, by World War II, in which he served as an officer in the Tank Destroyer Corps. After the war, he resumed writing and flooded the pulp magazines with his stories: detective and mystery tales, sports stories, aviation stories, and westerns. Finding that he had most success selling westerns, he decided to specialize in western fiction. He published his first novel, *Westward the Tide,* in 1948 at age 42.

L'Amour's books deal with residents of the American West—families, young men, seasoned cowboys, criminals, and outlaws. They range in theme from coming-of-age stories to tales of adventure in a harsh but rewarding land.

L'Amour went on to become the most prolific and popular writer of western fiction in history. In one year alone, one of his publishers sold 7,820,000 copies of his books, more than most writers dream of selling in a lifetime. In 1980, Bantam Books celebrated 100 million copies of L'Amour books in print around the world.

Despite this popularity, critical acclaim was slow in coming to L'Amour. His books were rarely even reviewed before the 1970s, when critics finally began to take notice of his work. Then, while still somewhat guarded in their praise, they gave L'Amour high marks for his lean, economical style and vivid, accurate descriptions.

The United States government was more generous, however. It awarded L'Amour the nation's two highest honors—the Congressional Gold Medal and the Presidential Medal of Freedom. L'Amour was the only novelist in the nation's history to receive either of these awards, let alone both of them.

Although self-educated, L'Amour read widely and throughout his life placed a high value on learning. He strove always to derive some lesson from all he encountered.

There are over 100 L'Amour titles currently in print. The list that follows represents a sample of some of the more popular ones. Additional titles may be found in *Books in Print.* Today's readers may find that L'Amour's stories of the American West are marred by his dated, stereotypical portrayals of American Indians.

NOVELS BY L'AMOUR

Bendigo Shafter (1978). Bantam 1983 $4.50. ISBN 0-553-26446-X Story of a young man's desire to be a writer and his initiation into the ways of the West.

Catlow (1963). Bantam 1984 $3.50. ISBN 0-553-42767-0 Story of two strong men on opposite sides of the law.

Comstock Lode (1981). Bantam 1982 $4.50. ISBN 0-553-26176-2 Historical novel about the discovery of silver in Nevada and the rise of Virginia City.

The Daybreakers (1960). Bantam 1984 $2.95. ISBN 0-553-24904-5 The first novel in the Sackett series, based on the exploits of several generations of the Sackett family.

Down the Long Hills (1968). Bantam 1984 $2.95. ISBN 0-553-25275-5 A seven-year-old boy and three-year-old girl survive a wagon-train massacre.

Flint (1960). Bantam 1985 $3.50. ISBN 0-553-25231-3 Hard-boiled story of concealed identity.

Heller with a Gun (1954). Bantam 1985 $3.50. ISBN 0-553-25206-2 Story of a wandering theatrical group and the man who protects them from weather, Indians, and outlaws; stereotypical portrayal of American Indians.

Hondo (1978). Bantam 1985 $2.95. ISBN 0-553-24757-3 Story of Hondo Lane and the help he gives a young woman and her son living in Indian territory; stereotypical portrayal of American Indians.

The Lonely Men (1969). Bantam 1984 $2.95. ISBN 0-553-25507-X When the wife of one of the Sacketts is murdered, the rest of the family comes to his aid.

Lonely on the Mountain (1980). Bantam 1986 $2.95. ISBN 0-553-25513-4 The Sackett family pulls together when one family member is unable to deliver a herd of cattle to a desperate town.

The Man from the Broken Hills (1975). Bantam 1986 $2.95. ISBN 0-553-25514-2 The adventures of Milo Sackett, who brings together the Talon and Sackett families.

Short Story Collections by L'Amour

The Strong Shall Live (1980). Bantam 1985 $3.50. ISBN 0-553-25200-3 Stories of physical and mental strength.

Yondering (1980). Bantam 1982 $2.95. ISBN 0-553-260391-1 Selection of some of L'Amour's favorite tales, with an introduction by L'Amour.

Nonfiction by L'Amour

Education of a Wandering Man. Bantam 1989 $16.95. ISBN 0-553-05703-0 L'Amour's recollections of his early years and his lifelong love affair with learning.

Book about L'Amour

Gale, Robert L. *Louis L'Amour.* G. K. Hall 1985 $15.95. ISBN 0-8057-7450-5 A good general introduction to L'Amour's life and works with an extensive discussion of how the two relate; includes a bibliography, chronology, and concise one-chapter biography.

LEE, HARPER (NELLE HARPER LEE)   1926–

Harper Lee was born in Monroeville, Alabama, where, like the narrator of her famous novel, she grew up the daughter of a lawyer. She attended Alabama's Huntington College in 1944 and 1945 and then went on to study law at the University of Alabama from 1945 to 1949. Her education also included a year at Oxford University in England.

After finishing school, Lee worked as an airlines reservations clerk in New York for a few years but left to devote herself full time to writing. In 1960, she published her acclaimed novel, *To Kill a Mockingbird,* a young girl's view of her father as he defends a black man accused of raping a white woman. Although Lee herself has said that she considers the novel to be a simple love story, focusing on a child's relationships with family and other children, the book immediately won praise for its incisive look at racial issues.

To Kill a Mockingbird has won many awards, including the Pulitzer Prize of 1961. It has been translated into 10 languages and was made into a 1962 movie starring Gregory Peck. The book continues to be widely read and taught today.

Lee still lives in the Alabama town where she was born. She is reportedly at work on a second novel.

Novel by Lee

To Kill a Mockingbird (1960). Warner Bks 1982 $3.95. ISBN 0-446-31486-2 Story of a young girl's childhood in the South as she watches her father defend a black man accused of raping a white woman.

LE GUIN, URSULA K.   1929–

Ursula Le Guin was born and raised in Berkeley, California, the daughter of an anthropologist, Alfred Kroeber, and a writer, Theodora Kroeber. She received a B.A. from Radcliffe College in 1951 and an M.A. from Columbia University in 1952. She then went to study in Paris on a Fulbright scholarship. While there she met and married historian Charles Le Guin. The couple and their three children currently live in Portland, Oregon.

Le Guin's unique blend of fantasy, science fiction, and social commentary give her stories the unmistakable flavor of intelligent, imaginative, poetic writing. While her tales may be set in outer space or distant times, they almost always reflect the problems of contemporary Earth. The plots emphasize personal relationships and human problems, and the themes suggest that the solutions to these problems will come through integration, the bringing together of things that are normally thought of as separate. For example, in one of Le Guin's short stories, a little girl survives a plane crash and is cared for by animals, but the girl sometimes sees the animals as human. Thus, Le Guin suggests the oneness of all life. Reality, she seems to say, is all in the way we see things, and we can overcome conflict if we choose to see similarities rather than differences.

Le Guin's works also explore other social and political concerns. She questions, for instance, whether fear and insecurity will undermine democracies and lead to dictatorship. She constantly calls attention to the creative power of language—the ability of words not only to describe reality but also to create or modify it. Le Guin is also very concerned with the concept of balance, the need for opposing forces to be brought into equilibrium with each other. But above all, as she noted in her acceptance speech for the National Book Award for *The Farthest Shore* (1972), she believes that the work of the fantasist is to talk "about human life as it is lived, and as it might be lived, and as it ought to be lived."

NOVELS BY LE GUIN

Always Coming Home (1985). Bantam 1987 $4.95. ISBN 0-553-26280-7 The history, adventures, customs, language, and art of the Kesh, an imaginary, ancient people discovered on the Pacific Coast.

The Dispossessed (1974). Avon 1976 $3.95. ISBN 0-380-00382-1 A fantasy set on an anarchist moon colony and its capitalist mother planet.

The Farthest Shore (1972). Bantam 1984 $3.50. ISBN 0-553-26847-3 Third book in the Earthsea trilogy; an aging leader sets off with a young prince to discover whether magic still remains in the land.

The Left Hand of Darkness (1969). Ace 1983 $3.95. ISBN 0-441-47812-3 Story of a planet populated by "androgynes," beings who periodically change from male to female.

The Tombs of Atuan (1971). Bantam 1984 $3.95. ISBN 0-553-27331-0 Second book in the Earthsea trilogy; Ged becomes the archmage (head magician) of the archipelago, and Arha gives up everything to become a high priestess.

Very Far Away from Anywhere Else (1976). Bantam 1982 $2.50. ISBN 0-553-25376-4 Story of a gifted, but lonely, high school boy who meets an equally gifted young woman.

A Wizard of Earthsea (1968). Bantam 1984 $3.95. ISBN 0-553-26250-5 Ged, the boy wizard, brings forth from the shadow a beast that wants to destroy his soul.

SHORT STORY COLLECTIONS BY LE GUIN

Buffalo Gals and Other Animal Presences (1987). Bantam 1987 $7.95. ISBN 0-452-26480-4 Collection of stories that presents our planet through the eyes of animals.

Orsinian Tales (1976). Harper 1987 $6.95. ISBN 0-06-091433-5 Tales of an alternate universe.

BOOKS ABOUT LE GUIN

Bloom, Harold (ed). *Ursula K. Le Guin.* Chelsea 1986 $27.50. ISBN 0-87754-659-2 A collection of modern critical essays encompassing a wide range of perspectives on Le Guin's work.

Spivak, Charlotte. *Ursula K. Le Guin.* G. K. Hall 1984 $7.95. ISBN 0-8057-7430-0 A general introduction to Le Guin's life and work, with extensive discussion of how the two relate; includes a one-chapter biography, chronology, and bibliography.

LESTER, JULIUS   1939–

The son of a Methodist minister, Julius Lester was born in St. Louis, Missouri. He moved to Kansas City, Missouri, when he was two years old and to Nashville, Tennessee, when he was 14. After graduating from high school in Nashville, he went on to receive a B.A. in English from Fisk University, in the same city.

In the early 1960s Lester was active in the civil rights movement, heading the photo department of the Student Non-Violent Coordinating Committee (a civil rights group) in 1966 and traveling to North Vietnam to photograph the effects of U.S. bombing in 1967. A talented musician, Lester has recorded albums for Vanguard Records and, with folksinger Pete Seeger, wrote *The Twelve-Stringed Guitar as Played by Leadbelly* (1965). He was the host of radio and television shows in New York City from 1969 to 1972. In 1971 he became a professor of Afro-American Studies at the University of Massachusetts in Amherst, where he still teachers.

Lester has written for both adult and young audiences. His first book for young readers, *To Be a Slave* (1968), was named a Newbery Honor Book and appeared on every recommended book list in 1969. His retelling of traditional black folktales, both African and American, and his ability to dramatize the lives of little-known historical figures have made him both a highly acclaimed and an extremely popular author of books for young readers.

NOVEL BY LESTER

Do Lord Remember Me (1984). Washington Square Pr 1986 $5.95. ISBN 0-671-60707-3

SHORT STORY COLLECTIONS BY LESTER

Black Folktales (1969). Grove 1984 $7.95. ISBN 0-8021-5022-7 Dramatic retelling of tales from Africa, from the American South, and from black urban centers in the United States.

Long Journey Home (1972). Scholastic 1988 $2.50. ISBN 0-590-41433-X Accounts of the lives and deeds of important but lesser-known African Americans.

More Tales of Uncle Remus: Further Adventures of Brer Rabbit, His Friends, Enemies, and Others (1988). Dial 1988 $15.00. ISBN 0-8037-0419-4 More modern retellings of the classic Uncle Remus tales.

The Tales of Uncle Remus: The Adventures of Brer Rabbit (1987). Dial 1987 $14.89. ISBN 0-8037-0272-8 New version of the classic Uncle Remus tales using contemporary references and modern black dialect.

This Strange New Feeling (1982). Dial 1982 $14.95. ISBN 0-8037-8491-0 Three stories about slave couples who find a measure of freedom through love.

NONFICTION BY LESTER

To Be a Slave (1968). Dial 1968 $13.95. ISBN 0-8037-8955-6 Accounts in slaves' own words of what it means to be in bondage.

LEWIS, SINCLAIR   1885–1951

Sinclair Lewis was born in Sauk Centre, Minnesota, the son of a doctor. In 1903, he entered Yale University but later left to join an experimental socialist community. After a short time as a writer and editor in New York City, he returned to Yale, where he received a B.A. degree in 1908. From 1914 to 1920, he published several undistinguished novels, including one for boys, *Hike and the Aeroplane* (1912).

Then, in 1920, Lewis published *Main Street.* This marked a turning point in Lewis's career, and the beginning of the series of novels about middle-class American life that would bring him fame and popularity.

Main Street is a satirical look at life in the small town of Gopher Prairie, Minnesota, which Lewis modeled on his hometown of Sauk Centre. He followed this successful work with *Babbit* (1922), a moving account of the life of a Middle America businessman. In *Arrowsmith* (1925), Lewis drew on his personal recollections of his father to contrast the idealism of a devoted scientist with the materialistic forces seeking to capitalize on his discoveries. For this book Lewis was offered the Pulitzer Prize, but he refused it. *Elmer Gantry* (1927) is a portrait of a dissolute but successful evangelist, and *Dodsworth* (1929) deals with a retired industrialist who marries an ambitious woman and finds that his material success does not bring the emotional fulfillment that he seeks.

Lewis faithfully portrayed the speech and actions of the middle classes in America's heartland. In fact, one critic called his books "a remarkable diary of the middle-class mind." Although some of the social conditions he describes now seem dated, his characters remain convincingly real. Their inability to break free from social conventions, from the expectations of those around them, and from the American dream of ever increasing wealth is as true today of many Americans as it was in Lewis's time.

In 1930, Sinclair Lewis became the first American to be awarded the Nobel Prize for literature. The honor seems to have inspired him to an even higher sense of social responsibility, and most of his later novels deal with specific social problems. While Lewis's later works were important social commentary when they were written, the passage of time has diminished their literary impact. Lewis's second wife was the well-known journalist Dorothy Thompson. He died of a heart attack in Rome.

NOVELS BY LEWIS

Arrowsmith (1925). Signet 1961 $4.95. ISBN 0-451-52225-7
Babbit (1922). Signet 1961 $4.95. ISBN 0-451-52366-0
Dodsworth (1929). Signet 1967 $4.95. ISBN 0-451-52177-3
Elmer Gantry (1927). Signet 1967 $4.50. ISBN 0-451-52251-6
It Can't Happen Here (1935). Signet 1970 $4.50. ISBN 0-451-15936-5
Main Street (1920). Signet 1961 $5.95. ISBN 0-451-52461-6

BOOKS ABOUT LEWIS

Bloom, Harold (ed). *Sinclair Lewis.* Chelsea 1987 $19.95. ISBN 0-87754-628-2 A collection of modern critical essays covering most aspects of Lewis's work.
Grebstein, Sheldon N. *Sinclair Lewis.* G. K. Hall 1987 $16.95. ISBN 0-8057-0448-5 A general study of Lewis's life and fiction, focusing on the relation of his life and works, and including a one-chapter biography, a chronology, and a bibliography.
Lundquist, James. *Sinclair Lewis.* Ungar 1974 $16.95. ISBN 0-8044-2563-0 A general introduction to Lewis's life and works, with extensive discussion of the major novels; includes chronology and bibliography.

LONDON, JACK   1876–1916

Jack London's life was every bit as dramatic as his fiction. He was born in San Francisco, California, to an astrologer father and a mother who came from a comfortable Ohio family. Growing up on the Oakland waterfront, London was in and out of schools as a child, and he eventually left school permanently at age 15. For two years he worked in a cannery, drank heavily, fought often, and barely managed to stay one step in front of the law. He also read every book he could get his hands on. At age 17, he signed on to the crew of a ship headed for the Arctic to hunt seals. He returned from the voyage to find the United States in a severe economic depression. Without a job, he joined a march on Washington to demand help for the unemployed. Just before he left for Washington, he won first prize in a newspaper short story contest.

During this period, London also discovered the writings of Karl Marx (*see* Marx, Vol. 2, Economics: Comparative Economic Systems) and became an active socialist. He attended the University of California for a semester in 1896, but decided he would rather educate himself. The following year he joined the Alaskan gold rush, carrying books of philosophy and poetry in his knapsack.

After a year in the Klondike, London returned to California and began to write stories based on his experiences. He published several short stories and a novel, mostly dealing with his Alaskan adventures, before publishing *The Call of the Wild* in 1903. This novel of the North was enormously successful, and London quickly published others like it that brought him fame and fortune. He was never entirely comfortable with his success, always comparing it with the misery he had seen and endured. He describes some of this discontent in his autobiographical novel *Martin Eden* (1909). London died young and unhappy, perhaps a suicide.

NOVELS BY LONDON

*The Call of the Wild and *White Fang* (1903, 1906). Bantam 1984 $2.50. ISBN 0-553-21233-8 Two of London's most famous dog stories; *The Call of the Wild,* about a sled dog that returns to his wild state, and *White Fang,* about a wild dog tamed by love.

Martin Eden (1909). Penguin 1984 $4.95. ISBN 0-14-039036-7

*The Sea Wolf (1904). Bantam 1984 $2.25. ISBN 0-553-21225-7 Story of a brutal sea voyage with Wolf Larson, the mad captain of the ship.

SHORT STORY COLLECTIONS BY LONDON

*Tales of the Pacific (1911). Penguin 1989 $4.95. ISBN 0-14-018358-2 Twelve stories of adventure in the South Seas.

*To Build a Fire and Other Stories. Bantam 1986 $4.50. ISBN 0-553-21335-0 Twenty-four stories spanning London's career as a writer, including 12 Klondike stories.

BOOKS ABOUT LONDON

Labor, Earle. *Jack London.* G. K. Hall 1977 $17.95. ISBN 0-8057-0455-8 A good, basic introduction to London's life and works.

Lundquist, James. *Jack London: Adventures, Ideas, and Fiction.* Ungar 1987 $16.95. ISBN 0-8044-2566-3 A general study of London's work, relating his personal exploits to his philosophy and fiction.

Perry , John. *Jack London: An American Myth.* Nelson-Hall 1981 $25.95. ISBN 0-88229-378-8 An intriguing portrait of this American writer and adventurer.

Stone, Irving. *Jack London: Sailor on Horseback.* Doubleday 1978 $12.95. ISBN 0-385-14084-3 A well-researched and highly readable biography of London by a noted novelist.

LOWELL, AMY   1874–1925

Amy Lowell was born in Brookline, Massachusetts, into a prominent New England family that included the nineteenth-century poet James Russell Lowell. (*See* J. Lowell, Vol. 1, American Literature: Romanticism and the American Renaissance.) She was educated privately and traveled widely in Europe while young.

Lowell began writing poetry while still in her teens and published her first volume, *A Dome of Many-Colored Glass,* in 1912. Although the poems in this collection are traditional in form and content, Lowell's later poetry was much more revolutionary. After meeting the expatriate American poet Ezra Pound (*see* Pound, Vol. 1, American Literature: The Twentieth Century) in England in 1913, she became a member of the school of poets who called themselves imagists. These poets—Lowell particularly—believed that poetry should focus on a single, concentrated moment of experience, use as few words as possible to express ideas, and employ sharp, concrete images. Lowell practiced these concepts so devotedly and became so identified with the movement that some critics called the movement "amygism." *Sword Blades and Poppy Seed* (1914) displays Lowell's experiments with this new writing style.

In her personal appearance and way of life, Lowell was anything but conventional. She was a large woman who enjoyed smoking cigars in public and seemed generally to delight in shocking her more traditional friends. However, her importance to American poetry went far beyond her unconventional habits. As critic Louis Untermeyer wrote in his introduction to her *Complete Poetical Works* (1955), "Her final place in the history of American literature has not yet been determined, but the importance of her influence remains unquestioned. Underneath her preoccupation with the need for novelty . . . she was a dynamic force."

POETRY BY LOWELL

A Critical Fable (1922). AMS (repr of 1922 ed) $17.50. ISBN 0-404-17126-5
A Dome of Many-Colored Glass (1912). AMS (repr of 1921 ed) $20.00. ISBN 0-404-17127-3
Pictures of the Floating World (1919). AMS (repr of 1919 ed) $24.50. ISBN 0-404-17128-1
Sword Blades and Poppy Seed (1914). AMS (repr of 1914 ed) $27.50. ISBN 0-404-17129-X

BOOKS ABOUT LOWELL

Benvenuto, Richard. *Amy Lowell.* G. K. Hall 1985 $18.95. ISBN 0-8057-7436-X A general study of Lowell's life and works, with a thorough discussion of how the two relate; also includes a chronology and a bibliography.
Flint, F. Cudworth. *Amy Lowell.* Univ of Minnesota Pr 1969 $1.25. ISBN 0-8166-0544-0 A pamphlet that provides a quick introduction to Lowell's poetry.

LOWELL, ROBERT 1917–1977

Robert Lowell was born in Boston, the great-grandnephew of James Russell Lowell (*see* J. Lowell, Vol. 1, American Literature: Romanticism and the American Renaissance) and distant cousin of Amy Lowell. (*See* A. Lowell, Vol. 1, American Literature: The Twentieth Century.) Thus Robert was a brilliant—though rebellious—member of one of New England's most distinguished families. He received his B.A. in 1940 from Kenyon College, where he had studied under critic and poet John Crowe Ransom. In 1940, he converted to Catholicism, a major turning point in his outlook on the world. During World War II, Lowell tried twice to enlist, but by the time he was actually called for service his strong feelings about the Allied bombing of European civilians had made him a conscientious objector (someone opposed on principle to fighting a war), and he refused to serve. As a result, he was sentenced to a year in jail.

That was not the last time that Lowell risked his freedom and reputation for his beliefs. He was bitterly opposed to the Vietnam War, and caused a sensation in 1965 when in protest he rejected a White House invitation to appear at an arts festival. In his letter to President Johnson, he wrote, "Every serious artist knows that he cannot enjoy public celebration without making subtle public commitments."

This sense of studied reflection on right and wrong, good and evil, runs through all of Lowell's poetry. In his collection of poems *For the Union Dead* (1964), he reflects on both his own past and that of the nation in examining contemporary values and morality. In many of his early poems, Lowell explores the history of his own family in search of the roots of modern morality. Frequently he arrives at a fierce opposition to the materialism of contemporary life and calls for more spiritual values. His late work gives off an uncanny glow of sadness and weary acceptance. These poems are the observations of a man who cares very much for his country and its citizens but who has come to despair that either would fulfill its promise.

POETRY BY LOWELL

The Collected Poems (1987). Farrar 1987 $25.00. ISBN 0-374-12625-9
Day by Day (1977). Farrar 1977 $5.95. ISBN 0-374-51471-2
For Lizzie and Harriet (1973). Farrar 1973 $2.95. ISBN 0-374-51291-4
Life Studies and *For the Union Dead* (1959, 1964). Farrar 1967 $7.95. ISBN 0-374-50628-0
Lord Weary's Castle and *The Mills of the Kavanaughs* (1946, 1951). Harcourt 1968 $3.95. ISBN 0-15-653500-9
Selected Poems (1976). Farrar 1976 $10.95. ISBN 0-374-51400-3

BOOKS ABOUT LOWELL

Hamilton, Ian. *Robert Lowell: A Biography.* Random 1983 $19.45. ISBN 0-394-50965-X
A massive work that sheds important light on Lowell's extremely troubled life.
Raffel, Burton. *Robert Lowell.* Ungar 1982 $16.95. ISBN 0-8044-2707-0 A solid, basic introduction to Lowell's life and work.
Rudman, Mark. *Robert Lowell: An Introduction to the Poetry.* Columbia Univ Pr 1983 $24.00. ISBN 0-231-04672-3 Makes ample use of the poems themselves to explain Lowell's art and vision.

McKAY, CLAUDE 1889–1948

Claude McKay was born in Jamaica, West Indies, the son of peasant farmers. Although his formal schooling was limited, he was influenced strongly by his brother Uriah, a schoolteacher, and by Walter Jekyll, an intellectual English neighbor, both of whom encouraged young Claude to read widely in the classics. Under their influence McKay began writing poetry while still very young. In an important move for McKay's career, Jekyll urged him to stop imitating the English poets he had read and to write instead in his native Jamaican dialect.

McKay took Jekyll's advice and soon achieved success. In 1912, he published two companion volumes of poetry: *Songs of Jamaica,* a collection celebrating the beauty and harmony of rural life, and *Constab Ballads,* a recollection of the bigotry and discord he found in urban Kingston. His poems won him a scholarship for study in the United States, but he soon became disillusioned by his college experiences at Tuskegee Institute, Alabama and Kansas State College, Emporia. After two years of higher education he moved to New York City to write.

In New York McKay quickly became known as a writer of promise, and was encouraged by several prominent editors. As both his poetry and politics became more radical, his work appeared more frequently in radical magazines. By 1922, he was on the editorial staff of *The Liberator,* a prominent left-wing journal of the time. He also became associated with a movement called the

Harlem Renaissance, which sought a rebirth in African-American literature and art.

In 1922, McKay left the United States for 12 years. He spent a year in the Soviet Union where, as a black leftist writer, he was considered a hero of the Russian Communist revolution. McKay spent most of the mid 1920s in Europe, primarily in France, where he wrote his first novel, *Home to Harlem* (1928). He then traveled to North Africa, where he completed his second novel, *Banjo* (1929); a collection of short stories, *Gingertown* (1932); and his third novel, *Banana Bottom* (1933). Throughout this entire period, McKay was considered a leader of the Harlem Renaissance movement, even though he lived far from Harlem. Nevertheless, he was writing about the African-American and African-Caribbean experience in new and influential ways.

Near the end of his life, McKay converted to Catholicism. He became quite conservative politically and attacked many of the causes that earlier he had embraced.

After a period of decline in the 1940s and 1950s, McKay's reputation is again on the rise. Both critics and readers admire anew the clear, powerful voice in which McKay spoke out against racial injustice and sang of the beauties of his native Jamaica and the black heritage of which he was so proud.

NOVELS BY MCKAY

Banana Bottom (1933). Harcourt 1974 $7.95. ISBN 0-15-610650-7
Banjo (1929). Harcourt 1970 $6.95. ISBN 0-15-610675-2
Home to Harlem (1928). Northeastern Univ Pr $10.95. ISBN 0-55553-024-9

SHORT STORY COLLECTION BY MCKAY

Gingertown (1932). Ayer (repr of 1932 ed) $16.00. ISBN 0-8369-4113-6

POETRY BY MCKAY

The Dialect Poetry of Claude McKay (includes *Songs of Jamaica* [1912] and *Constab Ballads* [1912]). Ayer (repr of 1912 ed) $21.00. ISBN 0-8369-8982-1
Selected Poems of Claude McKay (1953). Harcourt 1969 $3.95. ISBN 0-15-680649-5

NONFICTION BY MCKAY

A Long Way from Home. Harcourt 1970 $5.95. ISBN 0-15-653145-3 McKay's autobiography, detailing his travels and their importance in his life.

BOOKS ABOUT MCKAY

Cooper, Wayne C. *Claude McKay, Rebel Sojourner in the Harlem Renaissance: A Biography.* Louisiana State Univ Pr 1987 $29.95. ISBN 0-8071-1310-7 Traces McKay's life and identifies significant influences on him, both in and out of the Harlem Renaissance movement.
Wagner, Jean. *Black Poets of the United States: From Paul Laurence Dunbar to Langston Hughes.* Kenneth Douglas (tr). Univ of Illinois Pr 1973 $12.50. ISBN 0-252-00341-1 Contains a comprehensive chapter on McKay.

MacLEISH, ARCHIBALD   1892–1982

Archibald MacLeish was born in Glencoe, Illinois. He graduated from Yale University in 1915 and, after serving in World War I, he took a degree in law from Harvard University. He practiced law for only a short time, however, before leaving the United States for Paris to join the group of American artists and writers known as the "lost generation," so-called because they were "lost" and confused about American values after World War I. MacLeish remained in Paris from 1923 to 1928, writing four volumes of poetry while he was there. When he returned to the United States, he continued to write, while holding an editorial job at *Fortune* magazine. In 1939, he became Librarian of Congress, a post he held until 1944. In 1944, he became Assistant Secretary of State, and in 1945 he went to London as the head of the U.S. delegation to UNESCO. Four years later, MacLeish became a professor at Harvard, where he remained until 1962.

In his writing as well as in his personal and political life, MacLeish was a fearless fighter against censorship, government intimidation, and violations of civil liberties. Many of his shorter poems deal with questions of personal and political freedom. MacLeish also wrote highly successful plays in verse, exploring many of the same themes. *Panic* (1935) is a verse play about the stock market crash of 1929, relating the crash to America's lost sense of purpose. *The Fall of the City* (1937) is a radio play about democracy's need to defend itself against the threat of totalitarianism.

MacLeish won many honors for his work, including a Pulitzer Prize for *Conquistador* (1932), a long poem about the Spanish conquest of Mexico. He won a second Pulitzer for his *Collected Poems* (1952). *J.B.* (1958), a stage play in verse based on the biblical story of Job, won MacLeish his third Pulitzer Prize in 1959. Today, MacLeish is regarded as a first-rate poet who proved that a literary life can be effectively combined with a life of public service.

POETRY BY MACLEISH

Land of the Free (1938). Da Capo 1977 $7.95. ISBN 0-306-80080-2
New and Collected Poems, 1917–1982. Houghton 1985 $14.95. ISBN 0-395-26382-4

PLAYS BY MACLEISH

J. B. (1958). Houghton $6.95. ISBN 0-395-08353-2
Six Plays. Houghton 1980 $10.50. ISBN 0-395-28419-8

BOOKS ABOUT MACLEISH

Falk, Signi. *Archibald MacLeish.* New College & Univ Pr 1965 $10.95. ISBN 0-8084-0054-1 A general introduction to MacLeish's life and works, focusing on how the two relate and including a chronology and a bibliography.
Smith, Grover. *Archibald MacLeish.* Univ of Minnesota Pr 1971 $1.25. ISBN 0-8166-0618-8 A pamphlet providing a brief summary of MacLeish's life and works, with particular attention to his themes of political and personal freedom.

MALAMUD, BERNARD   1914–1986

Born in Brooklyn, New York, of immigrant Russian parents, Bernard Malamud graduated from the City College of New York and received an M.A. in English from Columbia University. He began teaching in 1939, eventually holding positions at Oregon State University and at Bennington College in Vermont.

In his first novel, *The Natural* (1952), which was made into a highly successful movie in 1983, Malamud tells the mythic story of baseball player Roy Hobbs and his homemade bat Wonderboy.

With the exception of *The Natural,* almost all of Malamud's books deal with Jewish characters. According to Malamud, that is so "because I know them. But more important I write about them because the Jews are the very *stuff* of drama." *The Assistant* (1957) takes place largely in a grocery store owned by a poor Jew. Like *The Natural,* it makes use of mythical themes, as does *The Fixer*

(1966), which was also made into a film. Malamud based *The Fixer* on an actual murder case that took place in Russia in 1911, in which a brickyard worker was falsely accused of the ritual murder of a child. *The Fixer* won both the National Book Award for fiction and the Pulitzer Prize in 1966.

In his later novels, Malamud became concerned with the relation of art to life and love. *Dubin's Lives* (1979) is about an aging New England biographer who finds himself challenged to live passionately when he starts to write a book about D. H. Lawrence. (*See* Lawrence, Vol. 1, British Literature: The Twentieth Century.) *God's Grace* (1982) is a fantasy on the theme of survival, which once again Malamud explores in a Jewish context.

Malamud's fiction is marked by a subtle complex humor, a strong compassion for human suffering, and a keen moral awareness. His special talent, however, is using the elements of fable and fantasy to enrich his stories with deep symbolic meaning.

NOVELS BY MALAMUD

The Assistant (1957). Avon 1980 $3.95. ISBN 0-380-51474-5 Moving and compassionate story of a poor Jewish grocer and the troubled young man he takes on as an assistant.
Dubin's Lives (1979). Farrar 1979 $10.00. ISBN 0-374-14414-1
The Fixer (1966). Pocket 1982 $3.95. ISBN 0-671-46075-7
God's Grace (1982). Avon 1983 $3.95. ISBN 0-380-64519-X
The Natural (1952). Avon 1960 $3.95. ISBN 0-380-50609-2 Story of a baseball player with extraordinary talents who must battle corruption and temptation.
A New Life (1961). Farrar 1988 $8.95. ISBN 0-374-52103-4
The Tenants (1971). Farrar 1988 $8.95. ISBN 0-374-52102-6

SHORT STORY COLLECTIONS BY MALAMUD

Idiots First (1963). Farrar 1963 $8.95. ISBN 0-374-52010-0
The Magic Barrel (1958). Farrar 1958 $14.95. ISBN 0-374-19576-5
Rembrandt's Hat (1973). Farrar 1986 $8.95. ISBN 0-374-52034-8
The Stories of Bernard Malamud (1983). Plume 1984 $9.95. ISBN 0-452-26354-9

BOOKS ABOUT MALAMUD

Field, Joyce, and Leslie Field. *Bernard Malamud: A Collection of Critical Essays.* Prentice 1975 $12.95. ISBN 0-13-548032-9 A collection of modern critical essays including consideration of Malamud as a Jewish writer.
Hershinow, Sheldon J. *Bernard Malamud.* Ungar 1980 $16.95. ISBN 0-8044-2377-6 A general survey of Malamud's life and works, with extensive discussion of how the life can be used to illuminate the work; includes a useful chronology and bibliography.

MASON, BOBBIE ANN   1940–

Born on a farm in Mayfield, Kentucky, Bobbie Ann Mason attended the University of Kentucky, where she received a B.A. in 1962. She continued her education at the State University of New York at Binghamton, from which she received an M.A. in 1966. In 1969, she married Roger B. Rawlings, a writer and editor. In 1972 she completed her Ph.D. at the University of Connecticut.

Mason began writing professionally while still an undergraduate, and contributed a steady stream of articles and stories to a variety of magazines throughout the 1960s. Most of the stories included in her first volume of fiction, *Shiloh and Other Stories* (1982), had originally appeared in such major national magazines as *The New Yorker* and *Atlantic Monthly*.

Since the publication of *Shiloh,* Mason has rapidly established a reputation as one of the United States's most important contemporary regional writers. Her technical skill has won particularly high praise from the critics. Mason's stories are almost always about the farmers and working-class families of the western Kentucky area she knows so well. Her characters are caught between two cultures—the sleepy agricultural world of the early twentieth-century South and the fast-paced modern world of high technology and rapid communication. Mason's characters struggle not to avoid this new world but to understand it and, most importantly, to find their place in it. They don't want to get left behind as a new society takes shape around them, yet they resist giving up the way of life that they have known and loved.

Mason's novel, *In Country* (1985), concerns a depressed Vietnam veteran and the young girl who helps him face his past. It was made into a film in 1990.

NOVELS BY MASON

*In Country (1985). Harper 1989 $4.95. ISBN 0-06-080959-0 Story of a 17-year-old girl's quest for the truth about her father's death in Vietnam through her relationship with her uncle, a despondent veteran.
Spence and Lila (1988). Harper 1989 $6.95. ISBN 0-06-09155-9

SHORT STORY COLLECTIONS BY MASON

*A Love Life: Stories (1989). Harper 1989 $17.95. ISBN 0-06-016042-X Stories of life in small-town America and of people trying to cope with a changing world.
*Shiloh and Other Stories (1982). Harper 1983 $7.95. ISBN 0-06-091330-4 Tales of ordinary people in western Kentucky; their hopes and dreams, frustrations and failures.

MASTERS, EDGAR LEE   1869–1950

Born in Kansas and raised in Illinois, Edgar Lee Masters practiced law in Chicago from 1891 to 1920. His first published volume of poetry, *A Book of Verses,* appeared in 1898. He went on to publish over 50 volumes of poetry, fiction, and biography. Masters's fame, however, rests on a single work, *Spoon River Anthology,* published in 1915. This book is a collection of poems supposedly spoken by the dead from their cemetery in a small Midwestern town. The poems function as epitaphs for their speakers, that is, commentary on the lives of the deceased and moral insights for the living. The poems in *Spoon River Anthology* together form a picture of life in small-town America at the turn of the century that is vastly different from the usual portrait of peaceful, neighborly, and honest small communities. With an irony that is often bitter, Masters depicts lives marked by broken dreams, frustrations, greed, and hypocrisy. He abandons the conventional verse forms that he uses elsewhere, employing instead a free-verse style combined with the colloquial speech of ordinary people. This was a style to which he never returned—and never again did his poetry ring as true.

POETRY BY MASTERS

A Book of Verses (1898). Gordon Pr (repr of 1898 ed) $59.95. ISBN 0-87968-761-4
Spoon River Anthology (1915). Buccaneer 1983 $19.95. ISBN 0-89966-456-3

BOOK ABOUT MASTERS

Wrenn, John H., and Margaret Wrenn. *Edgar Lee Masters.* G. K. Hall 1983 $16.95. ISBN 0-8057-7396-7 A useful introduction to Master's life and works for the general reader, discussing how Masters's life affected his poetry; includes a chronology and bibliography.

MICHENER, JAMES *c.* 1907–

The circumstances of James Michener's birth are a mystery, even to him. He knows he was raised by Mabel Michener, whom he refers to as his foster mother, near Doylestown, Pennsylvania, but he has never known exactly where or when he was born or anything of his family history.

The Micheners were a poor family, and James had few advantages as a child. At age 14, he decided to see the country and hitchhiked through most of the United States. When he returned to Doylestown, he became interested in sports and won an athletic scholarship to Swarthmore College.

After graduation, Michener went to Europe, where he studied at different institutions and on his own. When he returned to the United States, he took a master's degree from Colorado State College, where he also began to teach. In 1941, he left teaching to become an editor with the Macmillan Company, a New York publisher.

During World War II, Michener served as a naval lieutenant in the South Pacific, and toward the end of the war he began to write stories about his experiences there. When the war ended, he returned to New York, worked on his war stories, and in 1947 published them as *Tales of the South Pacific.* The book was an immediate success and was awarded the Pulitzer Prize in 1948. It later became the basis for a hit Broadway musical, *South Pacific,* and a popular film of the same name.

Michener went on to write many more novels, usually focused on a single geographic area and rich in the history of the locale and its people. Critic Webster Schott, writing in *The New York Times Book Review,* maintained that Michener "has found a formula. It delivers everywhere—Hawaii, Africa, Afghanistan, America, Israel, even outer space. The formula calls for experts, vast research, travel to faraway places and fraternizing with locals. And it calls for good guys and bad guys (both real and imagined) to hold the whole works together. It's a formula millions love. Mr. Michener gratifies their curiosity and is a pleasure to read." Despite some lukewarm praise from critics, Michener has remained one of the most popular authors of the late twentieth century.

NOVELS BY MICHENER

Alaska (1988). Random $22.50. ISBN 0-394-55154-0
The Bridges at Toko-Ri (1953). Fawcett 1988 $2.95. ISBN 0-449-20651-3 A naval task force must bomb heavily defended bridges to stop supplies from moving.
Centennial (1974). Fawcett 1989 $5.95. ISBN 0-449-21419-2
Chesapeake (1978). Fawcett 1989 $5.95. ISBN 0-449-21158-4
The Covenant (1980). Fawcett 1989 $5.95. ISBN 0-449-21420-6
The Drifters (1971). Fawcett 1989 $5.95. ISBN 0-449-21353-6
The Fires of Spring (1949). Fawcett 1989 $4.95. ISBN 0-449-21470-2 Story of a young boy's dangerous journey into manhood.
Hawaii (1959). Fawcett 1989 $5.95. ISBN 0-449-21335-8
Legacy (1987). Fawcett 1989 $4.95. ISBN 0-449-21641-1
Sayonara (1954). Fawcett 1983 $2.95. ISBN 0-449-20414-6
Space (1982). Fawcett 1989 $5.95. ISBN 0-449-20379-4 Story of a space mission to the dark side of the moon.
Tales of the South Pacific (1947). Fawcett 1987 $4.95. ISBN 0-449-20652-1
Texas (1985). Fawcett 1989 $5.95. ISBN 0-21092-8

NONFICTION BY MICHENER

Rascals in Paradise (1957). Fawcett 1987 $4.95. ISBN 0-449-21459-1 Biographical studies of 10 colorful pirates and scoundrels of the South Seas.
Sports in America (1976). Fawcett 1987 $4.95. ISBN 0-449-21450-8

BOOKS ABOUT MICHENER

Becker, George J. *James A. Michener.* Ungar 1983 $16.95. ISBN 0-8044-2044-0 A general study of Michener's life and works, with a concise biography and a useful chronology and bibliography.

Day, A. Grove. *James A. Michener.* G. K. Hall 1977 $16.95. ISBN 0-8057-7184-0 An introduction to Michener's life and works written by a friend and collaborator.

Hayes, John P. *James A. Michener: A Biography.* Macmillan 1984 $17.95. ISBN 0-672-52782-0 A complete and detailed account of Michener's life, with some attention to his works.

MILLAY, EDNA ST. VINCENT   1892–1950

Edna St. Vincent Millay was born in Rockland, Maine, the eldest of three girls. She was raised by her mother after her parents divorced. Millay began writing poetry while still in high school. One of her poems, "Renascence," was entered in a contest and drew the admiration of a sponsor, who then financed her education at Vassar College.

While at Vassar, Millay continued to write poetry as well as beginning a brief career as an actress. In 1919, she published her first collection, *Renascence and Other Poems.* The volume was highly praised, and Millay soon became the voice of the liberated female of the 1920s. Throughout the decade she led the fight for the right of a woman to be as sexually free as a man and followed her own principles by entering into several celebrated love affairs.

In her later years, Millay turned her attention toward other political and social problems. Her popularity remained high throughout the 1930s, but after World War II it began to decline. She still retains a faithful following, however, particularly among modern feminists.

POETRY BY MILLAY

Collected Lyrics (1943). Harper 1981 $8.95. ISBN 0-06-090863-7
Collected Poems (1981). Harper 1981 $14.95. ISBN 0-06-090889-0
Collected Sonnets (1941). Harper 1987 $6.95. ISBN 0-06-091091-7
Edna St. Vincent Millay's Poems Selected for Young People (1979). Harper 1979 $13.70. ISBN 0-06-024218 A selection particularly appropriate for grades 7–12.

BOOKS ABOUT MILLAY

Brittin, Norman A. *Edna St. Vincent Millay.* G. K. Hall 1982 $16.95. ISBN 0-8057-7362-2 Compact examination of Millay's life and work, including consideration of Millay's feminism and her relationship to "High Modernism."

*Daffron, Carolyn. *Edna St. Vincent Millay.* Chelsea 1989 $17.95. ISBN 1-55546-668-0 Highly readable overview of Millay's life and work designed for young adults, grades 7–12; contains a chronology and pictures.

MILLER, ARTHUR   1915–

Arthur Miller was born in New York City, the son of a prosperous Jewish manufacturer whose business failed during the Depression—a family tragedy that Miller never forgot. Miller was not a particularly enthusiastic student. He graduated from high school with poor grades and went to work in a warehouse. After two years, he decided to continue his education and enrolled in the University of Michigan to study journalism.

While at Michigan, Miller began writing plays and radio scripts, and he grew increasingly fond of the theater. His first published work, however, was a novel, *Focus* (1944), about anti-Semitism in America. Miller's first Broadway play, *The Man Who Had All the Luck* (1944), was a flop, but beginning with *All My Sons* in 1947, he had four hit plays in a row and came to be regarded as the most promising new voice in the American theater.

Miller's plays are deeply concerned with ethics and morality, especially in family and business relationships. In *All My Sons,* he dramatizes the conflicts facing a son, home from World War II, who learns that his flyer brother's death was caused by defective airplane parts manufactured by their profiteering father. *Death of a Salesman* (1949) examines the moral consequences of a man's inability to face his failure at work and at home. *The Crucible* (1953) looks at the Salem witch trials of 1692, comparing them to the political "witchhunts" of the early 1950s, when congressional committees, professional groups, and labor unions tried to find and punish anyone who might have had Communist sympathies. In *After the Fall* (1964), a highly autobiographical play, Miller questions his own moral integrity during his marriage to actress Marilyn Monroe. In his screenplay *The Misfits* (1961), based on one of his short stories and written especially for Monroe, he dramatizes the demise of the myth of the "old West."

None of Miller's more recent works has won the critical or financial success of his earlier plays, which continue to be produced on stage and television.

SHORT STORY COLLECTION BY MILLER

The Misfits and Other Stories (1961). Scribner's 1987 $5.95. ISBN 0-684-18779-5

PLAYS BY MILLER

After the Fall (1964). Penguin 1980 $3.95. ISBN 0-14-048162-1
The Creation of the World and Other Business (1972). Boulevard 1973 $12.95. ISBN 0-670-24616-0
The Crucible (1953). Penguin 1976 $9.95. ISBN 0-14-015507-4
Danger: Memory! (1987). Grove 1990 $5.95. ISBN 0-802-62353-3
Death of a Salesman (1949). Penguin 1985 $9.95. ISBN 0-14-015502-3
Incident at Vichy (1964). Penguin 1985 $4.95. ISBN 0-14-048193-1
The Price (1968). Penguin 1985 $3.95. ISBN 0-14-048194-X
A View from the Bridge (1955). Penguin 1985 $3.95. ISBN 0-14-048135-4

NONFICTION BY MILLER

Timebends. Grove 1988 $24.95. ISBN 0-8021-0015-5

BOOKS ABOUT MILLER

Bloom, Harold (ed). *Arthur Miller.* Chelsea 1987 $19.95. ISBN 0-87754-711-4 A selection of the best contemporary criticism on Miller; especially useful overview, introductory essay, and chronology.
Carson, Neil. *Arthur Miller.* Grove 1986 $6.95. ISBN 0-802-17966-8 A general study; opening chapter outlines Miller's life while subsequent chapters discuss his works.
*Glassman, Bruce. *Arthur Miller.* Silver 1990 $17.98. ISBN 0-382-09904-4 Very good biography that includes criticism of Miller's plays as well as details of his life.
Schlueter, June, and James K. Flanagan. *Arthur Miller.* Ungar 1987 $16.95. ISBN 0-8044-2797-6 A good general introduction to Miller's life and works, especially useful to the first-time reader of Miller, with a brief biography, a chronology, a bibliography, and extensive discussion of Miller's major plays.

MOHR, NICHOLASA   1935–

Nicholasa Mohr has won acclaim as a painter and as a writer of young adult novels and short stories. Her prize-winning works, which focus on young Puerto Ricans living in New York, are frequently anthologized in textbooks and other collections.

Mohr was born in New York in 1935. She attended the Art Students League from 1953 to 1956. In 1957, she married clinical psychologist Irwin Mohr, with whom she later had two children.

In 1959, Mohr resumed her study of art at the Brooklyn Museum Art School, while continuing to work as a painter and printmaker. From 1966 to 1969, she attended the Pratt Center for Contemporary Printmaking, while working as an artist and teaching in art schools in New York and New Jersey. Over the years she has taught art, writing, and Puerto Rican studies.

Mohr began her writing career with the publication in 1973 of *Nilda,* an award-winning young-adult novel that she illustrated herself. *Nilda* was honored as an outstanding work of juvenile fiction by the *New York Times* and the Jane Addams Peace Association. The book portrays the growth of a young Puerto Rican girl from childhood to adolescence as she faces poverty and racial intolerance in New York City.

In 1975 Mohr published *El Bronx Remembered: A Novella and Stories,* which received awards from the *New York Times* and *School Library Journal* and was also a 1976 National Book Award finalist for the most distinguished book in children's literature. Like *Nilda,* the collection focuses on Puerto Ricans living in New York, providing an intimate view of a world that is seldom portrayed in literature.

Mohr's work has sometimes been criticized as being too obvious in its efforts to portray a particular community. Some critics find that, rather than allowing her characters to emerge as real people, Mohr uses them to demonstrate the problems and strengths of New York Puerto Ricans. Other critics, however, praise the humor, sympathy, and profound optimism with which Mohr portrays the life of a community.

NOVELS BY MOHR

Felita (1979). Dial 1979 $9.89. ISBN 0-8037-3144-2 Story of a young girl's relationship with her family and friends in a Puerto Rican community in New York.
Going Home (1986). Dial 1986 $11.89. ISBN 0-8037-0270-1 Sequel to *Felita;* story of Felita's coming to terms with family and community as she travels to her family's home in Puerto Rico.
Nilda (1973). Harper Jr Bks 1973 $13.89. ISBN 0-06-024332-5 Tale of a young Puerto Rican girl's confrontation with racism and poverty in New York City.

SHORT STORY COLLECTION BY MOHR

El Bronx Remembered (1975). Harper Jr Bks 1975 $13.89. ISBN 0-06-024314-7 Fascinating group of portraits of Puerto Ricans living in the Bronx in New York City.

NONFICTION BY MOHR

Rituals of Survival: A Woman's Portfolio (1985). Arte Publico 1985 $7.50. ISBN 0-934770-39-5

BOOK ABOUT MOHR

Gallo, Donald R. (ed). *Speaking for Ourselves.* NCTE 1990 $12.95. ISBN 0-8141-4625-2 Collection of 87 autobiographical sketches of authors of young-adult books, including one of Mohr on the relationship between her painting and her writing.

MOORE, MARIANNE   1887–1972

Born in St. Louis, Marianne Moore graduated from Bryn Mawr College in 1909. She taught stenography and shorthand for five years before beginning to submit her poems to magazines. Some of her friends collected these poems and, without her knowledge, published them under the title *Poems* in 1921. That same year Moore became an assistant in the New York Public Library. When her poetry won critical acclaim, she went on to edit *The Dial,* one of the leading literary magazines of the time; Moore worked there from 1925 to 1929.

Moore's poetry is marked by unusual rhythmic patterns. "I tend to write," she once said, "in a patterned arrangement, with rhymes . . . to secure an effect of flowing continuity." She uses exceptionally long lines to achieve this effect, and her imagery is both sharp and unusual. "The firs stand in a procession, each with an emerald turkey-foot at the top," she wrote in "A Grave" (1924). Her poems, often witty and ironical, cover a wide range of subject matter—from current affairs to science and history to strange and exotic animals. Above all, Moore was interested in beauty and the purposes of art. Interestingly, she was opposed to teaching poetry in school, believing that it should be enjoyed for its own sake and never as the result of a school assignment.

POETRY BY MOORE

The Complete Poems of Marianne Moore. Penguin 1987 $8.95. ISBN 0-14-058016-6

BOOKS ABOUT MOORE

Bloom, Harold (ed). *Marianne Moore.* Chelsea 1986 $19.95. ISBN 0-87754-631-2 Eight essays which explore Moore's work and its contribution to the poetic tradition; contains an overview, introductory essay, and chronology.

Engel, Bernard F. *Marianne Moore.* G. K. Hall 1988 $19.95. ISBN 0-8057-7525-0 A solid general introduction to Moore's life and works.

Phillips, Elizabeth. *Marianne Moore.* Ungar 1982 $16.95. ISBN 0-8044-2698-8 A useful study of Moore's life and works with special attention to her poetic techniques; includes a chronology, bibliography, and concise biographical sketch.

MORRISON, TONI   1931–

Toni Morrison was born and raised in Lorain, Ohio, and attended Howard University, where she received a B.A. in 1953. After completing an M.A. at Cornell University in 1955, Morrison went on to teach English, first at Texas Southern University and later at Howard University. In 1965, she became an editor at Random House, where she continues to work, although in 1989 she was named to a one-year appointment as the Robert F. Goheen Professor of the Humanities at Princeton University.

Morrison's five novels all focus on certain basic themes. She is deeply concerned with the deception and betrayal of black people by whites and the white culture, as well as by other African Americans. She also returns frequently to the theme of the emerging self, to the individual searching for personal identity, sometimes thwarted by and sometimes aided by his or her community.

Morrison's first novel, *The Bluest Eye* (1970), is a tightly constructed experimental work that centers on the tragic story of Pecola Breedlove, a young black girl who becomes obsessed with having blue eyes, which she believes will solve all her problems. Morrison uses Pecola's and others' stories to show the pressures of racism on black women in particular, but also on the African-American community as a whole.

Sula (1973), Morrison's second novel, is the story of two women whose early friendship is severely tested when one of them returns home after a long absence. *Song of Solomon* (1977) is a complex work about one man's search for who he is and where he belongs within the long history of violence in his family. In all of these, as in her other novels, Morrison tells a gripping story while exploring difficult human and social questions. She is particularly concerned with the question of how black Americans can come to terms with their long and difficult history, and how they will take responsibility for their own responses to slavery and oppression.

NOVELS BY MORRISON

Beloved (1987). Plume 1988 $9.95. ISBN 0-452-26446-4
The Bluest Eye (1970). Washington Square Pr 1972 $3.95. ISBN 0-671-53146-8
Song of Solomon (1977). Signet 1978 $4.50. ISBN 0-451-15828-8
Sula (1973). Plume 1987 $6.95. ISBN 0-452-26010-8
Tar Baby (1981). Signet 1983 $4.95. ISBN 0-451-16639-6

BOOKS ABOUT MORRISON

Samuels, Wilfred D., and Clenora Hudson-Weems. *Toni Morrison.* G. K. Hall 1990 $17.95. ISBN 0-8057-7601-X A new and comprehensive study of Morrison's life and works, with extensive discussion of each novel and a concise biographical sketch; also includes chronology and bibliography.
Tate, Claudia (ed). *Black Women Writers at Work.* Crossroad 1984 $9.95. ISBN 0-8264-0243-7 Contains an excellent chapter on Morrison's works and literary principles based on conversations between Tate and Morrison.

MYERS, WALTER DEAN   1937–

Walter Dean Myers was born in Martinsberg, West Virginia, into a very poor family. When he was three years old, he was adopted by Herbert and Florence Dean, who moved to New York City. Thus Myers grew up in Harlem. He began writing stories while still in his teens but had little hope of becoming a professional writer because, coming from a family of laborers, he too was expected to work with his hands.

However, Myers refused to accept the notion that because he was black and poor he was restricted in what he could do. After high school he enlisted in the army, and while there he read everything he could. After completing his army service, he took what jobs he could get while continuing to write. He entered a contest for writers of books for young children, "more because I wanted to write *anything* than because I wanted to write a picture book." He won the contest, wrote several more books for young children, and then began writing novels for young adults.

Myers's novels for teenage readers have won high praise and several awards. Aside from telling good stories, Myers strives to convey what he learned while young. His message to black youth is that although growing up is not easy and reality can be harsh, young African Americans can succeed despite the odds against them. As he has said in an autobiographical essay, "I feel the need to show [black youngsters] the possibilities that exist for them that were never revealed to me as a youngster; possibilities that did not even exist for me then."

NOVELS BY MYERS

Brainstorm (1977). Dell 1979 $2.95. ISBN 0-440-90788-8 Story of a spaceship crew in the year 2076 sent to discover the nature of an alien force that is stealing people's minds.

Crystal (1987). Penguin 1987 $12.95. ISBN 0-670-80426-6 A young fashion model must decide whether fame is worth the price she has to pay for it.

Fast Sam, Cool Clyde, and Stuff (1975). Penguin 1975 $3.95. ISBN 0-14-032613-8 Novel about the value and meaning of true friendship.

Hoops (1981). Dell 1983 $2.95. ISBN 0-440-93884-8 Story of a gifted young basketball player who must make a choice on which his life depends.

The Legend of Tarik (1981). Scholastic 1982 $2.50. ISBN 0-590-41211-6 Novel about a young West African boy who vows to avenge the killing of his family.

Motown and Didi (1984). Dell 1987 $2.75. ISBN 0-440-95762-1 Two Harlem teenagers join forces to fight a drug dealer and end up falling in love.

The Outside Shot (1984). Dell 1987 $2.95. ISBN 0-440-96784-8 Story of a Harlem youth who wins a basketball scholarship to a Midwestern college and learns he can't get by on his street smarts alone.

Won't Know Till I Get There (1982). Penguin 1982 $3.95. ISBN 0-14-032612-X Story of a gang of black friends who are sentenced to work in a retirement home for the elderly.

The Young Landlords (1979). Flare 1980 $3.95. ISBN 0-380-52191-1 Five teenagers become landlords of a run-down Harlem apartment building.

O'CONNOR, FLANNERY   1925–1964

Flannery O'Connor was born in Savannah, Georgia. She had a quiet, bookish life as a child before attending Georgia State College for Women and going on to the Writers Workshop at the State University of Iowa, where she earned a Master of Fine Arts degree. Her 1949 dissertation consisted of six short stories, one of which she developed into her first novel, *Wise Blood* (1952).

Wise Blood is the story of a fanatical, wandering preacher who sets out to found a "church of truth without Jesus Christ crucified." The book introduces some of the religious themes that run throughout O'Connor's later work. Her second novel, *The Violent Bear It Away* (1960), is the story of a murder involving a Tennessee backwoods preacher and a small boy. Once again O'Connor explores unusual manifestations of religion and human eccentricities.

Although O'Connor produced only a small body of work during her relatively brief lifetime, she has received much critical attention. O'Connor suffered from lupus, an inherited disease, which crippled her and cut short her life, and so her creative work was largely compressed within the decade of the 1950s. She is frequently praised as being the most creative and distinctive writer of that period. The two most notable aspects of her fiction are its religious themes and its commentary on the oppressive traditions of the mid-twentieth-century Deep South.

SHORT STORY AND LETTER COLLECTION BY O'CONNOR

Collected Works: Wise Blood (1952); *A Good Man Is Hard to Find* (1955); *The Violent Bear It Away* (1960); *Everything That Rises Must Converge* (1965). Lib of America 1988 $35.00. ISBN 0-940450-37-2 Also contains all O'Connor's short stories and 259 letters.

BOOKS ABOUT O'CONNOR

Bloom, Harold (ed). *Flannery O'Connor.* Chelsea 1986 $19.95. ISBN 0-87754-637-0 Eleven critical essays that explore O'Connor's preoccupation with the violent, sacred, and grotesque; contains a chronology and bibliography.

McFarland, Dorothy T. *Flannery O'Connor.* Ungar 1976 $16.95. ISBN 0-8044-2609-0 A useful critical study of O'Connor's life and works, focusing on how the two are related; with chronology and bibliography.

Paulson, Suzanne M. *Flannery O'Connor.* G. K. Hall 1988 $18.95. ISBN 0-8057-8301-6 Based on unpublished letters and manuscripts; presents O'Connor as a modern moralist whose vision of humanity transcends the narrow labels previously assigned to her.

O'DELL, SCOTT 1903–1990

Born in Los Angeles, Scott O'Dell was educated at Occidental College, the University of Wisconsin, and Stanford University. He began his career in journalism, working as a photographer and book editor for a Los Angeles newspaper.

In 1934, O'Dell became a full-time writer. From 1934 to 1960, he wrote several novels for adults as well as a history of southern California. In 1960, he published his first novel for young adults, *Island of the Blue Dolphins.* The book was an immediate success, winning several major awards, including a John Newbery Medal and the Hans Christian Andersen award of merit. The book was made into a popular movie in 1964.

O'Dell has since written several more books for young readers that have been generally well received by the public and the critics. His stories frequently have historical settings, and their narrators are often young girls who tell their own stories. Because O'Dell bases his novels on extensive research, his plots and characters have an authentic period feeling. However, the rendering of historical detail always takes second place to the development of the characters, and O'Dell's books remain, above all, moving tales of very believable characters.

NOVELS BY O'DELL

*Alexandra (1984). Fawcett 1985 $2.95. ISBN 0-449-70290-1 Story of a teenage girl who decides to fish for sponge like her father—and runs into a gang of drug smugglers.

*The Black Pearl (1967). Dell 1977 $2.95. ISBN 0-440-90803-5 Ramon, a young pearl diver, must battle a giant manta ray to obtain the fabulous Pearl of Heaven.

*Black Star, Bright Dawn (1988). Fawcett 1990 $2.95. ISBN 0-449-70340-1 Story of Bright Dawn, a young girl who takes her father's place in a famous Alaskan dog-sled race.

*Carlotta (1977). Dell 1989 $2.95. ISBN 0-440-90928-7 The last days of the war between the Spanish Californians and the Anglo-Americans, told through the eyes of a teenage girl.

*The Castle in the Sea (1983). Fawcett 1984 $2.25. ISBN 0-449-70123-9 A young woman inherits the world's richest gold mines but begins to fear for her own safety.

*Island of the Blue Dolphins (1960). Dell 1978 $3.25. ISBN 0-440-94000-1 Karana, daughter of an Indian chief, is stranded alone for years on an island in the Pacific.

*The King's Fifth (1966). Houghton 1966 $14.95. ISBN 0-385-06963-7 Novel about the evil influence of the lust for gold on the Spanish conquistadors.

*The Road to Damietta (1985). Fawcett 1987 $2.95. ISBN 0-449-70233-2 The transformation of Francis Bernardone from playboy into St. Francis of Assisi, told through the eyes of a young girl.

*Sarah Bishop (1980). Scholastic 1988 $2.75. ISBN 0-590-42298-7 A young girl, orphaned in the Revolutionary War, flees to the wilderness, where she struggles to build a new life.

*The Serpent Never Sleeps (1987). Fawcett 1989 $2.95. ISBN 0-449-70328-2 Story of 17-year-old Serena Lynn, and the hardships she endures as an English colonist in the New World.

Sing Down the Moon (1970). Dell 1976 $2.95. ISBN 0-440-97975-7 Story of the 1864
    forced migration of the Navajos, told through the eyes of a young girl.
The Spanish Smile (1982). Fawcett 1983 $2.95. ISBN 0-449-70094-1 A young girl is kept
    isolated from the outside world by her father.
Streams to the River, River to the Sea (1986). Fawcett 1987 $2.95. ISBN 0-449-70244-8 The
    story of Sacajawea, the young Indian woman who accompanied Lewis and Clark
    on their famous expedition.
Zia (1976). Dell 1982 $2.95. ISBN 0-440-99904-9 A sequel to *Island of the Blue Dolphins*
    in which young Zia determines to find her lost aunt Karana.

BOOK ABOUT O'DELL

Gallo, Donald R. (ed). *Speaking for Ourselves.* NCTE 1990 $12.95. ISBN 0-8141-4625-2
    A fascinating collection of autobiographical sketches of 87 young-adult authors,
    including O'Dell; authors share stories of how they started to write and of signif-
    icant events that influenced them; includes complete list of published works and
    dates.

ODETS, CLIFFORD   1906–1963

Clifford Odets was born in Philadelphia, the son of immigrant Jewish parents.
When he was still very young, his family moved to New York City, where he
was raised. In 1923, Odets left school to become an actor, working mostly in
radio and with small theater companies outside of New York. In 1930, he
became a founding member of the Group Theater, an organization of writers
and actors who wanted to produce plays with social significance.

Joining the Group Theater was a turning point for Odets, since it was there
that he began writing plays. Beginning with *Waiting for Lefty* in 1935, Odets
wrote seven plays for the Group Theater before it disbanded in 1940. Most of
these concern poor New York Jewish families who are trying to cope with both
the economic hardships of the Depression and with anti-Semitism. Odets was
particularly skillful in capturing the speech of his working-class characters and
shaping it into a kind of dramatic poetry. Along with Lillian Hellman (*see*
Hellman, Vol. 1, American Literature: The Twentieth Century), Odets shares
the distinction of being the foremost American dramatist of the 1930s.

In both his art and his private life, Odets fought for greater rights and
opportunities for the poor. To him the world seemed to be divided into two
classes of people: the users and the used. His plays emphasize how difficult it
is for people to become mature, fully developed individuals in a world where
the only measure of success is money. This concern for the poor led him to join
the Communist Party, but he quickly became disillusioned with it and left after
a year.

Odets had mixed feelings about his own success. He worked for a time in
Hollywood and several of his plays became films. In 1948, however, he wrote
The Big Knife, about the corrupting influence of Hollywood success.

Odets's later plays lack the passion of his 1930s work. He remains one of
the most important American dramatists of the first half of the century.

PLAYS BY ODETS

Six Plays of Clifford Odets: Waiting for Lefty (1935), *Awake and Sing* (1935), *Golden Boy* (1937),
    Rocket to the Moon (1938), *Till the Day I Die* (1935), *Paradise Lost* (1935). Grove 1988
    $9.95. ISBN 0-394-17092-X

BOOK ABOUT ODETS

Miller, Gabriel. *Clifford Odets.* Continuum 1989 $18.95. ISBN 0-8044-2632-5. A comprehensive study of Odets and his plays, focusing on how Odets's fascination with socialism and political issues informed his work.

O'NEILL, EUGENE 1888–1953

Eugene O'Neill was born in New York City, the son of popular actors James O'Neill and Ellen Quinlan. As a young child, he frequently went on tour with his father and later attended a Catholic boarding school and a private preparatory school. He entered Princeton University but stayed for only a year. He took a variety of jobs, including prospecting for gold, shipping out as a merchant sailor, joining his father on the stage, and writing for newspapers. In 1912, he was hospitalized for tuberculosis and emotional exhaustion. While recovering, he read a great deal of dramatic literature and, after his release from the sanitarium, began writing plays.

O'Neill got his theatrical start with a group known as the Provincetown Players, a company of actors, writers, and other theater newcomers, many of whom went on to achieve commercial and critical success. His first plays were one-act works for this group, works that combined realism with experimental forms.

O'Neill's first commercial successes, *Beyond the Horizon* (1920) and *Anna Christie* (1921), were traditional realistic plays. *Anna Christie* is still frequently performed. It is the story of a young woman, Anna, whose hard life has led her to become a prostitute. Anna comes to live with her long-lost father, who is unaware of her past, and she falls in love with a sailor, who is also unaware. When Anna finds the two men fighting over her as though she were property, she is so angry and disgusted that she insists on telling them the truth. The man she loves rejects her at first, but later returns to marry her.

Soon O'Neill began to experiment more, and over the next 12 years used a wide variety of unusual techniques, settings, and dramatic devices. It is no exaggeration to say that, virtually on his own, O'Neill created a tradition of serious American theater. His influence on the playwrights who followed him has been enormous, and much of what is today taken for granted in modern American theater originated with O'Neill. A major legacy has been the nine plays he wrote between 1924 and 1931, tragedies that made heavy use of the new Freudian psychology just coming into fashion. His one comedy, *Ah, Wilderness* (1933), was the basis for the musical comedy *Oklahoma!*, itself a groundbreaking event in the American theater.

O'Neill's plays in the 1920s and early 1930s were highly successful, but then O'Neill abandoned the commercial theater to concentrate on a cycle of historical plays about the United States. Although O'Neill had originally projected an 11-play cycle spanning the story of a family from the eighteenth to the twentieth century, he only completed two of these works: *A Touch of the Poet* (1957) and *More Stately Mansions* (1962).

At about this time, O'Neill also began to write the intense, brooding, and highly autobiographical plays that are now considered his best work. *The Iceman Cometh* (1946) is set in a bar in Manhattan's Bowery, or skid-row district. In the course of the play, a group of apparently happy men are forced to recognize the true emptiness of their lives. In *A Long Day's Journey into Night* (1956), O'Neill examines his own family and their tormented lives, a subject he continues in *A Moon for the Misbegotten* (1957).

O'Neill's work was highly honored. He was awarded the Nobel Prize for literature in 1936 and Pulitzer Prizes for *Anna Christie, Beyond the Horizon, Strange Interlude* (1928), and *A Long Day's Journey Into Night,* which also received the New York Drama Critics Circle Award.

PLAYS BY O'NEILL

Complete Plays. Lib of America 1988 $100.00. ISBN 0-940450-62-3
The Iceman Cometh (1946). Random 1957 $5.95. ISBN 0-394-70018-X
A Moon for the Misbegotten (1957). Random 1974 $2.95. ISBN 0-394-71236-6
Three Plays: Desire Under the Elms (1924), *Strange Interlude* (1928), *Mourning Becomes Electra* (1931). Random 1959 $5.95. ISBN 0-394-70165-8

BOOKS ABOUT O'NEILL

Berlin, Normand. *Eugene O'Neill.* St. Martin's 1988 $10.95. ISBN 0-312-02125-9 A general study of O'Neill's life and works, relating events of his life to the incidents and characters of his plays.
Bloom, Harold (ed). *Eugene O'Neill.* Chelsea 1987 $27.50. ISBN 0-87754-633-9 A collection of modern critical essays examining O'Neill's work from a variety of perspectives, including work by such major critics as Lionel Trilling, giving an overview of O'Neill's work, C. W. E. Bigsby on the early plays, and Doris Falk on the late plays.
Carpenter, Frederick I. *Eugene O'Neill.* G. K. Hall 1984 $6.95. ISBN 0-8057-7428-9 Describes and criticizes O'Neill's best plays, attempts to outline his theory of tragedy, and relates his life to his works; contains a chronology and selected bibliography.

PARKER, DOROTHY   1893–1967

Dorothy Parker was born Dorothy Rothschild in West End, New Jersey. She was raised in New York City and educated at exclusive private schools. During her years of greatest fame, she was known primarily as a writer of light verse, a member of New York's literary elite, and a caustic and witty critic of literature and society. She is remembered now as an almost legendary figure of the 1920s and 1930s, and a writer of poignant, funny, and bitter short stories.

Parker's reviews and other contributions to three of the most influential U. S. magazines of this century—*Vanity Fair, The New Yorker,* and *Esquire*—were notable for their satire. She was also quite funny in person, and many bright remarks of the time were attributed to her. (For example, she supposedly commented on the huge luxury liner *Queen Elizabeth,* "When does this place get where it's going?")

Parker was very liberal in her political views, and the hard veneer of brittle toughness she showed to the world was often a shield for frustrated idealism and wounded sensibilities. The best of her fiction is marked by a balance of ironic detachment and sympathetic compassion, as in "Big Blonde," which won the 1929 O. Henry Award for the year's outstanding short story.

COLLECTION BY PARKER

The Portable Dorothy Parker (1944). Penguin 1976 $8.95. ISBN 0-14-015074-9

BOOKS ABOUT PARKER

Kinney, Arthur F. *Dorothy Parker.* G. K. Hall 1978 $15.95. ISBN 0-8057-7241-3 A comprehensive introduction to Parker's life and works, with extensive discussion of how the two relate; includes chronology and bibliography.

Meade, Marion. *Dorothy Parker: What Fresh Hell Is This?* Penguin 1989 $10.95. ISBN 0-14-011616-8 A very readable biography that explores the promises and frustrations of Parker's life.

PECK, RICHARD   1934–

Richard Peck was born in Decatur, Illinois, in 1934. After attending the University of Exeter from 1954 to 1955, he received his B.A. from DePauw University in 1956. Peck spent two years in the U.S. Army, serving in Stuttgart, Germany. Then he studied at Southern Illinois University and received his M.A. in 1959.

While going to school, Peck also taught English at Southern Illinois University at Carbondale. After further graduate study, he was a high school English teacher in Northbrook, Illinois, and then a textbook editor at Scott, Foresman in Chicago. Moving to New York, he taught English and education at Hunter College and Hunter College High School from 1965 to 1971.

Peck enjoyed teaching young people, but he eventually became overwhelmed by his inability to do more to help them. Leaving teaching, he turned to writing about the problems he had seen, producing more than a dozen novels for young adults and, eventually, best-selling adult novels as well.

Peck's first book was *Don't Look and It Won't Hurt* (1973), about a teenage pregnancy. Another well-known work, *Are You in the House Alone?* (1976), concerns a teenage girl who is raped. It won the Edgar Allan Poe Award from Mystery Writers of America for the best juvenile mystery novel.

Peck continues to write for young adults as well as to break ground in his adult novels. *Amanda/Miranda* (1980), about a heroic woman aboard the doomed ocean liner *Titanic*, was translated into nine languages and became a bestseller. *This Family of Women* (1983) won acclaim for its portrait of women who rise through their own abilities, rather than through associations with powerful men. In an interview with *Publishers Weekly*, Peck said that whichever age group he is writing for, he wants to "give readers leading characters they can look up to and reasons to believe that problems can be solved."

NOVELS BY PECK

Are You in the House Alone? (1976). Penguin 1976 $12.95. ISBN 0-670-13241-1 Story of a teenage girl who is raped and what happens afterward.

Blossom Culp and the Sleep of Death (1986). Dell 1987 $2.95. ISBN 0-440-40676-5 Teenage psychic Blossom Culp solves mysteries in the past and present; part of the Blossom Culp series, set in the 1910s.

Close Enough To Touch (1981). Dell 1989 $2.95. ISBN 0-440-91282-2 Story of Matt Moran, who tries to recover from the death of his first girlfriend by pursuing another, older woman.

The Dreadful Future of Blossom Culp (1983). Dell 1987 $2.95. ISBN 0-440-42154-3 Part of the Blossom Culp series; Blossom travels from her own time (1914) into the 1980s, encountering Valley Girls and video games as she tries to solve a mystery.

Dreamland Lake (1974). Dell 1990 $3.25. ISBN 0-440-92079-5 Story of two boys' discovery of a dead man and how the experience changes their lives.

Father Figure (1978). Dell 1988 $2.95. ISBN 0-440-20069-5 Story of Jim and Byron, who must go live with their long-absent father after their mother dies.

The Ghost Belonged to Me (1976). Dell 1987 $3.25. ISBN 0-440-42861-0 Part of the Blossom Culp series, set in the 1910s; Alexander Armsworth begins a series of adventures by making contact with the spirit world, helped by "spirit guide" Blossom Culp.

Ghosts I Have Been (1977). Dell 1987 $2.95. ISBN 0-440-42864-5 Part of the Blossom Culp series, set in the 1910s; Blossom discovers her second sight, time travel, and the power of history in this mystery tale.

Princess Ashley (1987). Dell 1988 $2.95. ISBN 0-440-20206-X Story of Chelsea's friend-ship with the popular—but dangerous—Ashley, leader of the "in" crowd.

Remembering the Good Times (1985). Dell 1986 $2.95. ISBN 0-440-97339-2 Story of a teenager's suicide and the impact it has on family and friends.

Representing Super Doll (1975). Dell 1989 $2.95. ISBN 0-440-97362-7 Story of a teenage beauty queen and her best friend as they travel to New York City to attend a beauty contest.

Secrets of the Shopping Mall (1979). Dell 1989 $3.25. ISBN 0-440-40270-0 Story of two teenage runaways and their escape into a suburban shopping mall.

Those Summer Girls I Never Met (1988). Dell 1988 $2.95. ISBN 0-440-20457-7 A 16-year-old boy's magical summer on a cruise ship.

Through a Brief Darkness (1975) Dell 1986 $2.95. ISBN 0-440-98809-8 Story of Karen's suspicions about the relatives she is sent to live with and of her fears that her father is really a criminal.

Voices After Midnight (1989). Dell 1990 $3.25. ISBN 0-440-40378-2 Story of 14-year-old Chad and his adventures in time travel.

NONFICTION BY PECK

Rock: Making Musical Choices (1985). Bob Jones Univ Pr 1985 $5.25. ISBN 0-89084-297-3

POETRY BY PECK

Sounds and Silences (1970) Dell 1990 $2.95. ISBN 0-440-98171-9

BOOK ABOUT PECK

Gallo, Donald R. (ed). *Speaking for Ourselves.* NCTE 1990 $12.95. ISBN 0-8141-4625-2 Collection of 87 autobiographical sketches of authors of young-adult books, including Peck's description of his childhood and his decision to become a writer.

PLATH, SYLVIA 1932–1963

Born in Boston and a graduate of Smith College, Sylvia Plath attended Newn-ham College, Cambridge University, on a Fulbright Fellowship and married the British poet Ted Hughes. (*See* Hughes, Vol. 1, British Literature, The Twentieth Century.) Her best poetry was produced as she pondered—in her poems as well as in her life—her own self-destruction. She eventually committed suicide, although many believe that she staged the suicide in such a way as to insure a rescue, which, through a series of unfortunate coincidences, came too late.

Of her first collection of poems, *The Colossus and Other Poems* (1962), the *Times Literary Supplement* remarked, "Plath writes from phrase to phrase as well as with an eye on the larger architecture of the poem; each line, each sentence is put together with a good deal of care for the springy rhythm, the arresting image and—most of all, perhaps—the unusual word."

Plath's second book of poetry, *Ariel,* written in a last burst of passionate creative activity in 1962, was published after her death. Her one novel, *The Bell Jar* (1963), about a troubled young woman's experience in New York City, is a revealing study of Plath's own personality, as well as of the limited choices open to women in the 1950s and early 1960s.

Plath is an extremely interesting figure who has been taken up by many feminist critics as exemplifying the plight of the woman artist. She was driven and ambitious, seeking always to excel in a world where such qualities were often attacked in women. She wrote bitterly about her father, whose approval she felt she could never win, but throughout her life she was troubled by his death, which took place when Plath was still a child. She developed close friendships with other women writers, including Anne Sexton, who herself committed suicide many years later.

Plath's stringent and uncompromising view of life, romantic relationships,

House by the Railroad.   Oil painting by Edward Hopper (1925).   Oil on canvas, 24 × 29". Collection, The Museum of Modern Art, New York. Given anonymously.

and family ties influenced her witty, imaginative, and often bitter poetry. That work, along with *The Bell Jar,* remain classics for all who are interested in the issues that concerned women at the beginning of the feminist movement.

NOVEL BY PLATH

The Bell Jar (1963). Bantam 1975 $4.50. ISBN 0-553-26008-1

POETRY BY PLATH

Collected Poems. Harper 1981 $11.95. ISBN 0-06-090900-5
The Colossus and Other Poems (1962). Random 1968 $3.95. ISBN 0-394-70466-5

COLLECTION OF PLATH'S WORK

Johnny Panic and the Bible of Dreams: Short Stories, Prose and Diary Excerpts (1979). Harper 1980 $7.95. ISBN 0-06-132062-5

NONFICTION BY PLATH

The Journals of Sylvia Plath. Ballantine 1987 $4.95. ISBN 0-345-35168-1 Edited journals that cover the poet's college years, her marriage, and her preparations for relocation to England with her husband in 1959.

BOOKS ABOUT PLATH

Bloom, Harold (ed). *Sylvia Plath.* Chelsea 1990 $22.50. ISBN 1-55546-280-4 A collection of modern critical essays on Plath's work and life, including such major critics as Hugh Kenner on Plath's treatment of the dangers of sincerity and an essay by Plath's estranged husband Ted Hughes on Plath's journals.

Stevenson, Anne. *Bitter Fame: A Life of Sylvia Plath.* Houghton 1990 $10.95. ISBN 0-395-53846-7 First authoritative biography of Plath as complete, balanced, and objectively written as the facts allow.

Wagner-Martin, Linda. *Sylvia Plath: A Biography.* St. Martin's 1988 $12.95. ISBN 0-312-02325-1 A detailed and readable biography—sympathetic to Plath without being sentimental.

POHL, FREDERIK   1919–

Frederik Pohl was born in New York City and attended public schools in Brooklyn. More interested in writing than in school, he dropped out of high school in his senior year and took a job with a publishing company. After serving in the United States Air Force from 1943 to 1945, he returned to publishing as an editor and literary agent. His first science fiction novels were published in the mid-1960s, some written in collaboration with other writers, others created alone. Since then he has produced a steady flow of novels.

Pohl describes his particular kind of science fiction as "cautionary": the novels he writes point out the negative, long-range consequences of present actions. Pohl takes some aspect of contemporary society and projects it into a future time as if to say, "If our society keeps doing this, here is what the result will be." He is particularly concerned with rapidly developing technology that is not matched by a corresponding improvement in the quality of living. According to Pohl, science fiction is "the only kind of writing . . . which takes into account the most important fact of life in the world today: change."

NOVELS BY POHL

The Annals of Heechee (1987). Del Rey 1988 $3.95. ISBN 0-345-32566-4 Fourth book in the Heechee Saga series; humans and Heechees join forces to repel the invaders known as the Foe.

Beyond the Blue Event Horizon (1980). Del Rey 1988 $3.95. ISBN 0-345-35046-6 Second book in the Heechee Saga series; Robinette Broadhead mounts an expedition to a Heechee food factory.

Bipohl: Two Novels, Drunkard's Walk (1960) *and The Age of the Pussyfoot* (1969). Ballantine 1982 $3.50. ISBN 0-345-35005-7 Tales of a society totally dependent on computers.

Gateway (1977). Del Rey 1988 $3.95. ISBN 0-345-34690-4 First book in the Heechee Saga series; the story of Bob Broadhead on an asteroid named Gateway, where an ancient race of aliens once lived.

Heechee Rendezvous (1984). Del Rey 1988 $3.95. ISBN 0-345-30056-6 Third book in the Heechee Saga series; Robinette Broadhead is forced to make another perilous space voyage to meet the Heechees.

Homecoming (1989). Ballantine 1989 $16.95. ISBN 0-345-33975-4 Sandy Washington, who was raised by aliens on their spaceship, is now coming home to Earth.

Narabedla Ltd. (1987). Ballantine 1989 $4.95. ISBN 0-345-36026-5 Nolly Stennis, a singer, is made a fabulous offer by Narabedla Ltd. and then mysteriously loses his voice.

The Space Merchants (1953). St. Martin's 1987 $3.95. ISBN 0-312-90655-2 A future society is dominated by rival advertising agencies.

The Starchild Trilogy (1965). (coauthored with Jack Williamson) Baen 1986 $3.95. ISBN 0-671-65558-2 An overpopulated world is rigidly controlled by a computer-directed plan.

SHORT STORY COLLECTION BY POHL

Yesterday's Tomorrows: Favorite Stories from Forty Years as a Science Fiction Writer (1982). Berkeley 1982 $9.95. ISBN 0-425-05648-1 Pohl's favorite tales of life in the future.

NONFICTION BY POHL

The Way the Future Was: A Memoir. Ballantine 1980 $1.95. ISBN 0-345-26059-7 Pohl's reflection on his life as a science fiction writer.

BOOK ABOUT POHL

Clareson, Thomas. *A Reader's Guide to Frederik Pohl.* Starmont 1987 $9.95. ISBN 0-930261-33-X Commentary on and interpretation and analysis of Pohl's major works.

PORTER, KATHERINE ANN   1890–1980

Katherine Ann Porter was born in Indian Creek, Texas, into a family descended from Daniel Boone, the Kentucky pioneer. After attending convent schools in Louisiana, she decided to set out on her own rather than go to college. She became a reporter and free-lance journalist and traveled widely in Europe and North America, living for a time in Mexico.

Porter's reputation was built on her short stories, which are generally regarded as being among the best of that genre by an American writer. Her most effective stories are inspired by her own southern American background. As a child of a proud family that was no longer as wealthy or powerful as it had been, she learned firsthand the resentment, anger, and sorrow of many Southerners who compared their declining present to their glorious past. These sentiments are most evident in Porter's excellent Miranda stories, published in *Pale Horse, Pale Rider* (1939) and *The Old Order* (1944). The life of Miranda, the main character, recalls Porter's own girlhood. In these tales, she subtly and skillfully shows the powerful influence of the past in shaping one's personality.

Porter's one novel, *Ship of Fools* (1962), took her 20 years to write. This study of the passengers on a ship sailing from Mexico to Germany in 1931 is really about the nature of German society shortly before Hitler came to power. Because the characters in *Ship of Fools* are representative "types" rather than fully developed personalities, the novel has a disappointing stiffness not found in Porter's shorter works. As a study of human weakness, social folly, and the origins of human evil, however, *Ship of Fools* is a powerful book that remains worthy of attention. It was made into a successful film.

Porter's *Collected Stories* (1965) won both the National Book Award and the Pulitzer Prize in 1966.

NOVEL BY PORTER

Ship of Fools (1962). Little 1984 $7.95. ISBN 0-316-71390-2

SHORT STORY COLLECTIONS BY PORTER

The Collected Stories of Katherine Ann Porter (1964). Harcourt 1979 $8.95. ISBN 0-15-618876-7
The Old Order: Stories of the South (1944). Harcourt 1955 $4.95. ISBN 0-668519-1
Pale Horse, Pale Rider (1939). Harcourt 1939 $15.95. ISBN 0-15-170750-2

BOOKS ABOUT PORTER

Bloom, Harold (ed). *Katherine Ann Porter.* Chelsea 1986 $19.95. ISBN 0-87754-657-0 Twelve respected essays that present a complete critical portrait of Porter; contains a chronology and bibliography.

Hendrick, George, and Willene Hendrick. *Katherine Ann Porter.* G. K. Hall 1988 $17.95. ISBN 0-8057-7513-7 A classic study, first published in 1965 and updated in 1988; provides a concise survey and analysis of Porter's life and writing.

Lopez, Enrique Hank. *Conversations with Katherine Anne Porter: Refugee from Indian Creek.* Little 1981. (o.p.). ISBN 0-316-53199-5 A fascinating chronicle of Porter's life, based on weeks of taped conversations.

POTOK, CHAIM   1929–

Chaim Potok was born in New York City in 1929. He graduated summa cum laude (with highest honors) from Yeshiva University in 1950, and received an advanced degree from Jewish Theological Seminary in 1954, when he also became an ordained Conservative rabbi. After two years of military service as a chaplain in Korea, Potok married Adena Sarah Mosevitzky in 1958. The couple had three children. Eventually, Potok returned to school and received his Ph.D. from the University of Pennsylvania in 1965.

Potok has held a variety of positions within the Jewish community, including directing a camp in Los Angeles, teaching at the University of Judaism in Los Angeles and at Jewish Theological Seminary in New York, and working as an editor on various religious publications.

Potok's first novel, *The Chosen,* was published in 1967, and he quickly won acclaim for this best-selling book about tensions within the Orthodox and Hasidic Jewish communities. This and later books have been both critically and popularly successful. Many of them explore the meaning of Judaism in the modern era, focusing on the conflict between traditional teachings and the pressures of modern life. *The Chosen* was nominated for a National Book Award in 1967 and made into a successful film in 1982. Its sequel, *The Promise* (1969), was the winner of an Athenaeum Award.

Potok is also the author of a nonfiction volume, *Wanderings: Chaim Potok's History of the Jews* (1978), as well as of several short stories and articles that have been published in both religious and secular magazines.

NOVELS BY POTOK

The Book of Lights (1981). Fawcett 1982 $4.95. ISBN 0-449-25469-1

The Chosen (1967). Simon 1987. (o.p.) Story of two boys in religious Jewish communities and of the conflicts between their religion and their individuality.

Davita's Harp (1985). Fawcett 1986 $4.50. ISBN 0-449-20775-3

In the Beginning (1975). Fawcett 1986 $4.50. ISBN 0-449-20911-3

My Name is Asher Lev (1972). Fawcett 1984 $4.95. ISBN 0-449-20714-5 A young artist growing up in a Hasidic community must choose between pursuing his artistic vision and preserving the traditions of his people.

The Promise (1969). Fawcett 1985 $4.95. ISBN 0-449-20910-5 Sequel to *The Chosen;* the boyhood friends of that book grow up, choose careers, and begin families.

NONFICTION BY POTOK

Wanderings: Chaim Potok's History of the Jews (1978). Knopf 1978 $40.00. ISBN 0-394-50110-1

BOOK ABOUT POTOK

Abramson, Edward A. *Chaim Potok.* G. K. Hall 1986 $17.95. ISBN 0-8057-7463-7 Concise critical introduction to Potok and his complete works; includes biographical and historical background.

RICH, ADRIENNE 1929–

Adrienne Rich was born in Baltimore, Maryland, and educated at Radcliffe College in Massachusetts. Her first book of poems, *A Change of World* (1951), was chosen by the prominent poet, W. H. Auden (*see* Auden, Vol. 1, British Literature: The Twentieth Century) for the prestigious *Yale Series of Younger Poets.* Both Auden and Rich's father, who had encouraged her writing throughout her childhood, strongly influenced her early poetry. This early work was traditional, largely in imitation of Auden.

When Rich's next book, *The Diamond Cutters* (1955), came out, she was married, had three children, and was struggling to balance the traditional roles of wife and mother with her desire to be a poet. Then, in the 1960s, Rich's poetry started to change remarkably. She began writing in her own female voice rather than in the mold of the male poets who came before her. Eventually, she moved to New York City, where she became involved in protests against the Vietnam War and in the developing women's movement. Her later poems display a merging of highly personal experience with social themes, and as Rich herself says, "at last the woman in the poem and the woman writing the poem become the same person."

POETRY BY RICH

Diving into the Wreck (1973). Norton 1973 $5.95. ISBN 0-393-04384-3
The Dream of a Common Language (1978). Norton 1978 $5.95. ISBN 0-393-04510-2
The Fact of a Doorframe: Poems Selected and New 1950–1984 (1984). Norton 1984 $9.70. ISBN 0-393-30204-0
Leaflets: Poems 1965–1968 (1969). Norton 1969 $4.95. ISBN 0-393-04191-3
Snapshots of a Daughter-in-Law (1963). Norton 1967 $4.95. ISBN 0-393-04146-8
Sources (1983). Heyeck 1983 $15.00. ISBN 0-940592-16-9
Time's Power (1989). Norton 1989 $7.70. ISBN 0-393-30575-9
A Wild Patience Has Taken Me This Far (1981). Norton 1981 $7.95. ISBN 0-393-00072-9

BOOKS ABOUT RICH

Gelpi, Barbara Charlesworth, and Albert Gelpi. *Adrienne Rich's Poetry.* Norton 1975. (o.p.) ISBN 0-393-09241-0 Three-part analysis of Rich and her work: the text of her major poems, commentary by the poet from essays of 1964–1974, and eight critical articles; includes a chronology and bibliography.
Keyes, Claire. *The Aesthetics of Power: The Poetry of Adrienne Rich.* Univ of Georgia Pr 1986 $22.50. ISBN 0-8203-0803-X A feminist interpretation of Rich's poetry, examining the accepted uses of power and the shape and scope of female aesthetics.
Warner, Craig. *Adrienne Rich.* Am Lib Assn 1988 $19.95. ISBN 0-8389-0487-4 An examination of Rich's poetry in the context of the criticism it has produced.

ROBINSON, EDWIN ARLINGTON 1869–1935

Edwin Arlington Robinson was born in Head Tide, Maine, and was raised in the city of Gardiner in that same state. His father was a mystic and spiritualist who spent much of his life experimenting with ways to contact the supernatural. Robinson began study at Harvard University but had to withdraw after two years because of his father's poor health. When his mother died suddenly from diphtheria, he felt his life had been shattered.

Robinson went to New York, where he continued his earlier practice of writing poetry, but he also began to drink heavily and became impoverished.

His fortunes changed when his poetry caught the attention of politician and later President Theodore Roosevelt. Roosevelt helped Robinson get a job at the New York City Custom House, a position he retained until his poetry became successful enough to enable him to write full-time. He also recovered from his alcoholism at this time, and his health improved.

Robinson's poetry is marked by clarity, honesty, and intelligence. His work stands in sharp contrast to much of the traditional romantic poetry that was still being written in the early part of the twentieth century. Much of his verse is ironic, contrasting pleasant surface appearances with the unhappiness and discord that lies beneath. Although his popularity has declined over the last 60 years, his critical reputation remains high. He is widely anthologized and is particularly well known for such narrative poems as "Richard Cory" (1896), the story of a man who seems to have everything—until he commits suicide—and "Miniver Cheevy" (1910), about a man who laments that he was born too late to enjoy the romance of medieval times—and who consoles himself with drink.

POETRY BY ROBINSON

Selected Poems of Edwin Arlington Robinson. Morton D. Zabel (ed). Macmillan 1966 $9.95. ISBN 0-02-070530-1

BOOKS ABOUT ROBINSON

Barnard, Ellsworth. *Edwin Arlington Robinson: A Critical Study.* Hippocrene 1969 $26.00. ISBN 0-374-90380-8 The best general introduction to Robinson's work.

Bloom, Harold (ed). *Edwin Arlington Robinson.* Chelsea 1987 $19.95. ISBN 1-55546-322-3 A collection of critical essays, including some by well-known poets, on Robinson's development and accomplishments; contains a chronology and a bibliography.

Redman, Ben. *Edwin Arlington Robinson.* Haskell 1974 $34.95. ISBN 0-8383-2045-7 A critical study of Robinson's poetry with special attention to his themes and longer works.

SALINGER, J. D. (JEROME DAVID)   1919–

J. D. Salinger was born in New York City of Jewish and Scots-Irish extraction. He was educated at Valley Forge Military Academy in Pennsylvania and then studied at New York and Columbia universities, although he never received a degree from either. He spent what he calls "a happy tourist year" in Europe just before World War II, and then served in the United States Army in the war.

During the 1940s, Salinger published some 20 short stories in such magazines as the *Saturday Evening Post* and *The New Yorker* without attracting much attention. In 1951, however, he published his first and only novel, *The Catcher in the Rye,* and very quickly became one of the most acclaimed writers of the 1950s. The novel is narrated by a character named Holden Caulfield, a teenager who leaves his prep school to spend a weekend in New York City. As Caulfield describes his trip to the city and his adventures there, he also comments on the hypocrisy and "phoniness" of the adult world through which he moves. The book was immediately extremely popular with college students and, later, with high school students as well.

In 1953 Salinger published *Nine Stories,* a collection of short stories that contained many of the themes that would characterize his later work. He produced two more short story collections, *Franny and Zooey* (1961) and *Raise High the Roof Beam, Carpenter* (1963), which center on the lives of members of the Glass family, some of whom appeared in *Nine Stories.*

Since 1963, Salinger has lived a life of quiet seclusion in Hanover, New Hampshire, and has not published anything. As a consequence his literary reputation has suffered somewhat. *The Catcher in the Rye,* however, continues to be taught in many schools, and admirers remain hopeful that Salinger may yet produce another book. His seclusion makes it difficult to find out much about his private life, but critics do know that he is married and has a son who is an aspiring actor.

NOVEL BY SALINGER

The Catcher in the Rye (1951). Bantam 1984 $2.95. ISBN 0-553-25025-6 Story of a teen-ager's efforts to make sense of the adult world.

SHORT STORY COLLECTIONS BY SALINGER

Franny and Zooey (1961). Bantam 1969 $2.95. ISBN 0-553-20348-7
Nine Stories (1953). Bantam 1984 $3.50. ISBN 0-553-26360-9
Raise High the Roof Beam, Carpenter and Seymour: An Introduction (1963). Bantam 1984 $3.95. ISBN 0-553-26255-6

BOOKS ABOUT SALINGER

Bloom, Harold (ed). *J. D. Salinger.* Chelsea 1987 $19.95. ISBN 0-87754-716-5 Collection of critical essays that examine Salinger's work thematically and structurally, including work by such major critics as Alfred Kazin, writing on Salinger's popularity, David D. Galloway on "The Love Ethic," and Bernice Goldstein and Sanford Goldstein on Salinger's treatment of Zen Buddhism.
French, Warren. *J. D. Salinger.* G. K. Hall 1988 $16.95. ISBN 0-8057-7522-6 The first structural analysis of Salinger's pre-1960 works; contains a useful overview of Salinger criticism.
Lundquist, James. *J. D. Salinger.* Ungar 1978 $16.95. ISBN 0-8044-2560-4 Penetrating and objective assessment of the writer and his ideas; focuses on the themes of alienation and isolation in Salinger's work.

SANDBURG, CARL   1878–1967

Carl Sandburg was born in Galesburg, Illinois, the son of Swedish immigrants. At the age of 13, he left school and became a wandering laborer, working his way west. During the Spanish-American War, he served in Puerto Rico. After the war he returned to Lombard College in Galesburg to complete his education. He graduated in 1902 and became a journalist, first in Milwaukee and later in Chicago.

Sandburg has been called the poet laureate of American labor. His poems celebrate American workers as the backbone of the nation. A lifelong socialist, Sandburg considered himself a poet of the common people and the voice of the ordinary worker. In the direct and simple language of everyday speech and without the usual refinements of rhyme and formal meter, Sandburg's verses are, as he says in the Introduction to his *Complete Poems* (1950), "simple poems for simple people."

Sandburg was also deeply tied to Chicago and the Midwest, and related imagery appears throughout his poetry. In his poem "Chicago" (1914, 1916) he calls the city "Hog Butcher for the World, / Tool Maker, Stacker of Wheat, / Player with Railroads and the Nation's Freight Handler; / Stormy, husky, brawling, / City of the Big Shoulders. . . ."

In addition to his poetry, Sandburg wrote a six-volume biography of

Abraham Lincoln. This widely read work continues to draw considerable critical praise.

Sandburg received the Pulitzer Prize for history in 1940 for his biography of Lincoln and was awarded the same honor for poetry in 1951. At Sandburg's death President Lyndon Johnson said of him, "Carl Sandburg was more than the voice of America, more than the poet of its strength and genius. He was America. . . . He gave us the truest and most enduring vision of our own greatness."

POETRY BY SANDBURG

Complete Poems. (1950). Harcourt 1970 $27.95. ISBN 0-15-270180-X
Harvest Poems: Nineteen Ten to Nineteen Sixty (1960). Harcourt 1960 $4.95. ISBN 0-15-639125-2
Honey and Salt (1963). Harcourt 1967 $2.95. ISBN 0-15-642165-8
*A Sandburg Treasury: Prose and Poetry for Young People (1970). Harcourt 1970 $24.95. ISBN 0-15-270180-X Sandburg's most accessible poems for young readers.

NOVEL BY SANDBURG

Remembrance Rock (1948). Harcourt 1990. ISBN 0-15-676390-7

NONFICTION BY SANDBURG

Abe Lincoln Grows Up (1928). Harcourt 1975 $16.95. ISBN 0-15-201037-8
Abraham Lincoln: The Prairie Years (1929) and *The War Years* (1939). Harcourt 1954 $49.95. ISBN 0-15-100638-5
*Always the Young Strangers. Harcourt 1953 $12.95. ISBN 0-15-105459-2 Sandburg's lively, interesting, and revealing autobiography; anecdotes about Sandburg's travels, his work, and the people he knew.
The American Songbag (1927). Harcourt 1970 $12.95. ISBN 0-15-605650-X
Prairie-Town Boy (1955). Harcourt 1977 $1.75. ISBN 0-15-673700-0

BOOKS ABOUT SANDBURG

**Allen, Gay W. *Carl Sandburg.* Univ of Minnesota Pr 1972 $1.25. ISBN 0-8166-0644-7 Useful booklet for beginners by a respected critic who briefly summarizes Sandburg's life and work.
Crowder, Richard. *Carl Sandburg.* G. K. Hall 1964 $15.95. ISBN 0-8057-0648-8 General study of Sandburg's poetry and prose and his role in American letters; contains a chronology and a bibliography.

SHEPARD, SAM   1943–

Born Samuel Shepard Rogers in Sheridan, Illinois, Sam Shepard spent most of his boyhood on a ranch in California. He moved to New York City before he was 20 years old, and his first play was produced off-Broadway soon after, in 1962. He won the first of his ten Obie awards (awards given to off-Broadway theater productions) when he was only 23. A rock lyricist and a major film actor as well as a dramatist, Shepard has written more than 40 plays, winning the Pulitzer Prize for drama in 1978 with his play *Buried Child.*

Shepard's plays show the impact of a variety of influences, including rock music, old movies, popular myths of the Old West, and the 1960s drug culture. His early plays, produced off-Broadway, are short, bizarre, nonrealistic pieces, which create impressions and moods rather than tell a coherent story. Shepard's later work has become more realistic and employs more traditional concepts of plot, character, and theme. Shepard has also become increasingly concerned with the collapse of the American dream, a theme only hinted at in his earlier work. Shepard's drama is often considered a chronicle of modern America—its myths, heroes, entertainments, values, and its confusion and loss of ideals.

PLAYS BY SHEPARD

Chicago and Other Plays (1984). Applause Theatre Bk 1988 $9.95. ISBN 0-317-65850-6
Fool for Love and Other Plays (1984). Bantam 1984 $7.95. ISBN 0-553-34339-4
Four Two-Act Plays (1980). Applause Theatre Bk 1988 $9.95. ISBN 0-317-65853-0
Motel Chronicles (1982). City Lights 1982 $5.95. ISBN 0-87286-143-0
Seven Plays (1981). Bantam 1981 $7.95. ISBN 0-553-3433-0
The Unseen Hand and Other Plays (1986). Bantam 1986 $8.95. ISBN 0-553-34263-0

BOOKS ABOUT SHEPARD   •

King, Kimball. *Sam Shepard: A Casebook.* Garland 1989 $34.00. ISBN 0-8240-4448-7 A varied collection of 12 new critical essays that assess Shepard's impact on twentieth-century drama.
Oumano, Ellen. *Sam Shepard: The Life and Work of an American Dreamer.* St. Martin's 1986 $12.95. ISBN 0-312-69839-9 A perceptive appraisal of Shepard's career with strong emphasis on the impact of his personal life on his work; contains photographs.

SILVERBERG, ROBERT   1935–

Robert Silverberg was born and raised in New York City, where he attended public schools. He completed his education at Columbia University, receiving a B.A. in 1956. As a boy Silverberg was an avid reader of science fiction and, while still a student at Columbia, he began publishing stories in the popular science fiction magazines of the 1950s. By the time he graduated, he was already so well known that he was given the Hugo Award for best new writer of 1956.

Silverberg then launched one of the most amazing bursts of productivity by any American writer. During the 1950s, he published hundreds of science fiction stories. When the demand for science fiction declined sharply in the early 1960s, Silverberg turned to writing nonfiction and in a few years had built a reputation as one of the nation's most skillful popularizers of scientific topics.

In 1966, health problems brought on by the frantic pace at which he worked forced Silverberg to slow down. He returned to writing science fiction with work of much higher literary quality than his earlier efforts, dealing with such mature themes as anxiety and alienation. Although these books received high critical praise and won awards, they did not sell well, and in 1975, disappointed by readers' cool reception to his work, Silverberg stopped writing science fiction.

The retirement last only four years. Then financial need forced him to write "one last book." In 1980 he produced *Lord Valentine's Castle,* a long work that combines science fiction with heroic fantasy. The book was a huge success, and Silverberg has gone on to write two related books, *The Majipoor Chronicles* (1982) and *Valentine Pontifex* (1983).

NOVELS BY SILVERBERG

At Winters End (1988). Warner Bks 1989 $4.95. ISBN 0-446-35397-3
*Lord Valentine's Castle (1980). Bantam 1981 $4.50. ISBN 0-553-25097-3 Story of a young prince's quest to regain his rightful throne.
*The Majipoor Chronicles (1982). Bantam 1983 $3.95. ISBN 0-553-25530-4 Story of the training of a street urchin to become a leader on the planet Majipoor.

Project Pendulum (1987). Walker 1987 $15.95. ISBN 0-8027-6712-5 A pair of twins enter a project that sends them separately into different time periods.

Son of Man (1971). Warner Bks 1987 $3.95. ISBN 0-446-34511-3 Series of surrealistic adventures that take place entirely in the world of the mind.

The Stochastic Man (1975). Warner Bks 1987 $3.95. ISBN 0-446-34507-5 Story of a statistician who discovers he has the ability to see into the future.

Tom O'Bedlam (1985). Warner Bks 1986 $3.95. ISBN 0-446-34002-2 Tale of a man who must pretend to be mad to keep the world from learning of his strange power.

Valentine Pontifex (1983). Bantam 1989 $4.50. ISBN 0-553-24494-9 Story of Lord Valentine, ruler of the planet Majipoor, who must prepare his planet for war after 14,000 years of peace.

SHORT STORY COLLECTIONS BY SILVERBERG

Beyond the Safe Zone: Collected Short Fiction of Robert Silverberg (1986). D I Fine 1986 $18.95. ISBN 0-917657-60-8 A recent collection of some of Silverberg's best stories.

Worlds Imagined (1988). Crown 1989 $8.98. ISBN 0-517-60829-7 Fifteen tales of the future.

BOOK ABOUT SILVERBERG

Clareson, Thomas D. *A Reader's Guide to Robert Silverberg.* Starmont 1983 $7.95. ISBN 0-916732-47-9 A guide to Silverberg's best novels and stories with discussion of the development of his craft.

SIMON, NEIL 1927–

Born in New York City, Neil Simon had childhood ambitions to be a doctor. After he attended New York University and the University of Denver without receiving a degree, however, he turned instead to radio and television, writing comedy for Sid Caesar, Phil Silvers, and other television stars of the 1950s and early 1960s. He also worked with other top comedy writers like Mel Brooks and Woody Allen (*see* Allen, Vol. 1, American Literature: The Twentieth Century). But Simon felt increasingly frustrated by the restrictions of writing to please network executives and advertising agencies and decided to try writing for the stage. His first play, *Come Blow Your Horn* (1958), is the partly autobiographical story of a young rebel who moves into the luxurious apartment of his older brother.

Ever since 1958, Simon has produced a steady stream of hit comedies, many of which have been made into hit movies. Throughout the 1970s and into the present, Simon has been the most successful comic writer in the American theater.

Most of Simon's early plays share certain elements: they are almost always set in New York City, with New York characters and the problems that normally spring from personal frustrations. Simon admits that he uses his own experiences as a source of ideas for his work. *Brighton Beach Memoirs* (1984), *Biloxi Blues* (1986), and *Broadway Bound* (1987) form a trilogy which traces Simon's life and career from his childhood in Brooklyn through his success as a Broadway playwright. These plays have received a more serious response from the critics, who had tended to dismiss Simon as little more than a skilled, but rather mechanical, gag writer. This recent work, while still hilarious, draws more humor from the complex interactions of characters, and it deals more directly with important issues.

PLAYS BY SIMON

Biloxi Blues (1986). Signet 1988 $2.95. ISBN 0-451-15392-8 Story of Eugene Morris Jerome's coming of age in a 1943 army training camp.

Brighton Beach Memoirs (1984). Signet 1986 $4.50. ISBN 0-451-16344-3 Story of 15-year-old Eugene Morris Jerome growing up in Brooklyn during the Depression years of the 1930s.

Broadway Bound (1987). Plume 1988 $6.95. ISBN 0-452-26148-1 Experiences of Eugene Morris Jerome and his brother Stan as they become comedy writers.

The Collected Plays of Neil Simon: Volume 1. Plume 1986 $12.95. ISBN 0-452-25870-7 Seven plays produced between 1960 and 1969.

The Collected Plays of Neil Simon: Volume 2. Plume 1986 $14.95. ISBN 0-452-26358-1 Eight plays produced between 1970 and 1979.

BOOKS ABOUT SIMON

Johnson, Robert K. *Neil Simon.* G. K. Hall 1985 $6.95. ISBN 0-8057-7446-7 Up-to-date introduction to Simon's work; first serious critical attention given to Simon.

McGovern, Edythe M. *Neil Simon: A Critical Study.* Ungar 1979 $16.95. ISBN 0-8044-2567-1 A useful study that contains summaries of Simon's plays through 1978.

SINCLAIR, UPTON   1878–1968

Born in Baltimore, Maryland, and educated at the City College of New York and Columbia University, Upton Sinclair was a prolific writer who began writing at the age of 15. Before he was 20 years old, he had published dozens of stories in magazines for young readers.

Sinclair, a lifelong socialist, gained national attention in 1906 with the publication of his novel *The Jungle,* which he published himself after five publishers had refused it. A moving and powerful novel that exposed the abuses and corruption in the Chicago meat-packing industry, the book became an immediate best-seller and led to the reform of the entire meat-packing industry. In 1967, Sinclair was invited by President Lyndon Johnson to witness the signing of the Wholesale Meat Act, a law that plugged the loopholes in the original Federal Meat Inspection Law (which had resulted from the outcry prompted by *The Jungle.*)

Although many of his books are fiction, Sinclair was not really a novelist but an intrepid and tireless journalist-crusader. All his early books are propaganda for social reform. Newspapers, colleges, schools, churches, and industries have all been the subject of attack by Sinclair.

Sinclair's 80 or so books have been translated into 47 languages, and his sales abroad, especially in the Soviet Union and Eastern Europe, have been enormous. In the United States, however, as the concept of government regulation of private industry has gone out of fashion, Sinclair's attacks on the abuses of large corporations have become similarly unfashionable, and, with the exception of *The Jungle,* his works are seldom read.

NOVELS BY SINCLAIR

Boston: A Documentary Novel of the Sacco-Vanzetti Case (1928). Bentley 1978 repr of 1928 ed $25.00. ISBN 0-8376-0420-6

The Jungle (1906). Penguin 1985 $2.95. ISBN 0-14-039031-6

King Coal: A Novel (1921). AMS 1980 repr of 1921 ed $30.00. ISBN 0-404-58469-1

NONFICTION BY SINCLAIR

Brass Check (1918). Ayer 1970 repr of 1918 ed $25.50. ISBN 0-405-01696-4

The Flivver King: A Study of Ford-America (1937). C. H. Kerr $7.95. ISBN 0-88286-054-2

Goose Step: A Study of American Education (1923). AMS (repr of 1923 ed) $31.50. ISBN 0-404-06068-4

The Goslings: A Study of American Schools (1924). AMS (repr of 1924 ed) $28.50. ISBN 0-404-06069-2

BOOKS ABOUT SINCLAIR

Bloodworth, William J. *Upton Sinclair.* G. K. Hall 1977 $17.95. ISBN 0-8057-7197-2
   Balanced analysis of Sinclair's place in American letters; contains a chronology
   and a bibliography.
Yoder, Jon A. *Upton Sinclair.* Ungar 1975 $16.95. ISBN 0-8044-2989-8 Sympathetic but
   objective exploration of Sinclair's major works with an emphasis on the role of
   socialism in his life.

STEINBECK, JOHN   1902–1968

John Steinbeck was born in Salinas, California, the son of a county official and
a former school teacher. In high school he was a good student, an athlete, and
president of his graduating class. Between 1920 and 1925 he attended Stanford
University off and on, but he never received a degree.

After a futile attempt to become a writer in New York City in 1926,
Steinbeck returned to California and worked in a fish hatchery while continuing to write. He published his first novel, *Cup of Gold,* in 1929; a collection of
related short stories, *The Pastures of Heaven* in 1932; and his second novel, *To a
God Unknown,* in 1933. None of these books was very successful, but Steinbeck's
third novel, *Tortilla Flat* (1935), established his reputation. It dealt with the lives
of *paisanos,* Californians of Mexican descent whose ancestors settled in the state
200 years ago.

Steinbeck's next work, *In Dubious Battle* (1936), is a powerful story of a labor
strike among migrant workers. He followed with *Of Mice and Men* (1937), an
experimental work, written almost entirely in dialogue, about a pair of migrant
farmhands. The story was dramatized in the year of its publication and won
the New York Drama Critics Circle Award, solidly establishing Steinbeck's
reputation as a formidable new writer.

A series of articles Steinbeck wrote about the migrant workers' camps in
California inspired his next—and probably greatest—work, *The Grapes of Wrath*
(1939). This novel recounts the odyssey of the Joad family, driven from their
farm in the Oklahoma dust bowl to seek a new life in California, only to be
forced to move from camp to camp. The powerful and moving saga of this
family touched a responsive chord in American readers still painfully aware of
the hardships of the Depressions. The book attracted a broad readership and
won the Pulitzer Prize in 1940, the same year it was made into a memorable
film.

Steinbeck's best and most ambitious novel is *East of Eden* (1952), a story of
two brothers based loosely on the biblical story of Cain and Abel. Three lighter
works—*Cannery Row* (1945), *The Wayward Bus* (1947), and *Sweet Thursday* (1955)—
find Steinbeck returning to the tone of *Tortilla Flat.* In 1961, Steinbeck produced
The Winter of Our Discontent, which deals with the destructive effect of materialism and greed on the human spirit. Steinbeck also wrote popular nonfiction,
including *Travels with Charley in Search of America* (1962), an account of his cross-
country journey to rediscover America. Steinbeck was awarded the Nobel Prize
for literature in 1962, but in the 1970s, his work fell out of favor.

Over the past decade, however, there has been a renewal of interest in
Steinbeck's work, and his literary reputation has risen considerably. He is now
regarded as one of the major American writers of his generation.

NOVELS BY STEINBECK

East of Eden (1952). Penguin 1979 $5.95. ISBN 0-14-004997-5
*The Grapes of Wrath: Text and Criticism (1939). Penguin 1977 $9.95. ISBN 0-14-015508-2
   Saga of the Joad family, which becomes a chronicle of Depression-era America.

In Dubious Battle (1936). Penguin 1979 $4.95. ISBN 0-14-004888-X

The Moon Is Down (1942). Penguin 1982 $3.95. ISBN 0-14-006222-X

Of Mice and Men (1937) and *Cannery Row* (1945). Penguin 1978 $3.95. ISBN 0-14-004891-X

*The Pearl (1947). Bantam 1986 $2.50. ISBN 0-553-26261-0 Enduring tale of a poor fisherman who finds a priceless pearl.

*The Red Pony (1933). Bantam 1986 $2.50. ISBN 0-553-26444-3 Story of a boy and his love for a sorrel colt.

Tortilla Flat (1935). Penguin 1977 $4.50. ISBN 0-14-004240-7

**Travels with Charley in Search of America* (1952). Penguin 1980 $4.95. ISBN 0-14-005320-4 Account of Steinbeck's cross-country journey to rediscover America.

The Wayward Bus (1947). Penguin 1979 $4.95. ISBN 0-14-005001-9

The Winter of Our Discontent (1961). Penguin 1982 $4.95. ISBN 0-14-006221-1

SHORT STORY COLLECTION BY STEINBECK

*The Long Valley (1938). Penguin 1986 $3.95. ISBN 0-14-008038-4 Thirteen short stories, including "The Chrysanthemums" and "Flight."

NONFICTION BY STEINBECK

Working Days: The Journals of The Grapes of Wrath. Penguin 1989 $18.95. ISBN 0-670-80845-8 Revealing account of Steinbeck's painful struggle to create his literary masterpiece.

BOOKS ABOUT STEINBECK

French, Warren (ed). *A Companion to The Grapes of Wrath.* Penguin 1990 $7.95. ISBN 0-14-011987-6 Criticism, newspaper articles, and essays elucidating the social, historical, and literary background of Steinbeck's classic novel.

French, Warren. *John Steinbeck.* G. K. Hall 1975 $16.95. ISBN 0-8057-0693-3 Relates Steinbeck's work to the literary and social criticism of the 1970s.

Steinbeck, Elaine, and Robert Wallsten (eds). *Steinbeck: A Life in Letters.* Penguin 1976 $14.95. ISBN 0-14-004288-1 Forty-five years of Steinbeck's letters presented as an autobiography.

TAYLOR, MILDRED 1943–

Mildred Taylor was born in Jackson, Mississippi, and was raised in Toledo, Ohio, where she attended public schools. She studied at the University of Toledo, and after graduation spent two years in the Peace Corps, teaching English and history in Ethiopia. After her return to the United States, she entered the University of Colorado and received a master's degree in journalism. She worked for a time as study skills coordinator for the Black Education Program at the University of Colorado and then moved to Los Angeles to begin writing.

Taylor's first novel, *Song of the Trees* (1975), was named Outstanding Book of the Year for 1975 by *The New York Times* and a Children's Book Showcase for 1976. Her second book, *Roll of Thunder, Hear My Cry* (1976), was even more highly honored, winning both the Newbery Medal and a Notable Book citation from the American Library Association in 1977. These two books focus on young Cassie Logan and her loving African-American family. Taylor continued her saga of the Logans in *Let the Circle Be Unbroken* (1981) and *The Friendship* (1987). These moving, vivid stories have been extremely well received and have established Taylor as a leading writer for young readers.

Novels by Taylor

*_The Friendship_ (1987). Dial 1987 $11.95. ISBN 0-8037-0417-8 Story about race relations in rural Mississippi during the Depression.

*_Gold Cadillac_ (1987). Dial 1987 $11.95. ISBN 0-8037-0342-2 Two black girls from the North take a Cadillac on a visit to Mississippi in the 1950s and experience racial prejudice for the first time.

*_Let the Circle Be Unbroken_ (1981). Bantam 1983 $2.95. ISBN 0-553-23436-6 Sequel to _Roll of Thunder, Hear My Cry,_ continuing the story of the Logan family's struggle against poverty and prejudice in Depression-era Mississippi.

*_Roll of Thunder, Hear My Cry_ (1976). Bantam 1984 $3.50. ISBN 0-553-25450-2 Story of the Logan family's struggle to maintain its dignity and independence in Depression-era Mississippi.

*_Song of the Trees_ (1975). Bantam 1984 $2.50. ISBN 0-553-27587-9 Story of the Logan family's fight to save the trees that surround their home.

THURBER, JAMES 1894–1961

James Thurber was born in Columbus, Ohio, into an eccentric family, whose members are sometimes featured in his stories. He attended Ohio State University and after graduation became a government clerk in Washington, D.C. He then joined the staff of the American embassy in Paris. In 1927, at the urging of his writer friend E. B. White, Thurber joined the staff of _The New Yorker_ magazine. Although he was a full-time staff member only until 1933, he contributed stories, essays, and unusual drawings and cartoons to this publication for the rest of his life.

Although equally talented in writing and drawing, Thurber preferred to think of himself as a writer who illustrated his own books. He published "fables" in the style of Aesop (_see_ Aesop, World Literature: Classical Greek Literature)—usually poking fun at some contemporary fad or fashion—as well as children's books, several plays, and numerous satires and parodies in short and full-length forms. "The Secret Life of Walter Mitty," included in _My World and Welcome to It_ (1942), is probably his best-known story.

Thurber's favorite topic was the plight of the decent, honest individual in the complex world of mass media, psychoanalysis, and sexual revolution. He had the ability to spot ideas or practices that were faddish or silly and hold them up to well-deserved ridicule. Poet T. S. Eliot (_see_ Eliot, Vol. 1, British Literature: The Twentieth Century) described Thurber's work as "a form of humor which is also a way of saying something serious."

Collections of Stories and Sketches by Thurber

*_The Best in Me and Other Animals: A Collection of Pieces and Drawings About Human Beings and Less Alarming Creatures_ (1948). Harcourt 1973 $5.95. ISBN 0-15-610850-X A good sampling of Thurber's fanciful humor and biting wit.

Fables of Our Time (1940). Harper 1983 $6.95. ISBN 0-06-090999-4

Is Sex Necessary? Or, Why You Feel the Way You Do (1929). (coauthored with E. B. White) Harper 1984 $6.95. ISBN 0-06-091102-6

James Thurber: 92 Stories. Crown 1985 $7.98. ISBN 0-517-45999-X

The Middle-Aged Man on the Flying Trapeze (1935). Amereon (repr of 1935 ed) $16.95. ISBN 0-89190-268-6

*_My World and Welcome to It_ (1942). Harcourt 1969 $7.95. ISBN 0-15-662344-7 Interesting sampling of Thurber's humorous fiction.

*_The Thurber Carnival_ (1945). Harper 1975 $8.95. ISBN 0-06-090445-3 Bitter but hilarious stories, fables, and sketches.

NONFICTION BY THURBER

My Life and Hard Times. Harper 1973 $3.95. ISBN 0-06-080290-1 Hilarious and revealing autobiography through 1932.
The Years with Ross. Penguin 1984 $7.95. ISBN 0-14-007380-9 A memoir of Thurber's years with *The New Yorker* and its editor, Harold Ross.

BOOKS ABOUT THURBER

Long, Robert E. *James Thurber.* Ungar 1988 $16.95. ISBN 0-8044-2546-9 A concise, reliable, and timely study of Thurber's life and work; contains a useful chronology and bibliography.
Morsberger, Robert E. *James Thurber.* G. K. Hall 1964 $16.95. ISBN 0-8057-0728-X Among the first book-length studies of his life and writing; still highly regarded.

TYLER, ANNE 1941–

Born in Minneapolis, Minnesota, Anne Tyler was raised in several Quaker communities in the Midwest and South. She attended high school in Raleigh, North Carolina, and then, at age 16, entered Duke University. She received a B.A. degree in 1961 and went on to graduate study at Columbia University. In 1963, she married Taghi Modarressi, an Iranian psychiatrist. After living and working in Canada for six years, she settled in Baltimore, a city that figures prominently in her writing.

Tyler published her first novel, *If Morning Ever Comes,* in 1964. Like her next two books, *The Tin Can Tree* (1965) and *A Slipping-down Life* (1970), *If Morning Ever Comes* deals with family life and the sadness of separation. Her growing concern with loneliness and the failure to communicate is most evident in *A Slipping-down Life,* the story of a teenage girl who believes the most important thing she has ever done is to slash the name "Elvis" on her forehead.

It was Tyler's fifth novel that brought her national attention. *Celestial Navigation* (1974) is the story of a timid, introspective artist who eventually withdraws from the world and his loving wife. With the subsequent publication of *Morgan's Passing* (1980), *Dinner at the Homesick Restaurant* (1982), and *The Accidental Tourist* (1985), all nominated for major book awards, Tyler has established herself as an important contemporary writer. *The Accidental Tourist* became a distinguished film, as well.

NOVELS BY TYLER

The Accidental Tourist (1985). Berkley 1988 $4.95. ISBN 0-425-11423-6
Breathing Lessons (1988). Berkley 1989 $5.50. ISBN 0-425-11774-X
Celestial Navigation (1974). Berkley 1985 $3.95. ISBN 0-425-09840-0
The Clock Winder (1972). Berkley 1987 $3.95. ISBN 0-425-09902-4
Dinner at the Homesick Restaurant (1982). Berkley 1989 $4.95. ISBN 0-425-09868-0
Earthly Possessions (1977). Berkley 1985 $3.95. ISBN 0-425-10167-3
If Morning Ever Comes (1964). Berkley 1987 $3.95. ISBN 0-425-09883-4
Morgan's Passing (1980). Berkley 1987 $4.50. ISBN 0-425-09872-9
Searching for Caleb (1976). Berkley 1987 $4.50. ISBN 0-425-09876-1
A Slipping-down Life (1970). Berkley 1989 $3.95. ISBN 0-425-10362-5
The Tin Can Tree (1965). Berkley 1987 $3.95. ISBN 0-425-09903-2

UPDIKE, JOHN 1932–

John Updike was raised in Shillington, Pennsylvania, a small town near Reading, where he was born. He was educated at Harvard University, from which he graduated with highest honors in 1954, and at the Ruskin School of Fine

Arts at Oxford University, where he studied for a year. After returning to the United States from England, Updike went to work for *The New Yorker* magazine, where his first stories appeared.

Updike's novels range widely in theme and setting. His first novel, *The Poorhouse Fair* (1959), is about a home for the aged that seems to represent society as a whole. *The Coup* (1978) concerns a revolution in Africa, and *The Witches of Eastwick* (1985) looks at suburban New England society through the eyes of three modern witches. *The Centaur* (1963) is a subtle and complicated novel about three days in the life of a small-town high school teacher, seen through the eyes of his son. It won the National Book Award.

Updike is best known for his biting look at suburban life. *Couples* (1968) looks at sexual relationships among a group of suburbanites in the 1960s, exploring the suburban lifestyle of that period. In the "Rabbit" novels, Updike traces the life and times of Harry "Rabbit" Angstrom, introducing him in *Rabbit Run* (1960) as a 26-year-old sales agent trapped in an unhappy marriage while looking back wistfully to his days as a high-school basketball star. *Rabbit Redux* (1971) takes up Harry's story 10 years later in the 1960s, giving Updike an opportunity to comment on that turbulent time. In *Rabbit Is Rich* (1981), Harry is comfortably middle-aged and a complacent member of the country-club set, whose shallow values Updike exposes.

Updike has also published eight collections of short stories and several volumes of poems, as well as many critical essays and reviews. Despite having been criticized for shifting direction with each new change in social attitudes, Updike is a serious artist whose versatility and solid achievement rank him among the major writers of his time.

NOVELS BY UPDIKE

Bech: A Book (1970). Random 1980 $5.95. ISBN 0-394-74509-4
Bech Is Back (1982). Fawcett 1983 $2.95. ISBN 0-449-20277-1
The Centaur (1963). Fawcett 1988 $4.95. ISBN 0-449-21522-9
The Coup (1978). Fawcett 1985 $4.50. ISBN 0-449-24259-5
Couples (1968). Fawcett 1985 $4.95. ISBN 0-449-20797-8
A Month of Sundays (1975). Fawcett 1985 $3.50. ISBN 0-449-20795-1
Of the Farm (1965). Fawcett 1987 $3.95. ISBN 0-449-21451-6
The Poorhouse Fair (1959). Fawcett 1985 $3.50. ISBN 0-449-21213-6
Rabbit Is Rich (1981). Fawcett 1982 $4.95. ISBN 0-449-24548-9
Rabbit Redux (1971). Fawcett 1985 $4.95. ISBN 0-449-20934-2
Rabbit, Run (1960). Fawcett 1983 $4.95. ISBN 0-449-20506-1
Roger's Version (1986). Fawcett 1987 $4.95. ISBN 0-449-21652-7
S (1988). Fawcett 1989 $4.95. ISBN 0-449-21652-7

SHORT STORY COLLECTIONS BY UPDIKE

Marry Me (1976). Fawcett 1983 $3.95. ISBN 0-449-20361-1
Museums and Women and Other Stories (1972). Random 1981 $7.95. ISBN 0-394-74762-3
The Music School (1966). Random 1980 $6.95. ISBN 0-394-74510-8
Pigeon Feathers and Other Stories (1962). Fawcett 1986 $3.95. ISBN 0-449-21132-0
Problems and Other Stories (1979). Fawcett 1985 $3.50. ISBN 0-449-21103-7
Same Door (1959). Random 1981 $7.95. ISBN 0-395-74763-1
Too Far to Go (1979). Fawcett 1982 $2.75. ISBN 0-449-20016-7
Trust Me (1987). Fawcett 1988 $4.95. ISBN 0-449-21498-2

POETRY BY UPDIKE

The Carpentered Hen (1982). Knopf 1982 $11.00. ISBN 0-394-52394-6
Midpoint and Other Poems (1969). Knopf 1969 $11.95. ISBN 0-394-40383-5
Telephone Poles and Other Poems (1963). Knopf 1963 $11.95. ISBN 0-394-40457-2
Tossing and Turning (1977). Knopf 1977 $11.50. ISBN 0-394-41090-4

Nonfiction by Updike

Self-Consciousness: Memoirs. Knopf 1989 $18.95. ISBN 0-394-57222-X Reflections by Updike on his life and works.

Books about Updike

Detweiler, Robert. *John Updike.* G. K. Hall 1977 $16.95. ISBN 0-8057-7422-X Apprecia-tive analysis of Updike's narrative art and its cultural significance.
Macnaughton, William R. *Critical Essays on John Updike.* G. K. Hall 1982 $36.50. ISBN 0-8161-8467-4 Well-chosen collection of essays by scholars and critics with differing viewpoints on Updike's art.

URIS, LEON 1924–

Leon Uris was born in Baltimore, the son of a Jewish immigrant father. The name Uris was derived from Yerushalami, which means "Jerusalemite." Uris attended public schools in Baltimore; Norfolk, Virginia; and Philadelphia, Pennsylvania. He was considered a poor student, failed English three times, and did not graduate from high school. He himself has commented, "It's a good thing English and writing have nothing to do with each other."

At age 17, Uris ran away from home and enlisted in the Marine Corps, serving throughout World War II. After the war he settled in San Francisco, determined to become a writer. His early efforts were failures, however, and he supported his family by driving a newspaper delivery truck.

Finally, in 1953, after being rejected nine times, Uris's first novel, *Battle Cry,* was published. Based on his experiences as a marine, the novel was well received, and Warner Brothers immediately bought the film rights. Uris was hired to write the screenplay, and stayed on in Hollywood as a film writer while working on his second novel, *The Angry Hills* (1955). During this period, he also wrote the screenplay for the classic film *Gunfight at the O.K. Corral.*

Uris then turned his attention to Israel. Consumed with a desire to write a book about the homeland of his ancestors, he went to Israel in 1956 and did extensive research on the new nation. The result was *Exodus* (1958), one of the top-selling novels in American publishing history. Uris also wrote the screen-play for the film version of his novel on the birth of Israel. Still fascinated by the history of the Jews, Uris wrote *Mila 18* in 1961, a novel about the uprising in the Jewish ghetto in Warsaw during World War II. His later books have also proved to be very popular, and Uris remains one of the best selling modern American novelists.

Novels by Uris

The Angry Hills (1955). Bantam 1972 $3.95. ISBN 0-553-24414-0
Armageddon (1964). Dell 1985 $5.95. ISBN 0-440-10290-1
Battle Cry (1953). Bantam 1982 $4.95. ISBN 0-553-25983-0
Exodus (1958). Bantam 1983 $4.95. ISBN 0-553-25847-8 Israel's establishment as a new nation after World War II, told through various people's stories.
The Haj (1984). Bantam 1985 $4.95. ISBN 0-553-24864-2
Mila 18 (1961). Bantam 1983 $4.95. ISBN 0-553-24160-5 Moving account of the Warsaw Ghetto and the heroic uprising of the Jews forced there.
Mitla Pass (1988). Doubleday 1988 $19.95. ISBN 0-385-18792-0
QB VII (1970). Bantam 1972 $4.95. ISBN 0-553-25957-1
Topaz (1967). Bantam 1981 $4.50. ISBN 0-553-26260-2
Trinity (1976). Bantam 1983 $4.95. ISBN 0-553-25846-X

VOIGHT, CYNTHIA 1942–

Cynthia Voight was born in Boston, Massachusetts. She received a B.A. from Smith College in 1963 and settled in Maryland, where she became a high school English teacher in Glen Burnie. In 1968, she moved to the Key School in Annapolis, Maryland, where she still teaches and serves as English department head. Rural Maryland is the setting for most of Voight's novels.

Voight published her first young-adult novel, *Homecoming,* in 1981, beginning the story of the Tillermans, four children without a father whose emotionally disturbed mother abandons them in a parking lot. The eldest, 13-year-old Dicey, must assume the role of parent and look after the other three. After a series of difficulties, the children make their way to their grandmother's house in Maryland, where they find a new home.

Voight continues the saga of the Tillerman children in *Dicey's Song* (1982), *A Solitary Blue* (1983), *Sons from Afar* (1988), and *Seventeen Against the Dealer* (1989). In a related novel, *The Runner* (1985), Voight tells the story of a Tillerman of a previous generation. *Dicey's Song* won the Newbery Medal in 1983. Another related novel, *Come a Stranger* (1986), explores the life of Dicey's African-American friend, Mina.

Voight's stories are marked by a concern for understanding and harmony between generations. Her characters move toward a resolution of their problems when they begin to communicate openly and freely with one another. While there are no contrived happy endings or quick solutions to difficult problems, there is an undercurrent of optimism that suggests that people can understand each other if they make the effort.

NOVELS BY VOIGHT

Building Blocks (1984). Fawcett 1988 $2.95. ISBN 0-449-44453-8 A 12-year-old boy goes back 30 years in time to discover why his father is a "loser."

The Callender Papers (1983). Fawcett 1984 $3.50. ISBN 0-449-70184-0 A young woman discovers a dangerous secret while sorting through the papers of a deceased friend.

Come a Stranger (1986). Fawcett 1987 $2.95. ISBN 0-449-70296-4 A young woman's love for ballet is threatened by the new awkwardness of her rapidly growing body.

Dicey's Song (1982). Fawcett 1989 $3.50. ISBN 0-449-70276-6 Thirteen-year-old Dicey learns to deal with life's problems with the help of her grandmother.

Homecoming (1981). Fawcett 1984 $2.95. ISBN 0-449-70254-5 Four children abandoned by their mother must find a new home.

Izzy, Willy-Nilly (1986). Fawcett 1988 $3.50. ISBN 0-449-70214-6 A 15-year-old girl loses a leg in a car accident.

Jackaroo (1985). Fawcett 1987 $3.50. ISBN 0-449-70187-5 Young girl aids oppressed peasants in medieval times.

The Runner (1985). Fawcett 1987 $3.95. ISBN 0-449-70294-4 An 18-year-old cross-country runner struggles with family problems.

Seventeen Against the Dealer (1989). Fawcett 1990 $3.95. ISBN 0-449-70375-4 Last part of the Tillerman saga, Dicey struggles to become a boat builder.

A Solitary Blue (1983). Fawcett 1985 $2.95. ISBN 0-449-70268-5 A young man's search for the mother he needs.

Sons from Afar (1988). Fawcett 1989 $3.50. ISBN 0-449-70293-6 Two brothers search for their long-missing father.

Tell Me If the Lovers Are Losers (1982). Fawcett 1985 $2.95. ISBN 0-449-70235-9 Story of three roommates at a women's college in the early 1960s.

Tree By Leaf (1988). Fawcett 1989 $3.50. ISBN 0-449-70334-7 A young girl learns to deal with the many problems that befall her family.

VONNEGUT, KURT, JR.   1922–

Kurt Vonnegut, Jr., was born in Indianapolis, Indiana. He attended Cornell University, but his college education was interrupted by World War II. Captured during the Battle of the Bulge and imprisoned in Dresden, Germany, he received a Purple Heart for what he calls a "ludicrously negligible wound." After the war, Vonnegut returned to Cornell and later earned his M.A. at the University of Chicago. He worked as a political reporter and in public relations before publishing short stories in popular magazines and beginning his career as a novelist.

Vonnegut's first novel, *Player Piano* (1952), is a highly believable account of a future society in which people count for far less than machines. *The Sirens of Titan* (1959) tells of a playboy whisked off to Mars to learn some humbling lessons about Earth's modest function in the total scheme of things. *Mother Night* (1962) is the chilling tale of an American writer and Allied undercover agent who broadcasts Nazi propaganda in Germany during World War II. *Cat's Cradle* (1963) is about the discovery of a special kind of ice that destroys the world. *God Bless You Mr. Rosewater* (1965) is a satirical account of a man who rushes about absurdly doing good deeds for useless people as he tries to save the world through love.

Vonnegut's most famous novel is *Slaughterhouse Five, or The Children's Crusade* (1969) about the massive firebombing of Dresden by the Allies in World War II. Through the time travels of the central character, Billy Pilgrim, Vonnegut offers ironic commentary on the inhumanity of war and the weapons of destruction that humans create. This book has often been the target of censors, who object to its language as inappropriate for young readers.

Breakfast of Champions (1973) is the story of a Pontiac dealer who goes crazy after reading a science fiction novel.

Slapstick (1976) is the memoir of a 100-year-old ex-president who thinks he can solve society's problems by giving everyone a new middle name.

Vonnegut's appeal may come in part from the fact that he is one of the few writers whose work has been acknowledged as both successful science fiction and "real literature." His popularity is also due to his sharp sense of humor and his biting satire, which he directs with unfailing accuracy at the flaws in modern technological society.

Many of Vonnegut's books have been attacked or even censored by those who see them as inappropriate for young readers. Vonnegut himself remains a strong supporter of intellectual freedom, ready to attack censorship or repression wherever it occurs.

Novels by Vonnegut

Bluebeard (1987). Dell 1988 $4.95. ISBN 0-440-20196-9
Breakfast of Champions (1973). Dell 1975 $4.95. ISBN 0-440-13148-0
Cat's Cradle (1963). Dell 1970 $4.95. ISBN 0-440-11149-8
Deadeye Dick (1982). Dell 1985 $3.95. ISBN 0-440-11765-8
Galapagos (1985). Dell 1986 $4.95. ISBN 0-440-12779-3
God Bless You Mr. Rosewater (1965). Dell 1978 $4.95. ISBN 0-440-12929-X
Jailbird (1979). Dell 1982 $4.95. ISBN 0-440-15473-1
Mother Night (1962). Dell 1988 $4.95. ISBN 0-440-15853-2
Player Piano (1952). Dell 1974 $4.95. ISBN 0-440-17037-0
The Sirens of Titan (1959). Dell 1970 $4.95. ISBN 0-440-17948-3
Slapstick (1976). Dell 1977 $4.95. ISBN 0-440-18009-0
Slaughterhouse Five, or The Children's Crusade (1969). Dell 1978 $4.95. ISBN 0-440-18029-5

SHORT STORY COLLECTION BY VONNEGUT

Welcome to the Monkey House (1968). Dell 1979 $4.95. ISBN 0-440-19478-4

PLAY BY VONNEGUT

Happy Birthday, Wanda Jean (1971). Delacorte 1971 $10.95. ISBN 0-385-28386-5

NONFICTION BY VONNEGUT

*Palm Sunday. Dell 1984 $4.95. ISBN 0-440-36906-1 Autobiographical collage of speeches, letters, fiction, and articles that reveal Vonnegut, the man.
*Wampeters, Foma and Granfallons (1974). Dell 1979 $4.95. ISBN 0-440-18533-5 Reviews, essays, and speeches.

BOOKS ABOUT VONNEGUT

Lundquist, James. *Kurt Vonnegut.* Ungar 1977 $16.95. ISBN 0-8044-2564-7 Critical study of Vonnegut's life and writings by a recognized scholar.
Schatt, Stanley. *Kurt Vonnegut, Jr.* G. K. Hall 1976 $17.95. ISBN 0-8057-7176-X Describes and analyzes Vonnegut's best-known works and relates his experiences to his writings.

WALKER, ALICE 1944–

Like so many characters in her fiction, Alice Walker was born into a family of sharecroppers in Eaton, Georgia. She began Spelman College on a scholarship and graduated from Sarah Lawrence College in 1965. While still in college, Walker became active in the civil rights movement and continued her involvement after she graduated, serving as a voter registration worker in Georgia. She also worked in a Head Start program in Mississippi and was on the staff of the New York City welfare department. She has lectured and taught at several colleges and universities and currently operates a publishing house, Wild Trees Press, of which she is a co-founder.

Walker began her literary career as a poet, publishing *Once: Poems* in 1968. The collection reflects her experiences in the civil rights movement and her travels in Africa. Her second collection of poetry, *Revolutionary Petunias and Other Poems* (1973), is a celebration of the struggle against oppression and racism. In between these two collections, she published her first novel, *The Third Life of Grange Copeland* (1970), the story of Ruth Copeland, a young black girl, and her grandfather, Grange, who brutalizes his own family out of the frustrations of racial prejudice and his own sense of inadequacy.

Walker's first collection of short stories, *In Love and Trouble: Stories of Black Women* (1973), established her special concern for the struggles, hardships, loyalties, and triumphs of black women, a powerful force in the rest of her fiction. *Meridian* (1976), her second novel, is the story of Meridian Hill, a civil rights worker. In her second collection of short stories, *You Can't Keep A Good Woman Down* (1981), Walker again portrays black women struggling against sexual, racial, and economic oppression.

Walker's third novel, *The Color Purple* (1982), brought her the national recognition denied her earlier works. Through this story of the sharecropper Celie and the abuses she endures, Walker draws together the themes that have run through her earlier work into a concentrated and powerful attack on racism and sexism, and produces a triumphant celebration of the spirit and endurance of black women. The book received the Pulitzer Prize and was made into a successful film.

Walker describes her most recent novel, *The Temple of My Familiar* (1989), as "a romance of the last 500,000 years." The book is a blend of myth and history revolving around three marriages. As the married couples tell their stories, they explore both their origins and the inner life of modern African Americans.

NOVELS BY WALKER

The Color Purple (1982). Harcourt 1982 $12.95. ISBN 0-15-119153-0
Meridian (1976). Harcourt 1976 $14.95. ISBN 0-15-159265-9
The Temple of My Familiar (1989). Harcourt 1989 $19.95. ISBN 0-15-188533-8
The Third Life of Grange Copeland (1970). Pocket 1988 $3.95. ISBN 0-671-66142-6

SHORT STORY COLLECTIONS BY WALKER

In Love and Trouble: Stories of Black Women (1973). Harcourt 1974 $3.95. ISBN 0-15-644450-X
You Can't Keep a Good Woman Down (1981). Harcourt 1982 $4.95. ISBN 0-15-699778-9

POETRY BY WALKER

Goodnight, Willie Lee, I'll See You in the Morning (1979). Harcourt 1984 $4.95. ISBN 0-15-636467-0
Horses Make a Landscape Look More Beautiful (1984). Harcourt 1986 $3.95. ISBN 0-15-642173-9
Once: Poems (1968). Harcourt 1976 $3.95. ISBN 0-15-668745-3
Revolutionary Petunias and Other Poems (1973). Harcourt 1973 $4.95. ISBN 0-15-676620-5

BOOK ABOUT WALKER

Bloom, Harold (ed). *Alice Walker.* Chelsea 1989 $22.50. ISBN 1-55546-314-4 Collection of critical essays by well-known scholars examining Walker's major themes.

WALKER, MARGARET 1915–

Margaret Walker was born in Birmingham, Alabama, the daughter of a minister from whom she learned that a good sermon could be a kind of poetry. She attended Northwestern University in Illinois, graduating in 1937. While there, she met a number of young writers, white and black, who had come to participate in government-sponsored writing projects. Her own interest in writing was strong, and this association stimulated her to produce her own work. In 1937, her poem "For My People" was published in the magazine *Poetry,* but it was not until five years later that her first volume of poetry, also titled *For My People,* was published by Yale University Press.

After completing her master's degree at the University of Iowa in 1940, Walker began teaching, first at Livingstone College in North Carolina and then at West Virginia State College before finally settling at Jackson State College in Mississippi. While teaching, raising her children, and caring for her disabled husband, Walker continued to work on her writing. In 1962, she returned to the University of Iowa to work on a Ph.D. in English, writing a novel to earn her degree. She was awarded the Ph.D. in 1965 and the novel, *Jubilee,* was published the following year. *Jubilee* tells the story of the Civil War and the Reconstruction period that followed through the eyes of the emancipated slave Vyry, a character based on Walker's great-grandmother.

In 1987, 45 years after the appearance of *For My People,* Walker published her second volume of poetry, *Apparitions,* and followed with a third collection, *This is My Century,* in 1989. Despite her relatively small body of published works, Walker has long been considered one of the most influential black writers of her time. She has served as an inspiration to a whole generation of younger writers who look to her pioneering work as a model for their own.

NOVEL BY WALKER

Jubilee (1966). Bantam 1975 $4.95. ISBN 0-553-27383-3 Story of Vyry, as she lives through slavery, the Civil War, and Reconstruction.

POETRY BY WALKER

Apparitions (1987). Jamestown 1987 $7.20. ISBN 0-89061-465-2
For My People (1942). Ayer 1969 repr of 1942 ed $9.95. ISBN 0-405-01902-5
This Is My Century: New and Collected Poems (1989). Univ of Georgia Pr 1989 $12.50. ISBN 0-8203-1135-9

NONFICTION BY WALKER

How I Wrote Jubilee and Other Essays on Life and Literature (1989). Feminist Pr 1989 $9.95. ISBN 1-55861-004-9
A Poetic Equation: Conversations Between Nikki Giovanni and Margaret Walker. (coauthored with Nikki Giovanni) Howard Univ Pr 1974 $9.95. ISBN 0-88258-003-5 Discussion of poetry, philosophy, and artistic attitudes by two major contemporary poets.

WARREN, ROBERT PENN   1905–1989

Robert Penn Warren was born in Guthrie, Kentucky, and educated at Vanderbilt University in Nashville, Tennessee. He enrolled at Vanderbilt intending to study science, but under the influence of famed critic and poet John Crowe Ransom decided to become a writer. At Vanderbilt he became a member of a group of Nashville intellectuals who met weekly to discuss literature and philosophy. The group also produced a magazine, *The Fugitive,* which Warren edited.

After graduating from Vanderbilt, Warren went to the University of California at Berkeley, where he received his M.A. in English in 1927. He did further graduate work at Yale University before being named a Rhodes Scholar and spending two years at Oxford University in England.

The versatile Warren has written almost every kind of literature and distinguished himself in all of them. He is most widely known, however, as a poet, critic, and novelist. Almost always writing about his native South, Warren has produced 10 novels and two collections of short stories. By far the most successful of his novels is *All the King's Men* (1946), the story of a southern politician based loosely on the turbulent career of Huey Long, governor of Louisiana during the 1930s. The novel won the Pulitzer Prize in 1947 and was made into a highly successful film in 1949.

Warren's distinguished career as a poet was crowned in 1986 when he was named the first United States Poet Laureate. (A poet laureate is a poet officially chosen to represent the nation.) Two of his collections of poetry, *Promises: Poems 1954–1956* (1957) and *Now and Then: Poems 1976–1978* (1978), were awarded Pulitzer Prizes. Warren's books of criticism, written with Cleanth Brooks, set the standard for the study of literature for an entire generation of American scholars and are still widely used today.

In 1989, a Center for the Study of Robert Penn Warren was established at Western Kentucky University.

Novels by Warren

All the King's Men (1946). Harcourt 1983 $6.95. ISBN 0-15-604762-4
At Heaven's Gate (1943). New Directions 1985 $9.95. ISBN 0-8112-0933-4
A Place to Come To (1977). Random 1977 $12.95. ISBN 0-394-73848-9

Short Story Collection by Warren

The Circus in the Attic and Other Stories (1947). Harcourt 1968 $5.95. ISBN 0-15-618002-2

Poetry by Warren

Brother to Dragons (1953). Random 1979 $12.95. ISBN 0-394-50551-4
Chief Joseph of the Nez Perce (1983). Random 1983 $5.95. ISBN 0-394-71356-7
New and Selected Poems (1985). Random 1985 $13.95. ISBN 0-394-73848-9
Now and Then: Poems 1976–1978 (1978). Random 1978 $5.95. ISBN 0-394-73575-3
Or Else: Poems 1968–1973 (1974). Random 1974 $10.95. ISBN 0-394-49448-2

Nonfiction by Warren

Portrait of a Father. Univ Pr of Kentucky 1988 $12.00. ISBN 0-8131-1655-4 Autobiographical essay and five poems about Warren's father.

Books about Warren

Bloom, Harold (ed). *Robert Penn Warren.* Chelsea 1986 $27.50. ISBN 0-87754-662-2 Collection of 17 critical essays, presenting a complete analysis of Warren's fiction, poetry, and criticism.
Bohner, Charles. *Robert Penn Warren.* G. K. Hall 1981 $16.95. ISBN 0-8057-7345-2 Revised and updated analysis of Warren's poetry and prose; contains a chronology and a bibliography.

WELTY, EUDORA   1909–

One of the most admired American writers, Eudora Welty was born in Jackson, Mississippi, and attended Mississippi State College for Women before going north to the University of Wisconsin and Columbia University. After completing her studies, Welty worked for a while in advertising, and then returned to Jackson to take a government publicity job. She has remained in Jackson ever since, living quietly with her family and pursuing a literary career that has brought her several awards and much critical attention.

Welty's short stories and novels are entirely original, sometimes melodramatic, occasionally fantastic, and often concerned with psychological abnormality. She has a fine ear for dialogue and a personal style that elevates her fiction above the ordinary. Although she has written five novels, she is probably best known for her short stories.

Welty is frequently classified as a southern writer, and her stories are certainly rich in the details of the Mississippi life she knows so well. But it would be wrong to consider her a regional writer; her fiction deals with basic human concerns that are not restricted to any time or place. One of her most powerful themes is the separation and isolation of individuals that can only be overcome through love.

Welty has been a strong influence on new writers such as Anne Tyler (*see* Tyler, Vol. 1, American Literature: The Twentieth Century), and her literary biography, *One Writer's Beginnings* (1984), was a best-seller, an unusual distinction for a serious work of its sort.

NOVELS BY WELTY

Delta Wedding (1946). Harcourt 1979 $5.95. ISBN 0-15-625280-5
Losing Battles (1970). Random 1978 $5.95. ISBN 0-394-72668-5
The Optimist's Daughter (1972). Random 1978 $4.95. ISBN 0-394-72667-7
The Ponder Heart (1954). Harcourt 1967 $5.95. ISBN 0-15-672915-6
The Robber Bridegroom (1942). Harcourt 1978 $4.95. ISBN 0-15-676807-0

SHORT STORY COLLECTION BY WELTY

The Collected Stories of Eudora Welty (1980). Harcourt 1982 $10.95. ISBN 0-15-614075-6

NONFICTION BY WELTY

One Writer's Beginnings (1984). Warner Bks 1985 $3.95. ISBN 0-446-34301-3 Welty's recollections of her start as a writer, based on a series of lectures she gave at Harvard University.

BOOKS ABOUT WELTY

Bloom, Harold (ed). *Eudora Welty.* Chelsea 1986 $27.50. ISBN 0-87754-718-1 Collection of 13 critical essays which examine Welty's fiction and assess her place in modern letters; includes an interview with Welty.
Kieft, Ruth M. *Eudora Welty.* G. K. Hall 1987 $18.95. ISBN 0-8057-7487-4 A comprehensive survey of Welty's work written by Welty's editor and close personal friend.

WEST, NATHANAEL (PSEUDONYM OF NATHAN WALLENSTEIN WEINSTEIN) 1904–1940

Nathanael West was born in New York City and educated at Brown University in Rhode Island. Between the two world wars, he built a reputation as a brilliant satirist of life in America. In his novel *Miss Lonelyhearts* (1933) West tells the story of a sensitive young advice columnist who becomes overwhelmed by the problems of his readers. *The Day of the Locust* (1939) grew out of West's own experiences as a screenwriter in Hollywood. It exposes the bizarre and meaningless life of the 1930s film world. The hatred and violence that lie buried beneath the glitter of Los Angeles erupt in a mob riot that results in the burning of the city.

In *A Cool Million* (1934), West parodies the all-American dream of success through the story of Lemuel Pitkin, a totally naive and trusting young man, who is manipulated by capitalists, Communists, and fascists alike.

While West himself is no longer widely read, his black humor and use of absurd and fantastic plot events as instruments of social satire has had a powerful impact on the writers who followed him.

NOVELS BY WEST

The Day of the Locust (1939). Signet 1983 $3.95. ISBN 0-451-52348-2
The Dream Life of Balso Snell (1931) and *A Cool Million* (1934). Farrar 1963 $5.95. ISBN 0-374-50292-7
Miss Lonelyhearts (1933) and *The Day of The Locust* (1939). New Directions 1989 $5.95. ISBN 0-8112-0215-1

BOOKS ABOUT WEST

Bloom, Harold (ed). *Nathanael West.* Chelsea 1987 $19.95. ISBN 1-55546-051-8 Fourteen outstanding essays tracing the modern critical response to West's novels.

Long, Robert E. *Nathanael West.* Ungar 1985 $16.95. ISBN 0-8044-2543-4 Critical study that examines West's themes and techniques.
Malin, Irving. *Nathanel West's Novels.* Southern Illinois Univ Pr 1972 $7.95. ISBN 0-8093-0577-1 The first chronological, chapter-by-chapter examination of West's novels.

WIESEL, ELIE (ELIEZER)   1928–

Elie Wiesel was born in Sighet, Romania, where he expected to spend his life studying the religious texts of Judaism and helping out in his family's grocery store. But in the spring of 1944, when Wiesel was 15, Nazis entered the region with the intention of exterminating 600,000 Jews in six weeks. The Jews of the region—including Wiesel and his family—were sent to death camps. Although Wiesel's parents and younger sister were killed in a camp, he survived. He later learned that his older sisters had also survived.

This experience would eventually become the foundation of Wiesel's many autobiographical novels and of his nonfiction accounts dealing with the Holocaust—the Nazis' attempt to exterminate the Jews of Europe. However, Wiesel was to remain silent about his experience for many years, feeling that it was not possible to communicate its full horror.

After the war, Wiesel went to France, where he worked at various jobs and eventually became successful as a reporter for French and Jewish newspapers. Finally, in 1956 he published the work translated into English as *Night,* an autobiographical novel about a teenage boy coming to terms with his guilt for having survived the camps when so many others did not and with his anger toward the God who had apparently allowed so many faithful Jews to be murdered.

In 1972, Wiesel began teaching at the City College of the City University of New York, and in 1976 he became Andrew Mellon Professor in the Humanities at Boston University. He continues to publish books and articles that explore the Holocaust from a religious perspective, seeking a basis for faith in a God who has permitted terrible things to happen.

In an interview with *People* magazine, Wiesel described his inner conflict between wanting to bear witness to the brutality he experienced and fearing to trivialize the events by reporting them. "You must speak," he said, "but how can you, when the full story is beyond language?" However, he concluded, "We [survivors] believe that if we survived, we must do something with our lives. The first task is to tell the tale. . . . The only way to stop the next holocaust—the nuclear holocaust—is to remember the last one. If the Jews were singled out then, in the next one we are all victims."

NOVELS BY WIESEL IN ENGLISH TRANSLATION

A Beggar in Jerusalem (1968). Schocken 1985 $8.95. ISBN 0-8052-0897-6
Dawn (1961). Bantam 1982 $2.85. ISBN 0-553-22536-7
The Fifth Son. Warner Bks 1986 $4.50. ISBN 0-446-35930-0
Gates of the Forest (1964). Schocken 1982 $13.00. ISBN 0-8052-0896-8
Night (1956). Bantam 1982 $2.95. ISBN 0-553-20807-1
Night, Dawn, Day. Aronson 1985 $17.95. ISBN 0-87668-877-0
The Night Trilogy: Night, Dawn, The Accident. Hill & Wang 1987 $9.95. ISBN 0-374-52140-9
The Oath (1973). Schocken 1986 $8.95. ISBN 0-8052-0808-9
Somewhere a Master: Further Tales of the Hasidic Masters (1981). Summit Bks 1984 $7.95. ISBN 0-671-50823-7

Souls on Fire (1972). Summit Bks 1982 $8.95. ISBN 0-671-44171-X
The Testament (1980). Bantam 1982 $3.95. ISBN 0-553-20810-1
The Town Beyond the Wall (1962). Schocken 1982 $7.95. ISBN 0-8052-0697-3
Twilight (1988). Warner Bks 1989 $9.95. ISBN 0-446-39066-6

NONFICTION BY WIESEL IN ENGLISH TRANSLATION

Five Biblical Portraits (1981). Univ of Notre Dame Pr 1983 $6.95. ISBN 0-268-00962-7
Four Hasidic Masters and Their Struggle Against Melancholy (1978). Univ of Notre Dame Pr 1978 $6.95. ISBN 0-268-00947-3
A Jew Today (1977). Random 1979 $4.95. ISBN 0-394-74057-2
The Jews of Silence (1987). Schocken 1987 $8.95. ISBN 0-8052-0826-7
Legends of Our Time (1966). Schocken 1982 $9.95. ISBN 0-8052-0714-7
Messengers of God: Biblical Portraits and Legends (1975). Summit Bks 1985 $8.95. ISBN 0-671-54134-X
One Generation After (1965). Schocken 1982 $6.95. ISBN 0-8052-0713-9

DRAMA BY WIESEL IN ENGLISH TRANSLATION

The Trial of God: A Play in Three Acts (1979). Schocken 1986 $9.95. ISBN 0-8052-0809-7
Zalmen, or the Madness of God (1966). Schocken 1985 $7.95. ISBN 0-8052-0777-5

BOOKS ABOUT WIESEL

Berenbaum, Michael. *The Vision of the Void: Theological Reflections on the Works of Elie Wiesel.* Univ Pr of New England 1979 $12.95. ISBN 0-8195-6189-4 Written by a Jewish theologian who served as Deputy Director on the Presidential Commission on the Holocaust; argues that Wiesel has a unique and radical vision in his treatment of the theological and social-historical aspects of the Holocaust.

Brown, Robert M. *Elie Wiesel: Messenger to All Humanity.* Univ of Notre Dame Pr 1989 $10.95. ISBN 0-268-00920-1 Written by a Protestant theologian who served with Wiesel on the U.S. Holocaust Memorial Council; examines Wiesel's treatment of the Holocaust as a moral journey from historical, theological, and literary perspectives.

Rittner, Carol. *Elie Wiesel: Between Memory and Hope.* New York Univ Pr 1990 $40.00. ISBN 0-8147-7410-5 Written by a Catholic scholar and director of the Elie Wiesel Foundation; looks at particular works and relates them to biographical material.

WILDER, THORNTON   1897–1975

Thornton Wilder was born in Madison, Wisconsin, but attended missionary schools in China, where his father served as a diplomat. He graduated from high school in California, earned a B.A. at Yale University, studied archaeology in Rome, and went on to complete an M.A. in French at Princeton University.

One of the most honored and versatile of modern writers, Wilder combined a career as a novelist with ground-breaking work for the theater. However, it was an early short novel, *The Bridge of San Luis Rey* (1927), that first brought him fame and won him the Pulitzer Prize in 1928. This story of a group of people who happen to be on a bridge in Peru when it collapses is ingeniously constructed and rich in questions about fate and destiny. Wilder's next novel, *The Woman of Andros* (1930), was set in ancient Greece shortly before the birth of Christ.

During the 1930s, Wilder turned his attention to the theater and wrote a number of radically experimental plays, culminating with *Our Town* (1938), which won him his second Pulitzer Prize. *Our Town* is about life in a small New Hampshire town, revealing the town people's simplicity and humor as well as their dark side. It has become one of the most popular and enduring works of the American theater. In 1942, Wilder received his third Pulitzer Prize for the play *The Skin of Our Teeth,* an experimental fantasy showing Adam and Eve as a suburban family, surviving the Great Flood and the Ice Age. His successful play *The Matchmaker* (1955) became even more successful in its musical version, *Hello, Dolly!* (1963).

In 1948, Wilder published *The Ides of March,* an historical novel about the last days of Julius Caesar. Wilder's last major novel, *The Eighth Day* (1967), is an intellectual thriller built around a murder case in southern Illinois; it won the National Book Award for fiction in 1968. Wilder's final novel, *Theophilus North* (1973), disappointed most reviewers and readers and stands as an ironically mild final statement of an exceptional literary career.

NOVELS BY WILDER

The Bridge of San Luis Rey (1927). Harper 1986 $5.95. ISBN 0-06-091341-X
The Eighth Day (1967). Carroll & Graf 1987 $4.95. ISBN 0-88184-339-3
The Ides of March (1948). Harper 1987 $7.95. ISBN 0-06-091403-3
Theophilus North (1973). Carroll & Graf 1988 $4.95. ISBN 0-88184-382-2

PLAY COLLECTION BY WILDER

Three Plays: Our Town (1938), *The Skin of Our Teeth* (1942), *and The Matchmaker* (1955). Harper 1985 $8.95. ISBN 0-06-091293-6

BOOKS ABOUT WILDER

Burbank, Rex J. *Thornton Wilder.* G. K. Hall 1978 $16.95. ISBN 0-8057-7223-5 Dated, but nonetheless useful, account of Wilder's life and work.
Castronovo, David. *Thornton Wilder.* Ungar 1986 $16.95. ISBN 0-8044-2119-6 A chronological study of Wilder's writings revealing the growth of his vision and artistry.
Harrison, Gilbert A. *The Enthusiastic: A Life of Thornton Wilder.* Fromm Intl 1986 $19.95. ISBN 0-88064-053-7 A candid account of Wilder, the creative performer vs. Wilder, the writer.

WILLIAMS, TENNESSEE   1911–1983

Tennessee Williams was born in Columbus, Missouri, in the rectory of the Episcopalian church where his grandfather was minister. When he was 12 years old, his family moved to St. Louis, where Williams had an unhappy childhood, enduring abuse by his father and constant worry about his emotionally disturbed sister. Williams briefly attended the University of Missouri but withdrew during the Depression to work as a clerk in a shoe company. After recovering from a mental breakdown, he enrolled at the University of Iowa, from which he graduated in 1938.

Williams's first plays were one-act works performed by student and amateur companies from 1936 to 1940. Many of these early plays were later collected in *Twenty-Seven Wagons Full of Cotton* (1946) and *Dragon Country* (1970). Williams's first major success was *The Glass Menagerie* (1944), a highly autobiographical play about the former Southern belle Amanda, who dreams of restoring her lost past by finding a suitor for her crippled daughter, while her son Tom dreams of escaping from the family problems. Williams's next play, *A Streetcar Named Desire* (1947), is the story of an emotionally fragile woman victimized by her brutish brother-in-law; it is considered Williams's masterpiece by many critics. Through the next two decades Williams produced a steady stream of successful plays, including *Cat on a Hot Tin Roof* (1955) and *Suddenly Last Summer* (1958).

Williams's plays focus on sensitive outcasts who are able to see the horror of the world but who nonetheless end up as its victims. Most often his central characters are lonely, vulnerable women, trapped in hellish lives, sustaining themselves by dreaming of a romantic past or a fanciful future. Williams has a gift for creating natural sounding yet poetic dialogue and a flair for comedy, especially ironic humor, and original theatrical effects.

Williams won Pulitzer prizes for *A Streetcar Named Desire* and *Cat on a Hot Tin Roof*. These two plays also won New York Drama Critics Circle Awards, as did *The Glass Menagerie* and *The Night of the Iguana* (1961).

NOVEL BY WILLIAMS

The Roman Spring of Mrs. Stone (1950). Ballantine 1985 $3.50. ISBN 0-345-32690-3

SHORT STORY COLLECTION BY WILLIAMS

Collected Stories (1985). New Directions 1985 $19.95. ISBN 0-8112-0952-0

PLAYS BY WILLIAMS

Camino Real (1953). New Directions 1970 $7.95. ISBN 0-8112-0218-6
Cat on a Hot Tin Roof (1955). Signet 1958 $3.95. ISBN 0-451-15869-5
Dragon Country: Eight Plays (1970). New Directions $7.95. ISBN 0-8112-0219-4
Four Plays: Summer and Smoke (1947), *Orpheus Descending* (1956), *Suddenly Last Summer* (1958),
  Period of Adjustment (1960). Signet 1976 $4.95. ISBN 0-451-52015-7
The Glass Menagerie (1944). Signet 1987 $3.50. ISBN 0-451-15170-4
A Streetcar Named Desire (1947). Signet 1986 $3.50. ISBN 0-451-15445-2
Sweet Bird of Youth (1959). New Directions 1975 $5.95. ISBN 0-8112-0596-7
Twenty-Seven Wagons Full of Cotton (1946). New Directions 1966 $7.95. ISBN 0-8112-
  0225-9

POETRY BY WILLIAMS

Androgyne, Mon Amour (1977). New Directions 1977 $8.50. ISBN 0-8112-0648-3
In the Winter of Cities (1956). New Directions 1964 $5.95. ISBN 0-8112-0222-4

BOOKS ABOUT WILLIAMS

Bloom, Harold (ed). *Tennessee Williams*. Chelsea 1987 $19.95. ISBN 0-87754-636-3
  Chronologically arranged collection of critical essays representing the modern
  critical responses to Williams and his plays.
Falk, Signi L. *Tennessee Williams*. G. K. Hall 1985 $15.95. ISBN 0-8057-7445-9 Scholarly
  examination of Williams's life and works.
Londre, Felicia H. *Tennessee Williams*. Ungar 1980 $16.95. ISBN 0-8044-2539-6 Lively,
  readable introduction to Williams and his work, showing the development of his
  art.

WILLIAMS, WILLIAM CARLOS 1883–1963

William Carlos Williams was born in Rutherford, New Jersey, the son of an English father and a Puerto Rican mother. He attended schools in Paris and Switzerland as well as in New Jersey. After graduating from Horace Mann High School in New York City, he went directly to medical school at the University of Pennsylvania. He received his medical degree in 1906 and became an intern at a New York City hospital. After his internship, he studied pediatrics for a year in Germany and then returned to begin his medical practice in Rutherford, New Jersey. While becoming one of the most influential American poets in the first half of this century, Williams continued to practice medicine until poor health forced him to retire in the mid-1950s.

Williams began publishing poetry in 1900 with a collection of verse he printed privately. Until the time of his death, Williams created poems that were both sensitive personal statements and technically imaginative constructions. He developed a concept called the "variable foot" that enabled him to produce lines of verse that sounded very much like ordinary American speech. His basic principle of "No ideas but in things" led him to find subjects for poems in ordinary objects like cold plums and wheelbarrows. Between 1946 and 1958, Williams published five books of his masterpiece, *Paterson,* a sequence of poems that traces the development of the New Jersey city from its founding by Alexander Hamilton in the eighteenth century to its industrial life in the middle of the twentieth century. Williams's influence on both the content and form of modern poetry has been substantial.

Williams also published prose: a collection of short stories called *The Farmers' Daughters* (1961); four novels; and a number of experimental plays, collected in *Many Loves and Other Plays* (1961).

NOVELS BY WILLIAMS

The Build-Up (1952). New Directions 1968 $9.95. ISBN 0-8112-0227-5
In the Money (1940). New Directions 1967 $7.45. ISBN 0-8112-0231-3
A Voyage to Pagany (1928). New Directions 1970 $8.25. ISBN 0-8112-0237-2
White Mule (1937). New Directions 1967 $9.95. ISBN 0-8112-0238-0

SHORT STORY COLLECTION BY WILLIAMS

The Farmers' Daughters (1961). New Directions 1961 $10.95. ISBN 0-8112-0228-3

POETRY BY WILLIAMS

Collected Poems of William Carlos Williams, 1909–1939. New Directions 1986 $35.00. ISBN 0-8112-0999-7
Collected Poems of William Carlos Williams, 1939–1962. New Directions 1988 $37.00. ISBN 0-8122-1063-4
Paterson, Books 1–5 (1946–1958). New Directions 1963 $8.95. ISBN 0-8112-0233-X

NONFICTION BY WILLIAMS

The Autobiography of William Carlos Williams. New Directions 1967 $10.95. ISBN 0-8112-0226-7 A candid and revealing self-portrait.
The William Carlos Williams Reader. New Directions 1969 $11.95. ISBN 0-8112-0239-9

BOOKS ABOUT WILLIAMS

Bloom, Harold (ed). *William Carlos Williams.* Chelsea 1986 $19.95. ISBN 0-87754-637-1 Collection of essays presenting a complete critical portrait of Williams.
Whitaker, Thomas. *William Carlos Williams.* G. K. Hall 1989 $18.95. ISBN 0-8057-7541-2 Comprehensive analysis of Williams's life and work with an emphasis on his poetry.

WOLFE, THOMAS   1900–1938

See also Wolfe, Vol. 1, Language Arts: Writing.

Thomas Wolfe was born in Asheville, North Carolina, where his father was a stonecutter and his mother ran a boarding house. A bright student, he was admitted to the University of North Carolina at age 15 and after receiving a B.A. there, went on to Harvard University for his master's degree. From 1924 to 1930, he taught at New York University, and then became a full-time writer.

As a novelist, Wolfe's one subject was his own life. In his short career he wrote one long autobiographical novel that was published in four parts, only two of them in his lifetime. The series begins with *Look Homeward, Angel* (1929), the story of a sensitive young man named Eugene Gant growing up in North Carolina. Wolfe's second book, *Of Time and the River* (1935), follows Gant as he goes to Harvard, has an unsuccessful love affair, and leaves for Europe. Shortly after the publication of this book, Wolfe changed publishers and, for legal reasons, had to change the name of his central character, who is now called George Webber. Wolfe had already written an enormous amount of material for the rest of this story, but it was still in rough form when he died as a result of complications from pneumonia.

Edward C. Ashwell, an editor at Harper and Company, Wolfe's new publisher, edited Wolfe's manuscripts into two final novels, *The Web and the Rock* (1939) and *You Can't Go Home Again* (1940). These final novels place George Webber in Europe before World War II, learning about the evils of Nazism and deciding to devote his career to writing novels of social protest.

In addition to these novels, Wolfe wrote some short stories that are collected in *From Death to Morning* (1935) and *The Hills Beyond* (1941). He also wrote several plays that were not very successful.

NOVELS BY WOLFE

Look Homeward, Angel (1929). Scribner's 1982 $8.94. ISBN 0-684-17616-5
Of Time and the River (1935). Scribner's 1971 $19.95. ISBN 0-684-16649-6
The Web and the Rock (1939). Harper 1986 $10.95. ISBN 0-06-019320-7
You Can't Go Home Again (1940). Harper 1973 $5.95. ISBN 0-06-080314-2

SHORT STORY COLLECTIONS BY WOLFE

The Complete Short Stories of Thomas Wolfe. Scribner's 1987 $24.95. ISBN 0-684-18743-4
From Death to Morning (1935). Scribner's 1935 $9.95. ISBN 0-684-71940-1

BOOKS ABOUT WOLFE

Bloom, Harold (ed). *Thomas Wolfe.* Chelsea 1987 $19.95. ISBN 0-87754-638-X Collection of eight essays probing the connection between Wolfe's life and work.
Donald, David H. *Look Homeward: A Life of Thomas Wolfe.* Little 1987 $24.95. ISBN 0-316-18952-9 Definitive and highly readable biography of Thomas Wolfe; contains photographs.
Evans, Elizabeth. *Thomas Wolfe.* Ungar 1984 $16.95. ISBN 0-8044-2188-9 Traces the influences, stylistic elements, and themes in Wolfe's novels.

WRIGHT, RICHARD   1908–1960

Richard Wright was born on a plantation near Natchez, Mississippi. His father left the family when Wright was only five years old, and he was raised first by his mother and then by a series of relatives. What little schooling he had ended with his graduation from ninth grade in Memphis, Tennessee. At age 15, he started work in Memphis, and later worked in Chicago before traveling across the country supporting himself with odd jobs.

When Wright finally returned to Chicago, he got a job with the federal Writer's Project, a government-supported arts program. He was quite successful, winning a $500 prize from a magazine for the best fiction written by a participant in that program. In Chicago he was also introduced to leftist politics and became a member of the Communist Party. In 1937, Wright left Chicago for New York, where he became Harlem editor for the Communist national newspaper, *The Daily Worker,* and where he met future novelist, Ralph Ellison. (*See* Ellison, Vol. 1, American Literature: The Twentieth Century.)

Wright became a celebrated author with the publication of *Native Son* (1940), a novel he wrote in only eight months. Based on the actual case of a young black murderer of a white woman, it was one of the first of the modern black protest novels, violent and shocking in its scenes of cruelty, hunger, rape, murder, flight, and prison. The novel brought Wright both fame and financial security. He followed it with his autobiography, *Black Boy* (1945), which was also successful. In 1942, Wright and his wife broke with the Communist Party, and in 1947, they moved to France, where Wright lived the rest of his life. His novel *The Outsider* (1953) is based on his experiences as a member of the Communist Party.

Wright is regarded as a major modern American writer, one of the first black writers to reach a large white audience, and thereby raise the level of national awareness of the continuing problem of racism in America. In many respects Wright paved the way for all the black writers who followed him.

NOVELS BY WRIGHT

The Long Dream (1958). Harper 1987 $5.95. ISBN 0-06-080864-1
Native Son (1940). Harper 1989 $4.95. ISBN 0-06-080977-9
The Outsider (1953). Harper 1989 $4.95. ISBN 0-06-080976-0

SHORT STORY COLLECTION BY WRIGHT

Uncle Tom's Children (1938). Harper 1989 $4.50. ISBN 0-06-080988-4

NONFICTION BY WRIGHT

*American Hunger (1977). Harper 1983 $7.95. ISBN 0-06-090991-9 Continuation of *Black Boy,* published posthumously.
*Black Boy (1945). Harper 1989 $4.95. ISBN 0-06-080987-6 Wright's autobiography covering his early years in the South.
Eight Men (1961). Thunder's Mouth 1987 $9.95.
White Man, Listen! (1957). Greenwood 1978 $35.00. ISBN 0-313-20533-7

BOOKS ABOUT WRIGHT

Bloom, Harold (ed). *Richard Wright.* Chelsea 1987 $24.95. ISBN 0-87754-639-8 Eleven excellent essays dealing with Wright's novels and short stories, as well as his role in the black literary tradition.
Felgar, Robert. *Richard Wright.* G. K. Hall 1980 $14.95. ISBN 0-8057-7320-7 Excellent general introduction to Wright's life and works.
*Urban, Joan. *Richard Wright.* Chelsea 1989 $17.95. ISBN 1-55546-618-1 Excellent introduction to Wright for young adult readers.

ZINDEL, PAUL 1936–

Paul Zindel was born in Staten Island in New York City. His father, a police officer, deserted the family when Zindel was only two years old. His mother worked at a variety of jobs to support Zindel and his older sister, but most often served as a live-in nurse to terminally ill patients. As a result, the family moved once or twice every year.

In his junior year in high school, Zindel contracted tuberculosis and had to spend a year and a half in a sanitarium where he was the only young person

in a world of sickly adults. After graduating from high school, Zindel entered
Wagner College on Staten Island, where he studied chemistry and also took
courses in creative writing. One of his teachers was playwright Edward Albee.
(*See* Albee, Vol. 1, American Literature: The Twentieth Century.)

After graduation, Zindel continued at Wagner for an additional year, earning an M.A. in education that enabled him to become a high school chemistry
teacher. He taught for 10 years, writing in his spare time, until the success of
his first play, *The Effect of Gamma Rays on Man-in-the-Moon Marigolds* (1965), enabled him to devote himself to writing full time.

Ironically, it was Zindel's success as a playwright that turned him into a
novelist. A book editor who saw *The Effect of Gamma Rays on Man-in-the-Moon
Marigolds* suggested to Zindel that he write novels for young adults. The result
was *The Pigman* (1968), a book that helped revolutionize the entire field of
young-adult fiction. Although it is over 20 years old, the book is still widely
read and has sold well over 1 million copies. In the years since *The Pigman,*
Zindel has written 10 more books for young adults and has established himself
as one of the leading writers in this field. He has also continued to write plays
for adult audiences.

Zindel's success as an author of young-adult fiction rests on his ability to
draw from his own experiences as an unhappy child and as a high school
teacher to "get inside" the minds of young people and express their concerns
and emotions. Zindel writes with sensitivity, honesty, and energy, and develops characters with whom young adults can identify.

NOVELS BY ZINDEL

The Amazing and Death-Defying Diary of Eugene Dingman (1989). Bantam 1989 $2.95. ISBN
0-553-27768-5 The diary of a 15-year-old boy who spends a summer as a waiter
at a ritzy Adirondack resort.

A Begonia for Miss Applebaum (1989). Harper 1989 $12.70. ISBN 0-06-026877-8 Teenag-
ers Henry and Zelda find their lives enriched by a favorite teacher, Miss Applebaum.

Confessions of a Teenage Baboon (1977). Bantam 1989 $2.95. ISBN 0-553-27190-3 A 15-
year-old misfit learns from another misfit how to take responsibility for his life.

The Girl Who Wanted a Boy (1981). Bantam 1985 $2.95. ISBN 0-553-26486-9 A 15-year-
old girl is a scientific whiz but can't figure out how to get boys interested in her.

Harry and Hortense at Hormone High (1984). Bantam 1985 $2.95. ISBN 0-553-25175-9 Two
high school students find a hero in a boy who says he is the reincarnation of the
Greek hero Icarus.

I Never Loved Your Mind (1971). Bantam 1972 $2.95. ISBN 0-553-27323-X Two high
school drop-outs search for something they can believe in.

My Darling, My Hamburger (1969). Bantam 1989 $2.95. ISBN 0-553-27324-8 Four con-
fused high school seniors look for intimacy and acceptance.

Pardon Me, You're Stepping on My Eyeball! (1976). Bantam 1983 $2.95. ISBN 0-553-
26690-X An emotionally fragile young man and the girl who helps him come to
grips with reality.

The Pigman (1968). Bantam 1983 $2.95. ISBN 0-553-26321-8 Two lonely high school
students befriend an old man.

The Pigman's Legacy (1980). Bantam 1984 $2.95. ISBN 0-553-26599-7 Sequel to *The
Pigman,* in which John and Lorraine discover their love for each other.

The Undertaker's Gone Bananas (1978). Bantam 1979 $2.95. ISBN 0-553-27189-X Two
high school students believe that their neighbor has murdered his wife.

PLAY BY ZINDEL

The Effect of Gamma Rays on Man-in-the-Moon Marigolds (1965). Bantam 1984 $2.95. ISBN
0-553-28028-7 Dramatizes the relationship of an eccentric, embittered woman
and her two daughters.

BOOK ABOUT ZINDEL

Forman, Jack J. *Presenting Paul Zindel.* G. K. Hall 1988 $18.95. ISBN 0-8057-8206-0 First full-length study of Paul Zindel; presents never-before published biographical information from interviews and a complete analysis of Zindel's works.

WORLD LITERATURE

Works in the World Literature section have been listed in two ways. In the listings of French, German, Italian, and Spanish and Latin American literature, publications in the native language or in bilingual editions have been listed, as well as those in English translation. For example, under French Language and Literature, the works of novelist Gustave Flaubert are first listed as "Novels by Flaubert in English Translation" and then as "Novels by Flaubert in French." In the case of these five literatures, as well as in Classical Greek Literature and Latin Literature, translators have been listed whenever possible. Other literatures, written in languages that are rarely taught at the junior or senior high school levels, include only bibliographic listings of works in English or in English translation.

For each of the four foreign languages commonly taught at these grade levels—French, Italian, Spanish, and German—there is a brief summary of the development and major characteristics of the language, followed by a list of books about the history and grammar of the language. The books listed for these four languages are intended to supplement those normally used in courses in each language and, therefore, do not include dictionaries or textbooks.

Black-figured Lekythos with women working wool.   Greek (Attic) terracotta oil jug attributed to the Amasis Painter (c. 540 B.C.).   Courtesy of The Metropolitan Museum of Art, Fletcher Fund, 1931. (31.11.10)

CLASSICAL GREEK LITERATURE

The thought and literature of ancient Greece lies at the very foundation of Western culture. From Geoffrey Chaucer's fourteenth-century poem, *Troilus and Criseyde* (*see* Chaucer, Vol. 1, British Literature: The Early Years) to John Updike's twentieth-century novel, *The Centaur* (*see* Updike, Vol. 1, American Literature: The Twentieth Century), all of Western literature—British, American, and European—abounds with references to the ideas, stories, and characters that sprang from the minds of the wonderfully imaginative people who lived in Greece 2,500 years ago.

The literature of ancient Greece grew directly out of its mythology. The stories of the 12 gods who lived on Mount Olympus and ruled the human race were an essential part of Greek life. So too were the tales of heroes of long ago—Hercules, Achilles, Odysseus, and all the other larger-than-life figures who had fought great battles and performed mighty deeds. The Greeks never tired of telling these stories, and their early lyric poetry, and later their drama, were filled with these accounts. They often told the same stories over and over, each time with a slightly different interpretation.

Unfortunately, what remains today of ancient Greek literature is only a tiny fraction of what once existed. Over the centuries, much has been lost or destroyed. Because Greek poetry was intended to be sung, not read silently, much of it was never written down. A great deal of what was written was destroyed in wars or fires, or simply allowed to decay as the Greek civilization went into decline. Of the many thousands of lyric poems composed over the centuries of Greek civilization, only a handful of these beautiful songs of love, death, joy, and sorrow remain. Many lyrics were composed to be sung by a chorus in celebration of such occasions as weddings or a god's feast day. It was from these choral poems that Greek drama developed.

One particular form of lyric poetry, called the dithyramb, was sung in honor of the god Dionysus during his festival each spring. At the festival Greek poets composed dithyrambs and competed in contests to see which poems were the best. Early in the sixth century BC, at the festival of Dionysus in Athens, a poet named Thespis of Icaria conceived the idea of having one singer leave the chorus to recite a dialogue with the remaining members. This "conversation" between actor and chorus was the beginning of Greek drama.

Later a poet named Aeschylus added a second actor to the dialogue, turning these actor-chorus poems into the first plays. The subjects of these first plays were taken from Greek mythology. Although the audience was already familiar with the stories, each play differed from the others in its interpretation of the familiar events and the presentation of the characters. These dramas, called *tragedies,* were serious plays about suffering, courage, and fate, and they inevitably ended with the destruction of the hero.

Greek *comedies*, on the other hand, were not based on myth, but dealt instead with daily life, although frequently in a fantastic or satirical manner. The only remaining examples of Greek comedy are the plays of Aristophanes, vulgar or bawdy plays that satirize political leaders and contemporary customs.

The fifth century BC saw the development of prose into an art form, capable of not only telling stories but of expressing profound ideas and moving people to action. The great speakers and thinkers of the time were honored both for what they said and how they said it. Elegance of expression became a prized art.

In the final period of Greek literature, dramatic comedy shifted away from the political and social satire characteristic of Aristophanes to concerns about family relationships, love, and marriage. Prose was used more widely to tell stories as well as to record history and philosophy. New forms of lyric poetry developed.

COLLECTIONS OF GREEK LITERATURE IN ENGLISH TRANSLATION

Auden, W. H. (ed). *The Portable Greek Reader.* Penguin 1977 $9.95. ISBN 0-14-015039-0 Includes works by 34 authors representing all of Greek literature and culture, comprising portions of more than 50 major writings.

Dover, K. J. *Ancient Greek Literature.* Oxford Univ Pr 1980 $9.95. ISBN 0-19-289124-3 Historical survey of Greek Literature from 700 BC to AD 500.

Grant, Michael (ed). *Greek Literature: An Anthology.* Penguin 1977 $6.95. ISBN 0-14-044323-1 Well-chosen selections covering the whole range of Greek poetry and prose.

Hadas, Moses (ed). *Greek Drama.* Bantam 1984 $3.95. ISBN 0-553-21221-4 Contains *Agamemnon* and *Eumenides* by Aeschylus; *Antigone, Oedipus the King,* and *Philoctetes* by Sophocles; *The Frogs* by Aristophanes; *Hippolytus, Medea,* and *Trojan Women* by Euripedes.

Howatson, M. C. *The Oxford Companion to Classical Literature.* Oxford Univ Pr 1989 $39.95. ISBN 0-19-866121-5 A useful reference work on Greek writers, works, and related subjects.

Jay, Peter (ed). *The Greek Anthology.* Penguin 1982 $6.95. ISBN 0-14-044285-5 Contains 850 Greek and Hellenic epitaphs, jokes, satires, pastoral epigrams, and poems of love and friendship arranged chronologically from the seventh century BC to the sixth century AD.

Oates, Whitney J., and Eugene O'Neill, Jr. (eds). *Seven Famous Greek Plays.* Vintage 1966 $7.95. ISBN 0-394-70125-9 Contains *Agamemnon* and *Prometheus Bound* by Aeschylus; *Oedipus the King* and *Antigone* by Sophocles; *Medea* and *Alcestis* by Euripedes; *The Frogs* by Aristophanes.

AESCHYLUS 524 BC–456 BC

Aeschylus was born in Eleusis, Greece, of a noble family. He fought at the battle of Marathon, Greece, where a small band of Greek soldiers heroically defeated the invading Persians (the territory of ancient Persia is today part of the country of Iran). The same love of country he showed at Marathon is evident in his surviving plays, all of which express strong patriotic sentiments.

Aeschylus' first triumph as a poet came at the festival of Dionysus in Athens in 485 BC, when he won the prize for tragedy. He went on to write between 60 and 90 plays (the exact number is disputed by scholars) and to win 12 more victories in dramatic competitions. Of these plays, only seven have survived in complete form. *The Orestia,* the only trilogy (group of three plays) in Greek drama that survives intact, includes *Agamemnon, The Libation Bearers,* and *The Eumenides* (or *The Furies*). His other four plays are *The Persians, Seven Against Thebes, The Supplicants,* and *Prometheus Bound.*

In 468 BC, after Aeschylus was defeated in a dramatic competition by Sophocles (*see* Sophocles, Vol. 1, World Literature: Classical Greek Literature), he left Athens, perhaps out of bitterness at his loss or perhaps because he had been accused of revealing religious secrets.

Aeschylus called his plays "dry scraps from Homer's banquet" because his plots and solemn language are derived from Homer, the great poet who wrote the epic poems the *Iliad* and the *Odyssey* (*see* Homer, Vol. 1, World Literature: Classical Greek Literature). But in many respects Aeschylus far outstrips Homer. The grandeur of his vision and the sweep of his tragedy go far beyond

Homer, as does the tragic dignity of his language. Because of his patriotism and belief in divine providence, there is a deep sense of order and justice in his plays. Despite the passion and power of his characters, they cannot pit their wills against those of the gods and succeed. Ultimately, divine justice prevails.

Aeschylus is aptly called the father of Greek tragedy. His introduction of the second actor made possible drama as it is known today, since now the two actors could speak to each other and enact their individual emotions. Playwrights who followed Aeschylus imitated his costumes, dances, spectacular effects, long descriptions, choral refrains, and dialogue.

PLAYS BY AESCHYLUS IN ENGLISH TRANSLATION

The Orestia: Agamemnon, The Libation Bearers, The Eumenides. W. B. Stanford (ed). Robert Fagles (tr). Penguin 1984 $3.95. ISBN 0-14-044333-9
Prometheus Bound and Other Plays. Philip Vellacott (tr). Penguin 1961 $4.50. ISBN 0-14-044112-3

BOOKS ABOUT AESCHYLUS

Conacher, D. J. *Aeschylus' Orestia: A Literary Commentary.* Univ of Toronto Pr 1987 $35.00. ISBN 0-8020-5716-0 Well-written, scholarly commentary on the *Orestia* by a respected scholar; too difficult for most students but a useful text for teachers.
Herington, John. *Aeschylus.* Yale Univ Pr 1986 $7.95. ISBN 0-300-03643-4 Excellent introduction to Aeschylus' times, his plays, and the early Athenian theater.
Spatz, Lois. *Aeschylus.* G. K. Hall 1982 $18.95. ISBN 0-8057-6522-0 Good general introduction to Aeschylus' plays and the period; includes chronology and bibliography.

AESOP   *c.* 620 BC-*c.* 560 BC

Very little is known about Aesop, the teller of fables. It is known that he lived during the second half of the sixth century BC, and references by Greek comic playwright Aristophanes (*see* Aristophanes, Vol. 1, World Literature: Classical Greek Literature) indicate that fables bearing Aesop's name were popular around the end of the fifth century BC.

Supposedly, Aesop was a slave, perhaps from the Greek region of Phrygia, who was later given his freedom. Legend places him on the Greek island of Samos from where he went to the court of King Croesus of Lydia, Greece, and became a valued messenger of the king. On one of his missions to the Greek shrine at Delphi, he supposedly angered the priests with his blasphemous wit and was thrown over a cliff to his death.

There is considerable doubt about how many, if any, of the fables attributed to Aesop were actually written by him. Many of their sources have been traced to earlier literature, suggesting that Aesop was more a collector and recorder of tales than an original composer of them. The collections known as *Aesop's Fables* were assembled in the second or third century AD, although the bulk of the material must have evolved several centuries earlier.

Aesop's stories of animals that talk and act like humans were very popular during the Middle Ages because of the moral instruction they provide. They have remained popular in modern times, mostly as stories for young children.

COLLECTION BY AESOP IN ENGLISH TRANSLATION

Fables of Aesop. S. A. Hanford (tr). Penguin 1954 $4.95. ISBN 0-14-044043-7 Collection of 207 very short tales about animals, each one illustrating a moral lesson.

BOOKS ABOUT AESOP

Jacobs, Joseph (ed). *The Fables of Aesop* (1889). Schocken 1966 $5.95. ISBN 0-8052-0138-6 Careful account of the transmission of the fables from antiquity through the Middle Ages to modern times.

Perry, Ben E., and Richard M. Dorson (eds). *Aesopica: A Series of Texts Relating to Aesop or Ascribed to Him or Closely Connected with the Literary Tradition That Bears His Name* (1952). Ayer 1981 $74.50. ISBN 0-405-13337-5 Valuable source book containing ancient testimonies about Aesop.

ARISTOPHANES   *c.* 448 BC–*c.* 388 BC

Almost nothing is known of Aristophanes' personal life except that he had three sons, all of whom, like their father, wrote comic plays. Eleven complete plays by Aristophanes and a few fragments of other plays of his are all that is left of the early Greek drama known as Old Comedy. These few examples, however, are enough to establish Aristophanes as a master comic writer.

Aristophanes' plays have three qualities that appear at first to be in conflict with one another. Their poetic language, especially that which is spoken by the chorus, is extremely beautiful; the plays preach the virtues of old-fashioned decency and morality; and the plays are grossly obscene and vulgar. About this last characteristic two things must be remembered: these plays were presented as part of the Festival of Dionysus, an occasion, much like the modern Mardi Gras, in which ordinary standards of behavior were suspended; and topics and language considered vulgar today were not necessarily considered so in ancient Greece.

Unlike the writers of tragedy, who dealt with lofty subjects and the deeds of kings and gods, comic dramatists dealt with the daily concerns of ordinary human beings. Thus, the plays of Aristophanes provide a revealing look at Greek culture and life. They show how Athenian theatergoers thought about war, taxes, political leaders, votes for women, education, contemporary literature, and a host of other topics that concern ordinary citizens. On all of these subjects, Aristophanes was always a strong conservative; he inevitably took the position that "it was better in the old days."

PLAYS BY ARISTOPHANES IN ENGLISH TRANSLATION

Four Plays. Meridian 1974 $5.95. ISBN 0-452-00717-8 Includes *The Birds, The Clouds, The Frogs,* and *Lysistrata.*

The Frogs and Other Plays. David Barrett (tr). Penguin 1964 $3.95. ISBN 0-14-044152-2 Includes *The Wasps, The Poet and the Women,* and *The Frogs.*

The Knights, The Peace, The Birds, The Assembly-Women, Wealth. Penguin 1974 $3.95. ISBN 0-14-044332-0

BOOKS ABOUT ARISTOPHANES

Dover, K. J. *Aristophanic Comedy.* Univ of California Pr 1972 $14.00. ISBN 0-520-02211-4 Useful and detailed analysis of the important characteristics and techniques of Aristophanes' works.

Lord, Louis E. *Aristophanes: His Plays and His Influence.* Cooper Square (repr of 1932 ed) $27.50. ISBN 0-8154-0140-X Scholarly and interesting discussion of the individual plays and of Aristophanes' influence on the art of comedy.

EURIPIDES   *c.* 485 BC–*c.* 406 BC

Euripides is the last of the three great classical Greek tragedians, coming after Aeschylus and Sophocles. (*See* Aeschylus *and* Sophocles, Vol. 1, World Literature: Classical Greek Literature.) Born in the area of ancient Greece known as

Attica, he lived most of his life in Athens, Greece. His first play was produced in 455 BC, and in 451 BC, he won the prize for tragedy, the first of five prizes that he would win during his career.

Out of some 92 plays that Euripides is known to have written, only 17 have survived in complete form. Euripedes seems not to have taken much part in public life, and he was generally moderate in his political views. Toward the end of his life, he grew weary of Athens and moved to Macedonia, a region in today's country of Yugoslavia. There he died at the court of King Archelaus.

Euripides' reputation has grown steadily over the years. In his own lifetime his plays were not among the most popular, and Aristophanes (*see* Aristophanes, Vol. 1, World Literature: Classical Greek Literature) ridiculed him in two of his comedies. However, after Euripides' death, his plays were performed more often than those of either Aeschylus or Sophocles. When Gilbert Murray's translations made Euripides available to the English-speaking public in the early twentieth century, readers were surprised to find how modern his plays seemed. His plots are far more exciting than those of other Greek tragedians, and his feeling for human pain and suffering, particularly that of women, is much closer to modern sensibilities than that of his contemporaries.

Euripides is responsible for several important technical advances in the development of the drama. He separated the chorus from the action of the play, paving the way for its later elimination. He developed a number of plot devices that have since become commonplace: the separation of infants from their rightful parents; the identification of characters by items of jewelry such as rings or necklaces; and surprise revelations of key characters' identities. He also used simple and direct language, unlike the lofty poetry of Aeschylus and Sophocles, which makes his dialogue sound more believable to modern ears.

Euripides has been criticized for his use of the *deus ex machina,* a plot device that has a god suddenly appear in the final scene to sort things out and resolve all problems. He has also been criticized for shortening the prologue, an introductory speech by the chorus that provided the audience with the background of the play. His concern, however, was with the passions of his characters, their problems and suffering. Providing background and plausible endings was less important to him.

PLAYS BY EURIPIDES IN ENGLISH TRANSLATION

Euripides: Four Tragedies, No. 1. David Greene and Richmond Lattimore (eds). Univ of Chicago Pr 1955 $6.50. ISBN 0-226-30780-8 Includes *Alcestis, Medea, Heracleidae,* and *Hippolytus.*

Euripides: Four Tragedies, No. 2. David Green and Richmond Lattimore (eds). Univ of Chicago Pr 1956 $6.50. ISBN 0-226-30781-6 Includes *Cyclops, Heracles, Iphigenia in Tauris,* and *Helen.*

Euripides: Four Tragedies, No. 3. David Greene and Richmond Lattimore (eds). Univ of Chicago Pr 1958 $6.50. ISBN 0-226-30782-4 Includes *Hecuba, Andromache, The Trojan Women,* and *Ion.*

Euripides: Four Tragedies, No. 4. David Greene and Richmond Lattimore (eds). Univ of Chicago Pr 1968 $6.50. ISBN 0-226-30783-2 Includes *Rhesus, The Suppliant Women, Orestes,* and *Iphigenia in Aulis.*

Euripides: Four Tragedies, No. 5. David Greene and Richard Lattimore (eds). Univ of Chicago Pr 1969 $6.50. ISBN 0-226-30784-0 Includes *Electra, The Phoenician Women,* and *The Bacchae.*

BOOKS ABOUT EURIPIDES

Halleran, Michael R. *Stagecraft in Euripides.* Barnes 1985 $27.50. ISBN 0-389-20512-3 Comprehensive, if somewhat technical, discussion of Euripides' stagecraft, with detailed studies of *Heracles, Troades,* and *Ion.*

Meagher, Robert. *Mortal Vision: The Wisdom of Euripides.* St. Martin's 1989 $29.95. ISBN 0-312-02720-6 Clear and well-written account of the principal themes in Euripides' plays; includes numerous comments on individual plays.

Michelini, Ann Noris. *Euripides and the Tragic Tradition.* Univ of Wisconsin Pr 1988 $32.75. ISBN 0-299-10760-4 Scholarly study of Euripides' central themes and his role as a commentaor on the culture of his time; includes discussions of *Hecuba, Electra, Herakles,* and *Hipplolytus.*

HOMER   *c.* 700 BC

Homer is generally regarded as the father of European literature. The Greeks believed that both the *Iliad* and the *Odyssey* were composed by a blind poet named Homer, but they were unsure of his date or place of birth. Seven cities in and around ancient Greece claimed him: Athens, Argos, Chios, Colophon, Rhodes, Salamis, and Smyrna. Today, it is conjectured that Homer was an Ionian, probably from Chios, and that he lived between 800 BC and 700 BC.

Scholars have long argued over whether one person composed both the poems traditionally ascribed to Homer, and the issue is far from settled. At the moment, however, there is general agreement that the *Iliad* was composed by a single author and that that author may well have composed the *Odyssey* also. Both poems were probably composed to be sung and were not written down until long after their composer's death. All of this, however, remains largely guesswork and is not likely ever to be definitively settled.

The *Iliad,* considered the earlier of Homer's two epic poems, tells the story of the Greek war with Troy, or Ilium, an ancient city in today's country of Turkey. The *Iliad* focuses on two heroes, the Greek Achilles and the Trojan Hector. The story begins in the middle of the Greek siege of the city of Troy and moves very rapidly toward its tragic conclusion (the total defeat of the Trojans and the burning of Troy). The language of the poem is magnificent, filled with beautiful images and metaphors drawn from nature and from Greek culture. In many ways the poetry of this epic has never been surpassed.

The *Odyssey,* which may have been written in Homer's old age, tells of the 10 years of wanderings and final homecoming of the Greek hero Odysseus after his participation in the Trojan War. Unlike the tragic *Iliad,* the *Odyssey* is largely an adventure story with comic overtones and a happy ending. Like the *Iliad* however, it is noteworthy for its beautiful poetry, its simplicity of language, and the nobility of its central characters.

The ancient Greeks revered the poems of Homer, considering them the sacred record of their cultural history and a source of wisdom. Homer's poetry shaped Greek values and Greek literature throughout the most glorious period in Greek history. The concept of the hero; the forms of tragedy and comedy; the techniques of beginning a story in the middle, of deliberately delaying the action for dramatic effect, of gods or divine forces interfering in human events; and the use of the flashback (going back to tell an earlier part of the story) all grew out of Homer's works.

POETRY BY HOMER IN ENGLISH TRANSLATION

The Iliad. W. H. D. Rouse (tr). Mentor 1975 $2.95. ISBN 0-451-62723-7 Story of the Trojan War told in an exceptionally smooth and easy-to-read prose translation.

The Odyssey. W. H. D. Rouse (tr). Mentor 1946 $3.50. ISBN 0-451-62805-5 Widely acclaimed prose translation; includes an index of pronunciation and an appendix on Homer's language.

BOOKS ABOUT HOMER

Bloom, Harold (ed). *Homer.* Chelsea 1986 $24.50. ISBN 0-87754-723-8 Collection of critical essays that aid the study of Homer's poems.
Michalopoulos, Andre. *Homer.* G. K. Hall 1975 $16.95. ISBN 0-8057-6432-X Good general introduction to Homer's epics; also contains a discussion of the authorship question.

SOPHOCLES   *c.* 496 BC–*c.* 406 BC

Sophocles was born to a wealthy family at Colonus, a suburb of Athens, Greece. As a youth, Sophocles was admired for his beauty and musical skill. However, he had to abandon his plans to become an actor because of a weak voice. Instead, he served Athens faithfully as a treasurer and a military general at a time when the city was expanding its influence. .

Sophocles won his first dramatic prize in 468 BC, defeating Aeschylus (*see* Aeschylus, Vol. 1, World Literature: Classical Greek Literature) at the great festival of Dionysus in Athens. He went on to become one of the most honored Athenian dramatists, winning the first prize for drama about 20 times and never falling below second place. Sophocles wrote approximately 123 plays, of which only seven complete tragedies remain.

Sophocles brought Greek tragedy to a higher, more complex level of development. He added a third actor, opening up new possibilities for both plot and dialogue; he also increased the size of the chorus; introduced painted scenery; made each play in a trilogy independent from the other two plays, shifted the focus from religious to more philosophical issues; and brought the majestic language and heroic characters somewhat closer to everyday life.

Before Sophocles there was little plot development in Greek tragedy. From the outset the hero was doomed by the will of the gods, and events moved steadily toward their inevitable conclusion. By introducing the idea of a *tragic flaw* in the character of the hero—a defect that contributes to his or her undoing—Sophocles shifted some of the responsibility for the outcome on to the heroes themselves. This innovation established an element of uncertainty in the plot and permitted the introduction of unexpected discoveries and surprises. Because Sophocles' characters are at least partly responsible for the tragedy that befalls them and because they accept their fate heroically, they gain even more sympathy from the audience than the heroes of the earlier tragedies.

Sophocles' best-known play is *Oedipus Rex* (Oedipus the King) (c. 429), which the Greek philosopher Aristotle considered the perfect tragedy. This story of a doomed prince who unknowingly kills his father and marries his own mother has been an inspiration to playwrights and a powerful experience for audiences for more than 2,000 years.

PLAYS BY SOPHOCLES IN ENGLISH TRANSLATION

Electra and Other Plays. E. F. Watling (tr). Penguin 1953 $3.50. ISBN 0-14-044028-3 Includes *Ajax, Electra, Women of Trachis,* and *Philoctetes.*
The Three Theban Plays: Antigone, Oedipus the King, Oedipus at Colonus. Robert Fagles (tr). Penguin 1984 $3.50. ISBN 0-14-044425-4

BOOKS ABOUT SOPHOCLES

Bloom, Harold (ed). *Sophocles.* Chelsea 1990 $26.50. ISBN 1-55546-323-1 Collection of critical essays by distinguished scholars examining Sophocles' works from a variety of perspectives.

Scodel, Ruth. *Sophocles.* G. K. Hall 1980 $17.95. ISBN 0-8057-6578-6 General introduction to Sophocles' work with a valuable discussion of the basic elements of Greek drama.

GREEK MYTHOLOGY

Greek mythology was in many ways unlike anything that had come before it. First of all it was a human mythology. All the other ancient civilizations had imagined their gods to be totally unlike anything seen on earth: part animal–part human or creatures with the features of many different animals, for example. The Greeks, however, imagined their gods to look like human beings—often physically perfect human beings, strong and beautiful.

Greek gods also acted like humans. They were jealous of one another or of humans who tried to be too much like them or who stole the affections of their loved ones. The Greek gods argued and fought among themselves. They drank too much and were unfaithful to their husbands and wives. To the Greeks, their gods might be powerful and fearsome, even unpredictable, but they were always understandable.

There is very little of the supernatural in Greek mythology. There are no ghosts or spirits. The gods could change shape or assume different forms, but they were real, natural forms—an animal, a waterfall, a tree. Nor did the Greeks look to the stars as guiding influences in their lives. There is very little magic and almost nothing mystical in Greek mythology. For the most part, these are stories of explanation, attempts to describe how natural things came to be and why people behave as they do.

Likewise, Greek myths do not present a divinely revealed code of ethical behavior; they have no equivalent of the Ten Commandments or the Sermon on the Mount. In fact, the opposite is true. The gods were expected to follow the same rules of behavior in their heaven that the Greeks followed on earth.

Nonetheless, myths were of enormous importance to the Greeks. They provided a common heritage and a cultural bond that helped hold the society together. They also provided a means by which the Greeks could identify and describe the place of humans in the universe. Further, they established the values that distinguished a worthwhile life from a wasted one. Without understanding Greek mythology, it was not then—and is not now—possible to understand Greek culture or literature.

The earliest record of the myths is in the works of Homer, which date to approximately 1000 BC. A more direct telling of the myths appears around 700 BC in the *Theogony* of Hesiod, in which Hesiod attempts to incorporate all of mythology into a single, ordered work, including both mythical genealogies and anecdotes about the gods. Much of what is now known about Greek mythology comes also from the plays of the great Greek tragedians Aeschylus, Sophocles, and Euripides, and from the poems of Pindar around the end of the sixth century BC.

BOOKS ABOUT GREEK MYTHOLOGY

Asimov, Isaac. *Words from the Myths.* Signet 1969 $4.50. ISBN 0-451-16686-8 Retelling of the Greek myths, each explained in terms of its influence on modern language and life.

Bulfinch, Thomas. *Bulfinch's Mythology* (1855). Crowell 1970 $17.95. ISBN 0-690-57260-3 Standard retelling of the myths, originally written in 1855 and somewhat dated in language.

*Bulfinch, Thomas. *Bulfinch's Mythology.* Edmund Fuller (ed). Dell 1959 $4.95. ISBN 0-440-30845-3 Abridged edition of the standard work, especially useful for young readers.

*Evslin, Bernard. *Heroes, Gods and Monsters of the Greek Myths.* Bantam 1984 $4.50. ISBN 0-553-25920-2 Twenty-six tales from Greek mythology retold in simple and dramatic language.

*Gibson, Michael. *Gods, Men, and Monsters from the Greek Myths.* Schocken 1989 $15.95. ISBN 0-805-20966-2 Twenty-six myths retold in modern language; includes the story of the Trojan War; color illustrations and maps.

Grant, Michael. *Myths of the Greeks and Romans.* Mentor 1964 $5.95. ISBN 0-451-62693-1 Retells the myths and describes their impact on creative arts through the ages.

*Graves, Robert. *Greek Gods and Heroes.* Dell 1965 $3.25. ISBN 0-440-93221-1 Very readable retelling of the myths and legends by a famous novelist and poet.

Graves, Robert. *The Greek Myths.* 2 vols. Penguin 1955. Vol. 1 $4.95. ISBN 0-14-020508-X Vol. 2 $4.95. ISBN 0-14-020509-8 Retells 170 different myths and records variations of each that help to determine religious or historical meanings; includes full references to classical sources as well as indexes and commentaries on each myth.

Hamilton, Edith. *Mythology.* Mentor 1953 $4.95. ISBN 0-451-62803-9 Highly respected and readable retelling and explanation of the myths; contains useful genealogical charts.

Holme, Bryan (ed). *Myths of Greece and Rome.* Penguin 1981 $19.95. ISBN 0-14-005643-2 Reworking of the standard *Bulfinch's Mythology* accompanied by many illustrations from ancient and modern art.

Kirk, G. S. *The Nature of Greek Myths.* Penguin 1975 $6.95. ISBN 0-14-021783-5 Examination of the nature of mythology followed by an account of the Greek myths and a discussion of the transition from the age of myth to that of philosophy.

*Renault, Mary. *The Bull from the Sea.* Random 1975 $4.95. ISBN 0-394-71504-7 Third book in the Theseus trilogy; all three novels are highly readable and scholarly.

*Renault, Mary. *The King Must Die.* Random 1988 $6.95. ISBN 0-394-75104-3 Second book in the Theseus trilogy; probably the best.

*Renault, Mary. *The Last of the Wine.* Random 1975 $4.95. ISBN 0-394-71653-1 First novel in a trilogy based on the myth of Theseus, the hero of Athens.

Rose, H. J. *A Handbook of Greek Mythology.* Dutton 1959 $8.95. ISBN 0-525-48414-0 Authoritative, abundantly annotated guide to the myths; includes a bibliography and indexes.

Rouse, W. H. D. *Gods, Heroes, and Men of Ancient Greece.* Mentor 1957 $4.95. ISBN 0-451-62800-4 Standard retelling of the myths by a classical scholar; includes useful charts and an index.

Tripp, Edward. *The Meridian Handbook of Classical Mythology.* Meridian 1974 $12.95. ISBN 0-452-00927-8 Comprehensive retelling of the Greek and Roman myths, arranged alphabetically and cross-referenced; includes all significant versions of each myth.

Wood, Michael. *In Search of the Trojan War.* Plume 1987 $14.95. ISBN 0-452-26364-6 Exploration of the modern search for the ancient city of Troy; sheds a great deal of light on Homer's epic.

*Zimmerman, J. E. *Dictionary of Classical Mythology.* Bantam 1983 $4.95. ISBN 0-553-25776-5 More than 2,000 entries containing concise descriptions of and background information on most Greek and Roman myths; lists heroes, authors, works, places, and symbols; includes names, spellings, and pronunciations.

LATIN LITERATURE

Latin literature must always be seen in the light of the Greek literature that preceded it, and it can be understood only in terms of contemporary Roman history. The early Roman poets—Livius Andronicus, Naevius, and Ennius—whose works survive only in fragments, adapted the poetry of Homer and the Greek tragedians into the Latin language. Their rich verse laid the foundations for the Latin literature that was to follow.

Then, toward the end of the third century BC, Plautus borrowed heavily from the New Comedy of the Greeks and became a popular playwright in a period when Rome was expanding its influence in the Mediterranean and developing a taste for Greek culture. As Greek fashions took hold in the second century BC, Terence was admired for his polished romantic comedies written in imitation of the style of Menander, the best of the Greek writers of New Comedy.

Despite serious civil wars at home, the first century BC was a time of great expansion and conquest for Rome, which then replaced Athens, Greece, and Alexandria, Egypt, as the intellectual and artistic center of the Mediterranean world. Cicero emerged as Rome's leading orator, philosopher, and politician, translating the works of the great Greek philosophers into Latin. Lucretius interpreted the works of the Greek philosopher Epicurus into poetry that is both skillful metrically and beautifully phrased.

With the assassination of the political leader Julius Caesar in 44 BC, the democratic government of the Roman republic came to an end. Out of it arose a new empire headed by the Emperor Augustus. With the empire began the Golden Age of Roman literature.

The brightest light of the Golden Age was Virgil, whose epic poem, the *Aeneid,* immortalized the Roman genius for administering law, maintaining peace, sparing the conquered, and subduing the proud. In poetry, Horace sang of the Roman virtues of moderation and patriotism with great technical skill and wry wit. Also at the court of the Emperor Augustus was the poet Ovid, whose fantastical *Metamorphoses* (retellings of Greek myths) and clever verses on the nature of love gently mocked imperial Rome. Phaedrus, a freed slave attached to Augustus' household, composed animal fables for moral instruction and for entertainment.

As the Roman emperors became more tyrannical, many writers paid the ultimate price for speaking out against the state. Petronius, author of the *Satyricon,* Seneca, the philosopher and popular playwright, and Lucian, a lyric poet, all died for their political offenses against an emperor. In response to these conditions, Persius and later Juvenal developed the satire, the only literary form the Romans did not borrow from the Greeks. Juvenal became especially skillful in this form of poetry and used it to attack the tyranny of the emperor Domitian. Other writers in the first century AD, known as the Silver Age of Latin literature, chose not to satirize their own era but to direct their attacks at the past. Suetonius looked back at the private lives of the early Caesars, and Statius wrote of mythological heroes and wars in epic verse. The famous emperor Julius Caesar himself wrote commentary on his campaigns in Gaul. These commentaries, *C. Juli Caesaris de Bello Gallico,* provided the prime source of information about the Gallic Wars. (*See* Caesar, Vol. 2, World History: Ancient Rome.)

During the second century, the time of the *pax romana,* or world peace under Roman rule, some writers turned their attention to more fanciful and philosophical writing. An example is Apuleius' *Metamorphoses.* Others, such as Donatus and Servius, wrote biographies and commentaries on the great people and events of Rome's past.

Christian ideals ruled the literary imagination from the rise of that new religion in the third century to the fall of Rome in the fifth century. Tertullian used his skill as a writer to champion the cause of Christianity, becoming the first Latin advocate of the new religion. The most classical of all the early supporters of the new doctrine was Lactantius, the Christian Cicero. Prudentius brought together the traditions of classical poetry and the beliefs of Christianity in his allegory of the soul, which he modeled on Virgil's epic the *Aeneid.*

After the fall of Rome in the fifth century, Latin continued to be the official language of the Western world. It survived after Greek was forgotten and remained the language of writers and thinkers well into the 1700s. In the areas of Europe that Rome had conquered, Latin developed into the romance languages of Italian, French, and Spanish. Ironically, the ideas and accomplishments of the Greeks endured largely because they had been copied by the Romans. For example, the mythology of the Romans was almost entirely derived from that of the Greeks, but it is the Latin names of the gods and heroes that have survived in the names given to the planets and constellations.

COLLECTIONS OF LATIN LITERATURE IN ENGLISH TRANSLATION

Davenport, Basil (ed). *The Portable Roman Reader.* Penguin 1977 $8.95. ISBN 0-14-015056-0

Grant, Michael (ed). *Latin Literature.* Penguin 1979 $6.95. ISBN 0-14-044389-4

Wedeck, Harry E. (ed). *Classics of Roman Literature.* Littlefield 1964 $9.95. ISBN 0-8226-0155-9

BOOKS ABOUT LATIN LITERATURE

Frank, Tenney. *Life and Literature in the Roman Republic.* Univ of California Pr 1930 $8.95. ISBN 0-520-00428-0

Ogilvie, R. M. *Roman Literature and Society.* Penguin 1980 $6.95. ISBN 0-14-022081-X

HORACE   65 BC–8 BC

See also Horace, Vol. 2, World History: Ancient Rome.

Horace was born in Venusia in southern Italy, the son of a former slave who had managed to become a property owner and send his son to Rome for the best available education. When Horace was about 18, he went to Athens to complete his schooling. While there he met Brutus, the man who would later lead the assassination conspiracy against the Roman leader Julius Caesar. (*See* Caesar, Vol. 2, World History: Ancient Rome.)

After Caesar's death, Horace joined Brutus' army and fought with him in a losing crusade against the army of Caesar's party. After the war he returned to southern Italy to find that his farm had been taken away by the new government. He became a clerk in the civil service and started writing.

Horace's writing brought him to the attention of the poet Virgil, who in turn introduced him to Maecenas, a wealthy man who often gave financial support to artists and poets. Maecenas gave Horace a farm, which supported him while he wrote.

Horace's early poetry was largely satirical, poking fun at various aspects of Roman society and at the works of other writers. But as he grew older and more prosperous, his verse became more mellow and lyrical, and he gained a reputation as the best lyric poet of his time. This reputation stands today, resting on the perfection of his verse technique, his wit (which he frequently directed at himself), his sincere patriotism, and his memorable phrases. Horace's poetry has supplied the world with more quotable phrases than all the rest of Latin literature combined.

POETRY BY HORACE IN ENGLISH TRANSLATION

The Essential Horace: Odes, Epodes, Satires, and Epistles. Burton Raffel (tr). North Point 1983 $22.50. ISBN 0-86547-112-6

Horace: Complete Odes and Epodes. W. G. Shepherd (tr). Penguin 1983 $7.95. ISBN 0-14-044422-X

BOOK ABOUT HORACE

Armstrong, David. *Horace.* Yale Univ Pr 1990 $9.95. ISBN 0-300-04573-5 Readable general introduction to Horace.

OVID   43 BC–AD 17

Ovid was born into a moderately wealthy family from Sulmo (now Sulmona) in the mountains of south-central Italy. Educated in Rome to be a lawyer and politician, he chose instead to become a poet.

Ovid's first literary success was his tragic play *Medea,* based on a Greek myth. He then wrote the *Heroides,* a series of imaginary love letters in verse, supposedly from women of the ancient past to their heroic lords. He went on to write more love poems, solidifying his reputation as a leading literary figure in Rome. Ovid's masterpiece, however, is the *Metamorphoses,* a marvelously imaginative collection of Greek myths and tales from Babylon and other lands of the East, in which every story involves a change in shape.

Although he became the leading poet of Rome, Ovid was banished from the city in AD 8 by an edict of the Roman emperor, Augustus, for reasons that remain unknown. He spent the last 10 years of his life as an unhappy exile in the city of Tomi on the Black Sea.

Ovid was admired and imitated throughout the Middle Ages and the Renaissance, and many British and Italian poets were strongly influenced by his works.

POETRY BY OVID IN ENGLISH TRANSLATION

The Erotic Poems. Peter Green (tr). Penguin 1983 $6.95. ISBN 0-14-044360-6

The Metamorphoses. Horace Gregory (tr). Mentor 1960 $4.95. ISBN 0-451-62622-2

POETRY BY OVID IN LATIN

Amores. Oxford Univ Pr 1961 $14.95. ISBN 0-19-814642-6

Ars Amatoria. Oxford Univ Pr 1989 $17.95. ISBN 0-19-814736-8

P. Ovidi Nasonis Metamorphoseon liber I. Books Demand $42.50. ISBN 0-317-27536-4

BOOK ABOUT OVID

Mack, Sara. *Ovid.* Yale Univ Pr 1988 $9.95. ISBN 0-300-04295-7 Readable and lively introduction to Ovid's works by a respected scholar; contains a close analysis of the *Metamorphoses.*

PLAUTUS, TITUS MACCIUS   *c.* 250 BC–184 BC

Plautus was born in the town of Sarsina in Umbria in central Italy. The details of his early life are uncertain, but he probably went to Rome while a young man and obtained something of an education there, including an excellent command of Latin. He worked in the theater, perhaps as an actor, before leaving Rome to enter foreign trade. His business was unsuccessful, however, and he returned to Rome in poverty, taking a job as a baker's assistant.

During this time, Plautus began writing plays, which brought him enough income to enable him to quit the bakery and live comfortably in Rome for the rest of his life. Although over 100 plays have been attributed to Plautus, it is uncertain how many of these he actually wrote and how many were mere revisions of the work of other writers. Twenty-one of his plays have survived.

Plautus modeled his plays on Greek New Comedy and sometimes even used long passages lifted directly from the original Greek plays. However, he brought to these Greek comedies his unique brand of wit and humor and an original understanding of human nature. Plautus used such stock characters as the tricky slave, the young lovers, the greedy and grumpy father, and the boasting soldier, as well as such standard plot devices as mistaken identity and confusing disguises. He used them so skillfully, however, that his comedies still retain a genuine sparkle and charm. Plautus was enormously popular during his lifetime, and his plays continued to be performed in Rome long after his death. A great many writers, including William Shakespeare (*see* Shakespeare, Vol. 1, British Literature: The Renaissance), have borrowed from Plautus.

PLAYS BY PLAUTUS IN ENGLISH TRANSLATION

The Pot of Gold and Other Plays. E. F. Watling (tr). Penguin 1965 $4.95. ISBN 0-14-044149-2 Includes *The Prisoners, The Brothers Menaechmus, The Swaggering Soldier,* and *Pseudolus.*

The Rope and Other Plays. E. F. Watling (tr). Penguin 1964 $4.95. ISBN 0-14-044136-0 Includes *The Ghost, A Three-Dollar Day,* and *Amphitryo.*

PLAYS BY PLAUTUS IN LATIN

Comoediae. 2 vols. Oxford Univ Pr 1904. Vol. 1 $29.95. ISBN 0-19-814628-0. Vol. 2 $32.50. ISBN 0-19-814629-9

BOOK ABOUT PLAUTUS

Segal, Erich. *Roman Laughter: The Comedy of Plautus.* Oxford Univ Pr 1987 $10.95. ISBN 0-19-504166-6 Readable commentary on Plautus' plays and comic techniques.

SENECA, LUCIUS ANNAEUS   *c.* 5 BC–AD 65

Lucius Annaeus Seneca was born in Spain into a wealthy Italian family of writers. His father, also named Lucius Annaeus Seneca and known as Seneca the Elder, wrote well-known collections of arguments used to train students in public speaking. Seneca's nephew Lucan was a famous poet who wrote about Rome's civil wars.

The younger Seneca studied public speaking and philosophy in Rome in preparation for a career in law. While a student, he became drawn to the Stoic philosophy, which taught that human conduct should be brought into agreement with nature by avoiding strong emotions, selfish thoughts, and personal indulgence. During his lifetime, he became a leading voice for this philosophy.

As a young man, Seneca became famous as a speaker and thinker, but his career was halted when he fell out of favor with Emperor Claudius and was exiled to Corsica in AD 41. Eight years passed before Seneca was recalled to Rome by Empress Agrippina to serve as tutor to her son Nero.

When Nero became emperor, Seneca became one of the most powerful men in Rome. But Nero's reign grew more murderous and corrupt, leading

Seneca to withdraw as much as possible from public life and devote himself to writing and philosophy. He was unable to escape Nero's displeasure, however, and, after Nero's attempt to poison him failed, Seneca was charged with treason and forced to commit suicide by opening his veins. He met his death with the calm befitting a Stoic philosopher.

Seneca's contribution to Roman literature consists of 10 tragedies, modeled after Greek drama and written to be recited rather than performed on stage. These include *Medea, Thyestes,* and *Hercules Furens.* The importance of these works in Roman times seems to have been limited, but their publication in England in 1581 had a powerful influence on the development of Elizabethan tragedy. Playwrights such as Christopher Marlowe (*see* Marlowe, Vol. 1, British Literature: The Renaissance), Thomas Kyd, and William Shakespeare (*see* Shakespeare, Vol. 1, British Literature: The Renaissance) were all influenced by Seneca's division of the tragedy into five acts, as well as by his use of horror, bloodshed, ghosts, and gloom.

PLAYS BY SENECA IN ENGLISH TRANSLATION

Seneca: Four Tragedies and Octavia. E. F. Watling (tr). Penguin 1966 $5.95. ISBN 0-14-044174-3 Includes *Phaedra, Oedipus, Thyestes,* and *The Trojan Women.*

PLAYS AND ESSAYS BY SENECA IN LATIN

Ad Lucilium Epistulae Morales. 2 vols. Oxford Univ Pr 1965. Vol. 1, Bks 1-13 $19.95. ISBN 0-19-814644-2. Vol. 2, Bks 14-20 $19.95. ISBN 0-19-814649-3
Apocolocyntosis. Cambridge Univ Pr 1984 $18.95. ISBN 0-521-28836-3
Phaedra. Cambridge Univ Pr 1990 $16.95. ISBN 0-521-33713-5

BOOK ABOUT SENECA

Pratt, Norman T. *Seneca's Drama.* Univ of North Carolina Pr 1983 $27.50. ISBN 0-8078-1555-1 Excellent, helpful critical study of Seneca's works.

TERENCE   *c.* 190 BC–159 BC

Terence was born at Carthage in North Africa and became the slave of Terentius Lucanus, a Roman senator who educated him and set him free. His first play, *Andria* (166 BC), was very successful and brought Terence into the inner circles of Roman literary society. He became close friends with some of the most famous poets of his day, and his six surviving plays were almost certainly written for this elite group, rather than for the Roman masses.

Terence adapted all of his plays from Greek comic playwright Menander and other writers of Greek New Comedy. His plays are polished, witty, and written at a high level of sophistication, with careful handling of plot and character. Though written in Latin, they are set in Greece, with Greek characters.

After several successful years in Rome, Terence went to Greece, where he died at an early age. His plays influenced such later writers as French comic playwright Molière (*see* Molière, Vol. 1, World Literature: French Language and Literature), and British playwrights Richard Brinsley Sheridan and William Congreve. (*See* Sheridan *and* Congreve, Vol. 1, British Literature: The Restoration and the Eighteenth Century.)

PLAYS BY TERENCE IN ENGLISH TRANSLATION

Terence: The Comedies. Betty Radice (tr). Penguin 1976 $6.95. ISBN 0-14-044324-X Includes *The Girl from Andros, The Self-Tormentor, The Eunuch, Phormio, The Mother-in-Law,* and *The Brothers.*

Plays by Terence in Latin

Comoediae. Oxford Univ Pr 1926 $19.95. ISBN 0-19-814636-1

Book about Terence

Forehand, Walter E. *Terence.* G. K. Hall 1985 $27.95. ISBN 0-8057-6593-X Useful introduction to Terence's comedy, containing a detailed discussion of each of the six surviving plays.

VIRGIL   70 BC–19 BC

See also Virgil, Vol. 2, World History: Ancient Rome.

Virgil, the greatest of all Latin poets, was born at Andes, near Mantua, in northern Italy. His father was a prosperous farmer who provided him with a good education. In 37 BC, after his studies in Rome and Naples, Virgil completed the *Eclogues,* 10 poems about the wonders and beauties of nature, which brought him great fame.

At that time Maecenas, a trusted counselor of the Roman emperor, Augustus, became Virgil's sponsor and protector. He provided the young poet with a villa at Naples and a country house in southern Italy. Virgil responded by composing the *Georgics,* a long poem on farming, which honored Maecenas. The *Georgics* was widely celebrated and confirmed Virgil's position as the leading poet of his age.

Virgil was then urged by Emperor Augustus to compose a long work on the history of Rome, with special attention to the emperor's family. Virgil devoted the rest of his life to this work, the *Aeneid.* This epic poem, derived from Homer's *Iliad* and *Odyssey* (*see* Homer, Vol. 1, World Literature: Classical Greek Literature), tells the story of the Trojan hero Aeneas and his wanderings and adventures after the fall of Troy. It describes how Aeneas, who embodies all of the personal qualities that Romans respected, finally landed in Italy and founded Rome.

Just as the poem was nearing completion, Virgil was taken ill, and he died before he could give the poem the polishing and revision he desired. His request that the imperfect manuscript be destroyed after his death was overruled by Emperor Augustus, who thus saved one of the true masterpieces of world literature.

Even during his lifetime, Virgil's works were considered classics, and after his death, his reputation grew even stronger. He was buried near Naples, and his tomb became the object of pilgrimages for people all over Europe. St. Paul is said to have wept before it. By the third century, Virgil's poems were treated as sacred texts, and the poet himself was revered by the Romans as part god, part magician. During the Renaissance this mantle of magic and divinity was stripped away, but Virgil's reputation as a poet continued to flourish. His poetry was a major influence on all subsequent European literature.

Poetry by Virgil in English Translation

*The Aeneid. Allen Mandelbaum (tr). Bantam 1981 $2.95. ISBN 0-553-21041-6 Story of the adventures of the Trojan hero Aeneas; the translation received the National Book Award; with glossary.

The Eclogues. Guy Lee (tr). Penguin 1984 $5.95. ISBN 0-14-044419-X

The Georgics. L. P. Wilkinson (tr). Penguin 1988 $5.95. ISBN 0-14-044414-9

POETRY BY VIRGIL IN LATIN

Aeneidos: Liber Primus. Oxford Univ Pr 1971 $15.95. ISBN 0-19-872117-X
Aeneidos: Liber Quartus. Oxford Univ Pr 1982 repr of 1955 ed $18.95. ISBN 0-19-872111-0
Aeneidos: Liber Secundos. Oxford Univ Pr 1964 $15.95. ISBN 0-19-872106-4
Aeneidos: Liber Sextus. Oxford Univ Pr 1986 $15.95. ISBN 0-19-872128-5
Eclogues "and" Georgics. St. Martin's 1983 $13.95. ISBN 0-312-84732-7

BOOKS ABOUT VIRGIL

Bloom, Harold (ed). *Virgil.* Chelsea 1986 $24.50. ISBN 0-87754-728-9 Varied collection of critical essays on Virgil's poetry with an emphasis on the *Aeneid.*
Camps, W. A. *An Introduction to Virgil's Aeneid.* Oxford Univ Pr 1969 $12.95. ISBN 0-19-872024-6 Solid and scholarly study of the epic in its Roman context.

FRENCH LANGUAGE AND LITERATURE

THE FRENCH LANGUAGE

French is one of the Romance languages that developed from the spoken Latin used in the different parts of the Roman Empire. In 51 BC, when the Romans conquered Gaul (the area of Europe that is now largely France), the inhabitants spoke a Celtic language called *Gaulish.* The native Gauls rapidly learned to speak the language of their conquerors, in large part because they believed that Roman culture was superior to their own. However, the soldiers from whom they learned the new language did not speak the pure, cultured Latin of educated Romans. They used a form of the Latin language called *vernacular* or *vulgar.* As they adopted vernacular Latin, the Gauls gave the words a "Gaulish" pronunciation. By the third or fourth century AD, Gaulish had all but disappeared, replaced by Gaulish Latin.

In the fifth century, the Roman Empire began to crumble. Northern Gaul was invaded and occupied by another people called the Salian Franks, who spoke a Germanic language. The Franks soon abandoned their native tongue in favor of the Gaulish Latin (called Romance) spoken by the people they conquered, but as they began to speak this language, they too changed the pronunciation and added new words. In southern Gaul, which was less affected by the Germanic invasions, the Romance language changed much less.

Nevertheless, by the ninth century, both forms of Romance had developed into a language so distinctive that its speakers could no longer read Latin. However, Latin was still the language of the educated, and the spoken language had no written form yet. This spoken language was Old French.

Old French existed in two distinct forms, or dialects: the *langue d'oil* dialect of the north and the *langue d'oc* dialect of the south. (The names came from the way the word *yes* was pronounced in each dialect.) The form of the *langue d'oil* spoken in Paris and at the French king's court nearby became the accepted form of Old French throughout the country by the end of the thirteenth century.

Beginning in the fifteenth century, Old French began to change substantially. New words from Greek and Latin came into the language, and poets began to write in French rather than in Latin, leading to a more uniform spelling and grammar. By the sixteenth century, a number of grammarians began analyzing and standardizing the language, a process that continued into the seventeenth century and resulted in the establishment of the French Academy in 1635.

The academy took on the task of regulating the spelling, grammar, and pronunciation of the French language and was instrumental in making modern French one of the most precise of the world's languages. For this reason and as a result of France's political power, French became the international language of culture and diplomacy throughout the seventeenth, eighteenth, and nineteenth centuries.

Today, in addition to being the language of France and its territories, French is an official language of Belgium, Canada, Haiti, Luxembourg, and Switzerland. There are approximately 115 million people who speak French as their native language, and many millions more who speak it as a second or third language.

Probably more than any other European people, the French have been proud and protective of their language and have taken steps to keep it pure and refined. In recent years, as the influence of other languages, especially English, has been felt on the development of contemporary French, the French Academy and large numbers of the French people have expressed alarm at what they see as the corruption of their language. At present, however, they seem unable to stem the flow of new "non-French" words into the French vocabulary.

BOOKS ABOUT THE FRENCH LANGUAGE

The following books provide an introduction to the history and grammar of modern French. The list does not include the many dictionaries and instructional textbooks that are widely available.

Cox, Thomas. *French Grammar.* Harcourt 1986 $8.95. ISBN 0-15-601611-7
Dumont, Francis (ed). *French Grammar.* Harper 1969 $8.95. ISBN 0-06-460035-1
Holmes, Urban, and Alexander H. Schutz. *A History of the French Language.* Biblo 1938 $15.00. ISBN 0-8196-0191-8
Ketteridge, J. O. *French Idioms and Figurative Phrases.* Saphrograph $17.50. ISBN 0-87557-024-0
Lupson, Peter, and Michael Pelissier. *Guide to French Idioms.* National Textbook 1987 $5.95. ISBN 0-8442-1502-3
Price, Glanville. *The French Language: Past and Present.* Longwood 1984 $11.95. ISBN 0-7293-0208-3
Rickard, Peter. *A History of the French Language.* Unwin 1989 $16.95. ISBN 0-04-445295-0
Tucker, G. *The French Speaker's Skill with Grammatical Gender.* Mouton 1977 $24.95. ISBN 90-279-3195-X

FRENCH LITERATURE

A major literature since the twelfth century, French literature blossomed during the Renaissance to become one of the most important literatures in Western civilization, a position it has continued to hold up to the present time. No other culture has attached so much importance to the purity and correct usage of its language, and no other literature has followed so consistently the principle that the quality of ideas and the quality of expression cannot be separated.

French literature has its roots in the stories of early Christian saints dating back to the fifth and sixth centuries and in the ancient Celtic tales of great heroes, such as King Arthur. These sources are evident most notably in the eleventh-century epic poem, the *Song of Roland,* and the early twelfth-century poems of Chrétien de Troyes. At about the same time, the troubadours—aristocratic poet-musicians from southern France—began composing their songs of love, war, chivalry, and nature in the southern dialect known as *langue d'oc.*

Later, in the early thirteenth century, Guillaume de Lorris began *Le Roman de la Rose,* a long poem about the nature of love that was finished later in the century by Jean de Meun. In the middle of the fifteenth century, François Villon, an outlaw and thief, wrote some of the most beautiful French lyric poetry of all time. The Middle Ages also saw the development of the miracle play, a form of religious drama that lasted well into the sixteenth century.

With the coming of the Renaissance in the sixteenth century, French writers looked to Italy for their models and to ancient Greece and Rome for their subjects. During this time François Rabelais, a Benedictine monk, wrote his famous stories of the lusty, gluttonous giants, Gargantua and Pantagruel. These wild, hilarious, often bawdy tales contain much wisdom and serious commentary. Later in the century, Michel Montaigne formulated his thoughts and feelings on a host of subjects and thus created the literary form known as the essay.

In the 1600s French literature entered the period known as classicism. It was a time when writers such as La Fontaine, Boileau, Pascal, Bousset, La Rochefoucauld, Mme de La Fayette, and Madame de Sévigné produced literature in a style that is clear, precise, refined, and restrained. Their primary subject was human nature and the behavior of people in society.

Also during this period, the French theater produced three of its greatest playwrights. Corneille and Racine wrote tragedies and Molière wrote comedies that remain popular to this day.

The eighteenth century is known as the Age of Enlightenment, when reason and logic were highly prized. From thinkers like Voltaire, Rousseau, Montesquieu, and others came some of the most powerful philosophical and political writing ever produced in Western culture. At the same time, Le Sage, Prévost, and Bernardin de Saint-Pierre gave new life and popularity to the novel, while Marivaux and Beaumarchais brought new direction to the theater.

The political and social turmoil of the French Revolution was accompanied by a similar revolution in literature as the rational Age of Enlightenment gave way to the emotional Romantic period. The most prominent of the Romantic writers was playwright, poet, and novelist Victor Hugo, whose career spanned the period. Other Romantics were Chateaubriand, Lamartine, Vigny, and Alfred de Musset. Novelists Balzac, Stendahl, and George Sand began the movement away from Romanticism toward a new realistic literature, exemplified by the works of Flaubert. A number of different literary movements sprang up during the nineteenth century, among them Symbolism, represented by the poet Arthur Rimbaud, and Naturalism, represented in the work of novelist Emile Zola.

The turmoil of two world wars, which were fought largely on French soil, disrupted the development of literature in the twentieth century. Nonetheless, novelists such as Marcel Proust, André Gide, André Malraux, Colette, Jean-

Paul Sartre, Albert Camus, and Claude Simon have developed the tradition of French literature and kept it vibrant and near the forefront of the literatures of the world.

ANOUILH, JEAN 1910–1987

During World War II, while Paris and most of France were under German occupation, a new play appeared based on the Greek legend of Antigone, a young woman who questioned the power of the state to force her to act against her conscience. The play was obviously a thinly disguised protest against the tyranny of the Germans, and it served as a rallying point for French youth against the occupying army. The playwright was Jean Anouilh.

Anouilh was born in Bordeaux in southern France and went to Paris when he was very young, where he began to study law and then worked for a time in an advertising agency. Always interested in the theater, in 1931 he became secretary to Louis Jovet, a famous actor–manager. Anouilh's first hit play was produced in 1935.

Anouilh had a distinct and highly original talent. His plays combine the serious with the fantastic, yet despite their unusual content, they are traditional in form. Anouilh's characters are most often symbolic, representing the forces of good and evil. His protagonists generally oppose life's compromises and seek salvation in love, which they then discover is no solution. Anouilh himself classifies his works as either *pièces roses* (pink plays), where the good triumph, or *pièces noires* (black plays), where evil is victorious.

Time Remembered (1942), a romantic love story with satiric overtones, was Anouilh's first Broadway hit. His moving dramatization of the trial of Joan of Arc in *The Lark* (1953), was also very well received when first presented in New York in 1955. To most Americans, Anouilh's best-known work is *Becket* (1959), about the courageous churchman Thomas à Becket and his resistance to his king. The play was made into an Academy award-winning film, starring Richard Burton and Peter O'Toole.

PLAYS BY ANOUILH IN ENGLISH TRANSLATION

Anouilh: Five Plays. Hill & Wang 1958 $7.95. ISBN 0-8090-0710-X Includes *Romeo and Jeannette, The Rehearsal, Ermine, Antigone, Eurydice.*
Anouilh: Five Plays. Heineman 1990 $9.95. ISBN 0-413-14030-X Includes *Leocadia, Antigone, Waltz of the Toreadors, Poor Bitos, The Lark.*
Becket (1959). Lucienne Hill (tr). Putnam 1960 $5.95. ISBN 0-698-10031-X
The Lark (1953). Christopher Fry (tr). Oxford Univ Pr 1956 $10.95. ISBN 0-19-500393-4

PLAYS BY ANOUILH IN FRENCH

Alouette (1953). Schoenhof 1963 $5.95. ISBN 0-685-10991-7
Antigone (1942). Schoenhof 1975 $8.95. ISBN 2-7103-0025-7
Cher Antoine on l'amour rote (1969). Schoenhof 1975 $5.95. ISBN 2-070-06697-9
Eurydice (1942) *et Medée* (1946). Basil Blackwell 1984 $15.95. ISBN 0-631-13692-4
L'invitation au château (1948). French and European 1962 $11.95. ISBN 0-685-11255-1
Le sauvage (1938). Schoenhof 1985 $7.95. ISBN 2-07-036874-2
Le voyageur sans bagages (1938). Schoenhof 1962 $6.95. ISBN 2-07-036759-2

BOOKS ABOUT ANOUILH

Archer, Marguerite. *Jean Anouilh.* Columbia Univ Pr 1971 $5.00. ISBN 0-231-03346-X
  Essay on Anouilh's dramatic art and his reinterpretation of Greek myths.
McIntire, H. G. *The Theatre of Jean Anouilh.* Barnes 1981 $23.50. ISBN 0-389-20182-0
  Study of Anouilh's plays in the context of mid-twentieth-century theater.

BALZAC, HONORE DE   1799–1850

Honoré de Balzac was born at Tours in southern France, educated at the Collège de Vendôme, and studied law at the Sorbonne University in Paris. Though he was born a peasant, he added the snobbish "de" to his name to pretend he was an aristocrat. In 1819, against his father's wishes, he left Tours for Paris and the life of a writer. His early literary efforts brought him little success, and he lived in abject poverty, accumulating heavy debts that were to plague him the rest of his life. He worked at a furious pace, turning out shoddy novels under pseudonyms in order to survive. It was not until 1829, 10 years after he left Tours, that he began to achieve genuine success as an author.

Many critics regard Balzac as the greatest of French novelists. His greatness is not only in the richness of his work, which is often compared to that of British writer Charles Dickens (*see* Dickens, Vol. 1, British Literature: The Victorian Age), but in its sheer volume. Even though he died at the age of 51, he left 92 novels (out of over 100 he had planned to write), most of which when taken together form what Balzac called *The Human Comedy.* His purpose in this gigantic undertaking was to present a complete picture of modern civilization, as well as a history of the manners and customs of French society in the first half of the nineteenth century. It is one of the most ambitious literary plans ever conceived; the books contain 2,000 distinctly drawn characters. Among the best known of the novels are *Le Père Goriot (Old Man Goriot)* (1834), *La Cousine Bette* (1846), and *Eugénie Grandet* (1833).

In 1849, in poor health, Balzac traveled to Poland to meet the Polish Countess Hanska, a wealthy woman with whom he had corresponded for 15 years. The following year they were married, and three months later Balzac died in Paris.

NOVELS BY BALZAC IN ENGLISH TRANSLATION

Cousin Bette (1846). Marion Ayton Crawford (tr). Penguin 1965 $4.95. ISBN 0-14-044260-X
Cousin Pons (1845). Herbert J. Hunt (tr). Penguin 1978 $6.95. ISBN 0-14-044205-7
Eugenie Grandet (1833). Marion Ayton Crawford (tr). Penguin 1955 $4.95. ISBN 0-14-044050-X
Lost Illusions (1843). Herbert J. Hunt (tr). Penguin 1976 $7.95. ISBN 0-14-044251-0
A Murky Business (1841). Herbert J. Hunt (tr). Penguin 1978 $6.95. ISBN 0-14-044271-5
Old Goriot (1834). Marion Ayton Crawford (tr). Penguin 1951 $3.95. ISBN 0-14-044017-8
Ursule Mirouet (1841). Donald Adamson (tr). Penguin 1976 $5.95. ISBN 0-14-044316-9
The Wild Ass's Skin (1831). Herbert J. Hunt (tr). Penguin 1977 $5.95. ISBN 0-14-044330-4

SHORT STORIES BY BALZAC IN ENGLISH TRANSLATION

Selected Short Stories. Sylvia Raphael (tr). Penguin 1977 $5.95. ISBN 0-14-044325-8

NOVELS BY BALZAC IN FRENCH

Les Chouans (1829). Schoenhof 1988 $7.95. ISBN 2-07-036084-7
La cousine Bette (1846). French and European $29.95. ISBN 0-685-34078-3
Le cousin Pons (1845). French and European $29.95. ISBN 0-685-34076-7
Eugénie Grandet (1833). Schoenhof 1965 $6.95. ISBN 2-07-036031-8
Le père Goriot (1834). French and European $29.95. ISBN 0-685-34092-9
Seraphita (1835). French and European 1950 $14.95. ISBN 0-686-53926-5

BOOKS ABOUT BALZAC

Festa-McCormick, Diane. *Honoré de Balzac*. G. K. Hall 1979 $15.95. ISBN 0-8057-6383-X Thoughtful and scholarly general introduction to Balzac's life and works.

Kanes, Martin (ed). *Critical Essays on Honoré de Balzac*. G. K. Hall 1990 $35.00. ISBN 0-8161-8845-9 Collection of superior critical essays representing the major streams of scholarship; includes a comprehensive index of titles, authors, and themes.

BAUDELAIRE, CHARLES   1821–1867

Born in Paris to a moderately wealthy family, Charles Baudelaire was educated in Lyon, France, and in Paris. He traveled to Asia before settling in Paris to live the life of a "literary gentleman" on an inheritance from his father. When his money ran out, he joined the bohemian (free-spirited) writers and artists living on the edge of poverty in Paris.

In 1846 Baudelaire discovered the American poet Edgar Allan Poe (*see* Poe, Vol. 1, American Literature: Romanticism and the American Renaissance), with whom he felt a mystical connection. For the rest of his life, he worked at brilliant translations of Poe's tales and poems.

Baudelaire was the poet of decadence of his period. His collected poems, *Les fleurs du mal (Flowers of Evil)* (1857), celebrate the pursuit of physical pleasure, the torment of love, and the freedom of moral anarchy. Their literary form is so polished as to be almost faultless. In 1857, Baudelaire was tried on charges of obscenity, and six of the more controversial poems had to be removed from *Les fleurs du mal* before it could be sold.

Baudelaire was also a perceptive literary and art critic. He died insane at the age of 46.

POETRY BY BAUDELAIRE IN ENGLISH TRANSLATION

Flowers of Evil (1857). Marthiel Mathews (tr). New Directions 1989 $16.95. ISBN 0-8112-1117-7

Invitation to a Voyage: Selected Poems. Kendall Lappin (tr). Black Swan Bks 1989 $20.00. ISBN 0-933806-59-0

Paris Spleen (1869). Louise Varese (tr). New Directions 1970 $5.95. ISBN 0-8112-0007-8

Selected Poems. Joanna Richardson (tr). Penguin 1975 $5.95. ISBN 0-14-042188-2

POETRY BY BAUDELAIRE IN FRENCH

Les fleurs du mal (1857). Basil Blackwell 1988 $15.95. ISBN 0-631-00410-6

Le spleen de Paris (1869). French and European 1973 $8.95. ISBN 0-686-51925-6

BOOKS ABOUT BAUDELAIRE

Bloom, Harold (ed). *Charles Baudelaire*. Chelsea 1987 $19.95. ISBN 0-87754-719-X Introductory collection of critical essays on Baudelaire's poetry; includes a bibliography and index.

Pichois, Claude. *Baudelaire*. Graham Robb (tr). Viking 1990 $24.95. ISBN 0-241-12458-1 Recent biography that uses new source material to draw parallels between Baudelaire's life and his work.

BECKETT, SAMUEL   1906–1989

Samuel Beckett was born in Dublin, Ireland, and educated there at Trinity College. He lectured in Paris at the Ecole Normale Supérieure and later at Dublin University. In 1937 he returned to settle in Paris permanently; he abandoned English and began writing in French.

Beckett is best known in the United States as the author of the play *Waiting for Godot* (1952). Other Beckett plays that have received critical acclaim are *Endgame* (1957) and *Krapp's Last Tape* (1959). Beckett also published several novels. His first novel, *Murphy* (1938), was written in English, but those that followed were written first in French and then tranaslated into English by Beckett himself.

Beckett's plays and novels portray life as essentially pointless and filled with misery, but he presents his message with a kind of black humor that makes use of slapstick and other low comedy techniques. His characters lead bleak lives, passive victims of an inscrutable fate. His style is highly original, hovering somewhere between tragedy and comedy. His characters tend to speak in a kind of shorthand, leaving out key words and ideas and underscoring the theme of the impossibility of real communication between people. Beckett was awarded the Nobel Prize for literature in 1969.

NOVELS BY BECKETT IN ENGLISH TRANSLATION

Molloy (1951), *Malone Dies* (1951), *The Unnamable* (1953). Samuel Beckett (tr). Grove 1989 $9.95. ISBN 0-8021-5091-8
Murphy (1938). Grove 1970 $9.95. ISBN 0-8021-5037-3
Watt (1958). Grove 1970 $10.95. ISBN 0-8021-5140-X

PLAYS BY BECKETT IN ENGLISH TRANSLATION

Collection of Shorter Plays by Samuel Beckett. Grove 1984 $12.95. ISBN 0-8021-5055-1
Endgame (1957). Samuel Beckett (tr). Grove 1983 $3.95. ISBN 0-394-17208-6
Ends and Odds. Samuel Beckett (tr). Grove 1976 $3.95. ISBN 0-394-17918-8
Krapp's Last Tape (1959) *and Other Dramatic Pieces.* Grove 1960 $7.95. ISBN 0-394-17223-X
Waiting for Godot (1952). Grove 1987 $4.50. ISBN 0-394-17204-3

NOVELS BY BECKETT IN FRENCH

Malone meurt (1951). French and European 1952 $28.95. ISBN 0-685-11337-X
Molloy (1951). French and European $15.95. ISBN 0-685-37199-9
Innomable (1953). French and European 1953 $27.95. ISBN 0-685-11252-7
Watt (1958). French and European $29.95. ISBN 0-685-37202-2

PLAYS BY BECKETT IN FRENCH

En attendant Godot (1952). French and European 1952 $19.95. ISBN 0-685-11159-8
Fin de partie (1957). French and European 1957 $11.95. ISBN 0-685-11186-5

BOOKS ABOUT BECKETT

Bair, Deirdre. *Samuel Beckett.* Summit Bks 1990 $14.95. ISBN 0-671-69173-2 Considered the most authoritative and complete biography of Beckett, examining the detailed chronology of both his life and his works.
Kennedy, Arthur K. *Samuel Beckett.* Cambridge Univ Pr 1989 $10.95. ISBN 0-521-25482-5 Scholarly survey of Beckett's works that seeks to identify key themes and patterns.
Topsfield, Valerie. *The Humor of Samuel Beckett.* St. Martin's 1988 $29.95. ISBN 0-312-01571-2 Examines Beckett's use of humor to accent key themes.

BOULLE, PIERRE 1912–

Pierre Boulle was born in Avignon and educated at the Ecole Supérieure d'Electricité, where he became a licensed engineer. In 1936, after working two years in France as an engineer, Boulle went to work on a rubber plantation in Malaysia. At the beginning of World War II, he joined the French Army there, and when France surrendered to Germany in 1940, Boulle joined the Free French resistance group and became a secret agent, posing as an Englishman.

Captured by the Germans and sent to a prison camp, he escaped after two years and rejoined the Free French forces for the rest of the war. After the war he returned to Malaysia to the rubber plantation, but he quickly grew dissatisfied and moved to Paris to write.

Boulle's early novels often use the settings in the East with which he was so familiar. One of his most popular books is *The Bridge over the River Kwai* (1954), on which the award-winning movie was based and for which Boulle wrote the screenplay. He later turned to science fiction, and one of these novels, *The Planet of the Apes* (1964), became the basis for several movies and a television series. His work is notable for the ironic contrast he points out between humanity's technological achievements and its spiritual and moral failures.

NOVELS BY BOULLE IN ENGLISH TRANSLATION

The Bridge over the River Kwai (1954). Bantam 1970 $2.95. ISBN 0-553-24850-2 Imprisoned British officer's passion for duty leads him to perform a feat of military genius for the Japanese army.
Garden on the Moon (1964). Vanguard 1965 $12.95. ISBN 0-8149-0063-1
The Good Leviathan (1978). Vanguard 1979 $14.95. ISBN 0-8149-0807-1
The Planet of the Apes (1964). Signet 1989 $3.95. ISBN 0-451-16016-9 After the devastation of a nuclear war, apes become masters of the earth.

SHORT STORIES BY BOULLE IN ENGLISH TRANSLATION

The Marvelous Palace and Other Stories (1977). Vanguard 1978 $12.95. ISBN 0-8149-0788-1

NOVELS BY BOULLE IN FRENCH

Le bon Leviathan (1978). French and European 1978 $14.95. ISBN 0-686-54097-2
Un métier de Seigneur (1960). French and European 1973 $9.95. ISBN 0-686-54106-5
Le planète des singes (1964). French and European $9.95. ISBN 0-686-54110-3
Le pont de la rivière Kwai (1954). French and European $9.95. ISBN 0-686-54111-1

SHORT STORIES BY BOULLE IN FRENCH

Histoires Charitables (1964). French and European 1965 $9.95. ISBN 0-686-54101-4
Histoires Perfides (1976). French and European 1976 $27.95. ISBN 0-686-54102-2

NONFICTION BY BOULLE IN ENGLISH TRANSLATION

My Own River Kwai. Vanguard 1967 $12.95. ISBN 0-8149-0061-5 Boulle's memoirs of his war days; funny, with moments of high excitement.

NONFICTION BY BOULLE IN FRENCH

Aux sources de la Kwai. French and European $9.95. ISBN 0-686-54096-4

CAMUS, ALBERT   1913–1960

Albert Camus was born in Algeria in North Africa, the son of a farm worker. He studied philosophy at the University of Algiers, where he was also active in student theater. After graduation he went to Paris as a journalist. During World War II, he joined the French Resistance and became one of the leading writers of the underground newspaper *Combat,* which became an important daily newspaper in France after the war.

Camus's fiction is built on the idea that when humans are confronted with the absurdities of life, they can do nothing more than courageously face up to them. His most famous novel, *The Stranger* (1942), the story of a Frenchman who kills an Arab, is a study of an absurd man in an absurd world. Camus's conviction of the essential meaninglessness of life saturates his social, philosophical, and literary points of view. In his novel *The Plague* (1947), he uses the plague-ridden city of Oran to symbolize human isolation and to argue for the concept of human dignity in the face of absurd conditions. The novel is also a representation of the French situation under the German occupation during World War II.

Although Camus shared the Existentialist views of some of his contemporaries, he did not agree that the only option for humans facing a meaningless existence is to surrender to nothingness. Instead he took the view that the search for purpose begins with confronting absurdity and dealing with it as best one can.

Camus was awarded the Nobel Prize for literature in 1957, less than two years before he was killed in an automobile accident. He was the second youngest man in history to receive the Nobel honor.

NOVELS BY CAMUS IN ENGLISH TRANSLATION

The Fall (1956). Justin O'Brien (tr). Vintage 1963 $6.95. ISBN 0-394-70223-9
The Plague (1947). Stuart Gilbert (tr). Vintage 1972 $5.95. ISBN 0-394-71258-7
The Stranger (1942). Vintage 1989 $7.95. ISBN 0-679-72020-0

PLAYS BY CAMUS IN ENGLISH TRANSLATION

Caligula and Three Other Plays. Stuart Gilbert (tr). Vintage 1962 $7.95. ISBN 0-394-70207-7

NOVELS BY CAMUS IN FRENCH

La chute (1956). Germaine Brée (ed). Schoenhof 1986 $9.95. ISBN 0-88332-465-2
L'etranger (1942). Schoenhof 1942 $5.95. ISBN 2-07-036002-4
La peste (1947). Schoenhof 1989 $6.95. ISBN 2-07-036042-3

PLAYS BY CAMUS IN FRENCH

Caligula (1945) *et Malentendu* (1945). Schoenhof 1990 $6.95. ISBN 2-07-036064-4

BOOKS ABOUT CAMUS

Rhein, Phillip H. *Albert Camus.* G. K. Hall 1989 $19.95. ISBN 0-8057-8253-2 General study of Camus's life and works with particular attention to his philosophy.
Thody, Philip. *Albert Camus.* St. Martin's 1989 $24.95. ISBN 0-312-02055-4 Useful introduction to Camus's life and works for students and general readers; with index and bibliography.

DUMAS, ALEXANDRE (PERE) 1802–1870

Perhaps the most popular of all French romantic novelists, Alexandre Dumas was born at Villers–Cotterêts, the son of a general in the French army. His youth was marked by idleness and feeble attempts at getting an education. At the age of 20, he went to Paris, where he obtained a minor position in the employ of the Duc d'Orléans and began to educate himself. In 1829 his play *Henri III* was a huge success and marked Dumas's entry into the world of French letters. He continued to write plays for several years before turning to the romantic and historical novels that were to bring him enduring fame. In 1844 he published *The Three Musketeers,* followed by its two sequels, *Twenty Years After* (1845) and *The Vicomte de Bragelonne* (1850). *The Count of Monte Cristo* appeared in 1845 and *The Man in the Iron Mask* in 1851.

During his lifetime Dumas published some 1,200 volumes, most of them with a group of collaborators known as Dumas & Co. The plots of some of his best-known works were stolen from other writers. *The Three Musketeers,* for example, was taken from the *Memoirs of Artagnan* by an eighteenth-century writer, and *The Count of Monte Cristo* came from an earlier work called *A Diamond and a Vengeance.* For these reasons, among others, critics tend to dismiss Dumas's novels in favor of his plays. However, Dumas was a genuine talent, as both playwright and novelist, and his popularity continues to remain high with the reading public.

Dumas's son was also a writer, so they are often referred to as Dumas's *père* (pronounced "pair") (father) and Dumas *fils* (pronounced "feess") (son).

NOVELS BY DUMAS IN ENGLISH TRANSLATION

*The Count of Monte Cristo (1845). Bantam 1986 $3.95. ISBN 0-553-21230-3 Story of a wrongly imprisoned man, who vows revenge on those who put him there.
*The Man in the Iron Mask (1851). Airmont 1967 $2.95. ISBN 0-8049-0150-3 Story of an aristocrat imprisoned in a dungeon while another rules in his place.
*The Three Musketeers (1844). Lowell Bair (tr). Bantam 1984 $5.95. ISBN 0-553-21337-7 Story of a country boy who finds adventure as a member of the king's guard.

NOVELS BY DUMAS IN FRENCH

Le comte de Monte Cristo (1845). French and European $19.90. ISBN 0-685-34891-1
Les trois mousquetaires (1844). French and European 1961 $9.95. ISBN 0-685-11605-0
Vingt ans après (1845). French and European 1961 $9.00. ISBN 0-685-11621-2

BOOK ABOUT DUMAS

Schopp, Claude. *Alexandre Dumas: Genius of Life.* A. J. Koch (tr). Watts 1988 $24.95. ISBN 0-531-15093-3 Lively biography that combines tragedy and farce in recounting Dumas's colorful life.

FLAUBERT, GUSTAVE   1821–1880

Gustave Flaubert was born in Rouen, the son of a surgeon. He studied law in Paris, where his friendship with French writer Victor Hugo and other literary Parisians influenced him to turn to writing. As a young man, he became afflicted with a rare nervous disorder that forced him to spend most of his life at Croisset (near Rouen) where his mother and niece lived. His disease may also have contributed to his bleak and pessimistic outlook on life. He never married; his most celebrated love affair was with poet Louise Colet.

Flaubert's masterpiece, *Madame Bovary* (1857), is a study of a woman with romantic dreams, trapped in an unhappy marriage, who destroys her life in a futile attempt to find love. After its publication the book was declared immoral because the narrator does not directly condemn any of the heroine's love affairs, and Flaubert was unsuccessfully prosecuted for obscenity.

His second novel, *Salammbô* (1862), is a story of sex and violence in ancient Carthage (a city in North Africa now part of Tunisia). Intended to shock, the novel tells a tale of sadistic and nightmarish brutality. In *The Sentimental Education* (1869), Flaubert explores a theme similar to that of *Madame Bovary* but with a male protagonist. *Bouvard and Pécuchet* (1881), a colossal satire, appeared a year after Flaubert's death, although he left it unfinished.

Flaubert was one of the most painstaking writers in all literature. He searched tirelessly for the right word and read every sentence aloud to be sure it had the right cadence and sound. His French phrase for the right word, *le mot juste* (luh moh zhust), has become a key literary term in English as well. Flaubert also prided himself on being a scrupulously objective realist who described life as he saw it.

Novels by Flaubert in English Translation

Bouvard and Pécuchet (1881). A. J. Krailsheimer (tr). Penguin 1976 $5.95. ISBN 0-14-044320-7

Madame Bovary (1857). Gerard M. Hopkins (tr). Oxford Univ Pr 1989 $2.95. ISBN 0-19-281564-4

Salammbô (1862). A. J. Krailsheimer (tr). Penguin 1977 $5.95. ISBN 0-14-044328-2

The Sentimental Education (1869). Douglas Parmee (tr). Oxford Univ Pr 1990 $4.95. ISBN 0-19-281731-0

Novels by Flaubert in French

Bouvard et Pécuchet (1881). French and European 1954 $9.95. ISBN 0-686-11054-0

L'Education sentimentale (1869). French and European 1961 $8.95. ISBN 0-685-11155-5

Madame Bovary (1857). French and European $9.95. ISBN 0-685-34900-4

Salammbô (1862). French and European 1961 $8.95. ISBN 0-685-11553-4

Books about Flaubert

Buck, Stratton. *Gustave Flaubert.* G. K. Hall 1966 $17.95. ISBN 0-8057-2312-9 Good introduction to the life and works of Flaubert; contains chronology and bibliography.

Lottman, Herbert. *Flaubert: A Biography.* Little 1988 $24.95. ISBN 0-316-53342-4 Vivid and detailed account of Flaubert's life using materials only recently available; highly readable.

Roe, David. *Gustave Flaubert.* St. Martin's 1989 $24.95. ISBN 0-312-02446-0 Introductory chapters on Flaubert's life, early writings, and literary ideas followed by longer sections on each of his novels.

FRANCE, ANATOLE (PSEUDONYM OF ANATOLE-FRANÇOIS THIBAULT) 1844–1924

Anatole France was the son of a bookseller, and his love of books is evident in both his fiction and his literary criticism. He began his career in the publishing business as a writer of advertisements for books. His first novel, *The Crime of Sylvester Bonnard* (1881) was very popular, and he quickly gained a reputation as a major writer. His fiction covers a wide range of subjects and historical periods. He became known as a free thinker who wrote skeptically about religion. Widely respected as a distinguished "prince of letters" and a leading example of French wit, intelligence, and intellectual prowess, he was elected to the French Academy. In 1921, Anatole France was awarded the Nobel Prize for literature.

Novels by France in English Translation

Penguin Island (1909). Random 1984 $6.95. ISBN 0-394-60516-0

Thais (1890). Basia Gulati (tr). Univ of Chicago Pr 1977 $3.95. ISBN 0-226-25989-7

Novels by France in French

L'île des pingouins (1909). French and European 1971 $9.95. ISBN 0-686-55864-2

Le livre de mon ami (1885). French and European 1956 $14.95. ISBN 0-686-55866-9

La révolte des anges (1914). French and European 1972 $9.95. ISBN 0-686-55875-8

Thais (1890). French and European 1960 $14.95. ISBN 0-685-11585-2

GIDE, ANDRE 1869–1951

Born in Paris, André Gide was a lifelong rebel against middle-class morality. He became one of the most controversial figures in modern European literature, partly because of his portrayal of homosexual relationships. He published his first book anonymously at age 18 and went on to become one of the most influential writers on the Parisian literary scene. He was a founder and editor of the respected journal *La Nouvelle Révue Française,* in which the works of many prominent European authors appeared. He remained a director of the magazine until 1941, when he resigned because the magazine passed into the hands of collaborationists (those who worked with the German army that occupied France during World War II). At first a strong supporter of Soviet communism, Gide became disillusioned with it after a trip to the Soviet Union.

Gide classified his fiction into three categories: satirical tales with elements of farce like *Lafcadio's Adventures* (1914); ironic stories narrated in the first person like *The Immoralist* (1902); and more complex narratives related from multiple points of view like *The Counterfeiters* (1925). One of his most famous works is the short story "The Pastoral Symphony," about a pastor who takes a blind orphan under his wing and in the process falls in love with her.

Gide was awarded the Nobel Prize for literature in 1947.

NOVELS BY GIDE IN ENGLISH TRANSLATION

The Counterfeiters (1925). Vintage 1973 $7.95. ISBN 0-394-71842-09
The Immoralist (1902). Richard Howard (tr). Vintage 1954 $6.95. ISBN 0-394-70008-2
Lafcadio's Adventures (1914). Vintage 1960 $5.95. ISBN 0-394-70096-1
Strait Is the Gate (1909). Dorothy Bussy (tr). Vintage 1956 $5.95. ISBN 0-394-70027-9

NOVELS BY GIDE IN FRENCH

Les caves du Vatican (1914). Schoenhof 1972 $6.95. ISBN 2-07-036034-2
Les faux-monnayeurs (1925). Schoenhof 1972 $7.95. ISBN 2-07-036879-3
L'immoraliste (1902). Waveland 1990 $7.95. ISBN 0-88133-474-X
La porte étroite (1909). Schoenhof 1972 $5.95. ISBN 2-07-036210-8

BOOK ABOUT GIDE

Rossi, Vinio. *André Gide.* Columbia Univ Pr 1968 $5.00. ISBN 0-231-02960-8 Brief introduction to Gide's life and works.

HUGO, VICTOR MARIE   1802–1885

Victor Hugo was born in Besançon, the son of a general in the French army. He was educated in Paris and in Madrid, Spain, finally completing his education at the Ecole Polytechnique in Paris. Something of a child prodigy, he produced a dramatic tragedy at the age of 14 and won three major poetry competitions before he was 20.

Hugo's figure dominates the landscape of French literary history, influencing writers throughout the nineteenth century and the entire French romantic movement. In the realms of poetry, criticism, drama, and fiction, he left an indelible mark. Hugo's poems are perhaps the greatest of his works and are among the greatest productions of world literature. It is unfortunate that his poetry has not been translated satisfactorily into English.

To English-speaking readers, Hugo is probably best known as the author of the novels *Nôtre Dame de Paris (The Hunchback of Notre Dame)* (1831) and *Les Misérables* (1862), an immense tale of human courage and social oppression set in the era of Napoleon. Both novels were made into classic films, and *Les Misérables* has recently been made into a popular musical.

Hugo spent much of his life actively engaged in politics. He was elected to national office several times and held important government positions. As a politician as well as as a writer, he was a champion of humanitarian causes.

Elected to the Academy in 1841, he was made a peer of France in 1845. When he died in 1885, all of France went into mourning; a national hero had passed from the scene.

NOVELS BY HUGO IN ENGLISH TRANSLATION

The Hunchback of Notre Dame (1831). Lowell Bair (tr). Bantam 1981 $2.95. ISBN 0-553-21370-9

Les Misérables (1862). Norman Denny (tr). Penguin 1982 $8.95. ISBN 0-14-044430-0

NOVELS BY HUGO IN FRENCH

Les misérables (1862). 3 vols. Schoenhof 1973 $13.80 each. ISBNs 2-07-036348-1, 2-07-03634-9-X, 2-07-036350-3

Nôtre Dame de Paris (1831). Schoenhof 1975 $8.95. ISBN 2-07-036549-2

BOOKS ABOUT HUGO

Bloom, Harold (ed). *Victor Hugo.* Chelsea 1987 $29.95. ISBN 155546-290-1 Collection of essays that approach Hugo's works from a variety of critical perspectives.

Houston, John R. *Victor Hugo.* G. K. Hall 1988 $19.95. ISBN 0-8057-8238-9 Good general introduction to Hugo's life and works; contains a chronology and a bibliography.

MAUPASSANT, GUY DE   1850–1893

Guy de Maupassant was born at the Norman castle of Miromesnil and was educated in Rouen, France. He worked as a government clerk in Paris, where he became part of the literary circle headed by French writer Emile Zola (*see* Zola, Vol. 1 World Literature: French Language and Literature). He was encouraged in his writing by French writer Gustave Flaubert (*see* Flaubert, Vol. 1, World Literature: French Language and Literature), who was a friend of Maupassant's mother, and was rumored to be Maupassant's father.

Maupassant is one of the early exponents of the modern genre of the short story. In addition to more than 360 short stories, Maupassant also wrote six novels, including *Bel Ami* (1885), the story of a selfish man's career, and *Pierre et Jean* (1888), about the hatred of two brothers. Among his most famous short stories are "The Necklace" and "Madame Fifi."

In a coldly objective style, free from sentimentality or preaching, Maupassant's stories expose the artificiality and vulgarity of the French middle class, which he viewed with a mixture of contempt and pity. Like his master Flaubert, Maupassant was a pessimist at heart, whose writing almost brutally dissects his characters. Some of his stories deal with terror and madness, a reflection of the mental illness that claimed his own life at the age of 43.

NOVELS BY MAUPASSANT IN ENGLISH TRANSLATION

Bel Ami (1885). Douglas Parmee (tr). Penguin 1975 $5.95. ISBN 0-14-044315-0

Pierre and Jean (1888). Leonard W. Tancock (tr). Penguin 1979 $4.95. ISBN 0-14-044358-4

Woman's Life (1883). H. N. Sloman (tr). Penguin 1978 $6.95. ISBN 0-14-044161-1

SHORT STORIES BY MAUPASSANT IN ENGLISH TRANSLATION

The Dark Side: Tales of Terror and the Supernatural. Arnold Kellett (tr). Carroll & Graf 1990 $8.95. ISBN 0-88184-596-5 Collection of chilling tales.

Selected Stories. Roger Colet (tr). Penguin 1971 $4.95. ISBN 0-14-044243-X Thirty stories, including "The Jewels" and "A Duel."

Selected Stories. Andrew R. MacAndrew (tr). Meridian 1984 $4.95. ISBN 0-452-00686-4 Twenty-four stories, including "The Necklace" and "A Piece of String."

Novels by Maupassant in French

Bel ami (1885). Schoenhof 1989 $7.95. ISBN 2-07-036865-3
Pierre et Jean (1888). Schoenhof 1962 $7.95. ISBN 2-07-037414-9

Short Stories by Maupassant in French

Contes fantastiques complets. French and European 1977 $9.95. ISBN 0-686-54786-1
Contes du jour et de la nuit. Schoenhof 1977 $7.95. ISBN 2-07-037558-7

Book about Maupassant

Sullivan, Edward D. *Maupassant the Novelist.* Greenwood 1978 $35.00. ISBN 0-313-20497-7 Explores basic themes in each of Maupassant's novels.

MOLIERE (PSEUDONYM OF JEAN-BAPTISTE POQUELIN) 1622–1673

Molière was born in Paris, the son of a successful upholsterer. He received a gentleman's education and studied for the law. At the age of 21, he received an inheritance and was able to embark on a life in the theater with financial security. For 12 years he struggled as an actor and director of his own theater company in the French provinces until, in 1659, his play *Les Précieuses Ridicules (The Pretentious Young Ladies)* won him the friendship and support of France's King Louis XIV.

The father of French comedy, Molière is by far the most popular of all French playwrights. A master of all comic forms, ranging from broad farce to subtle comedies of the intellect, Molière displays a knowledge of both dramatic technique and human nature. Beneath the laughter provoked by his plays, there is usually a serious theme. His plays advocate a balanced, practical approach to life, mocking any form of exaggeration or excess.

Molière's most important plays include *The Prententious Young Ladies* (1659), *The School for Wives* (1662), *Don Juan* (1665), *The Misanthrope* (1666), *Tartuffe* (1669), *The Would-Be Gentleman* (1670), *The Learned Women* (1672), and *The Imaginary Invalid* (1673). His influential play *The Miser* (1668) was the inspiration for U.S. author Thornton Wilder's play, *The Matchmaker,* which later became the basis for the musical *Hello, Dolly.* (*See* Wilder, Vol. 1, American Literature: The Twentieth Century.) Molière died in Paris while performing the title role in *The Imaginary Invalid.*

Plays by Moliere in English Translation

The Misanthrope (1666) *and Other Plays.* Donald M. Frame (tr). Signet 1968 $4.50. ISBN 0-451-52415-2 Includes *The Doctor in Spite of Himself, The Miser* (1668), *The Would-Be Gentleman* (1670), *The Mischievous Machinations of Scapin, The Learned Women* (1672), *The Imaginary Invalid* (1673).
Tartuffe (1669) *and Other Plays.* Donald M. Frame (tr). Signet 1960 $4.50. ISBN 0-451-52454-3 Includes *The Ridiculous Precieuses* (1659), *The School for Husbands, The School for Wives* (1662), *The Critique of the School for Wives, The Versailles Impromptu, Don Juan* (1665), *Tartuffe* (1669).

Plays by Moliere in French

Le bourgeois gentilhomme (1670). French and European 1975 $5.95. ISBN 0-686-54766-7
Don Juan (1665). French and European $5.95. ISBN 0-685-34236-0
L'ecole des femmes (1662). French and European 1964 $5.95. ISBN 0-685-11153-9

Le malade imaginaire (1673). French and European 1964 $5.95. ISBN 0-685-11335-3
Le misanthrope (1666). French and European 1965 $5.95. ISBN 0-685-11396-5
Les précieuses ridicules (1659). French and European 1965 $5.95. ISBN 0-685-11512-7
Le Tartuffe (1669). French and European $7.95. ISBN 0-685-34238-7

BOOKS ABOUT MOLIERE

Bulgakov, Mikhail. *The Life of Monsieur de Molière.* Mirra Ginsburg (tr). New Directions 1986 $9.95. ISBN 0-8112-0956-3 Scholarly and well-documented account of Molière's life.
Walker, Hallam. *Molière.* G. K. Hall 1989 $23.95. ISBN 0-8057-8258-3 Recently revised and updated general study of Moliere's life and works; a good introduction for students.

RACINE, JEAN   1639–1699

Jean Racine was born the son of a lawyer in La Ferté–Milon, France. He was educated at the convent of Port Royal, the center of a French Catholic movement called Jansenism that advocated a return to individual purity and less reliance on church doctrine. As his interest in the theater grew, Racine clashed with the Jansenists, who were opposed to theater in general.

Racine is considered the greatest of French tragic dramatists. His themes are taken from ancient Greek and Roman tragedies and are developed according to dramatic principles laid down by the Greek philosopher Aristotle. Following what he believed to be classical principles, Racine restricted himself to a few characters, limited the action to one location and a single day if possible, and wrote in precise verse. In his plays, Racine was interested in portraying human passions—particularly the passion of love—in a time of crisis. All the action of the play grows out of this central passion, and all other action is clearly secondary to it.

Racine's neoclassical drama is noted for the exceptional beauty of its poetry as well as for the technical brilliance of its structure. His major tragedies include *Andromache* (1667), *Britannicus* (1669), *Berenice* (1670), *Iphigenia* (1674), and *Phaedra* (1677), his greatest masterpiece. Racine married in 1677 and had seven children; he is buried in Port Royal.

PLAYS BY RACINE IN ENGLISH TRANSLATION

Four Greek Plays: Andromache (1667) *Iphigenia* (1674), *Phaedra* (1677), *Athalia* (1691). R. C. Knight (tr). Cambridge Univ Pr 1982 $15.95. ISBN 0-521-24415-3
Andromache (1667) *and Other Plays.* John Cairncross (tr). Penguin 1976 $5.95. ISBN 0-14-044195-6 Includes *Britannicus* (1669) and *Berenice* (1670).

PLAYS BY RACINE IN FRENCH

Andromaque (1667). French and European 1965 $5.95. ISBN 0-685-10999-2
Bérénice (1670). French and European 1964 $5.95. ISBN 0-685-11042-7
Britannicus. (1669). French and European 1964 $5.95. ISBN 0-685-11055-9
Iphigénie (1674). French and European 1965 $5.95. ISBN 0-685-11257-8
Phèdre (1677). French and European 1964 $5.95. ISBN 0-685-11490-2

BOOKS ABOUT RACINE

Goldman, Lucien. *Racine.* Alastair Hamilton (tr). Writers and Readers 1981 $4.95. ISBN 0-906495-77-6 A general introduction to Racine's plays.
Yarrow, P. J. *Racine.* Rowman 1978 $18.50. ISBN 0-87471-830-9 Studies Racine's dramatic talent in its neoclassical context.

SARTRE, JEAN-PAUL 1905–1980

Jean-Paul Sartre was born in Paris, educated at the prestigious Ecole Normale Supérieure, and taught philosophy at universities in France and Germany before World War II. During the war, he fought in the French army and was captured and imprisoned in Germany. Upon his release, he became an active member of the French Resistance until the end of the war.

Sartre was a major figure in the literary and intellectual circles of Europe beginning in the late 1930s. Widely known as the atheistic voice of the philosophy known as *Existentialism,* he believed that humans have no inherent identity at birth and become only what they choose to become. In his view, humans have no essences, or pre-existing natures—only *existence* itself, day-to-day life, determines who people are. Rejecting all notions of a supernatural force directing human lives, Sartre built his philosophy on the ideal of choice. In his view, without a God to guide humans, they must make their own moral decisions.

In his novels and plays, Sartre expresses his philosophy through characters who are confronted with difficult decisions and who gain a sense of personal freedom through their commitment to social and political action. His first play, *The Flies* (1943), was produced during the German occupation of France and is a strong call for defiance. In *No Exit* (1944), one of his most popular plays, he redefines the traditional concept of hell in existentialist terms. In 1964, Sartre was awarded the Nobel Prize for literature but refused to accept it, believing that the whole idea of giving prizes for literature was absurd.

Novels by Sartre in English Translation

The Age of Reason (1945). Vintage 1972 $6.95. ISBN 0-394-71838-0
Nausea (1938). H. Carruth (tr). New Directions 1959 $5.95. ISBN 0-8112-0188-0
The Reprieve (1945). Vintage 1972 $6.95. ISBN 0-394-71839-9
Troubled Sleep (1949). Vintage 1972 $6.95. ISBN 0-394-71840-2

Plays by Sartre in English Translation

No Exit (1944) *and Three Other Plays.* Vintage 1989 $7.95. ISBN 0-679-72516-4 Includes *The Flies* (1943), *Dirty Hands* (1948), and *The Respectful Prostitute* (1947).

Novels by Sartre in French

Age de raison (1945). Schoenhof 1976 $7.95. ISBN 0-686-54973-2
La nausée (1938). Schoenhof 1972 $6.95. ISBN 2-07-036805-X

Plays by Sartre in French

Les séquestrés d'altona (1956). Schoenhof 1972 $7.95. ISBN 2-07-036938-2
Théâtre, Tome I: Les mouches (1943), *Huis clos* (1944), *morts sans sepulture* (1945), *La putain respectueuse* (1947). Schoenhof 1947 $11.95. ISBN 0-685-35917-4

Books about Sartre

Brosman, Katherine Savage. *Jean-Paul Sartre.* G. K. Hall 1987 $16.95. ISBN 0-8057-6544-1 Good general introduction to Sartre's drama, fiction, and philosophy.
Hayman, Ronald. *Sartre: A Life.* Simon 1987 $22.95. ISBN 0-67145442-2 Detailed portrait of Sartre's professional and private life.

THE SONG OF ROLAND   END OF THE ELEVENTH CENTURY

The *Song of Roland* is the oldest and most famous of the surviving medieval *chansons de geste* or "songs of heroic exploits," a type of narrative poem written during the period extending from the end of the eleventh to the fourteenth century. The oldest of the seven existing manuscripts of the text is at Oxford University in England.

Composed by an unknown poet, (perhaps the Turoldus referred to at the end of the poem), the poem is considered to be the first great monument of French literature. Versions of the work also exist in other medieval languages. This epic poem is based on historical incidents going back to the year AD 778, when Charlemagne (a Frankish king who later became emperor of Western Europe) invaded Spain. In the poem, Roland and his friend Oliver are contrasted, with Roland as the rash and impetuous hero and Oliver as a more prudent soldier.

THE SONG OF ROLAND IN ENGLISH TRANSLATION

The Song of Roland. Glyn Burgess (tr). Penguin 1990 $4.50. ISBN 0-14-044532-3

THE SONG OF ROLAND IN FRENCH

Chanson de Roland. Basil Blackwell 1942 $15.95. ISBN 0-631-00390-8

STENDHAL (PSEUDONYM OF HENRI BEYLE)   1783–1842

One of the great French novelists of the nineteenth century, Stendhal describes his unhappy youth with sensitivity and intelligence in his autobiographical novel *The Life of Henri Brulard,* written in 1835 and 1836 but published in 1890, long after his death. Stendhal detested his father, a lawyer from Grenoble, France, whose only passion in life was making money. Therefore, Stendhal left home as soon as he could.

Stendhal served with Napoleon's army in the campaign in Russia in 1812, which helped inspire the famous war scenes in his novel *The Red and the Black* (1831). After Napoleon's fall, Stendhal lived for six years in Italy, a country he loved during his entire life. In 1821, he returned to Paris to a life of literature, politics, and love affairs.

Stendhal's novels feature heroes who reject any form of authority that would restrain their sense of individual freedom. They are an interesting blend of romantic emotionalism and eighteenth-century rationalism. Stendhal's heroes are sensitive, emotional individuals who are in conflict with the society in which they live, yet they have the intelligence and detachment to analyze their society and its faults.

Stendhal was a precursor of the realism of Flaubert. (*See* Flaubert, Vol. 1, World Literature: French Language and Literature.) He once described the novelist's function as that of a person carrying a mirror down a highway so that the mirror would reflect life as it was, for all society.

NOVELS BY STENDHAL IN ENGLISH TRANSLATION

The Charterhouse of Parma (1839). Meridian 1962 $4.95. ISBN 0-452-0089-3
The Life of Henri Brulard (1890). Jean Stewart and B. C. Knight (trs). Univ of Chicago Pr 1986 $12.95. ISBN 0-236-77251-9
The Red and the Black (1831). Bantam 1989 $3.95. ISBN 0-553-21357-1

NOVELS BY STENDHAL IN FRENCH

La chartreuse de Parme (1839). French and European $9.95. ISBN 0-685-35010-X
Le rouge et le noir (1831). French and European 1958 $9.95. ISBN 0-685-11543-7

BOOKS ABOUT STENDHAL

Bloom, Harold (ed). *Stendhal.* Chelsea 1987 $24.50. ISBN 1-55546-311-8 Collection of
   critical essays that provide different perspectives on Stendhal's works.
Hemmings, Frederick W. *Stendhal: A Study of His Novels.* Oxford Univ Pr 1964 $14.95.
   ISBN 0-19-815355-4 Scholarly analysis of the themes and psychological aspects
   of Stendhal's works.

VERNE, JULES   1828–1905

Jules Verne, the father of modern science fiction, was born in Nantes, France,
where he began his education before moving on to Paris to study law. Attracted
to the theater, he began writing stories for the opera in 1848.

Verne divided his time between his law practice and his writing until
1863. That year he wrote the novel *Five Weeks in a Balloon,* an adventure story
featuring the technical aspects of the still new science of ballooning. The
novel was extremely popular and encouraged Verne to continue writing stories that combined adventure and science. Verne wrote 50 such novels before
he died, giving birth to the new genre of science fiction, which has grown
steadily ever since.

Verne's best-known works are *A Journey to the Center of the Earth* (1864), *From
the Earth to the Moon* (1865), *Twenty Thousand Leagues Under the Sea* (1870), *Around*

The Discovery of the Chest.
Illustration by N. C. Wyeth (1918)
from *The Mysterious Island.*
Reprinted with permission of Charles
Scribner's Sons, an imprint of
Macmillan Publishing Company.
Copyright 1918 and 1946 by Charles
Scribner's Sons.

the World in Eighty Days (1873), and *The Mysterious Island* (1875). All of these have been made into films or television plays, some quite recently. Verne remains a popular author, especially with young readers.

NOVELS BY VERNE IN ENGLISH TRANSLATION

*Around the World in Eighty Days (1873). George M. Towle (tr). Bantam 1984 $2.25. ISBN 0-553-21145-5 Story of an Englishman, Philéas Fogg, his servant, Passepartout, and their attempt to circle the world in 80 days.
*Five Weeks in a Balloon (1863). Amereon (repr of 1869 ed) $21.95. ISBN 0-88411-907-6 Recounts a dangerous and exciting flight in the early days of ballooning.
*From the Earth to the Moon (1865). Airmont 1967 $1.75. ISBN 0-8049-0142-2 The tale of a voyage to the moon.
*Journey to the Center of the Earth (1864). Penguin 1986 $2.25. ISBN 0-14-035049-7 Story of a group of people who find adventure deep below the earth's crust.
* The Mysterious Island (1875). Signet 1986 $2.50. ISBN 0-451-52066-1 Adventurers stumble on the island home of the mysterious Captain Nemo.
*Twenty Thousand Leagues Under the Sea (1870). Bantam 1985 $2.50. ISBN 0-553-21252-4 Adventures of Captain Nemo and his marvelous ship *Nautilus* that sails under the sea.

NOVELS BY VERNE IN FRENCH

Cinq semaines en ballon (1863). French and European 1977 $8.95. ISBN 0-685-37131-X
De la terre à la lune (1865). French and European 1973 $10.95. ISBN 0-686-55042-0
L'ile mystérieuse (1875). French and European 1976 $10.95. ISBN 0-685-37134-4
Le tour du monde en 80 jours (1873). French and European 1976 $11.95. ISBN 0-686-55955-X
Vingt mille lieues sous la mer (1870). French and European 1977 $8.50. ISBN 0-685-37138-7
Voyage au centre de la terre (1864). Schoenhof $10.95. ISBN 0-685-37139-5

BOOK ABOUT VERNE

Evans, I. O. *Jules Verne and His Work.* Amereon 1976 $15.95. ISBN 0-88411-906-8 Detailed study of Verne's life and works, emphasizing his adventure novels.

VOLTAIRE (PSEUDONYM OF FRANÇOIS-MARIE AROUET) 1694–1778

Born in Paris the son of a government official, François-Marie Arouet was educated at the College Louis-le-Grand, a Jesuit seminary. He was educated to be a lawyer, but he had no taste for the law. When he was sent to Holland as a diplomat, an unwise love affair caused him to be sent back quickly to France. Shortly after returning, he was charged with writing a scathing satire of the nobility and was sent to prison for 11 months. While there, he assumed the name Voltaire and continued his writing.

Throughout his life, Voltaire was a progressive thinker and an opponent of political and religious oppression. He was instrumental in popularizing philosophical, religious, and scientific ideas that were frequently derived from liberal thinkers in England, where he lived for two years after his imprisonment. Probably more than anything else, Voltaire can be characterized as a "liberator," fighting always for man's freedom. Despite his many works of philosophy, plays, and political essays, Voltaire is best known to twentieth-century readers as the author of the novel *Candide* (1759), a masterpiece of satire on the overly optimistic views of the German philosopher Leibniz, for whom "all is for the best in this the best of all possible worlds." *Candide,* which has been called a "philosophical romance," was made into a musical by American composer and conductor Leonard Bernstein and played successfully in New York City on Broadway.

BOOK BY VOLTAIRE IN ENGLISH TRANSLATION

Candide (1759). Random 1985 $10.95. ISBN 0-394-60522-5

BOOK BY VOLTAIRE IN FRENCH

Candide (1759). French and European 1971 $3.95. ISBN 0-686-55740-9

BOOKS ABOUT VOLTAIRE

Andrews, Wayne. *Voltaire.* New Directions 1981 $6.95. ISBN 0-8112-0802-8 Brief study of Voltaire's philosophical positions within the context of the Enlightenment.

Richter, Peyton, and Ilona Ricardo. *Voltaire.* G. K. Hall 1980 $16.95. ISBN 0-8057-6425-9 Good general introduction to Voltaire's life and works; contains a chronology and bibliography.

ZOLA, EMILE   1840–1902

Emile Zola was born in Paris, the son of an Italian engineer. He began his literary career as a journalist but soon began writing short stories that were well received. With several other Parisian writers, including Gustave Flaubert (*see* Flaubert, Vol. 1, World Literature: French Language and Literature), he formed an informal literary society devoted to the discussion and analysis of literature. From this group Zola emerged as the champion of a literary philosophy called *Naturalism,* which focused on sociological detail to demonstrate how social forces inevitably shaped and often destroyed human beings. Thus Zola advocated what he called the scientific approach to literature. He described his theory in *Le roman expérimental (The Experimental Novel)* (1880). American author Theodore Dreiser's work was greatly influenced by these theories (*see* Dreiser, Vol. 1, American Literature: The Rise of Realism).

Zola was the author of a series of 20 novels called *The Rougon–Macquart,* in which he attempted to trace scientifically the effects of heredity through five generations of the Rougon and Macquart families. Three of the outstanding volumes are *L'assommoir* (1877), a study of alcoholism and the working class; *Nana* (1880), a story of a prostitute who destroys men; and *Germinal* (1885), a study of a strike at a coal mine. All provide an opportunity for Zola to display his gift for portraying crowds in turmoil, his passion for detail and his insight into environmental influences. Zola's novels continue to be read with enjoyment despite the fact that his literary theories have long been out of fashion.

NOVELS BY ZOLA IN ENGLISH TRANSLATION

L'Assommoir (1877). Penguin 1970 $6.95. ISBN 0-14-044231-6

La Bête Humaine (1890). Leonard W. Tancock (tr). Penguin 1977 $5.95. ISBN 0-14-044327-4

The Debacle (1892). Leonard W. Tancock (tr). Penguin 1973 $5.95. ISBN 0-14-044280-4

The Earth (1887). Douglas Parmee (tr). Penguin 1980 $5.95. ISBN 0-14-044387-8

Germinal (1885). Signet 1970 $3.95. ISBN 0-451-51975-2

Nana (1880). George Holden (tr). Penguin 1972 $6.95. ISBN 0-14-044263-4

Therese Raquin (1867). Leonard W. Tancock (tr). Penguin 1962 $5.95. ISBN 0-14-044120-4

Novels by Zola in French

L'assommoir (1877). Jacques Dubois (ed). French and European 1975 $4.95. ISBN 0-686-55765-4

La bête humaine (1890). Henri Mitterand (ed). French and European 1977 $4.95. ISBN 0-686-55769-7

La débâcle (1892). Schoenhof 1976 $10.95. ISBN 2-07-037586-2

Germinal (1885). Henri Guillmin (ed). French and European 1975 $4.95. ISBN 0-686-55781-6

Nana (1880). Henri Mitterand (ed). Schoenhof 1977 $7.95. ISBN 2-07-036956-0

La terre (1887). Marcel Girard (ed). Schoenhof 1973 $9.95. ISBN 2-07-037177-8

Thérèse Raquin (1867). Schoenhof 1970 $7.95. ISBN 2-07-037116-6

Books about Zola

Baguley, David, *et al. Critical Essays on Emile Zola.* G. K. Hall 1986 $35.00. ISBN 0-8161-8826-2 Collection of essays from 1868 to the present giving a variety of views on Zola's work.

Knapp, Bettina L. *Emile Zola.* Ungar 1980 $18.95. ISBN 0-8044-2482-9 Good general study of Zola's life and works; contains a bibliography and a chronology.

ITALIAN LANGUAGE AND LITERATURE

The Italian Language

In the third century BC, when the city of Rome was under the rule of the Roman Empire, the inhabitants of the Italian peninsula gradually adopted Rome's Latin language as their language. However, different sections of Italy developed slightly different pronunciations and vocabularies in the spoken, or vernacular, Latin that they used. With the decline and eventual fall of Rome in the fifth century AD, these vernacular versions of Latin became more important locally, even though pure Latin remained the language of the church and small groups of ruling aristocrats.

Over the centuries these spoken languages developed into varying forms, or dialects, that were recognizably different from the standard written Latin of the church and government. By about AD 1000, these dialects formed the beginning of the Italian language, although they remained quite different from one another.

Then, in the early thirteenth century, these dialects began to appear in writing, which previously had been entirely in Latin. As writers put their words on paper, they tended to make them conform to Latin grammar. Thus, the written dialects began to look somewhat alike, even though the spoken languages were still very different. Because Sicily and its court of Emperor Frederick II were the center of Italian culture during this period, the Sicilian dialect became the principal literary language.

With the death of Frederick II in 1250, Sicilian influence began to decline, and the city-states of Tuscany in central Italy began to gain power. By the late thirteenth century, the city of Florence was fast becoming the cultural center of Italy, and literature written in the Tuscan dialect began to come to the fore. When the great Florentine poet Dante Alighieri began to publish his works in the early fourteenth century, the Tuscan dialect in which he wrote became the literary language for all of Italy. Other great writers from Florence, most notably Petrarch and Boccaccio, followed Dante, assuring Tuscan its place as the primary Italian dialect and the basis of the modern Italian language.

By the middle of the sixteenth century, Italian had replaced Latin almost everywhere in Italy as both the spoken and written language, with the Tuscan dialect being considered the "pure" Italian of the educated classes. During the late sixteenth and seventeenth centuries, there were several challenges to the supremacy of the Tuscan dialect, but it retained its claim to being the legitimate Italian language.

Up to this point, the territory we now call Italy was actually made up of many small kingdoms, city-states, and separate territories. Finally, in the middle of the nineteenth century, Italy became united into one nation, whose center of power returned to Rome in 1870. The language that was taught in the new nation's schools was a modernized form of the Tuscan dialect.

Over the past 100 years, the Italian language has lost much of its original Tuscan character, so the Italian that is taught in today's schools and is used in writing and formal speech can be considered a truly national language. However, many local dialects are still spoken throughout Italy that bear only slight resemblance to "official" Italian and almost no resemblance to one another. A speaker of Piedmontese, from far northern Italy, would have much more difficulty conversing with a speaker of the dialect from the southern island of Sicily than would, for example, a speaker from the U.S. state of Maine, conversing with a speaker from southern Alabama.

Grammatically, Italian has remained much closer to its Latin roots than have the other Romance languages (those derived from Latin, such as French, Spanish, or Rumanian). In the conjugations, moods, and tenses of its verbs, in its vocabulary, and in its retention of the emphasis at the end of a sentence, Italian strongly reflects its Latin heritage.

BOOKS ON THE ITALIAN LANGUAGE

The books listed below provide an introduction to the history and grammar of modern Italian. The list does not include the many dictionaries and instructional textbooks that are widely available.

Burzio, Luigi. *Italian Syntax.* Kluwer Academic 1986 $24.95. ISBN 90-277-2015-0

Castiglione, Pierina B. *Italian Phonetics, Diction and Intonation.* Vanni 1986 $11.50. ISBN 0-913298-77-8

Devoto, Giacomo. *The Languages of Italy.* V. Louise Katainen (tr). Univ of Chicago Pr 1978 $30.00. ISBN 0-226-14368-6

Kibble, Lawrence, and Wayne Storey. *Italian Grammar.* Harper 1982 $5.95. ISBN 0-06-460199-4

Lepschy, Anne L., and Guido Lepschy. *The Italian Language Today.* New Amsterdam 1988 $16.95. ISBN 0-941533-22-0

ITALIAN LITERATURE

Italian literature can be divided into five major overlapping periods. The first period began in the late Middle Ages with the first significant use of an Italian dialect for literary purposes. During the twelfth and thirteenth centuries, literary centers flourished first at the court of Frederick II in Sicily and later in Perugia and Bologna, and finally in Florence. In Florence Dante produced his long poem, *The Divine Comedy* (1302–1321), the crowning achievement of the period.

Petrarch and Giovanni Boccaccio began the second period of Italian literature, which extends from the fourteenth through the sixteenth centuries. The literary masterpieces of this period are Petrarch's sonnets and songs, Boccaccio's *The Decameron* (1348–1353), Ariosto's *Orlando Furioso* (1532), Machiavelli's *The Prince* (1532) and *Mandragola* (1524), and Tasso's epic poem, *Gerusalema Liberata* (1575). When France and Spain marched their armies into Italy late in the fifteenth century, the Italian optimism of the Renaissance abruptly collapsed, setting the stage for a new movement in literature and art that did not really take hold for another 100 years.

The seventeenth century saw Italian literature become much more stylized and formal. Almost as if to compensate for the political upheaval brought on by the wars of the sixteenth century, seventeenth-century Italian writers became very rigid and orderly in their writing. Distinct literary styles were in fashion at different times, but the result was conformity to the prevailing style rather than expressions of individual genius. The most notable products of this period were the brilliant philosophical works of Giambattista Vico and the *commedia dell'arte,* a form of folk theater that remains popular today.

The fourth period of Italian literature began at the close of the seventeenth century with the radical changes in the Italian theater initiated by Italian playwrights Carlo Goldoni and Carlo Gozzi. However, these departures did not find their full expression until much later in the eighteenth century, in the drama of Vittorio Alfieri and the poetry of Giuseppe Parini. The message of this new movement was simple: if an Italy degraded by centuries of living under foreign rule was ever to assume a respected place among modern nations, Italians would have to become ashamed of the hypocritical lives they had learned to lead under their foreign masters. This nationalistic movement was fueled by the French Revolution at the end of the eighteenth century and by the political writings of such Italian theorists as Mazzini, Foscolo, Giusti, and de Sanctis. The giants of the early nineteenth century, however, were Alessandro Manzoni, whose novel *I Promessi Sposi* (1825–1826) remains an Italian classic; and Giacomo Leopardi, whose poetry ranks among the finest the world has produced.

After the unification of Italy in the late nineteenth century, Italian literature entered a period of searching for its identity. The early twentieth century saw the beginning of an array of "isms" that has extended into contemporary literature: Neobohemianism, Futurism, Hermeticism, Neorealism, and Experimentalism have each seen their day. Out of this turmoil, Italian literature has produced a host of twentieth-century literary talents. Since Giosuè Carducci won Italy's first Nobel Prize for literature in 1906, four other Italian writers have received this award: Grazia Deledda (1926), Luigi Pirandello (1934), Salvatore Quasimodo (1959), and Eugenio Montale (1975). In addition are such writers as Giorgio Bassani, who won world recognition with such works as *The Garden of the Finzi-Continis,* in which he analyzes the cloistered life of an aristocratic Jewish family that finally disappears in 1943 in the German concentration camps. Contemporary Italian literature shows its greatest promise in the experimental efforts of a new generation of novelists, playwrights, and poets.

Collections of Italian Literature in English Translation

Bassani, Giorgio. *Italian Stories.* Schocken 1989 $9.95. ISBN 0-8052-0877-1

Bentley, Eric (ed). *The Servant of Two Masters and Other Italian Classics.* Applause Theatre Bk 1986 $7.95. ISBN 0-936839-20-1

Bondanella, Julia Conway, and Mark Musa (eds). *The Italian Renaissance Reader.* Meridian 1987 $10.95. ISBN 0-452-01013-6

*Calvino, Italo. *Italian Folktales.* Pantheon 1981 $11.95. ISBN 0-394-74909-X Two hundred classic Italian tales, from the Middle Ages to the nineteenth century.

Smarr, Janet L. (tr). *Italian Renaissance Tales.* Solaris 1983 $13.95. ISBN 0-933760-03-5

Smith, Lawrence R. (ed). *The New Italian Poetry, 1945 to the Present: A Bilingual Anthology.* Univ of California Pr 1981 $12.95. ISBN 0-520-04411-8

Spatola, Adriano, and Paul Vangelisti (eds). *Italian Poetry, 1960–1980.* Invisible 1982 $7.50. ISBN 0-88031-060-X

Trevelyan, Raleigh (ed). *Italian Short Stories.* Penguin 1989 $6.95. ISBN 0-14-002196-5

Viglionese, Paschal C. *Italian Writers of the Seventeenth and Eighteenth Centuries.* McFarland 1988 $39.95. ISBN 0-89950-366-7

BOCCACCIO, GIOVANNI   1313–1375

Although a Tuscan—like famed Italian poets Petrarch and Dante Alighieri (*see* Dante *and* Petrarch, Vol. 1, World Literature: Italian Language and Literature)—Giovanni Boccaccio was raised and educated in Naples, Italy, where he wrote his first books. In 1340 he went to Florence, where in 1348 he witnessed the outbreak of the great plague, the so-called Black Death. This provided the setting for his most famous work, the prose masterpiece *Il Decamerone (The Decameron)* (1348–1353).

This classic work, written in Italian rather than in the customary Latin of the time, is a collection of 100 short stories told by 10 Florentines who leave plague-infested Florence for the safety of the country. In the neighboring hill town of Fiesole, the beauty of which is repeatedly described, each of the 10 tells a tale a day for a period of 10 days. Hence the name *decameron,* which is derived from the Greek word meaning "10 days."

Although many of these stories are retellings of medieval sermons or well-known folktales, Boccaccio gives them new life and meaning. It is possible to read *The Decameron* as an allegory, with the plague representing the "spiritual plague" of medieval Christianity as viewed by the humanistic Renaissance. *The Decameron* was enormously popular and had a major influence on much of European literature, including the *Canterbury Tales* of English writer Geoffrey Chaucer. (*See* Chaucer, Vol. 1, British Literature: The Early Years.)

SHORT STORIES BY BOCCACCIO IN ENGLISH TRANSLATION

The Decameron (1348–1353). G. H. McWilliam (tr). Penguin 1972 $6.95. ISBN 0-14-044269-3

SHORT STORIES BY BOCCACCIO IN ITALIAN

The Decameron: A Diplomatic Edition (1348–1353). Charles S. Singleton (ed). Johns Hopkins Univ Pr 1974 $95.00. ISBN 0-8018-1465-0

The Decameron: A Selection (1348–1353). St. Martin's 1988 $11.95. ISBN 0-7190-0934-0

BOOK ABOUT BOCCACCIO

Hutton, Edward. *Some Aspects of the Genius of Giovanni Boccaccio.* Gordon Pr 1977 $59.95. ISBN 0-8490-2625-3 Scholarly study of Boccaccio's works, with special attention to *The Decameron.*

CARDUCCI, GIOSUE   1835–1907

Giosuè Carducci was born the son of a physician in Valdicastello, near the Italian city of Pisa. A professor of Italian literature at the University of Bologna, he was elected to the Italian Parliament in 1876. By the time he received Italy's first Nobel Prize for literature in 1906, Carducci was not only Italy's leading poet, but also its first ranking critic and classical scholar.

Carducci has been called "the prophet of Italy in its finest hour" because of his prominence during Italy's early days as a modern nation. Carducci celebrated Italy's classical heritage and sought to return its literature to more traditional forms and subjects. His *Odes* (1873–1879) were experiments in the use of classical meters and structures within the modern Italian language.

POETRY BY CARDUCCI IN ENGLISH TRANSLATION

The Best Poems. Montgomery Trinidad (tr). 2 vols. American Classical Coll Pr 1979 $187.45. ISBN 0-89266-211-5
The Inspired Poetry by Joshua Carducci (1916). V. Corradini (tr). 2 vols. Found Class Repr 1982 $187.45. ISBN 0-89901-074-1

DANTE ALIGHIERI 1265–1321

Born in Florence, Dante Alighieri was the poet destined to give Italy both its greatest literary masterpiece and its national language. Almost all that is known about Dante's personal life is what is revealed in his works. It is, therefore, impossible to tell what is truth and what is fiction.

By far the most important of Dante's works is *The Divine Comedy* (1302–1321), a long poem in three books that describes Dante's imaginary visits to Hell, Purgatory, and Paradise (Heaven). At the literal level, the poem can be read as an epic journey through three wonderfully imaginative realms of the after-life. At a second level, the poem describes and comments on the life and politics of Dante's Florence. At yet another level, it can be read as a religious allegory, describing the journey of a Christian soul as it seeks to be united with God. In one of the great literary achievements of all time, Dante succeeds in combining all these levels in such a way that the reader is somehow aware of all of them simultaneously.

In addition to *The Divine Comedy,* Dante wrote *La Vita Nuova (The New Life)* (1292–1295), a collection of lyric poetry with prose commentary, as well as several prose works of philosophy.

Because of his political views, Dante was exiled from his beloved city of Florence for many years. This exile, however, made him a citizen of all Italy and not just of one city. Therefore, when he wrote his great poem, he chose Italian rather than Latin, giving his Tuscan dialect a special influence in the development of the new Italian language.

WORKS OF DANTE IN ENGLISH TRANSLATION

The Portable Dante. Penguin 1977 $8.95. ISBN 0-14-015032-3

POETRY BY DANTE IN BILINGUAL EDITIONS

Inferno (1302–c. 1310). Allen Mandelbaum (tr). Bantam 1982 $2.95. ISBN 0-553-21339-3
Purgatorio (c. 1309–1315). Allen Mandelbaum (tr). Bantam 1984 $2.95. ISBN 0-553-21344-X
Paradiso (c. 1316–1321). Allen Mandelbaum (tr). Bantam 1986 $2.95. ISBN 0-553-21204-4

BOOKS ABOUT DANTE

Bloom, Harold (ed). *Dante.* Chelsea 1986 $29.95. ISBN 0-87754-665-7 Collection of modern critical essays that assess the works of Dante from a variety of perspectives.

Holmes, George. *Dante*. Oxford Univ Pr 1987 $5.95. ISBN 0-19-287504-3 Good study of Dante's works, beliefs, and life.

Quinones, Ricardo J. *Dante*. G. K. Hall 1985 $7.95. ISBN 0-8057-6614-6 General introduction to Dante's life and works.

MORAVIA, ALBERTO 1907–1990

Born in Rome of Jewish-Catholic parents, Alberto Moravia published his first novel, *Time of Indifference* (1929), during the rule of Mussolini's fascists. In it he examines the decadent upper-middle class society of Rome, showing it to be apathetic and absorbed with sex and money.

The novel was enormously successful and marked Moravia as one of Italy's leading young writers. His popularity continued after World War II, when he published a series of novels that thrust him to the forefront of Italy's new wave of postwar authors. Among these books was the highly successful *Two Women* (1957), the story of a shopkeeper and her daughter learning to adapt to postwar life in Italy. Many consider *Two Women* Moravia's best novel, and it later became a popular film starring Sophia Loren.

NOVELS BY MORAVIA IN ENGLISH TRANSLATION

Nineteen Thirty-Four (1982). William Weaver (tr). Farrar 1983 $14.50. ISBN 0-374-22254-1

Time of Desecration (1978). Angus Davidson (tr). Farrar 1980 $12.95. ISBN 0-374-27781-8

SHORT STORIES BY MORAVIA IN ITALIAN

Racconti di Alberto Moravia. Vincenzo Traversa (ed). Irvington 1979 $12.95. ISBN 0-89197-368-0

Sette racconti. EMC 1981 $5.95. ISBN 0-88436-060-1

PETRARCH (FRANCESCO PETRARCA) 1304–1374

Son of an exiled Florentine clerk, Petrarch was born in Arezzo, Italy, but was raised at the court of the Pope in Avignon in southern France. He studied the classics in France and continued his education at the University of Bologna in Italy.

Less than a year after his return to Avignon in 1326, Petrarch fell in love with the woman he referred to as Laura in his most famous poetry. Although he never revealed her true name nor, apparently, ever expressed his love to her directly, he made her immortal with his *Canzoniere* (date unknown), or songbook, a collection of lyric poems and sonnets that rank among the most beautiful written in Italian, or in any other language.

Like the major Italian poet Dante Alighieri, Petrarch chose to write his most intimate feelings in his native Italian, rather than the Latin customary at that time. Petrarch used Latin for his more formal works, however. He incorrectly assumed that he would be remembered for the Latin works, but it was his Italian lyric poetry that influenced both the content and form of all subsequent European poetry, especially English poetry. Petrarch's sonnet form was prized by English poets as an alternative to English poet William Shakespeare's sonnet form.

POETRY BY PETRARCH IN ENGLISH TRANSLATION

Selections from the Canzoniere and Other Works. Mark Musa (tr). Oxford Univ Pr 1986 $12.50. ISBN 0-19-281707-8

BOOKS ABOUT PETRARCH

Bloom, Harold (ed). *Petrarch.* Chelsea 1989 $29.95. ISBN 1-55546-308-8 Collection of modern critical essays that approach Petrarch's poetry from a variety of viewpoints.

Mann, Nicholas. *Petrarch.* Oxford Univ Pr 1984 $12.95. ISBN 0-19-287610-4 Biographical study that looks at Petrarch's self-consciousness as a unifying force in his work.

PIRANDELLO, LUIGI   1867–1936

Born in Sicily, Luigi Pirandello attended the universities of Palermo and Rome in Italy and Bonn in Germany, before settling in Rome to teach and write. In all, Pirandello wrote six novels, some 250 short stories, and about 50 plays. It was a novel, *Il fu Mattia Pascal (The Late Mattia Pascal)* that first brought him fame in 1904. Not until 1920, however, when he was past 50 years old, did he turn seriously to writing plays, the work for which he is now best known.

Pirandello's plays tend to explore three topics: the nature of the theater; the complexities of human personality; and the relationship of the individual to society, religion, and art. Besides his world-famous play *Six Characters in Search of an Author* (1921), his best dramatic works include *It Is So (If You Think So)* (1917), *Henry IV* (1922), *Each in His Own Way* (1924), and *As You Desire Me* (1930). Another work, *The Mountain Giants,* was begun after Pirandello was awarded the Nobel Prize for literature in 1934 and left incomplete when he died two years later.

NOVEL BY PIRANDELLO IN ENGLISH TRANSLATION

The Late Mattia Pascal (1904). William Weaver (tr). Eridanos 1988 $23.00. ISBN 0-941419-09-6

SHORT STORIES BY PIRANDELLO IN ENGLISH TRANSLATION

Tales of Madness. Giovanni R. Bussino (tr). Dante Univ 1984 $14.50. ISBN 0-937832-26-X

Tales of Suicide. Giovanni R. Bussino (tr). Dante Univ 1988 $11.95. ISBN 0-937832-31-6

PLAYS BY PIRANDELLO IN ENGLISH TRANSLATION

Naked Masks: Five Plays. Eric Bentley (ed). Dutton 1957 $7.95. ISBN 0-525-48499-X

Pirandello's Major Plays. Eric Bentley (ed). Northwestern Univ Pr 1990 $9.95. ISBN 0-8101-0867-4

SHORT STORIES BY PIRANDELLO IN ITALIAN

Novelle per un anno. C. A. McCormick (ed). St. Martin's 1988 $12.95. ISBN 0-7190-0469-1

PLAYS BY PIRANDELLO IN ITALIAN

Three Plays: Enrico IV (1922), *Sei Personaggi in Cerca d'autore* (1921), *La Giara* (1927). F. Fifth (ed). St. Martin's 1988 $12.95. ISBN 0-7190-0346-6

BOOKS ABOUT PIRANDELLO

Basnett-McGuire. *Luigi Pirandello.* Grove 1968 $9.95. ISBN 0-394-62410-6 Examines Pirandello's theatrical range and contrasts key plays in each of the stylistic areas of his work.

Bloom, Harold (ed). Chelsea 1989 $24.95. ISBN 1-55546-307-X Collection of modern critical essays that examines Pirandello's life and work; a good general overview.

SPANISH LANGUAGE AND LITERATURE

THE SPANISH LANGUAGE

Spanish is a Romance language: a modern language that developed from ancient Latin. As the old Roman Empire expanded throughout Europe, the Romans conquered the Iberian peninsula (where modern Spain and Portugal are located) in the third and second centuries BC. The native Iberians learned the common, or vulgar, Latin spoken by the Roman soldiers who occupied their land and gradually adopted it as their own. By the time of the birth of Christ, almost the entire peninsula spoke this local form of Latin, which changed slowly over the next four centuries into a new language called Romance, still similar in many ways to Latin.

Early in the fifth century, the Iberian peninsula was again invaded, this time by Germanic tribes called Goths. Although they controlled the area for 300 years, the Goths had little influence on the Romance language. However, in 711, the Moors, an Arabic people, conquered almost the entire Iberian peninsula, and their effect on the local language and culture was significant. More than 4,000 modern Spanish words are Arabic in origin, and many place names in southern Spain are taken directly from the Arabic. Most of the new Arabic words added to the Romance language of medieval Spain had to do with the activities of the Moorish conquerors, such as warfare, administration, coins and money, weights and measures, and science. Certain grammatical features of the language also changed under Arabic influence, such as the practice of adding suffixes to adjectives.

By the year 1000, the language spoken on the Iberian peninsula had changed so much that no ancient Roman would have recognized it. There were in fact several forms, or dialects, of this language that were spoken in different parts of the peninsula. One of these regions, an area known as Castile, became very powerful during the thirteenth century. Because of its military, political, and cultural importance, its dialect, Castilian, became the dominant language of the Iberian peninsula.

During this same period, two other dialects developed into separate languages. The Galician–Portuguese dialect of the western part of the peninsula developed into Portuguese, and the Catalán dialect of the northeast became the Catalán language.

The language spoken by the Castilians from the middle of the thirteenth century to the end of the fourteenth is known as Old Spanish, and is the first literary, or written, form of the Spanish language. Over a period of 150 years, Old Spanish developed a somewhat regular spelling and rudimentary rules of grammar. It became the official language of Castilian Spain.

During the fourteenth and fifteenth centuries, Castilian Spanish spread rapidly throughout the country, both as a spoken and a literary language. During this period of "Middle Spanish," the language acquired more formal rules of grammar and spelling and became the standard language of the ruling classes and wealthy merchants.

Spanish exploration and colonization of North and South America in the sixteenth and seventeenth centuries spread the Castilian language throughout the Western Hemisphere. By then it was very similar to modern Spanish. Spanish, now spoken by 341 million people around the world, is the official language of Mexico and most nations of Central and South America (except Brazil), although the versions of the language used in the Americas vary somewhat from the language of Spain.

BOOKS ON THE SPANISH LANGUAGE

The following books provide an introduction to the history and grammar of modern Spanish. The list does not include the many dictionaries and instructional textbooks that are widely available.

Aldaraca, Bridget, and Edward Baker. *Spanish Grammar.* Harcourt 1986 $8.95. ISBN 0-15-601689-3

Canfield, D. Lincoln. *Spanish Pronunciation in the Americas.* Univ of Chicago Pr 1981 $4.95. ISBN 0-226-09263-1

Cortes, Carlos. *The Spanish and Portuguese Languages in the United States.* Ayer 1981 $33.50. ISBN 0-405-13181-X

Greenfield, Eric. *Spanish Grammar.* Harper 1972 $6.95. ISBN 0-06-460042-4

Ramboz, Ina W. *Spanish Verbs and Essentials of Grammar.* National Textbook 1983 $5.95. ISBN 0-8442-7214-0

Sole, Yolanda, and Carlos Sole. *Modern Spanish Syntax.* Heath 1976 $27.50. ISBN 0-669-00193-7

SPANISH LITERATURE

The Poem of the Cid (*c.* 1140) was widely considered to be the oldest surviving piece of Spanish literature until 1948, when some Hebrew poems discovered in Cairo, Egypt, were found to contain verses in Spanish. About 50 of these Hebrew poems, dated from around 1040, have been discovered, making up the oldest known lyric poetry in a Romance language. These anonymous verses, born out of a mixture of Arabic, Hebrew, and Spanish cultures, are an appropriate beginning for a Spanish literature that is characterized by its folk roots and deeply influenced by eight centuries of Arab rule and religious tolerance that, for a long period of time, extended to Jews.

Early in its history, Spain developed a tradition of popular ballads that told of such important events as battles, deaths, and weddings. Some of the ballads that have survived to the present day are apparently fragments of longer poems, probably epic tales of heroic adventures. The one Spanish epic that has survived intact is *The Poem of the Cid,* a narrative that relates the adventures of Rodrigo Díaz de Vivar, a Castilian soldier and aristocrat known as El Cid.

During the twelfth to the fourteenth centuries in the northwest section of Spain, a tradition of love poetry and satiric songs developed that also influenced the style and substance of later Spanish poetry. In addition to this tradition of ballads and songs, there was a smaller body of early literature developed by priests, one of whom, Gonzalo de Berceo, is the first Spanish author known by name.

Under the rule of King Ferdinand and Queen Isabella, Spain entered a period of literary achievement known as the Golden Age, lasting from 1530 to nearly the end of the sixteenth century. It included the development of the poetry of Garcilaso de la Vega and the dramas of Calderón de la Barca. The Golden Age also saw important developments in the novel and the theater. During this period, especially toward its end, Spanish poetry became very stylized and ornamental. Poets became increasingly concerned with saying things as elaborately and decoratively as possible, and less interested in what they said than in how they said it.

The Spanish novel was born during the Golden Age with *The Life of Lazarillo de Tormes* (1554), an anonymous work that describes the adventures of a young man as he makes his way in the world. This novel had many imitators, including some who satirized its form. The most successful of these satirists was Miguel de Cervantes, whose novel *Don Quixote* (1603) remains one of Spain's great classics.

In the theater at this time, Lope de Vega not only produced an extraordinary number of plays but laid the foundation for the development of a uniquely Spanish drama.

Another major development during the Golden Age was the writing of the mystics, whose colorful religious poetry and prose became a major influence on Spanish literature. Spain produced over 3,000 mystics, of whom the best known is probably Santa Teresa de Avila. Her humorous, colloquial style was widely admired and imitated. Her follower, Fray Luis de León, is considered one of Spain's greatest lyric poets.

During the 1600s, Spanish poetry became more flowery and ornamental under the leadership of Luis de Góngora y Argote. His elaborate, ornate style was so influential that it became known as gongorism and dominated Spanish poetry until the end of the seventeenth century.

The eighteenth and early nineteenth centuries were relatively quiet periods in the development of Spanish literature. The founding of the Royal Academy of Spain in the eighteenth century, modeled after the French Academy and intended to preserve the purity of the Spanish language, led only to the production of dull, lifeless, and stylistically "correct" literature.

The brief romantic period that followed in the early nineteenth century was concerned mostly with nationalism and emphasized Spain's literary and cultural history. During the second half of the nineteenth century, the Spanish novel began a period of explosive development led by the majestic realistic and historical works of Benito Pérez Galdós.

Spain's loss of Cuba in the Spanish–American War of 1898–1899 called the nation's attention to its decline over the centuries. A new group of writers, the Generation of 1898, dedicated themselves to rediscovering the true spirit of Spain, including the renewal of the Spanish language. Major writers in this group included novelist, playwright, and poet Miguel de Unomuno, dramatist Jacinto Benavente, novelist and playwright Ramón María del Valle-Inclán, and novelist Pío Baroja. These concerns led to a movement toward a new "pure poetry" in the early twentieth century.

The Spanish Civil War (1936–1939) slowed the development of Spanish literature to a halt, for many writers were killed, imprisoned, or exiled. Those who remained in Spain were silenced by severe censorship during the long rule of the Fascist dictator Francisco Franco. However, notable writers of the period include poet Juan Ramón Jiménez, who was awarded the Nobel Prize for literature in 1956, and poet Antonio Machado. Novelist José María Gironella is also known for his trilogy about life during and after the Spanish Civil War. Since the end of the fascist regime in 1978, many exiled writers have returned to Spain, and a renewal of Spanish literature has begun.

COLLECTIONS OF SPANISH LITERATURE IN ENGLISH TRANSLATION

Andrian, Gustave W. *Modern Spanish Prose: With a Selection of Poetry.* Macmillan 1987 $27.00. ISBN 0-02-303260-X

Bentley, Eric (ed). *Life Is a Dream and Other Spanish Dramas.* Roy Campbell (tr). Applause Theater Bk 1985 $8.95. ISBN 0-87910-244-6

Clark, B. H. *Masterpieces of Modern Spanish Drama.* Kraus 1969 $23.00. ISBN 0-527-17600-1

Crow, John A. *An Anthology of Spanish Poetry: From the Beginning to the Present Day.* Louisiana State Univ Pr 1979 $8.95. ISBN 0-8071-0483-3

O'Connor, Patricia W., and Anthony Pasquariello. *Contemporary Spanish Theater: Seven One-Act Plays* Macmillan 1980 $19.00. ISBN 0-02-388860-1

Pattison, Walter T., and Donald W. Bleznik. *Representative Spanish Authors.* 2 vols. Oxford Univ Pr 1971. Vol. 1 *From the Middle Ages Through the Eighteenth Century.* $22.00. ISBN 0-19-501433-2. Vol. 2 *The Nineteenth Century to the Present.* $24.00. ISBN 0-19-501433-2

Pott, Beatrice. *Spanish Literature 1700–1900.* Waveland 1989 $14.95. ISBN 0-88133-454-5

CALDERON DE LA BARCA, PEDRO   1600–1681

Pedro Calderón de la Barca, one of Spain's greatest dramatists, was born into an upper-class family in Madrid. He received his early schooling from an order of Catholic priests known as the Jesuits, and then studied law and philosophy at the University of Salamanca.

Calderón was master of the Spanish stage from the death of the Spanish dramatist Lope de Vega (*see* Lope de Vega, Vol. 1, World Literature: Spanish Language and Literature) in 1635 until his own death in 1681. Much of his work examines questions about free will, predestination, and other philosophical issues. He also dealt with themes that are traditional in Spanish drama, such as honor, religion, and loyalty to the monarchy. In *Life Is a Dream* (*c.* 1635) Calderón uses the idea, taken from Greek drama, of a prophecy telling a king that his son will someday kill him. *The Mayor of Zalamea* (*c.* 1642) is an adaptation of a play by Lope de Vega on the theme of honor. *Devotion to the Cross* (1633) is an example of a religious play of the sort Calderón perfected.

In 1651, Calderón became a priest and withdrew from the theater. After 10 years, however, he was recalled to the court of King Philip and urged to resume writing. He agreed but wrote only a few religious plays over the 20 remaining years of his life. Calderón is considered the last outstanding figure in the so-called golden age of Spanish literature.

PLAYS BY CALDERON IN ENGLISH TRANSLATION

Four Comedies by Pedro Calderón de la Barca. Kenneth Muir (tr). Univ Pr of Kentucky 1980 $26.00. ISBN 0-8131-1409-8

Life Is a Dream (*c.* 1635). William E. Colford (tr). Barron 1958 $5.95. ISBN 0-8120-0127-3

Love's No Laughing Matter. Don Cruikshank and Sean Page (trs). Humanities 1990 $18.50. ISBN 0-85668-366-3

Three Comedies by Pedro Calderón de la Barca. Kenneth Muir and Ann L. MacKenzie (trs). Univ Pr of Kentucky 1985 $9.00. ISBN 0-8131-016602

PLAYS BY CALDERON IN SPANISH

Calderón de la Barca: El alcalde de Zalamea (*c.* 1642). Longwood 1972 $3.95. ISBN 0-900411-38-4

BOOK ABOUT CALDERON

Aycock, Wendell M., and Sydney Cravens. *Calderón de la Barca at the Tercentenary: Comparative Views.* Texas Tech Univ Pr 1982 $12.00. ISBN 0-89672-101-9 Useful collection of essays developed from a seminar on Calderón's work on the three-hundredth anniversary of his death, presenting a variety of critical views.

CERVANTES SAAVEDRA, MIGUEL DE   1547–1616

The son of a poor medical practitioner, Miguel de Cervantes believed that "two roads lead to wealth and glory, that of letters and that of arms." He first tried arms, seeing service with the Spanish fleet in 1571 at the battle of Lepanto, in which he received a gunshot wound in the chest and his left hand was permanently crippled. After being captured by Turkish pirates, sold into slavery, and held for ransom, he returned to Spain, where he obtained work as a government purchasing agent and tax collector. He was imprisoned when a banker to whom he entrusted government funds went bankrupt.

Cervantes's first literary efforts were generally unsuccessful dramas, mildly interesting plays that could not compete with those of the master Spanish dramatist Lope de Vega. (*See* Lope de Vega, Vol. 1, World Literature: Spanish Language and Literature.) His next venture, however, would bring him the wealth and glory he sought. While in prison, he began writing a satirical novel about a man who has read so many romantic adventure stories that he can no longer tell the difference between the world of the novels and the real world. Don Quixote, as Cervantes called his hero, sets out on his bony horse, Rocinante, determined to restore justice to the world. With the pudgy peasant Sancho Panza as his squire and a barber's basin for a helmet, Don Quixote begins his series of highly amusing and sometimes touching adventures. Under Quixote's romantic gaze the most basic situations become idealized: A windmill becomes a giant, and a homely peasant girl is seen as a beautiful princess.

Don Quixote appeared in 1605 and was an immediate success. However, Cervantes continued to write plays and short stories (called *The Exemplary Novels*) rather than the sequel to *Don Quixote* that the public demanded. Finally, in 1615, he completed the second part of his novel, mostly to discourage imitators. This second book ends with the death of a disillusioned Quixote and a promise that Sancho Panza will continue the mission begun by Quixote.

Don Quixote is the world's first modern novel and a major influence on the development of European literature. It is also a marvelous story that continues to delight readers. The wild adventures which befall Don Quixote bring him into situations with many characters who represent the entire spectrum of human attitudes and personalities.

NOVELS BY CERVANTES IN ENGLISH TRANSLATION

Don Quixote (1605–1615). Walter Starkie (tr). Signet 1965 $6.96. ISBN 0-451-52507-9
The Trials of Persiles and Sigismunda (1616). Celia Weller and Clark Cohen (trs). Univ of California Pr 1989 $35.00. ISBN 0-520-06315-5

NOVEL BY CERVANTES IN SPANISH

El ingenioso hidalgo Don Quijote de la Mancha (1605–1615). 2 vols. Interbook 1968 $75.00. ISBN 0-317-00542-1

SHORT STORIES BY CERVANTES IN SPANISH

Novelas ejemplares (1613) Torres $7.95. ISBN 84-241-5613-7

BOOKS ABOUT CERVANTES

*Busoni, Rafaello. *The Man Who Was Don Quixote: The Story of Miguel de Cervantes*. Prentice 1902 $3.95. ISBN 0-13-548112-4 Well illustrated biography of the author that also depicts the life and background of the sixteenth and seventeenth centuries; appropriate for teenagers.
Byron, William. *Cervantes: A Biography*. Paragon Hse 1988 $12.95. ISBN 1-55778-006-4 Detailed and readable account of Cervantes' colorful life.
Durán, Manuel. *Cervantes*. G. K. Hall 1974 $17.95. ISBN 0-8057-2206-8 Carefully written general study of Cervantes' life and works.

El Saffar, Ruth. *Critical Essays on Cervantes.* G. K. Hall 1986 $35.00. ISBN 0-8161-8825-4 Collection of 18 wide-ranging articles on Cervantes' work, half of which are devoted to *Don Quixote* and the rest to other writings.
Russell, P. E. *Cervantes.* Oxford Univ Pr 1985 $17.95. ISBN 0-19-287570-1 Thorough biographical treatment with author's life related to *Don Quixote*.

GARCIA LORCA, FEDERICO 1899–1936

Federico García Lorca was born in the town of Fuente Vaqueros in the southern area of Spain known as Andalusia. He is perhaps the best known of modern Spanish writers, partly because of his brutal execution outside Granada by the Fascist army in the early days of the Spanish Civil War, but primarily because of his genius for poetry and drama.

In 1928 Lorca published *Gypsie Ballads,* a book of poetry that was immediately successful and still is considered one of the most important volumes of poetry of this century. Attracted to the Gypsies for what he saw as their exotic folklore, their "primitive" vitality, and their position as outcasts on the fringe of Spanish society, Lorca portrayed them in his poetry as larger than life, giving them almost mythical status. In these poems, nature takes on human form, and reality acquires a dreamlike quality as the lives and traditions of the Gypsies are given mythic form. This colorful, dramatic, and rhythmic verse contrasts sharply with that of Lorca's *Poet in New York* (1940), a pessimistic volume based on the poet's visit to New York in 1929.

Although Lorca was interested in drama throughout his life, he did not produce any plays of significance until the 1930s. His trilogy on Spanish family life in the provinces is his most important work. The three tragedies, *Blood Wedding* (1933), *Yerma* (1934), and *The House of Bernarda Alba* (1936), all have women as their central characters. In each play the fall of the protagonist pulls down those around her and is caused by the frustrations produced by a repressive family in a very conservative society. *The House of Bernarda Alba,* which dramatizes the destructive nature of the matriarch Bernarda's dictatorial rule of her household, remains one of Lorca's most popular plays.

POETRY BY GARCIA LORCA IN ENGLISH TRANSLATION

Gypsie Ballads (1928). Robert G. Harvard (tr). Humanities 1990 $19.95. ISBN 0-85688-491-0
Ode to Walt Whitman and Other Poems (1933). Carlos Bauer (tr). City Lights 1988 $6.95. ISBN 0-87286-212-7
Poet in New York (1940). Greg Simon (tr). Farrar 1988 $9.95. ISBN 0-374-52083-6
Selected Poems. Donald M. Allen (ed). New Directions 1990 $6.95. ISBN 0-8112-0091-4

PLAYS BY GARCIA LORCA IN ENGLISH TRANSLATION

Five Plays: Comedies & Tragicomedies. Richard L. O'Connell (tr). New Directions 1964 $8.95. ISBN 0-8112-0090-6
The Rural Trilogy: Blood Wedding (1933), *Yerma* (1934), *and The House of Bernarda Alba* (1936). Michael Dewell and Carmen Zapata (trs). Bantam 1980 $8.95. ISBN 0-553-34434-X

POETRY AND PLAYS BY GARCIA LORCA IN SPANISH

Libro de poemas (1921), *Poema del cante jondo* (1930), *Romancero Gitano* (1928), *Poeta en Nueva York* (1940), *Odas* (1931), *Llanto por Sanchez Mejias* (1935), *Bodas de sangre* (1933), *Yerma* (1934). Colton 1990 $4.50. ISBN 0-686-43211-8

POETRY BY GARCIA LORCA IN SPANISH

Romancero Gitano (1928). St. Martin's 1988 $11.00. ISBN 0-7190-1724-6

PLAYS BY GARCIA LORCA IN SPANISH

La casa de Bernarda Alba (1936). St. Martin's 1988 $12.95. ISBN 0-7190-0950-2
Yerma: A Tragic Poem in Three Acts and Six Scenes (1934). Humanities 1987 $19.95. ISBN 0-85688-338-8 In English and Spanish.
La zapatera prodigiosa (1927). Norton 1952. ISBN 0-393-09474-X

BOOKS ABOUT GARCIA LORCA

Gibson, Ian. *Federico García Lorca: A Life.* Pantheon 1989 $29.95. ISBN 0-394-50964-1
Colorful, articulate, and well-documented study of Lorca's life.
Londre, Felicia Hardison. *Federico García Lorca.* Ungar 1985 $13.50. ISBN 0-8044-2540-X
Study of Lorca's life and works intended for the general public.

LOPE DE VEGA CARPIO, FELIX   1562–1635

Félix Lope de Vega Carpio was born in Madrid and educated at Alcala in Spain. He spent much of his youth in the military, first in the army and then with the Spanish Armada (a fleet of ships). His early life was also marked by many love affairs. Then in 1614 he decided to become a priest. After his ordination he continued to write for the theater.

Lope de Vega was the creator of the national theater in Spain, and his achievements in drama are comparable in many respects to those of English poet and playwright William Shakespeare in England. (*See* Shakespeare, Vol. 1, British Literature: The Renaissance.) He embraced all of Spanish life in his drama, combining elements of previous Spanish drama, with aspects of Spanish history and tradition to produce plays with both intellectual and popular appeal. A prodigious writer, Lope de Vega is credited by his biographer with nearly 2,000 plays, of which about 500 survive.

Lope de Vega defined his primary purpose as entertaining his audience, and he gave the public what they wanted: ingeniously developed and fast-moving plots, plenty of action, and strong endings. He constructed three-act plays in which he withheld the outcome until the middle of the third act, after which events moved quickly to a conclusion. His major strength was the creation of plot; he did not create characters of the depth or complexity of Shakespeare's major figures. But his wide-ranging and exciting approach to drama revolutionized not only Spanish theater but that of all Europe.

PLAYS BY LOPE DE VEGA IN ENGLISH TRANSLATION

*La Dorotea (1632). Harvard Univ Pr 1985 $32.50. ISBN 0-674-50590-5 Autobiographical prose drama.
Justice Without Revenge (c. 1620). C. Davis (ed and tr). Humanities 1989 $18.50. ISBN 0-85668-424-4
Peribanez (c. 1610). Humanities 1989 $18.50. ISBN 0-85668-439-2

PLAYS BY LOPE DE VEGA IN SPANISH

Bella Malmaridada (c. 1617). Biblio Siglo 1986 $32.50. ISBN 0-84-599-1505-0
La Francesilla (c. 1619). Biblio Siglo 1981 $19.00. ISBN 84-499-4456-2
Fuente Ovejuna (c. 1621). Darien 1987 $11.95. ISBN 0-9625734-0-X
Triumfo de la fee en los reynos del Japon (c. 1630). Longwood 1965 $14.50. ISBN 0-900411-40-6

BOOK ABOUT LOPE DE VEGA

Gerstinger, Heinz. *Lope de Vega and Spanish Drama.* Samuel Rosenbaum (tr). Ungar 1974 $16.95. ISBN 0-8044-2227-3 Scholarly study of Lope de Vega's plays and their influence on the development of Spanish drama.

POEM OF THE CID   *c.* 1140

This poem recounts in 3,730 lines of verse the character and adventures of a Castilian soldier and nobleman, Rodrigo (or Ruy) Diaz de Vivar (called El Cid—the Chief), who died in 1099. According to the most widely accepted theory, the poem is actually a collection of many shorter songs celebrating El Cid's exploits. Scholars believe that around 1140, a Spaniard, thought to be a Christian living in Moorish-dominated Spain, brought the tales together to create the manuscript as it now exists.

In the poem, El Cid is sent into exile by King Alfonso VI after being accused of withholding some tribute money due to the king. He eventually recaptures the city of Valencia for Castile, thereby giving the Spaniards access to the Mediterranean. Depicted as a protective father, a loving husband, a loyal servant of the king, and a devout Christian, the Cid of the Spanish poem remains a human being, rather than becoming a superhuman or mythical figure, as do the heroes of many other epic poems. Although the real Cid's actual deeds are somewhat romanticized in the poem, the Spanish epic is considerably more grounded in reality than are most other early European epics.

POEM OF THE CID IN ENGLISH TRANSLATION

Poem of the Cid (*c.* 1140). R. Hamilton and J. Perry (trs). Penguin 1985 $5.95. ISBN 0-14-044446-7

POEM OF THE CID IN BILINGUAL EDITION

Poem of My Cid (Poema de mio Cid) (*c.* 1140). Peter Such and John Hodgkinson (eds). Humanities 1987 $16.50. ISBN 0-85668-322-1

BOOK ABOUT THE POEM OF THE CID

Smith, Colin. *The Making of the "Poema de Mio Cid."* Cambridge Univ Pr 1984 $52.50. ISBN 0-521-24992-9 Detailed study of the antecedents, historical background, and publishing history of the poem.

UNAMUNO Y JUGO, MIGUEL DE   1864–1936

The influential Spanish man of letters Miguel de Unamuno was born in Bilbao, Spain. He came of age during an important period of Spanish literature, when Spain was producing a generation of writers who had to come to terms with Spain's decline as a world power. Consequently, their works dealt with the political tragedy of their nation as well as with philosophical questions about the nature of reason, religion, and humanity. Unamuno, however, was a member of the group of intellectuals and writers known as the "Generation of 1898," a part of an all-encompassing patriotic, intellectual, and artistic Renaissance in Spain. The goal of the movement was to better the national life.

Professor of Greek and later rector of the University of Salamanca, Unamuno began writing in a philosophical style influenced by the German philosopher Friedrich Hegel, but in 1897 experienced a personal crisis that brought him to the religious view that people must accept God regardless of the lack of logical evidence. Despite his belief in the need for faith, Unamuno was opposed to what he saw as the dogmatic rules of Spain's official Catholic Church. He also was especially critical of the monarchy and of dictator Primo de Rivera. In 1920 this led him to be removed as rector of the university and in 1924 to be exiled from Spain for six years.

Most of Unamuno's philosophical works concern questions of doubt and faith and the issue of personal immortality, which he considered the most important question for humanity. His major poem, "El Cristo de Velazquez" ("The Velazquez Christ"), explores this issue.

Unamuno also was an essayist, and his six-volume *Ensayos* ("Essays") (1916–1918) are stimulating criticisms of such subjects as education, religion, literature, and politics. In addition, he wrote many innovative plays and novels. Among his major works are *Paz en la guerra* ("Peace in War") (1897); *Vida de Don Quijote y Sancho* ("Life of Don Quixote and Sancho," a reference to Miguel de Cervantes's famous novel *Don Quixote*) (1905); and *La agonia del cristianismo* ("The Agony of Christianity") (1928). Many critics consider his greatest work to be *Del sentimiento trágicode lavida en los hombres y en los pueblos* ("Tragic Sense of Life in Men and Nations"), written in 1913.

One of the major philosophers of the twentieth century, Unamuno died in 1936 in Salamanca, Spain.

FICTION AND DRAMA BY UNAMUNO IN ENGLISH TRANSLATION

Ficciones: Four Stories and a Play. Princeton Univ Pr 1987 $8.95. ISBN 0-691-01874-X
Novela-Nivola. Princeton Univ Pr 1987 $10.50. ISBN 0-691-01875-8
Selected Works: Our Lord Don Quixote. Vol. 3 Princeton Univ Pr 1968 $12.95. ISBN 0-691-01807-3

NONFICTION BY UNAMUNO IN ENGLISH TRANSLATION

Perplexities & Paradoxes. Greenwood 1968 $22.50. ISBN 0-8371-0253-7
The Private World: Selected Works of Miguel de Unamuno, Vol. 2 Princeton Univ Pr 1984 $36.50. ISBN 0-691-09927-8
Selected Works: Tragic Sense of Life in Men & Nations, Vol. 4 Princeton Univ Pr 1968 $13.95. ISBN 0-691-01820-0

FICTION BY UNAMUNO IN SPANISH

Dos novelas cortas. Wiley 1975 $18.50. ISBN 0-471-00597-5 With novella by Herbert E. Isar.
San Manuel Bueno, martir and la novela de Don Sandalio. Manchester Univ Pr 1988 $11.00. ISBN 0-7190-1092-6

See also Vol. 1, World Literature: Latin American Language and Literature.

GERMAN LANGUAGE AND LITERATURE

THE GERMAN LANGUAGE

German is the official language of the Federal Republic of Germany (including the former German Democratic Republic, or East Germany), Austria, and Liechtenstein, and is one of the official languages of Switzerland. Worldwide, about 150 million people speak modern German, making it one of the major international languages.

About 3,000 years ago, the peoples of northern and central Europe spoke varieties of an ancient Germanic language, generally classified into North, East, and West Germanic. North Germanic developed into what are now the Scandanavian languages of Norway, Sweden, and Denmark. East Germanic, sometimes called Old Norse, eventually died out altogether. West Germanic developed into two major dialects, Low German and High German.

The Low German dialect (sometimes known as Old Low German) gradually developed into several modern languages, including modern Low German, Flemish, Dutch, and English. The High German dialect developed into New High German, Swiss German, Alsatian (spoken in Alsace, on the French-German border), Swabian (spoken in the German region of Swabia), and Yiddish. Thus, German and English are related languages and share several common features in both grammar and vocabulary.

Today there are two major dialects spoken in Germany: modern Low German and New High German, generally called simply Low German and High German. The modern Low German dialect is spoken primarily by the people in the lowlands of northern Germany, while New High German is spoken by people living in the more mountainous central and southern sections of the country. The official German language used in schools, books, magazines, on radio and television, and by public officials is a variety of High German called Standard German.

New High German developed through four periods: the period of Old High German lasting from about AD 750 to about 1050; the Middle High German period stretching from about 1050 to about 1350; the Early New High German period beginning at approximately 1350 and lasting until around 1600; and the New High German period, from 1600 through the present. A major influence in the development of New High German was the decision by Martin Luther, the leader of the Protestant Reformation, to use the Saxon dialect of east-central Germany as the basis for his translation of the Bible. (*See* Luther, Vol. 2, World History: The Renaissance and Reformation.) As Luther's bible, hymns, and other writings spread throughout Germany in the early 1500s, the Saxon dialect became the language of religion, culture, and education.

One of the distinctive characteristics of the German language is its capacity to combine two or more words, or parts of words, into a single new word, which retains the sense but not necessarily the literal meaning of the words from which it is formed. For example, the word *Kindergarten* is composed of the words *Kinder* (children) and *Garten* (garden), which would give it the literal meaning of "garden of children." In fact, however, the word means "a place where children can be nurtured." At times this practice can produce quite a mouthful of syllables, as in the German word for streetcar stop, *Strassenbahnhaltestelle* (*strassen*—street + *Bahn*—track + *Halt*—stop + *Stelle*—place).

A second characteristic of German is the importance of word order. The order in which words are arranged in a German sentence is very precise, and a change in the word order can result in a significant change in meaning. Finally, in contrast to English, German pronunciation is very regular: few words are not pronounced according to the way they are spelled.

Because of its geographical position in central Europe, Germany has always been a politically important region. As a result, it has had long and frequent contact with most European countries and so has incorporated a sizeable number of foreign words into its language. Latin, French, Italian, English, Hungarian, and various Slavic languages have all made contributions to modern German.

BOOKS ABOUT THE GERMAN LANGUAGE

The following books provide an introduction to the history and grammar of modern German. The list does not include the many dictionaries and instructional textbooks that are widely available.

Brogyanyi, Bela, and Thomas Krommelbein. *Germanic Dialects.* Benjamins 1986 $105.00. ISBN 90-272-3526-0

D'Alquen, Richard. *Germanic Accent, Grammatical Change, and the Laws of Unaccented Syllables.* Peter Lang 1988 $31.20. ISBN 0-8204-0585-X

Fox, Anthony. *German Intonation: An Outline.* Oxford Univ Pr 1984 $29.95. ISBN 0-19-912048-0

Greenfield, Eric V. *German Grammar.* Harper 1968 $6.95. ISBN 0-06-460034-3

Hammond, Robin. *German Reference Grammar.* Oxford Univ Pr 1981 $11.95. ISBN 0-19-912048-X

Keller, Howard H. *German Root Lexicon.* Miami Univ Pr 1973 $10.95. ISBN 0-87024-244-X

Markey, T. L. *Germanic and Its Dialects.* Benjamins 1977 $75.00. ISBN 90-272-0981-2

Nielsen, Hans F. *Germanic Languages: Origins and Early Dialectual Interrelations.* Univ of Alabama Pr 1989 $12.50. ISBN 0-8173-0423-1

Taylor, Ronald J., and W. Gottschalk. *German-English Dictionary of Idioms.* Adlers 1973 $58.00. ISBN 3-19-006216-1

Wells, C. J. *German: A Linguistic History to Nineteen Forty-Five.* Oxford Univ Pr 1987 $29.95. ISBN 0-19-815809-2

GERMAN LITERATURE

The earliest examples of literature in German date from the early Middle Ages, around AD 750. The highest achievements of German medieval literature, however, are found in the so-called Middle High German period (*c.* 1000–1300). The literature of this era contains a wide variety of styles. Its lyric love poetry is best represented by the verses of Walther von der Vogelweide (*c.* 1200). Hartmann von Aue, Wolfram von Eschenbach, and Gottfried von Strassburg all contributed epic poems, based for the most part on earlier French epic romances.

Throughout the remainder of the Middle Ages, German literature gradually included more folk elements, reflecting the concerns of the rising merchant class. Toward the end of the fifteenth century, religious and moral concerns became much more evident.

During the sixteenth century, middle-class views and interests found expression in the poetry and plays of the Meistersinger, members of musical and poetical guilds (associations of craftworkers), who performed throughout Germany. The most famous Meistersinger was Hans Sachs, a comically earthy playwright about whom the composer Richard Wagner (*see* Wagner, Vol. 2, World History: The Arts in Nineteenth-Century Europe) later wrote an opera. Also during this century, Protestant religious leader Martin Luther (*see* Luther, Vol. 2, World History: The Renaissance and Reformation) translated the Bible from Latin into his native Saxon dialect. This act, more than any other single event, helped create a standard German literary language.

In the beginning of the seventeenth century, an important change took place in German poetry. Dissatisfied with the heavily stressed and accented poetry that had been traditional in Germany since the Middle Ages, poets turned to a new style of verse based on forms borrowed from ancient Greece and Rome. As a result of this movement, poetic forms such as the ode, the sonnet, and the elegy were introduced into German literature.

After the peaks of the seventeenth century, German literature changed little until the second half of the eighteenth century, when, in a new burst of creativity, German writers commanded the attention of all Europe. During this period there was a clash between the coolly rational and logical writers of the early part of the century and the writers of the new romantic school of *Sturm und Drang* (storm and stress). The latter produced works reflecting the emotional turmoil of the individual. The leaders of this movement were Wolfgang von Goethe and Friedrich Schiller, towering figures in German literature. The emotionalism and mysticism of the romantic movement that swept Europe during the late eighteenth and early nineteenth centuries had a stronger and more specific impact on German literature than on any other.

Goethe remained the most important force in German literature throughout the nineteenth century and into the twentieth. As a playwright, poet, and novelist, his influence was unmatched by any other writer. Although not as influential as Goethe, several German philosophers, notably Immanuel Kant, Friedrich Hegel, and Friedrich Nietzsche, also had an impact on the development of literature during this period. Other major German writers included the Brothers Grimm, whose renditions of German folktales and fairy tales continue to enjoy worldwide popularity.

The early twentieth century in Germany was marked by the emergence of a group of brilliant writers, including Rainer Maria Rilke, Thomas Mann, Franz Kafka, and Robert Musil. Most of the century, however, has been dominated by Germany's involvement in two world wars and the postwar shocks that each produced. With the exception of such writers as playwright Bertolt Brecht, strong new voices in German literature have been heard only in the past 30 years or so, as German writers began to come to terms with the legacy of World War II and the new era of postwar prosperity.

BOLL, HEINRICH   1917–1985

The son of sculptor Victor Böll, Heinrich Böll was born in Cologne, Germany. He was drafted into the German army shortly after he finished his schooling and served several years in the infantry during World War II.

Although Böll had won three literary prizes in Germany and translations of his earlier novels had been published in the United States, it was not until the publication of *Billiards at Half-Past Nine* (1959) that he became truly recognized outside his own country. Now considered one of the most important German novelists to have emerged since World War II, Böll's well-crafted novels tell a good story, and at the same time examine postwar German society. His trilogy—*And Never Said a Word* (1954), *The Unguarded House* (1955), and *The Bread of Those Early Years* (1959)—paints an unflattering picture of German life during and after the rule of the Nazis. In *The Clown* (1963), Böll's protagonist is a "loser" who fails constantly but keeps on trying. *The Lost Honor of Katharina Blum* (1974) focuses on the destructive conformist tendencies Böll sees in postwar Germany, where even the slightest deviation from doing what is expected becomes a serious social crime.

Böll was awarded the Nobel Prize for literature in 1972.

NOVELS BY BOLL IN ENGLISH TRANSLATION

Adam and the Train (1969). Leila Vennewitz (tr). McGraw 1974 $7.95. ISBN 0-07-006409-1
Billiards at Half-Past Nine (1959). McGraw 1971 $7.95. ISBN 0-07-006401-6
The Casualty (1986). Norton 1989 $7.95. ISBN 0-393-30599-6

Children Are Civilians Too (1970). Leila Vennewitz (tr). McGraw 1977 $5.95. ISBN 0-07-006430-X

The Clown (1963). Leila Vennewitz (tr). McGraw 1971 $6.95. ISBN 0-07-006-420-2

Group Portrait with Lady (1971). Avon 1976 $4.95. ISBN 0-380-00020-2

The Lost Honor of Katharina Blum (1974). Leila Vennewitz (tr). McGraw 1976 $6.95. ISBN 0-07-006429-6

SHORT STORIES BY BOLL IN ENGLISH TRANSLATION

The Stories of Heinrich Böll. Leila Vennewitz (tr). McGraw 1987 $9.95. ISBN 0-07-006422-9

NOVEL BY BOLL IN GERMAN

Und Sagte Kein Einziges Wort (1954). William Henson (ed). Routledge 1990 $16.95. ISBN 0-423-51640-X.

BOOK ABOUT BOLL

Reid, James H. *Heinrich Böll: A German for His Time.* St. Martin's 1988 $29.95. ISBN 0-85496-533-5 Study of Böll's life and works in the context of a changing German society.

BRECHT, BERTOLT   1898–1956

Bertolt Brecht, Germany's greatest modern playwright, was born in Augsburg, Germany, and studied medicine and philosophy at the universities of Munich and Berlin. He preferred the theater to medicine, however, and by 1922 had already established himself as a promising new playwright, winning the prestigious Kleist drama prize that year. Interested in the possibilities of combining drama and music, he collaborated with composer Kurt Weill on *The Threepenny Opera* (1928), a satire on contemporary materialistic society that remains popular today.

From the outset Brecht's work was experimental, and his early plays are marked by strong elements of social criticism presented in nonrealistic stage settings. Brecht eventually developed an approach to dramatic performance that he called "epic theater." His concept required that the audience be constantly aware that they were watching a performance and that the actors were merely playing parts, or in other words, that the illusion of reality, encouraged in realistic drama, be shattered. By the use of these distancing techniques, he sought to change the theater from a place of escapist entertainment to a place of entertaining instruction and inspiration that would lead audiences to think about their lives and then take action to change them. Although he claimed never to have been a member of the Communist party, Brecht was a dedicated Marxist, and the message of his epic theater was often a condemnation of capitalist exploitation of the poor.

A fervent opponent of German dictator Adolf Hitler (*see* Hitler, Vol. 2, World History: The Rise of Totalitarian States) and the Nazis, Brecht left Germany in 1933, eventually settling in the United States, where he continued to produce anti-Nazi and anticapitalist plays. After the war he accepted an offer from the East German government to run a theater in Berlin, a position he held until his death.

Brecht's most famous works include *The Good Woman of Setzuan* (1943), the story of a woman who disguises herself as a man in order to do the dirty deeds necessary for survival; *The Caucasian Chalk Circle* (1947), about a woman who faces difficulties taking care of a child; and *Galileo* (1942), a portrait of the committed scientist who challenged the church and political leaders of his time, insisting that the Earth moves around the sun.

PLAYS BY BRECHT IN ENGLISH TRANSLATION

Baal (1922), *A Man's a Man* (1926), *The Elephant Calf* (1926). Eric Bentley (tr). Grove 1989 $8.95. ISBN 0-8021-3159-X

The Caucasian Chalk Circle (1947). Eric Bentley (tr). Grove 1987 $5.95. ISBN 0-394-62372-X

Edward Second: A Chronicle Play (1924). Eric Bentley (tr). Grove 1970 $1.95. ISBN 0-394-17111-X

Galileo (1942). Charles Laughton (tr). Grove 1966 $5.95. ISBN 0-394-17112-8

The Good Woman of Setzuan (1943). Eric Bentley (tr). Grove 1966 $4.50. ISBN 0-394-17109-8

The Mother (1932). Lee Baxandall (tr). Grove 1989 $8.95. ISBN 0-8021-3160-3

Mother Courage and Her Children (1941). Eric Bentley (tr). Grove 1987 $5.95. ISBN 0-8021-3028-8

St. Joan of the Stockyards (1933). Frank Jones (tr). Univ of Indiana Pr 1970 $6.95. ISBN 0-253-21027-6

The Threepenny Opera (1928). Eric Bentley and Desmond Vesey (trs). Grove 1983 $4.95. ISBN 0-8021-5039-X

PLAYS BY BRECHT IN GERMAN

Leben des Galilei (1942). Heinemann 1981 $9.50. ISBN 0-435-38123-7

Mutter Courage und Ihre Kinder (1941). Heinemann 1960 $6.50. ISBN 0-435-38112-1

BOOKS ABOUT BRECHT

Bentley, Eric. *The Brecht Memoir.* PAJ 1985 $7.95. ISBN 0-933826-84-2 Account of Brecht's personal life by a long-time friend and translator of his plays.

Berlau, Ruth. *Living for Brecht: The Memoirs of Ruth Berlau.* Geoffrey Skelton (tr). Fromm Intl 1987 $19.95. ISBN 0-88064-071-5 Account of Berlau's theatrical and literary collaboration with Brecht.

Speirs, Ronald. *Bertolt Brecht.* St. Martin's 1987 $19.95. ISBN 0-312-00371-4 Clearly written, concise critical introduction to Brecht's development as a dramatist.

GOETHE, JOHANN WOLFGANG VON   1749–1832

Johann Wolfgang von Goethe was born in Frankfurt-am-Main, Germany, and was educated to be a lawyer, a profession in which he was never really interested. He began writing plays while continuing his law studies and, inspired by a love affair, began to write lyrical poetry.

Having completed his studies and qualified as a lawyer in 1771, Goethe returned to Frankfurt, where he took a position as a journalist. Two years later he produced his first successful play, *Götz von Berlichingen,* the story of a knight clinging to the code of chivalry in an age where honor is no longer valued. With this play and the novel *The Sorrows of Young Werther,* which followed in 1774, Goethe became the leading voice for the new *Sturm und Drang* ("storm and stress") movement, which represented a youthful, idealistic revolt against the constraints of the formal, highly rational approach to literature popular in Europe at that time.

In 1775, Goethe was invited to the court of Charles Augustus, Duke of the German region of Weimar. He became chief advisor and minister to the young Duke. For 10 years he served in this capacity while continuing to write and conduct experiments in all branches of the natural sciences. During this time he also began a friendship with Friedrich Schiller (*see* Schiller, Vol. 1, World Literature: German Language and Literature), a young poet with whom he entered into friendly competition in writing poetry.

In his later years Goethe produced creative work of amazing vitality and diversity: novels, narrative poems, autobiographical works, and the monumental poetic drama *Faust,* a play he worked on most of his life. This drama, which explores humankind's quest for knowledge and experience, is the single greatest work of German literature. In its breadth of vision and poetic grandeur, *Faust* outstrips anything written in German before or since.

Novels by Goethe in English Translation

Elective Affinities (1809). Penguin 1978 $6.95. ISBN 0-14-044242-1
The Sorrows of Young Werther (1774). Michael Hulse (tr). Penguin 1989 $4.95. ISBN 0-14-044503-X
Wilhelm Meister, Vol. 1: *The Years of Apprenticeship, Books 1–3* (1796). H. M. Waidson (tr). Riverrun 1982 $7.95. ISBN 0-7145-3675-X
Wilhelm Meister, Vol. 2: *The Years of Apprenticeship, Books 4–6* (1796). H. M. Waidson (tr). Riverrun 1982 $7.95. ISBN 0-7145-3699-7
Wilhelm Meister, Vol. 3: *The Years of Apprenticeship, Books 7–8* (1796). H. M. Waidson (tr). Riverrun 1982 $11.95. ISBN 0-7145-3928-7
Wilhelm Meister, Vol. 4: *The Years of Travel, Book 1* (1829). H. M. Waidson (tr). Riverrun 1982 $7.95. ISBN 0-7145-3827-2.
Wilhelm Meister, Vol. 5: *The Years of Travel, Book 2* (1829). H. M. Waidson (tr). Riverrun 1982 $7.95. ISBN 0-7145-3838-8
Wilhelm Meister, Vol. 6: *The Years of Travel, Book 3* (1829). H. M. Waidson (tr). Riverrun 1982 $7.95. ISBN 0-7145-3934-1

Poetry by Goethe in English Translation

The Eternal Feminine: Selected Poems of Goethe. Frederick Ungar (ed). Ungar 1980 $14.50. ISBN 0-8044-2256-7
Goethe: Selected Poems. Riverrun 1988 $17.95. ISBN 0-7145-4004-8
Roman Elegies and Other Poems (1794). Michael Hamburger (tr). Black Swan Bks 1983 $20.00. ISBN 0-933806-18-3

Plays by Goethe in English Translation

Dr. Henry Faust: The Tragedy's First and Second Parts (1808–1832). John A. Roth (tr). Univ Pr of America 1987 $15.00. ISBN 0-8191-6555-7
Egmont: A Play (1788). Charles E. Passage (tr). Ungar 1985 $5.95. ISBN 0-8044-6185-6
Faust (1808). Peter Salm (ed). Bantam 1985 $3.50. ISBN 0-553-21182-X
Torquato Tasso (1790). Alan Brownjohn (tr). Dufour 1986 $12.95. ISBN 0-946162-19-0

Nonfiction by Goethe in English Translation

The Autobiography of Johann Wolfgang von Goethe. John Oxenford (tr). 2 vols. Univ of Chicago Pr 1975. Vol. 1 $15.00. ISBN 0-226-30055-2. Vol. 2 $15.00. ISBN 0-226-30056-0

Novel by Goethe in German

Die Leiden des Jungen Werthers (1774). Basil Blackwell 1972 $9.95. ISBN 0-631-01900-6

Poetry by Goethe in German

Herman und Dorothea (1797). Daniel Coogan (tr). Ungar 1981 $7.95. ISBN 0-8044-6188-0 In German and English.

Plays by Goethe in German

Egmont (1788). Basil Blackwell 1974 $15.95. ISBN 0-631-01670-8
Faust (1808). Peter Salm (ed). Bantam 1985 $3.50. ISBN 0-553-21182-X

BOOK ABOUT GOETHE

Reed, T. J. *Goethe.* Oxford Univ Pr 1984 $3.90. ISBN 0-19-27502-7 Concise, readable, and careful handbook for the general reader that provides an excellent guide to Goethe's artistic and personal development.

GRASS, GUNTER   1927–

Günter Grass was born in Danzig (then part of Germany; today the city of Gdánsk in Poland), the son of a grocer. He was once a member of Hitler Youth, the youth group organized to support German dictator Adolf Hitler. At age 16 he was drafted into the German Army to fight in World War II. These experiences formed the basis for Grass's later anti-Nazi satires.

Taken prisoner and released after the war, Grass became first a farm laborer and stonecutter and eventually a sculptor and stage designer, until writing claimed all his time. He won an immediate and enormous audience in Europe and in the United States with his first novel, *Die Blechtrommel (The Tin Drum)* (1959). The novel tells the story of Oskar Matzerath, who decides at age three to stop growing, thereby avoiding the responsibility of making adult decisions. Oskar's story is a scathing indictment of how citizens in Nazi Germany likewise avoided their responsibilities.

In *Cat and Mouse* (1961), Grass tells another grotesque story, this time the tale of a young man who is a social outcast because of his huge Adam's apple. In *Hundejahre, Dog Years* (1963), he tells of a Jew who makes weird scarecrows, a tale that once again evolves into a grimly humorous picture of modern Germans violating all the standards of decency. These three novels form a kind of trilogy, commenting on German life just before, during, and after the Hitler years.

NOVELS BY GRASS IN ENGLISH TRANSLATION

Cat and Mouse (1961). Amereon 1990 $12.95. ISBN 0-8488-0112-1
Dog Years (1965). Harcourt 1989 $12.95. ISBN 0-15-626112-X
The Flounder (1977). Harcourt 1989 $11.95. ISBN 0-15-631935-7
Headbirths: Or the Germans Are Dying Out (1980). Ralph Manheim (tr). Harcourt 1990 $8.95. ISBN 0-15-639995-4
Local Anaesthetic (1970). Ralph Manheim (tr). Harcourt 1989 $9.95. ISBN 0-15-652940-8
The Meeting at Telgte (1978). Ralph Manheim (tr). Harcourt 1990 $8.95. ISBN 0-15-658575-8
The Rat (1986). Harcourt 1989 $9.95. ISBN 0-15-675830-X
The Tin Drum (1961). Ralph Manheim (tr). Vintage 1990 $9.95. ISBN 0-679-72575-X

POETRY BY GRASS IN ENGLISH TRANSLATION

In the Egg and Other Poems (1977). Michael Hamburger (tr). Harcourt 1977 $5.95. ISBN 0-15-672239-9

NOVEL BY GRASS IN GERMAN

Katz and Maus (1961). Heineman 1971 $10.50. ISBN 0-435-38370-1

POETRY BY GRASS IN GERMAN

Kinderlied (1982). Lord John 1983 $50.00. ISBN 0-935716-18-1

PLAY BY GRASS IN GERMAN

Die Plebejer Proben den Aufstand (1966). Heineman 1971 $6.50. ISBN 0-435-38372-8

BOOKS ABOUT GRASS

Keele, Alan. *Understanding Günter Grass.* Univ of South Carolina Pr 1988 $29.95. ISBN 0-87249-547-7 Study of Grass's works that deals with social context and Grass's disenchantment with German society.

Lawson, Richard. *Günter Grass.* Ungar 1985 $13.95. ISBN 0-8044-2500-0 Explication of Grass's work in all genres that seeks to explain Grass's ironic view of German life.

O'Neill, Patrick. *Critical Essays on Günter Grass.* G. K. Hall 1987 $35.00. ISBN 0-8161-8830-0 Collection of essays designed to trace Grass's critical reception from the 1960s through the 1980s.

HESSE, HERMANN 1877–1962

Born at Calw in Württemberg, Germany, Hermann Hesse was a bookseller before he published his first novel, *Peter Camenzind,* in 1904. When he publicly denounced the savagery and blind nationalism of World War I, he was considered a traitor in Germany and moved to Switzerland where he eventually became a naturalized citizen. Hesse warned of the coming of World War II and predicted that the cultureless Nazi state mindlessly devoted to efficiency would eventually destroy itself.

In all his novels Hesse was concerned with individuals who struggle with either conflicts within themselves or with their surroundings. *Steppenwolf* (1927) is the story of Haller, who struggles with the conflict of spiritual and worldly tendencies within himself. In *Narcissus and Goldmund* (1930), Hesse used the background of the Middle Ages to contrast a life of self-sacrifice with one of constant pleasure seeking. *Siddhartha* (1922), a novel inspired by Hesse's travels in India, profiles a man's search for self-knowledge, leading him past worldly temptations to final wisdom.

Hesse's sensitive and visionary works won him the Nobel Prize for literature in 1946.

NOVELS BY HESSE IN ENGLISH TRANSLATION

Demian (1919). Bantam 1981 $3.50. ISBN 0-553-26246-7
Magister Ludi: The Glass Bead Game (1943). Bantam 1982 $4.95. ISBN 0-553-26237-8
Narcissus and Goldmund (1930). Bantam 1984 $4.95. ISBN 0-553-27586-0
Peter Camenzind (1904). Michael Roloff (tr). Farrar 1969 $7.95. ISBN 0-374-50784-8
Siddhartha (1922). Bantam 1982 $2.95. ISBN 0-553-20884-5
Steppenwolf (1927). Bantam 1983 $4.50. ISBN 0-553-27990-4

BOOKS ABOUT HESSE

Field, George W. *Hermann Hesse.* G. K. Hall 1970 $16.95. ISBN 0-8057-2424-9 General introduction to Hesse's life and works; contains a chronology and a bibliography.

*Fleissner, Else M. *Hermann Hesse: Modern German Poet and Writer.* SamHar 1972 $2.50. ISBN 0-87157-026-2 Introduction to Hesse's life and works prepared especially for young readers.

KAFKA, FRANZ 1883–1924

Franz Kafka was born in Prague, Czechoslovakia, of middle-class Jewish parents. He apparently suffered a great deal of psychological pain at a young age at the hands of his domineering father. He took a law degree at the German University of Prague, then obtained a position in the workman's compensation division of the Austrian government.

Always neurotic, insecure, and filled with a sense of inadequacy, Kafka's writing is a search for personal fulfillment and understanding. He wrote very slowly and deliberately, publishing very little in his lifetime. At his death he asked a close friend to burn his remaining manuscripts, but the friend refused the request. Instead the friend arranged for publication of Kafka's longer stories, which have since brought him worldwide fame and have influenced many contemporary writers.

Kafka's stories are nightmarish tales in which a helpless central character's every move is controlled by heartless, impersonal forces. An example is his 1937 psychological thriller, "The Metamorphosis." The story centers around a salesman named Gregor, who wakes up one morning and finds he is no longer a man but a giant insect. In today's increasingly complex, technological, and bureaucratic societies, Kafka has found a growing audience of sympathetic readers who understand the feeling of powerlessness Kafka's heroes experienced.

NOVELS BY KAFKA IN ENGLISH TRANSLATION

Amerika (1927). Willa Muir and Edwin Muir (trs). Schocken 1987 $7.95. ISBN 0-8052-0417-2
The Castle (1926). Willa Muir and Edwin Muir (trs). Schocken 1987 $9.95. ISBN 0-8052-0415-6
The Trial (1925). Random 1969 $4.95. ISBN 0-394-70484-3

SHORT STORIES BY KAFKA IN ENGLISH TRANSLATION

*The Complete Stories: A Centennial Special Edition. Schocken 1987 $22.50. ISBN 0-8052-3863-8. Includes one of Kafka's most famous stories, "The Metamorphosis."

NOVELS BY KAFKA IN GERMAN

Der Prozess (1925). Heineman 1969 $9.00. ISBN 0-435-38501-1
Die Verwändlung (1916). Norton 1960 $5.95. ISBN 0-393-09533-9

SHORT STORIES BY KAFKA IN BILINGUAL EDITION

Parables and Paradoxes: Parabeln and Paradoxe. Schocken 1961 $8.95. ISBN 0-8052-0422-9

BOOKS ABOUT KAFKA

Citati, Pietro. *Kafka.* Knopf 1990 $22.95. ISBN 0-394-56840-0 Biography that reconstructs Kafka's experiences and explores his legendary complexity.
Lawson, Richard H. *Franz Kafka.* Ungar 1987 $16.95. ISBN 0-8044-2502-7 Concise, readable guide to Kafka's works.
Spann, Meno. *Franz Kafka.* G. K. Hall 1985 $18.95. ISBN 0-8057-6182-9 Good general introduction to Kafka's life and works.

MANN, THOMAS   1875–1955

Thomas Mann was born into a well-to-do upper-class family in Lübeck, Germany. His mother was a talented musician and his father a successful merchant. From this background Mann derived one of his dominant themes, the clash of views between the artist and the merchant.

Mann's first novel, *Buddenbrooks* (1901), traces the declining fortunes of a merchant family much like his own as it gradually loses interest in business but gains an increasing artistic awareness. Mann was only 26 years old when this novel made him one of Germany's leading writers.

Mann went on to write *The Magic Mountain* (1924), in which he studies the isolated world of a tuberculosis sanitarium. The novel was based on his wife's confinement in such an institution. *Doctor Faustus* (1947), his masterpiece, describes the life of a composer who sells his soul to the devil as the price for musical genius.

Mann is also well known for *Death in Venice* (1912) and *Mario the Magician* (1930), both of which portray the tensions and disturbances in the lives of artists. His last and unfinished work is *The Confessions of Felix Krull, Confidence Man* (1954), a brilliantly ironic story about a nineteenth-century swindler.

An avowed anti-Nazi, Mann left Germany (as Adolf Hitler came to power) and lived in the United States during World War II. He returned to Switzerland after the war and became a celebrated literary figure in both East and West Germany. In 1929 he was awarded the Nobel Prize for literature.

NOVELS BY MANN IN ENGLISH TRANSLATION

Buddenbrooks (1901). Vintage 1984 $5.95. ISBN 0-394-72637-5
The Confessions of Felix Krull, Confidence Man (1954). Vintage 1969 $6.95. ISBN 0-394-70496-7
Doctor Faustus: The Life of the German Composer, Adrian Leverkuhn, as Told by a Friend (1947). Vintage 1971 $6.95. ISBN 0-394-71297-8
The Holy Sinner (1951). Vintage 1983 $7.95. ISBN 0-394-71741-4
Lotte in Weimar: The Beloved Returns. H. T. Lowe-Porter (tr). Univ of California Pr 1990 $10.95. ISBN 0-520-07007-0
The Magic Mountain (1924). Vintage 1969 $10.95. ISBN 0-394-70497-5
Royal Highness (1909). Vintage 1983 $7.95. ISBN 0-394-71739-2

SHORT STORIES BY MANN IN ENGLISH TRANSLATION

Death in Venice and Other Stories. David Luke (tr). Bantam 1988 $4.50. ISBN 0-553-21333-4
Stories of Three Decades. Random 1979 $9.95. ISBN 0-394-60483-0

NOVELS BY MANN IN GERMAN

Der Tod in Venedig (1912). Oxford Univ Pr 1973 $4.95. ISBN 0-19-501688-2
Tonio Kröger (1913). Basil Blackwell 1968 $15.95. ISBN 0-631-01810-7

SHORT STORIES BY MANN IN GERMAN

Two Stories. Basil Blackwell 1971 $15.95. ISBN 0-631-01870-0 Includes "Unordnung und Frühes Leid" and "Mario und der Zäuberer."

BOOKS ABOUT MANN

Bloom, Harold (ed). *Thomas Mann.* Chelsea 1986 $34.95. ISBN 0-87754-725-4 Collection of modern critical essays that approach Mann's works from different critical perspectives.
Feuerlicht, Ignace. *Thomas Mann.* G. K. Hall 1968 $17.95. ISBN 0-8057-2584-9 General study of Mann's life and works.

RILKE, RAINER MARIA   1875–1926

Rainer Maria Rilke, the greatest modern poet in the German language, was born in Prague, Czechoslovakia, into a comfortable middle-class family. His early education at a military academy and business school were unhappy experiences, and he frequently clashed with his father. He studied art at the University of Prague as well as in Munich and Berlin in Germany. Rilke lived for many years in Paris, where he was secretary to Auguste Rodin, the famous sculptor, and later Rilke traveled widely throughout Europe.

In 1911, at the castle of Duino in Istria (in present-day Yugoslavia), Rilke began the 10 poems comprising his masterpiece, the *Duino Elegies* (1923). He followed with *Sonnets to Orpheus* (1923), which consists of 55 joyous and brilliant songs.

Rilke's themes are wide-ranging and not easy to summarize. His early poetry is very spiritual, gradually turning into a quest for knowledge of God. Later he became more interested in questions of beauty, art, and the role of the artist.

POETRY BY RILKE IN ENGLISH TRANSLATION

The Complete French Poems of Rainer Maria Rilke. W. D. Snodgrass (tr). Graywolf 1986 $12.00. ISBN 0-915308-83-5
The Duino Elegies and the Sonnets to Orpheus (1923). Houghton 1977 $10.95. ISBN 0-395-25058-7
The Lay of the Love and Death of Cornet Christopher Rilke (1906). Stephen Mitchell (tr). Graywolf 1985 $7.50. ISBN 0-915308-77-0
New Poems, Nineteen Hundred Seven (1907). North Point 1984 $9.95. ISBN 0-86547-415-X
New Poems: The Other Part (1908) Edward Snow (tr). North Point 1987 $9.95. ISBN 0-86547-416-8
Poems from the Book of Hours (1905). Babette Deutsch (tr). New Directions 1975 $4.95. ISBN 0-8112-0595-9
Selected Poems of Rainer Maria Rilke. Harper 1981 $9.95. ISBN 0-06-090727-4
The Selected Poetry of Rainer Maria Rilke. Stephen Mitchell (tr). Vintage 1989 $10.95. ISBN 0-679-72201-7

POETRY BY RILKE IN BILINGUAL EDITIONS

Duino Elegies (1923). Univ of California Pr 1961 $6.95. ISBN 0-520-01073-6
The Lay of the Love and Death of Cornet Christopher Rilke (1906). Norton 1963 $5.95. ISBN 0-393-00159-8
Selected Poems. C. F. McIntyre (tr). Univ of California Pr 1940 $6.95. ISBN 0-520-01070
Sonnets to Orpheus (1923). C. F. McIntyre (tr). Univ of California Pr 1960 $6.95. ISBN 0-520-01069-8
Stories of God (1904). Norton 1963 $6.95. ISBN 0-393-00154-7
Translations from the Poetry of Rainer Maria Rilke. M. Herter (tr). Norton 1962 $7.95. ISBN 0-393-00156-3

POETRY BY RILKE IN GERMAN

Geschichten vom Lieben Gott (1900). Irvington 1957 $29.50. ISBN 0-8057-5272-2

BOOKS ABOUT RILKE

Brodsky, Patricia Pollock. *Rainer Maria Rilke: The Theaters of Consciousness.* Christopher MacGowan (ed). G. K. Hall 1988 $24.95. ISBN 0-8057-8226-5 Highly informative, clearly written general study of Rilke's life and works; contains a bibliography and an index.
Prater, Donald A. *A Ringing Glass: The Life of Rainer Maria Rilke.* Oxford Univ Pr 1986 $27.50. ISBN 0-19-815755-X Comprehensive, detailed examination focusing on Rilke's life, with little analysis of his works; illustrated with indexes and bibliography.

SCHILLER, (JOHANN CHRISTOPH) FRIEDRICH VON   1759–1805

Friedrich Schiller was born in Marbach, Germany, the son of an army surgeon, a profession for which he himself was later educated. He never wanted to practice medicine, however, and found an outlet for his dissatisfaction in writing poetry and plays.

Schiller's first play to be performed was *The Robbers* (1781), a rallying cry for the freedom and idealism of youth against the tyranny and hypocrisy that Schiller saw all around him. The play was an immediate success, but Schiller, who had taken unauthorized leave from his regiment to watch the performance, was arrested and forbidden by the ruling Duke to write anything but medical books in the future. In defiance of the order, Schiller fled the duchy and, although suffering great poverty, continued to write. The remainder of Schiller's life was a struggle against poverty and, in his last years, against tuberculosis.

Each of Schiller's nine plays is a masterpiece of situation, characterization, subtle psychology, and brilliant dramatic technique. Most of his plays focus on historical subjects, such as Mary Queen of Scots, Joan of Arc, or the Swiss hero William Tell. Schiller uses these period characters and settings to suit his own themes, which center on individual freedom, justice, and heroism. He often sacrifices historical accuracy in order to make a point.

Schiller's place in German literature is very near the top. Among German dramatists there are none better, and perhaps only his friend German poet and playwright Goethe (*see* Goethe, Vol. 1, World Literature: German Language and Literature) can be called an equal.

PLAYS BY SCHILLER IN ENGLISH TRANSLATION

The Bride of Messina (1803), *William Tell* (1804), *Demetrius* (1806). Charles E. Passage (tr). Ungar 1967. (o.p.) $7.95. ISBN 0-8044-6817-6

Don Carlos, Infante of Spain (1785). Charles E. Passage (tr). Ungar 1959 $7.95. ISBN 0-8044-6817-6

Maiden of Orleans (1801). John T. Krupelmann (tr). AMS (repr of 1962 ed) $27.00. ISBN 0-404-50937-1

Mary Stuart (1801). Joseph Mellish (tr). Applause Theatre Bk 1986 $6.95. ISBN 0-936839-00-7

The Robbers (1781) *and Wallenstein* (1799). F. J. Lamport (tr). Penguin 1980 $6.95. ISBN 0-14-044368-1

Wilhelm Tell (1804). William F. Mainland (tr). Univ of Chicago Pr 1973 $8.95. ISBN 0-226-73801-9

BOOK ABOUT SCHILLER

Garland, Henry B. *Schiller.* Greenwood (repr of 1942 ed) $27.50. ISBN 0-8371-9084-3
   Superb general study of Schiller's life and works by a leading Schiller scholar.

WEISS, PETER   1916–1982

In December 1965, Peter Weiss's play *Marat/Sade,* in a brilliant presentation by England's Royal Shakespeare Company, stormed the Broadway stage, captivating audiences and critics alike. This "play about a play" is based on a fictional account of a theatrical performance given in an insane asylum early in the nineteenth century. In Weiss's drama, the play within the play has been written by one of the asylum's most notorious inmates, the Marquis de Sade, a torturer and murderer, and is performed by inmates of the asylum. This framework gives Weiss the opportunity to stage a political confrontation between the various inmates, who are playing leaders of the French Revolution, and the character de Sade, who represents the cynical individualist.

This play marked Weiss as one of the most innovative playwrights of postwar Germany. His plays, all about political subjects, deal with questions of individual loyalty to the state and the right of governments to control individual lives. He explores these themes vigorously in *The Investigation* (1965), a drama based almost entirely on the proceedings of the 1965 Frankfurt War Crimes Tribunal, which investigated the atrocities in the World War II concentration camp at Auschwitz.

PLAYS BY WEISS IN ENGLISH TRANSLATION

The Investigation: A Play (1966). Macmillan 1966 $8.95. ISBN 0-689-70569-7

The Persecution and Assassination of Jean-Paul Marat as Performed by the Inmates of the Asylum of Charenton Under the Direction of the Marquis de Sade (1964). Macmillan 1966 $6.95. ISBN 0-689-70568-9

Two Plays: The Story of the Lusitanian Bogey (1967) and *Discourse on the Progress of the Prolonged War in Vietnam* (1969). Macmillan 1970 $6.95. ISBN 0-689-10493-6

BOOK ABOUT WEISS

Ellis, Roger. *Peter Weiss in Exile: A Critical Study of His Works.* UMI 1987 $39.95. ISBN 0-8357-1764-X Clearly written, well-organized study of Weiss's life and work for the general reader.

SCANDINAVIAN LITERATURE

The earliest Scandinavian literature, Old Norse literature, survives mainly in the form of the Icelandic sagas. Toward the end of the ninth century, the island of Iceland was occupied by invaders from Norway who brought with them their oral tales of heroic adventures. These tales were passed from generation to generation by word of mouth until about AD 1000, when Christian missionaries introduced writing to Iceland. After about 1100, both the old tales and new sagas were written down.

Unlike its use in English, the word "saga" in Icelandic refers to any fictional or nonfictional account, not merely to stories of adventure. Thus not all of the Icelandic sagas are accounts of heroic exploits. Some, such as the *Laxdaela Saga* (*c.* 1250), which deals with family relationships and a love triangle, are much closer to romances than heroic adventures.

Sagas were written and collected in Iceland throughout the Middle Ages until about 1350. These include the later *Sagas of the Knights* and the *Sagas of the Kings,* which deal with twelfth- and thirteenth-century Icelandic history.

Until well into the nineteenth century, Scandinavian literature consisted mainly of folk tales, ballads, and religious writing, particularly Lutheran hymns, which became a major form of poetry. Danish and Swedish literature were largely dormant during this period, although during the seventeenth century Ludvig Holberg, a Danish writer of theatrical comedies, produced plays that are sometimes compared with those of France's major playwright, Molière (*see* Molière, Vol. 1, World Literature: French Language and Literature), and in the eighteenth century Sweden's Carl Michael Bellman wrote some fine poetry inspired by traditional Swedish songs. Prior to 1814, Norway was a province of Denmark and lacked any identifiable literature of its own.

During the early nineteenth century, two Danish writers, Soren Kierkegaard, a philosopher, and Hans Christian Andersen, a novelist and writer of fairy tales, produced enduring works. Then, toward the end of the nineteenth century and into the twentieth, there was a sudden flowering of Scandinavian literature. Two figures dominate the period, both playwrights. In Sweden, August Strindberg wrote pessimistic and bitter plays attacking various segments of Swedish society, including women. In Norway, Henrik Ibsen wrote more realistic plays about social issues that not only brought serious social problems to public attention but also helped to revolutionize the theater throughout Europe.

Meanwhile, Jens Peder Jacobsen was writing powerful naturalistic novels and stories designed to reveal human beings as mere creatures of nature, acting only in response to natural drives and impulses. His phrase "there is no God and man is his prophet" became something of a rallying cry for rebellious Scandinavian youth.

Throughout the twentieth century, Scandinavian literature has been characterized by strongly individualistic writers rather than by schools or movements. Novelists such as Sigrid Undset, Ole Rolvaag, Knut Hamsun, and Halldor Laxness developed their own approaches to life and writing. Although many Scandinavian writers in the twentieth century have been deeply concerned with the history and fate of working people in an industrial society, their concerns differ in detail and concept, and each one's work bears its own mark of originality.

Later writers such as Isak Dinesen, Gunnar Ekelöf, and Tarjei Vesaas have carried on this tradition of individuality. Twentieth-century Swedish film director Ingmar Bergman too can be seen as carrying out in his own way some of the theatrical innovations begun by Ibsen and Strindberg.

COLLECTIONS OF SCANDINAVIAN LITERATURE IN ENGLISH TRANSLATION

Asbjørnsen, Peter C., and Jørgen Moe. *Norwegian Folk Tales.* Pantheon 1982 $8.95. ISBN 0-394-7105-1

Billeskov, Jansen, and P. M. Mitchell (eds). *Anthology of Danish Literature: Middle Ages to Romantism.* Southern Illinois Univ Pr 1972 $13.95. ISBN 0-8093-0596-8

Billeskov, Jansen, and P. M. Mitchell (eds). *Anthology of Danish Literature: Realism to the Present.* Southern Illinois Univ Pr 1972 $14.95. ISBN 0-8093-0597-6

Christiansen, Reidar (ed). *Folktales of Norway.* Univ of Chicago Pr 1968 $12.00. ISBN 0-226-10510-5

Contemporary Danish Plays. Ayer 1977 $21.50. ISBN 0-8369-8211-8

Harding, Gunnar, and Stanley Barkan (eds). *Four Contemporary Swedish Poets.* Cross Cultural 1981 $5.00. ISBN 0-89304-609-4

Harding, Gunnar (ed). *Modern Swedish Poetry in Translation.* Univ of Minnesota Pr 1979 $15.00. ISBN 0-8166-8070-9

Haugen, Einar (ed). *Fire and Ice: Three Icelandic Plays.* Univ of Wisconsin Pr 1967 $7.95. ISBN 0-299-04484-X

Hollander, Lee M. (ed). *Saga of the Jomsvikings.* Univ of Texas Pr 1989 $6.95. ISBN 0-292-77623-3

Hollander, Lee M. *Viga-Glum's Saga.* American-Scandinavian 1972 $10.50. ISBN 0-89067-021-8

Matthias, John. *Contemporary Swedish Poetry.* Ohio Univ Pr 1980 $9.95. ISBN 0-8040-0812-4

Paulahorju, Samuli. *Arctic Twilight: Old Finnish Tales.* Finnish American 1982 $15.00. ISBN 0-943478-00-6

Stork, Charles W. (ed). *Anthology of Norwegian Lyrics.* Ayer 1977 $15.00. ISBN 0-8369-6043-2

Stork, Charles W. (ed). *Anthology of Swedish Lyrics: 1752 to 1925.* Roth (repr of 1930 ed) $29.50. ISBN 0-89609-170-8

Waidson, H. M. *Anthology of Modern Swedish Literature.* St. Martin's 1985 $29.95. ISBN 0-312-04227-2

ANDERSEN, HANS CHRISTIAN   1805–1875 (DANISH)

Hans Christian Andersen was born in Odense, Denmark, the son of a poor shoemaker. He received very little education as a child and left home at age 14 to find employment in Copenhagen, Denmark's capital.

Although Andersen showed an early gift for writing poetry, his lack of education prevented him from getting employment other than factory work. He tried acting but was unsuccessful. Finally, with the help of some generous friends, he received a grant from the Danish king that enabled him to get a higher education. While still in his teens, he published some of his poems and in 1829 published his first book, *A Walk to Amager,* a humorous literary satire. The following year his first volume of poetry appeared in print, and his career as an author was established.

Today Andersen is known worldwide as a writer of fairy tales, but these stories were only a small part of his life's work. In his own time, his novels and travel books were more warmly received by his contemporaries. He was also more esteemed in other countries than in his native Denmark. However, it was the fairy tales, the first of which were published in 1835, that survived; his novels and poetry have been long out of print.

In his old age, Andersen said about these famous stories: "My fairy tales are written as much for adults as for children. Children see only the trimmings, and not until they are mature will they see and comprehend the whole." In fact, Andersen's tales are marked by a yearning for love and acceptance, and a protest at the pain of being an outsider, that only a mature reader can fully appreciate. There is an intense autobiographical element in all of Andersen's writings; his memoirs were entitled *The Fairy Tale of My Life* (1855).

SHORT STORIES BY ANDERSEN IN ENGLISH TRANSLATION

The Complete Hans Christian Andersen Fairy Tales. Crown 1984 $11.98. ISBN 0-517-66718-5 Includes "The Emperor's New Clothes," "The Ugly Duckling," "Thumbelina," and the entire collection of Andersen favorites.

Tales and Stories by Hans Christian Andersen. Univ of Washington Pr 1980 $14.95. ISBN 0-295-95936-3 Includes the complete fairy tales and other stories not frequently published; an excellent translation.

BOOK ABOUT ANDERSEN

Conroy, Patricia, and Sven H. Rössel (eds). *The Diaries of Hans Christian Andersen.* Univ of Washington Pr 1990 $45.00. ISBN 0-295-96845-1 One-volume work excerpted from the 12-volume Danish edition published in the 1970s; provides good insights into Andersen's life and works.

DINESEN, ISAK (PSEUDONYM OF KAREN BLIXEN)   1885–1962 (DANISH)

Isak Dinesen was born into an aristocratic Danish family and educated in Denmark, England, Switzerland, Italy, and France. In 1914, she married her cousin, Baron Bror Blixen Finecke, and moved with him to Kenya, in East Africa, where she lived the happiest and most eventful years of her life.

From 1914 to 1931, Dinesen struggled to maintain a coffee plantation in Kenya, during which time she grew to love the people and the natural beauty of her adopted land. Her recollections of this experience, recorded in *Out of Africa* (1938) and its sequel, *Shadows on the Grass* (1961), are extraordinary memoirs. In them Dinesen is less interested in recording facts than in describing the spirit and beauty of a land where humanity and nature were still profoundly connected. After 1931 she returned to Denmark.

Dinesen's subsequent fiction was also influenced by her African experiences. In fact, all her writing contains strong undercurrents of the outlook on life she developed in Africa. Dinesen wrote primarily in a faultless, quite personal variety of English, and she found her most receptive audience in the

United States. Although her later stories are outwardly Gothic tales of mystery and terror, they conceal much wisdom and a deep sense of the sorrows that especially befall women.

SHORT STORIES BY DINESEN IN ENGLISH TRANSLATION

Babette's Feast and Other Anecdotes of Destiny (1958). Martha Levin (ed). Vintage 1988 $4.95. ISBN 0-394-75929-X *Babette's Feast* later became a motion picture.

Carnival: Entertainments and Posthumous Tales (1977). Univ of Chicago Pr 1979 $10.95. ISBN 0-226-15304-5

Last Tales (1957). Vintage 1985 $5.95. ISBN 0-394-74292-3

Seven Gothic Tales (1934). Vintage $6.95. ISBN 0-394-74291-5

Winter's Tales (1942). Vintage 1985 $8.95. ISBN 0-394-74293-1

NONFICTION BY DINESEN

Out of Africa (1938) *and Shadows on the Grass* (1961). Vintage 1989 $7.95. ISBN 0-679-72475-3 *Out of Africa* was made into a successful motion picture.

HAMSUN, KNUT (PSEUDONYM OF KNUT PEDERSEN) 1859–1952 (NORWEGIAN)

Knut Hamsun was born in Lom in the wilds of northern Norway. He had no formal schooling and as a boy worked with his uncle in the Lofoten Islands. As a young man he worked at a variety of jobs, including shoemaker and country schoolteacher. He immigrated twice to the United States, once working as a streetcar conductor in Chicago.

Hamsun became famous after the publication of his first novel, *Hunger* (1890), which depicted the struggles of a brilliant but poverty-stricken young writer who is filled with joy and emotional freedom while literally starving. Hamsun's most famous work is *Growth of the Soil* (1917), a novel that contrasts simple rural life with the corruption and exploitation of modern industrial society. Largely on the basis of this work, Hamsun was awarded the Nobel Prize for literature in 1920.

Hamsun introduced into Norwegian literature a focus on the emotional life of the individual without regard for underlying social concerns or larger moral "truths." Thus the hero of *Hunger* is depicted as a unique human being, not as the victim of some social injustice or the representative of some moral principle—an approach that had no precedent in Norwegian literature.

NOVELS BY HAMSUN IN ENGLISH TRANSLATION

August (1930). Fertig 1990 $45.00. ISBN 0-86527-374-X

Growth of the Soil (1917). Vintage 1972 $7.95. ISBN 0-394-71781-3

Hunger (1890). Farrar 1967 $7.95. ISBN 0-374-50520-9

Mysteries (1892). Carroll & Graf 1984 $8.95. ISBN 0-88184-031-1

Pan: From Lieutenant Thomas Glahn's Papers (1894). Farrar 1956 $8.95. ISBN 0-374-50016-9

SHORT STORIES BY HAMSUN IN ENGLISH TRANSLATION

Night Roamers and Other Stories. Fjord 1990 $9.95. ISBN 0-940242-19-2

BOOK ABOUT HAMSUN

Ferguson, Robert. *Enigma: The Life of Knut Hamsun.* Farrar 1988 $14.95. ISBN 0-374-52093-3 Detailed biography that demonstrates Hamsun's mastery of psychological fiction.

IBSEN, HENRIK   1828–1906 (NORWEGIAN)

Henrik Ibsen was born in Skien, Norway, into a poor family. His early education was limited, and he spent most of his youth in poverty. From 1844 to 1847, he was apprenticed to a pharmacist.

Ibsen's early efforts at playwriting were rejected, but he eventually obtained a position as a writer at Ole Bull's theater in Bergen, Norway. By 1857, he was producing significant work for the stage.

After some interesting but not exceptional early plays, including the poetic drama *Peer Gynt* (1867), Ibsen entered into the first of three major stages in his career with the 1877 production of *The Pillar of Society.* This was the first of his "social plays," which addressed themselves to specific social problems and issues. This early work was followed by *A Doll's House* (1879) the story of a woman who comes to reject traditional marriage; *Ghosts* (1881) about the evil effects of following convention; and *An Enemy of the People* (1882) about a man who must defend the truth against conventional society—all enduring works that are still produced today.

In his next phase Ibsen shifted his attention away from characters in conflict with social forces to characters facing conflicts within themselves. *The Wild Duck* (1884), *Rosmersholm* (1886), *The Lady from the Sea* (1888), and *Hedda Gabler* (1890) all belong to this period. *The Wild Duck*—about the conflict between harsh truth and necessary illusions—and *Hedda Gabler*—story of a woman

The Wyndam Sisters.   Detail of oil painting by John Singer Sargent (1900). Courtesy of The Metropolitan Museum of Art, Wolfe Fund, Catherine Lorillard Wolfe Collection, 1927. (27.67)

whose frustrations lead her to destroy herself and those around her—are still frequently produced.

Ibsen's last plays, written between 1892 and 1899, generally concern the self-destructive aspects of artistic ambition. Out of this period came *The Master Builder* (1892), *Little Eyolf* (1894), *John Gabriel Borkman* (1896), and *When We Dead Awaken* (1899).

Ibsen's influence on the modern theater was enormous. He was a writer so far ahead of his time that only in the last 50 years have his staging and theatrical innovations been fully appreciated. His concepts of social drama were powerful influences on such playwrights as George Bernard Shaw (*see* Shaw, Vol. 1, British Literature: The Twentieth Century) and Anton Chekhov. (*See* Chekhov, Vol. 1, World Literature: Russian Literature.)

PLAYS BY IBSEN IN ENGLISH TRANSLATION

Eight Plays. McGraw 1981 $6.95. ISBN 0-07-554342-7 Includes *A Doll's House* (1879), *Ghosts* (1881), *An Enemy of the People* (1882), *Rosmersholm* (1886), *Hedda Gabler* (1890), *The Master Builder* (1892), *The Wild Duck* (1884), and *The Lady from the Sea* (1888).

The Oxford Ibsen: Little Eyolf (1894), *John Gabriel Borkman* (1896), *When We Dead Awaken* (1899). Oxford Univ Pr 1977 $36.95. ISBN 0-19-211387-9

Peer Gynt (1867). Heinemann 1988 $6.95. ISBN 0-413-52250-4

POETRY BY IBSEN IN ENGLISH TRANSLATION

Henrik Ibsen's Poems. Oxford Univ Pr 1987 $32.50. ISBN 82-00-07455-2

BOOKS ABOUT IBSEN

May, Keith. *Ibsen and Shaw.* St. Martin's 1985 $25.00. ISBN 0-312-40371-2 *Choice* magazine found that this book "provides significant insights into the works of Ibsen and Shaw as well as into the major differences between them."

Meyer, Michael. *Ibsen.* Penguin 1985 $9.95. ISBN 0-14-058003-4 Comprehensive biography by a noted Ibsen scholar; provides insights into Ibsen's works as well as his life.

LAGERVIST, PAR   1891–1974 (SWEDISH)

In 1913 Pär Lagervist stated that his goal as a writer was to achieve a simplicity and dignity in his works similar to that found in the works of the Greek poet Homer, the Old Testament, and the Icelandic sagas. Over the following 60 years, Lagervist realized this aim in both plays and novels that are striking in their simple beauty and great power. These works are built on themes such as human curiosity and the search for knowledge, injustice and exploitation, the potential evil that lurks in all human beings, and the insecurity and uncertainty of the human condition.

There are no easy answers to the questions Lagervist poses. They are the nagging questions that most people brush aside because they are so unsettling. Lagervist, however, insists that they be faced. His novel *The Sibyl* (1956), a mystical work that expresses uncertainty about the nature of God, found a particularly enthusiastic audience in the United States. Lagervist was awarded the Nobel Prize for literature in 1951.

WORKS OF LAGERVIST IN ENGLISH TRANSLATION

Five Early Works. Roy Arthur Swanson (tr). Mellen 1989 $59.95. ISBN 0-88946-019-1

NOVELS BY LAGERVIST IN ENGLISH TRANSLATION

Barabbas (1950). Vintage 1989 $7.95. ISBN 0-679-72544-X
The Dwarf (1944). Hill & Wang 1958 $8.95. ISBN 0-374-52135-2
The Sibyl (1956). Vintage 1963 $4.95. ISBN 0-394-70240-9

PLAYS BY LAGERVIST IN ENGLISH TRANSLATION

Modern Theatre: Seven Plays and an Essay. Univ of Nebraska Pr 1966 $26.50. ISBN 0-8032-0098-6

RØLVAAG, OLE EDVART   1876–1931 (NORWEGIAN)

Ole Rølvaag was born in Donna, Norway, and immigrated to the United States in 1896. He was educated at St. Olaf College in Minnesota and at the University of Oslo in Norway. After completing his education he began to teach at St. Olaf, where he became head of the department of Norwegian in 1906, a position he held until his death in 1931. He became an American citizen in 1910.

Rølvaag's novels, written in Norwegian, brought him fame as an interpreter of the experiences of Norwegian immigrants in the United States, but his stories reflect the experiences of all the immigrants who came to the north-central United States at the close of the nineteenth century. His first, highly autobiographical, work, *The Third Life of Per Smevik,* was published in 1912 under the pseudonym Paal Morck. His major work, *Giants in the Earth* (1927), begins the story of Per Hansa's family, Norwegian settlers on the North Dakota prairie in the 1870s. The story is continued in *Peder Victorious* (1929) and *Their Father's God* (1931). These moving tales have given Rølvaag a solid place in both American and Norwegian literature.

NOVELS BY RØLVAAG IN ENGLISH TRANSLATION

The Boat of Longing (1933). Minnesota Hist Soc (repr of 1933 ed) $8.95. ISBN 0-87351-184-0
Giants in the Earth (1925). Harper 1985 $5.95. ISBN 0-06-083047-6
Peder Victorius: A Tale of the Pioneers Twenty Years Later (1928). Univ of Nebraska Pr 1982 $8.50. ISBN 0-8032-8906-5
Pure Gold (1930). Greenwood 1973 repr of 1930 ed $35.00. ISBN 0-8371-7070-2
Their Father's God (1931). Univ of Nebraska Pr 1983 $7.95. ISBN 0-8032-8911-1
The Third Life of Per Smevik (1912). Harper 1987 $6.95. ISBN 0-06-097076-6

BOOKS ABOUT RØLVAAG

Mosley, Ann. *Ole Edvart Rølvaag.* Boise State Univ Pr 1987 $2.95. ISBN 0-88430-079-X Fifty-page booklet with an excellent summary of critical opinion on Rølvaag's work and on the major themes of his stories; selected bibliography.
Reigstad, Paul. *Rølvaag: His Life and Art.* Univ of Nebraska Pr 1972 $16.50. ISBN 0-8032-0803-0 Detailed and scholarly general study of Rølvaag's life and works.

STRINDBERG, AUGUST   1849–1912 (SWEDISH)

Born in Stockholm, Sweden, into a poor family, August Strindberg suffered a hard and unhappy childhood. He studied for a while at the University of Uppsala in Sweden, but left without a degree.

Strindberg began to write while supporting himself at a variety of jobs, including journalist and librarian. The work that first brought him to public attention was the novel *The Red Room* (1879), a biting satire on Stockholm society that displayed his skill as both a literary stylist and a social commentator. Strindberg went on to write other novels, as well as stories and poems, but it is as a playwright that he is remembered. Sweden's greatest playwright, he ranks just behind Norway's playwright Henrik Ibsen as the leading Scandinavian dramatist. (*See* Ibsen, Vol. 1, World Literature: Scandinavian Literature.)

It is not easy to categorize Strindberg's plays. Many deal with social issues, but his own beliefs varied so often and so strongly that his works often contradict each other. Perhaps the only consistent theme in his plays is an abiding hatred of women, or more specifically, of women of strong will and character. *The Father* (1887), *Miss Julie* (1888), and *Creditors* (1888) contain his severest attacks on women. Strindberg himself was married and divorced three times, and his woman-hating plays may well reflect his own marital problems.

Fascination with Strindberg has not decreased since his death. His enormous influence on European and world literature can hardly be exaggerated, In general, however, his novels and biographical writings have not been popular with English-speaking readers. His plays, on the other hand, continue to be widely read and produced throughout Europe and the United States. They helped introduce greater attention to individual psychological disturbances as a subject for theater, as well as a poetic and surreal approach to violence, pain, and suffering.

NOVEL BY STRINDBERG IN ENGLISH TRANSLATION

By the Open Sea. Penguin 1987 $5.95. ISBN 0-14-044488-2

PLAYS BY STRINDBERG IN ENGLISH TRANSLATION

The Chamber Plays. Univ of Minnesota Pr 1981 $7.95. ISBN 0-8166-1031-2
The Post-Inferno Period. Univ of Minnesota Pr 1986 $10.95. ISBN 0-8166-1339-7 Includes plays written after 1897.
The Pre-Inferno Period. Univ of Minnesota Pr 1986 $10.95. ISBN 0-8166-1338-9 Includes plays written before 1897.
Selected Plays. Univ of Minnesota Pr 1986 $39.50. ISBN 0-8166-1506-3

BOOKS ABOUT STRINDBERG

Lagercrantz, Olof. *August Strindberg.* Anselm Hollo (tr). Farrar 1984 $12.95. ISBN 0-374-10685-1 General study of Strindberg's life and works by a leading Swedish scholar.
Strindberg, August. *Inferno: From an Occult Diary.* Penguin 1979 $6.95. ISBN 0-14-044364-9 Strindberg's account of a period of mental instability when he believed he was being pursued by creatures from another world.

UNDSET, SIGRID   1882–1949 (NORWEGIAN)

Sigrid Undset was born in Denmark, the daughter of a famous archaeologist, Ingvald Undset. From her father she gained both an interest in and knowledge of medieval Scandinavian culture. She used this knowledge to fashion her two literary monuments, *Kristin Lavransdatter* (1920–1922) and *The Master of Hestviken* (1925–1927), historical novels that depict in vivid detail the nature of life in the Norwegian Middle Ages.

Undset's earlier novels grew out of her experiences in an office where she was forced to work to support her sisters after the death of their father. For example, *Jenny* (1911), an idealistic and tragic love story, focuses on the problems of young middle-class women.

Undset became a Roman Catholic in 1924, shortly after completing *Kristin Lavransdatter,* and much of her life after that point is marked by intense religious devotion. Her medieval novels, however, bear no sign of religious dogmatism. Rather, they are vivid, realistic portrayals of medieval personalities, dealing with the full range of experiences of a young woman of that time and culture.

Undset's later works became increasingly autobiographical. They never achieved the scope or power of her medieval novels and are seldom read today. Nevertheless, Undset was awarded the Nobel Prize for literature in 1949, primarily for her earlier work.

NOVELS BY UNDSET IN ENGLISH TRANSLATION

Kristin Lavransdatter, Vol. I: The Bridal Wreath (1920). Vintage 1987 $8.95. ISBN 0-394-75299-6
Kristin Lavransdatter, Vol. II: The Mistress of Husaby (1921). Vintage 1987 $8.95. ISBN 0-394-75293-7
Kristin Lavransdatter, Vol. III: The Cross (1922). Vintage 1987 $8.95. ISBN 0-394-75291-0
The Master of Hestviken (1925–1927). Plume 1978 $14.95. ISBN 0-452-26034-5

SHORT STORIES BY UNDSET IN ENGLISH TRANSLATION

Four Stories. Greenwood 1978 repr of 1942 ed $35.00. ISBN 0-313-20566-3

BOOK ABOUT UNDSET

Brunsdale, Mitzi. *Sigrid Undset.* St. Martin's 1989 $25.00. ISBN 0-85496-027-9 Solid, readable biography that focuses on the sorrow in Undset's life: her unhappy marriage, loss of children, and mental illness.

EASTERN EUROPEAN AND YIDDISH LITERATURE

The literatures of Eastern Europe developed after the introduction of Christianity to the area in the Middle Ages, generally in the ninth and tenth centuries. The earliest writings, mostly in Latin, are primarily religious, such as prayers, hymns, lives of saints, and biblical stories. Although the different peoples of Eastern Europe had rich bodies of oral folktales and poetry, little exists in written form before the twelfth and thirteenth centuries. Constant wars and conquests by the Germans, Austrians, Russians, and Turks kept much of the area under foreign domination. In order to maintain their control, the foreign rulers almost always banned writing in the countries they occupied, thus retarding the growth of national literatures.

It was not until the eighteenth and nineteenth centuries that most of the nations of Eastern Europe began to develop what can truly be called national literatures. Even then, shifting political fortunes and occupations by foreign armies kept many of these nations from developing a national political identity. Such unified groups as existed were held together more by common language and culture than by a common government or by national boundaries.

It is not surprising, therefore, that a great deal of the writing produced in these countries during this period was highly patriotic and nationalistic. Inspired by the American and French revolutions, writers throughout Eastern Europe began to call for national identity and national independence. In Bulgaria, poet Christo Botev and novelist Ivan Vazov, in Czechoslovakia poets Jan Kollar and Karel Hynek Macha, and in Poland poet Adam Michiewicz all used their literary talents in the cause of national freedom. As political pressures in the region increased, many writers, particularly from Poland, were forced into exile. Nevertheless, they continued to press for national freedom and cultural identity.

The twentieth century saw Eastern Europe ravaged by two massive wars, both of which resulted in still more changes in national boundaries. The period between the wars saw a new burst of literary activity throughout the region, with a new generation of writers celebrating political and intellectual freedom. Czech writers Karel Capek, Jaroslav Hasek, and Jaroslav Seifert breathed new life and vigor into their new nation's literature, as did Mihaly Babits and Ferenc Molnar in Hungary. In Poland, new schools of poetry developed, led by such gifted writers as Julian Tuwin and Jan Przylos. New Bulgarian writers like Elin Pelin and Yordan Yovkov enlivened that nation's literature. Most of this activity was brought to a halt by World War II. The Communist regimes that came to power after the war drastically affected literary activity, requiring writers to work within and around official artistic policy. With the collapse of Communist rule in 1989, the writers of Eastern Europe began looking forward to new possibilities for freedom of expression. Perhaps the most dramatic symbol of this change is Czech playwright Vaclav Havel: jailed under the old regime, elected president under the new.

Yiddish literature, while not confined to Eastern Europe, experienced much of its growth and development in this region, especially in Poland and western Russia. Yiddish literature began in the Middle Ages and grew out of the spoken language of Ashkenazic Jews—those who settled in central and eastern Europe.

The Yiddish language, while technically a German dialect, is actually composed of elements of German, Hebrew, and Aramaic, as well as Slavic and Romance languages. In the mid-1930s, over 11 million people spoke Yiddish throughout the world. Today only 2 to 3 million people speak the language, and it is in danger of dying out. The primary reason for this sudden decline was the murder of millions of Yiddish-speaking Jews during the Nazi occupation of Europe. Interestingly, the one place where writers regularly publish literary and journalistic works in Yiddish is the Soviet Union.

Early Yiddish literature was largely religious—collections of Bible stories and commentaries. Much of the early literature was written for women who were traditionally not instructed in Hebrew and so needed religious writing in a language they could read.

By the middle of the nineteenth century, Yiddish literature had begun to lose its purely religious character as more and more tales of the lives and struggles of ordinary people were written. Toward the end of the century, three great writers brought Yiddish literature to a new height of popularity: I. L. Peretz; S. Y. Abromovitsh, who adopted the pen name Mendele Moykher Sforim; and Sholem Rabinowitz, better known as Sholom Aleichem.

In the twentieth century, there was another flowering of Yiddish literature after World War II as many Jewish writers tried to confront and explain the tragedy of the Holocaust, the Nazis' mass murder of European Jews during World War II. In 1978, Isaac Bashevis Singer, the greatest of the modern Yiddish writers, was awarded the Nobel Prize for literature.

COLLECTIONS OF EAST EUROPEAN AND YIDDISH LITERATURE IN ENGLISH TRANSLATION

Betsky, Sarah Z. (ed). *Onions and Cucumbers and Plums: Forty-Six Yiddish Poems in English.* Wayne State Univ Pr 1981 $12.95. ISBN 0-8143-1674-3

Busch, Marie, and Otto Rich (eds). *Selected Czech Tales.* Ayer (repr of 1925 ed) $15.00. ISBN 0-8369-3669-8

Gillon, Adam, and Ludwick Krzyzanowski (eds). *Introduction to Modern Polish Literature.* Hippocrene 1981 $12.95. ISBN 0-88254-516-7

Howe, Irving, and Eliezer Greenberg (eds). *A Treasury of Yiddish Poetry.* Schocken 1976 $10.95. ISBN 0-8052-0546-2

Howe, Irving, and Eliezer Greenberg (eds). *A Treasury of Yiddish Stories.* Schocken 1973 $13.95. ISBN 0-8052-0400-8

Howe, Irving, and Eliezer Greenberg (eds). *Yiddish Stories Old and New.* Holiday 1974 $5.95. ISBN 0-8234-0246-0

Leftwich, Joseph. *Anthology of Modern Yiddish Literature.* Mouton 1974 $20.75. ISBN 90-2793-496-7

Leihm, Antonin, and Peter Kussi (eds). *The Writing on the Wall: An Anthology of Czechoslovak Literature Today.* Karz-Cohl 1983 $19.95. ISBN 0-918294-19-3

Lenski, Branko (ed). *Death of a Simple Giant and Other Modern Yugoslav Stories.* Vanguard 1964 $10.00. ISBN 0-8149-0143-3

Mihailovich, Vasa D. (ed). *White Stones and Fir Trees: An Anthology of Contemporary Slavic Literature.* Fairleigh 1977 $35.00. ISBN 0-8386-1194-X

Mikasinovich, Branko (ed). *Modern Yugoslav Satire.* Cross Cultural 1979 $12.00. ISBN 0-89304-030-4

Rischling, Moses (ed). *Yiddish Tales.* Ayer 1975 repr of 1912 ed $47.50. ISBN 0-405-6755-0

ALEICHEM, SHOLEM (PSEUDONYM OF SHOLEM YAKOV RABINOWITZ)   1859–1916 (YIDDISH)

Sholem Aleichem, a pen name taken from the Hebrew greeting meaning "Peace be unto you," was born in the Russian Ukraine, where he lived until 1906, when he fled to America. The most popular and beloved of all Yiddish writers, he wrote with humor and tenderness about the Yiddish-speaking Jews of Eastern Europe and won the title of the Jewish Mark Twain. (*See* Twain, Vol. 1, American Literature: The Rise of Realism.) In his stories he adopts the role of sympathetic listener and reporter. He tells his tales as if they were told to him, and he is merely passing on what he has heard.

Some of Sholem Aleichem's characters have become world-famous through the stage and film versions of the musical *Fiddler on the Roof,* which is based on his "Tevye" stories. Although he also wrote plays and novels, Sholem Aleichem is best remembered for these and other brilliant, hilarious, and bittersweet stories.

SHORT STORIES BY SHOLEM ALEICHEM IN ENGLISH TRANSLATION

The Adventures of Menahem-Mendl (1892–1913). Putnam 1979 $4.95. ISBN 0-399-50396-X Stories of Menahem-Mendl, the clever but perpetually poor man always trying to make a deal.

Favorite Stories. Amereon $20.95. ISBN 0-8488-0414-7 Includes a variety of Sholem Aleichem's most memorable characters of the villages and cities of Eastern Europe.

Holiday Tales of Sholem Aleichem. Macmillan 1985 $5.95. ISBN 0-689-71034-8 Seven stories that center on the Jewish holidays of Passover, Purim, Chanukah, and Sukkoth.

More Favorite Stories. Amereon $20.95. ISBN 0-8488-0413-9 More tales of families, scholars, religious men; humorous and painful at the same time.

Tevye the Dairyman and the Railroad Stories (1949). Schocken 1988 $10.95. ISBN 0-8052-0905-0 Includes stories of Tevye and his rebellious daughters.

NONFICTION BY SHOLEM ALEICHEM IN ENGLISH TRANSLATION

From the Fair. Penguin 1986 $7.95. ISBN 0-14-008830-X Sholem Aleichem's autobiography describing his early life in the Ukraine.

BOOKS ABOUT SHOLEM ALEICHEM

Aarons, Victoria. *Author as Character in the Works of Sholem Aleichem.* Mellen 1985 $49.95. ISBN 0-88946-553-3 Study of Sholem Aleichem's literary techniques and the way in which his changing attitude toward Eastern European Jewish community life influenced them.

Halberstram-Rubin, Anna. *The Writer as Social Historian. American University Studies Series IX: History: Vol. 39.* Peter Lang 1989 $23.95. ISBN 0-8204-0675-9 Biography that draws on the original stories of the Yiddish humorist Sholem Aleichem and vividly portrays the situation of the Jews in czarist Russia.

Samuel, Maurice. *The World of Sholem Aleichem.* Macmillan 1986 $9.95. ISBN 0-689-70709-6 Tells of a pilgrimage through Sholem Aleichem's world, revealing a great man and an extraordinary civilization.

ANDRIC, IVO 1892–1975 (YUGOSLAV)

Ivo Andric was born near Travnik in the area of Yugoslavia known as Bosnia. He began to write short stories in 1923 and was one of the most respected writers in Yugoslav literature in the years before World War II, gaining the affectionate title of the Yugoslav Tolstoy. (*See* Tolstoy, Vol. 1, World Literature: Russian Literature.) After the war, Andric's novels, *The Bridge on the Drina* (1945) and *Bosnian Story* (1945), made him famous worldwide. In 1961, they won him the Nobel Prize for literature.

Andric wrote almost all his stories about his native Bosnia, a land that for centuries was isolated from the rest of the world and whose people lived hard lives, sustained only by their myths and dreams. What Andric found most interesting about his people was the attempt of different races and religions to live together in harmony amid a variety of forces that constantly tore at the fabric of their society. Along with these themes, Andric's skill at creating interesting and believable characters has helped make his stories among the most popular and admired of any modern Yugoslav author.

NOVEL BY ANDRIC IN ENGLISH TRANSLATION

The Bridge on the Drina (1945). Univ of Chicago Pr 1977 $9.95. ISBN 0-226-02045-2

CAPEK, KAREL 1890–1938 (CZECH)

Karel Capek—playwright, novelist, and biographer—is one of the most popular and respected Czech writers. In the United States he is best known as the author of *R.U.R* (1921)—Rossum's Universal Robots—a satirical play about an age during which technology has run wild and robots take over the world, leaving only one human alive. In fact, Capek gave the world the very word *robot,* coining it from the Czech word for work.

Capek's novels, like those of British author H.G. Wells (*see* Wells, Vol. 1, British Literature: Twentieth Century), are filled with startlingly accurate predictions of the impact of technology on society. *The Insect Play* (1921), in which the characters are actually insects, is both a comment on human weakness and a warning of the dangers of totalitarianism. Despite the apparent pessimism of his dire predictions and social satire, Capek's work has an enduring faith in the goodness of human nature, the triumph of justice, and the worth of democracy, which has maintained its popularity among Czechs during the postwar years.

NOVELS BY CAPEK IN ENGLISH TRANSLATION

The Absolute at Large (1922). Hyperion 1989 (repr of 1927 ed) $10.00. ISBN 0-88355-133-0

Krakatit (1924). Ayer 1975 repr of 1925 ed $23.00. ISBN 0-685-51338-6
Three Novels. Catbird 1990 repr of 1948 ed $13.95. ISBN 0-945774-08-7
The War with the Newts (1936). Catbird 1990 $9.95. ISBN 0-945774-10-9

SHORT STORIES BY CAPEK IN ENGLISH TRANSLATION

Money and Other Stories (1921). Ayer 1930 $18.00. ISBN 0-8369-3293-5
Nine Fairy Tales. Northwestern Univ Pr 1990 $24.95. ISBN 0-8101-0864-X
Toward the Radical Center: A Karel Capek Reader. Catbird 1990 $23.95. ISBN 0-945774-06-0

PLAYS BY CAPEK IN ENGLISH TRANSLATION

The Makropoulos Secret (1923). Branden 1991 $2.95. ISBN 0-8283-1447-0
R.U.R. and The Insect Play (1921). Oxford Univ Pr 1961 $7.95. ISBN 0-19-281010-3

BOOK ABOUT CAPEK

Harkins, William E. *Karel Capek.* Columbia Univ Pr 1962 $28.00. ISBN 0-231-02512-2
General study of Capek's life and works with emphasis on his basic themes and approaches to fiction.

KUNDERA, MILAN   1929– (CZECH)

Novelist, poet, and playwright, Milan Kundera is one of Czechoslovakia's foremost contemporary writers. His first novel, *The Joke* (1967), is a biting satire on political conditions under Communist rule in the 1950s. The book is the story of a young Communist party member who ruins his career—and his life—by writing a postcard to his girlfriend poking fun at her political enthusiasm. The novel was a huge success and was translated into a dozen languages and then made into a film, which Kundera himself wrote and directed.

Kundera's novel, *Life Is Elsewhere* (1974), was also widely acclaimed and won a major international book prize, the Prix de Medicis. In this story a somewhat self-deluded poet enters the rough-and-tumble world of politics with comically tragic results. *The Unbearable Lightness of Being* (1984) has likewise won Kundera a large readership and international acclaim, also becoming a motion picture.

Unable to express himself freely in Czechoslovakia, Kundera has lived and written in Paris for many years. His books are now being published in his native country for the first time.

NOVELS BY KUNDERA IN ENGLISH TRANSLATION

The Book of Laughter and Forgetting (1981). Penguin 1987 $7.95. ISBN 0-14-009693-0
The Farewell Party (1979). Penguin 1987 $7.95. ISBN 0-14-009694-9
The Joke (1967). Penguin 1987 $7.95. ISBN 0-14-009692-2
Life Is Elsewhere (1974). Penguin 1986 $8.95. ISBN 0-14-006470-2
The Unbearable Lightness of Being (1984). Harper 1985 $7.95. ISBN 0-06-091252-9

SHORT STORY BY KUNDERA IN ENGLISH TRANSLATION

Laughable Loves (1963). Penguin 1988 $7.95. ISBN 0-14-009691-4

PLAY BY KUNDERA IN ENGLISH TRANSLATION

Jacques and His Master (1981). Harper 1985 $7.95. ISBN 0-06-091222-7

LEM, STANISLAW   1921– (POLE)

Stanislaw Lem's broad and varied education—he is a graduate of the University of Cracow's medical school—makes him comfortable in both the sciences and philosophy. This breadth of learning has enabled Lem to become Poland's leading writer of science fiction and to give his writing a depth not frequently found in this genre. His work has become increasingly serious and philosophical as he speculates about possible tomorrows. Lem has also developed his gift as a storyteller, and his novels remain thoroughly engaging. Lem's solid worldwide reputation is testimony to both his skill as a novelist and his versatility as a thinker.

NOVELS BY LEM IN ENGLISH TRANSLATION

Chain of Chance (1976). Harcourt 1984 $2.95. ISBN 0-15-616500-7
Eden (1959). Harcourt 1989 $19.95. ISBN 0-15-127580-7
Fiasco (1986). Harcourt 1988 $6.95. ISBN 0-15-630630-1
The Futurological Congress (1971). Harcourt 1985 $5.95. ISBN 0-15-634040-2
His Master's Voice (1968). Harcourt 1984 $6.95. ISBN 0-15-640300-5
The Investigation (1959). Harcourt 1986 $4.95. ISBN 0-15-645158-1
Memoirs Found in a Bathtub (1961). Harcourt 1986 $7.95. ISBN 0-15-658585-5
Memoirs of a Space Traveler: Further Reminiscences of Ijon Tichy (1982). Harcourt 1983 $5.95. ISBN 0-15-658635-5
A Perfect Vacuum (1971). Michael Kandel (tr). Harcourt 1983 $6.95. ISBN 0-15-671686-0

SHORT STORIES BY LEM IN ENGLISH TRANSLATION

The Cyberiad: Fables for the Cybernetic Age (1965). Harcourt 1985 $7.95. ISBN 0-15-623550-1
More Tales of Prix the Pilot (1981). Harcourt 1983 $6.95. ISBN 0-15-662143-6
Tales of Prix the Pilot (1979). Harcourt 1990 $7.95. ISBN 0-15-688150-0

MILOSZ, CZESLAW   1911– (POLE)

Born in Lithuania, Czeslaw Milosz has been a published poet since 1933. In the mid-1930s, he was one of a number of Polish poets who sensed the coming of World War II, and his second volume of poetry, *Three Winters* (1936), conveys a strong sense of impending catastrophe. During World War II itself, Milosz continued to write as a member of the Polish underground. In 1951, unable to write freely under the Communist regime, he left Poland and eventually settled in the United States.

Milosz currently teaches at the University of California at Berkeley. His poetry, which is ironic, grotesque, and intellectual, has won a worldwide following. In 1978, Milosz received the Neustadt International Prize for Literature, and in 1980 he was awarded the Nobel Prize for his literary achievements.

NOVELS BY MILOSZ IN ENGLISH TRANSLATION

The Issa Valley (1955). Farrar 1981 $9.95. ISBN 0-374-51695-2
The Seizure of Power (1953). Farrar 1982 $6.95. ISBN 0-374-51697-9

POETRY BY MILOSZ IN ENGLISH TRANSLATION

The Collected Poems. Ecco 1990 $14.95. ISBN 0-88001-174-2

BOOK ABOUT MILOSZ

Czarnecka, Ewa, and Alexander Fiut. *Conversations with Czeslaw Milosz.* Harcourt 1987
$27.95. ISBN 0-15-122591-5 Transcribed conversations in which Milosz talks
about the suppression of freedom in Poland under communism and about his own
creative process.

SIENKIEWICZ, HENRYK   1846–1916 (POLE)

Henryk Sienkiewicz began his literary career as a journalist and built an early
reputation on his account of a two-year trip to the United States. Between 1882
and 1888, he published three historical novels dealing with political and military events in seventeenth-century Poland: *With Fire and Sword* (1882), *The Deluge*
(1886), and *Pan Michael* (1888). These works proved to be extremely popular
in other Slavic countries as well as in Poland.

Sienkiewicz's novel *Quo Vadis* (1896), about ancient Rome in the era of
Emperor Nero, was likewise extremely popular in his own time and spread his
fame to the rest of Europe and to the United States. Hollywood even used this
story as the basis for a 1950s epic film.

Although he is seldom read today, Sienkiewicz retains a position as one
of Poland's leading nineteenth-century authors. He was awarded the Nobel
Prize for literature in 1905.

NOVELS BY SIENKIEWICZ IN ENGLISH TRANSLATION

The Deluge: An Historical Novel of Poland, Sweden, and Russia (1886). AMS (repr of 1898 ed)
$24.50. ISBN 0-404-05995-3
Pan Michael: An Historical Novel of Poland, the Ukraine, and Turkey (1888). Greenwood 1969
repr of 1898 ed $69.50. ISBN 0-8371-0227-8
Quo Vadis (1896). Hippocrene 1990 $6.95. ISBN 0-87052-846-7

SINGER, ISAAC BASHEVIS   1904–1991 (YIDDISH)

Isaac Bashevis Singer was born in Poland, the son of a rabbi. He received a
traditional Jewish education, including training at a rabbinical seminary in
Warsaw. He began writing in Hebrew while he worked for 10 years as a
proofreader and translator in Warsaw. Although his early work was in Hebrew,
most of his fiction has been written in Yiddish.

In 1935, Singer immigrated to New York, where he became a journalist for
a Jewish newspaper. Most of his stories were originally published in this
newspaper in serial form. None of his works was translated into English until
1950.

Singer is above all a storyteller, and his tales of Jewish life in Poland,
Germany, and America are rich in vivid detail, humor, and drama. He is especially skillful at providing psychological insight into the characters he creates.
His vital and colorful characters have also been brought to the stage and screen
in such adaptations as the film *Enemies: A Love Story.*

In 1964, Singer was elected to the National Institute of Arts and Letters.
In 1978, he became the first Yiddish writer to win the Nobel Prize for literature.

NOVELS BY SINGER IN ENGLISH TRANSLATION

Enemies: A Love Story (1966). Farrar 1987 $8.95. ISBN 0-374-51522-0
The Family Moskat (1950). Farrar 1988 $12.95. ISBN 0-374-50392-3
King of the Fields (1987). Plume 1989 $8.95. ISBN 0-452-26312-3

The Magician of Lublin (1960). Fawcett 1985 $2.95. ISBN 0-449-20966-0
The Manor (1967). Farrar 1987 $12.95. ISBN 0-374-52080-1
The Penitent (1974). Fawcett 1984 $3.95. ISBN 0-449-20966-0
Satan in Goray (1935). Avon 1978 $1.65. ISBN 0-380-01538-2
Shosha (1976). Farrar 1988 $8.95. ISBN 0-374-52142-5
The Slave (1962). Avon 1978 $1.95. ISBN 0-380-01553-6

SHORT STORIES BY SINGER IN ENGLISH TRANSLATION

The Death of Methusela and Other Stories (1987). Farrar 1988 $17.95. ISBN 0-374-13564-9
Friend of Kafka and Other Stories (1970). Fawcett 1984 $4.95. ISBN 0-449-20695-5
Gimpel the Fool and Other Stories (1957). Farrar 1957 $8.95. ISBN 0-374-50052-5
Old Love and Other Stories (1979). Farrar 1979 $10.95. ISBN 0-374-22581-8
The Seance and Other Stories (1968). Fawcett 1981 $2.75. ISBN 0-449-24364-8
Short Friday and Other Stories (1964). Farrar 1964 $10.95. ISBN 0-374-26300-6
The Spinoza of Market Street and Other Stories (1961). Farrar 1961 $8.95. ISBN 0-374-26776-6

NONFICTION BY SINGER IN ENGLISH TRANSLATION

Love and Exile: A Memoir, A Little Boy in Search of God, A Young Man in Search of Love, Lost in America, and a New Introduction, The Beginning. Farrar 1986 $8.95. ISBN 0-374-51992-7 Singer's autobiography, covering his childhood through his immigration to America.

BOOKS ABOUT SINGER

Alexander, Edward. *Isaac Bashevis Singer.* G. K. Hall 1980 $17.95. ISBN 0-8057-6424-0 Excellent general introduction to Singer's life and works; contains chronology and bibliography.
*Kresh, Paul. *Isaac Bashevis Singer; The Story of a Storyteller.* Lodestar 1984 $13.95. ISBN 0-525-6424-0 Biography of Singer written for readers grade 6 and up.

RUSSIAN LITERATURE

Russian literature began with the conversion of the Russian people to Christianity in the tenth century. The earliest writings were almost entirely religious, consisting of accounts of the lives of the saints, prayers, or stories from the Bible. There were also historical records, most of which were little more than direct chronicles of events. The greatest literary accomplishment during this period was the unusual and complex *Tale of Igor's Campaign,* a dramatic story of the defeat of the Russian prince Igor early in the twelfth century.

There was little further development of Russian literature until the early eighteenth century, when Tsar Peter the Great made a monumental effort to westernize Russian culture and customs. As a result of Peter's reforms, the Russian language expanded greatly, with many new words from French, German, and other European languages. The Russian alphabet was revised as well.

Also at this time, Russian poets began using new verse forms, such as the ode and the epic, borrowed from Western Europe. Throughout the eighteenth century, Russian writers adopted Western literary forms to write about Russian subjects.

Early in the nineteenth century, Russian literature experienced a second burst of rapid development. New writers began to experiment with both literary forms and new themes. In poetry writers like Alexander Pushkin and Mikhail Lermontov brought a new vigor to traditional Russian subject matter. Strongly influenced by the British romantic poets, especially Lord Byron (*see*

Byron, Vol. 1, British Literature: The Romantic Period), the Russians built their poetry around nationalistic themes and heroic figures. One of Pushkin's most famous poems, *Eugene Onegin* (1828), owes much to Byron's earlier works. Pushkin also excelled in drama, and his plays helped create a new interest in the Russian theater.

Around the middle of the century, the literary emphasis in Russia moved from poetry to prose. Then a new generation of fiction writers ushered in Russian literature's Golden Age. The stories and novels written during this period, the last half of the nineteenth century, began a tradition that still sets Russian literature apart from the other literatures of Europe. Under the rigid and oppressive rule of the Russian czars (rulers), dissent was impossible and censorship of political activity—including political writing—was very restrictive. Thus, it fell to the novelists and short-story writers to become the voices for political reform as they cleverly built their works around urgent social issues and conditions, which they explored in disguised fictional forms.

However, the great writers of this age were not merely political activists who used their fiction to press for reform. They were genuine literary geniuses whose monumental works of art contained far more than political messages. Nikolai Gogol, Feodor Dostoevsky, Leo Tolstoy, Anton Chekhov, and Ivan Turgenev wrote about the Russian condition—and the human condition—in masterpieces of fiction that transcend national boundaries. In one generation they created a Russian literature that ranked with the best the world had to offer. Today their works are still widely read, their plays still performed, and their names inevitably included on any list of the world's greatest authors.

The twentieth century saw Russian literature again deeply affected by politics. During the Bolshevik revolution that began in 1917, many Russian writers were killed or left the country. The Communist leadership that came to power after the revolution soon began to exert political control over literature, and by the 1930s freedom of expression had virtually disappeared. From then through the 1970s, Soviet writers were expected to write within strict guidelines set by the state, and those who refused soon found they could not write for public audiences at all. Despite the fact that some authors were able to produce surprisingly good literature under these conditions, the major result was a stagnation of Russian literature.

The change in Soviet politics that took place during the mid-1980s brought new life to all the arts, and literary creativity and expression once again began to flower.

COLLECTIONS OF RUSSIAN LITERATURE IN ENGLISH TRANSLATION

Brown, Clarence (ed). *The Portable Twentieth-Century Russian Reader.* Penguin 1985 $7.95. ISBN 0-14-015100-1

Cooper, Joshua (ed). *Four Russian Plays.* Penguin 1972 $7.95. ISBN 0-14-044258-8

Fetzer, Leland (ed). *An Anthology of Pre-Revolutionary Russian Science Fiction.* Ardis 1982 $6.00. ISBN 0-88233-595-2

Glad, John, and Daniel Weissbort (eds). *Russian Poetry: The Modern Period.* Univ of Iowa Pr 1978 $12.50. ISBN 0-87745-084-6

Guerney, Bernard G. (ed). *A Treasury of Russian Literature.* Vanguard. (o.p.) $25.00. ISBN 0-8149-0113-1

Proffer, Carl R., and Ellendra Proffer (eds). *The Ardis Anthology of Russian Futurism.* Ardis 1980 $22.50. ISBN 0-931556-00-7

Proffer, Carl R. (ed). *From Karamzin to Bunin: An Anthology of Russian Short Stories.* Indiana Univ Pr 1969 $13.75. ISBN 0-253-32506-4

Reeve, F. D. (ed). *Nineteenth-Century Russian Plays.* Norton 1973 $12.95. ISBN 0-393-00683-2

Richards, David (ed). *The Penguin Book of Russian Short Stories.* Penguin 1981 $7.95. ISBN 0-14-004816-2

Zenkovsky, Serge A. (ed). *Medieval Russia's Epics, Chronicles, and Tales.* Dutton 1974 $15.95. ISBN 0-525-48366-7

BUNIN, IVAN   1870–1953

Ivan Bunin was relatively unknown in the United States until he became the first Russian writer to receive the Nobel Prize for literature in 1933. In the Soviet Union, however, he had been an active and popular writer for decades. Bunin was not a member of the many schools and movements that divided the ranks of Russian writers at the turn of the century. He went his own way, and his stories of the decline of the Russian nobility and the passing of a rural way of life are an interesting blend of realism and romanticism.

Bunin traveled abroad a great deal and frequently used foreign settings for his stories. His best-known story is "The Gentleman from San Fransisco" (1916), in which he emphasizes the emptiness of a life based only on the pursuit of earthly goods and pleasures. A staunch opponent of the Bolsheviks, Bunin moved to Paris after the Bolshevik revolution.

NOVELS BY BUNIN IN ENGLISH TRANSLATION

Grammar of Love (1934). Hyperion 1977 repr of 1934 ed $10.00. ISBN 0-88355-481-X
The Well of Days (1933). Hyperion 1977 repr of 1934 ed $10.00. ISBN 0-88355-483-6

SHORT STORIES BY BUNIN IN ENGLISH TRANSLATION

Dark Avenues and Other Stories (1949). Hyperion 1987 repr of 1949 ed $21.00. ISBN 0-88355-479-8
The Gentleman from San Fransisco and Other Stories (1934). Hippocrene 1980 repr of 1934 ed $22.00. ISBN 0-374-91093-6
Long Ago: Selected Stories. Dufour 1984 $13.95. ISBN 0-946162-11-5
Wolves and Other Love Stories. Capra 1989 $9.95. ISBN 0-88496-303-9

CHEKHOV, ANTON   1860–1904

Anton Chekhov began writing to support himself while studying medicine at Moscow University. After completing his studies, he continued to write. Ironically, this brilliant writer always considered himself a doctor, even though he actually practiced medicine very little.

Chekhov is best known as a playwright and is generally regarded as Russia's greatest dramatist. However, he began his career by writing stories, many of which rank among the world's best. His first collection, *Motley Stories,* was published in 1884, and by 1890, he was well established as a fiction writer and a member of Moscow's literary circles.

Chekhov's first attempt at writing for the stage, *Ivanov* (1887), was a failure. Despite some success with one-act plays, he was about to abandon playwriting when the Moscow Art Theater decided in 1898 to revive one of his earlier unsuccessful plays, *The Seagull.* This performance, produced by the famous actor and teacher Konstantin Stanislavsky, was very well received, and Chekhov agreed to write more plays for the company. He gave them *Uncle Vanya* (1900), *The Three Sisters* (1901), and *The Cherry Orchard* (1904), all masterpieces. So popular have these plays become that one of them is in production somewhere in the world every day of the year.

Chekhov drew his themes from all areas of Russian life, exploring them with sensitivity and insight. He was the first dramatist to show how tragedies can result from human beings' inability to communicate their thoughts and feelings. His plays always concern a group of Russian middle-class or aristocratic landowners whose inability to take meaningful action in their lives produces tragedy and farce. His drama is developed by having a series of seemingly minor incidents build in intensity to an emotional and psychological pitch that eventually sweeps up both his characters and the audience.

Novels by Chekhov in English Translation

Seven Short Novels. Norton 1971 $11.95. ISBN 0-393-00552-6
The Shooting Party: A Novel (1891). Univ of Chicago Pr 1987 $8.95. ISBN 0-226-10241-6

Short Stories by Chekhov in English Translation

A Doctor's Visit: Short Stories by Anton Chekhov. Bantam 1988 $3.50. ISBN 0-553-21322-9
Love and Other Stories. Ecco 1987 $9.50. ISBN 0-88001-060-6
The Party and Other Stories. Penguin 1986 $3.95. ISBN 0-14-044452-1
The Princess and Other Stories. Oxford Univ Pr 1990 $3.95. ISBN 0-19-282662-X
Ward Number Six and Other Stories. Oxford Univ Pr 1988 $3.95. ISBN 0-19-282174-1
A Woman's Kingdom and Other Stories. Oxford Univ Pr 1989 $3.95. ISBN 0-19-282209-8

Plays by Chekhov in English Translation

The Brute and Other Farces: Seven Short Plays. Applause Theatre Bk 1987 $5.95. ISBN 0-55783-003-7
Chekhov: Five Major Plays. Bantam 1984 $3.50. ISBN 0-553-21211-7

Books about Chekhov

Bill, Valentine Tschebotarioff. *Chekhov, the Silent Voice of Freedom.* Philosophical Lib 1987 $12.95. ISBN 0-8022-2514-4 Places Chekhov in historical context and analyzes themes and plots of many stories; includes plot summaries and useful insights for the general reader.
Eekman, Thomas A. *Critical Essays on Anton Chekhov.* G. K. Hall 1989 $38.50. ISBN 0-8161-8843-2 Excellent collection of contemporary essays on Chekhov's stories and plays; contains selected bibliography.
Pritchard, V. S. *Chekhov: A Spirit Set Free.* Random 1988 $17.95. ISBN 0-394-54650-4 Critical-biographical study of Chekhov by a noted novelist and short-story writer; readable discussion of the relationship between Chekhov's work and his life.

DOSTOEVSKY, FYODOR   1821–1881

One of the most powerful and significant authors in all of modern fiction, Fyodor Dostoevsky was the son of a harsh and domineering army surgeon who was murdered by his own serfs (slaves), an event that was extremely important in shaping Dostoevsky's view of social and economic issues. He studied to be an engineer and began work as a draftsman. However, his first novel, *Poor Folk* (1846), was so well received that he abandoned engineering for writing.

In 1849, Dostoevsky was arrested for being part of a revolutionary group that owned an illegal printing press. He was sentenced to be executed, but the sentence was changed at the last minute, and he was sent to a prison camp in Siberia instead. By the time he was released in 1854, he had become a devout believer in both Christianity and Russia—although not in its ruler, the Czar.

During the 1860s, Dostoevsky's personal life was in constant turmoil as the result of financial problems, a gambling addiction, and the deaths of his wife and his brother. His second marriage in 1867 provided him with a stable home life and personal contentment, and during the years that followed he produced his greatest novels: *Crime and Punishment* (1866), the story of Rodya Raskolnikov, who kills two old women in the belief that he is beyond the bounds of good and evil; *The Idiot* (1868), the story of an epileptic who tragically affects the lives of those around him; *The Possessed* (1872), the story of the effect of revolutionary thought on the members of one Russian community; *A Raw Youth* (1875), which focuses on the disintegration and decay of family relationships and life; and *The Brothers Karamazov* (1880), which centers on the murder of Fyodor Karamazov and the effect the murder has on each of his four sons. These works have placed Dostoevsky in the front rank of the world's great novelists. Dostoevsky was an innovator, bringing new depth and meaning to the psychological novel and combining realism and philosophical speculation in his complex studies of the human condition.

NOVELS BY DOSTOEVSKY IN ENGLISH TRANSLATION

The Adolescent (A Raw Youth) (1875). Norton 1981 $14.95. ISBN 0-393-00995-5
The Brothers Karamazov (1880). Signet 1986 $3.95. ISBN 0-451-52388-1
Crime and Punishment (1866). Norton 1989 $11.95. ISBN 0-393-95623-7
The Idiot (1868). Signet 1986 $4.50. ISBN 0-451-52094-7
Notes from the Underground (1864) *and The Double* (1846). Penguin 1972 $3.95. ISBN 0-14-044252-9
Poor Folk (1846). Ardis 1982 $4.50. ISBN 0-686-78410-3
The Possessed (1872). Signet 1962 $5.95. ISBN 0-451-51918-3

SHORT STORIES BY DOSTOEVSKY IN ENGLISH TRANSLATION

Best Short Stories of Dostoyevsky. Random 1979 $10.95. ISBN 0-394-60477-6
Great Short Works of Dostoevsky. Harper 1985 $7.95. ISBN 0-06-083081-6
Uncle's Dream and Other Stories. Penguin 1989 $6.95. ISBN 0-14-044518-8

BOOKS ABOUT DOSTOEVSKY

Kjetsaa, Geir. *Fyodor Dostoyevsky: A Writer's Life.* Siri Hustvedt and David McDuff (trs). Fawcett 1989 $10.95. ISBN 0-449-90334-6 Sensitive biography that looks at Dostoevsky's life in relation to his works and central themes.
Leatherbarrow, William J. *Feodor Dostoevsky.* G. K. Hall 1981 $17.95. ISBN 0-8057-6480-1 Excellent general study and introduction to Dostoevsky's life and works; contains a chronology and bibliography.

GOGOL, NIKOLAI 1809–1852

Nikolai Gogol, one of Russia's greatest writers, was born and raised in the Ukraine (a region of Russia near the Black Sea). After trying his hand at several professions without success, he turned to writing. Gogol achieved his first literary success with a volume of stories based on life in his native Ukraine; *Evenings on a Farm near Dikanka* (1831). He followed this success with two later collections, *Mirgorod* (1832) and *Arabesques* (1835), both of which also proved popular. In 1836, his hilariously satirical comedy, *The Inspector-General,* raised a storm of official protest from the bureaucracy it mocked, but it established Gogol as a dramatist of genius. His wit, combined with his flair for unusual, sometimes bizarre, plots give his plays and stories a flavor found in no other writer.

Gogol's personal life was in constant turmoil. He tried lecturing at Moscow University and briefly held a government position, but he grew increasingly dissatisfied. From 1836 to 1848, he lived outside Russia, mostly in Rome. During this time he wrote some of his most famous works, including "The Overcoat" (1842), one of the most influential of all Russian short stories, and

Dead Souls (1842), one of the great novels of world literature. In the latter, Gogol tells of a scoundrel who travels through Russia buying up "dead souls"—serfs who have died but whose names have not yet been taken off the tax register—as part of a scheme to swindle the government. The novel satirizes both bureaucracy and the inhumanity of Russian society.

Gogol's strengths as a writer lay in his imagination and powers of invention. His characters are generally caricatures, virtually without depth, but his ability to create comic situations and to tell meaningful stories is supreme.

NOVEL BY GOGOL IN ENGLISH TRANSLATION

Dead Souls (1842). Norton 1971 $12.95. ISBN 0-393-00600-X

SHORT STORIES BY GOGOL IN ENGLISH TRANSLATION

Arabesques (1835). Ardis 1982 $6.00. ISBN 0-88233-436-0
The Complete Tales of Nikolai Gogol: 1923–1985. 2 vols. Univ of Chicago Pr 1985. $10.95 each. ISBNs 0-226-30068-4, 0-30069-2
The Overcoat and Other Tales of Good and Evil. Bentley 1979 $14.00. ISBN 0-8376-0442-7

PLAYS BY GOGOL IN ENGLISH TRANSLATION

The Inspector-General and Other Plays (1836). Applause Theatre Bk 1987 $8.95. ISBN 0-936839-12-0

BOOKS ABOUT GOGOL

Maguire, Robert A. *Gogol from the Twentieth Century: Eleven Essays.* Princeton Univ Pr 1974 $15.95. ISBN 0-691-01326-8 Collection of modern essays by respected scholars interpreting Gogol's works in terms of contemporary critical theory.
Nabokov, Vladimir. *Nikolai Gogol.* New Directions 1961 $6.95. ISBN 0-8112-0120-1 Examination of Gogol's life, themes, and vision by a major contemporary Russian émigré novelist.

PASTERNAK, BORIS   1890–1960

Boris Pasternak was born in Moscow, the son of concert pianist Rosa Kaufman and Leonid Pasternak, a painter who had illustrated the novels of the famous author, Leo Tolstoy. (*See* Tolstoy, Vol. 1, World Literature: Russian Literature.) He studied law at the University of Moscow, then music under the noted composer Scriabin, and finally philosophy at the University of Marburg in Germany. He was a factory worker during World War I and later became a librarian for the Ministry of Education in Moscow.

Pasternak began writing poetry around 1909 and published his first collection in 1914. His first real success came with the volume *My Sister, Life,* published in 1922.

Although Pasternak was never really comfortable with the Communists who took power after the 1917 Russian Revolution, he tried to adapt to the new political restrictions on literature and wrote some patriotic poetry in the 1920s. By the 1930s, however, he had abandoned his own writing almost entirely and devoted himself to the translation into Russian of foreign literature, including classic works by the German poet and novelist Johann Wolfgang von Goethe (*see* Goethe, Vol. 1, World Literature: German Language and Literature) and the British dramatist and poet William Shakespeare. (*See* Shakespeare, Vol. 1, British Literature: The Renaissance.) With the death of the Soviet dictator Josef Stalin (*see* Stalin, Vol. 2, World History: Rise of Totalitarian States) in 1953, Pasternak, along with many other Russian writers, looked forward to a relaxation of the restrictions on literature.

In 1954 Pasternak wrote some poetry and then completed a novel he had been working on for several years, *Doctor Zhivago* (1957). A narrative set against the history of Russia from the 1905 revolution into World War II, the hero of the novel is a physician and poet who must confront the changes brought on by the Bolshevik revolution. The Soviet Union would not allow publication, so *Doctor Zhivago* was published first in Italy and then in the United States. The novel continued to be banned in the Soviet Union throughout Pasternak's lifetime because of its failure to endorse wholeheartedly the Communist revolution. Pasternak was expelled from the Soviet writer's union and shunned in public. When he was offered the Nobel Prize for literature in 1958, he was subjected to intense pressure from the Soviet government and the writer's union and eventually refused the award. He died shortly afterward. His work has since been restored to favor, and *Doctor Zhivago,* hailed as a masterpiece and made into a popular motion picture, is now available in the Soviet Union.

NOVEL BY PASTERNAK IN ENGLISH TRANSLATION

Doctor Zhivago (1957). Ballantine 1986 $5.95. ISBN 0-345-34100-7

SHORT STORY BY PASTERNAK IN ENGLISH TRANSLATION

Zhenia's Childhood (1924). Schocken 1987 $5.95. ISBN 0-8052-8129-0

POETRY BY PASTERNAK IN ENGLISH TRANSLATION

Second Nature: Forty-Six Poems. Dufour 1990 $32.00. ISBN 0-7206-0751-5
Selected Poems. Penguin 1984 $7.95. ISBN 0-14-042245-5
Seven Poems. Unicorn 1970 $6.95. ISBN 0-87775-005-X

NONFICTION BY PASTERNAK IN ENGLISH TRANSLATION

I Remember: Sketch for an Autobiography. Harvard Univ Pr 1983 $6.95. ISBN 0-674-43950-3 Pasternak's personal recollections of his early life; includes an essay on translating the works of William Shakespeare.

BOOK ABOUT PASTERNAK

Barnes, Christopher J., and Boris Leonidovich Pasternak. *Boris Pasternak.* Cambridge Univ Pr 1989 $69.50. ISBN 0-521-25957-6 Literary biography that presents Paternak's life in the context of the literary, social, and historical events of his times.

PUSHKIN, ALEKSANDR   1799–1837

Aleksandr Pushkin was born in Moscow into an established Russian noble family. He showed promise as a poet even while he was a student, but when he had completed his education in 1817, he chose to enter government service in St. Petersburg (then Russia's capital, now the city of Leningrad). He immediately embarked on the rather wild life that was more or less expected of young noblemen, and he also became close to leading members of St. Petersburg's literary set.

In 1820, Pushkin's *Ode to Liberty* and other revolutionary verses resulted in his exile to southern Russia as a political troublemaker. Ironically, the years of exile were very productive for Pushkin as a writer. The southern regions of the Caucasus, the Crimea, and Moldavia, with their wild scenery and Asian character, stimulated Pushkin to write some of his best works.

In 1824, Pushkin was allowed to return to his mother's estate, where he was confined for two more years. Finally, in 1826, the new czar (ruler), Nicholas I, pardoned Pushkin and allowed him to return to St. Petersburg. There he continued to write, but the watchful eye of the czar led him to restrict his subject matter.

In 1831, Pushkin married Nathalie Goncharova, an unhappy alliance that plunged him into the social life of the czar's court, which he detested. Finally, in 1837, Pushkin was obliged to engage in a duel with one of his wife's admirers and was killed.

Pushkin is acknowledged as the greatest Russian poet, a master of a variety of verse forms and of a simple but moving style that is universally admired. He frequently drew the subjects of his poetry from Russian history, celebrating the country he loved. In fact, he is credited with making enormous contributions to the development of a Russian national literature, as opposed to the imitations of European literature that previous writers had produced.

Pushkin's single greatest work, *Eugene Onegin* (1828), is a "novel in verse" about a dashing young member of St. Petersburg's society, and it offers a marvelously rich history of Russian social life in the period. Pushkin's works have been the basis for operas, plays, and films, and his influence on Russian poetry persists to this day.

SHORT STORIES BY PUSHKIN IN ENGLISH TRANSLATION

Complete Prose Tales of Pushkin. Norton 1968 $11.95. ISBN 0-393-00465-1

POETRY BY PUSHKIN IN ENGLISH TRANSLATION

The Bakhchesarian Fountain and Other Poems (1822). Ardis 1987 repr of 1849 ed $19.50. ISBN 0-88233-954-0
The Bronze Horseman (1833). Basil Blackwell $15.95. ISBN 0-631-14385-8
Eugene Onegin (1828). Dutton 1981 $7.95. ISBN 0-525-47591-5
Ruslan and Ludmila (1820). Imported 1987 $7.95. ISBN 5-05-000674-0

PLAYS BY PUSHKIN IN ENGLISH TRANSLATION

Boris Godunov (1831). Basil Blackwell $15.95. ISBN 0-900186-63-1
Mozart and Salieri: The Little Tragedies (1830). Dufour 1988 $10.95. ISBN 0-8023-1282-9

BOOKS ABOUT PUSHKIN

Bloom, Harold (ed). *Alexander Pushkin.* Chelsea 1987 $34.95. ISBN 0-55546-273-1 Collection of modern critical essays that approach Pushkin's poetry and prose from a variety of critical perspectives; a useful introduction.
Driver, Sam. *Pushkin: Literature and Social Ideas.* Columbia Univ Pr 1989 $25.00. ISBN 0-231-06848-4 Study of Pushkin's political ideas that traces his political development through a variety of sources while examining his poetry and prose.

SOLZHENITSYN, ALEXANDR, 1918–

Alexandr Solzhenitsyn's most famous novels grew out of his experiences during the years when dictator Josef Stalin (*see* Stalin, Vol. 2, World History: The Rise of Totalitarian States) was the leader of the Soviet Union, before, during, and after World War II. In 1945, while serving in the Soviet army, Solzhenitsyn was arrested for exchanging with a friend letters that criticized some of Stalin's war decisions. Solzhenitsyn was sentenced to eight years in prison, a term that he served in various places. One of these was a prison research institute, which he describes in his novel *The First Circle* (1968).

After his release from prison, Solzhenitsyn was exiled to Siberia, where he taught school. During this time he suffered from stomach cancer, and he later used this experience in his novel *The Cancer Ward* (1968).

In 1957, Solzhenitsyn was allowed to return to his home. He published his first novel, *One Day in the Life of Ivan Denisovich,* in 1962 during a period when censorship restrictions were relaxed briefly under Soviet Premier Nikita Krushchev. By the mid-1960s, the restrictive government policies had been reinstated, however, and Solzhenitsyn was again out of favor. He was no longer allowed to publish in the Soviet Union and in 1969 was expelled from the writer's union. Because he continued to publish his novels outside the Soviet Union, he was subjected to increased harassment by the Soviet government. After he was awarded the Nobel Prize for literature in 1970, the pressures relaxed briefly, but with the publication in Paris in 1973 of the first volume of *The Gulag Archipelago,* a scathing look at Soviet prison camps, he was again arrested and finally expelled from the Soviet Union. Since 1976 he has lived in the United States, in Vermont.

Solzhenitsyn's novels of life in the Soviet penal system during the repressive Stalin years have made him one of the most celebrated of modern Russian writers. He is currently working on a series of novels *(The Red Wheel)* dealing with World War I and the coming to power of the Bolsheviks. In 1971 the first novel in the series, *August 1914,* was published.

NOVELS BY SOLZHENITSYN IN ENGLISH TRANSLATION

August 1914: The Red Wheel I (1971). Farrar 1989 $19.95. ISBN 0-374-51999-4
The Cancer Ward (1968). Random 1989 $10.95. ISBN 0-394-60499-7
The First Circle (1968). Harper 1990 $14.95. ISBN 0-06-091683-4
The Gulag Archipelago, 1918–1956: An Experiment in Literary Investigation (1973). Harper 1974 $6.95. ISBN 0-06-080332-0
The Gulag Archipelago Two (1975). Harper 1975 $4.95. ISBN 0-06-080345-2
The Gulag Archipelago Three (1978). Harper 1979 $4.95. ISBN 0-06-080396-7
One Day in the Life of Ivan Denisovich (1962). Bantam 1984 $2.85. ISBN 0-553-24777-8

BOOKS ABOUT SOLZHENITSYN

Dunlop, John B., *et al* (eds). *Solzhenitsyn in Exile: Critical Essays and Documentary Materials.* Hoover Inst Pr 1985 $19.95. ISBN 0-8179-8051-2 Collection of essays by Western scholars of widely varied opinions, portraying Solzhenitsyn as "great," "a fascist," "a gloom-monger," and "the noblest man alive."
*Finke, Blythe F. *Alexandr Solzhenitsyn: Beleaguered Literary Giant of the U.S.S.R.* SamHar 1973 $3.95. ISBN 0-87157-560-4 Brief, 32-page review of Solzhenitsyn's life written for young readers.
Scammell, Michael. *Solzhenitsyn: A Biography.* Norton 1984 $14.95. ISBN 0-393-30378-0 Thorough and comprehensive study of Solzhenitsyn's life, amply documented and illustrated.

TOLSTOY, LEO 1828–1910

Leo Tolstoy is the author of *War and Peace* (1869), called by many the greatest novel ever written. He was born into an illustrious Russian noble family and educated at Karzan University, where he studied law and Asian languages but did not graduate. After leaving school, Tolstoy began living the usual carefree and fun-loving life expected of a man of his class, but he soon felt compelled to do something more with his life. In 1851 he became a soldier and began to write while serving in the Caucasus Mountain region in southern Russia. His experiences during the Crimean War and the siege of Sevastopol provided the background for *The Sevastopol Sketches* (1856), in which he describes human behavior in battle.

After the war, Tolstoy returned to St. Petersburg (today the city of Leningrad), traveled abroad, married, and eventually settled at his estate on the Volga River, taking up the life of author and landowner. During this period he wrote his greatest works: *War and Peace,* an epic story of several Russian aristocratic families during the era of Napoleon; and *Anna Karenina* (1876), the story of a woman's conflict between love and social and moral restrictions.

By 1879, Tolstoy's concern with moral behavior and religious questions led him to adopt an unusual view of Christianity that rejected the idea of a supernatural God and made moral behavior supremely important. He was eventually accused of blasphemy and excommunicated from the Russian Orthodox Church. He continued to be tormented by the burden of his own wealth and social position, which he found inconsistent with his moral beliefs in charity and equality, and he died in an unhappy flight from his wife and family.

Throughout his literary career, Tolstoy was profoundly concerned with the inner life of the individual, with family relationships, and with the forces that determine history. His works have won a permanent place among the outstanding classics of world literature.

NOVELS BY TOLSTOY IN ENGLISH TRANSLATION

Anna Karenina (1876). Bantam 1984 $3.50. ISBN 0-553-21346-6
Resurrection (1899). Penguin 1966 $4.95. ISBN 0-14-044184-0
War and Peace (1869). Oxford Univ Pr 1985 $14.95. ISBN 0-19-250898-9

SHORT STORIES BY TOLSTOY IN ENGLISH TRANSLATION

"Childhood," "Boyhood," and "Youth" (1852–56). Penguin 1964 $4.95. ISBN 0-14-044139-5
The Death of Ivan Ilych and Other Stories. Signet 1960 $2.50. ISBN 0-451-52380-6
The Kreutzer Sonata and Other Stories. Penguin 1986 $4.95. ISBN 0-14-044469-6
The Raid and Other Stories. Oxford Univ Pr 1982 $3.95. ISBN 0-19-281584-9
The Sebastapol Sketches (1856). Penguin 1986 $4.95. ISBN 0-14-044468-8

BOOKS ABOUT TOLSTOY

Bloom, Harold (ed). *Leo Tolstoy.* Chelsea 1986 $27.50. ISBN 0-87754-727-0 Collection of modern critical essays that examine Tolstoy's philosophy, religious beliefs, life, and works.
Rowe, William. *Leo Tolstoy.* G. K. Hall 1986 $14.95. ISBN 0-8057-6623-5 Comprehensive general study and introduction to Tolstoy's life and works; contains a chronology and a bibliography.

LATIN AMERICAN AND CARIBBEAN LITERATURE

The award of the 1990 Nobel Prize for literature to Octavio Paz of Mexico marks the fourth time since the end of World War II that this honor has gone to a writer from Latin America, a clear indication of the current strength and vigor of Latin American literature. Such was not always the case, however. The first writings to come from the southern portion of the New World were the journals and chronicles of the early explorers.

Since the struggles for survival by the early Spanish colonists left little time or desire for literary activity, it was not until the seventeenth and eighteenth centuries, as the colonies grew and prospered, that some original literature was produced in Latin America and the Caribbean. This literature, however, consisted almost entirely of feeble imitations of the writings being done in Spain, Portugal, and France. The one notable exception is Sor Juana

Ines de la Cruz, a Mexican nun of astonishing literary ability. Her poetry, filled with subtle satire and wit, towers above all other colonial Latin American literature.

At the start of the nineteenth century, the colonies of Latin America were beginning to take on a distinct cultural identity. The various ethnic groups—Native American, Spanish, Portuguese, and other European immigrants—all contributed elements to a new and distinctive Latin American culture. One major expression of this distinctive Latin American culture was the so-called gaucho literature celebrating the free-spirited cowboys, or gauchos, who drove cattle across the Argentine plains. When the gauchos began to be pushed off the plains with the coming of the railroads and a new farming culture at the end of the 1800s, José Hernández was inspired to write *Martín Fierro* (1872), a long epic poem in praise of the gauchos' manly heroism, which in turn inspired dozens of similar works in Argentina, Paraguay, Uruguay, and Brazil.

This period also saw the beginning of strong movements for freedom and independence with country after country waging revolutionary war to free itself from its colonial master.

The end of Spanish domination, however, did not bring the end of political oppression, as dictatorships arose in the former colonies. The political history of Latin America through the nineteenth and into the twentieth century is a history of struggle against political oppression and widespread poverty. The literary history of the region is largely one of protest and outrage. Many writers were exiled or killed because of their political beliefs or their outspoken defense of liberty. Although Latin America saw its share of purely literary movements during the nineteenth century, these pale in importance beside the pervasive concern for political, social, and economic justice.

The twentieth century saw the struggle for social justice continue, most dramatically in the Mexican Revolution of 1910–1920, but also in countless other revolutions and coups that often saw repressive governments fall, only to be replaced by other repressive governments. Once again, the literature of the region was profoundly influenced by these events. In addition, increasing numbers of Latin American writers began to sense a new threat as their rich neighbor, the United States, grew ever more powerful and began to dominate Latin America economically and to intervene in Latin American affairs. In addition, women writers such as Delmira Augustini and Gabriela Mistral began to press for greater freedom and rights for women.

Two events of the middle of the twentieth century had a major impact on Latin American literature. First, the Spanish Civil War of 1936–1939, a battle in which Fascists conquered those defending the elected government, brought disillusionment to many Latin Americans of Spanish descent and ended their sentimental attachment to Spain. More importantly, the Civil War brought to Latin America many immigrants from Spain who influenced and enriched the region's literature. Second, World War II produced an alliance between most Latin American countries and the United States and helped heal some of the wounds left by earlier American interventionist policies. The alliances also helped to awaken North Americans to the cultural richness of their southern neighbors. The result has been a postwar flowering of Latin American culture, especially literature, which has produced some of the world's best contemporary writers, such as Jorge Luis Borges, Carlos Fuentes, Gabriel García Márquez, Pablo Neruda, and Octavio Paz.

COLLECTIONS OF LATIN AMERICAN LITERATURE IN ENGLISH TRANSLATION

Bierhorst, John (ed). *Black Rainbow: Legends of the Incas and Myths of Ancient Peru.* Farrar 1976 $9.95. ISBN 0-374-30829-2

Colecchia, Francesca, and Julio Matas (trs). *Selected Latin American One-Act Plays.* Univ of Pittsburgh Pr 1974 $12.95. ISBN 0-8229-5241-6
Franco, Jean. *Introduction to Spanish-American Literature.* Cambridge Univ Pr 1975 $21.95. ISBN 0-521-09891-2
Franco, Jean (ed). *Spanish Short Stories.* Penguin 1966 $5.95. ISBN 0-14-002500-6
Frank, Waldo (ed). *Tales from the Argentine.* Anita Brenner (tr). Ayer (repr of 1930 ed) $17.00. ISBN 0-8369-3539-X
Howes, Barbara (ed). *Eye of the Heart: Short Stories from Latin America.* Avon 1974 $5.95. ISBN 0-380-00163-2
Mancini, Pat M. (ed). *Contemporary Latin American Short Stories.* Fawcett 1979 $1.95. ISBN 0-449-30844-8
Marazan, Julio (ed). *Inventing a Word: An Anthology of Twentieth Century Puerto Rican Poetry.* Columbia Univ Pr 1980 $14.00. ISBN 0-231-05011-9
Monegal, Emir Rodriguez (ed). *The Borzoi Anthology of Latin American Literature.* 2 vols. Knopf 1977 $18.95 ea. ISBNs 0-394-73301-0, 0-394-73366-5
Twentieth Century African and Latin American Verse Roth 1989 $49.95. ISBN 0-89609-271-2

BILINGUAL COLLECTIONS OF LATIN AMERICAN LITERATURE

Blackwell, Alice Stone (tr). *Some Spanish-American Poets.* Biblo 1968 (repr of 1937 ed) $20.00. ISBN 0-8196-0217-5
Flores, Angel, and Kate Flores. *The Defiant Muse: Hispanic Feminist Poems from the Middle Ages to the Present, a Bilingual Anthology.* Feminist Pr 1986 $11.95. ISBN 0-935312-54-4
Wagenheim, Kal (ed). *Cuentos: An Anthology of Short Stories from Puerto Rico.* Schocken 1979 $6.95. ISBN 0-8052-0608-6
Wieser, Nora J. (ed and tr). *Open to the Sun: A Bilingual Anthology of Latin American Women Poets.* Perivale 1980 $11.95. ISBN 0-912288-16-7

BORGES, JORGE LUIS 1899–1986 (ARGENTINE)

Born in Buenos Aires, Argentina, Jorge Luis Borges was educated by an English governess and studied in Europe. He returned to Buenos Aires in 1921, where he helped to establish several literary magazines. In 1955, he was appointed director of the Argentine National Library. In 1961, he won the International Publishers Prize, thus establishing himself as one of the most prominent writers in the world. Borges regularly taught and lectured throughout the United States and Europe, and his ideas have had a profound influence on writers worldwide.

Borges wrote both poetry and fiction, but he is best known for his short stories. He viewed literature as a combination of game and puzzle, and a central image in his work is the labyrinth—a maze which, he suggests, represents the confusing ways of a world that humans can never really understand. His stories almost always confront his readers with a problem, or a collection of problems, that deal with the efforts of people to find the center of life's labyrinth.

SHORT STORIES BY BORGES IN ENGLISH TRANSLATION

The Aleph and Other Stories (1952). Dutton 1979 $8.95. ISBN 0-525-47539-0
The Book of Sand (1977). Dutton 1979 $5.95. ISBN 0-525-47540-0
Dreamtigers (1977). Mildred Boyer and Harold Morland (trs). Univ of Texas Pr 1985 $6.95. ISBN 0-292-71549-8
Ficciones (1956). Grove 1963 $6.95. ISBN 0-8021-3030-5
Labyrinths: Selected Short Stories and Other Writings. Random 1983 $8.95. ISBN 0-394-60449-0

POETRY BY BORGES IN ENGLISH TRANSLATION

In Praise of Darkness (1969). Norman Giovanni (tr). Dutton 1974 $5.95. ISBN 0-525-03635-0

SHORT STORIES BY BORGES IN SPANISH

El aleph (1952). French and European 1982 $8.95. ISBN 0-8288-2502-5
Ficciones (1956). French and European $9.95. ISBN 0-8288-2556-X
El libro de arenas (1975). French and European 1981. ISBN 0-8288-2505-X

POETRY BY BORGES IN SPANISH

Obra poética (1964). French and European 1980 $27.50. ISBN 0-8288-2503-3

BOOKS ABOUT BORGES

Bloom, Harold (ed). *Jorge Luis Borges.* Chelsea 1986 $24.50. ISBN 0-87754-721-1 Collection of modern critical essays on Borges' life and works with special attention to his techniques.
Murray, George R. *Jorge Luis Borges.* Unger 1980 $16.95. ISBN 0-8044-2608-2 Useful general study of Borges's themes, fictional techniques, and critical reputation.

CARDENAL, FATHER ERNESTO   1925– (NICARAGUAN)

An ordained Roman Catholic priest who lives in Solentiname, a Nicaraguan community that he founded, Father Ernesto Cardenal is Latin America's best-known voice of what has been called the "literature of the theology of liberation." His poetry expresses his belief that the church must help the poor to bring about desperately needed social and political changes in Latin America.

Cardenal's poetry is explicitly written in order to teach and persuade. He often uses unusual sources such as newspapers, Native American texts, or local folklore as the subject matter of his poetry. He has also rewritten portions of the Bible in the contemporary language of the people to enable his congregation at Solentiname to better understand and discuss it.

POETRY BY CARDENAL IN ENGLISH TRANSLATION

Apocalypse and Other Poems (1976). New Directions 1977 $5.95. ISBN 0-8112-0662-9
Flights of Victory (1988). Marc Zimmerman (tr). Curbstone 1988 $9.95. ISBN 0-915306-74-3
From Nicaragua with Love: Poems 1979–1986 (1986). Jonathan Cohen (tr). City Lights 1986 $5.95. ISBN 0-87286-201-1
With Walker in Nicaragua and Other Early Poems (1985). Jonathan Cohen (tr). Wesleyan Univ Pr 1985 $9.95. ISBN 0-8195-6118-5
Zero Hour and Other Documentary Poems (1978). Paul Borgeson and Jonathan Cohen (trs). New Directions 1980 $6.95. ISBN 0-811-20767-6

NONFICTION BY CARDENAL IN ENGLISH TRANSLATION

In Cuba (1972). Donald D. Walsh (tr). New Directions 1974 $9.95. ISBN 0-8112-0538-X

CARPENTIER, ALEJO   1904–1980 (CUBAN)

Born in Havana, Cuba, Alejo Carpentier studied at the University of Havana. Professor of the history of music at the National Conservatory and a journalist in Havana and in Caracas, Venezuela, for many years he was director of Cuba's National Press, which, under his leadership, undertook an ambitious publishing program that produced millions of volumes. After the Cuban Revolution, he served in several different official government posts, including ambassador to France.

Carpentier's political activities seem to some to contrast with his literary work. In 1928 Carpentier had been forced to flee to Paris for political reasons, and while there he joined a group of surrealist poets. Their literary philosophy maintains that the best way to understand reality is through the unrestricted use of the imagination. Although many surrealist poets had leftist political leanings, many others saw political ideology as too restrictive. Carpentier, however, has used the conflict between political discipline and artistic freedom as a rich source of inspiration for his work.

A trained musician and composer, Carpentier combined principles of musical composition with elements of surrealism to produce novels with a strikingly different tone and structure. *The Kingdom of This World* (1949) deals with slave revolts in Haiti. *The Lost Steps* (1953) takes the form of a diary written by a Cuban musician and intellectual who seeks to escape from civilization during a trip to a remote Amazon village. *The Chase* (1956) explores the idea that time exists only in human minds and can vary from person to person. *Reasons of State* (1976) portrays a Latin American dictator while raising questions about the nature of revolution.

NOVELS BY CARPENTIER IN ENGLISH TRANSLATION

The Chase (1956). Alfred MacAdams (tr). Farrar 1989 $16.95. ISBN 0-374-12083-8
Concierto Barroco (1974). Asa Zatz (tr). Council Oak 1988 $7.95. ISBN 0-933031-12-2
Explosion in a Cathedral (1965). John Sturrock (tr). Farrar 1989 $7.95. ISBN 0-374-52198-0
The Kingdom of This World (1949). Harriet de Onis (tr). Farrar 1989 $7.95. ISBN 0-374-52197-2
The Lost Steps (1953). Harriet de Onis (tr). Farrar 1989 $8.95. ISBN 0-374-52199-9
Reasons of State (1976). Frances Partridge (tr). Writers and Readers 1981 $4.95. ISBN 0-904613-52-6

NOVELS BY CARPENTIER IN SPANISH

El reino de este mundo (1949). French and European $7.50. ISBN 0-8288-2557-2

DARIO, RUBEN (PSEUDONYM OF FELIX RUBEN GARCIA SARMIENTO)   1867–1916 (NICARAGUAN)

Born in Metapa, Nicaragua, Rubén Darío was a child prodigy who acquired an extensive knowledge of Spanish, French, and the other major European literatures through wide reading. He traveled widely in the Spanish-speaking world and abroad and acquired an excellent understanding of several different cultures. In addition to working as a journalist in Chile, he held various posts in different Latin American cities and in Paris and Madrid.

Darío is considered to be the founder of a poetic movement called modernism, which advocated an emphasis on poetic rhythm and precise diction rather than on the flowery expression of the earlier romantic poets. In his own poetry Darío constantly experimented with combinations of rhythms, sounds, accents, and meter as well as unusual and provocative subjects. He often invented new words in order to change the way language is used in poetry. Darío was opposed to the use of poetry to evade the realities of ordinary life and frequently chose to write about such unpleasant subjects as suffering and death. Among his most famous works are *Azul* (1888), *Prosas profanas* (1896), and *Cantos de vida y esperanza* (1905).

Darío was also very concerned about the growing power of the United States and its influence in Latin American affairs and was committed to the concept of Latin American unity in the search for freedom. Darío's influence on contemporary Spanish poetry, both in the Western Hemisphere and in Europe, was profound.

POETRY BY DARIO IN ENGLISH TRANSLATION

Eleven Poems of Rubén Darío. Thomas Walsh and Salomon de la Salva (trs). Gordon Pr 1977 $59.95. ISBN 0-8490-1758-0
Selected Poems of Rubén Darío. Lysander Kemp (tr). Univ of Texas Pr 1988 $6.95. ISBN 0-292-77615-2

POETRY BY DARIO IN SPANISH

El mundo de los sueños (Colección mente y palabra). Univ of Puerto Rico Pr $5.00. ISBN 0-8477-0503-X

BOOK ABOUT DARIO

Watland, Charles D. *Poet Errant: A Biography of Rubén Darío.* Philosophical Lib 1965 $5.95. ISBN 0-8022-1817-2 In-depth study of the life and thought of the unconventional poet.

FUENTES, CARLOS   1929– (MEXICAN)

Carlos Fuentes is almost certainly the most famous Mexican novelist of the twentieth century. Born in Panama City and educated at the Colegio Frances Morelos, the National University of Mexico, and the Instuit des Hautes Etudes Internationales in Geneva, Switzerland, Fuentes travelled extensively with his diplomat father. From 1950 to 1952 he served as cultural attaché to the Mexican Embassy in Geneva. He held a variety of other government posts as well, including that of Mexican ambassador to France from 1975 to 1977. All of Fuentes's works demonstrate his strong desire to interpret and understand Mexican culture and history. He finds Mexico's search for a national identity particularly difficult because of the Spanish conqueror's early mistreatment—in fact, annihilation—of the native Aztec population, acts that leave modern Mexicans with a sense of both guilt and confusion about their origins.

In *Where the Air Is Clear* (1958), Fuentes uses the whole of Mexico City as the central character as he presents a sweeping description of modern Mexico. He depicts a panorama of Mexican life since the 1920s through a wide range of characters drawn from various classes and professions. *The Death of Artemio Cruz* (1962), which made Fuentes' international reputation, tells the story of a dying man's reflections on the important decisions of his life.

Fuentes' other works have ranged from a parody of the spy novel (*The Hydra Head,* 1978) to an exploration of the effect of the persistence of the past on personality (*Aura,* 1962). Recently his story of the last days of American writer Ambrose Bierce (*see* Bierce, Vol. 1, American Literature: The Rise of Realism), *The Old Gringo* (1985), was made into a major Hollywood movie. Like all Fuentes's work, this novel also tries to unravel the complex ways in which the past shapes the present.

NOVELS BY FUENTES IN ENGLISH TRANSLATION

Aura (1962). Lysander Kemp (tr). Farrar 1975 $7.95. ISBN 0-374-51171-3
A Change of Skin (1968). Sam Hileman (tr). Farrar 1968 $9.95. ISBN 0-374-51427-5
The Death of Artemio Cruz (1962). Sam Hileman (tr). Farrar 1964 $8.95. ISBN 0-374-50540-3
Distant Relations (1982). Margaret S. Peden (tr). Farrar 1982 $8.95. ISBN 0-374-51813-0

The Good Conscience (1961). Sam Hileman (tr). Farrar 1987 $7.95. ISBN 0-374-50736-8
The Hydra Head (1978). Margaret S. Peden (tr). Farrar 1979 $8.95. ISBN 0-374-51563-8
The Old Gringo (1985). Harper 1989 $6.95. ISBN 0-06-097258-0
Terra Nostra (1975). Margaret Sayers (tr). Farrar 1976 $14.95. ISBN 0-374-51750-9
Where the Air Is Clear (1958). Sam Hileman (tr). Farrar 1971 $9.95. ISBN 0-374-50919-0

SHORT STORIES BY FUENTES IN ENGLISH TRANSLATION

Burnt Water (1982). Margaret S. Peden (tr). Farrar 1986 $7.95. ISBN 0-374-51988-9
Constancia and Other Stories for Virgins (1988). Thomas Christiansen (tr). Farrar 1990 $17.95. ISBN 0-374-12886-3

NOVELS BY FUENTES IN SPANISH

Aura (1962). French and European $5.95. ISBN 0-8288-2564-5
La muerte de Artemio Cruz (1962). French and European $9.95. ISBN 0-8288-2565-3

BOOKS ABOUT FUENTES

Brody, Robert, and Charles Rossman (eds). *Carlos Fuentes: A Critical View.* Univ of Texas Pr 1982 $25.00. ISBN 0-292-71077-1 Collection of essays and reviews that assess Fuentes' major works and evaluate his critical reputation.
Faris, Wendy B. *Carlos Fuentes.* Ungar 1983 $18.95. ISBN 0-8044-6143-0 General study and introduction to Fuentes' life and works; a good source for the general reader and student.

GARCIA MARQUEZ, GABRIEL   1928– (COLOMBIAN)

Gabriel García Márquez was born in Aracataca, Colombia. After studying law and journalism at the National University of Colombia in Bogotá, he became a journalist. In 1965, he left journalism to devote himself to writing. Acclaimed for both his craft and his imagination, he has been called a master of myth and magical realism (a style of literature that makes use of fantasical, highly improbable, and sometimes even supernatural events and characters). In his novels and stories he has created a fictional world out of his memories of the dust, rain, and boredom of life in an isolated Colombian community. His stories depict a world shaped by myth, history, politics, and nature. García Márquez first created Macondo, his fictional town, in his short story collections *Leaf Storm* (1955) and *No One Writes to the Colonel* (1961), but it was the novel *One Hundred Years of Solitude* (1967) that brought both Macondo and García Márquez to world attention.

One Hundred Years of Solitude traces a century in the town's history, from its founding through its destruction by a cyclone. Skillfully blending the fantastic, the mythical, and the commonplace in a humorous and powerful narrative, García Márquez tells a moving tale of people locked in an isolation, partly of their own making and partly due to U.S. and European cultural and political domination of Latin America. With this work García Márquez established himself internationally as a major novelist, and his reputation has continued to grow since he was awarded the Nobel Prize for literature in 1982.

NOVELS BY GARCIA MARQUEZ IN ENGLISH TRANSLATION

Autumn of the Patriarch (1976). Avon 1977 $4.50. ISBN 0-380-01774-1
Chronicle of a Death Foretold (1980). Ballantine 1984 $4.95. ISBN 0-345-31002-0
Clandestine in Chile: The Adventures of Miguel Littin (1986). Asa Zatz (tr). H. Holt 1988 $7.95. ISBN 0-8050-0945-0
In Evil Hour (1978). Avon 1980 $3.95. ISBN 0-380-52167-9
Love in the Time of Cholera (1987). Penguin 1989 $8.95. ISBN 0-14-011990-6

One Hundred Years of Solitude (1967). Gregory Rabassa (tr). Avon 1976 $4.95. ISBN 0-380-01503-X

The Story of a Shipwrecked Sailor (1985). Randolph Hogan (tr). Random 1989 $6.95. ISBN 0-679-72205-X

SHORT STORIES BY GARCIA MARQUEZ IN ENGLISH TRANSLATION

Innocent Erendira and Other Stories (1977). Gregory Rabassa (tr). Harper 1979 $6.95. ISBN 0-06-090701-0

Leaf Storm and Other Stories (1955). Gregory Rabassa (tr). Harper 1979 $6.95. ISBN 0-06-090699-5

No One Writes to the Colonel and Other Stories (1961). J. S. Bernstein (tr). Harper 1979 $7.95. ISBN 0-06-090700-2

NOVELS BY GARCIA MARQUEZ IN SPANISH

El Amor en los tiempos de Coléra (1987). French and European 1985 $19.95. ISBN 0-8288-2519-X

Cien años de soledad (1967). French and European $15.95. ISBN 0-8288-2567-X

Cronica de una muerte annunciada (1980). French and European 1981 $9.95. ISBN 0-8288-2518-1

El otoño del patriarca (1976). French and European 1986 $9.95. ISBN 0-8288-2517-3

SHORT STORIES BY GARCIA MARQUEZ IN SPANISH

El coronel no tiene quién le escriba (1961). French and European 1987 $9.95. ISBN 0-8288-2515-7

La increible y triste historia de la candida eredira y su abuela desalmada (1977). French and European 1983 $9.95. ISBN 0-8288-2514-9

BOOKS ABOUT GARCIA MARQUEZ

Bell-Villada, Gene H. *García Márquez: The Man and His Work.* Univ of North Carolina Pr 1990 $29.95. ISBN 0-8078-4264-8 Scholarly examination of the life and works of García Márquez.

McNerney, Kathleen. *Understanding Gabriel García Márquez.* Univ of South Carolina Pr 1989 $21.95. ISBN 0-87249-563-9 Guide for students to understanding the works of García Márquez.

Williams, Raymond L. *Gabriel García Márquez.* G. K. Hall 1984 $17.95. ISBN 0-8057-6597-2 General introduction to García Márquez's life and works.

HARRIS, WILSON   1921– (GUYANESE)

Harris Wilson was born in New Amsterdam, British Guiana (now Guyana). After completing his education at Queen's College, Georgetown, he worked for a time as a surveyor. In 1959 he moved to London, England, where he came to be regarded as one of the leading and most thought-provoking Caribbean writers. His novels typically deal with an actual voyage or journey that also serves as a means of self-discovery for the central character.

In *Palace of the Peacock* (1960), the journey is through the Guyanese hinterland. In *Da Silva's Cultivated Wilderness and Genesis of the Clowns* (1977), the "cultivated wilderness" is the city of London, where the hero undertakes a mental journey to discover his own ethnic history. Seeing a relationship between words as the raw material of literature and color as the raw material of painting, Harris tries to use words as some artists use paints—in layers of shocking contrasts. As a writer, he believes in freely exercising his imagination and rejects the idea that fiction must realistically portray life. Thus, his narratives often dwell on the thoughts and moods of his characters, and they frequently jump backward and forward in time.

Novels by Harris

The Angel at the Gate (1982). Faber & Faber 1983 $15.95. ISBN 0-571-11929-8
Carnival (1985). Faber & Faber 1985 $19.95. ISBN 0-571-13449-1
Da Silva's Cultivated Wilderness and Genesis of the Clowns (1977). Faber & Faber 1978 $9.95.
   ISBN 0-571-10819-9
Four Banks of the River of Space (1989). Faber & Faber 1990 $19.95. ISBN 0-571-14361-X
The Guyana Quartet (1985). Faber & Faber 1985 $11.95. ISBN 0-571-13679-6
The Infinite Rehearsal (1987). Faber & Faber 1987 $13.95. ISBN 0-571-14885-9

Book about Harris

Drake, Sandra E. *Wilson Harris and the Modern Tradition: A New Architecture of the World.*
   Greenwood 1986 $29.95. ISBN 0-313-24783-8 Scholarly, technical, and detailed
   study of Harris's fiction, appropriate for graduate students in English.

MISTRAL, GABRIELA (LUCILA GODOY DE ALCAYAGA)   1889–1957 (CHILEAN)

Gabriela Mistral was born in Vicuña, Chile. Although she was eventually to achieve fame as a stateswoman and Nobel Prize-winning poet, she began her career as a teacher in rural Chile, where she worked hard for school reform. Promoted to director of elementary and secondary schools throughout Chile, she had a profound impact on her country's public school system.

While Mistral was engaged to be married, her fiancé was discovered to be an embezzler. This discovery led to his suicide, a tragedy that inspired much of Mistral's writing. In 1914, her *Sonetos de la muerte (Sonnets About Death)* won first prize in the Chilean literary contest known as Juegos Florales, and her literary reputation was launched.

Later, Mistral was named honorary consul by her government. She served in Brazil, Spain, Portugal, and the United States. She continued to write poetry, which was collected in *Desolación* (1922), *Ternura* (1924), *Tala* (1938), and *Lagar* (1954). In addition to exploring her reactions to her fiancé's death, Mistral's poetry focuses on the oppression of peoples throughout the world. Her verse as well as her teaching expresses a love for children. Her passionate verse and powerful imagery continue to win her a wide readership throughout the world, and her poetry is frequently anthologized. In 1945, she became the first Latin American writer to receive the Nobel Prize for Literature.

Mistral died in 1957 in Hempstead, New York.

Poetry by Mistral in Spanish

Desolación—Ternura—Tala—Lagar. Editorial Porrúa 1981. (o.p.) $3.95. ISBN 968-432-
   280-1

Poetry by Mistral in Bilingual Edition

Selected Poems of Gabriela Mistral. Doris Dana (tr and ed). Johns Hopkins Univ Pr 1971.
   (o.p.) $10.00. ISBN 0-8018-1197-X

Books about Mistral

Arce de Vázquez, Margot. *Gabriela Mistral: The Poet and Her Work.* New York Univ Pr
   1964. (o.p.) $1.75. An affectionate catalogue of Mistral's achievements as well as
   a brief biographical sketch; useful introduction for the general reader.
Taylor, Martin C. *Gabriela Mistral's Religious Sensibility.* Univ of California Pr 1968. (o.p.)
   $7.00. A study of Jewish and Christian religious imagery in Mistral, with particu-
   lar attention to such resonant symbols as trees, wood, blood, water, and wine.

NAIPAUL, V. S. (VIDIADHAR SURAJPRASAD)   1932–
(TRINIDADIAN)

The grandson of emigrants from India to Trindad, V. S. Naipaul was born in
Chaguanas, Trinidad of Hindu parents. He was educated at Queen's Royal
College in Trinidad and then, from 1950 to 1954, at Oxford University in
England. Since then, he has lived in Britain, where he continues to write about
his native Trinidad and other West Indian countries.

Naipaul served as editor of "Caribbean Voices" for the British Broadcasting Company before publishing his first novel, *The Mystic Masseur,* in 1957. In
his novels Naipaul writes warmly, often humorously, of the lives of ordinary
West Indians and of the societies of which they are a part. He is particularly
skillful at capturing the sounds and rhythms of the West Indian dialects, and
the dialogues in his stories are especially delightful.

Naipaul's fiction, even when he appears to be analyzing a fascinating
character, is really an analysis of the entire society. Yet his observations are
always woven carefully and subtly into the narrative of the story, so that his
novels never seem like sociological studies but are always artful and fascinating
pieces of fiction.

Naipaul has also written powerful nonfiction books and essays based on
his international travels, including penetrating studies of India, the new nations
of Africa, and race relations in the United States.

NOVELS BY NAIPAUL

A Bend in the River (1979). Vintage 1989 $7.95. ISBN 0-679-72202-5
The Enigma of Arrival (1987). Vintage 1988 $6.95. ISBN 0-394-75760-2
In a Free State (1971). Vintage 1984 $5.95. ISBN 0-394-72205-1
Guerrillas (1975). Vintage 1990 $10.95. ISBN 0-679-73174-1
A House for Mr. Biswas (1961). Vintage 1984 $9.95. ISBN 0-394-72050-4
The Loss of El Dorado (1969). Vintage 1984 $5.95. ISBN 0-394-72124-1
Miguel Street (1959). Vintage 1984 $4.95. ISBN 0-394-72065-2
Mr. Stone and the Knight's Companion (1963). Vintage 1985 $4.95. ISBN 0-394-73226-X
The Mystic Masseur (1957). Vintage 1984 $4.95. ISBN 0-394-72073-3
The Suffrage of Elvira (1958). Vintage 1985 $4.95. ISBN 0-394-73216-2

BOOKS ABOUT NAIPAUL

Hassan, Dolly Z. *V. S. Naipaul and the West Indies.* Peter Lang 1989 $68.00. ISBN 0-8204-
    0750-X Detailed and scholarly examination of Naipaul's treatment of West Indian
    themes and settings.
Hughes, Peter. *V. S. Naipaul.* Routledge 1988 $9.95. ISBN 0-415-00654-6 Study of
    Naipaul's life and works for the general reader; puts particular emphasis on
    Naipaul's West Indian themes.

NERUDA, PABLO (PSEUDONYM OF NEFTALI RICARDO REYES)
1904–1973 (CHILEAN)

Pablo Neruda was born in southern Chile and educated at the University of
Santiago in the Chilean capital. In 1927, he entered Chile's diplomatic corps and
after an unpleasant tour in eastern Asia, he became consul, first to Barcelona,
Spain, and then, in 1935, to Madrid. During the Spanish Civil War in which
Fascist forces succeeded in overthrowing the left-wing Spanish Republic,
Neruda was a strong supporter of the Republic. When the Republicans were

defeated by the Fascist forces of General Francisco Franco, Neruda became an active Communist. His next diplomatic post was in Mexico, where he served until 1940, when he was recalled.

Back in his home country, Neruda joined the Chilean Communist Party and was elected to the Senate in 1945. He remained active in politics throughout the rest of his life.

Neruda first attracted attention as a poet in 1924 with the publication of *Twenty Poems of Love and a Song of Despair.* His later work became more political and socially conscious while retaining an amazing lyric power. His poetry is sometimes strikingly experimental in both form and subject matter.

Neruda's extraordinary poetic genius and his political activism made him a legendary and symbolic figure for many Latin American intellectuals, students, and artists. He was awarded the Nobel Prize for literature in 1971 "for poetry that, with the action of an elemental force, brings alive a continent's destiny and dreams."

POETRY BY NERUDA IN ENGLISH TRANSLATION

The Captain's Verses (1952). Donald Walsh (tr). New Directions 1972 $5.95. ISBN 0-8112-0457-X

Extravagaria (1958). Alastair Ried (tr). Farrar 1974 $8.95. ISBN 0-374-15126-1

Five Decades: Poems Nineteen Twenty-Five to Nineteen Seventy (1974). Grove 1987 $14.50. ISBN 0-8021-3035-6

Late and Posthumous Poems 1968–1974. Ben Belitt (tr). Grove 1989 $10.95. ISBN 0-8021-3145-X

POETRY BY NERUDA IN SPANISH

Canto general (1950). French and European 1968 $12.50. ISBN 0-8288-2532-7

Nuevas odas elementales (1964). French and European 1964 $9.95. ISBN 0-8288-2535-1

Odas elementales (1954). French and European 1970 $9.95. ISBN 0-8288-2534-3

Residencia en la tierra (1933). French and European 1958 $9.95. ISBN 0-8288-2530-0

Veinte poemas de amor y una cancion deseserada (1924). French and European 1958 $9.95. ISBN 0-8288-2529-7

BOOKS ABOUT NERUDA

Agosin, Marjorie. *Pablo Neruda.* G. K. Hall 1986 $19.95. ISBN 0-8057-6620-0 Good general introduction to Neruda's life and works that identifies the major influences on his poetry.

Bloom, Harold (ed). *Pablo Neruda.* Chelsea 1990 $29.95. ISBN 1-55546-298-7 Useful collection of modern critical essays that discuss Neruda's poetry from a variety of critical perspectives.

PAZ, OCTAVIO 1914– (MEXICAN)

Octavio Paz's poetry has been profoundly influenced by Mexican Indian mythology and Asian religious philosophy, particularly Tantric Buddhism, a form of Buddhism that focuses on the supernatural and on magic. The latter influence stems from the time that Paz served as Mexico's ambassador to India, a position he resigned in 1968 to protest the Mexican government's treatment of students who were demonstrating at the Olympic Games in Mexico City.

For Paz, poetry is always in conflict with government or established society because of poetry's potential to generate reform. Paz believes that the poetic imagination is a valuable tool for understanding society. He also thinks of poetry as a way of overcoming the barriers created by time, the physical world, and the individual self. He seeks in his work to achieve a state of innocence and a sense of psychological freedom bordering on the mystical.

Much of Paz's poetry sees women as the means through which humanity can achieve a connection with the universal. He constantly experiments with poetic form in an effort to overcome the limits of language and to describe a reality beyond the visible.

In 1990, Paz was awarded the Nobel Prize for literature in recognition of his long and rich contribution to poetic art.

POETRY BY PAZ IN ENGLISH TRANSLATION

The Collected Poems, 1957–1987. Eliot Weinberger, *et al* (trs). New Directions 1987 $37.50. ISBN 0-8112-1037-5

Conjunctions and Disconjunctions (1969). Helen R. Lane (tr). Seaver 1982 $7.95. ISBN 0-8050-0177-8

A Draft of Shadows and Other Poems (1978). Eliot Weinberger (tr). New Directions 1979 $8.95. ISBN 0-8112-0738-2

Eagle or Sun? (1973). Eliot Weinberger (tr). New Directions 1976 $5.95. ISBN 0-8112-0623-8

Early Poems 1935–1955. Muriel Rukeyser (tr). New Directions 1973 $6.95. ISBN 0-8112-0478-2

Selected Poems of Octavio Paz. Eliot Weinberger (tr). New Directions 1984 $7.95. ISBN 0-8112-0899-0

POETRY BY PAZ IN BILINGUAL EDITION

The Collected Poems, 1957–1987: Bilingual Edition. Eliot Weinberger, *et al* (trs). New Directions 1987 $37.50. ISBN 0-8112-1037-5

Configurations (1967). New Directions 1971 $5.95. ISBN 0-8112-0150-3

Eagle or Sun? (1973). Eliot Weinberger (tr). New Directions 1976 $5.95. ISBN 0-8112-0623-8

BOOKS ABOUT PAZ

Chiles, Frances. *Octavio Paz, the Mythic Dimension.* Peter Lang 1987 $33.50. ISBN 0-8204-0079-3 Scholarly study of myth and mythmaking in Paz's poetry that concentrates on the archetypal themes and symbols in his work.

Wilson, Jason. *Octavio Paz.* G. K. Hall 1986 $18.95. ISBN 0-8057-6630-8 Study of Paz's life and works that examines the poet's themes and techniques for the general reader.

PUIG, MANUEL   1932–1990 (ARGENTINE)

Manuel Puig has sometimes been called the novelist of popular culture, because so many of his novels are based on popular art forms. Puig is anything but a defender of popular culture, however. His stories invariably show the spiritual emptiness of characters who become strongly affected by popular or consumer culture. *Betrayed by Rita Hayworth* (1968) tells the story of a young Argentine boy who is obsessed with the movies and lives his life by identifying with characters on the screen. Here, as in many of Puig's works, he uses a variety of unusual narrative techniques to tell the story. One of these is the use of the techniques of pop art to communicate a vision of his world. According to one critic, Puig's novels are 'pop' because "he incorporates into his fiction elements of mass culture—radionovelas, comic books, glamour magazines, and in *Betrayed by Rita Hayworth,* commercial movies." He does this to show the role mass media plays in shaping contemporary life.

In *Heartbreak Tango* (1969), Puig depicts the emptiness of Argentine provincial life in the 1930s and the vulgarity of popular music and the soap opera.

In this work, he employs another technique—the bringing together of letters, diaries, newspapers, and conversations to reconstruct the lives of different Argentine women who loved the same man. In *The Buenos Aires Affair* (1972), he uses the form of the detective novel to parody pop fiction. *Kiss of the Spider Woman* (1979), which was made into a popular American movie, parodies modern novel forms that abandon traditional narrative techniques.

NOVELS BY PUIG IN ENGLISH TRANSLATION

Betrayed by Rita Hayworth (1968). Obelisk 1987 $7.95. ISBN 0-525-48285-7

Blood of Requited Love (1980). Jan L. Grayson (tr). Vintage 1984 $9.95. ISBN 0-394-72440-2

Eternal Curse of the Reader of These Pages (1981). Vintage 1983 $4.95. ISBN 0-394-71384-2

Heartbreak Tango: A Serial. (1973). Suzanne J. Levine (tr). Obelisk 1987 $7.95. ISBN 0-525-48228-1

Kiss of the Spider Woman (1979). Thomas Colchie (tr). Vintage 1985 $6.95. ISBN 0-394-74475-6

BOOKS ABOUT PUIG

Bacarisse, Pamela. *The Necessary Dream: A Study of the Novels of Manuel Puig.* Barnes 1988 $36.50. ISBN 0-389-20809-4 Detailed study of Puig's most important works, concentrating on his use of themes and techniques from popular culture.

Kerr, Lucille. *Suspended Fictions: Reading Novels by Manuel Puig.* Univ of Illinois Pr 1987 $21.95. ISBN 0-252-01329-8 Examines Puig's work from the premise that his novels both uphold and caricature the popular forms on which they are based.

AFRICAN LITERATURE

Modern African literature, rooted in oral tradition and steeped in folklore, is a reflection of the continent's rich culture and complex history. Traditionally, it was the duty of the village *griot,* or oral historian, to remember the history of the area and to recite it at various social and ceremonial gatherings such as births, weddings, and other tribal functions. By drawing on this body of local history and combining it with local folktales, legends, and proverbs, as well as with their own insights into contemporary politics, colonialism, and modern world history, contemporary African authors have produced a body of literature that has a distinctly African personality, despite the fact that most of it is written in the languages of the continent's former colonizers. Although Africa's population is composed of many different ethnic or tribal groups and African writers come from many different backgrounds, their works do reveal certain common themes: the effects of colonialism, the persistence of traditional culture, and the overwhelming importance of politics.

Modern African literature, as a distinct and identifiable body of writing, is still very young, emerging on the international scene in the 1950s. Among the pioneers of this period are Chinua Achebe, Amos Tutuola, and the late Guinean author Camara Laye.

Prior to the 1950s, however, several Africans writing in native languages had attracted large African audiences. One of the most important of these early writers was Thomas Mofolo, who is known primarily for his historical novel, *Chaka* (1931). Written in the Sesotho language and later translated into English, Mofolo's story of the great nineteenth-century Zulu warrior, Chaka, is famous throughout Africa. This novel may well be the first major African contribution to modern world literature.

Africa's best-known contemporary novelist is Chinua Achebe, whose nov-

Wooden mask.   Ivory Coast (Nineteenth Century).   Courtesy of Giraudon/Art Resource.

els and stories have captured a worldwide audience. Achebe's work laid the foundation for numerous other books depicting the total disruption of African traditions during the period of European colonization. Camara Laye is also among the first group of African novelists to gain recognition outside Africa. His semiautobiographical novel, *L'Enfant Noir (The Dark Child)* (1954), won an especially large non-African audience.

After the 1950s, when many African nations had gained independence, there was a sharp increase in the number of books dealing with politics. Some works expressed a pride in the continent's newly won independence; others were powerful attacks on various African governments, analyzing the ways in which the legacy of colonialism continued to corrupt African politics. In recent years there has been a small but noticeable increase in literary works by African women. Focusing generally on women's issues, these authors create characters who are, in the main, modern-day African women whose lives are not bound by tradition. Bessie Head and Flora Nwapa are two of these literary pioneers. Nwapa was the first Nigerian woman to have a novel—*Efury* (1966)—published.

One of the major concerns in African literature today is the language dilemma, a carry-over from colonial times when Africans were forced to adopt the language of their colonizers. Because the vast majority of contemporary African literature is written in either French or English, the audience is limited to Africa's educated elite. Desiring a wider audience, many contemporary African authors have begun to publish in native languages, and some are even calling for a single African language, perhaps Swahili, for the entire continent. The most outspoken of these writers is Kenya's Ngugi Wa Thiong'o, who has written several critically acclaimed works in the Kikuyu language.

In the last decade of the twentieth century, African literature is vibrant and flourishing. Younger authors like Kole Omotoso and Buchi Emecheta are building their reputations, while established writers like Wole Soyinka and Ngugi expand their literary output. The audience for African literature is steadily growing as African writers continue to share their continent's rich culture with the world.

COLLECTIONS OF AFRICAN LITERATURE

Abrahams, Roger D. *African Folktales: Traditional Stories of the Black World.* Pantheon 1983 $10.95. ISBN 0-394-72117-9
De Grandsaigne, J. *African Short Stories: An Anthology.* St. Martin's 1985 $29.95. ISBN 0-312-01029-X
Etherton, Michael. *African Plays for Playing.* Heinemann 1976 $7.00. ISBN 0-435-90179-6
Keidel, Eudene. *African Fables.* Herald 1978 $3.95. ISBN 0-8361-1842-1
Keidel, Eudene. *African Fables, Book 2.* Herald 1981 $3.95. ISBN 0-8361-1945-2
*Klein, Leonard S. (ed). *African Literatures in the Twentieth Century: A Guide.* Ungar 1986 $16.95. ISBN 0-8044-6362-X A good introduction to the major writers and their works, all arranged alphabetically by country.
Rodin, Paul. *African Folktales.* Schocken 1983 $11.95. ISBN 0-8052-0732-5
Twentieth Century African and Latin American Verse. Roth 1989 $49.95. ISBN 0-89609-271-2

ACHEBE, CHINUA 1930– (NIGERIAN)

Africa's most popular novelist, Chinua Achebe, received his B.A. degree from the University College at Ibadan, Nigeria. After graduation he pursued a successful career in broadcasting and served as Nigeria's Director of External Broadcasting from 1961 to 1966. Since 1971, Achebe has been the editor of *Okike: An African Journal of New Writing.* He currently teaches literature at the University of Nigeria at Nsukka.

Achebe achieved fame with his first novel, *Things Fall Apart* (1959), and he has been at the forefront of African literature ever since. He has written five novels as well as short stories, poetry, essays, and children's books. Achebe's works have been translated into more than 25 languages, and they are required reading in university courses in Africa, Europe, and the United States. Rich in the folklore and traditions of Nigeria's Ibo culture, Achebe's novels deal directly with the theme of cultures in conflict. While focusing primarily on Ibo society, his stories explore the impact on native Africans of Western culture brought by the colonial powers and by "been-to" Africans, those who have lived abroad and then returned home.

NOVELS BY ACHEBE

Anthills of the Savannah (1988). Anchor 1988 $16.95. ISBN 0-385-01664-6
Arrow of God (1964). Anchor 1989 $7.95. ISBN 0-385-01480-5
A Man of the People (1966). Anchor 1989 $6.95. ISBN 0-385-08616-4
No Longer at East (1961). Heinemann 1987 $7.00. ISBN 0-435-90528-7
Things Fall Apart (1958). Heinemann 1987 $4.00. ISBN 0-435-90526-0

SHORT STORIES BY ACHEBE

Girls at War and Other Stories (1973). Fawcett 1986 $3.50. ISBN 0-449-30046-3

POETRY BY ACHEBE

Beware Soul Brother (1971). Heinemann 1972 $7.50. ISBN 0-435-90120-6

BOOKS ABOUT ACHEBE

Carroll, David. *Chinua Achebe.* St. Martin's 1980 $16.95. ISBN 0-312-13386-3 Introduction to the life and works of Achebe with critical examination of his novels.

Innes, C. L. *Chinua Achebe.* Cambridge Univ Pr 1990 $34.50. ISBN 0-521-35623-7 Examines Achebe's life and works in the context of Nigerian culture and politics.
Njoku, Benedict C. *The Four Novels of Chinua Achebe: A Critical Study.* Peter Lang 1984 $20.00. ISBN 0-8204-0154-4 Careful examination of each of Achebe's first four novels with particular attention to cultural influences and major themes.

BETI, MONGO (PSEUDONYM OF ALEXANDRE BIYIDI) 1932– (CAMEROON)

Mongo Beti was born in M'Balmayo, Cameroon, and was educated at French missionary schools in Africa. He studied at the Sorbonne in Paris, and he continues to make his home in France, where he currently teaches classical Greek, Latin, and French literature in Rouen and edits the journal *Peuples Noirs, Peuples Africains (Black Peoples, African Peoples).* Beti published his first novel, *Ville Cruelle (Cruel City,* 1953), in French and has continued to write in that language.

One of Beti's favorite themes is the failure of colonial missionary efforts in Africa. He writes not so much against Christianity as against the futile Europeanization of Africans in the name of religion, and the failure of the colonizers to recognize the richness of African civilization. An active Marxist, Beti has also attacked government oppression of the poor, both by colonial rulers and by the new African governments that have been in power since independence. His more recent works have dealt with the issue of the subjugation of African women in post-colonial Africa.

NOVELS BY BETI IN ENGLISH TRANSLATION

King Lazarus (1958). Heinemann 1970 $7.00. ISBN 0-435-90077-3
Lament for an African Pol (1979). Richard Bjornson (tr). Three Continents 1985 $10.00. ISBN 0-89410-305-9
Mission to Kala (1957). Heinemann 1964 $7.00. ISBN 0-435-90013-7
Perpetua and the Habit of Unhappiness (1974). Heinemann 1978 $8.00. ISBN 0-435-90181-8
The Poor Christ of Bomba (1956). Heinemann 1971 $8.00. ISBN 0-435-90088-9
Remember Ruben (1973). Heinemann 1980 $9.00. ISBN 0-435-90214-8

COETZEE, J. M. (JOHN MICHAEL) 1940– (SOUTH AFRICAN)

J. M. Coetzee is among the best-known white South African novelists of his generation. Born in Capetown, South Africa, Coetzee was educated as a computer scientist and linguist. He received his M.A. in 1963 from the University of Capetown and his Ph.D. from the University of Texas in 1969.

From 1962 to 1963, Coetzee worked in London, England, for International Business Machines (IBM) as a computer programmer. From there he went to Bracknell, England, as a systems programmer for International Computers, where he stayed for several years. In 1968, he went to the United States. There, he joined the faculty of the State University of New York at Buffalo as an assistant professor of English. He stayed on the faculty until 1971. Coetzee then returned to South Africa, where in 1972, he took a position as a lecturer in English at the University of Capetown, where he has remained to the present.

Coetzee's opposition to the South African government's apartheid policies (strict institutional separation of the races) subjected him to considerable criticism in the past, but with the recent change in official attitude toward the rights of the black South African population, Coetzee is now being viewed more tolerantly by the white government of South Africa.

Coetzee is a powerful writer who relies heavily on specific details of time and place, but even though his works are clearly set in South Africa, they are universal in theme. In the novel *In the Heart of the Country* (1977), a lonely spinster on an isolated sheep farm writes in her diary of her love—and her hate—for her domineering father. *The Life and Times of Michael K.* (1983) looks closely at the moral cost of the policy of apartheid on both whites and blacks.

NOVELS BY COETZEE

Age of Iron (1989). Random 1990 $18.95. ISBN 0-394-58859-2
Dusklands (1974). Penguin 1985 $6.95. ISBN 0-14-007114-8
Foe (1987). Penguin 1988 $6.95. ISBN 0-14-009623-X
In the Heart of the Country (1977). Penguin 1982 $5.95. ISBN 0-14-006228-9
The Life and Times of Michael K. (1983). Penguin 1985 $6.95. ISBN 0-14-007448-1
Waiting for the Barbarians (1980). Penguin 1982 $6.95. ISBN 0-14-006110-X

EMECHETA, BUCHI 1944– (NIGERIAN)

Born near Lagos, Nigeria, Buchi Emecheta was educated at the Methodist Girls' High School in Lagos. From there she went to the University of London in England. Emecheta, who lives in London with her five children, has worked as a teacher, a librarian, and a social worker.

As one of the new generation of female African novelists, Emecheta has brought a strong new voice as well as a feminist point of view to modern African literature. In addition to her novels, she has published several children's books and numerous articles on the roles of African women. Her work focuses on the conflict facing African women between traditional and modern social roles and on the growing number of personal and social problems in the constantly changing scene of modern Africa.

Emecheta's first novel, *In the Ditch* (1972), is a largely autobiographical account of the struggle of Adah, a Nigerian mother of five, separated from her husband and living in London, where she tries to raise her children while earning an advanced degree. In her next book, *Second-Class Citizen* (1975), Emecheta takes her readers back in time to Adah's early years in Lagos, Nigeria, followed by her marriage and eventual move to London with her husband and two children. The title of the book refers to the sexual and racial discrimination Adah experiences in London.

Emecheta's later novels are set in Nigeria and usually revolve around a courageous woman who boldly challenges cultural traditions. Emecheta directs her strongest attacks on those customs that are hardest on women: arranged marriages, constant pregnancy and childbirth, polygamy, and widowhood. She rejects the stereotype of the obedient wife and mother and urges African women to build a sense of personal worth that does not depend on their roles in the family.

NOVELS BY EMECHETA

The Bride Price: Young Ibo Girl's Love; Conflict of Family and Tradition (1976). Braziller 1976 $6.95. ISBN 0-8076-0951-X
Destination Biafra (1982). Schocken 1988 $14.95. ISBN 0-8052-8119-3
Double Yoke (1982). Braziller 1983 $12.95. ISBN 0-8076-1128-X
The Family (1990). Braziller 1990 $8.95. ISBN 0-8076-1250-2
In the Ditch (1972). Schocken 1987 $4.95. ISBN 0-8052-8010-3
The Joys of Motherhood (1979). Braziller 1990 $6.95. ISBN 0-8076-0950-1
The Rape of Shavi (1983). Braziller 1985 $6.95. ISBN 0-8076-1118-2
Second-Class Citizen (1975). Braziller 1983 $6.95. ISBN 0-8076-1066-6
The Slave Girl (1977). Braziller 1977 $6.95. ISBN 0-8076-0952-8

GORDIMER, NADINE   1923– (SOUTH AFRICAN)

Winner of many international awards, South African Nadine Gordimer was born in Springs, Transvaal and received her education at a convent school and at the University of the Witersand, Johannesburg, South Africa.

Gordimer—novelist, short story writer, and essayist—is one of South Africa's best-known authors, and she is perhaps the country's most gifted contemporary novelist. In her fiction Gordimer consistently attacks the system of apartheid from the standpoint of the white middle class. Her stories show how some whites slowly awaken to the injustice and moral corruption of the system while others fail to see how the racial policy eats away at the moral basis of society.

Gordimer's narratives are rich in detail and precise observation. She frequently uses a single well-drawn event, incident, or scene to capture the sense of broad social decay she seeks to depict. In an early work *The Late Bourgeois World* (1966), she expresses some cautious hope for the future of South Africa. *A Sport of Nature* (1987), her most recent novel, shows the development of a young, middle-class, white woman into a political activist.

NOVELS BY GORDIMER

Burger's Daughter (1979). Penguin 1980 $8.95. ISBN 0-14-005593-2
The Conservationist (1974). Penguin 1983 $6.95. ISBN 0-14-004716-6
A Guest of Honor (1970). Penguin 1983 $6.95. ISBN 0-14-003696-2
July's People (1981). Penguin 1982 $5.95. ISBN 0-14-006140-1
The Late Bourgeois World (1966). Penguin 1983 $5.95. ISBN 0-14-005614-9
A Sport of Nature (1987). Penguin 1988 $7.95. ISBN 0-14-008470-3

SHORT STORIES BY GORDIMER

My Son's Song (1990). Farrar 1990 $19.95. ISBN 0-374-21751-3
Selected Stories (1975). Penguin 1983 $6.95. ISBN 0-14-006737-X
Six Feet of Country (1956). Penguin 1986 $6.95. ISBN 0-14-006559-8
A Soldier's Embrace (1980). Penguin 1982 $6.95. ISBN 0-14-005925-3
Something Out There (1984). Penguin 1986 $6.95. ISBN 0-14-007711-1

BOOKS ABOUT GORDIMER

Clingman, Stephen. *The Novels of Nadine Gordimer: History from the Inside.* Unwin 1986 $29.95. ISBN 0-04-800082-5 Study of Gordimer's increasingly radical novels as exercises in "the history of consciousness."
Newman, Judie. *Nadine Gordimer.* Routledge 1988 $9.95. ISBN 0-415-00660-0 Novel-by-novel study of Gordimer's development as a novelist and radical thinker.

LAYE, CAMARA   1928–1980 (GUINEAN)

Camara Laye was born in the Guinean city of Kouroussa, where he was raised in a strongly traditional African culture. He attended technical school in Conakry, Guinea, and then completed his education in France.

Laye's first novel, *The Dark Child* (1953), is based on memories of his childhood days in French Guinea, and is considered by many critics to be one of the best portraits of traditional African life ever written. The book brought him criticism from African nationalists, however, because it painted a picture of a happy child growing up under French colonial rule.

Laye's second novel, *Radiance of the King* (1954), is a much more ambitious and complex work that combines mysticism with wit and humor to tell a story of one man's search for God. His third book, *A Dream of Africa* (1966), explores the politics of Guinea in the years after independence. The book was considered politically dangerous by the Guinean government and resulted in Laye's being exiled to Senegal where he lived as the guest of President Leopold Sedar Senghor (*see* Senghor, Vol. 1, World Literature: African Literature), himself a noted poet. During his years in Senegal, where he died, Laye published his final novel, *The Guardian of the World* (1978), the story of the great Mali emperor Sundiata.

NOVELS BY LAYE IN ENGLISH TRANSLATION

The Dark Child (1953). Farrar 1954 $6.95. ISBN 0-374-50768-6
The Guardian of the World (1978). Vintage 1984 $7.95. ISBN 0-394-72441-0
Radiance of the King (1954). Vintage 1989 $9.95. ISBN 0-679-72200-9

NGUGI WA THIONG'O   1938– (KENYAN)

Born in Limuru, Kenya, Ngugi Wa Thiong'o attended both missionary schools and schools run by Kenya's Kikuyu tribe. In 1964, he graduated from Uganda's Makerere College and then did advanced work at the University of Leeds in England. In 1972, Ngugi became head of the literature department at the University of Nairobi in Kenya, a position he held until 1978, when he was arrested and imprisoned for writing a play that the government considered dangerous.

Novelist, playwright, and essayist, Ngugi is Kenya's best-known writer and one of East Africa's most outspoken social critics. His first novel, *Weep Not, Child* (1964), was a penetrating account of the Mau Mau uprising (a tribal revolt that occurred in colonial Kenya). It was the first English-language novel by an East African. Two subsequent works, *The River Between* (1965) and *A Grain of Wheat* (1967), are sensitive novels about the Kikuyu people caught between the old and the new Africa.

One of Ngugi's major concerns has been the lack of reading materials in native African languages. In an attempt to bring literature to African peasants and workers, he wrote and produced the play *I Will Marry When I Want* (1977) in his native Kikuyu language. The play, which shows the exploitation of Kikuyu workers and peasants, attracted a large audience of poor Kenyans. It also led to Ngugi's arrest and imprisonment. Since his release in 1979, he continues to write in Kikuyu, with a particular interest in children's books.

NOVELS BY NGUGI

Devil on the Cross (1980). Heinemann 1982 $7.50. ISBN 0-435-90844-8
A Grain of Wheat (1967). Heinemann 1987 $7.00. ISBN 0-435-90836-7
The River Between (1965). Heinemann 1965 $6.50. ISBN 0-435-90017-X
Weep Not, Child (1964). Heinemann 1988 $7.00. ISBN 0-435-90830-8

PLAYS BY NGUGI

The Black Hermit (1962). Heinemann 1968 $7.00. ISBN 0-435-90051-X
I Will Marry When I Want (1977). (coauthored with Ngugi Wa Miril) Heinemann 1982 $7.50. ISBN 0-435-90246-6
The Trial of Dedan Kimathi (1975). (coauthored with Micere Mubo) Heinemann 1977 $7.00. ISBN 0-435-90191-5

PATON, ALAN   1903–1988 (SOUTH AFRICAN)

A white South African writer and educator, Alan Paton was born in Pieter-maritzburg and educated at the University of Natal. He spent many years as a teacher, first at a native school, then at Pietermaritzburg College. A writer of novels, short stories, essays, and poetry, he was founder and president of the South African Liberal Party, a reformist anti-apartheid group no longer in existence.

Paton's best-known work—and perhaps the most popular novel to come out of South Africa—is *Cry, the Beloved Country,* published in 1948. This truly memorable work explores racial tensions in South Africa while appealing for universal brotherhood. It has been translated into more than 20 languages and has sold more copies in South Africa than any other book besides the Bible. The story centers on a Zulu minister who enters into the Johannesburg, South Africa, underworld to search for his son, who is accused of murdering a white man.

Paton's strong interest in race relations stems from his years as a principal of the Diepkloof Reformatory, a Johannesburg reform school for African youth, where he saw the results of enforced segregation and racial discrimina-tion and became known for the success of his enlightened methods of working with the troubled youngsters. His second novel, *Too Late the Phalarope* (1953), explores the tragic results of political and racial inflexibility on the part of white South Africans. In his short stories and essays, Paton has continued his call for freedom and dignity for black South Africans and an end to racial separation in South Africa.

NOVELS BY PATON

Ah, but Your Land Is Beautiful (1981). Macmillan 1983 $10.95. ISBN 0-684-17830-3
Cry, the Beloved Country (1948). Macmillan 1987 $4.95. ISBN 0-02-053210-5
Too Late the Phalarope (1953). Macmillan 1985 $4.50. ISBN 0-684-18500-8

SHORT STORIES BY PATON

Tales from a Troubled Land (1961). Macmillan 1977 $7.95. ISBN 0-684-18494-X

NONFICTION BY PATON

The Journey Continued. Macmillan 1990 $12.95. ISBN 0-02-035955-1 Paton's account of his later years including his political and literary activities.
Save the Beloved Country (1989). Macmillan 1989 $22.50. ISBN 0-684-19127-X
Towards the Mountain: An Autobiography. Macmillan 1987 $9.95. ISBN 0-684-18892-9 Paton's account of his early life through the publication of *Cry the Beloved Country.*

BOOK ABOUT PATON

Callan, Edward. *Alan Paton.* G. K. Hall 1982 $16.95. ISBN 0-8057-6512-3 Introduction to Paton's life and works; useful for the general reader and for students unfamiliar with his fiction.

SENGHOR, LEOPOLD SEDAR   1906– (SENEGALESE)

Born in the small village of Joal, Senegal, Leopold Sedar Senghor received a government scholarship in 1928 and left for France, where he graduated from the Sorbonne in 1932. He taught in French secondary schools until the start of

World War II, when he joined the French army. Captured by the Germans, he was a prisoner of war from 1940 to 1942. After the war, Senghor remained in France and began to publish poetry that reflected the concept of *negritude,* a belief in the beauty and value of African culture.

In 1947, Senghor returned to Senegal and became active in the Senegalese movement for political independence from France. When Senegal gained its independence in 1959, Senghor became the new nation's first president, a position he held until his retirement in 1981.

Senghor has won many literary honors and degrees, including an honorary doctorate from Oxford University. In 1983, he was elected to the Académie Française, France's most respected body of authors and scholars—the first black member of that body in its 349-year history.

Senghor has become known as the leading advocate of negritude, and his poems are filled with expressions of love and respect for African culture. His images are drawn from African life, and his themes come from African folklore and tradition. He is acknowledged as one of Africa's foremost literary figures and has often been mentioned as a candidate for the Nobel Prize in literature.

POETRY BY SENGHOR IN ENGLISH TRANSLATION

Collected Poems of L. S. Senghor. Univ Pr of Virginia 1991. ISBN 0-8139-1276-8
Selected Poems (1977). Cambridge Univ Pr 1977 $10.95. ISBN 0-521-29111-9

BOOK ABOUT SENGHOR

Spleth, Janice S. *Leopold Sedar Senghor.* G. K. Hall 1985 $24.95. ISBN 0-8057-6616-2
Comprehensive, detailed study of Senghor's life and works, tracing his development as a poet and politician in readable prose free of literary jargon.

SOYINKA, WOLE   1934– (NIGERIAN)

Distinguished playwright, novelist, poet, social critic, and political activist, Wole Soyinka is one of Africa's literary giants. Although his literary efforts cover a wide range of forms, Soyinka is best known outside Africa for his plays—social commentaries on the day-to-day problems of contemporary Africans.

Soyinka's plays are almost all comic in tone, ranging from the relatively light comedy of *The Lion and the Jewel* (1963) to the angry farce of *A Play of Giants* (1984). All of his works deal in some way with questions of political justice and freedom.

In fact, Soyinka's personal commitment to political activism caused him to be imprisoned and held in solitary confinement during the 1967–1969 Nigerian Civil War. Two of his works, *The Man Died: Prison Notes of Wole Soyinka* (1970) and *Poems from Prison* (1970), were secretly written on toilet paper and smuggled out of prison.

Soyinka's pioneering efforts and creative talent have been a major influence on the development of Nigerian drama. In the 1960s, he founded two Nigerian theater groups, and his plays have been widely performed in Nigeria and in England. His latest dramatic work, *A Play of Giants,* parodies African dictators. It premiered in 1984 at the Yale Repertory Theater in New Haven, Connecticut. Soyinka is currently on the faculty of Cornell University in Ithaca, New York.

NOVEL BY SOYINKA

The Interpreters (1965). Heinemann 1984 $8.00. ISBN 0-435-90076-5

POETRY BY SOYINKA

Idanre and Other Poems (1967). Hill & Wang 1987 $7.95. ISBN 0-8090-1352-5
Mandela's Earth and Other Poems (1988). Random 1988 $13.95. ISBN 0-394-57021-9

PLAYS BY SOYINKA

Collected Plays. (1973). Vol. 1 Oxford Univ Pr 1973 $9.95. ISBN 0-19-281136-3
Collected Plays. (1974). Vol. 2 Oxford Univ Pr 1974 $9.95. ISBN 0-19-281164-9
Death and the King's Horseman (1976). Hill & Wang 1987 $7.95. ISBN 0-8090-1252-9
A Play of Giants (1984). Heinemann 1988 $8.50. ISBN 0-413-55290-X

NONFICTION BY SOYINKA

Ake: The Years of Childhood. Vintage 1983 $8.95. ISBN 0-394-72219-1 Soyinka's autobi-
ography covering his first 11 years and offering insights into Yoruba culture and
its influence on his life.

MIDDLE EASTERN LITERATURE

Because of the Middle East's long history of political turmoil, religious rivalries,
conquest, and shifting national boundaries, Middle Eastern literature cannot be
described in terms of nationalities or geography. Rather it must be defined as
the written expression of peoples who speak a common language and share a
common culture, regardless of the name of the country they now call home.
Five major languages are spoken in the region, and thus, there are five major
literatures.

The dominant language of the area is Arabic, the primary tongue of more
than 100 million people. Because it is the language in which the Koran, the
sacred book of Islam, is written, it is an important language in all Islamic
societies. Consequently, Arabic writing is the most widespread of all the Middle Eastern literatures.

The region's other major languages are Farsi, spoken in Iran and portions
of Afghanistan; Turkish, spoken primarily in Turkey; Armenian, spoken in the
Soviet Republic of Armenia as well as by many thousands of Armenians living
in other parts of the world; and Hebrew, the official language of Israel and the
language of religious Judaism shared by many Jews worldwide. Each of these
languages has its own body of literature with its own historical development.

Ancient, or classical, Arabic literature consists mostly of religious writings
along with myths, fables, folktales, proverbs, and a type of very formal poetry
called *quasidah.* Modern Arabic literature began to take shape as early as the
sixteenth century, but it did not flower until the nineteenth century. It draws
many of its themes from the classical period but also uses newer forms that
have been borrowed from the West, such as the novel and the drama. In the
years following World War II, many Arab countries gained their independence
from European colonial powers. This led many Arabic writers to become increasingly concerned with social and political issues and less interested in the
romantic tales of love and adventure that characterized some earlier Arabic
literature.

The development of Armenian literature is also closely tied to the religious
and political history of the Armenian people. Begun in the early fourth century
as the expression of a people newly converted to Christianity, Armenian literature remained closely tied to the church through most of its early development.
Some of Armenia's rich oral tradition of poetry and folktales was written down
during this period as well. By the beginning of the eighteenth century, Ar-

menian literature had become noticeably less religious in theme and purpose. This trend continued through the nineteenth century, so that by the beginning of the twentieth century, little religious influence remained visible in the literature. The Turkish deportation of millions of Armenians to Syria in 1915 and the absorption of Armenia itself into the Soviet Union in 1920 brought literary development almost to a halt. Since 1920, much of Armenian literature has been produced by writers in exile. Recent changes in the Soviet Union, however, promise a rebirth of this important national literature.

Although Persia, now called Iran, was one of the most powerful nations of the ancient world, little is known about the literature of this early society. The Persian literature that is known is usually dated from the Islamic conquest of Persia in the seventh century, when the Arabic alphabet replaced the ancient Persian system of writing and the Muslim religion was adopted. During the eleventh and twelfth centuries, poets like Firdawsi, Omar Khayyam, and Farid Al-Din Attar produced beautiful and elegant verses that established the standards of Persian poetry for several centuries. Poetry continued to dominate Persian literature until the beginning of the twentieth century, when the desire for political and social change prompted many writers to use prose to argue their positions and express their ideas. For the past 50 years, Iranian literature has been subjected to severe political and religious censorship and has, therefore, experienced little growth and development.

Turkish literature has its roots in the oral folktales and poetry that reach back close to 2,500 years. However, during the time of the Ottoman Empire (*c.* 1400–1920), this folk tradition was ignored in favor of a more formal poetry, called Divan, that was modeled on Arabic and Persian poetic forms. With the founding of the modern Turkish republic in 1920, the old folk traditions were revived and modernized, and Turkish writers became more interested in the lives and concerns of ordinary people. During the past 50 years, there has been a growing British and American influence on Turkish literature. This is especially evident in the drama, where traditional Turkish forms such as the shadow play and the *Orta Oyunu*—an ancient form of broad comedy—have been almost completely abandoned in favor of adaptations of British and American dramatic forms.

Hebrew literature has also existed for more than 2,000 years, from the biblical period to the present. However, over the last 1,500 years, the primary use of the Hebrew language has been religious. When the Hebrew language ceased to be spoken toward the end of the biblical period, it was preserved in the religious rites, proverbs, and commentaries of Jews throughout the Middle East and Europe. By the Middle Ages, Hebrew was known to Jews as *leshon kodesh,* the sacred tongue.

Modern Hebrew literature has its beginnings in the seventeenth and eighteenth centuries when Jewish writers in central and eastern Europe again used the Hebrew language to write about nonreligious subjects. During the nineteenth century, Hebrew literature grew side by side with Yiddish literature (*see* Vol. 1, World Literature: Easter European Literature). Some Jewish authors, such as Mendele Moykher Sforim, wrote in both languages. Since the founding of the state of Israel in 1948, Hebrew literature has enjoyed a new burst of growth and development. As the official language of Israel, Hebrew once again became a spoken language in everyday life. A new generation of native Israeli writers, such as Moshe Shamir and Amos Oz, have begun to produce fiction and poetry in their national language.

COLLECTIONS OF MIDDLE EASTERN WRITING IN ENGLISH TRANSLATION

Arberry, A. J. *The Rubaiyat of Omar Khayyam and Other Persian Poems.* Biblio Dist 1977 $3.95. ISBN 0-460-00996-6

Badawi, M. M. (ed). *An Anthology of Modern Arabic Verse.* Oxford Univ Pr 1970 $9.95. ISBN 0-19-920032-7

Bargad, Warren, and Stanley F. Chyet (trs). *Israeli Poetry: A Contemporary Anthology.* Indiana Univ Pr 1988 $12.50. ISBN 0-253-20356-2

Carmi, T. (ed). *The Penguin Book of Hebrew Verse.* Penguin 1981 $13.95. ISBN 0-14-042197-1

Der Hovanessian, Diana, and Marzbed Margossian (eds). *An Anthology of Armenian Poetry.* Columbia Univ Pr 1978 $16.00. ISBN 0-231-04565-4

Downing, Charles. *Armenian Folktales and Legends.* Oxford Univ Pr 1978 $15.95. ISBN 0-19-274117-9

Etmekjian, James (ed). *An Anthology of Western Armenian Literature.* Caravan 1980 $30.00. ISBN 0-88206-026-0

Frank, Bernhard (tr). *Modern Hebrew Poetry.* Univ of Iowa Pr 1980 $11.95. ISBN 0-87745-107-9

Gibran, Kahlil. *A Treasury of Writings of Kahlil Gibran.* Book Sales 1989 $12.98. ISBN 0-89009-389-X

Halman, Talat S. *Contemporary Turkish Literature: Fiction and Poetry.* Fairleigh 1981 $39.50. ISBN 0-8386-1360-8

Halman, Talat S. *Modern Turkish Drama.* Bibliotheca 1976 $20.00. ISBN 0-88297-033-X

Iz, Fahir. *Anthology of Modern Turkish Short Stories.* Bibliotheca $11.95. ISBN 0-88297-039-9

Jayyusi, Salma K. *Modern Arabic Poetry: An Anthology.* Columbia Univ Pr 1987 $45.00. ISBN 0-231-05272-3

Johnson-Davies, Denys (ed). *Modern Arabic Short Stories.* Three Continents 1989 $7.00. ISBN 0-914478-75-3

Khouri, Mounah A., and Hamid Algar. *An Anthology of Modern Arabic Poetry.* Univ of California Pr 1974 $10.95. ISBN 0-520-02898-8

Kravitz, Nathaniel. *Three Thousand Years of Hebrew Literature: From the Earliest Times Through the Twentieth Century.* Ohio Univ Pr 1971 $20.00. ISBN 0-8040-0728-4

Kritzeck, James (ed). *An Anthology of Islamic Literature: From the Rise of Islam to Modern Times.* Meridian 1975 $12.95. ISBN 0-452-00783-6

Mahfuz, Nagib. *God's World: An Anthology of Short Stories.* Bibliotheca 1973 $12.00. ISBN 0-88297-031-3 A collection of Arabic short stories.

Nicholson, Reynold A. *Translations of Eastern Poetry and Prose.* Humanities 1987 $15.00. ISBN 0-391-03463-4

Pound, Omar (tr). *Arabic and Persian Poems.* New Directions 1970 $7.50. ISBN 0-8112-0358-1

Southgate, Minoo (ed, tr). *Modern Persian Short Stories.* Three Continents 1980 $9.00. ISBN 0-89410-033-5

Tolegian, Aram (tr). *Armenian Poetry Old and New.* Wayne State Univ Pr 1979 $22.95. ISBN 0-8143-1608-5

ASIAN LITERATURE

Asian literature can be divided into four major groups, each rich and diverse with a long literary tradition: the literature of South Asia, including India, Pakistan, Bangladesh, Nepal, and Sri Lanka; Chinese literature; Japanese literature; and the literature of Southeast Asia and Korea. For the most part, the writing from this part of the world, both ancient and modern, is barely known in the United States. Yet these literatures have flourished for thousands of years and contain some of the finest works produced by literary artists in any time or place. The following lists will provide American readers with only a general introduction to Asian literature.

THE LITERATURE OF SOUTH ASIA

The 1948 Constitution of the independent state of India recognizes 15 different languages as "official," but an additional 225 languages and dialects have been identified as widely used in different parts of the country. Likewise, in Pakistan, although Urdu is the official language, several other languages are spoken widely, such as Sindhi and Punjabi. Sri Lanka has two major tongues, Sinhalese and Tamil.

With such a wide range of languages, it is surprising that anything like a national literature ever developed in any of these three nations. Yet there is a single language that links all educated people in this vast area—English, the language of the British, who colonized and dominated the area for years. Although most people of South Asia do not speak English, it is the language of the educated elite. Much of the literature of the region is written originally in English, and most of what is written in other native languages is translated into English. Thus the literature of this region is easily available to English-speaking people the world over.

Early Indian literature is dominated by three great epics: the *Ramayana,* the *Mahabharata,* and the *Bhagavad-Gita.* These works have been reworked and modified over the centuries so that they provide a kind of code of social conduct for the Indian people as well as mythical stories of their past. They are also religious and philosophical writings; the *Bhagavad-Gita,* particularly, serves as a fundamental text of Hinduism, the religion of the majority of modern-day Indians.

Indian writing maintained its basically religious character throughout the Middle Ages. While the Muslim religion has maintained a presence in the Indian subcontinent since the eighth century, the literary and cultural influence of Islam did not become strong until the eleventh and twelfth centuries. In the thirteenth century, a great many Muslims came to India from the Near East, bringing a powerful impact on Indian culture and ideas. The Urdu language, a mixture of Hindustani, Persian, and Arabic, developed about this time, and by the sixteenth century, an Urdu literature was in full flower throughout India.

Modern Indian literature stems from the arrival of the British East India Company, which established trading stations throughout India in the 1600s. The British influence continued to grow, and with the establishment of British rule under the Empire in the middle of the eighteenth century, English language and culture began to dominate among the educated Indian classes. With the end of British rule in 1948 and the division of the subcontinent into the two nations of India and Pakistan, there was a strong movement toward the development of separate national cultures in each new country. Along with this came a movement to write in native languages. This movement has continued up to the present, with increasing numbers of Indian and Pakistani authors choosing to write in their native languages rather than in English. Now, although English still retains a powerful hold on the region's literature, there are written literatures in all the major languages of India and Pakistan. Major writers from the Indian subcontinent include Nobel Prize-winning Bengali poet Rabindranath Tagore and Pakistani author Salman Rushdie.

COLLECTIONS OF LITERATURE FROM SOUTH ASIA

Ali, Ahmed (ed and tr). *The Golden Tradition: An Anthology of Urdu Poetry.* Columbia Univ Pr 1973 $15.00. ISBN 0-231-03688-4
Buck, William (ed and tr). *Mahabharata.* Meridian 1979 $4.95. ISBN 0-452-00913-8

Buck, William (ed). *Ramayana.* Meridian 1977 $5.95. ISBN 0-452-00935-9

Cowasjee, Saros (ed). *Modern Indian Short Stories.* Oxford Univ Pr 1983 $6.95. ISBN 0-19-561563-8

Jamal, Mahmood (ed and tr). *The Penguin Book of Modern Urdu Poetry.* Penguin 1987 $6.95. ISBN 0-14-058512-5

King, Bruce. *Modern Indian Poetry in English.* Oxford Univ Pr 1987 $21.95. ISBN 0-19-561959-5

Lal, P. (ed). *Great Sanskrit Plays in Modern Translation.* New Directions 1957 $8.95. ISBN 0-8112-0079-5

Mahapatra, Sitalant (ed). *Anthology of Modern Oriya Poetry.* Advent 1984 $8.95. ISBN 0-7069-2583-1

Mascaro, Juan (tr). *The Bhagavad-Gita.* Penguin 1989 $3.95. ISBN 0-14-044121-2

Obeyesekere, Ranjini, and Chitra Fernando (eds). *Anthology of Modern Writing from Sri Lanka.* Univ of Arizona Pr 1981 $6.50. ISBN 0-8165-0703-1

Raina, Trilokinath (tr). *An Anthology of Modern Kashmiri Verse, 1930–1960.* Ind–US 1974 $12.50. ISBN 0-89158-181-2

Tagore, Rabindranath. *A Tagore Reader.* Amiya Chakravarty (ed). Beacon 1966 $14.95. ISBN 0-8070-5971-4

Van Buitenen, J. A. (tr). *Tales of Ancient India.* Univ of Chicago Pr 1968 $11.95. ISBN 0-226-84647-4

Vidyakara. *Anthology of Sanskrit Court Poetry: Vidyakara's "Subhasitartahosa."* Harvard Univ Pr 1965 $32.50. ISBN 0-674-03950-5

CHINESE LITERATURE

Chinese literature is among the world's most important and oldest literatures, with a history dating back more than 3,000 years. The oldest Chinese written records date from about 1400 BC, but writing was almost certainly developed long before then. The oldest surviving works of literature come from the period 500 BC to 200 BC, and they form the basis of one of China's major religions, Confucianism.

Because Chinese works were printed as early as the eighth century, a great deal of Chinese literature has survived to the present. This long history of printing also enabled the literary language—that is, the written language of China—to remain constant even while the spoken language changed. As a result, Chinese literature tends to be very imitative, with each new generation of writers basing their work on fixed models developed during the early years of China's literary history.

The principal form of Chinese literature is poetry, which developed into highly rigid and restrictive forms during the Tang dynasty (618–906). In these poems, each line is required to have a precise number of syllables and lines that rhyme exactly and that are nearly identical grammatically. Over the years, this type of poetic expression became so far removed from ordinary language that readers needed special dictionaries in order to decipher poetry.

Chinese short stories also have a long history. While not as stylized or restricted as poetry, they too tended to be of two types—tales of the supernatural or historical tales. Then, around the fourteenth century, longer stories, similar to modern novels, began to appear. These were written in the vernacular, or common language, and were read by ordinary people.

The long stories were treated with scorn by the literary masters, who continued to construct ever more polished and elaborate poetry and tales. As a result, only a few of these popular "novels" have survived. One of the survivors is *The Romance of the Three Kingdoms* (c. 1350), a story of chivalry and warfare. The somewhat later work, *The Dream of the Red Chamber,* tells the story of the economic decline of a wealthy family.

Chinese drama was probably established during the Mongol dynasty (1280–1368) and, like poetry, soon followed a fixed pattern. Chinese plays are presented without scenery or elaborate props, and they almost always involve singing, dancing, and acrobatics as well as acting. The plots are usually quite simple and direct, built around questions of conflicting loyalties, such as the son who wishes to be loyal to his parents but loves someone they do not want him to marry.

Contacts with the West during the nineteenth and twentieth centuries brought new literary forms to China. However, the unstable political climate in the early part of the twentieth century and the rigid censorship of the past 40 years, especially during the Cultural Revolution period in the 1960s, have retarded literary development. Now that China is undergoing still more political changes, we can expect its new literature to affect them.

COLLECTIONS OF CHINESE LITERATURE IN ENGLISH TRANSLATION

Birch, Cyril, and Donald Keene. *An Anthology of Chinese Literature from the Fourteenth Century to the Present.* Grove 1987 $14.95. ISBN 0-394-17766-5

Chang, H. C. (ed). *Chinese Literature. Vol. 1 Popular Fiction and Drama.* Columbia Univ Pr 1982 $20.00. ISBN 0-231-05367-3

Chang, H. C. (ed and tr). *Chinese Literature. Vol. 3 Tales of the Supernatural.* Columbia Univ Pr 1983 $24.00. ISBN 0-231-05794-6

Chang, H. C. (tr). *Chinese Literature. Vol. 2 Nature Poetry* Columbia Univ Pr 1977 $18.00. ISBN 0-231-04288-4

Chi-Chen Wang (tr). *Contemporary Chinese Stories.* Greenwood 1969 $4.95. ISBN 0-8371-8943-8

Gunn, Edward M. (ed). *Twentieth Century Chinese Drama: An Anthology.* Indiana Univ Pr 1983 $15.00. ISBN 0-253-20310-4

Kai-Yu Hsu (ed and tr). *Twentieth Century Chinese Poetry: An Anthology.* Cornell Univ Pr 1970 $14.95. ISBN 0-8014-9105-3

Jenner, W. J. (ed and tr). *Modern Chinese Stories.* Oxford Univ Pr 1974 $8.95. ISBN 0-19-519788-7

Lao Tzu. *The Way of Life: Tao Te Ching.* Mentor 1955 $3.95. ISBN 0-451-62674-5

Lau, Joseph (ed). *Modern Chinese Stories and Novellas, 1919–1945.* Columbia Univ Pr 1981 $20.00. ISBN 0-231-04203-5

Liu, Shih S. (tr). *Chinese Classical Prose: The Eight Masters of the T'ang-Sung Period.* Univ of Washington Pr 1980 $24.95. ISBN 0-295-95662-3

Li Xiou Ming (tr). *Chinese Fables.* Oyster River 1988 $6.95. ISBN 0-9617481-2-5

Rexroth, Kenneth (tr). *One Hundred Poems from the Chinese.* New Directions 1956 $5.95. ISBN 0-8112-0180-5

Robbins, Neal. *Contemporary Chinese Fiction: Four Short Stories.* Yale Univ Far Eastern Pubs 1986 $9.95. ISBN 0-88710-140-2

Roberts, Moss (ed). *Chinese Fairy Tales and Fantasies.* Pantheon 1980 $9.95. ISBN 0-394-73994-9

Shimer, Dorothy Blair (ed). *Rice Bowl Women: Writings by and About Women of China and Japan.* Meridian 1982 $4.95. ISBN 0-452-00827-1

Wai-lim Yip (tr). *Modern Chinese Poetry: Twenty Poets from the Republic of China.* Univ of Iowa Pr 1970 $19.95. ISBN 0-87745-004-8

Whincup, Greg. *The Heart of Chinese Poetry.* Anchor 1987 $8.95. ISBN 0-385-23967-X

See also Vol. 2, World History: Ancient India and China *and* Asia.

JAPANESE LITERATURE

Because early Japan had no written language of its own, Japanese literature was first written in Chinese, which was introduced into Japan in the third century. By the ninth century, however, a Japanese system of writing, based on the Chinese, was developed, and literature in the Japanese language began to develop. For the next five centuries (the period known as the classic age of Japanese literature), poets developed verse forms that continue to be used by Japanese poets today.

In addition to a large body of excellent poetry, early Japanese literature also contained important historical works and travel journals. During this classical period, several women writers made significant literary contributions. For example, Lady Murasaki Shikibu's *Tale of the Genji* (*c.* 1000), a novel about love, human frailty, and the uncertainty of life, is still considered one of Japan's greatest works. Some literary experts consider it to be the world's first novel. Shonagon Sei's *Pillow Book* (*c.* 975) vividly describes life at court in late tenth-century Japan.

The thirteenth through the sixteenth centuries saw the development of the four forms of Japanese theater: the spectacular *kabuki,* or popular theater; the classical *non* tragedies; the *kyogen,* or medieval comedies; and the *bunraku,* or puppet theater. These classic forms continue to occupy a prominent place in Japanese theater, and through the productions of Japanese touring companies *kabuki* has become known worldwide.

This period also saw a change in Japanese poetry. Until this time, most poetry was written in the form of the *tanka,* a five-line stanza with alternating lines of seven and five syllables. During the 1600s, the *tanka* was largely replaced by the *haiku,* a simpler verse form of three lines with five, seven, and five syllables respectively. This change was largely the result of the work of Bashō Matsuo, a poet who used the *haiku* with such skill that he made it Japan's most popular poetic form. Much of Bashō's work is in the form of poetic travel diaries, in which he records his observations as he moved about Japan.

The opening of Japan to the West in the 1800s had a major effect on Japanese literature. As the great works of Western literature were translated into Japanese, they had a powerful influence on Japanese writers, who began to use not only such Western forms as the novel, but also Western ideas and subjects, such as the notion of individual freedom and the search for personal identity.

The twentieth century has seen something of a reversal of this process. As Western writers became more familiar with traditional Japanese literature, they began to incorporate some of its features in their own work. For example, the imagist school of British and American poets in the early part of the twentieth century took many of its ideas from the Japanese haiku, in which an image, rather than an idea or story, is central to the poem. Japanese novelists and short story writers, such as Osamu Dasai, Yukio Mashima, and Yasunari Kawabata, have also gained worldwide recognition during this century and have been widely translated into English and other languages. Kawabata was awarded the Nobel Prize for literature in 1968, the first Japanese literary figure to be so honored.

COLLECTIONS OF JAPANESE LITERATURE IN ENGLISH TRANSLATION

Bashō. *The Narrow Road to the North and Other Travel Sketches.* Penguin 1967 $5.95. ISBN 0-14-044185-9

Bashō. *On Love and Barley: Haiku of Bashō.* Penguin 1986 $3.95. ISBN 0-14-044459-9

Bownas, Geoffrey, and Anthony Thwaite. *The Penguin Book of Japanese Verse.* Penguin 1986 $6.95. ISBN 0-14-058527-3

Darson, Richard M. *Folk Legends of Japan.* Tuttle 1962 $7.95. ISBN 0-8048-0191-6

Henderson, Harold G. (tr). *An Introduction of Haiku: An Anthology of Poems from Bashō to Shiki.* Anchor 1958 $2.50. ISBN 0-385-09376-4

Kawatake Toshio (ed). *Kabuki: Eighteen Traditional Dramas.* Chronicle 1985 $25.00. ISBN 0-87701-366-7

Keene, Donald (ed). *An Anthology of Japanese Literature: From the Earliest Era to the Mid-Nineteenth Century.* Grove 1988 $13.95. ISBN 0-8021-5058-6

Keene, Donald (ed). *Modern Japanese Literature: An Anthology.* Grove 1989 $10.95. ISBN 0-394-17254-X

Levy, Howard S. (tr). *Japanese Love Poems.* Oriental 1976 $8.00. ISBN 0-89986-304-3

Morris, Ivan. *Modern Japanese Stories.* Tuttle 1977 $9.50. ISBN 0-8048-1226-8

Morris, Ivan. *The World of the Shining Prince: Court Life in Ancient Japan.* Penguin 1985 $8.95. ISBN 0-14-055083-6

Murasaki, Shikibu. *The Tale of the Genji.* Vintage 1990 $7.95. ISBN 0-394-72921-8

Rexroth, Kenneth. *One Hundred Poems from the Japanese.* New Directions 1955 $6.95. ISBN 0-8112-0181-3

Shiffert, Edith, and Yuki Sawa (trs). *Anthology of Modern Japanese Poetry.* Tuttle 1971 $4.75. ISBN 0-8048-0672-1

Shimer, Dorothy Blair (ed). *Rice Bowl Women: Writings by and About the Women of China and Japan.* Meridian 1982 $4.95. ISBN 0-452-00827-1

Takaya, Ted T. (ed). *Modern Japanese Drama: An Anthology.* Columbia Univ Pr 1980 $17.00. ISBN 0-231-04685-5

Waley, Arthur. *Japanese Poetry: The Uta.* Univ of Hawaii Pr 1976 $3.95. ISBN 0-8248-0405-8

Waley, Arthur (ed). *The No Plays of Japan.* Grove 1957 $9.95. ISBN 0-394-17206-X

Wheeler, Post (ed). *Tales from the Japanese Storytellers as Collected in the Ho-Dan Zo.* Tuttle 1974 $3.95. ISBN 0-8048-1132-6

SOUTHEAST ASIAN AND KOREAN LITERATURE

Although Westerners consider Southeast Asia a distinct and unified geographical region, the many cultures, languages, and literatures of each country have developed out of a wide variety of traditions and as a result of many different influences. In early times it was primarily the impact of three major religions—Buddhism, Hinduism, and Islam—that produced marked differences among these countries. Later it was the influence of various Western colonial powers. During the nineteenth and twentieth centuries, all of the countries of this area except Thailand fell under the rule of some European nation. Such domination from outside directly affected the development of language and literature in each country. It is often said that the common bond among the Southeast Asian nations is the fact that so many other nations have so greatly influenced their historical, political, and cultural lives.

Myanma (Burma), for example, is closely linked to China by ethnic heritage and language, but it was dominated by India from the eleventh through the eighteenth centuries and by the British in the 1800s and early 1900s. Thus, Myanma's classical literature is primarily an expression of the religious and philosophical ideas of Indian Buddhism. Until the eighteenth century, virtually the only form of Mayanman literature was religious poetry written by Buddhist monks. Late in the century, some new forms of literature—popular dramas and long poems on nonreligious themes—began to appear. During the nineteenth century, under British rule, such Western forms as the novel and short story were adopted by Myanmanese writers.

In Indonesia and Malaya, the existence of over 200 languages—most with no written form—made the development of a native literature almost impossible. The earliest writings in those countries grew out of the Hindu religion, which was brought to the region from India. With the spread of Islam into the area in the fourteenth through the sixteenth centuries, a Malay literature, written in Arabic script, began to develop. With the arrival of the Dutch in Indonesia in the seventeenth century, Indonesian culture began to be influenced by Western ideas. This influence grew and remained strong well into the twentieth century, even though Indonesia achieved full independence from the Netherlands in the 1950s.

While the British never dominated Malaysia to the extent that the Dutch did Indonesia, their influence on Malaysian culture and literature was likewise substantial.

Korean literature was dominated by the Chinese, as was all Korean life, until well into the nineteenth century. Even though a workable Korean alphabet was developed in the 1440s, much of the literature of Korea continued to be written in Chinese. The first work published in the new Korean alphabet was "The Song of the Dragons Flying to Heaven" (c. 1450), a long poem in praise of the Yi dynasty. Some of the most famous Korean literature consists of poems, called *sijo*, which were written from the late sixteenth through the early nineteenth centuries. Early Korean prose consisted generally of novels written in imitation of Chinese forms and often written in the Chinese language as well. Modern Korean literature is marked by an effort to break away from classical tradition. Many modern Korean writers have adopted Western forms and are reflecting on such modern themes as the importance of social protest and the need for political justice.

China also strongly influenced the literatures of Vietnam, Cambodia, and Laos. This influence extended well into the nineteenth century. Although the French had been in the area since the 1500s, France did not become a true colonial power until late in the nineteenth century, when it assumed political rule over almost the entire region. The French influence on Vietnamese and Cambodian literature was powerful, since most writers from these countries received their educations in French schools. Even today, most Vietnamese literature is largely available only in French translation.

COLLECTIONS OF SOUTHEAST ASIAN AND KOREAN LITERATURE IN ENGLISH TRANSLATION

Aveling, Harry. *Contemporary Indonesian Poetry.* Univ of Queensland Pr 1975 $16.95. ISBN 0-7022-0932-5

Balaban, John (ed and tr). *Ca Dao Vietnam: Bilingual Anthology of Vietnamese Folk Poetry.* Unicorn Pr 1980 $8.95. ISBN 0-87775-129-3

Chung-Wa Chung (ed). *Modern Korean Short Stories.* Heinemann 1981 $9.00 ISBN 0-686-79035-5

Cocks, S. W. *Tales and Legends of Ancient Burma.* AMS (repr of 1916 ed) $17.00. ISBN 0-404-16068-9

Hendon, Rufus S. *Six Indonesian Short Stories.* Yale Univ Pr 1968 $5.50. ISBN 0-938692-17-8

Hollenbeck, Peter (ed). *Vietnam Literature Anthology.* American Poetry 1990 $10.95. ISBN 0-930933-14-1

Huynk S. Thong. *Tale of Kieu.* Yale Univ Pr 1987 $12.95. ISBN 0-300-04051-2

Lee, Peter H. (ed). *Anthology of Korean Literature: From Early Times to the Nineteenth Century.* Univ of Hawaii Pr 1981 $12.00. ISBN 0-8248-0756-1

Maung A. Htin. *Burmese Drama: A Study with Translations of Burmese Plays.* Greenwood 1978 (repr of 1957 ed) $35.00. ISBN 0-313-20381-4

Raffel, Burton (ed). *Anthology of Modern Indonesian Poetry.* SUNY 1968 $44.50. ISBN 0-87395-024-0

Stryk, Lucien, and Takashi Ihemoto (eds and trs). *The Penguin Book of Zen Poetry.* Penguin 1981 $6.95. ISBN 0-14-042247-1

Stryk, Lucien (ed). *World of the Buddha: An Introduction to Buddhist Literature.* Grove 1982 $12.95. ISBN 0-8021-3095-X

Toth, Marian. *Tales from Thailand: Folklore, Culture and History.* Tuttle 1983 $14.50. ISBN 0-8048-0563-6

U. Htin Aung. *Burmese Folk Tales.* AMS (repr of 1948 ed) $22.00. ISBN 0-404-16828-0

✨ LANGUAGE ARTS ✨

LANGUAGE

The history of American English begins with the first British colonists who came to North America early in the seventeenth century. Soon after their arrival, the English language they spoke began to undergo subtle changes. They adopted American Indian names for things they had never seen in their native country, and they developed new words for new aspects of colonial life. Throughout the 150 years of British colonial rule, this slow language change continued, so that by the time of the American Revolution, there were noticeable differences between American and British English. Independence increased the speed of the change, and by the two hundredth anniversary of American independence in 1976, the United States and Britain were, in the words of British dramatist and critic George Bernard Shaw, "two nations divided by a common language."

By the middle of the twentieth century, the state of English in America had become a subject of much criticism and commentary. Writers like Edwin Newman and William Safire have protested against the careless, pompous, and deceptive use of American English, while others like Hugh Rank have warned

Initial page of the Gospel of Matthew.
From *Lindisfarne Gospels* (Eighth Century).
Courtesy of Art Resource.

about the increasing pressures on American citizens from propaganda, advertising, and other forms of persuasive language. Noted linguistic scholar and politician S. I. Hayakawa has formed an organization devoted to having English proclaimed the official language of the United States. On the other hand, with the increasing influence of mass media in American life, many critics contend that the focus of English language instruction in American schools should shift away from an emphasis on "correctness" in written and spoken expression to an understanding of the ways language can be used to manipulate thought and behavior.

The writers and books presented in the Language section deal with such topics as the history of the English language, American dialects, jargon and slang, English grammar and usage, language and social class, how the English language conveys meaning, the power of words, advertising, propaganda, language and politics, and the varieties of English spoken around the world. Many of the writers deal with more than one of these topics in a single book and address other issues besides the ones listed. Because the study of language is intricate and complex, in its pursuit one thing invariably leads to another. The categories in this section reflect the changes taking place in English language instruction in American schools as the teaching of narrow "do and don't" rules of "correct" speech and writing gives way to broader instruction in the many shapes and uses of language. The sources included in this section represent a wide range of expert opinion on the way people use spoken and written language as well as on the changes taking place in American English.

PROCESSES: THE HISTORY OF MODERN ENGLISH

*Baron, Dennis. *The English-Only Question: An Official Language for Americans?* Yale Univ Pr 1990 $22.50. ISBN 0-300-04852-1 An analysis of the debate concerning English as the sole language of the United States; interesting to young adult students.

Baron, Dennis. *Grammar and Good Taste: Reforming the American Language.* Yale Univ Pr 1982 $10.95. ISBN 0-300-03080-0

Baugh, Albert, and Thomas Cable. *A History of the English Language.* Prentice 1978 $42.33. ISBN 0-13-389239-5

*Dillard, J. L. *Black English: Its History and Usage in the United States.* Random 1973 $7.95. ISBN 0-394-71872-0 Edition prepared especially for teens; explains why African-American English is more than a dialect and how it has developed its own unique grammar and vocabulary.

Kennedy, Arthur G. *Current English: A Study of Present-Day Usages and Tendencies, Including Pronunciation, Spelling, Grammatical Practice, Word-Coining, and the Shifting of Meanings.* Greenwood 1970 repr of 1935 ed $37.50. ISBN 0-8371-3543-5

Lindblad, K. E. *Noah Webster's Pronunciation and Modern New England Speech.* Kraus 1954 $15.00. ISBN 0-8115-0191-4

*Lowth, Robert. *Short Introduction to English Grammar.* Schol Facsimiles 1979 repr of 1775 ed $50.00. ISBN 0-8201-1332-8 The book that brought misery to generations by using Latin parts of speech to describe English grammar—a difficult fit at best; worth a look for historical interest.

*McCrum, Robert, William Cran, and Robert MacNeil. *The Story of English.* Penguin 1982 $14.95. ISBN 0-14-009435-0 The history of English in all its varieties from Anglo-Saxon England to high-tech American; a useful, readable, and comprehensive overview; the companion volume to Robert MacNeil's PBS television documentary series.

Meritt, H. D. *Old English Glosses: A Collection.* Kraus (repr of 1945 ed) $5.00. ISBN 0-527-03350-X

Millward, C. M. *Biography of the English Language.* Holt 1989 $20.00. ISBN 0-03-059431-6

*Murray, Lindley. *English Grammar.* Schol Facsimiles (repr of 1824 ed) $50.00. ISBN

0-8201-1369-7 Popularized false "rules" of grammar that still persist despite their awkwardness and inappropriateness, such as "Never end a sentence with a preposition"; worth a look for historical interest.

Smith, Jeremy. *The English of Chaucer: Essays on the Language of Late Medieval English Authors and Scribes.* Pergamon 1989 $31.50. ISBN 0-08-036403-9

Smitherman, Geneva. *Talkin and Testifyin: The Language of Black America.* Wayne State Univ Pr 1986 $14.50. ISBN 0-8143-1805-3

Stratmann, Francis. *Middle English Dictionary.* Oxford Univ Pr 1981 $68.00. ISBN 0-19-863106-5

WEBSTER, NOAH   1758–1843

Noah Webster was born in Hartford, Connecticut, and educated at Yale University. He began to teach immediately after graduating from Yale, then studied law and was admitted to the bar. However, Webster found he preferred teaching and returned to the classroom.

In 1783, Webster published *Webster's Spelling Book,* a text that sold over 80 million copies during the next 100 years. In 1828, he published *An American Dictionary of the English Language,* the book that made his name familiar to every subsequent generation of Americans. The dictionary has been through several revisions over the past 150 years; in the 1961 revision, its title was changed from "American" to "International."

Webster's influence on the history of American English can hardly be exaggerated. In an effort to promote distinctly "American" English, the spellings in Webster's books were made deliberately different from those used in Britain. Thus, for example, the British *cheque* became *check, colour* became *color, plough* became *plow,* and so·on. In addition, Webster designated the variety of English spoken in his native New England as "correct," with the result that every other American dialect was considered "incorrect," much to the dismay of generations of school children in all the other parts of the country.

Webster's dictionary and grammar books also established and reinforced a number of absurd grammatical "rules" that had nothing to do with the way English is actually written or spoken. For example, he maintained that sentences must not end in prepositions and infinitives must not be split, "rules" that were totally artificial creations, since some of the greatest writers in the English language did not observe them. Despite this, Webster's books did help to simplify and standardize American spelling and hastened the recognition of American English as a language significantly different from the English used in Britain.

BOOKS BY WEBSTER

An American Dictionary of the English Language (1828). Am Christian Pr 1967 facs of 1828 ed $32.00. ISBN 0-912498-03-X

An American Selection of Lessons in Reading and Speaking. Ayer 1975 $20.00. ISBN 0-405-06386-5

Collection of Papers on Political, Literary and Moral Subjects (1843). Burt Franklin 1968 repr of 1843 ed $24.50. ISBN 0-8337-3707-4

Elementary Spelling Book (1829). Beatty 1974 repr of 1873 ed $4.95. ISBN 0-87948-047-5

Grammatical Institute of the English Language (1785). Schol Facsimiles (repr of 1800 ed) $50.00. ISBN 0-8201-1351-4

The Webster Bible (1833). Baker Bk 1987 $29.95. ISBN 0-8010-9684-7

BOOK ABOUT WEBSTER

Commager, Henry. *Noah Webster's American Spelling Book.* Teachers College 1963 $5.00. ISBN 0-8077-1176-4 Details the influence of the "blue-backed speller" that replaced the *New England Primer* as the most common elementary school textbook; it established current American spellings and gave moral advice by means of little stories.

AMERICAN DIALECTS

Davis, Lawrence. *English Dialectology: An Introduction.* Univ of Alabama Pr 1983 $10.95. ISBN 0-8173-0114-3

Fisiak, Jacek (ed). *Historical Dialectology.* Mouton 1988 $167.50. ISBN 0-89925-434-9

*Hendrickson, Robert. *American Talk: The Words and Ways of American Dialects.* Penguin 1983 $7.95. ISBN 0-14-009421-0 Geographically arranged survey of popular speech, offering a grand tour of Americans' colorful ways with words.

Herman, Lewis, and Marguerite Herman. *American Dialects.* Theatre Arts 1959 $19.95. ISBN 0-87830-003-1

Reed, Carroll. *Dialects of American English.* Univ of Massachusetts Pr 1977 $7.95. ISBN 0-87023-233-9

*Shuy, Roger. *Discovering American Dialects.* NCTE 1967 $4.95. ISBN 0-8141-1206-4 Written for adults but useful for able student readers; concise and concrete introduction to the science of dialectology with many examples of regional vocabulary.

Each of the following books offers entertaining and concise looks at a particular regional dialect, and all are especially recommended for young people.

Chadbourn, W. R. *How to Speak L.A.* Price Stern 1984 $1.50. ISBN 0-8431-0949-1

Chadbourn, W. R. *How to Speak New York.* Price Stern 1986 $1.50. ISBN 0-8431-1573-4

Gates, Gary. *How to Speak Dutchified English.* Good Bks 1987 $5.95. ISBN 0-934672-58-X

Jacobs, Howard. *Cajun Night Before Christmas.* Pelican 1973 $11.95. ISBN 0-88289-002-6

Lewis, Gerald. *How to Talk Yankee.* Thorndike 1979 $1.95. ISBN 0-89621-054-5

Mitchell, Steve. *How to Speak Southern.* Bantam 1987 $2.95. ISBN 0-553-25667-X

Mohr, Howard. *How to Talk Minnesotan.* Penguin 1987 $7.95. ISBN 0-14-009284-6

Randolph, Vance, and George Wilson. *Down in the Holler: A Gallery of Ozark Folk Speech.* Univ of Oklahoma Pr 1979 $12.95. ISBN 0-8061-1535-1

Rosten, Leo. *Hooray for Yiddish.* Simon 1984 $8.95. ISBN 0-671-43026-2

Rosten, Leo. *The Joys of Yiddish.* Pocket 1991 $4.95. ISBN 0-317-568-76-0

Rosten, Leo. *The Joys of Yinglish.* NAL 1990 $14.95. ISBN 0-452-26543-6

Smith, Diann. *Down-Home Talk.* Macmillan 1988 $3.95. ISBN 0-02-045041-9

Sothern, James. *Cajun Dictionary: A Collection of Commonly Used Words and Phrases by the People of South Louisiana.* Marine Educ 1986 $5.50. ISBN 0-934114-79-X

Wilder, Roy, Jr. *You All Spoken Here.* Penguin 1987 $6.95. ISBN 0-14-008404-5

McDAVID, RAVEN I., JR.   1911–

Raven McDavid, Jr., was born and educated in Greenville, South Carolina. He did his undergraduate work at Furman University and completed his master's and doctoral degrees at Duke University. He then did additional study at the University of Michigan, the University of North Carolina, and Yale University. In 1957, after teaching English at a number of colleges and universities, McDavid joined the faculty of the University of Chicago in 1957.

In 1958, with fellow scholar W. Nelson Francis, McDavid published

Structure of American English, a basic work on the way American English is structured and used. He then began to write about the subject for which he is most famous—American dialects, that is, different patterns of speech that vary by region. With Hans Kurath he published *The Pronunciation of English in the Atlantic States* (1961), a study of the different pronunciation patterns along the eastern seaboard of the United States. In 1964, he served as editor for the massive *Linguistic Atlas of the Middle and South Atlantic States,* a work that maps the different dialects spoken in the states along the Atlantic coast from New York to Florida. He also edited a similar study of the north central states in 1952. In 1968, he edited a revised edition of U.S. critic and journalist H. L. Mencken's classic work *The American Language.* (See Mencken, Vol. 1, Language: American Dialects.) McDavid's more recent works have examined the relationship between dialect and culture in America and the use of dialect in American humor.

McDavid's studies of dialects have been a major contribution to an understanding of the wide variety of English spoken in the United States and of how each variety reflects the lives of the people who speak it.

BOOKS BY MCDAVID

Dialect Labels in the Merriam Third [Dictionary] (1967). Univ of Alabama Pr 1967 $2.75. ISBN 0-8173-0647-1

Dialects in Culture (1979). Univ of Alabama Pr 1979 $25.00. ISBN 0-87023-233-9

Linguistic Atlas of the Middle and South Atlantic States: Fascicles 1 and 2 (1980). (coauthored with Raymond O'Cain) Univ of Chicago Pr 1980 No. 1 $15.00. ISBN 0-226-55742-1. No. 2 $15.00. ISBN 0-226-55744-8

Mirth of a Nation: America's Great Dialect (1983). (coauthored with Walter Blair) Univ of Minnesota Pr 1983 $35.00. ISBN 0-8166-1022-3

The Pronunciation of English in the Atlantic States: Based on the Linguistic Atlas of the Eastern United States (1961). (coauthored with Hans Kurath) Univ of Alabama Pr 1982 $25.00. ISBN 0-8173-0129-1

Varieties of American English: Essays by Raven I. McDavid, Jr. (1980). Stanford Univ Pr 1980 $38.50. ISBN 0-8047-0982-3

ETYMOLOGY

*Ammer, Christine. *It's Raining Cats and Dogs . . . and Other Beastly Expressions.* Dell 1988 $5.95. ISBN 0-440-20507-7 Offers 1,000 short essays on widely used expressions involving animals, arranged in nine categories for easy access.

Ayers, Donald. *English Words from Latin and Greek Elements.* Univ of Arizona Pr 1986 $10.00. ISBN 0-8165-0978-6

Bauer, Laurie. *English Word-Formation.* Cambridge Univ Pr 1983 $14.95. ISBN 0-521-28492-9

Black, Donald Chain. *Spoonerisms, Sycophants, and Sops.* Harper 1989 $15.45. ISBN 0-06-015886-7

Cannon, Garland. *Historical Change and English Word-Formation: Recent Vocabulary.* Peter Lang 1987 $35.95. ISBN 0-8204-0403-9

Ciardi, John. *Good Words to You: An All-New Browser's Dictionary and Native's Guide to the Unknown American Language.* Harper 1987 $19.45. ISBN 0-06-015691-0

*Claiborne, Robert. *Loose Cannons and Red Herrings.* Ballantine 1989 $3.95. ISBN 0-345-36337-X Explains the origins of more than 1,000 common expressions that once were vivid figures of speech but have since become clichés.

Cole, Sylvia, and Abraham Lass. *The Facts on File Dictionary of Twentieth-Century Allusions.* Facts on File 1990 $21.95. ISBN 0-8160-1915-0

Feldman, David. *Who Put the Butter in Butterfly and Other Fearless Investigations into Our Illogical Language.* Harper 1989 $15.95. ISBN 0-06-016072-1

*Freeman, Morton. *The Story Behind the Word.* ISI Pr 1985 $14.95. ISBN 0-89495-047-9 Brief essays on the histories of common words; concise and packed with interesting facts.

*Funk, Charles E. *Heavens to Betsy and Other Curious Sayings.* Harper 1986 $5.95. ISBN 0-06-091353-3 Fascinating and amusing history of common expressions—a continuation of Funk's earlier *Hog on Ice.*

*Funk, Charles E. *Hog on Ice and Other Curious Expressions.* Harper 1985 $5.95. ISBN 0-06-091259-6 Fascinating history of common expressions such as "wet blanket," "in the bag," and "cock-and-bull story."

*Funk, Charles E. *Horsefeathers and Other Curious Words.* Harper 1986 $5.95. ISBN 0-06-091352-5 Continues Funk's sleuthing begun in *Thereby Hangs a Tale,* exposing the histories of many unusual words.

*Funk, Charles E. *Thereby Hangs a Tale: Stories of Curious Word Origins.* Harper 1985 $5.95. ISBN 0-06-091260-X Surprising, amusing etymologies of single words; an example is the evolution of "glamour" from "grammar."

Morris, William, and Mary Morris. *Morris Dictionary of Word and Phrase Origins.* Harper 1987 $24.50. ISBN 0-06-015862-X

*Robinson, Sandra. *Origins: Bringing Words to Life.* Teachers and Writers Coll Pr 1989 $16.95. ISBN 0-915924-90-0 Etymological dictionary prepared especially for young word sleuths.

*Rogers, James. *The Dictionary of Clichés.* Ballantine 1986 $3.95. ISBN 0-345-33814-6 Explains the roots of over 2,000 colorful clichés—amusing and informative.

*Sarnoff, Jane, and Reynold Ruffins. *Words: A Book About the Origins of Everyday Words and Phrases.* Macmillan 1981 $11.95. ISBN 0-684-16958-4 A simple introduction to the history of familiar words and phrases.

Shipley, Joseph T. *Dictionary of Word Origins.* Littlefield 1979 $10.50. ISBN 0-8226-0121-4

Weekley, Ernest. *Etymological Dictionary of Modern English.* 2 vols. Dover 1967 $17.00. ISBNs 0-486-21873-2, 0-486-21874-0

JARGON AND SLANG

Adorno, Theodor. *Jargon of Authenticity.* Northwestern Univ Pr 1973 $10.95. ISBN 0-8101-0657-4

*Artman, John. *Slanguage.* Good Apple 1980 $7.95. ISBN 0-916456-60-9 Most readable explanation available of the nature, purpose, limitations, and contributions of slang, especially as used among teens.

Berger, Melvin. *Space Talk.* Messner 1985 $9.29. ISBN 0-671-54290-7

*Chapman, Robert. *New Dictionary of American Slang.* Harper 1989 $23.45. ISBN 0-06-181157-2 Some 20,000 entries with examples of usage, etymologies, and notations regarding periods of popularity.

Green, Jonathan. *Newspeak: A Dictionary of Jargon.* Routledge 1984 $21.50. ISBN 0-7100-9685-2

Green, Jonathan. *Slang Thesaurus.* David and Charles 1988 $29.95. ISBN 0-241-11851-4

*James, P. T. *Military Jargon.* Beau Lac 1985 $1.50. ISBN 0-911980-15-6 Specialized vocabulary for military strategies, weapons, supplies, and other aspects of combat.

Lewin, Esther, and Albert Lewin. *The Thesaurus of Slang.* Facts on File 1988 $40.00. ISBN 0-8160-1742-5

Mulligan, William (ed). *Historical Dictionary of American Industrial Language.* Greenwood 1988 $55.00. ISBN 0-313-24171-6

*Richey, Jim. *Entertainment Language.* Janus Bks 1979 $3.95. ISBN 0-915510-34-0 Specialized vocabulary for people, activities, and equipment in the entertainment world, including show-biz slang.

*Rodlauer, Ruth. *Computer Tech Talk.* Childrens 1984 $14.60. ISBN 0-516-08252-3 Specialized vocabulary from the world of computer technology and its users.

Vasquez, Librado. *Regional Dictionary of Chicano Slang.* Jenkins 1975 $13.50. ISBN 0-8363-0083-1

ALL IN THE FAMILY: ENGLISH AROUND THE WORLD

*Bowles, Colin. *G'Day: Teach Yourself Australian in 20 Easy Lessons.* Salem Hse 1987 $5.95.
   ISBN 0-207-15431-7 Entertaining and instructive approach to the dialect popularized by Australian actor Paul Hogan in the movie *Crocodile Dundee.*
Brook, G. L. *English Dialects.* Basil Blackwell 1978 $34.95. ISBN 0-233-95641-7
Collins, Peter, and David Blair (eds). *Australian English: The Language of a New Society.* Univ
   of Queensland Pr 1989 $39.95. ISBN 0-7022-2110-4
*Crystal, David. *The English Language.* Penguin 1980 $8.95. ISBN 0-14-022730-X Al-
   though written for adults, a fascinating study for teens who know how to skim;
   examines the structures, history, and usage of English from Australia to Zimbabwe; a guided tour through the most widely spoken language in the world.
Schur, Norman. *British English, A to Zed.* Facts on File 1987 $35.00. ISBN 0-8160-1635-6
Smith, Larry. *English for Cross-Cultural Communication.* St. Martin's 1981 $37.50. ISBN
   0-312-25423-7

PRINCIPLES OF ENGLISH AND DESCRIPTIVE LINGUISTICS

Baker, C. L. *English Syntax.* MIT Pr 1989 $27.50. ISBN 0-262-02287-7
Fromkin, Victoria, and Robert Rodman. *An Introduction to Language.* Holt 1988 $12.95.
   ISBN 0-03-006532-1
Jesperson, Otto. *Growth and Structure of the English Language.* Univ of Chicago Pr 1982
   $8.00. ISBN 0-226-39877-3
Myers, Doris T. *Understanding Language.* Boynton 1984 $5.95. ISBN 0-86709-083-4
Parker, Frank. *Linguistics for Non-Linguists.* Pro Ed 1986 $16.50. ISBN 0-89079-275-5
Robins, R. H. *Short History of Linguistics.* Longman 1980 $14.95. ISBN 0-582-55288-5

CHOMSKY, NOAM   1928–

Noam Chomsky was born and educated in Philadelphia, Pennsylvania, and
went on to study at the University of Pennsylvania, where he received a Ph.D.
in linguistics in 1955. He then took a position as professor of linguistics at the
Massachusetts Institute of Technology, where he continues to teach.

Chomsky has had a substantial influence on modern theories of language
development and grammar. He has proposed two basic and extremely influential theories. First, he maintains that the structure of a language exists on two
levels, the surface level, which is what people say and hear, and on a deeper
level, where sentences are changed, or transformed, according to certain basic
principles that are the true underlying grammar of the language. Second,
Chomsky proposes that human beings are born with a built-in capacity to learn
language, so that language learning is not merely the result of a child hearing
words and repeating them.

Since Chomsky first argued these theories in the late 1950s and early 1960s,
he and others have accumulated much evidence that substantiates his ideas.
The vast majority of linguists now accept his propositions, although some
critics still doubt that Chomsky will ever be able to prove his theories completely.

Chomsky's theoretical work has had virtually no effect on language and
grammar teaching in the schools. School grammar, which deals only with the
surface level of language, continues to be based on 200-year-old definitions

and principles of "correct" and "incorrect" language that have long been discredited by linguistic scholars.

Chomsky has also engaged in political debate and has written several books on foreign policy that are not listed here.

BOOKS BY CHOMSKY

Aspects of the Theory of Syntax (1965). MIT Pr 1965 $8.95. ISBN 0-262-53007-4
The Knowledge of Language: Its Nature, Origin, and Use (1986). Praeger 1986 $11.95. ISBN 0-275-91761-4
Language and Politics (1989). Black Rose 1989 $16.95. ISBN 0-921689-34-9
Language and Responsibility (1978). Pantheon 1978 $4.95. ISBN 0-394-73619-2
Necessary Illusions: Thought Control in Democratic Societies (1989). South End 1989 $16.00. ISBN 0-89608-366-7
Reflections on Language (1975). Pantheon 1975 $7.95. ISBN 0-394-73123-9

BOOKS ABOUT CHOMSKY

Lyons, John. *Noam Chomsky.* Penguin 1978 $5.95. ISBN 0-14-004370-5 Good, readable account of and commentary on Chomsky's ideas and theories.
Smith, Neil, and Deirdre Wilson. *Modern Linguistics: The Results of Chomsky's Revolution.* Penguin 1991 $9.95. ISBN 0-14-013496-4 Clear evaluation of Chomsky's contributions to linguistic science in light of new knowledge about language acquisition, semantics, sound systems, and linguistic universals.

GRAMMAR AND USAGE

Bernstein, Theodore M. *Miss Thistlebottom's Hobgoblins: The Careful Writer's Guide to the Taboos, Bugbears and Outmoded Rules of English Usage.* Simon 1984 $6.95. ISBN 0-671-50404-5
Coe, Graham. *Colloquial English.* Routledge 1981 $14.95. ISBN 0-7100-0740-X
Follett, Wilson. *Modern American Usage: A Guide.* Hill & Wang 1966 $10.95. ISBN 0-8090-0139-X
Marckwardt, Albert H. *American English.* Oxford Univ Pr 1980 $8.60. ISBN 0-19-502609-8
Mencken, H. L. *The American Language.* Raven I. McDavid, Jr. (ed). Knopf 1977 $22.95. ISBN 0-394-73315-0
*Morris, William, and Mary Morris (eds). *Harper Dictionary of Contemporary Usage.* Harper 1987 $22.00. ISBN 0-06-181606-X Basic usage guide to slang, dialects, formal and informal words, word origins, and the differences between written and spoken language.
Pooley, Robert A. *The Teaching of English Usage.* NCTE 1974 $9.95. ISBN 0-8141-2778-6

MENCKEN, H. L. (HENRY LOUIS) 1880–1956

H. L. Mencken was born in Baltimore, Maryland, a city he considered home despite his many years in New York. As a child he attended Professor Friedrich Knapp's Institute, a private school for children of German descent. He completed his secondary education at Baltimore Polytechnic Institute, from which he graduated at the age of 16.

Mencken wanted to be a writer but was obligated to work in his father's cigar factory. When his father died suddenly in 1899, Mencken immediately sought a job at the Baltimore *Herald.* Though he began with no experience in journalism, he quickly learned every job at the newspaper and at age 25 became its editor.

Mencken went on to build himself a reputation as one of America's most brilliant writers and literary critics. His basic approach was to question everything and to accept no limits on personal freedom. He attacked organized religion, American cultural and literary standards, and every aspect of American life that he found shallow, ignorant, or false—which was almost everything. From the 1920s until his death, Mencken's sharp wit and penetrating social commentary made him one of the most highly regarded—and fiercely hated—of American social critics. He was later memorialized in the dramatic portrait of the cynical journalist in the play and film *Inherit the Wind*.

Shortly after World War I, Mencken began a project that was to fascinate him for the rest of his life: a study of the American language and how it had evolved from British English. In 1919 he published *The American Language: A Preliminary Inquiry into the Development of English in the United States.* To his and his publisher's surprise, the book sold out very quickly; its wit and nonscholarly approach attracted many readers who would not normally buy a book on such a subject. In 1936, a revised and enlarged edition was published, and in 1945 and 1948, supplements were added. The work shows not only how American English differs from British English, but how the 300-year American experience shaped the American dialect. Thus the book, still considered a classic in its field, is both a linguistic and a social history of the United States.

BOOKS BY MENCKEN

The American Language (1919). Raven I. McDavid, Jr. (ed). Knopf 1977 $22.95. ISBN 0-394-73315-0

The American Mercury: Facsimile Edition of Volume One 1924 (1924). (coedited with George Jean Nathan) Garber 1984 $50.00. ISBN 0-89345-050-2

The American Scene: A Reader. Knopf 1965 $20.00. ISBN 0-394-43594-X

A Choice of Days. Knopf 1980 $12.95. ISBN 0-394-50795-9

The Editor, the Bluenose, and the Prostitute: H. L. Mencken's History of the "Hatrack" Censorship Case. Rinehart 1988 $19.50. ISBN 0-911797-40-8

Prejudices: A Selection. Random 1958 $4.95. ISBN 0-394-70058-9

Vintage Mencken. Alistair Cooke (ed). Random 1955 $5.95. ISBN 0-394-70025-2

BOOKS ABOUT MENCKEN

Douglas, George. *H. L. Mencken: Critic of American Life*. Shoe String 1978 $27.50. ISBN 0-208-01693-7 Introduces a new generation to the man who wrote, "Democracy is the theory that the common people know what they want and deserve to get it good and hard."

Rodgers, Marion (ed). *Mencken and Sara: A Life in Letters*. McGraw 1987 $22.95. ISBN 0-07-041505-6 A record of the brief but loving marriage between the middle-aged Mencken and the young Sara that ended with Sara's death from tuberculosis in 1935; perhaps the best source for learning about Mencken's extraordinary wife.

Singleton, Marvin. *H. L. Mencken and the American Mercury Adventure*. Duke Univ Pr 1962 $14.95. ISBN 0-8223-0351-5 Examines Mencken's entry into mass-market publishing and his support of such young writers as Sinclair Lewis and Theodore Dreiser.

IDIOMS

Blumenfeld, Warren S. *Pretty Ugly: More Oxymorons and Other Illogical Expressions That Make Absolute Sense*. Putnam 1989 $4.95. ISBN 0-399-51493-7

Brock, Suzanne. *Idiom's Delight: Fascinating Phrases and Linguistic Eccentricities*. Times Bks 1988 $13.45. ISBN 0-8129-1722-7

*Collis, Harry. *Colloquial English*. Prentice 1987 $6.95. ISBN 0-13-150103-8 Explains idiomatic terms and phrases like "hot dog" and "step on it;" many examples provide much amusement and information.

Cowie, A. P., *et al. Oxford Dictionary of Current Idiomatic English.* 2 vols. Oxford Univ Pr. Vol. 1 *Verbs with Prepositions and Particles.* 1975 $19.95. ISBN 0-19-431145-7. Vol. 2 *Phrase, Clause and Sentence Idioms.* 1983 $19.95. ISBN 0-19-431150-3

Gulland, Daphne M., and David G. Hinds-Howell. *The Penguin Dictionary of English Idioms.* Penguin 1989 $7.95. ISBN 0-14-051135-0

Howard, Julie. *Idioms in American Life.* Prentice 1987 $6.95. ISBN 0-13-450207-8

*Reeves, George. *Idioms in Action.* Newbury Bks 1975 $12.50. ISBN 0-912066-63-6 Humorous and well-selected idioms explained in ways that make this special usage concept easy to grasp.

SOCIOLINGUISTICS

Brasch, Walter M. *Black English and the Mass Media.* Univ Pr of America 1984 $15.25. ISBN 0-8191-3978-5

Gregory, Michael, and Suzanne Carroll. *Language and Situation: Language Varieties and Their Social Contexts.* Routledge 1978 $12.95. ISBN 0-7100-8773-X

Labov, William. *Sociolinguistic Patterns.* Univ of Penn Pr 1973 $14.95. ISBN 0-8122-7657-4

Phillips, K. C. *Language and Class in Victorian England.* Basil Blackwell 1984 $29.95. ISBN 0-631-13689-4

Pride, Janet (ed). *Sociolinguistics.* Penguin 1986 $6.95. ISBN 0-14-022658-3

Trudgill, Peter. *Sociolinguistics: An Introduction to Language and Society.* Penguin 1983 $6.95. ISBN 0-14-022479-3

Williams, Raymond. *Keywords: A Vocabulary of Culture and Society.* Oxford Univ Pr 1976 $9.95. ISBN 0-19-520469-7

SEMANTICS

Chase, Stuart. *The Tyranny of Words.* Harcourt 1959 $7.95. ISBN 0-15-692394-7

Fabun, Don. *Communications: The Transfer of Meaning.* ISGS 1987 $3.85. ISBN 0-02-477490-1

Herman, Ethel, and Karen Everett. *Semantics for Teens.* LinguiSystems 1989 $19.95. ISBN 1-55999-070-8

Keffer, Christine, and Carolyn Long. *Semantic Fitness.* LinguiSystems 1986 $29.95. ISBN 1-55999-069-4

Lee, Irving. *How to Talk with People.* ISGS 1952 $9.00. ISBN 0-918970-30-X

Lee, Irving. *Language Habits in Human Affairs: An Introduction to General Semantics.* Greenwood 1979 $69.50. ISBN 0-313-20962-6

Lee, Irving (ed). *The Language of Wisdom and Folly.* ISGS 1977 $6.00. ISBN 0-918970-00-8

Lee, Irving, and Laura Lee. *Handling Barriers in Communication.* ISGS 1978 $7.50. ISBN 0-918970-01-6

Lutz, William. *Beyond Nineteen Eighty-Four: Doublespeak in a Post-Orwellian Age.* NCTE 1989 $10.95. ISBN 0-8141-0285-9

*Minteer, Catherine. *Words and What They Do to You: Beginning Lessons in General Semantics for Junior and Senior High School.* ISGS 1971 $6.00. ISBN 0-910780-06-4 Perhaps the best introduction to how people attach meaning to words and how the meanings in turn come to control the individual's thought and action.

Morain, Mary (ed). *Bridging Worlds Through General Semantics.* ISGS 1984 $12.00. ISBN 0-918970-34-2

Morain, Mary (ed). *Classroom Exercises in General Semantics.* ISGS 1980 $7.00. ISBN 0-918970-26-1

*Neaman, Judith, and Carole Silver. *Kind Words: A Thesaurus of Euphemisms.* Facts on File

1989 $22.95. ISBN 0-8160-1896-0 Useful compilation of euphemisms—"nice" or polite ways of talking about unpleasant subjects; readable and entertaining.

Ogden, Charles, and I. A. Richards. *The Meaning of Meaning.* Harcourt 1989 $8.95. ISBN 0-15-658446-8

Safire, William. *Safire's Political Dictionary: The New Language of Politics.* Random 1978 $17.95. ISBN 0-394-50261-2

Ullmann, Stephen. *Semantics: An Introduction to the Science of Meaning.* Barnes 1978 $9.95. ISBN 0-06-497076-0

HAYAKAWA, S. I. (SAMUEL ICHIYE)   1906–

S. I. Hayakawa was born in Vancouver, British Columbia, in Canada, where he attended school. He earned a bachelor's degree at the University of Manitoba and a master's from McGill University in Montreal before completing a Ph.D. at the University of Wisconsin in 1935. Hayakawa taught at several American colleges and universities before becoming a professor of English at San Francisco State College (now San Francisco State University) in 1955. He became President of San Francisco State in 1969. In 1977 he was elected to the United States Senate in which he served one term before retiring in 1983.

Hayakawa achieved national recognition in 1941 with the publication of *Language in Action.* The book is a readable but scholarly introduction to the branch of language study called semantics (the study of meaning). It received the unusual distinction for an academic book of being named a Book-of-the-Month Club selection. Through Hayakawa's book, millions of Americans became aware of how and why words mean what they do. Phrases like "The word is not the thing" (meaning that there is always a gap between what we say—the word—and what we mean—the thing) became fashionable all over America. The book made the best-seller list and continued to be popular for several years. In 1949, Hayakawa revised his work extensively and retitled it *Language in Thought and Action,* the title it retains today in its third revision.

As schools and colleges have become more concerned about teaching students how to understand the ways in which they are affected by language, Hayakawa's works are once again finding their way into the nation's classrooms.

BOOKS BY HAYAKAWA

Choose the Right Word: A Modern Guide to Synonyms. Harper 1987 $12.95. ISBN 0-06-091393-2

Language in Thought and Action (1949). (coauthored with Alan R. Hayakawa) Harcourt 1990 $14.00. ISBN 0-15-550120-8

Symbol, Status, and Personality (1963). Harcourt 1966 $5.95. ISBN 0-15-687611-6

NAMES AND THEIR ORIGINS

Alvarez–Altman, Grace, and Frederick Burelback (eds). *Names in Literature: Essays from Literary Onomastic Studies.* Univ Pr of America 1988 $26.50. ISBN 0-8191-6609-X

*Dickson, Paul. *What Do You Call a Person From . . .? A Dictionary of Residential Terms.* Facts on File 1990 $19.95. ISBN 0-8160-1983-5 Dictionary of terms to denote where a person lives; readable and entertaining for students who enjoy wordplay.

Eckler, A. Ross (ed). *Names and Games: Onomastics and Recreational Linguistics.* Univ Pr of America 1986 $28.75. ISBN 0-8191-5350-8

*Frumkes, Lewis. *Name Crazy: What Your Name Really Means.* Simon 1987 $5.95. ISBN

0-671-63187-X Explains what names mean; a pleasant reference book for curious browsers.

Gerrold, Henry. *Names, Handles, Monikers or Whatever They're Called—American Style.* Vantage 1988 $6.95. ISBN 0-533-07251-4

Harder, Kelsie. *Names and Their Varieties: A Collection of Essays in Onomastics.* Univ Pr of America 1986 $33.00. ISBN 0-8191-5232-3

*Room, Adrian. *Naming Names: Stories of Pseudonyms and Name Changes with a Who's Who.* McFarland 1981 $25.95. ISBN 0-89950-025-0 Stories of people taking new names; of particular interest to students who like literature and are familiar with some pseudonymous authors.

*Rydjord, John. *Indian Place-Names: Their Origin, Evolution, and Meanings, Collected in Kansas from the Siouan, Algonquian, Shoshonean, Caddoan, Iroquoian, and Other Tongues.* Univ of Oklahoma Pr 1982 $11.95. ISBN 0-8061-1763-X Explains American Indian place-names; fascinating introduction to Native American influences on the American English language.

*Stewart, George R. *American Given Names: Their Origin and History in the Context of the English Language.* Oxford Univ Pr 1986 $29.95. ISBN 0-19-502465-6 History of given names; interesting, readable, and often intriguing account.

*Stewart, George R. *American Place-Names: A Concise and Selective Dictionary for the Continental United States of America.* Oxford Univ Pr 1970 $29.95. ISBN 0-19-500121-4 Explains and locates place names; good for students who enjoy geography, wordplay, or both.

*Stewart, George R. *Names on the Land: A Historical Account of Placenaming in the United States.* Lexikos 1982 $10.00. ISBN 0-938530-02-X History of American place names; entertaining and readable account.

*Yonge, Charlotte. *A History of Christian Names.* Gordon Pr 1967 $75.00. ISBN 0-87968-368-6 History of given names; long and comprehensive; a useful reference work.

VOCABULARY DEVELOPMENT AND FUN WITH WORDS

*Agel, Jerome B. *Test Your Word Power.* Ballantine 1984 $2.95. ISBN 0-345-30897-2 Emphasizes etymology through games, quizzes, and essays by such well-known writers as Isaac Asimov.

Allen, F. Sturges. *Allen's Synonyms and Antonyms.* T. H. Van Motter (ed). Harper 1972 $4.95. ISBN 0-06-463328-4

*Brandreth, Gyles. *Word Games.* Harper 1986 $13.45. ISBN 0-06-055069-4 Anagrams, spoonerisms, palindromes, and other word games to play alone or with friends.

*Byrne, Josefa Heifetz. *Mrs. Byrne's Dictionary of Unusual, Obscure, and Preposterous Words, Gathered from Numerous and Diverse Authoritative Sources.* Robert Byrne (ed). Washington Square Pr 1984 $12.50. ISBN 0-8216-0203-9 Concise, informative, amusing definitions of odd words like *fard, jupe, giffgaff,* and *speigelschrift.*

*Cerf, Bennett (ed). *Out on a Limerick.* Harper 1985 $5.95. ISBN 0-06-091451-3 More than 300 of the best printable limericks from the pens of such notables as Mark Twain, Ogden Nash, and W. S. Gilbert.

*Espy, Willard. *Words to Rhyme With: A Rhyming Dictionary.* Facts on File 1986 $45.00. ISBN 0-8160-1237-7 Wonderful source for browsing and for playing word games as well as for writing poems and lyrics.

Evans, Bergen. *The Random House Word-A-Day Vocabulary Builder.* Ballantine 1982 $2.50. ISBN 0-345-30610-4

Facts on File Visual Dictionary. Facts on File 1987 $29.95. ISBN 0-8160-1544-9 Diagrams ordinary objects and machines, with the parts clearly labeled.

Hayakawa, S. I. *Choose the Right Word: A Modern Guide to Synonyms.* Harper 1987 $12.95. ISBN 0-06-091393-2

*Heacock, Paul. *Which Word When? The Indispensable Dictionary of 1,500 Commonly Confused Words.* Dell 1989 $4.95. ISBN 0-440-20388-0 Entertaining, reliable source for identifying and understanding modern misusage, in an easily used dictionary format.

Hellweg, Paul. *The Insomniac's Dictionary: The Last Word on the Odd Word.* Facts on File 1989 $19.95. ISBN 0-8160-1364-0

Lederer, Richard. *Get Thee to a Punnery.* Dell 1990 $5.95. ISBN 0-440-20499-2

*Lemay, Harold, Sid Lerner, and Marian Taylor. *The New New Words Dictionary.* Ballantine 1989 $2.95. ISBN 0-345-35696-9 More than 500 common words too new to have been included in other dictionaries.

Lewis, Norman. *Instant Word Power.* Signet 1982 $5.95. ISBN 0-451-16647-7

Lipton, James. *An Exaltation of Larks, or, The Venereal Game.* Penguin 1987 $8.95. ISBN 0-14-004536-8

Miller, Stuart. *Concise Dictionary of Acronyms and Initialisms.* Facts on File 1988 $22.95. ISBN 0-8160-1577-5

The New York Times *Everyday Reader's Dictionary of Misunderstood, Misused, and Mispronounced Words.* Signet 1987 $4.95. ISBN 0-451-15115-1

Robinson, Adam. *The Princeton Review Word Smart: Building an Educated Vocabulary.* Random 1988 $6.95. ISBN 0-394-75686-X

Salny, Abbie. *The Mensa Book of Words, Word Games, Puzzles, and Oddities.* Harper 1989 $5.95. ISBN 0-06-096208-9

Schur, Norman W. *1,000 Most Challenging Words.* Ballantine 1988 $4.95. ISBN 0-345-32165-0

*Schur, Norman. W. *1,000 Most Important Words.* Ballantine 1982 $3.50. ISBN 0-345-29863-2 Sharpens an awareness of what familiar words can convey; examples include "pedestrian" used as an adjective, "boomerang" as a verb.

Schur, Norman. W. *Practical English: 1,000 Most Effective Words.* Ballantine 1983 $3.50. ISBN 0-345-31038-1

*Urdang, Laurence (ed). *The Basic Book of Synonyms and Antonyms.* Signet 1984 $4.95. ISBN 0-451-16194-7 Easy to use, with examples of how sentences sometimes must be modified when a synonym is substituted for an original word.

Urdang, Laurence. *Dictionary of Confusable Words.* Facts on File 1985 $35.00. ISBN 0-8160-1650-X

COMMERCIAL AND POLITICAL PERSUASION

Albion, Mark. *Advertising's Hidden Effects.* Auburn 1983 $24.95. ISBN 0-86569-111-8

Arlen, Michael J. *Thirty Seconds.* Penguin 1981 $6.95. ISBN 0-14-005810-9

Boddeyn, J. *Advertising to Children.* Intl Advertising Assn 1984 $25.00. ISBN 0-318-14491-3

Boorstin, Daniel J. *The Image: A Guide to Pseudo-Events in America.* Macmillan 1988 $7.95. ISBN 0-689-70280-9

*De Bartolo, Dick, and Bob Clarke. *Mad Vertising.* NAL 1972 $1.25. ISBN 0-451-06739-8 *Mad Magazine*'s view of advertising; informs while it entertains; dated examples but timeless wisdom.

Dyer, Gillian. *Advertising as Communication.* Routledge 1982 $14.95. ISBN 0-416-74530-X

Ford, Nick (ed). *Language in Uniform: A Reader on Propaganda.* Odyssey Pr 1967 $4.68. ISBN 0-672-63054-0

Gold, Philip. *Advertising, Politics, and American Culture: From Salesmanship to Therapy.* Paragon Hse 1987 $18.95. ISBN 0-913729-35-3

Jowett, Garth, and Victoria O'Donnell. *Propaganda and Persuasion.* Sage 1986 $14.00. ISBN 0-8039-2399-6

Lee, Alfred, and Elizabeth Lee. *The Fine Art of Propaganda.* ISGS 1979 $7.00. ISBN 0-918970-25-3

Lutz, William. *Doublespeak: How Governments, Businesses, Advertisers, and Others Use Language to Deceive You.* Harper 1989 $17.45. ISBN 0-06-016134-5

Marchand, Roland. *Advertising the American Dream: Making Way for Modernity, 1920–1940.* Univ of California Pr 1985 $42.50. ISBN 0-520-05253-6

*Mitchell, Malcolm. *Propaganda, Polls and Public Opinion: Are the People Manipulated?* Prentice 1977 $16.97. ISBN 0-13-731109-5 Concrete analysis of a wide variety of influences brought to bear on the American public; timely, interesting, and useful.

NREL Staff. *Advertising Techniques and Consumer Fraud.* McGraw 1979 $13.96. ISBN 0-07-047308-0

Oxford English College Dictionary Staff. *Advertising Directed at Children: Endorsements in Advertising.* OECD 1982 $6.00. ISBN 0-92-64-12276-1

Packard, Vance. *The Hidden Persuaders.* McKay 1981 $4.95. ISBN 0-671-53149-2

Percy, Larry, and Arch Woodside. *Advertising and Consumer Psychology.* Lexington Bks 1983 $45.00. ISBN 0-669-05766-5

Sharp, Harold. *Advertising Slogans of America.* Scarecrow 1984 $39.50. ISBN 0-8108-1681-4

Short, K. R. *Film and Radio Propaganda in World War II.* Univ of Tennessee Pr 1983 $29.95. ISBN 0-87049-386-8

Shrank, Jeffrey. *Snap, Crackle, and Popular Taste: the Illusion of Free Choice in America.* Dell 1977 $6.95. ISBN 0-385-28810-7

*Skinner, Brian. *Advertisement Book.* McDougal 1976 $5.32. ISBN 0-88343-309-5 Explains the purposes, techniques, and target markets of a wide range of ads; with a wonderful introduction.

*Sobieszek, Robert. *Art of Persuasion: A History of Advertising Photography.* Abrams 1988 $40.00. ISBN 0-8109-1469-7 Close look at the art of advertising photography and a strong introduction to the language of images and forms.

Sylvester, Diane. *Advertising, Communication, Economics.* Learning Works 1986 $8.95. ISBN 0-88160-129-2

Taylor, Richard. *Film Propaganda: Nazi Germany and Soviet Russia.* Barnes 1979 $28.50. ISBN 0-06-496778-6

Thorson, Esther. *Advertising Age: The Principles of Advertising at Work.* National Textbook 1988 $11.95. ISBN 0-8442-3175-4

Ulanoff, Stanley. *Advertising in America: An Introduction to Persuasive Communication.* Hastings 1977 $19.95. ISBN 0-8038-0369-9

Wood, Richard (ed). *Film and Propaganda in America: A Documentary History.* 3 vols. Greenwood 1990 $75.00 each. Vol. 1 *World War I.* ISBN 0-313-20858-1. Vol. 2 *World War II, Part 1.* ISBN 0-313-20859-X. Vol. 3 *World War II, Part 2.* ISBN 0-313-20860-3

RANK, HUGH (DUKE)   1932–

Hugh Rank was born in Chicago, Illinois, and educated at the University of Notre Dame, from which he received a Ph. D. in English in 1969. He has been a professor of English at several colleges and universities and currently teaches at Governor's State University in Illinois.

Rank was instrumental in the creation of the National Council of Teachers of English Committee on Public Doublespeak in 1972, and he served as the Committee's first chair. "Doublespeak" was British author George Orwell's term for a word being used to mean its opposite, *e.g.* the Ministry of Peace being responsible for the conduct of war. (*See* Orwell, Vol. 1, British Literature: The Twentieth Century.) The Council's Committee on Public Doublespeak was formed to help "prepare children to cope with professional propaganda." As part of its work, Rank developed a technique to help young people analyze the sophisticated advertising and persuasive techniques with which they were being confronted every day.

Rank's major achievement was the creation of a simple pattern called Intensify/Downplay that "can be applied to verbal, nonverbal, and other symbolic human communication" to penetrate the techniques of persuasion used. He gave up copyright to his system so that it could be used more freely in schools and textbooks. The National Council of Teachers of English then made available a series of one-page teaching aids, based on Rank's work, for use in "teaching individuals the patterns of persuasion used by any persuader, commercial or political, left or right." In 1976, the Council gave Rank the George Orwell Award for his distinguished contribution toward integrity and clarity in public language.

During the 1980s, interest in the Council's materials decreased as schools concentrated on teaching basic skills rather than more systematic knowledge of language. Now, however, interest in Rank's work seems to be reviving.

BOOKS BY RANK

*Pep Talk: How to Analyze Political Language (1984). Counter Prop 1984 $11.95. ISBN 0-943468-01-9 Remarkably concrete explanations of how candidates and governments either intensify or downplay people's needs. Written for high school students but suitable for mature younger readers.

Persuasion Analysis: A Companion to Composition (1988). Counter Prop 1988 $10.00. ISBN 0-943468-02-7

The Pitch: How to Analyze Advertising (1982). Counter Prop 1982 $11.95. ISBN 0-943468-00-0

SAFIRE, WILLIAM 1929–

William Safire first came to national attention when he served as a special assistant and speech writer for President Richard M. Nixon from 1968 to 1973. Prior to working on the White House staff, Safire had been president of his own public relations firm in New York City. During his service in the Nixon administration, Safire was generally viewed as an extremely intelligent, resourceful, and articulate voice for the President's policies. After leaving Washington, Safire became a columnist for the *New York Times,* writing about politics and the English language.

Safire's columns and books on language are written from the standpoint of someone who understands public relations and who also cares very deeply about how language is used. Safire is particularly concerned about how meaning is distorted or obscured by careless or intentionally deceptive writers, advertisers, and politicians. His comments range from advice about the proper use of a particular word to critiques of the misuse of television advertising in political campaigns.

BOOKS BY SAFIRE

Freedom (1987). Doubleday 1987 $24.95. ISBN 0-385-15903-X

Fumblerules: A Lighthearted Guide to Grammar and Good Usage. Doubleday 1990 $15.00. ISBN 0-385-41301-7

I Stand Corrected: More on Language (1984). Times Bks 1984 $19.45. ISBN 0-8129-1097-4

Take My Word for It. (1986). Times Bks 1986 $22.00. ISBN 0-8129-1323-X

What's the Good Word? (1982). Times Bks 1982 $15.45. ISBN 0-8129-1006-0

Words of Wisdom: More Good Advice (1989). (coauthored with Leonard Safire) Simon 1989 $19.95. ISBN 0-671-67535-4

You Could Look It Up: More on Language (1988). Times Bks 1988 $22.00. ISBN 0-8129-1324-8

A CLOSER LOOK: LANGUAGE, IMAGE, AND POLITICS

Diamond, Edwin. *The Spot: The Rise of Political Advertising on Television.* MIT Pr 1988 $10.95. ISBN 0-262-54049-5

Foote, Joe S. *Television Access and Political Power: The Networks, the Presidency, and the "Loyal Opposition."* Praeger 1990 $40.00. ISBN 0-275-93438-1

McGinniss, Joe. *The Selling of the President 1968.* Penguin 1988 $7.95. ISBN 0-14-011240-5

Patterson, Thomas. *Mass Media Election: How Americans Choose Their President.* Praeger 1980 $15.95. ISBN 0-275-91502-6

Ranney, Austin. *Channels of Power: The Impact of Television on American Politics.* Basic 1983 $9.95. ISBN 0-465-00935-2

Robinson, Michael. *Over the Wire and on TV: CBS and UPI in Campaign '80.* Russell Sage 1983 $27.50. ISBN 0-87154-722-8

WORDSMITHS ON LANGUAGE: REFLECTIONS AND ADVICE

Daniels, Harvey. *Famous Last Words: The American Language Crisis Reconsidered.* Southern Illinois Univ Pr 1983 $19.95. ISBN 0-8093-1055-4

*MacNeil, Robert. *Wordstruck.* Viking 1990 $18.95. ISBN 0-670-81871-2 Journalist Mac-Neil's childhood memories of his growing love for the sound and sense of words; honest and often amusing.

Postman, Neil (ed). *Language in America: A Report on Our Deteriorating Semantic Environment.* Pegasus 1969 $10.83. ISBN 0-672-63552-6

Shaw, George Bernard. *On Language.* Carol 1964 $1.85. ISBN 0-685-19409-4

Tucker, Susie. *English Examined: Two Centuries of Comment on the Mother Tongue.* Shoe String 1961 $19.50. ISBN 0-208-01427-6

NEWMAN, EDWIN (HAROLD)   1919–

Edwin Newman was born and raised in New York City and educated at the University of Wisconsin. After several years as a reporter for a number of news services (including The International News Service and United Press), in 1947 Newman went to work for the Columbia Broadcasting System (CBS) as a news writer. In 1952, he joined the staff of the National Broadcasting Company (NBC) in London and spent several years in Europe as an NBC bureau chief and correspondent. In 1961, he returned to New York to work as an NBC television commentator and the host of a variety of news specials and documentaries.

In 1974, Newman generated considerable national interest with his book *Strictly Speaking: Will America Be the Death of English?* The book was a best-seller, an extremely rare achievement for a work on language. By using his ironic and sometimes biting wit to attack inaccurate, confusing, or deceptive language, Newman delighted millions of readers and sparked a national debate on the state of spoken and written language in America. Two years later, he followed with *A Civil Tongue* (1976), which was also very successful. Many of the examples of the absurd uses of language in Newman's second book were sent to him by readers of his first work.

Books by Newman

A Civil Tongue (1976). Warner Bks 1977 $3.95. ISBN 0-446-30758-0

I Must Say: On English, the News, and Other Matters (1988). Warner Bks 1988 $18.95. ISBN 0-446-51423-3

Strictly Speaking: Will America Be the Death of English? (1974). Warner Bks 1982 $4.95. ISBN 0-446-35528-3

HUMAN COMMUNICATION

At its most basic level, the act of communication involves one person sending a message and another receiving it, most frequently through direct speech and hearing. This simple process of speaking and listening is what underlies all the complex, technologically advanced communication systems that now tie the entire planet together. As basic and important as simple human communication is, it is often neglected in the modern rush to adopt the latest high-tech device.

The field of human communication has two basic aspects: verbal and nonverbal. Verbal communication includes such activities as conversation, group discussion, interviewing, public speaking, storytelling, and the oral interpretation—individual or group readings—of literature. Nonverbal communication is a relatively new field of study that examines the many ways people send messages to one another without using words, using instead body language, such as facial and hand gestures, eye movements, the distance they establish between them, and how they position their bodies while talking and listening.

Human communication also includes the study of sign languages and how they convey meaning. Sign languages include not only the formal systems used by the deaf, but intentional gestures used by people in various situations. These gestures range from the hitchhiker's use of the thumb to signal a passing car through the very specific hand and facial gestures used by southern Euro-

Writing on stone.   Egypt.   Courtesy of Giraudon/Art Resource.

peans in ordinary conversation to the elaborate signs used by baseball coaches to send messages to players.

Finally, the human communication field includes research in voice and diction, including pronunciation, the physical production of sound through the organs of human speech, and the improvement of speech patterns.

The writers profiled in the Human Communication section have studied the ways people talk to each other when face to face. Sources exploring the art and practice of conversation, group discussion, interviewing, public speaking, storytelling, and the oral interpretation of literature are presented. Because the human voice is not the only means by which people communicate, this section also includes works on nonverbal communication, covering everything from facial expressions to eye movements to the use of the hands in conversation and public speaking. Books that deal with the increasingly important topic of sign language as well as those that give advice on improving one's voice and diction are also included.

VERBAL MESSAGES

Adler, Mortimer J. *How to Speak—How to Listen: A Guide to Pleasurable and Profitable Conversation.* Macmillan 1983 $14.95. ISBN 0-02-500570-7

Beebe, Steven, and John Masterson. *Communicating in Small Groups: Principles and Practices.* Scott 1990 $10.00. ISBN 0-673-38874-3

Ehrlich, Eugene, and Raymond Hand, Jr. *NBC Handbook of Pronunciation.* Harper 1984 $15.45. ISBN 0-06-181142-4

Elgin, Suzette Haden. *The Gentle Art of Verbal Self-Defense.* Dorset 1985 $6.95. ISBN 0-88029-030-7

*Fleming, Alice. *What to Say When You Don't Know What to Say.* Fawcett 1982 $2.50. ISBN 0-449-70122-0 Helpful suggestions for teens who need to find the right words in pressure situations—on dates, at work, in interviews.

*Gabor, Don. *How to Start a Conversation and Make Friends.* Simon 1983 $7.95. ISBN 0-671-47421-9 Ideas for "openers"—questions, compliments, friendly comments—that invite a positive response.

Gumpert, Gary, and Robert Cathcart. *Inter/Media: Interpersonal Communication in a Media World.* Oxford Univ Pr 1982 $18.95. ISBN 0-19-503737-5

Hamlin, Sonya. *How to Talk So People Listen: The Real Key to Job Success.* Harper 1989 $17.45. ISBN 0-06-015669-4

Karant, Priscilla. *Storylines: Conversation Skills Through Oral Histories.* Newbury Hse 1988 $12.95. ISBN 0-06-632600-1

*Samovar, Larry, and Stephen King. *Communication and Discussion in Small Groups.* Gorsuch 1981 $3.00. ISBN 0-89787-308-4 Practical advice about listening, elaborating, probing, and restating—skills that lead to good communication in groups.

*Sarnoff, Dorothy. *Speech Can Change Your Life.* Dell 1971 $4.95. ISBN 0-440-18199-2 Useful advice for self-conscious young people who want to stop projecting a timid personality.

*Sternberg, Patricia. *Speak to Me: How to Put Confidence in Your Conversation.* Lothrop 1984 $6.50. ISBN 0-688-02694-X Emphasizes listening, attending to body language, and asking open-ended questions, with the goal of making conversation easier for shy people.

Tonnen, Deborah. *That's Not What I Meant! How Conversational Style Makes or Breaks Your Relations with Others.* Ballantine 1987 $2.95. ISBN 1-345-34090-6

Wood, Douglas, and Gerald Phillips. *Group Discussion: A Practical Guide to Participation and Leadership.* Harper 1985 $18.95. ISBN 0-06-045218-8

ALLEN, STEVE (STEPHEN VALENTINE PATRICK WILLIAM)   1921–

Writer, composer, musician, actor, and television host, Steve Allen was born in New York City, the son of a well-known vaudeville couple. As a child, Allen traveled extensively, attending 18 different schools. As a young man, he attended Duke University for a year in 1941 and then the University of Arizona before entering the army during World War II. After the war Allen resumed his career in radio, which he had begun in Phoenix in 1942. A talented musician and comedian, Allen performed on KFAC and KMTR in Los Angeles before becoming host of his own talk show—one of the first ever broadcast—in 1948.

In 1950, Allen joined the Columbia Broadcasting System (CBS) in New York and began a career in television. In 1954, he moved to the National Broadcasting Company (NBC) and began a new, late-evening variety and talk show, the first of its kind. Called the *Tonight Show,* it became a huge success and made Allen one of the most popular television personalities in the country. He went on to become the star of several other television shows, including *The Steve Allen Show, I've Got a Secret,* and *The Steve Allen Comedy Hour.*

One of Allen's most interesting television ventures was a program called *A Meeting of Minds,* a series he did for the Public Broadcasting System (PBS) from 1977 to 1981. A combination of talk show and historical review, the program presented a group discussion by famous historical figures (such as Julius Caesar, Abraham Lincoln, and Joan of Arc) of social and political issues with Allen acting as the moderator. The acting was convincing and the dialogue thought-provoking and often humorous. The show was critically acclaimed and established Allen as a creative and intelligent user of the television medium. It also showed the American public how a good group discussion should operate and what it can accomplish.

BOOKS BY ALLEN

How to Be Funny (1987). McGraw 1988 $7.95. ISBN 0-07-001217-2
How to Make a Speech. (1985). McGraw 1985 $15.95. ISBN 0-07-001164-8
Funny People (1981). Scarborough Hse 1982 $12.95. ISBN 0-8128-2764-3
A Meeting of Minds (1978). 4 vols. Prometheus Bks 1989 $49.95. ISBN 0-87975-561-X
More Funny People (1982). Scarborough Hse 1982 $14.95. ISBN 0-8128-2884-4
Ripoff: A Report on Moral Collapse and Corruption in America (1979). Carol 1979 $9.95. ISBN 0-8184-0249-0

BOMBECK, ERMA   1927–

It is estimated that Erma Bombeck, humorist, author, and writer of a thrice-weekly column for 700 newspapers throughout the world, is read by more than 31 million people. Bombeck's career began in Dayton, Ohio, where she was born, raised, and educated. She started by working as a copy girl for the *Dayton Journal Herald,* and in 1965, her column on domestic life went into national syndication.

A graduate of the University of Dayton, Bombeck also holds 14 honorary doctorates and is a member of The Society of Professional Journalists. In 1978, President Carter appointed her to serve on the President's Advisory Committee for Women. In 1979, she was named by The World Almanac to the list of the 25 Most Influential Women in America, and in 1986, she was named Grand Marshal of the Rose Parade. She is the author of numerous best-selling books. She lives today in Paradise Valley, Arizona with her husband and family.

BOOKS BY BOMBECK

At Wit's End. Fawcett 1986 $3.95. ISBN 0-449-21184-3

Aunt Erma's Cope Book: How to Get from Monday to Friday in Twelve Days. Fawcett 1985 $3.95. ISBN 0-449-220937-7

Four of a Kind: A Treasury of Favorite Works by America's Best-Loved Humorist. McGraw 1991 $16.95. ISBN 0-07-006456-3

*The Grass Is Always Greener Over the Septic Tank. Fawcett 1985 $3.95. ISBN 0-449-20759-5 A collection of skillful satire focusing on the frustrations of family life in suburbia.

*If Life Is a Bowl of Cherries—What Am I Doing in the Pits? McGraw 1978 $7.95. ISBN 0-07-006451-2 Treasury of wit and wisdom that manages to hit everybody's funny bone.

When You Look Like Your Passport Photo, It's Time to Go Home. Harper 1991 $19.95. ISBN 0-06-018311-X

INTERVIEWING

*Brady, John. *The Craft of Interviewing.* Random 1977 $6.95. ISBN 0-394-72469-0 Down-to-earth tips on planning and executing an interview, including researching, probing, pressing, taking notes and taping, verifying, and writing.

WALLACE, MIKE (MYRON LEON)   1918–

Known to millions of Americans for his work as a reporter and interviewer on the television program *60 Minutes,* Mike Wallace was born in Brookline, Massachusetts, where he attended local schools. After graduating from the University of Michigan in 1939, Wallace began his career in radio at stations WOOD and WASH in Grand Rapids, Michigan. In 1941, he moved to station WXYZ in Detroit and later worked for a number of stations in Chicago.

In 1951, Wallace joined the Columbia Broadcasting System (CBS) in New York, where he narrated documentaries and served as host and moderator for a number of radio and television programs. In 1956, he became an interviewer on *Night Beat* on WABD-TV in New York. His aggressive style as an interviewer won him a large audience, and he gained a reputation for asking uncomfortable questions of controversial guests.

The following year, the American Broadcasting Company (ABC) gave him his own interview show, *The Mike Wallace Interview,* which further established his image as a relentless, uncompromising questioner. Wallace returned to CBS in 1963 as a staff correspondent. In 1968, he became a co-editor and reporter/interviewer on the news magazine show *60 Minutes.*

Over the years Wallace has drawn criticism for his aggressive interviewing tactics and has been accused of being rude to those he interviews. His response has been that his goal is to get at the truth and to stimulate his audience to think. He also claims that many of those he interviews welcome the chance to discuss controversial questions and to air their own views in public.

BOOK BY WALLACE

Close Encounters: Mike Wallace's Own Story (1984). (coauthored with Gary Gates) Berkley 1985 $4.95. ISBN 0-425-08269-5

NONVERBAL LANGUAGE

Costello, Elaine. *Signing: How to Speak with Your Hands.* Bantam 1983 $13.95. ISBN 0-553-34612-1
*Fast, Julius. *Body Language.* Pocket 1984 $3.95. ISBN 0-671-63418-6 Popular explanation of what posture, facial expressions, and limb positions communicate.
*Greene, Laura, and Eva Dicker. *Sign Language Talk.* Watts 1988 $11.90. ISBN 0-531-10597-0 Comprehensive, illustrated guide that includes all the basics necessary for communicating with the deaf.
Hall, Edward. *Hidden Differences: Doing Business with the Japanese.* Doubleday 1987 $16.95. ISBN 0-385-23883-5
Hall, Edward. *Hidden Dimension.* Doubleday 1969 $5.95. ISBN 0-385-08476-5
*Hall, Edward. *The Silent Language.* Doubleday 1973 $5.95. ISBN 0-385-05549-8 Not always easy reading but a fascinating study of body language—especially the passage about changes in courtship customs and how a culture tends to expect old behaviors even under new circumstances.
Knapp, Mark. *Essentials of Nonverbal Communication.* Holt 1980 $18.95. ISBN 0-03-049861-9
*Patterson, Francine. *Koko's Kitten.* Scholastic 1987 $10.95. ISBN 0-590-40952-2 Story of how Koko the gorilla is taught sign language; fascinating study of how language is used by creatures that are not human.
*Patterson, Francine. *Koko's Story.* Scholastic 1987 $10.95. ISBN 0-590-40272-2 With *Koko's Kitten,* this book tells the story of Koko, the gorilla who learned to communicate through sign language.
Sternberg, Martin L. A. *American Sign Language: A Comprehensive Dictionary.* Harper 1981 $47.50. ISBN 0-06-014097-6

KELLER, HELEN   1880–1968

Helen Keller was born in Tuscumbia, Alabama, the daughter of a former captain in the Confederate army who had become a prosperous farmer. At the age of nine months, a serious fever left Helen Keller deaf and blind. By the time she was seven, she had developed into a difficult child. Unable to communicate except by a few hand signs, she grew increasingly wild and uncontrollable. On learning of the Perkins Institution for the Blind, which had developed methods for teaching such children, Helen's parents turned to the Institution for help. The school sent a recent graduate, Anne Sullivan, to become Keller's tutor. The story of Sullivan's work with the young girl—her difficulties, frustrations, and eventual success—are detailed in William Gibson's play *The Miracle Worker* (1959).

Because she lacked both sight and hearing, Keller depended on touch to communicate. She learned to communicate through the use of alphabet letters signed onto the palm of her hand (the sign language for the deaf communicated by touch instead of sight) and later learned to "read" lips by placing her hand over the speaker's mouth. She also used Braille and typewriting, and even learned to speak.

Eventually Keller entered Radcliffe College, from which she graduated with honors in 1904. She went on to publish 14 books and became proficient in several languages. She became a highly honored world celebrity, and even after her death she continues to remain an inspiration and proof of the power of silent communication.

BOOKS BY KELLER

Midstream: My Later Life (1929). Greenwood 1969 $41.50. ISBN 0-8371-0127-1
My Religion (1927). Swedenborg 1972 $3.50. ISBN 0-87785-103-4
The Story of My Life (1903). Doubleday 1954 $15.95. ISBN 0-385-04453-4
Teacher: Anne Sullivan Macy (1955). Greenwood 1985 $45.00. ISBN 0-313-24738-2

BOOKS ABOUT KELLER

*Davidson, Margaret. *Helen Keller's Teacher.* Scholastic 1972 $2.25. ISBN 0-590-02224-5
Comprehensive biography of Anne Sullivan Macy and her improvements on
Howe's methods for teaching the deaf–blind; details her life with her husband
John Macy, an editor, and her enduring friendship with Helen Keller.
*Gibson, William. *The Miracle Worker.* Knopf 1957 $12.95. ISBN 0-394-40630-3 Televi-
sion drama in 1957, stage play in 1959, and film in 1962 depicting Anne Sullivan's
initial breakthrough in teaching Helen Keller the manual alphabet and the concept of naming.
*Wepman, Dennis. *Helen Keller.* Chelsea 1989 $16.95. ISBN 1-55546-662-1 Warm, per-
sonal biography, offering a clear sense of the human being behind the stunning
achievements; written for young adults.

ORAL INTERPRETATION

Coger, Leslie, and Melvin White. *Readers Theatre Handbook.* Scott 1982 $21.25. ISBN
0-673-15270-7
Earley, Michael, and Philippa Keil. *Soliloquy: The Shakespeare Monologues.* 2 vols. Applause
Theatre Bk 1990 $6.95 each. Vol. 1 *Men.* ISBN 0-936839-78-3. Vol. 2 *Women.* ISBN
0-936839-79-1
Earley, Michael, and Philippa Keil. *Solo! The Best Monologues of the 80s.* 2 vols. Applause
Theatre Bk 1990 $5.95 each. Vol. 1 *Men.* ISBN 0-936839-65-1. Vol. 2 *Women.* ISBN
0-936839-66-X
Kleinau, Marion, and Janet McHughes. *Theatres for Literature.* Mayfield 1980 $16.95.
ISBN 0-87484-623-4
Lee, Charlotte, and Timothy Gura. *Oral Interpretations.* Houghton 1986 $42.76. ISBN
0-395-42440-2
*Poggi, Jack. *The Monologue Workshop: From Search to Discovery in Audition, Class and Performance.*
Applause Theatre Bk 1990 $8.95. ISBN 1-55783-031-2 Specific, clear guidelines
for selecting, cutting, interpreting, and performing monologues.
*Sloyer, Shirlee. *Reader's Theatre: Story Dramatization in the Classroom.* NCTE 1982 $12.95.
ISBN 0-8141-3838-1 Directions and examples—a useful guide for converting a
story to script and performing before peers.

PUBLIC SPEAKING

Allen, Steve. *How to Make a Speech.* McGraw 1985 $15.95. ISBN 0-07-001164-8
Humes, James C. *Instant Eloquence.* Harper 1986 $4.95. ISBN 0-06-463705-0
Johannesen, Richard, *et al. Contemporary American Speeches.* Kendall-Hunt 1988 $21.95.
ISBN 0-8403-4610-7
*Ryan, Margaret. *So You Have to Give a Speech!* Watts 1987 $11.90. ISBN 0-531-10337-4
Good advice about finding topics and interesting things to say as well as tips for
controlling anxiety and holding an audience's attention.

Wilbur, Perry. *Stand Up, Speak Up, or Shut Up: A Practical Guide to Public Speaking.* Dembner 1981 $12.95. ISBN 0-934878-05-6

Zannes, Estelle, and Gerald Goldhaber. *Stand Up, Speak Out: An Introduction to Public Speaking.* McGraw 1983 $18.50. ISBN 0-07-554833-X

MALCOLM X (MALCOLM LITTLE; EL-HAJJ MALIK EL-SHABAZZ) 1925–1965

See also Malcolm X, Vol. 2, United States History: The Turbulent Sixties.

Malcolm X was born in Omaha, Nebraska, the son of a Baptist minister, Earl Little, who was also a supporter of black separatism and the back-to-Africa movement. Driven from Omaha by the anti-black terrorist group, the Ku Klux Klan, Little and his family searched for several years for a community in which to settle. Finally they chose Lansing, Michigan, where their home was burned by a white supremacy group. Shortly afterward Earl Little's body was found, horribly butchered.

For a while the remainder of Little's family—his wife Louise and eight children, including Malcolm—lived on welfare, but the strain proved too much for Louise Little, and she suffered a mental collapse. Malcolm, along with the other children, was placed in a series of foster homes.

Although he was an excellent student, Malcolm was told by his teachers that his dream of becoming a lawyer was unrealistic because of his race, so the discouraged boy left school after the eighth grade. He soon drifted into a life of crime and drug-taking and was sent to prison in Massachusetts. There he educated himself, and upon his release he went to Chicago to become a minister in the Black Muslim religion, which advocated black separatism. The Muslims sent him to New York as a minister in Harlem.

It was in Harlem that Malcolm X built his reputation as a powerful public speaker. His dynamic platform presence and articulate, impassioned delivery moved his audiences with stunning effectiveness. He drew large crowds when he spoke, including people of all races and those who disagreed with his positions but came to listen to his brilliant oratory.

Malcolm X later broke with the Black Muslims and began to advocate black and white people working together to change a racist and unjust system. Shortly after this change of thinking, he was assassinated by gunmen believed to have been sent to silence him by the Black Muslims.

BOOKS BY MALCOLM X

Autobiography of Malcolm X (1965). Ballantine 1977 $3.95. ISBN 0-345-33920-7

By Any Means Necessary: Speeches, Interviews, and a Letter by Malcolm X. George Breitman (ed). Pathfinder Pr 1970 $7.95. ISBN 0-87348-150-X

Malcolm X on Afro-American History. Pathfinder Pr 1972 $4.95. ISBN 0-87348-085-6

Malcolm X: The Last Speeches. Pathfinder Pr 1989 $7.95. ISBN 0-87348-543-2

BOOKS ABOUT MALCOLM X

*Breitman, George. *The Last Year of Malcolm X: The Evolution of a Revolutionary.* Pathfinder Pr 1970 $7.95. ISBN 0-87348-004-X Well-documented analysis of the attitudes and actions of Malcolm X.

Breitman, George (ed). *Malcolm X Speaks: Selected Speeches and Statements.* Grove-Weidenfeld 1990 $8.95. ISBN 0-8021-3213-8

*Curtis, Richard. *The Life of Malcolm X.* Macrae Smith 1971 $4.95. ISBN 0-8255-2786-4 Biography for young people of the controversial black leader.

*Rummel, Jack. *Malcolm X.* Chelsea 1989 $16.95. ISBN 1-55546-600-1 Well-illustrated biography of the black leader, suitable for young readers.

STORYTELLING

Baker, Augusta, and Ellin Greene. *Storytelling: Art and Technique.* 2nd ed. Bowker 1987 $29.95. ISBN 0-8352-2336-1

*Grim, Gary, and Denny Dey. *Storytelling.* Good Apple 1979 $8.95. ISBN 0-916456-46-3 Discusses both the art of and the techniques for creating characters, building suspense, sustaining interest, and bringing closure.

Hutchinson, Duane. *Storyteller's Ghost Stories.* 2 vols. Foundation 1989 $5.95 each. ISBNs 0-934988-07-2, 0-934988-18-8

Hutchinson, Duane. *Storytelling Tips: How to Love, Learn and Relate a Story.* Foundation 1985 $5.95. ISBN 0-934988-13-7

Janssen, Dale, and Janice Beaty. *Storytelling Mark Twain Style.* Janssen 1988 $13.95. ISBN 0-9618217-1-X

VOICE AND DICTION

*Bloom, Harold (ed). *George Bernard Shaw's Pygmalion.* Chelsea 1988 $19.95. ISBN 1-55546-029-1 Inspiration for the musical *My Fair Lady* and a delightful play in its own right, dramatizing the transformation of a Cockney flower seller into a "duchess" by means of speech lessons.

Eisenson, John. *Voice and Diction: A Program for Improvement.* Macmillan 1985 $33.00. ISBN 0-02-331960-7

*Lerner, Alan J. *My Fair Lady.* NAL 1978 $2.95. ISBN 0-451-13890-2 A linguist teaches a young girl how to transform her Cockney dialect into standard British English and falls in love with her in the process.

Seidler, Ann, and Doris Bianchi. *Voice and Diction Fitness: A Comprehensive Approach.* Harper 1988 $23.95. ISBN 0-06-040665-8

*Skinner, Edith. *Speak with Distinction.* Applause Theatre Bk 1990 $29.95. ISBN 1-55783-047-9 Intended for actors but equally useful for anyone who wants to improve volume, clarity, emphasis, and style of speech.

MASS COMMUNICATION

The term *mass communication* refers to the ability to send the same message to large numbers of people at the same time. The invention of the printing press in Germany in the late fifteenth century was the beginning of mass communication, enabling the printing of the first newspapers. By the eighteenth century, newspapers were an established source of information in England, and a new form of printed communication, the magazine, had begun to appear.

In the middle of the nineteenth century, the steam-powered rotary press increased printing speed enormously. Improved railroad systems made it possible to deliver printed material over long distances in a relatively short time, and the spread of free public education provided a rapidly growing audience of readers. Thus mass communication took on a whole new importance.

Early in the twentieth century, radio was invented, and by 1920, America's first commercial radio station, KDKA, was on the air in Pittsburgh, Pennsylvania. It was now possible for the human voice to carry messages to large numbers of people, even those who could not read or see. During the same period, another invention, the moving picture, took the United States by storm.

Walt Disney and Donald Duck. © MCMLIV Walt Disney
Productions (1954).   Courtesy of UPI/Bettmann.

The first movie house opened in Pittsburgh in 1905, and by the 1920s, there
was barely a village in the country that did not have a movie house. Sound was
added to movies in 1927, and throughout the 1930s and 1940s, these two
media, radio and movies, were powerful influences on American life.

By 1945, television was available commercially and by the mid-1950s was
found in homes all across the country. By the 1960s, watching TV had become
a way of life for many people. In the decades that followed, television grew
to dominate mass communication in America.

The Mass Communication section includes authors who focus on the
nature of the mass media and the relationship between mass media and mass
culture. The section also includes studies of particular mass media, such as
magazines, cartoons and comic strips, radio, television, movies, and the various
news media, including newspapers and broadcast journalism. These writers,
most of whom work in the fields they write about, analyze the ways the media
operate and examine some of the questions that have developed over the years,
such as how the media have affected American politics, family life, and cultural
values.

MASS MEDIA, MASS CULTURE

*Bernards, Neal (ed). *Mass Media.* Greenhaven 1987 $15.95. ISBN 0-89908-425-7 Arti-
    cles showing both sides of key issues concerning the power and effects of mass
    media; an excellent introduction to the variety of current opinion on major ques-
    tions in this field.

Casty, Alan. *Mass Media and Mass Man.* Univ Pr of America 1982 $16.25. ISBN 0-8191-2261-0

Czitrom, Daniel. *Media and the American Mind: From Morse to McLuhan.* Univ of North Carolina Pr 1982 $8.95. ISBN 0-8078-4107-2

Flannery, Gerald. *Mass Media—Marconi to MTV: A Select Bibliography of New York Times Sunday Magazine Articles on Communication 1900–1988.* Univ of America Pr 1989 $42.50. ISBN 0-8191-7421-1

Seldes, Gilbert. *The New Mass Media: Challenge to a Free Society.* Public Affairs 1968 $4.50. ISBN 0-8183-0185-6

Toffler, Alvin. *The Third Wave.* Bantam 1981 $5.95. ISBN 0-553-14431-6

Ulloth, Dana, and Peter Klinge. *Mass Media: Past, Present, and Future.* West Pub 1983 $29.50. ISBN 0-314-69683-0

Wilson, S. Roy. *Mass Media—Mass Culture.* Random 1989 $18.95. ISBN 0-394-36655-7

McLUHAN, (HERBERT) MARSHALL   1911–1980

Marshall McLuhan was born in Edmonton, Alberta, in Canada and studied English literature at the University of Manitoba in Canada and later at Cambridge University in England. In 1946, he became a professor of English at St. Michael's College in Toronto, Ontario, and in 1963 the Director of the Centre for Culture and Technology at the University of Toronto.

In the 1960s, McLuhan created considerable controversy with the publication of his theories on the nature and effect of the communications media. In *The Gutenberg Galaxy: The Making of Typographic Man* (1962), he claimed that the invention of writing, followed by the invention of the printing press, caused people to become more individualistic and self-centered because they no longer had to depend on talking to each other to get information. Printed material also changed the way people thought and perceived, according to McLuhan: people now thought in the way that books provide information—in straightforward, sequential patterns.

McLuhan expanded on these ideas in *Understanding Media* (1964), in which he proposed that the medium itself, in the *way* it conveys information and ideas, rather than the information and ideas conveyed, changes society. This concept is expressed in McLuhan's much-quoted statement, "The medium is the message." McLuhan also saw the electronic media as pulling society together again, after the print media had pulled it apart, and uniting humanity in a "global village."

McLuhan's critics acknowledged that the ideas he proposed were important, but they complained that he did not develop his concepts fully or state them clearly. Despite these criticisms, McLuhan's effect on media analysts, communications theorists, and social commentators has been powerful. Virtually all contemporary commentary on the media begins with McLuhan.

Books by McLuhan

The Global Village: Transformations in World Life and Media in the Twenty-First Century (1989). (coauthored with Bruce R. Powers) Oxford Univ Pr 1989 $29.95. ISBN 0-19-505-444-X

The Gutenberg Galaxy: The Making of Typographic Man (1962). Univ of Toronto Pr 1962 $17.95. ISBN 0-8020-6041-2

Laws of Media: The New Science (1988). (coauthored with Eric McLuhan) Univ of Toronto Pr 1988 $27.50. ISBN 0-19-50544-X
Understanding Media: The Extensions of Man (1964). NAL 1966 $5.95. ISBN 0-451-62765-2

BOOKS ABOUT MCLUHAN

Czitrom, Daniel. *Media and the American Mind: From Morse to McLuhan.* Univ of North Carolina Pr 1982 $8.95. ISBN 0-8078-4107-2 Study of the ways media has changed American society, drawing in a small way on the theories of McLuhan.
Marchand, Philip. *Marshall McLuhan: The Medium and the Messenger.* Ticknor 1989 $19.95. ISBN 0-89919-485-0 Biography that proceeds step by step through the stages in McLuhan's life; comprehensive and informative, if not exceptionally revealing.
Sanderson, George, and Frank MacDonald. *Marshall McLuhan: The Man and His Message.* Fulcrum 1989 $17.95. ISBN 1-55591-035-1 Biography tracing McLuhan's life including the development of his ideas and theories.

NATURE AND EFFECTS

Altheide, David. *Media Power.* Sage 1985 $22.50. ISBN 0-8039-2410-1
Bagdikian, Ben. *The Media Monopoly.* Beacon 1984 $10.95. ISBN 0-8070-6171-9
Brody, E. W. *Communication Tomorrow: New Audiences, New Technologies, New Media.* Praeger 1990 $45.00. ISBN 0-275-93280-X
Didsbury, Howard, Jr. (ed). *Communications and the Future: Prospects, Promises, and Problems.* World Future 1982 $14.50. ISBN 0-930242-16-5
Greenfield, Patricia. *Mind and Media: The Effects of Television, Video Games, and Computers.* Harvard Univ Pr 1984 $5.95. ISBN 0-674-57621-7
Jamieson, Kathleen, and Karyl K. Campbell. *The Interplay of Influence: Mass Media and Their Public in News, Advertising, Politics.* Wadsworth 1982 $15.50. ISBN 0-534-08280-7
Katz, Elihu. *Mass Media and Social Change.* Sage 1981 $26.95. ISBN 0-8039-9807-4
Lazere, Donald (ed). *American Media and Mass Culture: Left Perspectives.* Univ of California Pr 1987 $15.95. ISBN 0-520-04496-7
Postman, Neil. *Amusing Ourselves to Death: Public Discourse in the Age of Show Business.* Penguin 1986 $6.95. ISBN 0-14-009438-5
Postman, Neil. *The Disappearance of Childhood.* Dell 1984 $3.95. ISBN 0-440-31945-5
Real, Michael. *Mass Mediated Culture.* Prentice 1977 $32.00. ISBN 0-13-559203-8
*Snow, Robert. *Creating Media Culture.* Sage 1983 $16.95. ISBN 0-8039-1995-6 Discussions of the grammar and syntax of newspapers, magazines, radio, film, and television; concrete examples will fascinate the younger reader who knows how to skim.
Toll, Robert. *The Entertainment Machine: American Show Business in the Twentieth Century.* Oxford Univ Pr 1982 $12.95. ISBN 0-19-503232-2

COPING

Berger, Arthur A. *Media Analysis Techniques.* Sage 1982 $9.95. ISBN 0-8039-0614-5
Key, Wilson Bryan. *Media Sexploitation.* Signet 1977 $5.95. ISBN 0-451-16193-9
*Littell, Joy (ed). *Coping with the Mass Media.* McDougal 1976 $8.76. ISBN 0-88343-302-8 Visually stunning, intellectually substantial book that helps the reader consider key questions about the nature and impact of each mass medium

through study of excerpts and artifacts from pop culture and the humanities.

*Schrank, Jeffrey. *Snap, Crackle and Popular Taste.* Dell 1977 $6.95. ISBN 0-385-28810-7 The best introduction to mass culture; introduces the concept of "pseudochoice" and covers television, sports, and advertising from a unique perspective; invaluable despite dated statistics.

MAGAZINES

Cutsinger, John (ed). *Magazine Fundamentals.* Columbia Scholastic 1984 $8.50 ISBN 0-916084

Jaspersohn, William. *Magazine: Behind the Scenes at Sports Illustrated.* Little 1983 $14.95. ISBN 0-316-45815-5

Life: The First Fifty Years 1936–1986. Little 1986 $50.00. ISBN 0-316-52613-4 Lavish volume of photographs and articles selected from our most popular mass-market magazine to capture the drama and comedy of American life from the Great Depression of the 1930s to the Great Greed of the 1980s.

*Mad Magazine Staff. *Mad About Mad.* Warner Bks 1990 $2.95. ISBN 0-446-30425-5 Inside look at *Mad*'s unique formula, mission, production, and place in the popular press.

Mahon, Gigi. *The Last Days of The New Yorker.* Plume 1989 $9.95. ISBN 0-452-26322-0

The New Yorker Album of Drawings. Penguin 1978 $16.95. ISBN 0-14-004968-1

The New Yorker Book of War Pieces. Ayer (repr of 1947 ed) $29.00. ISBN 0-8369-2470-3

The New Yorker Cartoon Album, 1975–1985. Penguin 1985 $20.00. ISBN 0-670-80677-3

The New Yorker Twenty-Fifth Anniversary Album, 1925–1950. Harper 1986 $15.95. ISBN 0-06-091357-6 Close look at the literature and artwork of *The New Yorker* in its heyday, giving a sense of what this literary institution was like before its recent sale.

Nourie, Alan, and Barbara Nourie (eds). *American Mass-Market Magazines.* Greenwood 1990 $79.95. ISBN 0-313-25254-8

Peterson, Theodore. *Magazines in the Twentieth Century.* Univ of Illinois Pr 1964 $22.50. ISBN 0-252-72537-9

Rivers, William. *Magazine Editing and Production.* Brown 1986 $24.90. ISBN 0-697-00278-0

Wainwright, Loudon. *A Great American Magazine: An Inside History of Life.* Knopf 1986 $19.45. ISBN 0-394-45987-3

JAFFEE, AL (ALLAN)   1921–

In the title of one of his books, cartoonist Al Jaffee describes himself as *Mad's Vastly Overrated Al Jaffee* (1983). Two generations of loyal readers of the satirical magazine, *Mad,* would disagree. Jaffee is the driving force behind *Mad* as well as one of its most creative cartoonists. He has also worked on Marvel Comics and other *Mad* publications. It is through *Mad* magazine, however, that Jaffee is best known to millions of Americans.

It is no exaggeration to say that many, if not most, American young adults have been introduced to social satire through *Mad.* The number who faithfully continue to read the magazine as adults attests to the high quality of its satire and artwork—the magazine is certainly *not* strictly for the young.

In an interview on the television program *60 Minutes,* Jaffee explained that he has always been interested in both drawing and satire and that the comic book format seemed a natural outlet for both these interests. The comic book format explains why young people were the first to appreciate his work. In its pages, the magazine has attacked virtually every aspect of modern American life, particularly the advertising industry, the entertainment media (especially television), and the political establishment.

In 1973, Jaffee received an award from the National Cartoonist society as best advertising and illustration artist.

BOOKS BY JAFFEE AND HIS STAFF

Al Jaffee's Mad Book of Magic and Other Dirty Tricks (1985). Warner Bks 1988 $2.95. ISBN 0-446-35027-3

Al Jaffee's Mad Inventions (1987). Warner Bks 1987 $2.95. ISBN 0-446-34628-4

Mad Blast (1988). Warner Bks 1988 $3.50. ISBN 0-446-35296-9

Mad in the Box (1989). Warner Bks 1989 $3.50. ISBN 0-446-35495-3

Mad's Al Jaffee Freaks Out (1982). Warner Bks 1988 $2.95. ISBN 0-446-35064-8

Mad's Vastly Overrated Al Jaffee (1983). Warner Bks 1983 $5.95. ISBN 0-446-37584-5

WHITE, E. B. (ELWYN BROOKS) 1899–1985

E. B. White was born in Mount Vernon, New York, the son of a piano manufacturer. He attended Cornell University, from which he graduated in 1921. White served in the United States Army during World War I. He began his career as a reporter for the *Seattle Times* from 1922 to 1923, and then left Seattle for New York, where he worked for an advertising agency for two years. In 1925, he joined the staff of *The New Yorker* magazine, for which he continued to write until his death.

Harold Ross had founded *The New Yorker* in 1925 with the idea of creating a high-quality magazine devoted to information about the intellectual and social life of New York City as well as providing a venue for first-rate literature. Joining White on the staff was James Thurber (*see* Thurber, Vol. 1, American Literature: The Twentieth Century), a talented cartoonist and essayist. Over the next two decades, Ross, White, Thurber, and a host of other talented writers and editors built *The New Yorker* into one of America's leading magazines, extending its influence far beyond New York City.

White's fame rests chiefly on his essays, many of which appeared in *The New Yorker*. His essays and stories were collected in *One Man's Meat* (1942) and *The Second Tree from the Corner* (1954). He also wrote children's books that are still extremely popular, most notably *Charlotte's Web* (1952). White is considered one of America's finest prose stylists and a master of the modern essay.

BOOKS BY WHITE

Charlotte's Web (1952). Harper 1952 $2.95. ISBN 0-06-440055-7

Essays of E. B. White (1977). Harper 1979 $8.95. ISBN 0-06-090662-6

Here Is New York (1949). Warner Bks 1988 $5.95. ISBN 0-446-38829-7

One Man's Meat (1942). Harper 1983 $9.95. ISBN 0-06-091081-X

The Second Tree from the Corner (1954). Harper 1984 $16.95. ISBN 0-06-015354-7

BOOK ABOUT WHITE

Elledge, Scott. *E. B. White: A Biography.* Norton 1984 $9.70. ISBN 0-393-30305-5 Describes White's childhood, undergraduate years at Cornell, and career at *The New Yorker,* including his relationships with publisher Harold Ross and writer James Thurber.

NEWS MEDIA

HISTORY AND OVERVIEW

*Chancellor, John, and Walter R. Mears. *The News Business.* NAL 1983 $3.95. ISBN 0-451-62309-6 Both a newswriting manual and an insider's view of the industry: sources, leads, news analysis, job-hunting and other topics; David Halberstam found it "the best primer for young journalists I have ever read."

David, Elmer. *A History of the New York Times 1851–1921.* Greenwood 1970 repr of 1921 ed $37.50. ISBN 0-8371-2578-2

Hartley, John. *Understanding News.* Methuen 1982 $11.95. ISBN 0-416-74550-4

Kenny, Herbert. *Newspaper Row: Journalism in the Pre-Television Era.* Globe Pequot 1987 $16.95. ISBN 0-87106-772-2

Kessler, Lauren. *The Dissident Press.* Sage 1984 $9.95. ISBN 0-8039-2087-3

*Manoff, Robert, and Michael Shudson. *Reading the News.* Pantheon 1990 $9.95. ISBN 0-394-74649-X Helps the newspaper reader understand how newspaper shapes the way its readers see the world around them.

Mirali, Robert. *Muckraking and Objectivity: Journalism's Colliding Traditions.* Greenwood 1990 $40.00. ISBN 0-313-27298-0

Moen, Daryl. *Newspaper Layout and Design.* Iowa State Univ Pr 1989 $26.95. ISBN 0-8138-1227-5

Pickett, Calder. *Voices of the Past: Key Documents in the History of American Journalism.* Macmillan 1977 $39.00. ISBN 0-02-395790-5

Schudson, Michael. *Discovering the News: A Social History of American Newspapers.* Basic 1981 $10.95. ISBN 0-465-01666-9

Stephens, Mitchell. *A History of News: From the Drum to the Satellite.* Penguin 1983 $24.95. ISBN 0-670-81378-8

Stephens, Mitchell. *A History of News: From Oral Culture to the Information Age.* Penguin 1988 $24.95. ISBN 0-670-81378-8

Sterling, Christopher, and John Kittross. *Stay Tuned: A Concise History of American Broadcasting.* Wadsworth 1989 $25.95. ISBN 0-534-11904-2

*Swanberg, W. A. *Citizen Hearst.* Scribner's 1961 $25.00. ISBN 0-684-14503-0 Comprehensive and objective examination of the long, bizarre life of William Randolph Hearst, founder of the vast Hearst publishing empire.

Yorke, Ivor. *The Technique of Television News.* Focal 1987 $29.95. ISBN 0-240-51253-7

NATURE AND EFFECTS

Altheide, David. *Creating Reality: How TV News Distorts Reality.* Sage 1976 $16.95. ISBN 0-8039-0672-2

*Crouse, Timothy. *The Boys on the Bus.* Ballantine 1976 $3.95. ISBN 0-345-34015-9 Reporter Timothy Crouse's behind-the-scenes coverage of the press corps during the 1972 Nixon–McGovern presidential campaign; photographs included.

Epstein, Edward. *News from Nowhere: Television and the News.* Random 1974 $3.96. ISBN 0-394-71998-0

Gans, Herbert J. *Deciding What's News: A Study of CBS Evening News, NBC Nightly News, Newsweek and Time.* Random 1980 $9.95. ISBN 0-394-74354-7

Graber, Doris. *Crime News and the Public.* Praeger 1980 $42.95. ISBN 0-275-90491-1

Koch, Tom. *The News as Myth: Fact and Context in Journalism.* Greenwood 1990 $38.00. ISBN 0-313-27268-9

Lang, Gladys. *The Battle for Public Opinion: The President, the Press, and the Polls During Watergate.* Columbia Univ Pr 1983 $16.00. ISBN 0-231-05549-8

*MacNeil, Robert. *The Right Place at the Right Time.* Penguin 1990 $8.95. ISBN 0-14-013120-5 An insider's view of television journalism; "a fascinating tale about a first-class reporter's education," according to television journalist Mike Wallace.

Matusow, Barbara. *The Evening Stars: The Making of the Network News Anchor.* Ballantine 1984 $3.95. ISBN 0-345-31714-9

Nimmo, Dan, and James Combs. *Nightly Horrors: Crisis Coverage in Television Network News.* Univ of Tennessee Pr 1985 $18.95. ISBN 0-87049-443-0

Shaw, David. *Press Watch: A Provocative Look at How Newspapers Report the News.* Macmillan 1984 $15.95. ISBN 0-02-610030-4

Tuchman, Gaye. *Making News: A Study in the Construction of Reality.* Free Pr 1978 $12.95. ISBN 0-02-932930-2

Woodward, Bob, and Carl Bernstein. *All the President's Men.* Simon 1987 $6.95. ISBN 0-671-64644-3

A Closer Look

Adler, Ruth. *A Day in the Life of the New York Times.* Ayer 1971 $22.00. ISBN 0-405-13782-6

Halberstam, David. *The Powers That Be.* Knopf 1979 $17.95. ISBN 0-394-50381-3

Merrill, John, and Harold Fisher. *The World's Great Dailies: Profiles of 50 Newspapers.* Hastings 1980 $10.50. ISBN 0-8038-8096-0

Prichard, Peter. *The Making of McPaper: The Inside Story of USA Today.* St. Martin's 1989 $5.95. ISBN 0-312-91168-8

Rosenberg, Jerry. *Inside the Wall Street Journal: The History and the Power of Dow Jones and Company and America's Most Influential Newspaper.* Macmillan 1982 $16.95. ISBN 0-02-604860-4

Wolseley, Roland. *Black Press, USA.* Iowa State Univ Pr 1989 $39.95. ISBN 0-8138-0494-9

PEARSON, DREW (ANDREW RUSSELL)   1897–1969

Columnist and investigative reporter Drew Pearson was born December 13, 1897, in Evanston, Illinois. After serving in the U.S. Army (1918), he received an A.B. degree from Swarthmore College in 1919.

Pearson's early career included time spent as the director of the American Friends Service Committee, a relief organization for which he worked in the war-torn Balkans, and as professor of industrial geography at the University of Pennsylvania in Philadelphia and at Columbia University in New York City. In 1925 he married Countess Felicia Gizycka, with whom he had one daughter. The couple were later divorced, and in 1936 Pearson married Luvie Moore.

Pearson began the work that was to win him national acclaim as a groundbreaking journalist and columnist in 1926. He was first a staff member on the *United States Daily* and then on the *Baltimore Sun.*

The reporter's first taste of fame came in 1931 when he was revealed as the coauthor (with fellow reporter Robert S. Allen) of *The Washington Merry-Go-Round,* a gossipy collection of behind-the-scenes stories that Allen's and Pearson's respective newspapers had refused to print. The book had been published anonymously, and both authors were fired when their identities were revealed. They soon began to collaborate on a syndicated column for United Features and for the next 10 years continued to report on Washington scandals.

When Allen went into the army in 1942, Pearson produced the column by himself. He was considered a somewhat self-righteous crusader who fearlessly sought to reveal scandals among the nation's political leaders. Although some criticized his ruthlessness and his tendency to attack certain figures without sufficient proof, all agreed that he created a new style of journalism: that of the relentless investigative reporter who stops at nothing to uncover the truth. He is credited as the forerunner of such investigative journalists as Bob Woodward and Carl Bernstein, whose aggressive reporting helped reveal the Watergate scandal that led to the resignation of President Richard M. Nixon in 1974.

In the late 1950s, Pearson again took on a co-writer, joining forces with one of his investigators, Jack Anderson. Anderson continued to write the column by himself after Pearson's death in 1969.

BOOK BY PEARSON

The Nine Old Men (1937). (coauthored with Robert S. Allen) Da Capo 1974 $45.00. ISBN 0-306-70609-1

CARTOONS

*Gould, Chester, and Herb Galewitz (eds). *Dick Tracy: The Thirties, Tommy Guns and Hard Times.* Chelsea 1978 $15.00. ISBN 0-87754-071-3 Reproduces Gould's famous *Dick Tracy* comic strips, adding commentary on the Great Depression of the 1930s as the context for stories about the "world's greatest detective," whose radio watch foreshadowed today's high-tech gear.
*Jacobs, Will, and Gerard Jones. *Comic Book Heroes: From the Silver Age to the Present.* Crown 1985 $11.95. ISBN 0-517-55440-2 Informative and amusing history of style, values, and heroism as depicted in the comics over several decades.
 Larson, Gary. *The Far Side Gallery.* Andrews 1984 $10.95. ISBN 0-8362-1200-2
 Larson, Gary. *The Far Side Gallery 2.* Andrews 1986 $10.95. ISBN 0-8362-2085-4
 Larson, Gary. *The Far Side Gallery 3.* Andrews 1988 $10.95. ISBN 0-8362-1831-0
 Larson, Gary. *Prehistory of the Far Side.* Andrews 1989 $12.95. ISBN 0-8362-1851-5
*O'Sullivan, Judith. *The Great American Comic Strip.* Bulfinch 1990 $40.00. ISBN 0-8212-1754-2 Fascinating critical history documented by reproductions of representative comic strips.
*Schulz, Charles. *You're a Knockout, Charlie Brown.* Fawcett 1989 $2.95. ISBN 0-449-21730-2 Most recent collection of Charlie Brown cartoons from Schulz's famous *Peanuts* comic strip.
 Scott, Randall. *Comic Books and Strips: An Information Sourcebook.* Oryx 1988 $30.00. ISBN 0-89774-389-X
 Sheridan, Martin. *The Comics and Their Creators: Life Stories of American Cartoonists.* Hyperion 1944 $12.00. ISBN 0-88355-525-5
 Trudeau, G. B. *Comic Relief: Drawings from the Cartoonists' Thanksgiving Day Hunger Project.* Holt 1986 $5.95. ISBN 0-03-009093-8
 Wood, Art. *Great Cartoonists and Their Art.* Pelican 1987 $19.95. ISBN 0-88289-476-5

SPECIAL TOPIC: EDITORIAL CARTOONS

 Block, Herbert. *Herblock at Large: Let's Go Back a Little and Other Cartoons from the Reagan Era.* Pantheon 1987 $16.95. ISBN 0-394-56569-X
 Brooks, Charles. *Best Editorial Cartoons of the Year: 1989 Edition.* Pelican 1989 $9.95. ISBN 0-88289-731-4.
 Forman, Maury, and Rick Marschall. *Cartooning Washington.* Melior 1989 $32.95. ISBN 0-9616441-7-6
 Press, Charles. *Political Cartoon.* Fairleigh 1981 $37.50. ISBN 0-8386-1901-0

Trudeau, G. B. *In Search of Reagan's Brain.* Holt 1981 $8.95. ISBN 0-03-059904
Trudeau, G. B. *Read My Lips, Make My Day, Eat Quiche and Die!* Andrews 1989 $6.95. ISBN 0-8362-1845-0

NAST, THOMAS 1840–1902

Born in Germany, Thomas Nast immigrated to America with his family when he was six years old. His father was a musician who found work in New York, where Nast attended local schools. Always interested in drawing, he left school at age 15 and began to study art. He eventually attended the National Academy of Design in New York.

From 1855 to 1859, Nast was a staff artist for *Frank Leslie's Illustrated Newspaper* in New York. Then he went to Italy, where he covered the campaign for Italian unification for newspapers in New York, London, and Paris.

Upon his return to the United States in 1862, Nast joined the staff of *Harper's Weekly* as a staff artist and political cartoonist. There he did most of the work for which he became famous.

Nast is frequently called the father of American political cartooning for the work he did at *Harper's* magazine, most notably the series of satirical cartoons that helped to bring down the corrupt New York politician known as Boss Tweed. As part of his campaign against Tweed, Nast drew a picture of a tiger to represent Tammany Hall, the New York political organization that Tweed headed. The tiger remained the symbol for the Tammany organization long after Tweed was gone. Nast was the first to use an elephant to represent the Republican party in the 1874 presidential campaign. He also originated the Democratic party donkey, Uncle Sam, and the white-bearded, red-suited man most Americans know as Santa Claus. He created the latter when he illustrated the text of Clement Clark Moore's immortal poem, "A Visit from St. Nicholas," better known as "The Night Before Christmas."

BOOKS BY NAST

Cartoons and Illustrations of Thomas Nast (1974). Dover 1974 $12.50. ISBN 0-486-23067-8
'Twas the Night Before Christmas: A Visit from St. Nicholas (1864). Illustrated by Thomas Nast, written by Clement Moore. Houghton 1912 $12.95. ISBN 0-395-06952-1

BOOKS ABOUT NAST

Callow, Alexander. *The Tweed Ring.* Greenwood 1981 $35.00. ISBN 0-313-22761-6 Details the rise of Boss Tweed's Tammany Hall (a corrupt political clique) and Nast's unique contribution to its decline.
Paine, Albert. *Thomas Nast: His Period and His Pictures.* Chelsea 1981 $8.95. ISBN 0-87754-169-8 Review of Nast's career with commentary on the politics of his period; amply illustrated with Nast's drawings.

TRUDEAU, GARY 1948–

As an undergraduate at Yale University, Gary Trudeau began drawing a comic strip for the *Yale Daily News.* In it he caricatured some of his friends and campus celebrities while satirizing both campus and world events. He created the name of the title character by combining the Yale slang term "doone," meaning a "good-natured fool," and the last name of one of his college roommates, a member of the famous flour-milling Pillsbury family.

Doonesbury was an immediate hit at Yale, and by 1970, it began to appear in newspapers all over the country. Over the years, the original cast of characters has grown older and a few new ones have been added, but the original irreverent satire has never faded. Although Trudeau's satire is social as well as political (California fads are among his favorite targets), many newspapers consider the strip to be primarily political and carry it on their editorial pages rather than in their comic sections.

Occasionally Trudeau's satire causes him trouble when, for example, targets of his wit threaten to sue or newspapers refuse to print strips they consider too controversial. But his fans remain numerous and loyal, and the strip shows no signs of losing its popularity. In fact, Trudeau caused something of a national outrage in 1982 when he decided to stop drawing *Doonesbury* in order to concentrate on other activities. His loyal fans breathed a sigh of relief when the strip returned to its 700 newspapers in 1984.

Trudeau was awarded the Pulitzer Prize for cartooning in 1974, and he has been widely praised by his fellow cartoonists and journalists. He is married to television news broadcaster Jane Pauley.

BOOKS BY TRUDEAU

Doonesbury (1971). McGraw 1971 $7.95. ISBN 0-07-065294-5
Doonesbury Chronicles (1975). Holt 1975 $12.95. ISBN 0-03-014906
Doonesbury Dossier: The Reagan Years (1984). Holt 1989 $22.95. ISBN 0-03-061729-4
Doonesbury's Greatest Hits (1978). Holt 1978 $12.95. ISBN 0-03-044851-4
Doonesbury: The Original Yale Cartoons (1973). Andrews 1973 $4.95. ISBN 0-8362-0550-2
Downtown Doonesbury (1987). H. Holt 1987 $5.95. ISBN 0-8050-0354-1

BOOK ABOUT TRUDEAU

Blair, Walter, and Hamlin Hill. *America's Humor from Poor Richard to Doonesbury.* Oxford Univ Pr 1980 $9.95. ISBN 0-19-502756-6 Valuable historical survey of the context of Trudeau's social humor but with little specific information about Trudeau.

RADIO

Archer, Gleason. *A History of Radio to 1926. History of Broadcasting: Radio to TV Ser.* Ayer 1971 repr of 1938 ed $28.00. ISBN 0-405-035557-8
Arnheim, Rudolf. *Radio. History of Broadcasting: Radio to TV Ser.* Ayer 1971 repr of 1936 ed $25.50. ISBN 0-405-03570-5
Bogosian, Eric. *Talk Radio.* Random 1988 $6.95. ISBN 0-394-75946-X
Busby, Linda, and Donald L. Parker. *The Art and Science of Radio.* Allyn 1984 $32.00. ISBN 0-205-08049-9
Cantor, Muriel, and Suzanne Pingree. *The Soap Opera.* Sage 1983 $19.95. ISBN 0-8039-2004-0
*Carter, Alden. *Radio: From Marconi to the Space Age.* Watts 1987 $10.40. ISBN 0-531-10310-2 Concise, concrete introduction to the history of radio and the innovative people who contributed to its social power and technological development.
Codel, Martin (ed). *Radio and Its Future. History of Broadcasting: Radio to TV Ser.* Ayer 1971 repr of 1930 ed $29.00. ISBN 0-405-03559-4
Dygert, Warren. *Radio as an Advertising Medium.* Garland 1985 $30.00. ISBN 0-8240-6752-5
Fornatale, Peter. *Radio in the Television Age.* Overlook Pr 1983 $9.95. ISBN 0-87951-172-9
Goffman, Erving. *Forms of Talk.* Univ of Penn Pr 1981 $8.95. ISBN 0-8122-1112-X
Huth, Arno. *Radio Today: The Present State of Broadcasting. History of Broadcasting: Radio to TV Ser.* Ayer 1971 repr of 1942 ed $14.00. ISBN 0-405-03585-3
Keillor, Garrison. *Lake Wobegone Days.* Penguin 1985 $17.95. ISBN 0-670-80514-9
Lazarsfeld, Paul. *Radio and the Printed Page: An Introduction to the Story of Radio and Its Role*

in the Communication of Ideas. History of Broadcasting: Radio to TV Ser. Ayer 1971 repr of 1940 ed $25.50. ISBN 0-405-03575-6

Levin, Murray. *Talk Radio and the American Dream.* Lexington Bks 1986 $10.95. ISBN 0-669-13217-9

Summers, Harrison (ed). *Radio Censorship. History of Broadcasting: Radio to TV Ser.* Ayer 1971 repr of 1939 ed $23.50. ISBN 0-405-03582-9

ROGERS, WILL (WILLIAM PENN ADAIR)   1879–1935

Will Rogers was born in Oolagh, Indian Territory (now part of Oklahoma), of Cherokee ancestry. In his youth, he traveled widely in the United States, Europe, and Africa, and in 1899, he worked as a horse-breaker for the British army during the Boer War in South Africa. In 1901, he returned to the United States and began working in rodeos and with a traveling wild west show. In 1904, he entered vaudeville as a rope twirler and comedian. By 1913, he had become famous enough to join the world-renowned Ziegfield Follies, and in 1919, he began making movies.

Known as "the cowboy philosopher," Rogers's humor was built around wry comments on the American political and social scene. His dry wit and easy manner were ideally suited to radio. His radio shows, like the newspaper columns he began writing in 1926, poked gentle fun at key political figures, fads, and big business.

In 1930, Rogers signed a contract to do 14 radio broadcasts, 15-minutes each, for the unheard of sum of $72,000. With the onset of the Depression, Rogers's radio broadcasts, filled with humorous messages of hope and informed by a "we're all in this together" attitude, were a source of comfort to millions of people. In 1933, he began a series of half-hour variety shows that aired every Sunday evening and became a weekly ritual for many American families.

In 1928, Rogers made a semiserious run for the United States presidency on the Anti-Bunk ticket using the slogan, "He chews to run," a parody of President Calvin Coolidge's famous remark, "I do not choose to run."

Rogers was also a pioneer in the field of aviation and commercial air travel. He was killed in an airplane crash in Alaska with famous aviator Wiley Post.

BOOKS BY ROGERS

Radio Broadcasts of Will Rogers (1983). Oklahoma State Univ Pr 1983 $10.95. ISBN 0-914956-24-8

Will Rogers' Daily Telegrams: 1926–1935 (1979). James Smallwood and Steven Gragert (eds). 4 vols. Oklahoma State Univ Pr 1979 $19.95 each. ISBNs 0-914956-10-8, 0-914956-11-6, 0-914956-12-4, 0-914956-13-2

Will Rogers Treasury: Reflections and Observations (1982). Crown 1986 $6.98. ISBN 0-517-62544-X

BOOKS ABOUT ROGERS

Musso, Louis. *Will Rogers: America's Cowboy Philosopher.* SamHar 1974 $3.95. ISBN 0-87157-574-4 Profiles Rogers's careers in radio and print journalism, highlighting his humility, humor, values, and political beliefs.

Rogers, Betty. *Will Rogers.* Univ of Oklahoma Pr 1982 $18.95. ISBN 0-8061-1526-2 Loving memoir written by Rogers's wife about her remarkable husband and their life together.

THOMAS, LOWELL   1892–1981

Radio and television commentator Lowell Thomas was born April 6, 1892, in Woodington, Ohio. He received his B.S. from the University of Northern Indiana in 1911 and his B.A. and M.A. from the University of Denver in 1912. After attending Kent College of Law from 1912 through 1914, Thomas received a second M.A. from Princeton University in 1916.

Lowell Thomas began his journalistic career as a reporter and editor on newspapers in Cripple Creek (Colorado), Denver, and Chicago. He also taught oratory briefly at Kent College of Law in Chicago. In 1917 he married Frances Ryan, with whom he later had one son.

Thomas first won world fame as the biographer of T. E. Lawrence, the so-called Lawrence of Arabia. At the end of World War I, Thomas was traveling with Allied forces as an observer and correspondent. In the course of his travels, he met Lawrence, a British Army officer who was leading a group of Arab tribes in their fight against the Turks. Thomas later toured the world with films of Lawrence accompanied by his own narration. He followed up the highly successful tours with the book *With Lawrence in Arabia* (1924).

In 1930, Thomas began to work as a radio journalist, a field in which he won numerous awards and was responsible for numerous firsts, including first broadcasts from a ship, from an airplane, from a coal mine, and from a submarine.

In 1939, Thomas broadcast the first news program on television, a medium in which he was also to win many awards. He continued to publish many books about his travels, to lecture, and to produce programs for films and television. His well-know resonant voice can be heard on almost 20 years of Twentieth Century-Fox Movietone newsreels—short films about current events shown in movie theaters.

One of Thomas's many famous exploits was his 1949 trip to Tibet to visit the Dalai Lama, the Tibetan religious leader. In the course of a dangerous trip through the Himalaya Mountains, Thomas fell from his horse and broke his leg, narrowly escaping, with the help of his son, a fatal fall down a cliff.

Thomas's first wife died in 1975, and he married Mariana Munn in 1977. He remained active until the end of his life, continuing to broadcast until 1976 and publishing a memoir, *From Quaker Hill to Kathmandu,* in 1977. He died of a heart attack in 1981.

NONFICTION BY THOMAS

Doolittle: A Biography (1976). (coauthored with Edward Jablonski) Da Capo 1976 $8.95. ISBN 0-306-80158-2
Old Gimlet Eye: Adventures of Smedley D. Butler (1933). Marine Corps 1981 $8.95. ISBN 0-940328-01-1
Ripley's Giant Believe It or Not! (1985). Crown 1985 $8.98. ISBN 0-517-49466-3 Fascinating collection of unusual and hard-to-believe facts.

WINCHELL, WALTER (WALTER WINCHEL)   1897–1972

Columnist Walter Winchell was born Walter Winchel (he later added the second *l*) on April 7, 1897, in New York City. His first job was as a newsboy. Then, at age 12, he began work in vaudeville, a popular live entertainment form of the time, featuring singers, dancers, and comedians.

While on the road with a vaudeville company, Winchell started his first column—a one-page bulletin in which he reported on such newsworthy items as which hotels had just fumigated their rooms as well as on various bits of gossip and scandal about his fellow performers. Eventually he began submitting these items to the major entertainment magazines of the time—the beginning of his work as a gossip columnist.

Winchell married vaudeville performer Rita Greene in 1920 and was divorced in 1922. The following year, he married dancer June Magee, with whom he had two children.

Throughout the 1920s, Winchell continued to work as a free-lance gossip columnist and as a journalist for various New York papers. He was given a regular position as columnist on the *New York Daily Mirror* in 1929, a position that launched him on an enormous wave of popularity that lasted through the 1950s.

Most observers recognize Winchell as the person who invented the gossip column—a chatty, personal type of journalism that combines items of interest about major personalities of the day with inside information about politics, business, and finance. Winchell's column also featured news of the underworld, taken from his personal acquaintances with many gangsters and mob figures.

At its peak, Winchell's column reached millions of Americans, as did his weekly radio broadcast, read in his famous "machine-gun-style" rapid-fire delivery. Mention by Winchell could make or break a book, a movie, or a movie star. He was also influential politically, supporting President Franklin D. Roosevelt's bid for a third term of office in 1940 and championing Wisconsin Senator Joseph McCarthy's anticommunist crusade in the 1950s. Many believe that Winchell destroyed the political career of Montana Senator Burton K. Wheeler.

Winchell narrated the popular television show *The Untouchables* in 1960, as well as appearing as a commentator on ABC-TV. He died of cancer in 1972.

BOOK ABOUT WINCHELL

Herr, Michael. *Walter Winchell.* Knopf 1990 $18.95. ISBN 0-394-58372-8 Fictional account of Winchell's life; lively, entertaining, dramatic.

TELEVISION

OVERVIEW AND HISTORY

*Barnouw, Erik. *Tube of Plenty: The Evolution of American Television.* Oxford Univ Pr 1982 $12.95. ISBN 0-19-503092-3 Single-volume, updated condensation of Barnouw's three-volume history.

*Brooks, Tim, and Earle Marsh. *The Complete Directory to Prime Time TV Shows, 1946–Present.* Ballantine 1985 $14.95. ISBN 0-345-35610-1 Guide to TV series premiering through 1981 with a list of the top 100 syndicated shows; includes an appendix listing series that came from radio.

Friendly, Fred. *Due to Circumstances Beyond Our Control.* Random 1967 $5.95. ISBN 0-394-70409-6

Henderson, Katherine Usher, and Joseph A. Mazzeo (eds). *Meanings of the Medium: Perspectives on the Art of Television.* Praeger 1990 $39.95. ISBN 0-275-93390-3

Inglis, Andrew. *A History of Broadcasting: Technology and Business.* Focal 1990 $34.95. ISBN 0-240-80043-5

*Kuney, Jack. *Take One: Television Directors on Directing.* Greenwood 1990 $39.95. ISBN 0-313-26384-1 Insights of 10 television directors, each a specialist in a different field, explaining the director's important, behind-the-scenes role.
MacDonald, J. Fred. *Blacks and White TV: Afro-Americans in Television Since 1948.* Nelson-Hall 1983 $14.95. ISBN 0-88229-816-X
*Oakey, Virginia. *Dictionary of Film and Television Terms.* Harper 1982 $8.95. ISBN 0-06-463566-X Defines 3,000 technical, artistic, and business terms as well as industry jargon; numerous examples and cross-references.
Reed, Marene. *Career Opportunities in TV, Cable and Video.* Facts on File 1986 $12.95. ISBN 0-8160-1534-1
Steinberg, Cobbett. *TV Facts.* Facts on File 1984 $35.00. ISBN 0-87196-733-2
*Wilkie, Bernard. *The Technique of Special Effects in Television.* Focal 1989 $32.95. ISBN 0-240-51284-7 Technical but informative; a great start toward demystifying the "magic" of special effects without detracting from the skills of the technicians.

CULTURAL AND SOCIAL IMPACT

Adler, Richard (ed). *Understanding Television: Essays on Television as a Cultural and Social Force.* Praeger 1981 $18.95. ISBN 0-275-91507-7
Arlen, Michael. *The Camera Age: Essays on Television.* Farrar 1981 $13.95. ISBN 0-374-11822-1
Cantor, Muriel. *Prime-Time Television: Content and Control.* Sage 1980 $9.95. ISBN 0-8039-1317-6
Cantor, Muriel, and Suzanne Pingree. *The Soap Opera.* Sage 1983 $9.95. ISBN 0-8039-2005-9
Cole, Barry (ed). *Television Today: A Close-Up View.* Oxford Univ Pr 1981 $12.95. ISBN 0-19-502799-X
Comstock, George. *Television in America.* Sage 1980 $9.95. ISBN 0-8039-1245-5
*Cross, Donna Woolfolk. *Mediaspeak: How Television Makes Up Your Mind.* NAL 1984 $5.95. ISBN 0-451-62802-0 Provocative analysis revealing how the viewer is manipulated by different types of programming from game shows, soap operas, and docudramas to newscasts, commercials, and political spots.
Esslin, Martin. *The Age of Television.* Freeman 1981 $12.95. ISBN 0-7167-1338-1
*Goldsen, Rose. *The Show and Tell Machine: How Television Works and Works You Over.* Dell 1978 $4.95. ISBN 0-385-28878-6 Exceptionally effective in depicting the power of TV to determine what viewers think *about* as well as what they think.
Greenberg, Bradley. *Life on Television: Content Analyses of United States TV Drama.* Ablex 1980 $24.95. ISBN 0-89391-062-7
Johnston, Jerome. *Positive Images: Breaking Stereotypes with Children's Television.* Sage 1982 $16.95. ISBN 0-8039-0385-5
Liebert, R. L. *The Early Window: Effects of Television on Children and Youth.* Pergamon 1988 $12.95. ISBN 0-08-034679-0
Mander, Jerry. *Four Arguments for the Elimination of Television.* Morrow 1978 $7.95. ISBN 0-688-08274-2
Marc, David. *Comic Visions: Television Comedy and American Culture.* Unwin 1989 $10.95. ISBN 0-04-445285-3
Miller, Mark Crispin. *Boxed-In.* Northwestern Univ Pr 1988 $14.95. ISBN 0-8101-0792-9
Mitroff, Ian, and Warren Bennis. *The Unreality Industry.* Birch Lane 1989 $17.95. ISBN 1-55972-014-X
Moody, Kate. *Growing Up on Television.* McGraw 1984 $6.95. ISBN 0-07-42871-9
Newcomb, Horace. *Television: The Critical View.* Oxford Univ Pr 1987 $16.95. ISBN 0-19-504175-5
Rader, Benjamin. *In Its Own Image: How Television Has Transformed Sports.* Free Pr 1984 $19.95. ISBN 0-02-925700-X
Sklar, Robert. *Prime-Time America: Life On and Behind the Television Screen.* Oxford Univ Pr 1980 $6.95. ISBN 0-19-503046-X

Turow, Joseph. *Entertainment, Education and the Hard Sell: Three Decades of Network Children's Television.* Praeger 1981 $31.95. ISBN 0-275-90735-X
Winn, Marie. *The Plug-In Drug: Television, Children, and the Family.* Penguin 1985 $6.95. ISBN 0-14-007698-0

A Closer Look

*Gitlin, Todd. *Inside Prime Time.* Pantheon 1985 $11.95. Using over 200 interviews with everyone from executives to actors, this book profiles the network's frantic search for the hit show.
Levinson, Richard, and William Link. *Stay Tuned: An Inside Look at the Making of Prime Time Television.* St. Martin's 1981 $11.95. ISBN 0-312-76136-8
*Whitfield, Stephen, and Gene Roddenberry. *The Making of Star Trek.* Ballantine 1979 $4.95. ISBN 0-345-34019-1 Detailed account of the development of the *Star Trek* series from its conception through the making of the pilot episode; published in 1968 and still the best study of the creation of a TV series.

MOYERS, BILL   1934–

Born Billy Don Moyers in Hugo, Oklahoma, Bill Moyers had his name legally changed to Bill when he became a journalist. He attended North Texas State University and the University of Texas, from which he graduated with honors in journalism in 1956. While still an undergraduate, Moyers became assistant news editor for KTBC radio and television in Austin, Texas. After graduation, Moyers studied for a year at the University of Edinburgh in Scotland before going on to Southwestern Baptist Theological Seminary, where he received a divinity degree in 1959.

In 1959, Moyers became special assistant to Senator Lyndon B. Johnson of Texas. In 1961, he went to work for the Peace Corps, becoming its deputy director in 1962. In 1963, Moyers returned to work for Johnson, who had become President, and from 1965 to 1967, he served as presidential press secretary.

In 1971, Moyers began his television career when he became host of the public affairs program *This Week* for National Educational Television. A year later he began hosting his own show, *Bill Moyers' Journal,* for which he received one of many Emmy Awards from the National Academy of Television Arts and Sciences. Moyers received another Emmy in 1974, when he was named outstanding broadcaster of the year.

Moyers has continued his career as reporter, commentator, and interviewer in both commercial and public television, and he is widely considered one of America's most intelligent and perceptive journalists. His recent programs, such as the highly acclaimed *Image and Reality in America with Bill Moyers,* which examined the impact of media on American thought, have won high critical praise as well as wide popularity.

BOOKS BY MOYERS

Moyers: Report from Philadelphia: The Constitutional Convention of 1787. Ballantine 1989 $3.95. ISBN 0-345-36160-1
The Power of Myth. (coauthored with Joseph Campbell) Doubleday 1988 $27.50. ISBN 0-385-24773-7
The Secret Government. Seven Locks 1988 $9.95. ISBN 0-932020-60-7
A World of Ideas: Conversations with Thoughtful Men and Women About American Life Today and the Ideas Shaping Our Future. Doubleday 1989 $29.95. ISBN 0-385-26278-7

MURROW, EDWARD R.   1908–1965

More than any other journalist, Edward R. Murrow has influenced the shape of television news broadcasting. As a reporter, commentator, and director of news for the Columbia Broadcasting System (CBS) in the early days of television, Murrow was a pioneer in the areas of live telecasts of news events, commentary on major issues, and face-to-face interviews. Above all, however, he established standards of integrity and accuracy for broadcast news that the entire industry still strives to meet.

After graduating from college, Murrow became president of the National Student Federation, and from 1929 to 1932, he traveled throughout the United States and Europe visiting schools and discussing student issues. He then spent three years with the Institute of International Education before joining the CBS radio network in 1935. Two years later, he became part of the network's European Bureau in London.

With the outbreak of World War II, Murrow began a series of on-the-scene broadcasts, the most famous being his live reports on the German bombing of London. For millions of Americans, Murrow's sign-on greeting, "This is London," signaled the start of their favorite news program.

After the war, Murrow returned to New York as a CBS vice president in charge of news. He was among the first to see the news potential of television, and in 1951, he began broadcasting a series called *See It Now* in which he used speeches, interviews, and visual images to put key news events in focus. In 1953, Murrow began to broadcast *Person to Person,* a weekly interview program in which he conversed with important public figures. When the show ended in 1959, he had interviewed more than 500 people.

Highly honored in his own lifetime, Murrow has become something of a legend since his death. Most critics agree with Murrow's colleague, commentator Eric Sevareid, who said that "We shall live in his afterglow—a very long time—we shall not see his like again."

BOOKS BY MURROW

In Search of Light: The Broadcasts of Edward R. Murrow (1967). Avon 1986 $1.95. ISBN 0-380-01279-0

This Is London (1941). Schocken 1989 $7.95. ISBN 0-8052-0882-8

BOOKS ABOUT MURROW

Lichello, Robert. *Edward R. Murrow: Broadcaster of Courage.* SamHar 1972 $2.50. ISBN 0-87157-004-1 Biography of the brilliant radio and TV journalist, recounting Murrow's unwillingness to be intimidated he helped end the McCarthy era, a period in the early 1950s during which took place a series of punitive congressional investigations of suspected Communists and sympathizers in public life, spearheaded by Senator Joseph McCarthy.

Persico, Joseph. *Edward R. Murrow: An American Original.* Dell 1990 $12.95. ISBN 0-440-50301-9 Exclusive sources from the private collection of Murrow's wife Janet make a historical biography rich in well-told, dramatic anecdotes.

Sperber, Ann. *Murrow: His Life and Times.* Freundlich 1986 $25.00. ISBN 0-88191-008-2 Comprehensive, probing biography using previously unavailable sources; the definitive work on Murrow.

REACTING TO TV

*DeBartolo, Dick, and Angelo Torres. *Mad Look at TV.* Warner Bks 1974 $2.95. ISBN 0-446-94436-X Outdated examples aside, *Mad Mazagine*'s satirical view of television is great fun and a first-rate reminder of TV's power to fool people.

Fiske, John, and John Hartley. *Reading Television.* Routledge 1978 $12.95. ISBN 0-416-85560-1
*Gitlin, Todd. *Watching TV.* Pantheon 1990 $9.95. ISBN 0-394-74651-1 Seven essays by leading critics of television help viewers decode or "read" TV screen messages.
Hunt, Albert. *The Language of Television.* Heinemann 1981 $6.95. ISBN 413-33740-5
*Lappe, Frances Moore. *What to Do After You Turn Off the TV.* Ballantine 1985 $7.95. ISBN 0-345-31660-6 "Author of *Diet for a Small Planet* shares the expertise she and dozens of other parents and families have developed as alternatives to watching television."—*Publisher's Weekly*
*Littell, Joy (ed). *Coping with Television.* McDougal 1973 $4.15. ISBN 0-88343-121-1 Visually appealing, with substantial information about content, ratings, production, impact, and advertising; designed for courses in visual literacy but interesting also for personal reading or research.
Schrank, Jeffrey. *TV Action Book.* McDougal 1974 $4.14. ISBN 0-88343-122-X
Winn, Marie. *Unplugging the Plug-In Drug.* Penguin 1987 $7.95. 0-14-008895-4

MOVIES

OVERVIEW AND HISTORY

Berger, Arthur. *Film in Society.* Transaction 1980 $12.95. ISBN 0-87855-245-6
*Blum, Daniel. *A New Pictorial History of the Talkies.* Putnam 1982 $9.95. ISBN 0-399-50666-7
Cook, David. *A History of Narrative Film, 1889–1979.* Norton 1988 $22.95. ISBN 0-393-95553-2
DeGrazia, Edward, and Roger Newman. *Banned Films: Movies, Censors and the First Amendment.* Bowker 1982 $24.95. ISBN 0-8352-1511-3
Doherty, Thomas. *Teenagers and Teenpics: The Juvenilization of American Movies in the 1950s.* Unwin 1988 $34.95. ISBN 0-04-445139-3
*Earley, Steven. *An Introduction to American Movies.* NAL 1990 $5.95. ISBN 0-451-62725-3 Comprehensive history beginning with Thomas Alva Edison's crude Kinetoscope through the futurism of *Star Wars;* includes glossary, index, photographs.
Fell, John. *Film Before Griffith.* Univ of California Pr 1983 $30.00. ISBN 0-520-04738-9
Fulton, Albert. *Motion Pictures: The Development of an Art from Silent Films to the Age of Television.* Univ of Oklahoma Pr 1980 $24.95. ISBN 0-8061-1633-1
Kane, Kathryn. *Visions of War: Hollywood Combat Films of World War Two.* Books Demand 1982 $48.40. ISBN 0-8357-1286-9
Kaplan, E. Anne. *Women and Film, Both Sides of the Camera.* Routledge 1983 $14.95. ISBN 0-416-31750-2
*Knight, Arthur. *The Liveliest Art: A Panoramic History of the Movies.* NAL 1979 $4.95. ISBN 0-451-62652-4 "An excellent introduction for interested YA's [young adults] . . . encourages critical viewing as well as appreciation for film as a medium."—*VOYA.*
*Kobal, John. *John Kobal Presents the Top 100 Movies.* Plume 1988 $9.95. ISBN 0-452-26146-5 Compilation of the top 100 favorite movies of film critics around the world; includes insightful history of each film with photos from Kobal's own collection.
*Konigsberg, Ira. *The Complete Film Dictionary.* NAL 1989 $24.95. ISBN 0-453-00564-0 Comprehensive reference with 3,000 entries covering all aspects of the film industry; defines practical and technical terms, historical terms, and the jargon of film criticism and theory; cross-references put definitions in proper context.
Life Goes to the Movies. Crown 1987 $19.95. ISBN 0-517-62585-7 Great selection of photographs and movie reviews from *Life* magazine going back nearly two generations; a perfect companion to any history of American cinema.
*Maltin, Leonard (ed). *The Whole Film Sourcebook.* Plume 1982 $9.95. ISBN 0-452-25361-6

Reference guide to the practical aspects of cinema, covering education and careers (schools and colleges, unions and guilds, grants, entry-level jobs); the film industry (studios and distributors, film festivals); and film resources (archives and libraries, nontheatrical distributors, film showcases, libraries, bookstores, and memorabilia dealers).

Mast, Gerald. *Short History of the Movies.* Macmillan 1986 $35.00. ISBN 0-02-580500-2

Monaco, James. *American Film Now: The People, the Power, the Money, the Movies.* New York Zoetrope 1984 $24.95. ISBN 0-918432-64-2

*Norman, Barry. *The Story of Hollywood.* Plume 1989 $9.95. ISBN 0-452-26299-2 Beginning with the sound revolution in 1927, Norman traces the development of the studio system, the depiction of sex in films, the impact of World War II, and the role of Hollywood today; tie-in to the 10-part series coproduced by the British Broadcasting Corporation (BBC) and Turner Broadcasting; includes more than 200 photos.

Oakes, Philip (ed). *Film Addicts Archive: Poetry and Prose of the Cinema.* Beekman 1966 $18.95. ISBN 0-8464-1190-3

Sanderson, Richard. *Historical Study of the Development of American Motion Picture Content and Techniques Prior to 1904.* Ayer 1977 $17.00. ISBN 0-405-09894-4

Schrank, Jeffrey. *The Guide to Short Films.* Boynton 1979 $10.00. ISBN 0-8104-6035-1

Torrence, Bruce. *Hollywood: The First One Hundred Years.* New York Zoetrope 1982 $24.95. ISBN 0-918432-44-8

ART

Boggs, Joseph. *Art of Watching Films.* Mayfield 1985 $22.95. ISBN 0-87484-712-5

Bordwell, David, and Kristin Thompson. *Film Art: An Introduction.* McGraw 1990 $23.95. ISBN 0-07-006439-3

*Cohen, Daniel. *Masters of Horror.* Houghton 1984 $12.95. ISBN 0-89919-221-1 Profiles of Stephen King, Boris Karloff, Bela Lugosi, Steven Spielberg, and many other horror-movie artists.

*Coynik, David. *Film: Real to Reel.* McDougal 1976 $8.50. ISBN 0-88343-304-4 How film artists create the fantasy images seen on the screen and why viewers often find real-life experience unappealing when compared to the movies.

Giannetti, Louis. *Understanding Movies.* Prentice 1987 $23.00. ISBN 1-13-936329-7

Huss, Roy, and Norman Silverstein. *The Film Experience.* Dell 1969 $3.95. ISBN 0-385-28280-X

Jacobs, Lewis (ed). *The Emergence of Film Art.* Norton 1979 $9.95. ISBN 0-393-95049-2

Kaminsky, Stuart. *American Film Genres.* Nelson-Hall 1984 $13.95. ISBN 0-88229-826-7

Perkins, V. T. *Film as Film: Understanding and Judging Movies.* Penguin 1972 $5.95. ISBN 0-14-021477-1

Solomon, S. J. *Beyond Formula: American Film Genres.* Harcourt 1976 $13.00. ISBN 0-15-505400-7

Stephenson, Ralph, and Guy Phelps. *The Cinema as Art.* Penguin 1990 $8.95. ISBN 0-14-011981-7

*Withers, Robert. *Introduction to Film.* Harper 1983 $7.95. ISBN 0-06-460202-8 Shows how image, soundtrack, script, producing, directing, acting, and editing combine to create the emotional and intellectual impact of film.

SCIENCE

*Clemens, Virginia Phelps. *Behind the Filmmaking Scene.* Westminster John Knox 1982 $12.95. ISBN 0-664-32691-9 Job descriptions of people behind the scenes (*e.g.* director, stunt person, sound mixer, editor, cinematographer) and information about the education, experience, and personality necessary for success.

Coe, Brian. *A History of Movie Photography.* New York Zoetrope 1982 $24.95. ISBN 0-904069-38-9

Fielding, Raymond. *Technique of Special Effects Cinematography.* Focal 1985 $29.95. ISBN 0-240-51234-0

Hutchinson, David. *Film Magic: The Art and Science of Special Effects.* Prentice 1987 $12.95. ISBN 0-13-314774-6

*LeBaron, John, and Philip Miller. *Portable Video: A Production Guide for Young People.* Prentice 1982 $7.95. ISBN 0-13-686519-4 Short history of video, descriptions of the various parts of a video system, hints on writing successful video programs, and activities that make learning about video enjoyable.

Maltin, Leonard. *Art of the Cinematographer: A Survey and Interviews with Five Masters.* Dover 1978 $7.95. ISBN 0-486-23686-2

*McDonough, Tom. *Light Years: Confessions of a Cinematographer.* Grove 1987 $17.95. ISBN 0-8021-0014-7 History and technological explanation of cinematography.

Pincus, Edward, and Steven Ascher. *The Filmmaker's Handbook.* Plume 1984 $12.95. ISBN 0-452-25526-0

Pincus, Edward, and J. Lincoln. *Guide to Film Making.* NAL 1969 $4.95. ISBN 0-451-15172-0

*Robinson, Richard. *The Video Primer: Equipment, Production, and Concepts.* Perigee Bks 1983 $10.95. ISBN 0-399-50698-5 "Each chapter covers a specific topic, such as lighting, and is well-illustrated with drawings of video systems and photographs of state-of-the-art equipment"—*Camera Age.* Includes a complete glossary of video terms and step-by-step instructions on the use of equipment.

REPRESENTATIVE DIRECTORS AND SPECIFIC FILMS

Bach, Steven. *Final Cut: Dreams and Disaster in the Making of Heaven's Gate.* Onyx 1987 $4.95. ISBN 0-451-40036-4

Brown, Karl. *Adventures with D. W. Griffith.* Da Capo 1976 $6.95. ISBN 0-306-80032-2

*Cox, Stephen. *The Munchkins Remember: The Land of Oz and Beyond.* Dutton 1989 $12.95. ISBN 0-525-48486-8 Actors and actresses who played Munchkins discuss the making of *The Wizard of Oz* and their lives afterward.

*Harmetz, Aljean. *The Making of the Wizard of Oz.* Delacorte 1989 $12.95. ISBN 0-385-29746-7

Leaming, Barbara. *Orson Welles: A Biography.* Penguin 1985 $19.95. ISBN 0-670-52895-1

Mabery, D. L. *George Lucas.* Lerner 1987 $8.95. ISBN 0-8225-1614-4

Marx, Groucho, and Richard Anobile. *Marx Brothers Scrapbook.* Harper 1989 $14.95. ISBN 0-06-097265-3

Mosley, Leonard. *Zanuck: The Rise and Fall of Hollywood's Last Tycoon.* McGraw 1985 $8.95. ISBN 0-07-043465-4

Mott, Donald, and Cheryl M. Saunders. *Steven Spielberg.* Twayne 1986 $18.95. ISBN 0-8057-9299-6

Phillips, Gene. *Alfred Hitchcock.* Twayne 1984 $18.95. ISBN 0-8057-9293-7

Phillips, Gene. *George Cukor.* Twayne 1982 $19.95. ISBN 0-8057-9286-4

Pogel, Nancy. *Woody Allen.* Twayne 1988 $19.95. ISBN 0-8057-9297-X

Quart, Barbara Koenig. *Women Directors: The Emergence of a New Cinema.* Praeger 1989 $15.95. ISBN 0-275-93477-2

Seidman, Steve. *The Film Career of Billy Wilder.* Redgrave 1978 $8.90. ISBN 0-913178-58-6

*Smith, Dian G. *Great American Film Directors.* Messner 1987 $9.95. ISBN 0-671-50231-X Lively look at such notables as Steven Spielberg, George Lucas, and Alfred Hitchcock; especially for younger fans.

Smith, Julian. *Chaplin.* Twayne 1984 $18.95. ISBN 0-8057-9294-5

Stowell, Peter. *John Ford.* Twayne 1986 $16.95. ISBN 0-8057-9305-4

Wexman, Virginia. *Roman Polanski.* Twayne 1985 $20.95. ISBN 0-8057-9296-1

Williams, Martin. *Griffith: First Artist of the Movies.* Oxford Univ Pr 1980 $19.95. ISBN 0-19-502685-3

ALLEN, WOODY (ALLEN STEWART KONIGSBERG)   1935–

See also Allen, Vol. 1, American Literature: The Twentieth Century.

Woody Allen was born December 1, 1935, in Brooklyn, New York. Although he attended both New York University and City College, he never graduated. Instead, he entered the entertainment world as a television comedy writer and went on to become a successful stand-up comedian. He has also written numerous short stories and several plays.

Today, however, Woody Allen is probably best known as a writer, director, and sometimes actor in some of the most sophisticated and stylish movies of his time. Allen's films have gone through a number of stylistic changes. Such early films as *Take the Money and Run* (1969) and *Bananas* (1971) were zany, madcap comedies, full of visual gags and featuring the hapless Allen persona. Allen then moved into the more sophisticated style of *Sleeper* (1973) and *Annie Hall* (1977) (both co-written with Marshall Brickman), explorations of romantic relationships that also featured satiric, incisive looks at politics and culture.

Later Allen works took on a darker tone, as Allen began to explore the existential anxieties about which he had written in his fiction and his plays. At this time he also began to make films in black and white, like the filmmakers he most admires, Swedish director Ingmar Bergman and Italian director Federico Fellini. *Stardust Memories* (1980) is a bitter look at the difficulties of being a well-known filmmaker. *Zelig* (1983) is the painful exploration of a man who has so little identity of his own that, chameleonlike, he becomes like any person he is near. Although these films are comedies, their bleak vision made many wonder about the direction of Allen's work.

Allen returned to glossier, funnier films with such works as *The Purple Rose of Cairo* (1985) and *Hannah and Her Sisters* (1986), although these films both have a darker underside as Allen explores painful family relationships in *Hannah* and the clash between illusion and reality in *Cairo.* His latest works, *Crimes and Misdemeanors* (1989) and *Alice* (1991), continue Allen's comic search for the meaning of life.

SCREENPLAYS BY ALLEN

Three Films of Woody Allen: Broadway Danny Rose, Zelig, The Purple Rose of Cairo. Random 1987 $12.95. ISBN 0-394-75304-6

BOOKS ABOUT ALLEN

Brode, Douglas. *Woody Allen: His Films and Career.* Citadel 1987 $14.95. ISBN 0-8065-1067-6 Good general overview of the many different phases of Allen's work and of his growth into a respected film artist.

Pogel, Nancy. *Woody Allen.* G. K. Hall 1988 $9.95. ISBN 0-8057-9309-7 Basic introduction to Allen's life and work, including a biographical sketch, a look at each of Allen's films, and a chronology.

HUSTON, JOHN   1906–1987

John Huston was born in Nevada, Missouri, the son of actor Walter Huston, who would later achieve stardom on Broadway and in Hollywood. As a child in an acting family, John Huston spent much of his childhood moving from place to place. Afflicted with poor health, he learned to box in order to build up his body and in his teens became an amateur champion. When he was barely 20 years old, Huston gained a commission in the Mexican cavalry, in which he served during the early 1920s. Returning to New York, he became a reporter for the *New York Graphic* and wrote stories for U.S. journalist and satirist H. L. Mencken's *American Mercury* magazine. (*See* Mencken, Vol. 1, Language Arts: Language.)

In 1938, John Huston moved to Hollywood, where he joined Warner Brothers as a scriptwriter. He soon moved into directing films, and his first film, *The Maltese Falcon* (1941), is considered one of the best detective movies ever made. In 1948, Huston wrote and directed *The Treasure of Sierra Madre,* in which his father Walter appeared. He received Academy Awards for both his direction and his script. In 1951, *The African Queen,* which Huston directed, received an Academy Award for best picture of the year. Huston directed 41 films in his 46-year career.

Huston also distinguished himself as an actor, frequently appearing in small character parts both in his own films and those of others. During his career Huston was nominated for 13 Academy Awards and won two. He received career achievement awards from the American Film Institute, the Film Society of Lincoln Center, and several other major industry organizations.

BOOK BY HUSTON

An Open Book (1980). Ballantine 1981 $3.95. ISBN 0-345-25444-9

BOOKS ABOUT HUSTON

Grobel, Lawrence. *The Hustons.* Avon 1990 $12.95. ISBN 0-380-71224-5 Hollywood gossip and filmmaking history. The definitive book about three generations of Hustons—Walter, John, and John's daughter, actress Anjelica Huston.
Hammen, Scott. *John Huston.* Twayne 1985 $20.95. ISBN 0-8057-9299-6 Critical appraisal of director Huston's major films; details his contributions to motion picture history.
Hepburn, Katharine. *The Making of the African Queen: Or How I Went to Africa with Bogart, Bacall and Huston and Almost Lost My Mind.* Plume 1988 $8.95. ISBN 0-452-26145-7 The actress's account of her jungle adventures with Huston and the cast as they made the Oscar-winning classic; includes photographs.

SPIELBERG, STEVEN   1947–

Steven Spielberg was born in 1947 in Cincinnati, Ohio. Although he never graduated from college, he attended California State College for a time. Soon, however, he found his way into the world of Hollywood filmmaking, where he has achieved enormous success.

Spielberg's career began as a director on such television series as *Marcus Welby, M.D.* and *Columbo.* He won acclaim for *Duel,* a television movie about a man pursued on the highway by a mysterious truck.

At the age of 26, Spielberg directed his first feature film. *The Sugarland Express* won critical praise for its blend of comedy, suspense, and fast-paced adventure in its portrayal of a young couple's attempt to kidnap their own child. The young director's next film was *Jaws,* the blockbuster story of a beach community terrorized by a huge shark. When *Jaws* became the leading money-making film up to its time, Spielberg's reputation and position in the filmmaking world were assured.

Many of Spielberg's later films went on to set new box-office records. His distinctive style frequently blends fantasy, science fiction, adventure, terrifying suspense, and touching moments of warmth. Such films as *Close Encounters of the Third Kind* and *E.T.* became the most talked-about films of their time, inspiring a host of imitators and setting the style for films for years to come.

Spielberg has also been influential as a producer, most notably of director George Lucas's *Raiders of the Lost Ark* and its sequels, fast-paced adventure comedies that have also influenced numerous other films. A whole generation of young filmmakers, including Chris Columbus and Joe Dante, have gotten their start in the so-called "Spielberg" factory, nurtured, promoted, and produced by Spielberg as they develop their own films within the style that he created.

Spielberg took on a different type of project when he directed *The Color Purple,* a film based on Alice Walker's prize-winning novel about a young black woman who suffers poverty and abuse before finally finding happiness in a reunion with her sister. The film was not particularly successful, however, and Spielberg was criticized for abandoning the fantasy style with which he has had so much success. He was likewise criticized for *Always,* a love story with fantasy elements.

Spielberg continues to take on a wide variety of projects and to produce a number of young directors. He remains a major figure in the entertainment world.

BOOKS ABOUT SPIELBERG

*Hargrove, Jim. *Steven Spielberg: Amazing Filmmaker.* Childrens 1988 $17.27. ISBN 0-516-03263-1 Lively account of Spielberg's work and life, written for a middle-school audience.

Kolker, Robert P. *A Cinema of Loneliness: Penn, Kubrick, Scorsese, Spielberg, Altman.* Oxford Univ Pr 1988 $16.95. ISBN 0-19-505390-7 Looks at Spielberg in the context of other major contemporary directors; interesting examination of Spielberg's often overlooked "darker side."

Mott, Donald R. and Cheryl M. Saunders. *Steven Spielberg.* G. K. Hall 1986 $18.95. ISBN 0-8057-9307-0 A good general introduction to Spielberg's life and work, with discussions of his major films, a biographical sketch, and a chronological listing of all films through 1985.

FILMS FROM LITERATURE

Boyum, Joy Gould. *Double Exposure: Fiction into Film.* NAL 1989 $4.95. ISBN 0-451-62695-8

Enser, A. G. *Filmed Books and Plays: A List of Books and Plays from Which Films Have Been Made 1928–1986.* Gower 1987 $59.95. ISBN 0-566-03564-2

Langley, Noel, *et al. The Wizard of Oz: The Screenplay.* Delacorte 1989 $9.95. ISBN 0-385-29760-2

*Pronzini, Bill, and Martin H. Greenberg (eds). *The Best of the West: Stories That Inspired Classic Western Films.* Signet 1989 $3.50. ISBN 0-451-15481-9 Contains: "The Bride Comes to Yellow Sky" *(Face to Face)* by Stephen Crane; *"The Tin Star" (High Noon)* by John M. Cunningham; *"3:10 to Yuma"* by Elmore Leonard; *"Jeremy Rodock" (Tribute to a Bad Man)* by Jack Shaefer; *"The Man Who Shot Liberty Valance"* by Dorothy M. Johnson; "The Outcasts of Poker Flat" by Bret Harte; *"The Caballero's Way" (The Cisco Kid);* *"Mission with No Record" (Rio Grande)* by James Warner Bellah; *"Town Tamer"* by Frank Gruber.

*Pronzini, Bill, and Martin H. Greenberg (eds). *The Best of the West II: Stories That Inspired Classic Western Films.* Signet 1990 $3.95. ISBN 0-451-16584-5 Contains: *"Command and Big Hunt" (She Wore a Yellow Ribbon)* by James Warner Bellah; *"Yankee Gold" (The Stranger Wore a Gun)* by John M. Cunningham; *"The Captives" (The Tall T)* by Elmore Leonard; "The Luck of Roaring Camp" by Bret Harte; *"The Passing of Black Eagle" (Black Eagle)* by O. Henry; *"My Brother Down There" (Running Target)* by Steve Frazee;

Back to God's Country" by James Oliver Curwood; *"Parson of Panamint"* by Peter B. Kyne; *"A Man Called Horse"* by Dorothy M. Johnson.

Sinyard, Neil. *Filming Literature: The Art of Screen Adaptation.* St. Martin's 1986 $27.50. ISBN 0-312-28939-1

*Wheeler, David (ed). *No, But I Saw the Movie: The Best Short Stories Ever Made Into Film.* Penguin 1989 $8.95. ISBN 0-14-011090-9 Contains: Mary Orr, *"The Wisdom of Eve"* (All About Eve); Howard Breslin, *"Bad Time at Honda"* (Bad Day at Black Rock); Julio Cortazar, *"Blow-up"*; Robert Louis Stevenson, *"The Body Snatchers"*; Daphne du Maurier, *"Don't Look Now"*; George Langelaan, *"The Fly"*; Tod Robbins, *"Spurs"* (Freaks); Damon Runyon, *"The Idyll of Miss Sarah Brown"* (Guys and Dolls); Bruce Jay Friedman, *"A Change of Plan"* (The Heartbreak Kid); John M. Cunningham, *"The Tin Star"* (High Noon); Samuel Hopkins Adams, *"Night Bus"* (It Happened One Night); Philip Van Doren Stern, *"The Greatest Gift"* (It's A Wonderful Life); Samson Raphaelson, *"The Day of Atonement"* (The Jazz Singer); Eric Hodgins, *"Mr. Blandings Builds His Castle"* (Mr. Blandings Builds His Dream House); Robert Bloch, *"The Real Bad Friend"* (Psycho); Cornell Woolrich, *"Rear Window"*; Ernest Haycox, *"Stage to Lordsburg"* (Stagecoach); Arthur C. Clarke, *"The Sentinel"* (2001: A Space Odyssey).

ANIMATION

Canemaker, John. *Animated Raggedy Ann and Andy: The Story Behind the Movie.* Macmillan 1977 $12.95. ISBN 0-672-52330-2

Culhane, Shamus. *Animation from Script to Screen.* St. Martin's 1988 $17.95. ISBN 0-312-02162-3

Hepworth, Cecil. *Animated Photography: The ABC of the Cinematograph.* Ayer (repr of 1900 ed) $7.50. ISBN 0-405-01615-8

Hoffer, Thomas W. *Animation: A Reference Guide.* Greenwood 1981 $36.95. ISBN 0-313-21095-0

Noake, Roger. *Animation Techniques.* Book Sales 1989 $22.98. ISBN 1-55521-331-6

Rubin, Susan. *Animation: The Art and the Industry.* Prentice 1984 $15.95. ISBN 0-13-037789-9

White, Tony. *Animator's Workbook.* Watson-Guptill 1988 $18.95. ISBN 0-8230-0229-2

DISNEY, WALT (WALTER ELIAS) 1901–1966

Walt Disney was born in Chicago, Illinois, one of five children of a building contractor. When Disney was five, the family moved to Missouri and began farming. Walt and his older brother, Roy, spent most of their time on farm chores, but Walt learned to amuse himself by drawing and painting. After several more moves, the Disney family returned to Chicago in 1917, and Walt completed his education at McKinley High School, where he contributed cartoons and pictures to the school paper.

After serving as an ambulance driver in France during World War I, Disney came home determined to become a commercial artist. In Kansas City, he met a gifted young Dutch artist named Ub Iwerks with whom he started a commercial art studio that promptly failed. Disney then took a job with the Kansas City Film Ad Service, a company that used the new technique of film animation to produce ads that were shown in movie theaters.

After learning how to make animated cartoon films, Disney and Iwerks set up their own company. In 1923, after several years of being on the verge of bankruptcy, they moved to Hollywood and began to produce cartoons for the growing movie industry. In 1928, Disney made an unsuccessful trip to New York to get financing to expand his business. On the train headed back to Los

Angeles, he got the idea for Mickey Mouse, and he never had to worry about money again.

The character of Mickey Mouse first appeared on the screen in 1928. In the 1930s, Mickey was joined by Minnie Mouse, Donald Duck, Pluto, Goofy, and several other memorable Disney characters. In 1937, the Disney Studios produced the first feature-length cartoon, *Snow White and the Seven Dwarfs,* and its success was followed by that of several other animated features. By the 1960s, Disney had become one of the richest and most powerful men in Hollywood and had received over 700 honors and awards, including 30 Oscars, the Presidential Medal of Freedom, and honorary degrees from Harvard and Yale universities.

Disney's fame lives on, not only in the movie studio that continues to make pictures under his name, but in the two gigantic amusement parks that bear his name.

BOOKS ABOUT DISNEY

Finch, Christopher. *The Art of Walt Disney: From Mickey Mouse to the Magic Kingdoms.* Abrams 1989 $39.95. ISBN 0-8109-8052-5 Exhaustive examination of the technological innovations and sophisticated engineering that Disney's vision and high standards required.

Ford, Barbara. *Walt Disney: A Biography.* Walker 1989 $15.95. ISBN 0-8027-6864-4 Account of the main events in Disney's life, his ideals, and the growth of his studio.

Hollis, Richard, and Brian Sibley. *The Disney Studio Story.* Crown 1988 $35.00. ISBN 0-517-57078-5 Story of Disney's studio and its powerful influence on quality and innovation in the movie industry; a balanced look at a unique and complex enterprise that also had its darker side.

Kinney, Jack. *Walt Disney and Assorted Other Characters: An Unauthorized Account of the Early Years at Disney's.* Crown 1988 $16.95. ISBN 0-517-57057-2 Unromanticized view of the personalities that made the studio great and working there interesting; of particular value for comparing authorized and unauthorized biographies.

Schickel, Richard. *The Disney Version.* Simon 1985 $10.95. ISBN 0-671-54714-3 Film critic's look at Disney's life in the context of American society, resulting in a highly critical picture of the famous cartoonist and filmmaker.

Thomas, Frank, and Ollie Johnson. *Disney Animation: The Illusion of Life.* Abbeville 1984 $39.98. ISBN 0-89659-698-2 Illustrated history and description of the Disney animation process by two animators who began their careers with Disney in the 1930s.

TYPES AND STEREOTYPES

Everson, William. *Bad Guys: A Pictorial History of the Movie Villain.* Carol 1968 $8.95. ISBN 0-8065-0198-7

Hilger, Michael. *The American Indian in Film.* Scarecrow 1986 $21.00. ISBN 0-8108-1905-8

Nesteby, James. *Black Images in American Films, 1896–1954: The Interplay Between Civil Rights and Film Culture.* Univ Pr of America 1982 $14.75. ISBN 0-8191-2168-1

New Jersey State Museum Staff. *Hollywood Indian: Stereotypes of Native Americans in Films.* New Jersey State Museum Pr 1981 $5.95. ISBN 0-938766-00-7

Rosen, Marjorie. *Popcorn Venus.* Avon 1974 $1.95. ISBN 0-380-001772

Russo, Vito. *The Celluloid Closet: Homosexuality in the Movies.* Harper 1987 $10.95. ISBN 0-06-096132-5

WRITING

Probably no other area of the language arts gets more attention in American education than written expression. Long after students are expected to be able to read and speak well, they are still taking courses in how to write—even at levels as advanced as graduate school. Yet despite all this instruction, employers, professors, and editorial writers continue to complain about the woeful state of writing in America.

In years past, much of this criticism was directed at such writing "errors" as incorrect spelling, faulty punctuation, grammatical lapses, and poor usage. More recently the critics have turned their attention to the content of what is being written, and they have concluded that most bad writing actually stems from unclear thinking. New approaches to teaching writing stress the thought processes that lead to good expression as well as the processes of composition and revision.

Current writing theory also recognizes that there are many different kinds of writing, each of which has to be approached in its own way. Writing a business letter does not involve exactly the same processes as writing a technical report, and neither of these is anything like writing a poem. Modern writing instruction also gives much more attention to the questions of audience and voice. It focuses on whom the writing is intended for, what it is supposed to achieve, and who is making the writing choices.

Some of the best sources of knowledge about writing are people who do it well. The final listing of books in this section consists of comments on the

Cover from *The Saturday Evening Post,* Jan. 17, 1920.
Painting by Norman Rockwell.
Printed by permission of The Norman Rockwell Family
Trust.   © 1920 The Norman Rockwell Family Trust.

process of writing by professional writers. Whether they find writing a joy, an agony, or both, all the writers have valuable advice to share with others who want to learn to write well.

If there is one topic that all writers seem to enjoy writing about it is the act of writing itself. The Writing section includes works by a variety of authors—from writers of children's books to Hollywood screenwriters—that deal with how the authors approach their work. The Writing section also lists books other than school composition textbooks that give aspiring writers advice on how to write better and how to find and address their audience. Also listed are books that provide models of different kinds of writing, as well as works on business and technical writing. Finally, there are books by writers who share their personal thoughts about the joys and agonies of writing professionally.

PRINCIPLES AND PROCESS

*Berbrich, Joan. *Writing Logically.* AMSCO 1978 $13.75. ISBN 0-87720-332-6 Principles of systematic thought, cause and effect, and connections among ideas explained in a clear, direct way.

Chicago Manual of Style. Univ of Chicago Pr 1982 $35.00. ISBN 0-226-10390-0

Corbett, Edward P. *Classical Rhetoric for the Modern Student.* Oxford Univ Pr 1971 $23.00. ISBN 0-19-501382-4

Costanzo, William. *Double Exposure: Composing Through Writing and Film.* Boynton 1984 $15.00. ISBN 0-86709-051-0

Elbow, Peter. *Writing with Power: Techniques for Mastering the Writing Process.* Oxford Univ Pr 1981 $8.95. ISBN 0-19-502913-5

Elbow, Peter. *Writing Without Teachers.* Oxford Univ Pr 1973 $6.95. ISBN 0-19-501679-3

Fahnestock, Jeanne, and Marie Secor. *A Rhetoric for Argument.* McGraw 1981 $17.95. ISBN 0-07-554826-7

Fearnside, W. Ward. *About Thinking.* Prentice 1980 $31.00. ISBN 0-13-000844-3

Flower, Linda. *Problem-Solving Strategies for Writing.* Harcourt 1989 $14.00. ISBN 0-15-571974-2

*Fuess, Billings, Jr. (ed). *How to Use the Power of the Printed Word.* Doubleday 1985 $6.95. ISBN 0-395-18216-3 Articles by Malcolm Forbes, Bill Cosby, Kurt Vonnegut, Steve Allen, Erma Bombeck, and others with advice for improving communication skills.

Garrison, Roger. *How a Writer Works.* Harper 1985 $8.50. ISBN 0-06-042242-4

Hacker, Diana, and Betty Renshaw. *Writing with a Voice: A Rhetoric and Handbook.* Scott 1989 $20.31. ISBN 0-673-39670-3

*Hawley, Robert, and Isabel Hawley. *Writing for the Fun of It: An Experience-Based Approach to Composition.* Ed Research 1974 $6.95. ISBN 0-913636-02-9 Emphasizes personal growth through thinking and writing about personal values and experiences.

*Lederer, Richard. *Anguished English: An Anthology of Accidental Assaults upon Our Language.* Dell 1987 $5.95. ISBN 0-440-20352-X Hilarious bloopers from ads, essays, letters, billboards, and official records, illustrating fundamental violations of writing processes and principles.

Levin, Gerald. *Writing and Logic.* Harcourt 1982 $12.00. ISBN 0-15-597788-1

Macrorie, Ken. *Telling Writing.* Boynton 1985 $14.00. ISBN 0-867-09133-9

Macrorie, Ken. *Writing to Be Read.* Boynton 1984 $12.50. ISBN 0-86709-133-9

*Meyer, Herbert E., and Jill M. Meyer. *How to Write.* Storm King 1986 $4.95. ISBN 0-394-75352-6 "The most helpful book the beginning writer can buy," according to columnist William Safire.

Rank, Hugh. *Persuasion Analysis: A Companion to Composition.* Counter Prop 1988 $10.00. ISBN 0-943468-02-7

Rico, Gabriele L. *Writing the Natural Way: Using Right-Brain Techniques to Release Your Expressive Powers.* Tarcher 1983 $15.95. ISBN 0-87477-186-2

Ruggerio, Vincent Ryan. *The Art of Thinking: A Guide to Critical and Creative Thought.* Harper 1987 $15.95. ISBN 0-06-045664-7

Schwartz, Mimi. *Writing for Many Roles.* Boynton 1985 $12.50. ISBN 0-86709-097-9

*Stillman, Peter. *Writing Your Way.* Boynton 1984 $10.00. ISBN 0-86709-067-7 Tips, examples, activities, and encouragement for the young writer; includes chapters on interviewing, storytelling, and keeping a journal.

Skillin, M., and R. Gay. *Words into Type.* 3rd edition Prentice 1986 $39.95. ISBN 0-13-964262-5

Zinsser, William. *Writing to Learn.* Harper 1989 $15.45. ISBN 0-06-015884-0

STYLE, USAGE, AND MECHANICS

Belanoff, Pat, *et al. The Right Handbook.* Boynton 1986 $12.50. ISBN 0-86709-167-3

Booher, Diana. *Good Grief, Good Grammar: The Business Person's Guide to Grammar and Usage.* Fawcett 1988 $3.95. ISBN 0-449-21681-0

Ebbitt, Wilma R., and David R. Ebbitt. *Writer's Guide and Index to English.* Scott 1982 $27.19. ISBN 0-673-15542-0

Gordon, Karen Elizabeth. *The Transitive Vampire: A Handbook of Grammar for the Innocent, the Eager, and the Doomed.* Times Bks 1984 $10.95. ISBN 0-8129-1101-6

Gordon, Karen Elizabeth. *The Well-Tempered Sentence: A Punctuation Handbook for the Innocent, the Eager, and the Doomed.* Ticknor 1983 $8.95. ISBN 0-89919-170-3

Montgomery, Michael, and John Stratton. *The Writer's Hotline Handbook.* NAL 1981 $5.95. ISBN 0-451-62639-7

Perrin, Porter G. *Reference Handbook of Grammar and Usage.* Morrow 1972 $12.95. ISBN 0-688-0061-4

*Queneau, Raymond. *Exercises in Style.* New Directions 1981 $12.95. ISBN 0-8112-0789-7 Encourages new ways of seeing and recombining old words by offering numerous activities and ideas for playing with word patterns.

Read, Herbert. *English Prose Style.* Pantheon 1981 $6.95. ISBN 0-394-74898-0

Strunk, William, Jr., and E. B. White. *Elements of Style.* Macmillan 1979 $8.95. ISBN 0-02-418190-0

*Tchudi, Susan, and Stephen Tchudi. *Young Writer's Handbook: A Practical Guide for the Beginner Who Is Serious About Writing.* Macmillan 1987 $4.95. ISBN 0-689-71170-0 Thorough but interesting guide to drafting, revising, and improving usage and mechanics for middle-school students.

Weathers, Winston. *An Alternate Style: Options in Composition.* Boynton 1980 $10.00. ISBN 0-8104-6130-7

WOLFE, TOM (THOMAS KENNERLY) 1931–

Tom Wolfe was born in Richmond, Virginia, and educated at Washington and Lee University, where he received a B.A. in 1951. In 1957, he was awarded a Ph.D. from Yale University.

From 1956 to 1959, Wolfe was a reporter for the Springfield, Massachusetts, *Union* before becoming Latin American correspondent for the *Washington Post.* He left the *Washington Post* in 1962 to become a staff writer and reporter for the Sunday magazine of the *New York Herald Tribune,* which became *New York* magazine in 1968. He is currently a contributing editor for *Esquire* magazine.

Wolfe is identified with a group of journalists, including Jimmy Breslin and Gay Talese, whose writing has been referred to as "new journalism," because they bring stylistic techniques to their nonfiction writing that had previously been used only in the novel and short story. Of all the practitioners of new journalism, Wolfe has received the most praise and the sharpest criticism. His flamboyant style—which involves unusual use of punctuation, shifting points of view, long dialogues, complex character development, and innovative language, including catchy slogans and names—has made his books and magazine articles enormously popular but has also drawn charges of triviality and vulgar showmanship. Phrases Wolfe invented, such as "Radical Chic" and "The Me Decade," have been widely adopted as descriptors of contemporary cultural trends.

Wolfe's keen reportorial eye and meticulous attention to detail have impressed even his severest critics, who may accuse him of poor taste, overelaborate style, and insensitivity but seldom charge him with inaccuracy of description. Wolfe unquestionably reports what he has seen. It is his interpretation of what he sees and the style in which he reports it that draws criticism.

BOOKS BY WOLFE

The Bonfire of the Vanities (1987). Farrar 1987 $19.95. ISBN 0-374-11534-6
The Electric Kool-Aid Acid Test (1968). Farrar 1987 $22.50. ISBN 0-374-14704-3
From Bauhaus to Our House (1981). Farrar 1981 $10.95. ISBN 0-374-15892-4
In Our Time (1980). Farrar 1980 $12.95. ISBN 0-374-17576-4
The Kandy Kolored Tangerine-Flake Streamline Baby (1965). Farrar 1987 $19.95. ISBN 0-374-18064-4
Mauve Gloves and Madman, Clutter and Vine (1976). Farrar 1976 $18.95. ISBN 0-374-20424-1
The New Journalism. (coauthored with E. W. Johnson) Harper 1973 $18.95. ISBN 0-06-047183-2
The Painted Word (1975). Farrar 1975 $12.95. ISBN 0-374-22878-7
The Pump House Gang (1968). Farrar 1968 $18.95. ISBN 0-374-23864-2
The Purple Decades: A Reader (1982). Farrar 1982 $17.50. ISBN 0-374-23927-4
Radical Chic, and Mau-Mauing the Flak Catchers (1971). Farrar 1987 $5.95. ISBN 0-374-52072-0
The Right Stuff (1979). Farrar 1983 $15.95. ISBN 0-374-25033-2

BOOK ABOUT WOLFE

Johnson, Michael. *New Journalism: The Underground Press, the Artists of Nonfiction, and Changes in the Established Media.* Univ Pr of Kansas 1971 $9.95. ISBN 0-7006-0085-X Comprehensive study of the changes in reporting and journalism that took place in the 1960s, with emphasis on Tom Wolfe, Jimmy Breslin, and the other "new journalists."

EDITING

Cook, Claire Kehrwald. *Line by Line.* Houghton 1986 $8.95. ISBN 0-395-89391-4
*Maggio, Rosalie. *Nonsexist Word Finder: A Dictionary of Gender-Free Usage.* Oryx 1987 $19.95. ISBN 0-89774-449-7 Dictionary format and comprehensive coverage help writers avoid sexist language.
Miller, Casey, and Kate Swift. *Handbook of Non-Sexist Writing.* Harper 1988 $15.45. ISBN 0-06-181602-7
Ross–Larson, Bruce. *Edit Yourself: A Manual for Everyone Who Works with Words.* Norton 1985 $5.70. ISBN 0-393-30268-7

MODELS OF WRITING

Anderson, Dave (ed). *The Red Smith Reader.* Random 1982 $6.95. ISBN 0-394-71750-3

Bombeck, Erma. *At Wit's End.* Fawcett 1986 $3.95. ISBN 0-449-21184-3

*Bombeck, Erma. *Family: The Ties That Bind—and Gag.* Fawcett 1988 $4.95. ISBN 0-449-21529-6 Hilarious look at everyday events from a mother's point of view; collected from Bombeck's syndicated column.

Campbell, Nelson (ed). *Grass Roots and Schoolyards: A High School Basketball Anthology.* Stephen Greene 1990 $8.95. ISBN 0-8289-0641-6

Dillard, Annie, and Robert Atwan (eds). *The Best American Essays 1988.* Ticknor 1988 $17.95. ISBN 0-89919-729-9

Goodman, Ellen. *At Large.* Summit Bks 1981 $12.95. ISBN 0-671-43306-7

Goodman, Ellen. *Making Sense.* Atlantic Monthly 1989 $17.95. ISBN 0-87113-281-8

Greene, Bob. *American Beat.* Penguin 1984 $7.95. ISBN 0-14-007320-5

Greene, Bob. *Johnny Deadline, Reporter: The Best of Bob Greene.* Nelson-Hall 1976 $21.95. ISBN 0-88229-361-3

Grizzard, Lewis. *Chili Dawgs Always Bark at Night.* Random 1989 $16.95. ISBN 0-394-57807-4

*Grizzard, Lewis. *Kathy Sue Laudermilk, I Love You.* Peachtree 1979 $11.95. ISBN 0-931948-05-3 Entertaining tales of the South, sharing Grizzard's love for down-home tradition and talk; collected from his syndicated column.

*Kael, Pauline. *Hooked.* Dutton 1989 $14.95. ISBN 0-525-48429-9 Distinguished film critic's reviews of 150 movies released since 1985, including *Top Gun* and *Blue Velvet;* crisply and elegantly written.

*Kael, Pauline. *State of the Art.* Dutton 1985 $12.95. ISBN 0-525-48186-9 Film critic for *The New Yorker* reviews more than 100 films made between 1983 and 1985, including *Beverly Hills Cop* and *Flashdance;* distinguished by Kael's forceful writing style.

Lapham, Lewis. *Money and Class: Notes and Observations on the American Character.* Weidenfeld 1987 $18.95. ISBN 1-55584-109-0

Lapham, Lewis. *Money and Class in America: Notes and Observations on a Civil Religion.* Ballantine 1989 $4.95. ISBN 0-345-35871-6

*Moffett, James, and Phyllis Tashlik. *Active Voices: A Writer's Reader.* 3 vols. Boynton 1987 $14.50 each. ISBNs 0-86709-091-X, 0-86709-205-X, 0-86709-207-6 Models of good writing by teen-agers about ideas and experiences they value.

*Rooney, Andrew. *Not That You Asked . . .* Random 1989 $15.95. ISBN 0-394-57837-6 Humorous yet pointed short essays on everyday experiences and common objects by a contributor to the television series *60 Minutes* and to the *Washington Post.*

Rooney, Andrew. *Word for Word.* G. K. Hall 1988 $12.95. ISBN 0-8161-4317-X

Royko, Mike. *Dr. Kookie, You're Right.* Dutton 1990 $18.95. ISBN 0-452-26515-0

*Royko, Mike. *Like I Was Sayin' . . .* Jove 1985 $3.95. ISBN 0-515-08416-6 Collection of short essays with the blunt humor and off-beat topics characteristic of Royko's newspaper columns.

*Siner, Howard (ed). *Sports Classics: American Writers Choose Their Best.* Coward 1983 $16.95. ISBN 0-698-11248-2 Splendid collection of sports writing from such sources as the *New York Post, Sports Illustrated,* and *Esquire.*

Will, George. *Men at Work* (1990). Macmillan 1990 $18.95. ISBN 0-02-628470-7

Will, George. *The Morning After: American Successes and Excesses 1981–1986* (1987). Macmillan 1987 $9.95. ISBN 0-02-055450-8

BAKER, RUSSELL 1925–

Russell Baker was born in Loudoun County, Virginia. His childhood and early years as a reporter are detailed beautifully and wittily in his two autobiographies, *Growing Up* (1982) and *The Good Times* (1989). After graduating from Johns Hopkins University in 1947, Baker took a job as a reporter with the *Baltimore*

Sun, becoming London bureau chief in 1953. In 1954, Baker joined the staff of the *New York Times,* where he continues to write the "Observer" column he began in 1962.

Baker is frequently described as a humorist, and there is no question that much of his writing is amusing, but he is much more than a funny writer. The term *satire* comes closer to describing Baker's work, but even it is inadequate. Like Mark Twain (*see* Twain, Vol. 1, American Literature: The Rise of Realism), with whom he is often compared, Baker is able to look at the world and see its faults and weaknesses with amazing clarity, and then to write about them with wit and humor.

Baker's style of writing simultaneously amuses, informs, and awakens the reader. His columns are really short essays that serve as models of fine English prose. He writes with clarity, purpose, and intelligence, yet his writing seems effortless. The reader never has to struggle to stay with a Baker essay or book despite its being crammed with ideas and observations.

Baker's work has won him numerous awards, including the Pulitzer Prize for distinguished commentary in 1979 and a second Pulitzer for *Growing Up* in 1982.

BOOKS BY BAKER

All Things Considered (1965). Greenwood 1981 $35.00. ISBN 0-313-22875-2
The Good Times (1989). Morrow 1989 $19.95. ISBN 0-688-06170-2
Growing Up (1982). NAL 1983 $18.95. ISBN 0-452-2550-3.
The Rescue of Miss Yaskell and Other Pipe Dreams (1983). NAL 1990 $8.95. ISBN 0-452-26458-8
So This Is Depravity (1980). Pocket 1984 $4.95. ISBN 0-671-55177-9
There's a Country in My Collar: The Best of Russell Baker (1990). Morrow 1990 $20.95. ISBN 0-688-09598-4

WRITERS ON WRITING: REFLECTION AND ADVICE

COLLECTIONS

*Charlton, James, and Lisbeth Mark (eds). *The Writer's Home Companion: Anecdotes, Comforts, Recollections, and Other Amusements for Every Writer, Editor, and Reader.* Penguin 1982 $4.95. ISBN 0-14-011012-7 Facts of literary life—rejections, writer's block, lost manuscripts—to amuse and encourage aspiring writers.

*Hancock, Geoff. *Canadian Writers at Work: Interviews with Geoff Hancock.* Oxford Univ Pr 1987 $19.95. ISBN 0-195-406-389 Conversations with such major Canadian writers as Jane Rule, Jack Hodgins, Mavis Gallant, Robert Kroetsch, Clark Blaise, Leon Rooke, Alice Munro, Josef Skvorecky, Margaret Atwood, and Bharati Mukherjee.

*Plimpton, George (ed). *Writers at Work. The Paris Review Interviews.* 8 vols. Viking 1986 $22.95 each. ISBN 0-670-80888-1 In-depth and revealing interviews with British, American, Australian, European, and South American writers from 1953 through 1985.

*Sternburg, Janet (ed). *The Writer on Her Work.* Norton 1981 $8.95. ISBN 0-393-00071-0 Essays on why and how they write by such major women writers as Anne Tyler, Joan Didion, Margaret Walker, and Maxine Hong Kingston.

*Tate, Claudia (ed). *Black Women Writers at Work.* Continuum 1984 $9.95. ISBN 0-8264-0243-7 Thoughtful, provocative interviews with such major black women writers as Toni Cade Bambara, Gwendolyn Brooks, Toni Morrison, and Alice Walker.

482   PART ONE   LITERATURE AND LANGUAGE ARTS

INDIVIDUAL WRITERS ON WRITING

*Gardner, John. *The Art of Fiction: Notes on Craft for Young Writers.* Vintage 1985 $4.95. ISBN 0-394-72544-1 Advice on technique and an inside look at how complex stories take shape, offered in a pleasant, personable tone.

Hemingway, Ernest. *Ernest Hemingway on Writing.* Scribner's 1984 $12.95. ISBN 0-684-18119-3

*LeGuin, Ursula K. *The Language of the Night: Essays on Fantasy and Science Fiction.* Berkley 1985 $5.95. ISBN 0-425-076-687 Discussion of where ideas for science fiction or fantasy begin, by a leading fantasy and science-fiction writer.

Murray, Don. *A Writer Teaches Writing.* Houghton 1984 $27.56. ISBN 0-395-35441-2

*Reed, Ishmael. *Writin' Is Fightin': Thirty-Seven Years of Boxing on Paper.* Macmillan 1988 $18.95. ISBN 0-689-11975-5 Honest, animated account of sorrows and successes; as much fun to read as one of the novels by this feisty, inventive black writer.

Rilke, Rainer Maria. *Letters to a Young Poet.* Random 1984 $11.95. ISBN 0-39453-762-9

Sarton, May. *Writings on Writing.* Puckerbush 1986 $6.95. ISBN 0-91300-620-3

Singer, Isaac Bashevis. *Conversations with Isaac Bashevis Singer.* Farrar 1986 $6.95. ISBN 0-37451-994-3

*Tolkien, J. R. R. *Tree and Leaf.* Houghton 1965 $8.95. ISBN 0-395-082-536 Essays revealing the importance the writer places on imagination and a fresh point of view; written by the author of *The Hobbit* and *The Ring* trilogy.

Ueland, Barbara. *If You Want to Write: A Book About Art, Independence and Spirit.* Graywolf 1987 $6.50. ISBN 0-91530-894-0

Walker, Alice. *In Search of Our Mothers' Gardens: Womanist Prose.* Harcourt 1984 $6.95. ISBN 0-15-644544-1

Welty, Eudora. *The Eye of the Story.* Random 1979 $6.95. ISBN 0-3944-72732-0

Welty, Eudora. *One Writer's Beginnings.* Warner Bks 1984 $3.50. ISBN 0-446-32983-5

DILLARD, ANNIE   1945–

Poet, novelist, and short story writer, Annie Dillard was born and raised in Pittsburgh, Pennsylvania, the city that is the setting for her charming and penetrating autobiography, *An American Childhood* (1987). She was educated at Hollins College in Virginia, from which she received a B.A. in 1967 and an M.A. the following year. She was a contributing editor to *Harper's* magazine from 1973 to 1982 and a professor of English at Wesleyan University in Middletown, Connecticut, from 1979 to 1982.

Dillard's first book, *Pilgrim at Tinker Creek* (1974), a personal narrative that she calls a "journal of the mind," won a Pulitzer Prize. That same year she also published her first volume of poetry, *Tickets for a Prayer Wheel.*

Widely considered one of America's finest contemporary writers, Dillard has produced two books on the art of writing. In *Living by Fiction* (1982), she reflects on the craft of the writer and meditates on her own experiences. The book is about how a writer feels about writing. In *The Writing Life* (1989), Dillard focuses on the actual process of writing, emphasizing how the writer's mind works when composing. She comments in the book, "At its best the sensation of writing is that of any unmerited grace. It is handed to you, but only if you look for it. You search, you break your heart, your back, your brain, and then—and only then—it is handed to you." These volumes provide instruction and inspiration for any writer, beginning or experienced.

BOOKS BY DILLARD

An American Childhood (1987). Harper 1987 $17.95. ISBN 0-06-015805-0
Holy the Firm (1988). Harper 1988 $6.95. ISBN 0-06-091543-9

Living by Fiction (1982). Harper 1988 $7.95. ISBN 0-06-091544-7
Pilgrim at Tinker Creek (1974). Harper 1988 $7.95. ISBN 0-06-091545-5
Teaching a Stone to Talk (1988). Harper 1988 $8.95. ISBN 0-06-091541-2
Tickets for a Prayer Wheel (1974). Harper 1988 $7.95. ISBN 0-06-091542-0
* *The Writing Life* (1989). Harper 1989 $15.45. ISBN 0-06-016156-6 Inspiring and instructive for serious readers; "fastens on the actual process of writing with an emphasis on the mind at work," according to reviewer Susan Cahill.

AUDIENCE AND PURPOSE

ACADEMIC WRITING

*Ehrlich, Eugene, and Daniel Murphy. *Writing and Researching Term Papers and Reports.* Bantam 1968 $3.95. ISBN 0-553-27046-X Comprehensive guide; includes an introduction to the use of reference libraries, an annotated sample research paper, and a brief bibliography of reference books.
Griffith, Kelley. *Writing Essays About Literature: A Guide and Style Sheet.* Harcourt 1986 $10.00. ISBN 0-15-597862-4
Hubbuch, Susan. *Writing Research Papers Across the Curriculum, 1984 MLA Version.* Holt 1987 $8.95. ISBN 0-03-012014-4
Macrorie, Ken. *The I-Search Paper.* Boynton 1988 $15.00. ISBN 0-86709-223-8
Wresch, William. *Writing for the Twenty-First Century: Computers and Research Writing.* McGraw 1988 $13.95. ISBN 0-07-072051-7

ADVERTISING COPY

Burton, Philip. *Advertising Copywriting.* Wiley 1984 $51.50. ISBN 0-471-84152-8
Higgins, Denis (ed). *Art of Writing Advertising.* National Textbook 1989 $9.95. ISBN 0-8442-3100-2

BIOGRAPHIES

Lomask, Milton. *The Biographer's Craft.* Harper 1987 $5.95. ISBN 0-06-091387-8
Pachter, Marc (ed). *Telling Lives: The Biographer's Art.* Univ of Penn Pr 1981 $12.95. ISBN 0-8122-1118-9

BUSINESS COMMUNICATIONS

*Booher, Dianna. *How to Write Your Way to Success in Business.* Harper 1985 $5.95. ISBN 0-06-463597-X Five easy steps to writing effective reports, letters, and memos.
Easton, Thomas. *How to Write a Readable Business Report.* Dow Jones 1983 $19.95. ISBN 0-87094-393-6
Paxson, William. *Business Writing Handbook.* Bantam 1981 $4.50. ISBN 0-553-27041-9
Reinold, Cheryl. *How to Write a Million Dollar Memo.* Dell 1988 $3.50. ISBN 0-440-20194-2

CHILDREN'S BOOKS

Aiken, Joan. *The Way to Write for Children.* St. Martin's 1982 $4.95. ISBN 0-312-85840-X
Sutherland, Zena (ed). *The Best in Children's Books: The University of Chicago Guide to Children's Literature, 1979–1984.* Univ of Chicago Pr 1986 $35.00. ISBN 0-226-78060-0
Woolley, Catherine (pseudonym of Jane Thayer). *Writing for Children.* NAL 1990 $17.95. ISBN 0-453-00707-4
Yolen, Jane. *Writing Books for Children.* Writers Digest 1988 $9.95. ISBN 0-87116-133-8

PATERSON, KATHERINE (WOMELDORF) 1932–

Katherine Paterson was born in Qing Jiang, Jiangsu, China, the daughter of missionary parents. Her early education was in China, but she returned to the United States in 1941 at the beginning of World War II, when she enrolled in the Calvin H. Wiley School in Winston-Salem, North Carolina. She later attended King College in Bristol, Tennessee, from which she graduated in 1954.

After several years as a missionary in Japan (1957–1961) and as a teacher in the United States (1963–1965), Paterson turned her attention to writing. Her first works were instructional materials and curriculum guides for schools. Then, in 1973, she published her first novel, *The Sign of the Chrysanthemum,* based on her experiences in Japan. Her second novel, *Of Nightingales That Weep* (1974), was highly praised, and her third, *The Master Puppeteer* (1976), won the National Book Award for children's literature in 1977. *Bridge to Terabithia* (1977) received the Newbery Medal from the American Library Association for best children's book of 1978. *The Great Gilly Hopkins* (1978) was honored by every major award-granting organization in the United States and by several abroad.

Paterson has been asked frequently why, with all her talent, she does not write books for adults. Her answer is that she not only enjoys writing for young readers but she considers writing for these readers to be among the most important tasks an author can attempt. Paterson has always been willing to share her writing knowledge with authors interested in writing for young adults.

FICTION BY PATERSON

Angels and Other Strangers: Family Christmas Stories (1979). Harper 1988 $3.50. ISBN 0-06-440283-5
Bridge to Terabithia (1977). Harper 1987 $12.89. ISBN 0-690-04635-9
Come Sing, Jimmy Go (1985). Avon 1986 $2.95. ISBN 0-380-70052-2
The Great Gilly Hopkins (1978). Harper 1978 $12.89. ISBN 0-690-03838-0
Jacob Have I Loved (1980). Harper 1980 $12.89. ISBN 0-690-04079-2
The Master Puppeteer (1976). Harper 1976 $13.70. ISBN 0-690-00913-5
Of Nightingales That Weep (1974). Harper 1974 $13.70. ISBN 0-690-00485-0
Park's Quest (1988). Lodestar 1988 $12.95. ISBN 0-525-67258-3
Rebels of the Heavenly Kingdom (1983). Lodestar 1983 $11.95. ISBN 0-525-66911-6

NONFICTION BY PATERSON

Gates of Excellence: On Reading and Writing Books for Children (1981). Dutton 1988 $9.95. ISBN 0-525-67249-4
The Spying Heart: More Thoughts on Reading and Writing Books for Children (1989). Dutton 1989 $8.95. ISBN 0-525-67269-9

COLLEGE APPLICATIONS

Bauld, Harry. *On Writing the College Application Essay.* Harper 1987 $14.95. ISBN 0-06-055076-7

Harvard Independent Staff. *100 Successful College Application Essays.* Plume 1988 $8.95. ISBN 0-452-26153-8

Schwartz, Mimi. *How to Write College Application Essays.* Petersons Guide 1982 $1.95. ISBN 0-87866-195-6

FILMSCRIPTS

Evans, Geoff. *How to Write a Film.* Schocken 1986 $5.95. ISBN 0-8052-8253-X

Field, Syd. *Screenplay: The Foundations of Screenwriting, Expanded Edition.* Dell 1984 $8.95. ISBN 0-440-57647-4

*King, Viki. *How to Write a Movie in 21 Days.* Harper 1988 $16.45. ISBN 0-06-055112-7 Step-by-step technique for bringing a movie from concept to actuality; how to be sure your idea is cinematic and how to develop it into a 120-page, 120-minute format, revising as you work.

Nash, Constance, and Virginia Oakey. *The Television Writer's Handbook.* Harper 1978 $6.95. ISBN 0-06-463455-8

Root, Wells. *Writing the Script: A Practical Guide for Films and Television.* H. Holt 1980 $8.95. ISBN 0-8050-0237-5

Walter, Richard. *Screenwriting: The Art, Craft, and Business of Film and Television Writing.* Plume 1988 $9.95. ISBN 0-452-26347-6

LEE, SPIKE (SHELTON JACKSON) 1957–

Spike Lee was born in Atlanta, Georgia, the son of a musician father and schoolteacher mother. He received a B.A. from Morehouse College in Atlanta, Georgia, in 1979 and did graduate work at New York University in 1982.

In just a few years, Lee established himself not only as a leading filmmaker but also as a talented writer and director.

In 1982, while still a graduate student, Lee made the short film *Joe's Bed-Stuy Barbershop: We Cut Heads,* about a barbershop that is a front for a gambling operation. The film was well reviewed and shown at international film festivals. In 1984, with virtually no money and with a small cast and crew that included himself and family members, Lee wrote and made *She's Gotta Have It,* about a woman and her three lovers. Released in 1986, the film was the sleeper of the year, receiving high critical praise and doing surprisingly well at the box office.

The success of his first feature enabled Lee to get financing from Columbia Pictures for his next venture, *School Daze,* a musical about rival factions at a black college. Lee again wrote, directed, and performed in the movie. The film was released in 1988 to mixed reviews, much of the criticism coming from black reviewers who found Lee's portrayal of divisions among black people insulting.

Lee's most recent films, *Do the Right Thing* (1989), *Mo' Better Blues* (1990), and *Jungle Fever* (1991), have received generally favorable reviews but have also provoked controversy over their portrayal of African Americans and black-white relations. Despite the controversy over the content of the films, however, there is no controversy over Spike Lee's extraordinary talent as a filmmaker.

BOOKS BY LEE

Do the Right Thing: The New Spike Lee Joint (1989). (coauthored with Lisa Jones) Simon 1989 $10.95. ISBN 0-671-68265-2

Uplift the Race: The Construction of School Daze (1988). (coauthored with Lisa Jones) Simon 1988 $9.95. ISBN 0-671-64418-1

Spike Lee's Gotta Have It: Inside Guerrilla Filmmaking (1987). Simon 1987 $9.95. ISBN 0-671-64417-3

SERLING, ROD (EDWARD RODMAN) 1924–1975

Rod Serling was born and raised in Columbus, Ohio. After completing high school, he entered the army, where he served as a paratrooper in the Pacific during World War II. After the war, he went to work as a writer for radio station WLW in Cincinnati, Ohio. In 1948, Serling began his career as a television writer with WKRC-TV, also in Cincinnati, where he worked until 1953.

Serling then became a free-lance writer and sold several scripts to television networks. In 1955 he became an overnight success with the production of his drama *Patterns,* which won him an Emmy award from the National Academy of Television Arts and Sciences. Two years later, he won his second Emmy for the highly acclaimed television play *Requiem for a Heavyweight,* which was also made into a movie.

After his success with *Patterns,* Serling began to feel restricted by the censorship he encountered from network officials and advertising agencies who objected to the content of some of his scripts. He therefore withdrew briefly from television writing.

Serling returned to television in 1959 with the highly successful fantasy series *The Twilight Zone,* for which he won another Emmy in 1959. He later received three more awards for plays written for the live television drama series *Playhouse 90.* Serling explained that he chose the fantasy genre because it permitted him to explore socially important topics, such as racial prejudice, without being censored.

It is a tribute to Serling's talent that episodes of *The Twilight Zone* are still broadcast on television. It is an even greater tribute that he is so widely imitated. His dramas are considered classics, not only because they were aired during the early days of television, but because they are still so good.

BOOKS BY SERLING

Into the Twilight Zone. Amereon $19.95. ISBN 0-89190-446-8

Rod Serling's Night Gallery Reader (1987). Dembner 1987 $15.95. ISBN 0-934878-93-5

The Twilight Zone Omnibus. Amereon $20.95.

BOOK ABOUT SERLING

Engel, Joel. *Rod Serling: His Life and Vision.* Contemporary Bks 1989 $16.95. ISBN 0-8092-4538-8 Biographical study of Serling's artistic development with attention to his disputes with networks and advertising agencies.

LETTERS

Hutchinson, Betty, and Warner A. Hutchinson. *Business Letters Made Simple.* Doubleday 1985 $8.95. ISBN 0-385-19427-7
*Mischel, Florence. *How to Write a Letter.* Watts 1988 $10.40. ISBN 0-531-10587-3 Introductory guide to writing letters for all occasions; explains why this ability is valued in an age of electronic communication.
New American Library editors. *The New American Handbook of Letter Writing and Other Correspondence.* Signet 1988 $4.50. ISBN 0-451-15414-2
Thomas, Del. *How to Write Powerful Complaint Letters and Others.* Boone-Thomas 1984 $7.00. ISBN 0-9611780-1-9
Watson, Lillian Eichler. *The Bantam Book of Correct Letter Writing.* Bantam 1963 $4.95. ISBN 0-553-27086-9

NEWS STORIES AND FEATURES

Block, Merv. *Writing Broadcast News: Shorter, Sharper, Stronger.* Bonus 1987 $22.95. ISBN 0-933893-20-5
Blundell, William E. *The Art and Craft of Feature Writing: The Wall Street Journal Guide.* Plume 1988 $8.95. ISBN 0-452-26158-9
Burkhardt, Ann. *Writing About Food and Families, Fashion and Furnishings.* Iowa State Univ Pr 1984 $10.95. ISBN 0-8138-1941-5
Fry, Don (ed). *The Best Newspaper Writing.* Poynster 1987 $9.95. ISBN 0-935742-14-X
Garvey, Daniel and William Rivers. *Newswriting for the Electronic Media: Principles, Examples, Applications.* Wadsworth 1982. (o.p.) $18.25. ISBN 0-534-01069-5
Harwood, William. *Writing and Editing School News.* Clark 1983 $11.45. ISBN 0-93104-11-7
Metz, William. *Newswriting: From Lead to "30."* Prentice 1991 $33.00. ISBN 0-13-622267-6
*Ruehlmann, William. *Stalking the Feature Story.* Vintage 1979 $7.56. ISBN 0-394-72849-1 How to get and write about the facts on the people, places, and events that make the news, with examples from columnist Russell Baker, essayist Joan Didion, investigative reporters Bob Woodward and Carl Bernstein, and others.

BUCHWALD, ART (ARTHUR)   1925–

Art Buchwald has been writing newspaper columns for over 40 years, and for 30 of those years, he has been regarded as one of America's foremost humorists and political and social commentators. Buchwald holds the day's news stories up to close scrutiny, revealing their hidden absurdities. His twice-weekly column, which appears in hundreds of newspapers across the country, regularly satirizes politics, politicians, and assorted fads, trends, and excesses in modern life.

Born in Mount Vernon, New York, Buchwald left high school in 1942 before graduating to join the Marines. After serving in World War II, he enrolled in the University of Southern California, but he left after three years to work in Paris. He joined the staff of the Paris edition of the *New York Herald Tribune,* and his two columns, "Paris After Dark" and "Mostly About People," were soon delighting thousands of European readers. In 1952, the two columns were combined into "Europe's Lighter Side," later called "Art Buchwald in Paris," for publication in America.

In 1962 Buchwald returned to the United States and took up residence in Washington, D.C., from where he has continued to comment on the American scene. Every morning Buchwald reads two or three newspapers and clips out stories that stimulate his interest or make him angry. He then thinks about the issues for a day or two before addressing them in his column.

From time to time Buchwald collects his columns and publishes them in book form. These collections almost always become best-sellers.

BOOKS BY BUCHWALD

The Bollo Caper: A Furry Tail for all Ages (1974). Putnam 1983 $4.95. ISBN 0-399-21003-2
Down the Seine and up the Potomac with Art Buchwald (1977). Fawcett 1980 $2.75. ISBN 0-449-23689-7
I Am Not a Crook (1974). Fawcett 1981 $2.50. ISBN 0-449-23404-5
I Think I Don't Remember (1987). Putnam 1987 $16.95. ISBN 0-399-13325-9
Laid Back in Washington (1982). Berkley 1984 $3.50. ISBN 0-425-07577-X
Washington Is Leaking (1976). Fawcett 1978 $2.95. ISBN 0-449-23294-8
While Reagan Slept (1983). Putnam 1983 $14.95. ISBN 0-399-12841-7
Whose Rose Garden Is It Anyway? (1989). Putnam 1989 $18.95. ISBN-0-399-13480-8
You Can Fool All of the People All of the Time (1985). Putnam 1985 $16.95. ISBN 0-399-13104-3

BOOK ABOUT BUCHWALD

Kiley, Frederick. *Satire: From Aesop to Buchwald.* Macmillan 1971 $23.00. ISBN 0-02-363590-8 A comprehensive history of satire through the ages.

NONFICTION

Evans, Glen (ed). *The Complete Guide to Writing Nonfiction.* Harper 1988 $10.95. ISBN 0-06-097135-5
Franklin, Jon. *Writing for Story: Craft Secrets of Dramatic Nonfiction.* Mentor 1987 $4.95. ISBN 0-451-62555-2
Garfinkel, Perry. *Travel and Writing for Profit and Pleasure.* Plume 1989 $8.95. ISBN 0-452-26159-7
Zinsser, William. *On Writing Well.* Harper 1988 $13.45. ISBN 0-06-015409-8

TERKEL, STUDS (LOUIS)   1912–

Studs Terkel was born in New York City and educated at the University of Chicago, where he received his bachelor's degree and completed law school. Terkel never practiced law, however. He worked first as a civil servant in Washington, D.C., and then as an actor and movie-house manager before finally becoming a radio and television broadcaster.

In 1945, Terkel returned to Chicago as host of an interview show on radio station WFMT. He had a television talk show called "Studs' Place" until 1953, when it was cancelled because of his appearance before the House Un-American Activities Committee (a congressional investigation into supposed Communists and their sympathizers). Like so many people called before the committee, Terkel had never been a Communist or even a Communist supporter, but he had allowed his name to be associated with causes, such as abolishing the poll tax, establishing rent control, and endorsing Social Security, that the committee took as evidence of Communist sympathy.

Out of work, Terkel took his skills as an interviewer on the road. Armed with a tape recorder, he began talking to Americans all over the country about their problems. (It has been said that the only person whose life was more affected by the tape recorder was President Richard Nixon.) The result of all these interviews has been a series of books by Terkel that capture different aspects of American life. One of his most famous, *Working: People Talk About What They Do All Day and How They Feel About What They Do* (1974), paints a dismal picture of Americans suffering through their jobs with little satisfaction. The book has since been made into a play and a musical. *American Dreams: Lost and Found* (1980) contains testimony from a group of people equally disillusioned about what they have gotten out of life in America.

As a writer of nonfiction, Terkel is unique. His ability to build interviews and conversations into a readable and informative narrative has been praised by his admirers and critics alike.

BOOKS BY TERKEL

American Dreams: Lost and Found (1980). Pantheon 1980 $14.95. ISBN 0-394-50793-2

Division Street: America (1967). Pantheon 1982 $5.95. ISBN 0-394-71009-6

The Good War: An Oral History of World War Two (1984). Pantheon 1984 $19.45. ISBN 0-394-53103-5

The Great Divide: Second Thoughts on the American Dream (1988). Pantheon 1988 $18.95. ISBN 0-394-57053-7

Hard Times: An Oral History of the Great Depression in America (1970). Pantheon 1986 $19.45. ISBN 0-394-42774-2

Talking to Myself (1977). State Mutual 1986 $44.75. ISBN 0-245-54376-7

Working: People Talk About What They Do All Day and How They Feel About What They Do (1974). Pantheon 1974 $7.95. ISBN 0-394-72953-6

PLAYS

Delgado, Ramón (ed). *Best Short Plays of 1988.* Applause Theatre Bk 1988 $21.95. ISBN 1-55783-025-8

*Grebanier, Bernard. *Playwriting.* Harper 1961 $7.95. ISBN 0-06-463498-1 Step-by-step guide to selecting a theme, developing the plot, building the structure, portraying the characters, and creating the dialogue.

Guernsey, Otis, and Jeffrey Sweet. *Best Plays of 1988–89.* Applause Theatre Bk 1989 $35.95. ISBN 1-55783-056-8

Hull, Raymond. *How to Write a Play.* Writers Digest 1988 $10.95. ISBN 0-89879-316-5

Pike, Frank, and Thomas G. Dunn. *The Playwright's Handbook.* Plume 1985 $9.95. ISBN 0-452-25688-7

POEMS

Dessner, Lawrence. *How to Write a Poem.* New York Univ Pr 1979 $12.50. ISBN 0-8147-1767-5

*Dunning, Stephen, *et al. For Poets.* Blanchard 1975 $7.95. Probably the best book for young poets; includes a brief anthology of great poems.

Higginson, William, and Penny Harter. *The Haiku Handbook.* McGraw 1985 $10.95. ISBN 0-07-028786-4

Kirby, David. *Writing Poetry: Where Poems Come from and How to Write Them.* Writer 1989 $12.95. ISBN 0-87116-159-1

Lehman, David (ed). *Best American Poetry 1988.* Scribner's 1988 $19.95. ISBN 0-684-18983-6

Padgett, Ron. *The Teachers and Writers Handbook of Poetic Forms.* Teachers and Writers Coll 1987 $19.95. ISBN 0-915924-24-2

*Stillman, Frances. *The Poet's Manual and Rhyming Dictionary.* Harper 1965 $15.45. ISBN 0-690-64572-4 Includes modern as well as traditional poetic forms; single, double, and even triple rhyming words; slang, colloquial, and common foreign words.

RESUMES

Block, Deborah. *How to Write a Winning Resumé.* National Textbook 1988 $6.95. ISBN 0-8442-6639-6

Cowan, Tom. *Resumés That Work.* Plume 1983 $12.95. ISBN 0-452-26213-5

Parker, Yana. *The Damn Good Resumé Guide.* Ten Speed 1989 $6.95. ISBN 0-89815-348-4

Parker, Yana. *The Resumé Catalog: 200 Damn Good Examples.* Ten Speed 1988 $11.95. ISBN 0-89815-219-4

Smith, Michael Holley. *The Resumé Writer's Handbook.* Harper 1987 $6.95. ISBN 0-06-463717-4

Yate, Martin J. *Resumés That Knock 'Em Dead.* Adams Inc MA 1988 $7.95. ISBN 1-55850-955-0

STORIES AND NOVELS

Card, Orson Scott. *The Elements of Fiction Writing: Characters and Viewpoint.* Writers Digest 1988 $12.95. ISBN 0-89879-307-6

Dihell, Ansen. *The Elements of Fiction Writing: Plot.* Writers Digest 1988 $13.95. ISBN 0-89879-303-3

Evans, Christopher. *Writing Science Fiction.* St. Martin's 1988 $10.95. ISBN 0-312-01849-5

Helprin, Mark, and Shannon Ravanel (eds). *Best American Short Stories 1988.* Houghton 1988 $17.95. ISBN 0-395-44257-5

Hills, Rust. *Writing in General and the Short Story in Particular.* Houghton 1987 $16.95. ISBN 0-395-44255-9

Jute, Andre. *Writing a Thriller.* St. Martin's 1987 $10.95. ISBN 0-312-001114-8

Keating, H. R. *Writing Crime Fiction.* St. Martin's 1987 $10.95. ISBN 0-312-01115-6

Martin, Rhona. *Writing Historical Fiction.* St. Martin's 1988 $10.95. ISBN 0-312-01848-7

*McCormick, Mona. *The Fiction Writer's Research Handbook.* Plume 1989 $9.95. ISBN 0-452-26444-8 Comprehensive, easy-to-use guide to reliable information on costumes, locales, events, weather, style, manners, morals, and other topics from ancient times to the present.

Meredith, Robert C., and John D. Fitzgerald. *Structuring Your Novel.* Harper 1972 $6.95. ISBN 0-06-463325-X

Newson, Michael. *How to Write Action–Adventure Novels.* Writers Digest 1989 $13.95. ISBN 0-89879-358-0

Pianka, Phyllis. *How to Write Romances.* Writers Digest 1988 $13.95. ISBN 0-89879-324-6

Reed, Kit. *The Elements of Fiction Writing: Revision.* Writers Digest 1989 $13.95. ISBN 0-89879-350-5

Turco, Lewis. *The Elements of Fiction Writing: Dialogue.* Writers Digest 1989 $12.45. ISBN 0-89879-344-1

Wlakowiak, J. *Adventure Game Writer's Handbook.* Abacus Soft 1985 $14.95. ISBN 0-916439-14-3

*Willis, Meredith S. *Personal Fiction Writing: A Guide to Writing from Real Life.* Teachers and

Writers Coll 1984 $11.95. ISBN 0-915924-13-7 Emphasizes the need for young writers to find their own writing voice; includes chapters on description, dialogue, and plot with examples of young people's work.

TECHNICAL REPORTS AND MANUALS

Anderson, Paul V. *Technical Writing: A Reader-Centered Approach.* Harcourt 1987 $20.00. ISBN 0-15-589680-6

Beason, Pamela. *Technical Writing for Business.* Scott 1989 $15.95. ISBN 0-673-38370-9

Beason, Pamela, and Patricia Williams. *Technical Writing in Today's Workplace.* Scott 1989 $17.95. ISBN 0-673-38730-5

Bly, Robert, and Gary Blake. *Technical Writing: Structure, Standards and Style.* McGraw 1982 $11.95. ISBN 0-07-006174-2

Weiss, Edmond. *How to Write a Usable User Manual.* ISI Pr 1985 $21.95. ISBN 0-89495-051-7

Path of Life 1
Woodcut in two colors by M. C. Escher
© 1958 M. C. Escher/Cordon Art-Baarn-Holland

PART TWO

MATHEMATICS

AND

COMPUTER SCIENCE

T he material in Part Two has been compiled to provide students, teachers, librarians, and other interested readers with a selection of resources that offers information on topics normally introduced in the mathematics and computer science courses offered in junior and in senior high school. These listings of sources will be useful in a variety of ways. Students can scan them when searching for a book on a particular subject or person. The profiles of notable individuals and the listings of their works will be of special help to students gathering sources for a research report.

Because a reference book must be selective, some key contributors or topics will inevitably be left out or treated more briefly than others. The problem of choosing what is to be included and what must be left out of a reference book is always a difficult one. Given the great wealth and evolving nature of the material, it was an especially challenging task to make such choices in mathematics and in computer science.

As is the case in Part One of *The Young Adult Reader's Adviser,* the books that are marked with an asterisk (*) are especially appropriate for younger readers, ages 12 to 14, in both reading level and content. Many of these books can be read with enjoyment and profit by older readers as well. Most of the remaining books listed are within the reading range of senior high school students, but there are a few that are suited primarily for the most able readers.

MATHEMATICS

To make the selections for the mathematics sections, the editors of *The Young Adult Reader's Adviser* studied the curriculum guides provided by numerous states to see which books are currently used in grades 6 through 12. The editors also consulted leading educators and a number of bibliographies of recommended readings for students ages 12 to 18 to find out which topics continue to be most popular with this age group. From this data, the editors chose to include those readings that received the best reviews and to profile those mathematicians with the strongest reputations.

Mathematics consists of a relatively small number of major fields, each with its own traditions, methods, classic problems, and assortment of practical applications. The most prominent of these areas are algebra, geometry, and analysis, the last of which includes calculus and function theory. Other important areas include probability, topology, symbolic logic, set theory, and number theory. There are related fields as well—recreational mathematics, the history of mathematics, and the philosophical foundations of mathematics.

Until modern times, mathematicians tended to cluster in just a few locations. One of the oldest centers of mathematical activity was the ancient city of Alexandria, Egypt, where Euclid, Apollonius, and Diaphantus lived and where Archimedes often visited. In the seventeenth century, Paris, France, became a center of mathematical activity. Here René Descartes and Blaise Pascal did their creative work between the years 1640 and 1660. Pierre de Fermat, who lived in the French city of Toulouse, was associated with this center as well. In the late seventeenth and early eighteenth centuries, Basel, Switzerland, became an active area for mathematics. Among its citizens was the Bernoulli family, many of whose members made important contributions to both mathematics and science.

In the nineteenth century, mathematically active centers tended to be concentrated at the great universities, such as the Ecole Polytechnique of Paris and the university at Göttingen, Germany. Among the mathematicians affiliated with the Ecole were Augustin Cauchy and Evariste Galois. The most famous mathematician associated with Göttingen was the great Carl Friedrich Gauss (1777–1855). Later, in the nineteenth century and in the early twentieth century, Göttingen included among its faculty such outstanding mathematicians as Felix Klein, David Hilbert, and Emmy Noether, who joined in an effort to unify much of the mathematics of the past.

Mathematical activity in this century has not been quite as geographically concentrated as it was in the past. In the English-speaking world, for example, outstanding mathematical work takes place at many institutions of higher learning, including Cambridge and Oxford universities in Great Britain and at Princeton, Yale, Harvard, the Massachusetts Institute of Technology, Columbia University, and the University of Chicago in the United States. At these and many other institutions, the research of the past has been continued. This research includes the attempt by Bertrand Russell, Kurt Gödel, and others to remove some of the boundaries that separate mathematics from logic.

In the mathematics section that follows, profiles of noteworthy contributors to the field appear at the end of their subsections. Profiles present basic information about a person's life, education, career, and major works. However, these are by no means complete accounts. For the most part, following a profile is a Books By section listing the works by a given writer that are currently in print.

The works included in the Books About sections have been selected to give additional information about an individual's life and work. In most cases the list has been limited in an effort to guide readers. The serious student, however, will find many more works about major mathematicians listed in Bowker's *Books in Print.* Brief descriptions of books that are out of print or especially important works have also been provided.

Whenever possible, the "books about" are readable, general discussions of an individual's background, major ideas, and major works. On occasion, more specialized and narrowly focused books have also been included because they have something special to offer. Every effort has been made to list books that are currently in print and available from major publishers, but this was not always possible.

COMPUTER SCIENCE

Because computer science is a rapidly evolving field of study, it is not possible here to treat its complex topics comprehensively. However, the subject breakdown does manage to include all the related areas of instruction covered in most American schools.

The story of today's computers begins with such aids to computation as the abacus and the more recent slide rule. Over the years since then, there have been a great number of inventions and discoveries by scientists and mathematicians. Many of these discoveries converged in the period from 1943 to 1946, when John Mauchly and J. Prosper Eckert designed and built ENIAC, the world's first all-electronic digital computer. Its 20,000 switching circuits were made of vacuum tubes and had a memory capacity of 20 numbers of 10 digits each. John Von Neumann, a well-known mathematician of the time, recommended a series of improvements to the design of ENIAC, improvements that were incorporated into a revamped version of the machine completed in 1946.

The next major development in the evolution of computers occurred in the early 1950s, when large commercial mainframes were developed for large organizations. Then, in the early 1960s came the minicomputer—the first alternative to mainframes. After that came the most familiar development of recent years—the microcomputer, or desktop computer.

Today, while not everyone has become a computer user, the ranks of users have expanded enormously. Wide accessibility of computers suggests some general questions about the essential nature of the computer, the stages in its development, the forces responsible for its dynamic growth, its benefits to individual users and to society, and the developments on the horizon.

.:. MATHEMATICS .:.

GENERAL REFERENCES AND HISTORIES IN MATHEMATICS

The references in this section are, as its name suggests, diverse, ranging from mathematical dictionaries to mathematical classics. Every attempt has been made to choose references and histories that are highly regarded. The reader is reminded that if a particular reference is not listed here, it may appear elsewhere in *The Young Adult Reader's Adviser*. For example, a history of geometry that is not found in this section might be listed under the geometry section.

*Abdelnoor, R. E. *The Silver Burdett Mathematical Dictionary.* Silver 1987 $7.95. ISBN 0-382-09309-7 Reference book for grades 5–12.

*Albers, Donald J., and G. L. Alexanderson (eds). *Mathematical People: Profiles and Interviews.* Birkhauser 1985 $26.95. ISBN 0-8176-3191-7 Collection of sketches on the century's leading mathematicians.

Aleksandrov, A. D., *et al* (eds). *Mathematics—Its Contents, Methods, and Meanings.* S. H. Gould (tr). 3 vols. MIT Pr 1983 $30.00. ISBN 0-262-51014-6

*Baker, Alan. *A Concise Introduction to the Theory of Numbers.* Cambridge Univ Pr 1985 $12.95. ISBN 0-521-28654-9 Short description of number theory (less than 100 pages).

Beiler, Albert H. *Recreations in the Theory of Numbers.* Dover 1964 $6.95. ISBN 0-486-21096-0

*Bell, Eric T. *Men of Mathematics.* Simon 1986 $13.95. ISBN 0-671-62818-6 Classic collection of chapter-length biographies of outstanding mathematicians.

Berggren, J. L. *Episodes in the Mathematics of Medieval Islam.* Springer-Verlag 1986 $29.00. ISBN 0-387-96318-9

Beth, E. W. *Mathematical Thought: An Introduction to the Philosophy of Mathematics.* Kluwer Academic 1965 $22.00. ISBN 90-277-0070-2

Boyer, Carl. *A History of Mathematics.* Princeton Univ Pr 1968 $16.95. ISBN 0-691-02391-3

Bronshtein, I. N., and K. A. Semendyayev. *Handbook of Mathematics.* K. A. Hirsch (tr). Van Nostrand 1985 $49.95. ISBN 0-442-21171-6

*Cajori, Florian. *A History of Mathematics.* Chelsea 1980 repr of 1938 ed $22.50. ISBN 0-8284-0329-6 Valuable reference and sourcebook that covers mathematical thought from ancient times to the end of World War I, with emphasis on the eighteenth to twentieth centuries.

*Chace, A. B. (ed). *The Rhind Mathematical Papyrus.* Classics Ser. Vol. 8 NCTM 1979 $17.00. ISBN 0-87353-133-7 Our major source of knowledge about early Egyptian mathematics.

*Chenier, Norman J. *Chenier Math Method: A Practical Math Dictionary and Workbook–Textbook.* Chenier 1989 $24.95. ISBN 0-9626061-0-3 Dictionary–textbook that presents general mathematics concepts and activities, from fractions to practical measurement tools, using a simplified table of contents.

*Courant, Richard, and Herbert Robbins. *What is Mathematics? An Elementary Approach to Ideas and Methods.* Oxford Univ Pr 1979 $16.95. ISBN 0-19-502517-2 Classic exploration into the nature and character of mathematics.

*Dalton, LeRoy C., and Henry D. Snyder. *Topics for Mathematics Clubs.* NCTM 1983 $7.00. ISBN 0-87353-208-2 Ideas and activities for mathematics clubs.

Davis, Martin. *Lectures on Modern Mathematics.* Notes on Mathematics and Its Applications Ser. 3 vols. Gordon & Breach 1967 $72.00. ISBN 0-677-00200-9

*Devlin, Keith. *Mathematics: The New Golden Age.* Viking 1988 $8.95. ISBN 0-14-022728-8 Popular treatment of mathematics achievements of the past 25 years including fractals, chaos theory, and the Four-Color Theorem solution.

Dickson, Leonard E. *History of the Theory of Numbers.* 3 vols. Chelsea 1971 $65.00. ISBN 0-8284-0086-5

*Downing, Douglas. *Dictionary of Mathematics Terms.* Barron 1987 $8.95. ISBN 0-8120-2905-4 Dictionary that explains mathematical terms taken from across the subdisciplines.

*Ecker, Michael W. *Getting Started in Problem Solving and Math Contests.* Watts 1987 $12.90. ISBN 0-531-10342-0 Designed to improve one's skills in mathematical thinking; could be helpful for preparation with SATs and other entrance exams.

*Fisher, Leonard Everett. *Number Art: Thirteen 1 2 3s from Around the World.* Macmillan 1982 $12.95. ISBN 0-590-07810-0 Illustrates and explains different numbering systems from around the world.

Fowler, D. H. *The Mathematics of Plato's Academy: A New Reconstruction.* Oxford Univ Pr 1987 $98.00. ISBN 0-19-853912-6

Gaffney, M. P., and L. A. Steen. *Annotated Bibliography of Expository Writing in the Mathematical Sciences.* Mathematical Assn 1976 $15.50. ISBN 0-88385-422-8

Gibson, Carol. *Facts on File Dictionary of Mathematics.* Facts on File 1990 $12.95. ISBN 0-8160-2365-4

Gillispie, Charles C. *Dictionary of Scientific Biography.* 8 vols. Scribner's 1970–1980 $750.00. ISBN 0-684-16962-2

Gow, James. *Short History of Greek Mathematics.* Chelsea 1968 $18.95. ISBN 0-8284-0218-3

Hardy, Godfrey H., and E. M. Wright. *Introduction to the Theory of Numbers.* Oxford Univ Pr 1979 $32.95. ISBN 0-19-853171-0

*Hershey, Robert L. *How to Think with Numbers.* Janson 1982 $7.95. ISBN 0-86576-014-4 Explains mathematical concepts such as percentage and interest through a series of puzzles and problems.

*Jacobs, Harold R. *Mathematics: A Human Endeavor (Teacher's Edition).* Freeman 1982 $12.95. ISBN 0-7167-1327-6 Textbook that also gives an overview of mathematics and examines its nature.

James, Glenn, and Robert C. James (eds). *Mathematics Dictionary.* Van Nostrand 1976 $39.95. ISBN 0-442-24091-0

√*Kasner, Edward, and James Newman. *Mathematics and the Imagination.* Microsoft 1989 $8.95. ISBN 1-55615-104-7 Classic book that deals with problems that motivate mathematicians.

Keenan, Edward P., and Anne X. Gantert. *Integrated Mathematics: Course 3.* AMSCO 1990 $11.00. ISBN 0-87720-277-X

Kline, Morris. *Mathematics: An Introduction to Its Spirit and Its Uses.* Freeman 1979 $14.95. ISBN 0-7167-0369-6

*Kline, Morris. *Mathematics for the Non-Mathematician. Popular Science Ser.* Dover 1985 $11.95. ISBN 0-486-24823-2 Basic account of what mathematics is all about.

Kline, Morris. *Mathematics in Western Culture.* Oxford Univ Pr 1964 $13.95. ISBN 0-19-500714-X

*Kogelman, Stanley, and Joseph Warren. *Mind Over Math.* McGraw 1978 $6.95. ISBN 0-07-035281-X Based on the author's series of workshops, this book helps one overcome math anxiety.

*Korner, Stephan. *The Philosophy of Mathematics: An Introductory Essay.* Dover 1986 $5.95. ISBN 0-486-25048-2 Introduction to the philosophy of mathematics.

Kramer, E. E. *The Nature and Growth of Modern Mathematics.* Princeton Univ Pr 1983. (o.p.) $18.95. ISBN 0-691-02372-7

Lang, Serge. *The Beauty of Doing Mathematics: Three Public Dialogues.* Springer-Verlag 1985 $24.00. ISBN 0-387-96149-6

Mathematics Encyclopedia. Macmillan 1989 $14.95. ISBN 0-02-689202-2 Intended for grades 4 and up.

Mikami, Y. *The Development of Mathematics in China and Japan.* Chelsea 1974 $19.95. ISBN 0-8284-0149-7

Millington, T. Alaric, and William Millington. *Dictionary of Mathematics.* Harper 1971 $7.95. ISBN 0-006-463311-X

*Newman, James R. *The World of Mathematics.* 4 vols. Microsoft 1988 $50.00. ISBN 1-55615-148-9 Classic compendium of mathematical literature and history that also presents explanations of mathematical concepts and personal viewpoints about mathematical issues.

North Carolina School of Science and Mathematics, Dept. of Mathematics and Computer Science Staff. *Matrices.* NCTM 1988 $10.00. ISBN 0-87353-270-8

*Osen, Lynn M. *Women in Mathematics.* MIT Pr 1974 $7.95. ISBN 0-262-65009-6 Book on eight significant women mathematicians.

*Pedoe, Dan. *The Gentle Art of Mathematics.* Dover 1973 $4.95. ISBN 0-486-22949-1 Popular book on mathematics that includes good puzzles.

Peet, T. Eric (tr). *The Rhind Mathematical Papyrus.* Kraus 1990 repr of 1923 ed $69.00. ISBN 3-262-00839-7

Rucker, Rudolf. *Infinity and the Mind: The Science and Philosophy of the Infinite.* Birkhauser 1982 $23.95. ISBN 0-8176-3034-1

Sawyer, W. W. *Prelude to Mathematics.* Dover 1983 $4.95. ISBN 0-486-24401-6

Scharlau, W., and H. Opolka. *From Fermat to Minkowski: Lectures on the Theory of Numbers and Its Historical Development. Undergraduate Texts in Mathematics Ser.* W. K. Buhler and G. Cornell (trs). Springer-Verlag 1984 $35.50. ISBN 0-387-90942-7

*Singh, Jagjit. *Great Ideas of Modern Mathematics.* Dover 1959 $6.50. ISBN 0-486-205-87-8 Examination of pivotal ideas of the mathematical revolution of the past 200 years.

*Smith, David E. *History of Mathematics.* Vol. 1 Dover (repr of 1923 ed) $10.00. ISBN 0-5486-20429-4 Story of elementary mathematics up to the mid-nineteenth century; includes a number of biographical sketches.

Smith, Karl J. *The Nature of Modern Mathematics.* Wadsworth 1987 $27.50. ISBN 0-534-06696-8

Steen, Lynn A. (ed). *Mathematics Today: Twelve Informal Essays.* Springer-Verlag 1984 $39.00. ISBN 0-387-90305-4

Steen, Lynn A. *Mathematics Tomorrow.* Springer-Verlag 1981 $29.80. ISBN 0-387-90564-2

*Struik, Dirk J. *A Concise History of Mathematics.* Dover 1987 $7.95. ISBN 0-486-60255-9 Brief but enlightening history by a mathematician who was a participant in some of the events at the Göttingen mathematical community in the 1920s, which he describes and assesses.

*Stwertka, Albert. *Recent Revolutions in Mathematics.* Watts 1987 $11.90. ISBN 0-531-10418-4 A report on recent advances in mathematics, with emphasis on practical applications and their effects on other sciences.

Swetz, Frank, and T. I. Kao. *Was Pythagoras Chinese? An Examination of Right Triangle Theory in Ancient China. Penn State Studies.* No. 39 Penn State Univ Pr 1977 $5.95. ISBN 0-271-01238-2

Szabo, Arprad. *The Beginnings of Greek Mathematics. Synthese Historical Library.* No. 17 Kluwer Academic 1978 $53.00. ISBN 90-277-0819-3

Theon of Smyrna. *Mathematics Useful for Understanding Plato or, Pythagorean Arithmetic, Music, Astronomy, Spiritual Disciplines. Secret Doctrine Reference Ser.* Robert Lawlor (tr). Wizards Bookshelf 1978 $14.00. ISBN 0-913510-24-6

Tod, M. N. *Ancient Greek Numerical Systems.* Ares 1979 $20.00. ISBN 0-89005-290-5

Van der Waerden, B. L. *Geometry and Algebra in Ancient Civilizations: From the Stone Age to Brahmagupta.* Springer-Verlag 1983 $63.50. ISBN 0-387-12159-5

Van Nostrand's Scientific Encyclopedia. 2 vols. Van Nostrand 1984 $195.00. ISBN 0-442-21750-1

Wang, Li-Chung. *Chinese Philosophy, Art, Life, and Mathematics.* L C Wang Pr 1987 $3.95. ISBN 0-9624242-0-X

*Wedberg, Anders. *Plato's Philosophy of Mathematics.* Greenwood 1977 repr of 1955 ed $35.00. ISBN 0-8371-9405-9 Explanation of the conception and role of mathematics in the larger scheme of Plato's philosophy of idealism.

Whitehead, Alfred North. *An Introduction to Mathematics.* Oxford Univ Pr 1959 $8.95. ISBN 0-19-500211-3

Yan, L., and Du Shiran. *Chinese Mathematics: A Concise History.* John N. Crossley and Anthony W. Lun (trs). Oxford Univ Pr 1987 $49.95. ISBN 0-19-858181-5

*Zingo, Laurie. *Mathematics Dictionary Made Simple.* Vantage 1988 $5.95. ISBN 0-533-07298-0

BOURBAKI, NICOLAS (PSEUDONYM FOR A GROUP OF TWENTIETH-CENTURY MATHEMATICIANS)

Nicolas Bourbaki is the name used by a group of mathematicians, mostly French, whose series of works on all aspects of modern mathematics, *Eléments de Mathématique,* treats mathematics from an abstract and axiomatic point of view. Since the appearance of the first volume of *Eléments* in 1939, a wide variety of topics has been covered, including set theory, algebra, general topology, functions of a real variable, topological vector spaces, and integration.

A major aim of the Bourbaki group is to make the logical structure of mathematical concepts as transparent and intelligible as possible. Each book starts at the logical beginning of its chosen topic and gives complete explanations. Working in this manner, the authors hope to develop a solid foundation for all of mathematics.

BOOKS BY BOURBAKI

Algebra One: Chapters 1–3 (1989). Springer-Verlag 1989 $69.00. ISBN 0-387-19373-1
Functions of a Real Variable (1982). Addison 1982. ISBN 0-201-00640-5
General Topology: Chapters 1–4 (1989). Springer-Verlag 1989 $69.00. ISBN 0-387-19374-X

BOOK ABOUT BOURBAKI

Fang, J. *Bourbaki. Towards a Philosophy of Modern Mathematics Ser.* Paideia 1970. (o.p.) Short history of modern mathematics that examines both Bourbaki and the "anti-Bourbakians."

CANTOR, GEORG   1845–1918

Georg Cantor was born in St. Petersburg, Russia, but was educated in and spent the rest of his life in Germany. He studied under Karl Weierstrass (*see* Weierstrass, Vol. 1, Calculus, Trigonometry, and Analysis: Analysis) and taught at the University of Halle from 1869 until 1913. He was the creator of set theory and the founder of the theory of transfinite numbers. His most important work appeared between 1895 and 1897. In addition to developing the philosophical implications of his transfinite set theory, Cantor was also concerned with the theological implications of his work. In 1891 he became the founder and first president of the German Mathematicians Union.

BOOK BY CANTOR

Contributions to the Founding of the Theory of Transfinite Numbers (1915). Philip E. Jourdain (tr). Dover 1955 repr of 1915 ed $5.95. ISBN 0-486-60045-9

BOOK ABOUT CANTOR

*Dauben, Joseph W. *George Cantor: His Mathematics and Philosophy of the Infinite.* Harvard Univ Pr 1979. (o.p.) $27.50. ISBN 0-674-34871-0 Account of Cantor's work that describes the social and academic context in which Cantor operated.

GODEL, KURT   1906–1978

Kurt Gödel was easily the most outstanding logician of the first half of the twentieth century. Born in Czechoslovakia, he studied at the University of Vienna, where he received his doctorate in 1930. In 1940 he came to the United States as a member of Princeton's Institute for Advanced Study. In 1953 he was made a professor at the institute, where he remained until his death in 1978.

Gödel is especially well known for his studies of the completeness of logic, the incompleteness of number theory, and the consistency of the axiom of choice and the continuum hypothesis. He is also known for his work on constructivity (the view that one must be able not only to define but also to build new mathematical objects in order for them to be mathematically valid), the decision problem (decidability), and the foundations of computation theory (used in computer theory and in algorithm analysis). In addition, he is recognized for his views on the philosophy of mathematics, especially his support of a strong form of Platonism in mathematics, that is, the belief that mathematical concepts and objects are "real" and exist independently, perhaps in a realm of abstract ideas.

BOOK BY GODEL

Collected Works of Kurt Gödel. Solomon Feferman, *et al* (eds). Vol. 1 Oxford Univ Pr 1986 $39.95. ISBN 0-1-9-503964-5

BOOKS ABOUT GODEL

Davis, M. (ed). *The Undecidable: Basic Papers on Undecidable Propositions, Unsolvable Problems and Computable Functions.* Raven 1965 $41.50. ISBN 0-911216-01-4 Presentation of Gödel's work on undecideable propositions.

Gensler, Harry J. *Gödel's Theorem Simplified.* Univ Pr of America 1984 $8.50. ISBN 0-8191-3869-X A simplified explanation of Gödel's Theorem, what it says, and what its significance is.

Schmettere, Leopold, and Paul Weingartner (eds). *Gödel Remembered. History of Logic Ser.* Vol. 4 Humanities 1987 $75.00. ISBN 0-88-7088-141-5 Collection of recollections and analyses of Gödel as a mathematical figure.

Smullyan, Raymond. *Forever Undecided: A Puzzle Guide to Gödel.* Knopf 1987 $17.95. ISBN 0-394-54943-0 Guide to the paradoxes implied by Gödel's work.

POINCARE, HENRI 1854–1912

Jules Henri Poincaré was a preeminent French mathematician, physicist, and author of the late nineteenth and early twentieth centuries. His academic credentials were of the highest. He was connected with the University of Paris from 1881, was elected to the Academy of Sciences in 1887 (becoming its president in 1906), and was elected to the Académie Française in 1909.

It has been claimed that Poincaré was the last of the great universalist mathematicians, one who could comprehend and make significant contributions to almost every branch of mathematics known in his day. Poincaré also did very important work in mathematical physics and astronomy. Above all, he opened many new fields, including algebraic topology, to mathematicians and made singular discoveries in the theory of complex variables (especially automorphic functions), differential equations, and celestial mechanics. Poincaré wrote for general audiences as well and made his own important contributions to both the philosophy and foundations of mathematics.

BOOK BY POINCARE

Papers on Fuchsian Functions. J. Stilwell (tr). Springer-Verlag 1985 $42.00. ISBN 0-387-96215-8

BOOK ABOUT POINCARE

Slosson, Edwin E. *Major Prophets of Today.* Ayer 1977 repr of 1914 ed $20.00. ISBN 0-8369-0882-1 Collection of biographies of turn-of-the-century personalities that, in the case of Poincaré, discusses the matter of creativity and the sources of scientific inspiration.

PYTHAGORAS *c.* 580 BC–*c.* 500 BC

Little is known of the life of the ancient Greek mathematician Pythagoras. This may be due to the influence of the mystical society that he founded, since its reclusive and communal nature discouraged the release of any information about its doings. Nevertheless, the influence of Pythagoras on mathematics is profound because of the famous theorem that carries his name—the Pythagorean Theorem. The theorem states that if a and b are the lengths of the two legs of a right triangle and if c is the length of the hypotenuse, then $a^2 + b^2 = c^2$.

It is unlikely that Pythagoras actually discovered the relationship that bears his name. But he may have been the first to prove it. The relationship was probably known and used by other ancients such as the Egyptians and the Babylonians. The Pythagorean approach to the right-triangle relationship, however, is fundamentally different from that of the Babylonians and the Egyptians. They were interested in the relationship as a means of solving certain specific problems in measurement, while Pythagoras and his followers were interested in the fact that the theorem expressed a fundamental geometric relationship that was true for *all* right triangles. It is this attitude that characterized the Pythagoreans as mathematicians in the modern sense of the word.

This mathematical attitude also can be seen in the way in which Pythagoras approached arithmetic—not as a computational skill but as the study of the properties of numbers. From the Pythagorean point of view, the proper role of arithmetic—and also of geometry, music, and astronomy—is to help a conscientious seeker of knowledge to attain a better appreciation of truth and beauty. The Pythagoreans regarded numbers, especially whole, or counting, numbers, as a supreme example of abstractions that are eternal and unchanging. This point of view is reflected in their overall mystical philosophy.

BOOK BY PYTHAGORAS

The Golden Verses of Pythagoras (late sixth century BC). *Sacred Texts Ser.* Concord Grove 1983 $8.75. ISBN 0-88695-009-0

BOOKS ABOUT PYTHAGORAS

Gorman, Peter. *Pythagoras: A Life.* Routledge 1978 $29.95. ISBN 0-7100-0006-5 Scholarly biography.

Hallam, Arthur F. *William Lloyd's Life of Pythagoras, with a New Thesis on the Origin of the New Testament.* Capitalist 1982 $8.50. ISBN 0-938770-01-2 Examination of William Lloyd's classic biography of Pythagoras.

Iamblicus *et al. The Pythagorean Sourcebook and Library: An Anthology of Ancient Writings Which Relate to Pythagoras and Pythagorean Philosophy.* Kenneth S. Guthrie (ed). Phanes 1987 $17.00. ISBN 0-933999-51-8 Collection of original writings from ancient Greek and Roman times that indicates the influence of Pythagoras' view of knowledge and traces the evolution of Pythagoreanism as a philosophy.

Levin, Flora R. *The Harmonics of Nicomachus and the Pythagorean Tradition.* Scholars Pr 1974 $10.95. ISBN 0-89130-241-7 Scholarly work focusing on the relation between the philosopher Nicomachus' work on harmonics and the influence of the Pythagorean outlook.

Loomis, Elisha S. *Pythagorean Proposition. Classics in Mathematics Education Ser.* NCTM 1968 $12.00. ISBN 0-87353-036-5 Discussion of the mathematics of Pythagoras.

McQuaid, Gary. *Pythagoras: The Reality of the New Computer Age.* Heridonius 1990 $24.95. ISBN 0-940539-11-X Pythagoras' viewpoint on numbers and its relevance to the computer age.

Oliver, George. *The Pythagorean Triangle. Secret Doctrine Reference Ser.* Wizards Bookshelf 1975 $13.00. ISBN 0-913510-17-3 Examination of the meaning and significance of the triangle and its relationships in Pythagorean philosophy and mathematics.

O'Meara, Dominic J. *Pythagoras Revived: Mathematics and Philosophy in Late Antiquity.* Oxford Univ Pr 1989 $49.95. ISBN 0-19-824485-1 Examines the process by which Pythagorean philosophy in general and Pythagorean mathematics in particular were reestablished in late antiquity.

Philip, James A. *Pythagoras and Early Pythagoreanism. Phoenix Ser Supplement.* Supplementary Vol. 7 Books Demand $58.00. ISBN 0-317-08752-5 Focuses on the origins and early development of Pythagorean philosophy.

Stanley, Thomas. *Pythagoras: His Life and Teachings.* Philos Res 1970 $16.95. ISBN 0-89314-408-8 Biography of Pythagoras and presentation of Pythagorean thought.

Taylor, Thomas. *Pythagorean Precepts.* Holmes Pub 1983 $6.95. ISBN 0-916411-00-1 Account of the principles of Pythagoras.

Taylor, Thomas. *The Theoretic Arithmetic of the Pythagoreans.* Wieser 1983 $12.50. ISBN 0-87728-558-6 Examination of Pythagoras' concept and theory of numbers and of arithmetic.

RAMANUJAN, SRINIVARA   1887–1920

Srinivara Ramanujan was an Indian worker in the Harbor Board office in Madras, India, during the early years of this century. What set him apart from his fellow workers was his extraordinary talent for mathematics. His teachers may well have recognized his ability while he was still in school, but his weakness in English deterred him from continuing his education at the university level. Nevertheless, Ramanujan attempted to improve his mathematical background, using the few books on modern mathematics available to him. As a result of his efforts, he not only taught himself mathematics but also reconstructed on his own, over a few years' time, much of Western mathematics for the 300 preceding centuries. Ramanujan's methods were unconventional, which gave his work a unique flavor. The details of his mathematical thought are recorded in his notebooks, which survive today.

Ramanujan's special interest was number theory, but he also was able to perform very competently in analysis. Wishing to extend his horizons, he wrote to the British mathematician G. H. Hardy, one of the leading mathematical figures of the day. On the basis of Ramanujan's mathematical accomplishments, which he described in his letter, Hardy invited the younger man to work with him at Cambridge University. Ramanujan accepted the invitation and sailed to join Hardy at Cambridge in 1917.

The collaboration between Hardy and Ramanujan benefited both parties. Hardy helped Ramanujan to fill the large gaps in his mathematical knowledge, while Ramanujan helped Hardy to understand his very individualistic approach to mathematical questions. The most fruitful result of their work together is a famous "partitioning" theorem about the number of ways a given number can be expressed as a sum of lesser whole numbers.

The relationship between Ramanujan and Hardy lasted for only two years. Ramanujan became increasingly dissatisfied with his strange surroundings, particularly with Western dietary customs. He began to suffer inner torments and painful dreams. His homesickness increased, his health deteriorated, and he began to experience a series of increasingly serious illnesses, the causes of which physicians could not easily determine. Eventually he returned to India, where he died less than a year later.

Ramanujan's special qualities and strengths were patience, power of calculation, an excellent memory, simplicity of formulation, a sense of good form, and the ability to modify his assumptions quickly when necessary. His story, including an interview with his widow, has been the subject of a television documentary on the Public Broadcasting System's *Nova* series.

BOOKS BY RAMANUJAN

Ramanujan's Notebooks, Part 1. B. C. Berndt (ed). Springer-Verlag 1985 $65.00. ISBN 0-387-96110-0

Ramanujan's Notebooks, Part 2. B.C. Berndt (ed). Springer-Verlag 1988 $79.80. ISBN 0-387-96794-X

BOOK ABOUT RAMANUJAN

Hardy, Godfrey H. *Ramanujan.* Chelsea 1978 $15.95. ISBN 0-8284-0136-5 Hardy's own account of Ramanujan's achievements and the story of their relationship.

RUSSELL, BERTRAND   1872–1970

Bertrand Russell was born in Wales and educated at Trinity College in Cambridge, England. During his long life, he concentrated his intellectual energies on philosophy, mathematics, and social reform. Among his mathematical works, *My Philosophical Development* and *Unpopular Essays* reflect his independence of mind.

Russell wrote his dissertation, which focused on the foundations of geometry, in 1897 at Cambridge University. He then went on to a special lectureship there in logic and the philosophy of mathematics. His primary scientific interest at the time was a general study of the principles of mathematics, which he believed could be reduced to a small set of fundamental principles. Eventually, in collaboration with his colleague Alfred North Whitehead, he produced the monumental *Principia Mathematica* (1910–1913). Russell's interest in the paradoxes of set theory and logic led him to advance a theory of types that was unsuccessful in saving mathematical logic from the proof, later given by Gödel (*see* Gödel, Vol. 1, General References and Histories in Mathematics), that no axiomatic system can be proved to be self-consistent—one of the goals Russell had set for himself in *Principia Mathematica.* A nontechnical exposition of the major intent and significance of *Principia Mathematica* was written by Russell in his *Introduction to Mathematical Philosophy* (1919).

BOOKS BY RUSSELL

An Essay on the Foundations of Geometry (1897). Dover 1956. (o.p.)
Essays in Analysis (1904–1913). D. Lackey (ed). Unwin 1973. (o.p.) $8.95.
Inquiry into Meaning & Truth. Unwin 1980 $7.95. ISBN 0-04-121019-0
Introduction to Mathematical Philosophy (1919). Simon 1971. (o.p.) $8.50.
The Philosophy of Leibniz (1900). Longwood 1989 $27.50. ISBN 0-89341-548-0
The Philosophy of Logical Atomism. Open Court 1985 $7.50. ISBN 0-87548-443-3
Principia Mathematica (1910–1913). (coauthored with Alfred North Whitehead) 3 vols. Cambridge Univ Pr 1925–1927 $400.00.
*The Principles of Mathematics (1903). Norton 1964 $12.95. ISBN 0-393-00249-7 Nontechnical treatment of Russell's mathematical philosophy, logicism.
The Problems of Philosophy (1911). Prometheus Bks 1988 $6.95. ISBN 0-87975-497-4

BOOKS ABOUT RUSSELL

Ayer, A. J. *Bertrand Russell.* Univ of Chicago Pr 1988 $9.95. ISBN 0-226-03343-0 Focuses on Russell as an analytic philosopher.
Brink, Andrew. *Bertrand Russell: A Psychobiography of a Moralist.* Humanities 1989 $12.50. ISBN 0-391-03605-X Psychological exploration of Russell's uncommon mixture of moral attitudes and principles.
Clark, Ronald. *The Life of Bertrand Russell.* Da Capo 1990 $17.95. ISBN 0-306-80397-6 Biography by the well-known biographer of Einstein.
Grattan-Guinness, Ivor. *Dear Russell–Dear Jourdain: A Commentary on Russell's Logic, Based on His Correspondence With Philip Jourdain.* Columbia Univ Pr 1977 $31.50. Presentation and discussion of the rich correspondence between two British philosopher-mathematicians about the paradoxes of set theory and related issues.
Hendley, Brian. *Dewey, Russell, Whitehead: Philosophers as Educators.* Southern Illinois Univ Pr 1985 $12.95. ISBN 0-8093-1243-3 Examination of the strongly held educational beliefs of these three scientifically oriented contemporaries.
Meyer, Samuel (ed). *Dewey and Russell: An Exchange.* Philosophical Lib 1985 $9.95. ISBN

0-8022-2406-7 Exchange of ideas between two great philosophers during the first half of the twentieth century.

Ryan, Alan. *Bertrand Russell: A Political Life.* Hill & Wang 1988 $19.95. ISBN 0-8090-2897-2 Examination of the role that political questions, and public stands on them, played in Russell's life.

GENERAL MATHEMATICS

General mathematics is the mathematics people use in their daily life—for example, when submitting a detailed bill for work done or preparing an accounting of volunteer funds spent. It helps people make such shopping decisions as choosing a particular brand of cat food from a wide selection of brands that have different sizes and prices. It shows people how to make financial plans wisely, whether purchasing a car, making an investment, starting a business, or planning for retirement. Its major focal points include arithmetic, word problems, consumer mathematics, business mathematics, and an introduction to topics from algebra and geometry.

Adams, W. *Fundamentals of Mathematics for Business, Social, and Life Sciences.* Prentice 1979 $53.00. ISBN 0-13-341073-0

Al-Hadad, Saba. *Agricultural Mathematics.* Kendall–Hunt 1981 $23.95. ISBN 0-8403-2450-2

*Ashlock, Robert, *et al.* *Merrill General Mathematics.* Merrill 1987 $22.20. ISBN 0-675-04800-1 Textbook with emphasis on computational skills plus preparation for business, technical, and academic mathematics.

*Dolciani, Mary P., *et al.* *Mathematics: Structure and Method Course 1.* Houghton 1988 $19.62. ISBN 0-395-43046-1 Textbook for Grade 7.

*Dolciani, Mary P., *et al.* *Mathematics: Structure and Method Course 2.* Houghton 1988 $19.62. ISBN 0-395-43048-8 Textbook for Grade 8.

*Dressler, Isidore. *Preliminary Mathematics.* AMSCO 1981 $9.70. ISBN 0-87720-242-7 Preparation for the formal study of algebra and geometry.

*Dritsas, *et al.* *HBJ Consumer Mathematics.* Harcourt 1989 $21.63. ISBN 0-15-353020-0 Textbook that teaches consumer skills and computation, using the Polya method of problem solving.

*Dritsas, *et al.* *HBJ Fundamentals of Mathematics.* Harcourt 1989 $21.63. ISBN 0-15-353001-4 Textbook that provides a consumer setting to teach computation, problem solving, and practical skills.

*Fogelman, Stanley, and Barbara R. Heller. *The Only Math Book You'll Ever Need.* Dell 1988 $6.95. ISBN 0-440-50007-9 Practical step-by-step solutions to everyday math problems.

*French, Francis G. *Consumer Mathematics.* Prentice 1989 $24.97. ISBN 0-13-166729-7 Textbook that deals with how to become an effective consumer and how to make real-world consumer decisions.

*Galerstein, David. *Mastering Fundamental Mathematics.* AMSCO 1976 $6.90. ISBN 0-87720-226-5 Textbook that uses simplified language and deals with *how* rather than *why.*

*Goozner, Calman. *Arithmetic Skills Worktext.* AMSCO 1988 $8.40. ISBN 0-87720-263-X Workbook that develops students' abilities in arithmetic computation and problem solving.

*Hogben, Lancelot. *Mathematics for the Millions.* Norton 1968 $22.50. ISBN 0-393-06361-5 Classic popular treatment of mathematics, written in the 1930s, that advocates that mathematics is both understandable and valuable for everyone.

*Price, Jack, *et al.* *Merrill Applications of Mathematics.* Merrill 1988 $22.80. ISBN 0-675-05717-5 Textbook directed toward applications; includes estimation, mental mathematics, and integrated use of calculators.

*Rich, Barnett. *Mathematics for the College Boards.* AMSCO 1987 $9.25. ISBN 0-87720-200-1 Well-organized, intensive textbook that prepares students for the mathematics section of the PSAT and SAT; includes five model examinations and teaches useful strategies, critical thinking skills, and problem-solving techniques.

*Stein, Edwin I. *Refresher Mathematics.* Prentice 1989 $24.97. ISBN 0-13-771122-0 Textbook that emphasizes problem-solving strategies and the skills of critical thinking and decision making.

*Usiskin, Zalman. *UCSMP-University of Chicago School Mathematics Project Transition Mathematics.* Scott 1990 $24.95. ISBN 0-673-45259-X Textbook that provides preparation for the systematic treatment of high school algebra and geometry.

ALGEBRA

Modern algebra is more than letter symbols, operation signs, and expressions, variables, and equations that can be used to solve problems. Algebra is a mathematical language that binds together all of the above ideas. It also is a mathematical system that focuses on the ways in which numbers can be combined and transformed according to certain rules. The symbols that now function as an integral part of algebra have not always existed. They came into being only in very gradual stages. During the early period in the development of algebra, when rudimentary algebraic concepts were developed, mathematical ideas were expressed using few special symbols at all. This period is sometimes called the "rhetorical" stage of algebra.

During the "intermediate" stage of development, in the first few centuries after the birth of Christ, some mathematicians, such as the Greek mathematician Diophantus, sometimes represented a mathematical idea by an abbreviation or by a symbol such as a letter. This stage, during which there was limited and crude use of mathematical symbols, lasted for centuries.

The third and last stage of development is the current one in which symbols are used extensively, with letters frequently representing numbers and superscript numbers symbolizing powers of numbers. However, as simple and familiar as these and other such symbols may be, more than 200 years passed before they were accepted by those who regularly worked with mathematics.

*Asimov, Isaac. *The Realm of Algebra.* Fawcett 1982 $3.50. ISBN 0-449-24396-2 Popular treatment and discussion of algebra for general audiences.

Bleau, Barbara. *Forgotten Algebra: A Refresher Course. Barron's Educational Ser.* Barron 1983 $9.95. ISBN 0-8120-2438-9

*Bramson, Morris. *Algebra: An Introductory Course.* AMSCO 1986 $15.17. ISBN 0-87720-261-3 Textbook intended for junior high school students who have difficulty with mathematics.

*Coxford, Arthur F., and Joseph N. Payne. *HBJ Algebra 1.* Harcourt 1990 $24.96. ISBN 0-15-353640-3 Textbook that builds connections to the real world and to geometry and statistics; includes historical digest feature and computer bank.

*Coxford, Arthur F., and Joseph N. Payne. *HBJ Algebra 2 with Trigonometry.* Harcourt 1990 $26.40. ISBN 0-15-353641-1 Textbook that continues the themes and formats of *HBJ Algebra 1* and builds connections to trigonometry and other subjects.

Dolciani, Mary P., *et al. Algebra: Structure and Method Book 1.* Houghton 1988 $21.99.

Dolciani, Mary P., *et al. Algebra and Trigonometry: Structure and Method Book 2.* Houghton 1988 $21.48.

Downing, Douglas. *Algebra the Easy Way. Easy Way Ser.* Barron 1989 $9.95. ISBN 0-8120-4194-1

*Dressler, Isidore. *Algebra I.* AMSCO 1966 $15.33. ISBN 0-87720-208-7 Textbook intended for average students; emphasizes problem solving and its related techniques.

*Dressler, Isidore, and Barnett Rich. *Modern Algebra Two.* AMSCO 1973 $16.73. ISBN 0-87720-233-8 Textbook that treats algebra as a deductive system, using well-phrased yet informal language and providing extensive treatments of verbal problems and of functions.

Fair, Jan, and Sadie Bragg. *Algebra 1.* Prentice 1990 $25.47. ISBN 0-13-021726-3

Fleming, Walter, and Dale Varberg. *College Algebra.* Prentice 1988 $29.50. ISBN 0-13-141656-1

*Foster, Alan G., *et al. Merrill Algebra Essentials.* Merrill 1988 $22.65. ISBN 0-675-05491-5 Slower-paced pre-algebra course for older students, with sufficient material for every ability level.

*Foster, Alan G., *et al. Merrill Algebra One.* Merrill 1990 $24.15. ISBN 0-675-05596-2 Textbook that emphasizes confidence building; includes use of scientific calculator and computers.

Hamilton, William R. *Mathematical Papers of Sir William Rowan Hamilton.* H. Halberstam and R. E. Ingram (eds). Vol. 3 Cambridge Univ Pr 1967 $140.00. ISBN 0-521-05183-5

*Harnadek, Anita. *How to Solve Algebra Word Problems. Algebra Word Problems Ser.* Midwest 1988 $5.95. ISBN 0-89455-315-1 Instructional workbook that breaks word problems into easily handled parts.

*Johnson, Mildred. *How to Solve Word Problems in Algebra: A Solved Problem Approach.* McGraw 1976 $4.95. ISBN 0-07-032620-7 Useful resource for solving word problems.

*Kasir, Daoud S. (ed). *The Algebra of Omar Khayyam.* AMS (repr of 1931 ed) $22.50. ISBN 0-404-55385-0 Classic study of algebra from medieval times.

*O'Daffer, Phares G., *et al. Pre-Algebra.* Addison 1987 $21.36. ISBN 0-201-29727-2 Textbook that includes number systems, equations and variables, equations in geometry, graphs of equations and statistics, data collection/analysis, and polynomials.

Research and Education Association Staff. *The High School Algebra Tutor.* Research & Education 1988 $10.95. ISBN 0-87891-564-8

Rosen, Frederic (tr). *The Algebra of Mohammed Ben Musa.* Coronet Bks (repr of 1831 ed) $57.50. ISBN 3-487-07722-1

*Smith, Stan, *et al. Algebra and Trigonometry.* Addison 1990 $24.90. ISBN 0-201-25383-6 Textbook that emphasizes problem understanding and solving.

*Usiskin, Zalman. *UCSMP-University of Chicago School Mathematics Project Advanced Algebra.* Scott 1990 $26.95. ISBN 0-673-45263-8 Textbook that follows multidimensional approach to understanding and emphasizes model-building tools (expressions and functions) and function graphers.

*Usiskin, Zalman. *UCSMP-University of Chicago School Mathematics Project Algebra.* Scott 1990 $23.95. ISBN 0-673-45275-1 Textbook that follows multidimensional approach to understanding by interlacing skills, properties, uses, and representations.

Van der Waerden, B. L. *A History of Algebra.* Springer-Verlag 1985 $69.00. ISBN 0-387-13610-X

Wooff, C., and D. Hodgkinson. *MuMath: A Microcomputer Algebra System.* Academic Pr 1987 $24.50. ISBN 0-12-763070-8

Yaglom, I. *Unusual Algebra.* Imported 1978 $1.95. ISBN 0-8285-0749-X

BOOLE, GEORGE 1815–1864

George Boole was a British mathematician and logician at Queens College in Cork, Ireland, where he taught and developed his theory of logic. In his everyday life Boole was well thought of by both those poorer than he and those who were more well-to-do. He had a reputation of being a kind of naive saint, who thought nothing of inviting a stranger to his home to continue a conversation that the two of them had begun on a train or in a shop. Boole's wife tolerated these interruptions fairly well, thus exhibiting some saintly behavior of her own.

Boole's development of symbolic logic had three major emphases. First, Boole believed that mathematicians of his day unnecessarily restricted themselves to the study of quantities and did not pay enough attention to abstract symbols. Second, he concerned himself with the relation between logic and language. Third, he studied the proper representation of mental operations. Thus Boole moved from quantity to symbols to language and finally to the rules of the thinking mind itself.

In 1847 Boole expressed his ideas in a pamphlet entitled *The Mathematical Analysis of Logic*. He is now remembered for using familiar symbols of algebra and arithmetic to help represent ideas of logic. The system he used is now known as Boolean algebra.

In creating his algebra of logic, Boole followed in the footsteps of the classical algebraists. Through careful analysis and resourcefulness, he developed a practical language for representing and solving a broad class of mathematical problems. Today Boole's contributions can be seen in the design of the modern digital computer.

BOOKS BY BOOLE

Logical Works. 2 vols. Vol. 1 *Studies in Logic and Probability* (1852). Open Court 1952 $29.95. ISBN 0-87548-038-1. Vol. 2 *Laws of Thought* (1854). Dover 1953 $9.95. ISBN 0-486-60028-9

DIOPHANTUS   *c.* 250

Diophantus lived in Greece in the third century AD. Little is known about his life, but since many of his writings have survived, it is known that he developed many algebraic concepts. These were translated into Latin, first in 1575 by Xylander and again in 1621 by the French mathematician Claude Gaspard de Bachet. Diophantus' major work is his multivolume *Arithmetica*. Six books of this 13-volume treatise have survived.

Diophantus is usually credited with initiating the long development of algebra as a symbol-based language. He used letters for unknowns and special symbols or symbol combinations for the concepts of square, minus, unit, and equal. However, he had no symbol for plus.

Diophantus also developed methods for solving several types of equations. The best known of these methods is that for solving indeterminate equations— equations in which the number of solutions is infinite. Diophantus imposed additional restrictions on the solutions; for example, he stipulated that they be rational numbers or even that they be integers. The resulting equations are called "Diophantine" equations. An example is $7x + 11y = 13$, which has, for example, $x = 5$, $y = -2$ as one of its many solutions.

BOOK BY DIOPHANTUS

Diophantus' Arithmetica: Books IV to VI in the Arabic Translation of Qusta ibn Luqa (late third century AD). *Sources in the History of Mathematics and the Physical Sciences Ser.* Vol. 3 Springer-Verlag 1982 $109.00. ISBN 0-387-90690-8

BOOK ABOUT DIOPHANTUS

Heath, Thomas L. *A History of Greek Mathematics*. 2 vols. Dover 1981. Vol. 1 $10.95. ISBN 0-486-24073-8. Vol. 2 $10.95. ISBN 0-486-24074-6 History that contains biographical information about Diophantus.

FERMAT, PIERRE DE   1601–1665

Pierre de Fermat was a quiet officeholder in the parliament of Toulouse in seventeenth-century France. In spite of this nonmathematical occupation, he found time to take part in mathematical pursuits, ultimately leaving a wealth of impressive private mathematical writings that includes correspondence with French philosopher and scientist René Descartes and other great mathematicians of the time. (*See* Descartes, Vol. 1, Geometry: Coordinate Geometry.) Fermat's correspondence reveals that he was involved in the exchange of some of the most important mathematical ideas of the day. If Fermat had published any of his discoveries, he may well have received credit for originating concepts eventually attributed to others. Instead, he is now remembered as perhaps the most gifted amateur in the history of mathematics.

Fermat was influenced by the Greek mathematician Diophantus, who lived about 1,300 years earlier. (*See* Diophantus, Vol. 1, Algebra.) In fact, Fermat's most famous theorem was inspired by an equation discussed by Diophantus. Like Diophantus, Fermat contributed to the theory of numbers, a branch of mathematics that examines the properties of special kinds of whole numbers such as prime numbers, "perfect" numbers, and Pythagorean triples. Fermat also contributed to the development of analytic geometry and the infinitesimal calculus.

Fermat distinguished himself in a number of mathematical areas. He stimulated the thinking of other mathematicians, not only those of his own time, but also those of today. His insights continue to challenge modern ideas about numbers. His best-known challenge to later generations is known as Fermat's last theorem. The theorem states that $x^n + y^n = z^n$ cannot be true if x, y, and z are positive integers and if n is an integer greater than 2. Even today, mathematicians do not know whether Fermat proved the theorem, nor even whether it is true.

Book about Fermat

Mahoney, Michael S. *The Mathematical Career of Pierre de Fermat (1601–1665)*. Books Demand $109.80. ISBN 0-317-08307-4 Comprehensive overview of Fermat's life and work.

GALOIS, EVARISTE   1811–1832

Evariste Galois was a brilliant, passionate, and tragic young man who contributed greatly to the foundations of group theory in his late teens and twentieth year. He lived in Paris, France, where his intense involvement in political causes twice led to imprisonment. His romantic life was also intense and entangled, leading to a duel that resulted in his death at the age of 20.

In the three or four years before his death, Galois created and developed mathematics at the highest level of intelligence and creativity. One of his major contributions is his work in group theory, which he developed in an attempt to find out under what conditions an algebraic equation can be solved by radicals. On the night before his death, he outlined his ideas in group theory in a long memo.

Galois was the first to apply the term *group* to a unified and interconnected system of numbers (or other objects or actions) in which certain special rules and conditions are satisfied. Although group theory was developed in the nineteenth century, it has many applications in modern society. For example, group theory is used in the study of crystals and in a theory of child development formulated by the Swiss psychologist Jean Piaget.

BOOKS ABOUT GALOIS

*Bell, Eric T. *Men of Mathematics.* Simon 1986 $13.95. ISBN 0-671-62818-6 Popular set of biographies that includes a dramatic, classic chapter on the life of Galois.
*Infeld, Leopold. *Whom the Gods Love: The Story of Evariste Galois. Classics in Mathematics Education Ser.: No. 7.* NCTM 1978 repr of 1948 ed $15.00. ISBN 0-87353-125-6 The tragic story of Galois.

NOETHER, EMMY 1882–1935

Emmy Noether, the most important woman mathematician of the early twentieth century, studied at Erlangen and Göttingen universities in Germany. She later taught at Göttingen, in Moscow, and in Frankfurt before coming to Bryn Mawr College in the United States in 1933.

In choosing to study mathematics, Noether emulated her father and her brother, who also were mathematicians. Following her undergraduate education at Erlangen, Noether took her doctorate at the same university. Afterward, she continued to study and do research at home, occasionally giving lectures in place of her father, who also taught at the university. After her father's retirement and the death of her mother, Noether responded to an invitation from David Hilbert to join him at Göttingen to study and lecture. (*See* Hilbert, Vol. 1, Geometry: Non-Euclidean, Transformational, and Abstract Geometry.) This pleased her greatly, because by this time she had already become interested in Hilbert's axiomatic approach to the construction of mathematical systems.

Impressed by her great ability, Hilbert attempted to help Noether obtain an official position on the faculty of the University of Göttingen. However, he encountered strong opposition because of the prejudice that the exclusively male institution harbored against women.

A compromise was finally worked out: the courses Noether taught would be listed under Hilbert's name. It was not until 1922, when she was already in her late thirties, that Noether was finally appointed to the academic position that she deserved. Even then, she received no pay for the position. In the late 1920s and early 1930s she also served as editor of the mathematics journal, *Mathematische Annalen.*

Noether did her most important mathematical work in abstract algebra. She developed the theory of primary ideals, a special kind of structure in the field of modern algebra. She also showed how this structure could be used to solve problems that had arisen in other areas of mathematics. Noether's mathematical research demonstrated a power to generalize quickly from the specific to the abstract by grasping the essence of a new mathematical entity or idea.

BOOK BY NOETHER

Collected Papers. Nathan Jacobson (ed). Springer-Verlag 1983 $88.00. ISBN 0-387-11504-8

BOOKS ABOUT NOETHER

Dick, Auguste. *Emmy Noether (1882–1935).* H. I. Blocher (tr). Birkhauser 1980 $17.50. ISBN 0-8176-3019-8 Personal and professional account of Noether's life and work, with limited mathematical detail and technical explanation.

Srinivasan, Bhama, and Judith D. Sally (eds). *Emmy Noether in Bryn Mawr: Proceedings of a Symposium Sponsored by the Association of Women in Mathematics in Honor of Emmy Noether's 100th Birthday.* Springer-Verlag 1983 $48.50. ISBN 0-387-90838-2 Historical articles about Noether's life and work, along with a collection of contemporary papers on topics that she developed.

Osen, Lynn M. *Women in Mathematics.* MIT Pr 1974 $7.95. ISBN 0-262-65009-6 Sensitively written, readable chapters on eight significant women mathematicians, including Emmy Noether.

GEOMETRY

The word *geometry* can be traced back to a practical problem that faced ancient peoples of the Near East, particularly Egypt and Mesopotamia. Because rivers flooded their banks annually, land boundaries were regularly erased and had to be restored. Thus great importance became attached to the theory and practice of surveying. With the passage of time, the ancient Greeks used the word *geometry,* which literally means "earth measure," to refer first to the practice of surveying and eventually to the study of figures in a plane or in space.

Modern geometry has many branches—Euclidean geometry of two and three dimensions (plane and solid geometry); coordinate geometry, also known as analytic geometry; non-Euclidean geometry; transformational geometry; topology; projective geometry; and abstract formal geometry—each of which has a central theme or focus. Many of the branches are applied to fields such as design and the visual arts.

Pattern of a woven carpet depicted in a miniature painting.   Baghdad (1396).

Euclidean geometry is the study of the geometry of the everyday world. Created by Euclid in the third century BC, it represents the first comprehensive model of a mathematical system based on proof.

In coordinate geometry, the theme is the correspondence between number pairs and points in the Euclidean plane, which enables shapes to be analyzed through the use of algebra and equations.

There are two kinds of non-Euclidean geometry—elliptical and hyperbolic. Hyperbolic geometry was developed in 1826 by Nikolai Lobachevsky, while elliptical geometry was developed in 1854 by Bernhard Riemann. At one time or another, each of these two geometries has been thought to be a better model of the universe than the one constructed by Euclid.

Projective geometry, developed by Victor Poncelet, has applications to many areas, including the analysis of language and the mechanism of vision, in which a three-dimensional object is projected onto a two-dimensional surface and then successfully interpreted.

Topology, first defined and developed in 1872 by Felix Klein, is the study of connectedness. It examines mapping rules to determine, for example, whether points near each other are mapped or transformed into points that remain near each other.

Transformational geometry focuses on the effects of mathematical changes known as transformations in which every point of the plane or space is mapped into some other point or into itself. The object is to find out and describe which properties of geometric figures are invariant, or left unaffected, by transformations.

Abstract formal geometry is the study of relations. It assumes the existence of two abstract sets called points and lines and the relations of membership and intersection associating them.

Abelson, Harold, and Andrea DiSessa. *Turtle Geometry: The Computer as a Medium for Exploring Mathematics. Artificial Intelligence Ser.* MIT Pr 1986 $26.50. ISBN 0-262-01063-1

Allman, George J. *Greek Geometry from Thales to Euclid. History of Ideas in Ancient Greece Ser.* Ayer 1976 repr of 1889 ed $18.00. ISBN 0-405-07287-2

Bezuska, Stanley, *et al. Applications of Geometric Series. Motivated Math Project Activity Books Ser.* Boston Coll Math 1976 $2.00. ISBN 0-917916-14-X

Bila, Dennis, *et al. Geometry and Measurement.* Worth 1976 $11.95. ISBN 0-87901-059-2

Blumenthal, Leonard M. *A Modern View of Geometry.* Dover 1980 $5.95. ISBN 0-486-63962-3

Bold, Benjamin. *Famous Problems of Geometry and How to Solve Them.* Dover 1982 $3.00. ISBN 0-486-24297-8

Bowyer, Adrian, and John Woodwark. *A Programmer's Geometry.* Butterworth 1983 $45.00. ISBN 0-408-01242-0

*Brownlee, Juanita. *Tangram Geometry in Metric.* Activity Resources 1976 $6.95. ISBN 0-918932-43-2 Activities for grades 5–10.

Brunes, Tons. *The Secrets of Ancient Geometry.* 2 vols. Humanities 1967 $99.00. ISBN 0-391-01117-0

Carus, Paul. *The Foundations of Mathematics: A Contribution to the Philosophy of Geometry.* AMS (repr of 1908 ed) $18.00. ISBN 0-404-59101-9

*Clemens, Sam, *et al. Addison-Wesley Geometry.* Addison 1990 $26.40. ISBN 0-201-21469-5 Textbook that encourages exploration of diverse geometric methods to arrive at similar results.

*Cox, Philip L. *Informal Geometry.* Prentice 1992 $25.97. ISBN 0-13-352451-5 Textbook that teaches geometric concepts by emphasizing induction, intuition, discovery, and critical thinking.

Coxeter, H. S. M. *Introduction to Geometry.* Wiley 1969 $64.95. ISBN 0-471-18283-4

*Cummins, Jerry J., *et al. Merrill Informal Geometry.* Merrill 1988 $23.40. ISBN 0-675-

05854-6 Textbook that develops geometric concepts by using discovery and hands-on methods.

*Dressler, Isidore. *Geometry.* AMSCO 1973 $8.85. ISBN 0-87720-234-6 Textbook that develops a series of insights into geometric relationships so that students can draw on each relationship to generate formal proofs.

Fetisov, A. *Proof in Geometry.* Imported 1979 $2.45. ISBN 0-8285-0742-2

*Fisher, Lyle. *Super Problems.* Seymour 1982 $11.95. ISBN 0-86651-101-6 Problem activities for grades 7–9.

Frieder, David. *Clear and Simple Geometry. Clear and Simple Study Guides Ser.* Arco 1986 $6.95. ISBN 0-671-62398-2

Golavina, L., and I. Yaglom. *Induction in Geometry.* Imported. (o.p.) $2.95. ISBN 0-8285-1534-4

*Jurgensen, Ray C., *et al. Geometry.* Houghton 1990 $24.97. ISBN 0-395-46146-4 Widely used geometry text that takes a developmental and hands-on approach.

*Jurgensen, Ray C., and Richard G. Brown. *Basic Geometry.* Houghton 1990 $23.40. ISBN 0-395-50120-2 Textbook that provides a simplified and informal approach with many worked-out examples.

*Kalin, Robert, and Mary Kay Corbitt. *Geometry.* Prentice 1990 $25.97. ISBN 0-13-352501-5 Textbook that includes systematic use of calculators and computers and applies algebraic problem-solving methods to creating geometric proofs.

Knorr, Wilbur. *Ancient Traditions of Geometric Problems. History of Science Ser.* Vol. 1 Birkhauser 1986 $74.50. ISBN 0-8176-3148-8

*Laycock, Mary, and Manuel Dominques. *Discover It!* Activity Resources 1986 $5.95. ISBN 0-918932-87-4 Geometric discovery material for grades 5–10.

*Leff, Lawrence. *Geometry the Easy Way. Easy Way Ser.* Barron 1984 $8.95. ISBN 0-8120-2718-3 Includes hundreds of step-by-step examples and practice exercises; ideal students' supplements for valuable overviews of course work and for extra help with difficult subject areas.

Piaget, Jean, *et al. A Child's Conception of Geometry.* E. A. Lunzer (tr). Norton 1981 $8.95. ISBN 0-393-00057-5

Moise, Edwin E. *Elementary Geometry from an Advanced Standpoint.* Addison 1990 $35.16. ISBN 0-201-50867-2

Oldknow, Adrian. *Microcomputers in Geometry. Mathematics and Its Applications Ser.* Halsted 1987 $28.95. ISBN 0-470-20814-7

Posamentier, Alfred. *Excursions in Advanced Euclidean Geometry.* Addison 1984 $10.36. ISBN 0-201-20359-6

Pottage, J. *Geometrical Investigations: Illustrating the Art of Discovery in the Mathematical Field.* Addison 1983 $55.95. ISBN 0-201-05733-6

Record, Robert. *The Path-Way to Knowledge, Containing the First Principles of Geometry.* Walter J. Johnson 1974 repr of 1551 ed $25.00. ISBN 0-90-221-0687-X

*Research and Education Association Staff. *The Geometry Problem Solver.* Research & Education 1989 $22.85. ISBN 0-87891-510-9 Tutorial study aid for geometry problem solving.

Research and Education Association Staff. *The Essentials of Topology.* Research & Education 1989 $4.95. ISBN 0-87891-685-7

*Ruchlis, Hy, and Harry Milgrom. *Math Projects: Mathematical Shapes. Science-Math Project Ser.* Book-Lab 1968 $3.95. ISBN 0-87594-015-3 Geometry projects for grades 4–9.

Saaty, Thomas L., and Paul G. Kainen. *The Four-Color Problem: Assaults and Conquests.* Dover 1986 $6.00. ISBN 0-486-65092-8

Shadler, Rubin. *Geometry Problems: One Step Beyond.* Seymour 1984 $14.50. ISBN 0-86651-227-6

*Stallings, Pat. *Puzzling Your Way into Geometry.* Activity Resources 1978 $6.95. ISBN 0-918932-58-0 Puzzle-solving approach to learning geometry.

*Ulrich, James F. *HBJ Geometry.* Harcourt 1987 $23.76. ISBN 0-15-353802-3 Textbook that includes plane, solid, coordinate, and transformational geometry.

Usiskin, Zalman. *UCSMP-University of Chicago School Mathematics Project Geometry.* Scott 1990 $28.95. ISBN 0-673-45269-7

Vasilyev, N., and V. Gutenmacher. *Straight Lines and Curves.* Imported 1980 $8.95. ISBN 0-8285-1792-4

*Vellozi, Joseph I. *Plane and Coordinate Geometry Study Aid.* Youth Education 1974 $2.50. ISBN 0-87738-040-6 Study aid for plane and coordinate geometry.

Weyl, Hermann. *Symmetry.* Princeton Univ Pr 1952 $7.95. ISBN 0-691-02374-3

Wiley, Larry. *Introductory Geometrics.* Trillium 1986 $14.95. ISBN 0-89824-065-4

Williams, Robert. *The Geometric Foundation of Natural Structure: A Source Book of Design.* Dover 1979 $9.95. ISBN 0-486-23729-X

*Yunker, Lee E., *et al.* *Merrill Geometry.* Merrill 1990 $24.81. ISBN 0-675-05928-3 Textbook that spans a wide variety of approaches to proof, including formal, informal, flow, coordinate, and paragraph.

EUCLIDEAN GEOMETRY

APOLLONIUS OF PERGA *fl.* 247 BC–205 BC

The ancient Greek Mathematician Apollonius of Perga built a foundation for the systematic study of the objects and operations of geometry. The "objects" were of all kinds, but the most significant were conic sections—shapes formed by cutting a cone at a given angle. The "operations" were the methods of geometric construction or drawing, as in the methods for making a line, circle, or square.

Historians of mathematics say that Apollonius may have consciously rejected the beginnings of algebraic notation when describing his knowledge of conic sections because he wanted to keep geometry pure and focused on simple methods. This emphasis on simplicity of methods may be the reason he required all constructions to be accomplished with only the aid of a compass to mark off distances and a straightedge, a ruler without number units. Until Apollonius' time, there was no such requirement in Greek mathematics.

According to one algebraic geometer, "Apollonius was the master of form and situation." The terms *form* and *situation* refer to Apollonius' ability to extract underlying characteristics of a geometric figure from the directly observed data.

BOOKS BY APOLLONIUS OF PERGA

Apollonius of Perga. Treatise on Conic Sections (late third century BC). T. L. Heath (ed). Dover 1971 repr of 1896 ed. (o.p.)

Apollonius on Cutting Off a Ratio (late third century BC). Edward Macierowski (tr). Golden Hind 1987 $30.00. ISBN 0-931267-00-5

EUCLID *fl. c.* 300 BC

Almost nothing is known with certainty of the life of the ancient Greek mathematician Euclid. Since it is known, however, that he was associated with the museum and library of Alexandria, Egypt, during the reign of the first Ptolemy (died 284 BC), he probably was in a position to collect, survey, and assess the mathematical knowledge of his time, and then to compile and synthesize it.

Euclid's 13 books, known as the *Elements,* accomplished two objectives. First, they summarized the known results of Greek mathematics. Second, they developed theorems of geometry in a systematic manner, out of which Euclid and his predecessors derived a long series of results. The most notable of the results is the Pythagorean Theorem, which describes the quantitative relationship between the three sides of a right triangle.

Euclid's system has survived for over 2,000 years with relatively little damage from the scrutiny that it has received. His organization of ancient geometry into a comprehensive axiomatic framework remains a model of rigorous reasoning.

BOOKS BY EUCLID

The Thirteen Books of Euclid's Elements (early third century BC). T. L. Heath (ed). 3 vols. Dover (repr of 1926 ed) Vol. 1 $8.95. ISBN 0-486-60088-2. Vol. 2 $8.95. ISBN 0-486-60089-0. Vol. 3. $8.95. ISBN 0-486-60090-4

Recipients, Commonly Called Data (early third century BC). Robert T. Schmidt (tr). Golden Hind 1988 $30.00. ISBN 0-0-318-35240-0

BOOKS ABOUT EUCLID

Frankland, F. W. *The Story of Euclid.* Gordon Pr $59.95. ISBN 0-8490-1132-9 Account of Euclid and his role in mathematics.

Greenberg, Marvin J. *Euclidean and Non-Euclidean Geometries: Development and History.* Freeman 1980 $26.95. ISBN 0-7167-1103-6 Explanation of how the discovery of non-Euclidean geometry led to a reformulation of the foundations of Euclidean geometry.

Mueller, Ian. *Philosophy of Mathematics and Deductive Structure in Euclid's "Elements."* MIT Pr 1981 $47.50. ISBN 0-262-13163-3 In-depth examination of what constitutes proof in Euclid's mathematics and of the strengths and shortcomings of his deductive process.

Smith, Thomas. *Euclid: His Life and His System. The Essential Library of the Great Philosophers Ser.* Found Class Repr 1983 repr of 1902 ed $127.75. ISBN 0-89901-092-X Conversational and relatively nontechnical discussion that stresses the exactness and significance of Euclid's methods and connects his great synthesis to many nonmathematical topics.

COORDINATE GEOMETRY

*Boyer, Carl B. *History of Analytic Geometry: Its Development from the Pyramids to the Heroic Age.* Scholars Bookshelf 1988 $12.95. ISBN 0-945726-12-0 Comprehensive and well-written text that traces the early developments of analytic geometry.

*Fuller, Gordon. *Analytic Geometry.* Addison 1986 $33.56. ISBN 0-201-10861-5 Classic textbook on analytic geometry.

*Middlemiss, Ross G., *et al. Analytic Geometry.* McGraw 1968 $45.95. ISBN 0-07-041896-9 Textbook on analytic geometry.

Salmon, George. *Analytic Geometry of Three Dimensions.* Vol. 2 Chelsea 1979 $15.95. ISBN 0-8284-0196-9

*Selby, Peter. *Analytic Geometry. College Outline Ser.* Harcourt 1986 $9.95. ISBN 0-15-601525-0 Review guide.

Smogorzhevsky, A. *Method of Coordinates.* Imported 1980 $2.95. ISBN 0-8285-1645-6

DESCARTES, RENE   1596–1650

Although best known as a philosopher, René Descartes also possessed one of the most prominent scientific and mathematical minds of his time. Born in the Touraine district of France, he was educated at a Jesuit college where, he later claimed, he learned little of importance. As a young man he moved to Holland where he served as an officer in the Dutch army and where he lived for most of his remaining years.

In mathematics Descartes is especially remembered for his development of analytic geometry, which makes use of a coordinate system with which it is possible to associate geometric curves with algebraic formulas. For example, a circle with its center at the point of intersection of the coordinate reference axes and a radius of 5 units has $x^2 + y^2 = 5^2$ as its equation. Descartes said that his analytic geometry method was an example of applying his general rational method. In fact, his work, *La Géométrie,* was published as an appendix to his longer and more general work, *Discours de la Méthode.*

Descartes also contributed extensively to the theory of algebraic equations and, in science, to meteorology, optics, and mechanics.

BOOKS BY DESCARTES

Discourse on Method and the Meditations. Great Books in Philosophy Ser (1637). John Veitch (tr). Prometheus Bks 1989 $5.95. ISBN 0-87975-526-1
Geometry (1637). D. E. Smith and M. L. Latham (tr). Dover 1954 repr of 1925 ed $6.00. ISBN 0-486-60068-8
Le Monde. Michael S. Mahoney (tr). Abaris 1979 $20.00. ISBN 0-913870-35-8

BOOKS ABOUT DESCARTES

Clarke, Desmond M. *Descartes' Philosophy of Science.* Penn State Univ Pr 1982 $22.50. ISBN 0-271-00325-1 Comprehensive treatment of Descartes's philosophy of science.
Scott, J. F. *The Scientific Work of René Descartes (1596–1650).* Garland 1987 $40.00. ISBN 0-8240-4672-2 Comprehensive treatment of Descartes's major discoveries and an evaluation of the importance of his work in the history of science.

GEOMETRY IN DESIGN, FORM, NATURE, AND THE VISUAL ARTS

Boles, Martha, and Rochelle Newman. *The Golden Relationship Art, Math, and Nature: Universal Patterns.* Book 1 Pythagorean Pr 1987 $24.95. ISBN 0-9614504-1-X
Cook, Theodore A. *The Curves of Life.* Dover 1979 $8.95. ISBN 0-0-486-23701-X
Ernst, Bruno. *The Magic Mirror of M. C. Escher.* Ballantine 1977. (o.p.) $6.95. ISBN 0-345-24243-2
Ghyka, Matila. *The Geometry of Art and Life.* Dover 1978 $3.95. ISBN 0-486-23542-4
Gordon, V. O., and M. A. Sementsov-Ogievskii. *Course in Descriptive Geometry.* Imported 1980 $10.00. ISBN 0-8285-1870-X
Ivins, William M., Jr. *Art and Geometry.* Dover 1946 $3.50. ISBN 0-486-20941-5
Locher, J. L. (ed). *M. C. Escher—His Life and Complete Graphic Work.* Abrams 1982 $65.00. ISBN 0-8109-8084-3
Locher, J. L. *The World of M. C. Escher.* Abrams 1988 $19.95. ISBN 0-8109-0858-1
Luckiesh, M. *Visual Illusions: Their Causes, Characteristics, and Applications.* Dover 1965 $4.95. ISBN 0-486-21530-X
Oliver, June. *Polysymetrics: The Art of Making Geometric Patterns.* Parkwest 1986 $6.95. ISBN 0-906212-09-X
Pedoe, Dan. *Geometry and the Visual Arts.* Dover 1983 $6.95. ISBN 0-486-24458-X
*Pohl, Victoria. *How to Enrich Geometry Using String Designs.* NCTM 1986 $10.00. ISBN 0-87353-227-9 For grades 6–10.
*Reitman, Edward. *Exploring the Geometry of Nature: Computer Modelling Projects.* TAB 1988 $24.95. ISBN 0-8306-9137-5 Expresses geometric patterns and processes in nature by means of computer models.
Schattschneider, Doris, and Wallace Walker. *M. C. Escher Kaleidocycles.* Pomegranate Artbooks 1987 $13.95. ISBN 0-87654-208-9
*Seymour, Dale. *Geometric Design.* Seymour 1988 $9.95. ISBN 0-866-51424-4 For grades 9–12.
*Stevens, Peter S. *Patterns in Nature.* Little 1974. (o.p.) $18.45. ISBN 0-316-81331-1 Book

with stunning photographs illustrating diversity of patterns and forms in nature, together with discussions of numerous spatial and structural concepts.

Stewart, Susan A. *Applied Descriptive Geometry.* Delmar 1986 $23.21. ISBN 0-8273-2377-8

Thompson, D'Arcy Wentworth. *On Growth and Form.* Cambridge Univ Pr 1952. (o.p.) $20.95. ISBN 0-521-09390-2

Yale, Paul B. *Geometry and Symmetry.* Holden-Day 1968 $28.00. ISBN 0-8162-9964-1

NON-EUCLIDEAN, TRANSFORMATIONAL, AND ABSTRACT GEOMETRY

Asanov, G. S. *Finsler Geometry, Relativity, and Gauge Theories.* Kluwer Academic 1985 $64.00. ISBN 0-90-277-1960-8

Barnsley, Michael. *The Desktop Fractal System.* Academic Pr 1989 $39.95. ISBN 0-12-079063-7

Barnsley, Michael. *Fractals Everywhere.* Academic Pr 1988 $39.95. ISBN 0-12-079062-9

*Coxeter, H. S. M., and S. L. Greitzer. *Geometry Revisited. New Mathematical Library: No. 19.* Mathematical Assn 1967 $11.75. ISBN 0-88385-619-0 Uses transformation concept to explore basic geometry; demonstrates links between geometry and other branches of mathematics.

Fejer, Paul H. *Time in Dynamic Geometry.* Bernadette Meier (ed). P. H. Fejer 1984 $60.00. ISBN 0-9607422-2-0

*Francis, G. K. *Topological Picturebook.* Springer-Verlag 1988 $35.00. ISBN 0-3987-96426-6 Picture-book treatment of topological figures and concepts.

Gleick, James. *Chaos: Making a New Science.* Penguin 1988 $11.95. ISBN 0-14-009250-1

Gleick, James *Nature's Chaos.* Penguin 1990 $29.95. ISBN 0-670-83532-3

Hess, Adrian L. *Four-Dimensional Geometry: An Introduction.* NCTM 1977 $3.00. ISBN 0-87353-117-5

Hocking, John G., and Gail S. Young. *Topology.* Dover 1988 $7.95. ISBN 0-486-65676-4

Krause, Eugene. *Taxicab Geometry: An Adventure in Non-Euclidean Geometry.* Dover 1986 $3.95. ISBN 0-486-25202-7

Mandelbrot, Benoit B. *The Fractal Geometry of Nature.* Freeman 1982 $39.95. ISBN 0-7167-1186-9

Monastyrsky, Michael. *Riemann, Topology and Physics.* Birkhauser 1987 $39.50. ISBN 0-8176-3262-X

Mukres, James. *Topology: A First Course.* Prentice 1975 $51.50. ISBN 0-13-925495-1

*Peitgen, Heinz O. *Fractals for the Classroom.* Springer-Verlag 1989 $29.00. ISBN 0-387-97041-X Educational treatment of fractal images and theory.

Peitgen, Heinz O., and Peter H. Richter. *The Beauty of Fractals: Images of Complex Dynamical Systems.* Springer-Verlag 1988 $39.00. ISBN 0-387-15851-0

Peitgen, Heinz O., and Dietmar Saupe. *The Science of Fractal Images.* Springer-Verlag 1989 $39.95. ISBN 0-387-96608-0

*Research and Education Association Staff. *The Essentials of Topology.* Research & Education 1989 $4.95. ISBN 0-87891-685-7 Tutorial study aid for topology.

*Rosenfeld, B. A. *The History of Non-Euclidean Geometry. Studies in the History of Mathematics and the Physical Sciences.* Vol. 12 Springer-Verlag 1988 $89.00. ISBN 0-387-96458-4 Account of the development of the various types of non-Euclidean geometry and of the evolution of new concepts about geometry itself.

Rucker, Rudolf. *Geometry, Relativity, and the Fourth Dimension.* Dover 1977 $3.95. ISBN 0-486-23400-2

Rucker, Rudy, *et al. The Fourth Dimension: A Guided Tour of Higher Universes.* Houghton 1985 $39.00. ISBN 0-395-39388-4

Runion, Garth E., and James R. Lockwood. *Deductive Systems: Finite and Non-Euclidean Geometries.* NCTM 1978 $5.50. ISBN 0-87353-129-9

Szmielev, Wanda. *From Affine to Euclidean Geometry.* Maria Maszynska (ed). Kluwer Academic 1983 $34.95. ISBN 0-90-277-1243-3

Von Neumann, John. *Continuous Geometry. Mathematics Ser.* Vol. 25 Princeton Univ Pr 1960 $39.00. ISBN 0-691-07928-5

HILBERT, DAVID   1862–1943

David Hilbert was born, like philosopher Immanual Kant, in Königsberg in East Prussia, Germany. However, unlike Kant, he left the town to establish his reputation at Göttingen, where he was to become a renowned professor of mathematics.

Hilbert was a mathematician's mathematician. A universalist, he was knowledgeable in every area of mathematics, making important contributions to each one. He was also a groundbreaker, laying a wholly new abstract foundation for geometry in which the words *points, lines,* and *planes* could stand for nongeometric objects. He also developed a wholly new understanding of the nature of axioms that emphasized consistency and independence of any given set of axioms.

At the 1900 International Conference of Mathematicians in Paris, Hilbert interpreted the past and future course of the whole of mathematics. In response to an invitation to forecast the direction of twentieth-century mathematics, he sketched out a list of 23 major unsolved problems and inadequately developed theories that the mathematicians of the new century ought to tackle and, if possible, solve.

The mathematical structure that bears his name—Hilbert spaces—deals with the nature and properties of abstract metrical spaces and infinite-dimensional coordinate systems or spaces. These have application, for example, to mathematical physics.

Books by Hilbert

Foundations of Geometry (1899). Leo Ungar (tr). Open Court 1980 $9.00. ISBN 0-87548-164-7

*Geometry and the Imagination. (coauthored with Stephan Cohn-Vossen) Chelsea 1952 $19.95. ISBN 0-8284-0087-3 Presents geometry as it stands today, in its visual, intuitive aspects, and contributes to a better appreciation of mathematics by a wider range of people than just the specialists.

Book about Hilbert

Reid, Constance. *Hilbert–Courant.* Springer-Verlag 1986 $38.00. ISBN 0-387-96256-5 Detailed and captivating biography that traces Hilbert's long and fruitful career, beginning with his childhood and arriving at his monumental work in the axiomatic and logical foundations of mathematics. Also includes a biography of Courant.

KLEIN, FELIX   1849–1925

Felix Klein began his academic career as an assistant to the geometrician Julius Plücker at the University of Bonn in Germany. After Plücker's death in 1868, Klein set his own course on a long, brilliant mathematical career.

Klein's mathematical life was linked to two centers of higher education, the universities of Erlangen and Göttingen. While still a young man, Klein made Erlangen the base for his mathematical research that revolutionized geometry. It was at Göttingen, however, that Klein established long and fruitful relationships with colleagues such as David Hilbert (*see* Hilbert, Vol. 1, Geometry: Non-Euclidean, Transformational, and Abstract Geometry) and students and protégés such as Emmy Noether. (*See* Noether, Vol. 1, Algebra.)

In 1872 at the age of 23 Klein presented his views on geometry in an address that became known as the *Erlanger Programm.* Its effect was to unify the various special geometries that had accumulated in the decades and centuries that preceded. In the scheme that Klein laid out, geometry is set forth as the study of those properties of figures that remain invariant (unchanged) under a certain group of transformations. For example, plane Euclidean geometry can be thought of as the study of properties, such as lengths and areas, that remain unchanged under the group of rigid transformations such as translations (shifts) and rotations in the plane.

Klein showed that a group of transformations can also be established for more general geometries that do not preserve lengths or area but do preserve other properties. For example, in the transformation group for projective geometry, an ellipse is not necessarily preserved as an ellipse, but it is preserved as a conic section, perhaps as a hyperbola or parabola.

As a result of Klein's vision, it became possible to create a kind of organization chart for geometry in which each existing branch of geometry fits above, below, or alongside each of the others. Klein's program also contains some surprises. It shows that Euclidean, hyperbolic, and elliptic geometries are all special cases of projective geometry. This fact in turn means that if the non-Euclidean geometries are ever shown to be inconsistent, as some opponents of those geometries were trying to prove, then the established projective geometry would be inconsistent also.

In his *Development of Mathematics in the Nineteenth Century* (1926–1927) Klein chronicles and interprets the rise of modern mathematics and its rich and many facets. This work is still regarded by some historians of mathematics as the finest such history ever written.

Klein had great vision for mathematics and for the academic community that lives it and encourages its growth. He pursued this vision in a number of ways, including actively working with Germany's recently centralized educational system to improve the mathematical sophistication of the nation's teachers. In this way he illuminated the mathematics of his own and earlier times and also prepared the way for mathematicians of the future.

BOOKS BY KLEIN

Development of Mathematics in the Nineteenth Century (1926–1927). LIE 1979 $60.00. ISBN 0-915692-28-7

*Famous Problems of Elementary Geometry and other Monographs (1894). (papers by Klein and others) Chelsea 1956 $14.95. ISBN 0-8284-0108-X The title paper, written by Klein for teachers, is suitable for grades 9–12.

LOBACHEVSKY, NIKOLAI IVANOVITCH   1793–1856

Nikolai Lobachevsky was a Russian mathematician who graduated from the University of Kazan and remained there, first as a teacher (1812) and later as a professor (1816) and rector (1827). Lobachevsky was one of three mathematicians who in the early and middle nineteenth century created internally consistent alternatives to the age-old framework of Euclidean geometry. The other two men were Janos Bolyai (1802–1860) and G. F. B. Riemann (1826–1866). Although Bolyai developed his ideas about non-Euclidean geometry before Lobachevsky did, Lobachevsky published his results first, in 1829.

Non-Euclidean geometry refers mainly to attempts to replace Euclid's fifth postulate, regarding parallel lines, with an alternative postulate on which a workable alternative system of geometry could be constructed.

The ideas of Lobachevsky, and also of Bolyai, came to the attention of Carl Friedrich Gauss (*see* Gauss, Vol. 1, Probability and Statistics), the greatest mathematician of his time. However, although he praised Lobachevsky's and

Bolyai's accomplishments in private correspondence, he never expressed his praise in print, where it would have reached a wider audience. As a result, the ideas of non-Euclidean geometry were slow to become generally known.

BOOKS ABOUT LOBACHEVSKY

Bonola, Roberto. *Non-Euclidean Geometry.* Dover 1954 $8.00. ISBN 0-486-60027-0

Kagan, V. *Lobachevsky and His Contribution to Science.* Foreign Language 1957. (o.p.)

Smogovzhevsky, A. *Lobachevskian Geometry.* Imported 1976 $1.95. ISBN 0-8285-0729-5

*Tarjemanov, J. *The Silver Horse-Shoe.* Imported $13.95. ISBN 5-03-001693-2 Historical novel about Nikolai Lobachevsky that describes the tremendous obstacles facing scholars in nineteenth-century Russia and Lobachevsky's passionate struggle for intellectual advancement.

PROJECTIVE GEOMETRY

Adams, George, and Olive Whicher. *The Plant Between Sun and Earth and the Science of Physical and Ethereal Spaces.* Anthroposophic 1980 $40.00. ISBN 0-85440-360-4

Coxeter, H. S. M. *Projective Geometry.* Springer-Verlag 1987 repr of 1964 ed $29.80. ISBN 0-387-96532-7

*Edwards, Lawrence. *Projective Geometry: An Approach to the Secrets of Space from the Standpoint of Artistic and Imaginative Thought.* Steiner 1985 $13.50. ISBN 0-317-40482-2 Based on the work of Rudolph Steiner, a nineteenth-century philosopher and educator who believed that the projective-geometry viewpoint could be used to build a scientific model of growth, development, and creativity processes in children and in nature.

Findley, A. M., *et al. The Geometry of Genetics. Monographs in Chemical Physics.* Wiley 1988 $44.95. ISBN 0-471-05617-0

Garner, L. E. *Outline of Projective Geometry.* Elsevier 1981 $49.75. ISBN 0-444-00423-8

Gray, J., and J. Field. *The Geometrical Work of Girard Desargues.* Springer-Verlag 1986 $79.50. ISBN 0-387-96403-7

Whicher, Olive. *Projective Geometry.* Anthroposophic 1986 $33.50. ISBN 0-85440-245-4

SOLID GEOMETRY AND SPACE

*Abbott, Edwin A. *Flatland.* Dover 1952 $2.25. ISBN 0-486-20001-9 Fiction; imaginative 1884 fantasy about the nature of barriers in a two-dimensional world.

*Bassetti, Fred, and Hy Ruchlis. *Math Projects: Polyhedral Shapes. Science–Math Project Ser.* Book-Lab 1968 $3.95. ISBN 0-87594-016-1 Geometry projects for grades 4–9.

Beskin, N. M. *Images of Geometric Solids.* Imported 1985 $2.95. ISBN 0-8285-3028-9

Burger, Dionys. *Sphereland.* Harper 1965 $7.95. ISBN 0-064-63574-0

Critchlow, Keith. *Order in Space.* Viking 1970. (o.p.) $12.95. ISBN 0-670-52830-7

Gray, Jeremy. *Ideas of Space: Euclidean, Non-Euclidean, and Relativistic.* Oxford Univ Pr 1979 $49.95. ISBN 0-19-853352-7

Henderson, Linda Dalrymple. *The Fourth Dimension and Non-Euclidean Geometry in Art.* Princeton Univ Pr 1983 $29.95. ISBN 0-691-10142-6

Hoffer, A. *A Model of the Universe.* Addison 1979 $23.76. ISBN 0-201-02958-8

Holden, Alan. *Shapes, Space, and Symmetry.* Columbia Univ Pr 1971. (o.p.) $13.00. ISBN 0-231-03549-7

Kastner, Bernice. *Space Mathematics.* Seymour 1988 $8.95. ISBN 0-86651-426-0

*Pedersen, Jean, and Peter Hilton. *Build Your Own Polyhedra.* Addison 1988 $22.00. ISBN 0-201-22060-1 Teacher's sourcebook for grades 6–12 that is also available in a student's edition.

*Pedersen, Jean, and Kent Pedersen. *Geometric Playthings: To Color, Cut, and Fold.* Seymour 1986 $8.95. ISBN 0-86651-351-5 Activity guide for grades 7–12.

Shargin, I. F. *Problems in Solid Geometry.* Imported. (o.p.) $4.95. ISBN 0-8285-3299-0

Smith, A. G. *Cut and Assemble 3-D Geometrical Shapes.* Dover 1986 $4.95. ISBN 0-486-25093-8

Stonerod, David. *Puzzles in Space.* Stokes 1982 $7.95. ISBN 0-914534-03-3

Wenninger, Magnus J. *Polyhedron Models.* Cambridge Univ Pr 1971 $21.95. ISBN 0-521-09859-9

Wolchonok, Louis. *Art of Three Dimensional Design: How to Create Space Figures.* Dover 1969 $6.50. ISBN 0-486-22201-2

ARCHIMEDES   *c.* 287 BC–212 BC

See also Archimedes, Vol. 2, Physics: Mechanics: Work, Energy, and Power.

Archimedes was born, lived, and died in the Hellenic island-colony of Syracuse that is now called Sicily and is part of Italy. He traveled widely in the Mediterranean world, in particular to Alexandria, the metropolis named after Alexander the Great and located on the Nile River in Egypt. One of Archimedes' colleagues in Alexandria was Eratosthenes, who was not only the official librarian of the great library there but also a fellow mathematician–geometer who devised an experiment that fairly accurately measured the size of the earth.

Archimedes possessed one of the most prolific and imaginative mathematical minds in all of the ancient world. He made a career out of solving problems, both practical and theoretical, serving Syracuse in a capacity that today might be called a one-person civil and military "think tank." More importantly, as a result of his service to his city–state, he created a useful body of methods and principles in geometry, number theory, and physics that constitute a lasting legacy for mathematics.

Archimedes engaged in a remarkably wide range of mathematical and scientific activities. These often reflected his ability to derive geometric insights from the principles of mechanics, and, in reverse, to apply mathematics to the development of mechanical knowledge. An example of the latter is his analysis and use of pulleys and levers. He is said to have demonstrated to his king how to lift a fully loaded ship using a rope attached to a system of pulleys. Archimedes' ability to establish connections between disciplines is also demonstrated by his work in optics. He is reported to have used a set of parabolic mirrors to focus the rays of the sun on attacking ships in the harbor during a siege, rendering them useless.

Perhaps the most famous story concerning Archimedes is associated with his discovery of the principle of buoyancy and the displacement of water. It is said that upon making his discovery, he ran from the public baths through the city streets shouting "Eureka!" ("I have found it!")

A final example of Archimedes' mathematical enthusiasm is the delight that he received in discovering a simple relationship between a right circular cylinder and its inscribed sphere. So great was his joy that he requested that a figure illustrating the relationship be inscribed on his tombstone.

Archimedes' versatility is exemplified by his many contributions to mathematics. In addition to those already mentioned, his contributions include work on conic sections, including the volumes of conic solids of rotation, on number systems and sequences, and on spirals.

According to legend Archimedes was killed by a Roman soldier during the siege of Syracuse. In one version of the legend, Archimedes was concentrating on a diagram that he was using as an aid to the solution of a difficult problem and did not see the approaching soldier.

BOOKS BY ARCHIMEDES

Geometrical Solutions Derived from Mechanics (late third century BC). J. L. Heiberg (ed). Lydia G. Robinson (tr). Open Court 1942 $2.95.
The Works of Archimedes with the Method of Archimedes (late third century BC). T. L. Heath (ed). Dover (repr of 1897 ed). (o.p.)

BOOKS ABOUT ARCHIMEDES

Clagett, Marshall. *Archimedes in the Middle Ages.* 5 vols. Am Philos 1964–1984. Comprehensive 20-year five-volume examination of the impact of the thought of Archimedes on thought during the Middle Ages (1,000 to 1,500 years after Archimedes) from seventh century Arab-Latin writings to thirteenth century geometry work.
Dijksterhuis, E. J. *Archimedes.* Princeton Univ Pr 1987 $50.00. ISBN 0-691-02400-6 Biographical study of Archimedes.
*Ipsen, D.C. *Archimedes: Greatest Scientist of the Ancient World.* Enslow 1989 $13.95. ISBN 0-89490-161-3 Short biography for grades 6–10.

FULLER, R. BUCKMINSTER (RICHARD)   1895–1983

Buckminster Fuller was an American architect and engineer who created a new approach to geometry, using that old subject to create new forms of design. In so doing, he solved some architectural problems that were as old as 2,000 years. Fuller accomplished this task by reinterpreting traditional Euclidean geometry, thereby creating a new field of study that he named "synergetics."

In formulating synergetics, Fuller criticized the usual perception and use of geometry. He believed, for example, that the geometry presented in textbooks is too far removed from the geometry reflected in nature. His greatest criticism was directed at the rectangular coordinate system regularly used to describe and build things. He pointed out that this system unduly discriminates against triangles and tetrahedra (solids consisting of four triangular faces), which in some contexts are more useful models than the more widely used right-angle figures such as squares and cubes. The contexts that Fuller had in mind include architectural design, the projection of three-dimensional global maps onto two-dimensional flat maps, and the analysis of packing problems.

An example of Fuller's thoughts on geometry is his observation that nature often prefers structures based on angles of 60° rather than 90°. To support this point, he cited the carbon atom, which is known to form bonds more easily with three additional carbon atoms to create a tetrahedral shape than with seven other carbon atoms to form a cube. (The angles involved are 60° for the tetrahedron and 90° for the cube.)

Using his insights into the properties of triangles and tetrahedra, Fuller invented new designs for automobiles, houses, and other structures, referring to these designs as "Dymaxion" designs. These designs of the 1930s and 1940s were not commercially successful, but they did attract public attention and influence other workers in the field of design.

One of Fuller's concepts—the geodesic dome, a polyhedron with a large number of triangular faces that has the approximate appearance of a hemisphere—was eventually very successful. Structures based on this design are easy to construct, disassemble, and transport to a new location. Since they do not require interior supporting pillars or beams, they allow more flexible use of the enclosed space. Among the early users of Fuller's design was the United States Air Force, which employed it as the basis for its portable arctic shelters and radar installations. Since that time, the design has also been incorporated into houses, stores, and even into playground climbing structures. Perhaps the most publicized application of the geodesic dome is the centerpiece building at Walt Disney World in Florida.

In his later years, Fuller was able to attract large crowds of young people to his public lectures and workshops and to enlist sizable numbers of them to work with him on his projects. These projects, pioneering efforts at the time, were often related to ecology, supporting the view that Earth can be compared to a spaceship that needs to be continually cared for and that should be appreciated for its finely tuned mechanisms.

BOOKS BY FULLER

The Artifacts of R. Buckminster Fuller—A Comprehensive Collection of His Designs and Drawings: The Dymaxion Experiment (1926–1943). William Marlin (ed). Vol. 1 Garland 1985 $190.00. ISBN 0-8240-5082-7

Cosmography: A Blueprint for the Science and Culture of the Future (1991). Macmillan 1991 $27.95. ISBN 0-02-541850-5

Critical Path (1981). St. Martin's 1982 $12.95. ISBN 312-17491-8

Intuition. Impact 1983. (o.p.) $6.95. ISBN 0-915166-20-8

*Inventions: The Patented Works of R. Buckminster Fuller. St. Martin's 1985 $18.95. ISBN 0-312-43479-0 Catalogs and describes the many invention and design patents that Fuller accumulated during his almost 70-year career.

Operating Manual for Spaceship Earth (1969). Dutton 1978 $8.95.

Synergetics: Explorations in the Geometry of Thinking (1975). (coauthored with Edgar J. Applewhite) Macmillan 1982 $19.95. ISBN 0-02-065320-4

Synergetics II: Further Explorations in the Geometry of Thinking. (coauthored with Edgar J. Applewhite) Macmillan 1983 $13.95. ISBN 0-02-092640-5

BOOKS ABOUT FULLER

*Edmonson, Amy C. *A Fuller Explanation: The Synergetic Geometry of R. Buckminster Fuller.* Birkhauser 1986 $39.95. ISBN 0-8176-3338-3 Clear explanation of Fuller's geometric concepts, including some synergetic concepts and methods previously unpublished; written by one of Fuller's close associates in the last decade of his life.

*Kenner, Hugh. *Bucky.* Morrow 1973. (o.p.) $7.95. ISBN 0-688-00141-6 Biography of Fuller with emphasis on his thinking.

*Marks, Robert W. *The Dymaxion World of Buckminster Fuller.* Doubleday 1983. (o.p.) $9.95. ISBN 0-385-01804-5 Well-illustrated tour of the things large and small that Fuller built, ranging from streamlined cars to prefabricated air-deliverable houses and giant geodesic domes.

Wagshall, Peter H., and Robert D. Kahn (eds). *R. Buckminster Fuller on Education.* Univ of Mass Pr 1979 $10.95. ISBN 0-87023-204-5 Discussion of Fuller's philosophy of education that emphasizes intuition, investigation, and electronic tools for access to global information.

CALCULUS, TRIGONOMETRY, AND ANALYSIS

Calculus, the study of continuous processes, and trigonometry, the study of triangles, are subjects that can be studied with little more background than algebra and geometry. However, both of these subjects are related, in different ways, to analysis, an important field not usually taught as a regular high-school course.

Analysis is concerned mainly with the nature and use of infinite processes, especially infinite processes that involve functions. Analysis uses mathematical functions to represent and solve problems, particularly those requiring the use of "limit processes," such as sums with an infinite number of terms. The process of using infinite sums to represent numbers can be extended to functions.

A surprising aspect of the use of functions in infinite series involves trigonometry. The traditional approach to trigonometry is to study trigonometric *ratios,* which are calculated by dividing the length of one side of a right triangle by the length of another.

The functional approach to trigonometry, however, is a more fruitful one for mathematicians. In this approach, a trigonometric *function* allows one to discover trigonometric properties that would otherwise be unknown.

Another example of the limit process occurs in calculus, the study of continuously changing processes. Its two branches, integral calculus and differential calculus, are complementary to one another, each being a kind of inverse of the other. Integral calculus shows how to separate the region under a curve into infinitely small pieces and to add the tiny areas together, using algebra and the limit process. Differential calculus is concerned with the rate of change of continuous functions, such as the time rate of change of temperature in a chemical reaction.

Calculus was invented in the late seventeenth century independently by Isaac Newton in England and Gottfried Wilhelm Leibniz in Germany. Although Newton's ideas on calculus were brilliant, the written form in which he expressed them was unwieldy for those who needed to use calculus as an everyday tool. Leibniz, on the other hand, expressed his calculus ideas in a clear, compact notation method that quickly became accepted across the continent of Europe and is used everywhere today.

CALCULUS AND PRECALCULUS

Benice, Daniel D. *Precalculus Mathematics.* Harcourt 1986 $28.00. ISBN 0-15-069550-2

*Cohen, Donald. *Calculus by and for Young People: Ages 7, Yes 7, and Up.* Donald Cohen 1989 $12.00. ISBN 0-9621674-1-X Treatment of the concepts of calculus for young students. Videocasette treatments of infinite series and sequences are also available.

Coughlin and Zitarelli. *Brief Calculus with Applications.* Harcourt 1989 $32.00. ISBN 0-15-031597-2

Coxford, Arthur F., and Joseph N. Payne. *HBJ Advanced Mathematics: A Preparation for Calculus.* Harcourt 1988 $26.40.

Crosswhite, F. Joe, *et al. Merrill Pre-Calculus Mathematics.* Merrill 1988 $27.90. ISBN 0-675-04978-4

Dressler, Robert, and Karl Stromberg. *Techniques of Calculus.* AMSCO 1982 $12.85. ISBN 0-87720-978-2

Goldstein, Larry Joel, *et al. Calculus and Its Applications.* Prentice 1990 $32.50. ISBN 0-13-011053-6

Newton, Isaac. *Mathematical Papers of Isaac Newton, Vol. 3: 1670–1673.* Cambridge Univ Pr 1969 $155.00. ISBN 0-521-07119-4

Oberle, William F. *Calculus and the Computer.* Addison 1986 $43.25. ISBN 0-201-15983-X

*Sawyer, W. W. *What is Calculus About? New Math Library.* No. 2 Mathematical Assn 1961 $10.50. ISBN 0-88385-602-6 Clear and imaginative treatment of an often repeated question.

Steen, Lynn A. *Calculus for a New Century: A Pump Not a Filter. MAA Notes Ser.* No. 8 Mathematical Assn 1988 $15.00. ISBN 0-88385-058-3

Thompson, Silvanus P. *Calculus Made Easy.* St. Martin's 1970 $7.95. ISBN 0-312-11410-9

TRIGONOMETRY

Cohen, Davis. *Precalculus: A Unit Circle Approach.* West Pub 1990 $32.96. ISBN 0-314-66813-6

Dressler, Isidore, and Barnett Rich. *Trigonometry.* AMSCO 1975 $7.20. ISBN 0-87720-219-2

Hayden, Jerome D., and Bettye C. Hall. *Trigonometry.* Prentice 1990 $26.97. ISBN 0-13-930835-0

Mergener, Robert J. *Trigonometry: A Functions Approach.* Kendall–Hunt 1989 $28.95. ISBN 0-8403-5308-1

Nielsen, Kaj L. *Modern Trigonometry.* Harper 1966 $7.95. ISBN 0-06-460047-5

Research and Education Association Staff. *The High School Trigonometry and Eleventh Year Math Problem Solver.* Research & Education 1988 $10.95. ISBN 0-87891-566-4

Thompson, J. E. *Trigonometry for the Practical Worker.* Van Nostrand 1982 $12.95. ISBN 0-442-28271-0

Zuckerman, Martin. *Algebra and Trigonometry: A Straightforward Approach.* Ardsley 1985 $29.95. ISBN 0-912675-49-7

ANALYSIS

Arya, Jagdish C., and Robin W. Lardner *Mathematical Analysis for Business and Economics.* Prentice 1985 $46.60. ISBN 0-13-561101-6

Bochner, Salomon, *et al. History of Analysis. Rice University Studies Ser.* Vol. 64, Nos. 2 and 3 Rice Univ Pr 1979 $10.00. ISBN 0-89263-236-4

Courant, R., and F. John. *Introduction to Calculus and Analysis.* 2 vols. Springer-Verlag 1989. Vol. 1 $45.00. ISBN 0-387-97151-3. Vol. 2 $59.00. ISBN 0-387-97152-1

Dolciani, Mary P., *et al. Introductory Analysis.* Houghton 1988 $26.58. ISBN 0-395-40655-2

Haeussler, Ernest F., Jr., and Richard S. Paul. *Introductory Mathematical Analysis.* Prentice 1990 $31.00. ISBN 0-13-050143-7

Jarnik, V. *Bolzano and the Foundations of Mathematical Analysis.* State Mutual 1981 $63.00. ISBN 317-52903-X

Polya, G., and G. Szego. *Problems and Theorems in Analysis I: Series, Integral Calculus, Theory of Functions.* Springer-Verlag 1989 $35.00. ISBN 0-387-90224-4

Rosenlicht, Maxwell. *Introduction to Analysis.* Dover 1986 $7.00. ISBN 0-486-65038-3

CAUCHY, AUGUSTIN LOUIS   1789–1857

Augustin Cauchy was educated to be a civil engineer, but because of health problems his friends convinced him to concentrate his efforts on mathematics, which demanded less physical exertion and outdoor exposure. He became one of the great figures of French science and mathematics in the early and middle nineteenth century and is remembered especially for his theoretical work in calculus and other forms of analysis. In particular, he developed rigorous proofs demonstrating that certain mathematical expressions with an infinite number of terms converge to a definite value.

Cauchy did important work in differential equations and functions of a complex variable, each of which is a major topic in analysis. He also made contributions to applied mathematics, including mathematical physics. Because of his early work as an engineer, he was able to use his knowledge of hydrodynamics to solve some theoretical problems in mathematics.

Cauchy's primary accomplishment in the field of applied mathematics is his concept of a hypothetical abstract fluid called the *ether*. In the eyes of many nineteenth-century physicists, a weightless "ether" fills all of space, serving as the medium through which electromagnetic waves such as light are propagated. Late in the century, the ether hypothesis was shown to be superfluous and was abandoned by scientists.

In 1816 Cauchy was made professor at the Ecole Polytechnique in Paris, France, where he assumed responsibility for the mathematical education of engineers and scientists. Although he generally showed himself to be sympathetic to the career goals of younger colleagues, he either lost or discarded the important mathematical papers of two young mathematicians, Evariste Galois (*see* Galois, Vol. 1, Algebra) and Niels Henrik Abel. As a result, neither could find sustained support for his ideas and discoveries.

Because of his political beliefs, Cauchy fled Paris for Italy in 1830, returning to Paris in 1838. While in exile, he continued to write on numerous mathematical topics, producing a body of works that in his day was exceeded in number only by the writings of Leonhard Euler. (*See* Euler, Vol. 1, Calculus, Trigonometry, and Analysis: Analysis.) In both his teaching and his writings, Cauchy supplied rigorous proofs to the mathematical arguments that he developed. This attention to rigor is one of the most important of Cauchy's legacies to the generations of mathematicians that followed him.

BOOK BY CAUCHY

Ordinary Differential Equations (1819–1824). Johnson Repr 1981 $24.50. ISBN 0-384-07950-4

BOOK ABOUT CAUCHY

Grabiner, Judith V. *The Origins of Cauchy's Rigorous Calculus.* MIT Pr 1981 $42.50. ISBN 0-262-07079-0 Account of the eighteenth-century search for rigorous proof in mathematics; shows how Cauchy's treatment of limit and convergence arose from the approximation techniques of Joseph Louis Lagrange (1736–1813) decades earlier.

EULER, LEONHARD 1707–1783

Leonhard Euler was a Swiss mathematician who was educated at Basel, where he knew members of the mathematically gifted Bernoulli family. (*See* Bernoulli, Vol. 1, Probability and Statistics.) In 1727 he became professor of mathematics at St. Petersburg. In 1761 he was invited to Berlin by Frederick the Great, where he remained until 1766, when he returned to St. Petersburg.

Euler was one of the most prolific mathematicians of all time. During his lifetime, he produced over 900 papers on a wide array of questions. He extended the frontiers of his field of study, engaged in voluminous scientific correspondence, and directly influenced a generation of young scientists and technicians.

Euler was adept at both pure and applied mathematics. In pure mathematics his areas of interest included algebra, calculus, number theory, the calculus of variations, and differential equations. In the area of applied mathematics, he contributed to mechanics, hydraulics, and astronomy.

Euler is especially remembered for his pioneering work in differential equations, equations in which the rate of change of a variable can itself be included as an equation variable. Such equations are used in many important physical applications, for example, in solving problems involving heat transfer through materials and current flow in electric circuits.

Euler wrote textbooks on algebra and calculus that have remained the standard introductions to these subjects for generations.

BOOKS BY EULER

Elements of Algebra (1770). Springer-Verlag 1984 $39.80. ISBN 0-387-96014-7

Introduction to the Analysis of the Infinite (1748). Book 1 Springer-Verlag 1988 $49.95. ISBN 0-387-96824-5

Letters of Euler on Different Subjects in Natural Philosophy. History, Philosophy and Sociology of Science Ser. 2 vols. Ayer 1975 $59.50. ISBN 0-405-06588-4

Opera Omnia. Secundia Ser. Vol. 17 Swiss Society of Natural Sciences, Euler Committee (ed). Birkhauser 1983 $85.00. ISBN 3-7643-1447-8

BOOKS ABOUT EULER

Truesdell, C. A. *Essays in the History of Mechanics.* Springer-Verlag 1968 $54.00. ISBN 0-387-04367-5 Essays on the history of mechanics, including Euler's rational mechanics.

Truesdell, C. A. *Six Lectures on Modern Natural Philosophy.* Springer-Verlag 1966 $19.00. ISBN 0-387-03684-9 Collection of essays that cover Euler's rational mechanics and other topics.

LEIBNIZ, GOTTFRIED WILHELM 1646–1716

Gottfried Leibniz was born in Leipzig, Germany to an academic family. His mother and father were both scholars. Their roots were Slavonic in origin, but their ancestors had lived in Germany for several hundred years.

Leibniz learned an enormous amount about the world because of his particular circumstances of life. He grew up in an academic tradition; he inherited his father's massive library through the intervention of his uncle when he was six; he was primarily self-taught and so followed his own interests, wherever they led, as to what to learn; and he took on a wide range of research and consulting assignments for the leading noblemen of the day, particularly the dukes of Hanover. These assignments ranged from diplomacy to mathematics to genealogy. He shifted back and forth between the great libraries of the day and the open road of scholarly travel throughout Europe, including England, France, Italy, Austria, and Russia. His contacts and conversations were extensive, and he was invited to join several national scholarly societies in succession. He was, in fact, the first foreigner to be asked to join the French Academy of Science, and he founded the Berlin Academy, being named its president for life.

Leibniz became a leading figure of the emerging Enlightenment, advocating the use of reason and method to both understand the world more deeply and to deal effectively with its problems. His primary achievements are in mathematics, philosophy, and computer science. All stem from what can be characterized as a talent for creating methods that in turn produce other methods. This to Leibniz was the way to solve a problem.

Operating with this approach, Leibniz produced a better calculus than Isaac Newton did. (*See* Newton, Vol. 2, Physics: Mechanics: Forces and Motion.) Leibniz's calculus was more natural and easy to use in its form and expression, and more general in conception than that of Newton. Leibniz's calculus was expressed more in terms of geometry, as in using the sides of a triangle to represent relative changes in quantity. He also designed a better mechanical calculator than Pascal did. Leibniz's version used binary numbers instead of decimal numbers, just as computers do today.

Leibniz invented calculus independently of Newton. He said he knew, via earlier correspondence with Newton, that Newton had succeeded in developing a tool for manipulating limit-oriented quantities, and what some of the conclusions were, and that a calculus tool was indeed possible to create. But he did not know the methods that Newton used, and so had to develop his own. He published his paper decades before Newton. A great controversy ensued, revolving around the charge of plagiarism by Leibniz, with much of the scientific world choosing sides, and with the mathematicians of Great Britain gradually isolating themselves from the mathematicians of Continental Europe.

A similar controversy took place in our own day, over who had first invented the electronic digital computer, Atasanoff or Mauchly and Eckert. Again, the controversy turned on whether discussions between them (several years before the latter group invented, designed, and built what is regarded as the first electronic digital computer) constituted unacknowledged copying of key techniques needed to implement an idea or goal. Eckert said he only saw conclusions, not methods. This enabled him to know what road to travel on, not how to get there. The same was true for Leibniz, whose formulation of calculus made it a more powerful and elegant tool than Newton's, a tool that propelled mathematics forward like nothing comparable for many hundreds of years.

Books by Leibniz

The Early Mathematical Manuscripts of Leibniz. J. M. Child (tr). Univ of Chicago Pr 1920. (o.p.)
General Investigators Concerning the Analysis of Concepts and Truths. Walter H. O'Briant (tr). Books Demand 1968 $32.30. ISBN 0-317-08968-4
Monadology and Other Philosophical Writings (1714). R. C. Sleigh (ed). Garland 1985 $55.00. ISBN 0-8246-6537-9
New Essays on Human Understanding (1705). Peter Remnant and Jonathan Bennett (eds). Cambridge Univ Pr 1982 $16.95. ISBN 0-521-28539-9
Theodicy (1710). Open Court 1985 $9.50. ISBN 0-87548-437-9

Books About Leibniz

Baron, Margaret E. *The Origins of the Infinitesimal Calculus*. Dover 1987 $7.95. ISBN 0-486-65371-4 A detailed account of both Newton's and Leibniz's efforts.
Dewey, John. *Leibniz's New Essays Concerning the Human Understanding: A Critical Exposition*. Gordon Pr 1977 $69.95. ISBN 0-8490-2148-0 A critical examination and discussion of Leibniz's theories and knowledge by the eminent American philosopher and educator, John Dewey.
Ishiguro, Hide. *Leibniz's Philosophy of Logic and Language*. Cambridge Univ Pr 1990 $16.95. ISBN 0-521-37781-1 A discussion of the key relationships between language and logic in Leibniz's philosophy.
*Leclerc, Ivor. *The Philosophy of Leibniz and the Modern World*. Vanderbilt Univ Pr 1973 $17.95. ISBN 0-8265-1181-3 Explores the relevance of Leibniz's thought to the modern world, and how Leibniz's ideas contributed to the development of modern computational tools.
Rescher, Nicholas S. (ed). *Leibniz: An Introduction to His Philosophy*. Univ Pr of America 1986 $12.25. ISBN 0-8191-5217-X An introductory approach to the philosophy of Leibniz, which in itself encompasses many aspects but has a core of methods in common.
*Russell, Bertrand. *The Philosophy of Leibniz*. Longwood 1989 $27.50. ISBN 0-89341-548-0 Examines Leibniz as a key figure in both mathematics and philosophy and as a forerunner of Einstein and Von Neumann, with respect to the general purpose of stored-program computers.
Woolhouse, R. S. *Leibniz: Metaphysics and Philosophy of Science. Oxford Readings in Philosophy*

Ser. Oxford Univ Pr 1981 $10.95. ISBN 0-19-875050-1 Explores the relationship in Leibniz's work between a systematic study of first principles in philosophy and the creation of an approach to learning systematically about the world through science.

WEIERSTRASS, KARL   1815–1897

As a young student, the German mathematician Karl Weierstrass showed great talent but was unable to complete his university education. However, he was able to obtain a license to teach secondary school mathematics based on his brilliant performance on a teacher's licensing examination.

After an unhappy period as a high school teacher and on the strength of a paper he wrote on Abelian functions, Weierstrass was offered a position teaching in Berlin, Germany. In 1864 he was appointed professor of mathematics at the University of Berlin, where he became the center of an important circle of younger mathematicians who sought to carry out his approach to "arithmeticizing" mathematics, an effort that was particularly influential in the latter part of the nineteenth century. In fact, supplying rigorous foundations to all mathematical arguments was one of Weierstrass's major preoccupations. Among the areas of research he pursued, the most important concern analytic functions, elliptic and hyperelliptic functions, Abelian functions, and the calculus of variations.

BOOKS BY WEIERSTRASS

Mathematische Werke (1894–1927). 7 vols. Johnson Repr 1967. (o.p.) $210.00. ISBN 0-384-66490-3

Einleitung in die Theorie der Analytischen Functionen (1878). *Dokumente zu Geschichte der Mathematik Ser.* Vol. 4 Ballen 1988 $36.00. ISBN 3-528-06334-3

BOOK ABOUT WEIERSTRASS

*Bell, Eric T. *Men of Mathematics.* Simon 1986 $13.95. ISBN 0-671-62818-6 Contains an excellent chapter devoted to both Weierstrass and his protégée, the brilliant mathematician Sonya Kovalevsky, and their major influence on each other.

PROBABILITY AND STATISTICS

Probability and statistics were first seriously discussed and written about in sixteenth- and seventeenth-century Europe. Since that time, both fields have grown in importance, slowly at first, more rapidly in recent years. In the modern world, the influence of both disciplines, especially statistics, is evident in such activities as forecasting the weather and election results, predicting the success of a new consumer product, and testing the efficacy and safety of a new medicine.

The systematic study of probability began in the middle of the seventeenth century as a result of some correspondence between two mathematicians, Blaise Pascal and Pierre de Fermat, concerning the proper strategy to follow in a game of chance. Out of this exchange evolved not only a determination of what game strategy to follow but, even more important, some principles of probability that lay behind the recommended strategy.

A colleague of Pascal published the ideas that he and Fermat had developed, but 50 years elapsed before a major treatment of probability was finally published. From this point on, probability was a firmly established mathematical area of inquiry.

The first serious attention to statistics also began in the seventeenth century, in the insurance business. As with probability, the attention grew slowly. Then, in the early eighteenth century, Abraham de Moivre prepared a table of annuities based on the principles of probability, principles that by that time were well known. Since then, the theory and application of statistics have advanced steadily, with the most rapid advances occurring in the last century. The range of statistical applications in present-day society and culture include application to the random motion of subatomic particles; statistical linguistics, a relatively new field that examines and analyzes the patterns of word frequencies in written texts; and a form of mathematical modeling called neural networks that uses statistical techniques and advanced computer technology to perform pattern-recognition tasks with a high degree of success. The procedure involves teaching a computer model gradually to improve its ability to discriminate "target" objects from other objects.

Cournot, Antoine A. *An Essay on the Foundations of Our Knowledge.* M. H. Moore (tr). Macmillan 1956 $3.95. ISBN 0-672-60400-0

Cramér, Harald. *Elements of Probability Theory and Some of Its Applications.* Krieger 1973 $17.50. ISBN 0-88275-144-1

*Danin D. *Probabilities and the Quantum World.* Imported 1983 $10.95. ISBN 0-8285-2739-3 Readable explanation of the counterintuitive nature of the quantum world.

Davison, Mark L. *Multidimensional Scaling.* Wiley 1983 $39.95. ISBN 0-471-86417-X

De Moivre, Abraham. *The Doctrines of Chance: A Method of Calculating the Probabilities of Events in Play, Including Treatise on Annuities.* Irvington 1967 repr of 1738 ed $7.50. ISBN 0-89197-736-8

*De Morgan, Augustus. *An Essay on Probabilities. Development of Science Ser.* Ayer 1981 $30.00. ISBN 0-405-13885-7 Nineteenth-century account that is a turning point in the evolution of the concept of probability.

Downing, Douglas, and Jeff Clark. *Statistics the Easy Way. Easy Way Ser.* Barron 1989 $9.95. ISBN 0-8120-4196-8

Fetzer, James H. (ed). *Probability and Causality.* Kluwer 1988 $27.50. ISBN 1-55608-052-2

Goldstein, Larry J., *et al. Finite Mathematics and Its Applications.* Prentice 1988 $34.50. ISBN 0-13-031735-4

Good, I. J. *Good Thinking: The Foundations of Probability and Its Applications.* Univ of Minnesota Pr 1983 $14.95. ISBN 0-8166-1141-6

Herdan, Gustav. *The Advanced Theory of Language as Choice and Chance. Communication and Cybernetics Ser.* Vol. 4 Springer-Verlag 1966 $55.00. ISBN 0-387-03584-2

Herdan, Gustav. *The Calculus of Linguistic Observations. Janus Linguarum, Ser Major* No. 9 Mouton 1962 $51.50. ISBN 90-2790-604-1

Hockett, Charles F. *Language, Mathematics, and Linguistics. Janus Linguarum, Ser Minor* No. 60 Mouton 1967 $28.00. ISBN 0-686-22442-6

Horwitz, Lucy, and Lou Ferleger. *Statistics for Social Change.* South End 1980 $30.00. ISBN 0-89608-033-1

*Huff, Darrell, and Irving Geis. *How to Lie with Statistics.* Norton 1954 $3.95. ISBN 0-393-09426-X Classic book that gives humorous examples of situations in which statistics can be very misleading.

*Kemeny, John G., *et al. Introduction to Finite Mathematics.* Prentice 1974 $52.00. ISBN 0-13-483834-3 Classic work that includes set theory, combinations, probability, and other topics.

Kendall, M. G., and W. R. Buckland *A Dictionary of Statistical Terms.* Wiley 1983 $31.95. ISBN 0-0-582-47008-0

*Marriott, F. H. (ed). *Dictionary of Statistical Terms.* Halsted 1990 $59.95. ISBN 0-470-21349-3 Useful reference work.

*Rastrigin, L. *This Chancy, Chancy, Chancy World.* Imported 1985 $5.95. ISBN 0-8285-

2900-0 Introduction to probability, chance, and random search, including the use of cybernetics and optimization in complex problems and decisions.

*Siskin, Bernard, *et al. What Are the Chances? Risks, Odds, and Likelihoods in Everyday Life.* Crown 1989 $16.95. ISBN 0-517-57260-5 A fascinating look at topics like sports, disasters, and health from the statistician's point of view.

Stigler, Stephen. *The History of Statistics.* Harvard Univ Pr 1986 $29.95. ISBN 0-674-40340-1

*Tankard, James W., Jr. *Statistical Pioneers.* Schenkman 1984 $11.95. ISBN 0-87073-409-1 Biographical profiles of the pragmatists and theorists who developed the field of statistics.

*Tarasov, L. *The World is Built on Probability.* Imported 1988 $10.95. ISBN 5-03-001124-2 Fundamental concepts of probability, such as events, choices, and random numbers, as well as derived concepts such as queues, games, and random searches; includes applications to physics and biology.

Travers, K., *et al. Using Statistics.* Addison 1985 $39.50. ISBN 0-201-20070-8

*Venttsel, Y. *Elements of Game Theory.* Imported 1984 $2.95. ISBN 0-8285-2899-3 Nonrigorous introduction to game theory and methods for solving matrix and finite games that includes strategies and approximation methods.

Vilenkin, N. Y. *Combinatorics.* A. Shenitzer and Sara Shenitzer (trs). Academic Pr 1971 $59.50. ISBN 0-12-721940-4

BERNOULLI, JAKOB   1654–1705

Jakob Bernoulli was among the most gifted of a mathematical family that over three generations provided the world with 10 mathematicians and scientists. The sons of a pharmacist in Basel, Switzerland, both Jakob and his younger brother Johann showed mathematical talent at an early age. Discouraged by their father from pursuing their mathematical interests, they began their careers along traditional lines, Jakob studying theology and Johann studying medicine. This all changed, however, after the brothers' attention was drawn to the professional writings of G. W. Leibniz, one of the codiscoverers of calculus. Under Leibniz's influence, the two brothers immediately decided to become mathematicians.

In due course, Jakob was invited to assume the chairmanship of the mathematics department at the University of Basel. In the years that followed, his mathematical achievements covered many areas. Prominent among these was the new field of polar coordinates; here he provided new insights concerning the logarithmic spiral and discussed a curve that now bears his name, the "lemniscate of Bernoulli."

Jakob Bernoulli's writings included a definitive set of textbooks for differential and integral calculus and a mathematical treatise, *Ars Conjectandi* (1713), which was published eight years after his death. Among its many contents was the first thorough exposition of probability theory. The treatise also provided a general formula for the coefficients (Bernoulli numbers) of the expanded form of $(a + b)^n$, even when the exponent n is a negative integer or a fraction rather than a positive number. It also contains the Bernoulli Law of Large Numbers, the basis of modern sampling theory in the field of statistics.

The two Bernoulli brothers strongly competed with one another. In 1697 Jakob offered a reward to anyone who could solve a fundamental problem concerning the path of a particle under certain conditions. Johann entered the competition, devising a solution to which Jakob responded by declaring it invalid, claiming that it would not work. Jakob then proceeded to offer his own solution to the problem, an action that led to a long and bitter dispute between the two brothers.

After Jakob's death in 1705, Johann was appointed to his brother's chair as head of the mathematics department at the University of Basel. He remained there for 43 years, doing very distinguished work in the field now known as analysis.

BOOK BY BERNOULLI

Die Gesammelten Werke. Vol. 3 *Wahrscheinlichkeitsrechnung.* Birkhauser 1975 $105.95. ISBN 3-7643-0713-7

BOOK ABOUT BERNOULLI

*Bell, Eric T. *Men of Mathematics.* Simon 1986 $13.95. ISBN 0-671-62818-6 Contains a chapter on the origins and development of the Bernoulli family of Belgium and Switzerland, featuring Jakob, Johann, and Daniel.

GAUSS, CARL FRIEDRICH   1777–1855

Carl Friedrich Gauss established the direction of mathematics for the nineteenth century, developing guiding principles in many fields of mathematics and mathematical physics.

The son of a gardener, Gauss was born in Brunswick, Germany. He was recognized as a child prodigy from at least the age of three. During his teens his talent came to the attention of the Duke of Brunswick, who thereupon agreed to finance and guide the boy's education. In 1795 Gauss enrolled at the University of Göttingen, where he spent most of his next 60 years. From 1807 until his death in 1855, he was director of the university's astronomical observatory.

Gauss's mathematical and scientific accomplishments had an extraordinarily wide range. A partial list of them covers such disparate fields as algebra, statistics, non-Euclidean geometry, number theory, electromagnetism, and the orbits of heavenly bodies.

Gauss's contribution to algebra was to prove the Fundamental Theorem of Algebra as his doctoral thesis. The theorem states that a polynomial equation with real coefficients has the same number of solutions, or roots, as the degree of the polynomial. His important achievements in statistics include the elaboration and widespread application of the Gaussian curve, also called the normal distribution and originally discovered by DeMoivre. This is the bell-shaped curve that depicts the distribution of statistical data, such as the heights of 35-year-old women and the lifetimes of electric light bulbs. He also laid the methodological groundwork for the field of non-Euclidean geometry. He did not publish his results, however, because he did not wish to face the predictable controversy and uproar. Instead, he left this field to others to claim as their discovery.

One of Gauss's most important fields of concentration was that of number theory. His major contributions in this area appeared in his *Disquisitiones Arithmeticae* (1801), which is remarkable not only for the quantity and difficulty of the problems it identifies and tackles but also for its continuing value as an introduction and guide to mathematicians developing number theory today. It includes his proof of the Fundamental Theorem of Arithmetic, which states that a positive integer can be represented as a product of prime numbers in only one way.

Among Gauss's other number-theory contributions that appear in the *Disquisitiones* is the concept of the algebra of congruences, an algebra that uses the relationship $\equiv$. Gauss developed the properties of algebraic congruences such as $ax \equiv b \bmod m$.

Gauss also made important contributions to physics, notably in developing the precise measurement of magnetism. The unit of flux density, the gauss, is named after him. From his model and data he predicted the location of the magnetic North Pole, a prediction later found to be surprisingly close to the actual location of the pole.

Gauss's work in astronomy was equally remarkable. In 1801 he used his method of least squares to calculate the orbit of the asteroid Ceres, using just a few data points that astronomers had been able to establish before the asteroid became lost from view. In 1818 he extended his earlier work to a theory of planetary motion that takes into account the effect that asteroids have on the orbit of planets. In 1846 his theory was used by others to predict and locate the orbit of the planet Neptune.

Some of Gauss's many other accomplishments include the solution (at the age of 19) of the problem of constructing a regular polygon of 17 sides, the recasting and simplification of the view of complex variables by representing them as two-coordinate points in a plane with real numbers on one axis and imaginary numbers on the other, and the introduction of the concept of an imaginary prime number, which he used to clarify previous results about real primes. He also wrote the first systematic study of convergence of an infinite series, the hypergeometric series.

BOOK BY GAUSS

Disquisitiones Arithmeticae (1801). W. C. Waterhouse, *et al* (eds). A. A. Clarke (tr). Springer-Verlag 1986 $75.00. ISBN 0-387-96254-9

BOOKS ABOUT GAUSS

Buehler, W. K. *Gauss: A Biographical Study.* Springer-Verlag 1987 $38.00. ISBN 0-387-10662-6 Account of the life of Gauss that also contains an indexed survey of his collected works.

Hall, T. *Carl Friedrich Gauss: A Biography.* A. Froderbart (tr). MIT Pr 1970. (o.p.) $10.00. ISBN 0-262-08040-0 Modestly technical mathematical biography of Gauss that helps the reader understand how Gauss solved the hard problems that he took on.

Merzbach, Uta C. (ed). *Carl Friedrich Gauss: A Bibliography.* Scholarly Res 1984 $100.00. ISBN 0-8420-2169-8 Comprehensive bibliography of primary and secondary sources that includes a guide to Gauss's correspondence.

PASCAL, BLAISE   1623–1662

French mathematician Blaise Pascal did much to set in motion what is known today as modern mathematics. An unusually creative mathematician, he developed a number of theorems and mathematical structures, including the beginnings of probability theory and a more sophisticated understanding of the geometry of conic structures.

At the age of 16, Pascal wrote a brilliant paper on conics; the paper consisted of one single printed page on which he states his major theorem—the opposite sides of any hexagon inscribed in a cone intersect in a straight line. This theorem led Pascal to develop several hundred related theorems in geometry.

Pascal's activities, however, were not confined to pure mathematics. When he was about 19 years old, he built a calculating machine that he demonstrated to the king of France. It worked well enough to allow him to build and sell about 50 of them over a few years' time. His work on problems in atmospheric pressure eventually resulted in an early version of the gas law.

At the age of 25, Pascal entered a Jansenist monastery to begin an ascetic life of study and argument. However, he continued his mathematical work.

With Pierre de Fermat, Pascal laid the foundation for the theory of probability. (*See* Fermat, Vol. 1, Algebra.) In 1654 Pascal's friend, the Chevelier de Méré, had asked him to analyze a problem arising from a game of chance. Pascal in turn exchanged a number of letters with Fermat about the problem. This correspondence became the starting point for a theory of probability. However, neither published the ideas developed in the correspondence. The letters did inspire one of Pascal's contemporaries, Christian Huygens of Holland, to publish in 1657 a short tract on the mathematics of games involving dice.

Pascal's name is now attached to "Pascal's Triangle" of binomial coefficients, which plays an important role in the study of combinations and probability. The triangle was known at least 600 years before Pascal became interested in it, but because of his contributions to its study, the triangle eventually became associated with his name.

A sensitive and temperamental man, Pascal was obsessed with religious philosophy, a subject on which he wrote extensively. In his general philosophy he was very much taken with the concept of the infinite, which unsettled him and inspired in him a sense of awe. Over a period of years, he wrote on many religious, philosophical, and mathematical subjects. His notes and letters were edited and published posthumously as his *Pensées*.

BOOKS BY PASCAL

Contradictions, Oppositions and Denials in the Life of the Mind. American Classical Coll Pr 1987 $157.45. ISBN 0-89266-605-6

The Nature of Man. Found Class Repr 1983 $117.50. ISBN 0-89901-113-6

**The Thoughts of Blaise Pascal* (1844). Greenwood 1978 $45.00. ISBN 0-313-20530-2 Pascal's collection of philosophical notes and thoughts *(Pensées)*.

The Provincial Letters (1656-1657). Penguin 1982 $5.95. ISBN 0-14-044196-4

BOOKS ABOUT PASCAL

*Cailliet, Emile. *Pascal: The Emergence of Genius.* Greenwood 1970 $22.50. ISBN 0-8371-2537-5 Portrayal of young Pascal as child prodigy and public figure.

MacKenzie, Charles S. *Pascal's Anguish and Joy.* Philosophical Lib 1973 $12.95. ISBN 0-8022-2117-3 Account of Pascal's spiritual and philosophical life.

MacKenzie, Louis A., Jr. *Pascal's Lettres Provinciales: The Motif and Practice of Fragmentation.* Summa 1988 $24.95. ISBN 0-917786-63-7 Short book that examines the role of fragmentation of thoughts in Pascal's letters and notes.

Renyi, Alfred. *Letters on Probability. Waynebooks Ser* No. 33 Wayne State Univ Pr 1973 $8.95. ISBN 0-8143-1465-1 Description of the development of Pascal's theory of probability as reflected in his correspondence.

Russell, Olga W. *Humor in Pascal.* Christopher 1977 $8.95. ISBN 0-8158-0343-5 Discussion of Pascal's use of humor in literary, philosophical, and research endeavors and the role it plays in his work.

Todhunter, Isaac. *A History of the Mathematical Theory of Probability from the Time of Pascal to That of Laplace.* Cambridge Univ Pr 1865. (o.p.) Classic historical work on Pascal and the early development of probability theory.

RECREATIONAL MATHEMATICS, PUZZLES, AND GAMES

Recreational mathematics and problem posing has a long history. Early Egyptian hieroglyphic writings, for example, include "think-of-a-number" word problems. In more modern times, recreational mathematics has often taken a surprisingly structured form that dates back at least 150 years to the *Journal of Recreational Mathematics,* which appeared in Great Britain in the 1840s.

The value of a "good problem" has always been a strong motivating force in mathematics and physics, but such problems can also have an inspiring influence for the average person as well. Problem posing and problem solving of the "famous problem" sort have periodically been accompanied by the offer of cash prizes in contests. These offers have often been made by patrons or mathematicians who wanted either to find a solution to a problem or to promote more intensive work in an area.

One hundred years ago the creators of puzzles and problems usually kept them within the range of the ability of anyone with a relatively elementary knowledge of mathematics. Today, however, puzzle writers often go far beyond this limit. Puzzle creators such as John Horton Conway and Piet Hein have attempted to meet the public's demands for more sophisticated and challenging puzzles. Conway's work is on a relatively high level. Piet Hein's innovative geometric puzzles like "Hex", on the other hand, cover a wider spectrum of ability and are designed to give someone other than the mathematician the same experience of creative struggle encountered by a practicing mathematician.

One of the most prolific writers on recreational mathematics is Martin Gardner, who for many years wrote a recreational mathematics column for *Scientific American* magazine. He has also written dozens of books on the subject and has been described by one reviewer as the "dean of mathematical recreationists."

*Adler, Irving. *The Impossible in Mathematics.* NCTM 1975. (o.p.) $1.70. ISBN 0-87-353062-4 Entertaining booklet with six familiar problems that have provoked mathematical interest for centuries.

Beck, Anatole, *et al. Excursions into Mathematics.* Worth 1969 $29.95. ISBN 0-87901-004-5

*Bell, Robbie, and Michael Cornelius. *Board Games Round the World: A Resource Book for Mathematical Investigations.* Cambridge Univ Pr 1989 $9.95. ISBN 0-521-35924-4 Cross-cultural resource book for games and their mathematical structures.

Bright, George, *et al. Learning and Mathematical Games.* NCTM 1985 $9.00. ISBN 0-87353-233-3

*Cundy, H. Martyn, and A. P. Rollett. *Mathematical Models.* Oxford Univ Pr 1961. (o.p.) $24.95. ISBN 0-198-325045 Explanation of the use of mathematical models that includes puzzles based on cross sections of geometric solids.

Daish, C. B. *Learn Science Through Ball Games.* Sterling 1972. (o.p.)

*Davidson, Jessica. *The Square Root of Tuesday.* Dutton 1971. (o.p.) Entertaining treatment of logic and clear thinking.

*Dudeney, Henry Ernest. *Amusements in Mathematics.* Dover 1917 $4.95. ISBN 0-486-20473-1 Classic work from another era.

*Dudeney, Henry Ernest. *Five Hundred Thirty-Six Puzzles and Curious Problems.* Scribner's 1983 $12.95. ISBN 0-684-71755-7 Classic collection of puzzles.

Eiffers, Joost, and Fleur Richter. *Geometric Games. Library of Visual Resources Ser.* Timken 1989 $35.00. ISBN 0-943221-04-8

Epstein, Richard A. *The Theory of Gambling and Statistical Logic.* Academic Pr 1977 $48.00. ISBN 0-12-240760-1

*Hemming, G. W. *Billiards, Mathematically Treated.* Macmillan 1904. (o.p.) Classic treatment of its subject.

*Jacobs, Harold R. *Geometry.* Freeman 1987 $31.95. ISBN 0-7167-1745-X Textbook with more than 700 pages of pictures, drawings, and cartoons; topics include non-Euclidean geometry, constructions, transformations, and inequalities.

Knuth, Donald E. *Surreal Numbers.* Addison 1974 $13.95. ISBN 0-201-03812-9

*May, Lola. *Supercube.* Harcourt 1973. (o.p.) Collection of activities that include geometry, topology, measurement, probability, and codes.

Murray, H. J. *A History of Board Games Other Than Chess.* Clarendon 1952. (o.p.)

Murray, H. J. *A History of Chess.* Benjamin Pr 1985 repr of 1913 ed $19.95. ISBN 0-936317-01-9

*Pallas, Norvin. *Calculator Puzzles, Tricks, and Games.* Sterling 1978 $4.95. ISBN 0-8069-7688-8 Discusses all sorts of activities—fun as well as practical—using the pocket calculator.

Paulos, John Allen. *Innumeracy: Mathematical Illiteracy and Its Consequences.* Hill & Wang 1989 $18.95. ISBN 0-8090-7447-8

Saaty, Thomas L., and Paul G. Kainen. *The Four-Color Problem: Assaults and Conquests.* Dover 1986 $6.00. ISBN 0-486-65092-8

*Scarne, John. *Scarne's Encyclopedia of Games.* Harper 1983 $13.95. ISBN 0-06-091052-6 Comprehensive collection of games, compiled by an expert writer on card games and gambling.

*Schaaf, William L. *A Bibliography of Recreational Mathematics.* Vol. 4 NCTM 1978 $10.00. ISBN 0-87353-128-0 Comprehensive compilation of recreational mathematics books and articles carefully grouped by topic and subtopic; ranges from sports to codes to anagrams to game and puzzle analysis, as well as problems and paradoxes in algebra, geometry, topology, and number theory.

*Schaaf, William L. *Mathematics and Science: An Adventure in Postage Stamps.* NCTM 1978 $9.00. ISBN 0-87353-122-1 Unusual portrait of the history of mathematics as reflected in the images of selected postage stamps.

Statistics: A Guide to the Unknown. NCTM 1972. (o.p.) $15.00. ISBN 0-816-28594-2 Forty-four nontechnical essays on the relevance and diversity of mathematics and statistics.

Tietze, Heinrich. *Famous Problems of Mathematics.* Graylock 1965 $20.00. ISBN 0-910670-11-0

*Trigg, Charles W. *Mathematical Quickies: Two Hundred Seventy Stimulating Problems with Solutions.* Dover 1985 $4.95. ISBN 0-486-24949-2 Collection of good mathematical problems.

Uspenskii, V. A. *Pascal's Triangle.* Univ of Chicago Pr 1975 $3.50. ISBN 0-226-84316-5

*Van Delft, Peter, and Jack Botermans. *Creative Puzzles of the World.* Abrams 1978. (o.p.) $19.95. ISBN 0-810-90765-8 Anthology of creative puzzles.

GARDNER, MARTIN   1914–

Martin Gardner was born in Tulsa, Oklahoma in 1914, the son of a wildcat oil prospecter. In 1936, he graduated from the University of Chicago, where he was known as a demon chess player. He quit the game, however, for the area of his degree and his greater love—philosophy. Interestingly, in his later writings, he continued to use chess as an abstract setting for bizarre philosophical problems.

Gardner started his career as a journalist and writer. While the serious Gardner published articles on logic and mathematics in such specialist quarterlies as *Scripta Mathematica,* the playful Gardner began in 1952 to compose games for *Humpty Dumpty's* magazine in New York. He became interested in mathematics by way of paper folding, an element that was a big part of his puzzle page at *Humpty.* A friend showed him a novel way to fold a strip of paper into a series of hexagons, which led to an article on combinatorial geometry in *Scientific American* in December 1956. He is probably best known, however, for his mathematical games column for the magazine *Scientific American* as well as for *The Annotated Alice,* one of more than 20 books of light verse, puzzles, and essays—books inspired by Gardner's love for wordplay.

Gardner's talent for combining math, science, philosophy, literature, and a passion for magic has resulted in the publication of a great many unusual books of diverse natures. His first book, *In the Name of Science,* was reviewed by the *San Francisco Chronicle,* which noted: "Mr. Gardner has written a highly critical and at times hilariously entertaining account of cults and fad sciences in various fields."

Gardner retired from *Scientific American* in 1981 and currently lives in Hendersonville, North Carolina.

Books by Gardner

Aha! Gotcha: Paradoxes to Puzzle and Delight. Freeman 1982 $10.95. ISBN 0-7167-1361-6
    Puzzles from *Scientific American* that involve mathematics and logic.
Aha! Insight. Freeman 1978 $11.95. ISBN 0-7167-1017-X Puzzles, paradoxes, and
    amusements.
The Ambidextrous Universe. Scribner's 1979. (o.p.)
Entertaining Mathematical Puzzles. Dover 1986 $2.95. ISBN 0-486-25211-6
Hexaflexagons and Other Mathematical Diversions. Univ of Chicago Pr 1988 $10.95. ISBN
    0-226-28254-6
Mathematical Carnival: A New Round-Up of Tantalizers and Puzzles from "Scientific American."
    Random 1977 $12.45. ISBN 0-394-72349-X
Mathematics, Magic, and Mystery. Dover 1956 $3.95. ISBN 0-486-20335-2
The Second Scientific American Book of Mathematical Puzzles and Diversions. Univ of Chicago Pr
    1987 $10.95. ISBN 0-226-28253-8 More puzzles taken from Gardner's magazine
    column.
Time Travel and Other Mathematical Bewilderments. Freeman 1987 $12.95. ISBN 0-7167-
    1925-8
Wheels, Life, and Other Mathematical Amusements. Freeman 1983 $13.95. ISBN 0-7167-
    1589-9 Puzzles and amusements.

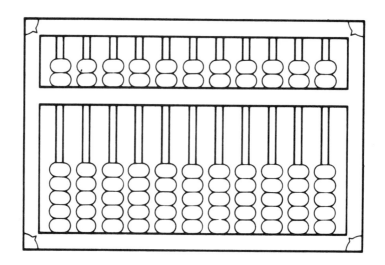

✨ COMPUTER SCIENCE ✨

GENERAL REFERENCES IN COMPUTER SCIENCE

The references in this section are of two kinds. The first consists of dictionaries of computer terminology, handbooks, and surveys. The rest are books of general interest within the computer-science field. If you are looking for a particular book that is not listed in this section, then you might find it under another heading such as "Social Impact of Computers" or "Computer Literacy."

*Amann, Dick, and Dick Smith. *Forgotten Women of Computer History.* Dick Whitson (ed). Prog Studies 1978 $49.95. ISBN 0-917194-09-8 Survey of the leading roles that women played in the development of several "breakthrough" computer languages and in the growth of the industry and the profession.

Andrews, Lincoln, *et al. The Art of Using Computers.* Boyd & Fraser 1986 $22.00. ISBN 0-87835-179-5

*Biermann, Alan W. *Great Ideas in Computer Science: A Gentle Introduction.* MIT Pr 1990 $27.95. ISBN 0-262-52148-2 Survey of the key developments and concepts in computer science.

*Brand, Stewart. *The Media Lab: Inventing the Future at MIT.* Viking 1987 $20.00. ISBN 0-670-81442-3 Description of the Media Lab at MIT, including custom-printed newspapers, compact disks for storing and retrieving vast amounts of text, and uses of "intensively" parallel computers.

Computer Books and Serials in Print, 1985–1986. Bowker 1985 $59.95. ISBN 0-8352-2044-3

*Dewdney, A. K. *The Armchair Universe: An Exploration of Computer Worlds.* Freeman 1989 $21.95. ISBN 0-7167-1939-8 Account of interactions with fantasy worlds created on the computer.

*Dewdney, A. K. *The Turing Omnibus: Excursions in Computer Science.* Freeman 1989 $24.95. ISBN 0-7167-8154-9 Imaginative look at the foundations and tools of computer science.

Dijkstra, Edsger W. *Selected Writings on Computing: A Personal Perspective. Texts and Monographs in Computer Science Ser.* Springer-Verlag 1982 $47.50. ISBN 0-387-90652-5

Encyclopedia of Computers and Electronics. Macmillan 1989 $14.95. ISBN 0-02-689200-6 Sourcebook for grade 4 and up.

*Forester, Tom. *The High-Tech Society: The Story of the Information Technology Revolution.* MIT Pr 1989 $24.95. ISBN 0-262-56044-5 Survey of the many aspects of the computer revolution, with a good bibliography.

Fransman, Martin. *The Market and Beyond: Co-Operation and Competition in Information Technology in the Japanese System.* Cambridge Univ Pr 1990 $54.50. ISBN 0-521-26803-6

Gersting, Judith L., and Michael Germignani. *The Computer: History, Working, Uses, and Limitations.* Ardsley 1988 $31.95. ISBN 0-912675-21-7

Glass, Robert L. *Computing Catastrophes.* Computing Trends 1983 $11.00. ISBN 0-686-35783-3

*Gonick, Larry, and Jay Hosler. *Cartoon Guide to Computer Science.* Harper 1983 $5.25. ISBN 0-06-460417-9 Elements of computer science as expressed in cartoons.

*Greene, Laura. *Computer Pioneers.* Watts 1985 $10.40. ISBN 0-531-04906-X Biographies of leading figures in the development and early days of the computer.

*Greenia, Mark W. *Consultant's Guide to Computer Abbreviations and Acronyms.* Lexikon 1988 $12.00. ISBN 0-944601-04-9 Helpful guide that includes both acronyms and abbreviations.

Grosch, Herb. *Computer: Bit Slices from a Life.* Underwood-Miller 1990 $24.95. ISBN 0-88733-085-1

*Heims, Steve V. *John Von Neumann and Norbert Wiener: From Mathematics to the Technologies of Life and Death.* MIT Pr 1980 $13.50. ISBN 0-262-58056-X Dual biography of two twentieth-century mathematicians who specialized in information technology.

*Hodges, Andrew. *Alan Turing: The Enigma.* Simon 1984 $10.95. ISBN 0-671-52809-2 Biography, later adapted as a drama on Broadway, of Turing, who helped to break the German code in World War II.

Jaki, Stanley L. *Brain, Mind and Computers.* Regnery 1989 $9.95. ISBN 0-89526-907-4

*Jespersen, James, and Jane Fitz-Randolph. *RAMS, ROMS, and Robots: The Inside Story of Computers.* Macmillan 1984 $13.95. ISBN 0-689-31063-3 A clear, well-organized introduction to uses and limitations of the computer.

Juliussen, Egil, and Karen Juliussen. *Computer Industry Almanac 1990.* Prentice 1991 $29.95. ISBN 0-13-155748-3

Kent, A., and James G. Williams. *Encyclopedia of Computer Science.* Vol. 21 Dekker 1989 $150.00. ISBN 0-8247-2271-X

*Lammers, Susan. *Programmers at Work: Interviews.* Microsoft 1986 $14.95. ISBN 0-914845-71-3 Interviews with 19 programmers of note who created classic software in the formative years of personal computers; includes interviews with Bill Gates, Dan Bricklin, Gary Kildall, John Warnock, and Scott Kim.

*Lundstrom, David E. *A Few Good Men from UNIVAC.* MIT Pr 1990 $10.95. ISBN 0-262-62075-8 Description of the early days of the UNIVAC computer and its creators.

*Martin, James. *An Information Systems Manifesto.* Prentice 1984 $59.60. ISBN 0-13-464769-6 Readable state-of-the-art advice to data-processing managers and decision makers on key issues in computer-systems development and operation.

*Martin, James. *Technology's Crucible.* Prentice 1986 $17.50. ISBN 0-13-902024-1 Short discussion on technology and computer tools and how they are tested to insure that their performance meets the expectations of their designers and sponsors.

MIT Staff and Stanford University Staff. *Bibliographic Guide to Computer Science.* G. K. Hall 1990 $150.00. ISBN 0-8161-7130-0

*Mollenhoff, Clark R. *Atanasoff, Forgotten Father of the Computer.* Iowa State Univ Pr 1988 $24.95. ISBN 0-8138-0032-3 Treatment of the pioneer of the vacuum-tube computing machine, a direct forerunner of the first general-purpose electronic computer.

Pioneers and Peers. Soc Computer Sim 1988 $28.00. ISBN 0-911801-37-5 Introduction to early and contemporary figures in the world of computers.

Red Feather Press and Scott Ladd. *The Computer and the Brain: Beyond the Fifth Generation.* Bantam 1986 $16.95. ISBN 0-553-34264-9

*Research and Education Association Staff. *Computer Science Problem Solver.* Research & Education 1989 $28.85. ISBN 0-87891-525-7 Study guide for learning to solve computer problems.

Rifkin, Glen, and George Harrar. *The Ultimate Entrepreneur: The Story of Ken Olsen and Digital Equipment Corporation.* Contemporary Bks 1988 $19.95. ISBN 0-8092-4559-0

*Ritchie, David. *The Computer Pioneers: The Making of the Modern Computer.* Simon 1986. (o.p.) $17.95. ISBN 0-671-52397-X Introduction to the development of computers, from their early days through the decades after World War II to the immediate present, as seen through the eyes of the people who made the computers.

Simon, A. R. *How To Be a Successful Computer Consultant.* McGraw 1985 $24.95. ISBN 0-07-057296-8

*Spencer, Donald D. *Famous People of Computing: A Book of Posters.* Camelot Pub Co 1987 $14.95. ISBN 0-89218-110-9 Informative posters of well-known figures in the computer field.

*Stockley, C., and L. Watts. *Computer Jargon. Computer and Electronics Ser.* EDC 1983 $2.95. ISBN 0-86020-737-4 Computer vocabulary explained.

Traub, J. F., *et al. Annual Review of Computer Science.* Vol. 4 Annual Reviews 1990 $45.00. ISBN 0-8243-3204-0

Tremblay, Jean-Paul, and Richard B. Bunt. *Introduction to Computer Science.* McGraw 1979 $44.95. ISBN 0-07-065163-9

*Vigil-Pinon, Evangelina. *The Computer Is Down.* Arte Publico 1987 $7.00. ISBN 0-317-

55289-9 Book of poems that deals with the theme of the increasing computerization of society and the problems that accompany it.

Webster's New World Dictionary of Computer Terms. Prentice 1990 $6.95. ISBN 0-13-949231-3 Comprehensive coverage of over 2,500 computer terms, with emphasis on the personal-computer environment.

Wiener, Norbert. *Cybernetics: Control and Communication in the Animal and the Machine.* MIT Pr 1961 $9.95. ISBN 0-262-73009-X

Wiener, Norbert. *The Human Use of Human Beings: Cybernetics and Society.* Da Capo 1988 $9.95. ISBN 0-306-80320-8

Wilkes, Maurice. *Memoirs of a Computer Pioneer. History of Computing Ser.* MIT Pr 1985 $22.50. ISBN 0-262-23122-0

HISTORY OF COMPUTERS

For a field with such a short span of existence, computer science has had a rich and intense history. It was less than fifty years ago that the world's first all-electronic digital computer was designed and built; it had a memory capacity of about 200 bytes. Within a decade after that a computer was developed that had about 20,000 bytes of memory. Since those early years, computer technology has advanced to the point where even a simple desktop computer has a memory capacity that is measured in the millions of bytes. More important, computers are now far more accessible to the average person—cheaper, lighter, more reliable, and easier to use. This trend will surely continue into the foreseeable future.

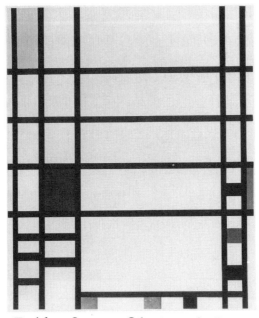

Trafalgar Square.   Oil painting by Piet Mondrian (1939–43).   Courtesy of The Bettmann Archive.

*Asimov, Isaac. *How Did We Find Out About Computers?* Walker 1984 $11.85. ISBN 0-8027-6533-5 A history of the development of computers, including an explanation of how they work.

*Burks, Alice R., and Arthur W. Burks. *The First Electronic Computer: The Atanasoff Story.* Univ of Michigan Pr 1988 $37.50. ISBN 0-472-10090-4 Story of John Atanasoff and Clifford Berry, who in 1940 successfully demonstrated the feasibility of making a computing device out of vacuum-tube switching elements.

Cortada, James W. (ed). *A Bibliographic Guide to the History of Computing, Computers and the Information Processing Industry.* Greenwood 1990 $65.00. ISBN 0-313-26810-X

*DeLamarter, Richard T. *Big Blue: IBM's Use and Abuse of Power.* Dodd 1986. (o.p.) $22.95. Account of the Justice Department's decade-long antitrust lawsuit against IBM.

*Fang, Irving E. *The Computer Story.* Rada 1988 $9.50. ISBN 0-9604212-4-6 Account of the history of computers.

Frank, Rose. *West of Eden: The End of Innocence at Apple Computer.* Penguin 1990 $8.95. ISBN 0-14-009372-9

*Freiberger, Paul, and Michael Swaine. *Fire in the Valley: The Making of the Personal Computer.* McGraw 1984 $9.95. Story of the personal-computer revolution from 1975–1983 written from an insider's point of view.

*Gassée, Jean-Louis. *The Third Apple: Personal Computers and the Cultural Revolution.* Harcourt 1987 $14.95. ISBN 0-15-189850-2 French view of the personal computer and its cultural revolution written by a former European executive for Apple computers.

*Greene, Laura. *Computer Pioneers.* Watts 1985 $10.40. ISBN 0-531-04906-X A history of computers and the men who invented them, from the seventeenth century to the late 1970s.

Hall, Mark, and John Barry. *Sunburst: The Ascent of Sun Microsystems.* Contemporary Bks 1990 $19.95. ISBN 0-8092-4368-7

*Levy, Steven. *Hackers: Heroes of the Computer Revolution.* Dell 1985 $17.95. ISBN 0-440-13405-6 Account of computer hackers of all kinds, from game addicts to those who gained unauthorized entry into sensitive systems.

Lindren, Michael. *Glory and Failure.* Craig G. McKay (tr). MIT Pr 1990 $45.00. ISBN 0-262-12146-8

McKenna, Regis. *Who's Afraid of Big Blue? How Companies are Challenging IBM—and Winning.* Addison 1988 $17.95. ISBN 0-201-15574-5

*Metropolis, N., *et al* (eds). *A History of Computing in the Twentieth Century.* Academic Pr 1980 $59.95. ISBN 0-12-491650-3 Collection of 39 papers presented at an international convention at Los Alamos in 1976; each written by a distinguished person in the computer field.

Mobley, Lou, and Kate McKeown. *Beyond IBM: The Real Story of Why IBM Has Worked, Why It Needs to Change and What Other Companies Can Learn.* McGraw 1989 $18.95. ISBN 0-07-042625-2

*Rodgers, Buck, and Robert Shook. *The IBM Way: Insights into the World's Most Successful Marketing Organization.* Harper 1987 $9.95. ISBN 0-06-091417-3 Explanation of the IBM corporate approach to marketing theory and employee relations and of the company's general corporate attitude.

*Schneiderman, Ron. *Computers: From Babbage to the Fifth Generation.* Watts 1986. (o.p.) $10.40. ISBN 0-531-10131-2 Account of important developments, from the 1830s onward in the evolution of the concepts and technologies of computing devices; for grades 4–9.

*Shurkin, Joel N. *Engines of the Mind: A History of the Computer.* Norton 1985 $4.95. ISBN 0-671-60036-2 Introductory work for the nontechnical reader.

Williams, Michael R. *A History of Computer Technology.* Prentice 1985 $37.00. ISBN 0-13-389917-9

BABBAGE, CHARLES   1791–1871

In the course of his life, Charles Babbage moved from designing and building *a* computer (a specialized calculating machine) to designing what we now call *the* computer (a general-purpose information processor). He and his brilliant friend and collaborator, Ada, countess of Lovelace (*see* Lovelace, Vol. 1, Computer Science: History of Computers), discovered most of the major characteristics and operating principles of a modern information processor, including programming. However, they were unable to build a working model of their conception with the existing technology of their day. Babbage devoted the greater part of his life and all of his fortune to creating and elaborating his concepts and to attempting to get his machines built.

The son of an upper-middle-class family, Babbage attended Cambridge University in Great Britain and became a successful and well-known mathematician. He was a cofounder in 1812 of the Analytical Society, a group of talented algebra reformers. In 1816 he became a member of the Royal Society, and in 1820 he cofounded the Royal Astronomical Society.

Babbage gradually became active in public policy issues regarding science and also did pioneering work in the branch of applied mathematics and statistics now known as operations research. In this work, he developed far more accurate methods for creating insurance actuarial tables. In addition, he successfully proposed a flat rate for the British postal system (the "penny post") regardless of the distance a letter was mailed, because it was cheaper to administer this type of system. The plan was adopted in 1840 and gradually spread to other countries, including the United States. Babbage was also an inventor. He designed the tachometer (speedometer for engines), the locomotive cowcatcher, and the ophthalmoscope for observing the eye's retina.

Babbage's serious entry into the design of computing equipment was sparked by anger at seeing so many errors in mathematical tables, such as astronomical tables. He knew that these errors were largely due to the slowness and unreliability of current computing methods. Taking matters into his own hands, he drew up a plan for a mechanical device called a Difference Engine that could more accurately calculate table entries.

His proposal was endorsed by the Royal Society, and a grant for scientific development soon came from the government (1823). The project was expected to be completed in three years. However, after 10 years, nothing had been completed, and funding was stopped in 1833. Nine years after that, the government officially terminated the project. Hostility had replaced good will on both sides during these years.

What had happened? Work went well for awhile, and then Babbage stopped everything, changed the design, and expanded the goals because he had developed greater insight and now knew how to make a better machine. This cycle of stopping work to improve the design of the machine was repeated, and Babbage never finished the device. A modest version was later completed by the Swede P. G. Scheutz with generous advice from Babbage. The Scheutz version of the Difference Engine was displayed in London in 1854. It worked well.

In 1833, Babbage shifted his attention to a new idea, his most brilliant insight of all, the Analytical Engine. It was general, not specialized, in computational scope, and it could be controlled by a set of punched instruction cards and data cards. It had a "mill" for computation (the original number-cruncher) and a "store" for holding data as well as intermediate results until they were needed again. There were also units to read punched cards and to print results. Essentially, Babbage was describing the nature of a 1950 computer, with its central processing unit, working memory, and card-based input-output stations.

For the next 40 years, Babbage elaborated on his ideas and drawings, using up his own inheritance and for a time receiving financial support from his friend and collaborator, Ada, countess of Lovelace.

After Babbage died in 1871, his son Henry arranged for the construction of the part of the Analytical Engine involving the mill and the printer. The machine, located in the Scientific Museum in London, still operates today.

BOOKS BY BABBAGE

Babbage's Calculating Machines (1889). Henry Babbage (ed). MIT Pr 1984 $55.00. ISBN 0-262-02200-1 Modern reprint of a classic collection of papers by Charles Babbage.

Charles Babbage: On the Principle and Development of the Calculator and other Seminal Writings (et al). Dover 1984 $8.95. ISBN 0-486-24691-4

The Exposition of Eighteen Fifty-One: Or Views of the Industry, the Science and the Government of England (1851). Gregg Intl (repr of 1851 ed) $90.00. ISBN 0-576-29115-3

Passages from the Life of a Philosopher (1864). Kelley 1969 repr of 1864 ed $49.50. ISBN 0-678-00479-X Babbage's famous autobiography, considered a fine literary work.

Reflections on the Decline of Science in England (1830). Kelley 1970 repr of 1830 ed $29.50. ISBN 0-678-00645-8

Science and Reform: Selected Works of Charles Babbage. Anthony Hyman (ed). Cambridge Univ Pr 1989 $59.50. ISBN 0-521-34311-9

BOOKS ABOUT BABBAGE

Bernstein, Jeremy. *The Analytical Engine: Computers—Past, Present, and Future.* Morrow 1981. (o.p.) $8.95. ISBN 0-688-00488-1 A series of articles on the history of computing, originally published in *The New Yorker* magazine.

Hyman, Anthony. *Charles Babbage: Pioneer of the Computer.* Princeton Univ Pr 1984 $14.95. ISBN 0-691-02377-8 An account of Babbage's life and times, with a bibliography of his published works.

GATES, WILLIAM   1955–

For 20 years William Henry ("Bill") Gates has searched for better tools for computer programmers and users. In this quest he has created and continues to create such innovative software as the Microsoft BASIC language for microcomputers, the MS DOS operating system for IBM-oriented microcomputers, and the Windows graphical user interface (pointing with a mouse at picture symbols on the screen to control the flow of actions and information).

As the head of what has grown to become the largest software company in the world, the Microsoft Corporation, Gates has played an influential and sometimes dominant role in determining the evolution of microcomputer software tools. This is a role he enjoys. He happily discusses new software products and controversies with audiences of computer users on a regular basis. In these dialogues, Gates projects an appreciation for the often puzzled computer user, who must wrestle with the choices among competing products for upgrading software tools and environments.

Gates's early experiences in microcomputer software development, at a time when the industry itself was being born (1973–1975), gave him the opportunity to grow into the software-industry leader he has become. While still in high school, he formed a computer service company called Traf-O-Data with a friend, Paul Allen, to analyze traffic patterns using a computer. Then Gates took a leave of absence from high school to work on a software project.

Following high school, in the fall of 1974, Gates entered Harvard. His friend Paul Allen had also moved to the Boston area. One day, when the January 1975 issue of *Popular Electronics* appeared on the newsstands with a picture of the first personal computer for sale (the Altair 8800), Gates and Allen decided to attempt to produce a BASIC compiler for the Altair's operating system. (A compiler is a program that converts an English-like representation of a program into the language of machine instructions that actually direct the computer's processing.) Gates and Allen contacted Ed Roberts, head of MITS, who said that he would buy the first compiler in the BASIC language that anyone produced that would actually run on his machine.

Early in 1975, Gates and Allen wrote the first BASIC compiler program for the 8800, based on experiences they had gained several years before during high school. Gates called the new compiler program Microsoft BASIC.

Soon after, in 1975, Gates and Allen founded Microsoft, a software development and marketing company, to market their new product and develop others. A short while later, as the business grew, Gates left Harvard to devote full time to managing this enterprise.

In 1980, IBM asked Microsoft to develop an operating system for the powerful new 16-bit personal computer it planned to announce in 1981. This operating system in its general form is called MS DOS. (The IBM PC version was called PC-DOS). Sales of the IBM PC soon skyrocketed, and each IBM PC contained (for a small additional price) PC-DOS from Microsoft.

From a tidal wave of small products, a software industry giant was born, and in 1982 Bill Gates became the embodiment of the personal computer "boy wonder." But far from riding a fad up and then down, Gates has steadily grown in power, wealth, and experience, while retaining a strong sense of commitment to his ideas and values. Through clear thinking, Gates has adeptly guided Microsoft and the computer industry to more complex and yet more useful forms of software tools.

Books about Gates

Freiberger, Paul, and Michael Swaine. *Fire in the Valley: The Making of the Personal Computer.* McGraw 1984 $11.95. ISBN 0-88134-121-5 Story of the personal-computer revolution from 1975 to 1983; includes a detailed account of Gates's transformation from teenage computer professional to software industry leader.
Lammers, Susan. *Programmers at Work: Interviews.* Microsoft 1986 $14.95. ISBN 0-914845-71-3 Interviews with 19 programmers of note, including Bill Gates.

HOLLERITH, HERMAN 1860–1929

Herman Hollerith was born to German immigrant parents in Buffalo, New York, and graduated as an engineer from Columbia University. He immediately went to work for the U.S. Census Office and later for the Patent Office, where he gained an understanding of the approaches that inventors were taking to equipment design. During this time, he himself was designing new kinds of tabulation devices.

As a capable young man with 10 years of valuable government service, Hollerith was asked to design and carry out the first automated U.S. Census analysis for the 1890 survey. The request came from John Shaw Billings, a director of vital statistics on loan to the Census Office from the Surgeon General's Office. Billings later became Hollerith's father-in-law. The two were an excellent team.

The method chosen for the census analysis was punched cards. This resourceful idea was the contribution of Billings. Hollerith devised the machines to deal with the cards. Their combined efforts produced a new approach to tabulation equipment. What had formerly been a seven-year analysis process was reduced to little more than two years. The simple population count took only six weeks. In addition, the opportunities for errors in counting, arithmetic, and transferring subtotals were greatly reduced.

The technology used by Hollerith and Billings resembled a much older approach to machine control, namely, Jacquard loom cards that were used to control weaving machines. But their design added a new ingredient—electricity. The technique involved pushing an array of metal pins through corresponding holes in each card. The pins that went through came into contact with liquid mercury underneath, completing an electric circuit. It worked incredibly well and was reliable.

Hollerith designed other devices, too, including time clocks to aid in administrative measurement and statistical work. In 1896 he founded the Tabulating Machine Company. This enterprise supplied the 1900 census with rental equipment and also served such clients as the governments of Canada and czarist Russia. Over time, Hollerith's company evolved and eventually produced tabulator-printers and other devices. In 1924 the company combined with three other data equipment companies to become the IBM Company. Thomas J. Watson, Sr., who had been part of Hollerith's company, took control of the new corporation.

Hollerith had made one resounding business mistake. He had failed to take out a patent on his census technology. A business rival, James Powers, later took out a patent on improvements he made to Hollerith's techniques and then received the government's 1910 census contract. Powers's company much later became part of the Remington Rand Corporation, IBM's chief rival in the 1950s in the growing computer market.

In 50 years, with the advent of the electronic circuit and the stored program, the clever but simple tabulating machines and data-handling methods of Hollerith and his business successors would evolve into unbelievably fast powerhouses of analytical and computational ability. These would be used to solve atomic equations, trace the dynamics of weather systems, and launch satellites into space. But one of their roots was Hollerith's solution to the problem of counting a growing nation and finishing the job before the next counting was to begin a decade later.

BOOK ABOUT HOLLERITH

Austrian, G. D. *Herman Hollerith: Forgotten Giant of Information Processing.* Columbia Univ Pr 1985 $15.50. Well-researched study by an IBM employee who had access to the Hollerith family papers.

HOPPER, GRACE MURRAY 1906–

From the early 1940s to the present, Grace Murray Hopper has had a remarkable career in computer science entwined with public service and professional leadership. Her story is a unique chapter in the history of technology policy development in our country.

Hopper studied mathematics at Vassar and Yale before teaching at Yale and then Barnard College during the 1930s and early 1940s. In 1944, she enlisted in the U.S. Navy and took part in programming the Mark I large-scale electromechanical computer at Harvard. Mark I was designed by Howard Aiken, a mathematics professor and an officer in the Naval Reserve.

Within five years, Hopper was to redefine the meaning and practice of programming by using the computer itself to automatically translate easier (to a human) programming commands into pure machine-level language. The tools that do this are called compilers and symbolic assemblers. Their purpose is similar to that of automatic transmission in an automobile: each simple action by the driver causes a much longer chain of individual mechanical events within the car.

Initially, there was widespread skepticism among Hopper's colleagues, who thought either that her system would not work or that the automatically generated program statements would not be efficient. In the introduction to her book *Breakthrough: Women in Science,* Diane Gleasner quotes Hopper on this issue: " 'Nobody believed it could be done,' she said. But she thought it was inefficient to start from scratch every time you wrote a program . . . Ms. Hopper's giant step in automatic programming helped launch the computer age." Hopper was not the first person to develop the concept of a compiler—Konrad Zuse had done so ten years earlier in Germany in connection with his electromechanical computers—but Hopper was the first to fully realize its potential and its generality.

After the war, Hopper stayed on at Harvard as a research fellow in the computation laboratory until she joined the Eckert-Mauchly Computer Corporation in Pennsylvania as senior mathematician in 1949. She was to work on and direct various projects, most notably the development of the computer language COBOL in the late 1950s.

Hopper, using her impressive skills in getting professionals to work together, also managed to secure the acceptance of COBOL as the standard language for administrative data processing by convincing a variety of government executives to treat it as the standard language for their own groups. Because the government was a large buyer of computers, no computer company could afford not to provide COBOL to its customers.

Hopper's second career began in 1971, when she was invited to plan and conduct conferences for government managers to promote the awareness of new developments in computers, especially the great potential of microcomputers. She also consulted on better use of computers in the government and served on the faculty of George Washington University.

In 1977 Hopper's work culminated in a request by the U.S. Navy for her to return to active duty in order to work more intensively on Navy applications of COBOL. She was on active duty from 1977 to 1986, when four months before her eightieth birthday she again retired, this time as a rear admiral, in a ceremony aboard the U.S.S. *Constitution.*

Hopper has continued to serve as a special consultant to the Secretary of the Navy and has also been a consultant to the Digital Equipment Corporation. She has written a popular nontechnical textbook on computers, yet another way of fostering an understanding of computers among the general public.

BOOK BY HOPPER

Understanding Computers. (coauthored with Steven L. Mandell) West Pub 1990 $38.75. ISBN 0-314-66590-0 Excellent description of computer literacy issues as well as profiles of people.

BOOKS ABOUT HOPPER

Amann, Dick, and Dick Smith. *Forgotten Women of Computer History.* Dick Whitson (ed). Prog Studies 1978 $49.95. ISBN 0-917194-09-8 Survey of the leading roles played by women in the development of several "breakthrough" computer languages and in the growth of the industry and the profession.

Greene, Laura. *Computer Pioneers.* Watts 1985 $10.40. ISBN 0-531-04906-X Biographies of leading figures in computer science; includes a short but clear account of Hopper's contributions to computer language development and of her skillful advocacy of better use of computers by government managers and professionals.

JOBS, STEVEN   1955–

In one sense or another, Steve Jobs has been a searcher for much of his life. At Reed College and afterwards on a meditation-oriented journey to the Himalayas, Jobs searched for a sense of personal identity and meaning. Later he sought fortune and fame by guiding Apple Computer, Inc., from its beginnings in a garage to a billion-dollar business. Jobs says that one of his proudest achievements is making millionaires of the more than 300 early employees, who received stock in the company when it was small.

Jobs also sought and found talent. A great motivator of people, he convinced some of the best technical people and marketing and management people from other companies that a better future lay with Apple's unorthodox approach to computers. Together Jobs and his recruits helped create a new kind of corporate culture as well as a new image for computers.

Apple began officially in 1976 as a partnership between Jobs and Stephen Wozniak. Wozniak was a wizard at electronic design, and Jobs had done some video game designing at Atari. They met through a mutual friend, and before long, they were running a small business designing and selling "blue boxes" that could generate free long-distance telephone calls. Using the boxes was illegal, but a "techie" subculture had grown up around the activity and was willing to pay for them. Wozniak designed the boxes and Jobs sold them.

When interest in personal computer kits began to grow in 1975, Jobs identified a new market, this time a fully legitimate one. Wozniak designed the Apple I single-board computer kit. About 600 were sold. Later, changes were suggested, and the fully assembled desktop computer known as the Apple II was born in 1977. Within two to three years, it revolutionized the world of computing and led IBM to produce its own approach to personal computing, the IBM PC. Like the Apple II, the IBM PC followed the open-architecture principle, meaning that the designs of the computers' operating systems were not kept a secret. The result was the development of software for these machines by companies not involved in making the computers. Therefore, much more software was available for these two computers than for other personal computers.

Before long, IBM had taken over much of Apple's potential business. The IBM PC was considerably more powerful than the Apple II and carried more clout with large corporations who were already IBM customers. Jobs countered this competition by producing the Lisa computer, which in turn spawned the Macintosh (1984). The goal of these new designs was to give users pictorial control over the computer, via a mouse, icons, and windows. This is known as the graphical user interface (GUI) approach. It was a tremendous corporate commitment, both in terms of cost and direction. Over the course of the next decade, the approach gradually caught on and was imitated by Microsoft Windows (for IBM) and other products.

In 1983, Jobs had brought John Sculley, the head of Pepsico, to Apple to help establish better management control over a company that in just a few years had gone from very small to very large. By 1985, Jobs had left Apple. He now runs a small computer hardware company called Next, Inc., which makes a relatively low-cost high-performance desktop computer product directed primarily at the higher-education market. Ever searching, Steve Jobs likes creating new realities in the market and in our culture.

BOOKS ABOUT JOBS

Butcher, Lee. *Accidental Millionaire: The Rise and Fall of Steve Jobs at Apple Computer.* Paragon Hse 1987 $9.95. ISBN 1-55778-143-5 Biography of Steve Jobs.

Sculley, John, and John A. Byrne. *Odyssey: Pepsi to Apple . . . A Journey of a Marketing Impresario.* Harper 1988 $10.95. ISBN 0-06-091527-7 Story of how Sculley made the transition from running Pepsico to running Apple Computer; includes Sculley's perceptions of and relationship with Steve Jobs.

LOVELACE, COUNTESS OF, ADA AUGUSTA 1815–1852

Ada, countess of Lovelace, can be called the mother of computer programming. According to Grace Hopper, one of the earliest and most creative programmers of the twentieth century, the countess "is now considered to be the first programmer because of her insight into the dynamics of the programming process. [In our own times,] a high-level programming language used mostly by the government was named Ada in honor of her achievements."

Ada, countess of Lovelace was born Ada Augusta Byron, the daughter of the British poet Lord Byron, who died a month after she was born. When she was about 20, she married Lord King. Later he was made an Earl, and her title became Ada, countess of Lovelace.

At the age of 15, young Ada had taken mathematics lessons from Augustus De Morgan, the accomplished mathematical logician. He taught her base-2 (binary) number notation and other number systems as well. She also taught herself geometry.

At some later point, through De Morgan's wife, the countess met Charles Babbage, designer of a computation machine. (*See* Babbage, Vol. 1, Computer Science: History of Computers.) She asked him to be her mathematics teacher. He was reluctant at first but finally relented. When Ada was shown his machine, she understood its nature immediately. Later, when an article about Babbage's machine appeared in French, the countess translated it into English on her own initiative. She added clarifying and enriching notes of her own, which were twice as long as the article. Her writing was so clear that Babbage said she explained his ideas better than he could.

Eventually, they became close friends and collaborators. She supported his project financially. She also devised additional properties for Babbage's Analytical Engine, his general-purpose computing machine. The most important among these was the ability to loop (to repeat a sequence of instructions), which in turn is related to the ability to branch (that is, to skip out of the sequence forward or backward to a desired point). This, of course, changed the whole strategy of programming the device, simplifying it immensely.

The countess could see Babbage's flaws clearly, and she did her best to get him to focus his work more. Laura Greene, author of *Computer Pioneers,* writes: "She found him impractical, careless in his work habits, and poor in dealing with people, and she did not hesitate to tell him so."

However, she also continued to give him encouragement and offered to coauthor new material. Before she could do so, however, she became ill and died at the age of 36. She attempted to leave Babbage an inheritance, but her mother prevented it.

BOOKS ABOUT LOVELACE

Baum, Joan. *The Calculating Passion of Ada Byron.* Shoe String 1986 $21.50. ISBN 0-208-02119 Biography of the countess of Lovelace, who conceptualized the programming of Charles Babbage's calculating machine.

Stein, Dorothy. *Ada: A Life and Legacy. Series in the History of Computing.* MIT Pr 1985 $27.50. ISBN 0-262-19242-X Story of Ada Byron (later the countess of Lovelace), who helped Charles Babbage develop his Analytic Engine.

MAUCHLY, JOHN   1907–1980

John Mauchly and his colleague and partner, J. Presper Eckert, created the first fully developed general-purpose electronic computer. Their work was completed in 1946. The task of designing, building, operating, repairing, and improving the computer was enormous and utilized the resources of the University of Pennsylvania, the U.S. Army, and talented scientists and mathematicians in nearby research centers.

Mauchly was born in Cincinnati, Ohio, and later moved with his family to the Washington, D.C., area, where his father, a physicist, was director of a section of the Carnegie Institution that did research on earth magnetism and electricity. As a youngster, Mauchly experimented with radio circuits (crystal sets and vacuum tubes). He also designed electrical wiring that would permit two different switches to control the same light, a problem requiring binary circuits as a solution.

After graduating from Johns Hopkins University as a physicist with a specialty in meteorology, Mauchly became interested in long-term weather forecasting. This entailed equations that required intensive calculations. He was struck by the need for faster and more powerful methods of machine-based calculation than could be realized with existing mechanical and electromechanical devices. Mauchly began experimenting with electronic approaches, which were much faster. He tried vacuum tubes, which were expensive, and small neon bulbs, which cost almost nothing and worked fine for the purpose of his early experiments. Mauchly had already seen vacuum tubes serving as particle counters in electromagnetic research, and he knew their computational use could be developed further.

Mauchly later became the head of the physics department at Ursinus College in Pennsylvania. In 1941, during World War II, he left his secure and relatively prestigious position in academic science and enrolled as a student in a special short course in electronic engineering at the University of Pennsylvania. Mauchly hoped this would give him the greater technical depth he needed in electronics. At the same time, he took part in special engineering projects related to the war effort. During this time, Mauchly talked to everyone about his ideas for building an electronics-based automatic computer, but few were interested until he met J. Presper Eckert, a graduate student.

Mauchly and Eckert were an interesting contrast. Mauchly had the broad vision, the conceptual framework for the project, good instincts and good temperament, and scientific grounding. Eckert was cooler and more controlled, brilliant and focused, thoroughly grounded in electronics, and unrelentingly practical in his approach to finding engineering solutions. He provided the engineering skill, the project strategy, and a great deal of energy. Still in his early twenties, Eckert firmly and intelligently directed the efforts of a former college department chairman and electronic visionary who was 12 years older. The relationship worked well, and the results started to flow. By the time the project was completed, the world of computation was forever changed.

A research and development proposal for Mauchly and Eckert's ENIAC (Electronic Numerical Integrator and Calculator) was made to the U.S. Army in 1943 and accepted. The army's chief need at that time was for a rapid computation device that could handle a serious backlog of calculations for artillery ballistics tables. Related activities were already being sponsored at the University of Pennsylvania and at MIT and were tied to the army's Ballistics Research Center in Aberdeen, Maryland. The center managed very advanced mathematical work overseen by a blue-ribbon panel of civilian scientists (including John von Neumann).

Mauchly and Eckert's ENIAC took two years to build. It was tested in 1945 and became fully operational in 1946. Soon it was being used for solving numerous nonmilitary problems. ENIAC had become a genuine general-purpose computer, as Mauchly and Eckert had intended. ENIAC was succeeded by the EDVAC, which Mauchly and Eckert designed in the mid-1940s and completed in 1951. It contained several far-reaching revisions recommended by Von Neumann.

Mauchly and Eckert left the University of Pennsylvania in 1946, so that they could retain the patents on their inventions. They formed their own company, which was eventually bought by Remington Rand (later Unisys), and designed UNIVAC computers. The first one appeared in 1951. Almost 30 years later, Mauchly and Eckert lost their patents and the accompanying license fees when John Atanasoff claimed that Mauchly had appropriated his prototype technology for an electronic computer in 1941. The lawsuit was brought in the mid-1950s but was not decided until 1973, when a judge placed the rights in the public domain.

Clearly, in the 1930s and 1940s many people were involved in the development of one form or another of an automatic computer. Just as clearly, the project of John Mauchly and J. Presper Eckert made the general-purpose, all-electronic automatic computer a reality.

BOOK ABOUT MAUCHLY

Ritchie, David. *The Computer Pioneers: The Making of the Modern Computer.* Simon 1986. (o.p.) $17.95. ISBN 0-671-52397-X Introduction to the development of computers that includes a detailed and very human sketch of how Mauchly's efforts and those of dozens of other computer pioneers gradually came together.

SHANNON, CLAUDE   1916–

Claude Shannon is considered the creator of information theory, a description of methods of sending messages from one place to another by the most efficient way possible. Information theory defines information in abstract terms and establishes laws that show how the terms relate to each other. The theorems of information theory were intended to be used with radio and telephone communications, but they can be extended to any system of sending messages. Information theory has been invaluable to computer design and to an understanding of the role of symbolic communication and information storage in DNA and other life systems.

The tool that Shannon used in developing information theory was Boolean logic, named after the mathematician George Boole (1815–1864). In this form of logic, all conditions are represented as being in one of two states: true or false, yes or no, 1 or 0. This two-state, or binary, logic allows information to be represented as a series of yes-no choices, known as *bits* (short for *bi*nary *digits*). Shannon saw that symbols could be transmitted as binary codes. The information content of these messages (the number of simple decisions being communicated) could be measured and the efficiency of different forms of transmission compared.

In 1936 Shannon received two bachelor's degrees from the University of Michigan, one in electrical engineering and the other in mathematics. While working on a thesis for his master's degree from 1936 to 1938, he fused together the most interesting ideas he had learned from each field. In his thesis, he demonstrated how the tools of Boolean logic could be embodied in existing electric switching circuits, such as those used in telephone networks.

Shannon's thesis project grew out of a simpler one assigned to him by his professor, Vannevar Bush, to analyze the logical structure of the Differential Analyzer, the famous analog computer Bush had earlier invented for scientific computational work. Because the gear-based machine had many difficulties associated with intensive use, Shannon began to speculate on what kind of mechanisms could replace it. He seized on the idea of on-off circuits, which were clean, simple, quick, and flexible in combination. Out of that insight came his famous thesis. Three other researchers (Atanasoff, Stibitz, and Zuse) in various other places at about the same time were to develop the same conclusion independently about the value of the Boolean approach to computers.

Shannon joined Bell Labs in 1941 and remained on staff there until 1956, when he moved to MIT. His major achievement came in 1948, at Bell Labs, when he published a paper entitled "A Mathematical Theory of Communication" in the *Bell System Technical Journal.* Shannon's ideas were also published the following year in book form, thus reaching a wider audience in science and technology.

It is said that the years immediately following World War II witnessed three great developments in conceptual thinking within the broad field of information science. One was the successful ENIAC project of John Mauchly (*see* Mauchly, Vol. 1, Computer Science: History of Computers) and J. Presper Eckert. The second was Norbert Wiener's theory of cybernetics (control and communications in machines and living systems). And the third was Shannon's mathematical theory of information.

BOOK BY SHANNON

The Mathematical Theory of Communication (1949). (coauthored with Warren Weaver) Univ of Illinois Pr 1963 $6.95. ISBN 0-252-72548-4

BOOKS ABOUT SHANNON

*Computer Basics. *Understanding Computers Ser.* Time-Life 1985 $19.93. ISBN 0-8094-5654-0 Well-illustrated, well-researched introduction to basic computer concepts and history that includes a short account of Shannon's contribution to computer science.

*Pierce, John R. *Introduction to Information Theory: Symbols, Signals, and Noise.* Dover 1980 $5.95. ISBN 0-486-24061-4 Excellent classic introduction to the information theory ideas of Shannon and to their various applications.

TURING, ALAN   1912–1954

British citizen Alan Turing attended Cambridge University, studying theoretical mathematics and philosophy. He was brilliant and unconventional in a deliberately challenging way.

In a class given by Max Newman, Turing became interested in the question of when a problem could be solved simply by doing enough calculation. He gradually developed the concept of a simple but universal machine that should be capable (from a logical, not a mechanical, point of view) of performing *any* computation. The machine would have its programs (instructions) and data stored on an endless tape. A device would move the tape, a frame at a time, to search for data, to erase old data, write new data, and get its next instructions. Each square on the tape could hold one symbol. This theoretical machine, which Turing called a universal automation, is now called a Turing machine. Having theorized the universal automation, Turing could then investigate its logical properties to help shed light on the computability problem he started with. His description of the machine was published in a paper called "On Computable Numbers" in 1936 when Turing was only 24 years old. The paper influenced many researchers in both mathematical logic and computation by computer, including John von Neumann. (*See* von Neumann, Vol. 1, Computer Science: History of Computers.)

During World War II (1939–1945), Turing and his former teacher, Max Newman, worked for the British wartime project at Bletchley Park, decoding German military messages transmitted between headquarters and field commanders. These codes were generated by an adapted teleprinter machine called an Enigma, which used a technique first developed by American Edward Hebern in 1915. Crucial to the Enigma were its five rotors. Depending on the initial rotated positions of each, a message could be scrambled in trillions of ways when the Enigma was combined with other simpler types of encoding. A given hybrid code was chosen by a combination of key and plug. The Germans changed these choices three times daily, so yesterday's decoding did not work today. To break the code, a method had to be devised to reanalyze messages rapidly at each new session. The Germans thought it was impossible for anyone to do this and so used their system with confidence.

The code-breaking team was a talented, varied, and somewhat eccentric group. It included Ian Fleming (later author of the James Bond novels) and Lewis Powell (later a U.S. Supreme Court justice). Turing's unforgettable contributions were first to design "speed-up" algorithms (methods of improving computation speed through program changes) for the group's eight-foot-high electromagnetic computers, called Bombes, and then to help design the computers that replaced Bombes. Unless these devices were fast enough to enable the Allies to make field decisions, they would be useless. A Turing colleague at Bletchley Park, I. J. Good, has said that the Allies might have lost the war without Turing's contributions, which are still classified as war secrets.

During the war, two different electronic computers were eventually built to cope with the decoding task and pick up where the Bombes left off. The first was the Heath Robinson, a highly improvised machine. The later one, the Colossus, had branching logic (a powerful tool in code breaking). Turing played a significant role in the development of the Colossus and got to see a real computer assembled and in operation for the first time, something he had envisioned and developed theoretically only 12 years earlier.

After the war, Turing played a major role in developing an advanced computer called the Pilot ACE (Automatic Computing Engine), which used a stored program. His choice of the word *engine* was a tip of the hat to Charles Babbage (*see* Babbage, Vol. 1, Computer Science: History of Computers), whose work he had become thoroughly familiar with much earlier in his career. Turing left the project before its completion in 1950.

In 1952, following conviction for homosexual behavior (a criminal act under British law at that time), rather than serve a jail sentence, Turing accepted an alternative and underwent "treatment" in the form of hormone injections and psychotherapy. In 1954 he apparently committed suicide by biting into an apple poisoned with cyanide.

BOOK BY TURING

The Automatic Computing Engine: Papers by Alan Turing and Michael Woodger (1936). *The Charles Babbage Institute Reprint Series for the History of Computing.* MIT Pr 1985 $22.00. ISBN 0-262-03114-0

BOOK ABOUT TURING

Hodges, Andrew. *Alan Turing: The Enigma.* Simon 1984 $10.95. ISBN 0-671-52809-2 Biography, later adapted as a drama on Broadway.

VON NEUMANN, JOHN   1903–1957

John von Neumann gave the definitive form to computing in the twentieth century. He was the kind of intellectual explorer in the world of science and technology who could go out to a new territory and come back with a map that captured it. He brought the emerging world of computer design into focus and sketched out, in various lectures and papers, its connection to the natural world of biology, brain "architecture," and self-replication.

This approach to new fields was characteristic of von Neumann. During his career he moved in succession from abstract mathematics to applied mathematics (including, in turn, quantum mechanics mathematics, hydrodynamics, ballistics, mathematical models of nuclear-weapons firing mechanisms, computational strategies for automated equipment, and the design of electronic computers).

Von Neumann was born in Budapest, Hungary. As a child, he possessed a photographic memory. Having read a book once, he could recite it back, in whole or in part, on demand. He also had a highly developed interest in history and in foreign languages. Later on, he loved to tell at gatherings some of the many stories he had acquired, aided in part by his extraordinary memory.

Von Neumann received a degree in chemical engineering from the Swiss Federal Institute of Technology in 1925 and his Ph.D. in mathematics from the University of Budapest in 1926, with top honors.

By 1927 he was already established in scientific circles as a distinguished mathematician and a young genius. In 1926 and 1927, he lectured at the University of Göttingen, working in a stimulating atmosphere with the best students from all over the world. Von Neumann then joined the faculty of the University of Berlin for three years, developing a worldwide reputation through papers written on algebra, set theory, and quantum mechanics. Each confronted a burning issue of the day. As an example, quantum physics contained two competing theories that both claimed to represent correctly the behavior of subatomic particles. These were the Schrödinger wave equation and the Neils Bohr quantum mechanics model. Flexing his mathematical muscles, von Neumann demonstrated that these two theories were in fact mathematically equivalent to each other.

From 1930 until his death in 1957, von Neumann worked in the United States, at Princeton University. At first he was a visiting professor, but by 1933 he had become a member of Princeton's prestigious and newly formed Institute for Advanced Studies, of which Albert Einstein was also a member.

In the early 1940s, when World War II had spawned wartime research, von Neumann's attention shifted to atomic energy research at Los Alamos, New Mexico, and to ballistics research in Maryland. For each project, he devised the mathematical analyses that clarified crucial issues. In the case of atomic weapons, he showed that the implosion (explosion inward) method of building a trigger for the nuclear reaction was theoretically sound. Until then no one knew for sure.

By the end of World War II, von Neumann was analyzing and revising the logical structure of the ENIAC computer and creating a proposal for a new computer, the EDVAC. When J. Presper Eckert, co-creator of ENIAC with John Mauchly (*see* Mauchly, Vol. 1, Computer Science: History of Computers) first met von Neumann, he said he immediately formed a great respect for von Neumann because his first questions were about the underlying logical organization of the ENIAC (how it was to function and how it was to represent data) and not about its electronics or wiring.

Von Neumann's most famous contribution to computer science was his advocacy of a stored program for the EDVAC in 1945. He did not originate this idea but refined it and gave it central importance within a real project. Alan Turing (*see* Turing, Vol. 1, Computer Science: History of Computers) had published the concept in 1936, and Eckert and Mauchly had also discussed the idea. Von Neumann had carefully read Turing's 1936 paper and even asked Turing to be his assistant in 1939, but Turing had declined the offer. When von

Neumann's paper on the topic appeared in 1945, it either spawned or directly influenced no fewer than five independent stored-program projects.

After 1946, von Neumann brought Herman Goldstine and other talented veterans of various electronic computation projects to the Institute for Advanced Studies at Princeton to develop the IAS computer.

In 1955 President Eisenhower appointed von Neumann to the Atomic Energy Commission. The scientist also developed a growing interest in linkages between brain function and computer design and gave lectures on his observations on the subject. At about this time he learned he had bone cancer. It became increasingly difficult for him to work on his projects, which included a lecture series to be given at Yale the following year. Nevertheless, von Neumann brought his notes to the hospital to continue some writing. He died in 1957.

He wife, Klara, who had herself been a computer programmer at Los Alamos, arranged for the publication of the parts of the Yale lectures that von Neumann had written but been unable to deliver in 1956. The lectures were published as a small paperback under the title *The Computer and the Brain.*

BOOKS BY VON NEUMANN

Collected Works (1963). A. W. Taub (ed). 6 vols. Pergamon (repr of 1963 ed). Vol. 1 *Logic, Theory of Sets, and Quantum Mechanics* $335.00. ISBN 0-08-009567-4. Vol. 5 *Design of Computers, Theory of Automata, and Numerical Analysis.* $275.00. ISBN 0-08-009561-2
*The Computer and the Brain. Silliman Lectures Ser. Yale Univ Pr 1958 $6.95. ISBN 0-300-02415-0 Short, clear, and brilliant presentation of von Neumann's speculations on how to make computers more brainlike and useful, written in the closing months of his life.

BOOKS ABOUT VON NEUMANN

Aspray, William, and Arthur Burks (eds). *Papers of John von Neumann on Computing and Computer Theory.* MIT Pr 1986 $35.00. ISBN 0-262-01121-2 Von Neumann's writings on computers with an explanatory essay by the noted computer-science researcher and writer Donald Knuth, as well as a general bibliography of writing by and about von Neumann.
Goldstine, Herman H. *The Computer from Pascal to von Neumann.* Princeton Univ Pr 1980 $12.95. ISBN 0-691-02367-0 Well-researched historical account of computer development by a leading participant.
Heims, Steve V. *John von Neumann and Norbert Wiener: From Mathematics to the Technologies of Life and Death.* MIT Pr 1980 $13.50. ISBN 0-262-58056-X Dual biography of two of the most brilliant and pioneering of twentieth-century mathematicians who specialized in information technology.

SOCIAL IMPACT OF COMPUTERS

Some commentators on the future of our society believe that the proliferation of computers throughout our economy is establishing the foundations of a "second industrial revolution." This viewpoint is based upon the fact that computers and computer networks have greatly facilitated the transmission of information, the basis of much of our modern service-dominated economy. Whether or not this conclusion is correct, it does serve as one example of the "social impact of computers." Among the references of this section are included some that address not only this issue but also many other issues related to the social consequences of the "computer explosion."

*Asimov, Isaac, *et al* (eds). *Computer Crimes and Capers.* Academy Chi Pubs 1983 $7.95. ISBN 0-89733-087-0 Survey of illegal and unauthorized dealings with computers.

Baber, Robert L. *Software Reflected: The Socially Responsible Programming of Computers.* Elsevier 1982 $51.50. ISBN 0-444-86372-9

*Bell, Daniel. *The Coming of Post-Industrial Society: A Venture in Social Forecasting.* Basic 1976 $15.95. ISBN 0-465-09713-8 Forecast of a "knowledge society" based on information technology and an "intellectual technology" that emphasizes complexity.

*Berger, Melvin. *Computers in Your Life.* Harper Jr Bks 1981 $12.89. ISBN 0-690-04101-2 Discussion of computers for students in grade 5 and up.

Bolter, J. David. *Turing's Man: Western Culture in the Computer Age.* Univ of North Carolina Pr 1984 $10.95. ISBN 0-8078-4108-0

Bradley, Gunilla. *Computers and the Psychosocial Work Environment.* Taylor & Francis 1989 $55.00. ISBN 0-85066-457-8

Brown, Geoffrey. *The Information Game: Ethical Issues in a Microchip World.* Humanities 1989 $39.95. ISBN 0-391-03575-4

*Cornish, Edward (ed). *The Computerized Society: Living and Working in an Electronic Age.* World Future 1985 $6.95. ISBN 0-930242-27-0 Overview of the benefits and trends in applying computer tools to the way we live and work.

*Crichton, Michael. *Electronic Life: How to Think About Computers.* Ballantine 1984. (o.p.) $3.95. ISBN 0-345-31739-4 Well-known novelist and physician's feelings about using a computer.

Donnelly, Denis (ed). *The Computer Culture: A Symposium to Explore the Computer's Impact on Society.* Fairleigh 1985 $27.50. ISBN 0-8386-3220-3

Dreyfus, Hubert L. *Mind Over Machine.* Free Pr 1988 $9.95. ISBN 0-02-908061-4

Dreyfus, Hubert L. *What Computers Can't Do: A Critique of Artificial Reason.* Harper 1979. (o.p.) $8.95. ISBN 0-06-090613-8

*Editors of Time-Life Books. *Computer Security. Understanding Computers Ser.* Time–Life 1990 $14.99. ISBN 0-8094-7567-7 Overview of computer security issues and problems and a look at the safeguards taken.

*Evans, Christopher. *The Micro Millenium.* Washington Square Pr 1982 $3.95. ISBN 0-671-46212-1 Entertaining projection of the future role of microcomputers.

Forester, Tom. *Computer Ethics Cautionary Tale.* MIT Pr 1990 $19.95. ISBN 0-262-06131-7

*Francis, Dorothy B. *Computer Crime.* Lodestar 1987 $12.95. ISBN 0-525-67192-7 A description of the various computer crimes and how they are detected.

*Freedman, Warren. *The Right of Privacy in the Computer Age.* Greenwood 1987 $39.95. ISBN 0-89930-187-8 Exploration of the privacy issue.

Garson, Barbara. *The Electronic Sweatshop: How Computers Are Transforming the Office of the Future into the Factory of the Past.* Penguin 1989 $7.95. ISBN 0-14-012145-5

*Gatlin, Lila. *Information Systems and the Living System. Molecular Biology Ser.* Columbia Univ Pr 1972. (o.p.) Application of information theory to DNA genetics considered as a channel of information; includes views of Francis Crick, John Von Neumann, and others.

Gerver, Elisabeth. *Humanizing Technology: Computers in Community Use and Adult Education.* Plenum 1986 $19.50. ISBN 0-306-42141-0

Graham, Neill. *The Mind Tool: Computers and Their Impact on Society.* West Pub 1985 $32.75. ISBN 0-314-93182-1

Hsu, Jeffrey, and Joseph Kusnan. *The Fifth Generation: The Future of Computer Technology.* TAB 1989 $16.95. ISBN 0-8306-9369-6

Kerr, Douglas M. *Science, Computers and the Information Onslaught: A Collection of Essays.* Academic Pr 1984 $45.00. ISBN 0-12-404970-2

*Lundell, Allan. *Virus! The Secret World of Computer Invaders That Breed and Destroy.* Contemporary Bks 1989 $9.95. ISBN 0-8092-4437-3 Discusses how destructive computer programs can ruin the world of information and what can and cannot be done about it.

*McAfee, J., and Colin Haynes. *Computer Viruses, Worms, Data Diddlers, Killer Programs and Other Threats to Your System.* St. Martin's 1989 $24.95. ISBN 0-312-03064-9 A description of various computer viruses, causes, and consequences.

*Martin, James. *The Telematic Society: A Challenge for Tomorrow.* Prentice 1981 $39.95. ISBN

0-13-902460-3 View of the emerging electronic future by one of its foremost developers and consultants.

Masuda, Yoneji. *The Information Society as Post-Industrial Society. Science and Engineering Policy Ser.* Transaction 1980 $12.50.

McGuire, Francis A. (ed). *Computer Technology and the Aged: Implications and Applications for Activity Programs. Activities, Adaptation and Aging Ser.* Vol. 8, No. 1 Haworth 1986 $29.95. ISBN 0-86656-481-0

McQuaid, Gary. *Pythagoras: The Reality of the New Computer Age.* Heridonius 1990 $24.95. ISBN 0-940539-11-X

*Miller, Richard K. (ed). *Fifth Generation Computers.* Fairmont 1986 $54.95. ISBN 0-88173-050-5 Review of the Japanese and American technological quest for a quasi-intelligent computer that can understand what its user says.

Moursand, Dave. *High Tech–High Touch: A Computer Education Leadership Development Workshop.* Intl Soc Tech Educ 1988 $18.00. ISBN 0-924667-52-4

Nelson, Theodor. *Computer Lib-Dream Machines.* Microsoft 1976 $18.95. ISBN 0-914845-49-7

*Nora, Simon, and Alain Minc. *The Computerization of Society: A Report to the President of France.* MIT Pr 1980. (o.p.) $8.95. ISBN 0-262-64020-1 Account of France's aggressive policy to make information technology a key industry in the growth of that country.

Nurminen, Marku. *People or Computers: Three Ways of Looking at Information Systems.* Krieger 1988 $17.50. ISBN 91-44-27251-0

Oakley, Brian, and Kenneth Owen. *Alvey: Britain's Strategic Computing Initiative.* MIT Pr 1990 $40.00. ISBN 0-262-15038-7

*Pagels, Heinz R. (ed). *Computer Culture: The Scientific, Intellectual, and Social Impact of Computers.* NY Acad Sci 1984 $66.00. ISBN 0-89766-245-8 Excellent collection of papers on the cultural impact of computer tools in our society written by leading figures for a major conference in 1984.

Pagels, Heinz R. *The Dreams of Reason: The Computer and the Rise of the Sciences and Complexity.* Simon 1988 $18.95. ISBN 0-671-62708-2

Penzias, Arno. *Ideas and Information: Managing in a High-Tech World.* Norton 1989 $17.95. ISBN 0-393-02649-3

*Riley, John T., and Judie L. Hurtz. *Organizing a Computer Club for Elementary School Children.* Computer Direct 1983 $7.95. ISBN 0-912007-00-1 Guide for organizing a computer club; can also be used to gain insight into organizing computer activities for older students.

Robinett, Jane, and Ramon Barquin (eds). *Computers and Ethics: A Source Book for Discussions.* Polytechnic Pr 1989. ISBN 0-918902-25-8

*Rossman, Peter. *Computers: Bridges to the Future.* Judson 1985 $6.95. ISBN 0-8170-1058-0 Introduction to the ever-changing world of computers with an emphasis on education and religion.

Roszak, Theodore. *The Cult of Information: The Folklore of Computers and the True Art of Thinking.* Pantheon 1987 $9.95. ISBN 0-394-75175-2

Schiller, Herbert I. *Information and the Crisis Economy.* Oxford Univ Pr 1986 $8.95. ISBN 0-19-520514-6

Shotton, Margaret. *Computer Addiction: Study of Computer Dependency.* Taylor & Francis 1989 $26.00. ISBN 0-85066-796-8

Simons, G. L. *Are Computers Alive? Evolution and New Life Forms.* Birkhauser 1983 $19.95. ISBN 0-8176-3144-5

Stern, Nancy B., and Robert A. Stern. *Computers in Society.* Prentice 1983 $37.00. ISBN 0-13-165282-6

Turkle, Sherry. *The Second Self: Computers and the Human Spirit.* Simon 1984 $17.95. ISBN 0-671-46848-0

*Vincent, Phillip. *Computer Ethics: A Philosophical Problem Book.* Trillium 1983 $9.95. ISBN 0-89824-082-4 Exercises in applied ethics.

Weinberg, Nathan. *Computers in the Information Society.* Westview 1990 $16.95. ISBN 0-8133-0985-9

Weizenbaum, Joseph. *Computer Power and Human Reason: From Judgment to Calculation.* Freeman 1976 $14.95. ISBN 0-7167-0463-3

Wessells, Michael G. *Computers, Self and Society.* Prentice 1989 $21.33. ISBN 0-13-171273-X

Witzell, Otto W., and J. K. Smith. *Closing the Gap: Computer Development in the People's Republic of China.* Westview 1988 $15.95. ISBN 0-8133-7692-0

Xu Kongshi (ed). *Advances in Chinese Computer Science.* Vol. 3 World Scientific 1990 $38.00. ISBN 981-02-0152-4

Yourdon, Edward. *Nations at Risk: The Impact of the Computer Revolution.* Prentice 1986 $19.95. ISBN 0-917072-04-9

Zenger, Chris. *Computer Health Hazards.* World Info Inst 1990 $97.50. ISBN 0-878492-50-0

Zuboff, Shoshana. *In the Age of the Smart Machine: The Future of Work and Power.* Basic 1988 $19.95. ISBN 0-465-03212-5

COMPUTER LITERACY

Computer Literacy is knowledge about and familiarity with computers whether or not this familiarity is accompanied by skills in operating a computer. The role of computer literacy in school curricula has expanded steadily in recent years. It began modestly in a number of ways, for example as a computer-concepts course featuring popular programming language such as BASIC and LOGO. Recently the area of computer literacy has expanded to include word processing, spreadsheets, and database systems. Computer literacy also manifests itself in classroom discussions of topics such as ease of access to information files and the ways in which computers can assist people with disabilities.

*Asimov, Isaac. *How Did We Find Out About Computers?* Walker 1984 $11.85. ISBN 0-8027-6533-5 Overview of computers for grades 5 and up.

*Bar-Lev, Zev. *Computer Talk for the Liberal Arts.* Prentice 1987 $29.80. ISBN 0-13-1163122-5 Computer jargon explained for the liberal-arts student and researcher.

Barlow, Michael. *Working with Computers: Computer Orientation for Foreign Students.* Athelstan 1987 $15.95. ISBN 0-940753-08-1

*Boy Scouts of America. *Computers.* Boy Scouts 1984 $1.50. ISBN 0-8395-3338-1 Overview of computers for grades 6–12.

*Brecher, Deborah L. *The Women's Computer Literacy Handbook.* NAL 1985 $9.95. ISBN 0-452-25565-1 Computer-literacy treatment that has as its goal helping women to feel comfortable with computers and to become motivated to use them.

*Buxton, Marilyn. *Beginning Projects for Children. Thinking-Learning-Creating: TLC for Growing Minds Ser.* Create Learn 1983 $11.95. ISBN 0-88193-101-2 Activities for grades 4–7.

*Calter, Paul. *Mathematics for Computer Technology.* Prentice 1986 $25.56. ISBN 0-13-562216-6 Presentation of the binary number system and other mathematics underlying computer systems for grades 11–12

*Cassel, Don. *Understanding Computers.* Prentice 1990 $30.67. ISBN 0-13-946120-5 Treatment of computer literacy.

*Chandler, Daniel. *Young Learners and the Microcomputer.* Taylor & Francis 1984 $24.00. ISBN 0-335-10578-5 Account of how personal computers can be used with young children.

*Curran, Susan, and Ray Curnow. *Overcoming Computer Illiteracy: A Friendly Introduction to Computers.* Penguin 1984 $12.95. ISBN 0-14-007159-8 Treatment of computer literacy.

*Darling, David. *Inside Computers: Hardware and Software.* Dillon 1986 $11.95. ISBN 0-87518-312-3 Overview of computers for grade 5 and up.

*D'Ignazio, Fred. *Small Computers.* Watts 1981 $11.90. ISBN 0-531-04269-3 Treatment of computer literacy by an author and researcher whose interests embrace family and community uses of computers as well as imaginative school projects.

*Dologite, Dorothy G., and R. Mockler. *Using Computers.* Prentice 1989 $34.67. ISBN 0-13-943309-0 Computer-literacy treatment that emphasizes the understanding of procedures and the accomplishment of useful data-handling and data-analysis tasks.

*Elting, Mary. *The Answer Book About Computers. The Answer Books Ser.* Putnam 1984 $2.95. ISBN 0-448-13803-4 Review of computer facts for grades 3–7.

*Graybill, Donald. *Computer Mathematics: Essential Math for Computer Proficiency.* Arco 1984 $8.95. ISBN 0-668-05845-5 Computer-mathematics study guide.

*Hopper, Grace M., and Steven L. Mandell. *Understanding Computers.* West Pub 1990 $38.75. ISBN 0-314-66590-0 Far ranging treatment of computer literacy issues.

*Luehrmann, Arthur, and Herbert D. Peckham. *Computer Literacy: A Hands-on Approach.* McGraw 1985 $35.52. ISBN 0-07-049186-0 Treatment of computer literacy by one of the founders of the personal-computer literacy movement.

*Rajaraman, Dharma. *Computer—A Child's Play.* Silicon 1989 $11.95. ISBN 0-9615336-9-2 Account of young children's explorations on the computer.

*Richman, Ellen. *Spotlight on Computer Literacy.* McGraw 1984 $14.00. ISBN 0-07-480653-X Introduction to computer literacy.

*Riley, John T., and Judie L. Hurtz. *Student Involvement-Implementing: A Computer Tutor Program.* Computer Direct 1983 $7.95. ISBN 0-912007-01-X Account of how students are encouraged to help other students learn how to use computers; also relates efforts with outside groups such as senior citizens.

Sanders, B. D. *Computer Confidence: A Human Approach to Computers.* Springer-Verlag 1983 $20.00. ISBN 0-387-90917-6

*Spencer, Donald D. *Computer Literacy Visual Masters.* Camelot Pub Co 1987 $15.95. ISBN 0-89218-104-4 Computer-literacy treatment presented in the medium of visual masters for overhead projectors.

*Spencer, Donald D. *An Introduction to Computers: Developing Computer Literacy.* Merrill 1983 $32.95. ISBN 0-675-20030-X Treatment of computer literacy.

Spencer, Donald D. *An Invitation to Computers.* Camelot Pub Co 1989 $19.95. ISBN 0-89218-210-5

*Tatchell, and N. Cutter *Practical Things to Do with a Microcomputer. Computer and Electronics Ser.* EDC 1983 $2.95. ISBN 0-88110-140-0 Discussion of computer applications for grade 6 and up.

*White, Jack R. *How Computers Really Work.* Dodd 1986 $11.95. ISBN 0-396-08768-X Introduction to computer literacy for grades 6–9.

*Wortham, A. William. *I Hate Computers.* Vantage 1987 $13.95. ISBN 0-533-06655-7 Some guidelines to how computers work.

COMPUTER SYSTEMS AND HARDWARE

Computers come in many sizes—as large as the supercomputer and as small as the laptop or palmtop computer. In between these extremes are the mainframe computer, the smaller minicomputer, and the smaller still microcomputer, also known as the personal computer. Inside today's computers the fairly large "central processing unit" of earlier generations has been miniaturized in the form of the microprocessor, a single chip an inch or two in length that now costs very little to produce. As a consequence, computer hardware is within the budgets of many people who would have been unable to afford a computer as recently as a generation ago. This section includes references for most of the major categories of computer, with special attention to both personal and advanced computers.

In everyday life we come into contact with or read about airline systems, traffic systems, television-network systems, economic systems, social systems, and health-care systems. Each of these systems is a group of things operating in an organized way. The systems concept applies also to computers, which are composed of many layers of subsystems, each of which is concerned with a specific process. The process may be as simple as moving a character of data to a monitor screen or as complex as scheduling and executing 400 program jobs. There are many professional fields that deal with computer systems, such as *systems programming, systems design,* and *systems analysis.* These fields, and others, are found in the references of this section.

*Beitman, K. (ed). *Buying Computers by Mail: A Directory of Mail Order Suppliers.* ARS 1989 $16.95. ISBN 0-938630-80-6 Product supplier directory.

*Bolt, Richard A. *The Human Interface Where People and Computers Meet.* Van Nostrand 1984 $20.95. ISBN 0-534-03387-3 Account of the human issues concerning computers; focuses on the frameworks that have been created to let people and systems communicate.

Burch, John L. (ed). *Computers: The Non-Technological (Human) Factors: A Recommended Reading List On Computer Ergonomics and User Friendly Design.* Ergosyst 1984 $17.50. ISBN 0-916313-00-X

Card, Stuart K., *et al. The Psychology of Human-Computer Interaction.* Erlbaum 1983 $29.95. ISBN 0-89859-859-1

Checkland, P. B. *Systems Thinking, Systems Practice.* Wiley 1981 $67.95. ISBN 0-471-27911-0

Currid, Cheryl C., and Craig A. Gillett. *Mastering Novell Netware.* Sybex 1990 $29.95. ISBN 0-89588-630-8

Dillon, John. *Foundations of General Systems Theory. Systems Inquiry Ser.* Intersystems 1982 $15.95. ISBN 0-914105-05-1

Eliason, Alan L. *Systems Development: Analysis, Design, and Implications.* Scott 1987 $34.00. ISBN 0-673-39038-1

Fitzgerald, Jerry, *et al. Fundamentals of Systems Analysis.* Wiley 1989 $45.95. ISBN 0-471-04968-9

Flood, Robert L., and Ewart R. Carson. *Dealing with Complexity: An Introduction to the Theory and Application of Systems Science.* Plenum 1988 $29.50. ISBN 0-306-42725-X

*Forester, Tom. *Computers in the Human Context: Information Technology, Productivity, and People.* MIT Pr 1989 $16.95. ISBN 0-262-56050-X Exposition of the view that computers and people need to work together more sensibly and naturally.

*Gall, John. *Systemantics: How Systems Work and How They Fail.* Random 1977. ISBN 0-8129-0674-8 Perceptive analysis of the nature of systems and the conditions under which they fail.

Gharajedaghi, Jashmid. *Toward a Systems Theory of Organization.* Intersystems 1985 $13.95. ISBN 0-914105-35-3

Gore, Marvin, and John W. Stubbe. *Elements of Systems Analysis.* Brown 1988 $31.60. ISBN 0-697-00738-3

*Hall, Vicki J. *Information Systems Analysis: Introduction to Fourth Generation Technology.* Prentice 1988 $36.00. ISBN 0-12-464363-1 Presentation of recent electronic tools that help the flow of information in organizations and society.

*Harriman, Cynthia, with Jack Hodgson. *The MS-DOS–Mac Connection.* Prentice 1988 $21.95. ISBN 0-13-449448-2 Discusses techniques for exchanging information (files, data, and electronic mail) between the Macintosh and IBM environments.

InfoWorld Consumer Product Review 1990. Vol. 2 *A Year of PC Hardware and Software Reviews.* Prentice 1990 $26.95. ISBN 0-13-453713-0 Compendium of product reviews taken from the 1990 issues of the magazine InfoWorld; includes the results of product testing conducted by the reviewers.

Kimble, Jim. *How to Get Started with Modems.* Comptr Pub 1989 $7.95. ISBN 0-945776-05-5

Laptop User's Guide. Abacus Soft 1990 $19.95. ISBN 0-55755-083-2

Lawrence, Bill. *Using Novell Netware.* Que 1990 $24.95. ISBN 0-88022-466-5

*Machin, Colin. *Computer Systems: Where Hardware Meets Software.* Krieger 1988 $13.50. ISBN 9144-23071-0 Examination of how hardware and software fit together.

Marshall, George R. *Systems Analysis in the Small Business Environment.* Prentice 1986 $41.00. ISBN 0-8359-7445-6-X

*Martin, James, and Simon Grant. *Telecommunications and the Computer.* Prentice 1990

$50.40. ISBN 0-13-902644-4 Advanced-level introductory textbook for learning the field of computer telecommunications.

Martin, James, and Joe Leben. *Principles of Data Communication.* Prentice 1988 $47.20. ISBN 0-13-709891-X

*Metropolis, N., *et al. Frontiers of Supercomputing. Los Alamos Ser. in Basic and Applied Sciences,* No. 7 Univ of California Pr 1985 $40.00. ISBN 0-520-05190-4 Account of super-computers and the purposes to which they can be put.

*Needleman, Raphael. *InfoWorld: Understanding Networks.* Prentice 1990 $24.95. ISBN 0-13-947474-9 Introduction to network concepts and products from the biweekly magazine Infoworld.

*Randall, Alex, and Steven J. Bennett. *Alex Randall's Used Computer Handbook.* Microsoft 1990 $14.95. ISBN 1-55615-267-1 Systematic discussion of the used-computer market by the director of a leading exchange service.

Teague, Lavette C., Jr., and Christopher W. Pidgeon. *Structured Analysis Methods for Computer Information Systems.* SRA 1984 $42.00. ISBN 0-574-21495-X

Weber, Doug. *NOVELL NetWare Commands and Installation Made Easy.* McGraw 1990 $21.95. ISBN 0-07-881614-9

Weinberg, Gerald M. *Rethinking Systems Analysis and Design.* Dorset Hse 1988 $26.00. ISBN 0-932633-08-0

Zaks, Rodney, and Alexander Wolfe. *From Chips to Systems.* Sybex 1987 $24.95. ISBN 0-89588-377-5

ADVANCED SYSTEMS

Chandy, K. Mani, and Jayadev Misra. *Parallel Program Design: A Foundation.* Addison 1988 $34.95. ISBN 0-201-05866-9

*Darling, David. *Fast, Faster, Fastest: The Story of Supercomputers.* Dillon 1986 $11.95. ISBN 0-87518-316-6 Overview 'of supercomputers for grade 5 and up.

Desrochers, George S. *Principles of Parallel and Multiprocessing.* McGraw 1987 $53.50. ISBN 0-07-016579-3

*Editors of Time-Life. *Alternate Computers. Understanding Computers Ser.* Time–Life 1989 $19.93. ISBN 0-8094-5745-8 Presentation of new approaches to computer design, such as the use of parallel computers.

Feitelson, Dror G. *Optical Computing.* MIT Pr 1988 $47.50. ISBN 0-262-06112-0

Kotov, V. E., and J. Miklosko (eds). *Algorithms, Software and Hardware of Parallel Computers.* Springer-Verlag 1986 $55.00. ISBN 0-387-13657-6

Lichnewsky, A., and Z. C. Sague. *Supercomputing: State of the Art.* Elsevier 1987 $97.50. ISBN 0-444-70320-9

Murdocca, Miles J. *Digital Design Methodology for Optical Computing.* MIT Pr 1990 $30.00. ISBN 0-262-13251-6

Uhr, Leonard, *et al.* (eds). *Evaluating Multicomputers for Image Processing.* Academic Pr 1987 $43.00. ISBN 0-12-706962-3

HISTORY OF PERSONAL COMPUTERS

*Aker, Sharon Z., and Arthur Naimen. *The Macintosh Bible.* Goldstein & Blair 1990 $25.00. ISBN 0-940235-11-0 Complete guide to the Macintosh.

*Daniels, Jerry, and Mary J. Mara. *Maclopedia: The Macintosh Hardware and Software Compendium.* Prentice 1990 $24.95. ISBN 0-13-541947-6 Up-to-date product guide.

*Egertson, Eric. *Developing Computer Skills: Operating Principles for Apple II, IIe and IIgs.* Inter Print Pubs 1989 $14.95. ISBN 0-8134-2792-4 Discussion of computer skills for grades 7–10.

Fenton, Erfert. *The Macintosh Font Book.* Peachpit 1989 $23.95. ISBN 0-938151-05-3

Goldstein, Larry Joel. *IBM PC: An Introduction to the Operating System: BASIC Programming, and Applications.* Brady Bks 1986 $20.00. ISBN 0-89303-620-X

*Heid, Jim, and Peter Norton. *Inside the Macintosh.* Prentice 1989 $22.95. ISBN 0-13-467622-X Survey of the Macintosh; includes material for both beginners and sophisticated users.

*Martin, James. *A Breakthrough in Making Computers Friendly: The Macintosh Computer.* Simon. (o.p.) $17.95. Analysis and description of the Macintosh and its operation.

Norton, Peter. *Inside the IBM PC.* Brady Bks 1985. ISBN 0-89303-583-1

*Pilgrim, Aubrey. *Build Your Own 80386 IBM Compatible and Save a Bundle.* TAB 1988 $17.95. ISBN 0-8306-3131-3 Description of how to assemble an IBM-compatible computer based on the Intel 80386.

*Poole, Lon, *et al. Apple II User's Guide for Apple II Plus and Apple IIe.* McGraw 1985 $18.95. ISBN 0-07-881176-7 Classic introduction to and reference for the Apple II.

*Spanik, Christian. *Amiga for Beginners.* Abacus Soft 1990 $16.95. ISBN 1-55755-021-2 Basic introduction to the Amiga.

Stallings, William. *Reduced Instruction Set Computers (RISC).* IEEE 1990 $54.50. ISBN 0-8186-8943-9

PERIPHERALS/INPUT-OUTPUT DEVICES

Computer peripherals, or input-output devices, enable a computer to exchange information with the world outside it. Examples are keyboards, monitors, modems, disk drives, and printers. A widely used peripheral attachment of recent years is the *mouse,* a device that can be moved about on a flat surface to control the cursor on a computer screen. Its ease of use appeals greatly to the average computer user, who increasingly chooses it over the keyboard as a way of communicating with his or her own programs.

*Boyd, John R., and Mary A. Boyd. *Input–Output.* Abaca 1989 $8.95. ISBN 0-933759-15-0 Introduction to computer peripherals for grades 7–12.

*Brey, Barry B. *Microprocessors and Peripherals: Hardware, Software, Interfacing and Applications.* Merrill 1988 $42.95. ISBN 0-675-20884-X Comprehensive treatment of personal-computer systems, with special coverage describing peripheral devices.

*Editors of Time-Life Books. *Input–Output. Understanding Computers Ser.* Time–Life 1986 $19.93. ISBN 0-8094-5666-4 Introduction to input–output concepts.

Herda, D. J. *Computer Peripherals.* Watts 1985 $10.40. ISBN 0-531-10036-7

*Rosch, Winn. *The Winn Rosch Hardware Bible.* Prentice 1989 $29.95. ISBN 0-13-160979-0 Comprehensive hardware product guide covering computers and every type of peripheral.

Sherr, Sol (ed). *Input Devices.* Academic Pr 1988 $59.00. ISBN 0-12-639970-0

INPUT DEVICES: KEYBOARDS, MOUSE POINTERS, AND HANDWRITING

*Fry, Edward B. *Computer Keyboarding For Children. Computers and Education Ser.* Teachers College 1984 $8.95. ISBN 0-8077-2754-7 An introduction to computer keyboarding; for grades 3–6 but may be useful for some older students as well.

*Hutchinson, Betty, and Warner A. Hutchinson. *Computer Typing Made Simple.* Doubleday 1985 $4.95. ISBN 0-385-19429-3 Introduction to the computer keyboard and its functions.

Microsoft Mouse Programmer's Reference. Microsoft 1989 $29.95. ISBN 0-55615-191-8

Plamondon, R., *et al. Computer Recognition and Human Production of Handwriting.* World Scientific 1989 $64.00. ISBN 9971-50-665-3

Radlauer, Steven. *Step-By-Step Keyboarding on the Personal Computer.* Barron 1984 $9.95. ISBN 0-8120-2628-4

OUTPUT DEVICES: PRINTERS

Bennett, Steven, and Peter Randall. *The LaserJet Handbook: A Complete Guide to Hewlett-Packard Printers.* Prentice 1990 $21.95. ISBN 0-13-387235-0
*Foerster, Scott. *The Printer Bible.* Que 1990 $24.95. ISBN 0-88022-512-2 Overview of the world of printers, with detailed coverage of most of them.
Ledin, Victor. *How to Buy and Use a Printer.* Environmental Design 1984 $12.00. ISBN 0-915250-11-X
Richter. *Laser Printer Bible.* Abacus Soft 1990 $24.95. ISBN 1-55755-095-6

OPERATING SYSTEMS

A computer operating system manages the resources of the computer's hardware by keeping a list of tasks to be done, allocating different parts of memory to these tasks, and overseeing the use of peripherals such as disk drives and printers. Some systems require the user to type operational commands into the computer while others merely have the user move a mouse about on a flat surface to indicate his or her choice of commands from a menu displayed on the monitor. This section includes references for all major operating systems, including MS-DOS, OS/2, UNIX, and Windows.

Banks, Michael. *Getting the Most out of DeskMate 3.* Prentice 1989 $21.95. ISBN 0-13-202334-2
Barron, D. W. *Computer Operating Systems: For Micros, Minis and Mainframes.* Routledge 1984 $18.95. ISBN 0-412-15630-X
Birnes, William J. (ed). *McGraw-Hill Personal Computer Programming Encyclopedia: Language and Operating Systems.* McGraw 1988 $95.00. ISBN 0-07-005393-6
Bull, Malcolm. *The Pick Operating System.* Routledge 1987 $29.50. ISBN 0-412-28050-7
Byrd, Joe, and Joe Guzaitas. *The World of GEM.* Prentice 1987 $25.95. ISBN 0-13-967696-1
Coffin, Stephen. *UNIX System V Release 4: The Complete Reference.* McGraw 1990 $29.95. ISBN 0-07-881653-X
Cortesi, David E. *The Programmer's Essential OS-2 Handbook.* M and T 1988 $24.95. ISBN 0-934375-82-8
*Cowart, Robert. *Mastering Windows 3.* Sybex 1990 $24.95. ISBN 0-89588-458-5 Introduction to Windows 3.0 for both beginning and experienced users; uses realistic illustrations and excellent representations of the graphics-based screens.
Deitel, Harvey M. *An Introduction to Operating Systems.* Addison 1989. ISBN 0-201-18038-3
DeVoney, Chris. *DOS Power Techniques.* Que 1990 $29.95. ISBN 0-88022-546-7
Dougherty, Dale, and Timothy O'Reilly. *UNIX Text Processing.* Sams 1987 $26.95. ISBN 0-672-46291-5
Fernandez, Judi, and Ruth Ashley. *The Power of OS/2: A Comprehensive User's Manual.* TAB 1989 $21.95. ISBN 0-8306-2993-9
Forney, James. *MS-DOS Expanded: Beyond the Boundary of 640K.* TAB 1989 $19.95. ISBN 0-8306-3239-5
Goldstein, Larry J. *IBM-PC: Introduction to Operating Systems, Basic Programming and Applications.* Prentice 1989 $24.95. ISBN 0-13-449521-7
Holland, R. C. *Microprocessors and Their Operating Systems: A Comprehensive Guide to 8, 16, and 32 Bit Hardware, Assembly Language and Computer Architecture. Applied Electricity and Electronics Ser.* Pergamon 1989 $30.00. ISBN 0-08-037189-2
Horner, Donald. *Operating Systems: Concepts and Implementations.* Scott 1989 $29.50. ISBN 0-673-38065-3
Jamsa, Kris. *DOS: The Pocket Reference.* McGraw 1988 $5.95. ISBN 0-07-881376-X

Kane, Gerry. *Guide to Popular Operating Systems.* MIT Pr 1988 $37.50. ISBN 0-673-18048-4

*Kerkloh, Ruediger, *et al.* *AmigaDOS Inside and Out.* Abacus Soft 1990 $19.95. ISBN 0-55755-041-7 Guide that includes DOS 2.0, the newer version of DOS.

*Kuveler. *UNIX for Beginners.* Abacus Soft 1989 $18.95. ISBN 0-55755-065-4 Treatment of UNIX for beginners.

LaFore, Robert, and Peter Norton. *Peter Norton's Inside OS/2.* Prentice 1988 24.95. ISBN 0-13-467895-8

Lane, Malcolm, and James Mooney. *A Practical Approach to Operating Systems.* Boyd & Fraser 1988 $40.00. ISBN 0-87835-300-3

Lawrence, Bill. *GEM Desktop Publisher.* Scott 1989. (o.p.) $23.95. ISBN 0-673-38147-1

*Libes, Don, and Sandy Ressler. *Life With UNIX: A Guide for Everyone.* Prentice 1990 $30.95. ISBN 0-13-536657-7 UNIX universe of help and resources, including books, groups, conferences, and so forth.

*LURNIX. *UNIX Made Easy.* McGraw 1989 $24.95. ISBN 0-07-881576-2 Step-by-step software-usage guide.

Murray, William H., III, and Chris H. Pappas. *Windows Programming: An Introduction.* McGraw 1990 $28.95. ISBN 0-07-881536-3

*Norton, Peter. *Peter Norton's DOS Guide.* Prentice 1989 $24.95. ISBN 0-13-662636-X Useful guide written by a leading expert on hard-disk management and other machine and operating-systems issues.

Peters, James F. *Introduction to VAX-VMS.* Prentice 1989 $25.00. ISBN 0-13-502808-6

Prochnow, Dave. *The GEM Operating System Handbook.* TAB 1987 $17.95. ISBN 0-8306-2742-1

*Sheldon, Tom. *Windows 3 Made Easy.* McGraw 1990 $19.95. ISBN 0-07-881537-1 Simplified usage guide.

Sisk, Jonathan E. *The Pick Pocket Guide. Pick Library Ser.* TAB 1989 $19.95. ISBN 0-8306-3245-X

Steiner, Josef, and Gerhardt Steiner. *GEM for the Atari 520 ST.* Susan Dom and Sean Moore (eds). Prog Peripherals $25.95. ISBN 0-941689-04-2

*Stinson, Craig, and Nancy Andrews. *Running Windows.* Microsoft 1990 $21.95. ISBN 0-55615-272-8 Well-organized guide published by the producer of Windows 3.0.

*Strong, Bryan, and Jay Hosler. *UNIX for Beginners: A Step-by-Step Introduction.* Wiley 1987 $29.95. ISBN 0-471-80666-8 Guide directed toward potential UNIX users who are also new to computer use.

*Topham, Douglas, and the Editors of InfoWorld. *InfoWorld: A DOS User's Guide to UNIX.* Prentice 1990 $27.95. ISBN 0-13-219098-2 Guide that builds on the user's knowledge of DOS.

Townsend, Carl. *The Best Book of Windows 3.* Sams 1990 $24.95. ISBN 0-672-22708-8

UNIX Quick Reference Guide. Abacus Soft 1988 $9.95. ISBN 0-55755-031-X

Vassilious, Marius. *Operating Systems and Languages.* McGraw 1989 $29.95. ISBN 0-07-067211-3

Waite, Michael T., *et al. UNIX Primer Plus.* Sams 1990 $22.95. ISBN 0-672-22028-8

*Wolverton, Van. *Running MS-DOS.* Microsoft 1989 $22.95. ISBN 1-55615-186-1 Excellent guide and explanation of DOS, with good examples and a comfortable format.

Worth, Don D., and Pieter M. Lechner. *Beneath Apple DOS.* Quality Soft 1984 $19.95. ISBN 0-912985-05-4

Yuen, C. K. *Essential Concepts of Operating Systems.* Addison 1986 $17.56. ISBN 0-201-12917-5

COMPUTER LANGUAGES

Over the past few decades, a number of computer languages have been developed, only a few of which have thrived. Among the older languages are BASIC, which has long been popular as an educational tool, and COBOL, which was designed for business use. The more recent languages, such as C, Pascal, and LOGO, are more highly structured and therefore easier to verify, test, and revise than the older languages. The references found in this section cover all the major languages as well as many of those less frequently encountered.

Adobe Systems. *Postscript Language Tutorial and Cookbook.* Addison 1991 $16.95. ISBN 0-201-18117-7

*Baron, Naomi. *Computer Languages: A Guide for the Perplexed.* Doubleday 1986 $27.50. ISBN 0-385-23214-4 Computer-language guide for the nontechnical person; gives a detailed review of each of 21 standard languages.

*Barstow, David R., *et al. Interactive Programming Environments.* McGraw 1983 $37.95. A look at software development from many perspectives.

Blum, Bruce I. *Tedium and the Software Process. Information Systems Ser.* MIT Pr 1989 $35.00. ISBN 0-262-02294-X

Carberry, M. Sandra, *et al. Principles of Computer Science: Concepts, Algorithms, Data Structures, and Applications.* Computer Science Pr 1986 $36.95. ISBN 0-7167-8128-X

*Chang, Shi-Kuo (ed). *Visual Languages.* Plenum 1987 $69.50. ISBN 0-306-42350-2 Comprehensive treatment of how the use of graphic images can, among other things, process Chinese characters.

Connell, John L., and Linda B. Shafer. *Structured Rapid Prototyping: An Evolutionary Approach to Software Development.* Prentice 1989 $38.00. ISBN 0-13-853573-6

*Dijkstra, Edsger W. *A Discipline of Programming.* Prentice 1976 $54.00. ISBN 0-13-215871-X Classic academic work that advocates top-down programming, including modular approaches.

Frank, A. L. *A Workbook for Software Entrepreneurs.* Prentice 1985 $40.00. ISBN 0-13-965302-3

Freeman, Peter. *Software Perspectives: The System Is the Message.* Addison 1987 $21.50. ISBN 0-201-11969-2

*Kernighan, Brian W., and P. J. Plauger. *The Elements of Programming Style.* McGraw 1978 $24.95. ISBN 0-07-034207-5 Classic textbook for programmers, giving standards for clarity and expression in programs.

*Kidder, Tracy. *The Soul of a New Machine.* Avon 1982 $3.95. ISBN 0-380-59931-7 Exciting and probing inside account of the successful programming of a very difficult commercial computer system in record time by a group of young programmers working for a corporation.

*Lampton, Christopher. *Computer Languages.* Watts 1983 $10.40. ISBN 0-531-04638-9 Description of computer languages for grade 5 and up.

*Martin, James. *Fourth Generation Languages.* Prentice 1985 $51.40. ISBN 0-13-329673-3 Description and analysis of some of the latest computer languages.

Moulton, Peter. *Introduction to Structured Programming.* Intl Soc Tech Ed 1987 $6.00. ISBN 0-924667-28-1

1–2–3 QuickStart: A Graphics Approach. Que 1988 $21.95. ISBN 0-88022-386-3

*Price, Jonathan. *How to Write a Computer Manual: A Handbook of Software Documentation.* Benjamin-Cummings 1985 $30.95. ISBN 0-8053-6870-1 Comprehensive textbook for writers and software people, showing by real examples how to schedule, write, edit, and evaluate for oneself the manuals and other documentation needed.

*Taft, David. *Computer Programming. Science in Action Ser.* Watts 1986 $11.90. ISBN 0-531-19007-2 Introduction to computer programming for grades 4–6.

*Tucker, Allen B. *Programming Languages. Computer Science Ser.* McGraw 1985 $47.95. ISBN 0-07-065416-6 Systematic, comprehensive treatment of 11 programming languages: Ada, APL, C, COBOL, FORTRAN, LISP, Pascal, PL/1, PROLOG, SNOBOL, and Modula-2.

Voss, Greg. *Object-Oriented Programming: An Introduction.* McGraw 1990 $29.95. ISBN 0-07-881682-3

*Weinstein, Cheryl, and Carol Harris. *Computer Programming for Young Children: A Step-By-Step Guide for Parents and Teachers.* Create Learn 1983 $12.95. ISBN 0-936-38621-5 Approach to program-writing computer activities for children.

*Wexelblat, Richard L. (ed). *History of Programming Languages.* Academic Pr 1981 $53.00. ISBN 0-12-745040-8 History of a number of programming languages, including several contributions by language authors and members of design teams.

Zafar, Z. *Object-Oriented Programming Systems.* Meghan-Kiffer 1990

Zimmer, J. A. *Abstraction for Programmers.* McGraw 1985 $22.95. ISBN 0-07-072832-1

ASSEMBLY LANGUAGES

Amiga Machine Language. Abacus Soft 1988 $19.95. ISBN 0-55755-025-5
Assembly Language Step By Step. Abacus Soft 1990 $34.95. ISBN 0-55755-096-4
Lichty, Ron, and David Eyes. *Programming the Apple IIGS in Assembly Language.* Prentice 1989 $21.95. ISBN 0-13-729559-6
Little, Gary. *Mac Assembly Language.* Brady Bks 1986 $24.95. ISBN 0-13-541434-2
Norton, Peter, and John Socha. *Peter Norton's Assembly Language Book for the IBM PC.* Prentice 1989 $29.95. ISBN 0-13-662479-0

BASIC

*Ault, Rosalie S. *BASIC Programming for Kids.* Houghton 1983 $10.95. ISBN 0-395-34920-6 Introduction to BASIC for grades 5 and up.
Bitter, Gary C. *Bitter's Introduction to Programming in BASIC for the Apple II–IIe–IIc.* Random 1985 $9.95. ISBN 0-676-39570-8
Downing, Douglas. *Computer Programming in BASIC The Easy Way. Easy Way Ser.* Barron 1989 $9.95. ISBN 0-8120-4253-0
Finkel, Leroy, and Jerald R. Brown. *Apple BASIC: Data File Programming.* Wiley 1982 $16.95. ISBN 0-471-09157-X
Golden, Neil. *Computer Programming in the BASIC Language.* Harcourt 1981 $16.71. ISBN 0-15-359090-4
*Kittner, M., and B. Northcutt. *Basic BASIC: A Structured Approach.* Addison 1984 $7.16. ISBN 0-805-34302-4 Learning guide for structured BASIC.
*Lampton, Christopher. *BASIC for Beginners.* Watts 1984 $11.90. ISBN 0-531-04745-8 Thoroughly examines the fundamentals of BASIC and outlines many projects.
*Mullish, Henry. *Basic Approach to Structured BASIC.* Wiley 1983 $27.24. ISBN 0-471-06071-2 Learning guide for structured BASIC.
*Norris, Cathleen A., and James L. Poirot. *BASIC Programming: Problem Solving with Structure and Style.* Heath 1985 $26.95. Learning guide for structured BASIC; emphasizes format and other elements of style.
Schoaff, Eileen. *Advanced BASIC: A Modular Approach.* West Pub 1986 $29.00. ISBN 0-314-98072-5
*Tracton, Ken. *The BASIC Cookbook.* TAB 1985 $7.95. ISBN 0-8306-1855-4 Serves as both a reference book and a guide to programming.
*Ventura, Fred. *Bite of BASIC for Apple II.* Seymour 1984 $7.50. ISBN 0-86651-211-X Learning guide for BASIC for grade 7 and up.

C

Berry, John. *Waite Group's Inside the AMIGA with C.* Sams 1988 $24.95. ISBN 0-672-22625-1
Dr. Dobb's Journal Staff. *Dr. Dobb's Toolbox of C.* Prentice 1986 $24.95. ISBN 0-89303-599-8
Feibel, Werner. *Using Quick C.* Prentice 1988 $21.95. ISBN 0-07-881595-9
*Hansen, Augie. *Learn C Now.* Microsoft 1988 $39.95. ISBN 1-55615-130-6 Well-written guide to learning the C language.
Kernighan, Brian W., and Dennis M. Ritchie. *The C Programming Language.* Prentice 1989 $28.00. ISBN 0-13-110362-8
Schildt, Herbert. *Artificial Intelligence Using C.* McGraw 1987 $21.95. ISBN 0-07-881255-0
Schildt, Herbert. *Born to Code in C.* McGraw 1989 $28.95. ISBN 0-07-881468-5
Schildt, Herbert. *Teach Yourself C.* McGraw 1989 $19.95. ISBN 0-07-881596-7
Schildt, Herbert. *Using C++.* McGraw 1990 $24.95. ISBN 0-07-881610-6

Traister, Robert J. *Learn C in Two Weeks with Run-C and Cbreeze.* Prentice 1986 $18.50. ISBN 0-13-527078-2

Waite Group and Mitchell Waite. *C Primer Plus.* Sams 1987 $24.95. ISBN 0-672-22582-4

COBOL

Popkin, Gary. *Comprehensive Structured COBOL.* Wadsworth 1986 $30.25. ISBN 0-534-06888-X

Rosendorf, Beverly. *Computer Programming in COBOL the Easy Way. Easy Way Ser.* Barron 1984 $9.95. ISBN 0-8120-2801-5

Spence, J. Wayne. *COBOL for Today.* West Pub 1989 $43.50. ISBN 0-314-68967-2

Vesely, Eric Garrigue. *COBOL: A Guide to Structured, Portable, Maintainable, and Efficient Program Design.* Prentice 1989 $39.00. ISBN 0-13-854050-0

LOGO

Abelson, H. *LOGO for the Apple II.* McGraw 1982 $18.95. ISBN 0-07-000426-9

*Bailey, Harold J., *et al. Apple LOGO: Activities for Exploring Turtle Graphics.* Brady Bks 1984 $14.95. ISBN 0-89303-312-X Activities for grade 5 and up.

*Mandell and Mandell. *Complete Apple LOGO Programming.* West Pub 1986 $16.96. ISBN 0-314-96234-4 Introduction to Apple LOGO programming for grades 7–9.

*Ruane, Pat, and Jane Hyman. *LOGO Activities for the Computer: A Beginner's Guide.* Messner 1984 $9.79. ISBN 0-671-50634-X Learning guide for LOGO activities.

*Thornburg, D. *Discovering Apple LOGO: An Introduction to the Art and Pattern of Nature.* Addison 1983 $11.80. ISBN 0-201-07769-8 Overview of patterns in nature, using LOGO on the Apple II.

**Understanding LOGO.* Manusoft 1984 $3.50. ISBN 0-88284-238-2 Introduction to LOGO for grades 4–9.

Watt, Daniel. *Learning with Apple LOGO.* McGraw 1983 $19.95. ISBN 0-07-068571-1

PASCAL

Austing, Richard H. *et al. Advanced Placement Test in Computer Science.* Arco 1985 $8.95. ISBN 0-668-06095-6

Downing, Douglas. *Computer Programming in Pascal the Easy Way. Easy Way Ser.* Barron 1984 $9.95. ISBN 0-8120-2799-X

Nameroff, Steven. *Using QuickPascal.* McGraw 1989 $24.95. ISBN 0-07-881520-7

Wood, Steven. *Using Turbo Pascal 5.* McGraw 1989 $22.95. ISBN 0-07-881496-0

OTHER LANGUAGES

Alam, S. S., and S. K. Sen. *The Computer and Computing with FORTRAN 77.* South Asia Bks 1988 $18.50. ISBN 81-804-0301-0

*Berk, A. A. *LISP: The Language of Artificial Intelligence.* Van Nostrand 1985 $33.95. ISBN 0-442-2074-6 Introduction to LISP that gives a comprehensive set of examples of how LISP serves as a platform for AI systems and applications design.

Bratko, Ivan. *Prolog Programming for Artificial Intelligence.* Addison 1990 $44.95. ISBN 0-201-41606-9

Bryan, Doug L., and Geoff O. Mendal. *Exploring Ada.* Prentice 1990 $31.80. ISBN 0-13-295684-5

Cohen, Norman. *Ada as a Second Language.* McGraw 1986 $40.95. ISBN 0-07-011589-3

Gilpin, Geoff. *Ada: A Guided Tour and Tutorial.* Prentice 1986 $21.95. ISBN 0-13-730599-0

Goldberg, Adele. *Smalltalk-80: The Interactive Programming Environment. Computer Science Ser.* Addison 1984 $38.75. ISBN 0-201-11372-4

Griswold, Ralph E., *et al. The SNOBOL4 Programming Language.* Prentice 1971 $28.00. ISBN 0-13-815373-6

Heilbrunner, S. *Ada in Industry. Ada Companion Ser.* Cambridge Univ Pr 1988 $42.95. ISBN 0-521-36347-0

Iverson, Kenneth E. *APL in Exposition.* APL Pr 1976 $3.50. ISBN 0-917326-02-4

Konigsberger, H., and F. De Bruyen. *Prolog from the Beginning.* McGraw 1990. ISBN 0-07-707216-2

Kreig, Arthur F., *et al. Computer Programming in Standard MUMPS.* MUMPS 1984 $26.00. ISBN 0-918118-28-X

Leff, Lawrence S. *Computer Programming in FORTRAN the Easy Way. Easy Way Ser.* Barron 1984 $9.95. ISBN 0-8120-2800-7

McKinley, Joe. *Beginning FORTRAN.* Weber Systems 1984 $19.95.

Rodgers, Jean B. *Prolog Primer.* Addison 1986 $21.50. ISBN 0-201-06467-7

Schutzer, Daniel. *An Applications-Oriented Approach to Artificial Intelligence.* Van Nostrand 1986 $39.95. ISBN 0-442-28034-3

Skansholm, Jan. *Ada from the Beginning.* Addison 1988 $29.95. ISBN 0-201-17522-3

*Touretsky. *LISP: A Gentle Introduction to Symbolic Computation.* Wiley 1984 $26.95. ISBN 0-47160349-X Beginner's treatment of LISP and associated concepts such as list processing and string handling.

Tracy, Martin, and Advanced MicroMotion, Inc. *Mastering FORTH.* Prentice 1988 $21.95. ISBN 0-13-559957-1

Winston, Patrick H. *LISP.* Addison 1985 $32.25. ISBN 0-201-08372-8

Wirth, Niklaus. *Programming in Modula-2. Texts and Monographs in Computer Science Ser.* Springer-Verlag 1985 $20.50. ISBN 0-387-15078-1

SOFTWARE APPLICATIONS

The term *software* is sometimes used to refer to systems software, such as operating systems and utility programs that are mainly of interest to programmers. For the general user, however, the word *software* refers to *applications software,* for example games and wordprocessing programs that help the user attain some goal that is unrelated to computers. This section begins with a few software references of a general kind, including surveys of software in the public domain. These are immediately followed by applications software listed under topical headings beginning with *Art, Music, and Literature,* and followed by *Business and Finance,* and so on.

Beizer, Boris. *The Frozen Keyboard: Living with Bad Software.* TAB 1988 $17.95. ISBN 0-8306-3146-1

*Bowker, R. R., Company. *Software Encyclopedia.* Bowker 1989 $179.95. ISBN 0-8352-2649-2 Software product guide.

*Brand, Stewart. *Whole Earth Software Catalog for 1986.* Doubleday 1985 $17.50. ISBN 0-385-23301-9 Useful resource for understanding and locating hardware, software, services, and books; includes short interviews with industry consultants and writers.

*De Maria, Rusel, and George R. Fontaine. *Public-Domain Software and Shareware: Untapped Resources for the PC User.* M and T 1988 $19.95. ISBN 1-55851-014-1 Guide to public-domain software and shareware.

Inscription from Saudi Arabia. (First Century B.C.). Courtesy of SEF/Art Resource.

*Eckhardt, Robert C. *Free (and Almost Free) Software for the Macintosh.* Crown 1987 $19.95. ISBN 0-517-56585-4 Product guide for public-domain software and shareware.
*Ford, Nelson. *Source Book of Free and Low-Cost Software.* PSL 1989 $19.95. ISBN 0-96223453-2-6 Guide to public-domain software and shareware.
The PC-SIG Encyclopedia of Shareware. PC-SIG 1990 $17.95. ISBN 0-915835-14-2

GAMES

*Ahl, David H. (ed). *Basic Computer Games: Microcomputer Edition.* Workman 1978 $7.95. ISBN 0-89480-052-3 Classic games from one of their earliest popularizers.
*Bonanni, Pete. *F-19 Stealth Air Combat.* McGraw 1990 $14.95. ISBN 0-07-881655-6 Aid to developing the necessary skills for playing this flight-simulation game well.
*Wilson, Johnny L. *The Sim City Planning Commission Handbook.* McGraw 1990 $19.95. ISBN 0-07-881660-2 Comprehensive handbook that presents real-life problems and current theories of urban design; intended to accompany the educational computer game of the same name.

HOME AND LEISURE

Computer Phone Book Guide to Using On-line Systems. NAL 1986 $14.95. ISBN 0-452-25652-6 Guide to on-line systems for grades 9–12.
*Cummings, Steve. *Mastering Quicken 3.* Sybex 1990 $21.95. ISBN 0-89588-662-6 Guidebook for Quicken, the home finance system.

*Darling, David. *Computers at Home: Today and Tomorrow.* Dillon 1986 $11.95. ISBN 0-87518-314-X Discussion of current and projected home uses of the computer for grade 5 and up.

*D'Ignazio, Fred. *Computing Together: A Parents and Teachers Guide to Computing with Young Children.* Compute Pubns 1984 $12.95. ISBN 0-942386-51-5 Presentation of the social dimension of computing, in the home as well as at school, and the special opportunities it presents for team efforts and learning together.

Grayson, Fred N. *Household Budgeting and Accounting on Your Home Computer.* Putnam 1984 $5.95. ISBN 0-399-50986-0

*Klitzner, Carol, and Herbert Klitzner. *Help Your Child Succeed with a Computer.* Simon 1984. (o.p.) $7.95. ISBN 0-671-49418-X Guide for parents of children ages 3–21 that shows in detail how to tailor the choice of hardware and software to a child's individual characteristics; contains examples of unexpected benefits.

Lyttle, Richard B. *Computers in the Home.* Watts 1984 $11.90. ISBN 0-531-04845-4

*Yourdon, Edward. *Coming of Age in the Land of Computers: A Parent's Guide to Computers for Children.* Prentice 1985 $17.95. ISBN 0-13-152125-X Parent's viewpoint that also is the viewpoint of a pioneer in the development of structured systems.

THE MILITARY

*Bellin, David (ed). *Computers in Battle: Will They Work?* Harcourt 1987 $14.95. ISBN 0-15-121232-5 Discussion of the military role of computers; deals with questions such as the reliability and practicality of computers under battlefield conditions.

*Lehner, Paul E. *Artificial Intelligence and National Defense: Opportunity and Challenge.* Petrocelli 1988 $34.95. ISBN 0-89433-286-4 Portrait and analysis of the role of artificial intelligence in national defense.

Lyttle, Richard B. *Computers in the Government and the Military.* Watts 1984 $11.90. ISBN 0-531-04844-6

*Seidel, R. J., and P. D. Weddle (eds). *Computer-Based Instruction in Military Environments.* Plenum 1988 $59.50. ISBN 0-306-42668-4 Collection of articles on uses of computers for training and education in the armed forces.

SPORTS AND HEALTH

*AAHPERD Research Consortium Computer Network Committee. *Directory of Computer Software with Applications to Physical Education, Exercise Science, Health, and Dance.* Ted A. Baumgartner and Charles F. Cicciarella (eds). AAHPERD 1987. (o.p.) $8.00. Useful list of resources for a wide range of software; published every few years.

*AAHPERD Staff. *Instructor's Guide to PHYSICAL BEST.* Karen Giuffre (coordinator). AAHPERD 1990 $6.95. ISBN 0-0-88314-452-2 Instructor's guide to children's fitness program; includes software and student educational kits.

*AAHPERD Staff. *PHYSICAL BEST Software System.* Karen Giuffre (coordinator). AAHPERD 1990 $34.95. ISBN 0-88314-444-1 Software component (IBM) for children's fitness program for schools (Apple II version also available).

Baumgartner, Ted A., and Andrew S. Jackson. *Measurement for Evaluation in Physical Education and Exercise Science.* Brown 1986 $28.00. ISBN 0-697-00916-5

Baumgartner, Ted A., and Andrew S. Jackson. *Measurement Evaluation in Physical Education.* Brown 1991 $41.03. ISBN 0-697-10067-7

*Christian, Janet L., and Janet L. Greger. *Nutrition for Living.* Addison 1991 $42.95. ISBN 0-8053-1013-4 Useful textbook resource that encourages students to think critically about nutrition; includes optional diet analysis software.

*Cicciarella, Charles F. *Microelectronics and the Sport Sciences.* Human Kinetics 1986 $16.00. ISBN 0-87322-056-0 Explains how to build low-cost electronic measuring equipment for research in the sport sciences.

*Dennison, Darwin. *DINE How to Improve Your Nutrition and Health Book.* AAHPERD 1990 $19.95. Accompanying text for DINE software system.

*Dennison, Darwin. *DINE System.* AAHPERD 1990 $190.00. Text and software for diet analysis and menu planning; includes a database of 5,600 foods.

*Donnelly, Joseph E. *Using Microcomputers in Physical Education and Sport Sciences.* Human Kinetics 1987 $32.00. ISBN 0-87322-083-8 Written for students and professionals in physical education and sport sciences; covers a wide range of sport sciences topics, including motor learning and control, exercise physiology, and biomechanics.

*Gray, Judith (ed). *Dance Technology: Current Applications and Future Trends.* AAHPERD 1989 $24.00. ISBN 0-88314-429-8 Applies such technologies as computers and video to the field of dance.

*Haggerty, Terry. *Developing Microcomputer Literacy: A Guide for Sport, Physical Education, and Recreation Managers.* Stipes 1985 $3.80. ISBN 0-87563-271-8 Role of computers in sports from the managers' point of view.

*Hamilton, Eva May, and Eleanor Whitney. *Nutrition Concepts and Controversies.* West Pub 1988 $44.25. ISBN 0-314-59743-3 Practical, colorful, and clearly written introductory textbook for non-health and non-science majors; includes optional diet analysis software.

Morrow, James R., Jr., and James M. Pivarnik. *Simulated Exercise Physiology Laboratories.* Human Kinetics 1989 $29.00. ISBN 0-87332-234-2

*Sandweiss, Jack H., and Steven L. Wolf (eds). *Biofeedback and Sports Science.* Plenum 1985 $29.50. ISBN 0-306-41995-5 Discusses biofeedback techniques in the context of sports research and training.

Schubert, Irmgard G., and Robert W. Douglass. *Choosing a Microcomputer for Parks and Recreation Administration.* Parks and Recreation Ser. Pub Horizons 1986 $16.95. ISBN 0-942280-17-2

*Sherrill, Claudine (ed). *Leadership Training in Adaptive Physical Education.* Human Kinetics 1988 $42.00. ISBN 0-87322-101-X Contains chapters on computer uses in observing, assisting, and enhancing handicapped students' experiences with exercise, sports, and physical development.

*Whitney, Eleanor, *et al. Understanding Nutrition.* West Pub 1989 $47.00. ISBN 0-314-57831-5 Science-intensive treatment of nutrition based on chemistry and physiology; includes course-related software called Diet Analysis 90.

COMPUTERS IN EDUCATION

The use of computers in the school environment has grown dramatically in the last few years. Not only has computer science itself become an integral part of the standard curriculum, but software for subject-specific applications has received widespread publication. In fact, in an effort to encourage self-directed learning at every level, some computer-assisted instruction is available for most fields of study, including special education.

Abelson, Harold, and Andrea A. diSessa. *Turtle Geometry: The Computer as a Medium for Exploring Mathematics.* MIT Pr 1981 $26.50. ISBN 0-262-01063-1

Balajthy, Ernest. *Computers and Reading: Lessons from the Past and the Technologies of the Future.* Prentice 1989 $24.60 ISBN 0-13-166562-6

Bedell, Kenneth. *The Role of Computers in Religious Education.* Abingdon 1986 $7.95. ISBN 0-687-36540-6

*Bitter, Gary. *Appleworks in the Classroom.* Knopf 1989. ISBN 0-394-39470-4 Learning guide for Appleworks.

Bowker, R. R., Staff. *Software for Schools, 1987–1988.* Bowker 1987 $49.95. ISBN 0-8352-2369-8

Budoff, Milton, *et al. Microcomputers in Special Education: An Introduction to Instructional Applications.* Brookline 1985 $17.95. ISBN 0-914797-18-2

Cameron, *et al. Computers and Modern Language Studies.* Prentice 1986 $46.95. ISBN 0-470-20343-9

Clemans, E. V. *Using Computers in Religious Education.* Abingdon 1986 $6.95. ISBN 0-687-43120-4

Cline, Hugh F., *et al. The Electronic Schoolhouse.* Erlbaum 1985 $19.95. ISBN 0-89859-795-1

Daiute, Colette. *Computers and Writing.* Addison 1985 $16.95. ISBN 0-201-10368-0

Educational Technology Magazine Staff (eds). *Expert Systems and Intelligent Computer-Aided Instruction. Anthology Ser.* Vol. 2 Educ Tech Pubns 1990 $27.95. ISBN 0-87778-224-5

Gerver, Elisabeth. *Humanizing Technology: Computers in Community Use and Adult Education. Approaches to Information Technology Ser.* Plenum 1986 $19.50. ISBN 0-306-42141-0

Grabinger, R. Scott, *et al. Building Expert Systems in Training and Education.* Greenwood 1990 $39.95. ISBN 0-275-93491-8

Hansen, Viggo P. (ed). *Computers in Mathematics Education: 1984 Yearbook.* NCTM 1984 $18.00. ISBN 0-87353-210-4

Harasim, Linda M. (ed). *Online Education: Perspectives on a New Environment.* Greenwood 1990 $41.95. ISBN 0-275-93448-9

Herring, James E. *The Microcomputer, the School Librarian and the Teacher.* ALA 1987 $22.95. ISBN 0-85157-399-1

Milheim, William (ed). *Artificial Intelligence and Instruction: A Selected Bibliography. Educational Technology Selected Bibliography Ser.* Vol. 1 Educ Tech Pubns 1989 $14.95. ISBN 0-87778-220-2

Montague, Marjorie. *Computers, Cognitive Processes, and Writing Instruction.* SUNY 1990 $14.95. ISBN 0-7914-0336-X

Moursand, Dave. *High Tech-High Touch: A Computer Education Leadership Development Workshop.* Intl Soc Tech Educ 1988 $18.00. ISBN 0-924667-52-4

Neill, Shirley B., and George W. Neill. *Only the Best, 1990: The Annual Guide to Highest-Rated Educational Software, Preschool–Grade 12.* Bowker 1989 $26.95. ISBN 0-8352-2766-9

*Nickerson, Raymond, and Philip Zodhiates. *Technology in Education: Looking Toward 2020.* Erlbaum $19.95. ISBN 0-201-11129-2 Projection of the influence of technology on education 30 years from now.

*Oettinger, Anthony G., and Sema Marks. *Run, Computer, Run: The Mythology of Educational Innovation—An Essay.* Harvard Univ Pr 1969 $24.50. ISBN 0-674-78041-8 Early criticism of narrow application of computers to school learning; includes a call for something better and more challenging, such as the LOGO approach.

Olsen, Solvig (ed). *Computer-Aided Instruction in the Humanities. Technology and the Humanities Ser.* MLA 1985 $16.50. ISBN 0-87352-553-1

*Pantiel, Mindy, and Becky Petersen. *Kids, Teachers, and Computers: A Guide to Computers in the Elementary School.* Prentice 1984 $25.00. ISBN 0-13-515396-4 Guide to elementary school programs using personal computers in 1984.

*Papert, Seymour. *Mindstorms: Children, Computers, and Powerful Ideas.* Basic 1982 $9.95. ISBN 0-465-04629-0 Presentation of an educational philosophy that led to the LOGO movement.

Poirot, James, and Cathleen Norris. *Computers and Mathematics.* Heath 1985 $27.95. ISBN 0-88408-424-8

Rooze, Gene E., and Terry Northrup. *Computers, Thinking, and Social Studies.* Libraries Unlimited 1990 $27.50. ISBN 0-87287-718-3

Russell, Susan, *et al. Beyond Drill and Practice: Expanding the Computer Mainstream.* Coun Exc Child 1989 $18.00. ISBN 0-86586-190-0

Schank, Roger C. *Reading and Understanding: Teaching from the Perspective of Artificial Intelligence.* Erlbaum 1982 $16.50. ISBN 0-89859-208-9

Schick, James B. *Teaching History with a Computer: A Complete Guide for College Professors.* Lyceum Bks 1990 $29.95. ISBN 0-925065-32-3

Schwartz, Helen J. *Interactive Writing.* Holt 1985 $15.95. ISBN 0-03-063073-8

Self, J. (ed). *Artificial Intelligence and Human Learning: Intelligent Computer-aided Instruction.* Routledge 1988 $42.50. ISBN 0-412-30130-X

Selfe, Cynthia L., *et al* (eds). *Computers in English and the Language Arts: The Challenge of Teacher Education.* NCTE 1989 $16.50. ISBN 0-8141-0817-2

Shillingburg, Patricia, *et al. The Teacher's Computer Book: Forty Student Projects to Use with Your Classroom Software. Computers and Education Ser.* Teachers College 1987 $15.95. ISBN 0-8077-2824-1

Sloane, Howard. *Evaluating Educational Software.* Prentice 1989 $16.20. ISBN 0-13-298571-3

*Snyder, Thomas, and Jane Palmer. *In Search of the Most Amazing Things: Children, Education and Computers.* Addison 1986 $10.53. ISBN 0-201-16437-X Nuts-and-bolts account of how children use personal computers to explore concepts and problems from the perspective of an early developer of this field.

Spaid, Ora A. *The Consummate Trainer.* Prentice 1986 $35.00. ISBN 0-8359-1003-2

Spencer, Donald D. *Cartoons for Computer Classes.* Camelot Pub Co 1988 $9.95. ISBN 0-89218-124-9

*Stotler, Donald W. *The Self-Learning Society.* Northwest Lib Service 1970. (o.p.) Readable description of self-directed community education that involves libraries and uses computers extensively.

Strickland, Dorothy, *et al. Using Computers in the Teaching of Reading. Computers and the Curriculum Ser.* Teachers College 1987 $16.95. ISBN 0-8077-2823-3

Terry, Patricia J. *How to Use Computers with Gifted Students: Creative Microcomputing in a Differentiated Curriculum.* Gifted Educ 1984 $10.00. ISBN 0-910609-06-3

Underwood, John H. *Linguistics, Computers, and the Language Teacher.* Newbury Hse 1984 $12.50. ISBN 0-88377-470-4

Wilkinson, Alex C. (ed). *Classroom Computers and Cognitive Science.* Academic Pr 1983 $29.00. ISBN 0-12-752070-8

Willis, Jerry, *et al. Computer Simulations: A Source Book to Learning in an Electronic Environment. Source Books on Education Reference Library of Social Science Ser.* Garland 1987 $56.00. ISBN 0-8240-8539-6

*Wold, Allen L. *Computer Science: Projects for Young Scientists.* Watts 1984. ISBN 0-531-04764-4 A guidebook showing how the computer can be applied to a scientific field of study; students can get ideas on how to use the computer in investigations and experiments.

Wresch, William (ed). *The Computer in Composition Instruction.* NCTE 1984 $15.95. ISBN 0-8141-0815-6

Wyatt, David H. *Computers and ESL. Language in Education Ser.* No. 56 Prentice 1986 $14.67. ISBN 0-13-165499-3

DISABLED USERS

Bradenburg, Sara A., and Gregg C. Vanderheiden (eds). *Communication, Control and Computer Access for Disabled and Elderly Individuals: Switches and Environmental Controls. Rehab-Education Resource Book Ser.* Bk. 2 College-Hill 1986 $27.00. ISBN 0-316-89615-2

*Cattoche, Robert J. *Computers for the Disabled.* Watts 1986 $10.40. ISBN 0-531-10212-2 Discussion for grades 7–9 of how disabled people use computers.

Hagen, Dolores. *Microcomputer Resource Book for Special Education: How to Use the Microcomputer with Handicapped Children.* Prentice 1984 $19.50. ISBN 0-8359-4344-5

McWilliams, Peter A. *Personal Computers and the Disabled.* Doubleday 1984 $9.95. ISBN 0-385-19685-7

COMPUTERS IN BUSINESS

Among all computer software applications available on the market, text systems, data systems, and utility tools are surely three of the most widely used. Wordprocessing and desktop publishing are examples of the first category; database and spreadsheet programs are examples of the second. An example of a utility tool is a file-recovery program such as that provided by

Norton Utilities. The references of this section include handbooks for the major programs on the market in the areas of text and data systems and utility tools.

BUSINESS AND FINANCE

Adams, Steve. *Quicken in Business.* Prentice 1989 $19.95. ISBN 0-13-165440-3

Adams, Steve. *Using Quicken on the Mac: Tips and Techniques to Enhance Your Business Productivity.* Prentice 1990 $19.95.

Chamberlain, Martin, *et al. Computers in Business.* Prentice 1987 $40.00. ISBN 0-13-164048-8

Nelson, Stephen L. *Business Planning and Forecasting with Microsoft Excel.* Microsoft 1988 $79.95. ISBN 1-55615-160-8

Schatt, Stan. *Microcomputers in Business and Society.* Merrill 1989 $32.95. ISBN 0-675-20862-9

*Schneider, J. Stewart, and Charles S. Bowen. *Microcomputers for Lawyers.* TAB 1983. (o.p.) $19.95. ISBN 0-8306-014-7 Presentation of law-office applications of computers, including preparation of court papers, correspondence, and legal research.

Thomas, Terry, and Marlene G. Weinstein. *Computer-Assisted Legal and Tax Research: A Professional's Guide to Lexis, Westlaw, and Phinet.* Prentice 1987 $40.00. ISBN 0-13-164468-8

DATABASE MANAGEMENT SYSTEMS

Chou, George Tsu-der, with W. Edward Tiley. *dBASE IV Handbook.* Que 1989 $23.95. ISBN 0-88022-380-4

Cobb, Douglas, and Brian Smith. *Paradox 3.0 Handbook. Business Productivity Library Ser.* Bantam 1989 $27.95. ISBN 0-553-34699-7

Dickler, Howard. *dBASE IV for the First Time User.* Prentice 1988 $21.95. ISBN 0-13-198748-8

Groff, James R., and Paul N. Weinberg. *Using SQL.* McGraw 1990 $26.95. ISBN 0-07-881524-X

Jones, Edward. *Foxpro Made Easy.* McGraw 1989 $22.95. ISBN 0-07-881609-2

*Jones, Edward. *Paradox 3 Made Easy.* McGraw 1989 $21.95. ISBN 0-07-881547-9 Software-usage guide.

Keogh, James. *Paradox 3: The Complete Reference.* McGraw 1989 $26.95. ISBN 0-07-881519-3

*Krumm, Rob. *Understanding and Using Paradox 3.5.* McGraw $29.95. ISBN 0-13-946328-3 Clear and well-developed presentation of Paradox.

*Liskin, Miriam. *dBASE IV Made Easy.* McGraw 1989 $19.95. ISBN 0-07-881464-2 Simplified but substantive discussion of dBASE IV.

Mahler, Paul. *Relational Databases and SQL.* Prentice 1990 $29.95. ISBN 0-13-772310-5

Parsaye, Kamran, *et al. Intelligent Databases.* Wiley 1989 $27.95. ISBN 0-471-50345-2

*Perry, Greg M. *Professional Write and File Made Easy.* McGraw $19.95. ISBN 0-07-881592-4 An introduction to a simple flat-file database integrated with a word processor.

*Ratliff, Wayne, *et al. dBASE IV for Everyone.* Prentice 1988 $21.95. ISBN 0-13-942814-3 Guidebook for dBASE.

*Simpson, Alan. *dBase IV User's Desktop Companion. Ready Reference Ser.* Sybex 1989 $26.95. ISBN 0-89588-523-9 Reference book for dBASE.

Simpson, Alan. *Understanding RBASE 5000.* Sybex 1985 $19.95. ISBN 0-89588-302-3

Smith, P., and G. M. Barnes. *Files and Databases: An Introduction.* Addison 1986 $29.56. ISBN 0-201-10746-5

Smith, P., and G. M. Barnes. *File Systems: Structures and Algorithms.* Prentice 1988 $40.00. ISBN 0-13-314709-6

Ullman, Jeffrey D. *Principles of Database Systems.* Freeman 1982 $39.95. ISBN 0-7167-8069-0

Watson, Jim. *Teaching Thinking Skills with Databases—AppleWorks Version.* Intl Soc Tech Educ 1988 $30.00. ISBN 0-924667-49-4

INFORMATION RETRIEVAL AND ON-LINE SERVICES

*Bowen, Charles, and David Peyton. *How to Get the Most Out of Compuserve.* Bantam 1986 $18.95. ISBN 0-553-34464-1 Guide that shows how to structure interactions with the Compuserve on-line service so that its use is effective and economical.

*Dvorak, John C., and Nick Anis. *Dvorak's Guide to Desktop Telecommunications.* McGraw 1991 $34.95. ISBN 0-07-881668-8 Useful guide that shows how to use network services and shareware to the best advantage.

*Glossbrenner, Alfred. *Glossbrenner's Guide to GEnie.* McGraw 1990 $29.95. ISBN 0-07-881659-9 Discussion of the installation and services of GEnie.

*Hedtke, John V. *Using Computer Bulletin Boards.* MIS Pr 1990 $24.95. ISBN 0-55828-020-0 Guide to the use of electronic bulletin-board services, large and small.

Marushkin. *OCLC, Inc. Its Governance, Function, Finance, and Technology.* Books in Library and Information Science Ser. Vol. 32 Dekker 1980 $55.00. ISBN 0-8247-1179-3

SPREADSHEETS

*Biow, Lisa. *Quattro PRO Made Easy.* McGraw 1990 $19.95. ISBN 0-07-881656-4 Software-usage guide.

*Campbell, Mary. *1–2–3 Release 3 Made Easy.* McGraw 1989 $19.95. ISBN 0-07-881541-X Software-usage guide for Lotus 1–2–3, Release 3.0.

*Cobb, Douglas. *Putting Microsoft Works to Work.* Microsoft 1988 $15.95. ISBN 1-55615-107-1 Guidebook for Microsoft Works, with applications.

*Jones, Edward. *Excel Made Easy for the Macintosh.* McGraw 1989 $19.95. ISBN 0-07-881523-1 Software-usage guide.

**Lotus 1–2–3 for Beginners.* Abacus Soft 1989 $18.95. ISBN 0-55755-066-2 Novice's guide to Lotus.

*McClure, Rhyder. *Fast Access-Lotus 1–2–3, Release 3.0.* Prentice 1989 $16.95. ISBN 0-13-307588-5 Short treatment of Lotus by a leading consultant and writer; includes easy-to-find help in running various kinds of tasks.

*Matthews, Carole Boggs. *AppleWorks Made Easy.* McGraw 1989 $19.95. ISBN 0-07-881587-8 Guide to the AppleWorks integrated package of writing tools and other software for the Apple II family.

Nelson, Stephen L. *Business Planning and Forecasting with Microsoft Excel.* Microsoft 1988 $15.95. ISBN 0-55615-160-8

*Nevison, Jack M. *The Elements of Spreadsheet Style.* Prentice 1987 $12.95. ISBN 0-13-08056-4 Introduction to spreadsheet style, including 22 rules for spreadsheet design and use.

*O'Brien, Bill. *Making Your Macintosh Excel!* Scott 1986 $19.95. ISBN 0-673-18370-X Excel guidebook for the novice; gives extra attention to business applications as well as techniques and hints of an advanced nature.

**1–2–3 QuickStart: A Graphics Approach.* Que 1988 $21.95. ISBN 0-88022-386-3 Short screen-oriented presentation of the essentials of Lotus 1–2–3.

*Schuchart. *Microsoft Works for Beginners.* Abacus Soft 1989 $18.95. ISBN 0-55755-063-8 Newcomer's guide to Microsoft Works.

*Schulman, Elayne Engelman, and Richard R. Page. *Spreadsheets for Beginners.* Watts 1987 $11.90. ISBN 0-531-10232-7 An account of how to produce these record-keeping devices and their various formats.

*Simpson, Alan (ed). *Best Book of Lotus 1–2–3.* Sams 1986 $21.95. ISBN 0-672-22563-8 Comprehensive treatment of Lotus and how to use it, edited by a respected commentator and consultant.

STATISTICS AND DATA ANALYSIS

Haux, Reinhold. *Expert Systems in Statistics.* VCH Pubs 1987 $37.50. ISBN 0-89574-235-7

Hill, MaryAnn. *BMDP Trainer's Manual.* BMDP Stat 1987 $15.00. ISBN 0-935386-05-X

*Jaffe, Jay. *Mastering the SAS System.* Van Nostrand 1988 $34.95. ISBN 0-442-24015-5 Comprehensive learning guide for the SAS system for statistical analysis.

*Norusis, Marija J. *SPSS-X Introductory Statistics Guide for SPSS-X Release 3.* SPSS 1988 $16.95. ISBN 0-918469-54-6 Introductory manual for SPSS-X.

SAS Applications Guide, 1987 Edition. SAS Inst 1987 $11.95. ISBN 1-55544-032-0 List of all the registered applications programs that have been written to run in the SAS framework and that are available for sale or sharing.

SAS Color Graphics Video Training Workbook, 1983 Edition. SAS Inst 1983 $10.95. ISBN 0-917382-41-2

SAS Introductory Guide for Personal Computers, Version 6 Edition. SAS Inst 1985 $12.95. ISBN 0-917382-81-1 Introductory manual for the personal-computer version of SPSS-X.

Soskin, Mark. *Using Minitab with Basic Statistics.* Norton 1987 $13.95. ISBN 0-393-95579-6

SPSS-PC Plus V2.0 Base. SPSS 1987 $29.95. ISBN 0-918469-55-4

Trower. *Using Minitab for Introductory Statistical Analysis.* Merrill 1989 $19.95. ISBN 0-675-21015-1

UTILITIES

*Berliner, Don. *Managing Your Hard Disk.* Que 1988 $22.95. ISBN 0-88022-348-0 Hard-disk management guide.

Bruce, Walter. *Using P.C. Tools Deluxe Version 6.* Que 1990 $24.95. ISBN 0-88022-579-3

*Cohen, F. *A Short Course on Computer Viruses.* ACM Press Ser. ASP 1990 $48.00. ISBN 1-878109-01-4 Standard reference work on viruses and related security issues.

Computer Viruses: A High-Tech Disease. Abacus Soft 1988 $18.95. ISBN 0-55755-043-3

Denning, Peter J. *Computers Under Attack: Intruders, Worms, and Viruses.* Addison 1990 $15.16. ISBN 0-201-53067-8

Dyson, Peter. *Mastering P.C. Tools Deluxe Version 6.* Sybex 1990 $24.95. ISBN 0-89588-700-2

*Elliott, Alan C. *Using Norton Utilities.* Que 1990 $24.95. ISBN 0-88022-580-7 Explanation of this well-known set of hard-disk and floppy-disk management routines that include the recovery of most erased files and the search for specific words in all files of a disk.

*Feibel, Werner. *Using SideKick Plus.* McGraw 1988 $21.95. ISBN 0-07-881345-X Guide to Sidekick, a multipurpose, instantly available program that performs such chores as storing notes, displaying a calendar, and providing a calculator.

Glossbrenner, Alfred, and Nick Anis. *Glossbrenner's Complete Hard Disk Handbook.* McGraw 1990 $39.95. ISBN 0-07-881604-1

Krumm, Rob. *Inside the Norton Utilities.* Prentice 1990 $24.95. ISBN 0-13-468406-0

Levin, Richard B. *The Computer Virus Handbook.* McGraw 1990 $24.95. ISBN 0-07-881647-5

Mace, Paul. *The Paul Mace Guide to Data Recovery.* Prentice 1988 $21.95. ISBN 0-13-654427-4

WORD PROCESSING AND DESKTOP PUBLISHING

Acerson, Karen L. *WordPerfect 5.1: The Complete Reference.* McGraw 1990 $24.95. ISBN 0-07-881634-3

*Anzovin, Steven. *Desktop Presentations.* Compute Pubns 1990 $19.95. ISBN 0-87455-200-1 General discussion of the art of desktop publishing.

Balint, John R. *Type, Graphics, and Macintosh: A Hands-On Instructional Manual Designed to Teach the Finer Points of Macintosh-Based Type and Graphics.* Computer Based Pubns 1987 $17.95. ISBN 0-941929-00-0

Bartel, Rainer. *Ventura Publisher for Beginners.* Abacus Soft 1989 $18.95. ISBN 0-55755-064-6

*Borland, Russell. *Working with Word for Windows.* Microsoft 1990 $21.95. ISBN 1-55615-163-2 Introduction to the Microsoft Word word processor in the graphic interface environment of Windows.

*Bove, Tony, *et al. The Art of Desktop Publishing: Using Personal Computers to Publish It Yourself.* Bantam 1987 $21.95. ISBN 0-553-34565-6 Introduction to the concepts and techniques of desktop publishing.

*Boyce, B., and Marilyn K. Popyk. *The Electronic Office and You: Word Processing Concepts.* McGraw 1985 $11.96. ISBN 0-07-006921-2 Textbook on the concepts of word processing, with emphasis on the "electronic office."

Clason, Kristy, and David Hansen. *WordPerfect Office: The Complete Reference.* McGraw 1991 $24.95. ISBN 0-07-881667-X

*Durbin, Harold C. *Word Processing Glossary.* Durbin Assoc 1984 $15.00. ISBN 0-936786-07-8 List of defined word-processing terms.

Ebel, P., and R. Retzlaff. *Word for Windows Know-How.* Abacus Soft 1990 $34.95. ISBN 0-55755-093-X

*Ettlin, Walter A. *WordStar 6.0 Made Easy.* McGraw 1990 $19.95. ISBN 0-07-881672-6 Software-usage guide.

*Hatsy-Thompson, Kate, *et al. Instant PageMaker (IBM Version 3.0): 20 Ready-To-Run Style Sheets.* Prentice 1989 $39.95. ISBN 0-13-46835-5 Guidebook for PageMaker.

*Heim, Michael. *Electric Language: A Philosophical Study of Word Processing.* Yale Univ Pr 1989 $12.95. ISBN 0-300-04610-3 Close examination of the nature and effects of writing via word processing.

*Hinckley, Dan. *Writing with a Computer: Using Your Word Processor for a New Freedom and Creativity in Writing.* Simon 1985 $12.95. ISBN 0-671-49197-0 Effort to show how to reach a high level of writing effectiveness and satisfaction through the use of word-processing tools.

Hoffman, Paul. *Microsoft Word 5 Made Easy.* McGraw 1989 $19.95. ISBN 0-07-881483-9

Holt, Marilyn, and Ricardo Birmele. *Ventura: The Complete Reference.* McGraw 1989 $27.95. ISBN 0-07-881462-6

*Holtz, M. (ed). *Mastering Ventura.* Sybex 1990 $26.95. ISBN 0-89588-703-7 Guidebook for Ventura.

Johnson, Richard D., and Harriet Johnson. *Macintosh Press: Desktop Publishing for Libraries.* Meckler 1989 $39.50. ISBN 0-88736-287-7

*Langman, Larry. *An Illustrated Dictionary of Word Processing.* Oryx 1986 $29.50. ISBN 0-89-774-286-9 Illustrated word-processing dictionary.

*Lee, Jo A. *Proofreading Skills for Word Processing.* Harcourt 1986 $6.45. ISBN 0-15-309002-2 Guide to proofreading in the computer word-processing environment.

Marshall, George R., and Ken Friedman. *The Manager's Guide to Desktop Electronic Publishing.* Prentice 1990 $27.95. ISBN 0-13-168584-8

*Matthews, Martin S. *PageMaker 4 for the Macintosh Made Easy.* McGraw 1990 $19.95. ISBN 0-07-881650-5 Software-usage guide.

McLaughlin, J. Richard. *MacIdeas.* Computer Pubns 1985 $16.95. ISBN 0-87455-015-7

*Mincberg, Mella. *WordPerfect 5.1: The Pocket Reference.* McGraw 1990 $6.95. ISBN 0-07-881662-9 Compact reference guide.

*Mitchell, Joan P. *The New Writer: Techniques for Writing Well with a Computer.* Microsoft 1987 $8.95. ISBN 1-55615-029-6 Introduction to new developments in word processing and their underlying concepts and technologies.

*Parker, Roger C. *From Writer to Designer: Twenty Steps from Word Processing to Mastering the Basics of Desktop Publishing.* Jesse Benst (ed). Xerox Pr 1990 $24.95. ISBN 1-878567-05-5 Detailed explanation of how the user familiar with word processing can learn desktop publishing.

Parker, Roger C. *Looking Good in Print: A Guide to Basic Design for Desktop Publishing.* Ventana 1990 $23.95. ISBN 0-940087-32-4

Provenzo, Eugene F. *Beyond the Gutenberg Galaxy: Microcomputers and the Emergence of Post-Typographic Culture.* Teachers College 1986 $9.95. ISBN 0-8077-2813-6

Que Corporation Staff. *Using MultiMate.* Que 1990 $22.95. ISBN 0-88022-548-3

*Que Corporation. *Using WordPerfect Library: Featuring WP Office.* Que 1990 $24.95. ISBN 0-88022-555-6 Guide to using the WordPerfect Office program.

*Que Corporation. *Using WordPerfect: Windows Version.* Que 1990 $24.95. ISBN 0-88022-556-4 Guidebook for a new version of WordPerfect written especially for the Windows environment.

*Que Corporation. *Using WordPerfect 5.1: Special Edition.* Que 1990 $24.95. ISBN 0-88022-554-8 Guidebook for WordPerfect.

Rothman, David H. *XYWrite Made Easier.* TAB 1988 $21.95. ISBN 0-8306-3040-6

*Rubin, Charles. *The Macintosh "What Do I Do Now!?" Book.* Goldstein & Blair 1990 $9.00. ISBN 0-940235-20-X Guide and troubleshooting book for the novice.

*Simpson, Alan. *Mastering WordPerfect 5.1.* Sybex 1989 $26.95. ISBN 0-89588-670-7 Guidebook for WordPerfect.

Sitarz, Daniel. *The Desktop Publisher's Legal Handbook: A Comprehensive Guide to Computer Publishing Law.* Nova Pub 1989 $19.95. ISBN 0-935755-02-0

*Vollnhals, Otto. *Elsevier's Dictionary of Word Processing: In English (with Definitions), French, and German.* Elsevier 1987 $136.00. ISBN 0-444-42608-X Multilingual word-processing dictionary especially valuable for foreign students.

*Will-Harris, Daniel. *Desktop Publishing in Style.* Peachpit 1990 $29.95. ISBN 0-938151-15-0 Presentation of the basics of desktop publishing, with emphasis on the pursuit of good visual style and how to achieve it.

Williams, Robin. *The Mac Is Not a Typewriter: A Style Manual for Creating Professional-Level Type on the Macintosh.* Performance Enhancement 1989 $9.95. ISBN 0-938-15131-2

Word 5.0 Know-How. Abacus Soft 1990 $24.95. ISBN 0-55755-088-3

Zorn, Karen L., and Kathy M. Berkmeyer. *How to Use Quark XPress.* FlipTrack 1990 $195.00. ISBN 0-917792-76-9

COMPUTERS IN THE ARTS

More and more graphic artists and musicians are using computers to perform specific artistic tasks. To meet these demands, a large software industry has developed. For example, many graphic artists use elaborate "paintbrush" programs that have been written for use with the Apple II series, the Macintosh, and the IBM PC and its clones. In the field of music, a number of music synthesizers are on the market in the form of software and hardware add-ons that allow a computer to imitate the sound of any instrument from a violin to a piano. These fields and others such as animation are represented in the listings of this section.

ANIMATION

Adams, Lee. *High Performance Graphics in C: Animation and Simulation.* TAB 1988 $27.95. ISBN 0-8306-9349-1
*Hayward, Stan. *Computers for Animation.* Focal 1984 $39.95. ISBN 0-240-51049-6 General treatment of the use of computers in animation work as of 1984; includes contributions of the microcomputer, mainframe, and supercomputer.
*Person, Ron. *Animation Magic with Your Apple IIe and IIc.* McGraw 1985 $15.95. ISBN 0-07-881161-9 Guide that shows how to animate your Apple II output.

ART, MUSIC, AND LITERATURE

Angell, Ian O. *Computer Geometric Art.* Dover 1985 $3.50. ISBN 0-486-24855-0
*Banks, Michael A., and Ansen Dibell. *Word Processing Secrets for Writers.* Writers Digest 1989 $14.95. ISBN 0-89879-348-3 Recommended for anyone involved in word processing; includes tips and shortcuts as well as some basics.
Bartles, Barton K. *Computer Software in Music and Music Education: A Guide.* Scarecrow 1987 $25.00. ISBN 0-8108-2056-0
Bigelow, Steven. *Making Music with Personal Computers.* Park Row 1987 $12.95. ISBN 0-935749-21-7
*Bolognese, Don, and Robert Thornton. *Drawing and Painting with the Computer.* Watts 1983 $10.90. ISBN 0-531-04653-2 An outline of techniques in using the computer to create artworks.
DeWeese, Gene. *Computers in Entertainment and the Arts.* Watts 1984 $11.90. ISBN 0-531-04843-8
Donaldson, Peter. *A Guide to Computer Music: An Introductory Resource.* Sound Mgmt 1988 $16.95. ISBN 0-9621514-0-8
*Flanagan, Floyd. *MacCats: 99 Ways to Paint a Cat with MacPaint.* Scott 1985 $5.95. ISBN 0-673-18143-X Presentation of MacPaint that shows how to make the most of this built-in Macintosh drawing and painting program.
Goodman, Cynthia. *Digital Visions: Computer and Art.* Abrams 1987 $29.95. ISBN 0-8109-1862-5
Grieman, April. *Hybrid Imagery: The Fusion of Technology and Graphic Design.* Watson-Guptill 1990 $45.00. ISBN 0-8230-2518-7
*Hofstetter, Fred T. *Computer Literacy for Musicians.* Prentice 1988 $34.00. ISBN 0-13-164477-7 Computer-literacy guide especially for the interests and needs of musicians.
Kozak, Donals. *Guide to Computer Music: Electronic Music Resource.* Sound Mgmt 1990 $19.95. ISBN 0-9621514-1-6
Lansdown, J., and R. A. Earnshaw (eds). *Computers in Art, Design, and Animation.* Springer-Verlag 1989 $79.80. ISBN 0-387-96896-2
Loveless, Richard L. (ed). *The Computer Revolution and the Arts.* Univ Presses FL 1989 $32.95. ISBN 0-8130-0912-X
Making Music on the Amiga. Abacus Soft 1990 $34.95. ISBN 0-55755-094-8
Prueitt, Melvin L. *Art and the Computer.* McGraw 1985 $39.95. ISBN 0-07-050899-2
Racter. *The Policeman's Beard is Half-Constructed: Computer Prose and Poetry.* Warner Bks 1984 $9.95. ISBN 0-446-38051-2

Wilson, Stephen. *Using Computers to Create Art.* Prentice 1986 $37.00. ISBN 0-13-938341-7

Winsor, Phil. *Computer Assisted Music Composition.* Petrocelli 1987 $29.95. ISBN 0-89433-262-7

GRAPHICS AND IMAGE PROCESSING

Association for Information and Image Management Staff and Jacqueline Virando. *Software for Information and Image Management.* Assn Inform & Image 1988 $30.00. ISBN 0-89258-131-X

*Baldwin, Margaret, and Gary Pack. *Computer Graphics.* Watts 1984 $10.40. ISBN 0-531-04704-0 Introduction to computer graphics for grades 6–8.

Basov, N.G. *Lasers and Holographic Data Processing.* Imported 1985 $7.95. ISBN 0-8285-2883-7

Berg, Brian, and Judith P. Roth. *Software for Optical Storage.* Meckler 1989 $47.50. ISBN 0-88736-379-2

Cathey, W. Thomas. *Optical Information Processing and Holography.* Krieger 1989 $49.95. ISBN 0-471-14078-3

*Curran, Susan, and Ray Curnow. *Games, Graphics and Sounds.* Simon 1983 $9.95. ISBN 0-671-49444-9 Focuses on controlling the graphics and sound capabilities of the computer in the game environment.

Danuloff, Craig. *Expert Adviser: Harvard Graphics.* Addison 1990 $22.95. ISBN 0-201-52369-8

Freeman, Raymond. *High Resolution NMR: A Handbook of Principles.* Wiley 1987 $54.95. ISBN 0-470-20812-0

Johnson, Nelson. *AutoCAD: The Complete Reference.* McGraw 1989 $39.95. ISBN 0-07-881614-9

*Kettelkamp, Larry. *Computer Graphics: How It Works, What It Does.* Morrow 1989 $12.95. Discussion of how computer graphics work, with investigation into their applications and important people and programs in the field.

*Masterson, Richard. *Exploring Careers in Computer Graphics. Exploring Careers Ser.* Rosen Grp 1990 $11.95. ISBN 0-8239-0632-9 Guide to careers in computer graphics for grades 11–12.

Matthews, Judy G., *et al. Clipart and Dynamic Designs for Libraries and Media Centers.* Vol. 2 *Computers and Audiovisual.* Libraries Unlimited 1989 $26.50. ISBN 0-87287-750-7

*Omura, George. *Mastering AutoCAD.* Sybex 1988 $29.95. ISBN 0-89588-574-8 Guidebook for AutoCAD.

Rice, Harbert, and Daniel Raker. *Inside AutoCAD: The Complete AutoCAD Reference Guide.* New Riders 1989 $29.95. ISBN 0-934035-49-0

Rogers, David F., and J. Alan Adams. *Mathematical Elements for Computer Graphics.* McGraw 1990 $39.85. ISBN 0-07-053529-9

Schmieman, Susan. *MacPaint: Drawing, Drafting, Design.* Prentice 1985 $15.95. ISBN 0-89303-648-X

*Schwartz, Roberta, and Michael Callery. *Apple Graphics: Tools and Techniques.* Prentice 1986 $23.95. ISBN 0-13-039512-9 Treatment of Apple II high-resolution graphics.

Sennrich, Bruno, *et al. Amiga 3D Graphic Programming in BASIC.* Abacus Soft 1990 $19.95. ISBN 0-55755-044-1

*Spencer, Donald D. *Illustrated Computer Graphics Dictionary.* Camelot Pub Co 1990 $24.95. ISBN 0-89218-117-6 Dictionary of computer graphics.

Thorell, Lisa G., and Wanda J. Smith. *Using Computer Color Effectively: An Illustrated Reference to Computer Color Interface.* Prentice 1989 $49.95. ISBN 0-13-930878-3

Traister, Robert J. *Programming Halo Graphics in C.* Prentice 1986 $21.95. ISBN 0-13-729310-0

Truckenbrod, Joan. *Creative Computer Imaging.* Prentice 1988 $29.80. ISBN 0-13-189309-2

Watt, Alan. *Fundamentals of Three-Dimensional Computer Graphics.* Addison 1989 $38.75. ISBN 0-201-15442-0
*Whitney, Patrick. *Computers in Design.* Random 1985 $12.00. ISBN 0-394-34305-0 Introduction to the use of computers as an adjunct to the design and drawing activities of artists, engineers, graphic designers, and industrial designers.
Zahoran, David G. *Harvard Graphics.* Wordware 1990 $21.95. ISBN 1-55622-164-9

SOUND AND VOICE PROCESSING

*Cater, John P. *Electronically Hearing: Computer Speech Recognition.* Sams 1983. (o.p.) Introduction to speech recognition.
*Cater, John P. *Electronically Speaking: Computer Speech Generation.* Sams 1983. (o.p.) Introduction to speech synthesis.
*Curtis, Jack F. *Introduction to Computers in Speech, Language, and Hearing.* College-Hill 1986 $20.00. ISBN 0-316-16551-4 Broad survey of computer applications in these fields, including research activities.
Flanagan, J. L. *Speech Analysis, Synthesis, and Perception.* Springer-Verlag 1983 $57.00. ISBN 0-387-05561-4
Holmes, J. N. *Speech Synthesis and Recognition.* Van Nostrand 1988 $41.95. ISBN 0-278-00013-4
*House, A. S. (ed). *The Recognition of Speech by a Machine—A Bibliography.* Academic Pr 1988 $49.95. ISBN 0-12-356785-8 Bibliography of speech-recognition books and articles.
Huber, David M. *The MIDI Manual.* Sams 1990 $24.95. ISBN 0-672-22757-6
Prochnow, Dave. *Chip Talk: Projects in Speech Synthesis.* TAB 1987 $24.95. ISBN 0-8306-2812-6
Teja, Ed, and Gary Gonnella. *Voice Technology.* Prentice 1983 $39.00. ISBN 0-8359-8417-6
*Witten, Ian H. *Making Computers Talk: An Introduction to Speech Synthesis.* Prentice 1986 $30.80. ISBN 0-13-545690-8 Introduction to the technologies and strategies behind the broad collection of activities called speech synthesis.
Yannakoudakis, E. J., and P. J. Hutton. *Speech Synthesis and Recognition Systems.* Prentice 1987 $54.95. ISBN 0-470-20959-3

MULTIMEDIA PROCESSING

*Anderson, Carol J., and Mark D. Velijkov. *Creating Interactive Multimedia: A Practical Guide.* Scott 1990 $27.95. ISBN 0-673-46141-6 Guide that shows how to use hypertext systems to control multimedia displays and interactions.
Anzovin, Steven. *Amiga Desktop Video.* Compute Pubns 1989 $19.95. ISBN 0-87455-171-4
*Bolter, J. *The Writing Space: The Computer and the History of Writing.* Erlbaum 1990 $17.50. ISBN 0-8058-0427-7 Account of the development of both writing and hypertext writing.
Bove, Tony. *Using Macromind Director.* Que 1990 $29.95. ISBN 0-88022-578-5
*Gluck, Myke. *Hypercard, Hypertext, and Hypermedia for Librarians.* Libraries Unlimited 1990 $28.50. ISBN 0-87287-723-X Presentation of general concepts and library applications for hypertext information structures and media.
Goodman, Denny. *The Complete Hyper-Card 2.0 Handbook.* Bantam 1990 $29.95. ISBN 0-553-34893-0
Hashim, Safaa H. *Exploring Hypertext Programming: Writing Knowledge Representation and Problem-Solving Programs.* TAB 1990 $22.95. ISBN 0-8306-3208-5

*Horton, William K. *Designing and Writing Online Documentation: Help Files to Hypertext.* Wiley 1989 $24.95. ISBN 0-471-50772-5 Discussion of techniques for augmenting hypertext systems.

*Jonassen, David H. *Hypertext–Hypermedia.* Educ Tech Pubns 1989 $24.95. ISBN 0-87778-217-2 Treatment of hypertexts as media.

Martin, James. *Hyperdocuments and How to Create Them.* Prentice 1990 $24.95. ISBN 0-13-447905-X

*McGrew, P. C., and W. D. McDaniel. *On-Line Text Management: Hypertext and Other Techniques.* McGraw 1989 $39.95 ISBN 0-07-046263-1 Description of how to store and manage a database of tailored, structured text that is intended to be read selectively by several people in an on-line environment.

Michel, Stephen L. *HyperCard: The Complete Reference.* McGraw 1988. (o.p.) $24.95. ISBN 0-07-881430-8

*Neilsen, Jacob. *Hypertext and Hypermedia.* Academic Pr 1990 $29.95. ISBN 0-12-518410-7 Comprehensive treatment of the concept of hypertext documents as a new style and structure of communication.

Schweir, Richard. *Interactive Video.* Educ Tech Pubns 1987 $36.95. ISBN 0-87778-206-7

*Seyer, Philip. *Understanding Hypertext: Concepts and Applications.* TAB 1989 $19.95 ISBN 0-8306-3308-1 Theory and practice of hypertext.

Wilson, Stephen. *Multimedia Design with Hypercard.* Prentice 1990 $24.95. ISBN 0-13-488891-X

Winkler, Dan. *HyperTalk the Book* Bantam 1990 $29.95 ISBN 0-553-34737-3

*Wright, Guy. *Amiga Desktop Video Guide.* Abacus Soft 1990 $19.95. ISBN 0-55755-057-3 Guide to "desktop video," the editing and processing of video with the aid of a desktop personal computer.

ARTIFICIAL INTELLIGENCE

The term *artificial intelligence* refers to machines that behave as if they were thinking. Two of its important branches are *expert systems* and *robotics.* The first has been applied to fields such as medical diagnosis and financial decision-making. The second involves the study of robots, their design, manufacture, and use—concerns that are prevalent in today's technological world. Each of these major aspects of artificial intelligence appears under its own heading in the listing of references that follow.

Aleksander, Igor, and Piers Burnett. *Thinking Machines: The Search for Artificial Intelligence.* Knopf 1987 $17.95. ISBN 0-394-74459-4

Angel, Leonard. *How to Build a Conscious Machine.* Westview 1989 $34.95. ISBN 0-8133-0944-1

Artificial Intelligence Systems in Government, 5th Conference. IEEE 1990 $60.00. ISBN 0-8186-2044-7

Beardon, Colin (ed). *Artificial Intelligence Terminology: A Reference Guide.* Prentice 1980 $29.95. ISBN 0-470-21601-8

Bellman, Richard. *An Introduction to Artificial Intelligence: Can Computers Think?* Boyd & Fraser 1978 $20.00. ISBN 0-87835-149-3

Born, Rainer. *Artificial Intelligence: The Case Against.* St. Martin's 1987 $29.95. ISBN 0-312-00439-7

*D'Ignazio, Fred, and Allen L. Wold. *Science of Artificial Intelligence.* Watts 1984 $10.40. ISBN 0-531-04703-2 Defines and explains artificial intelligence and compares it with human intelligence; robotics, pattern recognition, natural language, game playing, knowledge engineering, and human services are discussed.

*Forsyth, Richard. *Machines That Think.* Watts 1986 $10.90. ISBN 0-531-19017-X An introduction to artificial intelligence, how these machines work, and what they can and cannot do.

Hartnell, Tim. *Exploring Artificial Intelligence on Your Apple II.* Bantam 1985 $14.95. ISBN 0-553-34261-4

Haugeland, John. *Artificial Intelligence: The Very Idea.* MIT Pr 1989 $9.95. ISBN 0-262-58095-0

Herken, Rolf. *The Universal Turing Machine: A Half-Century Survey.* Oxford Univ Pr 1988 $115.00. ISBN 0-19-853741-7

Jackson, Philip C., Jr. *Introduction to Artificial Intelligence.* Dover 1985 $8.95. ISBN 0-486-24864-X

*Johnson, George. *Machinery of the Mind: Inside the New Science of Artificial Intelligence.* Microsoft 1987 $9.95. ISBN 1-55615-010-5 Survey of artificial intelligence, its movements, people, and controversies; includes a selective bibliography.

Kennedy, Noah. *Industrialization of Intelligence: Mind and Machine in the Modern Age.* Unwin 1990 $24.95. ISBN 0-04-440345-3

Kernoff, Alan (ed). *Who's Who in AI—A Guide to People, Products, Companies, Resources, Schools.* WWAI 1986 $95.00. ISBN 0-937287-00-8

Kott, L. (ed). *Automata, Languages and Programming. Lecture Notes in Computer Science Ser.* Vol. 226 Springer-Verlag 1986 $34.00. ISBN 0-387-16761-7

Kurzweil, Raymond. *The Age of Intelligent Machines.* MIT Pr 1990 $25.00. ISBN 0-262-11121-7

*McCorduck, Pamela. *Machines Who Think: A Personal Inquiry into the History and Prospects of Artificial Intelligence.* Freeman 1981 $14.95. ISBN 0-7167-1135-4 Introduction to artificial intelligence based on personal experience and interviews.

McCorduck, Pamela. *The Universal Machine: Confessions of a Technological Optimist.* McGraw 1985 $16.95. ISBN 0-07-044882-5

Mazurkiewicz, A. (ed). *Mathematical Foundations of Computer Science 1976. Lecture Notes in Computer Science Ser.* Springer-Verlag 1976 $29.00. ISBN 0-387-07854-1

Minsky, Marvin. *Finite and Infinite Machines.* Prentice 1967 $53.40. ISBN 0-13-165563-9

*Minsky, Marvin. *A Society of Mind.* Simon 1988 $12.95. ISBN 0-671-65713-5 Popular treatment of the significance of artificial intelligence.

*Mishkoff, Henry C. *Understanding Artificial Intelligence.* Sams 1988. ISBN 0-672-27271-7 Guidebook on artificial intelligence that gives an overview of the fundamentals, how it is used, and how it may affect our lives; easy-to-read material for students.

Platt, Charles. *Artificial Intelligence in Action.* Trillium 1985 $12.95. ISBN 0-89824-119-7

Praft, Vernon. *Thinking Machines: The Evolution of Artificial Intelligence.* Basil Blackwell 1987 $24.95. ISBN 0-631-14953-8

Raphael, Bertram. *The Thinking Computer: Mind Inside Matter.* Freeman 1976 $16.95. ISBN 0-7167-0723-3

*Shapiro, Stuart C. (ed). *The Encyclopedia of Artificial Intelligence.* 2 vols. Wiley 1990 $80.00. ISBN 0-471-52079-9 Articles by more than 200 contributors, each one accompanied by its own bibliography; over 5,000 entries.

*Simon, Herbert A. *Sciences of the Artificial.* MIT Pr 1981 $9.95. ISBN 0-262-69073-X Classic on the nature of the difference between the natural sciences and the design sciences, by the father of the process model in behavioral psychology.

Taylor, William A. *What Every Engineer Should Know About Artificial Intelligence.* MIT Pr 1988 $25.00. ISBN 0-262-20069-4

Turing, Alan, and Michael Woodger. *The Automatic Computing Engine: Papers by Alan Turing and Michael Woodger. The Charles Babbage Institute Reprint Series for the History of Computing.* MIT Pr 1985 $22.00. ISBN 0-262-03114-0

*Waldrop, M. Mitchell. *Man-Made Minds.* Walker 1987 $14.95. ISBN 0-8027-7297-8 Overall assessment of artificial intelligence; closely examines the attempts to teach computers to learn, reason, and use language.

Winston, Patrick. *Artificial Intelligence at MIT: Expanding Frontiers.* 2 vols. MIT Pr 1990. Vol. 1 $35.00. ISBN 0-262-23150-6. Vol. 2 $35.00. ISBN 0-262-23151-4

HUMAN, SOCIAL, AND PHILOSOPHICAL ISSUES

Bloomfield, Brian P. (ed). *The Question of Artificial Intelligence: Philosophical and Sociological Perspectives.* Routledge 1988 $59.00. ISBN 0-7099-3957-4

*Boden, Margaret. *Artificial Intelligence and Natural Man.* Basic 1987 $15.95. ISBN 0-465-00456-3 Textbook that gives an introduction to artificial intelligence from a philosopher's point of view.

Brink, J. R., and C. R. Haden (eds). *The Computer and the Brain: Perspectives on Human and Artificial Intelligence.* Elsevier 1989 $61.75. ISBN 0-444-88045-3

Campbell, Jerry. *The Improbable Machine: What the New Upheaval in Artificial Intelligence Research Reveals About How the Mind Really Works.* Simon 1989 $19.95. ISBN 0-671-65711-9

Carbonell, Jaime. *Machine Learning: Paradigms and Methods.* MIT Pr 1990 $27.50. ISBN 0-262-53088-0

Chiou, Wu Co, Sr. (ed). *Space Station Automation.* SPIE 1986 $50.00. ISBN 0-89252-764-1

Collins, Alan, and Edward Smith (eds). *Readings in Cognitive Science: A Perspective from Psychology and Artificial Intelligence.* Morgan Kaufmann 1988 $38.95. ISBN 0-55860-013-2

Collins, H. M. *Artificial Experts: Social Knowledge and Intelligent Machines. Inside Technology Ser.* MIT Pr 1990 $25.00. ISBN 0-262-03168-X

Feigenbaum, Edward A., and Pamela McCorduck. *The Fifth Generation: Artificial Intelligence and Japan's Computer Challenge to the World.* Addison 1983 $16.30. ISBN 0-201-11519-0

*Frude, Neil. *The Intimate Machine: Close Encounters with Computers and Robots.* NAL 1983 $14.95. ISBN 0-451-62322-3 Proposes the thesis that people tend to grant computers and robots roles that make them resemble people.

Gilbert, G. Nigel, and Christian Heath. *Social Actions and Artificial Intelligence.* Gower 1985 $45.00. ISBN 0-566-00768-1

Gill, Karamjit S. (ed). *Artificial Intelligence for Society.* Wiley 1986 $57.95. ISBN 0-471-90930-0

Glenn, Jerome C. *Future Mind: Artificial Intelligence: The Merging of the Mystical and the Technological in the 21st Century.* Acropolis 1989 $19.95. ISBN 0-87491-920-7

Grosz, Barbara, *et al.* (eds). *Readings in Natural Language Processing.* Morgan Kaufmann 1986 $38.95. ISBN 0-934613-11-7

*Haugeland, John C. (ed). *Mind Design: Philosophy, Psychology, and Artificial Intelligence.* MIT Pr 1981 $12.50. ISBN 0-262-58052-7 Textbook that contains a collection of articles, each dealing with a major conceptual issue or implication of artificial intelligence.

Hookway, Christopher (ed). *Mind, Machines and Evolution: Philosophical Studies.* Cambridge Univ Pr 1986 $14.95. ISBN 0-521-33828-X

Minsky, Marvin. *Semantic Information Processing.* MIT Pr 1969 $42.50. ISBN 0-262-13044-0

Reichman, Rachel. *Getting Computers to Talk Like You and Me: Discourse, Context, Focus, and Semantics; an ATN Model.* MIT Pr 1985 $27.50. ISBN 0-262-18118-5

Said, K. A., *et al.* (eds). *Modeling the Mind.* Oxford Univ Pr 1990 $39.95. ISBN 0-19-824973-X

*Schank, Roger C. *Tell Me a Story: A New Look at Real and Artificial Memory.* Macmillan 1991 $19.95. ISBN 0-684-19049-4 Description of the important role of scripts and memory linkages in modeling human behavior within the field of artificial intelligence.

*Staugaard, Andrew C. *Robotics and AI: An Introduction to Applied Machine Intelligence.* Prentice 1987 $47.20. ISBN 0-13-782269-3 Textbook that presents the technology of robotics, with emphasis on the use of artificial-intelligence techniques.

Torrance, S. *The Mind and the Machine: Philosophical Aspects of Artificial Intelligence.* Prentice 1984 $39.95. ISBN 0-470-20104-5

Trappi, R. (ed). *Impacts of Artificial Intelligence: Scientific, Technological, Military, Economic, Societal, Cultural and Political.* Elsevier 1986 $54.00. ISBN 0-444-87587-5

Unger, J. Marshall. *The Fifth Generation Fallacy: Why Japan Is Betting Its Future on Artificial Intelligence.* Oxford Univ Pr 1987 $24.95. ISBN 0-19-504939-X

Winograd, Terry, and Fernando Flores. *Understanding Computers and Cognition: A New Foundation for Design.* Addison 1987 $12.95. ISBN 0-317-62466-0

EXPERT SYSTEMS: SPECIFIC AREAS

Aluri, Rao, and Donald E. Riggs (eds). *Expert Systems in Libraries.* Ablex 1990 $52.50. ISBN 0-89391-589-0

Anderson, J. A. *What Neural Networks Can Do.* Erlbaum 1988 Manual $19.95. ISBN 0-8058-0446-3. Manual and video $250.00. ISBN 0-8058-0478-1. Demo video $10.00. ISBN 0-8058-0479-X

Barker, Donald, and Richard E. Eng. *Developing Business Expert Systems Using Level 5.* Merrill 1987 $24.95. ISBN 0-675-20951-X

Barrett, Michael L., and Annabel C. Beerel. *Expert Systems in Business: A Practical Approach. Information Technology Ser.* Prentice 1988 $38.95. ISBN 0-470-21083-4

*Berry, Dianne, and Anna Hart. *Expert Systems: Human Issues.* MIT Pr 1990 $35.00. ISBN 0-262-02307-5 Examination of the types of human issues involved in the design and use of expert systems.

*Bielawski, Larry, and Robert Lewant. *Expert Systems Development: Building PC-Based Applications.* QED Info Sci 1988 $34.50. ISBN 0-89435-239-3 Discussion of how to develop expert systems on the PC.

Bowerman, Robert G., and David E. Glover. *Putting Expert Systems into Practice.* Van Nostrand 1988 $44.95. ISBN 0-442-20842-1

Bramer, Max. *Practical Experience in Building Expert Systems.* Wiley 1990 $49.95. ISBN 0-471-92254-4

Building Expert Systems: Cognitive Emulation. Prentice 1987 $44.95. ISBN 0-470-20891-0

*Caudill, Maureen, and Charles Butler. *Naturally Intelligent Systems.* MIT Pr 1990 $19.95. ISBN 0-262-03156-6 Comprehensive look at neural nets and their applications, intended for general audiences without technical background; includes examples taken from biology.

Chadwick, Michael, and John Hannah. *Expert Systems for Microcomputers: An Introduction to Artificial Intelligence.* TAB 1987 $14.95. ISBN 0-8306-2838-X

Council for Science and Society Staff. *Benefits and Risks of Knowledge-Based Systems.* Oxford Univ Pr 1989 $14.95. ISBN 0-19-854743-9

Daly, Donal. *Expert Systems Introduced.* Krieger 1988 $19.50. ISBN 91-44-28541-8

Edmunds, Robert A. *The Prentice-Hall Guide to Expert Systems.* Prentice 1988 $39.95. ISBN 0-13-703241-2

Edwards, Alex, and N. A. Connell. *Expert Systems in Accounting.* Prentice 1989 $54.80. ISBN 0-13-295759-0

Feigenbaum, Edward, *et al. The Rise of the Expert Company: How Visionary Companies Are Using Artificial Intelligence to Achieve Higher Productivity and Profits.* Random 1990 $10.95. ISBN 0-679-72518-0

Forsyth, Richard (ed). *Expert Systems: Principles and Case Studies.* Routledge 1989 $27.50. ISBN 0-412-30470-8

Gale, William A. *Artificial Intelligence and Statistics.* Addison 1986 $43.25. ISBN 0-201-11569-7

Gallagher, John P. *Knowledge Systems for Business: Integrating Expert Systems and MIS.* Prentice 1988 $32.95. ISBN 0-13-516551-2

Gilmore, John. *Expert Visions Systems.* McGraw 1988 $44.95. ISBN 0-07-023308-X

Levine, Robert I., and Diane Drange. *Neural Networks: The Second AI Generation.* McGraw 1989 $24.95. ISBN 0-07-037486-4

Miller, P. L. *Expert Critiquing Systems. Series and Medicine.* Springer-Verlag 1986 $30.00. ISBN 0-387-96291-3

Minsky, Marvin, and Seymour A. Papert. *Perceptrons.* MIT Pr 1987 $13.50. ISBN 0-262-63111-3

Mumpower, J., *et al* (eds). *Expert Judgement and Expert Systems. NATO ASI Ser,* No. F35 Springer-Verlag 1987 $59.50. ISBN 0-387-17986-0

*Naylor, Chris. *Build Your Own Expert System: For the IBM PC and Compatibles.* Wiley $23.95. ISBN 0-470-20946-1 Guide to developing expert systems on the PC.

*Palmer, Marlene. *Expert Systems and Related Topics: A Selected Bibliography and Guide to Information Sources.* Idea Group 1990 $14.95. Information guide to and bibliography of expert systems.

Patterson, Dan W. *Introduction to Artificial Intelligence and Expert Systems.* Prentice 1990 $46.20. ISBN 0-13-477100-1

Pau, L. F., *et al.* (eds). *Expert Systems in Economics, Banking and Management.* Elsevier 1989 $97.50. ISBN 0-444-88060-7

Rienhoff, O., and B. Schneider (eds). *Expert Systems and Decision Support in Medicine. Lecture Notes in Medical Informations Ser.* Vol. 36 Springer-Verlag 1988 $88.00. ISBN 0-387-50317-X

Roysdon, Christine, and Howard White. *Expert Systems in Reference Services.* Haworth 1989 $39.95. ISBN 0-86656-839-5

Shafer, Daniel G. *Hands-On Expert Systems.* McGraw 1989 $24.95. ISBN 0-07-056372-1

Shapiro, Alen. *Structured Induction in Expert Systems.* Addison 1987 $28.95. ISBN 0-201-17813-3

*Siegel, Paul. *Expert Systems: A Non-Programmer's Guide to Development and Applications.* TAB 1986 $29.95. ISBN 0-8306-2738-3 Nonspecialist's learning guide to the methods of artificial intelligence.

Thierauf, Robert J. *Expert Systems in Finance and Accounting.* Greenwood 1990 $49.95. ISBN 0-89930-476-1

Van Lamsweerde, A. (ed). *Current Issues in Expert Systems. International Lecture in Computer Science Ser.* Academic Pr 1988 $42.50. ISBN 0-12-714030-1

Varsegi, Alex. *Fourth Generation Business Systems.* Wiley 1989 $34.95. ISBN 0-471-61548-X

Zeidenberg, Matthew. *Neural Networks in Artificial Intelligence. Ellis Horwood Series in Artificial Intelligence.* Prentice 1990 $43.95. ISBN 0-13-61218-4

ROBOTICS AND ROBOTS

*Darling, David. *Robots and the Intelligent Computer.* Dillon 1986 $11.95. ISBN 0-85418-315-8 Account of robots and intelligent computers for grade 5 and up.

*Hawkes, Nigel. *Robots and Computers.* Watts 1984 $11.90. ISBN 0-531-04816-0 Explains how robots are controlled by computers and the kinds of jobs they are currently performing.

*Liptak, Karen. *Robotics Basics.* Prentice 1984 $10.95. ISBN 0-13-782087-9 Tells what robots are, what they can do now, and predictions for the future.

*Moravec, Hans. *Mind Children: The Future of Robot and Human Intelligence.* Harvard Univ Pr 1988 $18.95. ISBN 0-674-57616-0 Discusses the human mind and that of the robot: how can these two exist in the future?

ADVANCED TOPICS IN COMPUTER SCIENCE

The formal study of computer science considers several important topics, some of which appear in the headings for the references that follow. For example, *algorithms* are step-by-step procedures that underlie most programming activities, *compiler design* refers to the creation of programs that can translate high-level languages into a language that a particular machine can understand, and *software engineering* refers to a formal and detailed way of specifying what a program should do and the testing of the program to see that it works. All of these topics are of interest primarily to those who want to learn about programming for its own sake rather than in order to accomplish a particular task using the computer.

Balcazar, J. L., and J. Diaz. *Structural Complexity I. EATCS Monographs on Theoretical Computer Science.* Vol. 11 Springer-Verlag 1988 $29.50. ISBN 0-387-18622-0

Berlioux, Pierre, and Philippe Bizard. *The Construction, Proof and Analysis of Programs.* Wiley 1986 $39.95. ISBN 0-471-90844-4

Biggerstaff, Ted. *Systems Software Tools.* Prentice 1990 $21.50. ISBN 0-13-881764-2

*Brooks, Frederick P., Jr. *The Mythical Man-Month.* Addison 1974 $20.50. ISBN 0-201-00650-2 Classic work on why software development projects usually take at least twice as long to complete as originally estimated and what can be done about it.

Dhamdhere, D. M. *Introduction to System Software.* Silicon 1989 $29.95. ISBN 0-9615336-7-6

Gane, Chris. *Computer-Aided Software Engineering.* McGraw 1988 $49.95. ISBN 0-07-022759-4

Gane, Chris. *Rapid System Development.* Prentice 1989 $41.00. ISBN 0-13-753070-6

Gurari, Eitan. *An Introduction to the Theory of Computation.* Freeman 1989 $41.95. ISBN 0-7167-8182-4

Humphrey, Watts S. *Managing the Software Process. SEI Ser in Software Engineering.* Addison 1989 $43.25. ISBN 0-201-18095-2

Ince, D. *Software Engineering.* Heath 1990 $29.95. ISBN 0-278-00079-7

International Conference on Distributed Computing Systems, Ninth. Comp Soc 1989 $100.00. ISBN 0-8186-1953-8

Martin, James. *Application Development Without Programmers.* Prentice 1982 $65.00. ISBN 0-13-038943-9

Martin, James. *Design and Strategy for Distributed Data Processing.* Prentice 1981 $69.80. ISBN 0-13-201657-5

Paul, M., and H. J. Seigert (eds). *Distributed Systems. Lecture Notes in Computer Science Ser.* Vol. 190 Springer-Verlag 1988 $33.00. ISBN 0-387-13216-4

Tischer, M. *PC System Programming for Developers.* Abacus Soft 1990 $59.95. ISBN 1-55755-036-0

Tourlakis, George J. *Computability.* Prentice 1983. (o.p.) $54.00. ISBN 0-8359-0877-1

Wilf, Herbert S. *Algorithms and Complexity.* Prentice 1986 $44.20. ISBN 0-13-021973-8

Yourdon, Edward (ed). *Classics in Software Engineering.* Prentice 1986 $43.20. ISBN 0-13-135179-6

ALGORITHMS

Adelson-Velsky, G. M., *et al. Algorithms for Games.* Springer-Verlag 1989 $59.50. ISBN 0-387-96629-3

Baase, Sara. *Computer Algorithms: Introduction to Design and Analysis.* Addison 1987 $38.75. ISBN 0-201-06035-3

Bellman, Richard E., *et al. Algorithms, Graphs and Computers. Mathematics in Science and Engineering Ser.* Vol. 62 Academic Pr 1970 $52.00. ISBN 0-12-084840-6

*Hatel, David. *Algorithmics: The Spirit of Computing.* Addison 1987 $24.75. ISBN 0-201-19240-3 Presentation of the central role of algorithmic methods in computer science and computer-software development.

*Hatel, David. *The Science of Computing: Exploring the Nature and Power of Algorithms.* Addison 1989 $17.95. ISBN 0-201-51723-X A view of algorithms and their applications.

Iverson, K. E. *Algebra: An Algorithmic Treatment.* APL Pr 1977 $15.00. ISBN 0-917326-09-1

Knuth, Donald E. *Art of Computer Programming: Semi-Numerical Algorithms.* Addison 1981 $34.36. ISBN 0-201-03822-4

*Research and Education Staff. *Essentials of Algorithms.* Research & Education 1990 $4.95. ISBN 0-87891-721-7 Study guide that deals with the essential elements of algorithms.

Sedgewick Robert. *Algorithms in C. Computer Science Ser.* Addison 1990 $46.95. ISBN 0-201-51425-7

Wetzel, Gregory F., and William G. Bulgren. *Pascal and Algorithms: An Introduction to Problem Solving.* SRA 1988 $12.00. ISBN 0-574-18632-8

COMPILERS

Aho, Alfred V., *et al. Compilers: Principles, Techniques, and Tools.* Addison 1986 $44.25. ISBN 0-201-10088-6

*Bornat, Richard. *Understanding and Writing Compilers: A Do It Yourself Guide.* Scholium 1989 $29.00. ISBN 0-333-21732-2 Self-study guide on how to fashion your own computer language and teach the computer to decipher it.

Brown, P. J. *Writing Interactive Compilers and Interpreters.* Wiley 1981 $32.95. ISBN 0-471-10072-2

*Calingaert, Peter. *Program Translation Fundamentals: Methods and Issues.* Freeman 1988 $41.-95. ISBN 0-7167-8146-8 Introduction to the ways in which a computer can be persuaded to translate its own instructions from English-sounding form into machine-symbol form.

*Farmer, Mick. *Compiler Physiology for Beginners.* Krieger 1985 $16.50. ISBN 1-944-22901-1 Intelligent introduction to compilers.

Holub, Allen I. *Compiler Design in C.* Prentice 1990 $42.20. ISBN 0-13-155045-4

Hunter, Robert. *Compilers: Their Design and Construction Using Pascal.* Wiley 1985 $36.95. ISBN 0-471-90720-0

Schreiner, Axel T., and H. George Friedman, Jr. *Introduction to Compiler Construction with UNIX.* Prentice 1985 $45.20. ISBN 0-13-474396-2

Tofte, M. *Compiler Generators.* Springer-Verlag 1990 $39.50. ISBN 0-387-51471-6

Tremblay, Jean-Paul, and Paul G. Sorenson. *An Implementation Guide to Compiler Writing.* McGraw 1983 $22.95. ISBN 0-07-065166-3

Tremblay, Jean-Paul, and Paul G. Sorenson. *The Theory and Practice of Compiler Writing.* McGraw 1985 $48.95. ISBN 0-07-065161-2

Von Neumann, John. *Collected Works.* A.W. Taub (ed). 6 vols. Vol. 5 *Design of Computers, Theory of Automata, and Numerical Analysis.* Pergamon (repr of 1963 ed) $275.00. ISBN 0-08-009561-2

Wulf, William A., *et al. The Design of an Optimizing Compiler. Programming Languages Ser, Elsevier Computer Science Library.* No. 2 Books Demand $43.80.

DATA STRUCTURES

Aho, Alfred V., *et al. Data Structures and Algorithms.* Addison 1983. ISBN 0-201-00023-7

*Barnett, M. P., and S. J. Barnett. *Animated Algorithms: A Self-Teaching Course in Data Structures and Fundamental Algorithms.* McGraw 1986 $31.95. ISBN 0-07-003792-2 Study guide for a useful subtopic in computer science.

Feldman, Michael B. *Data Structures with Modula-Two.* Prentice 1988 $45.20. ISBN 0-13-197334-4

Roski, Steve. *Data Structures on the IBM PC.* Prentice 1985 $21.95. ISBN 0-89303-481-9

Smith, Harry F., Jr. *Data Structures: Form and Function.* Harcourt 1987 $35.00. ISBN 0-15-516821-5

Van Amstel, J. J., and Poirters, J. A. *The Design of Data Structure and Algorithms.* Prentice 1989 $39.00. ISBN 0-13-199944-3

Van Leeuwen, J. (ed). *Graph-Theoretic Concepts in Computer Science. Lecture Notes in Computer Science Ser.* Vol. 344 Springer-Verlag 1989 $36.00. ISBN 0-387-50728-0
*Wirth, Niklaus. *Algorithms and Data Structures.* Prentice 1986 $48.20. ISBN 0-13-022005-1 Advanced treatment of the subject; may be interesting and helpful to students accustomed to the formal language and definitions used in software theory and formal mathematics.

APPENDIX:
LIST OF PUBLISHERS

The following list includes the abbreviations and full names of publishers whose titles appear in *The Young Adult Reader's Adviser*. The abbreviated form of a publisher's name as it appears throughout the two volumes is shown in boldface. The abbreviation is followed by the complete form of the name. The alphabetization method is word-by-word. Those university presses with standard abbreviations that need no further explanation have been omitted. For full information, addresses, and telephone and fax numbers, see the latest edition of *Books in Print*.

A

A & M A & M Books
AAHPERD American Alliance for Health, Physical Education, Recreation & Dance
Abaca Abaca Books
Abacus Pr Abacus Press
Abacus Pub Abacus Publishing Co.
Abacus Soft Abacus Software, Inc.
Abaris Abaris Books, Inc.
ABBE ABBE Publishers, Association of Washington, D.C.
Abbeville Abbeville Press, Inc.
ABC-Clio ABC-CLIO, Inc.
Aberdeen Aberdeen Group
Abingdon Abingdon Press
Ablex Ablex Publishing Corp.
Abner Schram Abner Schram, Ltd.
Abrams Harry N. Abrams, Inc.
Academia Academia Press
Academic Intl Academic International Press
Academic Pr Academic Press, Inc.
Academic Pubns Academic Publications
Academy Bks Academy Books
Academy Chi Pubs Academy Chicago Publishers, Ltd.
Acadia Acadia Publishing Co.
Ace Ace Books

Acropolis Acropolis Books
Activity Resources Activity Resources Co., Inc.
Adama Adama Publishers, Inc.
Adams Inc MA Bob Adams, Inc.
Adams Pr Adams Press
Addison Addison-Wesley Publishing Co., Inc.
Adlers Adlers Foreign Books, Inc.
Advent Advent Books, Inc.
Airmont Airmont Publishing Co., Inc.
ALA American Library Association
Alba Alba House
Aldine Aldine de Gruyter
Algonquin Algonquin Books of Chapel Hill
Allen Allen Press, Inc.
Allyn Allyn & Bacon, Inc.
Am Acad Pol Soc Sci American Academy of Politics and Social Science
Am Assn Physics American Association of Physics Teachers
Am Chemical American Chemical Society
Am Christian Pr American Christian Press
Am Enterprise Inst American Enterprise Institute for Public Policy Research

Am Inst Chem Eng   American Institute of Chemical Engineers

Am Inst Psych   The American Institute for Psychological Research

Am Jewish Comm   American Jewish Committee

Am Philos   American Philosophical Society

Am Red Cross   American Red Cross, Allen-Wells Chapter

Am Soc Pub Admin   American Society for Public Administration

Amer Mus of Nat Hist   American Museum of Natural History

Amereon   Amereon, Ltd.

American Assn of Retired Persons   American Association of Retired Persons

American Cancer Society   American Cancer Society, Inc.

American Classical Coll Pr   American Classical College Press

American Forestry   American Forestry Association

American Heritage   American Heritage

American Poetry   American Poetry & Literature Press

American Psychological Assn   American Psychological Association

American Public Health Assn   American Public Health Association Publications

American-Scandinavian   American-Scandinavian Foundation

AMS   AMS Press, Inc.

AMSCO   AMSCO School Publications, Inc.

Anchor   Anchor Press, *imprint of* Doubleday & Co., Inc.

Andrew Mountain   Andrew Mountain Press

Andrews   Andrews & McMeel

Andrews Univ Pr   Andrews University Press

Annual Reviews   Annual Reviews, Inc.

Antelope Island   Antelope Island Press

Anthroposophic   Anthroposophic Press, Inc.

Aperture   Aperture Foundation, Inc.

Aperture NW   Aperture Northwest, Inc.

APL Pr   APL Press

Applause Theatre Bk   Applause Theatre Book Publishers

Apt   Apt Books, Inc.

Arbor Hse   Arbor House, *imprint of* William Morrow & Co., Inc.

Arcade   Arcade Publishers

Archway   Archway Paperbacks, *imprint of* Pocket Books, Inc.

Arco   Arco Publishing, Inc.

Ardis   Ardis Publishers

Ardsley   Ardsley House Publishers, Inc.

Ares   Ares Publishers, Inc.

Argosy   Argosy

Aronson   Jason Aronson, Inc.

ARS   ARS Enterprises

Arte Publico   Arte Publico Press

Asia Bk Corp   Asia Book Corp. of America

Assn Amer Geographers   Association of American Geographers

Assn Inform & Image   Association for Information & Image Management

Assn Supervision   Association for Supervision & Curriculum Development

Assoc Faculty Pr   Associated Faculty Press, Inc.

Assoc Univ Pr   Associated University Presses

Athelstan   Athelstan Publications

Athenaeum   Athenaeum of Philadelphia

Atheneum   Atheneum, *imprint of* Macmillan Publishing Co., Inc.

Atlantic Monthly   Atlantic Monthly Press

Auburn   Auburn House Publishing Co., Inc., *imprint of* Greenwood Publishing Group, Inc.

Augsburg Fortress   Augsburg Fortress Publishers

Augustinian   Augustinian Press

Augustinian Coll Pr   Augustinian College Press

Auromere   Auromere, Inc.

Avery   Avery Publishing Group, Inc.

Avon   Avon Books

Avstar   Avstar Publishing Corp.

Ayer   Ayer Co. Publishers, Inc.

B

B & N Imports   Barnes & Noble Books—Imports

B. C. Scribe   B. C. Scribe Publications

Baen   Baen Books

Baker Bk   Baker Book House

Baker Pub   Baker Publishing

Ballantine   Ballantine Books, Inc.

Ballinger   Ballinger Publishing Co.

Banner of Truth   The Banner of Truth

Bantam   Bantam Books, Inc.

Barnes   Barnes & Noble Books

Barron   Barron's Educational Series, Inc.

Basic   Basic Books, Inc.

Basil Blackwell   Basil Blackwell, Inc.

Battery Pk   Battery Park Book Co.

Battery Pr   Battery Press

Battle Rd   Battle Road Press

Beacon   Beacon Press, Inc.

Bearly   Bearly, Ltd.

Beatty   R. W. Beatty

Beau Lac   Beau Lac Publishers

Beaufort   Beaufort Books, Publishers

Bedrick   Peter Bedrick Books

Beekman   Beekman Publishers, Inc.

Beil   Frederic C. Beil Publisher, Inc.

Bellerophon   Bellerophon Books

Benjamin Co.   Benjamin Co., Inc.

Benjamin-Cummings   Benjamin-Cummings Co. Publishing

Benjamin Pr   Benjamin Press

Benjamin Pub   Benjamin Publishing Co.

Benjamins   John Benjamins North America, Inc.

Bentley   Robert Bentley, Inc. Publishers

Bergin & Garvey   Bergin & Garvey Publishers, Inc., *imprint of* Greenwood Publishing Group, Inc.

Berkley   Berkley Publishing Group

Berkley West   Berkley West Publishing

Berkshire Traveller   Berkshire Traveller Press

Berle   Berle Books

Bess Pr   Bess Press, Inc.

Betterway Pubns   Betterway Publications

Biblio Dist   Biblio Distribution Center

Biblio Pub   Biblio Publishing

Biblio Pr   Biblio Press, the Jewish Women's Publisher

Biblio Siglo   Biblioteca Siglo de Oro

Bibliotheca   Bibliotecha Islamica, Inc.

Biblo   Biblo & Tannen Booksellers & Publishers, Inc.

Bilicki   Bilicki Publications

Birch Lane   Birch Lane Press, *imprint of* Carol Publishing Group

Birkhauser   Birkhauser Boston, Inc.

BJ Pubns   BJ Publications

Black Classic   Black Classic Press

Black Rose   Black Rose Books

Black Swan Bks   Black Swan Books, Ltd.

Black Swan Pr   Black Swan Press

BMDP Stat   BMDP Statistical Software

Bobbs   Bobbs-Merrill Co., *imprint of* Macmillan Publishing Co., Inc.

Bolchazy-Carducci   Bolchazy-Carducci Publishers

Bonus   Bonus Books, Inc.

Book-Lab   Book-Lab

Book Sales   Book Sales, Inc.

Books Demand   Books on Demand

Bookwrights   Bookwrights

Boone & Crockett   Boone & Crockett Club

Boone-Thomas   Boone-Thomas Enterprises

Boosey & Hawkes   Boosey & Hawkes, Inc.

Borden   Borden Publishing Co.

Borgo   Borgo Press

Boston Coll Math   Boston College Mathematics Institute

Boulevard   Boulevard Books

Bowker   R. R. Bowker

Boxwood   Boxwood Press

Boy Scouts   Boy Scouts of America
Boyd & Fraser   Boyd & Fraser
  Publishing Co.
Boyd Co   Boyd Co.
Boyd Deep Canyon   University of
  California at Riverside, Boyd
  Deep Canyon Desert Research
  Center
Boyd Griffin   Boyd Griffin, Inc.
Boydell & Brewer   Boydell &
  Brewer, *imprint of* Longwood
  Publishing Group, Inc.
Boynton   Boynton Cook
  Publishers, Inc.
Bradbury Pr   Bradbury Press
Brady Bks   Brady Books
Branden   Branden Publishing Co.
Braziller   George Braziller, Inc.
Brethren   Brethren Press
Broadside   Broadside Press
Brookings   Brookings Institution
Brookline   Brookline Books
Brooklyn Coll Pr   Brooklyn
  College Press
Brooks   Brooks Publishing Co.
Brooks-Cole   Brooks/Cole
  Publishing Co.
Brooks Ent   Brooks Enterprises
Brown   William C. Brown
  Publishers
Brunner-Mazel   Brunner/Mazel
  Publishers
Buccaneer   Buccaneer Books
Bulfinch   Bulfinch Press, *imprint of*
  Little, Brown & Co.
Bull   Bull Publishing Co.
Burt Franklin   Burt Franklin
  Publisher
Butterworth   Butterworth
  Publishers

C

C. Coolidge Memorial   Calvin
  Coolidge Memorial Foundation,
  Inc.
C. H. Kerr   Charles H. Kerr
  Publishing Co.
Cambridge   Cambridge Book
  Co.
Cambridge Univ Pr   Cambridge
  University Press
Camelot   Camelot Books, *imprint of*
  Avon Books

Camelot Consult   Camelot
  Consultants
Camelot Pr   Camelot Press, Ltd
Camelot Pub   Camelot Publishing
Camelot Pub Co   Camelot
  Publishing Co.
Camelot Pubs   Camelot Publishers
Camelot Self   Camelot Self
  Subsidy Publishers
Cameron   Cameron & Co., Inc.
Capitalist   Capitalist Press
Capra   Capra Press
Capricorn Bks   Capricorn Books
Capricorn Corp   Capricorn
  Corp.
Caravan   Caravan Books
Carcanet   Carcanet Press
Carlson   Carlson Publishing, Inc.
Carnegie Institution of Washington
  Carnegie Institution of
  Washington
Carol   Carol Publishing Group
Carolina Acad Pr   Carolina
  Academic Press
Carolina Biological   Carolina
  Biological Supply Co.,
  Publications Department
Carroll & Graf   Carroll & Graf
  Publishers
Carroll Coll   Carroll College Press
Carroll Pr   Carroll Press
Carroll Pub   Carroll Publishing Co.
Catbird   Catbird Press
Catholic Bk Pub   Catholic Book
  Publishing Co.
Caxton   Caxton Printers, Ltd.
Cayucos   Cayucos Books
Celo   Celo Press
Chandler & Sharp   Chandler &
  Sharp Publishers
Charles   Charles Press Publishers
Charles Pub   Charles Publishing
  Co.
Charles River   Charles River
  Books
Chelsea   Chelsea House Publishers
Chicago Review   Chicago Review
  Press, Inc.
Childrens   Children's Press
Chilton   Chilton Book Co.
China Bks   China Books &
  Periodicals, Inc.
China Hse Arts   China House of
  Arts
China Res   China Research

China West China West Books
Choice Pub Choice Publishing, Inc.
Christian Classics Christian Classics, Inc.
Christian Lit Christian Literature Crusade, Inc.
Christopher Christopher Publishing House
Chronicle Chronicle Books
Citadel Citadel Press, *imprint of* Carol Publishing Group
CITE Center for International Training & Education
City Lights City Lights Books
City Miner City Miner Books
Clarendon Clarendon Group, Inc.
Clarity Pr Clarity Press
Clarity Pub Clarity Publishing
Clark Clark Publishing, Inc.
Clark City Pr Clark City Press
Clark Davis Clark Davis Publishing Co.
Clark Univ Pr Clark University Press
Cleckley-Thigpen Cleckley-Thigpen Psychiatric Associates
College-Hill College-Hill Press, Inc.
Collins Collins Publishers
Colton Colton Book Imports
Columbia Scholastic Columbia Scholastic Press Association
Comptr Pub Computer Publishing Enterprises
Compute Pubns Compute! Publications, Inc.
Computer Based Pubns Computer Based Publications
Computer Direct Computer Directions for Schools
Computer-Prop Computer-Propaganda Press
Computer Science Pr Computer Science Press, Inc., *imprint of* W. H. Freeman & Co.
Computing Computing!
Computing Trends Computing Trends
Concord Grove Concord Grove Press
Congressional Quarterly Congressional Quarterly, Inc.

Connecticut Historical Soc The Connecticut Historical Society Press
Conservation Foundation Conservation Foundation
Consumer Reports Consumer Reports Books
Contact Contact/II Publications
Contemporary Bks Contemporary Books, Inc.
Continuum Continuum Publishing Co.
Cook David C. Cook Publishing Co.
Cooper Square Cooper Square Publishers, Inc.
Cordillera Cordillera Press, Inc.
Corner Corner House Publishers
Coronet Coronet, The Multimedia Co.
Coronet Bks Coronet Books
Coun Exc Child Council for Exceptional Children
Council Oak Council Oak Books
Council of State Governments Council of State Governments
Counter Prop The Counter-Propaganda Press
Coward Coward, McCann & Geoghegan, *imprint of* The Putnam Publishing Group
Crabtree Crabtree Publishing
Crabtree Pub Crabtree Publishing Co.
Create Learn Creative Learning Press, Inc.
Creative Ed Creative Education, Inc.
Creative Pubns Creative Publications
CRC Pr CRC Press, Inc.
CRC Pubns CRC Publications
Cromlech Cromlech Books, Inc.
Cross Cultural Cross-Cultural Communications
Crossing Pr The Crossing Press
Crossroad Crossroad Publishing Co.
Crowell Thomas Y. Crowell Co.
Crown Crown Publishers, Inc.
Crown Bks Crown Books
Crown Intle Crown Internationale
Crown Pub Crown Publishing Co., Inc.

Crown Pubns Crown Publications, Inc.
Ctr for Creative Photography Center for Creative Photography
Curbstone Curbstone Press

D

D I Fine Donald I. Fine, Inc.
Da Capo Da Capo Press, Inc.
Dallas Sandt Dallas Sandt Co.
Dante Univ Dante University of America Press, Inc.
Darien Darien House Books
Daring Daring Books
Daughters St. Paul Daughters of Saint Paul
David and Charles David & Charles, Inc.
Davida Davida Publications
Davis Pubns Davis Publications, Inc.
de Gruyter Walter de Gruyter, Inc.
Dekker Marcel Dekker, Inc.
Del Rey Del Rey Books, *imprint of* Ballantine Books, Inc.
Delacorte Delacorte Press
Dell Dell Publishing Co., Inc.
Delmar Delmar Publishers, Inc.
Dembner Dembner Books
Devin-Adair Devin-Adair Publishers, Inc.
Dial Dial Press, *imprint of* Doubleday & Co., Inc.
Dillon Dillon Press, Inc.
Documentary Pubns Documentary Publications
Dodd Dodd, Mead & Co.
Dodd-Blair Dodd-Blair & Associates
Donald Cohen Donald Cohen
Dorchester Dorchester Publishing Co., Inc.
Dorset Dorset Press
Dorset Hse Dorset House Publishing Co., Inc.
Dorset Pub Dorset Publishing Co., Inc.
Dorsett Dorsett
Doubleday Doubleday & Co., Inc.
Dover Dover Publications, Inc.
Dow Jones Dow Jones-Irwin
Dryden Dryden Press

Dufour Dufour Editions, Inc.
Durbin Assoc Durbin Associates
Dushkin Dushkin Publishing Group, Inc.
Dutton E. P. Dutton

E

E. Bowers Eddie Bowers Publishing Co.
E. J. Brill E. J. Brill (U.S.A.), Inc.
Eagle Bks Eagle Books
Eagle Cliff Eagle Cliff Publications
Eagle Comm Eagle Communications
Eagle North Eagle North Communications
Eagle Peak Pub Eagle Peak Publishing Co.
Eagle Pr Eagle Press
Eagle Pr Inc Eagle Press, Inc.
Eagle Pub Eagle Publishing Co.
Eagle Pub Corp Eagle Publishing Corp.
Eagle Pubn Co Eagle Publication Co.
Eagle Wing Bks Eagle Wing Books
Eakin Eakin Press
Eakins Eakins Press Foundation
Ecco Ecco Press
Ed Research Education Research Associates
Ed Solutions Educational Solutions, Inc.
Ed-U Pr Ed-U Press, Inc.
EDC EDC Publishing
Edins Hispamerica Ediciones Hispamerica
Editions Publisol Editions Publisol
Educ Tech Pubns Educational Technology Publications, Inc.
Eerdmans William B. Eerdmans Publishing Co.
Eisenbrauns Eisenbrauns
Elliots Elliot's Books
Elsevier Elsevier Science Publishing Co, Inc.
EMC EMC Publishing
Empak Empak Publishing Co.
Enslow Enslow Publishers, Inc.
Environmental Design Environmental Design & Research Center

Ergosyst   Ergosyst Associates, Inc.
Eridanos   Eridanos Press
Erlbaum   Lawrence Erlbaum
Associates, Inc.
Ethnology Monographs   Ethnology
Monographs
Eurasia   Eurasia Press

F

Faber & Faber   Faber & Faber, Inc.
Facts on File   Facts on File, Inc.
Fairleigh   Fairleigh Dickinson
University Press
Fairmont   Fairmont Press, Inc.
Farrar   Farrar, Straus & Giroux,
Inc.
Fawcett   Fawcett Book Group
Feminist Pr   Feminist Press at the
City University of New York
Fertig   Howard Fertig, Inc.
Finnish American   Finnish
American Literary Heritage
Foundation
Fireside   Fireside Paperbacks,
imprint of Simon & Schuster, Inc.
Fjord   Fjord Press
Flare   Avon Flare Books, *imprint of*
Avon Books
Fleet   Fleet Press Corp.
Flint Inst of Arts   Flint Institute of
Arts
FlipTrack   FlipTrack Learning
Systems
Focal   Focal Press
Focal Point   Focal Point Press
Focus Information   Focus
Information Group, Inc.
Folger   Folger Books
Folkcroft   Folkcroft
Follett   Follett Press
Foreign Language   Foreign
Language for Young Children
Foreign Policy Assn   Foreign
Policy Association
Forum Pr   Forum Press, Inc.
Found Amer Ed   The Foundation
for American Education
Found Class Repr   The Foundation
for Classical Reprints
Foundation   Foundation Books,
imprint of Doubleday & Co., Inc.
Foundation Bks   Foundation Books

Foundation Hse   Foundation
House Publications, Inc.
Foundation Pr   Foundation Press,
Inc.
Four Winds   Four Winds Press,
imprint of Macmillan Publishing
Co., Inc.
Free Pr   Free Press
Free Spirit   Free Spirit Publishing,
Inc.
Freeland   Freeland Press
Freeland Pubns   Freeland
Publications
Freeman   W. H. Freeman & Co.
French and European   French &
European Publications, Inc.
Friends Univ of Toledo   Friends of
the University of Toledo Library
Freundlich   Freundlich Books
Fromm Intl   Fromm International
Publishing Corp.
Fulcrum   Fulcrum, Inc.

G

G. K. Hall   G. K. Hall & Co.
Gale   Gale Research, Inc.
Garber   Garber Communications,
Inc.
Garden City   Garden City
Historical Society
Gardner   Gardner Press, Inc.
Gareth Stevens   Gareth Stevens,
Inc.
Garland   Garland Publishing, Inc.
Garrard   Garrard Publishing Co.
Garrett   Garrett Park Press
Garrett Ed   Garrett Educational
Corp.
Gateway   Gateway Press, Inc.
Gateway Pr   Gateway Press
Gaus   Theo Gaus, Ltd.
General Hall   General Hall, Inc.
Genesis   Genesis Publishing, Inc.
Genesis Pr   Genesis Press
Genesis Pub   Genesis Publishing
Co.
Gibbs Smith   Gibbs Smith
Publisher
Gifted Educ   Gifted Education
Press
Glenhurst   Glenhurst Publications,
Inc.

Glenmary Research Center
Glenmary Research Center
Globe Pequot Globe Pequot Press
Gloucester Gloucester Press, *imprint
of* Franklin Watts, Inc.
Gloucester Art Gloucester Art
Press
Godine David R. Godine
Publisher, Inc.
Golden Hind Golden Hind Press
Goldstein & Blair Goldstein &
Blair
Goldstein Soft Goldstein
Software, Inc.
Good Apple Good Apple, Inc.
Good Bks Good Books
Gordian Gordian Press, Inc.
Gordon & Breach Gordon &
Breach Science Publishers,
Inc.
Gordon Pr Gordon Press
Publishers
Gorsuch Gorsuch Scarisbrick
Publishers
Gower Gower Publishing Co.
Graylock Graylock Press
Graywolf Graywolf Press
Great Quotations Great
Quotations, Inc.
Greene Stephen Greene Press
Greenhaven Greenhaven Press
Greenleaf Bks Greenleaf Books
Greenleaf Classics Greenleaf
Classics, Inc.
Greenleaf Co Greenleaf Co.
Greenleaf Pub Greenleaf
Publishing Co.
Greenwillow Greenwillow Books
Greenwood Greenwood Press, Inc.,
imprint of Greenwood Publishing
Group, Inc.
Greenwood Hse Greenwood
House
Greenwood Pub Greenwood
Publishing
Gregg Gregg, Inc.
Gregg Intl Gregg International
Grey Fox Grey Fox Press
Grosset Grosset & Dunlap Inc.,
imprint of The Putnam Publishing
Group
Grove Grove Press
Groves Dict Music Groves
Dictionaries of Music, Inc.

Guilford Guilford Press
Gulf Pub Gulf Publishing Co.

H

H. Holt Henry Holt & Co.
Hacker Hacker Art Books
Hackett Hackett Publishing Co.,
Inc.
Halsted Halsted Press
Hammond Hammond, Inc.
Hampstead Hampstead Press,
imprint of Franklin Watts, Inc.
Harcourt Harcourt Brace
Jovanovich, Inc.
Harlan Davidson Harlan
Davidson, Inc.
Harper Harper & Row Publishers,
Inc.
Harper Jr Bks Harper & Row
Junior Books Group
Harper Pr Harper Press
Harper Sq Pr Harper Square Press
Harris H. E. Harris & Co., Inc.
Harris Acad Harris Academy
Harris Learn Syst Harris Learning
Systems, Inc.
Harris Pub Harris Publishing Co.
Harris Stonehouse Harris
Stonehouse Press
Harvard Common Pr Harvard
Common Press
Haskell Haskell Booksellers, Inc.
Hastings Hastings House
Publishers
Hastings Bks Hastings Books
Hastings Ctr Hastings Center
Hastings Pr Hastings Press
Haworth The Haworth Press,
Inc.
Hay Hay House, Inc.
Haynes Haynes Publications, Inc.
Hazelden Hazelden Foundation
Health Communications Health
Communications, Inc.
Heath D. C. Heath & Co.
Heineman James H. Heineman,
Inc., Publisher
Heinemann Heinemann
Educational Books, Inc.
Heisler Suzanne Heisler
Helene Obolensky Helene
Obolensky Enterprises, Inc.

Hemisphere Hemisphere
Publishing Corp.
Hendricks Hendricks House, Inc.
Herald Herald Press
Here's Life Here's Life Publishers,
Inc.
Heridonius Heridonius Foundation
Hermon Sepher-Hermon Press,
Inc.
Heyeck The Heyeck Press
Higginson Higginson Book Co.
High Plains High Plains
Publishing Co., Inc.
High Plains Pub High Plains
Publishing Co.
Hill & Wang Hill & Wang, Inc.
Hippocrene Hippocrene Books,
Inc.
Holden-Day Holden-Day, Inc.
Holiday Holiday House, Inc.
Holmes Holmes Book Co.
Holmes & Meier Holmes & Meier
Publishers, Inc.
Holmes Pub Holmes Publishing
Group
Holt Holt, Rinehart & Winston,
Inc.
Hoover Inst Pr Hoover Institution
Press
Hoover Lib Herbert Hoover
Presidential Library & Association
Inc.
Horton Thomas Horton &
Daughters
Houghton Houghton Mifflin Co.
House Fire Pr House of Fire Press
HP HP Books, *imprint of* Price Stern
Sloan, Inc.
Hudson Hills Hudson Hills Press,
Inc.
Human Kinetics Human Kinetics
Publishers
Human Relations Human
Relations Area Files Press, Inc.
Human Resource Human
Resource Development Press
Humanities Humanities Press
International, Inc.
Humanities Art Humanities &
Arts Press
Huntington Lib Huntington
Library Publications
Huntington Pr Huntington Press
Hyperion Hyperion Press, Inc.

I

ICS Bk ICS Books, Inc.
ICS Pr ICS Press
ICS Pubns ICS Publications,
Institute of Carmelite Studies
Ideals Ideals Publishing Corp.
IEEE IEEE Computer Society
Press
ILR Pr ILR Press
Imported Imported Publications,
Inc.
Ind-US Ind-US, Inc.
Indian Historian Pr Indian
Historian Press, Inc.
Indochina Curriculum Gp
Indochina Curriculum Group
Industrial Pr Industrial Press,
Inc.
Info Plus Information Plus
Inst Economic Pol Institute for
Economic & Political World
Strategic Studies
Inst for Economics and Finance
Institute for Economic & Financial
Research
Inst for Social Research
University of Michigan, Institute
for Social Research
Inst for Studies in Am Music
Institute for Studies in American
Music
Integrity Integrity Press
Inter Print Pubs Interstate Printers
& Publishers, Inc.
Inter-Varsity Inter-Varsity Press
Interbook Interbook, Inc.
Intersystems Intersystems
Publications
Intl Advertising Assn
International Advertising
Association
Intl Book International Book Co.
Intl Book Ctr International Book
Center
Intl City Management
International City Management
Association
Intl Defense & Aid International
Defense and Aid Fund for
Southern Africa
Intl Inst Garibaldian International
Institute of Garibaldian Studies,
Inc.

Intl Pub   International Publishing Corp.
Intl Pub Inc   International Publishing, Inc.
Intl Pubns   International Publications Service
Intl Pubs   International Publishers, Co.
Intl Specialized Bk   International Specialized Book Services
Intl Univ Pr   International University Press
Invisible   Invisible City/Red Hill Press
Irvington   Irvington Publishers
Irwin   Richard D. Irwin, Inc.
ISGS   International Society for General Semantics
ISI Pr   ISI Press
Island   Island Press
Ism Pr   Ism Press, Inc.
Ivy   Ivy Books

J

JAI   JAI Press, Inc.
James River   James River Press
Jamestown   Jamestown Publishers, Inc.
Janson   Janson Publications
Janssen   Janssen Education Enterprise, Inc.
Janus Bks   Janus Book Publishers, Inc.
Janus Lib   Janus Library, *imprint of* Abaris Books, Inc.
Janus Pr   Janus Press
JCEE   Joint Council on Economic Education
Jenkins   Jenkins Publishing Co.
Joelle   Joelle Publishing, Inc.
John Jay   John Jay Press
John Knox   John Knox Press, *imprint of* Westminster/John Knox Press
Johnson Inst   Johnson Institute
Johnson Repr   Johnson Reprint Corp.
Jonathan David   Jonathan David Publishers, Inc.
Jones & Bartlett   Jones & Bartlett Publishers, Inc.
Jossey-Bass   Jossey-Bass, Inc., Publishers

Jove   Jove Publications, Inc.
JPS   Jewish Publication Society
Judson   Judson Press

K

K. G. Saur   K. G. Saur
Karger   S. Karger, AG
Karz-Cohl   Karz-Cohl Publishers, Inc.
Katonah Gallery   Katonah Gallery
Kazi   Kazi Publications
Keats   Keats Publishing, Inc.
Kelley   Augustus M. Kelley Publishers
Kelley Comm Dev   Kelley Communication Development
Kelley Pubns   Kelley Publications
Kendall   Kendall Publishing Co.
Kendall Enterp   Kendall Enterprises, Inc.
Kendall-Hunt   Kendall/Hunt Publishing Co.
Kent   Kent Popular Press
Kern Intl   Kern International, Inc.
Kimbell Art   Kimbell Art Museum
Kingston   Kingston Ellis Press
Kipling   Kipling Press
Kluwer Academic   Kluwer Academic Publishers
Knopf   Alfred A. Knopf, Inc.
Kodansha   Kodansha International U.S.A., Ltd.
Kraus   Kraus Reprint & Periodicals
Kregel   Kregel Publications
Krieger   Robert E. Krieger Publishing Co., Inc.
Krishna   Krishna Press
Ktav   Ktav Publishing House, Inc.

L

L Hill Bks   Lawrence Hill Books
Landfall   Landfall Press, Inc.
Larlin   Larlin Corp.
LBJ Sch Pub Aff   Lyndon B. Johnson School of Public Affairs
Lea & Febiger   Lea & Febiger
League of Women Voters NYS   League of Women Voters of the City of New York
Learning Works   The Learning Works, Inc.

Leisure Pr Leisure Press
Lerner Lerner Publications, Co.
Lexikon Lexikon Services
Lexikos Lexikos Publishing
Lexington Lexington Center, Inc.
Lexington Bks Lexington Books
Lexington Data Lexington Data, Inc.
Lexington-Fayette Lexington-Fayette County Historic Commission
Lib of America The Library of America
Liberty Fund Liberty Fund, Inc.
Libraries Unlimited Libraries Unlimited, Inc.
Lightyear Lightyear Press, Inc.
Limelight Limelight, Ltd.
Limelight Edns Limelight Editions
LinguiSystems LinguiSystems, Inc.
Lion Lion Books
Lippincott J. B. Lippincott Co.
Little Little, Brown & Co.
Little Bks Little Books & Co.
Littlefield Littlefield Adams Quality Paperbacks
Liveright Liveright Publishing Corp.
Lodestar Lodestar Books
Longman Longman, Inc.
Longwood Longwood Publishing Group, Inc.
Longwood Cottage Longwood Cottage Publishing
Lord John Lord John Press
Lothrop Lothrop, Lee & Shepard Books
Lubrecht and Cramer Lubrecht & Cramer, Ltd.
Lucent Lucent Books
Lyceum Lyceum, *imprint of* Carlton Press, Inc.
Lyceum Bks Lyceum Books, Inc.
Lyceum Pr Lyceum Press
Lyon Pr Lyon Press
Lyon Prods Lyon Productions
Lyons & Burford Lyons & Burford Publishers, Inc.

M

M and T M & T Publishing, Inc.
M. Boyars Marion Boyars Publishers, Inc.
M. Evans M. Evans & Co., Inc.

McDougal McDougal, Littell & Co.
McFarland McFarland & Co., Inc., Publishers
McGraw McGraw-Hill Publishing Co.
McKay David McKay Co., Inc.
McKay Busn Systs McKay Business Systems
Macmillan Macmillan Publishing Co., Inc.
Madrona Madrona Publishers, Inc.
Main Street The Main Street Press
Manusoft Manusoft Corp.
Marine Corp Marine Corps Association
Marine Educ Marine Education Textbooks
Math Sci Pr Math-Sci Press
Mathematical Assn Mathematical Association of America
Maverick Maverick Publications
Mayfield Mayfield Publishing Co.
MECC Minnesota Educational Computing Corp.
Meckler Meckler Corp.
Meghan-Kiffer Meghan-Kiffer Press
Melior Melior Publications
Mellen The Edwin Mellen Press
Mentor Mentor Books, *imprint of* New American Library
Meredith Pr The Meredith Press, *imprint of* New Amsterdam Books
Meridian Meridian Books, *imprint of* New American Library
Merriam Webster Merriam-Webster, Inc.
Merrill Merrill Publishing Co.
Messner Julian Messner
Methuen Methuen, *imprint of* Heinemann Educational Books, Inc.
Metropolitan Mus of Art Metropolitan Museum of Art
Microsoft Microsoft
Mid Atlantic Middle Atlantic Press
Midwest Midwest Publications Co., Inc.
Military Affairs/Aerospace Historian Military Affairs/ Aerospace Historian Publishing

Minnesota Hist Soc Minnesota
Historical Society Press
Mirage Mirage Press, Ltd.
MIS Pr MIS Press
MIT Pr Massachusetts Institute of
Technology Press
MLA Modern Language
Association of America
Modern Lib Modern Library,
Inc.
Modern World Modern World
Publishing Co.
Monarch Pr Monarch Press
Monthly Review Monthly Review
Press
Moody Moody Press
Moon Moon Publications, Inc.
Moosehead Moosehead Products
Morgan Morgan & Morgan,
Inc.
Morgan Kaufmann Morgan
Kaufmann Publishers, Inc.
Morgan Pr Morgan Press
Morgan-Rand Morgan-Rand
Publications, Inc.
Morgan State Morgan State
University Press, English
Department
Morning Glory Morning Glory
Press, Inc.
Morrow William Morrow & Co.,
Inc.
Mosby Mosby/Multi-Media
Mott Media Mott Media
Mouton Mouton de Gruyter
Moyer Moyer Bell, Ltd.
MTL Materials for Today's
Learning, Inc./JV Corp.
MUMPS MUMPS Users Group
Music Sales Music Sales
Corp.
Mutual Mutual Publishing
Co.
Mysterious Mysterious Press

N

N Ross Norman Ross Publishing
Inc.
NAL New American Library
Namaste Namaste Publications
National Academy National
Academy Press

National Assn of Social Workers
National Association of Social
Workers
National Bk National Book Co.
**National Bureau of Economic
Research** Nation Bureau of
Economic Research, Inc.
National Gallery of Art National
Gallery of Art
National Geographic National
Geographic Society
National Journal National Journal
National Pr National Press, Inc.
National Textbook National
Textbook Co.
Natl Ctr Constitutional National
Center for Constitutional Studies
Naval Inst Pr Naval Institute Press
NCTE National Council of
Teachers of English
NCTM National Council of
Teachers of Mathematics
Neale Watson Neale Watson
Academic Publications, *imprint of*
Watson Publishing International
Nelson-Hall Nelson-Hall, Inc.
Network Network Publications
New Amsterdam New Amsterdam
Books
New College & Univ Pr The New
College & University Press
New Directions New Directions
Publishing Corp.
New Jersey State Museum New
Jersey State Museum
New Politics New Politics
Publishing
New Readers New Readers Press
New Riders New Riders
Publishing
New Society New Society
Publishers
New York Zoetrope New York
Zoetrope
Newbury Bks Newbury Books
Newbury Hse Newbury House
Publishers
Newmarket Newmarket Press
Newspaper Ent Newspaper
Enterprise Association, Inc.
Nightingale Nightingale-Conant
Corp.
Nilgiri Nilgiri Press
Noontide The Noontide Press

North Atlantic   North Atlantic Books
North Carolina Archives   North Carolina Division of Archives & History
North Point   North Point Press
North Point Hist Soc   North Point Historical Society
North River   North River Press, Inc.
Northland   Northland Press
Northland Bks   Northland Books
Northland Pub Co   Northland Publishing Co.
Northland Pubns   Northland Publications
Northland Winona   Northland Press of Winona
Northwest Pub   Northwest Publishing House
Norton   W. W. Norton & Co., Inc.
Nova Pub   Nova Publishing Co.
NY Acad Sci   New York Academy of Sciences

O

Oak Tree   Oak Tree Publications, Inc.
OAS   Organization of American States
Obelisk   Obelisk, *imprint of* E. P. Dutton
Occidental   Occidental Press
Oceana   Oceana Publications, Inc.
Octagon   Octagon Press
October   October House
Odyssey   Odyssey Publications, Inc.
Odyssey Pr   Odyssey Press
OECD   Organization for Economic Cooperation & Development
Ohio Hist Soc   Ohio Historical Society
Omnigraphics   Omnigraphics, Inc.
Onyx   Onyx, *imprint of* New American Library
Open Court   Open Court Publishing Co.
Open Hand   Open Hand Publishing, Inc.
Orbis   Orbis Books

Orbis Pubns   Orbis Publications, Inc.
Oregon Hist   Oregon Historical Society Press
Orient Bk Dist   Orient Book Distributors
Oriental   The Oriental Book Store
Oryx   Oryx Press
Outlet   Outlet Book Co.
Overlook Pr   Overlook Press
Ox Bow   Ox Bow Press
Oxford Univ Pr   Oxford University Press, Inc.
Oyster River   Oyster River Press
Ozer   Jerome S. Ozer Publisher, Inc.

P

P. H. Fejer   Paul Haralyi Fejer
Pacific   Pacific Press
Pacific Bk Supply   Pacific Book Supply, Co.
Pacific Bks   Pacific Books, Publishers
Pacific Edns   Pacific Editions
Pacific Gallery   Pacific Gallery Publishers
Pacific Hse   Pacific Publishing House
Pacific Info   Pacific Information, Inc.
Pacific Inst   Pacific Institute
Pacific Intl   Pacific International Publishing Co.
Pacific Pr   Pacific Press
Pacific Pr Pub Assn   Pacific Press Publishing Association
Pacific Pub   Pacific Publishing
Pagan   Pagan Press
Paganiniana   Paganiniana Publications, Inc.
Paideia   Paideia House, Publishers
PAJ   PAJ Publications
Paladin   Paladin Software Corp.
Paladin Hse   Paladin House Publishers
Paladin Pr   Paladin Press
Pantheon   Pantheon Books
Paperbacks   Paperbacks Plus Press
Paragon Benson   Paragon Associates/Benson Co., Inc.

Paragon Bk   Paragon Book Gallery, Ltd.
Paragon Group   The Paragon Group, Inc.
Paragon Hse   Paragon House Publishers
Paragon Pr   Paragon Press
Paragon Prodns   Paragon Productions
Paragon Pub   Paragon Publishing Co.
Paragon-Reiss   Paragon-Reiss
Park Row   Park Row Software
Parkwest   Parkwest Publications, Inc.
Pathfinder Fund   Pathfinder Fund
Pathfinder Pr   Pathfinder Press
Pathfinder Pub   Pathfinder Publishing
Pathfinder Pubns   Pathfinder Publications
Pathfinder Pubns Inc   Pathfinder Publications, Inc.
Patterson Smith   Patterson Smith Publishing Corp.
Paulist   Paulist Press
PBK   PBK Publications
PC-SIG   PC Software Interest Group
Peachpit   Peachpit Press
Peachtree   Peachtree Publishers, Ltd.
Peacock   F. E. Peacock Publishers, Inc.
Peak   Peak Press
Pegasus   Pegasus
Pegasus Bks   Pegasus Books, Ltd.
Pegasus Co   Pegasus Co.
Pegasus Pr   Pegasus Press
Pegasus Pub   Pegasus Publishing
Pegasus Pubns   Pegasus Publications
Pegus   Pegus Press
Pelican   Pelican Publishing Co., Inc.
Pendle Hill   Pendle Hill Publications
Pendulum   Pendulum Books
Penguin   Penguin Books
Penguin Comm   Penguin Communications Group
Performance Enhancement   The Performance Enhancements Products Press

Pergamon   Pergamon Press, Inc.
Perigee Bks   Perigee Books, *imprint of* The Putnam Publishing Group
Perigee Pr   The Perigee Press
Peripatetic   The Peripatetic Press
Perivale   Perivale Press
Persea   Persea Books, Inc.
Peter Lang   Peter Lang Publishing, Inc.
Peter Pauper   Peter Pauper, Inc.
Peter Smith   Peter Smith Publisher, Inc.
Petersons Guide   Peterson's Guides, Inc.
Petrocelli   Petrocelli Books
Phanes   Phanes Press
Pharos   Pharos Books
Phi Delta Kappa   Phi Delta Kappa Educational Foundation
Philadelphia Museum of Art   Philadelphia Museum of Art
Philomel   Philomel Books, *imprint of* The Putnam Publishing Group
Philos Res   Philosophical Research Society, Inc.
Philosophical Lib   Philosophical Library, Inc.
Pinnacle Bks   Pinnacle Books
Piper   Piper Publishing, Inc.
Plenum   Plenum Publishing Corp.
Plenum Pr   Plenum Press, *imprint of* Plenum Publishing Corporation
Plume   Plume Books, *imprint of* New American Library
Pocket   Pocket Books, Inc.
Polish Inst Art & Sci   Polish Institute of Arts & Sciences of America, Inc.
Pomegranate Artbooks   Pomegranate Artbooks, Inc.
Population Reference Bureau   Population Reference Bureau
Porcupine   Porcupine Press, Inc.
Portland House   Portland House, *imprint of* Outlet Book Co.
Poseidon   Poseidon Press, *imprint of* Pocket Books, Inc.
Poynster   Poynster Institute
Praeger   Praeger Publishers
Prentice   Prentice Hall
Presidential Acct   Presidential Accountability Group
Presidio   Presidio Press
Price Prodns   Price Productions

Price Pub   Price Publishing Co.
Price Stern   Price Stern Sloan, Inc.
Prima   Prima Publishing &
Communication
Pro Ed   Pro-Ed
Prog Peripherals   Prog Peripherals
& Software, Inc.
Prog Studies   Programmed Studies,
Inc.
Prometheus Bks   Prometheus
Books
Proscenium   Proscenium Press
PSL   PSL Computer Products
Pub Horizons   Publishing
Horizons, Inc.
Public Affairs   Public Affairs Press
Puckerbrush   Puckerbrush Press
Putnam   The Putnam Publishing
Group
Pythagorean Pr   Pythagorean Press

Q

QED Info Sci   QED Information
Sciences, Inc.
QED Pr   Q. E. D. Press of Ann
Arbor, Inc.
QED Pubns   Q. E. D. Publications
QED Research   QED Research,
Inc.
Quality Soft   Quality Software,
Inc.
Que   Que Corp.

R

R & E Pubs   R & E Publishers
RK Edns   RK Editions
Rada   Rada Press
Raintree   Raintree Publishers, Inc.
Rand   Rand McNally & Co.
Random   Random House, Inc.
Raven   Raven Press, Publishers
RCP   RCP Publications
Reader's Digest   Reader's Digest
Press
Redgrave   Redgrave Publishing Co.
Redpath   Redpath Press
Reed   Reed & Cannon Co.
Regina Bks   Regina Books
Regina Pr   Regina Press, Malhame
& Co.

Regnery   Regnery Gateway, Inc.
Reinhold   Reinhold Publishing
Corp., *imprint of* Van Nostrand
Reinhold
Reprint Services   Reprint Services
Corp.
Research   Research Publications
Research & Education   Research &
Education Association
Revisionist Pr   Revisionist Press
Reynal   Reynal, *imprint of* William
Morrow & Co., Inc.
Richard West   Richard West
Ridgeview   Ridgeview Publishing
Co.
Rienner   Lynne Rienner Publishers,
Inc.
Rinehart   Roberts Rinehart, Inc.,
Pubs.
Riverdale   The Riverdale Co., Inc.
Riverrun   Riverrun Press, Inc.
Rizzoli   Rizzoli International
Publications, Inc.
Rodale   Rodale Press, Inc.
Rosen   Rosen Publishing Group
Ross-Erikson   Ross-Erikson
Roth   Roth Publishing, Inc.
Rothman   Fred B. Rothman & Co.
Rourke   Rourke Corp.
Routledge   Routledge, Chapman &
Hall, Inc.
Rowman   Rowman & Littlefield
Publishers, Inc.
Running Pr   Running Press Book
Publishers
Russell Sage   Russell Sage
Foundation

S

Sabbot   Sabbot-Natural History
Books
Sage   Sage Publications, Inc.
Sage Creek Pr   Sage Creek Press
Sage Pr   Sage Press
Sage Pub   Sage Publishing Co.
Sage Pubns   Sage Publications
Saifer   Albert Saifer Publisher
St. Martin's   St. Martin's Press, Inc.
Salem Hse   Salem House
Publishers
Salem Pr   Salem Press, Inc.
Salem Pub   Salem Publishing Co.

SamHar SamHar Press
Sams Howard W. Sams & Co.
Saphrograph Saphrograph
Corp.
SAS Inst SAS Institute, Inc.
Saunders Saunders College
Publishing
Saybrook Pr The Saybrook Press
Saybrook Pub Co Saybrook
Publishing Co., Inc.
Scarborough Faire Scarborough
Faire, Inc.
Scarborough Hse Scarborough
House
Scarecrow Scarecrow Press, Inc.
Schenkman Schenkman Books,
Inc.
Schirmer Schirmer Books
Schocken Schocken Books, Inc.
Schoenhof Schoenhof's Foreign
Books, Inc.
Schol Am Res School of American
Research Press
Schol Facsimiles Scholars'
Facsimiles & Reprints
Scholarly Scholarly Press, Inc.
Scholarly Res Scholarly Resources,
Inc.
Scholars Bk Scholars Book Co.
Scholars Bks Scholars Books
Scholars Bookshelf Scholar's
Bookshelf
Scholars Ref Lib Scholar's
Reference Library
Scholars Pr Scholars Press
Scholars Pr Ltd. Scholars' Press,
Ltd.
Scholastic Scholastic, Inc.
Scholium Scholium International,
Inc.
Sci-Tech Pubns Sci Tech
Publications
Sci Tech Pubs Science Tech
Publishers
Scott Scott, Foresman & Co.
Scribner's Charles Scribner's Sons
Seaver Seaver Books
Seven Hills Seven Hills Book
Distributors
Seven Locks Seven Locks Press
Seymour Dale Seymour
Publications
Shambhala Shambhala
Publications, Inc.

Shapolsky Shapolsky Publishers,
Inc.
Sharon Sharon Publications, Inc.
Sharpe M. E. Sharpe, Inc.
Shaw Harold Shaw Publishers
Sheed & Ward Sheed & Ward
Shelter Shelter Publications, Inc.
Sheridan Med Bks Sheridan
Medical Books
Shoe String Shoe String Press, Inc.
Sierra Sierra Club Books
Signet Signet Books, *imprint of*
New American Library
Silicon Silicon Press
Silver Silver, Burdett & Ginn, Inc.
Simon Simon & Schuster, Inc.
Sinauer Sinauer Associates, Inc.
Slavica Slavica Publishers, Inc.
Smith W. H. Smith Publishers,
Inc.
Smith & Smith Smith & Smith
Publishing Co.
Smith & Varina Smith & Varina
Publishers
Smith Coll Smith College
Publications
Smith Coll Mus Art Smith
College Museum of Art
Smith Collins Smith Collins Co.
Smith Lib Warren Hunting Smith
Library
Smith Prod Smith Productions
Smithsonian Smithsonian
Institution Press
Smithsonian Bks Smithsonian
Books
Soc Computer Sim Society for
Computer Simulation
Society Tech Comm Society for
Technical Communication
Solaris Solaris Press, Inc.
Somerset Somerset Publishers, Inc.
Sophia Sophia Press
Sophia Inst Pr Sophia Institute
Press
Sound Mgmt Sound Management
Productions
South Asia Bks South Asia Books
South End South End Press
South-Western South-Western
Publishing Co.
Sovereign Sovereign Press
Spertus The Spertus College of
Judaica Press

Sphinx Sphinx Press
SPIE SPIE—International Society for Optical Engineering
Springer-Verlag Springer-Verlag New York, Inc.
SPSS SPSS, Inc.
SRA Science Research Associates
Stackpole Stackpole Books
Star Valley Star Valley Publications
Starmont Starmont House, Inc.
State Mutual State Mutual Book & Periodical Service, Ltd.
Station Hill Station Hill Press
Steck-Vaughn Steck-Vaughn Co.
Steiner Rudolf Steiner Institute
Stephen Greene Stephen Greene Press
Sterling Sterling Publishing Co., Inc.
Sterling & Selesnick Sterling & Selesnick
Stewart Tabori & Chang Stewart, Tabori, & Chang, Inc.
Stickley George F. Stickley Co.
Stipes Stipes Publishing Co.
Stoeger Stoeger Publishing Co.
Stokes Stokes Publishing Co.
Storm King Storm King Press
Stryker-Post Stryker-Post Publications
Sugden Sherwood Sugden & Co.
Summa Summa Publications
Summit Bks Summit Books
Sunrise Bks Sunrise Books
Sunrise Pr Sunrise Press
Swedenborg Swedenborg Foundation, Inc.
Swedenborg Sci Assn Swedenborg Science Association
Sybex Sybex, Inc.
Syracuse Univ Foreign Comp Syracuse University, Foreign & Comparative Studies Program

T

TAB TAB Books, Inc.
TAMS Token & Medal Society, Inc.
Taplinger Taplinger Publishing Co., Inc.
Tarcher Jeremy P. Tarcher, Inc.

Tavistock Tavistock Poetry Press
Taylor Taylor Publishing Co.
Taylor & Francis Taylor & Francis, Inc.
Taylor and Ng Taylor and Ng
Taylor-James Taylor-James, Ltd.
Taylor Taylor Taylor, Taylor & Taylor
Taylor Winnstead Pubs Taylor Winnstead Publishers
Teachers and Writers Coll Teachers & Writers Collaborative
Teachers College Teachers College Press
Templegate Templegate Publishers
Ten Speed Ten Speed Press
TeNeues TeNeues Publishing Co.
Territ Pr Territorial Press
Thames Hudson Thames & Hudson
Theatre Arts Theatre Arts Books
Third World Third World Book Shop
Thomas Charles C. Thomas Publisher
Thomasson-Grant Thomasson-Grant, Inc.
Thor Thor Publishing Co.
Thorndike Thorndike Press
Three Continents Three Continents Press
Thunder's Mouth Thunder's Mouth Press
Ticknor Ticknor & Fields
Timber Timber Press
Time-Life Time-Life Books
Times Bks Times Books
Timken Timken Publishers, Inc.
Torres Eliseo Torres & Sons
Touchstone Touchstone Books, *imprint of* Simon & Schuster, Inc.
Transaction Transaction Publications
Tree Bks Tree Books
Tree City Tree City Press
Tree Communications Tree Communications, Inc.
Tree Hse Tree House Press
Tree Life Tree of Life Publications
Triad Triad Press
Trillium Trillium Press
Troll Troll Associates
Tundra Tundra Books of Northern New York

Turtle Island Turtle Island Foundation, Netzahaulcoyotl Historical Society
Tuttle Charles E. Tuttle Co., Inc.
Twayne Twayne Publishers, *imprint of* G. K. Hall, & Co.
Twenty-First Pr Twenty-First Century Press

U

UCLA Lat Am Ctr University of California, Latin American Center
UMI UMI Research Press
UN United Nations
Underwood Barry Underwood
Underwood-Miller Underwood/ Miller
Ungar Ungar Publishing Co.
Unicorn Unicorn Press
Unicorn Bkshop Unicorn Bookshop
Unicorn Comm Unicorn Communications
Unicorn Ent Unicorn Enterprises
Unicorn Pub The Unicorn Publishing House, Inc.
Univ of California Inst of East Asian Studies University of California, Institute of East Asian Studies
Univ Place Bk Shop University Place Book Shop
Univ Pr of America University Press of America
Univ Presses FL University Presses of Florida
Universe Universe Books, Inc.
Universe Pub Universe Publishing Co.
Unwin Unwin Hyman, Inc.
Urban Inst Urban Institute Press
USGPO U. S. Government Printing Office

V

Valley Hill Valley Hill Publishing Company
Van Nostrand Van Nostrand Reinhold

Vance Biblios Vance Bibliographies
Vanguard Vanguard Press, Inc.
Vanguard Inst Vanguard Institutional Publishers
Vanni S. F. Vanni
Vantage Vantage Press, Inc.
Vantage Info Vantage Information
Vantage Printing Vantage Printing Co.
VCH Pubs VCH Publishers, Inc.
Ventana Ventana Press
Vienna Vienna House, Inc.
Viking Viking Penguin
Vintage Vintage Publications
Vintage America Vintage America Publishing Co.

W

Wadsworth Wadsworth Publishing Co.
Wadsworth Atheneum Wadsworth Atheneum
Walck Henry Z. Walck, Inc.
Walker Walker & Co.
Walker Ed Walker Educational Book Corp.
Walker, Evans, & Cogswell Walker, Evans, & Cogswell Co.
Walker Pub Walker Publishing Co., Inc.
Walker Pubns Walker Publications
Walter J. Johnson Walter J. Johnson, Inc.
Warner Bks Warner Books, Inc.
Warthog Warthog Press
Warwick Warwick Press, *imprint of* Franklin Watts, Inc.
Washington Square Pr Washington Square Press, Inc.
Watson Watson Publishing House
Watson-Guptill Watson-Guptill Publications, Inc.
Watson Pub Intl Watson Publishing International
Watts Franklin Watts, Inc.
Waveland Waveland Press, Inc.
Waverly Waverly Publishers
Waverly Comm Hse Waverly Community House, Inc.
Wayside Wayside Publishing

Weber Systems Weber Systems, Inc.
Wehman Wehman Brothers, Inc.
Weidenfeld Weidenfeld & Nicolson
Welstar Welstar Publications
West Pr West Press
West Pub West Publishing Co., College & School Division
Western Pub Western Publishing Co., Inc.
Westminster John Knox Westminster/John Knox Press
Westview Westview Press
White House Hist White House Historical Association
Whitston Whitston Publishing Co., Inc.
Wiener Markus Wiener Publishing, Inc.
Wieser Wieser & Wieser, Inc.
Wilderness Wilderness Press
Wiley John Wiley & Sons, Inc.
Williams and Wilkins Williams & Wilkins
Wilson H. W. Wilson
Wittenborn George Wittenborn, Inc.
Wizards Bookshelf Wizards Bookshelf
Wizards Pr Wizard's Press
Woodbridge Woodbridge Press Publishing Co.
Wordware Wordware Publishing, Inc.
Workman Workman Publishing Co., Inc.

World Book World Book, Inc.
World Eagle World Eagle, Inc.
World Future World Future Society
World Info Inst World Information Institute
World Scientific World Scientific Publishing Co., Inc.
World Without War World Without War Council
Worth Worth Publishers, Inc.
Writer Writer, Inc.
Writers and Readers Writers & Readers Publishing, Inc.
Writers Digest Writer's Digest Books
WWAI Who's Who in Artificial Intelligence

Y

Yale Univ Far Eastern Pubns Yale University, Far Eastern Publications
Year Bk Med Year Book Medical Publishers, Inc.
Youth Education Youth Education Systems, Inc.

Z

Zebra Zebra Books
Zenger Zenger Publishing Co., Inc.
Zondervan Zondervan Publishing House

PROFILE INDEX

This index appears in each of the two volumes of *The Young Adult Reader's Adviser.* It presents in alphabetical sequence the authors who are profiled in each volume. The number of the volume in which a profiled author appears is given with a colon followed by the page number on which the profile begins. For example, the entry **2:169** indicates that the profile of Abigail Adams can be found on page 169 of Volume 2.

The volume number and page number that immediately follow the author's name appear in boldface type. This always indicates the location of the profile, or biographical sketch. Some individuals are profiled twice (for example, Archimedes) and are followed by two boldface volume and page numbers. Sometimes more numbers in lightface may follow. These lightface numbers indicate additional secondary references to profiled authors, references that may occur in general introductions or in other biographical narratives.

A

Achebe, Chinua, **1:411**
Adams, Abigail, **2:169**
Adams, Ansel, **2:263**
Adams, Douglas, **1:64**
Adams, Henry, **2:214**
Adams, John, **2:170,** 2:169, 2:172, 2:214
Adams, John Quincy, **2:172,** 2:169, 2:170, 2:180, 2:181, 2:214
Addams, Jane, **2:208**
Aeschylus, **1:311,** 1:310, 1:314
Aesop, **1:312,** 1:290
Albee, Edward, **1:186,** 1:308
Alcott, Louisa May, **1:167,** 1:21
Aleichem, Sholem, **1:383**
Alexander, Lloyd, **1:187**
Alger, Horatio, Jr., **1:168**
Allen, Steve, **1:446**
Allen, Woody, **1:188, 1:471,** 1:286
Allport, Gordon W., **2:115**
Amis, Kingsley, **1:65,** 1:100
Andersen, Hans Christian, **1:374**
Anderson, Sherwood, **1:189,** 1:219
Andric, Ivo, **1:384**
Angelou, Maya, **1:190**

Anouilh, Jean, **1:328**
Antin, Mary, **2:208**
Apollonius of Perga, **1:513**
Archimedes, **1:520; 2:516**
Aristophanes, **1:313,** 1:311, 1:312
Aristotle, **2:286, 2:442,** 2:301, 2:302, 2:307
Armour, Richard, **1:192**
Armstrong, Louis, **2:263**
Arnold, Matthew, **1:40**
Arrow, Kenneth J., **2:64**
Asimov, Isaac, **1:193; 2:433**
Atwood, Margaret, **1:134**
Auden, W. H., **1:66,** 1:96, 1:100, 1:105, 1:281
Audubon, John James, **2:187**
Austen, Jane, **1:19**
Averroes, **2:301**

B

Babbage, Charles, **1:540,** 1:547
Bach, Johann Sebastian, **2:334**
Bacon, Sir Francis, **1:9; 2:435,** 2:498
Baker, Russell, **1:480**

Baldwin, James, **1:194**
Ballard, J. G., **1:66**
Balzac, Honoré de, **1:329**
Bambara, Toni Cade, **1:195**
Baraka, Amiri, **1:196**
Barrie, J. M., **1:67**
Barthelme, Donald, **1:197**
Bartok, Bela, **2:415**
Barton, Clara Harlowe, **2:193, 2:568**
Baudelaire, Charles, **1:330**
Baum, L. (Lyman) Frank, **1:198**
Beckett, Samuel, **1:330**
Behan, Brendan, **1:68**
Bell, Daniel, **2:149**
Bellow, Saul, **1:199**, 1:181
Benedict, Ruth, **2:43,** 2:44, 2:46
Benet, Stephen Vincent, **1:200**
Ben-Gurion, David, **2:412**
Bentham, Jeremy, **2:7**
Berlin, Irving, **2:264**
Berlioz, Hector, **2:346**
Bernoulli, Jakob, **1:530,** 1:525
Bernstein, Leonard, **2:265**
Bethune, Mary McLeod, **2:13**
Beti, Mongo, **1:412**
Bierce, Ambrose Gwinnett, **1:169**, 1:402
Binet, Alfred, **2:122**
Bismarck, Otto von, **2:341**
Blake, William, **1:31**
Blume, Judy, **1:201**
Boas, Franz, **2:44,** 2:43, 2:46, 2:134
Boccaccio, Giovanni, **1:348,** 1:6
Bohr, Neils Henrik David, **2:500,** 2:502, 2:521
Böll, Heinrich, **1:363**
Bolt, Robert, **1:68**
Bombeck, Erma, **1:446**
Bonaparte, Napoleon, **2:330,** 2:332
Boole, George, **1:506**
Borges, Jorge Luis, **1:399**
Boswell, James, **1:26,** 1:25
Boulle, Pierre, **1:331**
Bourbaki, Nicolas, **1:499**
Bowen, Elizabeth, **1:69,** 1:107
Bowman, Isaiah, **2:76**
Boyle, Robert, **2:498,** 2:501
Bradbury, Ray, **1:202**
Bradford, William, **1:151**
Bradstreet, Anne, **1:151**
Brahe, Tycho, **2:471,** 2:474
Brahms, Johannes, **2:348**
Brautigan, Richard, **1:203**
Brecht, Bertolt, **1:364**
Brezhnev, Leonid, **2:388**
Bridgers, Sue Ellen, **1:204**
Britten, Benjamin, **2:416**
Brontë, Charlotte, **1:41**
Brontë, Emily, **1:42,** 1:41
Brooke, Rupert, **1:70**
Brooks, Gwendolyn, **1:204**

Brown, Charles Brockden, **1:152**
Brown, Sterling, **1:205**
Brown, William Wells, **1:170**
Browning, Elizabeth Barrett, **1:43,** 1:44, 1:56, 1:132
Browning, Robert, **1:44,** 1:43
Bryan, William Jennings, **2:204,** 2:223
Bryant, William Cullen, **1:156**
Buchwald, Art, **1:487**
Buck, Pearl, **1:206**
Bunin, Ivan, **1:390**
Bunyan, John, **1:21**
Burgess, Anthony, **1:70**
Burke, Edmund, **2:8, 2:328,** 2:165
Burnford, Sheila, **1:136**
Burns, Robert, **1:32**
Burroughs, Edgar Rice, **1:207**
Burton, Sir Richard Francis, **2:363**
Bush, George Herbert Walker, **2:258**
Byron, Lord, George Gordon, **1:32,** 1:389

C

Cable, George Washington, **1:171**
Caesar, Julius, **2:291,** 1:319, 1:320; 2:293, 2:308
Calderón de la Barca, Pedro, **1:355**
Calhoun, John Caldwell, **2:180,** 2:182
Callaghan, Morley, **1:136,** 1:236
Calvin, John, **2:311**
Camus, Albert, **1:332**
Cantor, Georg, **1:499**
Capek, Karel, **1:384**
Cardenal, Father Ernesto, **1:400**
Carducci, Giosuè, **1:348**
Carnegie, Andrew, **2:205**
Carpentier, Alejo, **1:400**
Carroll, Lewis, **1:44**
Carson, Rachel, **2:242, 2:466**
Carter, James Earl, **2:255,** 2:253
Cary, Joyce, **1:71**
Cassat, Mary, **2:214**
Castro, Fidel, **2:409**
Cather, Willa, **1:208,** 1:180
Catlin, George, **2:188**
Cauchy, Augustin Louis, **1:524**
Cellini, Benvenuto, **2:312**
Cervantes Saavedra, Miguel de, **1:356**
Cezanne, Paul, **2:348**
Chagall, Marc, **2:417**
Chandler, Raymond, **1:209**
Chaucer, Geoffrey, **1:6,** 1:310, 1:348
Cheever, John, **1:210**
Chekhov, Anton, **1:390,** 1:378
Chesnutt, Charles W., **1:171**
Chesterton, G. K., **1:72**
Chief Joseph, **2:202**
Childress, Alice, **1:211**

Chisholm, Shirley Anita St. Hill, **2:33**
Chomsky, Noam, **1:434**
Chopin, Frédéric, **2:349**
Chopin, Kate, **1:172**
Christie, Dame Agatha, **1:73**
Churchill, Winston S., **2:385**
Cicero, Marcus Tullius, **2:292**
Clark, William, **2:176,** 2:175
Clarke, Arthur C., **1:74**
Clay, Henry, **2:181,** 2:173
Coetzee, J. M., **1:412**
Cohen, Leonard, **1:137**
Coleridge, Samuel Taylor, **1:33,** 1:22, 1:35, 1:38
Coles, Robert, **2:105**
Collins, Wilkie, **1:45**
Colum, Padraic, **1:75**
Columbus, Christopher, **2:159,** 2:309, 2:325
Comte, Auguste, **2:125**
Confucius, **2:282,** 2:283
Congreve, William, **1:21,** 1:323
Conrad, Joseph, **1:76,** 1:87, 1:173
Constable, John, **2:350,** 2:357
Cook, Captain James, **2:321**
Coolidge, Calvin, **2:227,** 2:230
Copernicus, Nicolaus, **2:513,** 2:471, 2:472
Cormier, Robert, **1:212**
Cortés, Hernán, **2:322**
Cousteau, Jacques–Yves, **2:487**
Coward, Sir Noel, **1:77**
Cowper, William, **1:22**
Crane, Stephen, **1:173,** 1:181
Crevecoeur, Michel-Guillaume Jean De, **1:152**
Crick, Francis Harry Compton, **2:439,** 2:440, 2:441, 2:505
Cronin, A. J., **1:78**
Cullen, Countee, **1:213**
Cummings, E. E., **1:214**
Cunningham, Merce, **2:265**
Curie, Marie, **2:509,** 2:504
Cushing, Harvey, **2:531**
Custer, George Armstrong, **2:202**

D

Dahl, Roald, **1:78**
Dalton, John, **2:501,** 2:503
Dante Alighieri, **1:349,** 1:117, 1:348
Darío, Rubén, **1:401**
Darwin, Charles Robert, **2:456,** 2:117, 2:459, 2:490
Davies, Robertson, **1:137**
Debussy, Achille Claude, **2:418**
Defoe, Daniel, **1:22**
Degas, Edgar, **2:351**
De Gaulle, Charles, **2:386**
Descartes, René, **1:514,** 1:508

Dewey, John, **2:219**
Dickens, Charles, **1:46,** 1:45, 1:61, 1:329
Dickey, James, **1:214**
Dickinson, Emily, **1:174**
Dillard, Annie, **1:482**
Dinesen, Isak, **1:375**
Diophantus, **1:507,** 1:508
Disney, Walt, **1:474**
Disraeli, Benjamin, **2:342,** 2:345, 2:368
Dollard, John, **2:116**
Donne, John, **1:10,** 1:154
Dostoevsky, Fyodor, **1:391**
Douglass, Frederick, **2:190**
Doyle, Sir Arthur Conan, **1:48**
Drabble, Margaret, **1:79**
Drake, Sir Francis, **2:323**
Dreiser, Theodore, **1:215,** 1:189, 1:344
Dryden, John, **1:23**
Du Bois, W. E. B., **2:210,** 2:213
Dulles, John Foster, **2:22,** 2:239
Dumas, Alexandre, **1:333**
Du Maurier, Daphne, **1:80**
Dunbar, Paul Laurence, **1:175**
Duncan, Isadora, **2:266**
Durer, Albrecht, **2:312**
Durkheim, Emile, **2:126**
Durrell, Lawrence, **1:81**

E

Edison, Thomas Alva, **2:522**
Edwards, Jonathan, **1:153**
Einstein, Albert, **2:519,** 2:521
Eisenhower, Dwight David, **2:239,** 2:22, 2:253
Eliot, George, **1:48,** 1:61
Eliot, T. S., **1:82,** 1:66, 1:134, 1:290
Ellington, Edward Kennedy, **2:266**
Ellison, Ralph, **1:217,** 1:307
Emecheta, Buchi, **1:413**
Emerson, Ralph Waldo, **1:156,** 1:153, 1:165, 1:167, 1:184
Engels, Friedrich, **2:58**
Erasmus, Desiderius, **2:314,** 2:313
Erikson, Erik H., **2:108**
Euclid, **1:513;** 2:517
Euler, Leonhard, **1:525**
Euripides, **1:313**

F

Faraday, Michael, **2:524**
Fast, Howard, **1:218**
Faulkner, William, **1:219,** 1:177, 1:190
Ferber, Edna, **1:220**
Ferlinghetti, Lawrence, **1:221,** 1:225
Fermat, Pierre de, **1:508,** 1:533

Fermi, Enrico, **2:528,** 2:503
Fielding, Henry, **1:24**
Fitzgerald, F. (Francis) Scott, **1:221,** 1:136, 1:236
Flaubert, Gustave, **1:334,** 1:337, 1:341, 1:344
Fleming, Alexander, **2:557**
Fleming, Ian, **1:83,** 1:65
Ford, Gerald R., **2:252,** 2:256
Forester, C. S., **1:84**
Forster, E. M., **1:85**
Fowles, John, **1:86**
Frame, Janet, **1:138**
France, Anatole, **1:335**
Frankfurter, Felix, **2:27**
Franklin, Benjamin, **2:167, 2:525,** 2:165
Freud, Sigmund, **2:117,** 2:10, 2:102, 2:108, 2:118, 2:119
Friedan, Betty, **2:243**
Friedman, Milton, **2:65**
Frisch, Karl von, **2:462,** 2:463, 2:465
Frost, Robert, **1:223**
Fry, Christopher, **1:86**
Fuentes, Carlos, **1:402**
Fuller, R. Buckminster, **1:521**

G

Gaines, Ernest J., **1:224**
Gainsborough, Thomas, **2:335**
Galbraith, John Kenneth, **2:66**
Galen, **2:546,** 2:548
Galileo, **2:471,** 2:498, 2:515
Gallant, Mavis, **1:139**
Galois, Evariste, **1:508,** 1:525
Galsworthy, John, **1:87**
Gandhi, Indira, **2:400**
Gandhi, Mohandas Karamchand, **2:365,** 1:165; 2:403
García Lorca, Federico, **1:357**
García Márquez, Gabriel, **1:403**
Gardner, Martin, **1:535**
Garfield, James Abram, **2:194**
Garibaldi, Giuseppi, **2:343**
Garrison, William Lloyd, **2:191**
Gates, William, **1:542**
Gauguin, Paul, **2:352**
Gauss, Carl Friedrich, **1:531,** 1:518
Gide, André, **1:335,** 1:231
Gilbert, Sir William Schwenk, **1:50**
Gilchrist, Ellen, **1:224**
Ginsberg, Allen, **1:225,** 1:221
Giovanni, Nikki, **1:225,** 1:230
Gladstone, William Ewart, **2:345,** 2:368
Glasgow, Ellen, **1:226**
Godden, (Margaret) Rumer, **1:88**
Gödel, Kurt, **1:499,** 1:503
Goethe, Johann Wolfgang von, **1:365,** 1:372, 1:393; 2:11

Gogol, Nikolai, **1:392**
Golding, William, **1:89**
Goldman, William, **1:227**
Goldsmith, Oliver, **1:25**
Goldwater, Barry Morris, **2:244,** 2:259
Goodall, Jane, **2:463**
Gorbachev, Mikhail Sergeyevich, **2:406**
Gordimer, Nadine, **1:414**
Gould, Stephen Jay, **2:457**
Grant, Ulysses S., **2:199**
Grass, Günter, **1:367**
Graves, Robert, **1:90,** 1:120, 1:231
Gray, Thomas, **1:25**
Greene, Bette, **1:227**
Greene, Graham, **1:91**
Gropius, Walter, **2:267**
Guy, Rosa, **1:228**
Guyot, Arnold, **2:80**

H

Haggard, Sir Henry Rider, **1:50**
Hakluyt, Richard, **2:324**
Halley, Edmond, **2:476**
Hamilton, Alexander, **2:173,** 2:171, 2:178
Hamilton, Virginia, **1:229**
Hammarskjold, Dag, **2:389**
Hammett, Dashiell, **1:231,** 1:210, 1:235
Hamsun, Knut, **1:376**
Handel, George Frederick, **2:336**
Hanrahan, Barbara, **1:139**
Hansberry, Lorraine, **1:232**
Hardy, Thomas, **1:51**
Harris, Marvin, **2:47**
Harris, Wilson, **1:404**
Harte, Bret, **1:176**
Harvey, William, **2:547**
Hawthorne, Nathaniel, **1:176,** 1:157, 1:160, 1:162
Hayakawa, S. I., **1:438**
Hayden, Robert, **1:232**
Haydn, Franz Joseph, **2:336**
Heaney, Seamus, **1:92**
Heinlein, Robert, **1:233**
Heller, Joseph, **1:234**
Hellman, Lillian, **1:235,** 1:272
Hemingway, Ernest, **1:236,** 1:136, 1:181, 1:190
Henry, Joseph, **2:483**
Henry, O., **1:178**
Hentoff, Nat, **1:237**
Herbert, Frank, **1:238**
Herbert, George, **1:10,** 1:154
Herodotus, **2:287**
Herrick, Robert, **1:11**
Herriot, James, **1:93**
Herschel, William, **2:477**
Hesse, Hermann, **1:368**

Heyerdahl, Thor, **2:410**
Highwater, Jamake, **1:239**
Hilbert, David, **1:517**, 1:509
Hilton, James, **1:93**
Hinton, S. E., **1:239**
Hippocrates, **2:532**, 2:547
Hitler, Adolf, **2:375**, 1:364
Hobbes, Thomas, **2:9**
Hollerith, Herman, **1:543**
Holmes, Oliver Wendell, **1:158**, 1:184; 2:28
Holmes, Oliver Wendell, Jr., **2:28**
Homer, **1:315**, 1:311; 2:270
Homer, Winslow, **2:215**
Hoover, Herbert Clark, **2:230**
Hopkins, Gerard Manley, **1:53**
Hopper, Grace Murray, **1:544**
Horace, **1:320**; **2:293**
Horney, Karen, **2:118**
Housman, A. E., **1:53**
Houston, Samuel, **2:185**
Hubble, Edwin Powell, **2:477**
Hughes, Langston, **1:240**, 1:232
Hughes, Ted, **1:94**, 1:276
Hugo, Victor Marie, **1:336**, 1:170
Humboldt, Friedrich Heinrich Alexander von, **2:77**
Humphrey, Hubert Horatio, **2:245**
Hurston, Zora Neale, **1:242**
Huston, John, **1:471**
Hutton, James, **2:489**, 2:490
Huxley, Aldous, **1:95**, 1:96

I

Ibn Batuta, **2:300**
Ibsen, Henrik, **1:377**, 1:380
Irving, Washington, **1:158**, 1:160
Isherwood, Christopher, **1:96**

J

Jackson, Andrew, **2:182**, 2:173, 2:180
Jackson, Shirley, **1:242**
Jacobs, W. W., **1:97**
Jaffee, Al, **1:455**
James, Henry, **1:178**, 1:173, 1:177, 1:182, 1:183; 2:96
James, P. D., **1:97**
James, Preston E., **2:78**
James, William, **2:96**
Jarrell, Randall, **1:243**
Jeffers, (John) Robinson, **1:244**
Jefferson, Thomas, **2:174**, 2:171, 2:176, 2:177, 2:178
Jewett, Sarah Orne, **1:180**
Jobs, Steven, **1:545**
Johanson, Donald Carl, **2:460**

Johnson, James Weldon, **1:245**
Johnson, Lyndon Baines, **2:245**, 2:25, 2:244, 2:245, 2:247, 2:248, 2:253
Johnson, Samuel, **1:26**, 1:25
Jonson, Ben, **1:11**
Jordan, Barbara Charline, **2:23**
Joyce, James, **1:98**, 1:136
Jung, Carl Gustav, **2:119**, 2:117

K

Kafka, Franz, **1:368**
Keats, John, **1:34**, 1:17
Keller, Helen, **1:448**
Kennan, George, **2:390**
Kennedy, John Fitzgerald, **2:246**, 1:130; 2:25, 2:245, 2:248, 2:251
Kennedy, Robert Francis, **2:248**
Kenyatta, Jomo, **2:394**, 2:210
Kepler, Johannes, **2:474**, 2:471, 2:472, 2:514
Kerouac, Jack, **1:246**
Kerr, M. E., **1:247**
Keynes, John Maynard, **2:67**, 2:60
Khrushchev, Nikita, **2:391**, 2:388
King, Martin Luther, Jr., **2:249**, 2:365
King, Stephen, **1:248**
Kipling, Rudyard, **1:54**, 1:65
Kissinger, Henry Alfred, **2:37**
Klein, Felix, **1:517**
Klein, Norma, **1:249**
Knowles, John, **1:251**
Koch, Robert, **2:444**, 2:445
Kohlberg, Lawrence, **2:109**
Krebs, Hans Adolf, **2:438**
Kroeber, Alfred Louis, **2:45**, 2:44
Kundera, Milan, **1:385**

L

La Follette, Robert Marion, **2:220**
Lagervist, Pär, **1:378**
Lamarck, Jean Baptiste De Monet De, **2:458**
Lamb, Charles, **1:35**
L'Amour, Louis, **1:251**
Lange, Dorothea, **2:231**
Lanier, Sidney, **1:159**
Lao-Tzu, **2:283**
Larkin, Philip, **1:99**
Lasswell, Harold D., **2:10**
Laurence, Margaret, **1:140**
Lavoisier, Antoine Laurent, **2:499**
Lawrence, D. H., **1:100**, 1:262
Lawrence, T. E., **2:372**
Laye, Camara, **1:414**
Leacock, Stephen, **1:140**
Leakey, Louis S. B., **2:49**, 2:463

Leakey, Mary, **2:49**
Leakey, Richard E. F., **2:49**
Le Carre, John, **1:102**
Le Corbusier, **2:419**
Lee, Harper, **1:253**
Lee, Robert Edward, **2:195**
Lee, Spike, **1:485**
Le Guin, Ursula K., **1:253**
Leibniz, Gottfried Wilhelm, **1:526**
Lem, Stanislaw, **1:386**
Lenin, Vladimir Ilyich, **2:377**, 2:379, 2:381, 2:409
Leonardo Da Vinci, **2:315**, 2:319
Lessing, Doris, **1:103**
Lester, Julius, **1:255**
Lévi-Strauss, Claude, **2:52**
Lewin, Kurt, **2:98**
Lewis, C. S., **1:104**
Lewis, Meriwether, **2:176**, 2:175
Lewis, Sinclair, **1:255**, 1:189, 1:231
Lincoln, Abraham, **2:196**, 2:15, 2:191, 2:198, 2:568
Lindsay, Norman, **1:141**
Linnaeus, Carolus, **2:442**
Liszt, Franz, **2:353**, 2:362, 2:424
Livingstone, David, **2:366**
Livy, **2:294**
Lloyd George, David, **2:373**
Lobachevsky, Nikolai Ivanovitch, **1:518**
Locke, John, **2:17**
London, Jack, **1:256**
Longfellow, Henry Wadsworth, **1:160**, 1:161, 1:176, 1:184
Lope de Vega Carpio, Félix, **1:358**, 1:355, 1:356
Lorenz, Konrad, **2:99**, 2:463, 2:462, 2:465
Lovelace, Countess of, Ada Augusta, **1:546**, 1:541
Lowell, Amy, **1:257**
Lowell, James Russell, **1:161**, 1:156, 1:257, 1:258
Lowell, Robert, **1:258**, 1:184
Luther, Martin, **2:316**, 1:361; 2:314
Lyell, Charles, **2:490**
Lynd, Helen Merrel, **2:131**
Lynd, Robert Staughton, **2:131**

M

McClintock, Barbara, **2:452**
McDavid, Raven I., Jr, **1:431**
McGovern, George Stanley, **2:251**
Machiavelli, Niccolò, **2:20**
McKay, Claude, **1:259**
Mackinder, Halford John, Sir, **2:78**
MacLeish, Archibald, **1:260**
McLuhan, (Herbert) Marshall, **1:453**
MacNeice, Louis, **1:105**, 1:66

Madison, James, **2:177**, 2:178
Mahler, Gustav, **2:354**
Maimonides, Moses, **2:302**
Malamud, Bernard, **1:261**
Malcolm X, **1:450; 2:250**
Malinowski, Bronislaw, **2:45**, 2:53
Malory, Sir Thomas, **1:7**
Malthus, Thomas Robert, **2:69**
Mandela, Nelson, **2:394**
Mann, Horace, **2:186**
Mann, Thomas, **1:369**
Mansfield, Katherine, **1:141**
Mao Zedong, **2:401**
Marlowe, Christopher, **1:12**, 1:323
Marryat, Captain Frederick, **1:56**
Marshall, Alfred, **2:56**
Marshall, George Catlett, **2:240**
Marshall, John, **2:29**
Martí, José, **2:370**
Marvell, Andrew, **1:13**
Marx, Karl, **2:59**, 1:257; 2:58, 2:73, 2:117, 2:143, 2:377, 2:381, 2:409
Mason, Bobbie Ann, **1:262**
Masters, Edgar Lee, **1:263**
Mauchly, John, **1:547**, 1:552
Maugham, W. (William) Somerset, **1:105**
Maupassant, Guy de, **1:337**
Maxwell, James Clerk, **2:527**
Mead, George Herbert, **2:139**
Mead, Margaret, **2:46**, 2:44, 2:134
Meir, Golda, **2:413**
Melville, Herman, **1:161**, 1:157, 1:177
Mencken, H. L., **1:435**, 1:432, 1:472
Mendel, Gregor Johann, **2:453**, 2:454
Mendeleev, Dimitri Ivanovich, **2:506**
Merton, Robert King, **2:140**
Metternich, Prince Klemens von, **2:332**
Michelangelo, **2:317**, 2:319, 2:338
Michener, James, **1:264**
Mill, John Stuart, **2:72**, 2:7
Millay, Edna St. Vincent, **1:265**
Miller, Arthur, **1:265**
Milosz, Czeslaw, **1:386**
Milton, John, **1:13**, 1:13
Mistral, Gabriela, **1:405**
Mitchinson, Naomi, **1:106**
Mohr, Nicholasa, **1:267**
Molière, **1:338**, 1:323, 1:373
Monroe, James, **2:178**, 2:172, 2:180
Montesquieu, Charles Louis de Secondat, Baron de la Brède et de, **2:18**
Montgomery, L. M., **1:142**
Moore, Marianne, **1:268**
Moravia, Alberto, **1:350**
More, Sir Thomas, **1:14**
Morgan, Thomas Hunt, **2:454**
Morrison, Toni, **1:268**
Mowat, Farley, **1:144**
Moyers, Bill, **1:466**

Muir, John, **2:220**
Muller, Hermann Joseph, **2:454**
Munro, Alice, **1:145**
Murdoch, Dame Iris, **1:107**
Murdock, George Peter, **2:51**
Murrow, Edward R., **1:467**
Myers, Walter Dean, **1:269**
Myrdal, Gunnar, **2:134,** 2:128

N

Naipaul, V. S., **1:406**
Nast, Thomas, **1:460**
Nehru, Jawaharlal, **2:403,** 2:400
Neruda, Pablo, **1:406**
Newman, Edwin, **1:443**
Newton, Isaac, **2:514,** 1:526; 2:474, 2:477, 2:519
Ngugi Wa Thiong'o, **1:415**
Nightingale, Florence, **2:569**
Nixon, Richard Milhous, **2:253,** 2:23, 2:247, 2:251, 2:252
Nkrumah, Kwame, **2:395,** 2:210
Noether, Emmy, **1:509,** 1:517
Norris, Frank, **1:180**
Nyerere, Julius, **2:396**

O

O'Casey, Sean, **1:108**
O'Connor, Flannery, **1:270**
O'Connor, Frank, **1:109**
O'Connor, Sandra Day, **2:31**
O'Dell, Scott, **1:271**
Odets, Clifford, **1:272**
O'Faolain, Sean, **1:110**
O'Keeffe, Georgia, **2:268**
O'Neill, Eugene, **1:273**
Oparin, Alexander Ivanovich, **2:461**
Orwell, George, **1:110,** 1:441
Osborne, John, **1:112**
Osler, William, **2:534,** 2:532
Ovid, **1:321**
Owen, Wilfred, **1:112,** 1:70, 1:116; 2:416

P

Paine, Thomas, **2:165**
Palestrina, **2:318**
Park, Mungo, **2:367**
Parker, Dorothy, **1:274**
Parsons, Talcott, **2:127**
Pascal, Blaise, **1:532**
Pasternak, Boris, **1:393**
Pasteur, Louis, **2:445**
Paterson, Katherine, **1:484**

Paton, Alan, **1:416**
Pauli, Wolfgang, **2:502**
Pauling, Linus Carl, **2:505**
Pavlov, Ivan Petrovich, **2:100, 2:464,** 2:101
Paz, Octavio, **1:407**
The Pearl Poet, **1:7**
Pearson, Drew, **1:458**
Peck, Richard, **1:275**
Pepys, Samuel, **1:27**
Perkins, Frances, **2:24**
Petrarch, **1:18, 1:350,** 1:9, 1:18, 1:348
Piaget, Jean, **2:110**
Picasso, Pablo, **2:420**
Pinter, Harold, **1:113**
Pirandello, Luigi, **1:351**
Planck, Max Karl Ernst Ludwig, **2:520,** 2:500, 2:519
Plath, Sylvia, **1:276,** 1:94
Plautus, Titus Maccius, **1:321**
Pliny the Younger, **2:295,** 2:296
Plutarch, **2:288**
Poe, Edgar Allan, **1:163,** 1:330
Pohl, Frederik, **1:278**
Poincaré, Henri, **1:500**
Polo, Marco, **2:308**
Pope, Alexander, **1:27**
Porter, Katherine Ann, **1:279**
Potok, Chaim, **1:280**
Priestley, J. B., **1:114**
Prokofiev, Sergei, **2:422**
Puig, Manuel, **1:408**
Purcell, Henry, **2:337,** 2:416
Pushkin, Aleksandr, **1:394**
Pythagoras, **1:500**

R

Racine, Jean, **1:339**
Radcliffe, Anne, **1:28**
Radcliffe-Brown, A. R., **2:53,** 2:45
Ramanujan, Srinivara, **1:502**
Rank, Hugh, **1:441**
Raphael, **2:319**
Ravel, Maurice, **2:423**
Rayburn, Sam, **2:34**
Reagan, Ronald Wilson, **2:259,** 2:31, 2:68, 2:256, 2:259
Redfield, Robert, **2:54**
Reynolds, Sir Joshua, **2:338,** 2:335
Ricardo, David, **2:73,** 2:7, 2:59
Rich, Adrienne, **1:281**
Richardson, Samuel, **1:28**
Richler, Mordecai, **1:145**
Riesman, David, **2:132**
Riis, Jacob August, **2:211**
Rilke, Rainer Maria, **1:370**
Rivlin, Alice Mitchell, **2:67**
Robespierre, Maximilien, **2:331**

Robinson, Edwin Arlington, **1:281**
Robinson, Joan, **2:60**
Rodin, Auguste, **2:355**
Rogers, Will, **1:462**
Rølvaag, Ole Edvart, **1:379**
Roosevelt, Anna Eleanor, **2:232**, 2:13,
    2:233
Roosevelt, Franklin Delano, **2:233**, 2:13,
    2:24, 2:27, 2:67, 2:230, 2:232, 2:236,
    2:245
Roosevelt, Theodore, **2:221**, 2:212, 2:220,
    2:223
Rossetti, Christina, **1:56**, 1:57
Rossetti, Dante Gabriel, **1:57**, 1:56
Rousseau, Jean Jacques, **2:11**
Rusk, Dean, **2:25**
Rusk, Howard Archibald, **2:564**
Russell, Bertrand, **1:503**
Rutherford, Ernest, **2:503**, 2:500, 2:509

S

Sadat, Anwar, **2:413**
Safire, William, **1:442**
Sagan, Carl, **2:479**
St. Augustine, **2:303**
Saint Bede, the Venerable, **2:307**
St. Thomas Aquinas, **2:306**
Saki, **1:115**
Salinger, J. D., **1:282**, 1:181, 1:227
Sandburg, Carl, **1:283**, 1:189
Sapir, Edward, **2:50**
Sartre, Jean-Paul, **1:340**
Sassoon, Siegfried, **1:115**
Sauer, Carl Ortwin, **2:79**
Sayers, Dorothy L., **1:116**
Schiller, (Johann Christoph) Friedrich von,
    1:371, 1:366
Schweitzer, Albert, **2:534**
Scott, Paul, **1:118**
Scott, Sir Walter, **1:36**
Seneca, Lucius Annaeus, **1:322**
Senghor, Leopold Sedar, **1:416**, 1:415
Serling, Rod, **1:486**
Service, Robert W., **1:146**
Shaffer, Peter, **1:118**
Shakespeare, William, **1:15**, 1:12, 1:322,
    1:323, 1:358, 1:393; 2:288, 2:397
Shannon, Claude, **1:549**
Shaw, George Bernard, **1:119**, 1:378
Shaw, William Napier, **2:484**
Shelley, Mary Wollstonecraft, **1:37**, 1:33
Shelley, Percy Bysshe, **1:37**, 1:33
Shepard, Sam, **1:284**
Sheridan, Richard Brinsley, **1:29**, 1:323
Shostakovich, Dmitri, **2:423**
Shute, Nevil, **1:146**
Sidney, Sir Philip, **1:16**, 1:17

Sienkiewicz, Henryk, **1:387**
Sillitoe, Alan, **1:120**
Silverberg, Robert, **1:285**
Simon, Neil, **1:286**
Sinclair, Upton, **1:287**
Singer, Isaac Bashevis, **1:387**
Skinner, B. F., **2:101**
Smith, Adam, **2:60**
Solzhenitsyn, Alexandr, **1:395**
Sophocles, **1:316**, 1:313, 1:314
Sousa, John Philip, **2:216**
Soyinka, Wole, **1:417**
Spark, Muriel, **1:121**
Spenser, Edmund, **1:17**
Spielberg, Steven, **1:472**
Spock, Benjamin McLane, **2:540**
Stalin, Joseph, **2:379**, 1:393, 1:395; 2:381,
    2:388, 2:392
Steichen, Edward, **2:269**
Steinbeck, John, **1:288**
Stendhal, **1:341**
Stevens, Thaddeus, **2:14**
Stevenson, Robert Louis, **1:57**
Stoker, Bram, **1:59**
Stoppard, Tom, **1:122**
Stouffer, Samuel A., **2:128**, 2:134
Strauss, Richard, **2:424**
Stravinsky, Igor, **2:425**
Strindberg, August, **1:379**
Suetonius, **2:296**
Sullivan, Louis Henry, **2:217**, 2:269
Swift, Jonathan, **1:29**
Swinburne, Algernon Charles, **1:59**
Synge, John Millington, **1:123**

T

Tacitus, Cornelius, **2:296**
Taft, William Howard, **2:222**, 2:205
Taylor, Edward, **1:154**
Taylor, Mildred, **1:289**
Tchaikovsky, Peter Ilyich, **2:356**
Tennyson, Lord, Alfred, **1:60**
Terence, **1:323**
Terkel, Studs, **1:488**
Thackeray, William Makepeace, **1:61**
Thatcher, Margaret, **2:407**
Thomas, Dylan, **1:124**
Thomas, Lowell, **1:463**
Thoreau, Henry David, **1:164**, 1:153, 1:157,
    1:167; 2:365
Thucydides, **2:289**
Thurber, James, **1:290**, 1:456
Tinbergen, Nikolaas, **2:464**, 2:462, 2:463
Tolkien, J. R. R., **1:125**
Tolstoy, Leo, **1:396**, 1:384, 1:393; 2:11,
    2:365
Trotsky, Leon, **2:381**

Trudeau, Gary, **1:460**
Truman, Harry S., **2:236,** 2:22, 2:24, 2:232, 2:240
Turing, Alan, **1:550,** 1:552
Turner, Joseph Mallord William, **2:357**
Tutu, Desmond, **2:397**
Twain, Mark, **1:181,** 1:141, 1:176, 1:383, 1:481
Tyler, Anne, **1:291,** 1:299

U

Ullman, Edward, **2:93**
Unamuno y Jugo, Miguel de, **1:359**
Undset, Sigrid, **1:380**
Updike, John, **1:291,** 1:310
Uris, Leon, **1:293**

V

Van Gogh, Vincent, **2:358**
Vaughan, Henry, **1:17**
Veblen, Thorstein, **2:145**
Verdi, Giuseppe, **2:360**
Verne, Jules, **1:342,** 1:128
Vesalius, Andreas, **2:548,** 2:546, 2:547
Vespucci, Amerigo, **2:325**
Victoria, Queen of Great Britain, **2:368**
Virgil, **1:324; 2:297**
Voight, Cynthia, **1:294**
Voltaire, **1:343**
Von Braun, Wernher, **2:482**
Vonnegut, Kurt, Jr., **1:295**
Von Neumann, John, **1:551,** 1:550

W

Wagner, Richard, **2:361,** 1:362; 2:353, 2:424
Walker, Alice, **1:296,** 1:230
Walker, Margaret, **1:297**
Wallace, Alfred Russel, **2:459,** 2:459
Wallace, Mike, **1:447**
Walsh, Gillian Paton, **1:126**
Ward, Barbara, **2:73**
Warren, Earl, **2:31**
Warren, Robert Penn, **1:298**
Washington, Booker T., **2:213**
Washington, George, **2:179,** 2:171, 2:173, 2:178
Watson, James Dewey, **2:440,** 2:439, 2:441
Watson, John B., **2:102,** 2:101

Waugh, Evelyn, **1:127,** 1:121
Weber, Max, **2:142**
Webster, Daniel, **2:183,** 2:181
Webster, John, **1:18**
Webster, Noah, **1:430**
Wegener, Alfred Lothar, **2:490**
Weierstrass, Karl, **1:528,** 1:499
Weiss, Peter, **1:372**
Weldon, Fay, **1:127**
Wells, H. G., **1:128,** 1:384
Welty, Eudora, **1:299**
West, Nathanael, **1:300**
Wharton, Edith, **1:182**
Wheatley, Phillis, **1:154**
White, E. B., **1:456**
White, Patrick, **1:147**
White, Paul Dudley, **2:562**
White, T. H., **1:129**
Whitman, Walt, **1:183,** 1:157, 1:162
Whittier, John Greenleaf, **1:165**
Whyte, William Foote, **2:149**
Wiesel, Elie, **1:301**
Wilde, Oscar, **1:62**
Wilder, Thornton, **1:302,** 1:338
Wilkins, Maurice Hugh Frederick, **2:441,** 2:439, 2:440, 2:505
Williams, Tennessee, **1:303**
Williams, William Carlos, **1:304**
Wilson, Woodrow, **2:224,** 2:22, 2:27, 2:205, 2:222, 2:223, 2:230, 2:233
Winchell, Walter, **1:463**
Wodehouse, P. G., **1:130**
Wolfe, Thomas, **1:305**
Wolfe, Tom, **1:478**
Woolf, Virginia, **1:132**
Wordsworth, William, **1:38,** 1:17, 1:22, 1:34, 1:66, 1:156
Wright, Frank Lloyd, **2:269,** 2:217
Wright, Richard, **1:306,** 1:217
Wundt, Wilhelm, **2:113**
Wyatt, Sir Thomas, **1:18**
Wyeth, Andrew, **2:270**

Y

Yeats, William Butler, **1:133,** 1:100, 1:105, 1:123

Z

Zindel, Paul, **1:307,** 1:247
Zola, Emile, **1:344,** 1:180, 1:216, 1:337; 2:349

AUTHOR INDEX

This index appears in both volumes of *The Young Adult Reader's Adviser.* It presents in alphabetical sequence the authors (both personal and corporate) of all books listed in the bibliographies. Names of the editors, compilers, and translators are also indexed.

The number of the volume in which a person's name appears is given with a colon followed by the page number on which the book title connected to that person can be found. For example, the entry 2:184 indicates that the book written by Thomas P. Abernethy can be found on page 184 of Volume 2.

A

AAHPERD Research Consortium
  Computer Network Committee, 1:568
AAHPERD Staff, 1:568
Aarons, Victoria, 1:384
Aaseng, Nathan, 2:431
Abba, Giuseppe C., 2:344
Abbas, K. A., 2:401
Abbey, Nancy, 2:555
Abbott, David (ed), 2:431
Abbott, Edwin A., 1:519
Abdelnoor, R. E., 1:496
Abel, Christopher (ed), 2:371
Abel, Elie, 2:404
Abelson, Harold, 1:511, 1:565
Aberle, David F., 2:52
Abernethy, Thomas P., 2:184
Aboulafia, Mitchell, 2:139
Abraham, Gerald, 2:346
Abraham, Henry J., 2:12
Abrahams, Israel, 2:303
Abrahams, Roger D., 1:411
Abrams, Philip, 2:124
Abramson, Edward A., 1:280
Abramson, Paul R., 2:39, 2:255
Abro, A., 2:512
Aburdene, Patricia, 2:51
Academy of Science of the U.S.S.R, 2:389
Acerson, Karen L., 1:575

Achebe, Chinua, 1:411
Ackerman, Bruce, 2:26
Ackrill, J. L. (ed), 2:442
Ada, Alma F., 2:409
Adair, Gene, 2:206
Adams, Abigail, 2:170
Adams, Ansel, 2:263
Adams, Cynthia H., 2:551
Adams, Douglas, 1:64–65
Adams, George, 1:519
Adams, Henry, 2:214
Adams, J. Alan, 1:578
Adams, John (ed), 2:71
Adams, John, 2:171
Adams, John Quincy, 2:173
Adams, Lee, 1:577
Adams, Samuel Hopkins, 2:225
Adams, Steve, 1:572
Adams, W., 1:504
Adams, Walter, 2:57
Adamson, Joy, 2:461
Addams, Jane, 2:208
Adelman, Gary, 1:77
Adelman, Jonathan R., 2:387
Adelman, M. A., 2:495
Adelson-Velsky, G. M., 1:585
Adderholdt-Elliott, Miriam, 2:536
Adkins, Robert K., 2:516
Adler, David A., 2:413, 2:468
Adler, Irving, 1:534

Adler, Irving, 2:437, 2:456, 2:461, 2:478
Adler, Kraig, 2:449
Adler, Mortimer J., 1:445; 2:16, 2:287
Adler, Richard (ed), 1:465
Adler, Ruth, 1:458
Adobe Systems, 1:563
Adorno, T. W., 2:114
Adorno, Theodor, 1:433
Adrian, Charles R., 2:40
Advanced MicroMotion, Inc., 1:566
Aers, David, 1:7
Aeschylus, 1:312
Aesop, 1:312
Agar, Michael H., 2:42
Agassi, Joseph, 2:525
Agay, Denes, 2:418
Agee, James, 2:228
Agel, Jerome B., 1:439
Aggeler, Geoffrey, 1:71
Agger, Robert E., 2:130
Aglion, Raoul, 2:387
Agmon, Tamir (ed), 2:71
Agnew, John A., 2:76
Agosin, Marjorie, 1:407
Agras, Stewart, 2:103
Agresto, John, 2:16, 2:26
Ahir, D. C., 2:281
Ahl, David H. (ed), 1:567
Ahmad, N., 2:76
Aho, Alfred V., 1:586
Aichele, Gary J., 2:29
Aiken, Joan, 1:484
Airhihenbuwa, Collins O., 2:566
Ajayi, J. F., 2:298
Ajayi, J. F. (ed), 2:272
Akbar, M. J., 2:404
Aker, Sharon Z., 1:559
Alam, S. S., 1:565
Albee, Edward, 1:186–87
Albers, Donald J. (ed), 1:496
Albion, Mark, 1:440
Albornoz, Miguel, 2:157
Alcott, Louisa May, 1:167–68
Aldaraca, Bridget, 1:353
Alden, John R., 2:327
Alderman, Clifford Lindsey, 2:161
Aldington, Richard, 2:373
Aldous, Joan (ed), 2:137
Aldred, Cyril, 2:279
Aldrich, Frank T., 2:92
Aleichem, Sholem, 1:383
Aleksander, Igor, 1:580
Aleksandrov, A. D. (ed), 1:496
Alexander, Charles C., 2:237
Alexander, Edward, 1:388
Alexander, H. T., 2:396
Alexander, Horace, 2:366
Alexander, Jeffrey C. (ed), 2:127
Alexander, Lloyd, 1:187–88

Alexander, Michael (tr), 1:6
Alexander, R. McNeill, 2:448
Alexander, Sidney, 2:418
Alexander, Yonah, 2:255
Alexanderson, G. L. (ed), 1:496
Al Faruqi, Isma'il, 2:272
Alford, Harold J., 2:135
Algar, Hamid, 1:420
Alger, Horatio, Jr., 1:169; 2:206
Al-Hadad, Saba, 1:504
Ali, Ahmed (ed and tr), 1:421
Ali, Sheikh R., 2:5, 2:33, 2:40
Ali, Tariq, 2:382
Aliber, Robert Z., 2:71
Alinder, Mary S. (ed), 2:263
Allaby, Michael, 2:495
Allan, Mea, 2:457
Allan, T., 2:279
Alland, Alexander, 2:48
Allen, F. Sturges, 1:439
Allen, Frederick Lewis, 2:225, 2:228, 2:237
Allen, Garland E., 2:438
Allen, Gay Wilson, 1:153, 1:157, 1:185, 1:284
Allen, John (ed), 2:81
Allen, Oliver E., 2:80, 2:484, 2:544
Allen, Steve, 1:446, 1:449
Allen, Walter, 2:142
Allen, Woody, 1:189, 1:471
Alliluyeva, Svetlana, 2:380
Allman, George J., 1:511
Allott, Miriam (ed), 1:38
Allport, Gordon W., 2:97, 2:104, 2:115, 2:135
Al-Magid Haridi, A. Abd (ed), 2:302
Alsop, Joseph, 2:234
Alter, Dinsmore, 2:468
Alter, Judy, 2:551
Alth, Charlotte, 2:484
Alth, Max, 2:484
Altheide, David, 1:454, 1:457
Altman, I. (ed), 2:105
Altshiller, Donald, 2:84
Aluko, Olajide (ed), 2:393
Aluri, Rao (ed), 1:583
Alvarez–Altman, Grace, 1:438
Amacher, Richard, 1:187
Amann, Dick, 1:537, 1:545
Ambati, Balamurali, 2:559
Ambati, Jayakrishna K., 2:559
Ambrose, Stephen E., 2:36, 2:203, 2:239
Amdur, Richard, 2:255
American Cancer Society, 2:556
American Educational Research Association, 2:122
American Historical Association, 2:16
American Medical Association Staff, 2:530, 2:561, 2:566
American Psychological Association, 2:122

American Red Cross, 2:566
American Political Science Association, 2:16
Amery, H., 2:290
Amey, Peter, 2:314, 2:316
Amin, Karmina, 1:205, 1:224, 1:230
Amin, Mohamed, 2:393
Amis, Kingsley, 1:65
Ammer, Christine, 1:432; 2:55
Ammer, Dean, 2:55
Andersen, Hans Christian, 1:374
Anderson, Carol J., 1:579
Anderson, Charles R., 1:175
Anderson, Dave (ed), 1:480
Anderson, Dwight, 2:196
Anderson, J. A., 1:583
Anderson, J. R., 2:103
Anderson, Kenneth, 2:549
Anderson, LaVere, 2:14
Anderson, Mac (ed), 2:123
Anderson, Madelyn Klein, 2:561, 2:565
Anderson, Martin, 2:68
Anderson, Modelyn Klein, 2:570
Anderson, Nancy S., 2:196
Anderson, Paul V., 1:491
Anderson, Roy R., 2:89, 2:411
Anderson, Sherwood, 1:190
Anderson, Terry L., 2:69
Andrade, E. N., 2:504
Andrae, Tor, 2:301
Andrews, Charles M., 2:163
Andrews, Elmer, 1:92
Andrews, Lincoln, et al, 1:537
Andrews, Nancy, 1:562
Andrews, Wayne, 1:344
Andrian, Gustave W., 1:354
Andric, Ivo, 1:384
Angel, Leonard, 1:580
Angeli, Helen R., 1:57
Angell, Ian O., 1:577
Angelo, Joseph A., Jr, 2:469
Angelou, Maya, 1:191–92
Angrosino, Michael, 2:42
Anis, Nick, 1:573, 1:574
Anobile, Richard, 1:470
Anouilh, Jean, 1:328
Ansermet, Ernest, 2:426
Antin, Mary, 2:210
Antonov-Ovseyeneko, Anton, 2:380
Anzovin, Steven, 1:575, 1:579
Apfel, Necia H., 2:469, 2:474, 2:497, 2:520
Apollonius of Perga, 1:513
Apostle, Richard A., 2:135
Appignanesi, Richard, 2:378
Aquila, Juan del, 2:408
Aquinas, St. Thomas, 2:307
Arberry, A. J., 1:419
Arce de Vázquez, Margot, 1:405
Archer, Gleason, 1:461
Archer, Jules, 2:241, 2:557

Archer, Marguerite, 1:328
Archimedes, 1:521
Arciniegas, German, 2:325
Arendt, Hannah, 2:374
Arensberg, Conrad M., 2:50
Argyle, Christopher, 2:371
Argyle, Michael, 2:104
Aries, Philippe, 2:136
Aristophanes, 1:313
Aristotle, 2:287, 2:442
Arjomand, Said A. (ed), 2:142
Arlen, Michael J., 1:440, 1:465
Armitage, Angus, 2:474
Armour, Richard, 1:192–93
Arms, Karen, 2:437
Arms, Thomas S., 2:237
Armstrong, David, 1:321
Armstrong, Donald, 2:559
Armstrong, Louis, 2:264
Armstrong, Scott, 2:27, 2:252
Armstrong, William, 2:228
Arndt, H. W., 2:62
Arnheim, Rudolf, 1:461
Arnheim, Rudolf, 2:113
Arnold, Caroline, 2:544, 2:561
Arnold, Denis, 2:152, 2:334
Arnold, Matthew, 1:41
Arnold, Peter, 2:566
Arnstein, Helene S., 2:538
Aron, Raymond, 2:36, 2:126
Aronsen, Lawrence, 2:387
Aronson, Elliot, 2:98
Aronson, Elliot (ed), 2:95
Aronson, Joseph, 2:260
Arrington, Karen, 2:152
Arrow, Kenneth J., 2:55, 2:64
Artman, John, 1:433
Artz, Frederick B., 2:304, 2:326, 2:333
Arundell, Dennis D., 2:338
Arvin, Newton, 1:161
Arya, Jagdish C., 1:524
Asanov, G. S., 1:516
Asbjørnsen, Peter C., 1:374
Ascher, Steven, 1:470
Ash, Mitchell G. (ed), 2:95
Ash, Timothy, G., 2:404
Ashabranner, Brent, 2:256
Ashby, Le Roy, 2:205
Asher, Herbert B., 2:39
Ashford, Janet I. (ed), 2:543
Ashley, Maurice, 2:326, 2:327
Ashley, Ruth, 1:561
Ashlock, Robert, 1:504
Ashlund, Anders, 2:407
Ashton, Thomas S., 2:339
Asimov, Isaac, 1:193–94, 1:318, 1:505,
    1:540, 1:556; 2:82, 2:272, 2:277, 2:284,
    2:431, 2:434, 2:438, 2:439, 2:447, 2:450,
    2:452, 2:456, 2:469, 2:474, 2:475, 2:478,

2:480, 2:484, 2:485, 2:493, 2:495, 2:497, 2:500, 2:506, 2:511, 2:512, 2:528
Asimov, Isaac (ed), 1:554
Aspray, William, 1:553
Asselineau, Roger, 1:153
Association for Information and Image Management Staff, 1:578
Atchley, Robert C., 2:129
Atchley, W. R., 2:456
Atkins, John, 1:115
Atkinson, Charles Milner, 2:8
Atmore, A., 2:276
Attenborough, David, 2:437, 2:456, 2:465
Atwan, Robert, 1:480
Atwood, Margaret, 1:135–36
Atwood, William G., 2:350
Auburn, Mark S., 1:29
Auden, W. H., 1:66
Auden, W. H. (ed), 1:311
Audouze, Jean, 2:469
Audubon, John James, 2:187
Audubon Society Staff, 2:448, 2:449
Auel, Jean M., 2:277
Auerbach, Paul S., 2:566
Aufderheide, Patricia, 2:414
August, Paul, 2:544
Augustine, St., 2:304
Ault, Rosalie S., 1:564
Austen, Jane, 1:20
Austin, William W., 2:187
Austing, Richard H., 1:565
Austrian, G. D., 1:544
Avakian, Bob, 2:402
Avallone, Michael, 2:413
Aveling, Harry, 1:426
Averroës, 2:302
Avery, James S., 2:94, 2:155
Aviad, Janet O., 2:142
Avraham, Regina, 2:450, 2:544, 2:554
Ayala, Francisco J., 2:456
Aycock, Wendell M., 1:355
Ayer, A. J., 1:503
Ayers, Donald, 1:432
Aylesworth, Thomas G., 2:493
Aylesworth, Virginia, 2:493
Ayling, Stanley, 2:9, 2:329

B

Baase, Sara, 1:585
Babbage, Charles, 1:542
Baber, Robert L., 1:554
Babkin, Boris P., 2:464
Bacarisse, Pamela, 1:409
Bach, Julie S., 2:12
Bach, Julie S. (ed), 2:81, 2:570
Bach, Robert L., 2:136
Bach, Steven, 1:470

Bachma, John E., 2:378
Bachman, David C., 2:551
Bacon, Donald, 2:35
Bacon, Sir Francis, 1:10; 2:435
Badawi, M. M. (ed), 1:420
Badcock, John, 2:291
Badt, Kurt, 2:349, 2:351
Baer, Michael, 2:504
Bagchi, Amiya Kumar, 2:71
Bagdikian, Ben, 1:454
Bagrow, Leo, 2:92
Baguley, David, 1:345
Bahera, K. S., 2:282
Bahree, Patricia, 2:366
Baigell, Matthew, 2:187, 2:260, 2:261
Bailey, Brian, 2:339
Bailey, Harold J., 1:565
Bailey, Helen M., 2:272
Bailey, Ronald H., 2:82, 2:492
Bailey, Thomas A., 2:152
Bailyn, Bernard, 2:163
Bailyn, Bernard (ed), 2:327
Bainbridge, William S., 2:142
Baines, John, 2:279
Bains, Rae, 2:194, 2:568
Bainton, Roland H., 2:301, 2:304, 2:310, 2:317
Bair, Deirdre, 1:331
Baker, Alan, 1:496
Baker, Augusta, 1:451
Baker, C. L., 1:434
Baker, Carlos, 1:237
Baker, David, 2:480
Baker, Edward, 1:353
Baker, Jeffrey W., 2:438
Baker, Kenneth, 2:414
Baker, Leonard, 2:28
Baker, Mary L., 2:449
Baker, Ray S., 2:198
Baker, Russell, 1:481
Baker, S., 2:549
Bakhash, Shaul, 2:411
Bakshi, S. R., 2:366
Balaban, John (ed and tr), 1:426
Balajthy, Ernest, 1:569
Balcazar, J. L., 1:585
Bald, R. C., 1:10
Baldini, Gabriele, 2:361
Baldwin, B., 2:296
Baldwin, James, 1:195
Baldwin, Leland D., 2:168
Baldwin, Louis, 2:477
Baldwin, Margaret, 1:578
Bales, Carol, 2:206
Bales, Robert F., 2:124
Balint, John R., 1:575
Ballard, J. G., 1:67
Ballard, Robert D., 2:82, 2:495
Balliett, Whitney, 2:225, 2:261
Ball-Rokeach, Sandra J., 2:129, 2:130

Balsdon, John, 2:290
Balzac, Honoré de, 1:329
Bambara, Toni Cade, 1:196
Bandura, Albert, 2:103, 2:105, 2:112
Banfield, Susan, 2:387
Banks, Ann, 2:228
Banks, Michael A., 1:561, 1:577
Baraka, Amiri, 1:197
Barash, David P., 2:133
Barbeau, Clayton C., 2:538
Barber, Benjamin, 2:12
Barber, Richard, 1:27
Bard, Allen J. (ed), 2:508
Bargad, Warren (tr), 1:420
Baritz, Loren (ed), 2:226
Bark, Joseph, 2:552
Barkan, Stanley (ed), 1:374
Barker, Daniel, 2:492
Barker, Donald, 1:583
Barker, Dudley, 1:73
Barker, James, 2:384
Barker, Lucius J., 2:256
Bar-Lev, Zev, 1:556
Barlow, Michael, 1:556
Barman, Roderick J., 2:369
Barnard, Chester I., 2:140
Barnard, Ellsworth, 1:282
Barnes, Christopher J., 1:394
Barnes, Clive, 2:261
Barnes, G. M., 1:572, 1:573
Barnes, Jonathan, 2:442
Barnes, LeRoy W. (ed), 2:124
Barnes, R. S. K., 2:465
Barnet, Sylvan, 1:16
Barnett, A. Doak, 2:398
Barnett, Correlli, 2:371
Barnett, Correlli (ed), 2:382
Barnett, George L., 1:35
Barnett, M. P., 1:586
Barnett, Rosalind (ed), 2:123
Barnett, S. A., 2:461
Barnett, S. J., 1:586
Barnouw, Erik, 1:464
Barnsley, Michael, 1:516
Baron, Dennis, 1:429
Baron, Jonathon, 2:110
Baron, Margaret E., 1:527
Baron, Naomi, 1:563
Baron, Robert (ed), 2:152
Barone, Michael, 2:4, 2:32
Barquin, Ramon (ed), 1:555
Barraclough, Geoffrey, 2:304, 2:404
Barraclough, Geoffrey (ed), 2:272
Barrett, G. W., 2:281
Barrett, Michael L., 1:583
Barrie, J. M., 1:67
Barro, Robert J. (ed), 2:57
Barron, D. W., 1:561
Barrow, Reginald H., 2:289

Barry, Elaine, 1:223
Barry, Iris, 2:277
Barry, John, 1:540
Barry, Kathleen, 2:206
Barry, Roger, 2:80, 2:483
Barstow, David R., 1:563
Bartel, Rainer, 1:575
Barthelemy-Madaule, Madeline, 2:459
Barthelme, Donald, 1:198
Bartke, Wolfgang, 2:398
Bartles, Barton K., 1:577
Bartlett, Richard A., 2:184
Bartók, Béla, 2:416
Barton, Clara Harlowe, 2:194, 2:568
Barton, Donald, 2:82
Barton, I. M., 2:298
Barton, William E., 2:568
Baryshnikov, Mikhail, 2:414
Barzini, Luigi, 2:87, 2:272
Barzun, Jacques, 2:261, 2:347
Bascom, Willard, 2:486
Basham, A. L. (ed), 2:272
Bashō, 1:424
Basnett-McGuire, 1:351
Basov, N. G, 1:578
Bassan, M. (ed), 1:174
Bassani, Ezio, 2:310
Bassani, Giorgio, 1:347
Bassetti, Fred, 1:519
Bastiat, Frederic, 2:55
Bataille, Gretchen M., 2:152
Batchelor, John E., 2:35
Bate, W. Jackson, 1:34
Bate, W. Johnson, 1:35
Bates, Robert L. (ed), 2:488
Bateson, Mary C., 2:47
Batson, Gary (ed), 2:123
Batson, Horace W. (ed), 2:123
Batten, Roger L., 2:495
Batterberry, Arianne, 2:152
Batterberry, Michael, 2:152
Batzing, Barry L., 2:443
Baudelaire, Charles, 1:330
Bauer, Laurie, 1:432
Baugh, Albert, 1:429
Bauld, Harry, 1:485
Baum, Joan, 1:547
Baum, L. (Lyman) Frank, 1:198–99
Baum, Lawrence, 2:4, 2:26
Baumann, Hans, 2:277
Baumert, John H., 2:476
Baumgartner, Ted A., 1:568
Baumol, William J., 2:55
Bavkis, Herman, 2:35
Baxter, Maurice G., 2:183
Beach, Joseph W., 1:180
Beaglehole, J. C., 2:321
Beal, Merrill D., 2:202
Bealer, Alex, 2:180

Bean, Frank D., 2:141
Beard, Annie E., 2:206
Beard, Charles A., 2:16, 2:21, 2:152, 2:166, 2:228, 2:339
Beard, Mary R. (ed), 2:272
Beardon, Colin (ed), 1:580
Beason, Pamela, 1:491
Beatty, Patricia, 2:192, 2:206
Beaty, Janice, 1:451
Beaumont, Peter, 2:89
Beazley, Charles R., 2:157
Beck, Anatole, 1:535
Beck, Charles B. (ed), 2:447
Beck, James, 2:320
Beck, Robert C., 2:112
Beck, Warren A., 2:160
Becker, Gary S., 2:136
Becker, George J., 1:101, 1:265
Becker, Peter, 2:85
Becker, Robert A., 2:169
Becker, Wayne M., 2:437
Beckett, Samuel, 1:331
Bedau, Hugo A. (ed), 2:133
Bede, St., 2:308
Bedell, Kenneth, 1:569
Bedford, Sybille, 1:96
Beebe, Steven, 1:445
Beerel, Annabel C., 1:583
Behan, Brendan, 1:68
Beiler, Albert H., 1:496
Beiser, Rudolph, 1:43
Beisner, Robert K., 2:218
Beit-Hallahmi, Benjamin, 2:138
Beitman, K. (ed), 1:558
Beizer, Boris, 1:566
Beja, Morris, 1:133
Belanoff, Pat, 1:478
Belaunde, Victor A., 2:369
Belin, David W., 2:247
Bell, Daniel, 1:554; 2:149
Bell, Eric T., 1:496, 1:509, 1:528, 1:531
Bell, Ian A., 1:23
Bell, Jack, 2:245
Bell, James B., 2:206
Bell, Louis, 2:435
Bell, Quentin, 1:133
Bell, Robbie, 1:535
Bell, Ruth, 2:542
Beller, Joel, 2:447
Bellin, David (ed), 1:568
Bellman, Richard E., 1:580, 1:585
Bello, José M., 2:408
Bellow, Saul, 1:200
Bell-Villada, Gene H., 1:404
Belmont, Thomas, 2:50
Belsky, Marvin S., 2:565
Bem, Daryl J., 2:97
Ben-Ari, E., 2:132
Bender, David L., 2:133, 2:144

Bender, David L. (ed), 2:62, 2:133, 2:137, 2:257
Bender, Thomas, 2:206
Bendersky, Joseph W., 2:382
Bendick, Jeanne, 2:480
Bendix, Reinhard, 2:143, 2:145
Benedict, Helen, 2:566
Benedict, Ruth, 2:44
Benet, Stephen Vincent, 1:200
Ben-Gurion, David, 2:412
Benice, Daniel D., 1:523
Benjamin, Ludy T., 2:95
Benjamin, Martin, 2:19
Benner, J., 2:556
Bennett, Joan, 1:133
Bennett, L. Claire, 2:557
Bennett, Leone, Jr, 2:152
Bennett, Norman R., 2:273
Bennett, Steven J., 1:559, 1:561
Bennett, William I., 2:530
Bennis, Warren, 1:465
Bensman, Joseph, 2:131
Benson, Herbert, 2:536
Benson, Kathleen, 2:241
Benson, Mary, 2:395
Benson, Philip G. (ed), 2:508
Benstock, Bernard, 1:99
Bent, Silas, 2:29
Bentham, Jeremy, 2:8
Bentley, Eric, 1:365
Bentley, Eric (ed and tr), 1:347, 1:354, 1:365
Benton, Michael, 2:456
Benvenuto, Richard, 1:43, 1:258
Benyo, Richard, 2:551
Berbrich, Joan, 1:477
Berdan, Frances F., 2:298
Berelson, Bernard R., 2:39
Berenbaum, Michael, 1:302
Berg, Brian, 1:578
Berg, Maggie, 1:42
Berg, Richard E., 2:521
Berger, Arthur A., 1:454, 1:468
Berger, Arthur V., 2:261
Berger, Charles R., 2:103
Berger, Gilda, 2:69, 2:147, 2:228, 2:241, 2:539, 2:554, 2:556
Berger, Kathleen S., 2:540
Berger, Melvin, 1:433, 1:554; 2:469, 2:475, 2:478, 2:480, 2:493, 2:494, 2:508, 2:544, 2:554, 2:565, 2:570
Berger, Peter L., 2:125
Berger, Raoul, 2:35
Berger, Thomas, 2:200
Berger, W., 2:488
Berggren, J. L., 1:496
Bergland, Richard, 2:545
Bergmann, Peter G., 2:512
Bergreen, Laurence, 2:264

Bergson, Abram, 2:68
Berk, A. A., 1:565
Berkin, Carol, 2:152
Berkmeyer, Kathy M., 1:576
Berland, Theodore, 2:561
Berlau, Ruth, 1:365
Berlay, Louise, 2:110
Berlin, Isaiah, 2:59, 2:339
Berlin, Isaiah (ed), 2:326
Berlin, Normand, 1:274
Berliner, Don, 1:574
Berlioux, Pierre, 1:585
Berlioz, Hector, 2:347
Berman, David R., 2:40
Berman, Edgar, 2:245
Berman, William, 2:434
Berman, William C., 2:237
Bernal, Ignacio, 2:298
Bernard, H. Russell (ed), 2:42
Bernard, Jessie, 2:147
Bernards, Neal (ed), 1:452; 2:129, 2:137
Bernkopf, Michael, 2:473
Bernoulli, Jakob, 1:531
Bernstein, Carl, 1:458; 2:22, 2:252
Bernstein, Irving, 2:69, 2:226, 2:228, 2:229
Bernstein, Jeremy, 1:542; 2:520
Bernstein, Leonard, 2:265
Bernstein, Richard B., 2:166
Bernstein, Richard J., 2:220
Bernstein, Theodore M., 1:435
Berry, Dianne, 1:583
Berry, Jeffrey M., 2:39
Berry, John, 1:564
Berry, John F., 2:63
Berry, L., 2:85
Berry, Louise A., 2:488, 2:570
Berry, Michael, 2:268
Berryman, John, 1:174
Bertram, John, 2:561
Beschloss, Michael R., 2:239
Beskin, N. M., 1:519
Besset, Maurice, 2:419
Beth, E. W., 1:496
Beti, Mongo, 1:412
Betsky, Sarah Z. (ed), 1:382
Bettancourt, Jeanne, 2:552
Bettelheim, Bruno, 2:97, 2:118
Bever, Thomas (ed), 2:103
Beyle, Thad L. (ed), 2:40
Bezuska, Stanley, 1:511
Bhagwati, Jagdish, 2:71
Bialer, Seweryn, 2:36
Bialer, Seweryn (ed), 2:380
Bianchi, Doris, 1:451
Biddle, Bruce J., 2:98
Bielawski, Larry, 1:583
Bierce, Ambrose Gwinnett, 1:169
Bierhorst, John, 2:298
Bierhorst, John (ed), 1:398; 2:298

Bierly, Paul E., 2:216
Bierly, Philip E., 2:216
Biermann, Alan W., 1:537
Biermann, June, 2:561
Biers, William R., 2:284
Bigelow, John, 1:156
Bigelow, Steven, 1:577
Biggerstaff, Ted, 1:585
Bila, Dennis, 1:511
Bill, Valentine Tschebotarioff, 1:391
Billeskov, Jansen (ed), 1:374
Billias, George A., 2:163
Billings, Malcolm, 2:304
Billington, Barry, 2:362
Billington, Ray A., 2:184
Bindoff, S. T., 2:326
Binet, Alfred, 2:110, 2:123
Bingham, Hiram, 2:298
Bingham, Marjorie W., 2:284
Bingham, Richard D., 2:40
Binkley, 2:511
Binstock, Robert H. (ed), 2:129
Binyon, Michael, 2:91
Biow, Lisa, 1:573
Biracree, Nancy, 2:152
Biracree, Tom, 2:152
Birch, Beverly, 2:445
Birch, Cyril, 1:423
Birch, Cyril (tr), 2:309
Birdsall, Stephen S., 2:90
Birkhead, Edith, 1:57
Birley, Anthony, 2:290
Birmele, Ricardo, 1:575
Birnbach, Lisa, 2:69
Birnes, William J. (ed), 1:561
Bishop, Jim, 2:198
Bishop, Morris, 2:305
Bishop, William W., Jr, 2:36
Bismarck, Otto von, 2:342
Bitossi, Sergio, 2:157; 2:359
Bitter, Gary C., 1:564, 1:569
Bizard, Philippe, 1:585
Bjork, Daniel W., 2:97
Black, Claudia, 2:555
Black, Cyril E., 2:404
Black, Donald Chain, 1:432
Black, Duncan, 2:39
Black, Elizabeth, 2:552
Black, Max (ed), 2:128
Blackmar, Frank W., 2:160
Blackmore, Stephen (ed), 2:448
Blackmur, R. P., 2:214
Blackwell, Alice Stone (tr), 1:399
Blackwood, Alan, 2:157
Blaedel, Niels, 2:501
Blaikie, William G., 2:367
Blair, Clay, Jr., 2:247
Blair, David (ed), 1:434
Blair, Joan, 2:247

Blair, Walter, 1:461
Blake, Charles A., 2:450
Blake, Gary, 1:491
Blake, Gerald H., 2:89
Blake, Peter, 2:419
Blake, Robert, 2:343
Blake, William, 1:32
Blanch, Robert J., 1:8
Blanchard, Kenneth, 2:63
Bland, Roger G., 2:448
Blandford, Percy W., 2:92
Blasingame, John W., 2:188
Blassingame, Wyatt, 2:380, 2:411
Blatt, Harry, 2:492
Blau, Justine, 2:244
Blau, Peter M., 2:140, 2:144, 2:148
Blau, Peter M. (ed), 2:144
Blau, Zena S., 2:106, 2:135, 2:137, 2:144, 2:148
Blau, Zena S. (ed), 2:106, 2:137
Blaug, Mark, 2:55, 2:69
Blaxter, Kenneth, 2:438
Bleaney, B. I., 2:522
Bleau, Barbara, 1:505
Bleifield, Maurice, 2:435, 2:436
Blesh, Rudi, 2:261
Blewett, John (ed), 2:220
Bleznik, Donald W., 1:355
Blinder, Alan S., 2:55
Bliss, Michael, 2:561
Block, Deborah, 1:490
Block, Herbert, 1:459
Block, Merv, 1:487
Blocksma, Mary, 2:435
Blodgett, E. D., 1:145
Blom, Margaret, 1:42
Bloodworth, William J., 1:288
Bloom, Harold, 1:17, 1:28, 1:44, 1:71, 1:134
Bloom, Harold (ed), 1:12, 1:23, 1:24, 1:25, 1:29, 1:33, 1:34, 1:35, 1:47, 1:61, 1:66, 1:77, 1:82, 1:86, 1:108, 1:109, 1:114, 1:187, 1:200, 1:209, 1:215, 1:241, 1:254, 1:256, 1:266, 1:268, 1:270, 1:274, 1:277, 1:279, 1:282, 1:283, 1:297, 1:299, 1:300, 1:304, 1:305, 1:306, 1:307, 1:316, 1:317, 1:325, 1:330, 1:337, 1:342, 1:349, 1:351, 1:370, 1:395, 1:397, 1:400, 1:407, 1:451; 2:11, 2:284, 2:298
Bloom, Lynn Z., 2:542
Bloomfield, Brian P. (ed), 1:582
Bloomfield, Leonard, 2:50
Blos, Joan, 2:184
Blos, Peter, 2:106
Blouet, Brian, 2:79
Bloyd, Sunni, 2:467
Blum, Bruce I., 1:563
Blum, Daniel, 1:468
Blum, John M., 2:218, 2:234
Blumberg, Rhoda, 2:184, 2:241, 2:488

Blume, Judy, 1:201; 2:542
Blumenfeld, Warren S., 1:436
Blumenson, John J., 2:261
Blumenthal, Leonard M., 1:511
Blumenthal, Sidney, 2:39
Blundell, William E., 1:487
Blunden, Caroline, 2:86, 2:273
Blunden, Edmund, 1:36
Blunt, Wilfrid, 2:443
Blus, S. (ed), 2:530
Bly, Robert, 1:491
Boardman, John (ed), 2:284, 2:290
Boardman, Tom W., 2:226
Boas, Franz, 2:44
Boatner, Mark M., III, 2:152, 2:163
Bobb, Dilip, 2:401
Bober, Natalie, 2:175
Boccaccio, Giovanni, 1:348
Bochner, Salomon, 1:524
Bockris, J. O., 2:508
Boddeyn, J., 1:440
Bode, Carl, 2:187
Boden, Margaret, 1:582; 2:110
Bodenhammer, Gregory, 2:554
Boehmer, Heinrich, 2:317
Boesen, Victor, 2:484
Bogart, Leo, 2:39, 2:129
Boggs, Jean Sutherland, 2:352
Boggs, Joseph, 1:469
Bogosian, Eric, 1:461
Bogue, Donald J., 2:142
Bohannan, Paul, 2:42, 2:393
Bohinski, 2:511
Bohman, S., 2:110
Bohner, Charles, 1:299; 2:176
Bohr, Neils Henrik David, 2:501
Bok, Bart J., 2:478
Bok, Priscilla F., 2:478
Bok, Sissela, 2:97
Bold, Benjamin, 1:511
Bold, Harold C., 2:447
Boles, Martha, 1:515
Böll, Heinrich, 1:363–64
Boller, Paul F., 2:39
Bolognese, Don, 1:577
Bolt, Richard A., 1:558
Bolt, Robert, 1:14, 1:69
Bolter, J. David, 1:554, 1:579
Bolton, Herbert E., 2:160
Bolton, Sarah K., 2:559
Bombeck, Erma, 1:447, 1:480
Bonaccorso, Richard, 1:110
Bonafoux, Pascal, 2:359
Bonanni, Pete, 1:567
Bonaparte, Napoleon, 2:330
Bondanella, Julia Conway, 1:347
Bonello, Frank J. (ed), 2:62
Bonner, Raymond, 2:398
Bonola, Roberto, 1:519

Bonomi, Patricia, 2:161
Bontemps, Arna, 2:188
Booher, Dianna, 1:478, 1:483
Bookchin, Murray, 2:12
Boole, George, 1:507
Boorstin, Daniel J., 1:440; 2:152, 2:161
Boorstin, Ruth F., 2:152
Booth, Martin, 2:342
Bordwell, David, 1:469
Bordwell, Sally, 2:556
Borges, Jorge Luis, 1:399–400
Borland, Russell, 1:575
Born, Rainer, 1:580
Bornat, Richard, 1:586
Bornet, Vaughn, 2:246
Bornstein, Jerry, 2:452
Bornstein, Marc H. (ed), 2:95
Bornstein, Sandy, 2:452
Bortolotti, Gary R., 2:465
Borysenko, Joan, 2:530
Boschke, F. L. (ed), 2:505
Bose, Mihir, 2:70
Boskin, Michael J., 2:257
Boskind-White, Marlene, 2:550
Boss, Valentin, 2:515
Boston Children's Hospital Staff, 2:543,
  2:549
Boston Women's Health Book Collective
  Staff, 2:542
Boswell, James, 1:26
Botermans, Jack, 1:535
Bott, Elizabeth, 2:52
Boucher, E. A., 2:507
Boudreau, Edward A., 2:506
Boulding, Kenneth, 2:71
Boulle, Pierre, 1:332
Bourbaki, Nicolas, 1:499
Bourdillon, Hilary, 2:530
Bourguignon, Erika (ed), 2:51
Bourne, Edward G. (ed), 2:157
Bourne, Peter G., 2:410
Bouwsma, William J., 2:311
Bove, Tony, 1:575, 1:579
Bowden, Mary W., 1:159
Bowder, Diana, 2:284, 2:290
Bowen, Catherine D., 2:16, 2:166, 2:435,
  2:526
Bowen, Charles S., 1:572, 1:573
Bowen, Elizabeth, 1:69–70
Bowen, Ezra, 2:465
Bowen-Woodward, Kathy, 2:550
Bower, Gordon H., 2:103, 2:112
Bower, Gordon H. (ed), 2:112
Bower, T. G., 2:106, 2:112, 2:113
Bowerman, Robert G., 1:583
Bowers, David G., 2:125
Bowker, R. R., Company, 1:566, 1:569
Bowles, Colin, 1:434
Bowman, Alan K., 2:279

Bowman, Isaiah, 2:77
Bowman, James S. (ed), 2:4, 2:19
Bowman, John, 2:206
Bownas, Geoffrey, 1:425
Bowyer, Adrian, 1:511
Boyce, B., 1:575
Boyd, John R., 1:560
Boyd, Mary A., 1:560
Boyd, Nancy, 2:570
Boyer, Carl B., 1:496, 1:514
Boyer, Jay, 1:203
Boyer, Rodney F., 2:511
Boyer, William H., 2:144
Boyle, R. Alexander, 2:81
Boyle, Robert, 2:499
Boyle, Robert H., 2:81
Boy Scouts of America, 1:556
Boyum, Joy Gould, 1:473
Bracken, Jeanne M., 2:561
Bradbrook, Muriel C., 1:18
Bradbury, Katherine L., 2:147
Bradbury, Ray, 1:202–203
Bradenburg, Sara A., 1:571
Bradford, G., 1:27
Bradford, Richard, 1:65
Bradford, Sarah, 2:343
Bradford, William, 1:151
Bradlee, Benjamin C., 2:247
Bradley, Brendan P., 2:121
Bradley, Gunilla, 1:554
Bradley, John, 2:91, 2:404
Bradshaw, Michael, 2:90
Bradstreet, Anne, 1:151
Brady, John, 1:447
Brady, Kathleen, 2:218
Bragg, Sadie, 1:506
Brahms, Johannes, 2:348
Brainerd, George W., 2:300
Bramer, Max, 1:583
Bramson, Morris, 1:505
Bramwell, Martyn, 2:492
Branch, Taylor, 2:12
Brand, Eric, 2:345
Brand, Stewart, 1:537, 1:566
Brandeis, Louis, 2:26
Brandes, Joseph, 2:206
Brandon, William, 2:157
Brandreth, Gyles, 1:439
Brandt, Keith, 2:163, 2:226
Brandt, Nat, 2:189
Branigan, Keith, 2:278
Branigan, Keith (ed), 2:273
Branley, Franklyn M., 2:435, 2:469, 2:475,
  2:478, 2:480, 2:484, 2:492
Brasch, Walter M., 1:437
Braskamp, Larry A., 2:112
Bratko, Ivan, 1:565
Braun, Aurel, (ed), 2:404
Brautigan, Richard, 1:203

Brazelton, T. Berry, 2:539
Breakstone (ed), 2:241
Brebner, John B., 2:157
Brecher, Deborah L., 1:556
Brecher, Kenneth, 2:469
Brecht, Bertolt, 1:365
Breckinridge, Sophonisba P., 2:152
Breen, Jennifer (ed), 1:113
Breen, William J., 2:223
Breit, William, 2:55
Breitman, George (ed), 1:450
Brennan, Bernard P., 2:97
Brent, Peter, 2:457
Breslauer, George W., 2:389, 2:392
Breslow, Ronald, 2:437
Brett, Philip (ed), 2:416
Brettell, Richard, 2:353
Breuil, Henri, 2:278
Brewster, Sir David, 2:516
Brey, Barry B., 1:560
Brezhnev, Leonid, 2:389
Brian, Denis, 1:237
Brickner, Philip, 2:567
Bridenbaugh, Carl, 2:161
Bridgers, Sue Ellen, 1:204; 2:237
Briggs, Asa, 2:339
Briggs, Carole S., 2:257, 2:480
Briggs, Geoffrey, 2:475
Bright, George, 1:535
Bright, Michael, 2:81, 2:461, 2:488
Brighthope, Ian, 2:559
Brightman, Frank H., 2:446, 2:447
Brightwell, Robin, 2:545
Brill, Alida, 2:12
Brim, Orville G., Jr. (ed), 2:106
Brink, Andrew, 1:503
Brink, J. R. (ed), 1:582
Brinkley, Alan, 2:229
Brinton, Clarence C., 2:329
Brinton, Crane, 2:273
British Library Staff, 2:157
Brittin, Norman A., 1:265
Brock, Suzanne, 1:436
Brock, Thomas D., 2:444
Brockington, J. L., 2:281
Brode, Douglas, 1:189, 1:471
Broderick, Francis (ed), 2:241
Brodhead, Richard (ed), 1:220
Brodie, Edmund, Jr., 2:450
Brodie, Fawn M., 2:364
Brodsky, Patricia Pollock, 1:371
Brody, E. W., 1:454
Brody, Jane, 2:450, 2:530, 2:549
Brody, Robert (ed), 1:403
Brogyanyi, Bela, 1:362
Brome, Vincent, 2:121
Bromwede, Martyn, 2:82
Bronshtein, I. N., 1:496
Brontë, Charlotte, 1:42

Brontë, Emily, 1:42
Brook, G. L., 1:434
Brooke, Rupert, 1:70
Brook-Little, John (comp), 2:277
Brooks, Charles, 1:459
Brooks, Cleanth, 1:220
Brooks, Frederick P., Jr, 1:585
Brooks, Gwendolyn, 1:205
Brooks, Polly S., 2:305
Brooks, Thomas R., 2:70, 2:237
Brooks, Tim, 1:464
Brosman, Katherine Savage, 1:340
Brown, A. S., 2:495
Brown, Calvin, 1:220
Brown, Charles Brockden, 1:152
Brown, Clarence (ed), 1:389
Brown, David, 2:357
Brown, Dee, 2:135, 2:200
Brown, Fern G., 2:561
Brown, Geoffrey, 1:554; 2:492
Brown, George H., 2:308
Brown, J. (ed), 2:518
Brown, Jerald R., 1:564
Brown, Karl, 1:470
Brown, Lauren, 2:465
Brown, Lester R., 2:36, 2:76, 2:81, 2:273
Brown, Lloyd A., 2:92
Brown, Maurice, 2:61
Brown, Michael S., 2:149
Brown, Milton W., 2:261
Brown, P. J., 1:586
Brown, Peter, 2:261, 2:304
Brown, Peter Lancaster, 2:469
Brown, R. Allen, 2:305
Brown, Richard G., 1:512
Brown, Robert M., 1:302
Brown, Seyom, 2:387
Brown, Sterling, 1:206
Brown, William Wells, 1:170
Browne, David, 2:554
Browne, Malcolm, 2:241
Brownell, David (ed), 2:273
Browning, Elizabeth Barrett, 1:43
Browning, Robert, 1:44
Browning, Robert, 2:301
Brownlee, Juanita, 1:511
Brownlow, Kevin, 2:226
Brownstein, Ronald, 2:257
Brownstone, David M., 2:432
Brubaker, Timothy H. (ed), 2:129
Bruce, Shelley, 2:561
Bruce, Walter, 1:574
Brumberg, Abraham, 2:405
Brumberg, Abraham (ed), 2:15
Brundage, Burr Cartwright, 2:298
Bruner, Jerome S., 2:112
Bruner, Jerome S. (ed), 2:112
Brunes, Tons, 1:511
Brunn, Bertal, 2:545

Brunn, Ruth Dowling, 2:545
Bruno, Frank J., 2:95
Bruns, Roger, 2:292
Bruns, Roger (ed), 2:33
Brunsdale, Mitzi, 1:381
Brush, Warren D., 2:447
Bruun, Bertel, 2:450
Bruun, Ruth D., 2:450
Bruyen, F. De, 1:566
Bryan, Doug L., 1:565
Bryan, William Jennings, 2:205
Bryant, William Cullen, 1:156
Buchan, Bruce, 2:21
Buchanan, James M., 2:71
Buchanan, John G., 2:165
Buchanan, Keith, 2:273, 2:281
Buchanan, Russell, 2:235
Buchsbaum, Ralph, 2:448
Buchwald, Art, 1:488
Buchwald, Jed Z., 2:527
Buck, Pearl, 1:207
Buck, Ross, 2:112
Buck, Stratton, 1:335
Buck, William (ed) and (tr), 1:421, 1:422
Buckland, W. R., 1:529
Buckman, Robert, 2:544
Budden, Julian, 2:361
Budge, Ernest A., 2:279
Budge, Ian, 2:405
Budoff, Milton, 1:569
Buehler, W. K., 1:532
Bugg, James L., Jr., 2:180
Buggey, J., 2:252
Bulfinch, Thomas, 1:318
Bulgakov, Mikhail, 1:339
Bulgren, William G., 1:586
Bull, Malcolm, 1:561
Bullard, E. John, 2:215
Bulliet, R. W., 2:516
Bunch, Bryan (ed), 2:432
Bundy, McGeorge, 2:238
Bunge, Frederica, 2:86
Bunge, M. A., 2:504
Bunin, Ivan, 1:390
Bunt, Richard B., 1:538
Bunyan, John, 1:21
Buranelli, Vincent, 1:164; 2:524
Burbank, Rex J., 1:303
Burch, John L. (ed), 1:558
Burckhardt, Jacob, 2:310
Burdman, Geri Marr, 2:544
Bureau of the Census, U.S. Department of
    Commerce, 2:4, 2:124
Burelback, Frederick, 1:438
Burford, Alison, 2:284
Burger, Dionys, 1:519
Burger, Ernst, 2:354
Burgess, Anthony, 1:71, 1:237
Burgess, Eric, 2:475

Burgess, Michael, 2:257
Burgess, Robert F., 2:278
Burk, Robert F., 2:239
Burke, Edmund, 2:9, 2:329
Burke, Kathleen, 1:168
Burkel, William E., 2:451
Burkhardt, Ann, 1:487
Burkholder, J. Peter, 2:261
Burkitt, M. C., 2:278
Burks, Alice R., 1:540
Burks, Ardath W., 2:86, 2:398
Burks, Arthur W., 1:540
Burks, Arthur W. (ed), 1:553
Burlingame, Roger, 2:203, 2:526
Burne, Glenn S., 2:364
Burne, Jerome (ed), 2:273
Burner, David, 2:229
Burnett, Constance, 2:223
Burnett, James, 2:355
Burnett, Piers, 1:580
Burnford, Sheila, 1:136
Burns, E. Bradford, 2:408
Burns, E. Bradford (ed), 2:369
Burns, James MacGregor, 2:40, 2:152
Burns, Robert, 1:32
Burns, Stewart, 2:241
Burrell, David B., 2:303, 2:307
Burris, Scott (ed), 2:560
Burroughs, Edgar Rice, 1:208
Burroughs, John, 2:188
Burrows, David, 2:521
Burt, Forrest D., 1:106
Burt, McKinley, Jr, 2:432
Burt, Olive W., 2:202, 2:495
Burton, David H., 2:223
Burton, Isabel, 2:364
Burton, Maurice, 2:449
Burton, Philip, 1:483
Burton, Sir Richard Francis, 2:364
Burzio, Luigi, 1:346
Busby, Linda, 1:461
Buscaglia, Leo F., 2:536
Buscall, R. (ed), 2:510
Busch, Hans (tr), 2:361
Busch, Marie (ed), 1:382
Busch, Moritz, 2:342
Bush, Catherine, 2:366
Bush, George Herbert Walker, 2:259
Bushman, Richard L., 2:161
Bushnell, David, 2:369
Busoni, Rafaello, 1:356
Butcher, Lee, 1:546
Butcher, Philip, 1:171
Butler, Charles, 1:583
Butler, Eamonn, 2:66
Butler, Francelia, 2:401
Butler, L. J., 1:52
Butler, Lord C. H., 2:404
Butlin, Martin, 2:358

Butson, Thomas G., 2:407
Butterworth, C. E. (ed), 2:302
Butterworth, Neil, 2:261, 2:337
Butts, R. Freeman, 2:12
Butts, Robert E. (ed), 2:473
Buvet, R., 2:447
Buxbaum, Melvin H., 2:526
Buxton, Marilyn, 1:556
Bylebyl, Jerome J., 2:547
Byrd, Joe, 1:561
Byrd, Peter (ed), 2:408
Byrne, John A., 1:546
Byrne, Josefa Heifetz, 1:439
Byrne, Katherine, 2:550
Byron, Lord, George Gordon, 1:33
Byron, William, 1:356

C

Cable, George Washington, 1:171
Cable, Mary, 2:298
Cable, Thomas, 1:429
Cadogan, Peter H., 2:475
Cady, John F., 2:398
Caen, Herb, 2:90
Caesar, Julius, 2:292
Cage, John, 2:261
Cahalan, Donn, 2:555
Cahill, Holger, 2:213
Cahill, Kevin M. (ed), 2:560
Cahn, Robert, 2:495
Cailliet, Emile, 1:533
Cain, Michael, 2:215
Cairns-Smith, A. G., 2:461
Cajori, Florian, 1:496
Calder, Alexander, 2:261
Calder, Nigel, 2:469, 2:475, 2:518
Calderón de la Barca, Pedro, 1:355
Caldwell, Dan (ed), 2:38
Caldwell, John C., 2:398
Caldwell, Lynton K., 2:81
Caldwell, Mark, 2:567
Calhoun, John Caldwell, 2:181
Calhoun, Richard J., 1:215
Califano, Joseph A., Jr, 2:567
Calingaert, Peter, 1:586
Callaghan, Morley, 1:137
Callahan, Daniel, 2:567
Callan, Edward, 1:416
Callender, Edward B., 2:15
Callery, Michael, 1:578
Callow, Alexander, 1:460
Calter, Paul, 1:556
Calvert, Patricia, 2:200
Calvin, John, 2:311
Calvino, Italo, 1:347
Calvocoressi, Michael D., 2:346
Calvocoressi, Peter, 2:36, 2:387
Cameron, Averil (ed), 2:273

Cameron, Charlotte, 2:369
Cameron, 1:570
Cameron, Robert, 2:87, 2:90
Cametti, Alberto, 2:319
Camp, Pamela S., 2:437
Campanella, Thomas, 2:473
Campbell, Andrew, 2:465
Campbell, Angus, 2:135
Campbell, Civardi, 2:320
Campbell, Colin, 2:70
Campbell, Jerry, 1:582
Campbell, John, 2:92, 2:488
Campbell, Joseph, 2:52
Campbell, Lewis, 2:527
Campbell, Mary, 1:573
Campbell, Nelson (ed), 1:480
Campbell, Norman R., 2:434
Campbell, Patricia, 1:213
Campbell, R., 2:465
Campbell, Rosemary, 2:70
Camps, W. A., 1:325
Camus, Albert, 1:333
Canemaker, John, 1:474
Canfield, D. Lincoln, 1:353
Cannon, Garland, 1:432
Cannon, John, 2:273
Cannon, Lou, 2:260
Cannon, Terry (ed), 2:86
Canon, Jill, 2:192
Canterbury, E. Ray, 2:55
Cantor, Georg, 1:499
Cantor, Milton, 2:5
Cantor, Muriel, 1:461, 1:465
Cantor, Norman F., 2:273
Cantrell, Jacqueline P., 2:298
Cantril, Hadley, 2:130
Cantu, Caesar C., 2:323
Capek, Karel, 1:384–85
Caplan, Frank, 2:540
Caplan, Theresa, 2:540
Caplovitz, David, 2:61
Caplow, Theodore, 2:130, 2:132, 2:142, 2:148
Caras, Roger, 2:461
Caravale, G. A. (ed), 2:73
Carberry, M. Sandra, 1:563
Carbonell, Jaime, 1:582
Carcopino, Jerome, 2:290
Card, Orson Scott, 1:490
Card, Stuart K., 1:558
Cardenal, Father Ernesto, 1:400
CARDRI Staff, 2:411
Carducci, Giosue, 1:349
Carey, Helen H., 2:92
Carey, John (ed), 1:90
Carlson, Allan, 2:135
Carmi, T. (ed), 1:420
Carnegie, Andrew, 2:206
Caro, Robert A., 2:246

Carola, R., 2:489
Carp, Robert A., 2:26
Carpenter, Finley, 2:102
Carpenter, Frederick I., 1:245, 1:274
Carpenter, Humphrey, 1:66, 1:126
Carpentier, Alejo, 1:401
Carper, Jean, 2:549
Carr, John (ed), 2:435
Carr, John D., 1:48
Carr, Raymond (ed), 2:374
Carr, Terry, 2:467
Carroll, David, 1:411
Carroll, Lewis, 1:45
Carroll, Suzanne, 1:437
Carruth, Ella K., 2:14
Carruth, Gorton (ed), 2:153
Carson, Ewart R., 1:558
Carson, James, 2:493
Carson, Neil, 1:266
Carson, Rachel Louise, 2:82, 2:243, 2:466,
    2:488
Carson, Rob, 2:493
Carson, Robert B., 2:57
Carson, S. L., 2:331
Carsten, F. L., 2:374
Carter, Alden, 1:461
Carter, Gwendolyn M., 2:393
Carter, Hodding, 2:260
Carter, Howard, 2:279
Carter, James Earl, 2:256
Carter, Jimmy C., Jr., 2:279
Carter, Margaret, 1:59
Carter, Paul A., 2:226
Carter, Rosalyn, 2:255
Carter, Sharon, 2:536, 2:538, 2:565, 2:567
Carterette, Edward C., 2:113
Carus, Paul, 1:511
Carver, Terrell, 2:59
Cary, Joyce, 1:72
Cary, Richard, 1:180
Caselli, Giovanni, 2:278, 2:279, 2:284,
    2:290, 2:305, 2:310
Casewit, Curtis W., 2:556
Casey, Jane C., 2:223
Cashman, Sean Dennis, 2:203
Casper, Barry M., 2:512
Cassat, Mary, 2:215
Cassel, Don, 1:556
Cassell, Carol, 2:543
Cassirer, Ernst, 2:50
Casson, Lionel, 2:273
Castiglione, Pierina B., 1:346
Castro, Fidel, 2:410
Castronovo, David, 1:303
Casty, Alan, 1:453
Cate, Curtis, 2:329
Cater, John P., 1:579
Cathcart, Robert, 1:445
Cather, Willa, 1:209; 2:200

Cathey, W. Thomas, 1:578
Catlin, George, 2:188
Cattell, Raymond B., 2:105
Cattoche, Robert J., 1:571
Catton, Bruce, 2:153, 2:189, 2:192, 2:199,
    2:200
Cauchy, Augustin Louis, 1:525
Caudill, Maureen, 1:583
Caufield, Catherine, 2:508
Caulaincourt, Armand, 2:330
Caulkins, Janet, 2:380
Cawson, Roderick, 2:553
Cecil, David, 1:20
Cellini, Benvenuto, 2:312
Ceram, C. W., 2:278
Cerf, Bennett (ed), 1:439
Cervantes Saavedra, Miguel de, 1:356
Ceserani, Gian P., 2:309
Cezanne, Paul, 2:349
Chace, A. B. (ed), 1:496
Chadbourn, W. R., 1:431
Chadwick, Henry (ed), 2:273, 2:290
Chadwick, Michael, 1:583
Chafe, William H., 2:238
Chagall, Marc, 2:417
Chaikin, Miriam, 2:382
Chakraborty, A. K., 2:404
Chaliand, Gerard, 2:36
Challener, Richard D. (ed), 2:388
Chalmers, David M., 2:226
Chamberlain, E. R., 2:310
Chamberlain, Martin, 1:572
Chambers, John W., II, 2:218
Chambers, Raymond W. (ed), 1:6
Chamot, Mary, 2:358
Champagne, Anthony, 2:35
Champigneulle, Bernard, 2:356
Chancellor, John, 1:457
Chandler, Daniel, 1:556
Chandler, Louis A., 2:123
Chandler, Raymond, 1:210
Chandler, William, 2:496
Chandler, William M., 2:35
Chandy, K. Mani, 1:559
Chang, David W., 2:398
Chang, H. C. (ed and tr), 1:423
Chang, K. C., 2:281
Chang, Shi-Kuo (ed), 1:563
Chaple, Glen F., Jr, 2:435
Chaplin, J. P., 2:95
Chapman, Gerald W., 2:9
Chapman, John J., 2:191
Chapman, Robert, 1:433
Chappuis, Adrien, 2:349
Charap, Stanley H., 2:522
Charlesworth, Edward A., 2:536
Charley, Richard J., 2:483
Charlier, Roger Henri, 2:486
Charlton, James (ed), 1:481

Charney, Maurice, 1:16
Charters, Ann, 1:247
Chartrand, Mark R., III, 2:469
Chase, Gilbert, 2:153
Chase, Stuart, 1:437
Chaucer, Geoffrey, 1:6
Chauvois, Louis, 2:547
Check, William A., 2:560
Checkland, P. B., 1:558
Cheever, John, 1:211
Cheever, Susan, 1:211
Cheilik, Michael, 2:273
Chekhov, Anton, 1:391
Cheney, Anne, 1:232
Cheney, Glenn A., 2:366, 2:495
Chenier, Norman J., 1:496
Cherlin, Andrew, 2:137
Cherrier, François, 2:504
Cherry, Sheldon H., 2:543
Chesnutt, Charles W., 1:172
Chesterman, Charles W., 2:492
Chesterton, G. K., 1:72–73; 2:307
Chew, Samuel C., 1:60
Chi-Chen Wang (tr), 1:423
Chiesa, Giulietto, 2:15
Chijioki, F. A., 2:299
Chikazumi, Sushin, 2:522
Childe, V. Gordon, 2:48
Childers, Peter G., 2:110
Childress, Alice, 1:212
Chiles, Frances, 1:408
Chilnick, Larry, 2:549
Chilton, John, 2:261, 2:264
Chiou, Wu Co, Sr. (ed), 1:582
Chippindale, Christopher, 2:305
Chiras, Daniel D., 2:467
Chirot, Daniel, 2:144
Chisholm, J., 2:273, 2:278
Chisholm, Shirley Anita St. Hill, 2:34
Chomsky, Noam, 1:435; 2:50
Chopin, Frederic, 2:350
Chopin, Kate, 1:173
Chorley, R. J., 2:80
Chou, George Tsu-der, 1:572
Chou, Hsiang-Kuang, 2:281
Christian, Janet L., 1:568
Christiansen, Reidar (ed), 1:374
Christianson, Gale E., 2:469, 2:516
Christie, Dame Agatha, 1:73–74
Chu, Daniel, 2:299
Chung-Wa Chung (ed), 1:426
Church, Clive, 2:332
Churchill, Winston S., 2:153, 2:192, 2:386
Chusid, Martin (ed), 2:361
Chute, Marchette, 1:11, 1:16
Chyet, Stanley F. (tr), 1:420
Ciardi, John, 1:432
Cicciarella, Charles F., 1:568
Cicero, Marcus Tullius, 2:293

Cikovsky, Nicolai, Jr. (ed), 2:216
Citati, Pietro, 1:369
Clagett, Marshall, 1:521; 2:518
Claghorn, Charles E., 2:153
Claiborne, Robert, 1:432
Clancy, Herbert J., 2:168
Clapp, Patricia, 2:161
Clareson, Thomas D., 1:234, 1:279, 1:286
Clark, B. H., 1:355
Clark, Beverly L., 1:45
Clark, Elizabeth, 2:357
Clark, Grenville, 2:36
Clark, Jeff, 1:529
Clark, Kenneth, 2:261, 2:316
Clark, Ronald W., 1:503; 2:457, 2:520,
    2:524, 2:526
Clark, Wilfrid E., 2:48, 2:278
Clark, William, 2:176
Clarke, Arthur C., 1:75
Clarke, Asa Bement, 2:200
Clarke, Bob, 1:440
Clarke, Desmond M., 1:515
Clarke, Ronald W., 2:378
Clason, Kristy, 1:575
Clay, Henry, 2:181
Claypool, Jane, 2:62, 2:70
Clayton, Alfred Stafford, 2:140
Cleary, Edward L., 2:408
Cleckley, Hervey M., 2:122
Clemans, E. V., 1:570
Clemens, John, 2:204
Clemens, Sam, 1:511
Clemens, Virginia Phelps, 1:469
Clemente, Carmine D. (ed), 2:450
Clements, Arthur L., 1:10
Clements, Frank, 2:373
Clifford, Mary L., 2:89
Clinard, Marshall B., 2:133
Cline, Hugh F., 1:570
Clingman, Stephen, 1:414
Clinton, Susan, 2:231
Cloudsley-Thompson, John, 2:449
Clout, Hough, 2:87
Cloward, Richard A., 2:40, 2:145, 2:258
Clynes, M. (ed), 2:121
Coale, Samuel, 1:71, 1:211
Coates, Henry, 2:319
Cobb, Douglas, 1:572, 1:573
Cobb, Jonathan, 2:144
Cobb, Vicki, 2:473, 2:498, 2:504
Cochran, Thomas C., 2:184, 2:204
Cochrane, Jennifer, 2:467
Cocks, S. W., 1:426
Codel, Martin (ed), 1:461
Coe, Brian, 1:469
Coe, Graham, 1:435
Coe, Michael D., 2:299
Coetzee, J. M., 1:413
Coffey, Wayne, 2:555

Coffin, Stephen, 1:561
Cogan, Marc, 2:289
Coger, Leslie, 1:449
Cohen, A. K., 2:133
Cohen, Arthur A., 2:402
Cohen, Bernard L., 2:496
Cohen, Daniel, 1:469; 2:110, 2:123, 2:279, 2:480, 2:536, 2:538, 2:561
Cohen, David (ed), 2:86
Cohen, Davis, 1:524
Cohen, Donald, 1:523
Cohen, F., 1:574
Cohen, I. Bernard, 2:507, 2:514
Cohen, Jeremy, 2:16, 2:26
Cohen, Leonard, 1:137
Cohen, Marcia, 2:148
Cohen, Mark Nathan, 2:47, 2:278
Cohen, Norman, 1:566
Cohen, Ronald J., 2:122
Cohen, Susan, 2:123, 2:536, 2:538
Cohen, Warren I., 2:26
Cohler, Anne M., 2:19
Cohn, Leigh, 2:551
Colbert, Edwin H., 2:495
Colbert, R. W. (ed), 2:376
Colburn, David R., 2:218
Cole, Barry (ed), 1:465
Cole, Bruce, 2:273, 2:305, 2:310
Cole, Don, 2:62, 2:257
Cole, J. P., 2:76, 2:91
Cole, Jonathan R., 2:144, 2:148
Cole, Michael, 2:103, 2:106
Cole, Sheila, 2:106
Cole, Stephen, 2:144
Cole, Sylvia, 1:432
Colecchia, Francesca (tr), 1:399
Coleman, James S., 2:130, 2:132, 2:135, 2:144
Coleman, Marion T., 2:138
Coleridge, Samuel Taylor, 1:34
Coles, Jane H., 2:137, 2:148
Coles, Robert, 1:70; 2:97, 2:105–106, 2:109, 2:137, 2:148, 2:241
Collaer, Paul, 2:261
Collcutt, Martin, 2:273
Collier, Christopher, 2:163, 2:166
Collier, James L., 2:163, 2:166, 2:264
Collier, Simon, 2:273
Collingham, H. A. C., 2:332
Collings, Virginia B., 2:113
Collingwood, G. H., 2:447
Collins, Alan (ed), 1:582
Collins, Donald, 2:486
Collins, H. M., 1:582
Collins, Michael, 2:480
Collins, P. M., 2:511
Collins, Peter (ed), 1:434
Collins, Randall, 2:132, 2:137
Collins, Wilkie, 1:45

Collis, Harry, 1:436
Colum, Padraic, 1:76
Columbus, Christopher, 2:159
Combs, James, 1:458
Commager, Henry S., 1:430; 2:5, 2:155, 2:166, 2:192, 2:294, 2:326
Commager, Henry S. (ed), 2:35
Compaine, Benjamin, 2:130
Commoner, Barry (ed), 2:84
Compton, Grant, 2:484
Comstock, George, 1:465
Comte, Auguste, 2:126
Conacher, D. J., 1:312
Conard, Henry S., 2:447
Conati, Marcello, 2:361
Conaway, Mary E., 2:43
Condie, Kent C. (ed), 2:82, 2:494
Condon, E. U., 2:500
Condon, Judith, 2:556
Confucius, 2:283
Congressional Quarterly, 2:5, 2:7, 2:16, 2:26, 2:32, 2:33, 2:36, 2:89, 2:257
Congreve, William, 1:21
Connah, Graham, 2:299
Connell, John L., 1:563
Connell, N. A., 1:583
Connolly, Peter, 2:284, 2:290
Connor, W. Robert, 2:290
Conquest, Robert, 2:405
Conrad, John P., 2:133
Conrad, Joseph, 1:76–77
Conrad, Pam, 2:200
Conrad, Peter, 2:138
Conradi, Peter J., 1:86
Conroy, Patricia (ed), 1:375
Constable, George (ed), 2:88
Constable, John, 2:351
Consumer Guide, 2:553
Consumer Reports Books Editors, 2:560
Conta, Marcia Maher, 2:12, 2:241
Conway, Moncure D., 2:165
Cook, Brian, 2:496
Cook, Chris, 2:273
Cook, Claire Kehrwald, 1:479
Cook, David, 1:468
Cook, Don, 2:387, 2:405
Cook, Fred J., 2:153, 2:241
Cook, Captain James, 2:321
Cook, Jan Leslie, 2:488
Cook, Theodore A., 1:515
Cooke, Alistair, 2:87
Cooke, Deryck, 2:355
Cooke, Jacob E. (ed), 2:166
Cooley, Charles H., 2:146
Coolidge, Calvin, 2:227
Cooper, Cary L., 2:536
Cooper, James Fenimore, 2:163, 2:168
Cooper, John D., 2:495
Cooper, John M., Jr, 2:218

Cooper, Joshua (ed), 1:389
Cooper, Kenneth H., 2:549, 2:551, 2:561
Cooper, Lettice, 1:58
Cooper, Mildred, 2:551
Cooper, Wayne C., 1:260
Copeland, Ian, 2:404
Copleston, F. C., 2:307
Corballis, Richard, 1:123
Corbett, Edward P., 1:477
Corbishley, Mike, 2:290
Corbitt, Mary Kay, 1:512
Corcoran, Neil, 1:92
Corden, W. M., 2:71
Cormier, Robert, 1:212–213
Cornelius, Michael, 1:535
Cornell, James, 2:469
Cornell, James (ed), 2:435, 2:480
Cornell, Tim, 2:290
Cornish, Edward (ed), 1:554
Corrick, James, 2:545
Corrick, James A., 2:437
Corson, John A., 2:123
Cortada, James W., 1:540
Cortes, Carlos, 1:353
Cortes, Hernan, 2:322
Cortesi, David E., 1:561
Corwin, Edward S., 2:16, 2:21
Coser, Lewis A., 2:125, 2:132
Coser, Lewis A. (ed), 2:141
Cosgrove, Margaret, 2:484
Cosner, Sharon, 2:153
Costa, Paul T., 2:116
Costa, Richard H., 1:129
Costanzo, William, 1:477
Costello, Elaine, 1:448
Costo, Jeannette H., 2:160
Costo, Rupert, 2:160
Cottam, Clarence, 2:448
Cotterell, Arthur, 2:273, 2:281
Cottrell, Alvin J., 2:89, 2:273
Coughlin, 1:523
Coulter, E. Merton, 2:198
Council for Science and Society Staff,
    1:583
Council of State Governments, 2:5
Couper, Heather, 2:475, 2:480
Courant, Richard, 1:496, 1:524
Cournot, Antoine A., 1:529
Cousteau, Jacques–Yves, 2:487
Cowan, Tom, 1:490
Coward, Sir Noel, 1:77–78
Cowart, Robert, 1:561
Cowasjee, Saros (ed), 1:422
Cowels, Michael, 2:122
Cowie, A. P., 1:437
Cowper, William, 1:22
Cox, Allan, 2:494
Cox, Archibald, 2:26
Cox, Barbara G., et al, 2:561

Cox, Catherine Bly, 2:242
Cox, Charles B. (ed), 1:124
Cox, Christopher, 2:232
Cox, Don R., 1:48
Cox, Harold, 2:129
Cox, Philip L., 1:511
Cox, Stephen, 1:470
Cox, Thomas, 1:326
Coxeter, H. S. M., 1:511, 1:516, 1:519
Coxford, Arthur F., 1:505, 1:523
Coynik, David, 1:469
Crabbe, Katharyn F., 1:126, 1:127
Crabtree, Adam, 2:121
Craft, Robert, 2:426
Craig, Albert M., 2:399
Craig, Warren, 2:153
Cramér, Harald, 1:529
Cran, William, 1:429
Crane, John K., 1:130
Crane, Julia, 2:42
Crane, Stephen, 1:173; 2:192, 2:207
Cranin, A. Norman, 2:552
Crankshaw, Edward, 2:326, 2:392
Cranston, Maurice, 2:18
Craven, Avery O., 2:189
Craven, Linda, 2:538
Craven, Wesley F., 2:166
Cravens, Sydney, 1:355
Craze, Dan S., 1:13
Creasy, Robert K., 2:543
Cremin, Lawrence, 2:161, 2:184
Crenson, Matthew A., 2:40
Cressey, Donald R., 2:133
Cressey, George B., 2:91
Crèvecoeur, Michel-Guillaume Jean De,
    1:153
Crichton, Jean, 2:544
Crichton, Michael, 1:554
Crick, Francis Harry Compton, 2:439
Critchfield, Howard J., 2:484
Critchlow, Keith, 1:519
Crockett, David, 2:184
Croll, Elisabeth (ed), 2:86, 2:398
Cronin, A. J., 1:78
Cronquist, Arthur, 2:447
Crosher, Judith, 2:284, 2:299
Cross, Donna Woolfolk, 1:465
Crosswhite, F. Joe (ed), 1:523
Crotty, William, 2:39
Crouse, Timothy, 1:457
Crow, John A., 1:355
Crowder, Michael, 2:298
Crowder, Michael (ed), 2:272, 2:276
Crowder, Richard, 1:284
Crowson, Philip, 2:492
Crowther, James G., 2:483
Cruise O'Brien, Maire, 2:305
Crummel, Alex, 2:273
Crump, Donald J., 2:461

Crump, Donald J. (ed), 2:82, 2:83, 2:90, 2:91, 2:278, 2:488, 2:493, 2:495
Crynes, B. L. (ed), 2:508
Crystal, David, 1:434
Cuff, David J., 2:92
Culbertson, John, 2:71, 2:257
Culhane, Shamus, 1:474
Cullen, Countee, 1:213–14
Culver, Raymond B., 2:187
Cummings, E. E., 1:214
Cummings, Paul, 2:261
Cummings, Steve, 1:567
Cummins, Jerry J., 1:511
Cundy, H. Martyn, 1:535
Cunliffe, Barry B., 2:305
Cunliffe, Marcus, 2:168, 2:179
Cunningham, Hugh, 2:184, 2:339
Cunningham, John D., 2:450
Cunningham, Merce, 2:266
Cuny, Hilaire, 2:445
Curie, Eve, 2:510
Curie, Marie, 2:510
Curnow, Ray, 1:556, 1:578
Curran, Susan, 1:556, 1:578
Current, Richard N., 2:180
Current-Garcia, Eugene, 1:178
Currid, Cheryl C., 1:558
Currimbhoy, Nayana, 2:401
Curtin, Philip D., 2:189, 2:393
Curtis, Jack F., 1:579
Curtis, Lindsay R., 2:567
Curtis, Richard, 1:450
Curtis, William, 2:419
Cushing, Harvey W., 2:532, 2:534
Cushman, Robert F., 2:12
Custer, George Armstrong, 2:203
Cutright, Paul R., 2:176
Cutsinger, John (ed), 1:455
Cutter, N., 1:557
Cwiklik, Robert, 2:520
Cyert, Richard M. (ed), 2:140
Czarnecka, Ewa, 1:387
Czitrom, Daniel, 1:453, 1:454

D

Dadd, Debra L., 2:570
Daffron, Carolyn, 1:265
Dahl, Roald, 1:79
Dahl, Robert A., 2:15, 2:40, 2:130
Dahlgren, R. M., 2:447
Dahlhaus, John, 2:362
Dahlmann, Friedrich C., 2:288
Dahrendorf, Ralf, 2:132, 2:405
Daintith, John (ed), 2:512
Daish, C. B., 1:535
Daiute, Colette, 1:570
Dal, E. (ed), 2:518

Dale, Alzina Stone, 1:73
Daley, William, 2:207
Dalhaus, Carl, 2:362
Dallek, Robert, 2:234
D'Alquen, Richard, 1:362
Dalton, George, 2:47
Dalton, Harlon (ed), 2:560
Dalton, Karen C., 2:216
Dalton, LeRoy C., 1:496
Daly, Donal, 1:583
Daly, Jay, 1:240
Dalzell, Robert F., Jr., 2:180
Dance, Stanley, 2:226, 2:267
Dangler, Sandy, 1:21
Daniel, Robert L., 2:153
Daniels, Jerry, 1:559
Danin D., 1:529
Danks, Susan M., 2:438
Dante Alighieri, 1:349
D'Antonio, William V. (ed), 2:137
Danuloff, Craig, 1:578
Danziger, Marlies, 1:25
Darby, Jean, 2:238
Da Rin, Doris, 1:109
Dario, Ruben, 1:402
Dark, Sidney, 1:50
Darling, David, 1:556, 1:559, 1:568, 1:584
Darling, David J., 2:480
Darlington, William, 1:29
Darson, Richard M., 1:425
Dartford, Gerald P., 2:329
Darwin, Charles Robert, 2:48, 2:457
Dauben, Joseph W., 1:499
Daugherty, James, 2:161
Daumier, Honore, 2:346
Davenport, Basil (ed), 1:320
Davenport, John, 2:105
David, A. Rosalie, 2:279
David, Elmer, 1:457
David, Hans T., 2:334
David, Heather M., 2:483
David, Richard, 2:324
David, Stephen, 2:94, 2:154
David, Stephen M., 2:85, 2:393
Davidovits, Joseph, 2:280
Davidowicz, Lucy S., 2:235
Davidshofer, Charles O., 2:122
Davidson, Arnold E., 1:146
Davidson, Art, 2:467
Davidson, Basil, 2:299, 2:320, 2:363, 2:393
Davidson, Jessica, 1:535
Davidson, Margaret, 1:449; 2:179
Davidson, Roger H. (ed), 2:5, 2:33
Davies, Eryl, 2:486
Davies, Jack, 2:33
Davies, Nigel, 2:299
Davies, Owen (ed), 2:480
Davies, P. C. (ed), 2:518
Davies, Robertson, 1:138

Davies, W. V., 2:280
Da Vinci, Leonardo. *See* Leonardo Da Vinci
Davis, Bertha, 2:64, 2:71, 2:257
Davis, Burke, 2:163, 2:192
Davis, Daniel S., 2:235
Davis, Derek R., 2:121
Davis, Joseph S., 2:63
Davis, Kenneth C., 2:153
Davis, Lawrence, 1:431
Davis, M. (ed), 1:500
Davis, Martin, 1:496
Davis, Patricia, 2:537
Davis, Ronnie J., 2:71
Davis, William C., 2:192
Davis, William S., 2:284, 2:290
Davison, Mark L., 1:529
Davison, Marshall B., 2:273
Dawood, Richard, 2:530
Dawson, Geraldine (ed), 2:121
Day, A. Grove, 1:265; 2:157
Day, James M. (ed), 2:114
Day, John A., 2:484
Day, Michael H., 2:460
Day, William, 2:461
Deal, Tara (ed), 2:129, 2:544
Deane, Phyllis, 2:55
Dearden, Seton, 2:364
De Bartolo, Dick, 1:440, 1:467
DeBeer, Gavin, 2:457
de Blij, Harm, 2:93
Debo, Angie, 2:153
DeBoer, J. (ed), 2:518
DeBroglie, Louis, 2:518
Debussy, Achille Claude, 2:418
Décarie, Thérèse G., 2:111
de Castillo, Bernal D., 2:323
Decker, Barbara, 2:83, 2:493
Decker, Robert, 2:83, 2:493
DeConde, Alexander, 2:153
De Duve, Christian, 2:437
Deegan, Mary J., 2:208
DeFleur, Melvin L., 2:130
Defoe, Daniel, 1:23; 2:557
Degas, Edgar, 2:352
De Gaulle, Charles, 2:387
De Grandsaigne, J., 1:411
DeGrazia, Edward, 1:468
DeGregorio, William A., 2:5, 2:21
De Haas, Cherie, 2:552
Deighton, Anne, 2:388
Deitel, Harvey M., 1:561
DeKruif, Paul, 2:443–446
Delgado, Ramón (ed), 1:489
De La Mare, W., 1:70
DeLamarter, Richard T., 1:540
de Lange, Nicholas, 2:280
Delanglez, Jean, 2:160
Del Castillo, Bernal, 2:320
DeLeiris, Alain, 2:346

Delf, George, 2:394
Deloria, Vine, Jr., 2:135, 2:241
Deltakron Institute Staff, 2:567
Delzell, Charles F. (ed), 2:340
De Marco, Joseph P., 2:211
De Maria, Rusel, 1:566
Dembo, L. S. (ed), 1:104
De Moivre, Abraham, 1:529
De Morgan, Augustus, 1:529
Dempsey, M. W. (ed), 2:89
Demuth, Norman, 2:423
DeNevi, Don, 2:160
Denhardt, David T., 2:439
Denisoff, R. Serge, 2:133
Denitch, Bogdan, 2:388
Denning, Peter J., 1:574
Dennis, Everette E., 2:130
Dennis, Henry C., 2:153
Dennison, Darwin, 1:569
Denzel, Justin F., 2:532
De Pauw, Linda G., 2:163
DePorte, Anton W., 2:388
Der Hovanessian, Diana (ed), 1:420
De Santis, Vincent, 2:204
Descartes, René, 1:515
Desloge, Edward A., 2:512
Desmond, Morris, 2:461
Desowitz, Robert S., 2:545
Desrochers, George S., 1:559
Dessner, Lawrence, 1:489
De Tolnay, Charles Q., 2:318
Detweiler, Robert, 1:293
Deutsch, Francine, 2:129
Deudney, Daniel, 2:496
Deutsch, Karl W., 2:15, 2:36, 2:130
Deutsch, Morton, 2:132
Deutsch, Otto E., 2:333, 2:336
Deutscher, Isaac, 2:380, 2:382
Devere, John, 2:394
De Vitis, A. A., 1:92
Devlin, Keith, 1:497
DeVoney, Chris, 1:561
DeVoto, Bernard, 2:160
Devoto, Giacomo, 1:346
Dewdney, A. K., 1:537
Dewdney, John C., 2:91
DeWeese, Gene, 1:577
Dewey, John, 1:527; 2:219
Dey, Denny, 1:451
Dhamdhere, D. M., 1:585
Diagram Group, 2:530, 2:545, 2:551
Diamond, Edwin, 1:442; 2:39
Diamond, Stanley, 2:42
Diaz, J., 1:585
Dibell, Ansen, 1:577
Dick, Auguste, 1:509
Dick, Bernard F., 1:90
Dick, Everett, 2:200
Dickens, Charles, 1:47; 2:329
Dickenson, Mollie, 2:257

Dicker, Eva, 1:448
Dickey, James, 1:215
Dickinson, Colin, 2:446
Dickinson, E., 2:507
Dickinson, Emily, 1:175
Dickinson, G. C., 2:92
Dickinson, John, 2:163
Dickler, Howard, 1:572
Dickson, Leonard E., 1:497
Dickson, Paul, 1:438
Dickson, William J., 2:149
Didsbury, Howard, Jr., (ed), 1:454
Diehl, Richard A., 2:299
Dienstag, Jacob I., 2:303
Dietrich, R.V., 2:492
Dietz, Mary G. (ed), 2:10
Digaetani, John L. (ed), 2:362
D'Ignazio, Fred, 1:556, 1:568, 1:580
Dihell, Ansen, 1:490
Dijksterhuis, E. J., 1:521
Dijkstra, Edsger W., 1:537, 1:563
Dilger, Robert J., 2:35
Dillard, Annie, 1:480, 1:482–83
Dillard, J. L., 1:429
Dillon, John, 1:558
Dilman, Ilham, 2:118
Dinesen, Isak, 1:375
Dinner, Sherry H., 2:538
Dinwiddy, John, 2:8
Diop, Cheikh A. (ed), 2:299
Diophantus, 1:507
Dippie, Brian W., 2:188
Dircks, Richard T., 1:24
DiSessa, Andrea, 1:511
Disraeli, Benjamin, 2:343
Ditlow, Clarence, 2:252
Divine, Robert A., 2:239
Dixon, Bernard, 2:432, 2:443, 2:446, 2:531
Dixon, Dougal, 2:495
Dobles, E. R., 2:522
Dobzhansky, Theodosius, 2:456
Dockerill, Michael, 2:223
Dr. Dobb's Journal Staff, 1:564
Dodd, Lawrence C., 2:33
Dodd, Robert T., 2:475
Doherty, Michael, 2:98
Doherty, Thomas, 1:468
Dolan, Edward F., Jr, 2:444
Dolan, Edwin G., 2:71
Dolan, Paul J. (ed), 2:252
Dolciani, Mary P., 1:504, 1:505,
    1:524
Dolger, Henry, 2:561
Dollard, John, 2:98, 2:103, 2:105,
    2:112, 2:116
Dologite, Dorothy G., 1:557
Dominguez, Jorge I., 2:408
Dominguez, Richard H., 2:551
Dominques, Manuel, 1:512
Domling, Wolfgang (ed), 2:335

Donald, David H., 1:306; 2:192
Donaldson, Frances, 1:127
Donaldson, Peter, 1:577
Donley, Carol, 2:520
Donne, John, 1:10
Donnelly, Denis (ed), 1:554
Donnelly, Joseph E., 1:569
Donno, Elizabeth S., 1:13
Donovan, Richard X., 2:432
Donovan, Robert, 2:237
Donovan, Robert J., 2:237, 2:238, 2:382
Dooley, Dennis, 1:231
Dorfman, Joseph, 2:146
Dorin, Henry, 2:500, 2:505, 2:507,
    2:508
Dorson, Richard M. (ed), 1:313
Dostert, Pierre E., 2:85, 2:88
Dostoevsky, Fyodor, 1:392
Dott, Robert H., Jr., 2:495
Dotto, Lydia, 2:81
Dougherty, Dale, 1:561
Douglas, Emily Taft, 2:226
Douglas, George, 1:436
Douglas, John H., 2:496
Douglas, Martin, 2:206
Douglas, Mary, 2:43, 2:47
Douglass, Frederick, 2:190
Douglass, Robert W., 1:569
Dover, K. J., 1:311, 1:313
Dowd, Douglas F., 2:146
Dowden, Anne O., 2:447
Dowling, Ann, 2:521
Downer, John, 2:461
Downing, Charles, 1:420
Downing, Douglas, 1:497, 1:505, 1:529,
    1:564, 1:565
Downs, Anthony, 2:147
Doyle, Sir Arthur Conan, 1:48
Doyle, Paul A., 1:207
Drabble, Margaret, 1:80
Drakakis-Smith, David, 2:85, 2:273
Drakakis-Smith, David (ed), 2:84, 2:274
Drake, Sir Francis, 2:323
Drake, Sandra E., 1:405
Drake, Stillman, 2:473
Dramer, Kim, 2:309
Drange, Diane, 1:583
Draper, Michael, 1:129
Dreiser, Theodore, 1:217
Dressler, Isidore, 1:504, 1:505, 1:506,
    1:512, 1:524
Dressler, Robert, 1:523
Drew, Elizabeth, 2:257
Dreyer, John L., 2:471
Dreyfus, Hubert L., 1:554
Dritsas, 1:504
Driver, Harold E., 2:157
Driver, Sam, 1:395
Drucker, Peter F., 2:63
Drury, Allen, 2:33

Druskin, Mikhail S., 2:426
Druyan, Ann, 2:476
Dryden, John, 1:23
Drysdale, Alasdair, 2:89
Dube, H. C., 2:443, 2:446
Dubofsky, Melvyn, 2:204
Du Bois, W. E. B., 2:135, 2:210–11
Dubos, René, 2:444, 2:445, 2:496
du Boulay, Shirley, 2:398
Duby, Georges, 2:305
Ducan, Kenneth, 2:88
Duckett, Margaret, 1:176, 1:182
Dudeney, Henry Ernest, 1:535
Dudley, Walter C., 2:486
Dudley, William, 2:133, 2:455
Duellman, William E., 2:449
Duff, James H., 2:271
Duffin, W. J., 2:522
Duffy, Karen G., 2:98
Duffy, Susan (comp), 2:34
Dugas, René, 2:512
Duggan-Cronin, Alfred M., 2:299
Dugger, Ronnie, 2:246
Duignan, Peter, 2:257
Duke, Dulcie, 2:305
Dulles, Foster R., 2:204
Dulles, John Foster, 2:23
Dumas, Alexandre, 1:334
Du Maurier, Daphne, 1:80–81
Dumont, Francis, 1:326
Dunbar, Leslie H., 2:12
Dunbar, Paul Laurence, 1:175
Dunbar, Robert E., 2:450
Duncan, Greg J., 2:68, 2:153
Duncan, Isadora, 2:266
Duncan, Otis D., 2:144, 2:148
Dundes, Alan, 2:43
Dunham, Montrew, 2:29
Dunlop, John B. (ed), 1:396
Dunlop, Storm, 2:469, 2:484, 2:485
Dunn, John, 2:18
Dunn, Ross E., 2:301
Dunn, Thomas G., 1:489
Dunne, Lavon J., 2:549
Dunner, David L. (ed), 2:121
Dunning, Stephen, 1:489
DuPlessix Gray, Francine, 2:405
Dupré, Catherine, 1:88
Duram, James C., 2:240
Durán, Manuel, 1:356
Durant, Ariel, 2:326, 2:329
Durant, Will, 2:280, 2:284, 2:305, 2:310, 2:326, 2:329
Durbin, Harold C., 1:575
Durer, Albrecht, 2:313
Durham, Philip, 2:200
Durkheim, Emile, 2:52, 2:126–27, 2:144
Durrant, Geoffrey H., 1:39
Durrell, Gerald, 2:437, 2:461

Durrell, Lawrence, 1:81
Durrell, Lee, 2:81, 2:437
Dusek, Dorothy, 2:554
Dusek, Jerome B., 2:542
Dusenberry, James S., 2:61
Dutt, Ashok K., 2:398
Dutt, Vishnu, 2:404
Dutton, Robert P., 1:200
Duxbury, Alison, 2:486
Duxbury, Alyn C., 2:486
Dvorak, John C., 1:573
Dwiggins, Don, 2:480
Dwyer, Frank, 2:171, 2:173
Dye, Thomas R., 2:40
Dyer, Gillian, 1:440
Dygert, Warren, 1:461
Dymally, M. M., 2:410
Dyson, Peter, 1:574
Dyson, Robert D., 2:438

E

Eade, J. C., 2:341
Eagles, Douglas A., 2:549, 2:560
Eagon, Andrea B., 2:97
Eames, Andrew, 2:398
Earhart, H. Byron, 2:274
Earle, Alice M., 2:161
Earle, Sylvia A., 2:486
Earley, Michael, 1:449
Earley, Steven, 1:468
Earnshaw, R. A., 1:577
East, W. Gordon, 2:93
Eastman, Carol M., 2:134
Eastman, Charles, 2:157
Easton, David, 2:7
Easton, Thomas, 1:483
Easwaran, Eknath, 2:366
Eaton, Clement, 2:192
Eban, Abba, 2:280, 2:411
Ebbighausen, Edwin B., 2:469
Ebbitt, David R., 1:478
Ebbitt, Wilma R., 1:478
Ebel, P., 1:575
Ebenstein, William, 2:5, 2:15, 2:274
Eble, Kenneth, 1:222
Ebon, Martin, 2:392
Ebrey, Patricia B. (ed and tr), 2:281
Eccles, John, 2:110
Echikson, William, 2:405
Ecker, Michael W., 1:497
Eckert, Allan W., 2:163, 2:168, 2:184
Eckhardt, Robert C., 1:567
Eckler, A. Ross (ed), 1:438
Edel, Leon, 1:180
Edelson, Edward, 2:544, 2:545, 2:549, 2:561
Edey, Maitland A., 2:48, 2:278, 2:456

Edie, James M., 2:97
Edison, Thomas Alva, 2:524
Editors of InfoWorld, 1:562
Editors of Time-Life Books, 1:554, 1:559,
    1:560; 2:83, 2:85–87, 2:90 2:91, 2:92,
    2:207, 2:226, 2:229, 2:235, 2:238, 2:241,
    2:274, 2:280, 2:301, 2:305, 2:309, 2:310,
    2:320, 2:326, 2:339, 2:363, 2:371, 2:382,
    2:383, 2:384, 2:393, 2:469, 2:475, 2:478,
    2:480, 2:544, 2:561
Edlin, Gordon, 2:531
Edminster, Joseph, 2:522
Edmonds, Walter D., 2:226
Edmonson, Amy C., 1:522
Edmunde, R. David, 2:168
Edmunds, Robert A., 1:583
Educational Technology Magazine Staff
    (eds), 1:570
Edwards, Alex, 1:583
Edwards, Chris, 2:71
Edwards, George C., III, 2:21
Edwards, Jonathan, 1:153
Edwards, Lawrence, 1:519
Edwards, R. G., 2:451
Eekman, Thomas A., 1:391
Egan, James P., 2:70
Egertson, Eric, 1:559
Ehlers, Ernest G., 2:492
Ehrenberg, Ralph E., 2:92
Ehrenhalt, Alan (ed), 2:5, 2:33
Ehrhart, W. D., 2:398
Ehrlich, Ann, 2:552
Ehrlich, Eugene, 1:445, 1:483
Ehrlich, Paul R., 2:85, 2:274
Eicher, Don L., 2:495
Eichner, James A., 2:40
Eiffers, Joost, 1:535
Einstein, Albert, 2:520
Eisdorfer, C., 2:561
Eisenhower, Dwight David, 2:239
Eisenson, John, 1:451
Eisenstadt, Samuel N., 2:129, 2:132, 2:144
Eisinger, Peter K., 2:147
Eisler, Colin, 2:415
Eisner, R. J., 2:97
Elazer, Daniel J., 2:16, 2:35
Elbow, Peter, 1:477
Eldredge, Niles, 2:456
Elgin, Suzette Haden, 1:445
Eliade, Mircea, 2:52
Eliason, Alan L., 1:558
Eliot, George, 1:49
Eliot, T. S., 1:82
Elisabeth L., 2:550, 2:551
Elkana, Yehuda (ed), 2:520
Elledge, Scott, 1:456
Ellen, Roy (ed), 2:46
Ellington, Edward Kennedy, 2:267
Ellington, Mercer, 2:267

Elliot, B. J., 2:342
Elliot, I. (ed), 2:177
Elliot, J. M., 2:410
Elliot, James, 2:475
Elliot, Jeffrey M., 2:5, 2:33, 2:40, 2:147
Elliot, Jeffrey M. (ed), 1:192
Elliott, Alan C., 1:574
Elliott, Martha H., 2:16
Ellis, George W., 2:161
Ellis, John, 2:371
Ellis, R. Robard, Jr., 2:500
Ellis, Richard, 2:449
Ellis, Roger, 1:373
Ellison, Ralph, 1:218
Elliston, Frederick A. (ed), 2:4, 2:19
Ellman, Michael, 2:58
Ellman, Richard, 1:62, 1:99
El Saffar, Ruth, 1:357
Elsen, Albert E., 2:356
Elster, John (ed), 2:59, 2:60
Elting, Mary, 1:557
Elvin, Mark, 2:86, 2:273
Elwood, Ann, 2:481
Emanuel, James A., 1:241
Ember, Carol R., 2:42
Ember, Melvin, 2:42
Emecheta, Buchi, 1:413
Emerson, Ralph Waldo, 1:157
Eng, Richard E., 1:583
Engberg, Robert (ed), 2:221
Engel, Bernard F., 1:268
Engel, Joel, 1:486
Engell, James, 1:26
Engelmayer, Sheldon D., 2:245
Engels, Friedrich, 2:58–59
England, R. W., Jr., 2:133
Englehart, Margaret, 2:207
Englemann, Bernt, 2:384
English, Diane, 2:553
Enser, A. G., 1:473
Ensminger, Audrey H., 2:549
Epstein, Beryl, 2:387, 2:525
Epstein, Edward, 1:457
Epstein, Richard A., 1:535
Epstein, Sam, 2:387, 2:525
Epstein, Samuel S., 2:496, 2:570
Erasmus, Charles J., 2:138
Erasmus, Desiderius, 2:314
Erdoes, Richard, 2:157
Erikson, Erik H., 2:108, 2:317
Ernst, Bruno, 1:515
Eron, Carol, 2:557
Erskine-Hall, Howard, 1:22
Esau, Katherine, 2:447
Eshag, Eprime, 2:71
Eshleman, Alan, 2:447
Espeland, Pamela, 2:555
Espenson, James H., 2:508
Espinosa, José M., 2:160

Esposito, John L., 2:274
Espy, Willard, 1:439
Esselin, Martin, 1:187
Esslin, Martin, 1:465
Etherton, Michael, 1:411
Etmekjian, James (ed), 1:420
Ettlin, Walter A., 1:575
Euclid, 1:514
Euler, Leonhard, 1:526
Euripides, 1:314
Evans, Barbara L., 1:16
Evans, Bergen, 1:439
Evans, Christopher, 1:490, 1:554; 2:255, 2:284
Evans, Elizabeth, 1:306
Evans, Gareth L., 1:16
Evans, Geoff, 1:485
Evans, Gillian R. (ed), 2:273, 2:290
Evans, Glen (ed), 1:488
Evans, Howard E., 2:91, 2:449
Evans, I. O., 1:343
Evans, Ifor, 2:437
Evans, J. A., 2:288
Evans, Mari (ed), 1:192
Evans, Mark, 2:226
Evans, Mary A., 2:91
Evans, Michael, 2:89, 2:411
Evans, Peter, 2:416, 2:461
Evans, Richard I., 2:112, 2:115
Evans, Richard I. (ed), 2:464
Evans, T. F., 1:120
Everdale, Carl P., 2:378
Everett, Karen, 1:437
Everson, William, 1:475
Evslin, Bernard, 1:318
Ewell, Barbara C., 1:173
Ewing, K. D., 2:408
Eyck, Erich, 2:342
Eyes, David, 1:564

F

Faber, Doris, 2:366, 2:408
Faber, Harold, 2:366
Fabun, Don, 1:437
Facer, G. S., 2:315
Facklam, Howard, 2:450, 2:455, 2:545, 2:565
Facklam, Margery, 2:450, 2:455, 2:545, 2:565
Fagan, Brian M., 2:278, 2:299, 2:300
Fage, J. D., 2:276, 2:299
Fagg, William, 2:310
Fahnestock, Jeanne, 1:477
Fain, Theodore C., 2:465
Fair, Jan, 1:506
Fair, Martha Harris, 1:16
Fairbanks, Carol, 2:200

Fairbridge, Rhodes W., 2:483
Fairchild, Henry P. (ed), 2:124
Fairfield, Sheila, 2:393, 2:398, 2:405, 2:408
Fairley, John, 1:75
Falk, Doris V., 1:235
Falk, Signi L., 1:261, 1:304
Falkof, Lucille, 2:200
Falls, Cyril, 2:371
Fancher, Raymond E., 2:95
Fang, Irving E., 1:540
Fang, J., 1:499
Fant, Maureen B., 2:285
Faraday, Michael, 2:525
Faris, Wendy B., 1:403
Farley, Reynolds, 2:135, 2:142
Farmer, Mick, 1:586
Farrand, Max, 2:16, 2:166
Farrison, William E., 1:170
Farwell, Byron, 2:364
Fasel, George, 2:9
Fasman, Gerald D. (ed), 2:511
Fast, Barbara, 2:538
Fast, Howard, 1:218; 2:163
Fast, Julius, 1:448; 2:538
Fauchereau, Serge, 2:415
Faulk, Laura E., 2:157
Faulk, Odie B., 2:157
Faulkner, Harold U., 2:218
Faulkner, P., 2:536
Faulkner, Robert K., 2:30
Faulkner, William, 1:219
Fausold, Martin L., 2:231
Fayer, Steve, 2:154
Fearnside, W. Ward, 1:477
Featherman, David L., 2:144
Feder, Georg, 2:337
Feeley, Malcolm M., 2:133
Fehlauer, Adolph, 2:317
Fehrenbach, T. R., 2:200
Fehrenbacher, Don E., 2:184, 2:189
Feibel, Werner, 1:564, 1:574
Feigenbaum, Edward A., 1:582, 1:583
Fein, Rashi, 2:566
Feirer, John, 2:435
Feirtag, Michael, 2:469
Feitelson, Dror G., 1:559
Feiwell, George R. (ed), 2:60, 2:64
Fejer, Paul H., 1:516
Feldman, Anthony, 2:432, 2:469
Feldman, David, 1:432
Feldman, Michael B., 1:586
Felgar, Robert, 1:307
Felix, Warner, 2:334
Fell, John, 1:468
Felsenthal, Carol, 2:537
Fenn, John B., 2:516
Fenton, Charles, 1:201
Fenton, Erfert, 1:559
Fenton, S. Martin, 2:5

Fenton, Steve, 2:127
Ferber, Edna, 1:220
Ferguson, Robert, 1:376
Ferguson, Thomas, 2:39
Ferguson, William M., 2:299
Ferlazzo, Paul J., 1:175
Ferleger, Lou, 1:529
Ferlinghetti, Lawrence, 1:221
Ferman, Barbara, 2:40
Fermi, Enrico, 2:528
Fermi, Laura, 2:528
Fernandez, Judi, 1:561
Fernandez-Armesto, Felipe, 2:414
Fernando, Chitra, 1:422
Fernea, Elizabeth Warnock, 2:89,
 2:411
Ferrar, H., 1:112
Ferraro, Geraldine A., 2:257
Ferrell, Keith, 1:111
Ferrell, Robert H., 2:237
Ferris, Ina, 1:61
Festa-McCormick, Diane, 1:330
Feste, Karen (ed), 2:257
Festinger, Leon, 2:123, 2:140
Fetisov, A., 1:512
Fetterman, David M., 2:42
Fettner, Ann Giudici, 2:560
Fetzer, James H. (ed), 1:529
Fetzer, Leland (ed), 1:389
Feuerlicht, Ignace, 1:370
Fialkov, Yu, 2:507
Fichman, Martin, 2:460
Fichter, George S., 2:438, 2:481
Fiedler, Jean, 1:194
Field, Frank, 2:80
Field, George W., 1:368
Field, J., 1:519
Field, Joyce, 1:262
Field, Leslie, 1:262
Field, Syd, 1:485
Fielding, Henry, 1:24
Fielding, Mantle, 2:261
Fielding, Raymond, 1:470
Fields, Mike, 2:552
Fiering, Norman, 2:161
Filler, Louis, 2:218
Fillingham, Patricia, 2:311
Filson, Brent, 2:536
Finberg, Alexander J., 2:358
Finch, Christopher, 1:475
Fincher, E. B., 2:36, 2:88, 2:257
Finck, Lila, 2:404
Findley, A. M., 1:519
Findling, John E., 2:257
Fine, Arthur, 2:518
Fine, John Christopher, 2:488
Fine, John V., 2:284, 2:305
Fine, Judylaine, 2:561
Finke, Blythe F., 1:396; 2:23, 2:238, 2:414

Finkel, Leroy, 1:564
Finkelstein, Norman, 2:160
Finley, M. I., 2:284
Finson, Jon W., 2:346
Finsterbusch, Kurt, 2:137, 2:144
Firth, Raymond, 2:52
Fischer, Claude S., 2:138, 2:147
Fischer, Fritz, 2:371
Fischer, Henry G., 2:280
Fischer, Louis, 2:378
Fischer-Pap, Lucia, 2:561
Fish, Carl R., 2:184
Fisher, David E., 2:475, 2:486
Fisher, Harold, 1:458
Fisher, Leonard Everett, 1:497; 2:204,
 2:207, 2:284
Fisher, Lyle, 1:512
Fisher, Maxine P., 2:42
Fisher, Robin (ed), 2:321
Fisher, Ron, 2:83
Fisher, Vardis, 2:169
Fishlock, Trevor, 2:401
Fisiak, Jacek (ed), 1:431
Fiske, John, 1:468
Fitzgerald, F. Scott, 1:222; 2:226
Fitzgerald, Hiram (ed), 2:95
Fitzgerald, Jerry, 1:558
Fitzgerald, John D., 1:490
Fitzgerald, Peter, 2:559
Fitzgibbon, Dan, 2:70
Fitzhardings, L. F., 2:284
Fitzpatrick, Joseph P., 2:134
Fitz-Randolph, Jane, 1:538; 2:479
Fiut, Alexander, 1:387
Fixx, James F., 2:551
Flach, Frederic (ed), 2:110, 2:123
Flanagan, Floyd, 1:577
Flanagan, J. L., 1:579
Flanagan, James K., 1:266
Flandermeyer, Kenneth, L., 2:552
Flannery, Gerald, 1:453
Flaubert, Gustave, 1:335
Flavin, Christopher, 2:496
Fleishman, Glen, 2:180
Fleissner, Else M., 1:368
Fleming, Alice, 1:445
Fleming, Ian, 1:84
Fleming, John, 2:154
Fleming, June, 2:92
Fleming, Robert S., 1:245
Fleming, Walter, 1:506
Fleming-Williams, Ian, 2:351
Fletcher, Miles, 2:374
Flexer, Abraham S., 2:562
Flexner, Eleanor, 2:12, 2:153
Flexner, James T., 2:161, 2:179, 2:187,
 2:213
Flink, James J., 2:218
Flint, F. Cudworth, 1:258

Flood, Robert L., 1:558
Flores, Angel, 1:399
Flores, Fernando, 1:583
Flores, Kate, 1:399
Florin, John W., 2:90
Flower, Linda, 1:477
Flower, Newman, 2:336
Flowers, Marilyn R., 2:71
Fluegge, S., 2:518
Flynn, Sarah, 2:154
Fodor, Ronald V., 2:492, 2:493, 2:494
Foelix, Rainer F., 2:449
Foerster, Scott, 1:561
Foged, Niels, 2:447
Fogel, Barbara R., 2:81
Fogel, Daniel, 2:160
Fogel, Robert W., 2:189
Fogelman, Edwin, 2:5, 2:15, 2:274
Fogelman, Stanley, 1:504
Folger, H. S. (ed), 2:508
Follett, Wilson, 1:435
Folse, Henry, Jr., 2:501
Foner, Eric, 2:189, 2:198
Foner, S., 2:522
Fontaine, George R., 1:566
Fonteyn, Margot, 2:415
Foote, Joe S., 1:442
Foote, Shelby, 2:192
Forbes, Esther, 2:164
Forbes, William, 2:411
Ford, Adam, 2:469
Ford, Alice, 2:188
Ford, Barbara, 1:475
Ford, Gerald R., 2:253
Ford, Nelson, 1:567
Ford, Nick (ed), 1:440
Ford, Peter, 2:432
Forehand, Walter E., 1:324
Foreign Policy Association, 2:36
Forer, Lucille K., 2:146
Forester, C. S., 1:84–85
Forester, Tom, 1:537, 1:554, 1:558
Forge, Andrew, 2:352
Forkel, Johann N., 2:334
Forman, Jack J., 1:309
Forman, James D., 2:241, 2:374
Forman, Maury, 1:459
Formi, Luigi, 2:257
Fornatale, Peter, 1:461
Forney, James, 1:561
Forrest, Gary G., 2:555
Forster, E. M., 1:85–86; 2:363
Forster, Margaret, 1:43
Forsyth, Elizabeth Held, 2:537, 2:560
Forsyth, Richard, 1:581
Forsyth, Richard (ed), 1:583
Fortey, Richard, 2:495
Fossey, Diane, 2:461
Foster, Alan G., 1:506

Foster, Robert, 1:126
Foster, Robert J., 2:489
Foundation for Public Affairs, 2:5, 2:39
Fowler, D. H., 1:497
Fowler, James W., 2:142
Fowler, Michael, 2:386
Fowler, Richard J., 2:522
Fowler, William W., 2:292
Fowles, John, 1:86
Fox, Anthony, 1:362
Fox, D. R. (ed), 2:229
Fox, Harrison W., Jr., 2:33
Fox, Mary Virginia, 2:257, 2:260, 2:481
Fox, Robin, 2:52
Fox, Sidney W., 2:456
Foyer, Christine H., 2:438
Fradin, Dennis B., 2:161, 2:170
Fraenkel, Eduard, 2:294
Frame, Janet, 1:138–39
France, Anatole, 1:335
Franchere, Ruth, 2:241
Francis, Dorothy B., 1:554; 2:537
Francis, G. K., 1:516
Francis, Peter, 2:489
Franck, Irene M., 2:432
Franck, Thomas M., 2:36
Francke, Linda B., 2:257
Franco, Jean (ed), 1:399
Frandsen, Kathryn J., 2:537, 2:538
Frank, A. L., 1:563
Frank, Arthur W., III (ed), 2:124
Frank, Bernhard (tr), 1:420
Frank, Frederick, 2:535
Frank, Katharine, 1:43
Frank, Robert G., Jr., 2:548
Frank, Rose, 1:540
Frank, Tenney, 1:320
Frank, Waldo (ed), 1:399
Frankfurter, Felix, 2:28
Frankl, Ron, 2:267
Frankl, Viktor E., 2:139
Frankland, F. W., 1:514
Franklin, Benjamin, 2:167–68, 2:526
Franklin, H. Bruce, 1:163
Franklin, John Hope, 2:153, 2:198
Franklin, Jon, 1:488
Franklin, Kenneth J., 2:548
Fransman, Martin, 1:537
Fraser, Antonia, 2:326, 2:327
Frassanito, William A., 2:196
Frazer, James George, 2:52
Frazier, Kendrick, 2:475
Fredman, Lionel E., 2:171
Freedman, Florence B., 2:189
Freedman, Milton, 2:153
Freedman, Russell, 2:200
Freedman, Warren, 1:554
Freeland, Richard M., 2:235
Freeman, Derek, 2:47

Freeman, Douglas S., 2:196
Freeman, Jo, 2:148
Freeman, Lucy, 2:118
Freeman, Morton, 1:433
Freeman, Peter, 1:563
Freeman, Raymond, 1:578
Freeman, Richard B., 2:70
Freese, Arthur S., 2:552, 2:566
Freiberger, Paul, 1:540, 1:543
Freidel, Frank, 2:223, 2:234
Fremont, John Charles, 2:184
French, Anthony P., 2:501, 2:520
French, Francis G., 1:504
French, John R. P., Jr., 2:148
French, Warren, 1:181, 1:283
French, Warren (ed), 1:289
Frenkel-Brunswik, Else, 2:114
Freud, Sigmund, 2:98, 2:117–18, 2:134,
    2:316
Freudenberg, Nicholas, 2:560
Fried, Lewis, 2:212
Friedan, Betty, 2:148, 2:244
Friedberg, Errol C., 2:562
Friedel, Frank, 2:153
Frieder, David, 1:512
Friedl, Ernestine, 2:52
Friedlander, Melvin A., 2:255, 2:414
Friedlander, Michael W., 2:469
Friedman, Alan J., 2:520
Friedman, Alan W., 1:220
Friedman, H. George, Jr., 1:586
Friedman, Herbert, 2:478
Friedman, Ken, 1:575
Friedman, Lenemaja, 1:243
Friedman, Leon (ed), 2:5
Friedman, Milton, 2:65–66, 2:257
Friedman, Morton P., 2:113
Friedman, Rose, 2:257
Friedman, Thomas L., 2:411
Friend, Llerena, 2:186
Friendly, Fred, 1:464
Friendly, Fred W., 2:16
Fries, James F., 2:566
Frieze, Irene, 2:148
Frisch, Karl von, 2:463
Frisch, Otto R., 2:518
Fritschner, Sarah, 2:549
Fritz, Jean, 2:166, 2:222
Fromkin, Victoria, 1:434
Fromm, Erich, 2:103, 2:118, 2:139
Frost, Lawrence A., 2:203
Frost, Robert, 1:223
Froude, James A., 1:21
Frude, Neil, 1:582
Frumkes, Lewis, 1:438
Fry, Christopher, 1:87
Fry, Don (ed), 1:487
Fry, Edward B., 1:560
Fry, Edward F., 2:415

Fry, Norman, 2:492
Frye, Northrup, 1:32
Fryxell, Greta A. (ed), 2:447
Fuchs, Thomas, 2:376
Fuentes, Carlos, 1:402–403
Fuess, Billings, Jr. (ed), 1:477
Fuess, Claude M., 2:228
Fuller, Gordon, 1:514
Fuller, Joseph V., 2:342
Fuller, R. Buckminster, 1:522
Fulton, Albert, 1:468
Fulton, James E., 2:552
Fulton, John F., 2:532
Funk, Charles E., 1:433
Furniss, Tim, 2:252, 2:257
Furth, Hans G., 2:112
Fusfeld, Daniel R., 2:56
Fussell, Paul (ed), 1:116

G

Gabbin, Joane V., 1:206
Gabin, Jane S., 1:160
Gabisch, Gunter, 2:57
Gabor, Don, 1:445
Gaddis, John L., 2:238, 2:388
Gaer, Joseph (ed), 1:169
Gaffikin, Frank, 2:408
Gaffney, M. P., 1:497
Gaffron, Norma, 2:106
Gage, Diane, 2:562
Gage, John, 2:358
Gahagan, D. D., 2:556
Gahagan, F. G., 2:556
Gaines, Ernest J., 1:224
Gaines, Steven, 2:261
Gainsborough, Thomas, 2:335
Gal, Hans, 2:348
Galambos, Nancy L., 2:107
Galbraith, James K., 2:63
Galbraith, John Kenneth, 2:66, 2:226,
    2:241, 2:274
Gale, Robert L., 1:253
Gale, William A., 1:583
Galen, 2:546
Galerstein, David, 1:504
Galewitz, Herb (ed), 1:459
Galileo, 2:473
Galinsky, Ellen, 2:543
Gall, John, 1:558
Gallagher, Hugh G., 2:234
Gallagher, John P., 1:583
Gallant, Mavis, 1:139
Gallant, Robert, 2:510
Gallant, Roy, 2:157, 2:299
Gallant, Roy A., 2:80, 2:103, 2:278, 2:456,
    2:469, 2:475, 2:479, 2:485, 2:493, 2:495,
    2:500

Gallavotti, G., 2:512
Gallenkamp, Charles, 2:299
Gallo, Donald R. (ed), 1:188, 1:201, 1:204,
    1:212, 1:213, 1:228, 1:229, 1:230, 1:238,
    1:240, 1:248, 1:250, 1:267, 1:272, 1:276
Gallo, Robert C., 2:560
Gallo, Rose A., 1:223
Galluzzi, Paolo (ed), 2:316
Galsworthy, John, 1:88
Galton, Lawrence, 2:567
Gambs, John S., 2:66
Gamlin, Linda, 2:461
Gamow, George, 2:518
Gandhi, Indira, 2:401
Gandhi, Mohandas Karamchand, 2:365–66
Gane, Chris, 1:585
Gans, Herbert J., 1:457; 2:131, 2:134, 2:147
Gantert, Anne X., 1:497
García Lorca, Federico, 1:357–58
García Márquez, Gabriel, 1:403–404
Gardiner, Stephen, 2:419
Gardner, Ernest A., 2:284
Gardner, Howard, 2:110
Gardner, John, 1:6, 1:84, 1:482
Gardner, John L. (ed), 2:299
Gardner, Martin, 1:536
Gardner, Philip, 1:65
Gardner, Robert, 2:481, 2:493, 2:516
Garfield, James Abram, 2:195
Garfinkel, Bernard, 2:408
Garfinkel, Perry, 1:488
Garibaldi, Giuseppi, 2:344
Garland, Hamlin, 2:198, 2:200
Garland, Henry B., 1:372
Garner, L. E., 1:519
Garnett, William, 2:527
Garraty, John A., 2:153
Garraty, John A. (ed), 2:16, 2:26
Garreau, Joel, 2:90
Garrels, Robert M., 2:83
Garrett, Elisabeth D., 2:184
Garrett, Henry E., 2:122
Garrison, Francis J., 2:191
Garrison, Roger, 1:477
Garrison, Wendell P., 2:191
Garrison, William Lloyd, 2:191
Garrow, David J. (ed), 2:250
Garson, Barbara, 1:554
Gartner, Carol B., 2:243, 2:466
Garvey, Daniel, 1:487
Garza, Hedda, 2:374, 2:382, 2:403
Gash, Norman, 2:332
Gaskell, Elizabeth, 1:42
Gasparini, Graziano, 2:299
Gassée, Jean-Louis, 1:540
Gastil, Raymond D., 2:12
Gates, Gary, 1:431
Gatland, Kenneth, 2:481
Gatlin, Lila, 1:554

Gattegno, Caleb, 2:516
Gauguin, Paul, 2:353
Gauss, Carl Friedrich, 1:532
Gaustad, John, 2:471
Gauthier, Howard L., 2:84
Gay, David, 2:56
Gay, Kathlyn, 2:41, 2:81, 2:93, 2:147,
    2:467, 2:486, 2:538, 2:570
Gay, Peter, 2:118, 2:326, 2:374, 2:384
Gay, R., 1:478
Gaylin, Willard, 2:103, 2:104, 2:536
Gealt, Adelheid, 2:273
Gearty, C. A., 2:408
Geertz, Clifford, 2:43, 2:52
Geiringer, Irene, 2:335, 2:337
Geiringer, Karl, 2:335, 2:337, 2:348
Geis, Irving, 1:529
Gelb, Harold, 2:561
Gelb, Norman, 2:388
Geldard, Frank A., 2:113
Gelderen, Dick van, 2:447
Gelinas, Paul J., 2:104
Gelman, Rita Golden, 2:88
Gelpi, Albert, 1:281
Gelpi, Barbara Charlesworth, 1:281
Gelya, Frank F., 2:42
Gennaro, Joseph, 2:436
Genovese, Eugene D., 2:189
Gensler, Harry J., 1:500
Gentilli, Joseph, 2:80
Gentry, Tony, 1:175
George, Linda K. (ed), 2:129
George, Margaret, 2:310
Gerber, Philip L., 1:209, 1:223
Gerberg, Mort, 2:166
Gerin, Winifred, 1:43
Germignani, Michael, 1:537
Gerrard, Jonathan, 2:465
Gerrold, Henry, 1:439
Gershey, Edward L., 2:570
Gerson, Leonard D. (ed), 2:378
Gerstenberger, Donna, 1:123
Gersting, Judith L., 1:537
Gerstinger, Heinz, 1:358
Gerver, Elisabeth, 1:554, 1:570
Gesell, A. Ames, 2:540
Getzoff, Ann, 2:538
Ghanayem, Ishaqi, 2:38
Gharajedaghi, Jashmid, 1:558
Ghougassian, Joseph P., 2:115
Ghyka, Matila, 1:515
Giannetti, Louis, 1:469
Giarini, Orio (ed), 2:68
Gibbon, Edward, 2:290
Gibbons, Don C., 2:139
Gibbons, John H., 2:496
Gibbs-Smith, Charles, 2:316
Giblin, James C., 2:184
Gibney, Frank, 2:86, 2:398

Gibran, Kahlil, 1:420
Gibson, Carol, 1:497
Gibson, Ian, 1:358
Gibson, James J., 2:113
Gibson, Michael, 1:318; 2:261
Gibson, William, 1:449
Giddens, Anthony, 2:125, 2:127, 2:143
Giddings, Al, 2:486
Gide, André, 1:336
Gies, Frances, 2:305
Gies, Joseph, 2:305
Giffen, Mary, 2:537
Gilbert, Bentley B., 2:374
Gilbert, G. Nigel, 1:582
Gilbert, Martin, 2:384
Gilbert, Neil, 2:57
Gilbert, Richard, 2:554
Gilbert, Sara, 2:536, 2:538
Gilbert, Scott, 2:451
Gilbert, Sir William Schwenk, 1:50
Gilchrist, Ellen, 1:225
Gill, Gillian, 1:74
Gill, Karamjit S. (ed), 1:582
Gillen, Charles H., 1:115
Gillett, Craig A., 1:558
Gillies, John, 2:544
Gilligan, Carol, 2:146
Gilling, Dick, 2:545
Gillispie, Charles C., 1:497
Gillon, Adam, 1:77, 1:383
Gilman, Sander L., 2:536
Gilmore, John, 1:583
Gilpin, Geoff, 1:566
Gilson, Etienne, 2:307
Gindin, James, 1:88, 1:90
Ginger, Ray, 2:204
Ginsberg, Allen, 1:225
Ginsburg, Herbert, 2:112
Ginzberg, Eli, 2:63, 2:257
Giovanelli, Ronald G., 2:475
Giovanni, Nikki, 1:226
Girdano, Daniel A., 2:554
Giroud, François, 2:510
Gitkin, Lisa S., 2:493
Gitlin, Todd, 1:468
Glackens, Ira, 2:153
Glad, John (ed), 1:389
Glad, Paul W., 2:205
Gladstone, William Ewart, 2:345
Glaser, Barney G., 2:137
Glasgow, Ellen, 1:227
Glass, Robert L., 1:537
Glassman, Bruce, 1:266
Glazer, Mark, 2:42
Glazer, Nathan, 2:136, 2:255
Glazer, Nathan (ed), 2:147
Gleick, James, 1:516
Glendenning, Victoria, 1:70
Glendinning, Sally, 2:369

Glenn, Jerome C., 1:582
Glenn, Norval D., 2:138
Glock, Charles Y., 2:136
Glossbrenner, Alfred, 1:573, 1:574
Glover, David E., 1:583
Glover, Michael, 2:329
Glubok, Shirley, 2:285
Gluck, Myke, 1:579
Gluckman, Max, 2:132
Glucksberg, Harold, 2:561
Goddard, Harold C., 1:16
Godden, Jon, 2:309
Godden, Rumer, 1:88–89; 2:309
Godel, Kurt, 1:500
Godman, Arthur, 2:432
Godoy, José F., 2:369
Goehlert, Robert, 2:5, 2:6, 2:33, 2:41
Goehlert, Robert (comp), 2:21
Goethe, Johann Wolfgang von, 1:366
Goff, Denise, 2:281
Goffman, Erving, 1:461; 2:50, 2:139
Gogol, Nikolai, 1:393
Golanty, Eric, 2:531
Golavina, L., 1:512
Gold, Philip, 1:440
Goldberg, Adele, 1:566
Goldberg, Jeanne P., 2:550
Goldberg, Joel, 2:522
Goldberg, Myron D., 2:561
Goldberg, Richard A., 2:80
Golden, Frederic, 2:83, 2:494
Golden, James R., et al, 2:405
Golden, Morris, 1:26
Golden, Neil, 1:564
Goldfarb, Theodore D. (ed), 2:81
Goldfinger, Stephen E. (ed), 2:531
Goldhaber, Gerald, 1:450
Goldin, Augusta, 2:81, 2:467, 2:486, 2:488, 2:496
Golding, William, 1:89–90
Goldman, Eric, 2:218, 2:238
Goldman, Lucien, 1:339
Goldman, Minton F., 2:92, 2:405
Goldman, William, 1:227
Goldscheider, Ludwig, 2:316
Goldsen, Rose, 1:465
Goldsmith, Maurice, 2:10
Goldsmith, Maurice (ed), 2:520
Goldsmith, Oliver, 1:25
Goldstein, E. Bruce, 2:113
Goldstein, Inge, 2:432
Goldstein, Joel K., 2:21
Goldstein, Kurt, 2:121
Goldstein, Larry Joel, 1:523, 1:529, 1:559, 1:561
Goldstein, Martin, 2:432
Goldstein, Michael, 2:257
Goldstein, Sue, 2:566
Goldstein, Thomas, 2:310

Goldstine, Herman H., 1:553
Goldthorpe, John H. (ed), 2:71
Goldwater, Barry Morris, 2:244
Goleman, Daniel, 2:536
Golombok, Susan, 2:122
Gompers, Samuel, 2:224
Gonick, Larry, 1:537
Gonnella, Gary, 1:579
Gonzalez, Edward (ed), 2:371
Good, I. J., 1:529
Goodall, Jane, 2:463
Goode, Stephen, 2:35, 2:241, 2:496
Goode, William J., 2:138, 2:144, 2:148
Goodenough, Judith E., 2:462
Goodheart, Barbara, 2:561
Goodin, J. R., 2:447
Goodman, Cynthia, 1:577
Goodman, Denny, 1:579
Goodman, Ellen, 1:480
Goodman, John C., 2:71
Goodman, Nancy, 1:47
Goodnough, David, 2:324
Goodstein, David L., 2:498, 2:518
Goodwin, Paul, 2:88
Goold, J. Douglas, 2:223
Gooneratne, Yasmine, 1:28
Goozner, Calman, 1:504
Gopal, Ram, 2:404
Gopal, S., 2:404
Goran, Marjorie, 2:451
Goran, Morris, 2:451
Gorbachev, Mikhail Sergeyevich, 2:406
Gordimer, Nadine, 1:414
Gordon, Burton, 2:88
Gordon, Donald E., 2:415
Gordon, Douglas, 2:516
Gordon, Jacquie, 2:563
Gordon, James S., 2:536
Gordon, Karen Elizabeth, 1:478
Gordon, Louis, 1:198
Gordon, Milton M., 2:125, 2:135
Gordon, Robert, 2:352
Gordon, Sarah, 2:376
Gordon, Sol, 2:542
Gordon, V. O., 1:515
Gore, Marvin, 1:558
Gorenstein, Paul, 2:480
Gorham, William (ed), 2:147
Gorman, Peter, 1:501
Gornick, Vivian, 2:432
Goslin, David A., 2:146
Gottleib, Milton, 2:518
Gottlieb, William P., 2:432
Gottschalk, W., 1:362
Gould, Chester (ed), 1:459
Gould, James L., 2:437
Gould, Lewis L., 2:218
Gould, Peter, 2:92
Gould, Roger, 2:106

Gould, Stephen Jay, 2:457–58
Gow, James, 1:497
Goya, 2:333
Graber, Doris, 1:457; 2:39, 2:257
Grabiner, Judith V., 1:525
Grabinger, R. Scott, 1:570
Grabo, Norman S., 1:154
Gradenwitz, Peter, 2:265
Graebner, Norman A., 2:153
Graff, Henry F. (ed), 2:6
Graham, Neill, 1:554
Graham, Otis L., Jr. (ed), 2:234
Graham, Richard, 2:369
Graham-Smith, Francis, 2:469
Granet, M., 2:278
Grannis, Gary E., 2:516
Grant, Daniel, 2:41
Grant, Matthew G., 2:202
Grant, Michael, 1:318, 2:274, 2:280, 2:285, 2:290
Grant, Michael (ed), 1:311, 1:320; 2:274
Grant, Ruth W., 2:18
Grant, Simon, 1:558
Grant, Ulysses S., 2:199
Grasha, Anthony F., 2:95
Grass, Günter, 1:367
Grattan-Guinness, Ivor, 1:503
Grave, Eric V., 2:435
Gravelle, Karen, 2:113, 2:537, 2:561
Graves, Robert, 1:8, 1:90–91, 1:318
Gray, Christopher, 2:353
Gray, Harry B., 2:505
Gray, Henry, 2:450
Gray, J., 1:519
Gray, Jeffrey A., 2:100, 2:464
Gray, Jeremy, 1:519
Gray, Judith (ed), 1:569
Gray, Randal, 2:371
Gray, Thomas, 1:26
Graybill, Donald, 1:557
Graymont, Barbara, 2:164
Grayson, Fred N., 1:568
Grebanier, Bernard, 1:489
Grebstein, Sheldon N., 1:256
Greeley, Andrew M., 2:135, 2:142
Green, Constance McLaughlin, 2:207
Green, Fitzhugh, 2:259
Green, Jonathan, 1:433
Green, Mark, 2:63
Green, Martin I., 2:567
Green, Peter, 2:274, 2:285
Green, Roger, 1:55
Green, Stanley, 2:154, 2:261
Greenaway, Frank, 2:502
Greenberg, Bradley, 1:465
Greenberg, Eliezer, 1:383
Greenberg, Harvey R., 2:536, 2:539, 2:566
Greenberg, Jerrold S., 2:536, 2:551
Greenberg, Joseph H. (ed), 2:50
Greenberg, Martin H., 1:75

Greenberg, Martin H. (ed), 1:473; 2:434
Greenberg, Marvin J., 1:514
Greenberg, Milton, 2:6
Greenberg, Stan, 2:274
Greenblatt, Miriam, 2:173, 2:234
Greene, Bette, 1:228
Greene, Bob, 1:480; 2:252
Greene, Carol, 1:168; 2:524
Greene, Ellin, 1:451
Greene, Graham, 1:91
Greene, Jack, 2:235
Greene, Laura, 1:448, 1:537, 1:540, 1:545
Greenfield, Eric V., 1:353, 1:362
Greenfield, Howard, 2:415
Greenfield, Kent R., 2:340
Greenfield, Patricia, 1:454
Greenhood, David, 2:92
Greenia, Mark W., 1:537
Greenland, David, 2:496
Greenwald, Martin L., 2:485
Greenwald, Maurine W., 2:224
Greenwood, John D. (ed), 2:95
Greger, Janet L., 1:568
Gregg, Charles T., 2:557
Gregory, Michael, 1:437
Greitzer, S. L., 1:516
Grene, Nicholas, 1:123
Grey, Rowland, 1:50
Grey, Vivian, 2:500
Gribbin, John, 2:486, 2:519
Gribbin, John (ed), 2:80, 2:485
Gridley, Mark C., 2:261
Grieman, April, 1:577
Griffin, Donald R., 2:462
Griffin, William, 1:104
Griffith, Elisabeth, 2:184
Griffith, Gwilym O., 2:340
Griffith, Kelley, 1:483
Griffiths, John, 2:88, 2:388
Griffiths, Paul, 2:154, 2:261
Griffiths, Ralph, 2:273
Grigg, John, 2:374
Grillone, Lisa, 2:436
Grim, Gary, 1:451
Grimaux, Edouard, 2:500
Grimm, Harold J., 2:310
Grimm, Herman F., 2:318
Grindstaff, Carl F., 2:142
Griswold, Ralph E., 1:566
Grizzard, Lewis, 1:480
Grizzard, Mary, 2:160
Grobel, Lawrence, 1:472
Grodzins, Morton, 2:16
Groff, James R., 1:572
Gropius, Walter, 2:268
Grosch, Herb, 1:538
Gross, Leonard, 2:565
Gross, M. Grant, 2:83
Gross, Susan H., 2:284

Grosz, Barbara, 1:582
Grout, Donald J., 2:154, 2:261
Groves, Paul A. (ed), 2:90
Grube, Joel W., 2:129
Grunfeld, Frederic V., 2:356
Grzimek, Bernhard (ed), 2:449
Guedes, M., 2:447
Guerlac, Henry, 2:500
Guerney, Bernard G. (ed), 1:389
Guernsey, Otis, 1:489
Guinness, Paul, 2:90
Gulland, Daphne M., 1:437
Gumpert, Gary, 1:445
Gumperz, John J. (ed), 2:50
Gunn, Edward M. (ed), 1:423
Gunn, James, 1:194
Gura, Timothy, 1:449
Gurari, Eitan, 1:585
Gúrko, Miriam, 2:184
Gurley, John C., 2:60
Gurney, Gene, 2:274
Gurvich, George (ed), 2:125
Gussow, Joan D., 2:549
Gutek, Gerald, 2:90
Gutek, Patricia, 2:90
Gutenmacher, V., 1:512
Gutman, Felix (ed), 2:508, 2:511
Gutmann, Amy (ed), 2:19
Gutnik, Martin J., 2:452, 2:465, 2:522
Guttmacher, Alan F., 2:543
Guy, Rosa, 1:229
Guyot, Arnold, 2:81
Guzaitas, Joe, 1:561
Gwynn, Stephen, 1:25
Gwynne, S. C., 2:70, 2:154

H

Haber, David, 2:567
Haber, Louis, 2:432
Hacker, Diana, 1:477
Hacker, Jeffrey H., 2:234
Hadas, Moses (ed), 1:311
Haden, C. R. (ed), 1:582
Haeussler, Ernest F., Jr., 1:524
Hafen, Brent Q., 2:531, 2:537, 2:538, 2:567
Haftmann, Werner, 2:261
Hagedorn, Hermann, 2:222, 2:535
Hagedorn, Robert B., 2:125
Hagen, Dolores, 1:571
Hagen, Osjkar, 2:360
Hagg, Thomas, 2:274
Haggard, Sir Henry Rider, 1:51
Haggerty, Terry, 1:569
Hagstrom, Jerry, 2:90, 2:155
Hague, David N., 2:508
Haig, Stanley, 2:157
Haight, Gordon S., 1:49

Haiman, Franklyn S., 2:12
Haines, Gail Kay, 2:432, 2:496
Hakluyt, Richard, 2:324
Halacy, Dan, 2:496, 2:528
Halacy, Daniel S., 2:434
Halberstam, David, 1:458; 2:21, 2:241
Halberstram-Rubin, Anna, 1:384
Hale, Edward Everett, 2:169
Hale, J. R. (ed), 2:310
Hale, Nathan G., Jr., 2:118
Hale, William H., 2:356
Hales, Dianne, 2:543
Haley, Alex, 2:252
Hall, Bettye C., 1:524
Hall, Calvin S., 2:95, 2:114
Hall, Daniel G., 2:398
Hall, Edward T., 1:448; 2:43
Hall, James, 2:154
Hall, John, 2:447
Hall, Kermit L. (ed), 2:35
Hall, Lindsey, 2:551
Hall, Lynn (ed), 2:81, 2:570
Hall, Mark, 1:540
Hall, Peter, 2:147
Hall, Robert A., Jr, 1:131
Hall, Robert E. (ed), 2:57, 2:63, 2:64, 2:68
Hall, Rupert, 2:516
Hall, T., 1:532
Hall, Trevor H., 1:117
Hall, Vicki J., 1:558
Hallam, Anthony, 2:491
Hallam, Arthur F., 1:501
Hallam, Elizabeth (ed), 2:305
Halleran, Michael R., 1:314
Halley, Edmond, 2:477
Halliday, Tim R., 2:449
Hallowell, A. Irving, 2:43
Halman, Talat S., 1:420
Halperin, John, 1:20
Halperin, Morton H., 2:36
Halstead, L. B., 2:495
Halvorson, Peter L., 2:142
Hamermesh, Daniel S., 2:70
Hamerow, Theodore S., 2:332, 2:340
Hamerow, Theodore S. (ed), 2:342
Hamilton, Alexander, 2:16, 2:35, 2:174
Hamilton, Edith, 1:318
Hamilton, Eva May, 1:569; 2:549
Hamilton, Ian, 1:259
Hamilton, Leni, 2:194
Hamilton, Nora (ed), 2:257
Hamilton, Peter, 2:128
Hamilton, Virginia, 1:230; 2:211, 2:257
Hamilton, William R., 1:506
Hamlin, Sonya, 1:445
Hamlin, Talbot, 2:261
Hamm, Charles, 2:154, 2:261
Hammacher, A. M., 2:360
Hammacher, Renilde, 2:360

Hammarskjold, Dag, 2:390
Hammen, Scott, 1:472
Hammett, Dashiell, 1:231
Hammond, Alan, 2:122
Hammond, Allen L. (ed), 2:453
Hammond, George P. (ed and tr), 2:157
Hammond, Robin, 1:362
Hammond, Susan W., 2:33
Hampden, John (ed), 2:324
Hampden-Turner, Charles, 2:95
Hampson, Norman, 2:331
Hampton, Henry, 2:154
Hamsun, Knut, 1:376
Hancock, Geoff, 1:481
Hancock, Ralph, 2:513
Hand, Raymond, Jr., 1:445
Handel, George Frederick, 2:336
Handlin, Lilian, 2:198
Handlin, Oscar, 2:198, 2:226
Handlin, Oscar (ed), 2:136
Haney, John, 2:378
Hanmer, Trudy, 2:41, 2:85, 2:93, 2:207
Hannah, John, 1:583
Hannerz, Ulf, 2:147
Hanrahan, Barbara, 1:140
Hans, James S., 2:97
Hansberry, Lorraine, 1:232
Hansen, Augie, 1:564
Hansen, David, 1:575
Hansen, Viggo P. (ed), 1:570
Hansen, William A., 2:85
Harasim, Linda M. (ed), 1:570
Harbison, Winfred A., 2:166
Harborne, J. B., 2:511
Harbutt, Fraser J., 2:386, 2:388
Hardeman, D. B., 2:35
Harder, Kelsie, 1:439
Hardine, Rosetta R., 2:123
Harding, Gunnar (ed), 1:374
Hardwick, Michael, 1:48
Hardy, Godfrey H., 1:497, 1:503
Hardy, Ralph, 2:485
Hardy, Thomas, 1:52
Hargrove, J., 2:395
Hargrove, Jim, 1:473
Harkins, William E., 1:385
Harlan, Judith, 2:243, 2:466
Harley, Ruth, 2:322
Harmetz, Aljean, 1:470
Harmo, Lois, 2:549
Harnadek, Anita, 1:506
Harpur, Brian, 2:475
Harrar, George, 1:538
Harré, Rom (ed), 2:498
Harrell, Mary Ann, 2:91
Harrigan, John J., 2:7
Harriman, Cynthia, 1:558
Harrington, John W., 2:494

Harrington, Michael, 2:39, 2:68, 2:144, 2:257
Harris, Carol, 1:563
Harris, Cyril M., 2:261
Harris, Geraldine, 2:280
Harris, H. A., 2:285
Harris, Jocelyn, 1:29
Harris, Jonathan, 2:88
Harris, Joseph, 2:299
Harris, Mark Jonathan, 2:235
Harris, Marvin, 2:48, 2:134
Harris, Nathaniel, 2:316, 2:330, 2:376
Harris, Susan E., 2:436, 2:471
Harris, William, 1:197
Harris, Wilson, 1:405
Harrison, Anthony, 1:57
Harrison, Gilbert A., 1:303
Harrison, James (ed), 2:432
Harrison, Richard, et al, 2:449
Harrison, Ross, 2:8
Harrisse, Henry, 2:157
Hart, Anna, 1:583
Hart, B. H., 2:373
Hart, Brian R., 2:494
Hart, Dudley, 2:561
Hart, Henry H., 2:309
Hart, Ivor B., 2:316
Hart, Jeffrey, 2:238
Hart, William B., 2:72, 2:257
Harte, Bret, 1:176; 2:201
Hartenian, Larry, 2:374
Harter, Penny, 1:489
Hartley, John, 1:457, 1:468
Hartman, David, 2:303
Hartman, Dick, 2:112
Hartman, William K., 2:476
Hartmann, Rudolf, 2:425
Hartmann, Susan M., 2:235
Hartnell, Tim, 1:581
Hartshorn, Truman, 2:93
Hartt, Frederick (ed), 2:318
Harty, John, III (ed), 1:123
Harvard Independent Staff, 1:485
Harvey, William, 2:547
Harwin, Judith (ed), 2:539
Harwood, William, 1:487
Hashim, Safaa H., 1:579
Hasken, Paul, 2:551
Haskins, Charles, 2:537
Haskins, James, 2:241, 2:401
Hassall, Christopher, 1:70
Hassan, Dolly Z., 1:406
Hassan, Salem K., 1:100
Hassett, John J., 2:409
Haste, Helen (ed), 2:112
Hastings, Max, 2:235, 2:238, 2:384, 2:388
Hastings, Michael, 1:82
Hatel, David, 1:585
Hatfield, Frederick C., 2:551

Hatsy-Thompson, Kate, 1:575
Hatterer, Lawrence J., 2:553
Haugeland, John, 1:581
Haugeland, John (ed), 1:582
Haugen, Einar (ed), 1:374
Hauner, Milan, 2:376
Haupt, Arthur, 2:85, 2:274
Hauptly, Denis J., 2:166, 2:241
Hauser, Robert M., 2:144
Hauser, Robert M. (ed), 2:145
Haux, Reinhold, 1:574
Haviland, William A., 2:42
Hawke, David Freeman, 2:432
Hawkes, Nigel, 1:584; 2:81, 2:481
Hawking, Stephen M., 2:469
Hawking, Stephen M. (ed), 2:516
Hawkins, Hugh, 2:213
Hawkins, Robert B., Jr. (ed), 2:35
Hawkins, Robert G. (ed), 2:36
Hawley, Isabel, 1:477
Hawley, Richard A., 2:542
Hawley, Robert, 1:477
Hawthorne, Nathaniel, 1:177
Hay, Edward A., 2:489
Hay, John, 2:198
Hay, Louise L., 2:560
Hayakawa, S. I., 1:438, 1:439
Hayden, Jerome D., 1:524
Hayden, Robert, 1:233
Hayden, Robert C., 2:432
Hayden, Robert C. (ed), 2:432
Haydn, Franz Joseph, 2:337
Hayes, E. Nelson (ed), 2:53
Hayes, Harold T., 2:496
Hayes, John, 2:335, 2:404
Hayes, John P., 1:265
Hayes, Nicky, 2:95
Hayes, Tanya (ed), 2:53
Hayman, LeRoy, 2:563
Hayman, Ronald, 1:340
Haynes, Colin, 1:554
Hays, Peter L., 1:237
Hayward, Stan, 1:577
Heacock, Paul, 1:439
Headings, Philip R., 1:83
Headlam-Morley, James, 2:342
Headon, Deirdre, 2:306
Heale, Elizabeth, 1:17
Heaney, Seamus, 1:92
Hearden, Patrick J., 2:234
Hearder, Harry, 2:340
Hearn, Charles R., 2:229
Heath, Christian, 1:582
Heath, Jim F., 2:241
Heath, Thomas L., 1:507
Hecht, Jeff, 2:519
Hedtke, John V., 1:573
Heer, Friedrick, 2:306
Heermance, J. Noel, 1:170, 1:172

Hefele, Bernhard, 2:274
Heid, Jim, 1:560
Heidel, William A., 2:533
Heidmann, Jean, 2:469
Heilbron, J. L., 2:521
Heilbroner, Robert L., 2:56, 2:57, 2:59, 2:60, 2:61, 2:63, 2:67, 2:339
Heilbroner, Robert L. (ed), 2:61
Heilbrunner, S., 1:566
Heim, Michael, 1:575
Heimlich, Henry J., 2:567
Heims, Steve V., 1:538, 1:553
Heinlein, Robert, 1:233–34
Helgren, David, 2:76
Heller, Barbara R., 1:504
Heller, Joseph, 1:234
Heller, Julek, 2:306
Heller, Walter, 2:63
Hellman, Lillian, 1:231, 1:235
Hellmuth, Jerome, 2:538
Hellweg, Paul, 1:440
Helprin, Mark (ed), 1:490
Hemenway, Robert E., 1:242
Hemingway, Albert, 2:235
Hemingway, Ernest, 1:236–37, 1:482; 2:224, 2:374
Hemingway, Mary Walsh, 1:237
Hemming, G. W., 1:535
Hemmings, Frederick W., 1:342
Henbest, Nigel, 2:470, 2:475, 2:480
Hench, John B. (ed), 2:327
Henderson, Harold G. (tr), 1:425
Henderson, Katherine Usher, 1:464
Henderson, Linda Dalrymple, 1:519
Henderson, Thomas F., 1:9
Henderson, W. O., 2:59
Henderson, W. O. (ed), 2:339
Henderson, William J., 2:362
Hendley, Brian, 1:503
Hendon, Rufus S., 1:426
Hendrek, Booraem V., 2:195
Hendrick, Burton J., 2:206
Hendrick, George, 1:280
Hendrick, Willene, 1:280
Hendrickson, Robert, 1:431; 2:486
Henig, Jeffrey R., 2:35
Henning, Margaret, 2:148
Henry, Jeannette (ed), 2:157
Henry, Nicholas, 2:41
Henry, O., 1:178
Henry, R. R., 2:549
Henslin, James M. (ed), 2:138
Hentoff, Nat, 1:237–38; 2:12, 2:16
Hentoff, Nat (ed), 2:262
Hentschel, U. (ed), 2:113
Hepburn, Katharine, 1:472
Heppenheimer, T. A., 2:494, 2:496
Hepworth, Cecil, 1:474
Herberg, Will, 2:142

Herbert, Brian, 1:239
Herbert, Eugenia W., 2:526
Herbert, Frank, 1:238
Herbert, George, 1:11
Herda, D. J., 1:560; 2:562
Herdan, Gustav, 1:529
Herington, John, 1:312
Herken, Rolf, 1:581
Herman, Ethel, 1:437
Herman, John, 2:80
Herman, Lewis, 1:431
Herman, Marguerite, 1:431
Hermann, Luke, 2:358
Hermes, Patricia, 2:537
Hernandez, Raphael, 2:408
Herodotus, 2:288
Herold, J. Christopher, 2:329, 2:330
Herr, Michael, 1:464
Herrick, Robert, 1:11
Herring, George C., 2:241, 2:252
Herring, James E., 1:570
Herriot, James, 1:93
Hersch, Giselle, 2:384
Hersey, John, 2:235, 2:253
Hersh, Seymour M., 2:38
Hershey, Philip, 2:435
Hershey, Robert L., 1:497
Hershinow, Sheldon J., 1:262
Hershovits, Melville, 2:44
Herzstein, Robert E., 2:376
Heslin, Jo-Ann, 2:550
Hess, Adrian L., 1:516
Hess, Beth B., 2:129, 2:146
Hess, Beth B. (ed), 2:148
Hess, Fred C., 2:504
Hesse, Hermann, 1:368
Hesse, Mary, 2:516
Hession, Charles H., 2:67
Hetherington, E. Morris (ed), 2:114
Heuer, Kenneth, 2:484
Hewett, Edgar L., 2:299
Heyerdahl, Thor, 2:411
Heywood, Vernon H. (ed), 2:447
Hibbard, Howard, 2:318
Hibbert, Christopher, 2:274, 2:310, 2:329, 2:344, 2:363
Hickey, Donald R., 2:169
Hicks, Edward, 1:7
Hicks, Florence, 2:14
Hicks, John D., 2:204
Hidaka, Rokuro, 2:398
Higgins, D. S., 1:51
Higgins, Denis (ed), 1:483
Higginson, Thomas W., 2:192
Higginson, William, 1:489
Higham, Charles, 2:280
Higham, John, 2:207
Highwater, Jamake, 1:239; 2:154, 2:261
Hilbert, David, 1:517

Hildesheimer, Wolfgang, 2:333
Hilgard, Ernest J., 2:112
Hilgard, Ernest R., 2:95
Hilger, Michael, 1:475
Hill, Christopher, 2:327, 2:378
Hill, David B., 2:39
Hill, Hamlin, 1:461
Hill, Martha (ed), 2:61
Hill, MaryAnn, 1:574
Hill, Robert W., 1:215
Hillard, John (ed), 2:67
Hillary, Edmund (ed), 2:81
Hilling, David, 2:86
Hills, Rust, 1:490
Hillway, Tyrus, 1:163
Hilton, James, 1:94
Hilton, Peter, 1:519
Hilton, Suzanne, 2:169, 2:179, 2:182, 2:231
Hinchliffe, Arnold P., 1:112, 1:114
Hinckley, A. D., 2:496
Hinckley, Dan, 1:575
Hinde, J. S., 2:462
Hinde, Robert A., 2:138, 2:462
Hinding, Andrea (ed), 2:148
Hindley, 2:306
Hinds, Harold E., Jr. (ed), 2:88, 2:274
Hinds-Howell, David G., 1:437
Hine, Darlene C., 2:154
Hinton, Harold C., 2:86
Hinton, S. E., 1:240
Hipple, Ted, 1:204
Hippocrates, 2:533
Hirschi, Travis, 2:133
Hirth, Friedrich, 2:281
Hitchcock, H. Wiley, 2:154
Hitchcock, H. Wiley (ed), 2:154, 2:187
Hitler, Adolf, 2:376
Hitti, Philip K., 2:274, 2:280
Hixson, Walter L., 2:391
Hoagland, Mahlon B., 2:439
Hobbes, Thomas, 2:10
Hobley, C. W., 2:299
Hobsbawn, Eric J., 2:332, 2:339
Hockachka, P. W. (ed), 2:511
Hockett, Charles F., 1:529
Hockey, Thomas A., 2:476
Hocking, John G., 1:516
Hodeir, Andre, 2:261
Hodgart, Matthew, 1:9
Hodge, Frederick W. (ed), 2:157
Hodge, Peter, 2:291
Hodges, Andrew, 1:538, 1:551
Hodges, J. C., 1:22
Hodgkinson, D., 1:506
Hodgson, Jack, 1:558
Hoehling, Adolph A., 2:224
Hoey Smith, Richard van, 2:447
Hoff, Darrel, 2:470
Hoff, Rhoda, 2:207

Hoffer, A., 1:519
Hoffer, Peter C. (ed), 2:162
Hoffer, Thomas, 2:130
Hoffer, Thomas W., 1:474
Hoffman, Daniel G., 1:174
Hoffman, Frederick J., 1:220
Hoffman, George, W., 2:88, 2:405
Hoffman, Paul, 1:575
Hoffmann, Banesh, 2:520
Hoff-Wilson, Joan (ed), 2:233
Hofstadter, Richard, 2:162, 2:164, 2:169, 2:204, 2:218
Hofstetter, Fred T., 1:577
Hogan, Michael J., 2:238
Hogben, Lancelot, 1:504
Hogwood, Christopher, 2:336
Hohler, Robert T., 2:481
Holbrook, Stewart H., 2:154, 2:204
Holden, Alan, 1:519
Holland, R. C., 1:561
Hollander, Jacob H., 2:73
Hollander, Lee M. (ed), 1:374
Hollenbeck, Peter (ed), 1:426
Holler, Frederick L., 2:6
Hollis, C., 1:24
Hollis, Richard, 1:475
Holloway, David, 2:176
Holloway, Robin, 2:418
Holme, Bryan (ed), 1:318
Holmes, Frederic, 2:500
Holmes, George, 1:350
Holmes, J. N., 1:579
Holmes, Oliver Wendell, 1:158
Holmes, Oliver Wendell, Jr., 2:29
Holmes, Richard, 1:34
Holmes, Urban, 1:326
Holoman, D. Kern, 2:347
Holst, Imogen, 2:338, 2:417
Holt, Marilyn, 1:575
Holton, Gerald (ed), 2:439, 2:440, 2:520
Holtsmark, Erling B., 1:208
Holtz, M. (ed), 1:575
Holub, Allen I., 1:586
Holum, John R., 2:511
Homans, George C., 2:104, 2:139
Homer, 1:315
Homer, Winslow, 2:216
Honan, Park, 1:20, 1:41
Hone, Ralph E., 1:118
Honour, Hugh, 2:154, 2:333
Hoobler, Dorothy, 2:241, 2:291, 2:320, 2:322, 2:380, 2:384, 2:398
Hoobler, Thomas, 2:241, 2:291, 2:320, 2:322, 2:380, 2:384, 2:398
Hood, Michael (ed), 2:393
Hook, Brian (ed), 2:87, 2:274
Hooks, William H., 2:226
Hookway, Christopher (ed), 1:582
Hoover, Herbert Clark, 2:231

Hopkins, Gerard Manley, 1:53
Hopper, Grace Murray, 1:545, 1:557
Hora, Bayard (ed), 2:447
Horace, 1:321; 2:294
Horgan, Paul, 2:198, 2:426
Horn, Pierre, 2:326
Hornback, Bert G., 1:47
Horne, A.D. (ed), 2:252
Horne, Jo, 2:544
Horner, Donald, 1:561
Horney, Karen, 2:98, 2:106, 2:119
Horowitz, Frances D. (ed), 2:106
Horton, William K., 1:580
Horwitz, Lucy, 1:529
Hosbaum, Phillip, 1:101
Hosen, Frederick E., 2:154
Hosler, Jay, 1:537, 1:562
Hourwich, Andrea T., 2:148
House, A. S. (ed), 1:579
Housman, A. E., 1:54
Houston, James D., 2:235
Houston, Jeanne W., 2:235
Houston, John R., 1:337
Houston, Samuel, 2:186
Hovde, Jane, 2:208
Howard, Donald R., 1:7
Howard, Jane, 2:47
Howard, Julie, 1:437
Howard, Leon, 1:163
Howard, Michael, 2:340
Howard, Neale E., 2:470
Howatson, M. C., 1:311
Howe, Irving, 1:52, 1:383
Howe, Mark De Wolfe, 2:29
Howells, William Dean, 2:207
Howes, Barbara (ed), 1:399
Hoxie, Frederick E. (ed), 2:157
Hoyle, Fred, 2:495, 2:514
Hoyt, Edwin P., 1:169
Hsu, Francis, 2:43
Hsu, Immanuel C., 2:363, 2:399
Hsu, Jeffrey, 1:554
Hubble, Edwin Powell, 2:478
Hubbuch, Susan, 1:483
Huber, David M., 1:579
Huber, Peter, 2:31
Hudson, Michael, 2:570
Hudson, Theodore, 1:197
Hudson-Weems, Clenora, 1:269
Huff, Darrell, 1:529
Hughes, Barbara, 2:554
Hughes, Langston, 1:241
Hughes, Libby, 2:408
Hughes, M. N., 2:511
Hughes, Peter, 1:406
Hughes, R. N., 2:465
Hughes, Ted, 1:95
Hughey, Pat, 2:465
Hugo, Victor Marie, 1:337

Huizinga, Johan, 2:43
Hull, Raymond, 1:489; 2:140
Hulliung, Mark, 2:19
Hultsch, David F., 2:129
Humboldt, Friedrich Heinrich Alexander
    von, 2:78
Humes, James C., 1:449
Hummel, Charles, 2:473
Humphrey, James H., 2:123, 2:540
Humphrey, Joy N., 2:540
Humphrey, Watts S., 1:585
Huneker, James G., 2:350
Hunger Project, The, 2:81
Hunt, Albert, 1:468
Hunt, Cynthia, 2:83
Hunt, Douglas, 2:536
Hunt, Frederick V., 2:521
Hunt, Irene, 2:192, 2:229
Hunt, Tina, 1:247
Hunter, Floyd, 2:131
Hunter, Nigel, 2:366
Hunter, Robert, 1:586
Hunting, Robert, 1:30
Hurston, Zora Neale, 1:242; 2:280
Hurt, R. Douglas, 2:229
Hurtz, Judie L., 1:555, 1:557
Huss, Roy, 1:469
Huston, John, 1:472
Hutcheson, Richard G., Jr., 2:258
Hutchings, William, 1:121
Hutchinson, Betty, 1:487, 1:560
Hutchinson, David, 1:470
Hutchinson, Duane, 1:451
Hutchinson, Warner A., 1:487,
    1:560
Huth, Arno, 1:461
Huttenbach, Henry, 2:207
Hutton, Edward, 1:348
Hutton, James, 2:490
Hutton, P. J., 1:579
Huxford, Marilyn (ed), 2:130
Huxley, Aldous, 1:95; 2:333
Huxley, Elspeth, 2:363, 2:393,
    2:570
Huynk S. Thong, 1:426
Hyde, Bruce G., 2:496
Hyde, Lawrence E., 2:455
Hyde, Margaret O., 2:98, 2:110, 2:145,
    2:455, 2:496, 2:537, 2:554, 2:556,
    2:560
Hyder, William D. (ed), 2:376
Hyland, William, 2:388
Hyman, Anthony, 1:542
Hyman, Dick, 2:41
Hyman, Herbert H., 2:146
Hyman, Jane, 1:565
Hymowitz, Carol, 2:154
Hyner, Gerald C., 2:551
Hynes, Samuel (ed), 1:92

I

Iacocca, Lee A., 2:63, 2:64, 2:258
Iamblicus, 1:501
Ibn Batuta, 2:301
Ibsen, Henrik, 1:378
Icek, Ajzen, 2:97
Igoe, James, 2:261
Igoe, Lynn Moody, 2:261
Igoe, Robert S., 2:549
Ihemoto, Takashi (ed) and (tr), 1:427
Ikime, Obaro (ed), 2:274
Illingworth, Valerie (ed), 2:470
Imbrie, John, 2:493
Imbrie, Katherine P., 2:493
Imelik, B., 2:507
Immerman, Richard H. (ed), 2:23
Immerwahr, Henry R., 2:288
Imperato, Pascal James, 2:557
Imperato, Pascal James (ed), 2:560
Ince, D., 1:585
Infeld, Leopold, 1:509
Inglehart, Ronald, 2:144
Inglis, Andrew, 1:464
Ingraham, Gloria D., 2:432
Ingraham, Leonard W., 2:432
Ingres, Jean A., 2:334
Inhelder, Barbel (ed), 2:112
Innes, C. L., 1:412
Insel, Paul, 2:531
Ipsen, D. C., 1:521; 2:285
Irons, Peter, 2:235
Irving, Washington, 1:159
Isherwood, Christopher, 1:96
Ishiguro, Hide, 1:527
Israel, Fred L., 2:38
Israel, Fred L. (ed), 2:5
Israel, Guy, 2:469
Israel, W. (ed), 2:516
Iverson, Kenneth E., 1:566, 1:585
Ives, Charles Edward, 2:261
Ivins, William M., Jr., 1:515
Iz, Fahir, 1:420
Izard, Carroll E., 2:103
Izard, Carroll E. (ed), 2:104

J

Jablonski, Edward, 2:154, 2:262
Jabor, William, 2:476
Jackall, Robert (ed), 2:148
Jackel, Eberhard, 2:376
Jackson, Andrew, 2:182
Jackson, Andrew S., 1:568
Jackson, Bob, 2:238
Jackson, Daphne F., 2:519
Jackson, David E., 2:301

Jackson, Helen Hunt, 2:201
Jackson, John G., 2:299, 2:300
Jackson, John S., III, 2:39
Jackson, Joseph H., 2:476
Jackson, Julia A. (ed), 2:488
Jackson, Philip C., Jr., 1:581
Jackson, Robert, 2:82
Jackson, Shirley, 1:243
Jackson, W. A., 2:92
Jacob, Herbert, 2:7, 2:26, 2:33
Jacobs, Francine, 2:559
Jacobs, George, 2:560
Jacobs, Harold R., 1:497, 1:535
Jacobs, Harriet A., 2:189
Jacobs, Howard, 1:431
Jacobs, Jane, 2:94
Jacobs, Joseph (ed), 1:313
Jacobs, Lewis (ed), 1:469
Jacobs, W. W., 1:97
Jacobs, Wilbur R., 2:162
Jacobs, Will, 1:459
Jacobs, William Jay, 2:207
Jacobson, Edmund, 2:536
Jacobson, Gary C., 2:39
Jacobson, Michael F., 2:549
Jacobson, Morris K., 2:449
Jaeger, Werner, 2:287
Jaffe, Jacquiline A., 1:48
Jaffe, Jay, 1:574
Jaffee, Al, 1:456
Jahn, Theodore L., 2:446
Jaki, Stanley L., 1:538
Jakoubek, Robert, 2:238, 2:250, 2:258
Jamal, Mahmood (ed and tr), 1:422
James, Everett L., 2:200
James, Glenn (ed), 1:497
James, Henry, 1:179
James, Leonard F., 2:326
James, Marquis, 2:186
James, P. D., 1:98
James, P. T., 1:433
James, Preston E., 2:78
James, Robert C. (ed), 1:497
James, William, 2:96
Jamsa, Kris, 1:561
Janis, Harriet, 2:261
Janis, Irving, 2:139
Janovy, John, 2:437
Janowitz, Morris, 2:145
Jansen, Marius B., 2:274
Janson, Anthony F., 2:154
Janson, H. W., 2:154
Janssen, Dale, 1:451
Jaques, H. E., 2:448
Jardim, Ann, 2:148
Jardin, André, 2:332
Jarnik, V., 1:524
Jarrell, Randall, 1:244
Jasen, David A., 1:131

Jaspersohn, William, 1:455
Jastrow, Robert, 2:456, 2:470, 2:479, 2:481
Jauch, Josef M., 2:519
Jay, Peter (ed), 1:311
Jayyusi, Salma K., 1:420
Jeans, D. N. (ed), 2:91
Jedlicka, Davor, 2:138
Jeffers, (John) Robinson, 1:244
Jefferson, Thomas, 2:175
Jefferys, William H., 2:470
Jeffrey, C., 2:441
Jelavich, Barbara, 2:340
Jencks, Charles, 2:415
Jenkens, Gwyn M., 2:510
Jenkins, Alan (ed), 2:86
Jenkins, E. N., 2:508
Jenkins, Marie M., 2:449
Jenkins, Reese V. (ed), 2:524
Jenner, W. J. (ed and tr), 1:423
Jennings, Gary, 2:300
Jennings, Jesse D. (ed), 2:157
Jensen, Joan M., 2:184
Jensen, Marilyn, 1:155
Jensen, Merrill, 2:17, 2:164, 2:169
Jensen, William B., 2:507
Jeremy, David J., 2:339
Jerome, John, 2:551
Jesperson, James, 1:538; 2:479
Jesperson, Otto, 1:434
Jessup, John E., 2:388
Jewell, Malcolm E., 2:41
Jewett, Sarah Orne, 1:180
Jezer, Marty, 2:243, 2:466
Jhabvala, Ruth P., 2:399
Joannides, Paul, 2:320
Johannesen, Richard, 1:449
Johannsen, Robert W., 2:189
Johanson, Donald Carl, 2:48, 2:278, 2:460
Johansson, Thomas B., 2:496
John, Bernard, 2:451, 2:452
John, Brian, 2:88
John, F., 1:524
Johnson, Colin, 2:553
Johnson, Eric W., 2:538
Johnson, G. Timothy, 2:530
Johnson, G. Timothy (ed), 2:531
Johnson, Gary L., 2:484
Johnson, Gaylord, 2:436
Johnson, George, 1:581
Johnson, Harriet, 1:575
Johnson, Jacqueline, 2:242
Johnson, James Weldon, 1:245
Johnson, Lee, 2:334
Johnson, Lyndon Baines, 2:246
Johnson, Michael, 1:479
Johnson, Mildred, 1:506
Johnson, Nelson, 1:578
Johnson, Oliver, 2:191
Johnson, Ollie, 1:475

Johnson, Peter, 2:19
Johnson, Rebecca, 2:467
Johnson, Regina E., 2:299
Johnson, Richard D., 1:575
Johnson, Robert, 2:518
Johnson, Robert K., 1:287
Johnson, Robert T., 2:220
Johnson, Samuel, 1:26
Johnson, Spencer, 2:283
Johnson, Sue, 2:542
Johnson, Sylvia, 2:446, 2:447, 2:451, 2:486
Johnson, T. H. (ed), 2:162
Johnson, Thomas H., 1:175
Johnson, Vernon E., 2:555
Johnson, W. W., 2:160
Johnson-Davies, Denys (ed), 1:420
Johnston, Hugh (ed), 2:321
Johnston, Jerome, 1:465
Johnston, Robert D. (ed), 1:57
Jokl, Peter, 2:551
Joll, Evelyn, 2:358
Joll, James, 2:371
Jonassen, David H., 1:580
Jones, Brian, 2:470
Jones, C. Eugene, 2:447
Jones, C. P., 2:289
Jones, Constance, 2:119
Jones, David W., 2:337
Jones, Edward, 1:572, 1:573
Jones, Elise F., 2:542
Jones, Ernest, 2:118
Jones, Francis C., 2:374
Jones, Gerard, 1:459
Jones, Gwyn, 2:306
Jones, J. Alfred, 2:566
Jones, Landon, 2:142, 2:144
Jones, Max, 2:264
Jones, R. Ben, 2:330
Jones, Roger, 2:320
Jonson, Ben, 1:12
Jordan, Barbara Charline, 2:24
Jordan, David P., 2:332
Jordan, Robert P., 2:193
Jordan, Winthrop D., 2:154
Jordon, Robert S. (ed), 2:390
Jordy, William H., 2:262
Jorgensen, Danny L., 2:42
Jorgensen, Donald G., Jr., 2:539
Jorgensen, June A., 2:539
Joseph, Joel D., 2:26
Josephson, Matthew, 2:204, 2:524
Josephy, Alvin M., 2:158, 2:184
Jovanovic, Lois, 2:545
Jowett, Garth, 1:440
Joy, Charles R., 2:535
Joyce, James, 1:99
Judd, Dennis R., 2:41
Judson, A. C., 1:17

Judson, Horace F., 2:434, 2:439, 2:440, 2:441
Juhasz, Vilmos, 2:416
Jules-Rosette, Bennetta (ed), 2:52, 2:142
Julien, Robert M., 2:553
Juliussen, Egil, 1:538
Juliussen, Karen, 1:538
Jullien, Adolphe, 2:362
Jump, John D., 1:60
Jung, Carl Gustav, 2:97, 2:121
Jurgensen, Ray C., 1:512
Justice, Blair, 2:531
Jute, Andre, 1:490

K

Kael, Pauline, 1:480
Kafka, Franz, 1:369
Kagan, Andrew, 2:418
Kagan, James (ed), 2:103
Kagan, Jerome, 2:95, 2:536, 2:540
Kagan, Jerome (ed), 2:103, 2:106
Kagan, V., 1:519
Kaganov, M. T., 2:522
Kahn, M. A. (ed), 2:510
Kahn, Robert D., 1:522
Kainen, Paul G., 1:512, 1:535
Kai-Yu Hsu (ed and tr), 1:423
Kalb, Bernard, 2:39
Kalb, Marvin, 2:39
Kalechofsky, Roberta, 1:111
Kalin, Robert, 1:512
Kalman, Bobbie, 2:399
Kalstone, David, 1:16
Kaltenmark, Max, 2:281
Kaminsky, Stuart, 1:469
Kane, Gerry, 1:562
Kane, Joseph N., 2:41
Kane, Kathryn, 1:468
Kane, Thomas T., 2:85, 2:274
Kanes, Martin (ed), 1:330
Kanitkar, Helen, 2:281
Kanitkar, Hemant, 2:281
Kanter, Rosabeth M., 2:139, 2:140
Kantor, MacKinley, 2:192
Kantor, Paul, 2:94, 2:154
Kao, T. I., 1:498
Kaplan, E. Anne, 1:468
Kaplan, Frederic M., 2:87, 2:274
Kaplan, Helen S., 2:560
Kaplan, Justin, 1:182
Kaplan, Lawrence S., 2:405
Kaplan, Leslie S., 2:538
Kaplan, Robert M., 2:122
Karant, Priscilla, 1:445
Karier, Clarence J., 2:95
Karnow, Stanley, 2:399, 2:403
Kart, Cary S., 2:544

Kartzer, David I. (ed), 2:137
Kasir, Daoud S. (ed), 1:506
Kasner, Edward, 1:497
Kastner, Bernice, 1:519
Katan, Norma J., 2:280
Katchadourian, Herant, 2:451
Katona, George, 2:61
Katz, Elihu, 1:454; 2:130
Katz, Elihu (ed), 2:130
Katz, Jacqueline H., 2:207
Katz, Lawrence, 2:122
Katz, Wendy R., 1:51
Katz, William L., 1:170; 2:201, 2:207
Kaufman, R. J. (ed), 1:120
Kaufman, William J., III, 2:470
Kaur, Harpinder, 2:366
Kavaler, Lucy, 2:447
Kavanagh, Dennis A. (ed), 2:408
Kavanagh, Michael, 2:449
Kawamura, K., 2:510
Kawatake Toshio (ed), 1:425
Kay, Dennis (ed), 1:16
Kay, Norman, 2:424
Kaye, Tony, 2:246
Keates, Jonathan, 2:336
Keating, Barry P., 2:63
Keating, H. R., 1:490
Keating, Maryann O., 2:63
Keats, John, 1:35
Keefe, William J., 2:33, 2:39, 2:41
Keegan, John, 2:235
Keegan, John (ed), 2:275
Keele, Alan, 1:368
Keen, Benjamin, 2:275
Keen, Benjamin (ed), 2:275
Keen, Martin L., 2:492
Keenan, Edward P., 1:497
Keene, Donald, 2:275
Keene, Donald (ed), 1:423, 1:425; 2:275
Keeton, William T., 2:437
Keffer, Christine, 1:437
Kegan, Robert, 2:106
Kehoe, Alice B., 2:158
Keidel, Eudene, 1:411
Keightley, David N. (ed), 2:282
Keightley, Moy, 2:415
Keigley, Peggy, 2:556
Keil, Philippa, 1:449
Keillor, Garrison, 1:461
Keim, Hugo A., 2:562
Keith, Harold, 2:193
Keith, Jennie (ed), 2:52
Keller, Edward A., 2:496
Keller, Evelyn F., 2:453
Keller, Helen, 1:449
Keller, Howard H., 1:362
Keller, Mollie, 2:386, 2:413, 2:510
Kelley, Amy, 2:306
Kelley, Donald R. (ed), 2:258

Kellner, Douglas, 2:396
Kelly, Alfred H., 2:166
Kelly, Gary F., 2:542
Kelly, George A., 2:114
Kelly, Regina Z., 2:247
Kelly, Richard, 1:45, 1:92
Kelman, Charles D., 2:552
Kelman, Harold, 2:119
Kelsey, Harry, 2:158
Kelsey, Larry, 2:470
Kemeny, John G., 1:529
Kendall, Alan (ed), 2:276
Kendall, M. G., 1:529
Kendall, Patricia L., 2:130
Kenen, Peter B., 2:72
Kennan, George F., 2:371, 2:374, 2:391
Kennedy, Arthur G., 1:429
Kennedy, Arthur K., 1:331
Kennedy, David M., 2:152, 2:224
Kennedy, DayAnn M., 2:432
Kennedy, John Fitzgerald, 2:247
Kennedy, Malcolm D., 2:374
Kennedy, Michael, 2:355, 2:417, 2:425
Kennedy, Noah, 1:581
Kennedy, P. J. (ed), 2:501
Kennedy, Paul, 2:275
Kennedy, Robert Francis, 2:248, 2:388
Kenner, Hugh, 1:522
Kenneth, Lee, 2:235
Kenney, Edwin J., 1:70
Kenny, Anthony, 1:14; 2:307
Kenny, Herbert, 1:457
Kent, A., 1:538
Kent, Zachary, 2:259
Kenyatta, Jomo, 2:394
Kenyon, Carl, 2:566
Kenyon, Cecelia M. (ed), 2:166
Kenyon Critics, 1:53
Keogh, James, 1:572
Kephart, William M., 2:131, 2:138
Kepler, Johannes, 2:474
Kerby, Mona, 2:562
Kerkloh, Ruediger, 1:562
Kerman, Joseph, 2:262
Kernighan, Brian W., 1:563, 1:564
Kernoff, Alan (ed), 1:581
Kerouac, Jack, 1:246–47
Kerr, Douglas M., 1:554
Kerr, Lucille, 1:409
Kerr, M. E., 1:247–48
Kerr, Richard, 2:475
Kerrins, Joseph, 2:560
Kerrod, Robin, 2:470
Kertzer, David L. (ed), 2:52
Kessler, Francis P., 2:21
Kessler, Lauren, 1:457
Ketcham, Ralph, 2:169
Kettelkamp, Larry, 1:578; 2:551
Ketteridge, J. O., 1:326

Kettner, James H., 2:7
Key, Wilson Bryan, 1:454
Keyes, Claire, 1:281
Keyfitz, Nathan, 2:142
Keynes, George, 2:548
Keynes, John Maynard, 2:67
Keynes, Milo (ed), 2:67
Keyzer, Hendrik (ed), 2:511
Khouri, Fred J., 2:89
Khouri, Mounah A., 1:420
Khourie, Fred J., 2:412
Khrushchev, Nikita, 2:392
Kibble, Lawrence, 1:346
Kidder, Rushworth M., 1:214
Kidder, Tracy, 1:563
Kidwell, David S., 2:70
Kiefer, Irene, 2:494
Kieft, Ruth M., 1:300
Kiehl, David W. (comp), 2:213
Kiernan, Brian, 1:148
Kiley, Frederick, 1:488
Killeffer, David H., 2:434
Killian, James R., 2:238
Killingray, David, 2:380, 2:397
Kim, C. I., 2:87, 2:277
Kimball, Warren F. (ed), 2:386
Kimbell, David R., 2:361
Kimble, Jim, 1:558
Kindleberger, Charles Poor, 2:72
King, Anthony (ed), 2:21, 2:33
King, Bruce, 1:422
King, Gary, 2:6
King, James, 1:22
King, Kimball, 1:285
King, Martin Luther, Jr., 2:12, 2:238, 2:250
King, Michael, 2:91
King, Perry S., 2:285
King, Robert C., 2:452
King, Stephen, 1:249
King, Stephen, 1:445
King, Viki, 1:485
Kinney, Arthur F., 1:274
Kinney, Jack, 1:475
Kinsley, Helen, 1:24
Kinsley, James, 1:24
Kipling, Rudyard, 1:55
Kirby, David, 1:489
Kirchherr, Eugene C., 2:85, 2:275
Kirk, G. S., 1:318
Kirk, John M., 2:371
Kirk, Russell, 2:329
Kirkland, Elizabeth, 1:16
Kirschmann, John D., 2:549
Kish, George (ed), 2:76
Kissinger, Henry Alfred, 2:38
Kitchen, Martin, 2:374, 2:387
Kitt, Howard, 2:156
Kittner, M., 1:564

Kitto, H. D., 2:285
Kittredge, Mary, 2:291, 2:450, 2:545, 2:553, 2:557, 2:565
Kittross, John, 1:457
Kitzinger, Rachel (ed), 2:274
Kjetsaa, Geir, 1:392
Klapper, Joseph, 2:130
Klapthor, Margaret Brown, 2:154
Klass, Perri, 2:531
Klebaner, Benjamin J., 2:70
Klee, Paul, 2:415
Klein, Aaron E., 2:432
Klein, Burton H., 2:57
Klein, David, 2:434, 2:539
Klein, Ethel, 2:148
Klein, Felix, 1:518
Klein, Holger, 1:115
Klein, J. Michael, 2:479
Klein, Lawrence, 2:56
Klein, Leonard S. (ed), 1:411
Klein, Marymae E., 2:434, 2:539
Klein, Michael J., 2:470
Klein, Norma, 1:250
Kleinau, Marion, 1:449
Kleinkauf, Horst (ed), 2:511
Kline, Morris, 1:497
Klingaman, William K., 2:229
Klinge, Peter, 1:453
Klipper, Miriam Z., 2:536
Klitzner, Carol, 1:568
Klitzner, Herbert, 1:568
Klosty, James (ed), 2:266
Kluckhohn, Clyde, 2:42
Knapp, Bettina L., 1:345
Knapp, Mark, 1:448
Knapp, Mona, 1:103
Knapp, Ron, 2:280
Knight, Allan, 2:562
Knight, Arthur, 1:468
Knight, David C., 2:521
Knight, David E., 2:443
Knight, James E., 2:164
Knill, Harry (ed), 2:273
Knollenberg, Bernhard, 2:164
Knorr, Wilbur, 1:512
Knowles, John, 1:251
Knox, Diana, 2:339
Knox, Paul L., 2:76
Knuth, Donald E., 1:535, 1:585
Kobal, John, 1:468
Kobler, J. F., 1:142
Koch, H. W., 2:371
Koch, Robert, 2:444
Koch, Tom, 1:457
Kocher, Paul, 1:126
Koestler, Arthur, 2:474
Koffka, Kurt, 2:113
Kogan, Barry S., 2:302
Kogelman, Stanley, 1:497

Kohl, Herbert, 2:462
Kohl, Judith, 2:462
Kohlberg, Lawrence, 2:97, 2:103, 2:109, 2:146
Kohler, Pierre, 2:494
Kohler, Wolfgang, 2:113
Kohn, Hans, 2:275, 2:374
Kohn, Melvin L., 2:145, 2:146
Kohn, Rita, 2:12
Kolker, Robert P., 1:473
Kolko, Gabriel, 2:207
Kolpas, Norman, 2:403
Kongold, Ralph, 2:15
Konigsberg, Ira, 1:468
Konigsberger, H., 1:566
Konvitz, Milton (ed), 1:158
Koop, C. Everett, 2:549
Korner, Stephan, 1:497
Kort, Michael, 2:392
Kortepeter, C. M. (ed), 2:89
Kosof, Anna, 2:145
Kostelanetz, Richard (ed), 2:262
Kostrubala, Thaddeus, 2:551
Kotov, V. E., 1:559
Kott, L., 1:581
Kozak, Donals, 1:577
Kraditor, Aileen S., 2:224
Kraehe, Enno E., 2:333
Kraft, Betsy Harvey, 2:496
Kramer, E. E., 1:497
Kramer, Samuel Noah, 2:280
Kramer, Samuel Noah (ed), 2:278
Kramnick, Isaac (ed), 2:9
Kratzner, Brice L., 2:549
Krause, Elliott, 2:125
Krause, Eugene, 1:516
Kraut, Alan M., 2:207
Kravitz, Nathaniel, 1:420
Krebs, Hans Adolf, 2:438
Kreig, Arthur F., 1:566
Kresh, Paul, 1:388
Kristeller, Paul O., 2:310
Kritzeck, James (ed), 1:420
Kroeber, Alfred L., 2:44, 2:45
Kroeber, Theodora, 2:45
Krohn, Marvin D., 2:139
Krommelbein, Thomas, 1:362
Krumm, Rob, 1:572, 1:574
Krutch, Joseph Wood, 1:165
Krzyzanowski, Ludwick, 1:383
Kübler-Ross, Elizabeth, 2:106, 2:107, 2:138
Kudlinski, Kathleen V., 2:243, 2:466
Kuhn, Thomas S., 2:514
Kuhrt, Amelie (ed), 2:273
Kuklin, Susan, 2:543
Kundera, Milan, 1:385
Kuney, Jack, 1:465
Kupchan, Charles A., 2:258
Kurelek, William, 2:207

Kurian, George T., 2:75, 2:76, 2:85, 2:88, 2:275, 2:393
Kurian, George T. (ed), 2:75
Kurland, Gerald, 2:171, 2:174, 2:238, 2:248, 2:392, 2:403, 2:405
Kurland, Morton L., 2:560
Kurzweil, Raymond, 1:581
Kusnan, Joseph, 1:554
Kussi, Peter, 1:383
Kuveler, 1:562
Kuznets, Simon, 2:63

L

Labarge, Margaret Wade, 2:310
Labor, Earle, 1:257
Labov, William, 1:437
Labovitz, Sanford I., 2:125
Lacey, W. K., 2:285
La Cour, Donna Ward, 2:275
Lacy, Robert, 2:63
Ladd, Scott, 1:538
LaFarge, Ann, 1:207
La Follette, Robert Marion, 2:220
LaFore, Robert, 1:562
Lagercrantz, Olof, 1:380
Lagervist, Par, 1:378–79
Laithwarte, Eric, 2:513
Lake, E., 2:295
Lal, P. (ed), 1:422
LaLoge, Bob, 2:554
Lamarck, Jean Baptiste De Monet De, 2:459
Lamb, Charles, 1:16, 1:35
Lamb, H. H., 2:80
Lamb, Harold, 2:306
Lamb, Mary, 1:16
Lamb, Michael E., 2:539
Lamb, Sharon (ed), 2:106
Lamberg, Lynn, 2:552
Lambert, David, 2:460, 2:485, 2:486, 2:489
Lambert, Mark, 2:495
Lambert, Richard D., 2:135
Lammers, Susan, 1:538, 1:543
L'Amour, Louis, 1:252–53
Lamphere, Louise (ed), 2:148
Lampton, Christopher, 1:563, 1:564; 2:455, 2:467, 2:470, 2:476, 2:479, 2:481, 2:483, 2:494
Landau, Elaine, 2:544, 2:551, 2:557, 2:559, 2:562, 2:567
Landon, Grelun, 2:156
Lane, Arthur L., 2:481
Lane, Malcolm, 1:562
Lane, N. Gary, 2:495
Lang, Gladys, 1:457
Lang, Paul H., (ed), 2:154
Lang, Serge, 1:497

Lange, Dorothea, 2:232
Langer, William L. (ed), 2:275
Langford, Gerald, 1:178
Langford, Jerome J., 2:473
Langley, Andrew, 2:248
Langley, Noel, 1:473
Langman, Larry, 1:575
Langness, L. L., 2:42
Langone, John, 2:537, 2:560
Lanham, Url N., 2:449
Lanier, Sidney, 1:160
Lansdown, J., 1:577
Lao-Tzu, 1:423; 2:283
Lapham, Lewis, 1:480
Lappe, Frances Moore, 1:468; 2:19
Laqueur, Walter, 2:6, 2:380, 2:405
Laqueur, Walter (ed), 2:12, 2:36
Lardner, Robin W., 1:524
Larkin, Philip, 1:100
Larkin, Robert P., 2:93
Larsen, Jens P., 2:337
Larsen, Otto N., 2:130
Larsen, Rachel, 2:235
Larsen, Rebecca, 2:254
Larson, David L., 2:242
Larson, Gary, 1:459
Larzelere, Alex, 2:410
Las Casas, Bartholomé de, 2:158
Lash, Joseph P., 2:233, 2:390
Lashi, Marghanita, 1:49
Laska, Shirley, 2:147
Lasky, Kathryn, 2:201, 2:207
Lass, Abraham, 1:432
Lasswell, Harold D., 2:10
Lasswell, Marcia, 2:138
Lasswell, Thomas E., 2:138
Latham, Peter, 2:348
Latham, Robert O., 2:367
Lathem, Edward C., 2:228
Lau, Joseph (ed), 1:423
Lauber, John, 1:36
Lauber, Patricia, 2:494
Laufer, William S. (ed), 2:114
Laure, Ettagale, 2:85, 2:393
Laure, Jason, 2:85, 2:393
Laurence, Margaret, 1:140
Lavoisier, Antoine Laurent, 2:499
Law, Dennis L., 2:496
Lawless, Joann A., 2:95
Lawrence, A. W. (ed), 2:373
Lawrence, Bill, 1:558, 1:562
Lawrence, D. H., 1:101
Lawrence, T. E., 2:372
Laws, Priscilla W., 2:566
Lawson, Don, 2:155, 2:218, 2:229, 2:242, 2:258, 2:399, 2:412
Lawson, Richard H., 1:368, 1:369
Lawson, V., 1:176
Laycock, George, 2:493

Laycock, Mary, 1:512
Laye, Camara, 1:415
Layton, Robert, 2:346
Lazarsfeld, Paul F., 1:461; 2:39, 2:130
Lazarsfeld, Paul F. (ed), 2:125, 2:129
Lazere, Donald (ed), 1:454
Leach, Douglas E., 2:162
Leach, Edmund, 2:53
Leach, Richard H., 2:41
Leach, William, 1:183
Leacock, Stephen, 1:141
Leakey, Louis S. B., 2:49
Leakey, Mary D., 2:49
Leakey, Richard E., 2:49–50, 2:460
Leaman, Oliver, 2:303
Leaming, Barbara, 1:470
Leary, Lewis, 1:166
Leatherbarrow, William J., 1:392
Leavell, Perry, 2:177, 2:225
Leavitt, Judith W., 2:567
LeBaron, John, 1:470
Leben, Joe, 1:559
Lebon, Gustave, 2:105, 2:139
Lebra, Takie S., 2:399
Lebra-Chapman, Joyce, 2:363
Le Carré, John, 1:102
Lechner, Pieter M., 1:562
Leckie, Robert, 2:193
Leclerc, Ivor, 1:527
Le Corbusier, 2:419
Leder, Jane M., 2:537
Lederer, Katherine, 1:235
Lederer, Richard, 1:440, 1:477
Ledin, Victor, 1:561
Lee, Alfred, 1:440
Lee, Betsy, 1:202
Lee, Charlotte, 1:449
Lee, Elizabeth, 1:440
Lee, Essie E., 2:536, 2:554
Lee, George L., 2:155
Lee, Harper, 1:253
Lee, Irving, 1:437
Lee, Irving (ed), 1:437
Lee, Jo A., 1:575
Lee, John J., 2:446
Lee, Laura, 1:437
Lee, Min, 2:486
Lee, Peter H. (ed), 1:426
Lee, Robert Edward, 2:196
Lee, Sally, 2:549, 2:565
Lee, Spike, 1:486
Lee, Stephen J., 2:374
Lee, Susan, 2:56
Leech, Clifford, 1:12
Leech, Margaret, 2:193
Leff, Lawrence S., 1:512, 1:566
Lefkowitz, Mary R., 2:285
Leftwich, Joseph, 1:383
Leftwich, Richard H., 2:56, 2:57, 2:65

Le Guin, Ursula K., 1:254, 1:482
Lehane, Brendan, 2:158
Lehman, David (ed), 1:490
Lehmann, Michael B., 2:57
Lehner, Paul E., 1:568
Lehninger, Albert L., 2:438, 2:511
Lehrer, Steven, 2:548
Leibniz, Gottfried Wilhelm, 1:527
Leihm, Antonin, 1:383
Leinwand, Gerald, 2:567
Leite, Evelyn, 2:555
Lekachman, Robert, 2:57, 2:58, 2:65
Lelyveld, Joseph, 2:393
Lem, Stanislaw, 1:386
Lemay, Harold, Sid Lerner, 1:440
Lenin, Vladimir Ilyich, 2:58, 2:378
Lenneberg, Eric H., 2:50
Lenski, Branko, 1:383
Lenski, Gerhard E., 2:145
Leonardo Da Vinci, 2:315
Leone, Bruno, 2:133
Leone, Bruno (ed), 2:15, 2:36, 2:58, 2:135,
    2:137, 2:144
Leopard, Donald D., 2:235
Lepre, J. P., 2:280
Lepschy, Anne L., 1:346
Lepschy, Guido, 1:346
Lerner, Alan J., 1:451
Lerner, Gerda, 2:148, 2:184
Lerner, Max (ed), 2:29
Lerner, Richard M., 2:107
Lerner, Richard M. (ed), 2:107
Lesko, Barbara S., 2:280
Lessa, William A., 2:52
Lessing, Doris, 1:103
Lester, Julius, 1:255; 2:189
Leuchtenburg, William E., 2:226
Le Vert, Suzanne, 2:560
Levi, Maurice, 2:56
Levi, Peter, 1:16; 2:275, 2:285, 2:306
Levich, Richard (ed), 2:71
Levin, Flora R., 1:501
Levin, Gerald, 1:477
Levin, Harry, 1:163, 1:164, 1:178
Levin, Henry M. (ed), 2:148
Levin, Milton (ed), 1:78
Levin, Murray, 1:462
Levin, Phyllis L., 2:170
Levin, Richard B., 1:575
Levine, Alan H., 2:13
Levine, Robert A. (ed), 2:43
Levine, Robert I., 1:583
Levine, Saul, 2:542, 2:566
Levinson, Daniel J., 2:107
Levinson, Nancy Snider, 2:12
Levinson, Richard, 1:466
Lévi-Strauss, Claude, 2:53
Levitan, Sar A., 2:68
Levitt, I. M., 2:470

Levy, Howard S. (tr), 1:425
Levy, Leonard W., 2:166, 2:169
Levy, Steven, 1:540
Lewant, Robert, 1:583
Lewin, Albert, 1:433
Lewin, Esther, 1:433
Lewin, Kurt, 2:97, 2:99, 2:104, 2:132
Lewin, Moshe, 2:379
Lewin, Roger, 2:460, 2:545
Lewis, Anthony, 2:12
Lewis, Bernard, 2:301
Lewis, C. S., 1:104
Lewis, David L., 2:226
Lewis, Dominic B., 1:27
Lewis, Gerald, 1:431
Lewis, I., 2:508
Lewis, Kenneth, 2:451, 2:452
Lewis, L. A., 2:85
Lewis, Meriwether, 2:176
Lewis, Norman, 1:440
Lewis, Oscar, 2:131
Lewis, Paul, 2:450
Lewis, Peter, 1:102
Lewis, R. W. B., 1:183
Lewis, Richard S., 2:481
Lewis, Sinclair, 1:256; 2:226
Lewis, Theodore H. (ed), 2:157
Ley, Charles D., 2:158
Ley, Willy, 2:498
Leymarie, Jean, 2:353
Li Xiou Ming (tr), 1:423
Libes, Don, 1:562
Libman, Lillian, 2:426
Lichello, Robert, 1:467; 2:390, 2:529
Lichnewsky, A., 1:559
Lichty, Ron, 1:564
Lickona, Thomas, 2:146
Liddell Hart, Basil H., 2:373
Lieberman, Jethro Koller, 2:17
Liebert, R. L., 1:465
Lightman, Alan P., (ed), 2:513
Lightman, Marjorie (ed), 2:233
Liliuokalani, 2:218
Lillegard, Dee, 2:195
Lillyquist, Michael J., 2:570
Lincoln, Abraham, 2:197
Lincoln, C. Eric, 2:136
Lincoln, J., 1:470
Lincoln, W. Bruce, 2:340, 2:371
Lindberg, Jan, 2:545
Lindblad, Jerri, 2:554
Lindblad, K. E., 1:429
Lindblad, Richard A., 2:554
Linden, Carl A., 2:392
Lindop, Edmund, 2:39
Lindren, Michael, 1:540
Lindsay, Alexander, 1:22
Lindsay, Jack, 2:335
Lindsay, Jeanne Warren, 2:542, 2:543

Lindsay, Maurice, 1:32
Lindsay, Norman, 1:141
Lindsey, Almont, 2:204
Lindsey, David, 2:181
Lindzey, Gardner (ed), 2:95
Ling, Roger, 2:285
Lingeman, Richard, 1:217
Link, Arthur S., 2:155, 2:218
Link, William, 1:466
Linnaeus, Carolus, 2:443
Linton, Ralph, 2:43
Lippard, Lucy R., 2:415
Lippman, Walter, 2:39
Lipset, Seymour M., 2:40, 2:145
Liptak, Karen, 1:584
Lipton, James, 1:440
Liroff, Richard A., 2:570
Lisio, Donald J., 2:231
Liskin, Miriam, 1:572
Lisle, Laurie, 2:268
List, Barbara A., 2:433
Liszt, Franz, 2:350, 2:354
Littell, Joy (ed), 1:454, 1:468
Little, Gary, 1:564
Little, Jeffrey B., 2:70
Little, R. John, 2:447
Liu, Shih S. (ed), 1:423
Livermore, Shaw, Jr., 2:169
Livesay, Harold, 2:204
Livingstone, David, 2:367
Livy, 2:295
Llerena, Mario, 2:410
Lloyd, Christopher, 2:324
Lloyd, Seton, 2:280
Lloyd George, David, 2:373
Locher, J. L. (ed), 1:515
Lockard, Duane, 2:17
Lockard, Duane (ed), 2:6
Locke, John, 2:18
Lockridge, Kenneth A., 2:162
Lockwood, James R., 1:516
Loeper, John J., 2:448
Loewe, Michael (ed), 2:282
Lofland, L., 2:147
Logsdon, Gene, 2:271
Lois, Lamya, 2:272
Lomask, Milton, 1:483; 2:166
London, Jack, 1:257
Londre, Felicia Hardison, 1:304, 1:358
Long, Carolyn, 1:437
Long, Robert E., 1:291, 1:301
Longfellow, Henry Wadsworth, 1:161
Longford, Elizabeth, 2:405
Longley, Edna, 1:105
Longstreet, Stephen (ed), 2:346
Looby, Christopher, 2:168
Loomis, Elisha S., 1:501
Loomis, Julia, 2:298
Loon, Brian Van, 2:456

Lope de Vega Carpio, Félix, 1:358
Lopez, Claude-Anne, 2:526
Lopez, Enrique Hank, 1:280
Lopez, George A., 2:36
Lopez, George A. (ed), 2:7
Lopez de Gomara, Francisco, 2:323
Loran, Erle, 2:349
Lorber, Judith, 2:148
Lorch, Robert S., 2:41
Lord, Louis E., 1:313
Lord, Walter, 2:218
Lorenz, Hans-Walter, 2:57
Lorenz, Konrad, 2:100, 2:103, 2:104, 2:464
Lory, Hillis, 2:375
Loss, Archie, 1:106
Loth, David G., 2:30
Lothrop, Gloria Ricci, 2:184
Lottman, Herbert, 1:335
Louchheim, Katie (ed), 2:229
Lounsbury, John F., 2:92
Lovallo, Len, 1:74
Love, John F., 2:63
Loveless, Richard L. (ed), 1:577
Lovell, Bernard, 2:469
Lovett, Gabriel H., 2:275
Lowder, Stella, 2:94
Lowe, Carl, 2:531
Lowe, John C., 2:84
Lowe, Kurt E., 2:492
Lowe, W. D., 2:288
Lowell, Amy, 1:258
Lowell, James Russell, 1:161
Lowell, Robert, 1:259
Lowi, Theodore J., 2:21
Lowrie, Robert H., 2:201, 2:251
Lowth, Robert, 1:429
Luard, Evan, 2:238
Lubetkin, Wendy, 2:240
Lucas, James, 2:340, 2:384
Lucas, John, 2:446
Luchetti, Cathy, 2:201
Luciano, Dorothy S., 2:451
Luckiesh, M., 1:515
Ludlum, David M., 2:485
Ludwig, Arnold M., 2:555
Ludwig, Emil, 2:376
Luehrmann, Arthur, 1:557
Lukas, J. Anthony, 2:238
Lukes, Bonnie L., 2:550
Lund, Henning (ed), 2:508
Lundberg, Ferdinand, 2:218
Lundell, Allan, 1:554
Lundquist, James, 1:217, 1:256, 1:257, 1:283, 1:296
Lundstrom, David E., 1:538
Lunt, Paul S., 2:51, 2:144
Lunt, Steven D., 2:58
Lupoff, Richard A., 1:208
Lupson, Peter, 1:326

Lupton, Kenneth, 2:368
LURNIX, 1:562
Lutgens, Frederick K., 2:489
Luther, Martin, 2:317
Luttbeg, Norman R., 2:39
Lutz, Alma, 2:185, 2:207
Lutz, William, 1:437, 1:440
Lydolph, Paul E., 2:80
Lye, Keith, 2:83, 2:85, 2:88, 2:90, 2:91, 2:275, 2:393, 2:405, 2:489
Lyell, Charles, 2:490
Lyman, Elizabeth, 2:226
Lynch, Dudley, 2:246
Lynch, Gerald, 1:141
Lynch, John, 2:369
Lynch, Kevin, 2:94
Lynd, Helen Merrell, 2:131–32
Lynd, Robert Staughton, 2:131–32
Lyons, David, 2:8
Lyons, John, 1:435
Lyons, Malcolm C., 2:301
Lyons, Thomas T. (ed), 2:21
Lyttle, Clifford, 2:135
Lyttle, Richard B., 1:568; 2:375, 2:421, 2:496
Lyttleton, Adrian, 2:375

M

Maalouf, Amin, 2:306
Mabbutt, J. A., 2:83
Mabery, D. L., 1:470
McAfee, J., 1:554
McAlester, A. Lee, 2:489
Macaulay, David, 2:280, 2:291, 2:306
Macaulay, Neill, 2:369
McAuley, Karen, 2:413
Mcbane, Robert C., 2:500, 2:504
McBurney, Donald H., 2:113
McCabe, John, 2:224
McCabe, Joseph, 1:120
McCaig, M., 2:522
McCall, Samuel W., 2:15
McCarthy, David J., Jr, 2:41
McClelland, D. C., 2:113
McClenahan, Carolyn, 2:538
McClintock, Jack, 2:76
McCloskey, Herbert, 2:12
McClure, Rhyder, 1:573
McConnaughey, Bayard H., 2:465
McConnell, Anita, 2:486, 2:489
McConnell, Campbell R., 2:56
McConnell, John, 2:56
McCord, A., 2:278
McCorduck, Pamela, 1:581, 1:582
McCormick, John, 2:82, 2:255
McCormick, Mona, 1:490
McCormick, Richard L., 2:218

McCoy, Donald R., 2:228, 2:237
McCoy, Kathy, 2:107
McCrum, Robert, 1:429
McCuen, Gary E., 2:82
McCuen, Gary E. (ed), 2:85, 2:89, 2:412, 2:531
McCullough, David, 2:218
McCurdy, David W., 2:43
McDaniel, W. D., 1:580
McDavid, Raven I., Jr., 1:432
MacDonald, David W., 2:449
Macdonald, Fiona, 2:324
McDonald, Forrest, 2:166
MacDonald, Frank, 1:454
MacDonald, George, 2:251
MacDonald, Hugh, 2:347
MacDonald, J. Fred, 1:465
MacDonald, Patricia, 2:422
MacDonald, William L., 2:291
McDonough, Tom, 1:470
McDougall, Derek, 2:10
McDougall William, 2:104
McDowell, Bart, 2:164
McDowell, Margaret B., 1:183
Mace, A. C., 2:279
Mace, Paul, 1:575
MacEachern, Diane, 2:82
McElroy, Richard L., 2:195
McElvaine, Robert S. (ed), 2:229
McEvedy, Colin, 2:88, 2:275, 2:278, 2:306
MacEwan, Arthur (ed), 2:57
McEwan, P. J. (ed), 2:363, 2:393
McFarland, Dorothy T., 1:209, 1:271
McFarland, Rhoda, 2:536
MacFarlane, Gwyn, 2:559
McFarlane, Ruth B., 2:447
McFreely, William S., 2:198, 2:200
McGilvery, Robert W., 2:511
McGinniss, Joe, 1:442; 2:40, 2:254
McGlinchee, Claire, 1:161
McGovern, Edythe M., 1:287
McGovern, George Stanley, 2:251
McGowen, Tom, 2:242, 2:509, 2:562
McGrath, Alice, 2:567
McGrath, Patrick, 2:176
McGrath, Susan, 2:512
McGraw, Thomas K., 2:65
McGraw-Hill Editors, 2:512
McGrew, P. C., 1:580
McGuire, Francis A., 1:555
McGuire, Meredith B., 2:142
McGuire, Paula, 2:539, 2:543
McGuirk, Carol, 2:343
Machiavelli, Niccolo, 2:20
Machin, Colin, 1:558
McHugh, Thomas K., 2:485
McHughes, Janet, 1:449
McInnis, Raymond G., 2:95
McIntire, H. G., 1:328

McIntosh, Jane, 2:278
Mack, Donald W., 2:379
Mack, Maynard, 1:28
Mack, Sara, 1:321; 2:291
Mack Smith, Denis. *See* Smith, Denis Mack
Mackail, Denis G., 1:68
McKay, Claude, 1:260
McKay, David, 2:405
McKay, David W., 2:481
MacKay, Ernest J., 2:282
McKay, Ian A., 2:92
McKeever, Porter, 2:238
McKendrick, Melveena, 2:275
MacKendrick, Paul, 2:285, 2:291, 2:300
McKenna, George, 2:125, 2:137, 2:144
McKenna, Regis, 1:540
MacKenzie, Charles S., 1:533
MacKenzie, Louis A., Jr., 1:533
Mackenzie, Norman H., 1:53
McKeown, Kate, 1:540
McKeown, Kieran, 2:72
McKhann, Charles F., 2:562
McKie, Robin, 2:516
McKillop, Beth, 2:282
Mackinder, Halford John, Sir, 2:79
McKinley, Joe, 1:566
McKinnell, Robert G., 2:451, 2:455
MacKinnon, L., 2:513
Mackintosh, N. J., 2:462
McKissack, Patricia C., 1:176; 2:229
McKnight, Gerald, 2:535
McKnight, Tom L., 2:93
Mack-Smith, Denis, 2:344
McKusick, Leon (ed), 2:560
McLaughlin, J. Richard, 1:576
McLanathan, Richard, 2:316
McLean, Albert F., Jr., 1:156
McLean, Hugh, 1:12
MacLeish, Archibald, 1:261
McLellan, Elizabeth, 2:285
McLellan, Tom, 2:537
McLuhan, Eric, 2:130
McLuhan, Marshall, 1:453–54; 2:130
McMahon, James A., 2:465
McMullen, Roy, 2:316, 2:352
McMullin, Ernan, 2:513
McMullin, Ernan (ed), 2:473
McNaugaher, Thomas L., 2:258
Macnaughton, William R., 1:293
MacNeice, Louis, 1:105
MacNeil, Robert, 1:429, 1:443, 1:458
McNerney, Kathleen, 1:404
McNulty, Paul J., 2:70
MacPherson, C. B., 2:9
McPherson, James M., 2:193
MacPherson, Myra, 2:242
McPhillips, Martin (ed), 2:485
McQuaid, Gary, 1:501, 1:555

MacRae, Donald S., 2:143
McReynolds, Ginny, 2:155
Macrorie, Ken, 1:477, 1:483
McTavish, Douglas, 2:516
McWilliams, Peter A., 1:571
Mad Magazine Staff, 1:455
Madaras, Area, 2:542
Madaras, Lynda, 2:542, 2:560
Madariaga, Salvador de, 2:408
Madden, James F., 2:92
Maddi, Salvatore R., 2:116
Maddow, Ben, 2:262
Madge, John H., 2:125
Madison, Arnold, 2:162
Madison, James, 2:177
Madsen, Axel, 2:488
Maehr, Martin L., 2:112
Magdaleno, Mauricio, 2:371
Maggio, Rosalie, 1:479
Magnuson, Norris, 2:207
Magoffin, Susan, 2:185
Magruder, Jeb, 2:252
Maguire, Robert A., 1:393
Mahapatra, Sitalant (ed), 1:422
Mahfuz, Nagib, 1:420
Mahler, Gustav, 2:355
Mahler, Paul, 1:572
Mahon, Gigi, 1:455
Mahoney, Dennis J., 2:166
Mahoney, Ellen Voelckers, 2:542
Mahoney, Michael S., 1:508
Mahoney, Olivia, 2:198
Mails, Thomas E., 2:201
Maimonides, Moses, 2:303
Main, Jackson T., 2:166
Mains, Karen B., 2:539
Makower, Joel, 2:92
Malamud, Bernard, 1:262
Malbin, Michael, 2:33
Malcolm, Andrew H., 2:90
Male, Emile, 2:306
Malek, Jaromir, 2:279
Malin, Irving, 1:301
Malinowski, Bronislaw, 2:46
Malinowsky, H. Robert, 2:560
Mallett, Philip, 1:55
Malory, Sir Thomas, 1:7
Malthus, Thomas Robert, 2:69
Maltin, Leonard, 1:470
Maltin, Leonard (ed), 1:468
Manach, Jorge, 2:371
Manchester, William, 2:248, 2:386
Man-ch'ing, Cheng, 2:284
Mancini, Pat M. (ed), 1:399
Mandel, Ernest, 2:382
Mandela, Nelson, 2:395
Mandela, Winnie, 2:395
Mandelbaum, Michael, 2:36, 2:260
Mandelbrot, Benoit B., 1:516
Mandell, 1:565

Mandell, Steven L., 1:557
Mander, Jerry, 1:465
Mandrou, Robert, 2:516
Mangan, John J., 2:315
Mango, Cyril, 2:301
Mann, Horace, 2:186
Mann, Mary, 2:187
Mann, Nicholas, 1:351
Mann, Peggy, 2:384
Mann, Stanley, 2:112
Mann, Thomas, 1:370
Manoff, Robert, 1:457
Mansfield, Katherine, 1:142
Mantoux, Paul, 2:339
Mao Zedong, 2:402
Mara, Mary J., 1:559
Marazan, Julio, 1:399
Marc, David, 1:465
March, James G., 2:140
March, Susan, 2:92
Marchand, Leslie, 1:33
Marchand, Roland, 1:440
Marckwardt, Albert H., 1:435
Marcus, Steven, 1:47; 2:118
Maren, Michael, 2:85, 2:393
Margolies, Luise, 2:299
Margossian, Marzbed (ed), 1:420
Margulis, Lynn, 2:441, 2:456
Marius, Richard, 1:14
Mark, Lisbeth (ed), 1:481
Markey, T. L., 1:362
Markham, Louis, 2:222
Marks, A., 2:291
Marks, Barry A., 1:214
Marks, Lawrence E., 2:113
Marks, Robert W., 1:522
Marks, Sema, 1:570
Markson, Elizabeth W., 2:129, 2:146
Marlin, Emily, 2:555
Marlin, John Tepper, 2:85, 2:94, 2:155,
    2:275
Marling, William, 1:210
Marlowe, Christopher, 1:12
Marples, David R., 2:82
Marrin, Albert, 2:169, 2:376, 2:380, 2:403
Marriott, F. H. (ed), 1:529
Marriott, McKim (ed), 2:131
Marrow, Alfred J., 2:99
Marryat, Captain Frederick, 1:56
Marsack, Robyn, 1:105
Marschall, Laurence A., 2:479
Marschall, Rick, 1:459
Marsh, Earle, 1:464
Marshall, Alfred, 2:57
Marshall, Dorothy, 2:369
Marshall, George Catlett, 2:240
Marshall, George R., 1:558, 1:575
Marshall, John, 2:30
Marshall, Michael, 2:304
Marshall, Roy, 2:70

Marshall, Roy K., 2:470
Marshall, S. L., 2:169, 2:201, 2:238, 2:371
Marshall, Brigadier General S.L.A., 2:224
Marston, Frank S., 2:224
Marten, Michael, 2:470
Martí, José, 2:370
Martin, Christopher, 1:129
Martin, David L., 2:41
Martin, Donald L., 2:70
Martin, E. A., 2:437
Martin, Fenton S., 2:21, 2:33
Martin, Geoffrey J., 2:77
Martin, George, 2:361
Martin, George W., 2:262
Martin, James, 1:538, 1:554, 1:558, 1:559,
    1:560, 1:563, 1:580, 1:585
Martin, Jo, 2:539
Martin, Joseph C., 2:555
Martin, Michael R., 2:275
Martin, Paul D., 2:432
Martin, Paul S., 2:158
Martin, Ralph G., 2:413
Martin, Rhona, 1:490
Martin, S. J., 2:443
Martin, Teri, 2:160
Martinez, Al (ed), 2:136
Martis, Kenneth C., 2:6
Martynov, Ivan I., 2:424
Marushkin, 1:573
Marvell, Andrew, 1:13
Marvin, Francis S., 2:126
Marx, Groucho, 1:470
Marx, Karl, 2:59
Mascaro, Juan (tr), 1:422
Maslow, Abraham H., 2:97, 2:114
Mason, Alpheus T., 2:223
Mason, Bobbie Ann, 1:263
Mason, H. A. (ed), 1:18
Mason, John, 2:476
Massie, Robert, 2:563
Massie, Suzanne, 2:563
Masson, Jeffrey Moussaieff, 2:118
Mast, Gerald, 1:469
Masters, Edgar Lee, 1:263
Masterson, John, 1:445
Masterson, Richard, 1:578
Masuda, Yoneji, 1:555
Matas, Julio (tr), 1:399
Math, Irwin, 2:522
Mathabane, Mark, 2:85, 2:393
Mathias, Marilynne, 2:518
Mathieson, John A., 2:258
Matlin, Margaret, 2:103, 2:113
Matsubara, T., 2:506
Matthew, H. C., 2:346
Matthews, Carole Boggs, 1:573
Matthews, Christopher, 2:19
Matthews, James, 1:109
Matthews, John, 2:290

Matthews, Judy G., 1:578
Matthews, Martin S., 1:576
Matthews, R. E. (ed), 2:441
Matthews, Rupert O., 2:90
Matthias, John, 1:374
Matthiessen, Francis Otto, 1:180, 1:217
Mattingly, Garrett, 2:310, 2:326
Mattoon, Mary-Ann, 2:121
Mattson, Mark T., 2:92
Matusow, Barbara, 2:458
Maugham, (William) Somerset,
    1:106
Maulitz, Russell C., 2:537
Maung A. Htin, 1:426
Maupassant, Guy de, 1:337–38
Maurois, André, 2:559
Mauss, Marcel, 2:47
Max, M. (ed), 2:540
Maxwell, James Clerk, 2:498, 2:518,
    2:527
Maxwell, John, 2:97
May, Elizabeth (ed), 2:262
May, Ernest, 2:218
May, Florence, 2:348
May, Henry F., 2:218
May, Keith, 1:378
May, Lola, 1:535
Mayer, Charles W., 2:71
Mayer, Gloria G., 2:566
Mayer, Jean, 2:550
Mayer, Thomas R., 2:566
Maynarde, Thomas, 2:158
Mayne, Richard (ed), 2:405
Mayr, Ernst, 2:456
Mazria, Edward, 2:485
Mazrui, Ali A., 2:393
Mazurkiewicz, A. (ed), 1:581
Mazuzan, George T., 2:231
Mazzenga, Isabel Burk, 2:539
Mazzeo, Joseph A., 1:464
Mead, George Herbert, 2:139
Mead, Margaret, 2:44, 2:46
Mead, Sidney E., 2:142
Meade, Marion, 1:275
Meadows, Jack, 2:433
Meagher, Robert, 1:315
Means, Barbara, 2:103
Mears, Walter R., 1:457
Medawar, J. S., 2:437
Medawar, Peter, 2:433, 2:437
Medland, William J., 2:388
Medoff, James L., 2:70
Medvedev, Roy A., 2:15, 2:392
Mee, Charles L., Jr., 2:167, 2:238
Meehan, Patrick J. (ed), 2:270
Meer, Fatima, 2:395
Meer, Jeff, 2:553
Meeuse, B. J. D., 2:452
Meier, August (ed), 2:153

Meier, Matt S., 2:155
Meinig, D. W., 2:90
Meinig, D. W. (ed), 2:93
Meir, Golda, 2:413
Melby, Christopher L., 2:551
Mele, Jim, 1:194
Melhem, D. H., 1:205
Mellers, Wilfrid, 2:155
Mellor, Anne K., 1:37
Mellow, James R., 1:178
Meltzer, Milton, 1:182; 2:14, 2:70, 2:133,
    2:155, 2:164, 2:179, 2:229, 2:232, 2:244,
    2:275, 2:526, 2:545
Melville, Arabella, 2:553
Melville, Herman, 1:162–63
Melville, Keith, 2:138
Mencken, H. L., 1:436
Mendal, Geoff O., 1:565
Mendel, Arthur, 2:334
Mendel, Gregor Johann, 2:453
Mendeleev, Dimitri Ivanovich, 2:507
Menshikov, Stanislav, 2:274
Menzel, Donald H., 2:470
Meredith, Martin, 2:85, 2:393
Meredith, Robert C., 1:490
Meredith, Roy, 2:193
Mergener, Robert J., 1:524
Meritt, H. D., 1:429
Meriwether, Louise, 2:238
Merk, Frederick, 2:185, 2:218
Merk, Lois B., 2:185, 2:218
Merril, Thomas F., 1:225
Merrill, John, 1:458
Merrill, Robert, 1:234
Merriman, Nick, 2:278
Merton, Robert, 2:98
Merton, Robert E., 2:144
Merton, Robert K., 2:145
Merton, Robert K. (ed), 2:129, 2:141
Merzbach, Uta C. (ed), 1:532
Metford, J. C., 2:369
Metos, Thomas H., 2:436, 2:557
Metropolis, N., 1:559
Metropolis, N. (ed), 1:540
Metternich, Prince Klemens von, 2:333
Metz, William, 1:487
Metzger, Larry, 2:198
Meyer, Herbert E., 1:477
Meyer, Jill M., 1:477
Meyer, Michael, 1:378
Meyer, Samuel (ed), 1:503
Meyers, Jeffrey, 1:142
Meyerson, A. Lee, 2:486
Michalopoulos, Andre, 1:316
Michel, Stephen L., 1:580
Michelangelo, 2:318
Michelini, Ann Noris, 1:315
Michener, James, 1:264
Middlemiss, Ross G., 1:514

Middleton, Alex L. (ed), 2:450
Middleton, Harry, 2:246
Miers, Earl S., 2:200
Mihailovich, Vasa D., 1:383
Mikami, Y., 1:497
Mikasinovich, Branko, 1:383
Mikhail, E. H., 1:68
Miklosko, J., 1:559
Milavsky, J. Ronald, 2:98, 2:130
Milford, Nancy, 1:223
Milgate, Jane, 1:36
Milgram, Stanley, 2:98, 2:104
Milgrom, Harry, 1:512
Milheim, William (ed), 1:570
Mill, James W., 2:537
Mill, John Stuart, 2:72
Millar, Fergus, 2:291
Millard, A., 2:278, 2:284, 2:285
Millay, Edna St. Vincent, 1:265
Miller, Arthur, 1:266
Miller, Casey, 1:479
Miller, Christina G., 2:488, 2:570
Miller, Chuck (ed), 1:249
Miller, David L., 2:140
Miller, David M., 1:14
Miller, Douglas T., 2:190
Miller, E. Willard, 2:93
Miller, G. Tyler, Jr, 2:465
Miller, Gabriel, 1:273
Miller, J. Hillis, 1:47
Miller, James, 2:11
Miller, John, 2:326, 2:327
Miller, John C., 2:164
Miller, Jonathan, 2:452, 2:456, 2:545
Miller, Mark Crispin, 1:465
Miller, Mary Ellen, 2:300
Miller, Merle, 2:237, 2:246
Miller, Neal E., 2:112
Miller, P. L., 1:583
Miller, Perry, 1:154
Miller, Perry (ed), 2:162
Miller, Philip, 1:470
Miller, Richard K. (ed), 1:555
Miller, Roger Leroy, 2:65
Miller, Ron, 2:476
Miller, Russell, 2:494
Miller, Stuart, 1:440
Millgate, Michael, 1:52
Millichap, Joseph R., 2:188
Millington, T. Alaric, 1:497
Millington, William, 1:497
Mills, C. Wright, 2:145
Mills, Dorothy, 2:306
Mills, Judie, 2:248
Mills, Theodore M., 2:104
Millward, C. M., 1:429
Milne, Hammish, 2:416
Milne, Lorus, 2:462, 2:466, 2:496, 2:509
Milne, Margery, 2:462, 2:466, 2:496, 2:509

Milner, Gulland R., 2:275
Milosz, Czeslaw, 1:386
Milton, John, 1:14
Milunsky, Aubrey, 2:543
Minc, Alain, 1:555
Mincberg, Mella, 1:576
Minear, Richard H., 2:399
Minelli, Giuseppe, 2:449
Minium, Edward W., 2:122
Minkin, Jacob, 2:303
Minsky, Marvin, 1:581, 1:582, 1:583
Minteer, Catherine, 1:437
Mintz, Barbara, 2:280
Mintz, Sidney (ed), 2:408
Minzhu, Han (ed), 2:16
Miquel, Pierre, 2:280, 2:291, 2:306, 2:320,
   2:326, 2:329, 2:371
Mirali, Robert, 1:457
Mischel, Florence, 1:487
Mishkoff, Henry C., 1:581
Misra, Jayadev, 1:559
Mistral, Gabriela, 1:405
MIT Staff, 1:538
Mitchell, Donald, 2:355
Mitchell, Donald (ed), 2:417
Mitchell, Joan P., 1:576
Mitchell, Malcolm, 1:440
Mitchell, P. M. (ed), 1:374
Mitchell, Robert D. (ed), 2:90
Mitchell, Steve, 1:431
Mitchinson, Naomi, 1:107
Mitchum, Hank, 2:201
Mitford, Jessica, 2:133
Mitroff, Ian, 1:465
Mobley, Lou, 1:540
Moche, Dinal L., 2:470
Mockler, R., 1:557
Modell, Judith, 2:44
Modigliani, Franco, 2:72
Moe, Jørgen, 1:374
Moen, Daryl, 1:457
Moffat, D. B., 2:451
Moffett, James, 1:480
Mogen, David, 1:203
Mohammed, Ovey N., 2:302
Moholy, Noel, 2:160
Mohr, Howard, 1:431
Mohr, Lillian H., 2:24
Mohr, Nicholasa, 1:267
Moise, Edwin E., 1:512
Molière, 1:338–39
Mollenhoff, Clark R., 1:538
Molyneux, John, 2:382
Momeni, Jamshid A. (ed), 2:145
Monaco, James, 1:469
Monastyrsky, Michael, 1:516
Monegal, Emir Rodriguez (ed), 1:399
Moner, John G., 2:438
Monnig, Judith, 2:565

Monroe, James, 2:178
Monsell, Helen A., 2:30
Montagna, William, 2:451, 2:545
Montagnier, Luc, 2:560
Montagu, Ashley, 2:98, 2:100
Montague, Marjorie, 1:570
Montaner, Carlos A., 2:410
Monte, Christopher F., 2:114
Montesquieu, Charles Louis de Secondat,
   Baron de la Brède et de, 2:19
Montgomery, Elizabeth R., 2:390
Montgomery, L. M., 1:143–44
Montgomery, Michael, 1:478
Moody, Kate, 1:465
Moon, Robert O., 2:533
Mooney, James, 1:562
Moore, Marianne, 1:268
Moore, Patrick, 2:470, 2:476
Moore, Ruth E., 2:439, 2:440, 2:446, 2:453;
   4:454, 4:455
Moore, Wilbert E. (ed), 2:125, 2:144
Moorman, Charles, 1:8
Moote, A. Lloyd, 2:327
Morain, Mary (ed), 1:437
Moran, Gary T., 2:551
Moravec, Hans, 1:584
Moravia, Alberto, 1:350
More, Sir Thomas, 1:14
Morecki, A. (ed), 2:513
Morehead, Joe, 2:6
Moreux, Serge, 2:416
Morgan, Cynthia, 2:556
Morgan, Edmund S., 2:175
Morgan, Ernest, 2:537
Morgan, Janet, 1:74
Morgan, Kenneth O., 2:374
Morgan, Kenneth O. (ed), 2:275
Morgan, R. P., 2:493
Morgan, Ted, 1:106; 2:234
Morgan, Thomas Hunt, 2:454
Morgan-Watts, Max, 2:557
Morgenthau, Hans J., 2:37
Morison, Samuel Eliot, 2:155, 2:158, 2:160,
   2:164, 2:320
Morison, Samuel Eliot (ed), 2:164
Morley, John M., 2:346
Morley, Sylvanus G., 2:300
Morner, Magnus, 2:88, 2:409
Morra, Marion, 2:545
Morrice, Polly, 2:160
Morris, Aldon D., 2:242
Morris, Arthur, 2:88, 2:409
Morris, Charles, 2:494
Morris, Desmond, 2:107
Morris, Ivan, 1:425
Morris, John E., 2:161
Morris, Margie, 2:280
Morris, Mary, 1:433
Morris, Mary (ed), 1:435

Morris, Richard B., 2:17, 2:167
Morris, Warren B., 2:375
Morris, William, 1:433
Morris, William (ed), 1:435
Morrison, Blake, 1:93
Morrison, Donald (ed), 2:407
Morrison, Hugh, 2:155
Morrison, Philip, 2:434
Morrison, Phylis, 2:434
Morrison, Toni, 1:269
Morrissey, Mike, 2:408
Morrow, James R., Jr., 1:569
Morsberger, Robert E., 1:291
Moryadas, S., 2:84
Moscovici, Serge, 2:104
Moser, Diane, 2:482
Moses, L. G. (ed), 2:155
Mosher, Michael, 1:112
Moskin, Marietta D., 2:476
Mosley, Ann, 1:379
Mosley, Leonard, 1:470
Moss, Alfred, 2:153
Moss, Howard A., 2:536, 2:540
Moss, Stephen J., 2:552
Mosse, George L., 2:340, 2:375
Mott, Donald R., 1:470, 1:473
Moulton, Peter, 1:563
Mount, Ellis, 2:433
Mountjoy, Alan, 2:86
Moursand, Dave, 1:555, 1:570
Mowat, Farley, 1:144–45
Mowery, David C. (ed), 2:140
Mowry, George E. (ed), 2:226
Moyers, Bill, 1:466; 2:52, 2:167
Moynihan, Daniel P., 2:136
Mucciolo, Gary, 2:542
Muchmore, Lynn R. (ed), 2:40
Mueller, Ian, 1:514
Muir, John, 2:221
Muirden, James, 2:436, 2:470
Mukres, James, 1:516
Mulder, John M., 2:225
Mulherin, Jennifer, 1:16
Mulherin, Jenny, 2:83
Muller, Hans W., 2:280
Muller, Hermann Joseph, 2:455
Muller, Peter O., 2:93
Muller, Robert A., 2:93
Mulligan, William (ed), 1:433
Mullineaux, A. W., 2:57
Mullins, Lisa C., 2:162
Mullish, Henry, 1:564
Mulvey, J. H. (ed), 2:498, 2:518
Mumford, Lewis, 2:94, 2:147, 2:207
Mumpower, J. (ed), 1:584
Mundy, 2:275
Munich, Adrienne, 1:44
Munro, Alice, 1:145
Munson-Williams-Proctor Institute, 2:415

Murasaki, Shikibu, 1:425
Murdin, Leslie, 2:479
Murdin, Paul, 2:479
Murdocca, Miles J., 1:559
Murdoch, Dame Iris, 1:107–108
Murdock, George Peter, 2:51, 2:300
Murphy, Daniel, 1:483
Murphy, E. Jefferson, 2:275, 2:300
Murphy, Kevin J., 2:539
Murphy, Kevin R., 2:122
Murphy, Paul C., 2:155
Murphy, Paul L., 2:12
Murphy, Walter F., 2:17
Murphy, Walter F. (ed), 2:6
Murphy, Wendy B., 2:270
Murray, Bruce C., 2:242
Murray, Charles, 2:242
Murray, Don, 1:482
Murray, Gene, 1:28
Murray, George R., 1:400
Murray, H. J., 1:535
Murray, Jocelyn (ed), 2:86, 2:275
Murray, Lindley, 1:429
Murray, Robert K., 2:226
Murray, William H., III, 1:562
Murrell, John N., 2:505, 2:507
Murrow, Edward R., 1:467
Musa, Mark, 1:347
Musgrave, Peggy, 2:71
Musgrave, Richard, 2:71
Mussen, Paul (ed), 2:95, 2:103, 2:107, 2:114
Musso, Louis, 1:462
Musto, Frederick W., 2:6, 2:41
Myers, Arthur, 2:537
Myers, Bernard S., 2:155
Myers, Doris T., 1:434
Myers, Elisabeth P., 2:190
Myers, Gerald E., 2:97
Myers, Irma, 2:537
Myers, Jeffrey, 1:112
Myers, Rollo H., 2:423
Myers, Walter Dean, 1:270
Myrdal, Gunnar, 2:87, 2:135, 2:399

N

Nabokov, Peter (ed), 2:155
Nabokov, Vladimir, 1:393
Nader, Ralph, 2:61, 2:252
Nafziger, George F., 2:331
Nagera, Humberto, 2:360
Naimen, Arthur, 1:559
Naipaul, V. S., 1:406
Naisbitt, John, 2:51, 2:255
Nameroff, Steven, 1:565
Nance, Guinevera, 1:96
Nanes, Allan, 2:255

Napier, John R., 2:449, 2:450
Napier, P. H., 2:450
Napoli, Maryann, 2:566
Nasatir, Abraham P., 2:272
Nash, Constance, 1:485
Nash, David T., 2:566
Nash, Dennison, 2:42
Nash, Gary B., 2:162
Nash, George H., 2:231
Nash, June (ed), 2:409
Nast, Thomas, 1:460
Nathan, Rhoda B., 1:142
Nathan, Ronald G., 2:536
National Geographic Society Staff, 2:193
National Research Council, 2:540
Nations, James D., 2:467
Natoli, Salvatore J. (ed), 2:76
Natow, Annette B., 2:550
Navarro, Peter, 2:40
Navazelskis, Ina, 2:389
Naylor, Chris, 1:584
Neal, H. K., 2:563
Neaman, Judith, 1:437
Nebenzahl, Kenneth, 2:158
Nechas, Jim, 2:531
Needell, Allan A. (ed), 2:481
Needleman, Raphael, 1:559
Nehru, Jawaharlal, 2:403
Neidle, Cecyle S., 2:207
Neill, George W., 1:570
Neill, Shirley B., 1:570
Neilsen, Jacob, 1:580
Nelkin, Dorothy, 2:149
Nelson, Helge, 2:160
Nelson, Joseph S., 2:450
Nelson, Robert A., 2:436
Nelson, Stephen L., 1:572, 1:573
Nelson, Theodor, 1:555
Neruda, Pablo, 1:407
Nesteby, James, 1:475
Nettl, Bruno, 2:262
Neu, Charles E., 2:235
Neubauer, Alfred, 2:504
Neurath, Hans, 2:511
Nevin, David, 2:185
Nevins, Allan, 2:155, 2:204
Nevison, Jack M., 1:573
New American Library editors, 1:487
Newcomb, Horace, 1:465
Newhall, Beaumont, 2:262, 2:275
Newhouse, John, 2:252
Newin, D., 2:193
New Jersey State Museum Staff, 1:475
Newman, Edwin, 1:443
Newman, James R., 1:497, 1:498
Newman, Judie, 1:414
Newman, Rochelle, 1:515
Newman, Roger, 1:468
Newman, Susan, 2:554, 2:555

Newman, William M., 2:142
Newmarch, Rosa H., 2:357
Newson, Michael, 1:490
Newton, David E., 2:433, 2:481
Newton, Isaac, 1:523
New York Times, 1:440
Ngugi Wa Thiong'o, 1:415
Nice, David C., 2:35
Nicholls, Peter, 2:438
Nichols, Roger (ed), 2:423
Nicholson, Alasdair, 2:238
Nicholson, Reynold A., 1:420
Nickerson, Raymond, 1:570
Nicolson, Harold, 2:332
Nicolson, Marjorie, 1:14
Niecks, Frederick, 2:350
Nielsen, Hans F., 1:362
Nielsen, Kaj L., 1:524
Nielson, Lawrence, 2:507
Nieman, David C., 2:550, 2:551
Niemi, Richard G., 2:6
Niering, William A., 2:466
Niesen, Thomas, 2:488
Niethammer, Carolyn, 2:155
Nightingale, Florence, 2:570
Nilsen, Alleen Pace, 1:248
Nilsson, Lennart, 2:545
Nimmo, Dan, 1:458
Nisbet, Robert, 2:384
Nisbet, Robert A., 2:127, 2:131
Nisbett, Alec, 2:464
Nixon, Richard Milhous, 2:254
Njoku, Benedict C., 1:412
Nkrumah, Kwame, 2:396
Noake, Roger, 1:474
Noer, Richard, 2:512
Noether, Emmy, 1:509
Nora, Simon, 1:555
Norbeck, Edward, 2:52
Nordby, Vernon J., 2:95
Nordham, George W., 2:180
Nordhaus, William D., 2:56
Norman, Barry, 1:469
Norris, Cathleen A., 1:564, 1:570
Norris, Christopher, 2:424
Norris, Frank, 1:180; 2:218
Norris, Jerrie, 1:229
North Carolina School of Science, 1:498
North, Douglas C., 2:65, 2:69, 2:185
North, John (ed), 2:272
Northcutt, B., 1:564
Northedge, F. S., 2:224
Northington, David K., 2:447
Northrup, Terry, 1:570
Norton, Mary B., 2:152
Norton, Peter, 1:560, 1:562, 1:564
Norusis, Marija J., 1:574
Nourie, Alan (ed), 1:455
Nourie, Barbara (ed), 1:455

Nourse, Alan E., 2:443, 2:451, 2:476, 2:543, 2:545, 2:559, 2:560
Novak, Michael, 2:69, 2:258
Novick, Nelson Lee, 2:552
Novick, Sheldon, 2:29
Noy, Dov, 2:276
Noyes, Russell, 1:39
NREL Staff, 1:441
Nugent, Jeffrey B. (ed), 2:89, 2:412
Null, Gary, 2:550
Numbers, Ronald L., 2:567
Nurminen, Marku, 1:555
Nutt, Mac, 2:161
Nuttin, Joseph R., et al, 2:113
Nye, Frank T., Jr, 2:231
Nye, Robert (tr), 1:6
Nyerere, Julius, 2:397
Nyrop, Richard F., 2:87, 2:88, 2:89
Myrop, Richard F. (ed), 2:88

O

Oakes, Philip (ed), 1:469
Oakey, Virginia, 1:465, 1:485
Oakley, Ann, 2:148
Oakley, Brian, 1:555
Oates, Joan, 2:280
Oates, K., 2:539
Oates, Stephen, 2:189
Oates, Whitney J. (ed), 1:311
Oberg, James E., 2:481
Oberlander, Theodore M., 2:93
Oberle, William F., 1:523
Obeyesekere, Ranjini, 1:422
O'Brien, Bill, 1:573
O'Brien, David M., 2:27
O'Brien, Eoin, 2:562
O'Brien, Marion (ed), 2:106
O'Brien, Steve, 2:174
O'Casey, Sean, 1:108–109
O'Connor, Edwin, 2:40
O'Connor, Flannery, 1:270
O'Connor, Frank, 1:109
O'Connor, Karen, 2:138, 2:145, 2:481
O'Connor, Patricia W., 1:355
O'Connor, R. F., 2:511
O'Connor, Thomas H., 2:198
O'Connor, William V., 1:72
Odabasi, H., 2:500
O'Daffer, Phares G., 1:506
O'Dea, Thomas S., 2:142
O'Dell, Scott, 1:271; 2:158, 2:162, 2:164, 2:169, 2:185
Odets, Clifford, 1:272
Odijk, Pamela, 2:280
O'Donnell, Charles P., 2:87
O'Donnell, James J., 2:304
O'Donnell, Victoria, 1:440

O'Driscoll, Gerald P., Jr., 2:61
Oettinger, Anthony G., 1:570
O'Faolain, Sean, 1:110
Ogden, Charles, 1:438
Ogden, Suzanne, 2:87, 2:399
Ogilvie, Marilyn Bailey, 2:433
Ogilvie, R. M., 1:320
Ogle, Carol, 2:399
Ogle, John, 2:399
O'Grada, Cormac, 2:276
Ogul, Morris S., 2:33, 2:41
O'Hern, Elizabeth Moot, 2:433
Ohrn, Karin B., 2:232
O'Keeffe, Georgia, 2:268
Okie, Susan, 2:481
Okubo, Miné, 2:235
Olander, Joseph D., 1:75
Olander, Joseph D. (ed), 2:434
Olby, Robert C., 2:439, 2:441, 2:453
Oldknow, Adrian, 1:512
Oleksy, Walter, 2:407
Oleszek, Walter J., 2:6
Oleszek, Walter J. (ed), 2:5, 2:33
Oliver, George, 1:501
Oliver, John E., 2:483
Oliver, June, 1:515
Oliver, Roland, 2:300
Oliver, Roland (ed), 2:276, 2:363
Olnek, Jay I., 2:72
Olsen, Solvig (ed), 1:570
Olsen, Victoria, 1:175
Olshen, Barry, 1:86
Olshen, Toni A., 1:86
Olson, James S. (ed), 2:229
Olson, Mancur, 2:63
Olwell, Carol, 2:201
O'Malley, C. D., 2:548
O'Malley, Kevin, 2:562
Omari, T. Peter, 2:396
Omdahl, Lloyd, 2:41
O'Meara, Dominic J., 1:501
O'Meara, Patrick, 2:393
Omura, George, 1:578
O'Neill, Cherry Boone, 2:551
O'Neill, Eugene, 1:274
O'Neill, Eugene, Jr. (ed), 1:311
O'Neill, Judith, 2:317
O'Neill, Patrick, 1:368
O'Neill, Terry, 2:138
O'Neill, Thomas (ed), 2:83
O'Neill, William L., 2:242
Oparin, Alexander Ivanovich, 2:461
Opfell, Olga S., 2:276
Opik, H., 2:448
Opolka, H., 1:498
Oppenheimer, Bruce J., 2:33
Opper, Sylvia, 2:112
Ordway, Frederick I., III, 2:483

O'Reilly, Timothy, 1:561
Orenstein, Arbie, 2:423
Orford, Jim (ed), 2:539
Orians, Gordon H., 2:437
Orlandi, Mario, 2:531, 2:537, 2:543, 2:550, 2:551
Orlandi, Mario (ed), 2:555
Orlov, Ann (ed), 2:136
Ornstein, Robert, 2:531
O'Rourke, Timothy G., 2:41
Orren, Gary, 2:145
Orrey, Leslie, 2:262
Orth, Samuel P., 2:204
Ortiz, Alfonso, 2:157
Ortiz, Victoria, 2:12, 2:88, 2:189
Orwell, George, 1:111; 2:7
Osborn, S., 2:550
Osborne, Angela, 2:170
Osborne, Cecil G., 2:537
Osborne, Charles, 2:362
Osborne, Harold (ed), 2:262
Osborne, John, 1:112
Osborne, Milton, 2:399
Osen, Lynn M., 1:498, 1:510
O'Shea, M.V. (ed), 2:540
Osler, William, 2:534
Osman, Tony, 2:481
Ostergaard-Christensen, L., 2:535
O'Sullivan, Judith, 1:459
O'Toole, Christopher (ed), 2:449
Oumano, Ellen, 1:285
Overvold, Amy Z., 2:543
Ovid, 1:321
Owen, Denis, 2:466
Owen, Kenneth, 1:555
Owen, Wilfred, 1:113
Oxford English College Dictionary Staff, 1:441
Oye, Kenneth A., 2:37
Oz, Amos, 2:89, 2:412

P

Pace, Mildred M., 2:280, 2:281
Pachai, Bridglal, 2:367
Pachter, Marc (ed), 1:483
Pacific War Research Society Staff (ed), 2:384
Pack, Gary, 1:578
Pack, Robert, 2:260
Packard, Vance, 1:441; 2:61, 2:258
Packer, Kenneth L., 2:543
Padget, Sheila, 2:486
Padgett, Ron, 1:490
Page, Richard R., 1:574
Pagels, Heinz R. (ed), 1:555
Paine, Albert, 1:460
Paine, Thomas, 2:165

Painter, Desmond, 2:160, 2:403
Pais, Abraham, 2:498
Pakenham, Thomas, 2:363
Paley, Alan L., 2:283, 2:375, 2:380
Pallas, Norvin, 1:535
Palmer, Alan, 2:276, 2:340
Palmer, Christopher (ed), 2:417
Palmer, Gladys L. (ed), 2:148
Palmer, Jane, 1:571
Palmer, John D., 2:462
Palmer, Marlene, 1:584
Palmer, R. R., 2:330
Palmer, R. R. (ed), 2:330
Palter, Robert (ed), 2:516
Pampe, William R., 2:496
Panati, Charles, 2:570
Pande, G. C., 2:282
Pang, Rosemary K., 2:449
Pangle, Thomas L., 2:19
Panksepp, J. (ed), 2:121
Panofsky, Erwin, 2:314
Pantiel, Mindy, 1:570
Papadaki, Stamo (ed), 2:420
Papert, Seymour A., 1:570, 1:583
Papp, Joseph, 1:16
Pappas, Chris H., 1:562.
Pardee, Arthur B., 2:562
Pardes, Herbert, 2:531
Parish, Peter J., 2:189
Park, Angela, 2:138
Park, Mungo, 2:368
Park, Robert E., 2:147
Parker, Donald L., 1:461
Parker, Dorothy, 1:274
Parker, Frank, 1:434
Parker, Henry S., 2:486
Parker, Roger C., 1:576
Parker, Steve, 2:545, 2:552
Parker, Sybil P. (ed), 2:433
Parker, W. H., 2:79
Parker, Yana, 1:490
Parkinson, Roger, 2:369
Parkinson, Sydney, 2:322
Parkman, Francis, 2:158, 2:161, 2:185
Parks, George B., 2:324
Parnes, Herbert S., 2:70
Parrinder, Geoffrey, 2:300
Parrinder, Geoffrey (ed), 2:276
Parrott, Fred J., 2:276
Parsaye, Kamran, et al, 1:572
Parsons, Frances T., 2:447
Parsons, Talcott, 2:47, 2:52, 2:127–28, 2:144
Pasachoff, Jay M., 2:470
Pascal, Blaise, 1:533
Pasquariello, Anthony, 1:355
Passell, Peter, 2:70

Pasternak, Boris Leonidovich, 1:393, 1:394
Pasteur, Louis, 2:445
Patai, Raphael, 2:301
Patent, Dorothy H., 2:449, 2:462
Paterson, Katherine, 1:484; 2:235
Patinkin, Mark, 2:86, 2:393
Patmore, K. A., 2:276
Paton, Alan, 1:416
Patten, Robert B., 2:94
Patterson, Dan W., 1:584
Patterson, Elizabeth C., 2:502
Patterson, Francine, 1:448
Patterson, James T., 2:7, 2:36
Patterson, Samuel C., 2:41
Patterson, Thomas E., 1:443; 2:40
Pattison, Walter T., 1:355
Pau, L. F. (ed), 1:584
Pauer, Gyuala, 2:400
Paul, M. (ed), 1:585
Paul, Oglesby, 2:563
Paul, Richard S., 1:524
Paulahorju, Samuli, 1:374
Pauli, Wolfgang, 2:501, 2:503
Pauling, Linus Carl, 2:506, 2:544
Paulos, John Allen, 1:535
Paulson, Suzanne M., 1:271
Pavlov, Ivan Petrovich, 2:100, 2:462, 2:464
Paxson, William, 1:483
Paxton, John (ed), 2:76
Payne, Joseph N., 1:505, 1:523
Payne, Robert O., 1:7
Paz, Octavio, 1:408
Peach, S., 2:285
Peacock, James L., 2:42
Peacocke, A. R., 2:511
Pearl, Bill, 2:551
The Pearl Poet, 1:8
Pearman, William A. (ed), 2:567
Pearsall, Robert B., 1:44
Pearson, Drew, 1:459
Pearson, Eileen, 2:376
Pearson, Hesketh, 1:50
Pearson, R. G. (ed), 2:508
Pease, Jane H., 2:189
Pease, William H., 2:189
Peavy, Linda S., 2:451, 2:550
Pechman, Joseph A. (ed), 2:71
Peck, Richard, 1:275–76
Peckham, Herbert D., 1:557
Pedersen, Jean, 1:519, 1:520
Pedersen, Kent, 1:520
Pedoe, Dan, 1:498, 1:515
Peet, T. Eric (tr), 1:498
Peitgen, Heinz O., 1:516
Pelham, David, 2:452
Pelissier, Michael, 1:326
Pellant, Chris, 2:492

Pelta, Kathy, 2:204
Pelto, Gretel H., 2:42
Pelto, Pertti J., 2:42
Penny, Nicholas, 2:320
Penny, Nicholas (ed), 2:339
Penrose, Roland, 2:415
Penzias, Arno, 1:555; 2:130
Peppin, 2:276
Pepys, Samuel, 1:27
Percy, Larry, 1:441
Perdue, Theda, 2:158
Perez, Alice J., 2:257
Perin, Constance, 2:94
Perkins, Edwin J., 2:162
Perkins, Frances, 2:24
Perkins, V. T., 1:469
Perkins, Whitney, 2:219
Perl, Lila, 2:162, 2:409
Perret, Jacques, 2:294
Perrin, D. D. (ed), 2:508
Perrin, Linda, 2:255
Perrin, Porter G., 1:478
Perrins, Christopher (ed), 2:450
Perrow, Charles, 2:140
Perry, Ben E. (ed), 1:313
Perry, Donald R., 2:466
Perry, Gerald J., 2:560
Perry, Greg M., 1:572
Perry, John, 1:257
Perry, Michael J., 2:20
Perry, Nicolette, 2:466
Persaud, T. V. N., 2:546, 2:548
Persico, Joseph, 1:467; 2:204
Person, Ron, 1:577
Persons, Albert C., 2:242
Peter, Laurence J., 2:140
Peterman, Michael, 1:138
Peters, Gary L., 2:93
Peters, James F., 1:562
Peters, Thomas J., 2:63
Petersen, Becky, 1:570
Petersen, H. Craig, 2:65
Petersen, William, 2:124
Peterson, Florence, 2:204
Peterson, Merril D., 2:181–183
Peterson, Richard L., 2:70
Peterson, Theodore, 1:455
Petrarch, 1:350
Petry, Ann, 2:189
Pettigrew, Thomas F., 2:136
Pevsner, Nikolaus, 2:262
Peyser, Joan, 2:265
Peyton, David, 1:573
Pfeffer, Cynthia R., 2:537
Pflaum, Rosalynd, 2:510
Phelan, Mary K., 2:164, 2:169
Phelps, Guy, 1:469
Philip, James A., 1:501
Phillips, Claude, 2:339

Phillips, E. D., 2:285
Phillips, Elizabeth, 1:268
Phillips, Gene, 1:470
Phillips, Gerald, 1:445
Phillips, K. C., 1:437
Phillips, Kevin, 2:7
Phillips, Roger, 2:492
Phy, Allene Stuart, 1:250
Piaget, Jean, 1:512; 2:111, 2:112, 2:146
Pianka, Phyllis, 1:490
Picasso, Pablo, 2:421
Pichois, Claude, 1:330
Pick, M., 2:513
Pickering, James S., 2:433
Pickett, Calder, 1:457
Pickett-Heaps, Jeremy, 2:447
Pickthal, Marmaduke, 2:301
Pickvance, Ronald, 2:360
Pidgeon, Christopher W., 1:559
Pierce, John R., 1:550
Pierce, Neal R., 2:90, 2:155
Piercy, Josephine K., 1:152
Pierre, Michel, 2:384
Pierson, Peter, 2:327
Pike, Frank, 1:489
Pike, Zebulon Montgomery, 2:169
Pilgrim, Aubrey, 1:560
Pimlott, John, 2:238
Pinchon, Edgcumb, 2:369
Pinchot, Gifford, 2:207
Pinciss, Gerald, 1:12
Pincus, Edward, 1:470
Pingree, Suzanne, 1:461, 1:465
Pinion, Frank B., 1:60
Pinter, Harold, 1:113, 1:114
Pirandello, Luigi, 1:351
Pirie, David, 1:38
Pitt, Barrie, 2:386
Pitts, Terence, 2:262
Pitzl, Gerald R. (ed), 2:76
Pivarnik, James M., 1:569
Piven, Frances F., 2:40, 2:145, 2:258
Place, Marian T., 2:494
Placksin, Sally, 2:262
Plamondon, R., 1:560
Planck, Max Karl Ernst Ludwig, 2:521
Plano, Jack C., 2:6
Plath, Sylvia, 1:277; 2:121
Platt, Charles, 1:581
Plauger, P. J., 1:563
Plautus, Titus Maccius, 1:322
Plessis, Alain, 2:340
Plessner, Donna R., 2:566
Plimpton, George (ed), 1:481
Pliny the Younger, 2:295–96
Plowden, Alice, 2:327
Plowden, Alison, 2:369
Plunka, Gene A., 1:119
Plutarch, 2:288–89

Pocs, Ollie, 2:138
Pode, J. S., 2:506
Poe, Edgar Allan, 1:164
Pogel, Nancy, 1:189, 1:470, 1:471
Poggi, Jack, 1:449
Pohl, Frederick J., 2:158, 2:325
Pohl, Frederik, 1:278–79
Pohl, Victoria, 1:515
Poincaré, Henri, 1:500
Poirier-Brode, Karen, 2:543
Poirot, James L., 1:564, 1:570
Poirters, J.A., 1:586
Polanyi, Karl (ed), 2:47
Polking, Kirk, 2:83, 2:488
Pollack, Jack Harrison, 2:32
Pollard, Arthur, 1:43
Pollard, Sidney, 2:276
Polley, Michael, 2:391
Pollock, Bruce, 2:262
Polo, Marco, 2:309
Polunin, Miriam, 2:552
Polya, G., 1:524
Pomeroy, Wardell B., 2:543
Poole, Frederick K., 2:403
Poole, Lon, 1:560
Poole, Robert M. (ed), 2:450
Pooley, Robert A., 1:435
Pope, Alexander, 1:27
Pope-Hennessey, John, 2:312, 2:320
Popescu, Julian, 2:405
Popkin, Gary, 1:565
Popyk, Marilyn K., 1:575
Porte, Joel, 1:158
Porter, Cedric L., 2:441
Porter, F., 2:295
Porter, Glenn, 2:204
Porter, Horace, 2:200
Porter, Katherine Ann, 1:279
Porter, Sylvia, 2:61
Porterfield, Kay Marie, 2:539, 2:555
Portes, Alejandro, 2:136
Posamentier, Alfred, 1:512
Possehl, Gregory L., 2:282
Possidius, 2:304
Postman, Neil, 1:454
Postman, Neil (ed), 1:443
Potok, Chaim, 1:280
Pott, Beatrice, 1:355
Pottage, J., 1:512
Potts, Eva, 2:545
Potts, Joseph C. (ed), 2:473
Pough, Frederick H., 2:492
Pound, Omar (tr), 1:420
Power, Thomas, 2:37
Powers, Bruce R., 2:130
Powers, Robert M., 2:476
Poynter, Margaret, 2:470, 2:479, 2:481, 2:486, 2:496
Pozzetta, George E., 2:218

Praft, Vernon, 1:581
Prager, Arthur, 2:384
Prager, Emily, 2:384
Prater, Donald A., 1:371
Pratt, Annis (ed), 1:104
Pratt, Julius, 2:219
Pratt, Norman T., 1:323
Preiss, Byron (ed), 2:17
Prescott, David M., 2:562
Prescott, William H., 2:323
Press, Charles, 1:459
Press, Frank, 2:489
Preston, Marilynn, 2:551
Preston-Mofham, Ken, 2:449
Preston-Mofham, Rod, 2:449
Previte-Orton, C. W. (ed), 2:276
Price, Glanville, 1:326
Price, Jack, 1:504
Price, Janet R., 2:13
Price, Jonathan, 1:563
Price, Roger, 2:332
Price, Sally (ed), 2:408
Prichard, Peter, 1:458
Pride, Janet (ed), 1:437
Priestley, J. B., 1:114
Pringle, Laurence, 2:82, 2:83, 2:255, 2:447,
    2:467, 2:493, 2:496, 2:497, 2:509
Prior, James, 2:329
Pritchard, V. S., 1:391
Prochnow, Dave, 1:562, 1:579
Proctor, William, 2:536
Proffer, Carl R. (ed), 1:389
Proffer, Ellendra (ed), 1:389
Prokofiev, Sergei, 2:422
Pronzini, Bill (ed), 1:473
Protheroe, W. M., 2:470
Prout, Christopher, 2:58
Provenzo, Eugene F., 1:576
Provost, Foster, 2:160
Prucha, Francis P., 2:201
Prudden, Bonnie, 2:552
Prue, Donald (ed), 2:555
Prueitt, Melvin L., 1:577
Prussen, Ronald W., 2:23
Pryce-Jones, David (ed), 1:127
Pryor, Elizabeth B., 2:194, 2:568
Public Citizen Health Research Group,
    2:566
Pugh, Martin, 2:374
Puig, Manuel, 1:409
Pula, James S., 2:161
Pulaski, Mary Ann Spencer, 2:112
Purcell, John, 2:235
Purves, William K., 2:437
Purvis, Ann, 2:485
Purvis, George, 2:485
Purvis, Hoyt (ed), 2:258
Pushkin, Aleksandr, 1:395
Putnam, R. J., 2:466

Pye, Lucian W., 2:87, 2:399
Pye, Mary W., 2:399
Pythagoras, 1:501

Q

Quandt, William B., 2:255
Quarles, Benjamin, 2:189
Quart, Barbara Koenig, 1:470
Que Corporation, 1:576
Queneau, Raymond, 1:478
Quigley, John M. (ed), 2:71
Quinlan, Maurice, 1:22
Quinley, Harold E., 2:136
Quinn, Edward, 2:262
Quinn, Edward (ed), 2:252
Quinn, Susa, 2:119
Quinones, Ricardo J., 1:350

R

Raat, W. Dirk (ed), 2:370
Rabin, A. I., 2:138
Rabinovitz, Rubin, 1:108
Raboff, Ernest, 2:314, 2:421
Rabushka, Alvin, 2:257
Raby, Peter, 1:63
Racine, Jean, 1:339
Racter, 1:577
Radcliffe, Anne, 1:28
Radcliffe, Michael, 2:379
Radcliffe-Brown, A. R., 2:54
Rader, Benjamin, 1:465
Radhakrishnan, S., 2:276, 2:282
Radlauer, Ruth, 2:493
Radlauer, Steven, 1:560
Raeburn, Michael (ed), 2:276
Raffel, Burton (ed), 1:259, 1:426
Ragan, John D., 2:370
Raghavan, G. N., 2:276, 2:399
Rahn, Joan Elma, 2:448
Raiffa, Howard, 2:132
Railey, Jay M., 2:510
Raina, Ashok, 2:401
Raina, Trilokinath, 1:422
Rajaraman, Dharma, 1:557
Raker, Daniel, 1:578
Ramanujan, Srinivara, 1:502
Ramboz, Ina W., 1:353
Ramm, Agatha, 2:340, 2:405
Ramraj, Victor J., 1:146
Ramsay, Cynthia, 2:91
Ramsey, Dan, 2:485
Ranahan, Demerris C., 2:531
Randall, Alex, 1:559
Randall, John A., Jr, 2:442
Randall, Peter, 1:561

Randall, Willard Sterne, 2:164
Randolph, Sallie G., 2:255
Randolph, Vance, 1:431
Rank, Hugh, 1:442, 1:477
Rankin, Chrissy, 2:452
Ranney, Austin, 1:443; 2:40
Ransford, Oliver, 2:367
Ransom, Roger L., 2:55, 2:193
Ransone, Coleman B., Jr, 2:41
Raphael, 2:320
Raphael, Bertram, 1:581
Rapson, E. J., 2:282
Raptis, Michael, 2:409
Rashkis, Harold A., 2:539
Rastrigin, L., 1:529
Rathjen, Gregory, 2:27
Ratliff, Wayne, 1:572
Rau, M., 2:404
Rausch, Friedrich, 2:95
Raval, M. H., 2:282
Ravanel, Shannon (ed), 1:490
Ravel, Maurice, 2:423
Ravitch, Diane (ed), 2:155
Rawls, James J., 2:158
Rawson, Elizabeth, 2:293
Rawson, Jessica, 2:282
Rayback, Joseph G., 2:204
Rayleigh, Strutt, 2:522
Raynak, Elton, 2:66
Raynor, Thomas P., 2:16, 2:258
Razuvaev, V., 2:370
Re, Richard N., 2:437
Read, Herbert, 1:478
Read, Peter B. (ed), 2:104
Reader, John, 2:278, 2:279, 2:460
Reader's Digest, 2:75, 2:300, 2:531
Reagan, Michael D., 2:36
Reagan, Ronald Wilson, 2:260
Real, Michael, 1:454
Record, Robert, 1:512
Red Feather Press, 1:538
Redfearn, Paul L., Jr., 2:447
Redfern, Ron, 2:91, 2:494
Redfield, Robert, 2:54, 2:370
Redman, Ben, 1:282
Redondi, Pietro, 2:473
Reed, Adolph L., Jr. 2:258
Reed, Adolph L., Jr. (ed), 2:242
Reed, Carroll, 1:431
Reed, John R., 1:129
Reed, Kit, 1:490
Reed, Marene, 1:465
Reed, T. J., 1:367
Rees, Albert, 2:65, 2:70
Rees, Anthony R., 2:438
Rees, Philip, 2:375
Reeve, F. D. (ed), 1:389
Reeves, George, 1:437
Reeves, Thomas C., 2:238

Reff, Theodore, 2:352
Regan, Richard J., 2:20
Regan, Robert (ed), 1:164
Regenstein, Lewis, 2:570
Rehnquist, William H., 2:27
Reichman, Rachel, 1:582
Reid, Constance, 1:517
Reid, James H., 1:364
Reigstad, Paul, 1:379
Reiman, Donald H., 1:38
Reinerman, Alan J., 2:333
Reinfeld, Nyles V., 2:565
Reinold, Cheryl, 1:483
Reischauer, Edwin O., 2:399
Reischauer, Edwin O. (ed), 2:399
Reisman, David, 2:57
Reiss, Ira, 2:138
Reitman, Edward, 1:515
Remarque, Erich M., 2:224, 2:371
Rembar, Charles, 2:17
Remini, Robert V., 2:180
Rempel, Gerhard, 2:377
Remy, Richard C., 2:13
Renault, Mary, 1:318
Renda, Gunsel (ed), 2:89
Renoir, Pierre A., 2:346
Rensberger, Boyce, 2:434
Renshaw, Betty, 1:477
Renyi, Alfred, 1:533
Rescher, Nicholas S. (ed), 1:527
Research and Education Association Staff, 1:506, 1:512, 1:516, 1:524, 1:538, 1:586
Resnick, Abraham, 2:379, 2:384, 2:405
Ressler, Sandy, 1:562
Retzlaff, R., 1:575
Rewald, John, 2:346, 2:349
Rex, John, 2:128
Rexroth, Kenneth, 1:425
Rexroth, Kenneth (tr), 1:423
Reynolds, 2:528
Reynolds, David, 2:235
Reynolds, Graham, 2:351, 2:358
Reynolds, Sir Joshua, 2:338
Reynolds, Lloyd G., 2:70
Reynolds, Peter J., 2:279
Rhein, Phillip H., 1:333
Rhodes, Frank H. T., 2:489
Rhoodie, Eschel M., 2:276
Riasanovsky, Nicholas V., 2:276, 2:327
Ribaroff, Margaret Flesher, 2:89, 2:409
Ricardo, David, 2:73
Ricardo, Ilona, 1:344
Rice, Edward E., 2:47, 2:276, 2:364, 2:403
Rice, Gerard T., 2:242
Rice, Harbert, 1:578
Rice, Kym S., 2:166
Rich, Adrienne, 1:281
Rich, Barnett, 1:505, 1:506, 1:524
Rich, Otto (ed), 1:382

Richard, Alison F., 2:450, 2:462
Richards, Alison, 2:433
Richards, David (ed), 1:390
Richards, G. C., 2:293
Richards, I. A., 1:438
Richards, N. V., 2:565
Richards, Vyvyan, 2:373
Richardson, Nigel, 2:384, 2:385
Richardson, Robert D., 1:165
Richardson, Samuel, 1:29
Richetti, John J., 1:23
Richey, Jim, 1:433
Richie, Donald, 2:87
Richler, Mordecai, 1:146
Richman, Ellen, 1:557
Richman, Irving B., 2:158
Richmond, Velma, 1:122
Richter, 1:561
Richter, Elizabeth, 2:538
Richter, Fleur, 1:535
Richter, Peter H., 1:516
Richter, Peyton, 1:344
Rickard, Peter, 1:326
Ricks, Christopher, 1:54
Rico, Gabriele L., 1:478
Ride, Sally K., 2:481
Rideout, Walter B., 1:190
Ridge, Martin, 2:184
Ridolfi, Roberto, 2:20
Ridpath, Ian, 2:470, 2:479
Rieber, Robert W., 2:114
Rieber, Robert W. (ed), 2:96
Riedman, Sarah R., 2:444, 2:446
Rienhoff, O. (ed), 1:584
Riesman, David, 2:51, 2:132, 2:146, 2:238
Rifkin, Glen, 1:538
Riggs, David, 1:12
Riggs, Donald E. (ed), 1:583
Rigney, Barbara H., 1:136
Riis, Jacob August, 2:212, 2:222
Riley, Eileen, 2:237
Riley, Glenda, 2:155, 2:201
Riley, John T., 1:555, 1:557
Riley, Peter, 2:436
Rilke, Rainer Maria, 1:370, 1:482;
  2:356
Rimell, Raymond L., 2:371
Rinear, Charles E., 2:559
Ringe, Donald A., 1:152
Rinzler, Carol A., 2:550
Rinzler, Jane, 2:543
Ripka, Hubert, 2:405
Ripley, C. Peter, 2:255
Risching, Moses, 1:383
Ritchie, David, 1:538, 1:549
Ritchie, Dennis M., 1:564
Rittner, Carol, 1:302
Rivera, Feliciana, 2:155
Rivers, William, 1:455, 1:487

Rivlin, Alice Mitchell, 2:68
Rivlin, Robert, 2:113
Roach, Hildreth, 2:155
Roach, James R., 2:87
Roan, Sharon L., 2:486
Roazen, Paul, 2:109
Robbins, Herbert, 1:496
Robbins, Neal, 1:423
Robbins, R. Robert, 2:470
Robbins, Thomas, 2:142
Robbins-Landon, H., 2:337
Roberts, Brad (ed), 2:36
Roberts, Elizabeth, 2:405
Roberts, Moss (ed), 1:423
Roberts, Paul C., 2:21
Roberts, Scott W., 2:531
Robertson, Nan, 2:555
Robertson, Priscilla, 2:332
Robespierre, Maximilien, 2:331
Robin, Gordon de Q., 2:493
Robinett, Jane (ed), 1:555
Robins, R. H., 1:434
Robinson, Adam, 1:440
Robinson, Daniel N., 2:110
Robinson, Edward, 2:373
Robinson, Edwin Arlington, 1:282
Robinson, Francis, 2:89
Robinson, Joan, 2:60
Robinson, Harlow, 2:422
Robinson, Michael, 1:443
Robinson, Richard, 1:470
Robinson, Roxana, 2:268
Robinson, Sandra, 1:433
Robinson, William H., 1:155
Roby, Kinley E., 1:72
Rochelle, Mercedes, 2:276
Rocher, Guy, 2:128
Rock, Irvin, 2:113
Roddenberry, Gene, 1:466
Rodgers, Buck, 1:540
Rodgers, Jean B., 1:566
Rodgers, Judith, 2:386
Rodgers, Marion (ed), 1:436
Rodin, Auguste, 2:355–56
Rodin, Paul, 1:411
Rodlauer, Ruth, 1:433
Rodman, Robert, 1:434
Roe, David, 1:335
Roethlisberger, F. J., 2:149
Rogers, Betty, 1:462; 2:229
Rogers, Carl, 2:114
Rogers, Colin, 2:70
Rogers, David F., 1:578
Rogers, Everett M., 2:144
Rogers, Jacquelyn, 2:556
Rogers, James, 1:433
Rogers, Joel, 2:39
Rogers, Will, 1:462; 2:230
Rogerson, John, 2:276

Roginskii, S. Z., 2:509
Rogow, Arnold A. (ed), 2:10
Rohr, Janelle (ed), 2:37, 2:393, 2:538
Rojo, Grinor, 2:409
Rokeach, Milton, 2:97
Rollett, A. P., 1:535
Roloff, Michael E., 2:103
Rølvaag, Ole Edvart, 1:379; 2:201
Romasco, Albert U., 2:231
Romer, John, 2:281
Ronan, Colin A. (ed), 2:471
Ronda, Bruce A., 2:106
Ronda, James P., 2:177
Room, Adrian, 1:439
Rooney, Andrew, 1:480
Roop, Connie, 2:476
Roop, Peter, 2:476
Roosevelt, Anna Eleanor, 2:232–33
Roosevelt, Franklin Delano, 2:233–34
Roosevelt, Theodore, 2:222
Root, Wells, 1:485
Rooze, Gene E., 1:570
Rosaldo, Michelle Zimbaliste (ed),
    2:148
Rosch, Winn, 1:560
Rose, Al, 2:262
Rose, H. J., 1:318
Rose, Jonathan, 2:342
Rose, Kenneth J., 2:441
Rose, Peter I., 2:136
Rose, Peter I. (ed), 2:146
Rosen, Charles, 2:346
Rosen, Frederic (tr), 1:506
Rosen, Marjorie, 1:475
Rosen, Winifred, 2:555
Rosenberg, Bruce A., 1:84; 2:203
Rosenberg, Charles E., 2:567
Rosenberg, Charles E. (ed), 2:570
Rosenberg, Jerome H., 1:136
Rosenberg, Jerry, 1:458
Rosenberg, Rosalind, 2:148
Rosenberg, Stephen N., 2:567
Rosenblum, Nancy L., 2:8
Rosendorf, Beverly, 1:565
Rosenfeld, B. A., 1:516
Rosenfield, Israel, 2:452
Rosenlicht, Maxwell, 1:524
Rosenthal, M. L., 1:244
Rosenthal, Michael, 2:351
Rosenthal-Schneider, Ilse, 2:521
Rosenthau, Ricky, 2:300
Rosin, Mark B., 2:539
Roski, Steve, 1:586
Rosmer, Alfred, 2:379
Rosow, Irving, 2:146
Ross, David A., 2:486
Ross, Irwin, 2:237
Ross, John A. (ed), 2:124
Ross, Julia, 2:538

Ross, Walter S., 2:226
Rossbocher, Lisa A., 2:489
Rössel, Sven H. (ed), 1:375
Rossett, Lisa, 1:195
Rossetti, Christina, 1:56
Rossetti, Dante Gabriel, 1:57
Rossi, Alice S. (ed), 2:148
Rossi, Vinio, 1:336
Rossing, Thomas D., 2:522
Rossiter, Clinton, 2:17, 2:164, 2:235
Ross–Larson, Bruce, 1:479
Rossman, Charles (ed), 1:403
Rossman, Peter, 1:555
Rostand, Claude, 2:354
Rosten, Leo, 1:431
Rostkowski, Margaret I., 2:224
Rostow, Walter, 2:72
Roszak, Theodore, 1:555
Roth, Guenther, 2:143
Roth, Judith P., 1:578
Roth, Leland M., 2:262
Roth, Walton, 2:531
Rothman, David H., 1:576
Rothman, Sheila M., 2:148
Rothschild, Joan (ed), 2:148
Rothschild, M., 2:335
Rothwell, William S., 2:512
Rouse, Blair, 1:227
Rouse, W. H. D., 1:318
Rousseau, Jean Jacques, 2:11
Roux, Georges, 2:281
Rovira, Luis J., 2:161
Rowe, John C., 2:214
Rowe, William, 1:397
Rowland-Entwistle, Theodore, 2:283,
    2:448, 2:493
Roy, Emil, 1:87
Royko, Mike, 1:480
Roysdon, Christine, 1:584
Rozental, S. (ed), 2:501
Rozgonyi, Tamas (ed), 2:140
Ruane, Pat, 1:565
Ruben, Samuel, 2:506
Rubenstein, David, 2:450
Rubin, Barry (ed), 2:12
Rubin, Charles, 1:576
Rubin, Julie, 2:561
Rubin, Susan, 1:474
Rubin, William S., 2:349, 2:415
Rubinfeld, Daniel L. (ed), 2:71
Rubins, Jack L., 2:119
Rubinstein, Charlotte S., 2:156
Ruchlis, Hy, 1:512, 1:519
Rucker, Rudolf, 1:498, 1:516
Rudman, Mark, 1:259
Rudolph, James (ed), 2:89, 2:409
Ruehlmann, William, 1:487
Ruffins, Reynold, 1:433
Rugg, Dean S., 2:405

Ruggerio, Vincent Ryan, 1:478
Ruiz, Ramon E., 2:219
Rule, John, 2:339
Rummel, Erika, 2:315
Rummel, Jack, 1:241, 1:450; 2:251
Rumney, Avis, 2:551
Rungeling, Brian, 2:70
Runion, Garth E., 1:516
Ruoff, A. Lavonne, 2:158
Rushforth, Keith D., 2:448
Rushton, Julian, 2:347
Rusinko, Susan, 1:123
Rusk, Dean, 2:26
Rusk, Howard Archibald, 2:565
Ruspoli, Mario, 2:279
Russell, Bertrand, 1:503, 1:527
Russell, Francis, 2:226
Russell, Olga W., 1:533
Russell, P. E., 1:357
Russell, Sharman, 2:190
Russell, Susan, 1:570
Russo, Vito, 1:475
Rust, John, 2:122
Rustow, Dankwart A., 2:252
Rutherford, Ernest, 2:504
Rutland, Jonathan, 2:285
Ryan, Alan, 1:504
Ryan, Elizabeth A., 2:539
Ryan, Halford R., 2:234
Ryan, Margaret, 1:449
Rybolt, Thomas R., 2:504
Rycroft, Michael, 2:481
Rydjord, John, 1:439
Ryf, Robert, 1:77

S

Saaty, Thomas L., 1:512, 1:535
Saavedra, Dane, 2:542
Sabato, Larry J., 2:40
Sabin, Lou, 2:183
Saccuzzo, Dennis P., 2:122
Sachar, Howard M., 2:276
Sachs, Curt, 2:262
Sackett, Russel, 2:466
Sadat, Anwar, 2:414
Sadat, Jehan, 2:412
Sadler, Lynn V., 1:80
Safa, Helen (ed), 2:409
Safire, William, 1:438, 1:442; 2:255
Sagal, Paul T., 2:102
Sagan, Carl, 2:476, 2:479–80
Sagan, Leonard A., 2:567
Sagar, Keith, 1:101
Sagar, Keith (ed), 1:95
Sagay, J. O., 2:276
Sague, Z. C., 1:559
Saha, B. P., 2:282

Sahakian, William S., 2:112
Said, Edward W., 2:89, 2:412
Said, K. A. (ed), 1:582
Sainsbury, Diana, 2:443, 2:446
St. Augustine. *See* Augustine, St.
Saint Bede, the Venerable. *See* Bede, St.
St. George, Judith, 2:185
Sakharov, Andrei, 2:405
Saki, 1:115
Salinger, J. D., 1:283
Salinger, Pierre, 2:87, 2:255
Salisbury, Harrison E., 2:340, 2:385,
  2:399
Sally, Judith D. (ed), 1:510
Salmen, L., 2:510
Salmon, George, 1:514
Salmore, Barbara G., 2:40
Salmore, Stephen A., 2:40
Salny, Abbie, 1:440
Salomon, Samuel R., 2:6, 2:41
Salwak, Dale, 1:78
Salwak, Dale (ed), 1:100
Salzinger, Kurt (ed), 2:96
Samovar, Larry, 1:445
Samson, Julia, 2:281
Samuel, Claude, 2:422
Samuel, Maurice, 1:384
Samuels, Andrew, 2:121
Samuels, Cynthia K., 2:13, 2:40
Samuels, Ernest, 2:214
Samuels, Wilfred D., 1:269
Samuelson, Paul A., 2:56
Sandberg, Peter S., 2:240
Sandburg, Carl, 1:284; 2:198
Sanders, B. D., 1:557
Sanders, Dennis, 1:74
Sanders, John E., 2:489
Sanderson, G. N. (ed), 2:363
Sanderson, George, 1:454
Sanderson, Richard, 1:469
Sandler, Martin, 2:156
Sandoz, Mari, 2:201
Sands, Kathleen N., 2:152
Sandweiss, Jack H., 1:569
Santillana, Giorgio de, 2:474
Santos, Richard G., 2:185
Sanzone, John G., 2:36
Sapinsley, Barbara, 2:71
Sapir, Edward, 2:50
Saposnik, Irving S., 1:58
Sarabande, William, 2:158
Sargent, Lyman T., 2:16
Sarin, Amita V., 2:399
Sarnoff, Dorothy, 1:445
Sarnoff, Jane, 1:433
Sarton, May, 1:482
Sartre, Jean-Paul, 1:340
Sassoon, Siegfried, 1:116
Sater, William F., 2:370

Sattler, Helen R., 2:485
Sauer, Carl Ortwin, 2:80
Saunders, Alan, 2:385
Saunders, Cheryl M., 1:470, 1:473
Saunders, Elijah, 2:562
Saunders, J. B. de C. M., 2:548
Saunders, Rubie, 2:552
Saunders, Tao I., 2:309
Saupe, Dietmar, 1:516
Sauts, William, 2:158
Sawa, Yuki (tr), 1:425
Sawyer, W. W., 1:498, 1:523
Sayen, Jamie, 2:520
Sayers, Dorothy L., 1:46, 1:117
Sayre, John R., 2:6, 2:33
Sayres, Sohnya (ed), 2:51, 2:242
Scammell, Michael, 1:396
Scarborough, John, 2:291
Scarne, John, 1:535
Scarre, Geoffrey, 2:310
Schaaf, Fred, 2:471
Schaaf, William L., 1:535
Schachner, Nathan, 2:169
Schaefer, Dick, 2:556
Schaefer, Vincent J., 2:484
Schafer, R. Murray, 2:522
Schank, Roger C., 1:570, 1:582; 2:110
Schapiro, Meyer, 2:349, 2:360
Scharlau, W., 1:498
Schatt, Stan, 1:572
Schatt, Stanley, 1:296
Schattschneider, Doris, 1:515
Scheader, Catherine, 2:34
Schele, Linda, 2:300
Schellenberg, James A., 2:99, 2:102, 2:118
Schellhase, Kenneth C., 2:297
Schelling, Thomas C., 2:37
Scherman, David E., 2:235, 2:385
Schick, James B., 1:570
Schickel, Richard, 1:475
Schildt, Herbert, 1:564
Schiller, Herbert I., 1:555
Schiller, (Johann Christoph) Friedrich von,
  1:372
Schlesinger, Arthur M., Jr., 2:7, 2:21, 2:33,
  2:40, 2:156, 2:180, 2:207, 2:248, 2:249
Schlesinger, Arthur M., Jr. (ed), 2:7, 2:13,
  2:33, 2:229, 2:260, 2:291
Schlink, F. J., 2:61
Schlissel, Lillian, 2:201
Schlueter, June, 1:266
Schmettere, Leopold, 1:500
Schmieman, Susan, 1:578
Schneider, B. (ed), 1:584
Schneider, David, 2:52
Schneider, J. Stewart, 1:572
Schneider, Joseph W., 2:138
Schneider, Stephen, 2:82, 2:486
Schneider, William, 2:40

Schneiderman, Ron, 1:540
Schoaff, Eileen, 1:564
Schoek, Richard, 1:7
Schoen, Celin V., 1:207
Schofield, Wilfred B., 2:448
Schooler, Carmi, 2:145
Schopflin, George (ed), 2:405
Schopp, Claude, 1:334
Schram, Stuart R., 2:403
Schramm, Wilbur, 2:130
Schrank, Jeffrey, 1:455, 1:468, 1:469
Schreeve, James, 2:48, 2:278
Schreiber, Flora R., 2:121
Schreiner, Axel T., 1:586
Schreuder, Yda, 2:161
Schroeder, Paul C., 2:449
Schroeder, Paul W., 2:333
Schubert, Irmgard G., 1:569
Schuchart, 1:573
Schuck, Peter H., 2:571
Schudson, Michael, 1:457
Schuh, Willi, 2:425
Schulke, Flip, et al, 2:481
Schulman, Elayne Engelman, 1:574
Schulz, Charles, 1:459
Schumacher, E. F., 2:63
Schumann, Clara J., 2:348
Schumpeter, Joseph A., 2:56–58, 2:63, 2:72
Schur, Norman. W., 1:434–1:440
Schurz, Carl, 2:182
Schutz, Alexander H., 1:326
Schutzer, Daniel, 1:566
Schwartz, Anna J., 2:153
Schwartz, Bernard, 2:32
Schwartz, Bernard (ed), 2:17
Schwartz, Helen J., 1:570
Schwartz, Karlene, 2:441
Schwartz, Mimi, 1:478, 1:485
Schwartz, Roberta, 1:578
Schwartz, Seymour I., 2:92
Schwarzbach, Martin, 2:492
Schweir, Richard, 1:580
Schweitzer, Albert, 2:535
Schwendowius, Barbara (ed), 2:335
Scientific American Editors, 2:562
Scodel, Ruth, 1:317
Scopes, John, 2:226
Scott, Andrew, 2:443, 2:557
Scott, J. F., 1:515
Scott, Joan W., 2:340
Scott, Joanna C., 2:399
Scott, John P., 2:98
Scott, Otto, 2:332
Scott, Paul, 1:118; 2:363
Scott, Randall, 1:459
Scott, Sharon, 2:556
Scott, Shirley L. (ed), 2:450
Scott, Sir Walter, 1:36
Screech, M. A., 2:315

Sculley, John, 1:546
Seaman, L. C., 2:276, 2:363
Seargent, David A., 2:476
Searl, Sarah, 2:557
Searle, Humphrey, 2:354
Sears, Francis W., 2:513
Sears, Robert R., 2:98, 2:103
Sebestyen, Quida, 2:198
Secor, Marie, 1:477
Sedge, Michael H., 2:82
Sedgewick Robert, 1:586
Seed, David, 1:235
Seeden, Margaret, 2:83
Seeley, Thomas, 2:462
Seeman, Bernard, 2:561
Sefton, James E., 2:198
Segal, Erich, 1:322; 2:291
Segal, Julius, 2:95
Seibenheller, Norma, 1:98
Seibold, E., 2:488
Seidel, R. J., 1:568
Seidler, Ann, 1:451
Seidman, Steve, 1:470
Seigert, H. J. (ed), 1:585
Seitz, Don C., 2:204
Seixas, Judith S., 2:540, 2:555
Selby, Peter, 1:514
Seldes, Gilbert, 1:453
Seldon, Anthony (ed), 2:408
Self, J. (ed), 1:570
Selfe, Cynthia L. (ed), 1:570
Seller, William Y., 2:294
Sellin, Thorsten, 2:133
Selz, Jean, 2:358
Selz, Peter, 2:262
Selznick, Gertrude J., 2:136
Semendyayev, K. A., 1:496
Sementsov-Ogievskii, M. A., 1:515
Sen, S. K., 1:565
Sen, Sailendra N., 2:282
Seneca, Lucius Annaeus, 1:323
Senghor, Leopold Sedar, 1:417
Sennett, Richard, 2:144
Sennrich, Bruno, 1:578
Serafini, Anthony, 2:506
Serenyi, Peter, 2:420
Serling, Rod, 1:486
Seroff, Victor I., 2:422, 2:424
Service, Elman R., 2:42
Service, Robert W., 1:146
Serwer-Bernstein, Blanche, 2:276
Seton-Watson, Hugh, 2:276, 2:340, 2:375
Seton-Watson, R. W., 2:371
Settle, Mary Lee, 2:486
Sevier, Raymond, 2:489
Seward, Desmond, 2:331
Sewell, John W., 2:258
Sewell, William H. (ed), 2:145
Sexton, James D., 2:409

Seybolt, Peter J., 2:399
Seyer, Philip, 1:580
Seymour, Charles (ed), 2:318
Seymour, Dale, 1:515
Shadegg, Stephen, 2:245
Shader, Laurel, 2:557
Shadler, Rubin, 1:512
Shafer, Daniel G., 1:584
Shafer, Linda B., 1:563
Shaffer, Peter, 1:119
Shakespeare, William, 1:15
Shankar, R., 2:519
Shanks, Hershel, 2:281
Shannon, Claude, 1:550
Shannon, David A., 2:229
Shapiro, Alen, 1:584
Shapiro, Cecile, 2:415
Shapiro, David, 2:415
Shapiro, Nat (ed), 2:262
Shapiro, Stuart C. (ed), 1:581
Shapiro, William E., 2:89, 2:236, 2:385,
    2:412
Shapland, David, 2:481
Shargin, I. F., 1:520
Sharp, Ansel, 2:65
Sharp, Harold, 1:441
Sharpe, Mitchell R., 2:483
Sharrock, Roger, 1:21
Shaw, Arnold, 2:156, 2:227, 2:262
Shaw, David, 1:458
Shaw, George Bernard, 1:120, 1:443
Shaw, Margery W. (ed), 2:565
Shaw, Samuel, 1:237
Shaw, William Napier, 2:484
Shea, William R., 2:504
Shearer, Benjamin F. (ed), 2:130
Shearman, Dierdre, 2:369
Shedd, C. W., 2:537
Sheehy, Gail, 2:107, 2:407
Sheldon, Eleanor B., 2:144
Sheldon, Richard, 2:390
Sheldon, Tom, 1:562
Shelley, Mary Wollstonecraft, 1:37
Shelley, Percy Bysshe, 1:38
Shelston, Alan, 2:339
Shelston, Dorothy, 2:339
Shelton, Suzanne, 2:262
Shemberg, Kenneth, 2:98
Shenkman, Richard, 2:156
Shepard, James, 1:151
Shepard, Sam, 1:285
Shepherd, William G., 2:65
Sheridan, Martin, 1:459
Sheridan, Richard Brinsley, 1:29
Sherman, Alan, 2:505
Sherman, Sharon J., 2:505
Sherr, Sol (ed), 1:560
Sherrill, Claudine (ed), 1:569
Sherry, Norman, 1:92

Sherwin, Martin J., 2:236
Shi, David E., 2:51
Shideler, Mary M., 2:96
Shiffert, Edith (tr), 1:425
Shillingburg, Patricia, 1:571
Shimer, Dorothy Blair (ed), 1:423, 1:425
Shine, Ian B., 2:454
Shipler, David K., 2:90, 2:406, 2:412
Shipley, Joseph T., 1:433
Shiran, Du, 1:498
Shirer, William L., 2:375, 2:377
Shirley, John W., 2:162
Shklar, Judith N., 2:11
Shnol', S. E., 2:509
Shoemaker, M. Wesley, 2:406
Shogan, Robert, 2:256
Shook, Robert, 1:540
Shor, Donnali, 2:331
Shore, Nancy, 2:229
Short, James F., Jr. (ed), 2:125
Short, K. R., 1:441
Short, Nicholas M., 2:92
Shorter, Edward, 2:567
Shostakovich, Dmitri, 2:422, 2:424
Shotland, Lance R., 2:98, 2:104
Shotton, Margaret, 1:555
Showerman, Grant, 2:294
Shrank, Jeffrey, 1:441
Shudson, Michael, 1:457
Shuker, Nancy F., 2:250
Shulman, Neil B., 2:562
Shurkin, Joel N., 1:540
Shute, Nevil, 1:147
Shuy, Roger, 1:431
Sibley, Brian, 1:475
Sica, Alan, 2:143
Sick, Gary, 2:37
Sidney, Sir Philip, 1:16
Siedel, Frank, 2:433
Siedel, James M., 2:433
Siegel, Beatrice, 2:162
Siegel, Mark A., 2:540, 2:566
Siegel, Paul, 1:584
Siegel, Paula M., 2:561
Sienkiewicz, Henryk, 1:387
Sigford, Ann E., 2:467
Silberman, Charles E., 2:133
Silk, Joseph, 2:471, 2:479
Silk, Leonard, 2:56
Silkett, John T., 2:169
Sillitoe, Alan, 1:121
Silver, Carole, 1:437
Silver, Donald M., 2:466
Silverberg, Robert, 1:285–86
Silverman, Dan P., 2:371
Silverstein, Alvin, 2:452, 2:545, 2:546, 2:553, 2:557, 2:560, 2:562
Silverstein, Arthur M., 2:546
Silverstein, Herma, 2:412, 2:556

Silverstein, Norman, 1:469
Silverstein, Virginia B., 2:452, 2:545, 2:546, 2:553, 2:560, 2:562
Simon, A. R., 1:538
Simon, Edith, 2:306
Simon, George T., 2:262
Simon, Herbert A., 1:581; 2:63, 2:140
Simon, Hilda, 2:448
Simon, Jacob (ed), 2:336
Simon, James F., 2:27, 2:28
Simon, Neil, 1:286
Simon, Nissa, 2:543
Simon, Noel, 2:497
Simon, Seymour, 2:471
Simonides, Carol, 2:562
Simons, G. L., 1:555
Simons, Richard C., 2:531
Simons, Robin, 2:563
Simpson, Alan, 1:572, 1:576
Simpson, Alan (ed), 1:574
Simpson, George E., 2:136
Simpson, Thomas D., 2:70
Sims, Naomi, 2:553
Sinclair, Andrew, 2:227
Sinclair, Upton, 1:287; 2:62, 2:219
Siner, Howard (ed), 1:480
Singer, Charles, 2:548
Singer, Isaac Bashevis, 1:387, 1:482
Singer, Jack W., 2:561
Singewood, Alan, 2:125
Singh, Jagjit, 1:498
Singleton, Marvin, 1:436
Singleton, Paul, 2:443, 2:446
Sinha, U., 2:443
Sinyard, Neil, 1:474
Siohan, Robert, 2:426
Sipiera, Paul, 2:253
Sisk, Jonathan E., 1:562
Siskin, Bernard, 1:530
Sisler, Harry H., 2:506
Sitarz, Daniel, 1:576
Sitkoff, Harvard, 2:229, 2:238
Sitwell, Sacheverell, 2:354
Sivin, Nathan (ed), 2:87, 2:276
Sjoberg, Gideon, 2:147
Skaggs, Peggy, 1:173
Skansholm, Jan, 1:566
Skeet, Ian, 2:252
Skelton, R. A., 2:92
Skelton, Robin, 1:123
Skillin, M., 1:478
Skinner, B. F., 2:101
Skinner, Brian, 1:441
Skinner, Edith, 1:451
Skinner, Elliot, 2:299
Skinner, Gordon B., 2:508
Skinner, Quentin, 2:20
Skinner, Robert E., 1:210, 1:231
Skipper, G. C., 2:377

Sklar, Robert, 1:465
Skolnick, Arlene S., 2:138
Skolnick, Jerome H., 2:138
Slack, Adrian, 2:448
Slater, Keith, 2:105
Slater, Peter J., 2:462
Slater, Philip, 2:134, 2:139
Slavin, Ed, 2:256
Sloane, Howard, 1:571
Slosson, Edwin E., 1:500
Slosson, Preston W., 2:224
Sloyer, Shirlee, 1:449
Slusser, Robert M., 2:392
Smakov, Gennady, 2:415
Small, Albion, 2:125
Small, Miriam R., 1:158
Smarr, Janet L.(tr), 1:347
Smelser, Neil J., 2:47, 2:139, 2:144
Smelser, Neil J. (ed), 2:124
Smith, A. G., 1:520
Smith, Adam, 2:61, 2:340
Smith, Ann, 2:552, 2:556
Smith, Anthony, 2:552
Smith, Anthony D., 2:341
Smith, Betsy C., 2:256
Smith, Bradley F., 2:385
Smith, Brian, 1:572
Smith, Bruce G., 2:481
Smith, Colin, 1:359
Smith, David, 1:112
Smith, David E., 1:498
Smith, Denis Mack, 2:341, 2:375
Smith, Dian G., 1:470
Smith, Diann, 1:431
Smith, Dick, 1:537, 1:545
Smith, Edward (ed), 1:582
Smith, Edward C., 2:6
Smith, Edward C. (ed), 2:17
Smith, G. E. Kidder, 2:262
Smith, Gene, 2:198
Smith, George H., 2:228
Smith, Grover, 1:261
Smith, Harry F., Jr., 1:586
Smith, Hedrick, 2:406
Smith, Henry Nash, 1:182
Smith, Hobart, 2:450
Smith, Howard E., 2:482
Smith, J. K., 1:556
Smith, Jeremy, 1:430
Smith, Julian, 1:470
Smith, Karl J., 1:498
Smith, Kathie, 2:175
Smith, Lacey B., 2:311, 2:327
Smith, Larry, 1:221, 1:434
Smith, Lawrence R. (ed), 1:348
Smith, Lendon, 2:550
Smith, Michael Holley, 1:490
Smith, Neil, 1:435
Smith, P., 1:572, 1:573

Smith, Page, 2:17, 2:164, 2:328, 2:340, 2:372
Smith, Peter J. (ed), 2:83
Smith, Ralph E. (ed), 2:148, 2:149
Smith, Richard N., 2:231
Smith, Stan, 1:66, 1:506
Smith, Thomas, 1:514
Smith, Ursula, 2:451, 2:550
Smith, Wanda J., 1:578
Smitherman, Geneva, 1:430
Smithsonian Institution, 2:156, 2:476
Smock, Raymond W. (ed), 2:213
Smogorzhevsky, A., 1:514, 1:519
Smullyan, Raymond, 1:500
Snipes, Katherine, 1:91
Snow, Robert, 1:454
Snowden, Frank M., Jr, 2:300
Snowden, Sheila, 2:471
Snyder, Henry D., 1:496
Snyder, Louis L., 2:385
Snyder, Thomas, 1:571
Sobel, David, 2:531
Sobel, Robert, 2:227, 2:258
Sobel, Robert (ed), 2:6
Sobieszek, Robert, 1:441
Sobin, Julian M., 2:87, 2:274
Socha, John, 1:564
Sohn, Louis, 2:36
Solberg, Carl, 2:245
Sole, Carlos, 1:353
Sole, Yolanda, 1:353
Solomon, Maynard, 2:334
Solomon, S. J., 1:469
Solzhenitsyn, Alexandr, 1:396
Sommer, Robin L., 2:422
Sonnett, Sherry, 2:556
Sootin, Harry, 2:453
Sophocles, 1:316
Sorensen, Theodore C., 2:21, 2:248
Sorenson, Paul G., 1:586
Sorokin, Pitirim, 2:144
Soskin, Mark, 1:574
Sothern, James, 1:431
Souchon, Edmond, 2:262
Sousa, John Philip, 2:216
Southern, David W., 2:135
Southern, Eileen, 2:156
Southgate, Minoo, 1:420
Sowell, Thomas, 2:69
Soyinka, Wole, 1:417–18
Spaeth, Harold J. (ed), 2:17
Spaid, Ora A., 1:571
Spain, Daphne, 2:147
Spangenberg, Ray, 2:482
Spanik, Christian, 1:560
Spann, Meno, 1:369
Spark, Muriel, 1:37, 1:121–22
Spatola, Adriano, 1:348
Spatz, Lois, 1:312

Speakes, Larry, 2:260
Spear, Margaret, 2:363
Spear, Percival, 2:363
Speare, Elizabeth, 2:162
Spearing, A. C., 1:8
Spector, Roy, 2:553
Speed, Peter, 2:340
Speirs, Ronald, 1:365
Spence, J. Wayne, 1:565
Spencer, Donald D., 1:538, 1:557, 1:571, 1:578
Spencer, Edgar W., 2:489
Spencer, William, 2:90, 2:412
Spenser, Edmund, 1:17
Sperber, Ann, 1:467
Spiegel, Steven L., 2:258
Spindler, George D., 2:43
Spivak, Charlotte, 1:254
Spleth, Janice S., 1:417
Spock, Benjamin McLane, 2:541
Spooner, Maggie, 2:485
Spradley, James P., 2:43
Sprigg, June, 2:187
Squadrito, Kathleen M., 2:18
Srinivasan, Bhama (ed), 1:510
Srivastava, S., 2:443
Staercke, André De (ed), 2:406
Stage, John Lewis, 2:156
Staines, David, 1:60
Stainsby, G., 2:507
Stalin, Joseph, 2:380
Stallings, Pat, 1:512
Stallings, William, 1:560
Stallworthy, James, 1:113
Stambler, Irwin, 2:156, 2:262
Stampp, Kenneth M., 2:193, 2:198
Stanford, Barbara Dodd, 1:205, 1:224, 1:230
Stanford University, 1:538
Stanley, David, 2:91
Stanley, Harold, 2:6
Stanley, Henry M., 2:367
Stanley, Sadie (ed), 2:154
Stanley, Steven M., 2:495
Stanley, Thomas, 1:502
Stansfield, William D., 2:452
Stansky, Peter, 2:346
Stanton, R. H. (ed), 2:510
Stare, Frederick J., 2:550
Stark, Rodney, 2:142
Starr, Chester G., 2:277, 2:279, 2:285, 2:291
Starr, Philip (ed), 2:567
Statt, David, 2:95
Staugaard, Andrew C., 1:582
Stead, Miriam, 2:281
Stearns, Marshall, 2:262
Stearns, Peter N., 2:332
Stearns, Peter N. (ed), 2:277

Steck, Frances B., 2:158
Stedman, Nancy, 2:557
Steed, Henry W., 2:327
Steen, Lynn A., 1:497, 1:523
Steen, Lynn A. (ed), 1:498
Steffens, Lincoln, 2:219
Stefoff, Rebecca, 2:172, 2:176, 2:178, 2:183, 2:400
Stegner, Wallace, 2:91, 2:201
Steichen, Edward, 2:269
Stein, Dorothy, 1:547
Stein, Edwin I., 1:505
Stein, Herbert, 2:65
Stein, Jean, 2:249
Stein, Maurice R., 2:147
Steinbeck, Elaine (ed), 1:289
Steinbeck, John, 1:288–89; 2:229, 2:242
Steinberg, Cobbett, 1:465
Steinberg, David J., 2:400
Steinberg, Laurence, 2:543
Steinberg, Stephen, 2:136
Steiner, Gerhardt, 1:562
Steiner, Gray A., 2:130
Steiner, Josef, 1:562
Steinglass, Peter, 2:540
Steinman, Michael, 1:109
Stelzer, Irwin M., 2:65, 2:156
Stendhal, 1:341–42
Stepanek, Sally, 2:311, 2:317
Stephens, Mark, 2:255
Stephens, Mitchell, 1:457
Stephens, Otis H., 2:27
Stephenson, Ralph, 1:469
Sterling, Christopher, 1:457
Sterling, John C., 2:183
Stern, Fritz R., 2:342
Stern, Jane, 2:242
Stern, Michael, 2:242
Stern, Nancy B., 1:555
Stern, Peter, 2:496
Stern, Robert A., 1:555
Sternberg, Martin L. A., 1:448
Sternberg, Michael J. E., 2:438
Sternberg, Patricia, 1:445
Sternburg, Janet, 1:196
Sternburg, Janet (ed), 1:481
Sternlicht, Sanford, 1:76
Stevens, Halsey, 2:416
Stevens, Irving L., 2:229
Stevens, Laurence, 2:466
Stevens, Paul, 2:320
Stevens, Peter S., 1:515
Stevens, Richard, 2:109
Stevenson, Anne, 1:278
Stevenson, Augusta, 2:203, 2:569
Stevenson, John, 2:273
Stevenson, Robert, 2:161
Stevenson, Robert Louis, 1:58
Stevenson-Hinde, Joan (ed), 2:138

Steward, Julian H., 2:43, 2:45, 2:48
Stewart, Ann H., 1:84
Stewart, Barbara J., 2:122
Stewart, George R., 1:439
Stewart, Hugh B., 2:57
Stewart, John, 2:277
Stewart, Michael, 2:72
Stewart, Peter, 2:180
Stewart, Stanley, 1:11
Stewart, Susan A., 1:516
Stick, David, 2:162
Stidham, Ronald, 2:26
Stigler, George, 2:56
Stigler, Stephen, 1:530
Stiller, Richard, 2:531
Stillman, Andrea G. (ed), 2:263
Stillman, Myra, 2:92
Stillman, Peter, 1:478
Stinchcombe, Arthur L., 2:133
Stine, G. Harry, 2:482
Stinson, Craig, 1:562
Stites, Frances N., 2:30
Stocking, George W., Jr., 2:44
Stockley, C., 1:538; 2:437
Stockton, William, 2:562
Stodelle, Ernestine, 2:262
Stohl, Michael S. (ed), 2:36
Stoker, Bram, 1:59
Stoler, Mark, 2:240
Stommel, Elizabeth, 2:485
Stommel, Henry, 2:485
Stone, Brian, 1:7
Stone, Doris M., 2:448
Stone, I. F., 2:285, 2:385, 2:400
Stone, Irving, 1:257; 2:201, 2:318, 2:360
Stone, Jeanne, 2:433
Stonerod, David, 1:520
Stoppard, Tom, 1:122
Storel, Nora, 1:80
Storey, Wayne, 1:346
Stork, Charles W. (ed), 1:374
Stork, David G., 2:521
Stotler, Donald W., 1:571
Stouffer, Samuel A., 2:128
Stover, Leon, 1:234
Stowe, Harriet Beecher, 2:189
Stowell, Peter, 1:470
Straayer, John, 2:41
Strachan-Davidson, James L., 2:293
Strachey, Lytton, 2:369, 2:570
Stradter, Philip A., 2:289
Strahler, Alan H., 2:93, 2:489
Strahler, Arthur N., 2:93, 2:489
Strange, Ian J., 2:89
Stratmann, Francis, 1:430
Stratton, Joanna, 2:201
Stratton, John, 1:478
Stratton, Peter, 2:95

Strauss, Anselm L., 2:137
Strauss, Richard, 2:425
Strauss, Richard H., 2:553
Strauss, Walter L. (ed), 2:314
Stravinsky, Igor, 2:426
Stravinsky, Theodore, 2:426
Stravinsky, Vera, 2:426
Strean, Herbert S., 2:118
Street, H., 2:448
Strickland, Dorothy, 1:571
Strindberg, August, 1:379, 1:380
Stromberg, Karl, 1:523
Strong, Bryan, 1:562
Stouffer, Samuel A., 2:128–29
Struik, Dirk J., 1:498
Strunk, William, Jr., 1:478
Stryk, Lucien (ed and tr), 1:427
Stuart, Gene S., 2:300
Stuart, George E., 2:300
Stubbe, John W., 1:558
Stwertka, Albert, 1:498; 2:436, 2:455
Stwertka, Eve, 2:96, 2:436, 2:455
Styron, William, 2:189
Subak-Sharpe, Genell J., 2:545
Suchard, Alan R., 1:214
Suckiel, Ellen Kappy, 2:97
Sue, Stanley, 2:121
Suelzle, Marijean, 2:135
Suetonius, 2:296
Sullivan, Edward D., 1:338
Sullivan, George, 2:255, 2:414
Sullivan, Jo, 2:86, 2:394
Sullivan, Julie, 2:82
Sullivan, Louis Henry, 2:217
Sullivan, Navin, 2:433
Sullivan, Walter, 2:479
Summers, Claude J., 1:96
Summers, David, 2:318
Summers, Harrison (ed), 1:462
Sumner, William G., 2:183
Sunstein, Emily W., 1:37
Sussex, Roland, 2:341
Sussman, Les, 2:556
Sussman, Marvin B., 2:531
Sussman, Marvin B. (ed), 2:148
Sutcliffe, Rosemary (tr), 1:6
Sutherland, Edwin H., 2:133
Sutherland, Edwin H. (ed), 2:133
Sutherland, Zena (ed), 1:484
Suttles, Gerald D., 2:131, 2:147
Swaine, Michael, 1:540, 1:543
Swanberg, W. A., 1:457
Swanson, Bert, 2:130
Swanson, Earl H., 2:300
Swartz, Thomas R. (ed), 2:62
Sweet, Jeffrey, 1:489
Sweet, William, 2:37
Sweetman, David, 2:360
Swetz, Frank, 1:498

Swift, Jonathan, 1:29
Swift, Kate, 1:479
Swinburne, Algernon Charles, 1:59
Swisher, Karen, 2:129, 2:544
Sydney, Sheldon B., 2:553
Sylvester, David W., 2:322
Sylvester, Diane, 1:441
Syme, Ronald, 2:297
Symons, Julian, 1:48
Synge, John Millington, 1:123
Szabo, Arprad, 1:498
Szego, G., 1:524
Szmielev, Wanda, 1:516
Sztompka, Piotr, 2:141
Szulc, Tad, 2:410
Szumski, Bonnie (ed), 2:133

T

Taaffe, Edward, 2:84
Tabb, William K. (ed), 2:57
Tacitus, Cornelius, 2:297
Tafel, Edgar, 2:270
Taft, David, 1:563
Taft, Donald R., 2:133
Taft, Lorado, 2:262
Taft, William Howard, 2:223
Tagore, Rabindranath, 1:422
Takaki, Ronald, 2:207
Takashi, Ihmeto (ed and tr), 1:427
Takaya, Ted T. (ed), 1:425
Talbot, Phillips, 2:400
Talbott, Strobe, 2:260
Tamarin, Alfred, 2:285
Tames, R., 2:368
Tames, Richard, 2:559, 2:570
Tandon, Prakash, 2:363, 2:400
Tanenhaus, Sam, 2:264
Taney, Roger B., 2:27
Tankard, James W., Jr., 1:530
Tannenbaum, Arnold S. (ed), 2:140
Tannenbaum, Beulah, 2:92
Tannenbaum, Percy H. (ed), 2:130
Tanner, Nancy M., 2:460
Taper, Bernard, 2:415
Tarasov, L., 1:530
Tarbuck, Edward J., 2:489
Tarjemanov, J., 1:519
Tarrant, V. E., 2:372
Tart, Charles T., 2:537
Tashjian, Levon D., 2:539
Tashlik, Phyllis, 1:480
Tatchell, 1:557
Tate, Claudia (ed), 1:96, 1:269, 1:481
Tatum, Charles M. (ed), 2:88, 2:274
Taubman, William, 2:380
Taute, Anne (comp), 2:277
Tavaka, Chester, 2:236

Tawney, Richard H., 2:47
Taylor, A. J., 2:341, 2:342, 2:372, 2:385
Taylor, Barbara, 2:513, 2:516
Taylor, Charles L., 2:37
Taylor, Edward, 1:154
Taylor, Fredric, 2:475
Taylor, G. Jeffrey, 2:476
Taylor, James C., 2:125
Taylor, Jerome, 1:7
Taylor, John Russell, 2:346
Taylor, L. B., Jr, 2:82
Taylor, Marian, 1:440
Taylor, Mark K., 2:48
Taylor, Martin C., 1:405
Taylor, Mildred D., 1:290; 2:229
Taylor, Richard, 1:441
Taylor, Ron, 2:456
Taylor, Ronald J., 1:362
Taylor, Thomas, 1:502
Taylor, Welford D., 1:190
Taylor, William A., 1:581
Tchaikovsky, Peter Ilyich, 2:357
Tchudi, Stephen, 1:478
Tchudi, Susan, 1:478
Teague, Lavette C., Jr., 1:559
Teasdale, Jim, 2:443, 2:446
Tegner, Bruce, 2:567
Teja, Ed, 1:579
Tennyson, Lord, Alfred, 1:60
Terence, 1:323–24
Terkel, Louis, 2:69, 2:70, 2:149
Terkel, Studs, 1:489; 2:229, 2:236, 2:252, 2:262
Terrill, Ross, 2:403
Terry, Patricia J., 1:571
Thackeray, William Makepeace, 1:61
Thackray, Arnold, 2:502
Thatcher, Margaret, 2:407
Thayer, James Bradley, 2:30
Thelen, David P., 2:220
Theodorson, Achilles A., 2:124
Theodorson, George A., 2:124
Theon of Smyrna, 1:498
Thernstrom, Stephan (ed), 2:124, 2:136
Theroux, Peter, 2:412
Thesiger, Wilfred, 2:90
Thieboux, Marcelle, 1:227
Thielens, Wayner, Jr., 2:125
Thierauf, Robert J., 1:584
Thigpen, Corbett, 2:122
Thody, Philip, 1:333
Thomas, Cyrus, 2:158
Thomas, Dana Lee, 2:433
Thomas, Del, 1:487
Thomas, Donald, 1:60
Thomas, Dylan, 1:124
Thomas, Frank, 1:475
Thomas, Gordon, 2:557
Thomas, Henry, 2:433

Thomas, Hugh S., 2:388
Thomas, Hugh S. (ed), 2:409
Thomas, Lewis, 2:438
Thomas, Lowell, 1:463
Thomas, Paul R., 2:549
Thomas, Terry, 1:572
Thomas, Theodore (ed), 2:89, 2:412
Thomas, William L. (ed), 2:82
Thompson, Chris, 2:121
Thompson, D'Arcy Wentworth, 1:516
Thompson, Dennis (ed), 2:19
Thompson, E. A., 2:306
Thompson, Edward P., 2:340
Thompson, Ida, 2:495
Thompson, J. E., 1:524
Thompson, J. L., 2:332
Thompson, J.M, 2:332
Thompson, Joseph, 2:368
Thompson, Kenneth, 2:126
Thompson, Kristin, 1:469
Thompson, Lawrence, 1:223
Thompson, Silvanus P., 1:523
Thompson, Virgil, 2:262
Thompson, Wayne C., 2:91
Thomson, Belinda, 2:353
Thomson, Elizabeth H., 2:532
Thoreau, Henry David, 1:165; 2:13
Thorell, Lisa G., 1:578
Thornburg, D., 1:565
Thorndike, Edward L., 2:110
Thorner, J. Lincoln, 1:234
Thornton, Richard C., 2:37
Thornton, Robert, 1:577
Thorpe, James, 1:14
Thorpe, Richard, 2:492
Thorson, Esther, 1:441
Thorton, Richard C., 2:252
Thrower, Norman J. (ed), 2:324
Thubron, Colin, 2:87, 2:90, 2:285, 2:400
Thucydides, 2:289
Thurber, James, 1:290
Thurman, Harold V., 2:487
Thurow, Lester, 2:56, 2:144
Thwaite, Anthony, 1:425
Tienda, Marta, 2:141
Tietze, Heinrich, 1:535
Tiley, W. Edward, 1:572
Tilly, Louise A., 2:340
Tilton, Eleanor M., 1:158
Timberlake, Lloyd, 2:86, 2:394
Timberlake, Michael, 2:94, 2:147
Timms, Howard, 2:436
Tinbergen, Elizabeth A., 2:122
Tinbergen, Niko, 2:122
Tinbergen, Nikolaas, 2:98, 2:465
Tindall, William Y., 1:124
Tingay, Graham I. F., 2:291
Tirion, Wil, 2:470
Tischer, M., 1:585

Tocci, Salvatore, 2:508
Tocqueville, Alexis de, 2:16, 2:180
Tod, M. N., 1:498
Todaro, Michael P., 2:72
Todd, John M., 2:317
Todhunter, Isaac, 1:533
Toffler, Alvin, 1:453; 2:62
Tofte, M., 1:586
Toland, John, 2:236, 2:375, 2:377, 2:385
Tolbert-Rouchaleau, Jane, 1:245
Tolegian, Aram (tr), 1:420
Tolkien, J. R. R., 1:125–26, 1:482
Toll, Robert, 1:454
Tollison, Robert D., 2:71
Tolstoy, Leo, 1:397
Tonnen, Deborah, 1:445
Toohey, Barbara, 2:561
Toor, Rachel, 2:233
Toothill, Elizabeth (ed), 2:437, 2:448
Tooze, John, 2:455
Topham, Douglas, 1:562
Topsfield, Valerie, 1:331
Tordjman, Nathalie, 2:485
Torrance, S., 1:582
Torrence, Bruce, 1:469
Torrents, Nissa (ed), 2:371
Torres, Angelo, 1:467
Toth, Emily, 1:173
Toth, Marian, 1:427
Toupence, William F., 1:203, 1:239
Touretsky, 1:566
Tourlakis, George J., 1:585
Tourtellot, Jonathan B. (ed), 2:76
Towns, Saundra, 1:235
Townsend, Carl, 1:562
Townsend, Kim, 1:190
Toye, Francis, 2:361
Tracton, Ken, 1:564
Tracy, Martin, 1:566
Trager, Oliver (ed), 2:37
Traister, Robert J., 1:565, 1:578; 2:436, 2:471
Trape, Augustine, 2:304
Trappi, R. (ed), 1:582
Trask, David F., 2:219
Traub, J. F., 1:538
Traubner, Richard, 2:263
Travers, K., 1:530
Traynor, John, 2:277
Treadgold, Donald W., 2:92, 2:277, 2:406
Treadgold, Warren, 2:301, 2:311
Trebilcock, Clive, 2:340
Trefil, James S., 2:479, 2:482
Trefousse, Hans L., 2:198
Tremblay, Jean-Paul, 1:538, 1:586
Trench, Richard, 2:90
Trenn, T. J., 2:509
Trevelyan, George M., 2:311, 2:327, 2:328, 2:345

Trevelyan, Raleigh (ed), 1:348
Tribe, Laurence H., 2:17, 2:27
Tricker, R. A. R., 2:527
Trigg, Charles W., 1:535
Trilling, Lionel, 1:41, 1:86
Tripp, Edward, 1:318
Trotsky, Leon, 2:379, 2:380, 2:381
Troupe, Quincy (ed), 1:195
Trower, 1:574
Truckenbrod, Joan, 1:578
Trudeau, Gary B., 1:459, 1:460, 1:461
Trudgill, Peter, 1:437
Trueb, Linda, 2:449
Truesdell, C. A., 1:526
Truman, Harry S., 2:237
Truman, Margaret, 2:237
Trump, Donald, 2:63
Tsukernik, V. M., 2:522
Tuchman, Barbara W., 2:164, 2:224, 2:306,
    2:341, 2:372, 2:400
Tuchman, Gaye, 1:458
Tuck, Jim, 2:370
Tuck, Richard, 2:10
Tucker, Allen B., 1:563
Tucker, Barbara M., 2:185
Tucker, G., 1:326
Tucker, Glenn, 2:196
Tucker, Robert C., 2:380
Tucker, Susie, 1:443
Tudesq, André-Jean, 2:332
Tufts, Eleanor, 2:334
Tumin, Melvin M., 2:145
Tunabe, Kozo, 2:508
Tunis, Edwin, 2:162, 2:169
Turco, Lewis, 1:490
Turing, Alan, 1:551, 1:581
Turkle, Sherry, 1:555
Turner, E. G., 2:285
Turner, Frederick, 2:221
Turner, Frederick Jackson, 2:156,
    2:201
Turner, Jonathan H., 2:124
Turner, Joseph Mallord William,
    2:357
Turner, Michael (ed), 2:69
Turow, Joseph, 1:466
Turton, Peter, 2:371
Tuttle, Sherwood, 2:83
Tutu, Desmond, 2:397
Tuveson, Ernest (ed), 1:30
Tver, David F., 2:497, 2:550
Twain, Mark, 1:182; 2:185, 2:204
Twitchett, Denis (ed), 2:282, 2:309
Twombly, Robert C., 2:217, 2:270
Tyler, Alice F., 2:185
Tyler, Anne, 1:291
Tyler, Charles M., 2:91
Tylor, Edward Burnett, 2:43
Tyson, Neil De Grasse, 2:471

U

Uchida, Yoshika, 2:236
Ueland, Barbara, 1:482
Uhr, Leonard (ed), 1:559
U. Htin Aung, 1:427
Ulack, Richard, 2:400
Ulam, Adam B., 2:375, 2:388
Ulanoff, Stanley, 1:441
Ulene, Art, 2:543
Ullman, Edward, 2:93
Ullman, Jeffrey D., 1:573
Ullmann, Stephen, 1:438
Ulloth, Dana, 1:453
Ulrich, James F., 1:512
Unamuno y Jugo, Miguel de, 1:360
Underwood, Benton J., 2:103
Underwood, John H., 1:571
Underwood, Tim (ed), 1:249
Undset, Sigrid, 1:381
Ungar, Sanford J., 2:86, 2:394
Unger, J. Marshall, 1:583
United Nations, 2:6, 2:37, 2:238
U.S. Department of Commerce, Bureau of
    the Census, 2:4, 2:124
U. S. Public Health Service, Department
    of Health, Office of the Surgeon
    General, 2:550
Unstead, R. J., 2:281
Unterrecker, John (ed), 1:134
Unwin, Timothy, 2:94
Updike, John, 1:292–93
Urban, George, 2:380
Urban, Joan, 1:307
Urdang, Laurence, 1:440
Urdang, Laurence (ed), 1:440
Uris, Leon, 1:293
Urquhart, Brian, 2:390
Usiskin, Zalman, 1:505, 1:506, 1:512
Uspenskii, V. A., 1:535
Utley, Robert M., 2:201

V

Vagts, Detlev, 2:21, 2:152
Vail, John, 2:166, 2:395, 2:412
Valentine, Lloyd M., 2:57
Vallas, Leon, 2:418
Vanags, P., 2:290
Van Amstel, J. J., 1:586
Van Buitenen, J. A. (tr), 1:422
Vance, Mary, 2:268
Van Delft, Peter, 1:535
VanDemark, Paul J., 2:443
Van den Berghe, Pierre L., 2:136
Van den Haag, Ernst, 2:133
Van den Toorn, Pieter C., 2:427

Vander, Arthur J., 2:451
Vanderheiden, Gregg C., 1:571
Van Der Post, Laurens, 2:86
Van der Waerden, B. L., 1:498, 1:506
Van Deusen, Glyndon G., 2:180
Vandiver, Frank E., 2:219
Van Doren, Carl, 2:17, 2:167, 2:168
Van Dusen, Albert E. (ed), 2:162
Van Dyne, Penny, 2:536
Vangelisti, Paul, 1:348
Van Gogh, Vincent, 2:359
Van Horn, Carl E. (ed), 2:6, 2:41
Van Lamsweerde, A. (ed), 1:584
Van Leeuwen, J. (ed), 1:587
Van Meter, Vandelia, 2:277
Van Moos, Stanlislaus, 2:420
Van Sertima, Ivan (ed), 2:433
Van Slyke, Lyman P., 2:87
Varberg, Dale, 1:506
Varey, Simon, 1:24
Varley, H. Paul, 2:87, 2:277, 2:309
Varsegi, Alex, 1:584
Vasilyev, N., 1:512
Vasquez, Librado, 1:433
Vassilious, Marius, 1:562
Vaughan, Alden, 2:163
Vaughan, Henry, 1:17
Vaughn, Edwin C., 2:224
Veblen, Thorstein, 2:62, 2:64, 2:69, 2:146
Vedral, Joyce L., 2:539, 2:543, 2:552
veer Reddy, G. P., 2:562
Velijkov, Mark D., 1:579
Vellozi, Joseph I., 1:513
Venino, S., 2:91
Venttsel, Y., 1:530
Ventura, Fred, 1:564
Verba, Sidney, 2:145
Verdi, Giuseppe, 2:361
Verne, Jules, 1:343
Vesely, Eric Garrigue, 1:565
Vespucci, Amerigo, 2:325
Vialls, Christine, 2:340
Vickery, Donald M., 2:566
Victoria, Queen of Great Britain, 2:369
Vidal, Gore, 2:198
Vidich, Arthur J., 2:131
Vidyakara, 1:422
Vigil-Pinon, Evangelina, 1:538
Viglionese, Paschal C., 1:348
Vilenkin, N. Y., 1:530
Villee, Claude A., 2:448
Villiers, Alan, 2:322
Vinaver, Eugene, 1:7
Vincent, George, 2:125
Vincent, Phillip, 1:555
Vining, Elizabeth Gray, 2:108
Viola, Herman, 2:345
Viola, Susan, 2:345
Viorst, Milton, 2:242

Virando, Jacqueline, 1:578
Virgil, 1:324–25; 2:298
Viroli, Maurizio, 2:11
Vlahos, Olivia, 2:300
Vogler, David J., 2:33
Vogt, Evon Z., 2:52
Vogt, Gregory, 2:476, 2:482, 2:522
Vogt, Thomas M., 2:531
Voight, Cynthia, 1:294
Vojta, George, 2:63, 2:257
Vollmer, Jurgen, 2:394
Vollnhals, Otto, 1:576
Voltaire, 1:344
Von Braun, Wernher, 2:482, 2:483
Von der Heide, John, 2:333
von Hagen, Victor Wolfgang, 2:78
von Hayek, Friedrich A., 2:72
Von Holst, Hermann E., 2:181
Vonnegut, Kurt, Jr., 1:295–96
Von Neumann, John, 1:516, 1:553, 1:586
Von Westernhagen, Curt, 2:362
Voorhees, Richard J., 1:131
Voss, Greg, 1:563
Voth, Alden H., 2:38
Voznesensky, Andrei, 2:418

W

Wabeke, Bertus H., 2:161
Waddell, Jack O. (ed), 2:136
Wade, Linda R., 2:256
Wagenheim, Kal (ed), 1:399
Wagenknecht, Edward C., 1:161
Wagman, Ellen, 2:555
Wagman, Robert J., 2:245
Wagner, Jean, 1:206, 1:260
Wagner, Richard, 2:362
Wagner-Martin, Linda, 1:278
Wagshall, Peter H., 1:522
Waidson, H. M., 1:374
Wai-lim Yip (tr), 1:423
Wainwright, Loudon, 1:455
Waisbren, Burton, 2:567
Waisbren, Charles J., 2:567
Waite Group, 1:565
Waite, Michael T., 1:562
Waite, Mitchell, 1:565
Waldeland, Lynne, 1:211
Waldheim, Kurt, 2:388
Waldrop, M. Mitchell, 1:581
Waldrup, Carole C., 2:156
Waley, Arthur, 1:425; 2:277
Waley, Arthur (ed), 1:425
Walker, Alan, 2:350
Walker, Alan (ed), 2:354
Walker, Alice, 1:296–97, 1:482
Walker, Bryce, 2:494
Walker, David B., 2:36
Walker, Dorothea, 1:122

Walker, Frank, 2:361
Walker, Hallam, 1:339
Walker, John, 2:351
Walker, Keith, 1:24
Walker, M. E., 2:444, 2:446
Walker, Margaret, 1:298
Walker, Philip L. (ed), 2:510
Walker, Robert, 2:346
Walker, Robert H., 2:204
Walker, Samuel, 2:13
Walker, Wallace, 1:515
Wallace, Alfred Russel, 2:459
Wallace, Anthony F., 2:52, 2:185
Wallace, Diane A., 2:435
Wallace, Mike, 1:447
Wallace, Ronald S., 2:311
Wallace-Hadrill, Andrew, 2:296
Wallbank, R. W., 2:285
Wallsten, Robert (ed), 1:289
Walraven, Michael G. (ed), 2:95
Walsh, Gillian Paton, 1:126
Waltar, 2:528
Walter, Alan J., 2:498
Walter, Mildred Pitts, 2:239
Walter, Richard, 1:485
Walterman, Robert H., Jr., 2:63
Walters, Alan, 2:408
Walters, Derek, 2:505, 2:508
Walters, Francis P., 2:224
Walton, Alan G., 2:507
Walworth, Arthur, 2:372
Walworth, Nancy Z., 2:291
Wander, Meghan Robinson (ed), 2:234
Wandersee, Winifred D., 2:156, 2:252
Wang, Li-Chung, 1:498
Ward, Barbara, 2:73
Ward, Brian R., 2:451, 2:452, 2:531, 2:550,
   2:552, 2:553, 2:555, 2:556, 2:564, 2:571
Ward, Geoffrey C., 2:193, 2:234
Ward, Harriet, 2:277
Ware, William, 2:291
Warmenhoven, Henri J., 2:88, 2:406
Warner, Charles D., 1:159
Warner, Craig, 1:281
Warner, Sylvia Townsend, 1:130
Warner, W. Lloyd, 2:51, 2:144
Warren, Earl, 2:31
Warren, Harris G., 2:229, 2:231
Warren, Joseph, 1:497
Warren, Mark D., 2:224
Warren, Robert Penn, 1:299
Washburn, Mark, 2:476
Washburn, Wilcomb E., 2:158
Washington, Booker T., 2:191, 2:213
Washington, George, 2:179
Wasserman, Burton, 2:277
Wasserman, Mark, 2:275
Wassing, Rene S., 2:277
Waterhouse, Ellis, 2:339

Waters, K. H., 2:288
Watland, Charles D., 1:402
Watrous, Hilda, 2:233
Watson, Derek, 2:362
Watson, James D., 2:435, 2:439, 2:440,
   2:441, 2:455
Watson, Jane W., 2:84
Watson, Jim, 1:573
Watson, John B., 2:102–103
Watson, Lillian Eichler, 1:487
Watson, Nancy, 2:494
Watson, O. Michael (ed), 2:136
Watson, Philip, 2:513
Watson, Robert I., 2:96
Watt, Alan, 1:579
Watt, Daniel, 1:565
Watts, Harold H., 1:96
Watts, L., 1:538
Waugh, Evelyn, 1:127
Wayne, Stephen J., 2:40
Ways, Peter, 2:531
Weatherby, W. J., 1:195
Weatherford, Doris, 2:207
Weatherford, Jack M., 2:156
Weathers, Winston, 1:478
Weaver, William (ed), 2:361
Webb, Robert N., 2:453
Webb, Walter P., 2:201
Weber, Doug, 1:559
Weber, Max, 2:56, 2:140, 2:143, 2:147
Webster, C. K., 2:333
Webster, Daniel, 2:183
Webster, John, 1:18
Webster, Noah, 1:430
Wechsler, Judith, 2:349
Wecter, Dixon, 2:230
Wedberg, Anders, 1:498
Weddle, P. D., 1:568
Wedeck, Harry E. (ed), 1:320
Weekley, Ernest, 1:433
Wegener, Alfred Lothar, 2:491
Wehr, Demaris S., 2:121
Wehr, Gerhard, 2:121
Weidhorn, Manfred, 2:331
Weidt, Margaret N., 1:202
Weierstrass, Karl, 1:528
Weil, Andrew, 2:531, 2:555
Weil, Robert (ed), 2:156
Weinberg, Gerald M., 1:559
Weinberg, Lawrence, 2:168
Weinberg, Nathan, 1:555
Weinberg, Paul N., 1:572
Weiner, Elliott A., 2:122
Weiner, Jonathan, 2:84
Weingartner, Paul, 1:500
Weinstein, Cheryl, 1:563
Weinstein, Marlene G., 1:572
Weintraub, Pamela (ed), 2:440
Weintraub, Stanley, 2:369

Weir, David, 2:571
Weisberger, Bernard A., 2:388
Weiss, Ann E., 2:258
Weiss, Edmond, 1:491
Weiss, Jeffrey, 2:567
Weiss, Malcolm E., 2:467
Weiss, Peter, 1:373
Weissberg, Robert, 2:6
Weissbort, Daniel (ed), 1:389
Weissman, Michaele, 2:154
Weitman, Lenore J., 2:138
Weitsman, Madeline, 2:242
Weitzenhoffer, Frances, 2:346
Weitzman, Martin L., 2:63
Weizenbaum, Joseph, 1:555
Welch, Holmes, 2:284
Weldon, Fay, 1:128
Welfare, Simon, 1:75
Wells, C. J., 1:362
Wells, Damon, 2:189
Wells, H. G., 1:129; 2:372
Wells, Harry K., 2:101
Wells, Reuben F., 2:292
Welty, Eudora, 1:300, 1:482
Wenar, Charles, 2:122
Wendell, Barrett, 2:163
Wenk, Arthur B., 2:418
Wenninger, Magnus J., 1:520
Wepman, Dennis, 1:449; 2:323, 2:370, 2:394
Werner, Rudolph, 2:511
Werstein, Irving, 2:363
Wertheimer, Barbara M., 2:156
Werthman, Michael S., 2:273
Wessells, Michael G., 1:556
West, John A., 2:281
West, Nathanael, 1:300
Westerby, Herbert, 2:354
Western Writers of America Staff, 2:202
Westfall, Richard, 2:516
Westkott, Marcia, 2:119
Westmoreland, William C., 2:242
Wetherbee, Winthrop, 1:7
Wetzel, Charles, 2:178
Wetzel, Gregory F., 1:586
Wexelblat, Richard L. (ed), 1:563
Wexler, Jerome, 2:448
Wexman, Virginia, 1:470
Weyl, Hermann, 1:513
Whalley, Paul, 2:449
Wharton, Edith, 1:183
Wharton, Mandy, 2:148
Wheatley, Phillis, 1:154
Wheeler, David (ed), 1:474
Wheeler, James O., 2:93
Wheeler, Post (ed), 1:425
Whelan, Elizabeth M., 2:550
Whicher, Olive, 1:519
Whicher, Stephen (ed), 1:158

Whincup, Greg, 1:423
Whipple, A. B., 2:485, 2:487
Whipple, Fred L., 2:476
Whitaker, Thomas, 1:305
Whitcomb, Ian, 2:265
White, Burton, 2:108
White, C. Langdon, 2:91
White, E. B., 1:456, 1:478
White, Eric W., 2:417
White, Ernest M., 2:225
White, Florence M., 2:242
White, Frederick, 2:522
White, G. Edward, 2:32
White, Harvey L., 2:36
White, Henry, 2:193
White, Howard, 1:584
White, J. Manchip, 2:281
White, Jack R., 1:557; 2:482, 2:522
White, K. D., 2:285
White, Leslie A., 2:43
White, Melvin, 1:449
White, Merry, 2:87, 2:400
White, Patrick, 1:147
White, Paul Dudley, 2:563
White, T. H., 1:130
White, Theodore H., 2:21, 2:252
White, Tony, 1:474
White, William A., 2:228
White, William C., Jr., 2:550
Whitecotton, Joseph W., 2:300
Whitehall, Walter M., 2:187
Whitehead, Alfred North, 1:498
Whitehead, Tony L., 2:43
Whitehouse, Ruth D. (ed), 2:279
Whitfield, Stephen, 1:466
Whitman, Walt, 1:184
Whitney, C. A., 2:477
Whitney, Eleanor N., 1:569; 2:549
Whitney, Patrick, 1:579
Whitney, Sharon, 2:156, 2:255
Whittaker, Ruth, 1:104
Whittall, Arnold, 2:417
Whittier, John Greenleaf, 1:166
Whorton, James C., 2:568
Whyman, Kathryn, 2:510
Whyte, Robert O., 2:93
Whyte, William Foote, 2:131, 2:150
Wicander, E. Reed, 2:492
Wickett, William H., Jr., 2:557
Wiebe, Robert H., 2:224
Wiener, Jonathan, 2:489
Wiener, Norbert, 1:539
Wiesel, Elie, 1:301; 2:385
Wieser, Nora J. (ed and tr), 1:399
Wievorka, Annette, 2:384
Wilbur, Perry, 1:450
Wilcox, Clair, 2:65
Wilcox, Kathleen, 2:542, 2:566
Wilde, Alan (ed), 1:96

Wilde, Oscar, 1:62
Wilder, Roy, Jr., 1:431
Wilder, Thornton, 1:303
Wiley, Larry, 1:513
Wiley, Roland J., 2:357
Wilf, Herbert S., 1:585
Wilford, John Noble, 2:92, 2:476
Wilford, John Noble (ed), 2:435
Wilkes, John, 2:323
Wilkes, Maurice, 1:539
Wilkie, Bernard, 1:465
Wilkins, Maurice Hugh Frederick, 2:441
Wilkinson, Alex C. (ed), 1:571
Wilkinson, Doris Y., 2:531
Wilkinson, J. Harvie, 2:27
Will, George, 1:480
Will-Harris, Daniel, 1:576
Williams, Cecil B,., 1:161
Williams, E. N., 2:277
Williams, Gordon F., 2:562
Williams, Greg H., 2:566
Williams, Guinevere, 2:538
Williams, Guy, 2:568
Williams, Hermine W., 2:261
Williams, James G., 1:538
Williams, Jerr S., 2:13
Williams, John E., 2:521
Williams, L. Pearce, 2:525
Williams, Lea E., 2:400
Williams, Martin, 1:470; 2:227
Williams, Michael R., 1:540
Williams, Oliver F., 2:86, 2:394
Williams, Patricia, 1:491
Williams, Raymond, 1:437; 2:134
Williams, Raymond L., 1:404
Williams, Robert, 1:513
Williams, Robin, 1:576
Williams, Tennessee, 1:304
Williams, William A. (ed), 2:242
Williams, William Carlos, 1:305
Williamson, George, 1:83
Willie, Charles V., 2:136, 2:138
Willie, Charles V. (ed), 2:136
Willis, David K., 2:92, 2:406
Willis, Jerry, 1:571
Willis, Meredith S., 1:490
Wills, Garry, 2:164, 2:260
Wilson, D. A., 2:276
Wilson, David, 2:504
Wilson, Deirdre, 1:435
Wilson, Dick, 2:403
Wilson, Edward O., 2:98, 2:105
Wilson, Francis, 2:484, 2:485
Wilson, George, 1:431
Wilson, J. M., 2:373
Wilson, Jason, 1:408
Wilson, Joan H., 2:230
Wilson, Johnny L., 1:567
Wilson, Raymond (ed), 2:155

Wilson, S. Roy, 1:453
Wilson, Stephen, 1:578, 1:580
Wilson, William J., 2:136
Wilson, Woodrow, 2:225
Windrow, Martin, 2:372
Winfree, Arthur T., 2:462
Winger, Hans, 2:268
Wingerson, Lois, 2:452
Winick, Charles, 2:43
Winkler, Allan M., 2:236
Winkler, Dan, 1:580
Winn, Marie, 1:466, 1:468
Winner, David, 2:398
Winograd, Terry, 1:583
Winslow, Susan, 2:230
Winsor, Phil, 1:578
Winston, Patrick H., 1:566, 1:581
Wirth, Arthur G., 2:220
Wirth, Louis, 2:131, 2:136, 2:147
Wirth, Niklaus, 1:566, 1:587
Wiser, Charlotte V., 2:400
Wiser, William, 2:400
Witcover, Paul, 1:242
Withers, Robert, 1:469
Witt, Elder, 2:6, 2:13, 2:27
Witten, Ian H., 1:579
Witter, Evelyn, 2:170
Wittington, W.A. (ed), 2:400
Witzell, Otto W., 1:556
Wlakowiak, J., 1:490
Wodehouse, P. G., 1:131
Woese, Carl R., 2:461
Wohlgelernter, Maurice, 1:109
Wohlstetter, Roberta, 2:236
Wolchonok, Louis, 1:520
Wold, Allen L., 1:571, 1:580; 2:482
Wolf, Josef, 2:279
Wolf, Steven L., 1:569
Wolf, Theta H., 2:123
Wolfe, Alexander, 1:559
Wolfe, Bertram D., 2:382
Wolfe, Peter, 1:102
Wolfe, Thomas, 1:306
Wolfe, Tom, 1:479; 2:242, 2:482
Wolff, Kurt H. (ed), 2:127
Wolfgang, Marvin E., 2:133
Wolfson, Martin H., 2:57, 2:156
Wolfson, Nicholas, 2:64
Wolpert, Lewis, 2:433
Wolseley, Roland, 1:458
Wolverton, Van, 1:562
Wood, Art, 1:459
Wood, Douglas, 1:445
Wood, E. J., 2:511
Wood, Erskine, 2:202
Wood, Gordon S., 2:7, 2:17
Wood, John C. (ed), 2:73
Wood, Laura N., 2:446
Wood, Linda C., 2:481

Wood, Marian, 2:156
Wood, Michael, 1:318; 2:279, 2:285, 2:306
Wood, Peter H., 2:216
Wood, Richard (ed), 1:441
Wood, Robert, 2:522
Wood, Steven, 1:565
Wood, W. J., 2:164
Woodburne, Russell T., 2:451
Woodford, Peggy, 2:363
Woodger, Michael, 1:581
Woodham-Smith, Cecil Blanche, 2:369, 2:570
Woodhead, A. Geoffrey, 2:290
Woodress, James, 1:209
Woodruff, David S., 2:456
Woods, Geraldine, 2:31, 2:468, 2:497, 2:555
Woods, Harold, 2:31, 2:468, 2:497
Woods, Samuel G., 2:559
Woods, Sylvia, 2:448
Woodside, Arch, 1:441
Woodward, Bob, 1:458; 2:22, 2:27, 2:252
Woodward, C. Vann, 2:156, 2:208
Woodward, William R. (ed), 2:95
Woodwark, John, 1:511
Wooff, C., 1:506
Woolf, Virginia, 1:43, 1:132
Woolhouse, R. S., 1:527
Woollcott, Alexander, 2:265
Woolley, Catherine, 1:484
Wooten, Anthony, 2:449
Worchester, J. H., Jr., 2:367
Worden, Robert L., 2:87
Wordsworth, William, 1:39
World Bank Staff, 2:56
World Health Organization, 2:560
Worrell, Arthur J., 2:163
Worth, Don D., 1:562
Worth, Richard, 2:129, 2:544
Wortham, A. William, 1:557
Wortman, Richard, 2:536
Woube, Mengistu, 2:85
Wratten, S. D., 2:466
Wrenn, John H., 1:263
Wrenn, Margaret, 1:263
Wresch, William, 1:483
Wresch, William (ed), 1:571
Wright, Arthur F., 2:277
Wright, Arthur F. (ed), 2:277
Wright, Deil S., 2:36, 2:41
Wright, E. M., 1:497
Wright, Esmond, 2:527
Wright, Frank Lloyd, 2:217, 2:270
Wright, Gordon, 2:236
Wright, Guy, 1:580
Wright, John M., Jr., 2:385
Wright, Louis B., 2:163
Wright, Olgivanna Lloyd, 2:270
Wright, Richard, 1:307

Wright, Thomas, 2:364
Wrigley, E. Anthony, 2:340
Wrobel, Sylvia, 2:454
Wrong, Dennis, 2:143
Wulf, William A., 1:586
Wundt, Wilhelm, 2:96, 2:114
Wuthnow, Robert, 2:142
Wyatt, David H., 1:571
Wyatt, Sir Thomas, 1:18
Wyden, Peter, 2:242, 2:388
Wyeth, Andrew, 2:271
Wynne, Michael J., 2:447

X

X, Malcolm, 1:450; 2:251
Xu Kongshi (ed), 1:556

Y

Yablonski, Lewis, 2:539
Yablonsky, Lewis, 2:104
Yaglom, I., 1:506, 1:512
Yale, Paul B., 1:516
Yan, L., 1:498
Yannakoudakis, E. J., 1:579
Yapp, Malcolm, 2:366
Yarrow, P. J., 1:339
Yartz, Frank J., 2:285
Yate, Martin J., 1:490
Yates, Elizabeth, 2:189
Yeats, William Butler, 1:134
Yellin, David, 2:303
Yep, Laurence, 2:208
Yergin, Daniel, 2:258
Yinger, Milton, 2:136
Yoder, Jon A., 1:288
Yogman, Michael W., 2:539
Yolen, Jane, 1:484
Yonge, Charlotte, 1:439
Yorke, Ivor, 1:457
Yoshihashi, Takehiko, 2:375
Young, Alida O., 2:202
Young, Bob, 2:531
Young, Gail S., 1:516
Young, Judy, 2:156
Young, Louise B., 2:494
Young, Patrick, 2:122, 2:555
Youngberg, Ruth T., 1:118
Youngs, Bettie B., 2:123
Yourdon, Edward, 1:556, 1:568
Yourdon, Edward (ed), 1:585
Yudkin, John, 2:550
Yuen, C. K., 1:562
Yuki, Sawa (tr), 1:425
Yunker, Lee E., 1:513

Z

Zacarian, Setrag A., 2:553
Zacher, Mark W., 2:390
Zadra, Dan, 2:202
Zafar, Z., 1:563
Zahoran, David G., 1:579
Zaks, Rodney, 1:559
Zander, Alvin, 2:104
Zangwill, Israel, 2:136
Zannes, Estelle, 1:450
Zeidenberg, Matthew, 1:584
Zeiger, Henry A., 2:249
Zeilik, Michael, 2:471
Zeitlin, Irving, 2:125
Zeldin, Theodore, 2:88
Zeldis, Yona, 2:553
Zelinsky, Wilbur, 2:91
Zenger, Chris, 1:556
Zenkovsky, Serge A. (ed), 1:390
Zerman, Melvyn B., 2:6
Zerner, Henri, 2:346
Zieger, Robert H., 2:230
Ziegler, David W., 2:37
Zim, Herbert S., 2:448, 2:485, 2:489
Zimbardo, Philip G., 2:122

Zimmer, Heinrich, 2:309
Zimmer, J. A., 1:563
Zimmerman, David R., 2:553
Zimmerman, Franklin B., 2:338
Zimmerman, J. E., 1:318
Zimmerman, Joseph F., 2:41
Zimor, Jonathan, 2:553
Zindel, Paul, 1:308
Zingo, Laurie, 1:498
Zinner, Stephen H., 2:559
Zinsser, William, 1:478, 1:488
Ziring, Lawrence, 2:87, 2:90, 2:277
Zirker, Jack B., 2:476
Zitarelli, 1:523
Zodhiates, Philip, 1:570
Zola, Emile, 1:344–45
Zonderman, Jon, 2:557
Zorbaugh, Harvey, 2:131
Zorn, Karen L., 1:576
Zottoli, Robert, 2:465
Zube, E. H. (ed), 2:105
Zuboff, Shoshana, 1:556; 2:149
Zubrick, James W., 2:510
Zuckerman, Martin, 1:524
Zurcher, Arnold, 2:6
Zweig, Paul, 1:185
Zysman, John, 2:65

TITLE INDEX

This index appears in each of two volumes of *The Young Adult Reader's Adviser.* It presents in alphabetical sequence the titles of all books listed in the bibliographies. It also includes notable books, poems, ballads, and essays that may be mentioned in general introductions and biographical narratives.

The number of the volume in which a title is cited is given with a colon followed by the page number on which the title can be found. For example, the entry 1:219 indicates that the title *Absalom, Absalom!* can be found on page 219 of Volume 1. Some titles refer to more than one page number. For example, the entry 1:284, 2:197 indicates that the title *Abe Lincoln Grows Up* can be found both on page 284 of Volume 1 (in American Literature) and on page 197 of Volume 2 (in United States History). When two or more identical titles by different authors appear, the last name of each author is given in parentheses following the title.

A

A. E. Housman: A Collection of Critical Essays, 1:54
A. J. Cronin, 1:78
Aaron Burr: A Biography, 2:169
Aaron Copland, 2:261
Aaron's Rod, 1:101
The Abbess of Crewe, 1:121
The ABC Murders, 1:73
ABC's of the Human Body, 2:531
Abe Lincoln Grows Up, 1:284; 2:198
Abigail Adams, 2:170
Abigail Adams: A Biography, 2:170
Abigail Adams: Advisor to a President, 2:170
Abigail Adams: First Lady of Faith and Courage, 2:170
Aboriginal Population of Northwestern Mexico, 2:80
The Abortion: An Historical Romance 1966, 1:203
About Thinking, 1:477
Above Hawaii, 2:90

Above London, 2:87
Above Paris, 2:87
Above San Francisco, 2:90
Abraham Lincoln, 2:198
Abraham Lincoln: Citizen of New Salem, 2:198
Abraham Lincoln: His Speeches and Writings, 2:197
Abraham Lincoln: The Prairie Years and the War Years, 1:284; 2:198
Abraham Lincoln and the Union, 2:198
Absalom, Absalom!, 1:219
The Absolute at Large, 1:384
Abstract Expressionism: A Critical Record, 2:415
Abstraction for Programmers, 1:563
Abundance for What? And Other Essays, 2:132
Abuse in the Family, 2:539
The Academic Mind: Social Scientists in Time of Crises, 2:125
The Academic Revolution, 2:132
The Academic Scribblers: Economists in Collision, 2:55

An Accidental Man, 1:107
Accidental Millionaire: The Rise and Fall of Steve Jobs at Apple Computer, 1:546
The Accidental Tourist, 1:291
Acculturation in Seven Indian Tribes, 2:43
The Accumulation of Capital, 2:60
Achievement Motive: With New Preface, 2:113
The Achievement of Ted Hughes, 1:95
The Achieving Society: With a New Introduction, 2:113
Acid Rain (Boyle and Boyle), 2:81
Acid Rain (Gay), 2:467, 2:486
Acid Rain (McCormick), 2:82, 2:255
Acid Rain: A Sourcebook for Young People, 2:570
Acquired Immunodeficiency Syndrome: Current Issues and Scientific Studies, 2:560
Across Five Aprils, 2:192
Across the Rhine, 2:382
Across the River and into the Trees, 1:236
Across the Wide Missouri, 2:160
The Action of Natural Selection on Man, 2:459
Active Voices: A Writer's Reader, 1:480
The Acts of King Arthur and His Noble Knights, 1:7
Acupuncture to Yoga: Alternative Methods of Healing, 2:531
Ad Lucilium Epistulae Morales, 1:323
Ada: A Guided Tour and Tutorial, 1:566
Ada: A Life and Legacy, 1:547
Ada as a Second Language, 1:566
Ada from the Beginning, 1:566
Ada in Industry, 1:566
Adam and the Train, 1:363
Adam Bede, 1:49
Adam or Ape: A Sourcebook of Discoveries About Early Man, 2:49
Adam Smith and Modern Political Economy: Bicentennial Essays on the Wealth of Nations, 2:61
Adam Smith's Economics: Its Place in the Development of Economic Thought, 2:61
Addiction: Its Causes, Problems, and Treatments, 2:554
Addison-Wesley Geometry, 1:511
Address to the Christian Nobility of the German Nation, 2:316
Adlai Stevenson: His Life and Legacy, 2:238
Administrative Behavior, 2:140
The Admirable Crichton, 1:67
Admiral Hornblower in the West Indies, 1:85
Admiral of the Ocean Sea: A Life of Christopher Columbus, 2:160

Adolescence, 2:543
The Adolescent (A Raw Youth), 1:392
Adolescent Development, 2:543
Adolescent Development and Behavior, 2:542
The Adolescent Passage: Developmental Issues, 2:106
Adolescent Pregnancy and Prenatal Care, 2:543
Adolf Hitler, 2:377
Adonais, 1:38
Adrienne Rich, 1:281
Adrienne Rich's Poetry, 1:281
Adult Development and Aging, 2:129
Advanced BASIC: A Modular Approach, 1:564
Advanced Placement Test in Computer Science, 1:565
The Advanced Theory of Language as Choice and Chance, 1:529
Advancement of Learning, 2:435
Advances in Chinese Computer Science, 1:556
Advances in Research and Theory, 2:112
Adventure Game Writer's Handbook, 1:490
Adventure with a Microscope, 2:444
Adventures for Another World: Jonathan Trumble's Commonplace Book, 2:162
The Adventures of Augie March, 1:199
The Adventures of George Washington, 2:179
The Adventures of Huckleberry Finn, 1:181, 1:182
The Adventures of Ibn Batuta: A Muslim Traveler of the Fourteenth Century, 2:301
The Adventures of Menahem-Mendl, 1:383
The Adventures of Sherlock Holmes, 1:48
The Adventures of Tom Bombadil, 1:125
The Adventures of Tom Sawyer, 1:181, 1:182
Adventures with Atoms and Molecules: Chemistry Experiments for Young People, 2:500, 2:504
Adventures with D. W. Griffith, 1:470
Advertisement Book, 1:441
Advertising Age: The Principles of Advertising at Work, 1:441
Advertising and Consumer Psychology, 1:441
Advertising as Communication, 1:440
Advertising, Communication, Economics, 1:441
Advertising Copywriting, 1:483
Advertising Directed at Children: Endorsements in Advertising, 1:441

Advertising in America: An Introduction to Persuasive Communication, 1:441

Advertising, Politics, and American Culture: From Salesmanship to Therapy, 1:440

Advertising Slogans of America, 1:441

Advertising Techniques and Consumer Fraud, 1:441

Advertising the American Dream: Making Way for Modernity, 1920–1940, 1:440

Advertising to Children, 1:440

Advertising's Hidden Effects, 1:440

Advice to a Young Scientist, 2:433

Advise and Consent, 2:33

Aeneid, 1:319, 1:320, 1:324; 2:297, 2:298

Aeneidos, 1:325

Aeschylus, 1:312

Aeschylus' Orestia: A Literary Commentary, 1:312

Aesopica: A Series of Texts Relating to Aesop or Ascribed to Him or Closely Connected with the Literary Tradition That Bears His Name, 1:313

Aesop's Fables, 1:312

The Aesthetics of Power: The Poetry of Adrienne Rich, 1:281

The Affluent Society, 2:66, 2:241

Africa (Dostert), 2:85

Africa (Lye), 2:393

Africa: Geography and Development, 2:86

Africa: Its People and Their Culture History, 2:51, 2:300

Africa: The People and Politics of an Emerging Continent, 2:86, 2:394

Africa, a Modern History: Eighteen Hundred to Nineteen Seventy Five, 2:276

Africa and Africans, 2:393

Africa and America, 2:273

Africa and Europe from Roman Times to National Independence, 2:273

Africa and the Great Powers in the 1980s, 2:393

Africa and the Renaissance: Art in Ivory, 2:310

Africa in the Iron Age, 2:300

Africa in the Roman Empire, 2:298

Africa Must Unite, 2:396

Africa Since Eighteen Hundred, 2:276

Africa South of the Sahara, 2:85

African Art: Its Backgrounds and Tradition, 2:277

African Beginnings, 2:300

African Civilizations: Precolonial Cities and States in Tropical Africa—An Archaeological Perspective, 2:299

African Environments and Resources, 2:85

African Fables, 1:411

African Folktales, 1:411

African Folktales: Traditional Stories of the Black World, 1:411

African Historical Biographies, 2:274

African Independence: The First Twenty-Five Years, 2:393

An African Journey, 2:86, 2:393

The African Kings, 2:298

African Literatures in the Twentieth Century: A Guide, 1:411

African Middle Ages, Fourteen Hundred to Eighteen Hundred, 2:276

African Mythology, 2:300

African Origin of Civilization: Myth or Reality, 2:299

African Plays for Playing, 1:411

The African Queen, 1:84

African Short Stories: An Anthology, 1:411

The African Slave Trade, 2:320, 2:363

African States and Rulers: An Encyclopedia of Native, Colonial and Independent States and Rulers Past and Present, 2:277

African Statistical Yearbook, 2:85, 2:89, 2:272

African Systems of Kinship and Marriage, 2:54

African Tightrope: My Two Years as Nkrumah's Chief of Staff, 2:396

The Africans: A Triple Heritage, 2:393

Africans and Their History, 2:299

Africans Become Afro-Americans: Selected Articles on Slavery in the American Colonies, 2:162

Afro-American Music, South Africa, and Apartheid, 2:261

After Barney Clark: Reflections on the Artificial Heart Program, 2:565

After Many a Summer Dies the Swan, 1:95

After the Dancing Days, 2:224

After the Fall, 1:266

After the Last Sky: Palestinian Lives, 2:89, 2:412

After the Tears: Parents Talk About Raising a Child with a Disability, 2:563

The Aftermath: Asia, 2:382

The Aftermath: Europe, 2:382

Against the Stream: Critical Essays on Economics, 2:135

Agamemnon, 1:105

Agatha Christie: A Biography, 1:74

Agatha Christie: An Autobiography, 1:74

An Agatha Christie Companion: The Complete Guide to Agatha Christie's Life and Work, 1:74

Agatha Christie: The Woman and Her Mysteries, 1:74

Age and Anthropological Theory, 2:52

The Age Care Sourcebook: A Resource Guide for the Aging and Their Families, 2:544

Age de raison, 1:340

The Age of Alexander, 2:288

The Age of Calamity: 1300–1400, 2:305

Age of Discovery, 2:320

Age of Empire, 2:339

Age of Enlightenment: The Eighteenth Century Philosophers, 2:326

Age of Faith, 2:305

Age of God–Kings: Time Frame 3000–1500 B.C, 2:280

Age of Improvement, 1783 to 1867, 2:339

The Age of Innocence, 1:183

The Age of Intelligent Machines, 1:581

The Age of Interdependence: Economic Policy in a Shrinking World, 2:72

Age of Iron, 1:413

The Age of Jackson, 2:180

Age of Louis Fourteenth, 2:326

The Age of Miracles: Medicine and Surgery in the Nineteenth Century, 2:568

The Age of Napoleon (Durant), 2:329

The Age of Napoleon (Herold), 2:329, 2:330

The Age of Nationalism: The First Era of Global History, 2:275

The Age of Reason (Paine), 2:165

The Age of Reason (Sarte), 1:340

Age of Reason Begins, 2:326

The Age of Reason, Being an Investigation of True and Fabulous Theology, 2:165

The Age of Reform: From Bryan to F.D.R, 2:218

Age of Revolution: Seventeen Eighty-Nine to Eighteen Forty-Eight, 2:332

The Age of Television, 1:465

The Age of the Cathedrals: Art and Society, 980–1420, 2:305

The Age of the Crowd: A Historical Treatise on Mass Psychology, 2:104

The Age of the Economist, 2:56

The Age of the Great Depression, 1929–1941, 2:229, 2:230

The Age of the Moguls, 2:204

Age of Voltaire, 2:326

The Age of Washington: George Washington's Presidency, 1789–1797, 2:180

Agent Orange on Trial: Mass Toxic Disasters in the Courts, 2:571

Aggression, 2:98

Aging, 2:544

Aging and Old Age: An Introduction to Social Gerontology, 2:129, 2:146

Aging: Continuity and Change, 2:129

Aging, Health, and Family: Long Term Care, 2:129

Aging, Health, and Society, 2:544

Aging in America: The Federal Government's Role, 2:32

The Agony and the Ecstasy, 2:318

The Agrarian Sociology of Ancient Civilizations, 2:143

The Agricola and The Germania, 2:297

Agricultural Mathematics, 1:504

Agricultural Thought in the Twentieth Century, 2:251

Ah, but Your Land Is Beautiful, 1:416

Ah, Wilderness, 1:273

Aha! Gotcha: Paradoxes to Puzzle and Delight, 1:536

Aha! Insight, 1:536

AIDS (Armstrong), 2:559

AIDS (Nourse), 2:560

AIDS: Deadly Threat, 2:560

AIDS: In Search of a Killer, 2:560

AIDS: Information Sourcebook, 2:560

AIDS: The Facts, 2:560

AIDS: Trading Fears for Facts: A Guide for Teens, 2:560

AIDS: What Does It Mean to You?, 2:560

AIDS and the Law: A Guide for the Public, 2:560

The AIDS Book: Creating a Positive Approach, 2:560

The AIDS Epidemic, 2:560

The AIDS Fighters, 2:559

The AIDS File: What We Need to Know About AIDS Now!, 2:560

AIDS Prevention and Control, 2:560

AIDS—The True Story: A Comprehensive Guide, 2:559

The Air War in Europe, 2:382

Airs, Waters and Places, 2:533

Aissa Saved, 1:71

Ake: The Years of Childhood, 1:418

Akhenaten: King of Egypt, 2:279

Al Jaffee's Mad Book of Magic and Other Dirty Tricks, 1:456

Al Jaffee's Mad Inventions, 1:456

Al Smith and His America, 2:226

Alan Paton, 1:416

Alan Sillitoe, 1:121

Alan Turing: The Enigma, 1:538, 1:551

Alaska, 1:264

The Albatross Muff, 1:140

Albert Camus, 1:333

Albert Einstein and the Theory of Relativity, 2:520

Albert Einstein, Creator and Rebel, 2:520

Albert Einstein: Historical and Cultural Perspectives: The Centennial Symposium in Jerusalem, 2:520

Albert Schweitzer, 2:535

Albrecht Dürer, 2:314
Albrecht Dürer: Sketchbook of His
  Journey to the Netherlands, 1520–1521,
  2:313
An Album of American Women: Their
  Changing Role, 2:432
Album of Space Flight, 2:242
An Album of the Vietnam War, 2:242
An Album of World War II, 2:384
Alcohol Abuse, 2:556
Alcohol and the Family, 2:539
Alcoholic Family, 2:540
Alcoholism, 2:556
Aldous Huxley, 1:96
The Aleph and Other Stories, 1:399
Alex Randall's Used Computer Handbook,
  1:559
Alexander Fleming, 2:559
Alexander Fleming: The Man and the
  Myth, 2:559
Alexander Graham Bell, 2:204
Alexander Hamilton, 2:174
Alexander Hamilton: Architect of
  American Nationalism, 2:174
Alexander Pope, 1:28
Alexander Pope: A Life, 1:28
Alexander Pushkin, 1:395
Alexander's Bridge, 1:209
Alexandr Solzhenitsyn: Beleaguered
  Literary Giant of the U.S.S.R, 1:396
Alexandra, 1:271
Alexandre Dumas: Genius of Life, 1:334
The Alexandria Quartet, 1:81
Alfred Binet, 2:123
Alfred Hitchcock, 1:470
Alfred Kroeber, 2:45
Alfred Kroeber: A Personal Configuration,
  2:45
Alfred Marshall: Progress and Politics,
  2:57
Alfred Russel Wallace, 2:460
Alfred Wegener: The Father of
  Continental Drift, 2:492
Algebra: An Algorithmic Treatment, 1:585
Algebra: An Introductory Course, 1:505
Algebra: Structure and Method Book 2,
  1:505
Algebra and Trigonometry, 1:506
Algebra and Trigonometry: A
  Straightforward Approach, 1:524
Algebra and Trigonometry: Structure and
  Method Book 1, 1:505
The Algebra of Mohammed Ben Musa,
  1:506
The Algebra of Omar Khayyam, 1:506
Algebra 1, 1:506
Algebra I, 1:505
Algebra One, 1:499
Algebra the Easy Way, 1:505

Algorithmics: The Spirit of Computing,
  1:585
Algorithms and Complexity, 1:585
Algorithms and Data Structures, 1:587
Algorithms for Games, 1:585
Algorithms, Graphs and Computers, 1:585
Algorithms in C, 1:586
Algorithms, Software and Hardware of
  Parallel Computers, 1:559
The Alhambra, 1:159
Alias O. Henry: A Biography of William
  Sydney Porter, 1:178
Alice Munro, 1:145
Alice Walker, 1:297
Alice's Adventures in Wonderland, 1:45
All About Health and Beauty for the
  Black Woman, 2:553
All About Maps and Mapmaking, 2:92
All About Your Money, 2:70
All Creatures Great and Small, 1:93
All Faithful People: Change and
  Continuity in Middletown's Religion,
  2:142
All Fall Down: America's Tragic Encounter
  with Iran, 2:37
All for Love, 1:23
All God's Children Need Traveling Shoes,
  1:191
All Men Are Brothers: Life and Thoughts
  of Mahatma Gandhi As Told In His
  Own Words, 2:365
All My Sons, 1:266
All Possible Worlds: A History of
  Geographical Ideas, 2:78
All Quiet on the Western Front, 2:224,
  2:371
All the Conspirators, 1:96
All the King's Men, 1:298, 1:299
All the President's Men, 1:458; 2:22, 2:252
All Things Bright and Beautiful, 1:93
All Things Considered, 1:481
All Things Wise and Wonderful, 1:93
All Times, All Peoples: A World History
  of Slavery, 2:275
All Together Now, 1:204; 2:237
Allan Quartermain, 1:51
Allen Ginsberg, 1:225
Allen's Synonyms and Antonyms, 1:439
Allergies, 2:561
Allies for Freedom: Blacks and John
  Brown, 2:189
Almanac of American Politics: 1990
  Edition, 2:32
Almanac of the American People, 2:152
Almanac of the Great War: A Chronology
  of the First World War, 2:371
Almayer's Folly, 1:76
Alnilam, 1:215
Aloneness, 1:205

Along This Way: The Autobiography of James Weldon Johnson, 1:245
Alouette, 1:328
The Alpine Christ and Other Poems, 1:244
The Alteration, 1:65
Alterations of Personality, 2:123
Altered Destinies, 2:562
Alternate Computers, 1:559
An Alternate Style: Options in Composition, 1:478
Alternative Health Maintenance and Healing Systems for Families, 2:531
Alvey: Britain's Strategic Computing Initiative, 1:555
Always Coming Home, 1:254
Always the Young Strangers, 1:284
Alzheimer's Disease, 2:562
Amadeus, 1:119
Amanda/Miranda, 1:275
The Amateur Astronomer's Handbook: A Guide to Exploring the Heavens, 2:470
The Amateur Naturalist, 2:437
The Amazing and Death-Defying Diary of Eugene Dingman, 1:308
The Amazing Universe, 2:478
The Amazing Voyage of the New Orleans, 2:185
Ambassador's Journal: A Personal Account of the Kennedy Years, 2:66
The Ambassadors, 1:179
The Ambidextrous Universe, 1:536
Ambrose Gwinnett Bierce: A Bibliography and Biographical Data, 1:169
Amelia Earhart, 2:229
The Amen Corner, 1:195
America Adopts the Automobile, 1895–1910, 2:218
America and Around the World: The First Logs of Columbus and Magellan, 2:159
America and the Jazz Age: A History of the Twenties, 2:226
America As a Multicultural Society, 2:135
America at Seventeen-Fifty: A Social History, 2:162, 2:164
America Enters the World: A People's History of the Progressive Era and World War I, 2:372
America Held Hostage, 2:255
America in the Gilded Age, 2:203
America in the Twentieth Century, 2:7
America in the World, 1962–1987: A Strategic and Political Reader, 2:36
America in Vietnam: A Documentary History, 2:242
The American, 1:179
American Aerial Close Up, 2:90
American and Soviet Intervention: Effects on World Stability, 2:257

American Art: Painting, Sculpture, Architecture, Decorative Arts, Photography, 2:261
American Art Posters of the 1890s, 2:213
American Beat, 1:480
American Beauty, 1:220
American Buildings and Their Architects, 2:262
American Capitalism: The Concept of Countervailing Power, 2:66
An American Childhood, 1:482
American Civil War, 2:192
American College Dictionary, 1:246
American Commercial Banking: A History, 2:70
American Constitution: Its Origin and Development, 2:166
American Constitutional Interpretation, 2:17
The American Constitutional Tradition, 2:16
The American Counties, 2:41
The American Country Women, 2:232
American Dialects, 1:431
An American Dictionary of the English Language, 1:430
An American Dilemma: The Negro Problem and Modern Democracy, 2:128, 2:134, 2:135
American Diplomacy, 2:391
American Domestic Priorities, 2:71
American Dream and Zoo Story, 1:186
The American Dream in the Great Depression, 2:229
American Dreams: Lost and Found, 1:489
American Education: The Colonial Experience, 1607–1783, 2:161
American Education: The National Experience, 1783–1896, 2:184
American English, 1:435
The American Environment, 2:82
An American Exodus: A Record of Human Erosion, 2:232
American Federalism: A New Partnership for the Republic, 2:35
American Federalism: A View from the States, 2:35
American Film Genres, 1:469
American Film Now: The People, the Power, the Money, the Movies, 1:469
American Folk Art: The Art of the Common Man in America 1750–1900, 2:213
American Foreign Policy, 2:38
American Foreign Policy: A Global View, 2:38
American Genesis: Captain John Smith and the Founding of Virginia, 2:163

American Given Names: Their Origin and History in the Context of the English Language, 1:439
The American Governorship, 2:41
American Heritage Book of Indians, 2:157
The American Heritage History of World War I, 2:224, 2:371
American Heritage Illustrated History of the United States, 2:157, 2:161, 2:163, 2:168, 2:184, 2:192, 2:200, 2:203, 2:218, 2:223, 2:228, 2:234, 2:237, 2:241, 2:382, 2:387
American Heritage Picture History of the Civil War, 2:153, 2:192
American Hunger, 1:307
American Ideals and Other Essays, Social and Political, 2:222
American Ideals versus the New Deal, 2:231
American Indian, 1492–1976: A Chronology and Fact Book, 2:153
The American Indian in Film, 1:475
The American Indian in Urban Society, 2:136
American Indian Literature, 2:158
American Indian Myths and Legends, 2:157
American Indian Reader: Anthology, 2:157
American Indian Women: Telling Their Lives, 2:152
American Individualism, 2:231
American Journey: The Times of Robert Kennedy, 2:249
American Kinship: A Cultural Account, 2:52
American Labor and the War, 2:224
The American Language, 1:432, 1:435, 1:436
American Leaders, 1789–1987: A Biographical Summary, 2:5
The American Legislative Process: Congress and the States, 2:33, 2:41
An American Life: One Man's Road to Watergate, 2:252
American Mass-Market Magazines, 1:455
American Media and Mass Culture: Left Perspectives, 1:454
The American Medical Association Encyclopedia of Medicine, 2:530
The American Medical Association Family Medical Guide, 2:530
The American Medical Association Handbook of First Aid and Emergency Care, 2:566
The American Medical Association Straight Talk No Nonsense Guide to Back Care, 2:561
The American Mercury: Facsimile Edition of Volume One 1924, 1:436

The American Music Miscellany, 2:187
American Musicians: Fifty-Six Portraits in Jazz, 2:261
The American Occupational Structure, 2:148
The American Pageant: A History of the Republic, 2:152
American Painting and Sculpture: 1862–1932, 2:213
American Parties in Decline, 2:39
American Phenomenon, 2:216
American Place-Names: A Concise and Selective Dictionary for the Continental United States of America, 1:439
The American Political Dictionary, 2:6
The American Political Tradition, 2:169, 2:204
The American Presidency: A Bibliography, 2:5
American Presidents: A Bibliography, 2:5
The American Reader: Words That Moved a Nation, 2:155
The American Revolution: How Revolutionary Was It?, 2:163
American Revolution: Seventeen Seventy-Five to Seventeen Eighty-Three, 2:327
The American Revolutionaries: A History in Their Own Words, 2:164
The American Scene: A Reader, 1:436
An American Selection of Lessons in Reading and Speaking, 1:430
American Sign Language: A Comprehensive Dictionary, 1:448
American Singers: Twenty-Seven Portraits in Song, 2:261
The American Soldier, 2:128
The American Songbag, 1:284
American State and Local Government, 2:41
The American System: A New View of Government in the United States, 2:16
American Talk: The Words and Ways of American Dialects, 1:431
An American Tragedy, 1:215, 1:216, 1:217
An American Vision: Three Generations of Wyeth Art, 2:271
The American Weather Book, 2:485
The American Wilderness, 2:263
American Women Artists: From Early Indian Times to the Present, 2:156
American Women in Jazz: Nineteen Hundred to the Present: Their Words, Lives, and Music, 2:262
American Women in the Twentieth Century, 2:153
Americanizing the American Indians: Writings by the "Friends of the Indians," 1880–1990, 2:201

The Americans, 2:161
Americans Before Columbus: Ice-Age
  Origins, 2:157
The Americas, 2:88, 2:90
America's Economy, 1989 Annual, 2:62,
  2:257
America's Future: Transition to the 21st
  Century, 2:144
America's Health Care Revolution: Who
  Lives? Who Dies? Who Pays?, 2:567
America's Hidden Wilderness, 2:90
America's Humor from Poor Richard to
  Doonesbury, 1:461
America's Immigrant Women, 2:207
America's Immigrants: Adventures in
  Eye-Witness History, 2:207
America's Longest War: The United States
  and Vietnam, 1950–1975, 2:241, 2:252
America's Magnificent Mountains, 2:82
America's Majestic Canyons, 2:83
America's Music: From the Pilgrims to the
  Present, 2:153
America's Outdoor Wonders, 2:90
America's Prisons, 2:133
America's Seashore Wonderlands, 2:83
America's Spectacular Northwest, 2:91
America's Wild and Scenic Rivers, 2:83
Amerigo and the New World, 2:325
Amerigo Vespucci, Pilot Major, 2:158,
  2:325
Amerika, 1:369
Amiable Autocrat: A Biography of Doctor
  Oliver Wendell Holmes, 1:158
Amiga Desktop Video, 1:579
Amiga Desktop Video Guide, 1:580
Amiga for Beginners, 1:560
Amiga Machine Language, 1:564
Amiga 3D Graphic Programming in
  BASIC, 1:578
AmigaDOS Inside and Out, 1:562
Amores, 1:321
Amoretti, 1:17
Amos Fortune, Free Man, 2:189
Amphibians, 2:449
Amusements in Mathematics, 1:535
Amusing Ourselves to Death: Public
  Discourse in the Age of Show Business,
  1:454
Amy Lowell, 1:258
The Analects of Confucius, 2:282,
  2:283
The Analysis of Behavior: A Program for
  Self-Instruction, 2:101
The Analysis of International Relations,
  2:36
Analytic Geometry (Fuller), 1:514
Analytic Geometry (Middlemiss), 1:514
Analytic Geometry (Selby), 1:514
Analytic Geometry of Three Dimensions,
  1:514

The Analytical Engine: Computers—Past,
  Present, and Future, 1:542
The Anatomy of American Popular
  Culture, 1840–1861, 2:187
Anatomy of an Epidemic, 2:557
The Anatomy of Racial Attitudes, 2:135
Anatomy of Seed Plants, 2:447
The Anatomy of Terror, 2:392
Ancient Africa, 2:299
Ancient Americas: The Making of the
  Past, 2:300
Ancient Architecture: Mesopotamia,
  Egypt, Crete, 2:280
Ancient Athens, 2:284
Ancient China, 2:281
Ancient China: Art and Archaeology,
  2:282
Ancient Civilizations: Four Thousand B.C.
  to Four Hundred A.D., 2:273
Ancient Egypt, 2:279
Ancient Egypt: Its Culture and History,
  2:281
Ancient Egyptian Calligraphy: A
  Beginner's Guide to Writing
  Hieroglyphs, 2:280
Ancient Egyptians, 2:280
Ancient Egyptians: Religious Beliefs and
  Practices, 2:279
Ancient Folktales from Around the World,
  2:276
Ancient Greece: An Illustrated History,
  2:274
Ancient Greek Literature, 1:311
Ancient Greek Numerical Systems, 1:498
Ancient Greek Philosophy: Sourcebook
  and Perspective, 2:285
Ancient Greek Town, 2:285
Ancient Greeks, 2:285
The Ancient Greeks: A Critical History,
  2:284
Ancient History: From Its Beginnings to
  the Fall of Rome, 2:273
Ancient History of China to the End of
  the Chou Dynasty, 2:281
Ancient History of India, 2:282
Ancient India: From the Earliest Times to
  the First Century A.D, 2:282
Ancient Indian History and Civilization,
  2:282
Ancient Indians: The First Americans,
  2:157, 2:299
Ancient Iraq, 2:281
Ancient Israel, 2:281
Ancient Judaism, 2:143
Ancient Life in Mexico and Central
  America, 2:299
Ancient Lives: Daily Life in Egypt of the
  Pharaohs, 2:281
The Ancient Mariners, 2:285
Ancient Maya, 2:300

The Ancient Mediterranean, 2:274
Ancient Mexico: Art, Architecture, and Culture in the Land of the Feathered Serpent, 2:298
Ancient North Americans, 2:157
Ancient Romans, 2:291
Ancient Traditions of Geometric Problems, 1:512
And I Heard a Bird Sing, 1:229
And Keep Your Powder Dry: An Anthropologist Looks at America, 2:46
And Never Said a Word, 1:363
And No Birds Sang, 1:144
And Still I Rise, 1:192
And the War Came: The North and the Secession Crises, 1860–1861; 2:193
Andaman Islanders, 2:53, 2:54
The Andean Past: Land, Societies, and Conflicts, 2:88, 2:409
Andersonville, 2:192
The Andes of Southern Peru, 2:77
André Gide, 1:336
Andreas Vesalius of Brussels, 1514–1564, 2:548
Andrew Carnegie, 2:206
Andrew Jackson, 2:183
Andrew Jackson: Seventh President of the United States, 2:183
Andrew Jackson, Frontier Patriot, 2:183
Andrew Johnson: A Biography, 2:198
Andrew Johnson and the Uses of Constitutional Power, 2:198
Andrew Marvell: The Critical Heritage, 1:13
Andrew Wyeth: The Helga Pictures, 2:271
Andria, 1:323
Androcles and the Lion, 1:120
Androgyne, Mon Amour, 1:304
Andromache, 1:339
Andromache (1667) and Other Plays, 1:339
Andromaque, 1:339
An Angel at My Table, 1:139
The Angel at the Gate, 1:405
Angel Face, 1:250
Angel Pavement, 1:114
Angels and Other Strangers: Family Christmas Stories, 1:484
The Anglo–Saxon Manner: The English Contribution to Civilization, 2:306
The Angry Hills, 1:293
Angry Waters: Floods and Their Control, 2:492
Anguished English: An Anthology of Accidental Assaults upon Our Language, 1:477
Animal Architecture, 2:463
The Animal Cell, 2:438
Animal Communication, 2:462
Animal Farm, 1:110, 1:111

The Animal in Its World, Explorations of an Ethologist, 1932–1972, 2:465
Animal Language, 2:461
Animal Sketching, 2:261
Animal Thinking, 2:462
Animals Without Backbones: An Introduction to the Invertebrates, 2:448
Animated Algorithms: A Self-Teaching Course in Data Structures and Fundamental Algorithms, 1:586
Animated Photography: The ABC of the Cinematograph, 1:474
Animated Raggedy Ann and Andy: The Story Behind the Movie, 1:474
Animation: A Reference Guide, 1:474
Animation: The Art and the Industry, 1:474
Animation from Script to Screen, 1:474
Animation Magic with Your Apple IIe and IIc, 1:577
Animation Techniques, 1:474
Animator's Workbook, 1:474
Ann Lee's, 1:69
Anna Christie, 1:273, 1:274
Anna Karenina, 1:397
The Anna Papers, 1:225
The Annals of Heechee, 1:278
The Annals of Imperial Rome, 2:297
The Annals, 2:297
Anne Bradstreet, 1:152
Anne Hutchinson: Fighter for Religious Freedom, 2:161
Anne of Avonlea, 1:142, 1:143
Anne of Green Gables, 1:142, 1:143
Anne of Ingleside, 1:143
Anne of the Island, 1:143
Anne of Windy Poplars, 1:143
Anne Radcliffe, 1:28
Anne's House of Dreams, 1:143
Annie Allen, 1:205
Annie Magdalene, 1:140
The Annotated Alice, 1:536
Annotated Bibliography of Expository Writing in the Mathematical Sciences, 1:497
The Annotated Sherlock Holmes: The Four Novels and the Fifty-six Short Stories Complete, 1:48
Annual Editions: Aging, 2:129
Annual Editions: Economics 89/90, 2:257
Annual Editions: Economics 90/91, 2:62
Annual Editions: Marriage and Family 89/90, 2:138
Annual Editions: Money and Banking 90/91, 2:70
Annual Editions: Personal Growth and Behavior 89/90, 2:98
Annual Editions: Psychology, 90/91, 2:95
Annual Editions: Social Problems 90/91, 2:124

Annual Editions: Sociology 90/91, 2:125
Annual Editions: Urban Society, 2:147
Annual Review of Computer Science, 1:538
The Annunciation, 1:225
The Annus Mirabilis of Sir Isaac Newton, 2:516
Another Country, 1:195
Another Part of the Forest, 1:235
Anouilh: Five Plays, 1:328
Anpao: An American Indian Odyssey, 1:239
Ansel Adams: An Autobiography, 2:263
Ansel Adams: Letters and Images, 1916–1984, 2:263
The Answer Book About Computers, 1:557
The Antagonists: Hugo Black, Felix Frankfurter and Civil Liberties in Modern America, 2:28
Anthills of the Savannah, 1:411
An Anthology of Armenian Poetry, 1:420
An Anthology of Chinese Literature from the Fourteenth Century to the Present, 1:423
Anthology of Danish Literature: Middle Ages to Romantism, 1:374
Anthology of Danish Literature: Realism to the Present, 1:374
An Anthology of Islamic Literature: From the Rise of Islam to Modern Times, 1:420
An Anthology of Japanese Literature: From the Earliest Era to the Mid-Nineteenth Century, 1:425; 2:275
Anthology of Korean Literature: From Early Times to the Nineteenth Century, 1:426
An Anthology of Modern Arabic Poetry, 1:420
An Anthology of Modern Arabic Verse, 1:420
Anthology of Modern Indonesian Poetry, 1:426
Anthology of Modern Japanese Poetry, 1:425
An Anthology of Modern Kashmiri Verse, 1930–1960, 1:422
Anthology of Modern Oriya Poetry, 1:422
Anthology of Modern Swedish Literature, 1:374
Anthology of Modern Turkish Short Stories, 1:420
Anthology of Modern Writing from Sri Lanka, 1:422
Anthology of Modern Yiddish Literature, 1:383
Anthology of Norwegian Lyrics, 1:374

An Anthology of Pre-Revolutionary Russian Science Fiction, 1:389
Anthology of Sanskrit Court Poetry: Vidyakara's "Subhasitartahosa, 1:422
An Anthology of Spanish Poetry: From the Beginning to the Present Day, 1:355
Anthology of Swedish Lyrics: 1752 to 1925, 1:374
Anthology of Western Armenian Literature, An, 1:420
Anthony Burgess, 1:71
Anthony Burns: The Defeat and Triumph of a Fugitive Slave, 1:230
The Anthropological Lens: Harsh Light, Soft Focus, 2:42
Anthropological Research: The Structure of Inquiry, 2:42
An Anthropologist at Work, 2:44, 2:46
Anthropology, 2:42
Anthropology: Culture, Patterns, and Processes, 2:45
Anthropology and Modern Life, 2:44
The Anti-Federalists, 2:166
The Anti-Federalists: Critics of the Constitution, Seventeen Eighty-One–Seventeen Eighty-Eight, 2:166
Antigone, 1:328
Anti-Semitism in America, 2:136
The Antislavery Harp, 1:170
Antoine Lavoisier: Chemist and Revolutionary, 2:500
Antony and Cleopatra, 2:288
Anwar Sadat, 2:414
Anwar Sadat, Egyptian Ruler and Peace Maker, 2:414
Anyone for Insomnia? A Playful Look at Sleeplessness, 1:192
Apache Devil, 1:208
The Apartheid Crisis: How We Can Do Justice in a Land of Violence, 2:86, 2:394
Apartheid's Rebels: Inside South Africa's Hidden War, 2:85, 2:393
Aphorisms, 2:533
Aphorisms from His Bedside Teachings and Writings, 2:534
APL in Exposition, 1:566
Apocalypse and Other Poems, 1:400
Apocolocyntosis, 1:323
Apollo: The Ten-Year Race to Put a Man on the Moon, 2:242
Apollonius of Perga. Treatise on Conic Sections, 1:513
Apollonius on Cutting Off a Ratio, 1:513
An Apology for Poetry, 1:16
An Apology for Printers, 2:167
Apparitions, 1:297, 1:298

Apple BASIC: Data File Programming, 1:564

The Apple Cart, 1:120

Apple Graphics: Tools and Techniques, 1:578

Apple LOGO: Activities for Exploring Turtle Graphics, 1:565

The Apple Tree, 1:80

Apple II User's Guide for Apple II Plus and Apple IIe, 1:560

Appleworks in the Classroom, 1:569

AppleWorks Made Easy, 1:573

Application Development Without Programmers, 1:585

Applications of Geometric Series, 1:511

An Applications-Oriented Approach to Artificial Intelligence, 1:566

Applied Descriptive Geometry, 1:516

The Apprenticeship of Duddy Kravitz, 1:145

Approaches to the Study of Social Structure, 2:144

April Morning, 1:218

Aquinas, 2:307

Ara Vos Prec, 1:82

Arab and Jew: Wounded Spirits in a Promised Land, 2:90, 2:412

The Arab Mind, 2:301

Arabesques, 1:392, 1:393

The Arabian Night: A Study of Sir Richard Burton, 2:364

The Arabian Nights, 2:364

Arabian Sands, 2:90

Arabic and Persian Poems, 1:420

The Arab-Israeli Dilemma, 2:89, 2:412

Arabs: A Short History, 2:280

Arabs in History, 2:301

Arcadia, 1:16

Archaeological Finds from Pre-Qin Sites in Guangdong, 2:278

Archaeology: A Brief Introduction, 2:278

The Archaeology of Ancient China, 2:281

The Archaeology of Greece: An Introduction, 2:284

Archibald MacLeish, 1:261

Archimedes, 1:521

Archimedes: Greatest Scientist of the Ancient World, 1:521; 2:285

Archimedes in the Middle Ages, 1:521; 2:518

The Architecture of Castles, 2:305

The Architecture of the Roman Empire: An Introductory Study, 2:291

The Architecture of the United States, 2:262

Arctic Twilight: Old Finnish Tales, 1:374

The Ardis Anthology of Russian Futurism, 1:389

Are Computers Alive? Evolution and New Life Forms, 1:555

Are Quanta Real? A Galilean Dialogue, 2:519

Are We to Be a Nation? The Making of the Constitution, 2:166

Are You in the House Alone?, 1:275

Are You There God? It's Me, Margaret, 1:201

Argonauts of the Western Pacific, 2:46

Ariel, 1:276

Arilla Sundown, 1:230

Aristocracy and People: Britain, Eighteen Fifteen to Eighteen Sixty-Five in Germany, 2:332

Aristophanes: His Plays and His Influence, 1:313

Aristophanic Comedy, 1:313

Aristotle (Barnes), 2:442

Aristotle (Jaeger), 2:287

Aristotle for Everybody, 2:287

Aristotle the Philosopher, 2:442

Aristotle to Zoos: A Philosophical Dictionary of Biology, 2:437

Aristotle's Constitution of Athens, 2:287

Aristotle's Physics, 2:442

Arithmetic Skills Worktext, 1:504

Arithmetica, 1:507

The Armada, 2:326

Armadale, 1:45

Armageddon, 1:293

The Armchair Universe: An Exploration of Computer Worlds, 1:537

Armed Truce: The Beginning of the Cold War, 1945–1946, 2:388

Armenian Folktales and Legends, 1:420

Armenian Poetry Old and New, 1:420

Armoury of Light Verse, 1:192

Arms and Oil: U. S. Military Strategy and the Persian Gulf, 2:258

Arms and the Man, 1:120

Army Life in a Black Regiment, 2:192

The Army of the Future, 2:386, 2:387

Around the World in Eighty Days, 1:342, 1:343

Arrow and the Foundations of the Theory of Economics Policy, 2:64

Arrow of God, 1:411

Arrowsmith, 1:256

Ars Amatoria, 1:321

Ars Conjectandi, 1:530

Art: Conversations with Paul Gsell, 2:355

Art and Artists of the Middle Ages, 2:306

The Art and Craft of Feature Writing: The Wall Street Journal Guide, 1:487

Art and Geometry, 1:515

The Art and Science of Negotiation, 2:132

The Art and Science of Radio, 1:461

Art and the Computer, 1:577

Art and Visual Perception: A Psychology of the Creative Eye—The New Version, 2:113

Art in Our Times: A Pictorial History, 1890–1980, 2:262

Art, Music, and Literature, 1:566

Art, Myth, and Ritual: The Path to Political Authority in Ancient China, 2:281

The Art of Cézanne, 2:349

Art of Computer Programming: Semi-Numerical Algorithms, 1:585

The Art of Desktop Publishing: Using Personal Computers to Publish It Yourself, 1:575

The Art of Fiction: Notes on Craft for Young Writers, 1:482

The Art of Loving, 2:103

The Art of Paul Gaugin, 2:353

Art of Persuasion: A History of Advertising Photography, 1:441

Art of Poetry, 2:294

Art of the Cinematographer: A Survey and Interviews with Five Masters, 1:470

Art of the Dance, 2:266

The Art of the Deal, 2:63

Art of the Western World: From Ancient Greece to Post-Modernism, 2:273

The Art of Thinking: A Guide to Critical and Creative Thought, 1:478

Art of Three Dimensional Design: How to Create Space Figures, 1:520

The Art of Understanding Yourself, 2:537

The Art of Using Computers, 1:537

The Art of Walt Disney: From Mickey Mouse to the Magic Kingdoms, 1:475

The Art of War, 2:20

Art of Watching Films, 1:469

Art of Writing Advertising, 1:483

Arthritis, 2:561

Arthur C. Clarke, 1:75

Arthur C. Clarke's World of Strange Powers, 1:75

Arthur Conan Doyle, 1:48

Arthur Mervyn, 1:152

Arthur Miller, 1:266

Articles of Confederation: An Interpretation of the Social Constitutional History of the American Revolution, 1774–1781, 2:17

The Artifacts of R. Buckminster Fuller—A Comprehensive Collection of His Designs and Drawings: The Dymaxion Experiment (1926–1943), 1:522

Artificial Experts: Social Knowledge and Intelligent Machines, 1:582

The Artificial Heart, 2:565

Artificial Intelligence, 2:110

Artificial Intelligence: The Case Against, 1:580

Artificial Intelligence: The Very Idea, 1:581

Artificial Intelligence and Human Learning: Intelligent Computer-aided Instruction, 1:570

Artificial Intelligence and Instruction: A Selected Bibliography, 1:570

Artificial Intelligence and National Defense: Opportunity and Challenge, 1:568

Artificial Intelligence and Natural Man, 1:582; 2:110

Artificial Intelligence and Statistics, 1:583

Artificial Intelligence at MIT: Expanding Frontiers, 1:581

Artificial Intelligence for Society, 1:582

Artificial Intelligence in Action, 1:581

Artificial Intelligence Systems in Government, 5th Conference, 1:580

Artificial Intelligence Terminology: A Reference Guide, 1:580

Artificial Intelligence Using C, 1:564

Artificial Satellites, 2:480

Artists in Quotation: A Dictionary of the Creative Thoughts of Painters, Sculptors, Designers, Writers, Educators, and Others, 2:275

Arts in Early American History, 2:187

As I Lay Dying, 1:219

As I Saw It, 2:26

As Thousands Cheer: the Life of Irving Berlin, 2:264

As You Desire Me, 1:351

Ash Wednesday, 1:82

Asia and Australasia, 2:91

Asian Drama: An Inquiry into the Poverty of Nations, 2:87, 2:134, 2:135, 2:399

The Asian Political Dictionary, 2:87, 2:277

Asian Power and Politics: The Cultural Dimensions of Authority, 2:399

Asimov on Astronomy, 2:469

Asimov on Chemistry, 2:497

Asimov on Physics, 2:512

Asimov's Biographical Encyclopedia of Science and Technology, 2:431, 2:434

Asimov's Chronology of Science and Discovery: How Science Has Shaped the World and How the World Has Affected Science from 4,000,000 B.C. to the Present, 2:272

Asimov's Guide to Halley's Comet: The Awesome Story of Comets, 2:474

Asimov's New Guide to Science, 2:431, 2:434

Asking Questions About Behavior: An Introduction to What Psychologists Do, 2:98

Asoka and Indian Civilization, 2:281

Aspects of Development and Underdevelopment, 2:60

Aspects of Greek Medicine, 2:285

Aspects of Language and Culture, 2:134
Aspects of Monet: A Symposium on the Artist's Life and Times, 2:346
Aspects of Nature in Different Lands and Different Climates, 2:78
Aspects of the Theory of Syntax, 1:435
Aspects of Verdi, 2:361
Assassination! Kennedy, King, Kennedy, 2:241
Assassination of President John F. Kennedy, 2:248
Assassination of Robert Kennedy, 2:248
The Assault on Truth: Freud's Suppression of the Seduction Theory, 2:118
Assembly Language Step By Step, 1:564
Assessing Individuals: Psychological and Educational Tests and Measurements, 2:122
Assessing Stress in Children, 2:123
The Assistant, 1:261, 1:262
The Association of American Geographers: The First Seventy-Five Years, 2:78
Asthma, 2:562
Asthma and Hay Fever: How to Relieve Wheezing and Sneezing, 2:562
Astronomy, 2:469
Astronomy: From Copernicus to the Space Telescope, 2:470
Astronomy: From Stonehenge to Quasars, 2:469
Astronomy: The Cosmic Perspective, 2:471
Astronomy and Planetology: Projects for Young Scientists, 2:469
Astronomy and Telescopes: A Beginner's Handbook, 2:436, 2:471
Astronomy from Space: Sputnik to Space Telescope, 2:480
The Astronomy Handbook, 2:470
Astronomy of the Ancients, 2:469
Astronomy Today: Planets, Stars, Space Exploration, 2:470
Astronomy with a Small Telescope, 2:436
Astronomy with Binoculars, 2:470
At Ease: Stories I Tell to Friends, 2:239
At Fault, 1:172
At Heaven's Gate, 1:299
At Home: The American Family, 2:184
At Large, 1:480
At the Summit: A New Start in U.S.–Soviet Relations, 2:406
At War in Nicaragua: The Reagan Doctrine and the Politics of Nostalgia, 2:408
At Winters End, 1:285
At Wit's End, 1:447, 1:480
At Work with Albert Schweitzer, 2:535
Atalanta in Calydon, 1:59
Atanasoff, Forgotten Father of the Computer, 1:538
Atlantic America, 1492–1800, 2:90

The Atlantic Frontier: Colonial American Civilization, 1607–1763, 2:163
Atlantic Slave Trade: A Census, 2:189
An Atlas of African History, 2:299
Atlas of Ancient America, 2:156, 2:299
Atlas of Ancient Egypt, 2:279, 2:280
The Atlas of Archaeology, 2:273
Atlas of Columbus and the Great Discoveries, 2:158
Atlas of Southeast Asia, 2:400
Atlas of the Arab World, 2:89
Atlas of the Bible, 2:276
Atlas of the Christian Church, 2:273, 2:290
Atlas of the Greek World, 2:285
Atlas of the Islamic World Since 1500, 2:89
Atlas of the Jewish World, 2:280
Atlas of the Lewis and Clark Expedition, 2:176
Atlas of the Roman World, 2:290
Atlas of the Third World, 2:75
Atlas of the World Today, 2:75
Atlas of Today, 2:75
Atlas of World Cultures, 2:51
Atmosphere, 2:80, 2:484
Atmosphere, Weather, and Climate, 2:80, 2:483
Atomic Structure, 2:500
Atomic Theory and the Description of Nature, 2:501
Atoms and Quanta, 2:519
Atoms in the Family: My Life with Enrico Fermi, 2:528
Atoms, Molecules, and Quarks, 2:508
Attila: King of the Huns, 2:291
Attitudes, Personality, and Behavior, 2:97
Attributes of Memory, 2:103
Audubon and His Journals, 2:187
The Audubon Society Encyclopedia of Animal Life, 2:448
The Audubon Society Field Guide to North American Fishes, Whales, and Dolphins, 2:449
The Audubon Society Field Guide to North American Fossils, 2:495
The Audubon Society Field Guide to North American Insects and Spiders, 2:448
The Audubon Society Field Guide to North American Reptiles and Amphibians, 2:449
The Audubon Society Field Guide to North American Rocks and Minerals, 2:492
August, 1:376
August 1914: The Red Wheel I, 1:396
August Strindberg, 1:380
Auguste Comte: The Foundation of Sociology, 2:126
Augustine, 2:304

Augustine of Hippo, 2:304
An Augustine Treasury: Selections from the Writings of St. Augustine, 2:304
"Auld Lang Syne," 1:32
Aunt Erma's Cope Book: How to Get from Monday to Friday in Twelve Days, 1:447
Aura, 1:402, 1:403
Aurora Leigh, 1:43
Australia, 2:91
Australia: A Geography, 2:91
Australia: A Natural History, 2:91
Australian English: The Language of a New Society, 1:434
Austria and the Papacy in the Age of Metternich: Between Conflict and Cooperation, 1809–1830, 2:333
Authentic Narrative of a Voyage Performed by Captain Cook and Captain Clerke in His Majesty's Ships Resolution and Discovery During the Years 1776–1780: In Search of a North-West Passage between the Continents of Asia and America (1782), 2:321
Author as Character in the Works of Sholem Aleichem, 1:384
The Authoritarian Personality, 2:114
Authority and Reward in Organizations: An International Research, 2:140
Autism: Nature, Diagnosis and Treatment, 2:121
Autistic Children: New Hope for a Cure, 2:122
An Autobiographical Sketch by John Marshall, 2:30
Autobiographies One (O'Casey), 1:109
Autobiographies Two (O'Casey), 1:109
Autobiography (Cellini), 2:312
Autobiography (T. Roosevelt), 2:222
The Autobiography and Other Writings (Franklin), 2:526
Autobiography and Selected Writings (Franklin), 2:167
The Autobiography of an Ex-Colored Man, 1:245
The Autobiography of an Idea, 2:217
The Autobiography of Andrew Carnegie, 2:206
The Autobiography of Benjamin Franklin, 2:167, 2:168, 2:526
The Autobiography of Calvin Coolidge, 2:228
Autobiography of Guiseppe Garibaldi, 2:344
The Autobiography of Harry S. Truman, 2:237
The Autobiography of Henry VIII, 2:310
The Autobiography of Johann Wolfgang von Goethe, 1:366

Autobiography of John Stuart Mill, 2:72
The Autobiography of LeRoi Jones/Amiri Baraka, 1:197
The Autobiography of Lincoln Steffens, 2:219
The Autobiography of Malcolm X, 1:450; 2:250, 2:251
The Autobiography of Mark Twain, 1:182
The Autobiography of Miss Jane Pittman, 1:224
The Autobiography of Sam Houston, 2:186
Autobiography of W. E. Burghardt Du Bois: A Soliloquy on Viewing My Life From the Last Decade of Its First Century, 2:210
The Autobiography of William Carlos Williams, 1:305
Autobiography: The Story of My Experiments with Truth, 2:365
AutoCAD: The Complete Reference, 1:578
The Autocrat of the Breakfast Table, 1:158
Automata, Languages and Programming, 1:581
The Automatic Computing Engine: Papers by Alan Turing and Michael Woodger, 1:551, 1:581
The Autumn Garden, 1:235
Autumn of the Patriarch, 1:403
Aux sources de la Kwai, 1:332
Avenues and the Metaphysics of Causation, 2:302
Averroes' Doctrine of Immortality: A Matter of Controversy, 2:302
Averroës on Plato's Republic, 2:302
Averroës's Middle Commentary on Aristotle's Topic, 2:302
The Avignon Quintet, 1:81
Awake and Sing, 1:272
The Awakening, 1:167, 1:172
The Awakening and Selected Stories, 1:173
Awareness of Dying, 2:137
Ayesha: The Return of She, 1:51
Azazel, 1:194
Aztec, 2:300
The Aztecs (Berdan), 2:298
The Aztecs (Crosher), 2:299
Azul, 1:401

B

Baal, 1:365
The Bab Ballads, 1:50
Babbage's Calculating Machines, 1:542
Babbit, 1:256
Babe Ruth, Home Run Hero, 2:226
Babe Zaharias, 2:226

Babette's Feast and Other Anecdotes of Destiny, 1:376
Baby and Child Care, 2:541
Babylon, 2:280
The Babylonian Captivity of the Church, 2:316
Babylonian Life and History, 2:279
Bach, 2:334
The Bach Reader, 2:334
The Bachelors, 1:121
Back to Methuselah, 1:120
Back to the City: The Making of a Movement, 2:147
A Backward Glance, 1:183
Bad Guys: A Pictorial History of the Movie Villain, 1:475
The Bagatelles from Passy, 2:168
Bahrain and the Gulf: Past Perspectives and Alternative Futures, 2:89, 2:412
The Bakhchesarian Fountain and Other Poems, 1:395
Balanchine: A Biography, 2:415
The Bald Eagle: Haunts and Habits of a Wilderness Monarch, 2:465
The Ballad in Literature, 1:9
The Ballad of Peckham Rye, 1:121
"The Ballad of Reading Gaol," 1:62
The Ballads, 1:9
Ballads and Other Poems, 1:160
Banana Bottom, 1:260
Bangladesh: Biography of a Muslim Nation, 2:87
Banjo, 1:260
Banned Films: Movies, Censors and the First Amendment, 1:468
The Banner of Battle: The Story of the Crimean War, 2:340
The Bantam Book of Correct Letter Writing, 1:487
Bantu Beliefs and Magic, 2:299
Bantu Tribes of South Africa, 2:299
The Baptism and The Toilet, Two Plays, 1:197
Barabbas, 1:379
"Babara Allen," 1:8
Barbarian Stories, 1:107
Barnaby Rudge, 1:46, 1:47
Barnes and Noble Thesaurus of Science, 2:432
Barren Ground, 1:226, 1:227
The Barretts of Wimpole Street, 1:43
Barrie: The Story of J. M. B., 1:68
Barry Goldwater: Freedom Is His Flight Plan, 2:245
Barsoom: Edgar Rice Burroughs and the Martian Vision, 1:208
Bartholomé de Las Casas: His Life, His Apostolate, and His Writings, 2:161
"Batleby the Scrivener," 1:162
Bartók: His Life and Times, 2:416

Bartók's Years in America, 2:416
Baryshnikov, 2:414
Basic Approach to Structured BASIC, 1:564
Basic BASIC: A Structured Approach, 1:564
The Basic Book of Synonyms and Antonyms, 1:440
Basic Cases in Constitutional Law, 2:6, 2:17
Basic Computer Games: Microcomputer Edition, 1:567
Basic Concepts in Sociology, 2:143
The BASIC Cookbook, 1:564
BASIC for Beginners, 1:564
A Basic Framework for Economics, 2:56
Basic Geometry, 1:512
Basic Luther, 2:317
BASIC Programming: Problem Solving with Structure and Style, 1:564
BASIC Programming for Kids, 1:564
Basic Research Resources in Political Science, 2:5
Basic Writings in the History of Psychology, 2:96
The Basic Writings of Sigmund Freud, 2:117
Battle: Story of the Bulge, 2:385
Battle Cry, 1:293
Battle Cry of Freedom: The Civil War Era, 2:193
The Battle for Public Opinion: The President, the Press, and the Polls During Watergate, 1:457
The Battle-Ground, 1:226
The Battle of Britain, 2:383
Battle of Little Big Horn, 2:201
The Battle of Normandy: Falaise Gap, 2:384
The Battle of the Atlantic, 2:383
The Battle of the Bulge, 2:383
The Battle with the Slum: A Ten Year War Rewritten, 2:212
Battles for Scandinavia, 2:383
Battles of the Revolutionary War, 1775–1781, 2:164
Baudelaire, 1:330
Bauhaus: Weimar, Dessau, Berlin, Chicago, 2:268
Bay of Pigs, 2:242
Bay of Pigs: A Firsthand Account of the Mission by a U. S. Pilot in Support of the Cuban Invasion Force in 1961, 2:242
The Beasts of Tarzan, 1:208
Beat to Quarters, 1:84, 1:85
The Beautiful and the Damned, 1:222
The Beauty of Doing Mathematics: Three Public Dialogues, 1:497
The Beauty of Fractals: Images of Complex Dynamical Systems, 1:516

Bech: A Book, 1:292
Bech Is Back, 1:292
Becket, 1:328
Beckonings, 1:205
Becoming: Basic Considerations for a
  Psychology of Personality, 2:115
Bede the Venerable, 2:308
Bees: Their Vision, Chemical Senses, and
  Language, 2:463
Beethoven, 2:334
Beetles and How They Live, 2:449
Before It's Too Late: A Scientist's Case for
  Nuclear Energy, 2:496
Before the Fall: An Inside View of the
  Pre-Watergate White House, 2:255
Before the Mayflower: A History of Black
  America, 2:152
Before the Sun Dies: The Story of
  Evolution, 2:456
Before the Trumpet: Young Franklin
  Roosevelt, 1882–1905, 2:234
A Beggar in Jerusalem, 1:301
The Beggar Maid, 1:145
The Beggar Queen, 1:187
The Beginner's Guide to Astronomy, 2:470
Beginner's Love, 1:250
Beginning FORTRAN, 1:566
Beginning Projects for Children, 1:556
The Beginnings of Greek Mathematics.
  Synthese Historical Library, 1:498
Beginnings of Human Life, 2:451
The Beginnings of Imperial Rome: Rome
  in the Mid-Republic, 2:291
Beginnings: The Story of Origins—of
  Mankind, Life, the Earth, the Universe,
  2:277, 2:434, 2:456
A Begonia for Miss Applebaum, 1:308
Behavior: An Introduction to Comparative
  Psychology, 2:102
The Behavior of Organisms, 2:101
Behavioral Economics and Business
  Organization, 2:63
Behaviorism, 2:102
Behind A Mask: The Unknown Thrillers
  of Louisa May Alcott, 1:167
Behind Barbed Wire: The Imprisonment of
  Japanese Americans During World War
  II, 2:235
Behind Mud Walls, Nineteen Thirty to
  Nineteen Sixty; With a Sequel: The
  Village in 1970, 2:400
Behind the Filmmaking Scene, 1:469
Behind the Mirror: A Search for a Natural
  History of Human Knowledge, 2:100,
  2:103, 2:464
Behind the Wall: A Journey Through
  China, 2:87, 2:400
Behold Man: A Photographic Journey of
  Discovery Inside the Body, 2:545

Being a Plant, 2:447
Being an Anthropologist: Fieldwork in
  Eleven Cultures, 2:43
Being Governor: The View from the
  Office, 2:40
Being Seventy: The Measure of a Year,
  2:108
Bel Ami, 1:337, 1:338
Bel Ria, 1:136
Béla Bartók, 2:416
Béla Bartók: Essays, 2:416
Belief, Attitudes, and Values: A Theory of
  Organization and Change, 2:97
Beliefs, Attitudes, and Human Affairs,
  2:97
The Bell, 1:107
The Bell Jar, 1:276, 1:277; 2:121
Bella Malmaridada, 1:358
Belonging in America: Reading Between
  the Lines, 2:94
Beloved, 1:269
Ben-Gurion Looks at the Bible, 2:412
Ben Jonson: A Life, 1:12
Ben Jonson: The Complete Poems, 1:12
Ben Jonson and the Cavalier Poets, 1:12
Ben Jonson's Plays and Masques, 1:12
A Bend in the River, 1:406
The Bender, 1:118
Bendigo Shafter, 1:252
Beneath Apple DOS, 1:562
Beneath the Mask: An Introduction to
  Theories of Personality, 2:114
Benedict Arnold: Patriot and Traitor,
  2:164
Benefits and Risks of Knowledge-Based
  Systems, 1:583
"Benito Cerino," 1:162
Benito Juárez, 2:370
Benito Mussolini, 2:374
Benito Mussolini: Fascist Dictator of Italy,
  2:375
Benjamin Britten: A Commentary on His
  Works from a Group of Specialists,
  2:417
Benjamin Britten: His Life and Operas,
  2:417
Benjamin Britten: Peter Grimes, 2:416
Benjamin Disraeli: Letters, 1815–1834,
  2:343
Benjamin Disraeli: Letters, 1835–1837,
  2:343
Benjamin Franklin, 2:168
Benjamin Franklin: A Biography, 2:526
Benjamin Franklin: An Autobiographical
  Portrait, 2:526
Benjamin Franklin: The New American,
  2:526
Benjamin Franklin, Envoy Extraordinary:
  The Secret Missions and Open Pleasures

of Benjamin Franklin in London and
Paris, 2:526
Bentham (Dinwiddy), 2:8
Bentham (Harrison), 2:8
Bentham's Theory of the Modern State,
2:8
Beowulf, 1:5, 1:6
Beowulf: An Introduction, 1:6
Bérénice, 1:339
Berlin Airlift, 2:238
Berlin Crisis of 1961: Soviet American
Relations and the Struggle for Power in
the Kremlin, June–November, 1961,
2:392
Berlin Diary: The Journal of a Foreign
Correspondent 1934–1941, 2:375
The Berlin Stories, 1:96
The Berlin Wall: Kennedy, Krushchev and
a Showdown in the Heart of Europe,
2:388
Berlioz, 2:347
Berlioz and His Century: An Introduction
to the Age of Romanticism, 2:347
Bernard Malamud, 1:262
Bernard Malamud: A Collection of Critical
Essays, 1:262
Bernardo O'Higgins, 2:370
Bernstein: A Biography, 2:265
Bernstein on Broadway, 2:265
Bert Breen's Barn, 2:226
Bertolt Brecht, 1:365
Bertrand Russell, 1:503
Bertrand Russell: A Political Life, 1:504
Bertrand Russell: A Psychobiography of a
Moralist, 1:503
The Best American Essays 1988, 1:480
Best American Poetry 1988, 1:490
Best American Short Stories 1988, 1:490
The Best and the Brightest, 2:21, 2:241
Best Book of Lotus 1–2–3, 1:574
The Best Book of Windows 3, 1:562
Best Editorial Cartoons of the Year: 1989
Edition, 1:459
The Best in Children's Books: The
University of Chicago Guide to
Children's Literature, 1979–1984, 1:484
The Best in Me and Other Animals: A
Collection of Pieces and Drawings
About Human Beings and Less
Alarming Creatures, 1:290
The Best Newspaper Writing, 1:487
The Best of Roald Dahl, 1:79
The Best of Robert Service, 1:146
The Best of Saki, 1:115
The Best of Simple, 1:241
The Best of the West: Stories That
Inspired Classic Western Films, 1:473
The Best of the West II: Stories That
Inspired Classic Western Films, 1:473

Best Plays of 1988–89, 1:489
The Best Poems, 1:349
The Best Science Fiction of Isaac Asimov,
1:194
Best Short Plays of 1988, 1:489
Best Short Stories of Dostoyevsky, 1:392
Best Short Stories of J. G. Ballard, 1:67
The Best Short Stories of O. Henry,
1:178
The Best Short Stories of Rudyard
Kipling, 1:55
Best-Kept Secret: The Story of the Atomic
Bomb, 2:235
Betrayal, 1:114
Betrayed by Rita Hayworth, 1:408,
1:409
Betty Friedan, 2:244
Betty Friedan: A Voice for Women's
Rights, 2:244
Between Elite and Mass Education:
Education in the Federal Republic of
Germany, 2:521
Between Planets, 1:233
Between the Acts, 1:132
Between the Wars: America, Nineteen
Nineteen to Nineteen Forty-One, 2:229
Beware Soul Brother, 1:411
Beyond a Reasonable Doubt: Inside the
American Jury System, 2:6
Beyond Boom and Crash, 2:57
Beyond Culture, 2:43
Beyond Drill and Practice: Expanding the
Computer Mainstream, 1:570
Beyond Expectation: Religious Dimensions
in Cultural Anthropology, 2:48
Beyond Formula: American Film Genres,
1:469
Beyond Freedom and Dignity, 2:101
Beyond Human Scale: Large Corporations
at Risk, 2:63, 2:257
Beyond IBM: The Real Story of Why IBM
Has Worked, Why It Needs to Change
and What Other Companies Can Learn,
1:540
Beyond Nineteen Eighty-Four:
Doublespeak in a Post-Orwellian Age,
1:437
Beyond Personality, 1:104
Beyond Punjab: A Sequel to Punjabi
Century, 2:400
Beyond Separate Spheres: Intellectual
Roots of Modern Feminism, 2:148
Beyond the Blue Event Horizon, 1:278
Beyond the Chocolate War, 1:212
Beyond the Divide, 2:201
Beyond the Gutenberg Galaxy:
Microcomputers and the Emergence of
Post-Typographic Culture, 1:576
Beyond the Horizon, 1:273, 1:274

Beyond the Hundredth Meridian: John Wesley Powell and the Second Opening of the West, 2:91, 2:201

Beyond the Melting Pot: The Negroes, Puerto Ricans, Jews, Italians, and Irish of New York City, 2:136

Beyond the Relaxation Response, 2:536

Beyond the Safe Zone: Collected Short Fiction of Robert Silverberg, 1:286

Beyond the Sea of Ice: The First Americans, 2:158

Beyond the Welfare State: Economic Planning and Its International Implications, 2:135

Beyond This Place, 1:78

The Bhagavad-Gita, 1:421, 1:422

The Bhopal Syndrome: Pesticides, Environment, and Health, 2:571

Bibliographic Guide to Computer Science, 1:538

A Bibliographic Guide to the History of Computing, Computers and the Information Processing Industry, 1:540

A Bibliography of Recreational Mathematics, 1:535

The Bicentennial Man and Other Stories, 1:194

The Big Bands, 2:262

The Big Bang, 2:471, 2:479

"Big Blonde," 1:274

Big Blue: IBM's Use and Abuse of Power, 1:540

The Big Change: America Transforms Itself, 1900–1950, 2:237

The Big Issues in the Passage to Adulthood, 2:542

The Big Knife, 1:272

The Big Knockover, 1:231

The Big Sea: An Autobiography, 1:241

The Big Sleep, 1:210

Big Sur, 1:246

The Bigelow Papers, 1:161

Billiards at Half-Past Nine, 1:363

Billiards, Mathematically Treated, 1:535

Billy Budd, 1:162

Billy Budd, Sailor, 1:162

Biloxi Blues, 1:286

Bioburst: The Impact of Modern Biology on the Affairs of Man, 2:437

Biochemistry: A Functional Approach, 2:511

Biochemistry: The Molecular Basis of Cell Structure and Function, 2:511

Biochemistry at Depth, 2:511

The Biochemistry of Viruses, 2:443

Biofeedback and Sports Science, 1:569

The Biographer's Craft, 1:483

Biographical Dictionary of Afro-American and African Musicians, 2:156

Biographical Dictionary of Jazz, 2:153

The Biographical Dictionary of Scientists: Astronomers, 2:431

The Biographical Dictionary of Scientists: Biologists, 2:431

The Biographical Dictionary of Scientists: Chemists, 2:431

The Biographical Dictionary of Scientists: Physicists, 2:431

Biographical Directory of the United States Executive Branch, 1774–1989, 2:6

Biography of Crèvecoeur: The Life of an American Farmer, 1:153

A Biography of George F. Kennan: The Education of a Realist, 2:391

Biography of the English Language, 1:429

Biological Foundations of Language, 2:50

Biological Rhythms and Living Clocks, 2:462

Biological Science, 2:437

Biology, 2:437

The Biology of Adolescence, 2:451

Biology of Amphibians, 2:449

Biology of Spiders, 2:449

Biomechanics of Motion, 2:513

Bipohl: Two Novels, Drunkard's Walk (1960) and The Age of the Pussyfoot (1969), 1:278

Bird Alone, 1:110

"The Birds," 1:80

The Bird's Nest, 1:243

The Birds of America, 2:187

The Birds of Paradise, 1:118

Birth and Growth, 2:452

The Birth of a New Physics, 2:514

The Birth of America, 2:156

Birth Order and Life Roles, 2:146

Birth to Maturity: A Study in Psychological Development, 2:536, 2:540

The Birthday Party, 1:113, 1:114

Bismarck, 2:342

Bismarck: The Kaiser and Germany, 2:342

Bismarck: The Man and the Statesman, 2:342

Bismarck and the Foundation of the German Empire, 2:342

Bismarck and the German Empire, 2:342

Bismarck in the Franco–German War, 1870–1871, 2:342

Bismarck's Diplomacy at Its Zenith, 2:342

Bite of BASIC for Apple II, 1:564

Bitter Fame: A Life of Sylvia Plath, 1:278

Bitter's Introduction to Programming in BASIC for the Apple II–IIe–IIc, 1:564

Bizou, 1:250

Black American Music Past and Present, 2:155

The Black Americans: A History in Their Own Words, 1619–1983, 2:155

Black Americans in World War II, 2:235
The Black Arrow, 1:58
Black Boy, 1:307
Black-Brown-White Relations: Race
  Relations in the 1970's, 2:136
The Black Cauldron, 1:187
Black Children–White Children:
  Competence, Socialization, and Social
  Structure, 2:135, 2:144
Black Comedy, 1:119
Black English: Its History and Usage in
  the United States, 1:429
Black English and the Mass Media, 1:437
Black Feeling, Black Talk, Black
  Judgement, 1:225, 1:226
The Black Folk Then and Now: An Essay
  in the History and Sociology of the
  Negro Race, 2:210
Black Folktales, 1:255
Black Genesis, African Roots, 2:394
The Black Hermit, 1:415
Black Heroes of the American Revolution,
  2:163
Black Holes: The Edge of Space, the End
  of Time, 2:479
Black Holes and Other Secrets of the
  Universe, 2:479
Black Images in American Films,
  1896–1954: The Interplay Between Civil
  Rights and Film Culture, 1:475
Black Inventors of America, 2:432
Black Jack: The Life and Times of John J.
  Pershing, 2:219
Black Judgement, 1:225
Black Leaders in the Twentieth Century,
  2:153
Black Literature for High School Students,
  1:205, 1:224, 1:230
Black Manhattan, 1:245
Black Market: A Study of White Collar
  Crime, 2:133
Black Mischief, 1:127
Black Mondays: Worst Decisions of the
  Supreme Court, 2:26
Black Music, 1:197
The Black Muslims in America, 2:136
Black Narcissus, 1:88
Black Night, White Snow: Russia's
  Revolutions 1905–1917, 2:340
Black North in 1901: A Social Study,
  2:210
The Black Pearl, 1:271
Black People Who Made the Old West,
  2:201
Black Pioneers of Science and Invention,
  2:432
Black Poets of the United States: From
  Paul Laurence Dunbar to Langston
  Hughes, 1:206, 1:260

Black Popular Music in America: From the
  Spirituals, Minstrels, and Ragtime to
  Soul, Disco, and Hip-Hop, 2:156
Black Press, USA, 1:458
The Black Prince, 1:107
Black Protest Thought in the Twentieth
  Century, 2:241
Black Rainbow: Legends of the Incas and
  Myths of Ancient Peru, 1:398, 2:298
Black Reconstruction in America,
  1860–1880, 2:210
Black Scientists of America, 2:432
Black Star, Bright Dawn, 1:271
The Black Tower, 1:98
The Black West, 2:201
Black Women in White America: A
  Documentary History, 2:148
Black Women Writers at Work, 1:269,
  1:481
Black Women Writers, 1950 to 1980: A
  Critical Evaluation, 1:192
Blackberry Winter: My Earlier Years,
  2:46
The Blacks, 1:191
Blacks and White TV: Afro-Americans in
  Television Since 1948, 1:465
Blacks in Antiquity: Ethiopians in the
  Greco–Roman Experience, 2:300
Blacks in Science: Ancient and Modern,
  2:433
Bleak House, 1:46, 1:47
Blind Fireworks, 1:105
Bliss and Other Short Stories, 1:142
Blithe Spirit, 1:77
The Blithedale Romance, 1:177
Blitzkrieg, 2:383
The Blood of Abraham: Insights into the
  Middle East, 2:279
The Blood of Kings: Dynasty and Ritual
  in Maya Art, 2:300
Blood of Requited Love, 1:409
The Blood of the Martyrs, 1:107
Blood Wedding, 1:357
Bloodline, 1:224
Blossom Culp and the Sleep of Death,
  1:275
Blubber, 1:201
The Blue and the Gray, 2:35, 2:192
The Blue Castle, 1:143
Blue Horizons: Paradise Isles of the
  Pacific, 2:83
Blue Jacket: War Chief of the Shawnees,
  2:168
The Blue Planet, 2:494
Bluebeard, 1:295
Bluebeard's Egg and Other Stories, 1:136
Blueprints: Solving the Mystery of
  Evolution, 2:456
Blues for Mr. Charlie, 1:195

Blues People: Negro Music in White America, 1:197
The Bluest Eye, 1:268, 1:269
BMDP Trainer's Manual, 1:574
Board Games Round the World: A Resource Book for Mathematical Investigations, 1:535
The Boat of Longing, 1:379
The Boat Who Wouldn't Float, 1:144
Bodily Harm, 1:135
The Body, 2:552
The Body in Question, 2:545
Body Language, 1:448
Body Maintenance, 2:451, 2:531
The Body Snatcher and Other Stories, 1:58
The Body Victorious: The Illustrated Story of Our Immune System and Other Defences of the Human Body, 2:545
The Boer War, 2:363
Bold Journey: West with Lewis and Clark, 2:176
Bolívar and the Political Thought of the Spanish–American Revolution, 2:369
The Bollo Caper: A Furry Tail for All Ages, 1:488
Bolsheviks, 2:375
Bolzano and the Foundations of Mathematical Analysis, 1:524
Bombers Over Japan, 2:383
Bonding and Structure, 2:505
The Bonfire of the Vanities, 1:479
The Book of Abigail and John: Selected Letters of the Adams Family, 1762–1784, 2:170, 2:171
The Book of Ages, 2:107
The Book of America: Inside 50 States Today, 2:90, 2:155
The Book of American City Rankings, 2:94, 2:155
The Book of Laughter and Forgetting, 1:385
The Book of Lights, 1:280
The Book of Lost Tales, 1:125
Book of Mercy, 1:137
The Book of Merlyn, 1:130
The Book of Sand, 1:399
The Book of Sir Marco Polo, the Venetian, Concerning the Kingdoms and Marvels of the East, 2:309
The Book of the Brotherhood, 1:107
The Book of the Moon: A Lunar Introduction to Astronomy, Geology, Space Physics, and Space Travel, 2:476
The Book of the States, 2:5
The Book of Three, 1:187
A Book of Verses, 1:263
The Book of Whales, 2:449

The Book of Women: The Code of Maimonides, 2:303
Book of World City Rankings, 2:85, 2:275
Booker T. Washington and His Critics, 2:213
Booker T. Washington in Perspective: Essays of Louis R. Harlan, 2:213
The Booker T. Washington Papers, 2:213
Boris Godunov, 1:395
Boris Pasternak, 1:394
Born Free: A Lioness of Two Worlds, 2:461
Born to Code in C, 1:564
Borstal Boy, 1:68
The Borzoi Anthology of Latin American Literature, 1:399
Bosnian Story, 1:384
Boss and the Machine, 2:204
Boston: A Documentary Novel of the Sacco-Vanzetti Case, 1:287
Boston Tea Party: Rebellion in the Colonies, 2:164
The Bostonians, 1:179
The Botanical World, 2:447
Both Ends of the Avenue: The Presidency, the Executive Branch and Congress in the 1980s, 2:21, 2:33
Bound with Them in Chains: A Biographical History of the Anti-Slavery Movement, 2:189
Bourbaki, 1:499
Bourbon and Stuart: Kings and Kingship in France and England in the 17th Century, 2:326
Bouvard and Pécuchet, 1:334, 1:335
Bouvard et Pécuchet, 1:335
Boxed-In, 1:465
The Boxer Rebellion, 2:363
Boy: Tales of Childhood, 1:79
Boys and Girls Together, 1:227
Boys and Sex, 2:543
Boy's Life on the Prairie, 2:200
The Boys on the Bus, 1:457
Brahms, 2:348
Brahms: His Life and Work, 2:348
The Brain: Magnificent Mind Machine, 2:450, 2:545
The Brain and Nervous System, 2:451
Brain Function. Encyclopedia of Psychoactive Drugs, 2:544
Brain, Mind and Computers, 1:538
Brainstorm, 1:270
Brandeis and Frankfurter: A Dual Biography, 2:28
Braque, 2:415
The Brass Butterfly, 1:90
Brass Check, 1:287
Brave New World, 1:95
Brave New World Revisited, 1:95

Brazil: The Forging of a Nation, 1798–1852, 2:369

Bread and Roses: The Struggle of American Labor, 2:70

The Bread of Those Early Years, 1:363

Breakfast of Champions, 1:295

Breaking New Ground, 2:207

Breaking the Connection: How Young People Achieve Drug-free Lives, 2:554

Breaking Up, 1:250

The Breaking Wave, 1:147

Breakthrough: The True Story of Penicillin, 2:559

Breakthrough: Women in Science, 1:544

A Breakthrough in Making Computers Friendly: The Macintosh Computer, 1:560

Breathing Lessons, 1:291

The Breathing Planet, 2:80, 2:485

The Brecht Memoir, 1:365

Brendan Behan: Interviews and Recollections, 1:68

The Brethren: Inside the Supreme Court, 2:27, 2:252

The Bride of Lammermoor, 1:36

The Bride of Messina, 1:372

The Bride Price: Young Ibo Girl's Love; Conflict of Family and Tradition, 1:413

Brideshead Revisited, 1:127

The Bridge of San Luis Rey, 1:302, 1:303

The Bridge on the Drina, 1:384

The Bridge over the River Kwai, 1:332

Bridge to Terabithia, 1:484

The Bridges at Toko-Ri, 1:264

Bridging Worlds Through General Semantics, 1:437

Brief Calculus with Applications, 1:523

A Brief History of Time from the Big Bang to Black Holes, 2:469

Briefing for a Descent into Hell, 1:103

Bright Stars, Red Giants, and White Dwarfs, 2:478

Brighton Beach Memoirs, 1:286, 1:287

Brighton Rock, 1:91

Bringing Your Employees into the Business: An Employee Ownership Handbook for Small Business, 2:149

Britain, 2:87

Britain and the British Seas, 2:78, 2:79

Britain's Economic Renaissance: Margaret Thatcher's Reforms, 1979–1984, 2:408

Britannicus, 1:339

British English, A to Zed, 1:434

British Foreign Policy Under Thatcher, 2:408

Britten, 2:417

The Britten Companion, 2:417

Broadway Bound, 1:286, 1:287

Broca's Brain: Reflections on the Romance of Science, 2:479

The Broken Fountain, 2:50

Broken Idols, Solemn Dreams, 2:406

Broken Soil, 1:76

The Brontës: Charlotte Brontë and Her Family, 1:42

Bronwen the Traw, the Shape-Shifter, 1:215

The Bronze Horseman, 1:395

Brother and Sister/Sisters and Brothers, 2:538

Brother, Can You Spare a Dime? The Great Depression, 1929–1933, 2:229, 2:230

Brother to Dragons, 1:299

Brothers, 1:227

The Brothers Karamazov, 1:392

Bruno's Dream, 1:107

The Brute and Other Farces: Seven Short Plays, 1:391

Bryan on Imperialism, 2:205

Bucky, 1:522

Buddenbrooks, 1:369, 1:370

Buddhism in Chinese History, 2:277

The Buenos Aires Affair, 1:409

Buffalo Gals and Other Animal Presences, 1:254

The Build-Up, 1:305

Build Your Own Expert System: For the IBM PC and Compatibles, 1:584

Build Your Own Polyhedra, 1:519

Build Your Own 80386 IBM Compatible and Save a Bundle, 1:560

Building Blocks, 1:294

Building Blocks of the Universe, 2:506

Building Expert Systems: Cognitive Emulation, 1:583

Building Expert Systems in Training and Education, 1:570

Building Sound Bones and Muscles, 2:544

Building the Future Order: The Search for Peace in an Interdependent World, 2:388

Bulfinch's Mythology, 1:318

Bulimarexia: The Binge–Purge Cycle, 2:550

The Bull from the Sea, 1:318

Bullet Park, 1:210, 1:211

Bully for You, Teddy Roosevelt!, 2:222

The Bumblebee Flies Anyway, 1:212

Bunyan, 1:21

Bureaucracy in Modern Society, 2:140

Burger's Daughter, 1:414

Buried Child, 1:284

Burke, 2:9

Burke's Politics: Selected Writings and Speeches on Reform, Revolution, and War, 2:9

Burma: A Country Study, 2:86

Burmese Days, 1:111

Burmese Drama: A Study with Translations of Burmese Plays, 1:426
Burmese Folk Tales, 1:427
The Burnt Ones, 1:148
Burnt Water, 1:403
Burton, 2:364
Bury My Heart at Wounded Knee, 2:135, 2:200
Business and Finance, 1:566
Business and Government, 2:65
The Business Cycle After Keynes: A Contempory Analysis, 2:57
Business Cycle Theory: A Survey of Methods and Concepts, 2:57
Business Cycles and Forecasting, 2:57
Business in American Life, 2:204
Business Letters Made Simple, 1:487
Business Planning and Forecasting with Microsoft Excel, 1:572, 1:573
Business Writing Handbook, 1:483
Busman's Honeymoon, 1:117
Butterflies of the World, 2:448
Butterfly Moth, 2:449
Buying Computers by Mail: A Directory of Mail Order Suppliers, 1:558
By a Single Vote! One-Vote Decisions That Changed American History, 2:39
By Any Means Necessary: Speeches, Interviews, and a Letter by Malcolm X, 1:450
By the Open Sea, 1:380
Byron: A Portrait, 1:33
Byron: Poems, 1:33
Byzantine Architecture, 2:301
The Byzantine Revival, 780–842, 2:301

C

C. G. Jung Speaking: Interviews and Encounters, 2:121
C. Juli Caesaris de Bello Gallico, 1:319
C Primer Plus, 1:565
The C Programming Language, 1:564
Ca Dao Vietnam: Bilingual Anthology of Vietnamese Folk Poetry, 1:426
Cabbages and Kings, 1:178
Caesar and Cleopatra, 1:120
Caffeine: The Most Popular Stimulant, 2:554
Cairo, 1:471
Cajun Dictionary: A Collection of Commonly Used Words and Phrases by the People of South Louisiana, 1:431
Cajun Night Before Christmas, 1:431
Cakes and Ale, 1:106
The Calculating Passion of Ada Byron, 1:547

Calculator Puzzles, Tricks, and Games, 1:535
Calculus and Its Applications, 1:523
Calculus and the Computer, 1:523
Calculus by and for Young People: Ages 7, Yes 7, and Up, 1:523
Calculus for a New Century: A Pump Not a Filter, 1:523
Calculus Made Easy, 1:523
The Calculus of Linguistic Observations, 1:529
Calder, 2:261
Calderón de la Barca: El alcalde de Zalamea, 1:355
Calderón de la Barca at the Tercentenary: Comparative Views, 1:355
Calendar of the Correspondence of James Madison, 2:177
Calhoun: Basic Documents, 2:181
California Women: A History, 2:184
Caligula, 1:333
Caligula and Three Other Plays, 1:333
Call for the Dead, 1:102
The Call of the Fife and Drum: Three Novels of the American Revolution, 2:163
The Call of the Wild and White Fang, 1:257
The Callender Papers, 1:294
Calvin Coolidge: The Man from Vermont, 2:228
Calvin Coolidge: The Quiet President, 2:228
Calvin, Geneva, and the Reformation: A Study of Calvin As Social Reformer, Churchman, Pastor, and Theologian, 2:311
The Cambridge Atlas of Astronomy, 2:469
The Cambridge Encyclopedia of Africa, 2:85, 2:276
The Cambridge Encyclopedia of China, 2:87, 2:274
The Cambridge History of Africa: 1870–1905, 2:363
The Cambridge History of China, 2:282, 2:309
The Camel and the Wheel, 2:516
The Camera, 2:263
The Camera Age: Essays on Television, 1:465
Camino Real, 1:304
Camouflage and Mimicry, 2:466
Camp David: Peacemaking and Politics, 2:255
Campaigning with Grant, 2:200
Campesino: The Diary of a Guatemalan Indian, 2:409
Canada, 2:90
Canada, 1988, 2:91

Canadian Writers at Work: Interviews with Geoff Hancock, 1:481
The Canadians, 2:90
Cancer, 2:562
Cancer: Can It Be Stopped?, 2:562
Cancer: The Misguided Cell, 2:562
Cancer Care: A Personal Guide, 2:561
Cancer, Fundamental Ideas, 2:562
The Cancer Ward, 1:395, 1:396
Candida, 1:120
Candidates, Parties, and Campaigns: Electoral Politics in America, 2:40
Candide, 1:343, 1:344
The Candle in the Wind, 1:130
Cannery Row, 1:288
Cannibals and Kings: The Origins of Cultures, 2:48
The Canterbury Tales, 1:6, 1:348
Canto general, 1:407
Cantos de vida y esperanza, 1:401
Canzoniere, 1:350
Cape Cod, 1:165
Capital, 2:59
Capital, Courthouse, and City Hall, 2:41
Capital Punishment in the United States, 2:133
Capitalism: Opposing Viewpoints, 2:15, 2:58
Capitalism and Freedom: With a New Preface, 2:65
Capitalism and Modern Social Theory: An Analysis of the Writings of Marx, Durkheim and Max Weber, 2:143
Capitalism and the Welfare State: Dilemmas of Social Benevolence, 2:57
Capitalism, Communism and Coexistence: From the Bitter Past to a Better Prospect, 2:66, 2:274
Capitalism for Beginners, 2:57, 2:58
Capitalism, Socialism, and Democracy, 2:58
The Captain, 1:130
Captain Cook and the Pacific, 2:322
Captain James Cook, 2:322
Captain James Cook and His Times, 2:321
Captain Sir Richard Francis Burton: The Secret Agent Who Made the Pilgrimage to Mecca, Discovered the Kama Sutra, and Brought the Arabian Nights to the West, 2:364
Captains Courageous, 1:55
The Captain's Verses, 1:407
Captured on Corregidor: Diary of an American P.O.W. in World War II, 2:385
Carbohydrates, 2:511
The Care of Strangers: The Rise of America's Hospital System, 2:567

Career Change in Midlife: Stress, Social Support and Adjustment, 2:148
Career Opportunities in TV, Cable and Video, 1:465
Careers in Geography, 2:76
Caregiving: Helping an Aged Loved One, 2:544
Caregiving: When Someone You Love Grows Old, 2:544
The Caretaker, 1:114
Cargoes: Famous Sea Stories, 1:97
Caribbean Contours, 2:408
Caring for the Disabled Elderly: Who Will Pay, 2:68
Carl Friedrich Gauss: A Bibliography, 1:532
Carl Friedrich Gauss: A Biography, 1:532
Carl Sagan: Superstar Scientist, 2:480
Carl Sandburg, 1:284
Carlos Fuentes, 1:403
Carlos Fuentes: A Critical View, 1:403
Carlotta, 1:271; 2:185
Carnival, 1:405
Carnival: Entertainments and Posthumous Tales, 1:376
The Carpathians, 1:138
The Carpentered Hen, 1:292
Carrie, 1:248, 1:249
Cartoon Guide to Computer Science, 1:537
Cartoon History of United States Foreign Policy, 1776–1976, 2:36
Cartooning Washington, 1:459
Cartoons and Illustrations of Thomas Nast, 1:460
Cartoons for Computer Classes, 1:571
Casear Augustus: Seven Aspects, 2:291
Cases in Civil Liberties, 2:12
Casino Royale, 1:84
Caste and Class Controversy, 2:136
Caste and Class in a Southern Town, 2:105, 2:116
The Castle (Kafka), 1:369
Castle (Macaulay), 2:306
Castle Corner, 1:71
The Castle in the Sea, 1:271
The Castle of Llyr, 1:187
Castles of the Middle Ages, 2:306
Castro's Ploy, America's Dilemma: The 1980 Cuba Boatlift, 2:410
The Casualty, 1:363
Cat and Mouse, 1:367
Cat on a Hot Tin Roof, 1:303, 1:304
Catalysis by Acids and Bases, 2:507
Cataracts: What You Must Know About Them, 2:552
Catch 22, 1:234
The Catcher in the Rye, 1:282, 1:283
Cathedral, 2:306
Cathedrals of France, 2:356

Catherine and Igor Stravinsky, 2:426
Catherine Cormier, 1:224
Catherine of Aragon, 2:310
Cathleen ni Houlihan, 1:133
The Catholic and Manichaean Ways of Life, 2:304
Catlin and His Contemporaries: The Politics of Patronage, 2:188
Catlin's North American Indian Portfolio: A Reproduction, 2:188
Catlow, 1:252
Cat's Cradle, 1:295
Cat's Eye, 1:135
The Caucasian Chalk Circle, 1:364, 1:365
Causes of Delinquency, 2:133
Cavalier in Buckskin: George Armstrong Custer and the Western Military Frontier, 2:201
Cavalry Scout, 2:200
Cave of Lascaux: The Final Photographs, 2:279
The Cave of Making: The Poetry of Louis MacNeice, 1:105
Caves, 2:493
Caves and Life, 2:489
The Caves of the Great Hunters, 2:277
Cavour: A Biography, 2:341
Cavour and Garibaldi Eighteen Sixty: A Study in Political Conflict, 2:344
"The Celebrated Jumping Frog of Calaveras County," 1:181
The Celebration of Heroes: Prestige As a Social Control System, 2:144
Celestial Navigation, 1:291
The Celestial Omnibus and Other Stories, 1:86
Cellini, 2:312
Cells, 2:438
The Celluloid Closet: Homosexuality in the Movies, 1:475
Celtic World: An Illustrated History of the Celtic Race, Their Culture, Customs and Legends, 2:305
The Centaur, 1:292, 1:310
Centennial, 1:264
Central Problems in Social Theory: Action, Structure, and Contradiction in Social Analysis, 2:125
Centuries of Childhood: A Social History of Family Life, 2:136
A Century of Controversy. Studies in Anthropology, 2:42
Century of Dishonor: A Sketch of the United States Government's Dealings, 2:201
The Century of Revolution, 1603–1714, 2:327
Century of Struggle: The Woman's Rights Movement in the United States, 2:12, 2:153

The Ceremony of Innocence, 1:239
Cervantes (Durán), 1:356
Cervantes (Russell), 1:357
Cervantes: A Biography, 1:356
Cesar Chavez, 2:241
Cesar Chavez: Man of Courage, 2:242
Cézanne: A Biography, 2:349
Cézanne: The Late Work, 2:349
A Cézanne Sketchbook: Figures, Portraits, Landscapes, and Still Lives, 2:349
Cézanne's Composition: Analysis of His Form with Diagrams and Photographs of His Motifs, 2:349
Chagall Discovered: From Russia and Private Collections, 2:418
Chagall in Chicago, 2:417
Chagall Lithographs VI (1978–1985), 2:417
Chaim Potok, 1:280
Chain of Chance, 1:386
A Chainless Soul: A Life of Emily Brontë, 1:43
Chaka, 1:409
The Challenge of Hidden Profits: Reducing Corporate Bureaucracy and Waste, 2:63
The Challenge to Liberty, 2:231
Challenger: The Final Voyage, 2:481
The Challenges of Our Time: Disarmament and Social Progress, 2:406
Challenges to Capitalism: Marx, Lenin, Stalin, and Mao, 2:60
The Chamber Plays, 1:380
"The Chambered Nautilus," 1:158
Chambers World Gazetteer: An A–Z of Geographical Information, 2:75
A Chance Child, 1:126
Change and Continuity in Seventeenth-Century England, 2:327
A Change of Skin, 1:402
A Change of World, 1:281
Changes and Choices: A Junior High Survival Guide, 2:107
Changing Bodies, Changing Lives. A Book for Teens on Sex and Relationships, 2:542
The Changing British Political System: Into the 1990s, 2:405
The Changing Culture of an Indian Tribe, 2:46
The Changing Families: Meeting Today's Challenges, 2:538
Channels of Power: The Impact of Television on American Politics, 1:443; 2:40
Chanson de Roland, 1:341
Chaos: Making a New Science, 1:516
Chaplin, 1:470
Chapterhouse: Dune, 1:238
Character and Culture, 2:98

Charles Babbage: On the Principle and Development of the Calculator and Other Seminal Writings, 1:542
Charles Babbage: Pioneer of the Computer, 1:542
Charles Baudelaire, 1:330
Charles Brockden Brown, 1:152
Charles Darwin: A Man of Enlarged Curiosity, 2:457
Charles Darwin: Evolution by Natural Selection, 2:457
Charles De Gaulle: A Biography, 2:387
Charles de Gaulle: Defender of France, 2:387
Charles Dickens, 1:47
Charles Dickens: Master Storyteller, 1:47
Charles Dickens: The World of His Novels, 1:47
Charles I and Cromwell, 2:327
Charles Ives: The Ideas Behind the Music, 2:261
Charles Lamb, 1:35
Charles Lamb and His Contemporaries, 1:36
Charles W. Chesnutt: America's First Great Black Novelist, 1:172
Charley Skedaddle, 2:192
Charlie and the Chocolate Factory, 1:79
Charlotte Brontë, 1:42
Charlotte's Web, 1:456
The Charterhouse of Parma, 1:341
The Chase, 1:401
Chaucer, 1:7
Chaucer: An Introduction, 1:7
Chaucer: His Life, His Works, His World, 1:7
Chaucer: The Canterbury Tales, 1:7
Chaucer Criticism: The Canterbury Tales, 1:7
The Cheerleader, 1:250
Chekhov: A Spirit Set Free, 1:391
Chekhov: Five Major Plays, 1:391
Chekhov, the Silent Voice of Freedom, 1:391
The Chemical Bond, 2:505
Chemical Bonds: An Introduction to Atomic and Molecular Structure, 2:505
The Chemical History of a Candle: Six Illustrated Lectures with Notes and Experiments, 2:525
Chemical Kinetics and Reaction Mechanisms, 2:508
Chemical Principles and Their Biological Implications, 2:511
Chemically Active! Experiments You Can Do at Home, 2:498, 2:504
Chemicals of Life, 2:511
The Chemist Who Lost His Head: The Story of Antoine Lavoisier, 2:500
Chemistry, 2:505, 2:508

Chemistry: The Study of Matter, 2:500, 2:505, 2:507, 2:508
Chemistry and Our Changing World, 2:505
Chemistry and Physics of Carbon, 2:510
Chemistry Around You, 2:508
Chemistry Made Simple, 2:504
Chemistry Today: The Portrait of a Science, 2:504
Chenier Math Method: A Practical Math Dictionary and Workbook–Textbook, 1:496
The Chequer Board, 1:147
Cher Antoine on l'amour rote, 1:328
Chernobyl and the Nuclear Power in the USSR, 2:82
The Cherokee, 2:158
Cherokee Removal, 1838: An Entire Nation Is Forced Out of Its Homeland, 2:180
Cherokees in Pre-Columbian Times, 2:158
The Cherry Orchard, 1:390
Chesapeake, 1:264
The Chessmen of Mars, 1:208
The Cheyenne, 2:157
Cheyenne Autumn, 2:201
"Chicago," 1:283
Chicago and Other Plays, 1:285
Chicago Manual of Style, 1:477
The Chicanos: A History of Mexican Americans, 2:155
Chief Joseph, 2:202
Chief Joseph: Boy of the Nez Percé, 2:202
Chief Joseph of the Nez Perce, 1:299
Chief Justice: John Marshall and the Growth of the Republic, 2:30
The Child: His Nature and His Needs, 2:540
Child Abuse, 2:138
Child Abuse and Neglect: What Happens Eventually?, 2:539
The Child and the Curriculum, 2:219
Child Development and Child Health, 2:540
Child Development During the Elementary School Years, 2:540
Child from Five to Ten, 2:540
Child Life in Colonial Days, 2:161
Child of Storm, 1:51
Child Psychology and Early Childhood Education: A Cognitive–Developmental View, 2:103, 2:109
Childe Harold's Pilgrimage, 1:33
Childhood and Society, 2:108
"Childhood," "Boyhood," and "Youth" (1852–56), 1:397
Childhood's End, 1:75
Children Are Civilians Too, 1:364
Children of Crisis, 2:105, 2:106
Children of Dune, 1:238

The Children of the Poor, 2:212
Children of the Tenements, 2:212
The Children of Violence, 1:103
Children with Cancer: A Comprehensive
  Reference Guide for Parents, 2:561
Children with Chronic Arthritis: A Primer
  for Patients and Parents, 2:562
The Children's Hour, 1:235
Child's Christmas in Wales, A, 1:124
A Child's Conception of Geometry, 1:512
The Child's Conception of the World,
  2:111, 2:146
A Child's Garden of Verses, 1:58
Chile: Dictatorship and the Struggle for
  Democracy, 2:409
Chile and the War of the Pacific, 2:370
Chili Dawgs Always Bark at Night, 1:480
The Chimpanzees of Gombe, 2:463
China (Buchanan), 2:273, 2:281
China (Hsu), 2:399
China (McKillop), 2:282
China: A Concise Cultural History, 2:281
China: A Country Study, 2:87
China: An Introduction, 2:87, 2:399
China: The March Toward Unity, 2:402
China After Mao: With Selected
  Documents, 2:398
China–Burma–India, 2:383
China—The People, 2:399
China's Civilization: A Survey of Its
  History, Arts, and Technology, 2:273
China's One Child Family Policy, 2:86,
  2:398
The Chinese Americans, 2:207
Chinese Civilization and Society: A
  Sourcebook, 2:281
Chinese Classical Prose: The Eight Masters
  of the T'ang-Sung Period, 1:423
Chinese Fables, 1:423
Chinese Fairy Tales and Fantasies, 1:423
Chinese Literature, 1:423
Chinese Mathematics: A Concise History,
  1:498
Chinese Philosophy, Art, Life, and
  Mathematics, 1:498
Chinese Women of America: A Pictorial
  History, 2:156
Chinua Achebe (Carroll), 1:411
Chinua Achebe (Innes), 1:412
Chip Talk: Projects in Speech Synthesis,
  1:579
Chiseling the Earth: How Erosion Shapes
  the Land, 2:492
The Chocolate War, 1:212, 1:213
A Choice of Days, 1:436
Choices and Consequences: What to Do
  When a Teenager Uses Alcohol–Drugs:
  A Step-by-Step System That Really
  Works, 2:556

The Cholera Years: The United States in
  1832, 1849, and 1866, 2:567
Choose the Right Word: A Modern Guide
  to Synonyms, 1:438, 1:439
Choosing a Microcomputer for Parks and
  Recreation Administration, 1:569
Chopin: The Man and His Music, 2:350
The Chopin Companion: Profiles of the
  Man and the Musician, 2:350
Choosing a Microcomputer for Parks and
  Recreation Administration, 1:569
Chopin's Letters, 2:350
The Chosen, 1:280
"Christabel," 1:34
Christian Instruction, Admonition, and
  Grace, the Christian Combat, Faith,
  Hope, and Charity, 2:304
The Christian Philosophy of St. Thomas
  Aquinas, 2:307
Christianity, 2:301
Christina Rossetti and Her Poetry, 1:57
Christina Rossetti in Context, 1:57
Christina's World, 2:271
Christine, 1:249
A Christmas Carol, 1:46, 1:47
Christopher Columbus, Mariner, 2:160
Christopher Fry, 1:87
Christopher Isherwood, 1:96
Christopher Marlowe, 1:12
Christopher Marlowe: Poet for the Stage,
  1:12
Chronicle of a Death Foretold, 1:403
Chronicle of a Revolution: A
  Western–Soviet Inquiry into Perestroika,
  2:15, 2:405
Chronicle of the World, 2:273
Chronicles of Avonlea, 1:144
The Chronicles of Clovis, 1:115
The Chronicles of Narnia, 1:104
A Chronology of Conflict and Resolution,
  1945–1985, 2:388
The Chrysanthemum and the Sword:
  Patterns of Japanese Culture, 2:43,
  2:44
"Church Going," 1:100
Churchill, 2:386
Churchill and Roosevelt, the Complete
  Correspondence, 2:386
Churchill and the Generals: Their Finest
  Hours, 2:386
Churchill Lecture, 2:253
Cicero, 2:293
Cicero: A Portrait, 2:293
Cicero and the Fall of the Roman
  Republic, 2:293
Cien años de soledad, 1:404
Cimaron (Mitchum), 2:201
Cimarron (Ferber), 1:220
The Cinema as Art, 1:469

A Cinema of Loneliness: Penn, Kubrick, Scorsese, Spielberg, Altman, 1:473
Cinq semaines en ballon, 1:343
The Circle Game, 1:135
Circle of Fire, 2:226
The Circulatory System, 2:450, 2:544
The Circus in the Attic and Other Stories, 1:299
The Citadel, 1:78
Cities of Tomorrow: An Intellectual History of Urban Planning and Design in the Twentieth Century, 2:147
Cities Under Stress: Can Today's City Systems Be Made to Work?, 2:41, 2:93, 2:147
Citizen Hearst, 1:457
Citizen of the Galaxy, 1:233
Citizen 13660, 2:235
Citizen Tom Paine, 1:218
Citizens and the Environment: Case Studies in Popular Action, 2:81
The Citizen's Presidency: Standards of Choice and Judgment, 2:21
Citizenship in the Nation, 2:12
The City, 2:147
City: A Story of Roman Planning and Construction, 2:291
The City in History: Its Origins, Its Transformations and Its Prospects, 2:94, 2:147
The City in the Stars, 1:75
City Life, 1:198
City of God, 2:303, 2:304
Civil Disobedience, 2:13
Civil Liberties, 2:12
Civil Rights: The Nineteen Sixties Freedom Struggle, 2:241
A Civil Tongue, 1:443
The Civil War (Caesar), 2:292
The Civil War (National Geographic Society Staff and Jordan), 2:193
The Civil War: Fort Sumter to Perryville, 2:192
The Civil War: Fredericksburg to Meridian, 2:192
The Civil War: Red River to Appomattox, 2:192
Civil War: Strange and Fascinating Facts, 2:192
The Civil War Dictionary, 2:152
Civil War Heroines, 2:192
Civilization and Its Discontents, 2:117, 2:134
Civilization of the Ancient Mediterranean, 2:274
Civilization of the Renaissance in Italy, 2:310
Civilized Man's Eight Deadly Sins, 2:464

Clamor at the Gates: The New American Immigration, 2:255
The Clan of the Cave Bear, 2:277
Clandestine in Chile: The Adventures of Miguel Littin, 1:403
Clara Barton, 2:194
Clara Barton: Angel of the Battlefield, 2:194, 2:568
Clara Barton: Founder of the American Red Cross, 2:569
Clara Barton, Professional Angel, 2:194, 2:568
Clara Howard, 1:152
The Clarendon Edition of the Philosophical Works of Thomas Hobbes, 2:10
Clarissa, 1:28, 1:29
Class and Class Conflict in Industrial Society, 2:132
Class and Conformity: A Study in Values, 2:146
Class Struggle in Africa, 2:396
The Classical Greeks, 2:285
Classical Mechanics, 2:512
Classical Rhetoric for the Modern Student, 1:477
Classics in Software Engineering, 1:585
Classics of Roman Literature, 1:320
The Classics Reclassified, 1:193
Classification and Nomenclature of Viruses, 2:441
Classification of the Animal Kingdom, 2:441
Classroom Computers and Cognitive Science, 1:571
Classroom Exercises in General Semantics, 1:437
Claude Debussy: His Life and Works, 2:418
Claude Debussy and the Poets, 2:418
Claude Lévi-Strauss, 2:53
Claude Lévi-Strauss: The Anthropologist as Hero, 2:53
Claude McKay, Rebel Sojourner in the Harlem Renaissance: A Biography, 1:260
Claudius the God, 1:90
Clear and Simple Geometry, 1:512
Clear Skin: A Step-by-Step Program to Stop Pimples, Blackheads, Acne, 2:552
Clearing Acne, 2:552
Cleopatra, 2:291
The Clergyman's Daughter, 1:111
Clifford Odets, 1:273
Climate, History, and the Modern World, 2:80
The Climate of the Earth, 2:80
Climates Past, Present and Future, 2:485
Clipart and Dynamic Designs for Libraries and Media Centers, 1:578

Clive Staples Lewis: A Dramatic Life, 1:104
The Clock Winder, 1:291
A Clockwork Orange, 1:71
The Clockwork Testament, 1:71
Cloning and the New Genetics, 2:455
Cloning of Frogs, Mice, and Other Animals, 2:451, 2:455
The Cloning of Joanna May, 1:128
Close Encounters: Mike Wallace's Own Story, 1:447
Close Enough To Touch, 1:275
Close Neighbors, Distant Friends: United States-Central American Relations, 2:257
Close Quarters, 1:89
Closing the Gap: Computer Development in the People's Republic of China, 1:556
Clotel: or, The President's Daughter, 1:170
Clouds of Witness, 1:117
The Clown, 1:363, 1:364
Coastal Rescue: Preserving Our Seashores, 2:488
Coastlines, 2:486
Coasts, 2:83
COBOL: A Guide to Structured, Portable, Maintainable, and Efficient Program Design, 1:565
COBOL for Today, 1:565
The Cockatoos, 1:148
The Cocktail Party, 1:82
The Code of the Woosters, 1:131
Cognition, 2:103
The Cognitive Computer: On Language, Learning and Artificial Intelligence, 2:110
The Coil of Life: The Story of the Great Discoveries of the Life Sciences, 2:439, 2:440, 2:446, 2:453, 2:454, 2:455
The Cold War, 2:238
The Cold War: From Iron Curtain to Perestroika, 2:388
Cold War, Cold Peace, 2:388
The Cold War Is Over, 2:388
Coleridge, 1:34
The Collapsing Universe: The Story of Black Holes, 2:478
Collected Articles and Speeches (Dulles), 2:23
Collected Correspondence of J. M. W. Turner with an Early Diary and a Memoir by George Jones, 2:358
Collected Lyrics (Millay), 1:265
Collected Nonsense and Light Verse, 1:73
Collected Papers (Noether), 1:509
Collected Papers of Enrico Fermi, 2:528
The Collected Papers of Franco Modigliani, 2:72
Collected Papers of Kenneth J. Arrow: Applied Economics, 2:64

Collected Plays (Soyinka), 1:418
Collected Plays (Yeats), 1:134
The Collected Plays of Lillian Hellman, 1:235
The Collected Plays of Neil Simon, 1:287
Collected Poems (Auden), 1:66
Collected Poems (Colum), 1:76
Collected Poems (Cummings), 1:214
Collected Poems (Durrell), 1:81
Collected Poems (Frost), 1:223
Collected Poems (Ginsberg), 1:225
Collected Poems (Hayden), 1:233
Collected Poems (Housman), 1:54
Collected Poems (Joyce), 1:99
Collected Poems (Lowell), 1:259
Collected Poems (MacLeish), 1:261
Collected Poems (Millay), 1:265
Collected Poems (Milosz), 1:386
Collected Poems (Owen), 1:113
Collected Poems (Plath), 1:277
Collected Poems (Pope), 1:27
Collected Poems (Thomas), 1:124
Collected Poems of L. S. Senghor, 1:417
The Collected Poems of Sterling A. Brown, 1:206
Collected Poems of William Carlos Williams, 1909–1939, 1:305
Collected Poems of William Carlos Williams, 1939–1962, 1:305
Collected Poems 1908–1956 (Sassoon), 1:116
The Collected Poems, 1957–1987 (Paz), 1:408
The Collected Poems, 1957–1987: Bilingual Edition (Paz), 1:408
Collected Poetry (Eliot), 1:82
Collected Scientific Papers (Pauli), 2:503
Collected Short Stories (Graves), 1:90
Collected Short Stories (Maugham), 1:106
Collected Short Stories of Sean O'Faolain, 1:110
Collected Sonnets (Millay), 1:265
Collected Stories (Bowen), 1:70
Collected Stories (Coward), 1:77
Collected Stories (Greene), 1:91
Collected Stories (Porter), 1:279
Collected Stories (Thomas), 1:124
Collected Stories (Williams), 1:304
The Collected Stories of Eudora Welty, 1:300
Collected Stories of Frank O'Connor, 1:109
The Collected Stories of Katherine Ann Porter, 1:279
Collected Stories of William Faulkner, 1:219
Collected Tales (Forster), 1:86
Collected Tales and Stories (Shelley), 1:37
Collected Verse (Coward), 1:77

The Collected Verse of Robert Service, 1:146
Collected Works (O'Connor), 1:270
Collected Works (von Neumann), 1:553, 1:586
Collected Works of Kurt Gödel, 1:500
Collected Works of Phillis Wheatley, 1:154
Collecting and Preserving Plants for Science and Pleasure, 2:447
Collection of Papers on Political, Literary and Moral Subjects (Webster), 1:430
Collection of Shorter Plays by Samuel Beckett, 1:331
Collection of the Facts and Documents Relative to the Death of Major-General Alexander Hamilton, 2:174
The Collector, 1:86
College Algebra, 1:506
Colloids in Food, 2:507
Colloquial English (Coe), 1:435
Colloquial English (Collis), 1:436
Colloquies, 2:314
Colonel Sun, 1:65
The Colonel's Dream, 1:172
Colonial Architecture of the Mid-Atlantic, 2:162
The Colonial Background of the American Revolution, 2:163
Colonial Craftsmen: The Beginnings of American Industry, 2:162
The Colonial Experience, 2:161
The Colonial Overlords: 1850–1900, 2:363
Colonial Women and Domesticity: Selected Articles on Gender in Early America, 2:162
Color, 1:214
Color and Democracy: Colonies and Peace, 2:210
The Color Line and the Quality of Life in America, 2:142
The Color of the Light, 1:227
The Color Purple, 1:296, 1:297
The Colossus and Other Poems, 1:276, 1:277
Columbus, 2:160
Columbus Dictionary, 2:160
Comanches, 2:200
Combat, 1:332
Combinatorics, 1:530
Come a Stranger, 1:294
Come Along with Me, 1:243
Come Back, Dr. Caligari, 1:197, 1:198
Come Blow Your Horn, 1:286
Come My Beloved, 1:207
Come Sing, Jimmy Go, 1:484
The Comedians, 1:91
The Comedies of William Congreve, 1:21
Comet, 2:476, 2:479
The Comet Is Coming! The Feverish Legacy of Mr. Halley, 2:475

Comets: Vagabonds of Space, 2:476
Comets and Meteors, 2:475
Comets, Meteors, and Asteroids, 2:475
The Comforters, 1:121
Comic Book Heroes: From the Silver Age to the Present, 1:459
Comic Books and Strips: An Information Sourcebook, 1:459
Comic Relief: Drawings from the Cartoonists' Thanksgiving Day Hunger Project, 1:459
The Comic Style of P. G. Wodehouse, 1:131
Comic Visions: Television Comedy and American Culture, 1:465
The Comics and Their Creators: Life Stories of American Cartoonists, 1:459
Coming Apart: An Informal History of America in the 1960s, 2:242
The Coming Century of Peace, 2:406
The Coming Fury, 2:189
Coming of Age in Samoa, 2:46
Coming of Age in the Land of Computers: A Parent's Guide to Computers for Children, 1:568
The Coming of Post-Industrial Society: A Venture in Social Forecasting, 1:554; 2:149
The Coming Quake: Science and Trembling on the California Earthquake Frontier, 2:494
Coming to America: Immigrants from the Far East, 2:255
Coming Up for Air, 1:110, 1:111
The Commandos, 2:383
A Commentary on Plutarch's Pericles, 2:289
Commentary on the Lao Tzu, 2:284
Commentary on the Lord's Sermon on the Mount with Seventeen Related Sermons, 2:304
Commerce and Community: Selected Articles on the Middle Atlantic Colonies, 2:162
The Commerce Clause Under Marshall, Taney, and Waite, 2:28
The Commercialization of Space, 2:82
The Commercialization of the Oceans, 2:82
The Commission on Civil Rights (Arrington), 2:152
The Commission on Civil Rights (Schlesinger), 2:13
Commitment and Community: Communes and Utopias in Sociological Perspective, 2:139
Commodore Hornblower, 1:85
The Common Cold, 2:557
The Common Cold and Influenza, 2:557

Common Ground: A Turbulent Decade in the Lives of Three American Families, 2:238
The Common Law, 2:28, 2:29
The Common Sense Book of Baby and Child Care, 2:541
Common Sense, The Rights of Man, and Other Essential Writings of Thomas Paine, 2:165
Communicable Disease Handbook, 2:557
Communicable Diseases, 2:557
Communicating in Small Groups: Principles and Practices, 1:445
Communicating with Your Doctor: Rx for Good Medical Care, 2:566
Communication and Discussion in Small Groups, 1:445
Communication, Control and Computer Access for Disabled and Elderly Individuals: Switches and Environmental Controls, 1:571
Communication Tomorrow: New Audiences, New Technologies, New Media, 1:454
Communications: The Transfer of Meaning, 1:437
Communications and Society: A Bibliography on Communications Technologies and Their Social Impact, 2:130
Communications and the Future: Prospects, Promises, and Problems, 1:454
Communism: Opposing Viewpoints, 2:15, 2:58
Communism, Conformity, and Civil Liberties, 2:129
Communism of Mao Tse-tung, 2:402
The Communist Manifesto, 2:58, 2:59
Community Conflict, 2:130, 2:132
Community Power Structure: A Study of Decision Makers, 2:131
Comoediae (Plautus), 1:322
Comoediae (Terence), 1:324
A Companion to The Grapes of Wrath, 1:289
Comparative Government: Politics of Industrialized and Developing Nations, 2:15
Comparative Methods in Psychology, 2:95
Comparative Studies of How People Think: An Introduction, 2:103
Compiler Design in C, 1:586
Compiler Generators, 1:586
Compiler Physiology for Beginners, 1:586
Compilers: Principles, Techniques, and Tools, 1:586
Compilers: Their Design and Construction Using Pascal, 1:586

The Compleat Naturalist: A Life of Linnaeus, 2:443
Complete Annals of Thomas Jefferson, 2:175
Complete Apple LOGO Programming, 1:565
The Complete Book of Food: A Nutritional, Medical, and Culinary Guide, 2:550
The Complete Book of Running, 2:551
The Complete Book of Sports Medicine, 2:551
The Complete Book of United States Presidents, 2:5, 2:21
The Complete Directory to Prime Time TV Shows, 1946–Present, 1:464
The Complete Eater's Digest and Nutritional Scoreboard, 2:549
The Complete English Poems of John Donne, 1:10
The Complete Engravings, Etchings, and Dry Points of Albrecht Dürer, 2:313, 2:314
The Complete Etchings of Goya, 2:333
The Complete Father Brown, 1:72
The Complete Film Dictionary, 1:468
The Complete French Poems of Rainer Maria Rilke, 1:371
The Complete Guide to Health and Nutrition, 2:550
The Complete Guide to Middle-Earth from The Hobbit to the Silmarillion, 1:126
A Complete Guide to Monkeys, Apes, and Other Primates, 2:449
The Complete Guide to Sherlock Holmes, 1:48
The Complete Guide to Writing Nonfiction, 1:488
The Complete Hans Christian Andersen Fairy Tales, 1:375
The Complete Hyper-Card 2.0 Handbook, 1:579
Complete Jefferson, 2:175
The Complete Letters of Vincent Van Gogh, 2:359
Complete London Symphonies, 2:337
The Complete Madison: His Basic Writings, 2:177
The Complete Manual of Fitness and Well-Being, 2:530
The Complete Memoirs of George Sherston, 1:116
The Complete Novels of Jane Austen, 1:20
Complete Oxford Shakespeare, 1:15
The Complete Paintings of Cézanne, 2:349
The Complete Paintings of Michelangelo, 2:318

The Complete Paintings of Raphael (Abrams), 2:320
Complete Paintings of Raphael (Penguin), 2:320
The Complete Plays (Behan), 1:68
Complete Plays (Marlowe), 1:12
Complete Plays (O'Neill), 1:274
Complete Plays and Poems (Marlowe), 1:12
The Complete Plays of Gilbert and Sullivan, 1:50
Complete Plays of John M. Synge, 1:123
Complete Poems (Cummings), 1:214
Complete Poems (Dunbar), 1:175
Complete Poems (Hardy), 1:52
Complete Poems (Jarrell), 1:244
The Complete Poems (Keats), 1:35
Complete Poems (Kipling), 1:55
The Complete Poems (Lawrence), 1:101
The Complete Poems (Marvell), 1:13
Complete Poems (Sandburg), 1:283, 1:284
Complete Poems and Selected Letters of Michelangelo, 2:318
The Complete Poems of Emily Dickinson, 1:175
Complete Poems of Emily J. Brontë, 1:42
The Complete Poems of Henry Vaughan, 1:17
The Complete Poems of Marianne Moore, 1:268
The Complete Poems of Rupert Brooke, 1:70
Complete Poetical Works (Byron), 1:33
Complete Poetical Works (Lowell), 1:258
Complete Poetical Works (Scott), 1:36
Complete Poetry and Selected Prose (Whitman), 1:184
The Complete Poetry and Selected Prose of John Donne, 1:10
The Complete Poetry of John Milton, 1:14
The Complete Poetry of Robert Herrick, 1:11
Complete Prose Tales of Pushkin, 1:395
The Complete Short Stories (Lawrence), 1:101
The Complete Short Stories (Twain), 1:182
Complete Short Stories (Wells), 1:129
The Complete Short Stories of Ambrose Bierce, 1:169
The Complete Short Stories of Thomas Wolfe, 1:306
Complete Shorter Fiction (Woolf), 1:132
The Complete Stories: A Centennial Special Edition (Kafka), 1:369
The Complete Tales of Nikolai Gogol: 1923–1985, 1:393
The Complete War Memoirs of Charles de Gaulle: 1940–1946, 2:387
Complete Works (Carroll), 1:45

Complete Works (Shakespeare), 1:15
Complete Works (Tacitus), 2:297
The Complete Works of Aristotle: The Revised Oxford Translation, 2:442
The Complete Works of Oliver W. Holmes, 2:29
The Complete Works of Oscar Wilde, 1:62
The Complete Works of Raphael, 2:320
Complete Works of Saki, 1:115
Complete Writings of William Blake, 1:32
Complex Organizations, 2:140
Composite Systems from Natural and Synthetic Polymers, 2:510
Comprehensive Structured COBOL, 1:565
Compromise or Confrontation: Dealing with the Adults in Your Life, 2:539
Computability, 1:585
Computer: Bit Slices from a Life, 1:538
The Computer: History, Working, Uses, and Limitations, 1:537
Computer—A Child's Play, 1:557
Computer Addiction: Study of Computer Dependency, 1:555
Computer-Aided Instruction in the Humanities, 1:570
Computer-Aided Software Engineering, 1:585
Computer Algorithms: Introduction to Design and Analysis, 1:585
The Computer and Computing with FORTRAN 77, 1:565
The Computer and the Brain, 1:553
The Computer and the Brain: Beyond the Fifth Generation, 1:538
The Computer and the Brain: Perspectives on Human and Artificial Intelligence, 1:582
Computer-Assisted Legal and Tax Research: A Professional's Guide to Lexis, Westlaw, and Phinet, 1:572
Computer Assisted Music Composition, 1:578
Computer-Based Instruction in Military Environments, 1:568
Computer Basics, 1:550
Computer Books and Serials in Print, 1985–1986, 1:537
Computer Confidence: A Human Approach to Computers, 1:557
Computer Crime, 1:554
Computer Crimes and Capers, 1:554
The Computer Culture: A Symposium to Explore the Computer's Impact on Society, 1:554
Computer Culture: The Scientific, Intellectual, and Social Impact of Computers, 1:555
Computer Ethics: A Philosophical Problem Book, 1:555

Computer Ethics Cautionary Tale, 1:554
The Computer from Pascal to von
    Neumann, 1:553
Computer Geometric Art, 1:577
Computer Graphics, 1:578
Computer Graphics: How It Works, What
    It Does, 1:578
Computer Health Hazards, 1:556
The Computer in Composition Instruction,
    1:571
Computer Industry Almanac 1990, 1:538
The Computer Is Down, 1:538
Computer Jargon, 1:538
Computer Keyboarding for Children,
    1:560
Computer Languages, 1:563
Computer Languages: A Guide for the
    Perplexed, 1:563
Computer Lib-Dream Machines, 1:555
Computer Literacy: A Hands-on
    Approach, 1:557
Computer Literacy for Musicians, 1:577
Computer Literacy Visual Masters, 1:557
Computer Mathematics: Essential Math
    for Computer Proficiency, 1:557
Computer Operating Systems: For Micros,
    Minis and Mainframes, 1:561
Computer Peripherals, 1:560
Computer Phone Book Guide to Using
    On-line Systems, 1:567
Computer Pioneers, 1:537, 1:540, 1:545,
    1:547
The Computer Pioneers: The Making of
    the Modern Computer, 1:538, 1:549
Computer Power and Human Reason:
    From Judgment to Calculation, 1:555
Computer Programming, 1:563
Computer Programming for Young
    Children: A Step-By-Step Guide for
    Parents and Teachers, 1:563
Computer Programming in BASIC the
    Easy Way, 1:564
Computer Programming in COBOL the
    Easy Way, 1:565
Computer Programming in Pascal the Easy
    Way, 1:565
Computer Programming in Standard
    MUMPS, 1:566
Computer Programming in the BASIC
    Language, 1:564
Computer Recognition and Human
    Production of Handwriting, 1:560
The Computer Revolution and the Arts,
    1:577
Computer Science: Projects for Young
    Scientists, 1:571
Computer Science Problem Solver, 1:538
Computer Security, 1:554
Computer Simulations: A Source Book to

Learning in an Electronic Environment,
    1:571
Computer Software in Music and Music
    Education: A Guide, 1:577
The Computer Story, 1:540
Computer Systems: Where Hardware
    Meets Software, 1:558
Computer Talk for the Liberal Arts, 1:556
Computer Tech Talk, 1:433
Computer Technology and the Aged:
    Implications and Applications for
    Activity Programs, 1:555
Computer Typing Made Simple, 1:560
The Computer Virus Handbook, 1:575
Computer Viruses: A High-Tech Disease,
    1:574
Computer Viruses, Worms, Data Diddlers,
    Killer Programs and Other Threats to
    Your System, 1:554
The Computerization of Society: A Report
    to the President of France, 1:555
The Computerized Society: Living and
    Working in an Electronic Age, 1:554
Computers, 1:556
Computers: Bridges to the Future, 1:555
Computers: From Babbage to the Fifth
    Generation, 1:540
Computers: The Non-Technological
    (Human) Factors: A Recommended
    Reading List On Computer Ergonomics
    and User Friendly Design, 1:558
Computers and Audiovisual, 1:578
Computers and ESL, 1:571
Computers and Ethics: A Source Book for
    Discussions, 1:555
Computers and Mathematics, 1:570
Computers and Modern Language Studies,
    1:570
Computers and Reading: Lessons from the
    Past and the Technologies of the Future,
    1:569
Computers and the Psychosocial Work
    Environment, 1:554
Computers and Writing, 1:570
Computers at Home: Today and
    Tomorrow, 1:568
Computers, Cognitive Processes, and
    Writing Instruction, 1:570
Computers for Animation, 1:577
Computers for the Disabled, 1:571
Computers in Art, Design, and Animation,
    1:577
Computers in Battle: Will They Work,
    1:568
Computers in Business, 1:572
Computers in Design, 1:579
Computers in English and the Language
    Arts: The Challenge of Teacher
    Education, 1:570

Computers in Entertainment and the Arts, 1:577
Computers in Mathematics Education: 1984 Yearbook, 1:570
Computers in Society, 1:555
Computers in Space, 2:482
Computers in the Government and the Military, 1:568
Computers in the Home, 1:568
Computers in the Human Context: Information Technology, Productivity, and People, 1:558
Computers in the Information Society, 1:555
Computers in Your Life, 1:554
Computers, Self and Society, 1:556
Computers, Thinking, and Social Studies, 1:570
Computers Under Attack: Intruders, Worms, and Viruses, 1:574
Computing Catastrophes, 1:537
Computing Together: A Parents and Teachers Guide to Computing with Young Children, 1:568
Comstock Lode, 1:252
Comte: The Founder of Sociology, 2:126
Comus, A Masque, 1:13
Conan Doyle: Portrait of an Artist, 1:48
The Concept of Cultural Systems: A Key to Understanding Tribes and Nations, 2:43
The Concept of the Corporation, 2:63
Concepts and Theories of Human Development, 2:107
Concerning the Most Certain Fundamentals of Astrology, 2:474
Concierto Barroco, 1:401
Concise Dictionary of Acronyms and Initialisms, 1:440
Concise Dictionary of Physics, 2:512
Concise Encyclopedia of the Italian Renaissance, 2:310
The Concise Handbook of Astronomy, 2:470
A Concise History of American Architecture, 2:262
A Concise History of American Painting and Sculpture, 2:260
A Concise History of Mathematics, 1:498
A Concise History of the American People, 2:155
A Concise Introduction to the Theory of Numbers, 1:496
Concrete Island, 1:67
The Condition of the Working Class in England, 2:58
Conditioned Reflexes: An Investigation of the Physiological Activity of the Cerebral Cortex, 2:462, 2:464

Conditioned Reflexes: An Investigation of the Psychological Activity of the Cerebral Cortex, 2:100
Conditioning and Associative Learning, 2:462
"Coney Island of the Mind," 1:221
The Confessions, 2:303
Confessions of a Teenage Baboon, 1:308
Confessions of an English Opium Eater, 2:347
The Confessions of Felix Krull, Confidence Man, 1:370
The Confessions of Jean Jacques Rousseau, 2:11
The Confessions of Nat Turner, 2:189
The Confidence Gap: Business, Labor and Government in the Public Mind, 2:40
The Confidence Man: His Masquerade, 1:163
The Confidential Agent, 1:91
The Confidential Clerk, 1:82
A Confidential Matter: The Letters of Richard Strauss and Stefan Zweig, 1931–1935, 2:425
Configurations, 1:408
Configurations of Culture Growth, 2:45
Conflict and Crisis: The Presidency of Harry S. Truman, 1945–1948, 2:237
Conflict, Decision, and Dissonance, 2:123
Conflict Sociology: Toward an Explanatory Science, 2:132
Conflicts and Comprise: The Political Economy of Slavery, Emancipation, and the American Civil War, 2:193
The Confucian Persuasion, 2:277
Confucianism and Chinese Civilization, 2:277
Confucius: Ancient Chinese Philosopher, 2:283
Confucius and Ancient China, 2:283
Congress A to Z: Congressional Quarterly's Ready Reference Encyclopedia, 2:5, 2:32
Congress and Its Members, 2:33
Congress and Law-Making: Researching the Legislative Process, 2:33
Congress and the American People, 2:33
Congress Investigates: A Documented History, 1792–1974, 2:33
Congress of Vienna: A Study of Allied Unity 1812–1822, 2:332
Congress Reconsidered, 2:33
Congress Shall Make No Law: Oliver Wendell Holmes, the First Amendment and Judicial Decision-Making, 2:16, 2:26
Congressional Government: A Study in American Politics, 2:225
Congressional Procedures and the Policy Process, 2:6, 2:33

Congressional Staffs: The Invisible Force in American Lawmaking, 2:33
Congressman Sam Rayburn, 2:35
Congreve: The Critical Heritage, 1:22
Conifers (Gelderen and Smith), 2:447
Conifers (Rushforth), 2:448
Conjunctions and Disconjunctions, 1:408
The Conjure Woman, 1:172
A Connecticut Yankee in King Arthur's Court, 1:182
Conquering Back Pain: A Comprehensive Guide, 2:561
The Conquerors, 2:163
The Conquest of Gaul, 2:292
The Conquest of Mexico, 2:323
The Conquest of Peru, 2:323
Conquistador, 1:261
Conscience of a Conservative, 2:244
Consciencism: Philosophy and the Ideology for Decolonization, 2:396
Consciousness and Unconsciousness in the Behavior of the Crowds, 2:139
Consensus and Disunity: The Lloyd George Coalition Government, 1918–1922, 2:374
The Conservationist, 1:414
Conservatism in America, 2:235
Conspiracy at Mukden: The Rise of the Japanese Military, 2:375
Constab Ballads, 1:259
Constable, 2:351
Constable: The Natural Painter, 2:351
Constable: The Painter and His Landscape, 2:351
Constable Landscape Watercolours and Drawings, 2:351
Constable Paintings, Drawings and Watercolours, 2:351
Constance, 1:81
Constance: A Story of Early Plymouth, 2:161
Constancia and Other Stories for Virgins, 1:403
Constancy and Change in Human Development, 2:106
Constantine the Great: Roman Emperor, 2:291
The Constellations: How They Came to Be, 2:479
The Constitution: A Documentary and Narrative History, 2:17
Constitution: Keepsake Edition, 2:17
The Constitution: That Delicate Balance, 2:16
The Constitution of the United States: Bicentennial Edition, 2:17
Constitutional Choices, 2:17
A Constitutional History of the United States, 2:166

Constitutional Opinions: Aspects of the Bill of Rights, 2:169
Constraint of Empire: The United States and Caribbean Interventions, 2:219
Construction of Reality in the Child, 2:111
The Construction, Proof and Analysis of Programs, 1:585
Consultant's Guide to Computer Abbreviations and Acronyms, 1:537
Consumer Mathematics, 1:504
Consumer Response to Income Increases, 2:61
A Consumer's Guide to Emergency Medical Services, 2:566
The Consummate Trainer, 1:571
"Contemplations," 1:151
Contemporary American Speeches, 1:449
Contemporary Atlas of China, 2:87, 2:276
Contemporary Chinese Fiction: Four Short Stories, 1:423
Contemporary Chinese Stories, 1:423
Contemporary Danish Plays, 1:374
Contemporary Indonesian Poetry, 1:426
The Contemporary International Economy: A Reader, 2:71
Contemporary Latin American Short Stories, 1:399
Contemporary Political Ideologies: A Comparative Analysis, 2:16
Contemporary Spanish Theater: Seven One-Act Plays, 1:355
Contemporary Swedish Poetry, 1:374
Contemporary Turkish Literature: Fiction and Poetry, 1:420
Contes du jour et de la nuit, 1:338
Contes fantastiques complets, 1:338
The Continental Operative, 1:231
Continents in Collision, 2:494
Continuities in Social Research: Studies in the Scope and Method of the American Soldier, 2:129, 2:141
Continuity, Chance, and Change: The Character of the Industrial Revolution in England, 2:340
Continuous Geometry, 1:516
Contradictions, Oppositions and Denials in the Life of the Mind, 1:533
Contribution to the Theory of Natural Selection, 2:459
The Contributions of Faraday and Maxwell to Electrical Science, 2:527
The Contributions of Lenin and Mao Tse-tung to the Communist Theories Advanced by Marx and Engels, 2:378
Contributions of Women: Medicine, 2:531
Contributions to the Founding of the Theory of Transfinite Numbers, 1:499
Control, 1:227

The Control of Water Balance by the Kidney, 2:451

Controlling Cholesterol: Dr. Kenneth H. Cooper's Preventive Medicine Program, 2:549

A Convention of Delegates: The Creation of the Constitution, 2:166

Conversations with Czeslaw Milosz, 1:387

Conversations with Igor Stravinsky, 2:426

Conversations with Isaac Bashevis Singer, 1:482

Conversations with Katherine Anne Porter: Refugee from Indian Creek, 1:280

Conversations with Kennedy, 2:247

Conversations with Maya Angelou, 1:192

A Cool Million, 1:300

Cooperation and Competition Among Primitive Peoples, 2:46

The Copernican Revolution: Planetary Astronomy in the Development of Western Thought, 2:514

Coping Through Assertiveness, 2:536

Coping Through Friendship, 2:538

Coping with a Hospital Stay, 2:565

Coping with a Negative Body Image, 2:550

Coping with AIDS: Facts and Fears, 2:560

Coping with an Alcoholic Parent, 2:539

Coping with Anger, 2:104

Coping with Beauty, Fitness and Fashion: A Girl's Guide, 2:553

Coping with Medical Emergencies, 2:567

Coping with Parents, 2:538

Coping with Peer Pressure, 2:538

Coping with Stress: A Guide to Living, 2:537

Coping with Stress: A Practical Guide, 2:536

Coping with Television, 1:468

Coping with the Mass Media, 1:454

Coping with Your Emotions, 2:104

Coping with Your Fears, 2:104

Coping with Your Image, 2:536

Coral Reefs, 2:486

Core Concepts in Health, 2:531

Coriolanus, 2:288

Coronado's Quest: Discovery of the American Southwest, 2:157

Correspondence and Papers of Edmond Halley, 2:477

The Correspondence Between Richard Strauss and Hugo von Hofmannsthal, 2:425

Correspondence of Wagner and Liszt, 2:362

The Corrida at San Feliu, 1:118

The Corridors of Deceit: The World of John Le Carré, 1:102

Cortés: The Life of the Conqueror of Mexico by His Secretary, Francisco Lopez de Gomara, 2:323

Cortés and the Conquest of Mexico by the Spaniards in 1521, 2:323

Cortés and the Fall of the Aztec Empire, 2:323

The Cosmic Connection: An Extraterrestrial Perspective, 2:480

Cosmic Quest: Searching for Intelligent Life Among the Stars, 2:470, 2:479

Cosmography: A Blueprint for the Science and Culture of the Future, 1:522

Cosmos (Sagan), 2:480

The Cosmos (Time-Life), 2:469

Costume of Colonial Times, 2:161

Cotton Candy on a Rainy Day, 1:226

Cotton Mather, 2:163

Count Belisarius, 1:90

The Count of Monte Cristo, 1:333, 1:334

Countee Cullen, 1:214

The Counterfeiters, 1:336

A Country Doctor, 1:180

"The Country Husband," 1:211

The Country of the Pointed Firs, 1:180

The Coup, 1:292

Couples, 1:292

Course in Descriptive Geometry, 1:515

The Court Martial of Daniel Boone, 2:184

The Courtship of Miles Standish, 1:160

Cousin Bette, 1:329

Cousin Pons, 1:329

Cousteau: An Unauthorized Biography, 2:488

The Covenant, 1:264

Cover Her Face, 1:97, 1:98

Cowboys of the Wild West, 2:200

Cows, Pigs, Wars, and Witches: The Riddles of Culture, 2:48, 2:134

Crack and Cocaine, 2:554

Crack—The New Drug Epidemic, 2:554

The Craft of Interviewing, 1:447

Craftsmen in Greek and Roman Society, 2:284

Crash, 1:67

Crash! A New Money Crisis, 2:70

Crazy Horse and Custer: The Parallel Lives of Two American Warriors, 2:203

CRC Handbook of Chemistry and Physics, 2:512

CRC Practical Handbook of Biochemistry and Molecular Biology, 2:511

Creating Interactive Multimedia: A Practical Guide, 1:579

Creating Media Culture, 1:454

Creating Reality: How TV News Distorts Reality, 1:457

The Creation of the American Republic, 1776–1787, 2:7, 2:17

The Creation of the Anglo-American
Alliance, 1937–1941: A Study in
Competitive Cooperation, 2:235
The Creation of the World and Other
Business, 1:266
Creative Computer Imaging, 1:578
The Creative Mind, 2:110
The Creative Process in the Autograph
Musical Documents of Hector Berlioz,
2:347
Creative Puzzles of the World, 1:535
Creditors, 1:380
"The Cremation of Sam McGee," 1:146
Creoles and Cajuns: Stories of Old
Louisiana, 1:171
The Crest of the Wave: Adventures in
Oceanography, 2:486
Cries for Democracy, 2:16
Crime and Criminals: Opposing
Viewpoints, 2:133
Crime and Punishment, 1:392
Crime and Punishment: Changing
Attitudes in America, 2:133
Crime in America, 2:133
Crime News and the Public, 1:457
The Crime of Galileo, 2:474
The Crime of Sylvester Bonnard, 1:335
Criminal Justice, 2:133
Criminal Violence, Criminal Justice, 2:133
Criminology, 2:133
Crimsoned Prairie: The Indian Wars,
2:169, 2:201
The Crisis, 2:165
Crisis and Change: The Church in Latin
America Today, 2:408
Crisis in Central America: Regional
Dynamics and U. S. Policy in the 1980s,
2:257
The Crisis in Economic Theory, 2:149
Crisis in Industry: Can America Compete?,
2:71, 2:257
Crisis in the Population Question, 2:134
A Critical Dictionary of Jungian Analysis,
2:121
Critical Essays on Anton Chekhov, 1:391
Critical Essays on Benjamin Franklin,
2:526
Critical Essays on Cervantes, 1:357
Critical Essays on Emile Zola, 1:345
Critical Essays on Günter Grass, 1:368
Critical Essays on Honoré de Balzac,
1:330
Critical Essays on John Updike, 1:293
Critical Essays on Virginia Woolf, 1:133
A Critical Fable, 1:258
Critical Path, 1:522
The Critical Writing by Desiderius
Erasmus on the Spiritual Conditions of
His Times and the Psychological

Impulses Motivating the Actions of
Men, 2:314
Crocodiles and Alligators, 2:449
Cromwell: The Lord Protector, 2:327
Cronica de una muerte annunciada, 1:404
The Cross and the Crescent: A History of
the Crusades, 2:304
Crossing the Shadow Line: Travels in
Southeast Asia, 2:398
Crow, 1:95
The Crow Indians, 2:51
The Crowd: A Study of the Popular
Mind, 2:105
Crucial Decade and After: America,
Nineteen Forty-Five to Nineteen Sixty,
2:238
The Crucible, 1:266
The Crucible of Europe: The Ninth and
Tenth Centuries in European History,
2:304
Cruel City, 1:412
Crusade for Kindness: Henry Bergh and
the ASPCA, 2:448
Crusade in Europe, 2:239
Crusaders for Fitness: The History of
American Health Reformers, 2:568
The Crusades: The Flame of Islam, 2:306
The Crusades Through Arab Eyes, 2:306
A Cry for Help, 2:537
Cry, the Beloved Country, 1:416
Crying in the Wilderness, 2:397
Crystal, 1:270
The Crystal World, 1:67
Cuba: Dilemmas of a Revolution, 2:408
Cuba: Order and Revolution, 2:408
Cuba: The Making of a Revolution, 2:219
The Cuban Crisis of Nineteen Sixty-Two:
Selected Documents, Chronology, and
Bibliography, 2:242
Cuban Missile Crisis, 2:388
The Cuban Missile Crisis, October 1962:
The United States and Russia Face a
Nuclear Showdown, 2:241
Cuban Missile Crisis of Nineteen
Sixty-Two: Needless or Necessary, 2:388
The Cuban Revolution Twenty-five Years
Later, 2:409
Cubism, 2:415
Cuentos: An Anthology of Short Stories
from Puerto Rico, 1:399
Cujo, 1:249
The Cult of Information: The Folklore of
Computers and the True Art of
Thinking, 1:555
Cultural Anthropology (Ember and
Ember), 2:42
Cultural Anthropology (Harris), 2:48
Cultural Atlas of Africa, 2:86, 2:275
Cultural Atlas of China, 2:86, 2:273

Cultural Atlas of Islam, 2:272
Cultural Atlas of Japan, 2:273
Cultural Atlas of Russia and the Soviet
  Union, 2:275
The Cultural Background of Personality,
  2:43
The Cultural Contradiction of Capitalism,
  2:149
The Cultural Experience: Ethnography in
  Complex Society, 2:43
The Cultural Geography of the United
  States, 2:91
A Cultural History of India, 2:272
Cultural Materialism: The Struggle for a
  Science of Culture, 2:47
Cultural Patterns and Technical Change,
  2:46
Culture and Experience, 2:43
Culture and Nationalism in
  Nineteenth-Century Eastern Europe,
  2:341
Culture and Self: Asian and Western
  Perspectives, 2:43
Culture, Behavior and Personality, 2:43
Culture, Conflict and Crime, 2:133
The Culture of Cities, 2:207
The Culture of the Twenties, 2:226
Culture, People, Nature: An Introduction
  to General Anthropology, 2:48
Culture Shift in Advanced Industrial
  Society, 2:144
Cup of Gold, 1:288
Cured to Death: The Effects of
  Prescription Drugs, 2:553
Curious Naturalist, 2:465
Current American Government, 2:5, 2:32
Current English: A Study of Present-Day
  Usages and Tendencies, Including
  Pronunciation, Spelling, Grammatical
  Practice, Word-Coining, and the
  Shifting of Meanings, 1:429
Current Issues in Expert Systems, 1:584
Current Perspectives on Aging and the
  Life Cycles, 2:106
Currents of Space, 1:193
Curtain, 1:73
The Curves of Life, 1:515
Custer and the Epic of Defeat, 2:203
Custer Battlefield, a History and Guide to
  the Battle of the Little Bighorn, 2:201
Custer Died for Your Sins: An Indian
  Manifesto, 2:241
Custer Legends, 2:203
Custom and Conflict in Africa, 2:132
The Custom of the Country, 1:183
Customs and Fashions in Old New
  England, 2:161
Cut and Assemble 3-D Geometrical
  Shapes, 1:520

The Cyberiad: Fables for the Cybernetic
  Age, 1:386
Cybernetics: Control and Communication
  in the Animal and the Machine, 1:539
The Cycles of American History, 2:156
Cycles, Value, and Employment:
  Responses to the Economic Crisis,
  2:68
The Cynic's Word Book, 1:169
Cytochromes and Cell Respiration, 2:438
Czechoslovakia, 2:405
Czechoslovakia Enslaved: The Story of the
  Communist Coup D'Etat, 2:405
Czechoslovakian Crisis of 1968, 2:405

D

D. H. Lawrence, 1:101
A D. H. Lawrence Handbook, 1:101
Da Silva's Cultivated Wilderness and
  Genesis of the Clowns, 1:404, 1:405
Dada, Surrealism and Their Heritage,
  2:415
Dag Hammarskjold, 2:390
Dag Hammarskjold: A Giant in
  Diplomacy, 2:390
Dag Hammarskjold: Custodian of the
  Brushfire Peace, 2:390
Dag Hammarskjold: Peacemaker for the
  United Nations, 2:390
Dag Hammarskjold Revisited: The United
  Nations Secretary-General As a Force in
  World Politics, 2:390
Dag Hammarskjold's United Nations,
  2:390
The Daguerreotype in America, 2:262
Daily Life in Ancient Rome: The People
  and the City at the Height of the
  Empire, 2:290
Daisy Miller, 1:179
The Damn Good Resumé Guide, 1:490
The Dance Language and Orientation of
  Bees, 2:463
The Dance of Life: The Other Dimension
  of Time, 2:43
Dance of the Continents: Adventures with
  Rocks and Time, 2:494
Dance of the Happy Shades and Other
  Stories, 1:145
Dance Technology: Current Applications
  and Future Trends, 1:569
The Dancer and the Dance: Merce
  Cunningham in Conversation with
  Jacqueline Lesschaeve, 2:266
Dandelion Wine, 1:202
Danger: Memory, 1:266
Danger and Survival: The Political History
  of the Nuclear Weapon, 2:238

Dangerous Currents: The State of
Economics, 2:56
Dangling Man, 1:199
Daniel Defoe, 1:23
Daniel Deronda, 1:49
Daniel Martin, 1:86
Daniel Webster and a Small College, 2:183
Daniel Webster and the Rise of National
Conservatism, 2:180
Daniel Webster and the Supreme Court,
2:183
Daniel Webster and the Trial of American
Nationalism, 1843–1852, 2:180
Dante (Bloom), 1:349
Dante (Holmes), 1:350
Dante (Quinones), 1:350
Dante Gabriel Rossetti, 1:57
Daring the Unknown: A History of
NASA, 2:482
Dark Avenues and Other Stories, 1:390
The Dark Child, 1:414, 1:415
The Dark Half, 1:249
Dark Harvest, 2:256
The Dark Is Light Enough, 1:87
The Dark Labyrinth, 1:81
Dark Laughter, 1:190
The Dark Side: Tales of Terror and the
Supernatural, 1:337
The Dark Tower: The Gunslinger, 1:249
Darkness Visible, 1:89
Darwin and His Flowers: The Key to
Natural Selection, 2:457
Darwin for Beginners, 2:456
Darwinism: An Exposition of the Theory
of Natural Selection with Some of Its
Applications, 2:459
Das Kapital (Capital), 2:58
Dashiell Hammett, 1:231
Dashiell Hammett: Five Complete Novels,
1:231
Data Structures: Form and Function, 1:586
Data Structures and Algorithms, 1:586
Data Structures on the IBM PC, 1:586
Data Structures with Modula-Two, 1:586
Daughter Buffalo, 1:138
Daughters of the Earth, 2:155
David Ben-Gurion, 2:412
David Copperfield, 1:46, 1:47
David Livingstone, 2:367
David Livingstone: The Dark Continent,
2:367
David Lloyd George: A Political Life,
2:374
David Lloyd George: Welsh Radical As
World Statesman, 2:374
David Ricardo: A Centenary Estimate,
2:73
David Ricardo: Critical Assessments, 2:73
Davita's Harp, 1:280

Dawn, 1:301
The Dawn of Man, 2:279
Dawn of Modern Science, 2:310
Day by Day, 1:259
Day in Old Athens, 2:284
Day in Old Rome, 2:290
A Day in the Life of America, 2:90
A Day in the Life of Australia, 2:91
A Day in the Life of Canada, 2:90
A Day in the Life of China, 2:86
A Day in the Life of Japan, 2:86
A Day in the Life of the New York
Times, 1:458
The Day Lincoln Was Shot, 2:198
The Day of Creation, 1:67
The Day of the Locust, 1:300
The Day of the Scorpion, 1:118; 2:363
The Day They Came to Arrest the Book,
1:237
The Daybreakers, 1:252
Days of Knights and Castles, 2:306
The Days of the French Revolution: The
Day-to-Day Story of the Revolution,
2:329
The Days of the Musketeers, 2:306
Days to Come, 1:235
Days with Albert Schweitzer: A
Lambaréné Landscape, 2:535
Days with Chief Joseph: Diary,
Recollections & Photos, 2:202
dBASE IV for Everyone, 1:572
dBASE IV for the First Time User, 1:572
dBASE IV Handbook, 1:572
dBASE IV Made Easy, 1:572
dBase IV User's Desktop Companion,
1:572
De Cive: The English Version, 2:10
De Gaulle, 2:387
De humani corporis fabrica (On the
Structure of the Human Body), 2:548
De la terre à la lune, 1:343
De methodo medendi (Method of
Healing), 2:546
De Motu Cordis: Anatomical Studies on
the Motion of the Heart and Blood,
2:547
De Revolutionibus Orbium Coelestium,
2:514
"The Deacon's Masterpiece," 1:158
Dead End: A Book About Suicide,
2:537
The Dead Father, 1:198
Dead Serious: A Book for Teenagers
About Teenage Suicide, 2:537
Dead Souls, 1:393
Deadeye Dick, 1:295
Dealing Creatively with Death: A Manual
of Death Education and Simple Burial,
2:537

Dealing with Complexity: An Introduction to the Theory and Application of Systems Science, 1:558

Dealing with Death, 2:106

Dean Rusk, 2:26

Dean Rusk: A Seventy-Fifth Birthday Celebration—A Commemorative Record, 2:26

The Dean's December, 1:199

Dear Cherry: Questions and Answers on Eating Disorders, 2:551

Dear Doctor, 2:542, 2:566

Dear Judas, 1:244

Dear Russell–Dear Jourdain: A Commentary on Russell's Logic, Based on His Correspondence With Philip Jourdain, 1:503

Dear Theo: The Autobiography of Vincent Van Gogh, 2:359

Death: The Final Stage of Growth, 2:106

Death and Dying: Opposing Viewpoints, 2:538

Death and Dying Annual 1989, 2:137

The Death and Life of Great American Cities, 2:94

Death and the King's Horseman, 1:418

Death Comes for the Archbishop, 1:209

The Death Penalty in America, 2:133

Death in the Castle, 1:207

Death in the Woods and Other Stories, 1:190

Death in Venice and Other Stories, 1:370

Death of a Lady's Man, 1:137

Death of a Naturalist, 1:92

Death of a Salesman, 1:266

Death of a Simple Giant and Other Modern Yugoslav Stories, 1:383

Death of an Expert Witness, 1:98

The Death of Artemio Cruz, 1:402

The Death of Bessie Smith, 1:186

Death of Hitler, 2:377

The Death of Ivan Ilych and Other Stories, 1:397

The Death of Methusela and Other Stories, 1:388

"The Death of the Ball Turret Gunner," 1:244

The Death of the Heart, 1:69

"Death of the Hired Man," 1:223

Death on the Nile, 1:73

The Death Penalty: A Debate, 2:133

The Debacle, 1:344

Debussy and Wagner, 2:418

Debussy Letters, 2:418

Decade by Decade: Twentieth Century American Photography from the Collection of the Center for Creative Photography, 2:262

Decade of Disillusionment: The Kennedy–Johnson Years, 2:241

A Decade of Revolution, 1789–1799, 2:329

The Decameron, 1:6, 1:347, 1:348

The Decameron: A Diplomatic Edition, 1:348

The Decameron: A Selection, 1:348

Deciding What's News: A Study of CBS Evening News, NBC Nightly News, Newsweek and Time, 1:457

Deciphering the Senses: The Expanding World of Human Perception, 2:113

Decision in Philadelphia: The Constitutional Convention 1787, 2:166

Decision-Making in the White House: The Olive Branch or the Olives, 2:21

The Decision to Intervene: Soviet–American Relations, 1971–1972, 2:371, 2:391

Decline and Fall, 1:127

The Decline and Fall of the Roman Empire, 2:290

The Decline of Bismarck's European Order: Franco–Russian Relations, 1875–1890, 2:391

The Decline of Laissez-Faire, 1897–1917, 2:218

The Declining Significance of Race: Blacks and Changing American Institutions, 2:136

Deductive Systems: Finite and Non-Euclidean Geometries, 1:516

Deenie, 1:201

The Deep Range, 1:75

Deep Song: The Dance Story of Martha Graham, 2:262

Deephaven and Other Stories, 1:180

The Defense of Galileo, 2:473

A Defense of Poesie, 1:16

The Defiant Muse: Hispanic Feminist Poems from the Middle Ages to the Present, a Bilingual Anthology, 1:399

The Deficits: How Big? How Long? How Dangerous?, 2:149

Defoe's Fiction, 1:23

Degas (Boggs), 2:352

Degas (Gordon and Forge), 2:352

Degas: His Life, Times, and Work, 2:352

Degas: The Artist's Mind, 2:352

A Degas Sketchbook: The Halevy Sketchbook, 1877–1883, 2:352

"Dejection: An Ode," 1:34

Del sentimiento trágicode lavida en los hombres y en los pueblos, 1:360

A Delicate Balance, 1:186

Delicate Fire, 1:107

Delineations of American Scenery and Character, 2:187

Delinquent Behavior, 2:139

Delinquent Boys, 2:133
Deliverance (Dickey), 1:215
The Deliverance (Glasgow), 1:226
Delta Wedding, 1:300
The Deluge: An Historical Novel of
    Poland, Sweden, and Russia, 1:387
Demetrius, 1:372
Demian, 1:368
Democracy, 2:175
Democracy, an American Novel, 2:214
Democracy and Education: An
    Introduction to the Philosophy of
    Education, 2:219
Democracy and Its Critics, 2:15
Democracy and Social Ethnics, 2:208
Democracy in America, 2:16, 2:131, 2:180
Democratic Ideals and Reality, 2:79
The Democratic Party: Jefferson to
    Jackson, 2:168
Dental Care, 2:553
The Dependent City: The Changing
    Political Economy of American Urban
    Politics Since 1789, 2:94, 2:154
The Deptford Trilogy, 1:138
Der Prozess, 1:369
Der Tod in Venedig, 1:370
Descartes' Philosophy of Science, 1:515
The Descent of Man and Selection in
    Relation to Sex, 2:457
The Description of the World, 2:309
Desert Landforms, 2:83
Desert Trails of Atacama, 2:77
Deserts (Lye), 2:83
Deserts (McMahon), 2:465
Deserts of the World: Future Threat or
    Promise, 2:84
Design and Strategy for Distributed Data
    Processing, 1:585
The Design of an Optimizing Compiler,
    1:586
The Design of Data Structure and
    Algorithms, 1:586
Designing and Writing Online
    Documentation: Help Files to
    Hypertext, 1:580
Designs for "The Three-Cornered Hat,"
    2:421
Desire Caught by the Tail, 2:421
The Desktop Fractal System, 1:516
Desktop Presentations, 1:575
The Desktop Publisher's Legal Handbook:
    A Comprehensive Guide to Computer
    Publishing Law, 1:576
Desktop Publishing in Style, 1:576
Desmond Tutu: The Courageous and
    Eloquent Archbishop Struggling Against
    Apartheid in South Africa, 2:398
Desolacíon—Ternura—Tala—Lagar, 1:405
Desolation Angels, 1:246
The Desperate People, 1:144

Desperate Remedies, 1:51, 1:52
Destination Biafra, 1:413
Developing Business Expert Systems
    Using Level 5, 1:583
Developing Computer Skills: Operating
    Principles for Apple II, IIe and IIgs,
    1:559
Developing Microcomputer Literacy: A
    Guide for Sport, Physical Education,
    and Recreation Managers, 1:569
Developing Person Through Childhood
    and Adolescence, 2:540
The Developing Person Through the Life
    Span, 2:540
Development During Middle Childhood,
    2:540
The Development of American
    Citizenship, 1608–1870, 2:7
The Development of Children, 2:106
The Development of Intelligence in
    Children, 2:110
The Development of Mathematics in
    China and Japan, 1:497
Development of Mathematics in the
    Nineteenth Century, 1:518
Developmental Biology, 2:451
Developmental Psychology: Historical and
    Philosophical Perspectives, 2:107
Developmental Psychopathology from
    Infancy Through Adolescence, 2:122
Deviance and Medicalization: From
    Badness to Sickness, 2:138
The Devil and Daniel Webster and Other
    Stories, 1:200
The Devil Drives: A Life of Sir Richard
    Burton, 2:364
Devil on the Cross, 1:415
The Devil's Dictionary (The Cynic's Word
    Book), 1:169
The Devil's Disciple, 1:120
The Devil's Law Case, 1:18
Devotion to the Cross, 1:355
Dewey and Russell: An Exchange, 1:503
Dewey, Russell, Whitehead: Philosophers
    as Educators, 1:503
Dharma Bums, The, 1:247
Diabetes, 2:561
The Diabetic's Total Health Book, 2:561
Dialect Labels in the Merriam Third, 1:432
The Dialect Poetry of Claude McKay,
    1:260
Dialectical and Historical Materialism,
    2:380
Dialects in Culture, 1:432
Dialects of American English, 1:431
Dialogue Concerning the Two Chief
    World Systems, Ptolemaic and
    Copernican, 2:473
A Dialogue Concerning the Two Principal
    Systems of the World, 2:473

Dialogue on Oratory, 2:296
Dialogue with Gordon Allport, 2:115
Dialogues (Stravinsky), 2:426
Dialogues Concerning Two New Sciences, 2:473
A Diamond and a Vengeance, 1:334
The Diamond Cutters, 1:281
The Diamond Smugglers, 1:84
Diamonds Are Forever, 1:84
The Diaries of Hans Christian Andersen, 1:375
Diaries, 1748–1799 (Washington), 2:179
The Diaries of Tchaikovsky, 2:357
The Diario of Christopher Columbus' First Voyage to America, 1492–1493, 2:159
Diary and Sundry Observations of Thomas Alva Edison, 2:524
A Diary in the Strict Sense of the Term, 2:46
The Diary of John Quincy Adams: 1794–1845, 2:173
The Diary of One of Garibaldi's Thousand, 2:344
Diary of Samuel Pepys, The, 1:27
Diatoms in Alaska, 2:447
Dicey's Song, 1:294
Dick Tracy: The Thirties, Tommy Guns and Hard Times, 1:459
Dickens: From Pickwick to Dombey, 1:47
Dictionary of American Art, 2:261
Dictionary of American Painters, Sculptors, and Engravers, 2:261
Dictionary of American Politics, 2:6
A Dictionary of American Pop-Rock, 2:156
Dictionary of Anthropology, 2:43
A Dictionary of Architecture, 2:262
Dictionary of Architecture and Construction, 2:261
Dictionary of Biology: The Facts You Need to Know—At a Glance, 2:437
A Dictionary of Botany, 2:447
Dictionary of Business and Economics, 2:55
Dictionary of Classical Mythology, 1:318
The Dictionary of Clichés, 1:433
Dictionary of Confusable Words, 1:440
Dictionary of Contemporary American Artists, 2:261
Dictionary of Dangerous Pollutants, Ecology, and Environment, 2:497
Dictionary of Demography, 2:124
Dictionary of Film and Television Terms, 1:465
Dictionary of Food Ingredients, 2:549
A Dictionary of Genetics, 2:452
Dictionary of Geologic Terms, 2:488
Dictionary of Key Words in Psychology, 2:95
Dictionary of Life Sciences, 2:437

Dictionary of Mathematics, 1:497
Dictionary of Mathematics Terms, 1:497
Dictionary of Microbiology and Molecular Biology, 2:443, 2:446
Dictionary of Physics, 2:512
The Dictionary of Physics, 2:512
Dictionary of Politics, 2:6
Dictionary of Psychology, 2:95
Dictionary of Science and Engineering, 2:433
Dictionary of Scientific Biography, 1:497
Dictionary of Sociology and Related Sciences, 2:124
Dictionary of Space Technology, 2:469
A Dictionary of Statistical Terms (Kendall), 1:529
Dictionary of Statistical Terms (Marriott), 1:529
Dictionary of Subjects and Symbols in Art, 2:154
The Dictionary of the English Language, 1:26
Dictionary of the Environment, 2:495
Dictionary of Word Origins, 1:433
Did Molly Pitcher Say That?: The Men and Women Who Made American History, 2:153
Die Blechtrommel (The Tin Drum), 1:367
Die Gesammelten Werke, 1:531
Die Leiden des Jungen Werthers, 1:366
Die Plebejer Proben den Aufstand, 1:367
Die Verwändlung, 1:369
Diet and Nutrition, 2:550
Different Like Me: A Book for Teens Who Worry About Their Parents' Use of Alcohol/Drugs, 2:555
Different People: Pictures of Some Japanese, 2:87
Difficulties with Girls, 1:65
The Diffusion of Innovations, 2:144
The Digestive System, 2:450, 2:544
Digital Design Methodology for Optical Computing, 1:559
Digital Visions: Computer and Art, 1:577
The Dilemmas of an Upright Man: Max Planck as Spokesman for German Science, 2:521
The Dilemmas of Presidential Leadership: Of Caretakers and Kings, 2:21
Dimensions of the Holocaust, 2:385
Dimensions of Tolerance: What Americans Believe About Civil Liberties, 2:12
DINE How to Improve Your Nutrition and Health Book, 1:569
DINE System, 1:569
Dinky Hooker Shoots Smack, 1:247
Dinner at the Homesick Restaurant, 1:291
Diophantus' Arithmetica: Books IV to VI in the Arabic Translation of Qusta ibn Luqa, 1:507

Directory of Computer Software with Applications to Physical Education, Exercise Science, Health, and Dance, 1:568
Dirk Gently's Holistic Detective Agency, 1:64
Dirty Hands, 1:340
The Disappearance, 1:229
The Disappearance of Childhood, 1:454
Disastrous Hurricanes and Tornadoes, 2:484
Disastrous Volcanoes, 2:493
A Discipline of Programming, 1:563
Disclosing the Past, 2:49
Discours de la Méthode, 1:515
The Discourse of Western Planting, 2:324
Discourse on Free Will, 2:314
Discourse on Method and the Meditations, 1:515
Discourse on the Inequalities of Men, 2:11
Discourse on the Progress of the Prolonged War in Vietnam, 1:373
The Discourses (Machiavelli), 2:20
Discourses (Reynolds), 2:338
Discover It, 1:512
Discover the Invisible: A Naturalist's Guide to Using the Microscope, 2:435
Discovering American Dialects, 1:431
Discovering Apple LOGO: An Introduction to the Art and Pattern of Nature, 1:565
Discovering Archaeology: Stonehenge, 2:277
Discovering Astronomy, 2:470
Discovering the News: A Social History of American Newspapers, 1:457
Discovery: The Search for DNA's Secrets, 2:439
The Discovery and Conquest of Mexico 1517–1521, 2:320
The Discovery of India, 2:404
The Discovery of Insulin, 2:561
The Discovery of Our Galaxy, 2:477
The Discovery of the Elements, 2:498
The Discovery of the Tomb of Tutankhamen, 2:279
Discrimination Against Women: A Global Survey of the Economic, Educational, Social and Political Status of Women, 2:276
Disney Animation: The Illusion of Life, 1:475
The Disney Studio Story, 1:475
The Disney Version, 1:475
The Dispossessed, 1:254
Dispossessing the American Indian: Indians and Whites on the Colonial Frontier, 2:162
A Disquisition on Government, 2:181

Disquisitiones Arithmeticae, 1:531, 1:532
Disraeli, 2:343
The Dissenting Opinions of Mr. Justice Holmes, 2:28, 2:29
The Dissident Press, 1:457
Distant Encounters: The Exploration of Jupiter and Saturn, 2:476
A Distant Mirror: The Calamitous 14th Century, 2:306
Distant Relations, 1:402
Distant Thunder: A Photographic Essay on the American Civil War, 2:192
The Distracted Preacher and Other Tales, 1:52
Distributed Systems, 1:585
The Disunited States: The Era of Civil War and Reconstruction, 2:198
Divers Voyages Touching the Discovery of America and the Islands Adjacent, 2:324
The Divine Campaigns: 1100–1200, 2:305
The Divine Comedy, 1:38, 1:117, 1:160, 1:346, 1:349
Divine Dancer: A Biography of Ruth St. Denis, 2:262
The Diviners, 1:140
Diving into the Wreck, 1:281
Division and Reunion: 1829–1889, 2:225
The Division of Labor in Society, 2:126, 2:144
A Division of the Spoils, 1:118; 2:363
Division Street: America, 1:489
The Divorce Revolution: The Unexpected Social and Economic Consequences for Women and Children in America, 2:138
Dmitri Shostakovich: The Life Background of a Soviet Composer, 2:424
Dmitri Shostakovich, the Man and His Work, 2:424
DNA and the Creation of New Life, 2:455
DNA for Beginners, 2:452
The DNA Story: A Documentary History of Gene Cloning, 2:440, 2:455
Do Lord Remember Me, 1:255
"Do Not Go Gentle into That Good Night," 1:124
Do the Right Thing: The New Spike Lee Joint, 1:486
Dr. Dobb's Toolbox of C, 1:564
Doctor Faustus: The Life of the German Composer, Adrian Leverkuhn, as Told by a Friend, 1:370
Dr. Frank Field's Weather Book, 2:80
Dr. Heimlich's Home Guide to Emergency Medical Situations, 2:567
Dr. Henry Faust: The Tragedy's First and Second Parts, 1:366
The Doctor Is Sick, 1:71

Dr. Jean Mayer's Diet and Nutrition Guide, 2:550
Dr. Jekyll and Mr. Hyde, 1:58
Dr. Kenneth H. Cooper's Preventive Medicine Program: Preventing Osteoporosis, 2:561
Dr. Kookie, You're Right, 1:480
Dr. No, 1:84
Doctor Spock: Biography of a Conservative Radical, 2:542
Dr. Spock on Parenting, 2:541
Doctor Zhivago, 1:394
Doctor Zimor's Guide to Clearer Skin, 2:553
The Doctor's Dilemma, 1:120
A Doctor's Visit: Short Stories by Anton Chekhov, 1:391
The Doctrines of Chance: A Method of Calculating the Probabilities of Events in Play, Including Treatise on Annuities, 1:529
A Documentary History of the First Federal Elections: 1788–1790, 2:169
Documents in World History, 2:277
Documents of American History, 2:5
Documents Relating to the Sentimental Agents in the Volyen Empire, 1:103
Dodsworth, 1:256
Does This School Have Capital Punishment, 1:238
The Dog It Was That Died, 1:122
The Dog Who Wouldn't Be, 1:144
Dog Years, 1:367
Doing Something About the Weather, 2:484
A Doll's House, 1:377
The Dolphin Crossing, 1:126
Dolphins and Porpoises, 2:449
Dom Pedro: The Struggle for Liberty in Brazil and Portugal, 1798–1834, 2:369
Dombey and Son, 1:46, 1:47
A Dome of Many-Colored Glass, 1:258
Domestic Violence: No Longer Behind the Curtains, 2:540
Don Carlos, Infante of Spain, 1:372
Don Juan (Byron), 1:33,
Don Juan (Moliere), 1:338
Don Quixote, 1:354, 1:356, 1:360
Donald Barthelme, 1:198
Donor Banks: Saving Lives with Organ and Tissue Transplants, 2:565
Don't Know Much About History: Everything You Need to Know About American History But Never Learned, 2:153
Don't Look and It Won't Hurt, 1:275
Don't Ride the Bus on Monday: The Rosa Parks Story, 2:238

Don't Worry, You're Normal: A Teenager's Guide to Self-Health, 2:543
Doolittle: A Biography, 1:463
Doonesbury, 1:460, 1:461
Doonesbury: The Original Yale Cartoons, 1:461
Doonesbury Chronicles, 1:461
Doonesbury Dossier: The Reagan Years, 1:461
Doonesbury's Greatest Hits, 1:461
The Door into Summer, 1:233
Door into the Dark, 1:92
Doors of Opportunity: The Life and Legacy of Herbert Hoover, 2:231
Doris Lessing (Knapp), 1:103,
Doris Lessing (Whittaker), 1:104
Doris Lessing: Critical Studies, 1:104
Dorothea Lange, 2:232
Dorothea Lange: Life Through the Camera, 2:232
Dorothea Lange and the Documentary Tradition, 2:232
Dorothy and the Wizard in Oz, 1:198
Dorothy L. Sayers: A Literary Biography, 1:118
Dorothy L. Sayers: A Reference Guide, 1:118
Dorothy L. Sayers: Nine Literary Studies, 1:117
Dorothy Parker, 1:274
Dorothy Parker: What Fresh Hell Is This?, 1:275
Dos novelas cortas, 1:360
DOS: The Pocket Reference, 1:561
DOS Power Techniques, 1:561
The Double, 1:392
The Double Dealer, 1:21
Double Exposure: Composing Through Writing and Film, 1:477
Double Exposure: Fiction into Film, 1:473
The Double Helix: A Personal Account of the Discovery of the Structure of DNA, 2:435, 2:439, 2:441
Double Life: Newly Discovered Thrillers of Louisa May Alcott, A, 1:168
Double Sin and Other Stories, 1:74
Double Star, 1:233
Double Yoke, 1:413
Doublespeak: How Governments, Businesses, Advertisers, and Others Use Language to Deceive You, 1:440
Douglas MacArthur, 2:238
Dove: A Novel, 1:140
The Dove and the Bear: Did They Avert the Third World War?, 2:257
"Dover Beach" 1:39
The Dow Jones-Irwin Guide to Using "The Wall Street Journal," 2:57
Down Among the Women, 1:128

Down and Out in Paris and London, 1:110
Down and Out in the Great Depression: Letters from the Forgotten Man, 2:229
Down-Home Talk, 1:431
Down in the Holler: A Gallery of Ozark Folk Speech, 1:431
Down Is Not Out: Teenagers and Depression, 2:536
Down the Long Hills, 1:252
Down the Sante Fe Trail and into Mexico: The Diary of Susan Shelby Magoffin, 1846–1847, 2:185
Down the Seine and up the Potomac with Art Buchwald, 1:488
The Downside of Drugs, 2:554
Downtown Doonesbury, 1:461
The Drackenburg Adventure, 1:187
Dracula, 1:59
Dracula: The Vampire and the Critics, 1:59
A Draft of Shadows and Other Poems, 1:408
Dragon Country: Eight Plays, 1:303, 1:304
The Dragon Wakes: China and the West, 1793–1911, 2:363
Dragons, Gods, and Spirits from Chinese Mythology, 2:309
The Dragons of Eden, 2:479, 2:480
Dragonwings, 2:208
Drake and the Armada, 2:324
Dramatic Works (Dryden), 1:23
Drawing and Painting with the Computer, 1:577
The Drawing of the Three (The Dark Tower II), 1:249
Drawings (Degas), 2:352
Drawings of Cézanne, 2:349
Drawings of Daumier, 2:346
Drawings of Degas, 2:352
Drawings of Edouard Manet, 2:346
Drawings of Gauguin, 2:353
Drawings of Goya, 2:333
Drawings of Ingres, 2:334
Drawings of Matisse, 2:346
The Drawings of Paul Cézanne: A Catalogue Raisonne, 2:349
Drawings of Paul Klee, 2:415
Drawings of Raphael, 2:320
The Drawings of Raphael: With a Complete Catalog, 2:320
Drawings of Renoir, 2:346
Drawings of Rodin, 2:356
Drawings of Thomas Gainsborough, 2:335
The Dreadful Future of Blossom Culp, 1:275
The Dream, 2:474
The Dream Keeper, 1:241
The Dream Life of Balso Snell, 1:300
The Dream of a Common Language, 1:281

A Dream of Africa, 1:415
The Dream of the Red Chamber, 1:423
Dreaming of Babylon, 1:203
Dreamland Lake, 1:275
Dreams of a Perfect Earth, 2:496
The Dreams of Reason: The Computer and the Rise of the Sciences and Complexity, 1:555
Dreamtigers, 1:399
The Dred Scott Case: Its Significance in American Law and Politics, 2:189
The Drifters, 1:264
The Driver's Seat, 1:121
The Drought, 1:67
The Drowned World, 1:67
Drug Abuse, 2:554
Drug Abuse: The Impact on Society, 2:554
Drug Abuse A–Z, 2:554
Drug Education, 2:554
Drug Free: The Back in Control Program for Keeping Your Kids Off Drugs, 2:554
Drug-Related Diseases, 2:554
Drug Use and Drug Abuse (Hughes), 2:554
Drug Use and Drug Abuse (Ward), 2:555
Drugs and Drug Abuse, 2:555
Drugs and Medicines: A Consumers' Guide, 2:553
Drugs and Performance in Sports, 2:553
Drugs and Pregnancy, 2:555
Drugs and Sports, 2:553
Drugs and the Body in Health and Disease, 2:553
Drugs and the Family, 2:539
Drugs and Your Child: What Can a Parent Do?, 2:554
Drum Taps, 1:162, 1:184
Drunk with Love, 1:225
Dryden, 1:24
Dryden: Poems, 1:23
Dryden: The Critical Heritage, 1:24
Dubin's Lives, 1:262
Dubliners, 1:98, 1:99
The Duchess of Malfi, 1:18
Due to Circumstances Beyond Our Control, 1:464
The Duino Elegies and the Sonnets to Orpheus, 1:371
Duke Ellington, 2:267
Duke Ellington in Person: An Intimate Memoir, 2:267
Dune, 1:238
Dune Messiah, 1:238
Durkheim and Modern Sociology, 2:127
Durkheimian Sociology: Cultural Studies, 2:127
Dusklands, 1:413
The Dust Bowl: An Agricultural and Social History, 2:229

Dustland, 1:230
Dutch Catholic Immigrant Settlement in Wisconsin, 2:161
Dutch Emigration to North America, 1624–1860, 2:161
Dutchman and The Slave, Two Plays, 1:197
Dvorak's Guide to Desktop Telecommunications, 1:573
The Dwarf, 1:379
Dwight D. Eisenhower, 2:240
Dwight D. Eisenhower: Hero and Politician, 2:239
The Dying Sea, 2:81, 2:488
Dying to Please: Anorexia Nervosa and Its Cure, 2:551
Dylan Thomas: A Collection of Critical Essays, 1:124
The Dymaxion World of Buckminster Fuller, 1:522
Dymer, 1:104
Dynamical Theory of the Electromagnetic Field, 2:527
The Dynamics of Bureaucracy, 2:140
The Dynamics of Culture Change, 2:46

E

E. B. White: A Biography, 1:456
E. E. Cummings, 1:214
E. E. Cummings: An Introduction to the Poetry, 1:214
E. M. Forster, 1:86
Each in His Own Way, 1:351
The Eagle and the Dragon: The History of U.S.–China Relations, 2:155
Eagle or Sun?, 1:408
Eagle Resurgent: The Reagan Era in American Foreign Policy, 2:37
The Ear and Hearing, 2:552
Earl Warren: A Public Life, 2:32
Earl Warren: The Judge Who Changed America, 2:32
The Earliest Farmers and the First Cities, 2:280
Early American Architecture: From the First Colonial Settlements to the National Period, 2:155
The Early Asimov, 1:194
Early Childhood Years: The Two to Six Year Old, 2:540
Early China (Goff), 2:281
Early China (Keightley), 2:282
Early Christianity, 2:301
Early Forerunners of Man, 2:48, 2:278
Early Greece: The Bronze and Archaic Ages, 2:284

Early History of Human Anatomy: From Antiquity to the Beginning of the Modern Era, 2:546, 2:548
The Early History of Rome, 2:295
Early Humans, 2:278
Early Life, 2:456
Early Man, 2:278
Early Man: Prehistory and the Civilizations of the Ancient Near East, 2:279
Early Man and the Ocean: A Search for the Beginnings of Navigation and Seaborne Civilizations, 2:411
The Early Mathematical Manuscripts of Leibniz, 1:527
The Early Medieval Balkans: A Critical Survey from the Sixth to the Late Twelfth Century, 2:305
Early Novels and Stories of Willa Cather, 1:209
Early Poems 1935–1955 (Paz), 1:408
Early Psychoanalytic Writings (Freud), 2:117
Early Window: Effects of Television on Children and Youth, The, 1:465
The Early Works of J. M. W. Turner, 2:358
Ears, Hearing, and Balance, 2:448
The Earth (Lye), 2:489
Earth (Press), 2:489
The Earth (Smith), 2:83
The Earth (Zola), 1:344
The Earth: A Topical Geography, 2:93
The Earth: An Introduction to Physical Geology, 2:489
Earth Afire! Volcanoes and Their Activity, 2:493
Earth and Life Through Time, 2:495
Earth and Man: Lectures on Comparative Physical Geography in Its Relation to the History of Mankind, 2:80, 2:81
Earth in Motion: The Concept of Plate Tectonics, 2:494
Earth, Sea, and Sky, 2:489
Earthly Possessions, 1:291
Earthquake, 2:494
Earth's Changing Climate, 2:80, 2:278, 2:485
East Africa, 2:85, 2:393
East Asia and the Western Pacific, 2:86
East of Eden, 1:288
East Wind: West Wind, 1:206
Easter Island, 2:411
Eastern Europe (Rugge), 2:405
Eastern Europe (Time-Life), 2:87
Eastern Europe Between the Wars: 1918–1941, 2:375
Eat, Drink and Be Wary: Getting and Spending: A Consumer's Dilemma, 2:61

Eating Disorders: Managing Problems with Food, 2:551
Eating Without Fear: A Guide to Understanding and Overcoming Bulimia, 2:551
The Ebony Tower, 1:86
The Ecclesiastical History of England, 2:308
Ecclesiastical History of the English People, 2:308
Echoes from the Macabre, 1:81
The Eclipse of Community: An Interpretation of American Studies, 2:147
The Eclogues, 1:324; 2:297, 2:298
Eclogues "and" Georgics, 1:325
Ecological Energetics, 2:465
Ecology Basics, 2:466
Ecology Projects for Young Scientists, 2:465
Ecology 2000, 2:81
The Economic and Social Growth of Early Greece, 800–500 BC, 2:285
The Economic Base of American Cities, 2:93
Economic Choices, 2:68
The Economic Consequences of the Peace, 2:67
Economic Co-operation Among Negro Americans, 2:210
Economic Development: The History of an Idea, 2:62
Economic Development in the Third World, 2:72
The Economic Effects of Multinational Corporations, 2:36
Economic Geography, 2:93
Economic Growth and Urbanization in Developing Areas, 2:84, 2:274
Economic Growth of Nations: Total Output and Production Structure, 2:63
Economic Growth of the United States, 1790–1860, 2:185
Economic History and the History of Economics, 2:55
An Economic Interpretation of the Constitution of the United States, 2:16, 2:166
Economic Issues Today: Alternative Approaches, 2:57
The Economic Problem, 2:63
Economic Problems of Socialism in the U.S.S.R, 2:380
Economic Systems and Society, 2:47
Economic Theory and Econometrics, 2:56
Economic Theory in Retrospect, 2:55, 2:69
The Economic Theory of Organizations and the Firm, 2:140
Economic Thought and the Problem of the Unity of the World, 2:58

Economics, 2:56
Economics: Principles and Policy, 2:55
Economics and Liberalism in the Risorgimento: A Study of Nationalism in Lombardy, 1814–1848, 2:340
Economics in Plain English: Updated and Expanded, 2:56
The Economics of Imperfect Competition, 2:60
Economics of Labor, 2:70
The Economics of Public Issues, 2:65
Economics of Public Policy: The Micro View, 2:71
Economics of Social Issues, 2:65
The Economics of Trade Unions, 2:70
The Economics of Work and Pay, 2:70
Economy and Society: A Study in the Integration of Economic and Social Theory, 2:47
The Economy of Colonial America, 2:162
Eden, 1:386
Edgar Allan Poe, 1:164
Edgar Huntly, 1:152
Edgar Lee Masters, 1:263
Edgar Rice Burroughs, 1:208
The Edge of the Sea, 2:82, 2:243, 2:466
The Edge of the Sword, 2:386, 2:387
The Edible Woman, 1:135
Edison, 2:204, 2:524
Edison: The Man Who Made the Future, 2:524
Edit Yourself: A Manual for Everyone Who Works with Words, 1:479
Edith Jackson, 1:228
Edith Wharton, 1:183
Edith Wharton: A Biography, 1:183
The Editor, the Bluenose, and the Prostitute: H. L. Mencken's History of the "Hatrack" Censorship Case, 1:436
Edmond Halley and His Comet, 2:477
Edmund Burke (Fasel), 2:9
Edmund Burke (Kramnick), 2:9
Edmund Burke: A Genius Reconsidered, 2:329
Edmund Burke: His Life and Opinions, 2:9, 2:329
Edmund Burke: The Practical Imagination, 2:9
Edmund Spenser, 1:17
Edmund Spenser's Poetry, 1:17
Edna St. Vincent Millay, 1:265
Edna St. Vincent Millay's Poems Selected for Young People, 1:265
Educated Guesses: Light-Serious Suggestions for Parents and Teachers, 1:193
Education of a Wandering Man, 1:253
The Education of Black People. 1906–1960: Ten Critiques, 2:210
The Education of Henry Adams, 2:214

Edward Albee, 1:187
Edward R. Murrow: An American
  Original, 1:467
Edward R. Murrow: Broadcaster of
  Courage, 1:467
Edward S. Corwin's Constitution and
  What It Means Today, 2:16
Edward Second: A Chronicle Play, 1:365
Edward Taylor, 1:154
Edward Weston: His Life, 2:262
Edwin Arlington Robinson, 1:282
Edwin Arlington Robinson: A Critical
  Study, 1:282
The Effect of Gamma Rays on
  Man-in-the-Moon Marigolds, 1:308
The Effective Executive, 2:63
Effective Listening: Hearing What People
  Say and Making It Work for You, 2:539
The Effects of Mass Communication,
  2:130
Efforts for Social Betterment Among
  Negro Americans, 2:211
Efury, 1:410
Egmont: A Play, 1:366
Ego Tripping and Other Poems for Young
  People, 1:226
Egypt After the Pharaohs, 2:279
Egyptian Art, 2:279
An Egyptian Craftsman, 2:279
Egyptian Hieroglyphs, 2:280
Egyptian Life, 2:281
The Egyptian Pyramids: A
  Comprehensive, Illustrated Reference,
  2:280
Egyptian Town, 2:281
The Egyptians, 2:279
Eight Black American Inventors, 2:432
Eight Chapters of Maimonides on Ethics,
  2:303
Eight Cousins, or The Aunt Hill, 1:168
Eight Men, 1:307
Eight Mules from Monterey, 2:206
Eight Plays (Ibsen), 1:378
Eight Plus One, 1:213
Eighteen Forty-Eight: The Revolutionary
  Tide in Europe, 2:332
Eighteen Twelve: The War Nobody Won,
  2:169
Eighteenth Century Europe, 2:326
The Eighth Day, 1:303
The Eighth Day of Creation: Makers of
  the Revolution in Biology, 2:439, 2:440,
  2:441
Einleitung in die Theorie der Analytischen
  Functionen, 1:528
Einstein, 2:520
Einstein: A Centenary Volume, 2:520
Einstein: The First Hundred Years, 2:520
Einstein: The Life and Times, 2:520
Einstein as Myth and Muse, 2:520

Einstein in America, 2:520
Einstein's Universe, 2:518
Eisenhower, 2:239
Eisenhower: A Centennial Life, 2:239
Eisenhower and the Cold War, 2:239
The Eisenhower Diaries, 2:239
El aleph, 1:400
El Amor en los tiempos de Coléra, 1:404
El Bronx Remembered: A Novella and
  Stories, 1:267
"El Cristo de Velazquez," 1:360
El coronel no tiene quién le escriba, 1:404
The El Dorado Adventure, 1:188
El ingenioso hidalgo Don Quijote de la
  Mancha, 1:356
El libro de arenas, 1:400
El mundo de los sueños (Colección mente
  y palabra), 1:402
El otoño del patriarca, 1:404
El reino de este mundo, 1:401
The Elderly, 2:544
The Elderly: Opposing Viewpoints,
  2:129
Eleanor: The Years Alone, 2:233
Eleanor and Franklin: The Story of Their
  Relationship Based on Eleanor
  Roosevelt's Private Papers, 2:233
Eleanor of Aquitaine and the Four Kings,
  2:306
Eleanor Roosevelt, 2:233
Eleanor Roosevelt's My Day: Her
  Acclaimed Columns, 1936–1945, 2:232
Election Journal: The Political Events of
  1987–1988, 2:257
Elective Affinities, 1:366
Electra and Other Plays, 1:316
The Electric Kool-Aid Acid Test, 1:479
Electric Language: A Philosophical Study
  of Word Processing, 1:575
Electricity: From Faraday to Solar
  Generators, 2:522
Electricity: Principles and Applications,
  2:522
Electricity and Magnetism, 2:522, 2:527
Electrochemistry: The Past Thirty and the
  Next Thirty Years, 2:508
Electrodynamics, 2:503
Electronic Life: How to Think About
  Computers, 1:554
The Electronic Office and You: Word
  Processing Concepts, 1:575
The Eletronic Schoolhouse, 1:570
Electronic Structures and Properties and
  the Periodic Law, 2:506
The Electronic Sweatshop: How
  Computers Are Transforming the Office
  of the Future into the Factory of the
  Past, 1:554
Electronically Hearing: Computer Speech
  Recognition, 1:579

Electronically Speaking: Computer Speech Generation, 1:579
"Elegy Written in a Country Churchyard," 1:25
Elementary Aspects of Chemical Periodicity, 2:506
The Elementary Forms of the Religious Life, 2:52, 2:127
Elementary Geometry from an Advanced Standpoint, 1:512
Elementary Particles, 2:528
Elementary Spelling Book, 1:430
The Elementary Structures of Kinship, 2:53
Elementary Treatise on Chemistry, 2:499
Elements, 1:513
Eléments de Mathématique, 1:499
Elements of Algebra, 1:526
Elements of Chemistry, 2:499
The Elements of Fiction Writing: Characters and Viewpoint, 1:490
The Elements of Fiction Writing: Dialogue, 1:490
The Elements of Fiction Writing: Plot, 1:490
The Elements of Fiction Writing: Revision, 1:490
Elements of Game Theory, 1:530
Elements of General and Biological Chemistry, 2:511
The Elements of Law: Natural and Politic, 2:10
The Elements of Mechanics, 2:512
Elements of Physical Geography, 2:93, 2:489
Elements of Probability Theory and Some of Its Applications, 1:529
The Elements of Programming Style, 1:563
Elements of Social Organization, 2:52
The Elements of Spreadsheet Style, 1:573
Elements of Style, 1:478
Elements of Systems Analysis, 1:558
The Elephant Calf, 1:365
Eleven Poems of Rubén Darío, 1:402
Elia and The Last Essays of Elia, 1:35
Elie Wiesel: Between Memory and Hope, 1:302
Elie Wiesel: Messenger to All Humanity, 1:302
Elizabeth Barrett Browning, 1:43
Elizabeth Bowen, 1:70
Elizabeth Tudor: Biography of a Queen, 2:327
Elizabeth Tudor and Mary Stewart: Two Queens in One Isle, 2:327
Ellen Glasgow, 1:227
Ellis Island: Gateway to the New World, 2:207

Ellis Island: New Hope in a New Land, 2:207
Elmer Gantry, 1:256
Elsevier's Dictionary of Word Processing: In English (with Definitions), French, and German, 1:576
Elsie Venner, 1:158
The Elusive Executive: Discovering Statistical Patterns of the Presidency, 2:6
The Emerald City of Oz, 1:198
The Emerald Realm: Earth's Precious Rain Forests, 2:83
The Emergence of Film Art, 1:469
The Emergence of Latin America in the Nineteenth Century, 2:369
The Emergence of Life: Darwinian Evolution from the Inside, 2:456
The Emergence of Morality in Young Children, 2:106
The Emergence of Rome: As a Ruler of the Western World, 2:291
Emergency Handbook: A First-aid Manual for Home and Travel, 2:566
Emergency Medical Procedures for the Home, Auto, and Workplace, 2:567
Emergent Mind and Education: A Study of George H. Mead's Bio-Social Behaviorism from an Educational Point of View, 2:140
Emerson: A Collection of Critical Essays, 1:158
Emerson: Prospect and Retrospect, 1:158
Emile, 2:11
Emile Durkheim, 2:127
Emile Durkheim, 1858–1917: A Collection of Essays, with Translations and a Bibliography, 2:127
Emile Zola, 1:345
Emiliano Zapata, 2:370
Emily Brontë, 1:43
Emily Climbs, 1:143
Emily Dickinson, 1:175
Emily Dickinson: An Interpretive Biography, 1:175
Emily Dickinson's Poetry: Stairway of Surprise, 1:175
Emily of New Moon, 1:143
Emily's Quest, 1:143
Eminent Victorians, 2:570
Emma, 1:20
Emma McChesney and Co, 1:220
Emma Willard: Pioneer Educator of American Women, 2:185
Emmy Noether in Bryn Mawr: Proceedings of a Symposium Sponsored by the Association of Women in Mathematics in Honor of Emmy Noether's 100th Birthday, 1:510
Emmy Noether (1882–1935), 1:509

Emotional Illness in Your Family: Helping Your Relatives, Helping Yourself, 2:536, 2:539

Emotions and Psychopathology, 2:121

Emotions, Cognition, and Behavior, 2:103

Emperor's Winding Sheet, The, 1:126

Empire of Business, 2:206

The Empire of Reason: How Europe Imagined and America Realized the Enlightenment, 2:326

Empire of the Inca, 2:298

Empire of the Sun, 1:66, 1:67

Empire on the Pacific: A Study in American Continental Expansion, 2:153

En attendant Godot, 1:331

Encounters, 1:69

Encounters with Stravinsky: A Personal Record, 2:426

Encounters with Verdi, 2:361

Encyclopedia Africana, 2:210

The Encyclopedia of American Facts and Dates, 2:153

The Encyclopedia of American Music, 2:154

Encyclopedia of Animal Behavior, 2:462

The Encyclopedia of Animal Biology, 2:448

The Encyclopedia of Aquatic Life, 2:465

The Encyclopedia of Artificial Intelligence, 1:581

The Encyclopedia of Birds, 2:450

Encyclopedia of China Today, 2:87, 2:274

The Encyclopedia of Climatology, 2:483

Encyclopedia of Computer Science, 1:538

Encyclopedia of Computers and Electronics, 1:537

Encyclopedia of Electrochemistry of the Elements, 2:508

The Encyclopedia of Folk, Country, and Western Music, 2:156

Encyclopedia of Furniture, 2:260

Encyclopedia of Geographic Information, 2:76

The Encyclopedia of Insects, 2:449

Encyclopedia of Latin-American History, 2:275

The Encyclopedia of Mammals, 2:449

The Encyclopedia of Mushrooms, 2:446

Encyclopedia of Physics, 2:512

The Encyclopedia of Pop, Rock, and Soul, 2:156, 2:262

Encyclopedia of Religion, 2:52

The Encyclopedia of Reptiles and Amphibians, 2:449

Encyclopedia of Science and Technology, 2:433

Encyclopedia of the American Revolution, 2:152, 2:163

Encyclopedia of the Cold War, 2:237

Encyclopedia of the Musical Theatre, 2:154

Encyclopedia of the Third World, 2:275

Encyclopedia of World History, 2:275

Encyclopedic Dictionary of Economics, 2:56

The Encyclopedic Dictionary of Psychology, 2:95

The Encyclopedic Dictionary of Science, 2:432

Encyclopedic Dictionary of Sociology, 2:124

The End of American Innocence: A Study of the First Years of Our Own Time, 1912–1917, 2:218

The End of Eternity, 1:193

The End of Ideology: On the Exhaustion of Political Ideas in the Fifties, 2:149

The End of the Battle, 1:127

The End of the Cold War: European Unity, Socialism, and the Shift in Global Power, 2:388

Endangered Species, 2:467

Endangered Species: Our Endangered Planet, 2:467

Enderby, 1:71

Enderby Outside, 1:71

Enderby's Dark Lady, 1:71

Endgame, 1:331

Ending Hunger: An Idea Whose Time Has Come, 2:81

Endless Life: Selected Poems, 1:221

Ends and Odds, 1:331

The Enduring Constitution: An Exploration of the First Two Hundred Years, 2:17

Endymion, 1:34

Enemies: A Love Story, 1:387

An Enemy of the People, 1:377, 1:378

The Enemy Within, 2:248

Energy, 2:516

Energy: The Conservation Revolution, 2:496

Energy and Human Welfare: A Critical Analysis, 2:84

Energy and Power, 2:516

Energy Choices for the Future, 2:81

Energy Crisis: What Are Our Choices?, 2:252

Energy Metabolism in Animals and Man, 2:438

Energy Projects for Young Scientists, 2:516

Energy Resources in an Uncertain Future: Coal, Gas, Oil, and Uranium Supply Forecasting, 2:495

The Engineers and the Price System, 2:146

Engines, Energy and Entropy: A Thermodynamics Primer, 2:516

Engines of the Mind: A History of the Computer, 1:540
England in the Age of Wycliffe, 2:311
England in the Eighteen-Eighties: Toward a Social Basis for Freedom, 2:131
"England in 1819," 1:38
England Under Queen Anne, 2:328
England Under the Stuarts, 2:327
The English: A Social History, 1066–1956, 2:274
English and Scottish Popular Ballads, 1:8
The English Ballad, 1:8
English Dialectology: An Introduction, 1:431
English Dialects, 1:434
English Examined: Two Centuries of Comment on the Mother Tongue, 1:443
English for Cross-Cultural Communication, 1:434
English Grammar, 1:429
The English Language, 1:434
The English of Chaucer: Essays on the Language of Late Medieval English Authors and Scribes, 1:430
The English-Only Question: An Official Language for Americans?, 1:429
The English Poems of George Herbert, 1:11
English Prose Style, 1:478
English Revolution Sixteen Eighty-Eight to Sixteen Eighty-Nine, 2:328
English Syntax, 1:434
English Word-Formation, 1:432
English Words from Latin and Greek Elements, 1:432
Enigma: The Life of Knut Hamsun, 1:376
The Enigma of Arrival, 1:406
Enjoying Racket Sports, 2:551
Enjoying Skating, 2:551
Enjoying Swimming and Diving, 2:551
Enjoying Track and Field Sports, 2:551
The Enlightenment: An Interpretation—The Science of Freedom, 2:326
Enlightenment in France, 2:326
"The Enormous Radio," 1:211
The Enormous Room, 1:214
Ensayos, 1:360
Enterprises: An Introduction to Business, 2:57
The Entertainer, 1:112
Entertaining Mathematical Puzzles, 1:536
Entertainment, Education and the Hard Sell: Three Decades of Network Children's Television, 1:466
The Entertainment Functions of Television, 2:130
Entertainment Language, 1:433

The Entertainment Machine: American Show Business in the Twentieth Century, 1:454
The Enthusiastic: A Life of Thornton Wilder, 1:303
The Environment and Health, 2:571
Environment 1989–1990, 2:81
The Environmental Crisis: Opposing Viewpoints, 2:81, 2:570
Environmental Diseases, 2:565, 2:570
Environmental Geology, 2:496
Environmental Science, 2:467
Environmental Stress and Behavioral Adaptation, 2:105
The Envoy from Mirror City, 1:139
Enzymes: The Machines of Life, 2:437
Epic of the Wheat, 1:180
Epidemic! The Story of the Disease Detective, 2:557
Epidemics, 2:533
Epilepsy, 2:562
An Episode of Sparrows, 1:88
Episodes in the Mathematics of Medieval Islam, 1:496
Epithalamion, 1:17
Equal Justice: A Biography of Sandra Day O'Connor, 2:31
The Equal Rights Amendments: The History and the Movements, 2:156, 2:255
Equality in America: The View from the Top, 2:145
Equality of Educational Opportunity, 2:135
Equus, 1:119
Era of Excess: A Social History of the Prohibition Movement, 2:227
Era of Reconstruction: Eighteen Sixty-Five to Eighteen Seventy-Seven, 2:198
Erasmus: Ecstasy and the Praise of Folly, 2:315
Erasmus and His Times: Selections from the Letters of Erasmus and His Circle, 2:315
Erasmus as Translator of the Classics, 2:315
Erasmus of Christendom, 2:310
Erik Erikson: An Introduction, 2:109
Erik H. Erikson: The Growth of Work, 2:109
Erik H. Erikson: The Power and Limits of a Vision, 2:109
Erlanger Programm, 1:517
Ernest Hemingway, 1:237
Ernest Hemingway: A Life Story, 1:237
Ernest Hemingway and His World, 1:237
Ernest Hemingway on Writing, 1:482
The Erotic Poems, 1:321
Escape from Anxiety and Stress, 2:537

Escape from Freedom, 2:103, 2:139
The Escape, or A Leap for Freedom, 1:170
The Eskimo of Baffin Land and Hudson
  Bay, 2:44
An Essay Concerning Human
  Understanding, 2:17, 2:18
Essay on Criticism, 1:27
An Essay on Marxian Economics, 2:60
An Essay on Probabilities, 1:529
An Essay on the Foundations of
  Geometry, 1:503
An Essay on the Foundations of Our
  Knowledge, 1:529
An Essay on the Principles of Population,
  2:69
The Essays (Bacon), 1:10
Essays (Emerson), 1:157
Essays and Lectures (Emerson), 1:157
Essays Before a Sonata, the Majority, and
  Other Writings, 2:261
Essays in Analysis, 1:503
Essays in International Economic Theory,
  2:71
Essays in Physics, 2:520
Essays in Positive Economics, 2:65
Essays in Sociological Theory, 2:127
Essays in the Earlier History of American
  Corporations, 2:63
Essays in the History of Mechanics, 1:526
Essays in the Theory of Employment, 2:60
Essays of E. B. White, 1:456
Essays of Elia, 1:35
Essays of Ralph Waldo Emerson, 1:157
Essays on Atomic Physics and Human
  Knowledge, Nineteen Fifty-eight to
  Nineteen Sixty-two, 2:501
Essays on Atomic Physics and Human
  Knowledge, Nineteen Thirty-three to
  Nineteen Fifty-seven, 2:501
Essays on Behavioral Economics, 2:61
Essays on John Maynard Keynes, 2:67
Essays on Shelley, 1:38
Essays, Physical and Chemical, 2:499
The Essential Adam Smith, 2:61
Essential Concepts of Operating Systems,
  1:562
The Essential Guide to Nonprescription
  Drugs, 2:553
The Essential Horace: Odes, Epodes,
  Satires, and Epistles, 1:321; 2:294
Essential Human Anatomy, 2:451
The Essential Jung, 2:121
The Essential Piaget, 2:111
The Essential T. E. Lawrence: Selections
  from His Writings, 2:372
Essentials of Algorithms, 1:586
Essentials of Cell Biology, 2:438
Essentials of Geology, 2:489
The Essentials of Lenin, 2:378

Essentials of Modern Biochemistry, 2:511
Essentials of Nonverbal Communication,
  1:448
Essentials of Oceanography, 2:487
The Essentials of Topology, 1:512, 1:516
Eternal Curse of the Reader of These
  Pages, 1:409
The Eternal Feminine: Selected Poems of
  Goethe, 1:366
The Eternal Moment and Other Stories,
  1:86
Ethan Frome, 1:183
Ethical and Legal Issues of Social
  Experimentation, 2:68
Ethics: An Investigation of the Facts and
  Laws of the Moral Life, 2:114
Ethics and Politics: Cases and Comments,
  2:19
Ethics, Government, and Public Policy: A
  Reference Guide, 2:19
Ethiopia and the Origin of Civilization,
  2:299
The Ethnic Myth: Race, Ethnicity and
  Class in America, 2:136
The Ethnic Phenomenon, 2:136
The Ethnographic Interview, 2:43
Ethnography: Step by Step, 2:42
The Etruscans, 2:290
Etymological Dictionary of Modern
  English, 1:433
Euclid: His Life and His System, 1:514
Euclidean and Non-Euclidean Geometries:
  Development and History, 1:514
Eudora Welty, 1:300
Eugene Onegin, 1:389, 1:395
Eugene O'Neill, 1:274
Eugene V. Debs: A Biography, 2:204
Eugénie Grandet, 1:329
The Eumenides, 1:313
Euripides: Four Tragedies, 1:314
Euripides and the Tragic Tradition, 1:315
Europe, 2:88, 2:275, 2:405
Europe Between the Superpowers: The
  Enduring Balance, 2:388
Europe Between the Wars, 2:374
Europe in Eighteen Thirty, 2:332
Europe in the Nineteenth Century, 2:340
Europe in the Twentieth Century, 2:405
Europe, 1992, 2:405
Europe Since Hitler: The Rebirth of
  Europe, 2:405
The European Dictatorships, 1918–1945,
  2:374
The European Discovery of America: The
  Northern Voyages, 2:158, 2:320
The European Discovery of America: The
  Southern Voyages, 2:158, 2:320
The European Emergence: 1500–1600,
  2:310

The Europeans, 2:87, 2:272
Eurydice, 1:328
Eva Trout, 1:69
Evaluating Educational Software, 1:571
Evaluating Multicomputers for Image
Processing, 1:559
Evangeline, 1:160
"The Eve of St. Agnes," 1:34
The Eve of St. Venus, 1:71
Evelyn Waugh, 1:127
Evelyn Waugh: Portrait of a Country
Neighbor, 1:127
Evelyn Waugh and His World, 1:127
The Evening Stars: The Making of the
Network News Anchor, 1:458
Evenings on a Farm near Dikanka, 1:392
Ever Since Darwin: Reflections on Natural
History, 2:457
Every Four Years: The American
Presidency, 2:156
Every Good Boy Deserves Favor and
Professional Foul, 1:122
Everyday Reader's Dictionary of
Misunderstood, Misused, and
Mispronounced Words, 1:440
Everyone's Trash Problem: Nuclear
Wastes, 2:496
Everyone's United Nations, 2:6, 2:37, 2:238
Everything in Its Place: Social Order and
Land Use in America, 2:94
Everything Is Somewhere: The Geography
Quiz Book, 2:76
Everything That Rises Must Converge,
1:270
Everything to Gain: Making the Most of
the Rest of Your Life, 2:256
Everything You Need to Know About
Birth Control, 2:542
Everything You Need to Know About
Sexually Transmitted Disease, 2:559
The Evidence of Things Not Seen, 1:195
Evolution and Ecology: Essays on Social
Transformation, 2:48
The Evolution and Modification of
Behavior, 2:100, 2:464
Evolution and Speciation, 2:456
The Evolution of a Revolt: Early Postwar
Writings of T. E. Lawrence, 2:372
The Evolution of Economic Ideas, 2:55
The Evolution of Societies, 2:127
Evolution of the Earth, 2:495
The Evolving Self: Problem and Process in
Human Development, 2:106
An Exaltation of Larks, or, The Venereal
Game, 1:440
Examples: The Making of Forty
Photographs, 2:263
Excel Made Easy for the Macintosh, 1:573
Except the Lord, 1:72

Excursions in Advanced Euclidean
Geometry, 1:512
Excursions into Mathematics, 1:535
The Executive Branch of the United States
Government: A Bibliography, 2:5, 2:21
Exemplary Novels, The, 1:356
Exercise, 2:551
Exercise and Fitness, 2:552
Exercise and Physical Fitness: A
Personalized Approach, 2:551
The Exercise Fix, 2:551
Exercises in Style, 1:478
Exercitatio anatomica de motu cordis et
sanguinis in animalibus (An Anatomical
Treatise on the Movement of the Heart
and Blood in Animals), 2:547
Exercitationes de generatione animalium
(On the Generation of Living Things),
2:547
The Exile, 1:207
Exiles, 1:99
Exodus, 1:293
Expansionists of Eighteen Ninety-Eight:
The Acquisition of Hawaii and the
Spanish Islands, 2:219
Expedition to Earth, 1:75
The Expeditions of John Charles Fremont,
2:184
The Expeditions of Zebulon Montgomery
Pike, 2:169
Experience and Education, 2:219
Experience and Nature, 2:219
The Experience of Science: An
Interdisciplinary Approach, 2:432
Experiencing Adolescence: A Sourcebook
for Parents, Teachers, and Teens, 2:107
Experimenting with a Microscope, 2:435
Experimenting with Plants, 2:447
Experiments in Plant-Hybridisation,
2:453
Expert Adviser: Harvard Graphics, 1:578
Expert Critiquing Systems, 1:583
Expert Judgement and Expert Systems,
1:584
Expert Systems: A Non-Programmer's
Guide to Development and
Applications, 1:584
Expert Systems: Human Issues, 1:583
Expert Systems: Principles and Case
Studies, 1:583
Expert Systems and Decision Support in
Medicine, 1:584
Expert Systems and Intelligent
Computer-Aided Instruction, 1:570
Expert Systems and Related Topics: A
Selected Bibliography and Guide to
Information Sources, 1:584
Expert Systems Development: Building
PC-Based Applications, 1:583

Expert Systems for Microcomputers: An Introduction to Artificial Intelligence, 1:583
Expert Systems in Accounting, 1:583
Expert Systems in Business: A Practical Approach, 1:583
Expert Systems in Economics, Banking and Management, 1:584
Expert Systems in Finance and Accounting, 1:584
Expert Systems in Libraries, 1:583
Expert Systems in Reference Services, 1:584
Expert Systems in Statistics, 1:574
Expert Systems Introduced, 1:583
Expert Visions Systems, 1:583
The Exploding Suns: The Secrets of the Supernovas, 2:478
Explorations of Captain James Cook in the Pacific, as Told by Selections of His Own Journals, 1768–1779, 2:321
Explorations of the Highlands of Brazil, with a Full Account of the Gold and Diamond Mines, 2:364
Explorers of North America, Fourteen Ninety-Two to Eighteen Hundred Six, 2:157
Explorers of the Atom, 2:500
Explorers of the Body, 2:548
Exploring Ada, 1:565
Exploring America's Scenic Highways, 2:91
Exploring America's West, 2:90
Exploring Artificial Intelligence on Your Apple II, 1:581
Exploring Careers in Computer Graphics, 1:578
The Exploring Expedition to the Rocky Mountains, 2:184
Exploring Hypertext Programming: Writing Knowledge Representation and Problem-Solving Programs, 1:579
Exploring Our Living Planet, 2:82, 2:495
Exploring the City: Inquiries Toward an Urban Anthropology, 2:147
Exploring the Deep Frontier: The Adventure of Man in the Sea, 2:486
Exploring the Geometry of Nature: Computer Modelling Projects, 1:515
Exploring the Mind and Brain, 2:544
Exploring the Oceans: An Introduction for the Traveler and Amateur Naturalist, 2:486
Exploring the Sun, 2:476
Exploring the Universe, 2:470
Exploring the Visual Arts, 2:277
Exploring with a Telescope, 2:435
Explosion in a Cathedral, 1:401

The Exposition of Eighteen Fifty-One: Or Views of the Industry, the Science and the Government of England, 1:542
Expositions and Developments, 2:426
The Expression of Attitude, 2:97
Expressionism: Art and Idea, 2:415
An Ex-smoker's Survival Guide: Positive Steps to a Slim, Tranquil, Smoke-free Life, 2:556
Extragalactic Adventure: Our Strange Universe, 2:469
Extraordinary Groups: An Examination of Unconventional Life-Styles, 2:131
Extraordinary Properties of Ordinary Solutions, 2:507
Extraterrestrial Civilizations, 2:434
Extravagaria, 1:407
The Eye and Seeing, 2:552
Eye-Deep in Hell: Trench Warfare in World War I, 2:371
Eye of the Heart: Short Stories from Latin America, 1:399
The Eye of the Storm, 1:147
The Eye of the Story, 1:482
Eyeless in Gaza, 1:95
Eyes of Darkness, 1:239
The Eyes of the Dragon, 1:249

F

F-19 Stealth Air Combat, 1:567
F. Scott Fitzgerald (Eble), 1:222
F. Scott Fritzgerald (Gallo), 1:223
The Faber Book of Ballads, 1:8
A Fable, 1:219
A Fable for Critics, 1:161
The Fables of Aesop, 1:312, 1:313
Fables of Our Time, 1:290
The Fabric of Mind, 2:545
Face of Emotion, 2:104
Faces in the Crowd: Individual Studies in Character and Politics, 2:132
Faces in the Water, 1:138
Facing Mount Kenya, 2:394
The Fact of a Doorframe: Poems Selected and New 1950–1984, 1:281
The Factories, 2:204
Factors Determining Human Behavior, 2:98
The Facts About Cancer, 2:562
Facts and Figures on Smoking, 1976–1986, 2:556
The Facts of Life, 2:452
The Facts on File Dictionary of Archaeology, 2:279
The Facts on File Dictionary of Astronomy, 2:470

The Facts on File Dictionary of Biology, 2:437
The Facts on File Dictionary of Botany, 2:448
Facts on File Dictionary of European History: 1485–1789, 2:277
Facts on File Dictionary of Mathematics, 1:497
The Facts on File Dictionary of Physics, 2:512
The Facts on File Dictionary of Twentieth-Century Allusions, 1:432
The Facts on File Dictionary of Twentieth-Century History, 2:276
Facts on File National Profile: Benelux Countries, 2:88
Facts on File National Profile: East Africa, 2:85, 2:393
Facts on File National Profile: Mexico and Central America, 2:88
Facts on File National Profile: Scandinavia, 2:88
Facts on File Visual Dictionary, 1:439
Fade, 1:213
The Faerie Queene, 1:17
The Faerie Queene: A Reader's Guide, 1:17
Fahrenheit 451, 1:202
Fair Science: Women in the Scientific Community, 2:148
The Fairy Tale of My Life, 1:375
A Faithful Narrative of the Surprising Work of God, 1:153
Falconer, 1:210, 1:211
The Falklands: South Atlantic Islands, 2:89
Falkner: A Novel, 1:37
The Fall, 1:333
The Fall of Hyperion, 1:34
The Fall of Japan, 2:383
The Fall of the City, 1:261
The Fall of the House of Hapsburg, 2:326
"The Fall of the House of Usher," 1:164
Fall of the Peacock Throne: The Story of Iran, 2:411
The Fall of the Roman Republic: Six Roman Lives, 2:288
Familiar Letters of John Adams and His Wife Abigail Adams During the Revolution, 2:170, 2:171
Families and Religions: Conflict and Change in Modern Society, 2:137
The Families of the Monocotyledons, 2:447
The Family (Emecheta), 1:413
The Family (Goode), 2:138
Family: The Ties That Bind—and Gag, 1:480
Family and Property in Sung China: Yuan Ts'ai's Precepts for Social Life, 2:281

Family and Social Network: Roles, Norms, and External Relationships, 2:52
The Family First-aid Handbook, 2:567
The Family in Classical Greece, 2:285
Family in Transition: Rethinking Marriage, Sexuality, Child Rearing, and Family Organization, 2:138
Family Letters of Richard Wagner, 2:362
The Family Moskat, 1:387
The Family of Man, 2:269
Family Pictures, 1:205
Family Relations: A Reader, 2:138
Family Relations in the Life Course Perspective, 2:137
Family Relationships in Later Life, 2:129
The Family Reunion, 1:82
Family Secrets, 1:250
Family, Socialization, and Interaction Process, 2:127
The Family, Society, and the Individual, 2:138
Famine in Africa, 2:86, 2:394
Famous American Men of Science, 2:483
Famous Astronomers, 2:433
Famous Last Words: The American Language Crisis Reconsidered, 1:443
Famous Men of Science, 2:559
Famous People of Computing: A Book of Posters, 1:538
Famous Problems of Elementary Geometry and other Monographs, 1:518
Famous Problems of Geometry and How to Solve Them, 1:511
Famous Problems of Mathematics, 1:535
Famous Speeches of Abraham Lincoln, 2:198
Fancy Free, 2:265
The Fanfarlo, 1:121
Fanshawe, 1:177
Fantastic Voyage, 1:193
Fantastic Voyage II: Destination Brain, 1:193
Far as Human Eye Could See, 2:431
A Far Cry from Kennsington, 1:121
Far from Home: Families of the Westward Journey, 2:201
Far from the Madding Crowd, 1:52
The Far Planets, 2:475
The Far Side Gallery, 1:459
The Far Side Gallery 2, 1:459
The Far Side Gallery 3, 1:459
Faraday: A Biography, 2:525
Faraday as a Natural Philosopher, 2:525
Farewell, Great King, 1:126
Farewell, My Lovely, 1:210
The Farewell Party, 1:385
A Farewell to Arms, 1:236; 2:224
Farewell to Manzanar, 2:235
Farmer in the Sky, 1:233

The Farmers' Daughters, 1:305
The Farthest Shore, 1:254
Fascinating Experiments in Chemistry, 2:504
Fascism: The Meaning and Experience of Reactionary Revolution, 2:374
Fascism and Pre-Fascism in Europe, Eighteen Ninety to Nineteen Forty-Five: A Bibliography of the Extreme Right, 2:375
Fast Access-Lotus 1–2–3, Release 3.0, 1:573
Fast Breeder Reactors, 2:528
Fast, Faster, Fastest: The Story of Supercomputers, 1:559
The Fast Food Nutrition Guide: What's Good, What's Bad and How to Tell the Difference, 2:549
Fast Reactions, 2:508
Fast Sam, Cool Clyde, and Stuff, 1:270
The Fat Woman's Joke, 1:128
The Fateful Alliance: France, Russia, and the Coming of the First World War, 2:371
The Father, 1:380
Father Figure, 1:275
Father Goose: His Book, 1:198
Fathers and Sons, 2:539
Fathers of the Constitution, 2:166
Faulkner: A Collection of Critical Essays, 1:220
Faust, 1:366
The Favorite Game, 1:137
Favorite Stories, 1:383
FDR: A Biography, 2:234
FDR: A Centenary Remembrance, 1882–1945, 2:234
FDR's New Deal, 2:229
FDR's Splendid Deception, 2:234
Fear in Battle, 2:103, 2:116
Fear Itself: The Horror Fiction of Stephen King, 1:249
Fearful Symmetry: A Study of William Blake, 1:32
The Federal Courts, 2:26
The Federal Government: How It Works, 2:7
Federalism: A Nation of States, 2:35
Federalism: The Founders' Design, 2:35
Federalism and Intergovernmental Relations, 2:36
Federalism and the Role of the State, 2:35
Federalism: The Politics of Intergovernmental Relations, 2:35
The Federalist, 2:166, 2:173, 2:177
The Federalist Papers, 2:16, 2:35, 2:174
Federico García Lorca, 1:358
Federico García Lorca: A Life, 1:358

A Feeling for the Organism: The Life and Work of Barbara McClintock, 2:453
Feelings: Our Vital Signs, 2:103, 2:536
Felita, 1:267
Felix Frankfurter Reminisces, 2:28
Felix Holt, the Radical, 1:49
Fell, 1:247
Female Friends, 1:128
The Female World, 2:147
Female World from a Global Perspective, 2:147
The Feminine Mystique, 2:148, 2:243, 2:244
Feminine Psychology, 2:119
Feminism: Opposing Viewpoints, 2:148
The Feminist Legacy of Karen Horney, 2:119
Feodor Dostoevsky, 1:392
Ferdinand and Isabella, 2:320
Ferdinand Magellan, 2:157
Fermi: Father of the Atomic Bomb, 2:529
"Fern Hill," 1:124
Ferraro: My Story, 2:257
A Few Good Men from UNIVAC, 1:538
Fiasco, 1:386
Ficciones, 1:399, 1:400
Ficciones: Four Stories and a Play, 1:360
The Fiction of Joseph Heller: Against the Grain, 1:235
The Fiction Writer's Research Handbook, 1:490
Fidel, 2:410
Fidel: A Critical Portrait, 2:410
Fidel and Religion: Castro Talks on Revolution and Religion with Frei Betto, 2:410
Fidel by Fidel: A New Interview with Dr. Fidel Castro Ruz, President of the Republic of Cuba, 2:410
Fidel Castro: Nothing Can Stop the Course of History, 2:410
Fidel Castro and the Cuban Revolution: Age, Position, Character, Destiny, Personality, and Ambition, 2:410
Fidel Castro Speeches: Building Socialism in Cuba, 2:410
Fidel Castro Speeches, Nineteen Eighty-Four to Nineteen Eighty-Five: War and Crisis in the Americas, 2:410
The Field Description of Igneous Rocks, 2:492
The Field Description of Metamorphic Rocks, 2:492
The Field Guide to Early Man, 2:460
Field Guide to Geology, 2:489
A Field Guide to Rocks and Minerals, 2:492
A Field Guide to the Atmosphere, 2:484

Field Guide to the Birds of North America, 2:450

A Field Guide to the Stars and Planets, 2:470

Field Projects in Anthropology: A Student Handbook, 2:42

Field Studies, 2:465

Field Theory in Social Science, 2:99

Field Work, 1:92

Fifth Business, 1:137, 1:138

The Fifth Child, 1:103

The Fifth Column, 1:236

The Fifth Column and Four Stories of the Spanish Civil War, 2:374

The Fifth Generation: Artificial Intelligence and Japan's Computer Challenge to the World, 1:582

The Fifth Generation: The Future of Computer Technology, 1:554

Fifth Generation Computers, 1:555

The Fifth Generation Fallacy: Why Japan Is Betting Its Future on Artificial Intelligence, 1:583

The Fifth Letter of Hernando Cortés to the Emperor Charles 5th Containing an Account of His Expedition to Honduras, 2:322

The Fifth Son, 1:301

The Fifth String, 2:216

Fifth Sun: Aztec Gods, Aztec World, 2:298

Fifty Basic Civil War Documents, 2:192

50 Simple Things You Can Do to Save the Earth, 2:81

Fifty Years and Other Poems, 1:245

Fighting Angel, 1:207

Fighting Cancer, 2:561

A Fighting Man of Mars, 1:208

Fighting Troops of the Austro-Hungarian Army, 1868–1914, 2:340

File Systems: Structures and Algorithms, 1:573

Files and Databases: An Introduction, 1:572

Film: Real to Reel, 1:469

Film Addicts Archive: Poetry and Prose of the Cinema, 1:469

Film and Propaganda in America: A Documentary History, 1:441

Film and Radio Propaganda in World War II, 1:441

Film Art: An Introduction, 1:469

Film as Film: Understanding and Judging Movies, 1:469

Film Before Griffith, 1:468

The Film Career of Billy Wilder, 1:470

The Film Experience, 1:469

Film in Society, 1:468

Film Magic: The Art and Science of Special Effects, 1:470

Film Propaganda: Nazi Germany and Soviet Russia, 1:441

Filmed Books and Plays: A List of Books and Plays from Which Films Have Been Made 1928–1986, 1:473

Filming Literature: The Art of Screen Adaptation, 1:474

The Filmmaker's Handbook, 1:470

Fin de partie, 1:331

Final Cut: Dreams and Disaster in the Making of Heaven's Gate, 1:470

Final Days, 2:22

Final Disclosure: The Full Truth About the Assassination of President Kennedy, 2:247

Final Harvest: Emily Dickinson's Poems, 1:175

Final Lectures (Horney), 2:119

Financial Crises: Understanding the Postwar U.S. Experience, 2:57, 2:156

Financial Institutions, Markets, and Money, 2:70

The Financier, 1:216, 1:217

The Fine Art of Propaganda, 1:440

Finite and Infinite Machines, 1:581

Finite Mathematics and Its Applications, 1:529

Finnegan's Wake, 1:99

Finsler Geometry, Relativity, and Gauge Theories, 1:516

Fire and Ice: The Greenhouse Effect, Ozone Depletion, and Nuclear Winter, 2:486

Fire and Ice: Three Icelandic Plays, 1:374

Fire Down Below, 1:89

Fire in the Streets: America in the Nineteen Sixties, 2:242

Fire in the Valley: The Making of the Personal Computer, 1:540, 1:543

The Fire Next Time, 1:195

Fire of Life: The Smithsonian Book of the Sun, 2:475, 2:476

The Fires of Jubilee: Nat Turner's Fierce Rebellion, 2:189

The Fires of Spring, 1:264

Firestarter, 1:249

Fireweed, 1:126

Fireworks, Picnics, and Flags: The Story of the Fourth of July Symbols, 2:184

First Aid and Emergency Care: Procedure and Practice, 2:566

First Aid for Health Emergencies, 2:567

The First American Revolution: The American Colonies on the Eve of Independence, 2:164

First Americans, 2:158

First Americans: Forbidden Land, 2:158

First Battle, 2:205

The First Book of Local Government, 2:40

The First Circle, 1:395, 1:396
The First Civilizations (Caselli), 2:278
First Civilizations (Millard), 2:278
The First Class Temperament: The
    Emergence of Franklin Roosevelt, 2:234
The First Dance of Freedom: Black Africa
    in the Postwar Era, 2:85, 2:393
The First Electronic Computer: The
    Atanasoff Story, 1:540
The First Emperor of China, 2:281
The First Freedom: The Tumultuous
    History of Free Speech in America, 2:12,
    2:16
The First Ladies, 2:154
First Lady from Plains, 2:255
The First Men in the Moon, 1:129
The First Men on the Moon, 2:252
First Men to the Moon, 2:483
First-Person America, 2:228
The First Salute: A View of the American
    Revolution, 2:164
The First Stargazers: An Introduction to
    the Origins of Astronomy, 2:469
The First Three Years of Life, 2:108
The First Travel Guide to the Bottom of
    the Sea, 2:488
The First 25 Years in Space: A
    Symposium, 2:481
First Women Who Spoke Out, 2:12
First World War: An Illustrated History,
    2:372
Fiscal and Monetary Policies and Problems
    in Developing Countries, 2:71
Fishbones: Hoboing in the 1930s, 2:229
The Fishes, 2:449
Fishes of the World, 2:450
Five Biblical Portraits, 1:302
Five Black Scholars: An Analysis of
    Family Life, Education, and Career,
    2:138
Five Decades: Poems Nineteen
    Twenty-Five to Nineteen Seventy, 1:407
Five Early Works (Lagervist), 1:378
Five Finger Exercise, 1:118
Five for Freedom: Lucretia Mott, Elizabeth
    Cady Stanton, Lucy Stone, Susan B.
    Anthony, Carrie Chapman Catt, 2:223
Five Hundred Thirty-Six Puzzles and
    Curious Problems, 1:535
Five Ideas That Change the World, 2:74
Five Kingdoms: An Illustrated Guide to
    the Phyla of Life on Earth, 2:441
Five Letters of Cortés, 2:322
Five Plays: Comedies & Tragicomedies
    (Garcia Lorca), 1:357
Five Plays by Langston Hughes, 1:241
Five Slave Narratives: A Compendium,
    1:170
Five Weeks in a Balloon, 1:342, 1:343

The Fixer, 1:261, 1:262
Flagons and Apples, 1:244
The Flamingo's Smile: Reflections on
    Natural History, 2:458
Flannery O'Connor (Bloom), 1:270
Flannery O'Connor (McFarland), 1:271
Flannery O'Connor (Paulson), 1:271
Flappers and Philosophers, 1:222
Flatland, 1:519
Flaubert: A Biography, 1:335
Flaws in the Glass: A Self Portrait, 1:148
"The Flesh and the Spirt," 1:151
The Flies, 1:340
The Flight from the Enchanter, 1:107
Flights of Victory, 1:400
Flint, 1:252
The Flivver King: A Study of
    Ford-America, 1:287
The Floating Light Bulb, 1:189
Florence, 1:211
Florence in the Time of the Medici, 2:310
Florence Nightingale, 2:570
Florence Nightingale, 1820–1910, 2:570
Florence Nightingale on Hospital Reform,
    2:570
The Flounder, 1:367
The Flow of Information: An Experiment
    in Mass Communication, 2:130
Flowering Cherry, 1:68
Flowering Plants of the World, 2:447
Flowers of Evil, 1:330
Flush: A Biography, 1:43, 1:132
Flying Colors, 1:85
Flying the Frontiers of Space, 2:480
Flying to the Moon and Other Strange
    Places, 2:480
Focus, 1:266
Foe, 1:413
Folk and Traditional Music of the
    Western Continents, 2:262
Folk Legends of Japan, 1:425
Folklore in the Old Testament, 2:52
Folktales of Norway, 1:374
Following the Color Line, 2:198
Food and Digestion, 2:451
Food and Population: The World in Crisis,
    2:251
The Food Book: The Complete Guide to
    the Most Popular Brand-name Foods in
    the United States, 2:549
The Food Crisis in Prehistory:
    Overpopulation and Origins of
    Agriculture, 2:47, 2:278
Food for Health, 2:549
Food in Chinese Culture: Anthropological
    and Historical Perspectives, 2:281
Food in the Social Order: Studies of Food
    and Festivities in Three American
    Communities, 2:47

Food, Nutrition, and You, 2:451, 2:550
The Food of the Gods, 1:129
The Food Pharmacy: Dramatic New
  Evidence That Food Is Your Best
  Medicine, 2:549
Foods and Nutrition Encyclopedia, 2:549
Foods for Healthy Kids, 2:550
Fool for Love and Other Plays, 1:285
Footprints on the Planet: A Search for an
  Environmental Ethic, 2:495
For Lizzie and Harriet, 1:259
For My People, 1:297, 1:298
For Poets, 1:489
For the Union Dead, 1:259
For Whom the Bell Tolls, 1:236
For Your Eyes Only, 1:84
Forbidden Sands: A Search in the Sahara,
  2:90
Force and Movement, 2:513
Force: The Power Behind Movement,
  2:513
Forces and Fields, 2:516
Ford: The Men and the Machine, 2:63
Foreign and Female: Immigrant Women in
  America, 1840–1930, 2:207
Forest Physiography, 2:76
Forever, 1:201
Forever Undecided: A Puzzle Guide to
  Gödel, 1:500
Forging the Alliance: NATO, 1945–1950,
  2:405
Forgotten Algebra: A Refresher Course,
  1:505
Forgotten Women of Computer History,
  1:537, 1:545
Form and Thought in Herodotus, 2:288
The Formation and Properties of
  Precipitates, 2:507
Forms of Energy, 2:516
Forms of Talk, 1:461; 2:50
The Forsyte Saga, 1:87, 1:88
The Fortunes of Perkin Warbuck: A
  Romance, 1:37
Forty Stories (Barthelme), 1:198
The Fossil Evidence for Human Evolution:
  An Introduction to the Study of
  Paleoanthropology, 2:48, 2:278
The Fossil History of Man, 2:460
Fossils, 2:495
Fossils: The Key to the Past, 2:495
Foundation and Earth, 1:193
The Foundation Trilogy, 1:193
Foundation's Edge, 1:193
The Foundations of Chemical Kinetics,
  2:508
The Foundations of Ethology, 2:464
Foundations of General Systems Theory,
  1:558
Foundations of Geometry, 1:517
Foundations of Leninism, 2:380

The Foundations of Mathematics: A
  Contribution to the Philosophy of
  Geometry, 1:511
Foundations of the Republic, 2:228
Founders of Modern Medicine, 2:444,
  2:445
Founding Mothers: Women of America in
  the Revolutionary Era, 2:163
The Fountains of Paradise, 1:75
Four Arguments for the Elimination of
  Television, 1:465
Four Aspects of Civic Duty, 2:223
Four Banks of the River of Space, 1:405
The Four Basic Psychological Functions of
  Man and the Establishment of
  Uniformities in Human Structures and
  Human Behavior, 2:121
The Four-Color Problem: Assaults and
  Conquests, 1:512, 1:535
Four Comedies by Pedro Calderón de la
  Barca, 1:355
Four Contemporary Swedish Poets,
  1:374
Four-Dimensional Geometry: An
  Introduction, 1:516
Four Families of Karimpur, 2:400
The Four-Gated City, 1:103
The Four Gothic Kings: The Turbulent
  History of Medieval England and the
  Plantagenet Kings (1216–1377)—Henry
  III, Edward I, Edward II, Edward
  III—Seen Through the Eyes of Their
  Contemporaries, 2:305
Four Great Makers of Modern
  Architecture: Gropius, Le Corbusier,
  Mies van der Rohe, Wright, 2:268
Four Greek Plays (Racine), 1:339
Four Guineas: A Journey Through West
  Africa, 2:393
Four Hasidic Masters and Their Struggle
  Against Melancholy, 1:302
Four Hundred Centuries of Cave Art,
  2:278
The Four Novels of Chinua Achebe: A
  Critical Study, 1:412
Four of a Kind: A Treasury of Favorite
  Works by America's Best-Loved
  Humorist, 1:447
Four Plays (Aristophanes), 1:313
Four Plays (Williams), 1:304
Four Quartets, 1:82
Four Russian Plays, 1:389
Four Short Novels (Love Among the
  Haystacks, The Ladybird, The Fox, The
  Captain's Doll), 1:101
Four Stories (Undset), 1:381
Four Two-Act Plays (Shepard), 1:285
Four Voyages to the New World, 2:159
The Fourth Dimension and Non-Euclidean
  Geometry in Art, 1:519

The Fourth Dimension: A Guided Tour of Higher Universes, 1:516
Fourth Generation Business Systems, 1:584
Fourth Generation Languages, 1:563
Foxpro Made Easy, 1:572
The Fractal Geometry of Nature, 1:516
Fractals Everywhere, 1:516
Fractals for the Classroom, 1:516
A Fragment on Government, 2:8
The Fragmented World: Competing Perspectives on Trade, Money and Crisis, 2:71
Frames of Mind: The Theory of Multiple Intelligences, 2:110
The Framing and Ratification of the Constitution, 2:166
The Framing of the Constitution of the United States, 2:16
Frances Perkins: That Woman in FDR's Cabinet, 2:24
Francis Bacon: A Selection of His Works, 1:10
Francis Bacon: His Career and His Thought, 1:10
Francis Bacon: The Temper of a Man, 2:435
Francis Drake, 2:324
Francis Drake Privateer: Contemporary Narratives and Documents, 2:324
Francis Scott Key and the History of the Star Spangled Banner, 2:169
Francisco Franco, 2:374
The Franco-Prussian War: The German Invasion of France, 1870–71, 2:340
The Frangipani Garden, 1:139, 1:140
Frank Herbert, 1:239
Frank Lloyd Wright, 2:270
Frank Lloyd Wright: An Interpretive Biography, 2:270
Frank Lloyd Wright: His Life, His Work, His Words, 2:270
Frank Lloyd Wright: His Living Voice, 2:270
Frank Norris, 1:181
Frank O'Connor, 1:109
Frank O'Connor: An Introductory Study, 1:109
Frank O'Connor at Work, 1:109
Frankenstein, 1:37
Franklin D. Roosevelt, 2:234
Franklin D. Roosevelt: A Rendezvous with Destiny, 2:234
Franklin D. Roosevelt: Thirty-Second President of the United States, 2:234
Franklin D. Roosevelt and American Foreign Policy, 1932–1945, 2:234
Franklin D. Roosevelt and Foreign Affairs, 2:233
Franklin D. Roosevelt and Foreign Affairs: Second Series 1937–1939, 2:234

Franklin D. Roosevelt, His Life and Times, 2:234
Franklin D. Roosevelt's Rhetorical Presidency, 2:234
Franklin of Philadelphia, 2:527
Franny and Zooey, 1:282, 1:283
Franz Boas, 2:44
Franz Boas: Eighteen Fifty-Eight to Nineteen Forty-Two, 2:44
A Franz Boas Reader: Shaping of American Anthropology, 1883–1911, 2:44
Franz Kafka, 1:369
Franz Liszt: A Chronical of His Life in Pictures and Documents, 2:354
Franz Liszt: The Virtuoso Years, 1811–1847, 2:354
Fray Juan Crespi, Missionary Explorer on the Pacific Coast, 1769–1774, 2:160
Frederic Chopin, 2:350
Frederic Chopin as a Man and Musician, 2:350
Frederick Douglass (Russell), 2:190
Frederick Douglass (Washington), 2:191
Frederick Douglass: Boy Champion of Human Rights, 2:190
Frederick Douglass: The Narrative and Selected Writings, 2:190
Frederick Douglass and the Fight for Freedom, 2:190
Free (and Almost Free) Software for the Macintosh, 1:567
Free Enterprise in America, 2:58
Free Fall, 1:89
Free Soil, Free Labor, Free Men: The Ideology of the Republican Party Before the Civil War, 2:189
Free to Choose: A Personal Statement, 2:65, 2:257
Freedom, 1:442
Freedom and Civilization, 2:46
Freedom and Development—Uhuru Na Maendeleo, 2:397
Freedom and Socialism, 2:397
Freedom and the Court: Civil Rights and Liberties and Rights in the United States, 2:12
Freedom and Unity, 2:397
Freedom in the World: Political Rights and Civil Liberties, 2:12
The Freedom of a Christian Man, 2:316
Freedom Under Thatcher: Civil Liberties in Modern Britain, 2:408
Freedom's Blood, 2:241
Freedom's Ferment: Phases of American Social History from the Revolution to the Outbreak of the Civil War, 2:185
The French, 2:88
The French Americans, 2:160
French Grammar, 1:326

French Idioms and Figurative Phrases, 1:326
French in America, 1488–1974: A Chronology and Fact Book, 2:161
French Jesuits in Lower Louisiana (1700–1763), 2:160
The French Language: Past and Present, 1:326
The French Lieutenant's Woman, 1:86
The French Lieutenant's Woman and Other Screenplays, 1:114
The French Revolution, 2:329
The French Speaker's Skill with Grammatical Gender, 1:326
Frenchman's Creek, 1:80
Frenzied Fiction, 1:141
Freud: A Life for Our Time, 2:118
Freud and Man's Soul, 2:118
Freud and the Americans: The Origin and Foundation of the Psychoanalytic Movement in America, 1876–1918, 2:118
Freud and the Culture of Psychoanalysis: Studies in the Transition from Victorian Humanism to Modernity, 2:118
Freud and the Mind, 2:118
Freud and Women, 2:118
Freud, Jews, and Other Germans: Masters and Victims in Modernist Culture, 2:384
Friedrich Engels: His Life and Thought, 2:59
Friend of Kafka and Other Stories, 1:388
The Friends, 1:228, 1:229
Friends and Relations, 1:69
"Friendship," 1:157
The Friendship, 1:289, 1:290
The Frogs and Other Plays, 1:313
From a Surgeon's Journal, 1915–1918, 2:532
From Affine to Euclidean Geometry, 1:516
From Alexander to Cleopatra: The Hellenistic World, 2:285
From Bauhaus to Our House, 1:479
From Beirut to Jerusalem, 2:411
From Boy to Man, from Delinquency to Crime, 2:133
From Brown to Bakke: The Supreme Court and School Integration 1954–1978, 2:27
From Cell to Clone: The Story of Genetic Engineering, 2:455
From Cells to Atoms: An Illustrated Introduction to Molecular Biology, 2:438
From Chips to Systems, 1:559
From Chocolate to Morphine: Understanding Mind-active Drugs, 2:555
From Cortés to Castro: An Introduction to the History of Latin America, 2:273
From Death to Morning, 1:306

From Fermat to Minkowski: Lectures on the Theory of Numbers and Its Historical Development, 1:498
From Flower to Fruit, 2:447
From Frontier to Plantation in Tennessee: A Study in Frontier Democracy, 2:184
From Galileo to Newton, 2:516
From Generation to Generation: Age Groups and Social Structure, 2:129
From Humanism to Science, 1480–1700, 2:516
From Karamzin to Bunin: An Anthology of Russian Short Stories, 1:389
From Lenin to Khrushchev: The History of World Communism, 2:276
From LeRoi Jones to Amiri Baraka: The Literary Works, 1:197
From Maxwell to Microphysics: Aspects of the Electromagnetic Theory in the Last Quarter of the Nineteenth Century, 2:527
From Nationalism to Revolutionary Islam: Essays on Social Movements in the Contemporary Near and Middle East, 2:142
From Nicaragua with Love: Poems 1979–1986, 1:400
From Plotzk to Boston, 2:209, 2:210
From Prague After Munich: Diplomatic Papers, 1938–1939, 2:391
From Quaker Hill to Kathmandu, 1:463
From Quarks to Quasars: A Tour of the Universe, 2:479
From Russia with Love, 1:84
From Slavery to Freedom: A History of Negro Americans, 2:153
From Spore to Spore: Ferns and How They Grow, 2:448
From the Deep Woods to Civilization: Chapters in the Autobiography of an Indian, 2:157
From the Earth to the Moon, 1:342, 1:343
From the Fair, 1:383
From the Fifteenth District, 1:139
From the Middle Ages Through the Eighteenth Century, 1:355
From the Old Diplomacy to the New, 1856–1900, 2:218
From the Renaissance to Romanticism: Trends in Style in Art, Literature, and Music, 2:333
From Vienna to Versailles, 2:276
From Writer to Designer: Twenty Steps from Word Processing to Mastering the Basics of Desktop Publishing, 1:576
Front Lines: Soldiers' Writings from Vietnam, 2:241
The Frontier in American History, 2:156, 2:201

Frontier Living, 2:169
The Frontier, the Union, and Stephen A.
   Douglas, 2:189
Frontiers of Change: Early
   Industrialization in America, 2:184
Frontiers of Economics, 2:64
The Frontiers of Paradise: A Study of
   Monks and Monasteries, 2:306
Frontiers of Supercomputing, 1:559
The Frontiersman, 2:168
Frozen Earth: Explaining the Ice Ages,
   2:493
The Frozen Keyboard: Living with Bad
   Software, 1:566
Frustration and Aggression, 2:98, 2:103,
   2:116
Frustration and Aggression: An
   Experiment with Young Children, 2:99
Fryderyk Chopin: Pianist from Warsaw,
   2:350
Fuel Resources, 2:495
Fuente Ovejuna, 1:358
A Fuller Explanation: The Synergetic
   Geometry of R. Buckminster Fuller,
   1:522
Fumblerules: A Lighthearted Guide to
   Grammar and Good Usage, 1:442
Fun with Physics, 2:512
Functions of a Real Variable, 1:499
The Functions of Social Conflict, 2:132
The Functions of the Executive, 2:63,
   2:140
Fundamentals of Electricity, 2:522
Fundamentals of Mathematics for
   Business, Social, and Life Sciences, 1:504
Fundamentals of Systems Analysis, 1:558
Fundamentals of Three-Dimensional
   Computer Graphics, 1:579
Funny People, 1:446
Fur Trappers and Traders: The Indians,
   the Pilgrims, and the Beaver, 2:162
The Furies, 1:313
"The Furnished Room," 1:178
Further Chronicles of Avonlea, 1:144
Further Letters of Queen Victoria from
   the Archives of the House of
   Brandenburg–Prussia, 2:369
The Future Comes: A Study of the New
   Deal, 2:228
Future Indefinite: An Autobiography, 1:78
Future Mind: Artificial Intelligence: The
   Merging of the Mystical and the
   Technological in the 21st Century, 1:582
The Future of Religion: Secularization,
   Revival, and Cult Formation, 2:142
The Future of the International Monetary
   System, 2:71
The Future of the Past, 2:156
Future Shock, 2:62

The Future World of Energy, 2:496
The Futurological Congress, 1:386
Fyodor Dostoyevsky: A Writer's Life,
   1:392

G

G. B. Shaw: A Collection of Critical
   Essays, 1:120
G. K. Chesterton, 1:73
Gabriel García Márquez, 1:404
Gabriela Mistral: The Poet and Her Work,
   1:405
Gabriela Mistral's Religious Sensibility,
   1:405
Gaffer Samson's Luck, 1:126
Gainsborough: His Life and Art, 2:335
Gainsborough's Landscape Paintings: A
   Critical Text and Catalogue Raisonne,
   2:335
Galapagos, 1:295
Galaxies, 2:478
The Galbraith Reader, 2:66
Galen on Bloodletting, 2:546
Galen on Respiration and the Arteries,
   2:546
Galen on the Affected Parts: Translation
   from the Greek Text with Explanatory
   Footnotes, 2:546
Galen on the Usefulness of the Parts of
   the Body, 2:546
Galileo, 1:365
Galileo: Heretic, 2:473
Galileo: Man of Science, 2:473
Galileo at Work: His Scientific Biography,
   2:473
The Galileo Connection, 2:473
Galileo, Science, and the Church, 2:473
Games, Graphics and Sounds, 1:578
Gandhi, 2:366
Gandhi and Civil Disobedience
   Movement, 2:366
Gandhi, Nehru and the Challenge, 2:404
Gandhi Reader: A Source Book of His Life
   and Writings, 2:365
Gandhi Remembered, 2:366
Gandhi the Man, 2:366
Gandhi Through Western Eyes, 2:366
Gandhi's Concept of Civil Disobedience:
   A Study with Special Reference to
   Thoreau's Influence on Gandhi, 2:366
Gandhi's Truth: On the Origins of
   Militant Nonviolence, 2:108
García Márquez: The Man and His Work,
   1:404
The Garden of the Finzi-Continis, 1:347
Garden on the Moon, 1:332

The Garden Party: Katherine Mansfield's New Zealand Stories, 1:142

Garibaldi and His Enemies: The Clash of Arms and Personalities in the Making of Italy, 2:344

Garibaldi and the Making of Italy, 2:345

Garibaldi and the Thousand, 2:345

Garibaldi's Memoirs from the Manuscript, Personal Notes, and Authentic Sources, 2:344

The Garrick Year, 1:79, 1:80

Gas, 2:496

Gates of Excellence: On Reading and Writing Books for Children, 1:484

Gates of the Forest, 1:301

Gateway, 1:278

Gateway to Empire, 2:168

Gather Together in My Name, 1:190, 1:191

A Gathering of Days: A New England Girl's Journal, 1830–1832, 2:184

A Gathering of Old Men, 1:224

Gaudy Night, 1:117

Gauguin, 2:353

Gauguin: Watercolors, Pastels, Drawings, 2:353

Gauss: A Biographical Study, 1:532

The Gawain-Poet, 1:8

G'Day: Teach Yourself Australian in 20 Easy Lessons, 1:434

GEM Desktop Publisher, 1:562

GEM for the Atari 520 ST, 1:562

The GEM Operating System Handbook, 1:562

Gemini: An Extended Autobiographical Statement on My First Twenty-Five Years of Being a Black Poet, 1:226

Gender and Stress, 2:123

Gender and the Life Course, 2:148

Gender Politics, 2:148

General Chemistry, 2:506

General Climatology, 2:484

General Economic History, 2:56

General Geology, 2:489

General Grant's Letters to a Friend, 1861–1880, 2:199

General Investigators Concerning the Analysis of Concepts and Truths, 1:527

General Principles of Quantum Mechanics, 2:503

General Selections from the Works of Sigmund Freud, 2:118

The General Theory of Employment, Interest, and Money, 2:67

General Topology: Chapters 1–4, 1:499

General Zoology, 2:448

The Generals: Ulysses S. Grant and Robert E. Lee, 2:196

Generation of Animals, 2:442

Genes, Medicine, and You, 2:546

Genesis on Planet Earth: The Search for Life's Beginnings, 2:461

Genetic Engineering, 2:455

Genetic Engineering: Opposing Viewpoints, 2:455

Genetics and Heredity, 2:545

Genetics and the Origin of Species, 2:456

The Genetics Explosion, 2:452

Genetics Projects for Young Scientists, 2:452

The "Genius," 1:217

Genius and the Mobocracy, 2:217

The Genius of the People: The Constitutional Convention of 1787, 2:167

The Gentle Art of Mathematics, 1:498

The Gentle Art of Verbal Self-Defense, 1:445

The Gentle Tamers: Women of the Old Wild West, 2:200

Gentlehands, 1:247

The Gentleman from San Fransisco and Other Stories, 1:390

Geo-Data: The World Almanac Gazetteer, 2:75

Geoffrey Chaucer, 1:7

The Geographer at Work, 2:92

Geography: An Introduction to Concept and Method, 2:92

Geography: Inventory and Prospect, 2:78

Geography and Cartography: A Reference Handbook, 2:76

Geography as Spatial Interaction, 2:93

Geography Behind History, 2:93

Geography 89/90, 2:76

Geography of Climate, 2:80

Geography of Contemporary China: The Impact of the Past Mao Decade, 2:86

Geography of Europe: Problems and Prospects, 2:88, 2:405

Geography of Hunger: Some Aspects of the Causes and Impacts of Hunger, 2:85

Geography of Modern Africa, 2:85

Geography of Movement, 2:84

Geography of the Ozark Highland of Missouri, 2:80

Geography of the Soviet Union, 2:91

The Geography of the World Economy, 2:76

Geography of Third World Cities, 2:94

Geography of Transportation, 2:84

Geography of Urban Rural Interaction in Developing Countries, 2:94

Geography of World Affairs, 2:76

Geological Disasters: Earthquakes and Volcanoes, 2:493

Geological Evidence of the Antiquity of Man, 2:490

Geology, 2:489

Geometric Design, 1:515

The Geometric Foundation of Natural
   Structure: A Source Book of Design,
   1:513
Geometric Games, 1:535
Geometric Playthings: To Color, Cut, and
   Fold, 1:520
Geometrical Investigations: Illustrating the
   Art of Discovery in the Mathematical
   Field, 1:512
Geometrical Solutions Derived from
   Mechanics, 1:521
The Geometrical Work of Girard
   Desargues, 1:519
Geometry (Descartes), 1:515
Geometry (Dressler), 1:512
Geometry (Jacobs), 1:535
Geometry (Jurgensen), 1:512
Geometry (Kalin), 1:512
Geometry and Algebra in Ancient
   Civilizations: From the Stone Age to
   Brahmagupta, 1:498
Geometry and Measurement, 1:511
Geometry and Symmetry, 1:516
Geometry and the Imagination, 1:517
Geometry and the Visual Arts, 1:515
The Geometry of Art and Life, 1:515
The Geometry of Genetics, 1:519
The Geometry Problem Solver, 1:512
Geometry Problems: One Step Beyond,
   1:512
Geometry, Relativity, and the Fourth
   Dimension, 1:516
Geometry Revisited, 1:516
Geometry the Easy Way, 1:512
George Bernard Shaw, 1:120
George Bernard Shaw's Pygmalion, 1:451
George Bush, 2:259
George C. Marshall: Soldier-Statesman of
   the American Century, 2:240
George Cantor: His Mathematics and
   Philosophy of the Infinite, 1:499
George Catlin, 2:188
George Catlin: Episodes from "Life
   Among the Indians" and "Last
   Rambles," 2:188
George Cukor, 1:470
George Custer: Boy of Action, 2:203
George Eliot, 1:49
George F. Kennan: Cold War Iconoclast,
   2:391
George Gordon, Lord Byron, 1:33
George Herbert, 1:11
George Herbert Mead: Self, Language, and
   the World, 2:140
George Herbert Mead on Social
   Psychology, 2:139
George Lucas, 1:470
George M. Cohan: The Man Who Owned
   Broadway, 2:224
George Marshall, 2:240

George Meany: Modern Leader of the
   American Federation of Labor,
   2:238
George Orwell, 1:111
George Orwell: The Political Pen, 1:111
George Orwell for Beginners, 1:112
George W. Cable, 1:171
George Washington: Man and Monument,
   2:179
George Washington and the Birth of Our
   Nation, 2:179
George Washington Carver, 2:206
Georgia, Georgia, 1:191
Georgia O'Keeffe, 2:268
Georgia O'Keeffe: A Life, 2:268
The Georgics, 1:324; 2:297, 2:298
Geothermal Energy: A Hot Prospect,
   2:496
Gerald Ford, 2:253
Geraldine Ferraro: The Woman Who
   Changed American Politics, 2:258
Gerard Manley Hopkins, 1:53
German: A Linguistic History to Nineteen
   Forty-Five, 1:362
German-English Dictionary of Idioms,
   1:362
German Grammar, 1:362
The German Ideology, 2:58
German Intonation: An Outline, 1:362
German Reference Grammar, 1:362
German Root Lexicon, 1:362
The Germania, 2:296
Germanic Accent, Grammatical Change,
   and the Laws of Unaccented Syllables,
   1:362
Germanic and Its Dialects, 1:362
Germanic Dialects, 1:362
Germanic Languages: Origins and Early
   Dialectual Interrelations, 1:362
Germany Declares for Peace, 2:376
Germany's Aims in the First World War,
   2:371
Germany's First Bid for Colonies,
   1884–1885: A Move in Bismarck's
   European Policy, 2:341, 2:342
Germinal, 1:344, 1:345
Gershwin: A Biography, 2:262
Gerusalema Liberata, 1:347
Geschichten vom Lieben Gott, 1:371
Gestalt Psychology, 2:113
Get Help: Solving the Problems in Your
   Life, 2:536
Get on out of here, Philip Hall, 1:228
Get Thee to a Punnery, 1:440
Getting Better All the Time: Inside
   Alcoholics Anonymous, 2:555
Getting Computers to Talk Like You and
   Me: Discourse, Context, Focus, and
   Semantics; an ATN Model, 1:582
Getting Even, 1:189

Getting It Together: The Black Man's Guide to Good Grooming and Fashion, 2:552

Getting Started in Problem Solving and Math Contests, 1:497

Getting Stronger: Weight Training for Men and Women, 2:551

Getting the Most out of DeskMate 3, 1:561

Gettysburg: The Final Fury, 2:192

Ghana: Autobiography of Kwame Nkrumah, 2:396

The Ghetto, 2:131, 2:136

The Ghost Belonged to Me, 1:275

The Ghost in the Atom: A Discussion of the Mysteries of Quantum Physics, 2:518

Ghosts, 1:377, 1:378

Ghosts I Have Been, 1:275

G.I. The American Soldier in World War II, 2:235

Giant, 1:220

The Giant Planets, 2:476

Giants from the Past: The Age of Mammals, 2:495

Giants in the Earth, 1:379; 2:201

Giants of Jazz, 2:262

Gideon's Trumpet, 2:12

Gift: The Form and Reason for Exchange in Archaic Societies, 2:47

The Gift of Black Folk, 2:211

The Gift of the Magi, 1:178

The Gifted and Talented: Developmental Perspectives, 2:106

Gigolo, 1:220

Gilbert and Sullivan, 1:50

Gilded Age, 1:181

The Gilded Age: A Tale of Today, 1:182; 2:204

Gilded Age, Eighteen Seventy-Five to Eighteen Ninety-Six, 2:204

The Gilded Six-Bits, 1:242

Gilgamesh, 2:280

Gimpel the Fool and Other Stories, 1:388

Gingertown, 1:260

Giotto and Florentine Painting, 1280–1375, 2:305

Giovanni's Room, 1:195

A Girl in Winter, 1:100

The Girl on the Outside, 2:239

The Girl Who Wanted a Boy, 1:308

Girls and Sex, 2:543

Girls at War and Other Stories, 1:411

The Girls of Slender Means, 1:121

Giselle, Save the Children, 2:384

Giuseppe Garibaldi, 2:345

Giuseppe Verdi: His Life and Works, 2:361

Give Me One Wish: A True Story of Courage and Love, 2:563

Glacier, 2:492

Glaciers, 2:82

Glaciers and Ice Caps, 2:492

Glaciers and Ice Sheets, 2:493

Gladstone: A Progress in Politics, 2:346

Gladstone. Eighteen Nine to Eighteen Seventy-Four, 2:346

Glanmore Sonnets, 1:92

The Glass Key, 1:231

The Glass Menagerie, 1:303, 1:304

Glasses and Contact Lenses: Your Guide to Eyes, Eyewear, and Eye Care, 2:553

Gleanings of Past Years, 1843–1878: And Later Gleanings, 2:345

Glimpses of World History, 2:404

Glinda of Oz, 1:199

Global Issues, 1989–1990, 2:82

A Global Jigsaw Puzzle: The Story of Continental Drift, 2:494

Global Rivals, 2:36

Global Studies: Africa, 2:86, 2:394

Global Studies: China, 2:87, 2:399

Global Studies: Latin America, 2:88

Global Studies: Middle East, 2:90, 2:412

Global Studies: Soviet Union and Eastern Europe, 2:92, 2:405

Global Studies: Western Europe, 2:88, 2:406

The Global Village: Transformations in World Life and Media in the Twenty-First Century, 1:453; 2:130

Global Warming, 2:82

Global Warming: Are We Entering the Greenhouse Century?, 2:486

A Glorious Age in Africa, 2:299

Glory and Failure, 1:540

A Glossary of Faulkner's South, 1:220

Glossbrenner's Complete Hard Disk Handbook, 1:574

Glossbrenner's Guide to GEnie, 1:573

Go Down Moses and Other Stories, 1:219

Go for Broke: A Pictorial History of the Japanese American 100th Infantry Battalion and the 442nd Regimental Combat Team, 2:236

Go Tell It on the Mountain, 1:194, 1:195

Goblin Market, 1:56

God and the Astronomers, 2:470

God Bless You Mr. Rosewater, 1:295

God Emperor of Dune, 1:238

God in the White House: How Religion Has Changed in Modern Presidency, 2:258

God Knows, 1:234

God Save This Honorable Court: How the Choice of Supreme Court Justices Shapes Our History, 2:27

Gödel Remembered, 1:500
Gödel's Theorem Simplified, 1:500
God's Englishman: Oliver Cromwell and the English Revolution, 2:327
God's Grace, 1:262
Gods, Graves, and Scholars: The Story of Archaeology, 2:278
Gods, Heroes, and Men of Ancient Greece, 1:318
Gods, Men, and Monsters from the Greek Myths, 1:318
Gods of Mars, 1:208
The Gods Themselves, 1:194
God's Trombones, 1:245
God's World: An Anthology of Short Stories, 1:420
Goethe, 1:367
Goethe: Selected Poems, 1:366
Gogol from the Twentieth Century: Eleven Essays, 1:393
Going Back: An Ex-Marine Returns to Vietnam, 2:398
Going Backwards, 1:250
Going Home, 1:267
Going Like Sixty: A Lighthearted Look at the Later Years, 1:193
Going Solo, 1:79
Going to Meet the Man, 1:195
Going to the Territory, 1:218
Going to Work: A Unique Guided Tour Through Corporate America, 2:69
Gold and Iron: Bismarck, Bleischroder, and the Building of the German Empire, 2:342
The Gold Bat and Other School Stories, 1:131
Gold Cadillac, 1:290
The Gold Coast and the Slum: A Sociological Study of Chicago's Near Northside, 2:131
Golda Meir, 2:413
Golda Meir: The Romantic Years, 2:413
The Golden Ball and Other Stories, 1:74
The Golden Bough, 2:52
The Golden Bowl, 1:179
Golden Boy, 1:272
The Golden Notebook, 1:103
The Golden Relationship Art, Math, and Nature: Universal Patterns, 1:515
The Golden Road, 1:143
The Golden Tradition: An Anthology of Urdu Poetry, 1:421
The Golden Verses of Pythagoras, 1:501
Goldengrove, 1:126
Goldfinger, 1:84
Goldwater, 2:244
Good as Gold, 1:234
The Good Companions, 1:114
The Good Conscience, 1:403

The Good Earth, 1:206, 1:207
The Good Fight, 2:34
Good Grief, Good Grammar: The Business Person's Guide to Grammar and Usage, 1:478
Good Grooming for Boys, 2:552
Good Grooming for Girls, 2:552
The Good Leviathan, 1:332
A Good Man Is Hard to Find, 1:270
The Good Natured Man, 1:25
Good Neighbors?, 2:258
Good Old Cause: English Revolution of 1640–1660, 2:327
The Good Terrorist, 1:103
Good Thinking: The Foundations of Probability and Its Applications, 1:529
The Good Times, 1:480, 1:481
The Good War: An Oral History of World War Two, 1:489; 2:236
The Good Woman of Setzuan, 1:364, 1:365
Good Words to You: An All-New Browser's Dictionary and Native's Guide to the Unknown American Language, 1:432
Good-bye Mr. Chips, 1:94
Goodbye to All That, 1:90, 1:91
Goode's World Atlas, 2:75
Goodnight, Willie Lee, I'll See You in the Morning, 1:297
Goose Step: A Study of American Education, 1:287
Gorbachev: A Biography, 2:407
Gorbachev: The Man Who Changed the World, 2:407
Gorbachev's Struggle for Reform, 2:407
Gordon W. Allport's Ontopsychology of the Person, 2:115
Gorilla, My Love, 1:196
Gorillas in the Mist, 2:461
The Goslings: A Study of American Schools, 1:287
Götz von Berlichingen, 1:365
Governing: Readings and Cases in American Politics, 2:5
Governing at the Grassroots: State and Local Politics, 2:41
Governing the Five Trillion Dollar Economy: A Twentieth Century Fund Essay, 2:65
Governing the Ungovernable City: Political Skill, Leadership and the Modern Mayor, 2:40
Government by the People: National, State and Local Politics, 2:40
Governments, Markets, and Growth: Financial Systems and the Politics of Industrial Change, 2:65

Governor William Bradford and His Son Major William Bradford, 1:151
The Governors of the American States, Commonwealths, and Territories: 1900–1980, 2:6, 2:41
Graham Greene, 1:92
Graham Greene: A Collection of Critical Essays, 1:92
A Grain of Wheat, 1:415
Grammar and Good Taste: Reforming the American Language, 1:429
Grammar of Love, 1:390
Grammatical Institute of the English Language, 1:430
Grand Obsession: Madame Curie and Her World, 2:510
The Grand Tour: A Traveler's Guide to the Solar System, 2:476
Grandchildren of Alcoholics, 2:556
The Grandissimes, 1:171
Grant: A Biography, 2:200
Grant and Lee: The Virginia Campaigns, 1864–1865, 2:196
Grant Moves South, 2:199
Grant Takes Command, 2:199
The Grapes of Wrath, 1:288; 2:229
The Grapes of Wrath: Text and Criticism, 1:288
Graph-Theoretic Concepts in Computer Science, 1:587
The Grass Is Always Greener Over the Septic Tank, 1:447
The Grass Is Singing, 1:103
Grass Roots and Schoolyards: A High School Basketball Anthology, 1:480
Grasslands, 2:465
Grasslands and Tundra, 2:465
"A Grave," 1:268
Gray Fox: Robert E. Lee and the Civil War, 2:192
Gray's Anatomy, 2:450
Gray's Anatomy of the Human Body, 2:450
The Great American Comic Strip, 1:459
Great American Film Directors, 1:470
The Great American Gold Rush, 2:184
The Great American Guide to Diet and Health, 2:550
A Great American Magazine: An Inside History of Life, 1:455
The Great American Values Test: Influencing Behavior and Belief Through Television, 2:129
The Great Betrayal: Assassination of Indira Gandhi, 2:401
Great Bull Market: Wall Street in the 1920s, 2:227
Great Cartoonists and Their Art, 1:459
Great Constitution, 2:166
Great Crash of 1929, 2:226

The Great Crusade and After, 1914–1928, 2:224
Great Days, 1:198
Great Dinosaur Hunters and Their Discoveries, 2:495
The Great Divide: Second Thoughts on the American Dream, 1:489
Great Economists Since Keynes: An Introduction to the Lives and Works of One Hundred Modern Economists, 2:55
Great Expectations, 1:47
Great Expectations: A Novel of Friendship, 1:47
Great Expectations: America and the Baby Boom Generation, 2:142, 2:144
Great Experiments in Psychology, 2:122
The Great Explorers: The European Discovery of America, 2:158, 2:320
The Great Gatsby, 1:222; 2:226
Great Geological Controversies, 2:491
The Great Gilly Hopkins, 1:484
Great Ideas in Computer Science: A Gentle Introduction, 1:537
Great Ideas of Modern Mathematics, 1:498
Great Issues 79–80. A Forum on Important Questions Facing the American Public, 2:259
The Great Journey: The Peopling of Ancient America, 2:299
Great Music of Duke Ellington, 2:267
The Great Mutiny: India, Eighteen Fifty-Seven, 2:363
The Great Nuclear Power Debate, 2:496
Great Patriotic War of the Soviet Union, 2:380
The Great Plains, 2:201
The Great Psychologists, 2:96
The Great Rehearsal: The Story of the Making and Ratifying of the Constitution of the United States, 2:17, 2:167
Great Rivers of the World, 2:83
The Great Russian Dancers, 2:415
Great Sanskrit Plays in Modern Translation, 1:422
The Great Scientists, 2:433
Great Short Works (Conrad), 1:77
Great Short Works of Dostoevsky, 1:392
Great Short Works of Edgar Allan Poe, 1:164
Great Slave Narratives, 2:188
The Great Triumvirate: Webster, Clay, and Calhoun, 2:181–183
The Great War at Sea: A History of Naval Action, 1914–1918, 2:224
The Great War, 1914–1918, 2:371
The Greatness and Limitations of Freud's Thought, 2:118
Greed Is Not Enough: Reaganomics, 2:65
Greek and Norse Legends, 2:284

Greek and Roman Technology, 2:285
The Greek Anthology, 1:311
The Greek Armies, 2:284
Greek Classical Byzantine, 2:301
Greek Drama, 1:311
Greek Geometry from Thales to Euclid, 1:511
Greek Gods and Heroes, 1:318
Greek Literature: An Anthology, 1:311
Greek Medicine: Being Extracts Illustrative of Medical Writing from Hippocrates to Galen, 2:546
The Greek Myths, 1:91, 1:318
Greek Myths and Legends, 2:284
Greek Papyri: An Introduction, 2:285
The Greek Potter, 2:284
Greek Revival Architecture in America, 2:261
The Greek Stones Speak: The Story of Archaeology in Greek Lands, 2:285
The Greek World, 2:285
The Greeks (Crosher), 2:284
The Greeks (Kitto), 2:285
Greeks: A Great Adventure, 2:284
The Greeks Overseas: Their Early Colonies and Trade, 2:284
The Green Hills of Africa, 1:237
Green Magic: Algae Rediscovered, 2:447
The Green Man, 1:65
The Green Years, 1:78
The Greengage Summer, 1:88
The Greenhouse Effect, 2:81, 2:467, 2:486
Greenhouse Effect: Life on a Warmer Planet, 2:467
Gregor Mendel: Father of the Science of Genetics, 2:453
Gregor Mendel and Heredity, 2:453
Grendel, 1:6
Grey Seas Under, 1:144
Griffith: First Artist of the Movies, 1:470
The Grimké Sisters from South Carolina: Pioneers for Women's Rights and Abolition, 2:184
Group Discussion: A Practical Guide to Participation and Leadership, 1:445
The Group Mind, 2:104
Group Portrait with Lady, 1:364
Groupthink: Psychological Studies of Policy Decision, 2:139
Growing Old in America, 2:544
Growing Up, 1:480, 1:481
Growing Up on Television, 1:465
Growth and Structure of the English Language, 1:434
Growth and Welfare in the American Past, 2:69
The Growth of a Medieval Town, 2:305
The Growth of an American Village in the Early Industrial Revolution, 2:185
The Growth of Cities, 2:41, 2:93, 2:207
Growth of the American Revolution, 1766–1775, 2:164
"The Growth of the Poet's Mind," 1:39
Growth of the Soil, 1:376
Grzimek's Encyclopedia of Mammals, 2:449
The Guardian Angel, 1:158
The Guardian of the World, 1:415
Guatemala: A Country Study, 2:88
Guerrillas, 1:406
A Guest of Honor, 1:414
The Guggenheim Correspondence, 2:270
Guide for the Perplexed, 2:302, 2:303
A Guide to Computer Music: An Introductory Resource, 1:577
Guide to Computer Music: Electronic Music Resource, 1:577
Guide to Film Making, 1:470
Guide to French Idioms, 1:326
Guide to Information Sources in the Geographical Sciences, 2:76
Guide to Mars, 2:476
Guide to Places of the World: A Geographical Dictionary of Countries, Cities, National and Man-made Wonders, 2:75
Guide to Popular Operating Systems, 1:562
A Guide to Psychologists and Their Concepts, 2:95
The Guide to Short Films, 1:469
Guide to the 1988 Presidential Election, 2:257
Guide to the U.S. Supreme Court, 2:26
Guide to the Worlds of Robert A. Heinlein, A, 1:234
Guide to U.S. Elections, 2:5
Guide to U.S. Supreme Court, 2:5
A Guided Tour of the Living Cell, 2:437
Guidelines for Modern Resource Management, 2:496
The Gulag Archipelago, 1:396
The Gulag Archipelago, 1918–1956: An Experiment in Literary Investigation, 1:396
The Gulag Archipelago Three, 1:396
The Gulag Archipelago Two, 1:396
The Gulf Crisis, 2:89, 2:411
Gulliver's Travels, 1:30
Gulliver's Travels and Other Writings, 1:30
Gunfight at the O.K. Corral, 1:293
Gunnar Myrdal and Black-White Relations: The Use and Abuse of "An American Dilemma," 1944–1969, 2:135
The Guns of August, 2:224, 2:372
Günter Grass, 1:368
Gustav Mahler: An Introduction to His Music, 2:355
Gustav Mahler: The Early Years, 2:355

Gustav Mahler and Richard Strauss Correspondence, 1888–1911, 2:425
Gustave Flaubert, 1:335
The Gutenberg Galaxy: The Making of Typographic Man, 1:453
Guy Domville, 1:179
The Guyana Quartet, 1:405
Gwendolyn Brooks: Poetry and the Heroic Voice, 1:205
Gypsie Ballads, 1:357

H

H. G. Wells, 1:129
H. H. Munro (Saki), 1:115
H. L. Mencken and the American Mercury Adventure, 1:436
H. L. Mencken: Critic of American Life, 1:436
The Habit of Loving, 1:103
Hackers: Heroes of the Computer Revolution, 1:540
The Haiku Handbook, 1:489
The Haj, 1:293
Hakluyt's Voyages, 2:324
Halford Mackinder: A Biography, 2:79
"Half-Way Covenant," 1:153
Halfway to Anywhere, 1:141
Hamlet, 1:122
The Hamlet, 1:219
Hammarskjold, 2:390
Hammond Physical World Atlas, 2:75
Handbook for Space Colonists, 2:482
Handbook of Aging and the Social Sciences, 2:129
Handbook of Basic Citizenship Competencies, 2:13
Handbook of Child Psychology, 2:95
Handbook of Child Psychology: Cognitive Development, 2:103
Handbook of Child Psychology: Infancy and Developmental Psychobiology, 2:107
Handbook of Child Psychology: Socialization, Personality, and Social Development, 2:114
A Handbook of Greek Mythology, 1:318
The Handbook of International Financial Management, 2:71
Handbook of Latin American Popular Culture, 2:88, 2:274
Handbook of Mathematics, 1:496
Handbook of Model Rocketry, 2:482
Handbook of Non-Sexist Writing, 1:479
Handbook of Perception, 2:113
Handbook of Political and Social Indicators, 2:10
Handbook of Revolutionary Warfare, 2:396

The Handbook of Social Psychology, 2:95
Handbook of Socialization Theory and Research, 2:146
Handbook of Sociology, 2:124
Handbook of the Elements, 2:506
Handel, 2:336
Handel: A Celebration of His Life and Times, 1685–1759, 2:336
Handel: A Documentary Biography, 2:336
Handel: His Personality and His Times, 2:336
Handel: The Man and His Music, 2:336
A Handful of Dust, 1:127
Handling Barriers in Communication, 1:437
The Handmaid's Tale, 1:135
Hands-On Expert Systems, 1:584
Hanging In: What You Should Know About Psychotherapy, 2:566
Hangman's Holiday, 1:117
Hannah and Her Sisters, 1:189
Hannibal and the Enemies of Rome, 2:290
Hapgood, 1:122
Happy Birthday, Wanda Jean, 1:296
The Happy Life and Other Works, 2:304
The Happy Prince and Other Stories, 1:62
The Happy Valley, 1:147
Hapsburg Monarchy, 2:327
Harappan Civilization and Rojdi, 2:282
Hard and Soft Acids and Bases, 2:508
The Hard Boiled Explicator: A Guide to the Study of Dashiell Hammett, Raymond Chandler, and Ross Macdonald, 1:210, 1:231
Hard Times, 1:46, 1:47
Hard Times: An Oral History of the Great Depression in America, 1:489; 2:69, 2:229
Hardball: How Politics Is Played—Told by One Who Knows the Game, 2:19
Harding Era: Warren G. Harding and His Administration, 2:226
Hare and the Tortoise: Culture, Biology, and Human Nature, 2:133
The Harmonics of Nicomachus and the Pythagorean Tradition, 1:501
Harmony and Unity: The Life of Niels Bohr, 2:501
Harold D. Lasswell and the Study of International Relations, 2:10
Harold Pinter, 1:114
Harper Dictionary of Contemporary Usage, 1:435
Harriet Tubman: Conductor on the Underground Railway, 2:189
Harry and Hortense at Hormone High, 1:308
Harry S. Truman, 2:237
Harry S. Truman and the Modern American Presidency, 2:237

Harvard Encyclopedia of American Ethnic Groups, 2:124, 2:136
Harvard Graphics, 1:579
The Harvard Medical School Health Letter Book, 2:531
The Harvest of Sorrow: Soviet Collectivization and the Terror-Famine, 2:405
Harvest Poems: Nineteen Ten to Nineteen Sixty, 1:284
Harvey and the Oxford Physiologists: A Study of Scientific Ideas, 2:548
Harvey Cushing, 2:532
Harvey Cushing: A Biography, 2:532
Harvey Cushing: Surgeon, Author, Artist, 2:532
Hatter's Castle, 1:78
The Haunting of Hill House, 1:243
Have His Carcase, 1:117
Have Spacesuit Will Travel, 1:233
Hawaii, 1:264
Hawaii's Story by Hawaii's Queen, 2:218
The Hawk in the Rain, 1:94, 1:95
The Hawkline Monster: A Gothic Western, 1:203
Hay Fever, 1:77
Haydn: A Creative Life in Music, 2:337
Haydn: Chronicle and Works, 2:337
Haydn: His Life and Music, 2:337
Haydn: His Life and Times, 2:337
Hazardous Substances: A Reference, 2:570
Hazardous Waste in America: Our Number One Environmental Crisis, 2:496, 2:570
HBJ Advanced Mathematics: A Preparation for Calculus, 1:523
HBJ Algebra 1, 1:505
HBJ Algebra 2 with Trigonometry, 1:505
HBJ Consumer Mathematics, 1:504
HBJ Fundamentals of Mathematics, 1:504
HBJ Geometry, 1:512
Headaches: All About Them, 2:562
Headbirths: Or the Germans Are Dying Out, 1:367
The Healing Brain: Breakthrough Medical Discoveries About How the Brain Manages Health, 2:531
Health, a Concern for Every American, 2:566
The Health and Fitness Handbook, 2:552
Health and Healing: Understanding Conventional and Alternative Medicine, 2:531
Health and Wellness: A Holistic Approach, 2:531
Health Care for an Aging Society, 2:567
Health Care of Homeless People, 2:567
The Health Century, 2:567
Health Facts. A Critical Evaluation of the Major Problems, Treatments, and

Alternatives Facing Medical Consumers, 2:566
Health Insurance Alternative: A Guide to Health Maintenance Organizations, 2:566
Health, Medicine, and the Human Body, 2:531
The Health of Nations: The True Causes of Sickness and Well-Being, 2:567
Health–Wellness: An Introductory Approach, 2:531
Healthful Aging, 2:544
The Healthy Body: A Maintenance Manual, 2:530
Hear Me Talkin' to Ya: The Story of Jazz by the Men Who Made It, 2:262
Hear That Lonesome Whistle Blow: Railroads in the West, 2:200
The Heart and Blood, 2:545
The Heart and Circulatory System, 2:450
Heart Disease, 2:561, 2:563
The Heart of a Woman, 1:191
The Heart of Chinese Poetry, 1:423
Heart of Darkness, 1:76
Heart of Darkness: Search for the Unconscious, 1:77
The Heart of Midlothian, 1:36
The Heart of the Country, 1:128
The Heart of the Matter, 1:91
Heart-Shape in the Dust, 1:232
Heart to Heart: A Cleveland Clinic Guide to Understanding Heart Disease and Open Heart Surgery, 2:565
Heartbreak House, 1:120
Heartbreak Tango: A Serial, 1:408, 1:409
The Hearts and Lives of Men, 1:128
Heat, 1:227
The Heat of the Day, 1:69
Heaven and Other Poems, 1:247
Heavens to Betsy and Other Curious Sayings, 1:433
Hector Berlioz: Selections from His Letters, and Aesthetic, Humorous and Satirical Writings, 2:347
Hedda Gabler, 1:377
Heechee Rendezvous, 1:278
Heinrich Böll: A German for His Time, 1:364
Helen Keller, 1:449
Helen Keller's Teacher, 1:449
The Hellenistic World, 2:285
Heller with a Gun, 1:252
Help Your Child Succeed with a Computer, 1:568
Helping People: Karen Horney's Psychoanalytic Approach, 2:119
The Hemingway Reader, 1:237
Henderson the Rain King, 1:199, 1:200
Henri III, 1:333
Henrietta Temple, 2:342

Henrik Ibsen's Poems, 1:378
Henry Adams, 2:214
Henry Adams and Henry James: The
  Emergence of a Modern Consciousness,
  2:214
Henry Clay, 2:182
Henry David Thoreau, 1:165
Henry David Thoreau: A Life of the
  Mind, 1:165
Henry VIII: The Mask of Royalty, 2:311
Henry Esmond, 1:61
Henry Fielding, 1:24
Henry IV, 1:351
Henry James: A Life, 1:180
Henry Kissinger, 2:38
Henry Kissinger: His Personality and
  Policies, 2:38
Henry Purcell, 2:338
Henry Purcell: His Life and Times,
  1659–1695, 2:338
Henry Wadsworth Longfellow, 1:161
Henry Wadsworth Longfellow: His Poetry
  and Prose, 1:161
Hen's Teeth and Horse's Toes: Further
  Reflections on Natural History, 2:458
Her, 1:221
Herbert Hoover, 2:231
Herbert Hoover: The Forgotten
  Progressive, 2:230
Herbert Hoover: The Public Life, 2:229
Herbert Hoover and the Great Depression,
  2:229, 2:231
Herbert Hoover and the Reconstruction
  Finance Corporation, 1931–1933, 2:229
Herblock at Large: Let's Go Back a Little
  and Other Cartoons from the Reagan
  Era, 1:459
Hercules Furens, 1:323
Hercules, My Shipmate, 1:90
Here Are My Lectures and Stories, 1:141
Here I Stand: A Life of Martin Luther,
  2:317
Here Is New York, 1:456
Hereditary Diseases, 2:561
Heretics of Dune, 1:238
Heritage: Civilization and the Jews, 2:280
Heritage of Buddhism, 2:281
Heritage of Music, 2:276
Herman Hollerith: Forgotten Giant of
  Information Processing, 1:544
Herman Melville, 1:163
Herman Melville: A Biography, 1:163
Herman und Dorothea, 1:366
Hermann Hesse, 1:368
Hermann Hesse: Modern German Poet
  and Writer, 1:368
Hernán Cortés, 2:323
Hernán Cortés: Conquistador in Mexico,
  2:323

Hernando De Soto: Knight of the
  Americas, 2:157
A Hero Ain't Nothin' but a Sandwich,
  1:212
Herodotus, 2:288
Herodotus: The Wars of Greece and
  Persia, 2:288
Herodotus the Historian: His Problems,
  Methods, and Originality, 2:288
Heroes, Gods and Monsters of the Greek
  Myths, 1:318
Heroides, 1:321
Herpes: Cause and Control, 2:557
Herself Surprised, 1:72
Herzog, 1:199, 1:200
The Herzogenberg Correspondence, 2:348
Hesperides and Noble Numbers, 1:11
Hexaflexagons and Other Mathematical
  Diversions, 1:536
Hiawatha, 1:160
The Hidden Contributors: Black Scientists
  and Inventors in America, 2:432
Hidden Differences: Doing Business with
  the Japanese, 1:448
Hidden Dimension, 1:448
The Hidden History of the Korean War,
  1950–1951, 2:400
Hidden Injuries of Class, 2:144
The Hidden Persuaders, 1:441
The Hidden World of Forces, 2:522
Hidden Worlds, 2:436
Hieroglyphs: The Writing of Ancient
  Egypt, 2:280
High Blood Pressure, 2:562
High Blood Pressure: What It Means for
  You and How to Control It, 2:562
High Crimes and Misdemeanors: The
  Impeachment and Trial of Andrew
  Johnson, 2:198
The High King, 1:187, 1:188
High Performance Graphics in C:
  Animation and Simulation, 1:577
High Points in Anthropology, 2:42
High Resolution NMR: A Handbook of
  Principles, 1:578
High Rise, 1:67
The High School Algebra Tutor, 1:506
The High School Trigonometry and
  Eleventh Year Math Problem Solver,
  1:524
High Spirits, 1:138
High Tech–High Touch: A Computer
  Education Leadership Development
  Workshop, 1:555, 1:570
The High-Tech Society: The Story of the
  Information Technology Revolution,
  1:537
The High Window, 1:210
High Windows, 1:100

The Higher Learning in America, 2:146
Higher Than Hope: The Biography of Nelson Mandela, 2:395
Hike and the Aeroplane, 1:255
Hilbert–Courant, 1:517
The Hills Beyond, 1:306
Him She Loves, 1:247
Him with His Foot in His Mouth and Other Stories, 1:200
The Hindu View of Life, 2:282
Hippocrates, 2:533
Hippocrates and His Successors in Relation to the Philosophy of Their Time, 2:533
Hippocrates Latinum: Repertorium of Hippocratic Writings in the Latin Middle Ages, 2:533
Hippocratic Medicine, 2:533
Hippocratic Writings, 2:533
Hiroshima, 2:235
His Master's Voice, 1:386
The Hispanic Population of the United States. The Population of the United States in the 1980's: A Census Monograph, 2:141
Histoires Charitables, 1:332
Histoires Perfides, 1:332
Historical Atlas of Africa, 2:272
The Historical Atlas of United States Congressional Districts, 1789–1983, 2:6
Historical Change and English Word-Formation: Recent Vocabulary, 1:432
Historical Dialectology, 1:431
Historical Dictionary of American Industrial Language, 1:433
Historical Dictionary of the New Deal: From Inauguration to Preparation for War, 2:229
The Historical Significance of Desiderius Erasmus in the Light of the Protestant Revolution and the Catholic Church as Revealed by His Most Famous Pronouncements, 2:314
Historical Sociology, 2:124
Historical Study of the Development of American Motion Picture Content and Techniques Prior to 1904, 1:469
Histories (Herodotus), 2:288
The Histories (Tacitus), 2:297
Historical Art Index, A.D. 400–1650: People, Places, and Events Depicted, 2:276
History, 2:287
History Begins at Sumer: Thirty-Nine "Firsts" in Man's Recorded History, 2:280
A History of Africa, 2:299

History of African Civilization, 2:275, 2:300
A History of Algebra, 1:506
A History of American City Government: The Emergence of the Metropolis, 1920–1945, 2:40
A History of American Foreign Policy, 2:153
History of American Labor, 2:204
History of American Painting, 2:161, 2:187, 2:213
History of American Presidential Elections, 1972–1984, 2:40
History of American Sculpture, 2:262
History of Analysis, 1:524
History of Analytic Geometry: Its Development from the Pyramids to the Heroic Age, 1:514
The History of Ancient Israel, 2:280
A History of Art: From Twenty-Five Thousand B.C. to the Present, 2:273
History of Art for Young People, 2:154
A History of Board Games Other Than Chess, 1:535
A History of Broadcasting: Technology and Business, 1:464
History of Cartography, 2:92
A History of Chess, 1:535
A History of Chinese Buddhism, 2:281
A History of Christian Names, 1:439
A History of Civilization: 1815 to the Present, 2:273
A History of Civilization: Prehistory to 1300, 2:273
A History of Civilization: 1300 to 1815, 2:273
A History of Computer Technology, 1:540
A History of Computing in the Twentieth Century, 1:540
History of Economic Analysis, 2:56, 2:72
A History of Greek Mathematics, 1:507
The History of Henry Esmond, 1:61
A History of Immunology, 2:546
The History of Impressionism, 2:346
A History of Israel: From the Aftermath of the Yom Kippur War, 2:276
A History of Israel: From the Rise of Zionism to Our Time, 2:276
The History of King Richard III and Selections from the English and Latin Poems, 1:14
A History of Latin America, 2:275
The History of Manned Space Flight, 2:480
A History of Mathematics, 1:496
A History of Mechanics, 2:512
A History of Mexican Archaeology: The Vanished Civilizations of Middle America, 2:298

History of Modern Brazil, 1889–1964, 2:408

A History of Movie Photography, 1:469

The History of Mr. Polly, 1:129

A History of Narrative Film, 1889–1979, 1:468

A History of Nazi Germany, 2:382

History of New York, 1:159

A History of News: From Oral Culture to the Information Age, 1:457

A History of News: From the Drum to the Satellite, 1:457

The History of Non-Euclidean Geometry, 1:516

A History of Our Time: Readings on Postwar America, 2:238

The History of Pendennis, 1:61

The History of Photography: From 1839 to the Present Day, 2:275

History of Programming Languages, 1:563

A History of Psychology: Original Sources and Contemporary Research, 2:95

A History of Radio to 1926, 1:461

History of Rome (Grant), 2:290

History of Rome (Livy), 2:294, 2:295

A History of Russia, 2:276

A History of Southeast Asia, 2:398

The History of Statistics, 1:530

A History of the American Revolution, 2:327

A History of the Ancient World, 2:279

History of the Balkans: Eighteenth and Nineteenth Centuries, 2:340

History of the Bank of New York and Trust Company, 1784–1934, 2:155

History of the Conquest of Mexico, 2:323

The History of the Earth's Crust, 2:495

A History of the English Language, 1:429

A History of the English Speaking Peoples, 2:153

A History of the English-Speaking Peoples (1956–1958), 2:386

History of the Expedition Under the Command of Lewis and Clark, 2:176

A History of the French Language, 1:326

A History of the Indians of the United States, 2:153

A History of the League of Nations, 2:224

A History of the Mathematical Theory of Probability from the Time of Pascal to That of Laplace, 1:533

A History of the New York Times 1851–1921, 1:457

History of the Peloponnesian War, 2:289

A History of the Physical Sciences Since Antiquity, 2:498

History of the Theory of Numbers, 1:497

A History of the United Nations. Nineteen Forty-Five to Fifty-Five: The Cold War Years, 2:238

History of the United States During the Administrations of Jefferson and Madison, 2:214

A History of the Vikings, 2:306

History of West Africa, 2:298

A History of West Africa, One Thousand to Eighteen Hundred, 2:299

A History of Western Music, 2:154

History of Women in America, 2:154

History Will Absolve Me, 2:410

The Hitchhiker's Guide to the Galaxy, 1:64

Hitler, 2:376

Hitler: A Chronology of His Life and Time, 2:376

Hitler: A Portrait of a Tyrant, 2:376

The Hitler Fact Book, 2:376

Hitler, Germans, and the "Jewish Question," 2:376

Hitler in History, 2:376

Hitler's Children: The Hitler Youth and the SS, 2:377

Hitler's Generals, 2:382

Hitler's Reich, 2:376

Hobbes, 2:10

The Hobbit, 1:125

Hog on Ice and Other Curious Expressions, 1:433

Holding the Line: The Eisenhower Era, 1952–1961, 2:237

The Hole in the Sky: Man's Threat to the Ozone Layer, 2:486

Holiday Tales of Sholem Aleichem, 1:383

Hollywood: The First One Hundred Years, 1:469

Hollywood: The Pioneers, 2:226

Hollywood Indian: Stereotypes of Native Americans in Films, 1:475

The Holmes Reader, 2:29

The Holocaust, 2:384

The Holocaust: The History of the Jews of Europe During the Second World War, 2:384

The Holy Sinner, 1:370

Holy the Firm, 1:482

Home Before Dark, 1:204

Home Before Dark: A Biographical Memoir of John Cheever, 1:211

The Home Front: Germany, 2:383

The Home Front: USA, 2:383

The Home Front and Beyond: American Women in the 1940s, 2:235

Home Front U.S.A. America During World War II, 2:236

Home Life in Colonial Days, 2:161

Home Sweet Home: My Canadian Album, 1:146
Home to Harlem, 1:260
Home Truths, 1:139
The Homecoming (Pinter), 1:114
Homecoming (Pohl), 1:278, 1:294
Homecoming (Voight), 2:94
Homecoming: When the Soldiers Returned from Vietnam, 2:252
The Homefront: America During World War II, 2:235
The Homeless (Bender), 2:144
The Homeless (Landan), 2:567
Homeless: Profiling the Problem, 2:145
Homeless Children, 2:138, 2:145
Homeless in America, 2:145
Homeless in the United States, 2:145
Homer, 1:316
Homer's Daughter, 1:90
Homo Ludens: A Study of the Play Element in Culture, 2:43
Hondo, 1:252
Honduras: A Country Study, 2:89, 2:409
Honey and Salt, 1:284
Honey for the Bears, 1:71
Honeybee Ecology: A Study of Adaptation in Social Life, 2:462
Honkers and Shouters, 2:262
Honorable Justice: The Life of Oliver Wendell Holmes, 2:29
Honoré de Balzac, 1:330
The Honourable Schoolboy, 1:102
Hooded Americanism: The History of the Klu Klux Klan, 2:226
Hooked, 1:480
Hoops, 1:270
Hooray for Yiddish, 1:431
The Hoover Presidency: A Reappraisal, 2:231
Hope: New Choices and Recovery Strategies for Adult Children of Alcoholics, 2:555
Hope and Suffering: Sermons and Speeches, 2:397
Horace (Armstrong), 1:321
Horace (Fraenkel), 2:294
Horace (Perret), 2:294
Horace: Complete Odes and Epodes, 1:321
Horace and His Influence: Our Debt to Greece and Rome, 2:294
Horace Mann and Religion in the Massachusetts Public Schools, 2:187
Horace Talks: The Satires, 2:294
Horace's Satires and Epistles, 2:294
Horatio's Boys: The Life and Works of Horatio Alger, Jr, 1:169
The Horizon Concise History of Spain, 2:275

Hormones: The Woman's Answer Book, 2:545
Hornblower and the Atropos, 1:85
Hornblower and the Hotspur, 1:85
Horsefeathers and Other Curious Words, 1:433
Horses Make a Landscape Look More Beautiful, 1:297
The Horse's Mouth, 1:72
Hortus Cliffortianus, 2:443
Hosni Mubarak: President of Egypt, 2:411
The Hostage, 1:68
The Hotel, 1:69
The House Behind the Cedars, 1:172
A House Divided, 1:207
A House Divided: America in the Age of Lincoln, 2:198
A House for Mr. Biswas, 1:406
The House in Paris, 1:69
The House of Bernarda Alba, 1:357
A House of Children, 1:71, 1:72
The House of Dies Drear, 1:230
The House of Medici: Its Rise and Fall, 2:310
The House of Mirth, 1:183
"House of the One Father," 2:209
The House of the Seven Gables, 1:177
The House of Tudor, 2:327
A House with Four Rooms, 1:89
Household Budgeting and Accounting on Your Home Computer, 1:568
The Householder, 2:399
How a Writer Works, 1:477
How and Why: The Third Reich, 2:384
How Animals Behave, 2:461
How Computers Really Work, 1:557
How Congress Works, 2:32
How Did We Find Out About Atoms?, 2:500
How Did We Find Out About Black Holes?, 2:478
How Did We Find Out About Blood?, 2:450
How Did We Find Out About Coal?, 2:495
How Did We Find Out About Comets?, 2:474
How Did We Find Out About Computers?, 1:540, 1:556
How Did We Find Out About DNA?, 2:439
How Did We Find Out About Earthquakes?, 2:493
How Did We Find Out About Nuclear Power?, 2:434, 2:528
How Did We Find Out About Oil?, 2:495
How Did We Find Out About Our Genes?, 2:452

How Did We Find Out About Outer Space?, 2:480
How Did We Find Out About Photosynthesis?, 2:438, 2:447
How Did We Find Out About Solar Power?, 2:485
How Did We Find Out About the Atmosphere?, 2:484
How Did We Find Out About the Brain?, 2:450
How Did We Find Out About the Universe?, 2:469
How Did We Find Out About Volcanoes?, 2:82, 2:493
How Did You Think of That? An Introduction to the Scientific Method, 2:434
How Do You Know It's True?, 2:434
How I Found Livingstone, 2:367
How I Wrote Jubilee and Other Essays on Life and Literature, 1:298
How It Was, 1:237
How It Was: The War and Post-War Reconstruction in the Soviet Union, 2:389
How Life Began, 2:437, 2:456, 2:461
How Life Begins, 2:452
How the Colonists Lived, 2:162
How the Other Half Lives, 2:212
How the World Works: A Guide to Science's Greatest Discoveries, 2:434
How to Avoid Ripoffs at the Dentist, 2:566
How to Be a Reasonably Thin Teenage Girl (Without Starving, Losing Your Friends, or Running Away from Home), 2:550
How To Be a Successful Computer Consultant, 1:538
How to Be Funny, 1:446
How to Build a Conscious Machine, 1:580
How to Buy and Use a Printer, 1:561
How to Care for Your Back, 2:562
How to Choose and Use Your Doctor, 2:565
How to Cope with a Teenage Drinker: New Alternatives and Hope for Parents and Families, 2:555
How to Dissect: Exploring with Probe and Scalpel, 2:434
How to Enrich Geometry Using String Designs, 1:515
How to Forecast Weather, 2:485
How to Get Started with Modems, 1:558
How to Get the Most Out of Compuserve, 1:573
How to Handle Stress, 2:123
How to Have the Healthiest Baby You Can, 2:543
How to Know the Ferns, 2:447

How to Know the Insects, 2:448
How to Know the Mosses and Liverworts, 2:447
How to Know the Protozoa, 2:446
How to Know the Seed Plants, 2:447
How to Lie with Statistics, 1:529
How to Live Longer and Feel Better, 2:544
How to Live with a Single Parent, 2:538
How to Live with Diabetes, 2:561
How to Live with Parents and Teachers, 2:538
How to Make a Speech, 1:446, 1:449
How to Master Science Labs, 2:435
How to Protect Yourself from STD's, 2:559
How to Raise Parents: Questions and Answers for Teens and Parents, 2:538
How to Read Shakespeare: A New Guide to the Plays, 1:16
How to Read the Financial Pages, 2:70
How to Save a Life Using CPR: Cardiopulmonary Resuscitation, 2:567
How to Say No and Keep Your Friends: Peer Pressure Reversal, 2:556
How to Solve Algebra Word Problems, 1:506
How to Solve Word Problems in Algebra: A Solved Problem Approach, 1:506
How to Speak Dutchified English, 1:431
How to Speak L.A., 1:431
How to Speak New York, 1:431
How to Speak Southern, 1:431
How to Speak—How to Listen: A Guide to Pleasurable and Profitable Conversation, 1:445
How to Start a Conversation and Make Friends, 1:445
How to Stay Healthy Abroad, 2:530
How to Stay Healthy While Traveling: A Guide for Today's World Traveler, 2:531
How to Survive in America the Poisoned, 2:570
How to Talk Minnesotan, 1:431
How to Talk So People Listen: The Real Key to Job Success, 1:445
How to Talk with People, 1:437
How to Talk Yankee, 1:431
How to Think with Numbers, 1:497
How to Use an Astronomical Telescope: A Beginner's Guide to Observing the Cosmos, 2:436, 2:470
How to Use Computers with Gifted Students: Creative Microcomputing in a Differentiated Curriculum, 1:571
How to Use Maps and Globes, 2:92
How to Use Quark XPress, 1:576
How to Use the Power of the Printed Word, 1:477
How to Write, 1:477

How to Write a Computer Manual: A Handbook of Software Documentation, 1:563
How to Write a Film, 1:485
How to Write a Letter, 1:487
How to Write a Million Dollar Memo, 1:483
How to Write a Movie in 21 Days, 1:485
How to Write a Play, 1:489
How to Write a Poem, 1:489
How to Write a Readable Business Report, 1:483
How to Write a Usable User Manual, 1:491
How to Write a Winning Resumé, 1:490
How to Write Action–Adventure Novels, 1:490
How to Write College Application Essays, 1:485
How to Write Powerful Complaint Letters and Others, 1:487
How to Write Romances, 1:490
How to Write Your Way to Success in Business, 1:483
How We Think: A Restatement of the Relation of Reflective Thinking to the Educative Process, 2:219
Howard's End, 1:85
Howl, 1:225
The Hubble Atlas of Galaxies, 2:478
Hubert: The Triumph and Tragedy of the Humphrey I Knew, 2:245
Hubert Humphrey: A Political Biography, 2:245
Hubert Humphrey: The Man and His Dream, 1911–1978, 2:245
The Huddled Masses: The Immigrant in American Society, 1880–1921, 2:207
Huis clos, 1:340
Human Associative Memory, 2:103
Human Biological Rhythms, 2:462
Human Biology, 2:450
The Human Body, 2:450, 2:545
The Human Body: An Overview, 2:450
The Human Body on File, 2:545
The Human Brain, 2:545
The Human Brain: Mind and Matter, 2:545
The Human Comedy, 1:329
Human Comfort, 2:105
Human Development: A Life-Span Perspective, 2:107
Human Evolution: An Illustrated Introduction, 2:460
The Human Group, 2:104, 2:139
The Human Interface Where People and Computers Meet, 1:558
Human Motivation, 2:113
Human Motivation and Emotion, 2:112
Human Nature: Darwin's View, 2:48

Human Nature and the Social Order, 2:146
Human Nature, Class, and Ethnicity, 2:135
Human Physiology: The Mechanisms of Body Function, 2:451
The Human Rights Reader, 2:12
The Human Senses, 2:113
Human Sexuality, 2:543
Human Sexuality Annual 1989, 2:137
Human Skin, 2:451, 2:545
The Human Thing: The Speeches and Principles of Thucydides' History, 2:289
The Human Use of Human Beings: Cybernetics and Society, 1:539
Humanism in Personology: Allport, Maslow and Murray, 2:116
Humanizing Technology: Computers in Community Use and Adult Education, 1:554, 1:570
Humboldt's Gift, 1:200
Humor and the Presidency, 2:253
Humor in Pascal, 1:533
The Humor of Samuel Beckett, 1:331
The Hunchback of Notre Dame, 1:337
Hundejahre, Dog Years, 1:367
Hunger, 1:376
Hunger and Malnutrition in America, 2:567
Hungerfield and Other Poems, 1:244
Hungry Hill, 1:80
The Hunting of the Snark, 1:45
Hunting with the Microscope, 2:436
The Hustons, 1:472
Hybrid Imagery: The Fusion of Technology and Graphic Design, 1:577
The Hydra Head, 1:402, 1:403
HyperCard: The Complete Reference, 1:580
Hypercard, Hypertext, and Hypermedia for Librarians, 1:579
Hyperdocuments and How to Create Them, 1:580
Hyperspace! Facts and Fun from All Over the Universe, 2:468
HyperTalk the Book, 1:580
Hypertext and Hypermedia, 1:580
Hypertext–Hypermedia, 1:580

I

I Am a Camera, 1:96
I Am a Woman Worker: A Scrapbook of Autobiographies, 2:148
I Am Not a Crook, 1:488
I Am the Cheese, 1:213
I Can Not Get You Close Enough, 1:225
I, Claudius, 1:90

I Don't Know What to Say . . . How to
Help and Support Someone Who Is
Dying, 2:544
I Hate Computers, 1:557
I Have Done My Duty: Florence
Nightingale in the Crimean War,
1854–56, 2:569
I Hear the Morning Star, 1:239
I Know Why the Caged Bird Sings, 1:190,
1:191
I Love Myself When I Am Laughing and
Then Again When I Am Looking Mean
and Impressive: A Zora Neale Hurston
Reader, 1:242
I Must Say: On English, the News, and
Other Matters, 1:443
I Never Loved Your Mind, 1:308
I Promessi Sposi, 1:347
I Remember: Sketch for an
Autobiography, 1:394
I, Robot, 1:193, 1:194
I Sing the Body Electric, 1:202
I Stand Corrected: More on Language,
1:442
I Stay Near You, 1:247
I Think I Don't Remember, 1:488
"I Touch the Future": The Story of
Christa McAuliffe, 2:481
"I Wandered Lonely as a Cloud," 1:39
I Will Fight No More Forever, 2:202
I Will Marry When I Want, 1:415
Iacocca: An Autobiography, 2:63
Ian Fleming, 1:84
Ian Fleming's James Bond: The Illustrated
Sherlock Holmes Treasury, 1:84
IBM PC: An Introduction to the
Operating System: BASIC Programming,
and Applications, 1:559
IBM-PC: Introduction to Operating
Systems, Basic Programming and
Applications, 1:561
The IBM Way: Insights into the World's
Most Successful Marketing
Organization, 1:540
Ibsen, 1:378
Ibsen and Shaw, 1:378
The Ice Age, 1:80
The Ice Ages (Gallant), 2:278, 2:493
Ice Ages: Solving the Mystery, 2:493
Ice Palace, 1:220
The Iceman Cometh, 1:273, 1:274
Ida Tarbell: Portrait of a Muckraker, 2:218
Idanre and Other Poems, 1:418
The Idea of a Party System: The Rise of
Legitimate Opposition in the United
States, 1780–1840, 2:169
The Idea of Social Structure: Papers in
Honor of Robert K. Merton, 2:141
The Ideal Husband, 1:62

Ideas and Information: Managing in a
High-Tech World, 1:555; 2:130
Ideas and Institutions, 2:340
Ideas and Opinions, 2:520
Ideas of Le Corbusier: Architecture and
Urban Planning, 2:419
The Ideas of Psychology: Conceptual and
Methodological Issues, 2:95
Ideas of Space: Euclidean, Non-Euclidean,
and Relativistic, 1:519
Ideas of the Great Economists, 2:56
The Ideas of the Woman Suffrage
Movement, 1880–1920, 2:224
Identifying American Architecture, 2:261
Identity and the Life Cycle, 2:108
Ideological Origins of the American
Revolution, 2:163
Ideology and Social Change in Latin
America, 2:409
Ideology and the Development of
Sociology Theory, 2:125
The Ides of March, 1:303
Idiom's Delight: Fascinating Phrases and
Linguistic Eccentricities, 1:436
Idioms in Action, 1:437
Idioms in American Life, 1:437
The Idiot, 1:392
Idiots First, 1:262
The Idylls of the King, 1:60
If Beale Street Could Talk, 1:195
If Blessing Comes, 1:196
If I Love You, Am I Trapped Forever,
1:247
If Life Is a Bowl of Cherries—What Am I
Doing in the Pits?, 1:447
If Morning Ever Comes, 1:291
If You Love Somebody Who Smokes:
Confessions of a Nicotine Addict,
2:556
If You Want to Write: A Book About Art,
Independence and Spirit, 1:482
Iggie's House, 1:201
Igneous Rocks, 2:492
Ignore Your Teeth . . . & They'll Go
Away: The Patient's Complete Guide to
Prevention and Treatment of
Periodontal (Gum) Disease, 2:553
Igor Stravinsky: An Autobiography,
2:426
Igor Stravinsky: His Personality, Works,
and View, 2:426
The Ikons and Other Poems, 1:81
Il Decamerone (The Decameron), 1:348
Il Duce: The Rise and Fall of Benito
Mussolini, 2:375
Il fu Mattia Pascal (The Late Mattia
Pascal), 1:351
Il Penseroso, 1:13
The Iliad, 1:27, 1:156, 1:311, 1:315, 1:324

I'll Never Walk Alone: The Inspiring Story of a Teenager's Struggle Against Cancer, 2:562

The Ill-Made Knight, 1:130

Illustrated Computer Graphics Dictionary, 1:578

An Illustrated Dictionary of Word Processing, 1:575

The Illustrated Encyclopedia of Space Technology, 2:481

Illustrated Facts and Records Book of Animals, 2:448

An Illustrated Guide to the Protozoa, 2:446

The Illustrated Man, 1:202

The Illustrated Naked Ape: A Zoologist's Study of the Human Animal, 2:461

The Illustrations from the Works of Andreas Vesalius of Brussels, 2:548

The Illyrian Adventure, 1:188

I'm Really Dragged, but Nothing Gets Me Down, 1:237

The Image: A Guide to Pseudo-Events in America, 1:440

The Image of Peter the Great in Russian History and Thought, 2:327

Image of the City, 2:94

Images of America: A Panorama of History in Photographs, 2:154

Images of Earth, 2:489

Images of Geometric Solids, 1:519

Images of Women in Antiquity, 2:273

The Imaginary Invalid, 1:338

The Immigrants, 1:218

The Immigrant's Daughter, 1:218

Immigrants to Freedom: Jewish Communities in Rural New Jersey Since 1882, 2:206

The Immoralist, 1:336

The Immune System, 2:545

The Impact of Technological Change on Employment and Economic Growth, 2:140

Impacts of Artificial Intelligence: Scientific, Technological, Military, Economic, Societal, Cultural and Political, 1:582

Imperial Democracy: The Emergence of America as a Great Power, 2:218

Imperial Earth, 1:75

Imperial Germany and the Industrial Revolution, 2:146

Imperial Hearst, 2:218

The Imperial Presidency, 2:21

Imperial Rockefeller, 2:204

Imperialism, the Highest Stage of Capitalism, 2:378

The Imperiled Union: Essays of the Background of the Civil War, 2:193

An Implementation Guide to Compiler Writing, 1:586

Implicit Meanings: Essays in Anthropology, 2:43

The Importance of Being Earnest and Other Plays, 1:62

The Importance of Being Earnest, 1:62

The Impossible in Mathematics, 1:534

The Impossible Peace: Britain, the German Problem, and the Origins of the Cold War, 2:388

Impressionist Dreams: The Artists and the World They Painted, 2:346

The Improbable Machine: What the New Upheaval in Artificial Intelligence Research Reveals About How the Mind Really Works, 1:582

In a Different Voice: Psychological Theory and Women's Development, 2:146

In a Free State, 1:406

In a German Pension, 1:141

In Country, 1:263

In Cuba, 1:400

In Defense of American Liberties: A History of the ACLU, 2:13

In Defense of Freedom, 2:407

In Defense of Socialism: Four Speeches on the 30th Anniversary of the Cuban Revolution, 2:410

In Defense of the Body: An Introduction to the New Immunology, 2:545

In Defense of the Indians, 2:158

In Dubious Battle, 1:288, 1:289

In Evil Hour, 1:403

In God We Trust: New Patterns of Religious Pluralism in America, 2:142

In Her Own Right: The Life of Elizabeth Cady Stanton, 2:184

In Hitler's Germany: Everyday Life in the Third Reich, 2:384

In Its Own Image: How Television Has Transformed Sports, 1:465

In Joy Still Felt: An Autobiography of Isaac Asimov, 1954–1978, 2:434

In League with Eleanor: Eleanor Roosevelt and the League of Women Voters, 1921–1962, 2:233

In Love and Trouble: Stories of Black Women, 1:296, 1:297

In Memory Yet Green: An Autobiography of Isaac Asimov, 1920–1954, 2:434

In My Father's House, 1:224

In Our Time, 1:479

In Praise of Darkness, 1:399

In Search of Excellence: Lessons from America's Best Run Companies, 2:63

In Search of Identity: An Autobiography, 2:414

In Search of Liberty: The Story of the Statue of Liberty and Ellis Island, 2:206

In Search of Light: The Broadcasts of Edward R. Murrow, 1:467

In Search of Our Mothers' Gardens: Womanist Prose, 1:482

In Search of Reagan's Brain, 1:460

In Search of Southeast Asia: A Modern History, 2:400

In Search of the Big Bang: Quantum Physics and Cosmology, 2:519

In Search of the Common Good: Utopian Experiments Past and Future, 2:138

In Search of the Dark Ages, 2:306

In Search of the Most Amazing Things: Children, Education and Computers, 1:571

In Search of the Primitive: A Critique of Civilization, 2:42

In Search of the Trojan War, 1:318; 2:285

In Support of Families, 2:539

In the Age of Mankind: A Smithsonian Book of Human Evolution, 2:460

In the Age of the Smart Machine: The Future of Work and Power, 1:556; 2:149

In the Arena, 2:254

In the Beginning (Hamilton), 1:230

In the Beginning (Potok), 1:280

In the Cause of Architecture, 2:270

In the Ditch, 1:413

In the Egg and Other Poems, 1:367

In the Heart of the Country, 1:413

In the Interest of the Governed: A Study in Bentham's Philosophy of Utility and Law, 2:8

In the Land of Dreamy Dreams, 1:224, 1:225

In the Land of Israel, 2:89, 2:412

In the Land of the Olmec, 2:299

In the Money, 1:305

In the Most of Life, 1:169

In the Name of Apartheid: South Africa in the Postwar Era, 2:393

In the Name of Science, 1:536

In the Presence of the Creator: Isaac Newton and His Times, 2:516

In the Shadow of Man, 2:463

In the Shadow of the Glen, 1:123

In the Teeth of the Evidence, 1:117

In the Wake of the Exxon Valdez: The Devastating Impact of the Alaska Oil Spill, 2:467

In the Wet, 1:147

In the Winter of Cities, 1:304

In the World of Sumer: An Autobiography, 2:280

In This House of Brede, 1:88

In This Our Life, 1:226, 1:227

In Transit, 1:139

In Vietnam, 2:241

In War's Dark Shadow: The Russians Before the Great War, 2:340

In Watermelon Sugar, 1:203

Inadmissible Evidence, 1:112

Inaugural Addresses of the Presidents of the United States from George Washington, 1789, to George Bush, 1989, 2:154

Inca Architecture, 2:299

Incident at Vichy, 1:266

Incidents in the Life of a Slave Girl Written by Herself, 2:189

Income, Saving and the Theory of Consumer Behavior, 2:61

Incongruities, Inconsistencies, Absurdities and Outright Stupidities in Scientific Economics, 2:55

Incredible Era: The Life and Times of Warren Gamaliel Harding, 2:225

The Incredible Journey, 1:136

The Incredible Sixties: The Stormy Years That Changed America, 2:241

Independence and After, 2:404

Independence in Latin America, 2:369

Independent Journey: The Life of William O. Douglas, 2:27

India (Caldwell), 2:398

India (Time-Life), 2:86

India: A Country Study, 2:87

India: An Ancient Land, A New Nation, 2:399

India in the 1980s, 2:400

India Remembered, 2:363

India Two Thousand: The Next Fifteen Years, 2:87

India under Indira and Rajiv Gandhi, 2:401

Indian Chiefs, 2:200

The Indian Frontier of the American West, 1846–1890, 2:201

Indian Givers: How the Indians of the Americas Transformed the World, 2:156

Indian Heritage of America, 2:158

The Indian in America, 2:158

Indian Lives: Essays on Nineteenth and Twentieth Century Native American Leaders, 2:155

Indian Place-Names: Their Origin, Evolution, and Meanings, Collected in Kansas from the Siouan, Algonquian, Shoshonean, Caddoan, Iroquoian, and Other Tongues, 1:439

Indian Religions, 2:276

Indian, Soldier, and Settler: Experiences in the Struggles for the American West, 2:201

Indians and Europeans: Selected Articles on Indian-White Relations in Colonial North America, 2:162
Indians Before Columbus: Twenty Thousand Years of North American History Revealed by Archaeology, 2:158
Indians in American History, 2:157
Indians of California: The Changing Image, 2:158
Indians of North America, 2:157
Indians of the Plains, 2:51, 2:201
India's Foreign Policy, 2:404
India's Quest: Being Letters on Indian History, 2:404
Indicators of Social Change: Concepts and Measurements, 2:144
Indira Gandhi, 2:401
Indira Gandhi: The Last Post, 2:401
Indira Gandhi—Selected Speeches and Writings, 1972–77, 2:401
Individual and Community: The Rise of Polis, 800–500 BC, 2:285
The Individual and the Social Self: Unpublished Work of George Herbert Mead, 2:139
Individual Differences in Response to Stress, 2:123
Individual Interests and Collective Action: Selected Essays, 2:144
Individualism Reconsidered, 2:132
Indochina's Refugees: Oral Histories from Laos, Cambodia and Vietnam, 2:399
Indonesia: A Country Study, 2:86
Induction in Geometry, 1:512
Indus Civilization, 2:282
Industrial and Commercial Correspondence of Alexander Hamilton Anticipating His Report on Manufactures, 2:174
The Industrial City, 1820–1870, 2:339
The Industrial Heritage of Britain, 2:339
Industrial Revolution, 2:339
Industrial Revolution in the Eighteenth Century: An Outline of the Beginnings of the Modern Factory System in England, 2:339
Industrial Revolution on the Continent: Germany, France, Russia 1800–1914, 2:339
The Industrial Revolution, Seventeen-Sixty to Eighteen-Thirty, 2:339
Industrialization of Intelligence: Mind and Machine in the Modern Age, 1:581
The Industrialization of the Continental Powers 1780–1914, 2:340
Industry and Empire, 2:339
Inequality and Heterogeneity: A Primitive Theory of Social Structure, 2:144

Infamy: Pearl Harbor and Its Aftermath, 2:385
Inferno, 1:349
Inferno: From an Occult Diary, 1:380
The Infinite Rehearsal, 1:405
Infinite Vistas: New Tools for Astronomy, 2:435
Infinity and the Mind: The Science and Philosophy of the Infinite, 1:498
Inflation: Causes and Effects, 2:63, 2:64, 2:68
Inflation, Exchange Rates, and the World Economy: Lectures on International Monetary Economics, 2:71
The Influence of Geography Upon the History of Mankind, 2:81
The Influence of Sea Power on Ancient History, 2:277
Informal Geometry, 1:511
Information and the Crisis Economy, 1:555
The Information Game: Ethical Issues in a Microchip World, 1:554
The Information Society as Post-Industrial Society, 1:555
Information Sources of Political Science, 2:6
Information Systems Analysis: Introduction to Fourth Generation Technology, 1:558
Information Systems and the Living System, 1:554
An Information Systems Manifesto, 1:538
InfoWorld: A DOS User's Guide to UNIX, 1:562
InfoWorld: Understanding Networks, 1:559
InfoWorld Consumer Product Review 1990, 1:558
Inherit the Wind, 1:436
The Inheritors, 1:89
The Inland Sea, 2:87
An Inland Voyage, 1:58
Innocent Blood, 1:98
Innocent Erendira and Other Stories, 1:404
The Innocents Abroad, 1:181
Innomable, 1:331
Innumeracy: Mathematical Illiteracy and Its Consequences, 1:535
The Inorganic Chemistry of Biological Processes, 2:511
Input Devices, 1:560
Input–Output (Boyd), 1:560
Input–Output (Time-Life), 1:560
Inquiry into Meaning & Truth, 1:503
An Inquiry into the Nature and Causes of the Wealth of Nations, 2:60, 2:61
An Inquiry into the Nature and Causes of the Wealth of Nations: Glasgow Edition, 2:340

Insect-Eating Plants and How to Grow Them, 2:448
The Insect Play, 1:384
Insects, 2:448
Insects of the World, 2:449
Inside an Egg, 2:451
Inside AutoCAD: The Complete AutoCAD Reference Guide, 1:578
Inside Computers: Hardware and Software, 1:556
Inside Nicaragua: Young People's Dreams and Fears, 2:88
Inside Prime Time, 1:466
Inside the Atom, 2:500
Inside the IBM PC, 1:560
Inside the Macintosh, 1:560
Inside the Norton Utilities, 1:574
Inside the Wall Street Journal: The History and the Power of Dow Jones and Company and America's Most Influential Newspaper, 1:458
The Inside Tract: The Complete Guide to Digestive Disorders, 2:561
Insight Guide to Thailand, 2:87
The Insomniac's Dictionary: The Last Word on the Odd Word, 1:440
The Inspector-General and Other Plays, 1:392, 1:393
The Inspired Poetry by Joshua Carducci, 1:349
Instability and Change in the World Economy, 2:57
Instant Eloquence, 1:449
Instant PageMaker (IBM Version 3.0): 20 Ready-To-Run Style Sheets, 1:575
Instant Word Power, 1:440
Instinct and Intelligence, 2:462
The Institutes of the Christian Religion, 2:311
Instructor's Guide to PHYSICAL BEST, 1:568
Integrated Mathematics: Course 3, 1:497
Intellect and Spirit: The Life and Work of Robert Coles, 2:106
Intellectual Origins of the English Revolution, 2:327
Intelligence and Affectivity in Early Childhood: An Experimental Study of Jean Piaget's Object Concept and Object Relationships, 2:111
Intelligence—What Is It, 2:110
Intelligent Databases, 1:572
Intelligent Life in the Universe, 2:480
The Intelligent Universe, 2:495
Intensive Care, 1:138
Interaction Process Analysis, 2:124
Interaction Ritual: Essays in Face-to-Face Behavior, 2:139
Interactive Programming Environments, 1:563

Interactive Video, 1:580
Interactive Writing, 1:570
The Interest Group Society, 2:39
Interesting People: Black American History Makers, 2:155
Inter/Media: Interpersonal Communication in a Media World, 1:445
International Conference on Distributed Computing Systems, Ninth, 1:585
The International Economic Order: Essays on Financial Crisis and International Public Goods, 2:72
International Economics: A Self-Teaching Introduction to the Basic Concepts, 2:71
The International Economy, 2:72
International Encyclopedia of Population, 2:124
International Law: Cases and Materials, 2:36
The International Money Game, 2:71
International Peacekeeping, 1918–86, 2:277
International Relations: Contemporary Theory and Practice, 2:7, 2:36
Internationalism, 2:36
The Interplay of East and West, 2:74
The Interplay of Influence: Mass Media and Their Public in News, Advertising, Politics, 1:454
The Interpretation of Cézanne, 2:349
The Interpretation of Cultures, 2:43
The Interpretation of Dreams, 2:117
Interpretation of Ordinary Landscapes, 2:93
The Interpreters, 1:417
Interpreting the City: An Urban Geography, 2:93
Intervention: How to Help Someone Who Doesn't Want Help, 2:555
The Intimate Journals of Paul Gauguin, 2:353
The Intimate Life of Ancient Rome from the Personal Letters of the Younger Pliny, 2:295
The Intimate Machine: Close Encounters with Computers and Robots, 1:582
Into the Twilight Zone, 1:486
Into the Unknown: The Story of Exploration, 2:76
Introducing India, 2:276
Introduction of African Art of Kenya, Zaire, and Nigeria, 2:276
An Introduction of Haiku: An Anthology of Poems from Bashō to Shiki, 1:425
Introduction to African Civilization, 2:300
An Introduction to American Movies, 1:468
Introduction to Analysis, 1:524
Introduction to Artificial Intelligence, 1:581

Introduction to Artificial Intelligence and Expert Systems, 1:584
An Introduction to Artificial Intelligence: Can Computers Think, 1:580
An Introduction to Bacteria, 2:443
Introduction to Bryology, 2:448
Introduction to Calculus and Analysis, 1:524
An Introduction to Cancer Biology: Readings from Scientific American, 2:562
Introduction to Chemical Kinetics, 2:508
Introduction to Compiler Construction with UNIX, 1:586
Introduction to Computer Science, 1:538
An Introduction to Computers: Developing Computer Literacy, 1:557
Introduction to Computers in Speech, Language, and Hearing, 1:579
Introduction to Ecological Biochemistry, 2:511
An Introduction to Electrochemical Science, 2:508
Introduction to Film, 1:469
Introduction to Finite Mathematics, 1:529
Introduction to Geographic Field Methods and Techniques, 2:92
Introduction to Geometry, 1:511
Introduction to Information Theory: Symbols, Signals, and Noise, 1:550
An Introduction to Language, 1:434
Introduction to Marine Biology, 2:465
Introduction to Marine Ecology, 2:465
Introduction to Mathematical Philosophy, 1:503
An Introduction to Mathematics, 1:498
Introduction to Modern Polish Literature, 1:383
Introduction to Money and Banking, 2:70
Introduction to Oceanography, 2:486
An Introduction to Operating Systems, 1:561
An Introduction to Plant Taxonomy, 2:441
Introduction to Positive Philosophy, 2:126
An Introduction to Psychology, 2:96, 2:114
An Introduction to Psychopathology, 2:121
Introduction to Sensation Perception, 2:113
Introduction to Social Research, 2:125
Introduction to Spanish-American Literature, 1:399
Introduction to Structured Programming, 1:563
Introduction to System Software, 1:585
Introduction to the Algae, 2:447
Introduction to the Analysis of the Infinite, 1:526
Introduction to the Code of Maimonides (Mishneh Torah), 2:303

An Introduction to the Physical Chemistry of Biological Organization, 2:511
An Introduction to the Principles of Morals and Legislation, 2:7
An Introduction to the Psychology of Learning, 2:112
An Introduction to the Study of Society, 2:125
An Introduction to the Study of Speech, 2:50
An Introduction to the Theory of Computation, 1:585
Introduction to the Theory of Employment, 2:60
Introduction to the Theory of Numbers, 1:497
An Introduction to the World's Oceans, 2:486
Introduction to Theories of Personality, 2:114
An Introduction to Thermal Physics, 2:516
Introduction to United States Public Documents, 2:6
Introduction to VAX-VMS, 1:562
An Introduction to Virgil's Aeneid, 1:325
Introduction to World Peace Through World Law, 2:36
Introductory Analysis, 1:524
Introductory Cartography, 2:92, 2:488
Introductory Geometrics, 1:513
Introductory Mathematical Analysis, 1:524
Intruder in the Dust, 1:219
Intuition, 1:522
The Invasion from Mars, 2:130
Invasion of Poland. Turning Points in World War II, 2:385
Inventing a Word: An Anthology of Twentieth Century Puerto Rican Poetry, 1:399
Inventing America: Jefferson's Declaration of Independence, 2:164
Inventing the American Woman: A Perspective on Women's History, 2:155
Inventions: The Patented Works of R. Buckminster Fuller, 1:522
The Inventions of Leonardo da Vinci, 2:316
The Inventors: Nobel Prizes in Chemistry, Physics, and Medicine, 2:431
Inventors and Discoverers: Changing Our World, 2:154
Investigating Art: A Practical Guide for Young People, 2:415
The Investigation (Lem), 1:386
The Investigation: A Play (Weiss), 1:372, 1:373
Investigations on the Theory of the Brownian Movement, 2:520
The Invincible Armada and Elizabethan England, 2:326

The Invincibles, 1:109
The Invisible Hand: How Free Trade Is
  Choking the Life Out of America, 2:72
The Invisible Man (Ellison), 1:217, 1:218
The Invisible Man (Wells), 1:129
Invitation to a Voyage: Selected Poems,
  1:330
An Invitation to Computers, 1:557
Invitation to Sociology: A Humanistic
  Perspective, 2:125
Inward Bound: Of Matter and Forces in
  the Physical World, 2:498
Ionization Constants of Inorganic Acids
  and Bases in Aqueous Solutions, 2:508
Iphigenia, 1:339
Iphigénie, 1:339
Ira Hayes: Pima Marine, 2:235
The Iran-Contra Arms Scandal, 2:37
The Iran-Iraq War, 2:89, 2:412
Ireland Before and After the Famine:
  Explorations in Economic History,
  1800–1925, 2:276
Iris Murdoch, 1:108
The Irish Countryman: An
  Anthropological Study, 2:50
Iron and the Industrial Revolution, 2:340
Iron Bridge to Crystal Palace: Impact and
  Images of the Industrial Revolution,
  2:339
The Iron Curtain: Churchill, America, and
  the Origins of the Cold War, 2:386,
  2:388
Irony in the Mind's Life, 1:70
Iroquois in the American Revolution,
  2:164
Irving Berlin and Ragtime America, 2:265
Is Sex Necessary? Or, Why You Feel the
  Way You Do, 1:290
Is That You, Miss Blue, 1:248
Is This Kid "Crazy"? Understanding
  Unusual Behavior, 2:98
Isaac Asimov (Fiedler), 1:194
Isaac Asimov (Olander and Martin), 2:434
Isaac Asimov: The Foundations of Science
  Fiction, 1:194
Isaac Bashevis Singer, 1:388
Isaac Bashevis Singer; The Story of a
  Storyteller, 1:388
Isaac Newton, 2:516
Isadora Speaks, 2:266
The I-Search Paper, 1:483
Ishi, Last of His Tribe, 2:45
Islam: The Straight Path, 2:274
Islam and the West: A Historical Cultural
  Survey, 2:274
Island, 1:95
Island Fighting, 2:383
Island of Cuba, 2:78
The Island of Dr. Moreau, 1:129
Island of the Blue Dolphins, 1:271

The Island World of the Pacific Ocean,
  2:91
Ismaelillo, 2:370
Isotopes in Biochemistry, 2:509
Israel: A Political History, 2:412
Israel: Years of Challenge, 2:412
Israeli Poetry: A Contemporary
  Anthology, 1:420
The Issa Valley, 1:386
Issues in New Information Technology,
  2:130
It, 1:249
It All Started with Stones and Clubs,
  1:192
It Can't Happen Here, 1:256
It Changed My Life, 2:243
It Is So (If You Think So), 1:351
It Will Never Happen to Me, 2:555
It Won't Happen to Me: Teenagers Talk
  About Pregnancy, 2:543
It Won't Happen to Me: True Stories of
  Teen Alcohol & Drug Abuse, 2:555
The Italian, 1:28
Italian Art, 1250–1550: The Relation of
  Art to Life and Society, 2:310
The Italian Campaign, 2:383
Italian Folktales, 1:347
The Italian Girl, 1:108
Italian Grammar, 1:346
The Italian Language Today, 1:346
Italian Phonetics, Diction and Intonation,
  1:346
Italian Poetry, 1960–1980, 1:348
The Italian Renaissance Reader, 1:347
Italian Renaissance Tales, 1:347
Italian Short Stories, 1:348
Italian Stories, 1:347
Italian Syntax, 1:346
Italian Writers of the Seventeenth and
  Eighteenth Centuries, 1:348
Italy at War, 2:383
Italy in the Age of the Risorgimento
  1790–1870, 2:340
Itch, Sniffle, and Sneeze, 2:562
It's a Free Country! A Young Person's
  Guide to Politics and Elections, 2:13,
  2:40
It's All Elementary, 2:497
It's All Relative: Einstein's Theory of
  Relativity, 2:520
It's Nation Time, 1:197
It's Not the End of the World, 1:201
It's Raining Cats and Dogs: All Kinds of
  Weather and Why We Have It, 2:484
It's Raining Cats and Dogs . . . and Other
  Beastly Expressions, 1:432
It's Snowing, 2:484
Ivan P. Pavlov: Toward a Scientific
  Psychology and Psychiatry, 2:101
Ivan Pavlov, 2:100, 2:464

Ivanhoe, 1:36
Ivanov, 1:390
Izzy, Willy-Nilly, 1:294

J

J. B., 1:261
J. B. Priestley, 1:115
J. B. Priestley's Plays, 1:115
J. D. Salinger, 1:283
J. M. Keynes in Retrospect: The Legacy of the Keynesian Revolution, 2:67
J. M. Synge, 1:123
J. M. W. Turner: A Wonderful Range of Mind, 2:358
J. R. R. Tolkien, 1:126
J. S. Bach, 2:534, 2:535
Jack London, 1:257
Jack London: Adventures, Ideas, and Fiction, 1:257
Jack London: An American Myth, 1:257
Jack London: Sailor on Horseback, 1:257
Jackaroo, 1:294
Jackson and Calhoun, 2:181
Jacksonian Democracy, 2:180
Jacksonian Era: Eighteen Twenty-Eight to Eighteen Forty-Eight, 2:180
Jacob Faithful, 1:56
Jacob Have I Loved, 1:484; 2:235
Jacob's Room, 1:132
Jacques and His Master, 1:385
Jacques Cousteau's Calypso, 2:487
The Jade Steps: A Ritual Life of the Aztecs, 2:298
Jailbird, 1:295
Jake's Thing, 1:65
Jamaica Inn, 1:80
James A. Garfield, 2:195
James A. Garfield—His Life & Times: A Pictorial History, 2:195
James A. Michener, 1:265
James A. Michener: A Biography, 1:265
James Baldwin, 1:195
James Baldwin: Artist on Fire, 1:195
James Baldwin: The Legacy, 1:195
James Boswell: A Short Life, 1:27
James Bradley Thayer, Oliver Wendell Holmes, and Felix Frankfurter on John Marshall, 2:30
James Carter, 2:256
James Dickey, 1:215
James Herriot's Dog Stories, 1:93
James Herriot's Yorkshire, 1:93
James Joyce, 1:99
James Madison, 2:177
James Madison, 1751–1836: Chronology, Documents, Bibliographical Aids, 2:177
James Monroe, 2:178

James Monroe: Fifth President of the United States, 2:178
James Russell Lowell, 1:161
James Russell Lowell: Portrait of a Many Sided Man, 1:161
James Thurber, 1:291
James Thurber: 92 Stories, 1:290
James Weldon Johnson, 1:245
Jamestown, Fifteen Forty-Four to Sixteen Ninety-Nine, 2:161
Jane Addams: Social Reformer Feminist, 2:208
Jane Addams and the Men of the Chicago School, 1892–1918, 2:208
Jane Austen: Her Life, 1:20
Jane Brody's Good Food Book, 2:450
Jane Brody's Nutrition Book, 2:549
Jane Brody's The New York Times Guide to Personal Health, 2:530
Jane Eyre, 1:41, 1:42
Jane Eyre: Portrait of a Life, 1:42
Jane of Lantern Hill, 1:143
Jane Talbot, 1:152
Japan (Reischauer), 2:399
Japan (Stefoff), 2:400
Japan (Time-Life), 2:274
Japan: A Country Study, 2:86
Japan: A Postindustrial Power, 2:86, 2:398
Japan: The Fragile Superpower, 2:86, 2:398
Japan: The Story of a Nation, 2:399
Japan: Tradition and Transformation, 2:399
Japan and Its World: Two Centuries of Change, 2:274
Japan at War, 2:383
Japanese Culture, 2:87, 2:277, 2:309
The Japanese Educational Challenge: A Commitment to Children, 2:87, 2:400
Japanese Love Poems, 1:425
Japanese Models of Conflict Resolution, 2:132
Japanese Poetry: The Uta, 1:425
Japanese Religion: Unity and Diversity, 2:274
Japanese Today, 2:399
Japanese Women: Constraint and Fulfillment, 2:399
Japan's Longest Day: Surrender—The Last Twenty-Four Hours Through Japanese Eyes, 2:384
Japan's Military Masters: The Army in Japanese Life, 2:375
Japan's New Order in East Asia: Its Rise and Fall, 1937–1945, 2:374
Jargon of Authenticity, 1:433
Jawaharlal Nehru, 2:404
Jawaharlal Nehru: An Anthology, 2:404
Jawaharlal Nehru of India, 1889–1964, 2:404
Jawaharlal Nehru's Writings, 2:404

Jazz: Its Evolution and Essence, 2:261
The Jazz Age: Popular Music in the 1920s, 2:227
Jazz Bibliography: An International Literature on Jazz, Blues, Spirituals, Gospel, and Ragtime Music with a Selected List of Works on the Social and Cultural Background from the Beginning to the Present, 2:274
Jazz Country, 1:237, 1:238
Jazz Styles: History and Analysis, 2:261
The Jazz Tradition, 2:227
Je Suis Le Cahier: The Sketchbooks of Picasso, 2:421
Jean Anouilh, 1:328
Jean Carper's Total Nutrition Guide: The Complete Official Report on Healthful Eating, 2:549
Jean-Jacques Rousseau, 2:11
Jean-Paul Sartre, 1:340
Jean Piaget: The Man and His Ideas, 2:112
The Jedera Adventure, 1:188
Jefferson Davis, 2:192
Jelly Roll, Jabbo, and Fats: Nineteen Portraits in Jazz, 2:225
Jennie Gerhardt, 1:217
Jenny, 1:380
Jeremy Bentham: His Life and Work, 2:8
Jerusalem, 2:90
Jerusalem the Golden, 1:80
Jesse Jackson, 2:258
The Jesse Jackson Phenomenon: The Crisis of Purpose in Afro-American Politics, 2:258
The Jesuits in North America, 2:161
A Jew Today, 1:302
The Jewel in the Crown, 1:118; 2:363
The Jewish Americans, 2:207
The Jews in Their Land, 2:412
The Jews of Silence, 1:302
Jill, 1:100
Jim Fixx's Second Book of Running, 2:551
Jimmy Carter, 2:256
Jimmy Carter, President, 2:256
Jimmy's Blues: Selected Poems, 1:195
Joan Robinson and Modern Economic Theory, 2:60
Johann Sebastian Bach, 2:334
Johann Sebastian Bach: His Life, Art and Work, 2:334
Johann Sebastian Bach: Life, Times, Influence, 2:335
Johann Sebastian Bach: The Culmination of an Era, 2:335
Johannes Brahms: His Work and Personality, 2:348
John Adams, 2:171
John Adams: American Revolutionary Leader and President, 2:171

John Adams: Second President of the United States, 2:172
John Brown's Body, 1:200
John Bunyan, 1:21
John Bunyan: The Writer of Pilgrim's Progress, 1:21
John C. Calhoun, 2:181
John Cabot: The Discoverer of North America and Sebastian His Son: A Chapter in Maritime History of England Under the Tudors, 1496–1557, 2:157
John Cage, 2:262
John Calvin, 2:311
John Calvin: A Sixteenth-Century Portrait, 2:311
John Cheever, 1:211
John Constable's Clouds, 2:351
John Constable's Correspondence, 2:351
John Dalton: Critical Assessments of His Life and Science. Monographs in the History of Science, 2:502
John Dalton and the Atom, 2:502
John Dalton and the Atomic Theory, 2:502
John Dewey, 2:220
John Dewey: His Thought and Influence, 2:220
John Dewey as Educator: His Design for Work in Education (1894–1904), 2:220
John Donne: A Life, 1:10
John Donne's Poetry: An Annotated Text with Critical Essays, 1:10
John Dryden, 1:24
John F. Kennedy (Kelly), 2:247
John F. Kennedy (Langley), 2:248
John Ford, 1:470
John Foster Dulles: Master of Brinkmanship and Diplomacy, 2:23
John Foster Dulles: The Road to Power, 2:23
John Foster Dulles and the Diplomacy of the Cold War, 2:23
John Fowles, 1:86
John Galsworthy: A Biography, 1:88
John Galsworthy's Life and Art: An Alien's Fortress, 1:88
John Greenleaf Whittier, 1:166
John Huston, 1:472
John James Audubon, 2:188
John Keats, 1:35
John Kenneth Galbraith, 2:66
John Kenneth Galbraith and His Critics, 2:67
John Kepler, 2:474
John Kobal Presents the Top 100 Movies, 1:468
John L. Lewis: Labor Leader, 2:230
John Le Carré, 1:102
John Locke, 2:18
John Locke: A Biography, 2:18

John Locke's Liberalism, 2:18
John Marshall: Boy of Young America, 2:30
John Marshall: Defender of the Constitution, 2:30
John Millington Synge, 1:123
John Milton: A Reader's Guide to His Poetry, 1:14
John Milton: Complete Poems and Major Prose, 1:14
John Milton: Poetry, 1:14
John Milton: The Inner Life, 1:14
John Muir to Yosemite and Beyond: Writings from the Years 1863–1875, 2:221
John Osborne, 1:112
John Paul Jones: A Sailor's Biography, 2:164
John Paul Jones: Hero of the Seas, 2:163
John Philip Sousa, American Phenomenon, 2:216
John Quincy Adams, 2:173
John Quincy Adams: Sixth President of the United States, 2:173
John Steinbeck, 1:289
John Updike, 1:293
John Von Neumann and Norbert Wiener: From Mathematics to the Technologies of Life and Death, 1:538, 1:553
John Webster, 1:18
Johnny Deadline, Reporter: The Best of Bob Greene, 1:480
Johnny Panic and the Bible of Dreams: Short Stories, Prose and Diary Excerpts, 1:277
Johnny Tremain, 2:164
Johnson: Selected Writings, 1:26
Johnson and His Age, 1:26
The Johnson & Johnson First Aid Book, 2:567
The Joke, 1:385
The Joliet-Marquette Expedition, 1673, 2:158
Jomo Kenyatta, 2:394
Jomo Kenyatta: Towards Truth About "The Light of Kenya," 2:394
Jonathan Edwards, 1:154
Jonathan Edwards' Moral Thought and Its British Context, 2:161
Jonathan Swift, 1:30
Jordan: A Country Study, 2:89
Jorge Luis Borges (Bloom), 1:400
Jorge Luis Borges (Murray), 1:400
Jo's Boys, 1:168
José Martí, 2:371
José Martí: Architect of Cuba's Freedom, 2:371
José Martí: Major Poems, 2:370

José Martí: Mentor of the Cuban Nation, 2:371
José Martí: Revolutionary Democrat, 2:371
José Martí and the Cuban Revolution Retraced, 2:371
Joseph Andrews, 1:24
Joseph Conrad, 1:77
Joseph Heller, 1:234
Joseph Pulitzer, His Life and Letters, 2:204
Joseph Stalin, 2:380
Joseph Stalin and Communist Russia, 2:380
Joshua Then and Now, 1:146
Journal (During His First Voyage, 1492–1493): And Documents Relating to the Voyages of John Cabot and Gaspar Corte Real, 2:159
Journal of a Mission to the Interior of Africa, 2:368
Journal of a Tour to the Hebrides with Samuel Johnson, 1:26
Journal of a Voyage to the South Seas in H.M.S. Endeavour, 2:322
Journal of H.M.S. Endeavour, 1768–1771, 2:321
The Journal of Major George Washington, Sent by the Hon. Robert Dinwiddie to the Commandant of the French Forces, 1754, 2:179
Journal of the Federal Convention, 2:177
Journal of the First Voyage to America, 2:159
A Journal of the Plague Year, 1:22, 1:23; 2:557
Journal of the Proceedings of the President: 1793–1797, 2:179
Journal to Stella, 1:30
Journals of Lewis and Clark: A New Selection, 2:176
Journals of Susanna Moodie: Poems, 1:135, 1:136
The Journals of Sylvia Plath, 1:277
Journey, 2:563
The Journey Continued, 1:416
Journey Home, 2:236
Journey into Sexuality: An Exploratory Voyage, 2:138
Journey Into Space: The First Thirty Years of Space Exploration, 2:242
Journey to a War, 1:96
Journey to the Center of the Earth, 1:342, 1:343
Journey to the Stars: Space Exploration—Tomorrow and Beyond, 2:481
The Joy of Claude Debussy, 2:418
The Joy of Music, 2:265
The Joy of Running, 2:551
Joyce Cary, 1:72

The Joys of Motherhood, 1:413
The Joys of Yiddish, 1:431
The Joys of Yinglish, 1:431
Juan Rodriguez Cabrillo, 2:158
Jubilee, 1:297, 1:298
Jude the Obscure, 1:52
Judy Blume's Story, 1:202
Jules Verne and His Work, 1:343
The Julian Messner Illustrated Dictionary
   of Science, 2:433
Julius Caesar (Bruns), 2:292
Julius Caesar (Shakespeare), 2:288,
   2:397
Julius Caesar and the Foundation of the
   Roman Imperial System, 2:292
The July Monarchy: A Political History of
   France 1830–1848, 2:332
The July Plot, 2:385
July's People, 1:414
Jumpers, 1:122
Jung: A Biography, 2:121
Jung: Man and Myth, 2:121
Jung and Feminism: Liberating
   Archetypes, 2:121
Jung and the Post-Jungians, 2:121
Jungian Psychology in Perspective,
   2:121
The Jungle, 1:287; 2:62, 2:219
The Jungle Book, 1:55
Junípero Serra: God's Pioneer, 2:160
Junípero Serra: The Illustrated Story of the
   Franciscan Founder of California's
   Missions, 2:160
Junípero Serra, the Vatican, and
   Enslavement Theology, 2:160
Junius Over Far, 1:230
Juno and the Paycock, 1:108
Jupiter: King of the Gods, Giant of the
   Planets, 2:475
The Jurisprudence of John Marshall,
   2:30
Just Above My Head, 1:195
Just Give Me a Cool Drink of Water 'fore
   I Diiie, 1:191, 1:192
Just So Stories, 1:55
Justice and Her Brothers, 1:230
Justice at War: The Inside Story of the
   Japanese American Internment, 2:235
Justice in America: Courts, Lawyers, and
   the Judicial Process, 2:26
Justice Oliver Wendell Holmes: A
   Biography, 2:29
Justice Oliver Wendell Holmes: The
   Proving Years 1870–1882, 2:29
Justice Sandra Day O'Connor, 2:257
Justice Without Revenge, 1:358
The Justices of the United States Supreme
   Court, 1789–1978, 2:5
Justinian and Theodora, 2:301

K

Kabuki: Eighteen Traditional Dramas,
   1:425
Kaffir Boy, 2:85, 2:393
Kafka, 1:369
Kaiser vs. Bismarck, 2:342
Kalevala, 1:160
The Kandy Kolored Tangerine-Flake
   Streamline Baby, 1:479
Kangaroo, 1:101
Kangaroos, Opossums, and Other
   Marsupials, 2:449
Karel Capek, 1:385
Karen Horney, 2:119
Karen Horney: Gentle Rebel of
   Psychoanalysis, 2:119
Karl Marx: A Reader, 2:59
Karl Marx: His Life and Environment,
   2:59, 2:339
Kate Chopin, 1:173
Katherine Ann Porter (Bloom), 1:279
Katherine Ann Porter (Hendrick), 1:280
Katherine Mansfield, 1:142
Katherine Mansfield: A Biography, 1:142
Katherine Mansfield: A Study of the Short
   Fiction, 1:142
Kathy Sue Laudermilk, I Love You, 1:480
Katz and Maus, 1:367
Keep the Aspidistra Flying, 1:111
Keeping Promises: The Challenge of a
   Sober Parent, 2:555
Kenilworth, 1:36
Kennedy, 2:248
Kenya: The Magic Land, 2:393
Kepler's Dream, 2:474
Kerouac: A Biography, 1:247
Kerouac's Crooked Road: Development of
   a Fiction, 1:247
The Kestrel, 1:188
The Keys of the Kingdom, 1:78
Keywords: A Vocabulary of Culture and
   Society, 1:437
Khrushchev: A Career, 2:392
Khrushchev: The Years in Power, 2:392
Khrushchev and Brezhnev as Leaders:
   Building Authority in Soviet Politics,
   2:389, 2:392
Khrushchev and the Soviet Leadership,
   1957–1964, 2:392
Khrushchev Remembers, 2:392
Khrushchev Speaks: Selected Speeches,
   Articles and Press Conferences,
   1949–1961, 2:392
Kidnapped, 1:58
Kids, Teachers, and Computers: A Guide
   to Computers in the Elementary School,
   1:570

Killing Pain Without Prescription: A New and Simple Way to Free Yourself from Headache, Backache, and Other Sources of Chronic Pain, 2:561
Kilmeny of the Orchard, 1:143
Kim, 1:55
Kind and Unusual Punishment: The Prison Business, 2:133
Kind Words: A Thesaurus of Euphemisms, 1:437
Kindergarten Chats and Other Writings, 2:217
Kinderlied, 1:367
King and People in Provincial Massachusetts, 2:161
King Arthur, 2:338
King Arthur and His Knights, 1:7
King Coal: A Novel, 1:287
King Jesus, 1:90
King Lazarus, 1:412
The King Must Die, 1:318
King of the Fields, 1:387
King Philip's War, 2:161
King Solomon's Mines, 1:50, 1:51
King Solomon's Ring, 2:100, 2:464
Kingdom of Fear: The World of Stephen King, 1:249
The Kingdom of This World, 1:401
Kingdoms of Asia, the Middle East, and Africa: An Illustrated Encyclopedia of Ruling Monarchs from Ancient Times to the Present, 2:274
Kingdoms of Europe: An Illustrated Encyclopedia of Ruling Monarchs from Ancient Times to the Present, 2:274
Kings and Queens of England, 2:273
Kings and Queens of Great Britain: A Genealogical Chart Showing Their Descent and Relationship, 2:277
The King's Fifth, 1:271; 2:158
The King's General, 1:80
Kingsley Amis, 1:65
Kinship and Marriage: An Anthropological Perspective, 2:52
Kipling: The Critical Heritage, 1:55
Kipling Considered, 1:55
Kipps: The Story of a Simple Soul, 1:129
Kiss, Kiss, 1:79
Kiss of the Spider Woman, 1:409
Kissinger, 2:39
The Kissinger Legacy: American Middle East Policy, 2:38
Klass: How Russians Really Live, 2:92, 2:406
Klemens von Metternich, 2:333
The Knight in History, 2:305
Knights, 2:306
Knights and Castles, 2:306

The Knights, The Peace, The Birds, The Assembly-Women, Wealth, 1:313
Know About Smoking, 2:556
Knowing the Atomic Nucleus, 2:500
Knowing the Unknowable God: Ibn-Sina, Maimonides, Aquinas, 2:303, 2:307
Knowing Your Trees, 2:447
Knowledge for What? The Place of Social Science in American Culture, 2:131
The Knowledge of Language: Its Nature, Origin, and Use, 1:435; 2:50
Knowledge Systems for Business: Integrating Expert Systems and MIS, 1:583
Kodansha Encyclopedia of Japan, 2:275
Koko's Kitten, 1:448
Koko's Story, 1:448
Kommando: German Special Forces of World War II, 2:384
Konrad Lorenz, 2:464
Konrad Lorenz: The Man and His Ideas, 2:464
Kon-Tiki: Across the Pacific by Raft, 2:411
The Korean War, 2:238, 2:388
Kosmos, 2:77
Krakatit, 1:385
Krapp's Last Tape, 1:331
The Kreutzer Sonata and Other Stories, 1:397
Kristin Lavransdatter, 1:380, 1:381
The Ku Klux Klan: America's Recurring Nightmare, 2:153
"Kubla Khan," 1:34
Kublai Khan: Mongol Emperor, 2:309
A Kurt Goldstein Reader: The Shaping of Neuropsychology, 2:121
Kurt Vonnegut, 1:296
Kurt Vonnegut, Jr, 1:296
Kwame Nkrumah: The Anatomy of an African Dictatorship, 2:396

L

La agonía del cristianismo, 1:360
La Bête Humaine, 1:344, 1:345
La casa de Bernarda Alba, 1:358
La chartreuse de Parme, 1:342
La chute, 1:333
La cousine Bette, 1:329
La débâcle, 1:345
La Dorotea, 1:358
La Follette's Autobiography: A Personal Narrative of Political Experiences, 2:220
La Francesilla, 1:358
La Giara, 1:351

La increíble y triste historia de la cándida Erendira y su abuela desalmada, 1:404
La muerte de Artemio Cruz, 1:403
La nausée, 1:340
La peste, 1:333
La porte étroite, 1:336
La révolte des anges, 1:335
La Salle and the Discovery of the Great West, 2:158
La terre, 1:345
La ville radieuse (The Radiant City), 2:419
La Vita Nuova (The New Life), 1:349
La zapatera prodigiosa, 1:358
Labor and the Common Welfare, 2:224
Labor Economics, 2:70
Labor Economics and Labor Relations, 2:70
Labor in America, 2:204
The Labor Injunction, 2:28
Laboratory Experiments and General Papers, 2:465
The Labouring Classes in Early Industrial England 1750–1850, 2:339
Labyrinths: Selected Short Stories and Other Writings, 1:399
The Ladies of Seneca Falls: The Birth of the Woman's Rights Movement. Studies in the Life of Women, 2:184
Lady Frederick, 1:106
The Lady from Dubuque: A Play in Two Acts, 1:186
The Lady from the Sea, 1:377
The Lady in the Lake, 1:210
The Lady of the Lake, 1:36
The Lady of the Shroud, 1:59
Lady Oracle, 1:135
Lady Windermere's Fan, 1:62
Lady's Maid, 1:43
The Lady's Not for Burning, 1:87
Lafcadio's Adventures, 1:336
Lagar, 1:405
Laid Back in Washington, 1:488
The Lair of the White Worm, 1:59
"The Lake Isle of Innisfree," 1:133
The Lake Region of Central Africa: A Picture of Exploration, 2:364
Lake Wobegone Days, 1:461
Lakes, Peaks, and Prairies, 2:83
L'Allegro, 1:13
Lamarck, the Mythical Precursor: A Study of the Relations Between Science and Ideology, 2:459
Lamb's Poetry for Children, 1:35
Lament for an African Pol, 1:412
The Land, 1:76
Land and Labor in Latin America, 2:88
Land and Life: A Selection from the Writings of Carl Ortwin Sauer, 2:80
Land and People of Afghanistan, 2:89

Land and People of Cuba, 2:88
Land and People of France, 2:88
Land and People of Kenya, 2:85, 2:393
The Land of Oz, 1:198
Land of the Free, 1:261
Land of the Iron Dragon, 2:202
Landforms and Landscapes, 2:83
The Landing of the Pilgrims, 2:161
Landlocked, 1:103
The Landmark History of the American People, 2:152
The Landscape of Memory, 2:545
The Landscape of the Brontës, 1:43
Langston Hughes, 1:241
The Langston Hughes Reader, 1:241
Language, 2:50
Language and Class in Victorian England, 1:437
Language and Myth, 2:50
Language and Politics, 1:435
Language and Responsibility, 1:435
Language and Situation: Language Varieties and Their Social Contexts, 1:437
Language and Social Identity, 2:50
The Language and Thought of the Child, 2:111
Language Habits in Human Affairs: An Introduction to General Semantics, 1:437
Language in Action, 1:438
Language in America: A Report on Our Deteriorating Semantic Environment, 1:443
Language in Thought and Action, 1:438
Language in Uniform: A Reader on Propaganda, 1:440
Language, Mathematics, and Linguistics, 1:529
The Language of Social Research: A Reader in the Methodology of Social Research, 2:125
The Language of Television, 1:468
The Language of the Night: Essays on Fantasy and Science Fiction, 1:482
The Language of Wisdom and Folly, 1:437
The Languages of Italy, 1:346
Lao-Tzu: My Words Are Very Easy to Understand, 2:284
Lao Tzu and Taoism, 2:281
Laptop User's Guide, 1:558
The Lark, 1:328
The Larousse Guide to Weather Forecasting, 2:484
Laser Printer Bible, 1:561
The LaserJet Handbook: A Complete Guide to Hewlett-Packard Printers, 1:561
Lasers and Holographic Data Processing, 1:578

L'Assommoir, 1:344, 1:345
The Last Circle, 1:200
The Last Crusade: The War on
    Consumption, Eighteen Seventy-two to
    Nineteen Fifty-four, 2:567
The Last Days of The New Yorker, 1:455
Last Days of the Sioux Nation, 2:201
Last Days of the Third Reich: Collapse of
    Nazi Germany, 2:384
The Last Half Century: Societal Change
    and Politics in America, 2:145
The Last Hero: Charles A. Lindberg, 2:226
The Last Hurrah, 2:40
Last Journals of David Livingstone in
    Central Africa from 1865 to His Death,
    2:367
The Last Leaf, 1:178
The Last Lion: Winston Spencer Churchill
    Visions of Glory, 1874–1932, 2:386
The Last Nine Days of the Bismarck, 1:85
The Last of the Mohicans, 2:163
The Last of the Wine, 1:318
The Last One Hundred Days, 2:385
The Last Place on Earth, 2:496
Last Poems (Housman), 1:53
Last Rambles Amongst the Indians of the
    Rocky Mountains and the Andes, 2:188
The Last Ride of Wild Bill and Eleven
    Narrative Poems, 1:206
The Last September, 1:69
Last Tales, (Dinesen), 1:376
The Last Tycoon, 1:222
The Last Year of Malcolm X: The
    Evolution of a Revolutionary, 1:450
Late and Posthumous Poems 1968–1974
    (Neruda), 1:407
The Late Bourgeois World, 1:414
The Late Mattia Pascal, 1:351
Late Picasso: Paintings, Sculpture,
    Drawings, Prints 1953–1972, 2:421
Later Collected Verse (Service), 1:146
Latin America, 2:78
Latin America: A Concise Interpretive
    History, 2:408
Latin America: Between the Eagle and the
    Bear, 2:408
Latin America: Economic Development
    and Regional Differences, 2:88, 2:409
Latin America: The Development of Its
    Civilization, 2:272
Latin America in the Twentieth Century,
    2:88
Latin America, 1987, 2:88
Latin American Civilization: History and
    Society, 1492 to the Present, 2:275
Latin Journey: Cuban and Mexican
    Immigrants in the United States, 2:136
Latin Literature, 1:320
Laugh with Leacock, 1:141

Laughable Loves, 1:385
Laughing to Keep from Crying, 1:241
Lavoisier: Seventeen Forty-three to
    Seventeen Ninety-four, 2:500
Lavoisier and the Chemistry of Life: An
    Exploration of Scientific Creativity,
    2:500
Law and Politics, 2:28
Law and Politics in the United States: An
    Introduction, 2:7, 2:33
Lawrence Ferlinghetti: Poet at Large, 1:221
Lawrence of Arabia, 2:373
Lawrence of Arabia: A Biographical
    Enquiry, 2:373
Lawrence: The Story of His Life, 2:373
Laws of Media: The New Science, 1:454;
    2:130
The Laws of the Land: The Evolution of
    Our Legal System, 2:17
Laws of Thought, 1:507
Laxdaela Saga, 1:373
The Lay of the Last Minstrel, 1:36
The Lay of the Love and Death of Cornet
    Christopher Rilke, 1:371
The Lays of Beleriand, 1:125
LBJ: The White House Years, 2:246
Le bon Leviathan, 1:332
Le bourgeois gentilhomme, 1:338
Le comte de Monte Cristo, 1:334
Le Corbusier, 2:419
Le Corbusier: Architect, Painter, Writer,
    2:420
Le Corbusier: Elements of a Synthesis,
    2:420
Le Corbusier: Ideas and Forms, 2:419
Le Corbusier in Perspective, 2:420
Le Corbusier Sketchbooks, 2:419
Le cousin Pons, 1:329
Le livre de mon ami, 1:335
Le malade imaginaire, 1:339
Le misanthrope, 1:339
Le Monde, 1:515
Le Morte D'Arthur, 1:5, 1:7
Le Père Goriot (Old Man Goriot), 1:329
Le planète des singes, 1:332
Le pont de la rivière Kwai, 1:332
Le Roman de la Rose, 1:327
Le roman expérimental (The Experimental
    Novel), 1:344
Le rouge et le noir, 1:342
Le sauvage, 1:328
Le spleen de Paris, 1:330
Le Tartuffe, 1:339
Le tour du monde en 80 jours, 1:343
Le voyageur sans bagages, 1:328
Leader of the Band, 1:128
Leaders, 2:254
Leadership Training in Adaptive Physical
    Education, 1:569

Leaf Storm and Other Stories, 1:403, 1:404
Leaflets: Poems 1965–1968, 1:281
The League of Nations: Its Life and Times, 1920–1946, 2:224
The Lean Years: A History of the American Worker 1920–1933, 2:226
Learn C in Two Weeks with Run-C and Cbreeze, 1:565
Learn C Now, 1:564
Learn Science Through Ball Games, 1:535
The Learned Women, 1:338
Learning About Sex: A Contemporary Guide for Young Adults, 2:542
Learning and Mathematical Games, 1:535
Learning with Apple LOGO, 1:565
The Leatherstocking Tales, 2:168
Leaven of Malice, 1:137, 1:138
Leaves from the Journal of Our Life in the Highlands, 1848–1861, 2:369
Leaves of Grass, 1:155, 1:184
Lebanon, 2:89, 2:412
Leben des Galilei, 1:365
L'ecole des femmes, 1:338
Lectures on Conditioned Reflexes, 2:100
Lectures on Education, 2:186
Lectures on Human and Animal Psychology, 2:114
Lectures on Modern Mathematics, 1:496
L'Education sentimentale, 1:335
Lee: In His Own Words and Those of His Contemporaries, 2:196
Lee and Longstreet at Gettysburg, 2:196
The Left Hand of Darkness, 1:254
The Legacy (Fast), 1:218
Legacy (Michener), 1:264
The Legacy of Ricardo, 2:73
Legend Days, 1:239
The Legend of Sleepy Hollow and Other Selections from Washington Irving, 1:159
The Legend of Tarik, 1:270
The Legend of the Founding Fathers, 2:166
Legends, Lies, and Cherished Myths of American History, 2:156
Legends of Our Time, 1:302
Legislative Law and Process in a Nutshell, 2:33
The Legislative Process, 2:41
Leibniz: An Introduction to His Philosophy, 1:527
Leibniz: Metaphysics and Philosophy of Science, 1:527
Leibniz's New Essays Concerning the Human Understanding: A Critical Exposition, 1:527
Leibniz's Philosophy of Logic and Language, 1:527

Leisure in the Industrial Revolution, Seventeen Eighty to Eighteen Eighty, 2:184, 2:339
The Lemon Book: Auto Rights, 2:61, 2:252
Lendon Smith's Diet Plan for Teenagers, 2:550
L'Enfant Noir (The Dark Child), 1:410
Lenin (Clark), 2:378
Lenin (Rawcliffe), 2:379
Lenin: Founder of the Soviet Union, 2:379
Lenin: Notes for a Biographer, 2:379
Lenin and the Russian Revolution, 2:378, 2:379
Lenin and the Twentieth Century: A Bertram D. Wolfe Retrospective, 2:378
Lenin and Trotsky, 2:378
Lenin for Beginners, 2:378
Lenin on Politics and Revolution: Selected Writings, 2:378
Lenin's Last Struggle, 2:379
Leo Tolstoy, 1:397
Leon Trotsky, 2:382
Leon Trotsky's Theory of Revolution, 2:382
Leonard Bernstein, 2:265
Leonardo and the Renaissance, 2:316
Leonardo da Vinci, 2:316
Leonardo da Vinci: Engineer and Architect, 2:316
Leonardo da Vinci: Life and Work, Paintings and Drawings, 2:316
Leonardo Da Vinci and a Memory of His Childhood, 2:316
Leonardo Da Vinci Drawings, 2:315
Leonid Brezhnev, 2:389
Leonid I. Brezhnev: His Life and Work, 2:389
Leonid I. Brezhnev: Pages from His Life, 2:389
Leopold Sedar Senghor, 1:417
Les caves du Vatican, 1:336
Les Chouans, 1:329
Les faux-monnayeurs, 1:336
Les fleurs du mal (Flowers of Evil), 1:330
Les Misérables, 1:336, 1:337
Les Précieuses Ridicules (The Pretentious Young Ladies), 1:338, 1:339
Les séquestrés d'altona, 1:340
Les trois mousquetaires, 1:334
The Lesson of Quantum Theory, 2:518
Let the Circle Be Unbroken, 1:289, 1:290
Let the Oppressed Go Free, 1861–1867, 2:191
Let the Word Go Forth: The Speeches, Statements, and Writing of John F. Kennedy, 1946–1963, 2:21
Let Us Now Praise Famous Men, 2:228
L'etranger, 1:333
"Letter from Birmingham," 2:249

Letter on the China Root, 2:548

Letter to Louis Kossuth, Concerning Freedom and Slavery in the United States in Behalf of the American Anti-Slavery Society, 2:191

Letter to Rafael Sanchez, 2:159

Letter to Washington, 2:165

Letters (Gainsborough), 2:335

Letters (Pliny the Younger), 2:296

Letters and Writings of George Frideric Handel, 2:336

Letters by Joshua Reynolds, 2:338

Letters Eighteen Fifty-Three to Eighteen Ninety-Six (Schumann and Brahms), 2:348

Letters from a Farmer in Pennsylvania to the Inhabitants of the British Colonies, 2:163

Letters from an American Farmer and Sketches of Eighteenth-Century America, 1:152, 1:153

Letters from Egypt: A Journey on the Nile, 1849–1850, 2:569

Letters from Mexico, 2:322

Letters of Amerigo Vespucci and Other Documents Illustrative of His Career, 2:325

Letters of Euler on Different Subjects in Natural Philosophy, 1:526

Letters of Franz Liszt, 2:354

Letters of Grover Cleveland, 1850–1908, 2:204

Letters of John Calvin, 2:311

Letters of Louis D. Brandeis, 2:26

The Letters of Randall Jarrell, 1:244

Letters of Runnymede, 2:343

Letters of the Lewis and Clark Expedition, with Related Documents, 1783–1854, 2:176

The Letters of the Younger Pliny, 2:296

Letters of Ulysses S. Grant to His Father and His Youngest Sister, 2:199

The Letters of Vincent Van Gogh, 2:359

Letters on Probability, 1:533

Letters to a Niece and Prayer to the Virgin of Chartres, 2:214

Letters to a Young Poet, 1:482

Letters to His Family: An Autobiography, 2:357

Letters to Judy: What Kids Wish They Could Tell You, 2:542

Leviathan, 2:9, 2:10

The Levittowners: Ways of Life and Politics in a New Suburban Community, 2:131

The Lewis Acid–Base Concepts: An Overview, 2:507

Lewis and Clark: Pioneering Naturalists, 2:176

Lewis and Clark Among the Indians, 2:177

Lewis and Clark and the Crossing of North America, 2:176

The Lewis and Clark Expedition, 2:176

Lewis Carroll, 1:45

Liber Studiorum, 2:357

Liberation, 2:383

The Liberator, 1:259

Library of Nations, 2:274

Libro de poemas, 1:357

Libya and Qaddafi, 2:412

Lieutenant Hornblower, 1:85

Life: The First Fifty Years 1936–1986, 1:455

Life: The Science of Biology, 2:437

Life Above the Jungle Floor: A Biologist Explores a Strange and Hidden Treetop World, 2:466

Life Among the Savages, 1:243

Life and Art of Albrecht Dürer, 2:314

The Life and Art of Thomas Gainsborough, 2:335

Life and Faith of Martin Luther, 2:317

Life and Gabriella, 1:226

The Life and Letters of Charles Darwin, 2:457

Life and Literature in the Roman Republic, 1:320

The Life and Loves of a She-Devil, 1:128

The Life and Lyrics of Andrew Marvell, 1:13

Life and Music of Béla Bartók, 2:416

Life and Opinions of Maximilien Robespierre, 2:331

Life and Selected Writings (Jefferson), 2:175

The Life and Speeches of the Hon. Henry Clay, 2:181

The Life and Thought of Isaiah Bowman, 2:77

Life and Times of Frederick Douglass, 2:190

The Life and Times of Michael K, 1:413

The Life and Times of Victoria, 2:369

The Life and Times of William and Mary, 2:327

The Life and Times of William Shakespeare, 1:16

The Life and Work of Sigmund Freud, 2:118

The Life and Writings of Frederick Douglass, 2:190

The Life, as Written by Himself in His Letters and Memoirs (Berlioz), 2:347

Life, Character, and Influence of Desiderius Erasmus of Rotterdam, 2:315

Life Cycle Completed: A Review, 2:108

Life Goes to the Movies, 1:468

Life Goes to War: A Pictorial History of World War II, 2:235, 2:385
Life History of Surface Air Currents, 2:484
Life in a Medieval Castle, 2:305
Life in a Medieval Village, 2:305
Life in a Mexican Village: Tepoztlàn Restudied, 2:131
Life in Ancient Rome, 2:291
A Life in Our Times: Memoirs, 2:66
Life in Russia, 2:91
Life in Space, 2:480
Life in the Age of Enterprise, 2:204
Life in the Iron Age, 2:279
Life Is a Dream and Other Spanish Dramas, 1:354, 1:355
Life Is Elsewhere, 1:385
Life Itself, 2:439
Life, Letters, and Journals (Lyell), 2:490
Life, Letters, and Poetry (Michelangelo), 2:318
The Life of Andrew Carnegie, 2:206
The Life of Bertrand Russell, 1:503
The Life of Captain James Cook, 2:321
The Life of Captain Sir Richard Burton, 2:364
The Life of Charlotte Brontë, 1:42
Life of Clara Barton, 2:568
Life of General Sam Houston: A Short Autobiography, 2:186
A Life of George Herbert, 1:11
The Life of Graham Greene, 1:92
Life of Greece, 2:284
The Life of Henri Brulard, 1:341
The Life of Herbert Hoover: The Engineer 1874–1914, 2:231
The Life of Herbert Hoover: The Humanitarian, 1914–1917, 2:231
The Life of Herodotus, 2:288
Life of Horace Mann, 2:187
The Life of J. M. W. Turner, 2:358
Life of James C. Maxwell, 2:527
The Life of Jane Austen, 1:20
The Life of Johannes Brahms, 2:348
The Life of Lazarillo de Tormes, 1:354
The Life of Lenin, 2:378
The Life of Malcolm X, 1:450
Life of Michelangelo, 2:318
The Life of Monsieur de Molière, 1:339
The Life of Niccolò Machiavelli, 2:20
The Life of Saint Augustine, 2:304
The Life of Samuel Johnson, 1:26
The Life of Samuel Johnson, LL.D, 1:26
The Life of Sir Alexander Fleming, Discoverer of Penicillin, 2:559
The Life of Sir Arthur Conan Doyle, 1:48
Life of Sir Richard Burton, 2:364
Life of Sir William Osler, 2:532, 2:534
Life of the Past, 2:495
Life of William Ewart Gladstone, 2:346
The Life of William Harvey, 2:548

Life on a Little-Known Planet, 2:449
Life on Earth: A Natural History, 2:437, 2:456
Life on Earth: Biology Today, 2:466
Life on Television: Content Analyses of United States TV Drama, 1:465
Life on the Mississippi, 1:181, 1:182; 2:185
Life Studies and For the Union Dead, 1:259
Life, the Universe and Everything, 1:64
Life With UNIX: A Guide for Everyone, 1:562
Liftoff: The Story of America's Adventure in Space, 2:480
Light Can Be Both Wave and Particle, 1:225
Light in August, 1:219
Light in the East: 1000–1100, 2:309
The Light of China: Selections, 2:283
The Light That Failed, 1:55
Light Years: Confessions of a Cinematographer, 1:470
Lighting the Night: Revolution in Eastern Europe, 2:405
Like Birds, Like Fishes, and Other Stories, 2:399
Like I Was Sayin', 1:480
L'ile des pingouins, 1:335
L'ile mystérieuse, 1:343
Lillian Hellman, 1:235
Limited War in the Nuclear Age, 2:36
Limits of Land Settlement: A Report on Present-Day Possibilities, 2:77
The Limits of Organization, 2:64
L'immoraliste, 1:336
Lincoln, 2:198
Lincoln and the Civil War in the Diaries and Letters of John Hay, 2:198
Lincoln-Douglas Debates of Eighteen Fifty-Eight, 2:189
Lincoln Reconsidered: Essays on the Civil War Era, 2:192
Line by Line, 1:479
"Lines Written on Westminster Bridge," 1:39
Linguistic Atlas of the Middle and South Atlantic States, 1:432
Linguistics, Computers, and the Language Teacher, 1:571
Linguistics for Non-Linguists, 1:434
Linus Pauling: A Man and His Science, 2:506
L'invitation au château, 1:328
The Lion and the Jewel, 1:417
LISP, 1:566
LISP: A Gentle Introduction to Symbolic Computation, 1:566
LISP: The Language of Artificial Intelligence, 1:565

Listen to the Hunger: Why We Overeat, 2:550

Liszt, 2:354

Liszt, Composer, and His Piano Works, 2:354

Literary Lapses, 1:140, 1:141

Literature and Revolution, 2:381

A Little Anthropology, 2:42

Little Big Man, 2:200

The Little Community and Peasant Society and Culture, 2:54, 2:370

Little Dorrit, 1:47

The Little Drummer, 1:102

Little Eyolf, 1:378

The Little Foxes, 1:235

The Little Girls, 1:69

A Little Love, 1:230

Little Men, 1:167, 1:168

The Little Minister, 1:67

Little Red Book, 2:402

The Little Sister, 1:210

Little Women, 1:21, 1:167, 1:168

Live and Let Die, 1:84

The Liveliest Art: A Panoramic History of the Movies, 1:468

Lively Experiment: The Shaping of Christianity in America, 2:142

Lives: An Anthropological Approach to Biography, 2:42

The Lives and Loves of a She-Devil, 1:128

Lives at Stake: The Science and Politics of Environmental Health, 2:496

The Lives of a Cell: Notes of a Biology Watcher, 2:438

Lives of Girls and Women, 1:145

Lives of Illustrious Men, 2:296

The Lives of Plants: Exploring the Wonders of Botany, 2:448

The Lives of Spiders, 2:449

Lives of the Abbots, 2:308

Lives of the Caesars, 2:296

Lives on the Boundary: A Moving Account of the Struggles and Achievements of America's Educational Underclass, 2:136

Livia: or, Buried Alive, 1:81

The Living and the Dead, 1:147

Living Biographies of Great Scientists, 2:433

Living by Fiction, 1:482, 1:483

Living City, 2:270

Living for Brecht: The Memoirs of Ruth Berlau, 1:365

Living in Space, 2:482

Living in the Environment: An Introduction to Environmental Science, 2:465

Living in the Maniototo, 1:138

Living Minstrelsy: The Poetry and Music of Sidney Lanier, A, 1:160

The Living Planet: A Portrait of the Earth, 2:437, 2:465

The Living Sea, 2:487

Living with a Disability, 2:565

Living with a Parent Who Takes Drugs, 2:540, 2:555

Living with Death and Dying, 2:106, 2:138

Living with Lung Cancer: A Guide for Patients and Their Families, 2:561

Living with Stress, 2:536

Living with Your Allergies and Asthma, 2:561

Livingstone, Man of Africa: Memorial Essays, 1873–1973, 2:367

Livingstone's Africa, 2:367

Livy: Hannibal the Scourge of Rome, 2:295

Liza of Lambeth, 1:105

Lloyd George, 2:374

Lloyd George: From Peace to War, 1912–1916, 2:374

Lloyd George: The People's Champion, 1902–1911, 2:374

Loading Mercury with a Pitchfork, 1:203

Lobachevskian Geometry, 1:519

Lobachevsky and His Contribution to Science, 1:519

Lobbying for the People: The Political Behavior of Public Interest Groups, 2:39

Local Anaesthetic, 1:367

Local Government Election Systems, 2:24

Local Government Law in a Nutshell, 2:41

Locke, 2:18

Logic: The Theory of Inquiry, 2:219

The Logic of Perception, 2:113

Logical Works, 1:507

LOGO Activities for the Computer: A Beginner's Guide, 1:565

LOGO for the Apple II, 1:565

The Loneliest Campaign: The Truman Victory of 1948, 2:237

The Loneliness of the Long-Distance Runner, 1:120, 1:121

The Lonely Crowd: A Study of the Changing American Character, 2:51, 2:132, 2:238

The Lonely Men, 1:252

Lonely on the Mountain, 1:252

Long Ago: Selected Stories, 1:390

The Long Dark Tea Time of the Soul, 1:64

The Long Day Wanes, 1:71

A Long Day's Journey into Night, 1:273, 1:274

The Long Dream, 1:307

The Long Goodbye, 1:210

Long Journey Home, 1:255

The Long March, 2:399

The Long Peace: Inquiries into the History of the Cold War, 2:388

Long Time Passing, 2:242

The Long Valley, 1:289
A Long Way from Home, 1:260
The Longest Journey, 1:85
Longfellow: His Life and Work, 1:161
Longman Dictionary of Geography:
    Human and Physical, 2:75
The Longman Handbook of Modern
    European History 1763–1985, 2:273
Look Back in Anger, 1:112
Look Homeward: A Life of Thomas
    Wolfe, 1:306
Look Homeward, Angel, 1:306
Look to the Night Sky: An Introduction to
    Star Watching, 2:471
Looking at Microscopes, 2:436
Looking Forward, 2:234, 2:259
The Looking Glass War, 1:102
Looking Good in Print: A Guide to Basic
    Design for Desktop Publishing, 1:576
Loose Cannons and Red Herrings, 1:432
Lope de Vega and Spanish Drama, 1:358
The Lopsided World, 2:74
The Lord God Made Them All, 1:93
Lord Hornblower, 1:85
Lord Jim, 1:76
Lord Malguist and Mr. Moon, 1:122
Lord of the Flies, 1:89
The Lord of the Rings, 1:125
Lord Peter: A Collection of All the Lord
    Peter Stories, 1:117
Lord Peter Views the Body, 1:117
"Lord Randal," 1:8
Lord Valentine's Castle, 1:285
Lord Weary's Castle and The Mills of the
    Kavanaughs, 1:259
Lords of Cuzco: A History and
    Description of the Inca People in Their
    Final Days, 2:298
Lorraine Hansberry, 1:232
Lorraine Hansberry: The Collected Last
    Plays, 1:232
Losing Battles, 1:300
Losing Someone You Love: When a
    Brother or Sister Dies, 2:538
The Loss in China and the Revolutionary
    Legacy of Mao Tse-tung, 2:402
The Loss of El Dorado, 1:406
The Loss of Self: A Family Resource for
    the Care of Alzheimer's Disease and
    Related Disorders, 2:561
Lost City of the Incas, 2:298
The Lost Honor of Katharina Blum, 1:363,
    1:364
Lost Horizon, 1:94
Lost Illusions, 1:329
Lost in the Barrens, 1:144
A Lost Lady, 1:209
The Lost Princess of Oz, 1:198, 1:199
The Lost Road and Other Writings, 1:125

The Lost Steps, 1:401
The Lost Tales of Horatio Alger, 1:169
Lost World: Last Poems, 1:244
The Lost World of the Kalahari, 2:86
Lotte in Weimar: The Beloved Returns,
    1:370
The Lottery, 1:243
Lotus 1–2–3 for Beginners, 1:573
Louis: The Louis Armstrong Story,
    1900–1971, 2:264
Louis Armstrong, 2:264
Louis Armstrong: An American Success
    Story, 2:264
Louis XIV, 2:326
Louis L'Amour, 1:253
Louis MacNeice: A Study, 1:105
Louis Napoleon and the Second Empire,
    2:332
Louis Pasteur, 2:446
Louis Pasteur: Free Lance of Science,
    2:445
Louis Pasteur: The Man and His Theories,
    2:445
Louis Pasteur: The Scientist Who Found
    the Cause of Infectious Disease and
    Invented Pasteurization, 2:445
Louis Sullivan: His Life and Work, 2:217
Louis the Fourteenth and the Greatness of
    France, 2:326
Louis XIII, The Just, 2:327
Louis Wirth on Cities and Social Life,
    2:147
Louisa May Alcott, 1:168
Louisa May Alcott: Author, Nurse,
    Suffragette, 1:168
Love, 2:536
Love Among the Chickens, 1:130
Love and Exile: A Memoir, A Little Boy in
    Search of God, A Young Man in Search
    of Love, Lost in America, and a New
    Introduction, The Beginning, 1:388
Love and Mr. Lewisham, 1:129
Love and Other Euphemisms, 1:250
Love and Other Stories, 1:391
Love for Love, 1:21
Love in the Days of Rage, 1:221
Love in the Time of Cholera, 1:403
Love Is a Missing Person, 1:248
A Love Life: Stories, 1:263
The Love Pavillion, 1:118
Love Poems and Others, 1:101
"The Love Story of J. Alfred Prufrock,
    1:82
The Love You Make: An Insider's Story of
    the Beatles, 2:261
The Loved One, 1:127
Love's No Laughing Matter, 1:355
The Loving Spirit, 1:80
The Loving Tree, 1:80

Low-Level Radioactive Waste: From Cradle to Grave, 2:570
Low Vision: What You Can Do to Preserve—And Even Enhance—Your Usable Sight, 2:563
Luck and Pluck, 1:169
The Luck of Roaring Camp, 2:201
Lucky Jim, 1:65, 1:100
Lucy: The Beginnings of Human Kind, 2:48, 2:278, 2:460
Lucy's Child: The Search for Our Origins, 2:48, 2:278, 2:460
Luigi Pirandello, 1:351
Luis Melendez: Eighteenth-Century Master of the Spanish Still Life, with a Catalogue Raisonne, 2:334
The Lungs and Breathing, 2:451, 2:545
Lupercal, 1:95
Lure of Longevity: The Art and Science of Living Longer, 2:451
Lusitania, 2:224
Lust for Life, 2:360
Luther, 1:112
Luther: A Life, 2:317
Luther and the Reformation in the Light of Modern Research, 2:317
Luther, Erasmus, and Loyola, 2:314
Luther's Ninety-Five Theses, 2:317
Lycidas, 1:13
Lying: Moral Choice in Public and Private Life, 2:97
Lyme Disease, 2:557
Lyme Disease: The Great Imitator, 2:557
Lynda Madaras Talks to Teens About AIDS: An Essential Guide for Parents, Teachers, and Young People, 2:560
Lyndon: An Oral Biography, 2:246
Lyndon B. Johnson, 2:246
The Lyre of Orpheus, 1:138
The Lyrical Ballads, 1:30, 1:34, 1:38, 1:39
Lyrics of Lowly Life, 1:175
Lyrics of Noel Coward, 1:77
Lytton Strachey's Queen Victoria, 2:369

M

M. C. Escher—His Life and Complete Graphic Work, 1:515
M. C. Escher Kaleidocycles, 1:515
M. C. Higgins, the Great, 1:229, 1:230
Mac Assembly Language, 1:564
The Mac Is Not a Typewriter: A Style Manual for Creating Professional-Level Type on the Macintosh, 1:576
McCarthyism, 2:238
MacCats: 99 Ways to Paint a Cat with MacPaint, 1:577
McDonald's: Behind the Arches, 2:63
McGraw-Hill Dictionary of Art, 2:155
McGraw-Hill Dictionary of Earth Sciences, 2:489
McGraw-Hill Encyclopedia of Astronomy, 2:470
McGraw-Hill Encyclopedia of Geological Sciences, 2:489
McGraw-Hill Encyclopedia of Ocean and Atmospheric Sciences, 2:483, 2:486
McGraw-Hill Personal Computer Programming Encyclopedia: Language and Operating Systems, 1:561
Machiavelli, 2:20
Machina ex Dea: Feminist Perspectives on Technology, 2:148
Machine Learning: Paradigms and Methods, 1:582
Machinery of the Mind: Inside the New Science of Artificial Intelligence, 1:581
Machines That Built America, 2:203
Machines That Think, 1:581
Machines Who Think: A Personal Inquiry into the History and Prospects of Artificial Intelligence, 1:581
Machu Picchu: A Citadel of the Incas, 2:298
MacIdeas, 1:576
The Macintosh Bible, 1:559
The Macintosh Font Book, 1:559
Macintosh Press: Desktop Publishing for Libraries, 1:575
The Macintosh "What Do I Do Now!?" Book, 1:576
Mackinder: Geography as an Aid to Statecraft, 2:79
Maclopedia: The Macintosh Hardware and Software Compendium, 1:559
The Macmillan Book of Astronomy, 2:469
The Macmillan Illustrated Encyclopedia of Dinosaurs and Prehistoric Animals: A Visual Who's Who of Prehistoric Life, 2:495
Macmillan Illustrated Encyclopedia of Myths and Legends, 2:273
Macmillan Practical Guides: Astronomy, 2:469
MacPaint: Drawing, Drafting, Design, 1:578
McTeague, 1:180, 1:181
Mad About Mad, 1:455
Mad Blast, 1:456
Mad in the Box, 1:456
Mad Look at TV, 1:467
Mad Vertising, 1:440
Madam Prime Minister: A Biography of Margaret Thatcher, 2:408
Madame Bovary, 1:334, 1:335
Madame Curie, 2:510

"Madame Fifi," 1:337
The Madrid Codices of Leonardo Da Vinci, 2:315
Mad's Al Jaffee Freaks Out, 1:456
Mad's Vastly Overrated Al Jaffee, 1:455, 1:456
Magazine: Behind the Scenes at Sports Illustrated, 1:455
Magazine Editing and Production, 1:455
Magazine Fundamentals, 1:455
Magazines in the Twentieth Century, 1:455
Maggie: A Girl of the Streets, 1:167, 1:173; 2:207
A Maggot, 1:86
The Magic Barrel, 1:262
Magic for Marigold, 1:143
The Magic Lantern: The Revolution of 1989 Witnessed in Warsaw, Budapest, Berlin, and Prague, 2:404
The Magic Mirror of M. C. Escher, 1:515
The Magic Mountain, 1:369, 1:370
The Magic of Dance, 2:415
The Magic of Oz, 1:199
The Magic of the Mind, 2:110
Magic, Science and Religion and Other Essays, 2:46
The Magician of Lublin, 1:388
Magister Ludi: The Glass Bead Game, 1:368
Magnetism: Selected Topics, 2:522
Magnificent Microbes, 2:443, 2:446
The Magus, 1:86
Mahabharata, 1:421
Mahatma Gandhi, 2:366, 2:404
Mahler, 2:355
Mahler's Unknown Letters, 2:355
Maiden of Orleans, 1:372
Maimonides: His Life and Works, 2:303
Maimonides and St. Thomas Aquinas, 2:303
Maimonides-Torah and Philosophic Quest, 2:303
Main Currents in Sociological Thought: Montesquieu, Comte, Marx, Tocqueville, the Sociologist, and the Revolution of 1848, 2:126
Main Street, 1:256; 2:226
Main-Travelled Roads, 2:198
The Maine Woods, 1:165
Maintaining Good Health, 2:531
Majestic Island Worlds, 2:83
The Majipoor Chronicles, 1:285
Major Barbara, 1:120
Major Prophets of Today, 1:500
The Majority Finds Its Past: Placing Women in History, 2:148
The Makers of Rome: Nine Lives by Plutarch, 2:288

Makers of the City, 2:212
Making a Photograph, 2:263
Making Computers Talk: An Introduction to Speech Synthesis, 1:579
Making Groups Effective, 2:104
Making Health Decisions: An Epidemiologic Perspective on Staying Well, 2:531
Making His Way: Frank Courtney's Struggle Upward, 2:206
Making Mondragon: The Growth and Dynamics of the Worker Cooperative Complex, 2:150
Making Music on the Amiga, 1:577
Making Music with Personal Computers, 1:577
Making News: A Study in the Construction of Reality, 1:458
The Making of a Continent, 2:91, 2:494
The Making of America: Industry and Finance, 2:220
The Making of America: Labor, 2:220
The Making of an American, 2:212
The Making of an Inventor, February 1847–June 1873, 2:524
The Making of Economics, 2:55
The Making of McPaper: The Inside Story of USA Today, 1:458
The Making of Modern India: Rammohun Roy to Gandhi and Nehru, 2:399
The Making of Star Trek, 1:466
The Making of the African Queen: Or How I Went to Africa with Bogart, Bacall and Huston and Almost Lost My Mind, 1:472
The Making of the American Constitution, 2:17
The Making of the Constitution, 2:17
Making of the English Working Class, 2:340
The Making of the Micro: A History of the Computer, 2:255
The Making of the New Deal: The Insiders Speak, 2:229
The Making of the "Poema de Mio Cid," 1:359
The Making of the President, Nineteen Seventy-Six, 2:21
The Making of the President, Nineteen Seventy-Two, 2:21, 2:252
The Making of the President, Nineteen Sixty: A Narrative History of American Politics in Action, 2:21
The Making of the President, Nineteen Sixty-Eight, 2:21
The Making of the President, Nineteen Sixty-Four, 2:21
The Making of the Representative for Planet Eight, 1:103

The Making of the Wizard of Oz, 1:470

Making Our Way: America at the Turn of the Century in the Words of the Poor and Powerless, 2:207

Making Sense (Bruner and Haste), 2:112

Making Sense (Goodman), 1:480

Making Sense of Marx, 2:60

Making Things Right When Things Go Wrong: Ten Proven Ways to Put Your Life in Order, 2:536

Making Your Macintosh Excel, 1:573

The Makropoulos Secret, 1:385

The Malay Archipelago, 2:459

Malaysia: A Country Study, 2:86

Malcolm, 2:251

Malcolm X, 1:450; 2:251

Malcolm X: The End of White World Supremacy: Four Speeches, 2:251

Malcolm X: The Last Speeches, 1:450; 2:251

Malcolm X on Afro-American History, 1:450; 2:251

Malcolm X Speaks: Selected Speeches and Statements, 1:450; 2:251

Malcolm X Talks to Young People, 2:251

A Male Child, 1:118

Male/Female Roles Annual 1989, 2:137

Male/Female Roles: Opposing Viewpoints, 2:138

Malinowski Between Two Worlds: The Polish Roots of an Anthropological Tradition, 2:46

Malone meurt, 1:331

Malory, 1:7

The Maltese Falcon, 1:231

Malthus and His Time, 2:69

The Mammoth Hunters, 2:277

Man: 12,000 Years Under the Sea, 2:278

Man and Aggression, 2:98, 2:100

Man and Superman, 1:120

The Man Died: Prison Notes of Wole Soyinka, 1:417

A Man for All Seasons, 1:14, 1:68, 1:69

The Man from the Broken Hills, 1:252

Man in Nature: America Before the Days of the White Man, 2:80

The Man in the Iron Mask, 1:333, 1:334

Man-Made Minds, 1:581

The Man-Made Sun: The Quest for Fusion Power, 2:496

Man Makes Himself, 2:48

Man Meets Dog, 2:464

A Man of Property, 1:87

A Man of the People, 1:411

The Man Verdi, 2:361

The Man Who Had All the Luck, 1:266

The Man Who Invented Sin, 1:110

The Man Who Was Don Quixote: The Story of Miguel de Cervantes, 1:356

The Man Who Was Thursday, 1:72

The Man with the Golden Gun, 1:84

A Man Without a Country, 2:169

Management and the Worker: An Account of a Research Program Conducted by Western Electric Co, 2:149

The Managerial Woman, 2:148

The Manager's Guide to Desktop Electronic Publishing, 1:575

Managing the Software Process, 1:585

Managing Your Doctor: How to Get the Best Possible Medical Care, 2:566

Managing Your Hard Disk, 1:574

Mandate for Change, 2:239

Mandela's Earth and Other Poems, 1:418

Mandragola, 1:347

Manifest Destiny and Mission in American History: A Reinterpretation, 2:185, 2:218

Manifest Destiny and the Coming of the Civil War, 1840–1861, 2:184

Manners, Customs, and Condition of the North American Indians, 2:188

The Manor, 1:388

A Man's a Man, 1:365

Man's Future Birthright: Essays on Science and Humanity, 2:455

Man's Role in Changing the Face of the Earth, 2:82

Man's Search for Meaning, 2:139

Mansfield Park, 1:20

The Manticore, 1:137, 1:138

Manual of Meteorology, 2:484

Many Loves and Other Plays, 1:305

Mao: A Biography, 2:403

Mao and China: From Revolution to Revolution, 2:403

Mao Tse-Tung, 2:403

Mao Tse-Tung: Founder of Communist China, 2:403

Mao Tse-tung and His China, 2:403

Mao Tse-tung on Revolution and War, 2:402

Mao Zedong, 2:403

Mao Zedong: A Preliminary Reassessment, 2:403

Mao's Way, 2:403

The Map Catalog: Every Kind of Map and Chart on Earth and Even Some Above It, 2:92

The Mapmakers, 2:92

Mapping, 2:92

Mapping Our Genes: The Genome Project and the Future of Medicine, 2:452

The Mappings of America, 2:92

Maps and Air Photographs: Images of the Earth, 2:92

Maps and Compass: A User's Handbook, 2:92

Maps of the Mind, 2:95
Maps on File, 2:75
Marat/Sade, 1:372
Marathon Man, 1:227
The Marble Faun, 1:177
Marc Antony, 2:291
Marc Chagall (Greenfield), 2:415
Marc Chagall (Kagan), 2:418
Marc Chagall: An Intimate Biography, 2:418
The March of Islam: 600–800, 2:301
Marching Along, 2:216
Marching Men, 1:189
Marco Polo, 2:309
Marco Polo: Venetian Adventurer, 2:309
Marcos and the Philippines, 2:399
Marcus Aurelius, 2:290
Margaret Atwood, 1:136
Margaret Atwood: A Critical Inquiry, 1:136
Margaret Drabble, 1:80
Margaret Drabble: Symbolic Moralist, 1:80
Margaret Mead and Samoa: The Making and Unmaking of an Anthropological Myth, 2:47
Margaret Mead: A Life, 2:47
Margaret Mead: A Portrait, 2:47
Margaret Sanger: Pioneer of the Future, 2:226
Margaret Thatcher, 2:408
Margaret Thatcher: Britain's Iron Lady, 2:408
Margot Fonteyn: Autobiography, 2:415
Maria Theresa, 2:326
Marianne Moore, 1:268
Marie Curie, 2:510
Marie Curie: A Life, 2:510
The Marine Biology Coloring Book, 2:488
Mario the Magician, 1:370
Mark Twain: A Writer's Life, 1:182
Mark Twain: The Development of a Writer, 1:182
Mark Twain and Bret Harte, 1:176, 1:182
The Market and Beyond: Co-Operation and Competition in Information Technology in the Japanese System, 1:537
Market Socialism in Yugoslavia, 2:58
Markets and Minorities, 2:69
Markings, 2:389, 2:390
Marmion, 1:36
Marriage a la Mode, 1:23
Marriage and Family in a Changing Society, 2:138
Marriage and Family Today, 2:138
Marriage and the Family, 2:138
Marriage and the Family in the Middle Ages, 2:305
Marriage, Divorce, Remarriage, 2:137

The Marriages Between Zones Three, Four and Five, 1:103
The Marrow of American Divinity: Selected Articles on Colonial Religion, 2:162
The Marrow of Tradition, 1:172
Marry Me, 1:292
Mars: Our Future on the Red Planet, 2:476
Mars and the Inner Planets, 2:476
Mars Beckons, 2:476
The Mars Project, 2:483
Mars, the Red Planet, 2:475
Marshall McLuhan: The Man and His Message, 1:454
Marshall McLuhan: The Medium and the Messenger, 1:454
The Marshall Plan, 2:238
The Marshall Plan: America, Britain, and the Reconstruction of Western Europe, 1947–1952, 2:238
Marshall's Mission to China: December 1945 to January 1947, 2:240
"The Marshes of Glynn," 1:159
Martha Quest, 1:103
Martí: Apostle of Freedom, 2:371
Martí on the U.S.A, 2:370
The Martian Chronicles, 1:202
Martin Chuzzlewit, 1:46, 1:47
Martin Eden, 1:257
Martín Fierro, 1:398
Martin Luther, 2:317
Martin Luther King Jr, 2:250
Martin Luther King, Jr. Civil Rights Leader, Theologian, Orator, 2:250
The Marvelous Palace and Other Stories, 1:332
Marx and Engels: The Intellectual Relationship, 2:59
Marx and Engels and the English Workers and Other Essays, 2:59
Marx Brothers Scrapbook, 1:470
Marxism and the Problems of Linguistics, 2:380
Marxism in Our Time, 2:381
Marxist Political Economy and Marxist Urban Sociology: A Review and Elaboration of Recent Developments, 2:72
Mary Anne, 1:80
Mary Cassatt, 2:215
The Mary Cassatt Datebook, 2:215
Mary Cassatt, Oils and Pastels, 2:215
Mary McLeod Bethune, 2:14
Mary McLeod Bethune: Teacher with a Dream, 2:14
Mary McLeod Bethune, A Great American Educator, 2:229
Mary Queen of Scots, 2:326

Mary Shelley, 1:37
Mary Shelley: Her life, Her Fiction, Her Monsters, 1:37
Mary Shelley: Romance and Reality, 1:37
Mary Stuart, 1:372
Masaccio and the Art of Early Renaissance Florence, 2:310
Masques of God: Forms and Theme in the Poetry of Henry Vaughan, 1:17
Mass Media, 1:452; 2:129
Mass Media: Past, Present, and Future, 1:453
Mass Media and American Politics, 2:39, 2:257
Mass Media and Mass Man, 1:453
Mass Media and Social Change, 1:454; 2:130
Mass Media Election: How Americans Choose Their President, 1:443
The Mass Media Elections: How Americans Choose Their Presidents, 2:40
Mass Media—Marconi to MTV: A Select Bibliography of New York Times Sunday Magazine Articles on Communication 1900–1988, 1:453
Mass Media—Mass Culture, 1:453
Mass Mediated Culture, 1:454
The Master Architect: Conversations with Frank Lloyd Wright, 2:270
The Master Builder, 1:378
The Master Builders: Le Corbusier, Mies van der Rohe, Frank Lloyd Wright, 2:419
The Master of Ballantrae, 1:58
The Master of Hestviken, 1:380, 1:381
Master of Middle-Earth: The Fiction of J. R. R. Tolkien, 1:126
The Master Puppeteer, 1:484
Mastering AutoCAD, 1:578
Mastering FORTH, 1:566
Mastering Fundamental Mathematics, 1:504
Mastering Novell Netware, 1:558
Mastering P.C. Tools Deluxe Version 6, 1:574
Mastering Quicken 3, 1:567
Mastering the SAS System, 1:574
Mastering Ventura, 1:575
Mastering Windows 3, 1:561
Mastering WordPerfect 5.1, 1:576
Masterman Ready, 1:56
Masterpieces of Modern Spanish Drama, 1:355
Masters of Horror, 1:469
Masters of Russian Music, 2:346
Masters of Social Psychology: Freud, Mead, Lewin, and Skinner, 2:99, 2:102, 2:118

Masters of Sociological Thought: Ideas in Historical and Social Context, 2:125
The Matchmaker, 1:303, 1:338
Math Projects: Mathematical Shapes, 1:512
Math Projects: Polyhedral Shapes, 1:519
Mathematical Analysis for Business and Economics, 1:524
The Mathematical Analysis of Logic, 1:507
The Mathematical Career of Pierre de Fermat (1601–1665), 1:508
Mathematical Carnival: A New Round-Up of Tantalizers and Puzzles from "Scientific American," 1:536
Mathematical Elements for Computer Graphics, 1:578
Mathematical Foundations of Computer Science 1976, 1:581
Mathematical Models, 1:535
Mathematical Papers of Isaac Newton, 1:523
Mathematical Papers of Sir William Rowan Hamilton, 1:506
Mathematical People: Profiles and Interviews, 1:496
Mathematical Quickies: Two Hundred Seventy Stimulating Problems with Solutions, 1:535
The Mathematical Theory of Communication, 1:550
Mathematical Thought: An Introduction to the Philosophy of Mathematics, 1:496
Mathematics: A Human Endeavor, 1:497
Mathematics: An Introduction to Its Spirit and Its Uses, 1:497
Mathematics: Structure and Method, 1:504
Mathematics: The New Golden Age, 1:497
Mathematics and Science: An Adventure in Postage Stamps, 1:535
Mathematics and the Imagination, 1:497
Mathematics Dictionary, 1:497
Mathematics Dictionary Made Simple, 1:498
Mathematics Encyclopedia, 1:497
Mathematics for Computer Technology, 1:556
Mathematics for the College Boards, 1:505
Mathematics for the Millions, 1:504
Mathematics for the Non-Mathematician, 1:497
Mathematics in Western Culture, 1:497
Mathematics—Its Contents, Methods, and Meanings, 1:496
Mathematics, Magic, and Mystery, 1:536
The Mathematics of Plato's Academy: A New Reconstruction, 1:497
Mathematics Today: Twelve Informal Essays, 1:498
Mathematics Tomorrow, 1:498

Mathematics Useful for Understanding
Plato or, Pythagorean Arithmetic,
Music, Astronomy, Spiritual Disciplines,
1:498
Mathematische Werke, 1:528
The Mating Season, 1:131
Matrices, 1:498
Matter and Energy, 2:518
Matter, Energy, and Life: An Introduction
to Chemical Concepts, 2:438
A Matter of Life and Death: A Discussion
About Death for Young People, 2:538
Matthew Arnold, 1:41
Matthew Arnold: A Life, 1:41
Maud Martha, 1:205
Maugham: A Biography, 1:106
Maupassant the Novelist, 1:338
Mauve Gloves and Madman, Clutter and
Vine, 1:479
Max, 1:218
Max Weber (MacRae), 2:143
Max Weber (Wrong), 2:143
Maximilien Robespierre, 2:331
Maxwell on Molecules and Gases, 2:498,
2:518
The Maya (Coe), 2:299
Maya (Gallenkamp), 2:299
Maya: The Riddle and Rediscovery of a
Lost Civilization, 2:299
Maya: Treasures of an Ancient
Civilization, 2:299
Mayflower, 1:151
The Mayor of Casterbridge, 1:52
The Mayor of Zalamea, 1:355
"The Maypole at Marymont," 1:177
Mazzini: Prophet of Modern Europe, 2:340
Me Me Me Me Me: Not a Novel, 1:248
The Meaning of Independence: John
Adams, George Washington, Thomas
Jefferson, 2:175
The Meaning of Meaning, 1:438
The Meaning of Shakespeare, 1:16
Meaning of the Glorious Koran, 2:301
Meanings of the Medium: Perspectives on
the Art of Television, 1:464
The Measure of a Man, 2:250
Measurement and Prediction, 2:129
Measurement Evaluation in Physical
Education, 1:568
Measurement for Evaluation in Physical
Education and Exercise Science, 1:568
The Measurement of Intelligence, 2:110
Measuring and Computing, 2:436
Measuring Emotions in Infants and
Children, 2:104
Mechanics and Motion, 2:513
Mechanics, Heat, and Sound, 2:513
The Mechanism of Mendelian Heredity,
2:454, 2:455

Medallic Portraits of Adolf Hitler, 2:376
Medea (Ovid), 1:321
Medea (Seneca), 1:323
Media Analysis Techniques, 1:454
Media and the American Mind: From
Morse to McLuhan, 1:453, 1:454
The Media Lab: Inventing the Future at
MIT, 1:537
The Media Monopoly, 1:454
Media Power, 1:454
Media Power in Politics, 2:39
Media Sexploitation, 1:454
Mediaspeak: How Television Makes Up
Your Mind, 1:465
The Mediating Self: Mead, Sartre, and
Self-Determination, 2:139
Medical and Psychological Stress:
Guidebook for Reference and Research,
2:123
Medical Care, Medical Costs: The Search
for a Health Insurance Policy, 2:566
Medical Mayhem: How to Avoid It and
Get the Best Possible Care from Your
Doctor and Hospital, 2:566
Medicare: A Handbook in the History and
Issues of Health Care Services for the
Elderly, 2:567
Medicine for the Outdoors: A Guide to
Emergency Medical Procedures and First
Aid for Wilderness Travelers, 2:566
The Medieval Church, 2:304
A Medieval Monk, 2:305
The Medieval Papacy, 2:304
Medieval Russia's Epics, Chronicles, and
Tales, 1:390
Medieval World: Europe Eleven Hundred
to Thirteen Fifty, 2:306
The Mediterranean, 2:383
The Meeting at Telgte, 1:367
Megatrends: Ten New Directions
Transforming Our Lives, 2:51, 2:255
Megatrends 2000: Ten New Directions for
the 1990's, 2:51
Mein Kampf, 2:375, 2:376
The Meiotic Mechanism, 2:451, 2:452
The Melting Pot: A Drama in Four Acts,
2:136
Members of Congress Since Seventeen
Eighty-Nine, 2:33
Memoir of Roger B. Taney: Chief Justice
of the Supreme Court of the United
States, 2:27
Memoir of the Life and Character of the
Right Honorable Edmund Burke, 2:329
Memoir on Heat, 2:499
Memoirs (Ben-Gurion), 2:412
Memoirs (Berlioz), 2:347
Memoirs (Brezhnev), 2:389
Memoirs (Hoover), 2:230, 2:231

Memoirs (Sakharov), 2:405
Memoirs Found in a Bathtub, 1:386
Memoirs, 1925–1950 (Kennan), 2:391
Memoirs of a Computer Pioneer, 1:539
Memoirs of a Fox-Hunting Man, 1:116
Memoirs of a Space Traveler: Further
    Reminiscences of Ijon Tichy, 1:386
Memoirs of an Infantry Officer, 1:116
Memoirs of an Unregulated Economics,
    2:56
Memoirs of Artagnan, 1:334
The Memoirs of Barry Lyndon, 1:61
Memoirs of Harry S. Truman: Years of
    Trial and Hope, 2:237
Memoirs of John Quincy Adams,
    Comprising Portions of His Diary from
    1795–1848, 2:173
Memoirs of Many in One, 1:147
Memoirs of Prince Metternich, 1773–1835,
    2:333
The Memoirs of Sherlock Holmes, 1:48
Memoirs of the Life, Writings, and
    Discoveries of Sir Isaac Newton, 2:516
Memoirs of William Jennings Bryan, 2:205
The Memorial, 1:96
Memories and Adventures, 2:386
Memories and Commentaries, 2:426
Memories, Dreams, Reflections, 2:120,
    2:121
Memory: How It Works and How to
    Improve It, 2:103
Men and Citizens: A Study of Rousseau's
    Social Theory, 2:11
Men and Women of the Corporation,
    2:140
Men at Arms, 1:127
Men at Work, 1:480
Men of Mathematics, 1:496, 1:509, 1:528,
    1:531
Men to Match My Mountains, 2:201
The Men Who Kept the Secrets: Richard
    Helms and the C.I.A, 2:37
The Menace of AIDS, 2:560
Menachem Begin, 2:255
Mencken and Sara: A Life in Letters,
    1:436
Mendelssohn and Schumann: Essays on
    Their Music and Its Context, 2:346
The Mensa Book of Words, Word Games,
    Puzzles, and Oddities, 1:440
Menstruation, 2:543
Merce Cunningham, 2:266
Merchant of Venice, 2:397
Mere Christianity, 1:104
Mere Literature and Other Essays, 2:225
Meridian, 1:296, 1:297
The Meridian Handbook of Classical
    Mythology, 1:318
Merlin's Tour of the Universe, 2:471

Merrill Algebra Essentials, 1:506
Merrill Algebra One, 1:506
Merrill Applications of Mathematics, 1:504
Merrill General Mathematics, 1:504
Merrill Geometry, 1:513
Merrill Informal Geometry, 1:511
Merrill Pre-Calculus Mathematics, 1:523
Mesoamerica's Ancient Cities, 2:299
Messengers of God: Biblical Portraits and
    Legends, 1:302
Metamorphoses (Apuleius), 1:320
The Metamorphoses (Ovid), 1:319, 1:321
"The Metamorphosis," 1:369
Meteorological Observations and Essays,
    2:501
Method of Coordinates, 1:514
Method of Henry James, 1:180
Methods of Chemical Nomenclature, 2:499
Methods of Research in Social
    Psychology, 2:95
Metternich's Diplomacy at Its Zenith,
    1820–1823, 2:333
Metternich's German Policy: The Congress
    of Vienna, 1814–1815, 2:333
Mexican and Central American Population
    and U.S. Immigration Policy, 2:141
Mexican War, 2:185
Mexico (Coe), 2:88
Mexico (Constable), 2:299
Mexico: A Country Study, 2:89, 2:409
Mexico: From Independence to
    Revolution, 1810–1910, 2:370
Mexico and the United States: Their
    Linked Destinies, 2:36, 2:88, 2:257
Mexico and the United States Today:
    Issues Between Neighbors, 2:89, 2:409
Mexico in Revolution, 2:369
Michael Faraday: Apprentice to Science,
    2:525
Michelangelo, 2:318
Michelangelo: A Record of His Life As
    Told in His Own Letters and Papers,
    2:318
Michelangelo: The Sistine Chapel, 2:318
Michelangelo and the Language of Art,
    2:318
The Micro Millenium, 1:554
Microbe Hunters, 2:443–446
Microbes, 2:443, 2:446
The Microbes: An Introduction to Their
    Nature and Importance, 2:443
Microbial Ecology, 2:465
Microcomputer Resource Book for Special
    Education: How to Use the
    Microcomputer with Handicapped
    Children, 1:571
The Microcomputer, the School Librarian
    and the Teacher, 1:570
Microcomputers for Lawyers, 1:572

Microcomputers in Business and Society, 1:572

Microcomputers in Geometry, 1:512

Microcomputers in Special Education: An Introduction to Instructional Applications, 1:569

Microelectronics and the Sport Sciences, 1:568

Micronesia Handbook: A Guide to the Caroline, Gilbert, Marianas, 2:91

Microprocessors and Peripherals: Hardware, Software, Interfacing and Applications, 1:560

Microprocessors and Their Operating Systems: A Comprehensive Guide to 8, 16, and 32 Bit Hardware, Assembly Language and Computer Architecture, 1:561

The Microscope: How to Use It and Enjoy It, 2:436

Microsoft Mouse Programmer's Reference, 1:560

Microsoft Word 5 Made Easy, 1:575

Microsoft Works for Beginners, 1:573

The Middle-Aged Man on the Flying Trapeze, 1:290

Middle Ages (Bishop), 2:305

The Middle Ages (Casselli), 2:305

The Middle Ages (Mills), 2:306

The Middle East, 2:36, 2:89

The Middle East and North Africa: A Political Geography, 2:89

Middle East Geographical Study, 2:89

Middle East Political Dictionary, 2:90, 2:277

Middle English Dictionary, 1:430

Middle Ground, 1:80

Middlemarch: A Study of Provincial Life, 1:49

Middletown, 2:131, 2:132

Middletown Families: Fifty Years of Change and Continuity, 2:130, 2:132

Middletown in Transition: A Study in Cultural Conflicts, 2:131, 2:132

The MIDI Manual, 1:579

Midpoint and Other Poems, 1:292

Midstream: My Later Life, 1:449

Midsummer Night's Dream, 2:338

Midsummer Night's Madness, 1:110

The Mighty Aztecs, 2:300

Miguel Street, 1:406

Mikhail Gorbachev, 2:407

Mikhail Gorbachev: A Leader for Soviet Change, 2:407

Mikhail S. Gorbachev: An Intimate Biography, 2:407

Mila 18, 1:293

Milestones in Science and Technology: The Ready Reference Guide to Discoveries, Inventions, and Facts, 2:433

Military Jargon, 1:433

The Military Side of Japanese Life, 2:374

The Milky Way, 2:478

The Mill on the Floss, 1:49

The Miller of Old Church, 1:226

The Millstone, 1:80

Milton Friedman: A Guide to His Economic Thought, 2:66

The Mind and Faith of Justice Holmes: His Speeches, Essays, Letters, and Judicial Opinions, 2:29

Mind and Media: The Effects of Television, Video Games, and Computers, 1:454

The Mind and the Machine: Philosophical Aspects of Artificial Intelligence, 1:582

Mind Children: The Future of Robot and Human Intelligence, 1:584

Mind Design: Philosophy, Psychology, and Artificial Intelligence, 1:582

Mind Drugs, 2:554

Mind, Machines and Evolution: Philosophical Studies, 1:582

A Mind of Her Own: The Life of Karen Horney, 2:119

The Mind of Jawaharlal Nehru, 2:404

The Mind of Mahatma Gandhi, 2:366

The Mind of Napoleon: A Selection of His Written and Spoken Words, 2:329

The Mind of Primitive Man, 2:44

The Mind of the Middle Ages: An Historical Survey: AD 200–1500, 2:304

Mind Over Machine, 1:554

Mind Over Math, 1:497

Mind, Self, and Society: From the Standpoint of a Social Behaviorist, 2:139

A Mind to Murder, 1:98

The Mind Tool: Computers and Their Impact on Society, 1:554

Minding the Body, Mending the Mind, 2:530

Mindstorms: Children, Computers, and Powerful Ideas, 1:570

Mine-Land Rehabilitation, 2:496

Mineral Resources, 2:495

Minerals Handbook: 1984–1985, 2:492

Minerals, Rocks, and Fossils, 2:492

Minimalism: Art of Circumstance, 2:414

"The Minister's Black Veil," 1:177

"Miniver Cheevy," 1:282

Minoan Crete, 2:285

Minority Report: What's Happened to Blacks, Hispanics, American Indians and Other American Minorities in the 1980s, 2:12

The Mint, 2:372

Miracle at Philadelphia: The Story of the Constitutional Convention, May to September 1787, 2:16, 2:166

The Miracle Worker, 1:448, 1:449

Mirgorod, 1:392
Mirror for Man: The Relation of Anthropology to Modern Life, 2:42
Mirror of Her Own, 1:229
Mirth of a Nation: America's Great Dialect, 1:432
The Misanthrope (1666) and Other Plays, 1:338
Miscellaneous Writings (Carnegie), 2:206
The Miser, 1:338
Misery, 1:249
The Misfits, 1:266
The Misfits and Other Stories, 1:266
Mishneh Torah, 2:302
The Mismeasure of Man, 2:458
Miss Julie, 1:380
Miss Lonelyhearts, 1:300
Miss Marple: The Complete Short Stories, 1:74
Miss Thistlebottom's Hobgoblins: The Careful Writer's Guide to the Taboos, Bugbears and Outmoded Rules of English Usage, 1:435
Missing Links: The Hunt for Earliest Man, 2:278, 2:460
Mission to Earth: Landsat Views the World, 2:92
Mission to Kala, 1:412
Missionary Travels and Researches in South Africa, 2:367
Missions of California: A Legacy of Genocide, 2:160
Mr. Clemens and Mark Twain, 1:182
Mr. Conservative: Barry Goldwater, 2:245
Mister Johnson, 1:72
Mr. Justice Brandeis, 2:26
Mr. Midshipman Easy, 1:56
Mr. Midshipman Hornblower, 1:85
Mister President: The Story of Ronald Reagan, 2:260
Mr. Sammler's Planet, 1:200
Mr. Stone and the Knight's Companion, 1:406
Mrs. Byrne's Dictionary of Unusual, Obscure, and Preposterous Words, Gathered from Numerous and Diverse Authoritative Sources, 1:439
Mrs. Dalloway, 1:132
Mistress Masham's Repose, 1:130
Mistress Pat, 1:143
Mitla Pass, 1:293
A Mixture of Frailties, 1:137, 1:138
Moby-Dick, or The White Whale, 1:155, 1:162, 1:163
A Model of the Universe, 1:519
Model Rockets, 2:482
Modeling the Mind, 1:582
Models of Bounded Rationality, 2:63

A Moderate Among Extremists: Dwight D. Eisenhower and the School Desegregation Crisis, 2:240
Modern Africa, 2:393
Modern Algebra Two, 1:506
Modern American Usage: A Guide, 1:435
The Modern American Vice Presidency: The Transformation of a Political Institution, 2:21
Modern Arabic Poetry: An Anthology, 1:420
Modern Arabic Short Stories, 1:420
Modern Bioelectrochemistry, 2:511
Modern Business Cycle Theory, 2:57
Modern Carbohydrate Chemistry, 2:511
Modern Chinese Poetry: Twenty Poets from the Republic of China, 1:423
Modern Chinese Stories, 1:423
Modern Chinese Stories and Novellas, 1919–1945, 1:423
A Modern Comedy, 1:88
The Modern Concept of Nature, 2:455
Modern Concepts in Biochemistry, 2:511
The Modern Corporation: Free Markets versus Regulation, 2:64
A Modern Dictionary of Sociology, 2:124
Modern Ethology: The Science of Animal Behavior, 2:461
Modern Experimental Biochemistry, 2:511
The Modern Family Guide to Dental Health, 2:552
Modern Hebrew Poetry, 1:420
Modern Ideas about Children, 2:123
Modern Indian Poetry in English, 1:422
Modern Indian Short Stories, 1:422
Modern Japanese Drama: An Anthology, 1:425
Modern Japanese Literature: An Anthology, 1:425
Modern Japanese Stories, 1:425
Modern Korean Short Stories, 1:426
Modern Linguistics: The Results of Chomsky's Revolution, 1:435
Modern Music: The Avant Garde Since 1945, 2:261
Modern Persian Short Stories, 1:420
Modern Power Mechanics, 2:516
Modern Psychometrics: The Science of Psychological Assessment, 2:122
The Modern Social Conflict: An Essay on the Politics of Liberty, 2:132
Modern Spanish Prose: With a Selection of Poetry, 1:354
Modern Spanish Syntax, 1:353
Modern Sports Science, 2:551
Modern Swedish Poetry in Translation, 1:374
Modern Theatre: Seven Plays and an Essay, 1:379
Modern Trigonometry, 1:524

Modern Turkish Drama, 1:420
A Modern Utopia, 1:129
A Modern View of Geometry, 1:511
Modern Yugoslav Satire, 1:383
A Modest Proposal, 1:30
The Modocs, 2:157
The Modulor and Modulor 2, 2:419
Mohammed: The Man and His Faith, 2:301
Mohandas Gandhi, 2:366
Mohandas K. Gandhi, 2:366
The Molecular Biology of the Gene, 2:440
Molière, 1:339
Moll Flanders, 1:22, 1:23
Molloy, 1:331
Mom, the Wolf Man and Me, 1:250
Mona Lisa: The Picture and the Myth, 2:316
Monadology and Other Philosophical Writings, 1:527
Monarch Notes on Virgil's Aeneid and Other Works, 2:298
Monetary History of the United States, 1867–1960, 2:66, 2:153
Monetary Nationalism and International Stability, 2:72
Monetary Theory and Stabilization Policies, 2:72
Monetary Trends in the United States and the United Kingdom: Their Relations to Income, Prices, and Interest Rates, 1867–1975, 2:66
Monetary versus Fiscal Policy, 2:66
Money and Class in America: Notes and Observations on a Civil Religion, 1:480
Money and Class: Notes and Observations on the American Character, 1:480
Money and Motivation: An Analysis of Incentives in Industry, 2:150
Money and Other Stories, 1:385
Money, Banking and Economic Analysis, 2:70
Money, Credit and Commerce, 2:57
Money, Interest, and Capital: A Study in the Foundations of Monetary Theory, 2:70
Money, Whence It Came, Where It Went, 2:66
The Mongol Conquests: 1200–1300, 2:309
The Monkey's Paw, 1:97
"Monna Innominata," 1:56
The Monologue Workshop: From Search to Discovery in Audition, Class and Performance, 1:449
Mononucleosis and Other Infectious Diseases, 2:557
Monsieur, 1:81
Montesquieu and the Old Regime, 2:19

Montesquieu's Comparative Politics and the Spirit of American Constitutionalism, 2:19
Montesquieu's Philosophy of Liberalism: A Commentary on the Spirit of the Laws, 2:19
Montezuma's Daughter, 1:51
A Month of Sundays, 1:292
Mont-Saint-Michel and Chartres, 2:214
The Moon: Our Sister Planet, 2:475
The Moon and Its Exploration, 2:474
The Moon and Sixpence, 1:106
A Moon for the Misbegotten, 1:273, 1:274
The Moon Is Down, 1:289
The Moons of Jupiter, 1:145
The Moonstone, 1:45
Moortown, 1:95
The Moral Dimensions of Politics, 2:20
The Moral Judgment of the Child, 2:111
The Moral Life of Children, 2:97, 2:106
Moral Principles in Education, 2:219
Morality, Politics and Law: A Bicentennial Essay, 2:20
Morals and Manners Among Negro Americans, 2:211
Mordecai Richler, 1:146
More Collected Verse (Service), 1:146
More Die of Heartbreak, 1:200
More Favorite Stories, 1:383
More Funny People, 1:446
More Poems (Housman), 1:54
More Stately Mansions, 1:273
More Tales of Prix the Pilot, 1:386
More Tales of Uncle Remus: Further Adventures of Brer Rabbit, His Friends, Enemies, and Others, 1:255
Morgan's Passing, 1:291
The Morning After: American Successes and Excesses 1981–1986, 1:480
Morning Is a Long Time Coming, 1:228
Morphology of Seed Plants, 2:447
Morris Dictionary of Word and Phrase Origins, 1:433
A Mortal Antipathy, 1:158
Mortal Vision: The Wisdom of Euripides, 1:315
Mosby's Memoirs and Other Stories, 1:200
Moscow Under Lenin, 2:379
Moses: Man of the Mountain, 2:280
Moses Maimonides, 2:303
Moses' Rock: A Play in Three Acts, 1:109
Mosses, 2:447
Mosses from an Old Manse, 1:177
The Most Dangerous Man in America: Scenes From the Life of Benjamin Franklin, 2:526
Most of P. G. Wodehouse, 1:131
Most Secret, 1:147

Motel Chronicles, 1:285
The Mother, 1:365
Mother and Daughter: The Letters of Eleanor and Anna Roosevelt, 2:233
Mother Courage and Her Children, 1:365
Mother Night, 1:295
Motion Pictures: The Development of an Art from Silent Films to the Age of Television, 1:468
Motivating the Unmotivated, 2:112
Motivation: Theories and Principles, 2:112
Motivation and Economic Mobility, 2:61
Motivation Factor: A Theory of Personal Investment, 2:112
Motivation, Planning, and Action, 2:113
Motives and Goals in Groups, 2:104
Motives, Personality, and Society, 2:113
Motley Stories, 1:390
Motown and Didi, 1:270
Mount St. Helens, 2:494
Mount St. Helens: The Eruption and Recovery of a Volcano, 2:493
The Mount St. Helens Disaster: What We've Learned, 2:493
The Mountain Giants, 1:351
Mountains, 2:83
Mountains of California, 2:221
Mourning Becomes Electra, 1:274
The Mousetrap and Other Plays, 1:74
The Mousetrap, 1:73
Move Your Shadow: South Africa Black and White, 2:393
Moyers: Report from Philadelphia: The Constitutional Convention of 1787, 1:466; 2:167
Mozart, 2:333
Mozart: A Documentary Biography, 2:333
Mozart and Salieri: The Little Tragedies, 1:395
MS-DOS Expanded: Beyond the Boundary of 640K, 1:561
The MS-DOS–Mac Connection, 1:558
"MS Found in a Bottle," 1:163
The Muckrakers, 2:218
Muckraking and Objectivity: Journalism's Colliding Traditions, 1:457
Muir Among the Animals: The Wildlife Writings of John Muir, 2:221
Mulliner Nights, 1:131
Multidimensional Scaling, 1:529
Multimedia Design with Hypercard, 1:580
Multiple Exposures: Chronicles of the Radiation Age, 2:508
Multiple Man: Explanations in Possession and Multiple Personality, 2:121
MuMath: A Microcomputer Algebra System, 1:506
The Munchkins Remember: The Land of Oz and Beyond, 1:470

Mungo Park, 2:368
Mungo Park: The African Traveler, 2:368
Mungo Park and the Niger, 2:368
Municipal Yearbook, 2:41
Murder at the Vicarage, 1:73
Murder in the Cathedral, 1:82
Murder Must Advertise, 1:117
A Murder of Quality, 1:102
The Murder of Roger Ackroyd, 1:73
Murder on the Orient Express, 1:73
Murder Trials, 2:293
"The Murders in the Rue Morgue," 1:164
Muriel Spark, 1:122
A Murky Business, 1:329
Murphy, 1:331
Murrow: His Life and Times, 1:467
Museums and Women and Other Stories, 1:292
Mushrooms, 2:446
The Music: Reflections on Jazz and Blues, 1:197
Music at the Close: Stravinsky's Last Years, 2:426
Music in a New Found Land: Themes and Developments in the History of American Music, 2:155
Music in the Life of Albert Schweitzer, 2:535
Music in the New World, 2:154
Music in the United States: A Historical Introduction, 2:154
Music Is My Mistress, 2:267
The Music of Aaron Copland, 2:261
The Music of Benjamin Britten, 2:416
The Music of Black Americans, 2:156
The Music of Britten and Tippett: Studies in Themes and Techniques, 2:417
The Music of Gustav Mahler, 2:355
The Music of Igor Stravinsky, 2:427
Music of Liszt, 2:354
Music of the Americas, 2:261
The Music School, 1:292
Music with Words: A Composer's View, 2:262
The Musical Language of Berlioz, 2:347
Musics of Many Cultures: An Introduction, 2:262
Muslim Contributions to Geography, 2:76
Mussolini: A Biography, 2:375
The Mute Stones Speak: The Story of Archaeology in Italy, 2:291
Mutter Courage und Ihre Kinder, 1:365
My Antonía, 1:209; 2:200
My Bondage and My Freedom, 2:190
My Brother Sam Is Dead, 2:163
My Country 'Tis of Me: Helping Children Discover Citizenship Through Cultural Heritage, 2:12
My Cousin Rachel, 1:80

My Darling, My Hamburger, 1:308
My First Summer in the Sierra, 2:221
My Friends, the Wild Chimpanzees, 2:463
My House, 1:226
My Life (Chagall), 2:417
My Life (Duncan), 2:266
My Life (Meir), 2:413
My Life (Trotsky), 2:381
My Life (Wagner), 2:362
My Life, a Record of Events and Opinions (Wallace) 2:459
My Life and Hard Times (Thurber), 1:291
My Life and Medicine: An Autobiographical Memoir (White), 2:563
My Life as a Body, 1:250
My Life on the Plains, 2:203
My Love, My Love, or the Peasant Girl, 1:229
My Mark Twain, 1:181
My Mortal Enemy, 1:209
My Name is Asher Lev, 1:280
My Oedipus Complex, 1:109
My Own River Kwai, 1:332
My Parents Are Driving Me Crazy, 2:539
My People, 2:411
My Philosophical Development, 1:503
My Religion, 1:449
My Sister, Life, 1:393
My Son's Song, 1:414
My Southern Home: The South and Its People, 1:170
My Talks with the Arabs, 2:412
My Uncle Oswald, 1:79
My World and Welcome to It, 1:290
Mysteries, 1:376
Mysteries of Life on Earth and Beyond, 2:478
Mysteries of Outer Space, 2:480
Mysteries of the Ancient Americas, 2:299, 2:300
Mysteries of the Ancient World, 2:278
Mysteries of the Mind, 2:95
Mysteries of the Satellites, 2:475
The Mysteries of Udolpho, 1:28
The Mysterious Affair at Styles, 1:73
The Mysterious Island, 1:343
The Mysterious Maya, 2:300
The Mysterious Undersea World, 2:488
Mysterium cosmographicum, 2:474
The Mystery of Drear House: The Conclusion of the Dies Drear Chronicle, 1:230
The Mystery of Edwin Drood, 1:47
The Mystery of the Bog Forest, 2:466
The Mystic Masseur, 1:406
Mystic Warriors of the Plains, 2:201
The Mythical Man-Month, 1:585
Mythologies of the Ancient World, 2:278
Mythologiques (Mythologies), 2:53

Mythology, 1:318
Myths and Symbols in Indian Art and Civilization, 2:309
Myths of Greece and Rome, 1:318
Myths of Religion, 2:142
Myths of the Greeks and Romans, 1:318

N

The Nabobs: A Study of the Social Life of the English in Eighteenth Century India, 2:363
Nada the Lily, 1:51
Nadine Gordimer, 1:414
The Naive and Sentimental Lover, 1:102
The Naked God, 1:218
Naked Masks: Five Plays, 1:351
Name Crazy: What Your Name Really Means, 1:438
Names and Games: Onomastics and Recreational Linguistics, 1:438
Names and Their Varieties: A Collection of Essays in Onomastics, 1:439
Names, Handles, Monikers or Whatever They're Called—American Style, 1:439
Names in Literature: Essays from Literary Onomastic Studies, 1:438
Names on the Land: A Historical Account of Placenaming in the United States, 1:439
Naming Names: Stories of Pseudonyms and Name Changes with a Who's Who, 1:439
Nana, 1:344, 1:345
Napoleon (Harris), 2:330
Napoleon (Weidhorn), 2:331
Napoleon: Man and Myth, 2:330
Napoleon and Hitler: A Comparative Biography, 2:331
Napoleon Bonaparte, 2:331
Napoleonic Wars: Illustrated History 1792–1815, 2:329
Napoleon's Europe, 2:329
Napoleon's Invasion of Russia, 2:331
Napoleon's Memoirs, 2:330
Narabedla Ltd, 1:278
Narcissus and Goldmund, 1:368
Narrative and Writings of Andrew Jackson of Kentucky, 2:182
Narrative of an Expedition to the Zambesi and Its Tributaries: And of the Discovery of Lakes Shirwa and Nyasa, 1858–1864, 2:367
Narrative of the Life of David Crockett of the State of Tennessee, 2:184
Narrative of the Life of Frederick Douglass, an American Slave, 2:190

A Narrative of Travels on the Amazon and Rio Negro, 2:459

The Narrative of William W. Brown, A Fugitive Slave, 1:170

Narratives of the Career of Hernando De Soto in the Conquest of Florida As Told by a Knight of Elvas, 2:157

Narratives of the Coronado Expedition, 1540–1542, 2:157

The Narrow Road to the North and Other Travel Sketches, 1:424

Nathanael West, 1:300, 1:301

Nathanael West's Novels, 1:301

Nathaniel Hawthorne in His Times, 1:178

Nathaniel Hawthorne's Tales, 1:177

Nation Against Nation: What Happened to the U.N. Dream and What the U.S. Can Do About It, 2:36

A Nation of Immigrants, 2:247

Nation Takes Shape: 1789–1837, 2:168

The National Atlas of the United States of America, 2:90

The National Debt, 2:64, 2:257

National Geographic Atlas of the World, 2:75

National Geographic Picture Atlas of Our Universe, 2:75, 2:475

National Patriotic and Typical Airs of All Lands, 2:216

National Security Strategy of the United States, 2:259, 2:260

Nationalism: Its Meaning and History, 2:275

Nationalism and Ideology, 2:74

Nationalism and Realism, 2:275

Nationalism in the Soviet Union, 2:374

The Nationalization of the Masses: Political Symbolism and Mass Movements in Germany, from the Napoleonic Wars Through the Third Reich, 2:340

Nations and States: An Enquiry into the Origins of Nations and the Politics of Nationalism, 2:340

Nations at Risk: The Impact of the Computer Revolution, 1:556

The Nations Within: The Past and Future of American Indian Sovereignty, 2:135

Native American Testimony: An Anthology of Indian and White Relations, 2:155

Native Argosy, 1:136, 1:137

Native Son, 1:307

N.A.T.O. and the United States: The Enduring Alliance, 2:405

NATO at Forty: Change, Continuity, and Prospects for the Future, 2:405

NATO's Anxious Birth: The Prophetic Vision of the 1940s, 2:406

The Natural, 1:261, 1:262

A Natural Curiosity, 1:80

The Natural History of H. G. Wells, 1:129

The Natural History of the Primates, 2:450

Natural House, 2:270

Natural Skin Care: All You Need to Know for Healthy Skin, 2:552

Naturally Intelligent Systems, 1:583

Nature, 1:157

The Nature and Growth of Modern Mathematics, 1:497

The Nature and Logic of Capitalism, 2:57

The Nature of Culture, 2:45

The Nature of Greek Myths, 1:318

The Nature of Magnetism, 2:522

The Nature of Man, 1:533

The Nature of Matter, 2:518

The Nature of Matter: Wolfson College Lectures, 1980, 2:498, 2:518

The Nature of Modern Mathematics, 1:498

The Nature of Personality: Selected Papers, 2:115

The Nature of Prejudice, 2:97, 2:104, 2:115, 2:135

The Nature of the Chemical Bond and the Structure of Molecules and Crystals, 2:505, 2:506

Nature of the Child, 2:106

Nature's Chaos, 1:516

Nature's Great Carbon Cycle, 2:466

Nature's Weather Forecasters, 2:485

Nature's World of Wonders, 2:83

Nausea, 1:340

The Nazis, 2:383

Nazism: A Historical and Comparative Analysis of National Socialism, 2:375

NBC Handbook of Pronunciation, 1:445

The Necessary Dream: A Study of the Novels of Manuel Puig, 1:409

Necessary Illusions: Thought Control in Democratic Societies, 1:435

"The Necklace," 1:337

The Needle's Eye, 1:79, 1:80

Nefertiti and Cleopatra—Queen-Monarchs of Ancient Egypt, 2:281

The Negative, 2:263

Negotiation: The Alternative to Hostility, 2:256

Negro Americans: What Now, 1:245

The Negro Artisan, 2:211

The Negro Caravan, 1:205, 1:206

The Negro Cowboys, 2:200

The Negro in American Fiction and Negro Poetry and Drama, 1:206

The Negro in Business, 2:211

The Negro in the American Rebellion: His Heroism and His Fidelity, 1:170

The Negro in the South, 2:213

Nehru: The Making of India, 2:404
Nehru for Children, 2:404
Nehru on World History, 2:404
"Neighbor Rosicky," 1:209
Neighborhood Politics, 2:40
Neil Simon, 1:287
Neil Simon: A Critical Study, 1:287
Nelson and Winnie Mandela, 2:395
Nelson Mandela: I Am Prepared to Die, 2:395
Nelson Mandela: Pictorial History, 2:395
Nelson Mandela: South Africa's Silent Voice of Protest, 2:395
Nelson Mandela: The Man and His Movement, 2:395
Nemesis, 1:194
Neo-Classism, 2:333
Nero, 2:290
The Nerves of Government, 2:130
A Nest of Simple Folk, 1:110
Networks and Places: Social Relations in the Urban Setting, 2:147
Neural Networks: The Second AI Generation, 1:583
Neural Networks in Artificial Intelligence, 1:584
Neurosis and Human Growth, 2:106, 2:119
The Neurotic Personality of Our Time, 2:98, 2:119
The Neutrals, 2:383
Never at Rest: A Biography of Isaac Newton, 2:516
Never Cry Wolf, 1:144
The New Aerobics for Women, 2:551
A New Age Now Begins: A People's History of the American Revolution, 2:164, 2:328
The New American Handbook of Letter Writing and Other Correspondence, 1:487
The New American Poverty, 2:68, 2:257
New and Collected Poems (MacLeish), 1917–1982, 1:261
New and Selected Poems (Warren), 1:299
New Architecture and the Bauhaus, 2:268
The New Astronomy, 2:470
The New Atlas of the Universe, 2:470
New Book of World Rankings, 2:76, 2:275
New Consensus on Family and Welfare: A Community of Self-Reliance, 2:69, 2:258
The New Country: A Social History of the American Frontier, 1776–1890, 2:184
The New Deal and the States: Federalism in Transition, 2:36
The New Deal Collective Bargaining Policy, 2:228
A New Deal for Blacks: The Emergence of Civil Rights as a National Issue: The Depression Decade, 2:229

New Dictionary of American Slang, 1:433
New Dimensions of Political Economy, 2:63
The New Earth Book: Our Changing Planet, 2:494
New England Frontier: Indians and Puritans, 1620–1675, 2:163
The New England Mind: The Seventeenth Century, 2:162
A New England Town: The First Hundred Years, 2:162
New Essays on Human Understanding, 1:527
New Essays on the Psychology of Art, 2:113
The New Eyes of the Scientist, 2:436
The New Face of War, 2:241
The New Federalism (Goode), 2:35
The New Federalism (Reagan and Sanzone), 2:36
New Forces, Old Forces, and the Future of World Politics, 2:387
New Frontiers in Genetics, 2:452
The New Grove Dictionary of American Music, 2:154
The New Grove Haydn, 2:337
The New Grove Wagner, 2:362
New Guide to the Moon, 2:476
New Guys Around the Block, 1:229
A New History of England: 410–1975, 2:276
The New Holistic Health Handbook, 2:530
New Hope for Problem Pregnancies: Helping Babies BEFORE They're Born, 2:543
New Hope for the Handicapped, 2:565
The New Industrial State, 2:66
New International Atlas, 2:75
The New Italian Poetry, 1945 to the Present: A Bilingual Anthology, 1:348
The New Journalism, 1:479
New Journalism: The Underground Press, the Artists of Nonfiction, and Changes in the Established Media, 1:479
New Letters of Berlioz, 1830–1868, 2:347
A New Life, 1:262
New Light on the Green Algae, 2:447
New Maps of Hell, 1:65
The New Mass Media: Challenge to a Free Society, 1:453
New Mexico: A History of Four Centuries, 2:160
New Money Book For the 80's, 2:61
The New Nation: A History of the United States During the Confederation, 1781–1789, 2:164
The New Nationalism, 2:222
The New New Words Dictionary, 1:440
New Orleans Jazz: A Family Album, 2:262

The New Oxford Companion to Music, 2:152
New Perspectives on Galileo, 2:473
The New Philippines, 2:399
A New Pictorial History of the Talkies, 1:468
New Poems: The Other Part (Rilke), 1:371
New Poems, Nineteen Hundred Seven (Rilke), 1:371
The New Race for Space: The U.S. and Russia Leap to the Challenge for Unlimited Rewards, 2:481
New Reign of Terror in the Slaveholding States, for 1859–1860, 2:191
The New Religions of Africa, 2:52, 2:142
New Selected Poems (Hughes), 1:95
The New State of the World Atlas, 2:75
New System of Chemical Philosophy, 2:502
New Theories on Diet and Nutrition, 2:549
New Ways in Psychoanalysis, 2:119
New Worlds: Discoveries from Our Solar System, 2:483
The New Writer: Techniques for Writing Well with a Computer, 1:576
The New Yorker Album of Drawings, 1:455
The New Yorker Book of War Pieces, 1:455
The New Yorker Cartoon Album, 1975–1985, 1:455
The New Yorker Twenty-Fifth Anniversary Album, 1925–1950, 1:455
New Zealand in Color, 2:91
Newer Ideals of Peace, 2:208
The News as Myth: Fact and Context in Journalism, 1:457
The News Business, 1:457
News from Nowhere: Television and the News, 1:457
Newspaper Layout and Design, 1:457
Newspaper Row: Journalism in the Pre-Television Era, 1:457
Newspeak: A Dictionary of Jargon, 1:433
Newswriting: From Lead to "30," 1:487
Newswriting for the Electronic Media: Principles, Examples, Applications, 1:487
Newton and Russia: The Early Influence 1698–1796, 2:515
Newton on Matter and Activity, 2:513
Newtonian Mechanics, 2:512
The Next Left: The History of a Future, 2:39
The Next Million Years, 2:48
The Nez Percé Indians and the Opening of the Northwest, 2:184
Nicaragua: A Country Study, 2:89, 2:409
The Nice and the Good, 1:107, 1:108

Nicholas Nickleby, 1:46, 1:47
The Nick Adams Stories, 1:237
Nicolas Copernicus: An Essay on His Life and Work, 2:514
Niels Bohr: A Centenary Volume, 2:501
Niels Bohr: His Life and Work as Seen by His Friends and Family, 2:501
Niels Bohr and the Development of Physics: Essays Dedicated to Bohr on the Occasion of his Seventieth Birthday, 2:501
The Nigger of the Narcissus, 1:77
Night, 1:301; 2:385
Night and Day, 1:132
Night, Dawn, Day, 1:301
The Night Journey, 2:207
Night Kites, 1:248
The Night of the Iguana, 1:304
Night Roamers and Other Stories, 1:376
Night Shift, 1:249
Night to Remember, 2:218
The Night Trilogy: Night, Dawn, The Accident, 1:301
Night Watches, 1:97
Nightfall and Other Stories, 1:194
Nightly Horrors: Crisis Coverage in Television Network News, 1:458
A Nightmare in History: The Holocaust 1933–1945, 2:382
Nikita Khrushchev (Ebon), 2:392
Nikita Krushchev (Kort), 2:392
Nikita Sergeievich Khrushchev: Modern Dictator of the U.S.S.R, 2:392
Nikolai Gogol, 1:393
Nilda, 1:267
Nile Basin, 2:364
The Nine Billion Names of God, 1:75
Nine Fairy Tales, 1:385
The Nine Hundred Days: The Siege of Leningrad, 2:385
The Nine Nations of North America, 2:90
The Nine Old Men, 1:459
Nine Stories (Salinger), 1:282, 1:283
The Nine Tailors, 1:117
Nine Tomorrows, 1:194
1984, 1:111; 2:229
Nineteen Eighty-Four: Commemorative Edition, 2:7
Nineteen Ninety-Nine: The Global Challenges We Face in the Next Decade, 2:254
Nineteen Ninety-Nine: Victory Without War, 2:254
Nineteen Thirty-Four, 1:350
Nineteenth-Century Africa, 2:363
Nineteenth-Century Russian Plays, 1:389
Nixon, 2:255

The Nixon–Kissinger Years: The
Reshaping of American Foreign Policy,
2:37, 2:252
Nkrumah, 2:396
No, But I Saw the Movie: The Best Short
Stories Ever Made Into Film, 1:474
No Easy Walk to Freedom, 2:395
No Exit, 1:340
No Laughing Matter: Chalk Talks About
Alcohol, 2:555
No Longer at East, 1:411
No More Fears, 2:536
No More Saturday Nights, 1:250
No More Vietnams, 2:254
No More War!, 2:506
No Name, 1:45
No-Nonsense Nutrition for Kids, 2:550
No One Writes to the Colonel and Other
Stories, 1:403, 1:404
No Peace with Napoleon, 2:330
The No Plays of Japan, 1:425
No Promises in the Wind, 2:229
No Way to Treat a Lady, 1:227
Noa Noa: The Tahitian Journal, 2:353
Noah Webster's American Spelling Book,
1:430
Noah Webster's Pronunciation and
Modern New England Speech, 1:429
Noam Chomsky, 1:435
Nobody Knows My Name, 1:195
Noel Coward, 1:78
Non-Euclidean Geometry, 1:519
None Died in Vain: The Saga of the
American Civil War, 2:193
Nonsexist Word Finder: A Dictionary of
Gender-Free Usage, 1:479
The Nontoxic Home: Protecting Yourself
and Your Family from Everyday Toxics
and Health Hazards, 2:570
Nontraditional Families: Parenting and
Child Development, 2:539
Normans and the Norman Conquest,
2:305
North, 1:92
North Africa, 2:272
The North African Stones Speak, 2:300
North America: A Human Geography,
2:90
North America: The Historical Geography
of a Changing Continent, 2:90
North American Indians: A
Comprehensive Account, 2:158
The North Ship, 1:100
The North Star, 2:190
Northern Ireland: The Thatcher Years,
2:408
Northwest Passage, 2:158
Norwegian Folk Tales, 1:374
Nostromo, 1:77

A Not Entirely Benign Procedure: Four
Years as a Medical Student, 2:531
Not-for-Profit, 2:63
Not Honor More, 1:72
Not So Free to Choose: The Political
Economy of Milton Friedman and
Ronald Reagan, 2:66
Not That You Asked, 1:480
Not Without Laughter, 1:241
The Notebooks of Frank Herbert's Dune,
1:239
The Notebooks of Leonardo Da Vinci,
2:315
Notes for Another Life, 1:204
Notes from the Underground, 1:392
Notes of a Native Son, 1:195
Notes of Debates in the Federal
Convention of 1787, 2:177
Notes on Genesis, 2:259
Notes on Hospitals, 2:569
Notes on Matters Affecting the Health,
Efficiency and Hospital Administration
of the British Army, 2:569
Notes on Nursing: What It Is and What It
Is Not, 2:569, 2:570
Notes on the Life of Edmund Spenser,
1:17
Nothing like the Sun, 1:71
Nothing to Be Ashamed of: Growing up
with Mental Illness in Your Family,
2:538
Nothing to Fear, 2:234
Nôtre Dame de Paris (The Hunchback of
Notre Dame), 1:336, 1:337
Novela-Nivola, 1:360
Novelas ejemplares, 1:356
NOVELL NetWare Commands and
Installation Made Easy, 1:559
Novelle per un anno, 1:351
The Novels of Dashiell Hammett, 1:231
The Novels of Nadine Gordimer: History
from the Inside, 1:414
Novum Organum and Related Writings,
2:435
Now and at the Hour, 1:212
Now and Then: Poems 1976–1978, 1:298,
1:299
Now You've Got Your Period, 2:542
Nubian Culture: Past and Present, 2:274
The Nuclear Age: Atomic Energy,
Proliferation, and the Arms Race, 2:37
The Nuclear Arms Race—Can We Survive
It?, 2:258
The Nuclear Delusion: Soviet–American
Relations in the Atomic Age, 2:391
Nuclear Energy, 2:496, 2:528
The Nuclear Energy Controversy, 2:496
Nuclear Physics, 2:528
The Nuclear Question, 2:467

Nuevas odas elementales, 1:407
Number Art: Thirteen 1 2 3s from Around the World, 1:497
Numquam, 1:81
Nureyev, 2:261
Nutrition, 2:550
Nutrition: Where Have All These Labels Been? The "Secret" Nutrition Labels for Over 1200 Common Foods, 2:549
Nutrition Almanac, 2:549
Nutrition and Dental Health, 2:552
Nutrition and Health Encyclopedia, 2:550
Nutrition and the Brain, 2:549
Nutrition Concepts and Controversies, 1:569; 2:549
The Nutrition Debate: Sorting Out Some Answers, 2:549
Nutrition for Living, 1:568
Nutrition for the Prime of Your Life, 2:550
Nutritional Diseases, 2:549
Nuts & Bolts of the Past: A History of American Technology 1776–1860, 2:432
Nyerere and Nkrumah, 2:397

O

O. Henry, 1:178
O Pioneers, 1:209; 2:200
Oak and Ivy, 1:175
The Oath, 1:301
Object-Oriented Programming: An Introduction, 1:563
Object-Oriented Programming Systems, 1:563
Obra poética (Borges), 1:400
Observations: Selected Speeches and Essays, 1982–1984, 2:38
"An Occurrence at Owl Creek Bridge," 1:169
The Ocean Almanac, 2:486
Ocean Frontiers, 2:486
The Ocean Realm, 2:83, 2:488
Oceanography, 2:83
The Oceans, 2:82
Oceans in Peril, 2:488
Oceans of Energy: Reservoir of Power for the Future, 2:488
Oceans of the World: Our Essential Resource, 2:83, 2:488
OCLC, Inc. Its Governance, Function, Finance, and Technology, 1:573
Octavio Paz, 1:408
Octavio Paz, the Mythic Dimension, 1:408
The October Country, 1:202
The Octopus, 1:180, 1:181; 2:218
Octopussy, 1:84
Odas elementales (Neruda), 1:407

"Ode on a Grecian Urn," 1:35
"Ode to a Nightingale," 1:35
Ode to Liberty, 1:394
Ode to Walt Whitman and Other Poems, 1:357
Odes (Carducci), 1:349
The Odes of Horace: A Critical Study, 2:294
The Odyssey, 1:27, 1:156, 1:311, 1:315, 1:324
Odyssey: Pepsi to Apple . . . A Journey of a Marketing Impresario, 1:546
Oedipus Rex, 1:316
Oeuvres de Maximilien Robespierre, 2:331
Of Human Bondage, 1:106
Of Love and Dust, 1:224
Of Mice and Men, 1:288, 1:289
Of Nightingales That Weep, 1:484
Of Plymouth Plantation: Sixteen Twenty to Sixteen Forty Seven, 1:151
Of the Farm, 1:292
Of Time and the River, 1:306
Officers and Gentlemen, 1:127
The Official Halley's Comet Book, 2:475
Oh Pray My Wings Are Gonna Fit Me Well, 1:192
Oh What a Paradise It Seems, 1:211
Oil and Natural Gas, 2:496
Oil and Turmoil: America Faces OPEC and the Middle East, 2:252
Okike: An African Journal of New Writing, 1:411
The Old Bachelor, 1:21
The Old Century and Seven More Years, 1:116
Old Creole Days, 1:171
The Old Curiosity Shop, 1:46, 1:47
The Old Devils: A Novel, 1:65
Old English Glosses: A Collection, 1:429
Old Gimlet Eye: Adventures of Smedley D. Butler, 1:463
Old Goriot, 1:329
The Old Gringo, 1:402, 1:403
"Old Ironsides," 1:158
Old Love and Other Stories, 1:388
The Old Man and the Sea, 1:236
Old Myths and New Realities in United States-Soviet Relations, 2:258
The Old Order: Stories of the South, 1:279
Old Possum's Book of Practical Cats, 1:82
Old Times, 1:114
Older Men, 1:250
Olduvai Gorge, 2:49
Ole Edvart Rølvaag, 1:379
Oliphaunt, 1:125
Oliver Goldsmith, 1:25
Oliver Goldsmith and Richard Brinsley Sheridan, 1:25

Oliver Twist, 1:46, 1:47
Oliver Wendell Holmes, 1:158
Oliver Wendell Holmes, Jr., 2:29
Oliver Wendell Holmes, Jr. Boy of Justice, 2:29
The Olmec World, 2:298
Olympians: Great Gods and Goddesses of Ancient Greece, 2:284
Olympic Games: The Records 776 B.C. to A.D. 1988, 2:274
Olympic Games in Ancient Greece, 2:285
Olympics in Art: An Exhibition of Works Related to Olympic Sports, 2:415
The Omni Book of Space, 2:480
The Omni Future Almanac, 2:156
The Omni Interviews, 2:440
Omoo: A Narrative of Adventures in the South Seas, 1:162, 1:163
On Aggression, 2:99, 2:100, 2:104, 2:464
On Anatomical Procedure, 2:546
On Becoming a Biologist, 2:437
On Becoming a Person, 2:114
On Becoming Human, 2:460
"On Civil Disobedience," 1:165
On Double Consciousness, 2:123
On Education: Articles on Educational Theory and Pedagogy, and Writings for Children from the Age of Gold, 2:370
On Geography: Selected Writings of Preston E. James, 2:78
On Growth and Form, 1:516
On Her Majesty's Secret Service, 1:84
On Higher Education: The Academic Enterprise in an Era of Rising Student Consumerism, 2:132
On Knowing: Essays for the Left Hand, 2:112
On Land and Sea with Caesar, 2:292
On Language, 1:443
On Liberty: With the Subjection of Women and Chapters on Socialism, 2:72
On Life and Living: Konrad Lorenz in Conversation with Kurt Mundl, 2:464
On-Line Text Management: Hypertext and Other Techniques, 1:580
On Love and Barley: Haiku of Bashō, 1:424
"On Melancholy," 1:35
On Nuclear War and Peace, 2:535
On Our Way, 2:234
On the American Revolution, 2:329
On the Beach, 1:147
On the Move: American Women in the 1970s, 2:252
On the Origin of Species by Means of Natural Selection, 2:48
On the Peoples Democratic Dictatorship, 2:402

On the Razzle, 1:122
On the Road, 1:246, 1:247
On the Shoulders of Giants: A Shandean Postscript, 2:141
On Writing the College Application Essay, 1:485
On Writing Well, 1:488
Once: Poems, 1:296, 1:297
The Once and Future King, 1:130
Once Around the Galaxy, 2:469
One Brief Shining Moment: Remembering Kennedy, 2:248
One Church, Many Cultures: The Challenge of Diversity, 2:134
One Day in the Life of Ivan Denisovich, 1:396
One Fat Englishman, 1:65
One for the Road, 1:114
One Generation After, 1:302
One Half of Robertson Davies, 1:138
The One-Hundred-Percent Natural, Purely Organic, Cholesterol-Free, Megavitamin, Low-Carbohydrate Nutrition Hoax, 2:550
One Hundred Poems from the Chinese, 1:423
One Hundred Poems from the Japanese, 1:425
One Hundred Selected Poems, 1:214
100 Successful College Application Essays, 1:485
One Hundred Years of Music in America, 2:154
One Hundred Years of Solitude, 1:403, 1:404
The One in the Middle Is the Green Kangaroo, 1:201
One Life: An Autobiography, 2:49
One Man's Meat, 1:456
The One Minute Manager, 2:63
One of Ours, 1:209
One Small Step: The Apollo Missions, the Astronauts, the Aftermath, 2:252
One Thousand and One Things Everyone Should Know About American History, 2:153
1,000 Most Challenging Words, 1:440
1,000 Most Important Words, 1:440
1–2–3 QuickStart: A Graphics Approach, 1:563, 1:573
1–2–3 Release 3 Made Easy, 1:573
One Way to Heaven, 1:213
One World Divided: A Geographer Looks at the Modern World, 2:78
One Writer's Beginnings, 1:299, 1:300, 1:482
Onions and Cucumbers and Plums: Forty-Six Yiddish Poems in English, 1:382

Online Education: Perspectives on a New Environment, 1:570

The Only Math Book You'll Ever Need, 1:504

Only One Earth: The Care and Maintenance of a Small Planet, 2:74

The Only Problem, 1:121

Only the Best, 1990: The Annual Guide to Highest-Rated Educational Software, Preschool–Grade 12, 1:570

Only the Names Remain: The Cherokees and the Trail of Tears, 2:180

Only Yesterday, 2:225

Ontogeny and Phylogeny, 2:458

Ontogeny, Cell Differentiation, and Structure of Vascular Plants, 2:447

OPEC: Twenty-Five Years of Prices and Politics, 2:252

"The Open Boat," 1:173

An Open Book, 1:472

Open Heart Surgery: A Second Chance, 2:565

Open to the Sun: A Bilingual Anthology of Latin American Women Poets, 1:399

"The Open Window," 1:115

Opening the Space Frontier, 2:482

Opera: A Concise History, 2:262

Opera as Drama, 2:262

The Opera Companion, 2:262

Opera Omnia, 1:526

The Operas of Verdi, 2:361

Operating Manual for Spaceship Earth, 1:522

Operating Systems: Concepts and Implementations, 1:561

Operating Systems and Languages, 1:562

Operetta: A Theatrical History, 2:263

Oppenheimer and The Atomic Bomb, 2:235

Opportunity and Change, 2:144

The Opposite Sex Is Driving Me Crazy: What Boys Think About Girls, 2:543

Optical Computing, 1:559

Optical Information Processing and Holography, 1:578

Opticks, 2:515

Optics and the Theory of Electrons, 2:503

The Optimist's Daughter, 1:300

Options for Tax Reform, 2:71

Or Else: Poems 1968–1973, 1:299

Oral Interpretations, 1:449

Orbiting the Sun: Planets and Satellites of the Solar System, 2:476

Ordeal By Ice, 1:144

The Ordeal of Gilbert Pinfold, 1:127

Ordeal of Total War, 1939–1945, 2:236

Order and Conflict in Contemporary Capitalism, 2:71

Order in Space, 1:519

Ordinary Differential Equations, 1:525

Oregon Trail, 2:185

The Orestia: Agamemnon, The Libation Bearers, The Eumenides, 1:311, 1:312

Organ Transplants, 2:565

The Organic Chemistry Laboratory Survival Manual, 2:510

Organizations, 2:140

Organizing a Computer Club for Elementary School Children, 1:555

Organon, 2:442

Origin and Evolution of Gymnosperms, 2:447

Origin of Continents and Oceans, 2:491

The Origin of Life, 2:461

The Origin of Species by Means of Natural Selection, 2:456, 2:457, 2:490

The Origin of the Family: Private Property and the State, 2:59

The Origin of Totalitarianism, 2:374

The Original Hitchhiker's Radio Scripts, 1:65

The Originality of Japanese Civilization, 2:277

Origins: Bringing Words to Life, 1:433

Origins: What New Discoveries Reveal About the Emergence of Our Species and Its Possible Future, 2:49, 2:460

The Origins and Development of Labor Economics, 2:70

Origins in Acoustics: The Science of Sound from Antiquity to the Age of Newton, 2:521

The Origins of Cauchy's Rigorous Calculus, 1:525

The Origins of Chinese Civilization, 2:282

Origins of Life, 2:461

Origins of Mendelism, 2:453

The Origins of Modern Germany, 2:404

Origins of Scientific Sociology, 2:125

Origins of the American Revolution: With a New Introduction and Bibliography, 2:164

The Origins of the Civil Rights Movement: Black Communities Organizing for Change, 2:242

Origins of the Cold War in Comparative Perspective: American, British, and Canadian Relations with the Soviet Union, 1941–48, 2:387

The Origins of the First World War (Joll), 2:371

Origins of the First World War (Koch), 2:371

The Origins of the Infinitesimal Calculus, 1:527

The Origins of the Second World War, 2:385

Orlando, 1:132

Orlando Furioso, 1:347
Ormond, 1:152
Orsinian Tales, 1:254
Orson Welles: A Biography, 1:470
The Orwell Reader, 1:111
Oscar Wilde (Ellman), 1:62
Oscar Wilde (Raby): 1:63
The Other America, 2:144
The Other Arab-Israeli Conflict: Making America's Middle East Policy, from Truman to Reagan, 2:258
Other Bells for Us to Ring, 1:213
The Other 1492: Jewish Settlement in the New World, 2:160
The Other Paris, 1:139
Other People's Money: A Study in the Social Psychology of Embezzlement, 2:133
The Other Place and Other Stories of the Same Sort, 1:114
Otto von Bismarck, 2:342
Otto Von Bismarck: A Historical Assessment, 2:342
Otto Warburg: Cell Physiologist, Biochemist, and Eccentric, 2:438
Our Accoustic Environment, 2:522
Our America: Writings on Latin America and the Struggle for Cuban Independence, 2:370
Our Awesome Earth, 2:83
Our Bodies, Ourselves, 2:542
Our Endangered Atmosphere: Global Warming and the Ozone Layer, 2:82
Our Fiery Trial: Abraham Lincoln, John Brown, and the Civil War Era, 2:189
Our Foreign-Born Citizens, 2:206
Our Forty-First President: George Bush, 2:259
Our Freedoms: Rights and Responsibilities, 2:13
Our Golda: The Story of Golda Meir, 2:413
Our Inner Conflicts, 2:119
Our Kind: Who We Are, Where We Came From, Where We Are Going, 2:48
Our Man in Havana, 1:91
Our National Parks, 2:221
Our Oriental Heritage, 2:280
Our Primitive Contemporaries, 2:51
Our Restless Earth, 2:493
Our Time Has Come: A Delegate's Diary of Jesse Jackson's 1984 Presidential Campaign, 2:256
Our Town, 1:302
Our Violent Earth, 2:494
Ourselves and Other Animals, 2:461
Out in the Midday Sun: My Kenya, 2:393
Out of Africa, 1:375, 1:376
Out of Mulberry Street, 2:212

Out of My Later Years, 2:520
Out of the Night: A Biologist's View of the Future, 2:455
Out of the Silent Planet, 1:104
Out of the Whirlpool, 1:121
Out on a Limerick, 1:439
The Outcast of the Islands, 1:76, 1:77
The Outcasts of Poker Flat and Other Stories, 1:176
Outline of Cultural Materials, 2:51
An Outline of Geography, 2:78
Outline of Projective Geometry, 1:519
The Outline of Sanity: A Biography of G. K. Chesterton, 1:73
Outline of World Cultures, 2:51
Outre-Mer: A Pilgrimage Beyond the Sea, 1:160
The Outside Shot, 1:270
The Outsider (Fast), 1:218
The Outsider (Wright), 1:307
The Outsiders, 1:239, 1:240
Over Here: The First World War and American Society, 2:224
"The Over-Soul," 1:157
Over the Teacups, 1:158
Over the Wire and on TV: CBS and UPI in Campaign '80, 1:443
Over There: The Story of America's First Great Overseas Crusade, 2:223
Over to You, 1:79
The Overcoat and Other Tales of Good and Evil, 1:393
Overcoming Arthritis, 2:561
Overcoming Computer Illiteracy: A Friendly Introduction to Computers, 1:556
Overcoming Disability, 2:564
Overcoming Stress: Everything You Ever Need to Know, 2:123
Overheard in a Balloon, 1:139
Overlord: D-Day and the Battle of Normandy, 2:235, 2:384
Overnight to Many Distant Cities, 1:198
Ovid, 1:321; 2:291
Owls Do Cry, 1:138
An Ownership Theory of the Trade Union: A New Approach, 2:70
The Oxford Book of Flowerless Plants, 2:446, 2:447
The Oxford Companion to Classical Literature, 1:311
The Oxford Companion to Twentieth-Century Art, 2:262
Oxford Dictionary of Current Idiomatic English, 1:437
The Oxford Encyclopedia of Trees of the World, 2:447
The Oxford History of the American People, 2:155

The Oxford History of the Classical World: Greece and the Hellenistic World, 2:284

The Oxford History of the Classical World: The Roman World, 2:290

The Oxford Ibsen, 1:378

The Oxford Illustrated History of Britain, 2:275

The Oxford Illustrated History of the British Monarchy, 2:273

The Oz Series, 1:198

Ozma of Oz, 1:198

Ozone Crisis: The Fifteen Year Evolution of a Sudden Global Emergency, 2:486

P

P. D. James, 1:98

P. G. Wodehouse, 1:131

P. G. Wodehouse: A Portrait of a Master, 1:131

P. Ovidi Nasonis Metamorphoseon liber I, 1:321

Pablo Neruda, 1:407

Pablo Picasso, 2:421, 2:422

Pablo Picasso: The Man and the Image, 2:421

Pablo Picasso Eighteen Eighty-One to Nineteen Seventy-Three, 2:415

PAC Power: Inside the World of Political Action Committees, 2:40

Pack, Band, and Colony: The World of Social Animals, 2:462

Padraic Colum, 1:76

Pagan Priests: Religion and Power in the Ancient World, 2:272

A Pageant and Other Poems, 1:56

PageMaker 4 for the Macintosh Made Easy, 1:576

The Painted Word, 1:479

Painting in the Twentieth Century, 2:261

The Paintings and Drawings of J. M. W. Turner, 2:358

Paintings in the Hermitage, 2:415

Paintings of Eugene Delacroix, 2:334

The Paintings of J. M. W. Turner, 2:358

A Pair of Blue Eyes, 1:51, 1:52

Pakistan: A Country Study, 2:87

Palace of the Peacock, 1:404

The Palace of Truth, 1:50

Pale Horse, Pale Rider, 1:279

Palestrina, 2:319

Palm Sunday, 1:296

Palmerston, Metternich and the European System: 1830–1841, 2:333

Pamela, 1:24, 1:28, 1:29

Pan: From Lieutenant Thomas Glahn's Papers, 1:376

Pan Michael: An Historical Novel of Poland, the Ukraine, and Turkey, 1:387

Panama: A Country Study, 2:88

A Panama Forest and Shore, 2:88

Pancho Villa and John Reed: Two Faces of Romantic Revolution, 2:370

The Panda's Thumb: More Reflections in Natural History, 2:458

Panic, 1:261

Panic: Facing Fears, Phobias, and Anxiety, 2:103

Panic on Wall Street: A Classic History of America's Financial Disasters—with a Timely Exploration of the Crash of 1987, 2:258

The Pantheon Story of American Art: For Young People, 2:152

The Panther and the Lark, 1:241

Panzer Army Africa, 2:384

The Paper Men, 1:89

The Papers of George Catlett Marshall, 2:240

Papers of John von Neumann on Computing and Computer Theory, 1:553

The Papers of Thomas Alva Edison, 2:524

The Papers of Woodrow Wilson, 2:225

Papers on Fuchsian Functions, 1:500

Parables and Paradoxes: Parabeln and Paradoxe, 1:369

Parables of Sun Light: Observations on Psychology, the Arts, and the Rest, 2:113

Paradise Lost, 1:13

Paradise Regained, 1:13

Paradiso, 1:349

Paradox 3: The Complete Reference, 1:572

Paradox 3 Made Easy, 1:572

Paradox 3.0 Handbook, 1:572

Parallel Lives of Greeks and Romans, 2:288

Parallel Program Design: A Foundation, 1:559

The Parasites, 1:81

A Parcel of Patterns, 1:126

Pardon Me, You're Stepping on My Eyeball!, 1:308

Parent's Guide to Anorexia and Bulimia. Understanding and Helping Self-Starvers and Binge-Purgers, 2:550

Parent's Guide to Nutrition: Eating from Birth Through Adolescence, 2:549

Paris Spleen, 1:330

Park's Quest, 1:484

A Part of My Soul Went with Him, 2:395

Participant Observation: A Methodology for Human Studies, 2:42

Participation and Political Equality: A Seven-Nation Comparison, 2:145

Particulars of My Life: The Shaping of a Behaviorist—A Matter of Consequences, 2:101

Parties, Politics and Public Policy in America, 2:39

Parting the Waters: America in the King Years, 2:12

Partisans, 2:383

The Party and Other Stories, 1:391

The Party's Just Begun: Shaping Political Parties for America's Future, 2:40

Pascal: The Emergence of Genius, 1:533

Pascal and Algorithms: An Introduction to Problem Solving, 1:586

Pascal's Anguish and Joy, 1:533

Pascal's Lettres Provinciales: The Motif and Practice of Fragmentation, 1:533

Pascal's Triangle, 1:535

Passage Through Armageddon: The Russians in War and Revolution 1914–1918, 2:371

A Passage to India, 1:85; 2:363

Passages, 2:107

Passages from the Life of a Philosopher, 1:542

A Passion for Science, 2:433

A Passion to Know, 2:453

Passionate Attachments, 2:103

The Passive Solar Energy Book, 2:485

Pasteur and Modern Science, 2:445

The Pastures of Heaven, 1:288

The Pat Hobby Stories, 1:222

Pat of Silver Bush, 1:143

The Patchwork Girl of Oz, 1:198

Paterson, 1:305

The Path Between the Seas: The Creation of the Panama Canal, 1870–1914, 2:218

The Path to the Double Helix, 2:439, 2:441

The Pathfinders: A Saga of Exploration in Southern Africa, 2:85

The Path-Way to Knowledge, Containing the First Principles of Geometry, 1:512

Pathways to the Universe, 2:469

Patience, 1:8

Patrick White, 1:148

The Patriot, 1:207

A Patriot for Me, 1:112

Pattern for Industrial Peace, 2:150

Patterns, 1:486

Patterns in Comparative Religion, 2:52

Patterns in Criminal Homicide, 2:133

Patterns in Nature, 1:515

Patterns in Pluralism: A Portrait of American Religion, 2:142

Patterns of Culture, 2:43, 2:44

Patterns of Emotions, 2:104

Paul Cézanne, 2:349

Paul Cézanne: The Watercolors—A Catalogue Raisonne, 2:349

Paul Cézanne, Letters, 2:349

Paul Gauguin: Letters to His Wife and Friends, 2:353

Paul Laurence Dunbar, 1:175

Paul Laurence Dunbar: A Poet to Remember, 1:176

Paul Laurence Dunbar Critically Examined, 1:176

The Paul Mace Guide to Data Recovery, 1:575

Paul Revere and the World He Lived In, 2:164

"Paul Revere's Ride," 1:160

Pauli Lectures on Physics, 2:503

Pauline, 1:44

"Paul's Case," 1:209

Pavlov: A Biography, 2:464

Payment Deferred, 1:84

Paz en la guerra, 1:360

PC System Programming for Developers, 1:585

The PC-SIG Encyclopedia of Shareware, 1:567

Peace and Bread in Time of War, 2:208

Peace and War: A Theory of International Relations, 2:36

Peace Breaks Out, 1:251

Peace Conference of Nineteen Nineteen: Organization and Procedure, 2:224

Peace Corps, 2:242

Peace Corps in the Eighties, 2:242

Peace Has No Alternative: Speeches, Articles, Interviews, 2:406

Peace with Justice, 2:239

Peace Without Promise: Britain and the Peace Conferences 1919–1923, 2:223

Peaceful Conquest: The Industrialization of Europe, 1760–1970, 2:276

The Peach Grove, 1:140

The Peacock Spring, 1:88

Peanuts, 1:459

The Pearl (Pearl Poet), 1:7

The Pearl (Steinbeck), 1:289

Pearl: A New Verse Translation, 1:8

Pearl Buck, 1:207

Pearl Buck: Famed American Author of Oriental Stories, 1:207

Pearl Harbor, 2:236, 2:385

Pearl Harbor: Warning and Decision, 2:236

Pearl Poems: An Omnibus Edition, 1:8

The Pearl Poet, 1:8

Pearl S. Buck, 1:207

A Pebble in the Sky, 1:194

Peder Victorius: A Tale of the Pioneers Twenty Years Later, 1:379

Peer Gynt, 1:377, 1:378

The Pegnitz Junction, 1:139

Pelican Economic History of Britain, 2:339

The Pelican History of Greek Literature, 2:275

The Peloponnesian War, 2:289
Penetrating Wagner's Ring: An Anthology, 2:362
The Penguin Atlas of Ancient History, 2:278
The Penguin Atlas of Medieval History, 2:306
The Penguin Atlas of North American History to 1870, 2:275
The Penguin Atlas of Recent History: Europe Since 1815, 2:88
The Penguin Book of Hebrew Verse, 1:420
The Penguin Book of Japanese Verse, 1:425
The Penguin Book of Modern Urdu Poetry, 1:422
The Penguin Book of Russian Short Stories, 1:390
The Penguin Book of Zen Poetry, 1:427
The Penguin Dictionary of English Idioms, 1:437
The Penguin Encyclopedia of Ancient Civilizations, 2:273
The Penguin Encyclopedia of Nutrition, 2:550
Penguin Island, 1:335
The Penitent, 1:388
Pensées, 1:533
People and Nations of Africa, 2:393
People and Nations of Asia, 2:398
People and Nations of Europe, 2:405
People and Nations of the Americas, 2:408
People and Nations of the Far East and the Pacific, 2:398
People at Work in India, 2:399
The People Could Fly: American Black Folk Tales, 1:230
The People Look at Television, 2:130
People Need People: The Importance of Relationships to Health and Wellness, 2:538
The People of the Deer, 1:144
People of the Earth: An Introduction to World Prehistory, 2:278
People of the Lake, 2:50
People or Computers: Three Ways of Looking at Information Systems, 1:555
The People, the Sovereigns, 2:178
The People's Choice: How the Voter Makes Up His Mind in a Presidential Campaign, 2:39
The People's Emergency Guide, 2:567
The People's Emperor: A Biography of Mao Tse-tung, 2:403
The People's Guide to Sports and Fitness, 2:551
The Peopling of a World: Selected Articles on Immigration and Settlement Patterns in British North America, 2:162

Pep Talk: How to Analyze Political Language, 1:442
A Pepys Anthology, 1:27
Perceptrons, 1:583
The Perceptual World of the Child, 2:106, 2:113
Percy Bysshe Shelley, 1:38
Perelandra, 1:104
Perestroika: New Thinking for Our Country and the World, 2:406
A Perfect Spy, 1:102
A Perfect Vacuum, 1:386
Perfectionism: What's Bad About Being Too Good, 2:536
Peribanez, 1:358
Pericles, 2:285
Perils of Prosperity: Nineteen Fourteen to Nineteen Thirty-Two, 2:226
The Periodic Table: Experiments and Theory, 2:506
Permanent Connections, 1:204
Permanent Magnets in Theory and Practice, 2:522
Perpetua and the Habit of Unhappiness, 1:412
Perplexities & Paradoxes, 1:360
The Persecution and Assassination of Jean-Paul Marat as Performed by the Inmates of the Asylum of Charenton Under the Direction of the Marquis de Sade, 1:373
The Persian Gulf and the West: Dilemmas of Security, 2:258
The Persian Gulf States: A General Study, 2:89, 2:273
Persian Gulf States: Country Studies, 2:89
The Persian Wars, 2:288
The Persians, 1:311
Personal Computers and the Disabled, 1:571
Personal Fiction Writing: A Guide to Writing from Real Life, 1:490
Personal Influence: The Part Played by People in the Flow of Mass Communications, 2:130
Personal Life of David Livingstone, 2:367
Personal Memoirs of U. S. Grant, 2:199
Personal Narrative of Travels to Equinoctial Regions of America During the Years 1799–1804, 2:78
The Personal President: Power Invested, Promise Unfulfilled, 2:21
Personality: A Psychological Interpretation, 2:115
Personality and Learning Theory: The Structure of Personality in Its Environment, 2:105
Personality and Social Encounter: Selected Essays, 2:115
Personality Plus, 1:220

Personality Theory, Moral Development, and Criminal Behavior, 2:114

Persons, Behavior, and the World: The Descriptive Psychology Approach, 2:96

Perspectives in Biochemistry, 2:511

Perspectives on Brazilian History, 2:369

Persuasion Analysis: A Companion to Composition, 1:442, 1:477

Pet Sematary, 1:249

Peter Camenzind, 1:368

Peter Norton's Assembly Language Book for the IBM PC, 1:564

Peter Norton's DOS Guide, 1:562

Peter Norton's Inside OS/2, 1:562

Peter Pan, 1:67

The Peter Principle: Why Things Always Go Wrong, 2:140

Peter Shaffer: Roles, Rites, and Rituals in the Theater, 1:119

Peter Simple, 1:56

Peter Weiss in Exile: A Critical Study of His Works, 1:373

Peterson First Guide to Astronomy, 2:470

Petrarch, 1:351

Petroleum: How It Is Found and Used, 2:496

Petrology: Igneous, Sedimentary, and Metamorphic, 2:492

Peuples Noirs, Peuples Africains (Black Peoples, African Peoples), 1:412

The Peyote Religion Among the Navajo, 2:52

Phaedra, 1:323, 1:339

The Phantom Ship, 1:56

Pharaohs and Pyramids, 2:279

Phèdre, 1:339

The Philadelphia Negro: A Social Study, 2:211

Philip Hall likes me. I reckon maybe, 1:228

Philip Larkin: The Man and His Work, 1:100

Philip Larkin and His Contemporaries: An Air of Authenticity, 1:100

Philip Second of Spain, 2:327

Philippics, 2:293

Philippines: A Country Study, 2:86

Phillis Wheatley: Negro Slave of John Wheatley, 1:155

Phillis Wheatley and Her Writings, 1:155

Philosophia Botanica, 2:443

Philosophiae Naturalis Principia Mathematica, 2:515

Philosophy of Civilization, 2:535

The Philosophy of Leibniz, 1:503, 1:527

The Philosophy of Leibniz and the Modern World, 1:527

The Philosophy of Logical Atomism, 1:503

The Philosophy of Mathematics: An Introductory Essay, 1:497

Philosophy of Mathematics and Deductive Structure in Euclid's "Elements," 1:514

The Philosophy of Moral Development: Essays in Moral Development, 2:97, 2:109

The Philosophy of Niels Bohr: Framework of Complementarity, 2:501

Phoenicians, 2:280

A Phoenix Too Frequent, 1:87

A Photographic Atlas of the Planets, 2:475

Photographs of the Southwest, 2:263

Photosynthesis, 2:438

Photosynthetic Systems: Structure, Function, and Assembly, 2:438

PHYSICAL BEST Software System, 1:568

Physical Fitness, 2:551

Physical Geography: A Landscape Appreciation, 2:93

Physical Geography: Earth Systems and Human Interaction, 2:93

Physical Geography Today: Portrait of a Planet, 2:93

Physical Geology, 2:489

Physical Geology: Principles and Perspectives, 2:489

The Physical, Political, and International Value of the Panama Canal, 2:223

Physical Properties of Hydrocarbons, 2:510

Physics of Magnetism, 2:522

The Physics of Sound, 2:521

The Physiology of Flowering Plants, 2:448

Piaget and His School: A Reader in Developmental Psychology, 2:112

Piaget and Knowledge: Theoretical Foundations, 2:112

Piaget's Theory of Intellectual Development, 2:112

The Piazza Tales and Other Prose Pieces, 1839–1860, 1:162

Picasso: Photos Nineteen Fifty-One to Nineteen Seventy-Two, 2:262

Picasso Line Drawings and Prints, 2:421

Picasso Lithographs: Sixty-One Works, 2:421

The Pick Operating System, 1:561

The Pick Pocket Guide, 1:562

Picket Lines and Bargaining Tables: Organized Labor Comes of Age, 1935–1955, 2:70, 2:237

The Pickwick Papers, 1:46, 1:47

Pictorial Astronomy, 2:468

Pictorial Guide to the Planets, 2:476

The Picture of Dorian Gray, 1:62

Picture This, 1:234

Pictures of the Floating World, 1:258

"Pied Beauty," 1:53

Pierre and Jean, 1:337

Pierre Curie, 2:510
Pierre et Jean, 1:337, 1:338
Pierre, or the Ambiguities, 1:162, 1:163
Pigeon Feathers and Other Stories, 1:292
The Pigman, 1:247, 1:308
The Pigman's Legacy, 1:308
Pilgrim at Tinker Creek, 1:482, 1:483
The Pilgrim's Progress, 1:21
The Pilgrim's Progress in Today's English, 1:21
The Pillar of Society, 1:377
Pillow Book, 1:424
Piñatas and Paper Flowers—Piñatas y Flores de Papel: Holidays of the Americas in English and Spanish, 2:409
Pincher Martin, 1:89
Pioneer Astronomers, 2:433
The Pioneer Fringe, 2:76, 2:77
Pioneer Trails West: Great Stories of the Westering Americans and the Trails They Followed, 2:202
Pioneer Women, 2:201
Pioneers and Peers, 1:538
Pioneers in Psychology, 2:95
Pioneers in Science, 2:433
Pioneers of Public Health: The Story of Some Benefactors of the Human Race, 2:444, 2:446
Pirandello's Major Plays, 1:351
Pirates of the Cell: The Story of Viruses from Molecule to Microbe, 2:443, 2:557
The Pit, 1:180
The Pit: A Study of Chicago, 2:218
"The Pit and the Pendulum," 1:164
The Pitch: How to Analyze Advertising, 1:442
The Pituitary Gland, 2:450
Place Names of Africa, 1935–1986: A Political Gazetteer, 2:85, 2:275
A Place to Come To, 1:299
The Plague, 1:333
Plain Speaking: An Oral Biography of Harry S. Truman, 2:237
Plain Tales from the Hills, 1:55
Plain Verses, 2:370
The Plains of Passage, 2:277
Plane and Coordinate Geometry Study Aid, 1:513
Planet Earth (Lampton), 2:494
Planet Earth (Weiner), 2:84, 2:489
Planet Earth in Jeopardy: Environmental Consequences of Nuclear War, 2:81
The Planet of Junior Brown, 1:229, 1:230
The Planet of the Apes, 1:332
The Planets: Exploring the Solar System, 2:475
The Planets: The Next Frontier, 2:480
Planned Variation in Education: Should We Give Up or Try Harder, 2:68

Planning Ahead for Pregnancy, 2:543
The Plant Between Sun and Earth and the Science of Physical and Ethereal Spaces, 1:519
Plant Cell Structure and Metabolism, 2:447
Plant Facts and Fancies, 2:448
The Plantagenet Chronicles, 2:305
Planters and Yeomen: Selected Articles on the Southern Colonies, 2:162
Plastics, 2:510
Plate Tectonics: How It Works, 2:494
Plate Tectonics and Crustal Evolution, 2:82, 2:494
Plato's Philosophy of Mathematics, 1:498
Play, Dreams, and Imitation in Childhood, 2:111, 2:112
Play It Again, Sam, 1:189
A Play of Giants, 1:417, 1:418
Playback, 1:210
The Playboy of the Western World, 1:123
Player Piano, 1:295
Playhouse 90, 1:486
The Plays (Albee), 1:186
The Playwright's Handbook, 1:489
Playwriting, 1:489
The Pleasure Addicts: The Addictive Process—Food, Sex, Drugs, Alcohol, Work, and More, 2:553
Pleasures of Music: An Anthology of Writings About Music and Musicians from Cellini to Bernard Shaw, 2:261
The Pledge, 1:218
The Plough and the Stars, 1:108
The Plug-In Drug: Television, Children, and the Family, 1:466
Plutarch and His Times, 2:289
Plutarch and Rome, 2:289
Plutarch's Historical Methods: An Analysis of the Mulierum Virtues, 2:289
Plutarch's Lives, 2:289
A Pocket History of the United States, 2:155
The Pocket Mirror, 1:139
Poe: A Collection of Critical Essays, 1:164
Poem of My Cid (Poema de mio Cid), 1:359
Poem of the Cid, 1:353, 1:359
Poems (E. Browning), 1:43
The Poems (R. Browning), 1:44
Poems (Dickey), 1:215
Poems (Eliot), 1:82
Poems (Moore), 1:268
Poems (D. Rosetti), 1:51
Poems (Shelley), 1:38
Poems (Wordsworth), 1:39
The Poems (Wordsworth), 1:39
Poems and Ballads and Atalanta in Calydon (Swinburne), 1:59

Poems and Prose (Coleridge), 1:34
Poems and Songs (Burns), 1:32
Poems by Robert Frost: A Boy's Will and North of Boston, 1:223
Poems by Two Brothers, 1:60
Poems, Chiefly in the Scottish Dialect, 1:32
Poems from Prison, 1:417
Poems from the Book of Hours, 1:371
Poems of Gerard Manley Hopkins, 1:53
Poems of Horace, 2:294
The Poems of Katherine Mansfield, 1:142
Poems of Matthew Arnold, 1:41
Poems of Philip Sidney, 1:16
Poems of Samuel Taylor Coleridge, 1:34
The Poems of Yeats, 1:134
The Poet at the Breakfast Table, 1:158
Poet Errant: A Biography of Rubén Darío, 1:402
Poet in New York, 1:357
Poeta en Nueva York, 1:357
The Poetic Debussy: A Collection of His Song Texts and Selected Letters, 2:418
A Poetic Equation: Conversations Between Nikki Giovanni and Margaret Walker, 1:226, 1:298
Poetical Works (E. Browning), 1:43
Poetical Works (Swift), 1:30
The Poetical Works of Edward Taylor, 1:154
The Poetical Works of Longfellow, 1:161
The Poetical Works of Lowell, 1:161
The Poetical Works of Oliver Wendell Holmes, 1:158
The Poetical Works of Tennyson, 1:60
The Poetical Works of Whittier, 1:166
The Poetical Works of William Cowper, 1:22
Poetical Works of William Cullen Bryant, 1:156
Poetics, 2:287
Poetics of Music in the Form of Six Lessons, 2:426
Poetry and Criticism of Matthew Arnold, 1:41
The Poetry and Poetics of Amiri Baraka: The Jazz Aesthetic, 1:197
Poetry and the Age, 1:244
The Poetry of Robert Frost, 1:223
The Poetry of Seamus Heaney, 1:92
Poetry of Stephen Crane, 1:174
The Poet's Manual and Rhyming Dictionary, 1:490
Point Counter Point, 1:95
Poison Plants, 2:447
Pol Pot: Cambodian Prime Minister, 2:399
The Polar Passion, 1:144
Polaris and Other Stories, 1:128

The Policeman's Beard is Half-Constructed: Computer Prose and Poetry, 1:577
The Policy Game: How Special Interests and Ideologies Are Stealing America, 2:40
The Political and Economic Doctrines of John Marshall, 2:30
Political Attitudes in America, 2:39, 2:255
Political Cartoon, 1:459
Political Change in the Metropolis, 2:7
Political Economy and Risk in World Financial Markets, 2:71
The Political Economy of Underdevelopment, 2:71
Political Essay on the Kingdom of New Spain, 2:78
The Political Life of Children, 2:106
Political Parties and Elections in the United States, 2:370
Political Socialization: A Study in the Psychology of Political Behavior, 2:146
The Political System: An Inquiry into the State of Political Science, 2:7
Political Writings (Shelley), 1:38
Political Writings of John Adams, 2:171
The Politician: The Life and Times of Lyndon Johnson, 2:246
Politics, 2:287
Politics: A Handbook for Students, 2:6
Politics: Who Gets What, When, and How, 2:10
Politics Among Nations, 2:37
Politics and Change in the Middle East: Sources of Conflict and Accommodation, 2:89, 2:411
Politics and Policy in States and Communities, 2:7
Politics and the American Future, 2:7
Politics in America: The 100th Congress, 2:5, 2:33
Politics in States and Communities, 2:40
Politics, Innocence and the Limits of Goodness, 2:19
The Politics of American Cities: Private Power and Public Policy, 2:41
The Politics of Civil Rights in the Truman Administration, 2:237
The Politics of Congress, 2:33
The Politics of Displacement: Racial and Ethnic Transition in Three American Cities, 2:147
The Politics of Rich and Poor: Wealth and the American Electorate in the Reagan Aftermath, 2:7
Politics, Personality and Social Science in the Twentieth Century: Essays in Honor of Harold D. Lasswell, 2:10

Politics, Power and People: Four Governments in Action, 2:16
Pollination, 2:452
Polls and the Awareness of Public Opinion, 2:39
Polls, Politics, and Populism, 2:204
Pollution, 2:468, 2:497
Polyhedron Models, 1:520
Polymeric Carbons—Carbon Fibre, Glass, and Charcoal, 2:510
Polysymetrics: The Art of Making Geometric Patterns, 1:515
Pomp and Circumstance, 1:77
The Ponder Heart, 1:300
Poor and Minority Health Care, 2:531
The Poor Christ of Bomba, 1:412
Poor Folk, 1:391, 1:392
The Poor Pay More: Consumer Practices of Low Income Families, 2:61
Poor People's Movements: Why They Succeed, How They Fail, 2:145
Poor Richard: The Almanack for the Years 1733–1758, 2:526
Poor Richard's Almanac, 2:167
Poor Robin's Almanac, 2:167
Poor White, 1:190
The Poorhouse Fair, 1:292
Pop Art, 2:415
Popcorn Venus, 1:475
Pope: Poetry and Prose, 1:27
Pope Joan, 1:81
Poppy, Nineteen Twenty-Seven, 2:268
Popular Culture and High Culture: An Analysis and Evaluation of Taste, 2:134
Popular Government: Its Essence, Its Performance, Its Perils, 2:223
Population: The First Essay, 2:69
Population and Society: A Sociological Perspective, 2:142
Population Bomb, 2:85, 2:274
Population Change and Social Policy, 2:142
Population Geography, 2:93
The Population Handbook, 2:85
The Population of the United States: Historical Trends and Future Projections, 2:142
The Population Reference Bureau's Population Handbook: International Edition, 2:85, 2:274
The Populist Revolt: A History of the Farmer's Alliance and the People's Party, 2:204
Porfirio Diaz, 2:369
Pork Chop Hill: The American Fighting Man in Action: Korea, Spring 1953, 2:238
The Portable Charles Lamb, 1:35
The Portable Chaucer, 1:6

The Portable Coleridge, 1:34
The Portable Dante, 1:349
The Portable Dorothy Parker, 1:274
The Portable Emerson, 1:157
The Portable Greek Reader, 1:311
The Portable Henry James, 1:179
The Portable Milton, 1:14
The Portable Poe, 1:164
The Portable Roman Reader, 1:320
The Portable Saul Bellow, 1:200
The Portable Sherwood Anderson, 1:190
The Portable Swift, 1:30
The Portable Thomas Jefferson, 2:175
The Portable Thoreau, 1:165
The Portable Twentieth-Century Russian Reader, 1:389
The Portable Veblen, 2:146
Portable Video: A Production Guide for Young People, 1:470
The Portable Whitman, 1:184
The Portfolios of Ansel Adams, 2:263
Portrait of a Father, 1:299
The Portrait of a Lady, 1:179
Portrait of an Artist: A Biography of Georgia O'Keeffe, 2:268
A Portrait of Jane Austen, 1:20
Portrait of T. E. Lawrence, 2:373
A Portrait of the Artist as a Young Dog, 1:124
A Portrait of the Artist as a Young Man, 1:98, 1:99
Portuguese Voyages, 1498–1663, 2:158
The Positive History of the New Social Order, 2:126
Positive Images: Breaking Stereotypes with Children's Television, 1:465
The Positive Philosophy, 2:126
The Possessed, 1:392
Post-Impressionism: From Van Gogh to Gauguin, 2:346
The Post-Inferno Period, 1:380
Post-Modernism: The New Classicism in Art and Architecture, 2:415
Postscript Language Tutorial and Cookbook, 1:563
The Pot of Gold and Other Plays, 1:322
The Pothunters and Other Stories, 1:131
Poverty of Abundance: Hoover, the Nation, the Depression, 2:231
The Poverty of Progress: Latin America in the Nineteenth Century, 2:369
Power and Privilege: A Theory of Social Stratification, 2:145
The Power and the Glory, 1:91
Power Elite, 2:145
The Power of Blackness: Hawthorne, Poe, Melville, 1:163, 1:164, 1:178
The Power of Ice, 2:493
The Power of Myth, 1:466; 2:52

The Power of OS/2: A Comprehensive User's Manual, 1:561
The Powerful Consumer: Psychological Studies of the American Economy, 2:61
Powers of Nature, 2:493
Powers of the Crown: 1600–1700, 2:326
The Powers That Be, 1:458
Practical Applications of Psychology, 2:95
A Practical Approach to Operating Systems, 1:562
The Practical Archaeologist, 2:278
Practical Biochemistry for Colleges, 2:511
Practical English: 1,000 Most Effective Words, 1:440
Practical Experience in Building Expert Systems, 1:583
A Practical Guide to Psychodiagnostic Testing, 2:122
Practical Quantum Mechanics, 2:518
Practical Solar Energy Technology, 2:485
The Practical Theorist: The Life and Work of Kurt Lewin, 2:99
Practical Things to Do with a Microcomputer, 1:557
The Pragmatic Philosophy of William James, 2:97
Pragmatism, 2:96
Prairie Songs, 2:200
Prairie-Town Boy, 1:284
Prairie Women: Images in American and Canadian Fiction, 2:200
Praise of Folly, 2:314
Prayers for Dark People, 2:211
Pre-Algebra, 1:506
Precalculus: A Unit Circle Approach, 1:524
Precalculus Mathematics, 1:523
Predicting the Properties of Mixtures, 2:507
Pregnancy, Birth, and Family Planning, 2:543
Prehistory, 2:278
Prehistory of the Far Side, 1:459
The Preindustrial City: Past and Present, 2:147
The Pre-Inferno Period, 1:380
Prejudices: A Selection, 1:436
Preliminary Mathematics, 1:504
The Prelude, 1:39
Prelude to Foundation, 1:194
Prelude to Mathematics, 1:498
Prelude to the Cold War: The Tsarist, Soviet, and U.S. Armies in the Two World Wars, 2:387
Prelude to War, 2:383
"The Premature Burial," 1:164
The Prententious Young Ladies, 1:338
The Prentice-Hall Dictionary of Nutrition and Health, 2:549
The Prentice-Hall Guide to Expert Systems, 1:583

Prescription and OTC Drugs, 2:553
Prescription Drugs, 2:553
Present Indicative: An Autobiography, 1:78
Presentation of Self in Everyday Life, 2:139
Presenting Judy Blume, 1:202
Presenting M. E. Kerr, 1:248
Presenting Norma Klein, 1:250
Presenting Paul Zindel, 1:309
Presenting Robert Cormier, 1:213
Presenting Rosa Guy, 1:229
Presenting S. E. Hinton, 1:240
Presenting Sue Ellen Bridgers, 1:204
The Presidency: A Research Guide, 2:5, 2:21
The Presidency of Harry S. Truman, 2:237
The Presidency of Lyndon B. Johnson, 2:246
The President: A Minute-by-Minute Account of a Week in the Life of Gerald Ford, 2:253
The President: Office and Powers, 2:21
The President: Preacher, Teacher, Salesman: Selected Presidential Speeches, 1933–1983, 2:21
The President and Protest: Hoover, Conspiracy, and the Bonus Riot, 2:231
The President from Texas: Lyndon Baines Johnson, 2:246
Presidential Addresses and State Papers, 2:222
Presidential Campaigns, 2:39
The Presidential—Congressional Political Dictionary, 2:5, 2:33
Presidential Economics: The Making of Economic Policy from Roosevelt to Reagan and Beyond, 2:65
Presidential Elections and American Politics: Voters, Candidates, and Campaigns Since 1952, 2:39
Presidential Primaries and Nominations, 2:39
The Presidents: A Reference, 2:6
Presidents Above Party: The First American Presidency, 1789–1829, 2:169
Presidents in American History, 2:21, 2:152
Presidents of the United States of America, 2:153
Presidents' Wives: The Lives of Forty-Four American Women of Strength, 2:156
The Press and Public: Who Reads What, Where, and Why in American Newspapers, 2:129
The Press and the American Revolution, 2:327
Press Watch: A Provocative Look at How Newspapers Report the News, 1:458

Pretty Ugly: More Oxymorons and Other Illogical Expressions That Make Absolute Sense, 1:436

Preventing AIDS: A Guide to Effective Education for the Prevention of HIV Infection, 2:560

The Price, 1:266

The Price of Affluence: Dilemmas of Contemporary Japan, 2:398

The Price of Power: Kissinger in the Nixon White House, 2:38

The Price of the Ticket: Collected Nonfiction 1948–1985, 1:195

The Price System and Resource Allocation, 2:57

Prices, Wages, and Business Cycles: A Dynamic Theory, 2:57

Pride and Prejudice, 1:20

Primary Education, 2:209

Primate Ecology and Social Organization, 2:462

Primates and Their Adaptations, 2:449

Primates in Nature, 2:450

The Prime of Miss Jean Brodie, 1:121

Prime-Time America: Life On and Behind the Television Screen, 1:465

Prime-Time Television: Content and Control, 1:465

A Primer of Freudian Psychology, 2:114

Primitive Art, 2:44

Primitive Classification, 2:127

The Primitive World and Its Transformations, 2:54

The Prince, 1:347; 2:20

The Prince and the Pauper, 1:182

Prince Henry the Navigator, the Hero of Portugal and of Modern Discovery, 1394–1460, 2:157

The Prince's Progress and Other Poems, 1:56

The Princess and Other Stories, 1:391

Princess Ashley, 1:276

The Princess Bride, 1:227

The Princess Casamassima, 1:179

A Princess of Mars, 1:208

The Princeton Review Word Smart: Building an Educated Vocabulary, 1:440

Principal Navigations, Voyages, Traffiques and Discoveries of the English Nation, 2:324

Principia, 2:477, 2:515, 2:516

Principia Mathematica, 1:503

The Principles and Practice of Medicine, 2:534

Principles of Biochemistry, 2:438

Principles of Chemistry, 2:506, 2:507

Principles of Computer Science: Concepts, Algorithms, Data Structures, and Applications, 1:563

Principles of Data Communication, 1:559

Principles of Database Systems, 1:573

Principles of Ecology, 2:466

Principles of Economics, 2:56, 2:57

Principles of Geology, 2:490

Principles of Gestalt Psychology, 2:113

The Principles of Mathematics, 1:503

The Principles of Morals and Legislation, 2:8

Principles of Parallel and Multiprocessing, 1:559

Principles of Physical Geology, 2:489

Principles of Physiological Psychology, 2:114

Principles of Political Economy, 2:69, 2:72

Principles of Political Economy and Taxation, 2:73

The Principles of Psychology, 2:96

Principles of Public Finance, 2:71

Principles of Quantum Mechanics, 2:519

The Principles of Relativity, 2:520

The Print, 2:263

The Printer Bible, 1:561

Printing and Publishing in Medieval China, 2:309

Prisoner of Grace, 1:72

Prisoners of War, 2:383

Prisons We Choose to Live Inside, 1:103

Private Correspondence of Henry Clay, 2:181

The Private Ear, 1:118

The Private Franklin: The Man and His Family, 2:526

Private Lives, 1:77

The Private Lives of Animals, 2:461

Private Lives of the Stars, 2:479

The Private World: Selected Works of Miguel de Unamuno, 1:360

The Prize: The Epic Quest for Oil, Money, and Power, 2:258

Probabilities and the Quantum World, 1:529

Probability and Causality, 1:529

Problem Book in Relativity and Gravitation, 2:513

Problem-Solving Strategies for Writing, 1:477

Problems and Other Stories, 1:292

Problems and Theorems in Analysis I: Series, Integral Calculus, Theory of Functions, 1:524

Problems in Solid Geometry, 1:520

Problems of Africa, 2:86, 2:393

Problems of Lasting Peace, 2:231

The Problems of Philosophy, 1:503

The Process Is the Punishment: Handling Cases in a Lower Criminal Court, 2:133

Professional Ethics and Civic Morals, 2:127

The Professional Stranger: An Informal Introduction to Ethnography, 2:42

Professional Thief, 2:133
Professional Write and File Made Easy, 1:572
The Professor, 1:41
The Professor at the Breakfast Table, 1:158
The Professor's House, 1:209
Profiles in Courage, 2:247
Profiles in Stress, 2:123
Profiles of Pioneer Women Scientists, 2:433
Program Translation Fundamentals: Methods and Issues, 1:586
Programmers at Work: Interviews, 1:538, 1:543
The Programmer's Essential OS-2 Handbook, 1:561
A Programmer's Geometry, 1:511
Programming Halo Graphics in C, 1:578
Programming in Modula-2, 1:566
Programming Languages, 1:563
Programming the Apple IIGS in Assembly Language, 1:564
Programs in Aid of the Poor, 2:68
Progress for a Small Planet, 2:74
The Progress of Love, 1:145
The Progressive Era, 2:218
The Progressive Movement, Nineteen Hundred to Nineteen Fifteen, 2:218
Progressivism, 2:218
Project Pendulum, 1:286
Projective Geometry, 1:519
Projective Geometry: An Approach, 1:519
Prokofiev, 2:422
Prokofiev by Prokofiev: A Composer's Memoir, 2:422
Prolog from the Beginning, 1:566
Prolog Primer, 1:566
Prolog Programming for Artificial Intelligence, 1:565
Prometheus Bound and Other Plays, 1:311, 1:312
Prometheus Unbound, 1:38
The Promise, 1:280
The Promised Land: The Autobiography of a Russian Immigrant, 2:209, 2:210
Promises: Poems 1954–1956, 1:298
Promises to Keep: Carter's First 100 Days, 2:256
The Pronunciation of English in the Atlantic States: Based on the Linguistic Atlas of the Eastern United States, 1:432
Proof in Geometry, 1:512
Proofreading Skills for Word Processing, 1:575
Propaganda and Persuasion, 1:440
Propaganda, Polls and Public Opinion: Are the People Manipulated, 1:440

Propaganda Techniques in the World War, 2:10
A Proper Marriage, 1:103
Properties of Liquids and Solutions, 2:507
The Prophet Armed: Trotsky, 1879–1921, 2:382
Prophet in the Wilderness: The Story of Albert Schweitzer, 2:535
The Prophet Outcast: Trotsky, 1929–1940, 2:382
The Prophet Unarmed: Trotsky, 1921–1929, 2:382
Prophets of Regulation, 2:65
Prosas profanas, 1:401
Prose and Poetry (Crane), 1:173
Protestant, Catholic, Jew: An Essay in American Religious Sociology, 2:142
The Protestant Ethic and the Spirit of Capitalism, 2:143
The Proud and the Free, 1:218
The Proud Peoples: The Heritage and Culture of Spanish-Speaking Peoples in the United States, 2:135
Proud Tower, 2:341
The Provincial Letters, 1:533
Prufrock and Other Observations, 1:82
Prydain Chronicles: The Book of Three, 1:187
Psmith: Journalist, 1:131
Psychoanalysis: From Freud to the Age of Therapy, 2:96
Psychodrama: Resolving Emotional Problems Through Role-Playing, 2:104
Psychological Care of Infant and Child, 2:103
Psychological Perspectives in Psychiatry, 2:121
Psychological Testing: An Introduction to Tests and Measurement, 2:122
Psychological Testing: Principles and Applications, 2:122
Psychological Testing: Principles, Applications, and Issues, 2:122
Psychology: An Introduction, 2:95
Psychology and Religion, 2:97, 2:121
Psychology from the Standpoint of a Behaviorist, 2:103
Psychology in America: A Historical Survey, 2:95
Psychology in Twentieth-Century Thought and Society, 2:95
The Psychology of Human-Computer Interaction, 1:558
The Psychology of Interpersonal Behavior, 2:104
The Psychology of Learning and Motivation, 2:112
The Psychology of Moral Development, 2:97, 2:109

The Psychology of Reasoning, 2:123
Psychology of the Child, 2:111
Psychology; or, a View of the Human
 Soul, Including Anthropology, 2:95
Psychopathology and Politics, 2:10
Puberty: The Story of Growth and
 Change, 2:543
Public and Private High Schools: The
 Impact of Communities, 2:130
Public and Private Papers, 2:175
The Public Eye, 1:118
Public-Domain Software and Shareware:
 Untapped Resources for the PC User,
 1:566
Public Finance in Theory and Practice,
 2:71
Public Finances, 2:71
Public Interest Profiles, 1988–1989, 2:5,
 2:39
Public Investment, the Rate of Return,
 and Optimum Fiscal Policy, 2:64
Public Opinion, 2:39
The Public Papers (Sullivan), 2:217
The Public Papers of Chief Justice Earl
 Warren, 2:32
Public Papers of the Secretaries-General of
 the United Nations (1953–1961), 2:390
Public Philosopher: Selected Letters of
 Walter Lippman, 2:218
Public Policies Toward Business, 2:65
Public Policy and Federalism: Issues in
 State and Local Politics, 2:35
The Public Presidency: The Pursuit of
 Popular Support, 2:21
Public Spaces and Places, 2:105
Pudd'nhead Wilson, 1:182
Pueblo Sites in Southeastern Arizona,
 2:80
Puerto Rican Americans: The Meaning of
 Migration to the Mainland, 2:134
The Pullman Strike, 2:204
The Pulse of Enterprise, 2:339
The Pump House Gang, 1:479
Punctured Poems: Famous First Lines and
 Infamous Second Lines, 1:192
Punjabi Century, 1857–1947, 2:363
Pure Gold, 1:379
Purgatorio, 1:349
Puritan in Babylon: The Story of Calvin
 Coolidge, 2:228
The Puritanical Society and the Growth of
 Capitalism, 2:47
Puritans: A Sourcebook of Their Writings,
 2:162
Puritans Among the Indians: Accounts of
 Captivity and Redemptions, 1676–1724,
 2:163
Purity, 1:8
The Purple Decades: A Reader, 1:479

The Purposes of Groups and
 Organizations, 2:104
The Pursuit of Loneliness: American
 Culture at the Breaking Point, 2:134,
 2:139
Pushkin: Literature and Social Ideas, 1:395
Put Out More Flags, 1:127
Putting Expert Systems into Practice,
 1:583
Putting It Together: Teenagers Talk About
 Family Breakups, 2:539
Putting Microsoft Works to Work, 1:573
Puzzles in Space, 1:520
Puzzling Your Way into Geometry, 1:512
Pygmalion, 1:119, 1:120
The Pyramid (Golding), 1:89
Pyramid (Macaulay), 2:280
Pyramid Builders of Ancient Egypt: A
 Modern Investigation of Pharaoh's
 Workforce, 2:279
The Pyramids: An Enigma Solved, 2:280
Pyramids: Tombs for Eternity, 2:280
Pythagoras: A Life, 1:501
Pythagoras: His Life and Teachings, 1:502
Pythagoras: The Reality of the New
 Computer Age, 1:501, 1:555
Pythagoras and Early Pythagoreanism,
 1:501
Pythagoras Revived: Mathematics and
 Philosophy in Late Antiquity, 1:501
Pythagorean Precepts, 1:502
Pythagorean Proposition, 1:501
The Pythagorean Sourcebook and Library:
 An Anthology of Ancient Writings
 Which Relate to Pythagoras and
 Pythagorean Philosophy, 1:501
The Pythagorean Triangle, 1:501

Q

QB VII, 1:293
Quakers in the Colonial Northeast, 2:163
Quality Street, 1:67
The Quare Fellow, 1:68
Quarrels That Have Shaped the
 Constitution, 2:16, 2:26
Quattro PRO Made Easy, 1:573
The Queen: The Life of Elizabeth II, 2:405
Queen and Mister Gladstone, 2:369
Queen Eleanor: Independent Spirit of the
 Medieval World: A Biography of
 Eleanor of Aquitaine, 2:305
Queen Victoria, 2:369
Queen Victoria: English Empress, 2:369
Queens, Empresses, Grand Duchesses and
 Regents: Women Rulers of Europe, A.D.
 1328–1989, 2:276
Quentin Durward, 1:36

The Quest for Community: A Study in
the Ethics of Order and Freedom, 2:131
Quest for the Past: Great Discoveries in
Archaeology, 2:278
The Quest of the Historical Jesus, 2:534
The Question of Artificial Intelligence:
Philosophical and Sociological
Perspectives, 1:582
The Question of Value: Thinking Through
Nietzsche, Heidegger, and Freud, 2:97
Questions and Answers on Death and
Dying, 2:107, 2:138
Quicken in Business, 1:572
The Quiet American, 1:91
Quinx: Or the Ripper's Tale, 1:81
Quit and Win: The War of Cigarette
Withdrawal Once and for All, 2:556
Quit Smoking: Forty Major Techniques to
Help You Stop Smoking, 2:556
Quo Vadis, 1:387

R

R. Buckminster Fuller on Education, 1:522
Rølvaag: His Life and Art, 1:379
Ra, 2:411
Ra Expeditions, 2:411
Rabbit Is Rich, 1:292
Rabbit Redux, 1:292
Rabbit, Run, 1:292
Racconti di Alberto Moravia, 1:350
Race: Science and Politics, 2:44
Race, Class, and Politics: Essays on
American Colonial and Revolutionary
Society, 2:162
Race, Language, and Culture, 2:44
Race, Politics, and Culture: Critical Essays
on the Radicalism of the 1960s, 2:242
Race, Religion and the Continuing
American Dilemma, 2:136
Rachel Carson, 2:243, 2:466
Rachel Carson: Pioneer of Ecology, 2:243,
2:466
Rachmaninoff: His Life and Times, 2:346
Racial and Cultural Minorities: An
Analysis of Prejudice and
Discrimination, 2:136
Racine, 1:339
Racism: Opposing Viewpoints, 2:135
Radiance of the King, 1:414, 1:415
The Radiant City (La ville radieuse), 2:419
The Radiant Way, 1:80
Radiation: Waves and Particles, 2:509
Radical Chic, and Mau-Mauing the Flak
Catchers, 1:479
Radio, 1:461
Radio: From Marconi to the Space Age,
1:461

Radio and Its Future, 1:461
Radio and the Printed Page: An
Introduction to the Story of Radio and
Its Role in the Communication of Ideas,
1:461; 2:130
Radio as an Advertising Medium, 1:461
Radio Broadcasts of Will Rogers, 1:462
Radio Censorship, 1:462
Radio in the Television Age, 1:461
Radio Listening in America: The People
Look at Radio Again, 2:130
Radio Today: The Present State of
Broadcasting. History of Broadcasting,
1:461
Radioactive Substances, 2:510
Radioactive Wastes from Nuclear Power
Plants, 2:496
Radioactivité, 2:510
Radioactivity: A Science in Its Historical
and Social Context, 2:508
Radioactivity: From the Curies to the
Atomic Age, 2:509
Radioactivity and Atomic Theory, 2:509
The Rage Within: Anger in Modern Life,
2:103
Ragged Dick and Struggling Upward,
1:168, 1:169
The Raid and Other Stories, 1:397
Rain of Troubles: The Science and Politics
of Acid Rain, 2:467
The Rainbow, 1:101
The Rainbow and the Rose, 1:147
The Rainbow Effect: Interracial Families,
2:538
Rainbow Jordan, 1:212
Rainbow Valley, 1:143
Rainbows, Halos, and Other Wonders:
Light and Color in the Atmosphere,
2:484
Rainbows, Mirages, and Sundogs: The Sky
As a Source of Wonder, 2:475
Rainer Maria Rilke: The Theaters of
Consciousness, 1:371
Raise High the Roof Beam, Carpenter and
Seymour: An Introduction, 1:282, 1:283
Raise Race Rays Raze: Essays Since 1965,
1:197
A Raisin in the Sun and The Sign in
Sidney Brustein's Window, 1:232
The Raj Quartet, 1:118
Ralph Bunche: Diplomat, 2:238
Rama II, 1:75
Ramanujan, 1:503
Ramanujan's Notebooks, 1:502
Ramayana, 1:421, 1:422
RAMS, ROMS, and Robots: The Inside
Story of Computers, 1:538
Ranch Life and the Hunting Trail, 2:222
Rand McNally Atlas of the Oceans, 2:75

Rand McNally Atlas of World History, 2:276
Rand McNally World Atlas of Nations, 2:75
Randall Jarrell, 1:244
Random Harvest, 1:94
The Random House Word-A-Day Vocabulary Builder, 1:439
The Rani of Jhansi: A Study of Female Heroism in India, 2:363
"The Ransom of Red Chief," 1:178
The Rape of Shavi, 1:413
The Rape of the Lock, 1:27
Raphael, 2:320
Raphael: Tables of Houses, 2:320
Rapid System Development, 1:585
Rascals in Paradise, 1:264
The Rat, 1:367
The Rate of Interest and Other Essays, 2:60
Rate of Reaction, Sensitivity, and Chemical Equilibrium, 2:508
The Rational Infant: Learning in Infancy, 2:106, 2:112
Rationality and Intelligence, 2:110
Ravel, 2:423
Ravel: His Life and Works, 2:423
Ravel: Man and Musician, 2:423
Ravel Remembered, 2:423
"The Raven," 1:164
The Raven: A Biography of Sam Houston, 2:186
A Raw Youth, 1:392
Ray Bradbury, 1:203
Rayburn: A Biography, 2:35
Raymond Chandler, 1:210
The Razor's Edge, 1:106
Re: Colonized Planet 5—Shikasta, 1:103
Reach for Tomorrow, 1:75
Reaction and Reconstruction in English Politics, 1832 to 1852, 2:332
Read My Lips, Make My Day, Eat Quiche and Die, 1:460
Reader in Comparative Religion: An Anthropological Approach, 2:52
A Reader's Guide to D. H. Lawrence, 1:101
A Reader's Guide to Dylan Thomas, 1:124
A Reader's Guide to Frederik Pohl, 1:279
A Reader's Guide to George Orwell, 1:112
A Reader's Guide to Gerard Manley Hopkins, 1:53
A Reader's Guide to Robert Silverberg, 1:286
A Reader's Guide to T.S. Eliot, 1:83
Reader's Theatre: Story Dramatization in the Classroom, 1:449
Readers Theatre Handbook, 1:449
Reading and Understanding: Teaching from the Perspective of Artificial Intelligence, 1:570
Reading Television, 1:468
Reading the News, 1:457
Reading the Numbers: A Survival Guide to the Measurements, Numbers, and Sizes Encountered in Everyday Life, 2:435
Readings in Cognitive Science: A Perspective from Psychology and Artificial Intelligence, 1:582
Readings in Natural Language Processing, 1:582
Readings on Human Behavior: The Best of Science '80–'86, 2:122
Reagan, 2:260
Reagan and Gorbachev, 2:260
Reagan and the Economy: The Successes, Failures, and Unfinished Agenda, 2:257
The Reagan Years, 2:260
Reagan's America: Innocents at Home, 2:260
Reagan's Ruling Class: Portraits of the President's Top 100 Officials, 2:257
The Real Inspector Hound, 1:122
Real Peace, 2:254
The Real Thing, 1:122
The Real Truth About Women and AIDS, 2:560
The Real War, 2:254
Reality and Scientific Truth: Discussions with Einstein, von Laue, and Planck, 2:521
The Realm of Algebra, 1:505
The Realm of the Nebulae, 2:478
Realms of Gold, 1:80
Reasons of State, 1:401
Rebecca, 1:80, 1:81
The Rebel Angels, 1:137, 1:138
Rebels and Yankees: The Fighting Men of the Civil War, 2:192
Rebels of the Heavenly Kingdom, 1:484
Recent Issues in the Analysis of Behavior, 2:101
Recent Revolutions in Anthropology, 2:42
Recent Revolutions in Astronomy, 2:470
Recent Revolutions in Biology, 2:437
Recent Revolutions in Geology, 2:489
Recent Revolutions in Mathematics, 1:498
Recipients, Commonly Called Data, 1:514
The Recognition of Speech by a Machine—A Bibliography, 1:579
Recollecting the Future: A View of Business, Technology, and Innovation in the Next 30 Years, 2:57
Recollections and Reflections, 2:425
Recombinant DNA: A Short Course, 2:440
Reconstructing American Law, 2:26

Reconstructing Europe After the Great War, 2:371
Reconstruction: America's Unfinished Revolution, 1863–1877, 2:198
Reconstruction After the Civil War, 2:198
The Records of the Federal Convention of Seventeen Eighty-Seven, 2:166
Recreations in the Theory of Numbers, 1:496
The Red and the Black, 1:341
The Red and the Green, 1:108
Red Army Resurgent, 2:383
The Red Badge of Courage, 1:166, 1:167, 1:173; 2:192
The Red Badge of Courage and Other Writings, 1:173
The Red Cross: A History of This Remarkable International Movement in the Interest of Humanity, 2:194
The Red Cross in Peace and War, 2:194
Red Giants and White Dwarfs, 2:479
Red Harvest, 1:231
Red Planet, 1:233
The Red Pony, 1:289
"A Red, Red Rose," 1:32
The Red Room, 1:379
Red Scare: A Study in National Hysteria, 1919–1920, 2:226
The Red Smith Reader, 1:480
The Red Wheel, 1:396
Red, White, and Black: The Peoples of Early America, 2:162
Redburn: His First Voyage, 1:163
Redheap, 1:141
Rediscovering America: John Muir in His Time and Ours, 2:221
Rediscovering America's Values, 2:19
Rediscovering Love, 2:104
Reduced Instruction Set Computers (RISC), 1:560
Reference Handbook of Grammar and Usage, 1:478
Reflections on Language, 1:435
Reflections on the Decline of Science in England, 1:542
Reflections on the Revolution in Europe, 2:405
Reflections on the Revolution in France, 2:8, 2:328, 2:329
Reform and Reformers in the Progressive Era, 2:218
Reformation, 2:310
A Reformation Debate, 2:311
The Reformation Era: 1500–1650, 2:310
Reformation of the Sixteenth Century, 2:310
Reforming Air Pollution Regulation: The Toil and Trouble of EPA's Bubble, 2:570
Refresher Mathematics, 1:505

Reggae or Not, 1:197
Reginald, 1:115
Regional Dictionary of Chicano Slang, 1:433
Regional Geography of Anglo-America, 2:91
Regional Landscapes of the United States and Canada, 2:90
Reign of the Ayatollahs: Iran and the Islamic Revolutions, 2:411
Relational Databases and SQL, 1:572
Relationships and Mechanisms in the Periodic Table, 2:506
Relationships Within Families: Mutual Influences, 2:138
Relatives at Risk for Mental Disorders, 2:121
Relativity: The Special and General Theory, 2:520
The Relaxation Response, 2:536
Religion: An Anthropological View, 2:52
Religion: The Social Context, 2:142
Religion in Human Life: Anthropological Views, 2:52
The Religion of China, 2:143
The Religion of India, 2:143
The Religion of Java, 2:52
Religions, Values, and Peak Experiences, 2:97
Religious Change in America, 2:142
Religious Origins of the American Revolution, 2:328
Remains of Elmet, 1:95
Remarkable Women of Ancient Egypt, 2:280
Rembrandt's Hat, 1:262
Remember Me, 1:128
Remember Ruben, 1:412
Remembering the Good Times, 1:276
Remembrance Rock, 1:284
Reminiscences and Reflections, 2:438
Renaissance, 2:310
The Renaissance and the New World, 2:310
The Renaissance Artist at Work: From Pisano to Titian, 2:310
Renaissance Before the Renaissance: Cultural Revivals of Late Antiquity and the Middle Ages, 2:311
Renaissance Diplomacy, 2:310
Renaissance Europe: The Individual and Society, 1480–1520, 2:310
Renaissance Thought and Its Sources, 2:310
Renascence and Other Poems, 1:265
Rendezvous with Destiny: A History of Modern American Reform, 2:218
Rendezvous with Rama, 1:75

Renewable Energy: The Power to Choose, 2:496
Renewable Resources in Our Future, 2:496
Replication of DNA, 2:439
Report from Part I, 1:205
Report from Xun wu, 2:402
Report on Planet Three and Other Speculations, 1:75
Representative Opinions of Mr. Justice Holmes, 2:29
Representative Spanish Authors, 1:355
Representing Super Doll, 1:276
The Reprieve, 1:340
The Reproductive System, 2:544
Reptiles of North America, 2:450
Requiem for a Heavyweight, 1:486
The Rescue of Miss Yaskell and Other Pipe Dreams, 1:481
Rescued! America's Endangered Wildlife on the Comeback Trail, 2:495
Research Guide for Psychology, 2:95
Research Methods in Cultural Anthropology, 2:42
Researches into the Early History of Mankind and the Development of Civilization, 2:43
Residencia en la tierra, 1:407
Resilience: Discovering a New Strength at Times of Stress, 2:123
The Resistance, 2:383
The Resolution of Conflict: Constructive and Destructive Processes, 2:132
Resolving Social Conflicts, 2:97, 2:99, 2:104, 2:132
The Respectful Prostitute, 1:340
The Respiratory System, 2:545
The Restaurant at the End of the Universe, 1:64
The Restless Heart: The Life and Influence of St. Augustine, 2:304
Restless Oceans, 2:487
Restoration and Reaction, 1815–1848, 2:332
Restoration, Revolution, Reaction: Economics and Politics in Germany, 1815–1871, 2:332
Restoring Our Earth, 2:255
The Resumé Catalog: 200 Damn Good Examples, 1:490
The Resumé Writer's Handbook, 1:490
Resumés That Knock 'Em Dead, 1:490
Resumés That Work, 1:490
Resurrection, 1:397
Rethinking Systems Analysis and Design, 1:559
The Return of Halley's Comet, 2:476
The Return of Sherlock Holmes, 1:48
The Return of Tarzan, 1:208
The Return of the Native, 1:52

The Return of the Shadow, 1:125
Return to the Philippines, 2:383
Reveille in Washington, 1860–1865, 2:193
Revenge of the Lawn: Stories 1962–1970, 1:203
The Revival of Civic Learning: A Rationale for Citizenship Education in American Schools, 2:12
Revolt in the Desert, 2:372
Revolution and Counter Revolution in Chile, 2:409
Revolution and Counterrevolution: Change and Persistence in Social Structure, 2:145
Revolution and Red Tape: The French Ministerial Bureaucracy, 1770–1850, 2:332
Revolution in Physics: A Non-Mathematical Survey of Quanta, 2:518
Revolution in the Third World: Currents and Conflicts in Asia, Africa, and Latin America, 2:36
The Revolutionary Age of Andrew Jackson, 2:180
The Revolutionary Career of Maximilien Robespierre, 2:332
Revolutionary Petunias and Other Poems, 1:296, 1:297
Revolutionary War: America's Fight for Freedom, 2:164
Revolutions in Physics, 2:512
Revolutions of 1848, 2:332
Revolutions of 1848: A Social History, 2:332
Reynolds, 2:339
A Rhetoric for Argument, 1:477
The Rhind Mathematical Papyrus, 1:496, 1:498
Rice Bowl Women: Writings by and About Women of China and Japan, 1:423, 1:425
Rich Countries and Poor Countries: Reflections from the Past, Lessons for the Future, 2:72
Rich Lands and Poor, 2:134
The Rich Nations and the Poor Nations, 2:74
Richard Brautigan, 1:203
"Richard Cory," 1:282
Richard F. Burton, 2:364
Richard Hakluyt and the English Voyages, 2:324
Richard M. Nixon: President, 2:255
Richard Nixon: Rise and Fall of a President, 2:254
Richard Strauss, 2:425
Richard Strauss: A Chronicle of the Early Years, 1864–1898, 2:425

Richard Strauss: The Staging of His
  Operas and Ballets, 2:425
Richard Wagner: A Biography, 2:362
Richard Wagner: His Life and His
  Dramas, 2:362
Richard Wagner: His Life and Works,
  2:362
Richard Wagner and His World, 2:362
Richard Wright, 1:307
The Riddle of Gravitation, 2:512
Rider Haggard: A Biography, 1:51
Rider Haggard and the Fiction of Empire,
  1:51
Riders in the Chariot, 1:147
Riders to the Sea, 1:123
Riemann, Topology and Physics, 1:516
Rifles for Watie, 2:193
The Right Handbook, 1:478
The Right of Privacy in the Computer
  Age, 1:554
The Right Place at the Right Time, 1:458
The Right Stuff, 1:479; 2:242, 2:482
Right Turn: The Decline of the Democrats
  and the Future of American Politics,
  2:39
The Rights of Man, 2:165
The Rights of Students: The Basic ACLU
  Guide to a Student's Rights, 2:13
Rights of Women, 2:148
Rilla of Ingleside, 1:143
The Rime of the Ancient Mariner, 1:34,
  1:38
The Ring of the Nibelung, 2:361, 2:362
The Ring of Truth: An Inquiry into How
  We Know What We Know, 2:434
A Ringing Glass: The Life of Rainer Maria
  Rilke, 1:371
Rings: Discoveries from Galileo to
  Voyager, 2:475
Rinkitink in Oz, 1:199
"Rip Van Winkle," 1:158
Ripley's Giant Believe It or Not, 1:463
Ripoff: A Report on Moral Collapse and
  Corruption in America, 1:446
Ripple from the Storm, 1:103
The Rise and Decline of Nations:
  Economic Growth, Stagflation, and
  Social Rigidities, 2:63
The Rise and Fall of Adolf Hitler, 2:377
The Rise and Fall of Athens: Nine Greek
  Lives, 2:289
The Rise and Fall of Economic Growth: A
  Study in Contemporary Thought, 2:62
The Rise and Fall of Great Powers:
  Economic Change and Military Conflict
  from 1500 to 2000, 2:275
The Rise and Fall of the Second Empire,
  1852–1871, 2:340
The Rise and Fall of the Third Reich,
  2:375

Rise of Big Business, 2:204
The Rise of Fascism, 2:374
Rise of Industrial America, 2:340
The Rise of Life: The First 3.5 Billion
  Years, 2:279
The Rise of Mammals, 2:495
The Rise of Modern China, 2:363
The Rise of Political Consultants: New
  Ways of Winning Elections, 2:40
The Rise of Silas Lapham, 2:207
Rise of the City: 1878–1898, 2:207
The Rise of the Common Man: Eighteen
  Thirty to Eighteen Fifty, 2:184
The Rise of the Counter-Establishment:
  From Conservative Ideology to Political
  Power, 2:39
The Rise of the Expert Company: How
  Visionary Companies Are Using
  Artificial Intelligence to Achieve Higher
  Productivity and Profits, 1:583
The Rise of the New Physics, 2:512
The Rise of the Raj, 2:363
The Rise of Urban America, 2:207
The Rise of Urbanization and the Decline
  of Citizenship, 2:12
Rise to Globalism: American Foreign
  Policy Since 1938, 2:36
The Rising Son, 1:170
The Rising Sun, 2:383
Rising Sun: The Decline and Fall of the
  Japanese Empire: 1936–1945, 2:236,
  2:375, 2:385
Rising Voices, 2:136
Rites of Passage, 1:89
Rituals of Survival: A Woman's Portfolio,
  1:267
Rivalry, Reason, and Revolution, 2:326
The Rivals, 1:29
The Rivals: America and Russia Since
  World War II, 2:388
River, 1:95
The River Between, 1:415
Rivers and Lakes (Bailey), 2:82
Rivers and Lakes (Bromwede), 2:82
Rivers and Lakes (Mulherin), 2:83
Rivers and Lakes (Pringle), 2:493
The Road to Cibola, 2:80
The Road to Damietta, 1:271
The Road to Oz, 1:198
The Road to Respectability: James A.
  Garfield & His World, 1844–1852, 2:195
The Road to the White House: The
  Politics of Presidential Elections, 2:40
Road to Tokyo, 2:383
Roald Dahl's Book of Ghost Stories, 1:79
Roald Dahl's Tales of the Unexpected,
  1:79
Roanoke Island: The Beginning of English
  America, 2:162
Roast Beef Medium, 1:220

The Robber Barons, 2:204
The Robber Bridegroom, 1:300
The Robbers, 1:372
Robert A. Heinlein, 1:234
Robert Browning, 1:44
Robert Browning: A Collection of Critical
    Essays, 1:44
Robert Burns: The Man, His Works, the
    Legend, 1:32
Robert E. Lee, 2:196
Robert E. Lee (Freeman), 2:196
Robert E. Lee and the Southern
    Confederacy, 2:193
Robert F. Kennedy: A Biography, 2:249
Robert Frost, 1:223
Robert Frost: A Biography, 1:223
Robert Graves, 1:91
Robert K. Merton: An Intellectual Profile,
    2:141
Robert Kennedy and His Times, 2:249
Robert Koch: A Life in Medicine and
    Bacteriology, 2:444
Robert Louis Stevenson (Cooper), 1:58
Robert Louis Stevenson (Saposnik), 1:58
Robert Lowell, 1:259
Robert Lowell: A Biography, 1:259
Robert Lowell: An Introduction to the
    Poetry, 1:259
Robert M. La Follette and the Insurgent
    Spirit, 2:220
Robert M. La Follette, Jr. and the Decline
    of the Progressive Party in Wisconsin,
    2:220
Robert Penn Warren, 1:299
Robertson Davies, 1:138
Robespierre, 2:332
Robespierre: The Reign of Terror, 2:332
Robinson, 1:121
Robinson Crusoe, 1:19, 1:22, 1:23, 1:56;
    2:557
Robinson Jeffers, 1:245
The Robot Trilogy, 1:194
Robotics and AI: An Introduction to
    Applied Machine Intelligence, 1:582
Robotics Basics, 1:584
Robots and Computers, 1:584
Robots and Empire, 1:193, 1:194
Robots and the Intelligent Computer,
    1:584
Rock: Making Musical Choices, 1:276
Rock and Hawk: Shorter Poems, 1:244
Rock Paintings of Southern Andalusia: A
    Description of a Neolithic and Copper
    Age Art Group, 2:278
Rocket Ship Galileo, 1:233
The Rocket Team, 2:483
Rocket to the Moon, 1:272
The Rocket's Red Glare: An Illustrated
    History of Rocketry Through the Ages,
    2:483

The Rockin' Fifties, 2:262
Rocks, Minerals, and Fossils of the World,
    2:492
Rod Serling: His Life and Vision, 1:486
Rod Serling's Night Gallery Reader, 1:486
The Rodgers and Hammerstein Story,
    2:261
Rodin, 2:356
Rodin: A Biography, 2:356
Rodin on Art and Artists: With Sixty
    Illustrations of His Work, 2:356
Rodin's Thinker and the Dilemmas of
    Modern Public Sculpture, 2:356
Roger's Version, 1:292
The Role of Computers in Religious
    Education, 1:569
The Role of Unions in the American
    Economy, 2:70
Role Theory: Expectations, Identities, and
    Behaviors, 2:98
Roll, Jordan, Roll: The World the Slaves
    Made, 2:189
Roll of Thunder, Hear My Cry, 1:289,
    1:290; 2:229
Roman Elegies and Other Poems, 1:366
The Roman Emperors: A Biographical
    Guide to the Rulers of Imperial Rome:
    31 BC–AD 476, 2:290
The Roman Empire and the Dark Ages,
    2:290
The Roman Empire, Twenty-Seven BC to
    Four Hundred Seventy-Six AD: A
    Study in Survival, 2:291
Roman Fever and Other Stories, 1:183
Roman Laughter: The Comedy of Plautus,
    1:322
Roman Literature and Society, 1:320
Roman Medicine, 2:291
Roman Poets of the Augustan Age:
    Horace and the Elegiac Poets, 2:294
Roman Polanski, 1:470
A Roman Soldier, 2:290
The Roman Spring of Mrs. Stone, 1:304
Roman Towns, 2:291
Roman Women, Their History and Habits,
    2:290
Roman World, 2:290
The Romance of a Plain Man, 1:226
The Romance of the Three Kingdoms,
    1:422
The Romans, 2:291
Romanticism and Realism: The Mythology
    of Nineteenth-Century Art, 2:346
Rome and Italy, 2:295
Rome and Romans, 2:290
Rome and the Mediterranean, 2:295
Romola, 1:49
Ronald Reagan: U.S. President, 2:260
Ronald Reagan Talks to America, 2:260
A Room with a View, 1:85

Roosevelt and De Gaulle: Allies in Conflict: A Personal Memoir, 2:387
Roosevelt and Hitler: Prelude to War, 2:376
Roosevelt and Stalin: The Failed Courtship, 2:384
Roosevelt Confronts Hitler: America's Entry into World War II, 2:234
The Roosevelt I Knew, 2:24
Roots, 2:252
The Roots of American Psychology: Historical Influences and Implications for the Future, 2:96
Roots of Conflict: British Armed Forces and Colonial Americans, 1677–1763, 2:162
The Roots of Modern Biochemistry: Fritz Lipmann's Squiggie and Its Consequences, 2:511
The Roots of Perception: Individual Differences in Information Processing Within and Beyond Awareness, 2:113
The Roots of the Bill of Rights: An Illustrated Source Book of American Freedom, 2:17
The Rope and Other Plays, 1:322
Rosencrantz and Guildenstern Are Dead, 1:122
Rosmersholm, 1:377, 1:378
A Roster of Civilizations and Culture, 2:45
Rough Crossing, 1:122
The Rough Riders (Hagedorn), 2:222
Rough Riders (Roosevelt), 2:222
Roughing It, 1:181, 1:182
The Rougon–Macquart, 1:344
Rousseau: Dreamer of Democracy, 2:11
Rousseau and Revolution, 2:326
Rousseau and the "Well-Ordered Society," 2:11
Royal Charles: Charles II and the Restoration, 2:327
Royal Highness, 1:370
The Royal House of Windsor, 2:405
The Royal Hunt of the Sun, 1:119
The Rubaiyat of Omar Khayyam and Other Persian Poems, 1:419
Ruby, 1:228
Rudyard Kipling, 1:65
Rulers and the Ruled, 2:130
The Rules of Life, 1:128
The Rules of Sociological Method, 2:127
Rumble Fish, 1:240
Rumer Godden, 1:89
Run, Computer, Run: The Mythology of Educational Innovation—An Essay, 1:570
The Runner, 1:294
Running City Hall: Municipal Administration in America, 2:41

Running MS-DOS, 1:562
Running Windows, 1:562
Rupert Brooke: A Biography, 1:70
Rupert Brooke and the Intellectual Imagination, 1:70
R.U.R. and The Insect Play, 1:384, 1:385
The Rural Trilogy: Blood Wedding, 1:357
Ruslan and Ludmila, 1:395
Russia and the West Under Lenin and Stalin, 2:374, 2:391
Russia Beseiged, 2:383
Russia 1472–1917, 2:277
The Russia House, 1:102
Russia in the Shadows, 2:372
Russia Leaves the War, 2:371, 2:391
Russia, the Atom, and the West, 2:391
The Russian Empire: Eighteen Hundred One to Nineteen Seventeen, 2:340
Russian Poetry: The Modern Period, 1:389
The Russian Revolution: The Overthrow of Tzarism and the Triumph of the Soviets, 2:381
The Russians, 2:406
Ruth Benedict, 2:44
Ruth Benedict: Patterns of a Life, 2:44
Rutherford: Simple Genius, 2:504
Rutherford and Boltwood: Letters on Radioactivity, 2:504
Rutherford and Physics at the Turn of the Century, 2:504
Rutherford and the Nature of the Atom, 2:504

S

S, 1:292
Sacco and Vanzetti: The Case Resolved, 2:226
The Sacred Cow and the Abominable Pig: Riddles of Food and Culture, 2:48
Sacred Cows and Other Edibles, 1:226
Sacred Thread: Hinduism in Continuity and Diversity, 2:281
Sadat: The Man Who Changed Mid-East History, 2:255, 2:414
Sadat and Begin: The Domestic Politics of Peacemaking, 2:255, 2:414
Sadat and His Statecraft, 2:414
Saddam's Iraq: Revolution or Reaction, 2:411
Sadness, 1:198
Safe Sex in a Dangerous World, 2:543
Safe, Strong, Streetwise: The Teenager's Guide to Preventing Sexual Assaults, 2:566
Safire's Political Dictionary: The New Language of Politics, 1:438

Saga of the Jomsvikings, 1:374
Sagas of the Kings, 1:373
Sagas of the Knights, 1:373
"Sailing to Byzantium," 1:133
St. Augustine: Man, Pastor, Mystic, 2:304
St. Augustine: The Greatness of the Soul, 2:304
St. Joan, 1:120
St. Joan of the Stockyards, 1:365
St. Peter Relates an Incident: Selected Poems, 1:245
St. Thomas Aquinas, 2:307
Saint Urbain's Horseman, 1:145
Saladin: The Politics of the Holy War, 2:301
Salammbô, 1:334, 1:335
Sally Ride and the New Astronauts, 2:481
The Salt Eaters, 1:196
The Salterton Trilogy, 1:138
A Salute to Black Scientists and Inventors, 2:432
Salvation in the Slums: Evangelical Social Welfare Work, 1865–1920, 2:207
Sam Adams: Pioneer in Propaganda, 2:164
Sam Houston: The Great Designer, 2:186
Sam Shepard: A Casebook, 1:285
Sam Shepard: The Life and Work of an American Dreamer, 1:285
Same Door, 1:292
Samson Agonistes, 1:13
Samuel Beckett, 1:331
Samuel de Champlain: Father of New France, 2:158
Samuel Gompers and Organized Labor in America, 2:204
Samuel Pepys, 1:27
Samuel Pepys, Esq, 1:27
Samuel Richardson, 1:29
Samuel Slater and the Origins of the American Textile Industry, 1790–1860, 2:185
Samuel Taylor Coleridge, 1:34
The San Francisco Calamity by Earthquake and Fire, 2:494
San Manuel Bueno, martir and la novela de Don Sandalio, 1:360
San Martin the Liberator, 2:369
The Sandbox and The Death of Bessie Smith, 1:187
The Sandbox, Fam and Yam, The American Dream, 1:186
A Sandburg Treasury: Prose and Poetry for Young People, 1:284
The Sandcastle, 1:108
Sandra Day O'Connor, 2:31
The Sands of Mars, 1:75
Sandstorms: Days and Nights in Arabia, 2:412

Santa Anna's Campaign Against Texas, 1835–1836, 2:185
Sara Will, 1:204
Sarah Bishop, 1:271; 2:164
Sarah Orne Jewett, 1:180
Sarajevo: A Study in the Origins of the Great War, 2:371
Saratoga Trunk, 1:220
Sartre: A Life, 1:340
SAS Applications Guide, 1987 Edition, 1:574
SAS Color Graphics Video Training Workbook, 1983 Edition, 1:574
SAS Introductory Guide for Personal Computers, Version 6 Edition, 1:574
Satan in Goray, 1:388
Satchmo: My Life in New Orleans, 2:264
Satellites of Today and Tomorrow, 2:482
Satire: From Aesop to Buchwald, 1:488
Saturday Night and Sunday Morning, 1:120, 1:121
Saturdee, 1:141
Saturn: The Spectacular Planet, 2:475
Satyricon, 1:319
Saudi Arabia: A Country Study, 2:89
Saul Bellow, 1:200
Save Our Planet: 750 Everyday Ways You Can Help Clean Up the Earth, 2:82
Save the Beloved Country, 1:416
The Saxon Shillin', 1:75
Say No to Alcohol, 2:555
Sayings of Confucius, 2:283
The Sayings of Poor Richard: The Prefaces, Proverbs and Poems of Benjamin Franklin, 2:168
Sayonara, 1:264
Scandinavia: A New Geography, 2:88
The Scapegoat, 1:80, 1:81
The Scarecrow of Oz, 1:199
The Scarlet Letter, 1:155, 1:177
Scarne's Encyclopedia of Games, 1:535
Scattered Poems, 1:247
Scavengers and Decomposers: The Clean-Up Crew, 2:465
The Scent of Eucalyptus, 1:139
Scented Gardens for the Blind, 1:138
The Sceptical Chemist, 2:498
Schaum's Outline of Electromagnets, 2:522
Schiller, 1:372
Schizophrenia, 2:122
Scholarship and Partisanship: Essays on Max Weber, 2:143
School and Society, 2:219
The School for Scandal and Other Plays, 1:29
The School for Wives, 1:338
Schooling and Achievement in American Society, 2:145
Science: It's Changing Your World, 2:432

The Science Almanac 1985-86, 2:432

Science and Reform: Selected Works of Charles Babbage, 1:542

Science and Serendipity: Great Discoveries by Accident, 2:434

Science and Technology in Fact and Fiction: A Guide to Young Adult Books, 2:432

Science and Technology of Polymer Colloids, 2:510

Science, Computers and the Information Onslaught: A Collection of Essays, 1:554

Science Ethics, 2:433

Science Facts You Won't Believe, 2:432

Science Now, 2:432

The Science of AIDS: Readings from Scientific American Magazine, 2:560

Science of Artificial Intelligence, 1:580

The Science of Computing: Exploring the Nature and Power of Algorithms, 1:585

The Science of Culture: A Study of Man and Civilization, 2:43

The Science of Fractal Images, 1:516

Science of Galileo, 2:473

The Science of Sound: Musical, Electronic, Environmental, 2:522

Science, Technology and Society in Seventeenth Century England, 2:141

Sciences of the Artificial, 1:581

Scientific Autobiography and Other Papers, 2:521

The Scientific Work of René Descartes (1596–1650), 1:515

Scientists and Inventors, 2:432

Scientists and Technologists, 2:432

Scientists at Work: The Creative Process of Scientific Research, 2:435

Scientists of the Mind: Intellectual Founders of Modern Psychology, 2:95

Scoop, 1:127

The Scope of Sociology, 2:125

The Scope of Total Architecture, 2:268

The Scorpion God, 1:90

Scott Joplin and the Ragtime Years, 2:226

Scoundrel Time, 1:231, 1:235

Screenplay: The Foundations of Screenwriting, Expanded Edition, 1:485

Screenwriting: The Art, Craft, and Business of Film and Television Writing, 1:485

The Screwtape Letters, 1:104

Sculpture and Ceramics of Paul Gauguin, 2:353

The Sculpture of Auguste Rodin: The Collection of the Rodin Museum, Philadelphia, 2:356

The Sea Around Us, 2:82, 2:243, 2:466, 2:488

The Sea Birds Are Still Alive, 1:196

The Sea Cook, 1:58

The Sea Floor: An Introduction to Marine Biology, 2:488

Sea Green, 1:139

Sea of Slaughter, 1:144

Sea Stories, 1:77

The Sea, The Sea, 1:107, 1:108

The Sea Wolf, 1:257

The Seagull, 1:390

Seamus Heaney, 1:93

Seamus Heaney: A Faber Student Guide, 1:92

Sean O'Casey, 1:109

Sean O'Faolain's Irish Vision, 1:110

The Seance and Other Stories, 1:388

The Search for a New Order: Intellectuals and Fascism in Prewar Japan, 2:374

The Search for JFK, 2:247

The Search for Order: 1877–1920, 2:224

The Search for Solutions, 2:434

The Search for the Past: Fossils, Rocks, Tracks, and Trails, the Search for the Origin of Life, 2:495

Searching for Caleb, 1:291

The Searching Wind, 1:235

Seas and Oceans, 2:486

Seascape; Counting the Ways; Listening; All Over, 1:186, 1:187

Seasons in Full Score, 2:337

The Seasons of a Man's Life, 2:107

Seawater: A Delicate Balance, 2:486

The Sebastapol Sketches, 1:397

Sebastian, or the Ruling Passions, 1:81

Second-Class Citizen, 1:413

"The Second Coming," 1:133

The Second Front, 2:383

Second Nature: Forty-Six Poems, 1:394

The Second Scientific American Book of Mathematical Puzzles and Diversions, 1:536

The Second Self: Computers and the Human Spirit, 1:555

The Second Stage, 2:244

The Second Tree from the Corner, 1:456

The Second Victory: The Marshall Plan and the Postwar Revival of Europe, 2:238, 2:382

The Second World War (Pierre and Wievorka), 2:384

The Second World War: An Illustrated History, 2:385

The Second World War (1948–1954), (Churchill), 2:385, 2:386

The Second Year: The Emergence of Self-Awareness, 2:106

The Secret Adversary, 1:73

The Secret Agent, 1:77

The Secret Government, 1:466

"The Secret Life of Walter Mitty," 1:290
The Secret Meaning of Things, 1:221
The Secret of Chimneys, 1:73
The Secret Pilgrim, 1:102
The Secret War, 2:384
The Secrets of Ancient Geometry, 1:511
Secrets of the Heart, 1:207
Secrets of the Shopping Mall, 1:276
Secrets of the Sun, 2:475
Secrets Told By Children of Alcoholics, 2:539
Seeing the Insane, 2:536
Sei Personaggi in Cerca d'autore, 1:351
Seize the Day, 1:200
The Seizure of Power, 1:386
The Seizure of Power: Fascism in Italy, 1919–1929, 2:375
Selected Antitrust Cases: Landmark Decisions, 2:65, 2:156
Selected Czech Tales, 1:382
Selected Essays: 1963–1975 (Sauer), 2:80
Selected Essays from the Rambler, Adventurer and Idler, 1:26
Selected Essays on Atheism, 1:38
Selected Latin American One-Act Plays, 1:399
Selected Letters (Cicero), 2:293
Selected Letters of Edmund Burke, 2:9, 2:329
Selected Letters of Gustav Mahler, 2:355
Selected Plays (Fry), 1:87
Selected Plays (Strindberg), 1:380
Selected Plays of Padraic Colum, 1:76
Selected Poems (Atwood), 1:136
Selected Poems (Baudelaire), 1:330
Selected Poems (Brooks), 1:205
Selected Poems (Gray), 1:26
Selected Poems (Garcia Lorca), 1:357
Selected Poems (Herrick), 1:11
Selected Poems (Hughes), 1:241
Selected Poems (Jarrell), 1:244
Selected Poems (Lanier), 1:160
Selected Poems (Lowell), 1:259
Selected Poems (MacNiece), 1:105
Selected Poems (Pasternak), 1:394
Selected Poems (Rilke), 1:371
Selected Poems (Rosetti), 1:56
Selected Poems (Senghor), 1:417
Selected Poems (Swinburne), 1:59
Selected Poems of Claude McKay, 1:260
Selected Poems of Edwin Arlington Robinson, 1:282
Selected Poems of Gabriela Mistral, 1:405
Selected Poems of Octavio Paz, 1:408
Selected Poems of Rainer Maria Rilke, 1:371
Selected Poems of Rubén Darío, 1:402
Selected Poetry (Blake), 1:32
The Selected Poetry and Prose (Poe), 1:164

The Selected Poetry of Rainer Maria Rilke, 1:371
Selected Political Speeches (Cicero), 2:293
Selected Prose (Arnold), 1:41
Selected Readings (Mao Zedong), 2:402
Selected Short Fiction (Dickens), 1:47
Selected Short Stories (Balzac), 1:329
Selected Speeches and Statements of General of the Army George C. Marshall, 2:240
Selected Stories (Gordimer), 1:414
Selected Stories (Maupassant), 1:337
Selected Tales and Sketches (Hawthorne), 1:177
Selected Topics in Field Quantization, 2:503
Selected Works (Burke), 2:329
Selected Works (Cicero), 2:293
Selected Works (Lenin), 2:378
Selected Works: Our Lord Don Quixote, 1:360
Selected Works: Tragic Sense of Life in Men & Nations, 1:360
Selected Works of Mao Tse-tung, 2:402
Selected Works of Washington Irving, 1:159
Selected Writings: George Herbert Mead, 2:139
Selected Writings and Speeches (Burke), 2:329
Selected Writings and Speeches (Lincoln), 2:198
Selected Writings of Edward Sapir in Language, Culture, and Personality, 2:50
The Selected Writings of John and John Quincy Adams, 2:173
Selected Writings of Jonathan Edwards, 1:153
Selected Writings of St. Thomas Aquinas, 2:307
Selected Writings on Computing: A Personal Perspective, 1:537
Selections from the Canzoniere and Other Works, 1:350
Self-Analysis, 2:119
Self-Consciousness: Memoirs, 1:293
Self-defense and Assault Prevention for Girls and Women, 2:567
The Self-Learning Society, 1:571
"Self-Reliance," 1:157
Self, Sex, and Gender in Cross-Cultural Fieldwork, 2:43
Selling Money: A Young Banker's Account of the Great International Lending Boom and Bust, 2:70, 2:154
The Selling of the President, 2:40, 2:254
The Selling of the President 1968, 1:442
Semantic Fitness, 1:437
Semantic Information Processing, 1:582

Semantics: An Introduction to the Science of Meaning, 1:438
Semantics for Teens, 1:437
Send These to Me: Immigrants in Urban America, 2:207
Seneca: Four Tragedies and Octavia, 1:323
Seneca's Drama, 1:323
Sensation and Perception, 2:113
A Sense of Detachment, 1:112
The Sense of the Seventies: A Rhetorical Reader, 2:252
The Sense of Wonder, 2:243, 2:466
The Senses Considered as Perceptual Systems, 2:113
The Sentimental Education, 1:334, 1:335
Sentiments and Activities: Essays in Social Science, 2:104
A Separate Peace, 1:251
The Seraphim and Other Poems, 1:43
Seraphita, 1:329
Sergei Prokofiev: A Biography, 2:422
Sergei Prokofiev: A Soviet Tragedy, 2:422
Sergei Prokofiev: Materials, Articles, Interviews, 2:422, 2:424
Serpent in the Sky: The High Wisdom of Ancient Egypt, 2:281
The Serpent Never Sleeps, 1:271; 2:162
The Serpent's Coil, 1:144
The Servant of Two Masters and Other Italian Classics, 1:347
Sette racconti, 1:350
Setting Limits: Medical Goals in an Aging Society, 2:567
Settlers of Kenya, 2:363
Seurat: A Biography, 2:346
The Sevastopol Sketches, 1:396
Seven Against Thebes, 1:311
Seven Black American Scientists, 2:432
Seven Clues to the Origin of Life: A Scientific Detective Story, 2:461
Seven Edwards of England, 2:276
Seven Famous Greek Plays, 1:311
Seven Gothic Tales, 1:376
The Seven Pillars of Wisdom, 2:372
Seven Plays (O'Casey), 1:108
Seven Plays (Shepard), 1:285
Seven Poems (Pasternak), 1:394
Seven Short Novels (Chekhov), 1:391
Seven States of Matter, 2:518
Seventeen Against the Dealer, 1:294
Seventeen Eighty-Seven: The Grand Convention, 2:17
A Severed Head, 1:107
Sex and Temperament in Three Primitive Societies, 2:46
Sex and the American Teenager, 2:137
Sex, Gender, and Society, 2:148
Sex Hormones, 2:544

Sexually Transmitted Diseases (Landau), 2:559
The Sexually Transmitted Diseases (Rinear), 2:559
Shadow and Act, 1:218
The Shadow of a Gunman, 1:108
Shadow of Dictators: 1925–1950, 2:384
The Shadow of the Parthenon: Studies in Ancient History and Literature, 2:285
Shadows on the Grass, 1:375, 1:376
Shadows on the Rock, 1:209
Shaker: Masterworks of Utilitarian Design Created Between 1800 and 1875 by the Master Craftsmen and Craftswomen of America's Foremost Communal Religious Sect, 2:187
Shakespeare, 1:16
Shakespeare Alive!, 1:16
The Shakespeare Companion, 1:16
Shakespeare for Everyone, 1:16
Shakespeare of London, 1:16
Shakespeare's Plays for Young People, 1:16
Shakespeare's Sonnets, 1:15
The Shaky Game: Einstein, Realism, and the Quantum Theory, 2:518
Shale Oil and Tar Sands: The Promises and Pitfalls, 2:496
Shamela, 1:24
Shannon's Way, 1:78
Shapes, Space, and Symmetry, 1:519
The Shaping of America, 2:90
The Shaping of Middle-Earth, 1:125, 1:126
The Share Economy: Conquering Stagflation, 2:63
The Shattered Bloc: Behind the Upheaval in Eastern Europe, 2:404
Shaw: The Critical Heritage, 1:120
She, 1:51
She Stoops to Conquer, 1:25
She Wanted to Read: The Story of Mary McLeod Bethune, 2:14
Shelley, 1:38
The Sheltered Life, 1:226, 1:227
The Shepheardes Calendar, 1:17
Sheridan, 1:29
Sheridan's Comedies: The Contexts and Achievements, 1:29
Sherlock Holmes: The Complete Novels and Stories, 1:48
Sherman's March, 2:193
Sherwood Anderson, 1:190
Sherwood Anderson: A Collection of Critical Essays, 1:190
Shh! We're Writing the Constitution, 2:166
Shiloh and Other Stories, 1:262, 1:263
The Shining, 1:249
Ship of Fools, 1:279

A Ship of the Line, 1:85
Ships and Seamanship in the Ancient
World, 2:273
Shirley, 1:42
Shirley Chisholm: A Bibliography of
Writings by & about Her, 2:34
Shirley Chisholm: Teacher and
Congresswoman, 2:34
Shirley Jackson, 1:243
Shiva's Pigeons: An Experience of India,
2:309
"The Shooting of Dan McGrew," 1:146
The Shooting Party: A Novel, 1:391
A Short Course on Computer Viruses,
1:574
Short Friday and Other Stories, 1:388
A Short Guide to Shakespeare, 1:16
A Short History of Africa, 2:276
Short History of Anatomy and
Physiology: From the Greeks to Harvey,
2:548
A Short History of Biology, 2:434
Short History of Greek Mathematics,
1:497
Short History of Linguistics, 1:434
A Short History of Opera, 2:261
A Short History of Sociological Thought,
2:125
Short History of the Movies, 1:469
Short Introduction to English Grammar,
1:429
The Short Stories of Ernest Hemingway,
1:237
The Short Stories of Katherine Mansfield,
1:142
The Shorter Cambridge Medieval History,
2:276
Shosha, 1:388
Shostakovich, 2:424
Shostakovich: About Himself and His
Times, 2:424
Shostakovich: The Man and His Music,
2:424
Shots Without Guns: The Story of
Vaccination, 2:444, 2:446
The Show and Tell Machine: How
Television Works and Works You Over,
1:465
Show Boat, 1:220
Showdown at Little Big Horn, 2:200
The Shrapnel Academy, 1:128
A Shropshire Lad, 1:53, 1:54
Shroud for a Nightingale, 1:98
SI: The International System of Units,
2:436
SI Metric Handbook, 2:435
Sibelius, 2:346
Siberia and the Soviet Far East:
Unmasking the Myths, 2:405

The Siberians, 1:144
The Sibyl, 1:378, 1:379
Sickness and Health in America: Readings
in the History of Medicine and Public
Health, 2:567
Siddhartha, 1:368
Side Effects, 1:189
Sidelights on Relativity, 2:520
Sidereus Nuncius (The Sidereal
Messenger), 2:473
Sidnee Poet Heroical, 1:197
Sidney's Poetry, 1:16
Siegfried Sassoon's Long Journey:
Selections from the Sherston Memoirs,
1:116
Siegfried's Journey, 1:116
Sienese Painting in the Age of the
Renaissance, 2:310
A Sigh of Relief: First Aid Handbook
for Childhood Emergencies,
2:567
Sight and Seeing: A World of Light and
Color, 2:448
The Sign in Sidney Brustein's Window,
1:232
Sign Language Talk, 1:448
The Sign of the Chrysanthemum,
1:484
Significance of the Frontier in American
History, 2:156
Signing: How to Speak with Your Hands,
1:448
Sigrid Undset, 1:381
Silas Marner, 1:49
Silence: Lectures and Writings of John
Cage, 2:261
The Silent Intruder: Surviving the
Radiation Age, 2:570
Silent Killers: Radon and Other Hazards,
2:570
The Silent Language, 1:448
Silent Sound: The World of Ultrasonics,
2:521
Silent Spring, 2:243, 2:466
The Silent World, 2:487
Silex Scintillans, 1:17
The Silmarillion, 1:125
The Silver Box, 1:87
The Silver Burdett Mathematical
Dictionary, 1:496
The Silver Horse-Shoe, 1:519
The Sim City Planning Commission
Handbook, 1:567
Simón Bolívar, 2:370
The Simple Life: Plain Living and High
Thinking in American Culture, 2:51
Simple's Uncle Sam, 1:241
Simulated Exercise Physiology
Laboratories, 1:569

Since Yesterday: The Nineteen-Thirties in America: Sept. 3, 1929–Sept. 3, 1939, 2:228

Sinclair Lewis, 1:256

Sing Down the Moon, 1:272; 2:185

Singin' and Swingin' and Gettin' Merry like Christmas, 1:192

"Sinners in the Hands of an Angry God," 1:153

Sir Francis Drake, 2:157, 2:324

Sir Francis Drake and the Famous Voyage, 1577–1580: Essays Commemorating the Quadricentennial of Drake's Circumnavigation of the Earth, 2:324

Sir Francis Drake, His Voyage, Fifteen Ninety-Five, 2:158

Sir Gawain and the Green Knight, 1:5, 1:8

Sir Gawain and the Green Knight: A Reference Guide, 1:8

Sir Joshua Reynolds, 2:339

Sir Philip Sidney: An Anthology of Modern Criticism, 1:16

Sir Thomas Malory: His Turbulent Career, 1:7

Sir Thomas Wyatt: A Literary Portrait, 1:18

Sir Thomas Wyatt: The Complete Poems, 1:18

Sir Walter Raleigh and the New World, 2:162

Sir Walter Scott, 1:36

The Sirens of Titan, 1:295

The Sirian Experiments, 1:103

Sister Carrie, 1:215, 1:216, 1:217

The Sisterhood: The True Story of the Women Who Changed the World, 2:148

Six Armies in Normandy: From D-Day to the Liberation of Paris, 2:235

Six Characters in Search of an Author, 1:351

Six Comedies (Maugham), 1:106

Six Feet of Country, 1:414

Six Indonesian Short Stories, 1:426

Six Lectures on Modern Natural Philosophy, 1:526

Six Plays (MacLeish), 1:261

Six Plays by Lillian Hellman: The Children's Hour, Days to Come, The Little Foxes, Watch on the Rhine, Another Part of the Forest, The Autumn Garden, 1:235

Six Plays of Clifford Odets: Waiting for Lefty, 1:272

The Six Stages of Parenthood, 2:543

Sixteenth-Century North America: The Land and the People as Seen by Europeans, 2:80

Sixties People, 2:242

The Sixties Reader, 2:241

The Sixties, Without Apology, 2:51, 2:242

Sixty Stories (Barthelme), 1:198

Skeleton Crew, 1:249

The Sketch Book, 1:159, 1:160

Sketches by Boz, 1:46

Sketches from a Life, 2:391

Sketches from a Life's Journey, 2:391

Sketches of Places and People Abroad, 1:170

Skin Care for Teens, 2:552

Skin Disorders, 2:552

The Skin of Our Teeth, 1:303

Skin Secrets: A Dermatologist's Prescription for Beautiful Skin at Any Age, 2:552

The Skinner Primer: Behind Freedom and Dignity, 2:102

Skinner's Philosophy, 2:102

The Skull Beneath the Skin, 1:98

Sky Dragons and Flaming Swords: The Story of Eclipses, Comets, and Other Strange Happenings in the Skies, 2:476

The Sky Watcher's Handbook, 2:471

Skyguide: A Field Guide for Amateur Astronomers, 2:469

Slang Thesaurus, 1:433

Slanguage, 1:433

Slapstick, 1:295

Slaughterhouse Five, or The Children's Crusade, 1:295

The Slave, 1:388

The Slave Community: Plantation Life in the Ante-Bellum South, 2:188

The Slave Girl, 1:413

Slavery, History, and Historians, 2:189

Slavery, Law, and Politics: The Dred Scott Case in Historical Perspective, 2:189

Slavery, Letters and Speeches, 2:186

Sleeper, 1:189

Sleeping Murder, 1:73

Sleuth, 1:119

A Slipping-down Life, 1:291

Slumps, Grunts, and Snickerdoodles: What Colonial America Ate and Why, 2:162

Small Computers, 1:556

Small Is Beautiful: Economics as if People Mattered, 2:63

A Small Sound of the Trumpet: Women in the Medieval Life, 2:310

A Small Town in Germany, 1:102

Small Town in Mass Society: Class, Power, and Religion in a Rural Community, 2:131

Small Worlds Close Up, 2:436

Smalltalk-80: The Interactive Programming Environment, 1:566

Smile! How to Cope with Braces, 2:552

Smiley's People, 1:102

Smith of Wooten Major, 1:125

The Smoke Problem of Our Great Cities, 2:484

Smoking, 2:556

Smoking and Health, 2:556

Smoking Cigarettes: The Unfiltered Truth: Understanding Why and How to Quit, 2:556

Smoking Not Allowed, 2:556

Snap, Crackle, and Popular Taste: the Illusion of Free Choice in America, 1:441, 1:455

Snapshots, 1:250

Snapshots of a Daughter-in-Law, 1:281

The SNOBOL4 Programming Language, 1:566

The Snow Walker, 1:144

Snow White, 1:197

The Snowbird, 2:200

Snow-Bound: A Winter Idyll, 1:166

The Snows of Kilimanjaro and Other Stories, 1:237

So Big, 1:220

So Long and Thanks for all the Fish, 1:64

So This Is Depravity, 1:481

So You Have to Give a Speech, 1:449

So You're Getting Braces, 2:553

The Soap Opera, 1:461, 1:465

Social Actions and Artificial Intelligence, 1:582

Social and Cultural Dynamics: A Study of Changes in Major Systems of Art, Truth, Ethics, and Social Relationships, 2:144

The Social Animal, 2:98

Social Behavior in Animals: With Special Reference to Vertebrates, 2:465

Social Change in Rural Societies: An Introduction to Rural Sociology, 2:144

Social Change in the Industrial Revolution, 2:144

Social Change in the Modern Era, 2:144

Social Choice and Individual Values, 2:55, 2:64

Social Cognition and Communication, 2:103

The Social Construction of Communities, 2:131

The Social Contract, 2:11

Social Contract: Essays by Locke, Hume, and Rousseau, 2:7

Social Darwinism in American Thought, 2:204

Social Forces and Aging: An Introduction to Social Gerontology, 2:129

Social Foundations of German Unification, 1858–1871, 2:340

The Social Foundations of Thought and Action: A Social Cognitive Theory, 2:103, 2:105

The Social Importance of Self-Esteem, 2:139

Social Learning and Imitation, 2:112, 2:116

Social Learning Theory, 2:105, 2:112

The Social Life of a Modern Community, 2:51, 2:144

Social Mobility in Industrial Society, 2:145

Social Movements of the 1960s, 2:241

Social Order of the Slum, 2:147

The Social Organization of Australian Tribes, 2:53

Social Problems of the Industrial Revolution, 2:340

Social Research and the Practicing Professions, 2:141

Social Research to Test Ideas: Selected Writings, 2:129

The Social Sciences Since the Second World War, 2:149

Social Security and Retirement: Private Goals and Public Policy, 2:7, 2:33

Social Statistics and Social Dynamics: The Theory of Order and the Theory of Progress, 2:126

Social Stratification: The Forms and Functions of Inequality, 2:145

Social Stratification in Science, 2:144

Social Structure, 2:51

Social Structure and Personality, 2:52

The Social System, 2:127, 2:144

The Social Theories of Talcott Parsons: A Critical Examination, 2:128

Social Theory and Modern Sociology, 2:125

Social Theory and Social Structure, 2:141, 2:145

Social Thought of Jane Addams, 2:208

The Social Thought of W. E. B. Du Bois, 2:211

Socialism: Opposing Viewpoints, 2:15, 2:58

Socialism: Utopian and Scientific, 2:59

Socialist Planning, 2:58

Socialization and the Life Cycle, 2:146

Socialization to Old Age, 2:146

Society, Culture and Urbanization, 2:144

A Society of Mind, 1:581

Sociobiology: The New Synthesis, 2:98, 2:105

Sociobiology and Behavior, 2:133

Socioeconomic Background and Achievement, 2:144

Sociolinguistic Patterns, 1:437

Sociolinguistics, 1:437

Sociolinguistics: An Introduction to Language and Society, 1:437

Sociological Theory and Modern Society, 2:127

Sociological Traditions from Generation to Generation: Glimpses of the American Experience, 2:141

Sociology: A Student Handbook, 2:124

The Sociology of Culture, 2:134

The Sociology of Emile Durkheim, 2:127

Sociology of Marriage and the Family, 2:137

The Sociology of Race Relations: Reflection and Reform, 2:136

The Sociology of Religion, 2:142, 2:143

The Sociology of Science: Theoretical and Empirical Investigations, 2:141

The Sociology of Small Groups, 2:104

The Sociology of Work, 2:148

The Sod-House Frontier, 1854–1890: A Social History of the Northern Plains from the Creation of Kansas and Nebraska to the Admission of the Dakotas, 2:200

Software Encyclopedia, 1:566

Software Engineering, 1:585

Software for Information and Image Management, 1:578

Software for Optical Storage, 1:578

Software for Schools, 1987–1988, 1:569

Software Perspectives: The System Is the Message, 1:563

Software Reflected: The Socially Responsible Programming of Computers, 1:554

Soil Erosion and Its Control, 2:493

Sojourner Truth, 2:12, 2:189

The Solar Energy Almanac, 2:485

Solar System, 2:475

The Solar System: Opposing Viewpoints, 2:476

Soldier in the Rain, 1:227

A Soldier Reports, 2:242

A Soldier's Embrace, 1:414

Soldiers' Pay, 1:219

Solid Acids and Bases: Their Catalytic Properties, 2:508

Solid Gold: The Popular Record Industry, 2:133

The Solid Mandala, 1:147

Soliloquy: The Shakespeare Monologues, 1:449

A Solitary Blue, 1:294

The Solitary Singer: A Critical Biography of Walt Whitman, 1:185

Solo! The Best Monologues of the 80s, 1:449

Solzhenitsyn: A Biography, 1:396

Solzhenitsyn in Exile: Critical Essays and Documentary Materials, 1:396

Somatic Cell Division, 2:451

Some Aspects of the Genius of Giovanni Boccaccio, 1:348

Some Desperate Glory: The World War I Diary of a British Officer, 2:224

Some Letters from Livingstone, 1840–1872, 2:367

Some Spanish-American Poets, 1:399

Something Happened, 1:234

Something in Common and Other Stories, 1:241

Something I've Been Meaning to Tell You, 1:145

Something Out There, 1:414

Something Wicked This Way Comes, 1:202

Somewhere a Master: Further Tales of the Hasidic Masters, 1:301

Somnium: The Dream, or Posthumous Work on Lunar Astronomy, 2:474

Son of Man, 1:286

The Son of Someone Famous, 1:248

The Son of Tarzan, 1:208

Soñetos de la muerte (Sonnets About Death), 1:405

The Song of Roland, 1:327, 1:341

A Song of Sixpence, 1:78

Song of Solomon, 1:269

"The Song of the Chattahoochee," 1:160

"The Song of the Dragons Flying to Heaven," 1:426

The Song of the Lark, 1:209

Song of the Trees, 1:289, 1:290

Songs of Experience, 1:32

Songs of Innocence, 1:31, 1:32

Songs of Jamaica, 1:259

The Sonnets and Narrative Poems: The Complete Non-Dramatic Poetry (Shakespeare), 1:15

The Sonnets by Dante Gabriel Rossetti, 1:57

Sonnets from the Portuguese and Other Love Poems, 1:43

Sonnets to Orpheus, 1:371

Sons, 1:207

Sons and Lovers, 1:100, 1:101

Sons from Afar, 1:294

Sophocles (Bloom), 1:317; 2:284

Sophocles (Scodel), 1:317

The Sorcerer's Apprentice: A Journey Through East Africa, 2:363

The Sorrows of Young Werther, 1:365, 1:366

The Soul Catcher, 1:238

The Soul of a New Machine, 1:563

Soul of America, 2:152

The Souls of Black Folk, 2:210, 2:211

Souls on Fire, 1:302

Sound and Sources of Sound, 2:521

The Sound and the Fury, 1:219

Sound, Speech, and Music, 2:521

Sounder, 2:228

Sounding the Alarm: A Biography of Rachel Carson, 2:243, 2:466
Sounds and Silences, 1:276
Source Book in Geography, 2:76
Source Book of Free and Low-Cost Software, 1:567
Sources, 1:281
Sources and Documents Illustrating the American Revolution, 1764–1788, and the Formation of the Federal Constitution, 2:164
Sources of Shang History: The Oracle-Bone Inscriptions of Bronze Age China, 2:282
Sousa's Great Marches in Piano Transcription, 2:216
South Africa: Coming of Age Under Apartheid, 2:85, 2:393
South America, 2:88
South America Called Them; Explorations of the Great Naturalists: La Condamine, Humboldt, Darwin, Spence, 2:78
The South During the Reconstruction, 1865–1877, 2:198
South of Yosemite: Selected Writings of John Muir, 2:221
Southeast Asia (Time-Life), 2:86
Southeast Asia (Wittington), 2:400
Southeast Asia: A History, 2:400
Southeast Asia: An Illustrated Introductory History, 2:399
Southeast Asia: Realm of Contrasts, 2:398
The Southeast Asian World, 2:398
Southern Road, 1:206
Soviet-American Relations, 1917–1920, 2:371, 2:391
The Soviet-East European Relationship in the Gorbachov Era: The Prospects for Adaptation, 2:404
Soviet Foreign Policy: Nineteen Seventeen to Nineteen Forty-One, 2:391
The Soviet Juggernaut, 2:384
Soviet Potentials: A Geographic Appraisal, 2:91
The Soviet Union (Congressional Quarterly), 2:36
Soviet Union (Time-Life), 2:92
The Soviet Union: Will Perestroika Work?, 2:91, 2:404
The Soviet Union and Eastern Europe (Schopflin), 2:405
Soviet Union and Eastern Europe (Shoemaker), 2:406
Soviet Women: Walking the Tightrope, 2:405
Space (Feldman), 2:469
Space (Michener), 1:264
Space (Ridpath), 2:479
Space: Frontier of the Future, 2:481

Space Cadet, 1:233
Space Colony: Frontier of the 21st Century, 2:480
Space Flight: The Records, 2:257
Space Frontier, 2:483
Space History, 2:481
Space Log: A Chronological Checklist of Manned Space Flights, 1961–1990, 2:257
Space Mathematics, 1:519
The Space Merchants, 1:278
Space Probes and Satellites, 2:480
Space Satellites, 2:482
Space Science Projects for Young Scientists, 2:481
Space Sciences, 2:470
Space Shots, Shuttles, and Satellites, 2:480
The Space Shuttle (Fichter), 2:481
Space Shuttle (Hawkes), 2:481
Space Shuttles: Projects for Young Scientists, 2:482
Space Station Automation, 1:582
Space Talk, 1:433; 2:469
Space Telescope (Branley), 2:435
The Space Telescope (Lampton), 2:481
Space, Time, Infinity: The Smithsonian Views the Universe, 2:479
Space Travel, 2:480
Space Travel: A History, 2:482, 2:483
Spacelab: Research in Earth Orbit, 2:481
Spaceship Earth, 2:74, 2:469
Spanish-American Revolutions 1808–1826, 2:369
The Spanish-American War and President McKinley, 2:218
The Spanish and Portuguese Languages in the United States, 1:353
Spanish Civil War, 2:375
The Spanish Civil War: A History in Pictures, 2:374
Spanish Colonial Art and Architecture of Mexico and the U.S. Southwest, 2:160
Spanish Colonization in the Southwest, 2:160
Spanish Conquerors, 2:158
Spanish Explorers in the Southern United States, 1528–1543, 2:157
Spanish Folk-Tales from New Mexico, 2:160
Spanish Grammar, 1:353
Spanish Literature 1700–1900, 1:355
Spanish Music in the Age of Columbus, 2:161
Spanish Pronunciation in the Americas, 1:353
Spanish Proverbs: A Survey of Spanish Culture and Civilization, 2:161
Spanish Short Stories, 1:399
The Spanish Smile, 1:272

Spanish Verbs and Essentials of Grammar, 1:353

Spanish West, 2:160

Spare Parts for People, 2:565

Spartacus, 1:218

The Spartans, 2:284

Spatial Geography, 2:93

Speak to Me: How to Put Confidence in Your Conversation, 1:445

Speak with Distinction, 1:451

Speaking for Ourselves, 1:188, 1:201, 1:204, 1:212, 1:213, 1:228–230, 1:238, 1:240, 1:248, 1:250, 1:267, 1:272, 1:276

Speaking My Mind: Selected Speeches, 2:260

Speaking Out: The Reagan Presidency from Inside the White House, 2:260

Specimen Days, 1:184

Speech Analysis, Synthesis, and Perception, 1:579

Speech and Law in a Free Society, 2:12

Speech Can Change Your Life, 1:445

Speech for Conciliation with America, 2:328

Speech on American Taxation, 2:328

Speech Synthesis and Recognition, 1:579

Speech Synthesis and Recognition Systems, 1:579

The Speeches of Adolf Hitler, 2:376

The Spell of the Yukon, 1:146

Spence and Lila, 1:263

Sphereland, 1:519

Spiders of the World, 2:449

Spike Lee's Gotta Have It: Inside Guerrilla Filmmaking, 1:486

Spill! The Story of the Exxon Valdez, 2:467

The Spinoza of Market Street and Other Stories, 1:388

The Spire, 1:89

The Spirit of Seventeen Eighty-Seven: The Making of Our Constitution, 2:166

The Spirit of the Laws, 2:18, 2:19

The Spirit of Youth and the City Streets, 2:208

Spiritual Life of Children, 2:106

The Splendor That Was Africa, 2:300

Splendors of the Past: Lost Cities of the Ancient World, 2:277

Splitting the Difference: Compromise and Integrity in Ethics and Politics, 2:19

Spock on Spock: A Memoir of Growing Up with the Century, 2:541

Spoon River Anthology, 1:263

Spoonerisms, Sycophants, and Sops, 1:432

Sport in Greece and Rome, 2:285

A Sport of Nature, 1:414

Sports Classics: American Writers Choose Their Best, 1:480

Sports Fitness and Training, 2:551

Sports in America, 1:264

The Sports Medicine Fitness Course, 2:551

The Spot: The Rise of Political Advertising on Television, 1:442; 2:39

Spotlight on Computer Literacy, 1:557

Spreadsheets for Beginners, 1:574

SPSS-PC Plus V2.0 Base, 1:574

SPSS-X Introductory Statistics Guide for SPSS-X Release 3, 1:574

Spunk: The Selected Stories of Zora Neale Hurston, 1:242

Sputnik, 2:482

Sputnik, Scientists, and Eisenhower: A Memoir of the First Special Assistant to the President for Science and Technology, 2:238

The Spy Who Came in from the Cold, 1:102

The Spy Who Loved Me, 1:84

The Spying Heart: More Thoughts on Reading and Writing Books for Children, 1:484

The Square Root of Tuesday, 1:535

Squaring the Circle, 1:122

Sri Lanka: A Country Study, 2:87

Stagecraft in Euripides, 1:314

The Stages of Ethical Development: From Childhood Through Old Age, 2:109, 2:146

Stages of Faith: The Psychology of Human Development and the Quest for Meaning, 2:142

Stalin, 2:380

Stalin: A Political Biography, 2:380

Stalin: An Appraisal of the Man and His Influences, 2:380

Stalin: The Glasnost Revelations, 2:380

Stalin: The Iron Fisted Dictator of Russia, 2:380

Stalin: The Man and His Era, 2:375

Stalin: Russia's Man of Steel, 2:380

Stalin and His Generals: Soviet Military Memoirs of World War II, 2:380

Stalin as Revolutionary, 1879–1929: A Study in History and Personality, 2:380

Stalinism, 2:380

Stalin's American Policy, 2:380

Stalking the Feature Story, 1:487

The Stand, 1:249

Stand Up, Speak Out: An Introduction to Public Speaking, 1:450

Stand Up, Speak Up, or Shut Up: A Practical Guide to Public Speaking, 1:450

The Standard Edition of the Complete Psychological Works of Sigmund Freud, 2:118

Standard First Aid and Personal Safety, 2:566
Standard Handbook for Telescope Making, 2:470
Standards for Educational and Psychological Testing, 2:122
Stanley and the Women, 1:65
The Star Beast, 1:234
Star Gazing, Comet Tracking, and Sky Mapping, 2:469
Star Guide, 2:469
Star Maps for Beginners, 2:470
Star Trek, 1:466
Star Wars, 1:468
The Starchild Trilogy, 1:278
Stargazing: Astronomy Without a Telescope, 2:470
Starring Sally J. Freedman as Herself, 1:201
The Starry Room: Naked Eye Astronomy in the Intimate Universe, 2:471
Stars, 2:478
The Stars: Decoding Their Messages, 2:478
Stars and Planets, 2:470
The Stars, like Dust, 1:194
State and Local Government: The Third Century of Federalism, 2:41
State and Local Government in America, 2:41
State and Local Government in an Urban Society, 2:40
The State and Local Government Political Dictionary, 2:40
State and Local Politics, 2:40
State and Local Politics: The Great Entanglement, 2:41
The State and Revolution, 2:378
State Government: C.Q.'s Guide to Current Issues and Activities, 1988–1989, 2:40
The State in Its Relations with the Church, 2:345
State Legislatures: A Bibliography, 2:6, 2:41
The State of Afro-American History: Past, Present, and Future, 2:154
State of Revolution, 1:69
A State of Siege, 1:138
The State of Sociology: Problems and Prospects, 2:125
State of the Ark: An Atlas of Conservation in Action, 2:81
State of the Art, 1:480
The State of the States, 2:6, 2:41
State of the World, 1988, 2:76, 2:273
State of the World, 1989: A Worldwatch Institute Report on Progress Toward a Sustainable Society, 2:36
State of the World, 1991, 2:81

State Papers and Other Public Writings, 2:231
State Surveys, 2:145
State-Local Relations: A Partnership Approach, 2:41
States of Matter, 2:498, 2:518
States' Rights, 2:35
Statesman's Year-Book and World Gazetteer, 2:75
The Statesman's Year-Book, 1989–1990, 2:76
Station Island, 1:92
Statistical Abstract of the United States, 2:4, 2:124
Statistical Mechanics, 2:503
Statistical Pioneers, 1:530
Statistical Reasoning in Psychology and Education, 2:122
Statistics: A Guide to the Unknown, 1:535
Statistics for Social Change, 1:529
Statistics in Psychology: A Historical Perspective, 2:122
Statistics the Easy Way, 1:529
Stay Tuned: A Concise History of American Broadcasting, 1:457
Stay Tuned: An Inside Look at the Making of Prime Time Television, 1:466
Staying Found: The Complete Map and Compass Handbook, 2:92
Staying On, 1:118
Staying Supple, 2:551
Steichen: A Life in Photography, 2:269
Steichen at War, 2:269
Steinbeck: A Life in Letters, 1:289
Stendhal, 1:342
Stendhal: A Study of His Novels, 1:342
Step-By-Step Keyboarding on the Personal Computer, 1:560
Stepfamilies: New Patterns of Harmony, 2:538
Stepfathering: Stepfathers' Advice on Creating a New Family, 2:539
Stephen Crane: A Collection of Critical Essays, 1:174
Stephen Crane: A Critical Biography, 1:174
Stephen Douglas: The Last Years, 1857–1861, 2:189
Stephen Leacock: Humor and Humanity, 1:141
Stephen Vincent Benét: The Life and Times of an American Man of Letters, 1:201
Stepkids: A Survival Guide for Teenagers in Stepfamilies, 2:538
Steppenwolf, 1:368
Sterling A. Brown: Building the Black Aesthetic Tradition, 1:206
Steven Spielberg, 1:470, 1:473

Steven Spielberg: Amazing Filmmaker, 1:473
A Stillness at Appomattox, 2:192, 2:199
Stilwell and the American Experience in China 1911–1945, 2:400
The Stochastic Man, 1:286
Stokely Carmichael: the Story of Black Power, 2:242
A Stolen Past, 1:251
Stone Age Africa: An Outline of Prehistory in Africa, 2:49
The Stone Angel, 1:140
Stonehenge Complete, 2:305
Stones: Their Collection, Identification, and Uses, 2:492
Stoppard: The Mystery and the Clockwork, 1:123
"Stopping by Woods on a Snowy Evening," 1:223
The Store, 1:216
Stories (Lessing), 1:103
Stories (Mansfield), 1:142
Stories from a Ming Collection, 2:309
The Stories of Bernard Malamud, 1:262
The Stories of F. Scott Fitzgerald, 1:222
Stories of God, 1:371
The Stories of Heinrich Böll, 1:364
The Stories of John Cheever, 1:211
Stories of Muriel Spark, 1:122
Stories of Three Decades, 1:370
Storm, 2:485
Storm Center: The Supreme Court in American Politics, 2:27
Storming Eagles: German Airborne Forces in World War Two, 2:384
The Story Behind the Word, 1:433
The Story Girl, 1:143
The Story of a Shipwrecked Sailor, 1:404
Story of American Railroads, 2:154, 2:204
The Story of English, 1:429
The Story of Euclid, 1:514
Story of Evolution, 2:456
The Story of Giuseppe Verdi, 2:361
The Story of Hollywood, 1:469
The Story of Human Communication: Cave Painting to Microchip, 2:130
The Story of Ireland, 2:305
The Story of Irving Berlin, 2:265
Story of Jazz, 2:262
The Story of Life on Earth, 2:456
The Story of Maps, 2:92
Story of Music, 2:275
Story of My Boyhood and Youth, 2:221
The Story of My Childhood, 2:194, 2:568
The Story of My Life, 1:449
Story of Painting, 2:276
The Story of the Boston Massacre, 2:164
The Story of the Louisiana Purchase, 2:169

A Story of the Red Cross, 2:568
A Story of the Red Cross: Glimpses of Field Work, 2:194
The Story of the Thirteen Colonies, 2:161
Storylines: Conversation Skills Through Oral Histories, 1:445
Storyteller's Ghost Stories, 1:451
Storytelling, 1:451
Storytelling: Art and Technique, 1:451
Storytelling Mark Twain Style, 1:451
Storytelling Tips: How to Love, Learn and Relate a Story, 1:451
Straight From the Heart: How to Talk to Your Teenagers About Love and Sex, 2:543
Straight Lines and Curves, 1:512
Straight Talk About Drinking: Teenagers Speak Out About Alcohol, 2:555
Straight Talk About Parents, 2:539
Strait Is the Gate, 1:336
The Strange Career of Jim Crow, 2:208
Strange Fugitive, 1:136
Strange Interlude, 1:274
The Stranger, 1:332, 1:333
Stranger in a Strange Land, 1:234
Strangers from a Different Shore: A History of Asian Americans, 2:207
Strangers in the Land: Patterns of American Nativism, 1860–1925, 2:207
Strategic Interaction, 2:139
Strategy and Arms Control, 2:37
The Strategy of Peace, 2:247
Stravinsky, 2:426
Stravinsky: In Pictures and Documents, 2:426
The Strayed Reveller and Other Poems, 1:40
Streams to the River, River to the Sea: A Novel Of Sacagawea, 1:272, 2:169
Street Corner Society: The Social Structure of an Italian Slum, 2:131, 2:150
A Street in Bronzeville, 1:205
A Streetcar Named Desire, 1:303, 1:304
Strength to Love, 2:250
Stress and Its Management, 2:123
Stress and Mental Health, 2:537
Stress Management, 2:536
Stress Management: A Comprehensive Guide to Wellness, 2:536
A Stress Management Guide for Young People, 2:123
Stretch! The Total Fitness Program, 2:552
Strictly Speaking: Will America Be the Death of English, 1:443
Stride Toward Freedom: The Montgomery Story, 2:12, 2:238, 2:250
Strikes in the United States, 2:204
Striking a Balance: Making National Economic Policy, 2:65

Strong Democracy: Participatory Politics for a New Age, 2:12
Strong Poison, 1:117
The Strong Shall Live, 1:253
Structural Anthropology, 2:53
Structural Complexity I, 1:585
Structure and Function in Primitive Societies, 2:54
The Structure and Properties of Matter, 2:506
Structure of American English, 1:432
The Structure of American Industry, 2:57
The Structure of Social Action, 2:128
Structured Analysis Methods for Computer Information Systems, 1:559
Structured Induction in Expert Systems, 1:584
Structured Rapid Prototyping: An Evolutionary Approach to Software Development, 1:563
Structuring Your Novel, 1:490
The Struggle for America's Soul: Evangelicals, Liberals, and Secularism, 2:142
The Struggle Is My Life, 2:395
Student Involvement-Implementing: A Computer Tutor Program, 1:557
The Student-Physician: Introductory Studies in the Sociology of Medical Education, 2:141
A Student's Dictionary of Psychology, 2:95
Studies in Animal and Human Behavior, 2:464
Studies in Hysteria, 2:117
Studies in Logic and Probability, 1:507
Studies in Social and Emotional Development, 2:104
Studies in the Origin of Buddhism, 2:282
Studies in the Quantity Theory of Money, 2:66
Studies on Fermentation, 2:445
A Study in Courage and Fear, 2:105
A Study in Scarlet, 1:48
The Study of Folklore, 2:43
The Study of Instinct, 2:98, 2:465
A Study of Thinking, 2:112
Substance Abuse, 2:555
Substance Abuse: Prevention and Treatment, 2:554
The Subterraneans, 1:247
The Subtle Revolution: Women at Work, 2:148, 2:149
Suddenly Last Summer, 1:303
Suetonius: The Biographer of the Caesars, 2:296
Suetonius: The Scholar and His Caesars, 2:296
The Suffrage of Elvira, 1:406

Suicidal Adolescents, 2:537
The Suicidal Child, 2:537
Suicide, 2:126, 2:127
Suicide: The Hidden Epidemic, 2:537
Suicide, a Preventable Tragedy, 2:537
Sula, 1:269
Sumerian Mythology: A Study of Spiritual and Literary Achievement in the Third Millennium B.C, 2:280
Sumerians: Their History, Culture, and Character, 2:280
Summa Theologiae, 2:307
Summa Theologiae—A Concise Translation, 2:307
A Summer Bird-Cage, 1:79, 1:80
Summer of My German Soldier, 1:228
The Summing Up, 1:106
The Sun (Couper), 2:475
The Sun (Lampton), 2:476
The Sun Also Rises, 1:236
Sun Dogs and Shooting Stars: A Skywatcher's Calendar, 2:469
The Sun, He Dies, 1:239
Sun, Weather and Climate, 2:80
The Sunbelt–Snowbelt Controversy: The War over Federal Funds, 2:35
Sunburst: The Ascent of Sun Microsystems, 1:540
The Sundial, 1:243
Sunlight and Health: The Positive and Negative Effects of the Sun on You, 2:570
Sunpower Experiments: Solar Energy Explained, 2:485
Sunshine Sketches of a Little Town, 1:141
Super Chief: Earl Warren and His Supreme Court, a Judicial Biography, 2:32
Super Motion, 2:513
Super Problems, 1:512
Supercomputing: State of the Art, 1:559
Supercube, 1:535
Superfudge, 1:201
Supernova!, 2:479
The Supernova Story, 2:479
Supernovae, 2:479
Supersense: Perception in the Animal World, 2:461
The Supplicants, 1:311
The Supply-Side Revolution: An Insider's Account of Policymaking in Washington, 2:21
Suppression of the African Slave Trade, 1638–1870, 2:211
The Supreme Court, 2:26
The Supreme Court: The Way It Was—the Way It Is, 2:27
The Supreme Court and Constitutional Democracy, 2:16, 2:26

The Supreme Court and Individual Rights, 2:6, 2:13, 2:27

The Supreme Court and the Allocation of Constitutional Powers, 2:27

Supreme Instants: The Photography of Edward Weston, 2:262

Surfacing, 1:135

The Surgeon General's Report on Nutrition and Health, 2:550

The Surgeon General's Report on Nutrition and Health: Summary and Recommendations, 2:549

Surprising Lands Down Under, 2:91

Surreal Numbers, 1:535

Surrogate Parenting: Personal, Medical, and Legal Aspects of One of the Most Dramatic Biomedical Developments of Our Time, 2:543

Survey of Organizations, 2:125

The Survival Book, 2:567

The Survival of Charles Darwin: A Biography of a Man and an Idea, 2:457

Survival Strategies of the Algae, 2:447

Surviving Exercise: Judy Alter's Safe and Sane Exercise Program, 2:551

Susan B. Anthony: Rebel, Crusader, Humanitarian, 2:207

Susan B. Anthony, A Biography: A Singular Feminist, 2:206

Susan Lee's ABZs of Money and Finance, 2:56

Susanna, "Jeanie," and "The Old Folks at Home": The Songs of Stephen C. Foster from His Time to Ours, 2:187

Suspended Fictions: Reading Novels by Manuel Puig, 1:409

Swan Song, 1:87

Swedes and the Swedish Settlements in North America, 2:160

The Swedish Experiment in Family Politics: The Myrdals and the Interwar Population Crisis, 2:135

Sweeney Astray, 1:92

Sweet and Lowdown: America's Popular Song Writers, 2:153

Sweet Bird of Youth, 1:304

The Sweet Grass Lives On: Fifty Contemporary North American Indian Artists, 2:261

Sweet Thursday, 1:288

Sweet Whispers, Brother Rush, 1:230, 2:257

Swift: A Collection of Critical Essays, 1:30

Swinburne, 1:60

Swinburne: The Poet of His World, 1:60

Swing That Music, 2:264

Switch Down and Quit: What the Cigarette Companies Don't Want You to Know About Smoking, 2:556

Sword Blades and Poppy Seed, 1:258

The Sword in the Stone, 1:129, 1:130

Sword of Honor, 1:127

The Swordbearers: Supreme Command in the First World War, 2:371

Sybil, 2:121

Sylvia Plath, 1:277

Sylvia Plath: A Biography, 1:278

Symbiosis: Close Encounters of the Natural Kind, 2:466

Symbol, Status, and Personality, 1:438

Symmetry, 1:513

Synergetics: Explorations in the Geometry of Thinking, 1:522

Synergetics II: Further Explorations in the Geometry of Thinking, 1:522

Synge: A Critical Study of the Plays, 1:123

Systema Naturae, 2:443

Systemantics: How Systems Work and How They Fail, 1:558

Systematic Thinking for Social Action, 2:68

Systematics and the Origin of Species, 2:456

Systems Analysis in the Small Business Environment, 1:558

Systems Development: Analysis, Design, and Implications, 1:558

Systems of Positive Polity, 2:126

Systems Software Tools, 1:585

Systems Thinking, Systems Practice, 1:558

T

T. E. Lawrence: A Reader's Guide, 2:373

T. E. Lawrence by His Friends, 2:373

T. E. Lawrence in Arabia and After, 2:373

T. H. White, 1:130

T. S. Eliot, 1:82, 1:83

Tacitus, 2:297

Tacitus in Renaissance Political Thought, 2:297

Taft Papers on the League of Nations, 2:223

A Tagore Reader, 1:422

Take Care of Yourself: The Consumer's Guide to Medical Care, 2:566

Take Charge of Your Health: The Guide to Personal Health Competence, 2:531

Take Heart: The Life and Prescription for Living of Dr. Paul Dudley White, 2:563

Take My Word for It, 1:442

Take One: Television Directors on Directing, 1:465

Taking Sides: Clashing Views on Controversial Economic Issues, 2:62

Taking Sides: Clashing Views on Controversial Social Issues, 2:125, 2:137, 2:144
Taking Sides: Clashing Views on Environmental Issues, 2:81
Tala, 1:405
Talcott Parsons, 2:128
Talcott Parsons and American Sociology, 2:128
Talcott Parsons and the Social Image of Man, 2:128
Talcott Parsons on Institutions and Social Evolution: Selected Writings, 2:128
A Tale of a Tub, 1:30
Tale of Igor's Campaign, 1:388
Tale of Kieu, 1:426
The Tale of the Genji, 1:424, 1:425
A Tale of Two Cities, 1:47; 2:329
Tale of Valor, 2:169
Tales and Legends of Ancient Burma, 1:426
Tales and Stories by Hans Christian Andersen, 1:375
Tales from a Troubled Land, 1:416
Tales from Shakespeare, 1:35
Tales from Thailand: Folklore, Culture and History, 1:427
Tales from the Argentine, 1:399
Tales from the Japanese Storytellers as Collected in the Ho-Dan Zo, 1:425
Tales of a Fourth Grade Nothing, 1:201
Tales of Ancient India, 1:422
Tales of Henry James, 1:179
Tales of Madness, 1:351
Tales of Prix the Pilot, 1:386
Tales of Suicide, 1:351
Tales of Ten Worlds, 1:75
Tales of the Elders: A Memory Book of Men and Women Who Came to America as Immigrants, 1900–1930, 2:206
Tales of the Grotesque and Arabesque, 1:164
Tales of the Pacific, 1:257
Tales of the South Pacific, 1:264
The Tales of Uncle Remus: The Adventures of Brer Rabbit, 1:255
Tales of Unrest, 1:77
Talk Radio, 1:461
Talk Radio and the American Dream, 1:462
Talk Sex, 2:542
Talkin and Testifyin: The Language of Black America, 1:430
Talking Between the Lines: How We Mean More Than We Say, 2:538
Talking Minds: The Study of Language in Cognitive Sciences, 2:103
Talking Straight, 2:63, 2:64, 2:258

Talking to Myself, 1:489
Tall Grass and Trouble, 2:467
"Tam O'Shanter," 1:32
Tamburlaine, 1:12
Tamerlane, 1:163
Taming the Star Runner, 1:240
A Tangled Web, 1:143
Tangram Geometry in Metric, 1:511
Tanzania After Nyerere, 2:393
Tao Te Ching, 2:283
Taoism: The Parting of the Way, 2:284
Taos Pueblo, 2:263
Tar Baby, 1:269
Taran Wanderer, 1:187, 1:188
Tarnished Gold: The Record Industry Revisited, 2:133
Tartuffe (1669) and Other Plays, 1:338
Tarzan and the Jewels of Opar, 1:208
Tarzan and Tradition: Classical Myth in Popular Literature, 1:208
Tarzan of the Apes, 1:208
Tarzan the Untamed, 1:208
The Task Ahead, 2:401
A Taste for Death, 1:98
Tattered Tom, 1:169
Taxes, 2:71
Taxicab Geometry: An Adventure in Non-Euclidean Geometry, 1:516
Taxonomy of Flowering Plants, 2:441
Tchaikovsky, 2:357
Tchaikovsky: His Life and Works with Extracts from His Writings and the Diary of His Tour Abroad in 1888, 2:357
Tchaikovsky: The Crisis Years, 2:357
Tchaikovsky: The Early Years, 1840–1874, 2:357
Tchaikovsky: The Years of Wandering, 1878–1885, 2:357
Tchaikovsky's Ballets: Swan Lake, Sleeping Beauty, Nutcracker, 2:357
Teach Yourself C, 1:564
Teacher: Anne Sullivan Macy, 1:449
The Teacher, the Free Choice of the Will, Grace, and Free Will, 2:304
The Teachers and Writers Handbook of Poetic Forms, 1:490
The Teacher's Computer Book: Forty Student Projects to Use with Your Classroom Software, 1:571
Teaching a Stone to Talk, 1:483
Teaching History with a Computer: A Complete Guide for College Professors, 1:570
The Teaching of English Usage, 1:435
Teaching Thinking Skills with Databases—AppleWorks Version, 1:573
The Teachings of Maimonides, 2:303

Technical Writing: A Reader-Centered Approach, 1:491

Technical Writing: Structure, Standards and Style, 1:491

Technical Writing for Business, 1:491

Technical Writing in Today's Workplace, 1:491

Technique of Special Effects Cinematography, 1:470

The Technique of Special Effects in Television, 1:465

The Technique of Television News, 1:457

Techniques of Calculus, 1:523

Technology in Education: Looking Toward 2020, 1:570

Technology's Crucible, 1:538

Tecumseh and the Quest for Indian Leadership, 2:168

Tedium and the Software Process, 1:563

Teen Guide to Safe Sex, 2:559

The Teenage Body Book Guide to Dating, 2:107

Teenage Competition: A Survival Guide, 2:538

Teenage Fitness, 2:552

Teenage Marriage: Coping with Reality, 2:542

Teenage Pregnancy in Industrialized Countries, 2:542

Teenage Sexuality, 2:137

Teenage Stress, 2:536

Teenage Stress: Understanding the Tensions You Feel at Home, at School, and Among Your Friends, 2:123

The Teenage Survival Book: The Complete, Revised, Up-dated Edition of You, 2:542

Teenagers and Teenpics: The Juvenilization of American Movies in the 1950s, 1:468

Teenagers Face to Face with Bereavement, 2:537

Teenagers Face-to-Face with Cancer, 2:561

Teens Parenting: The Challenge of Babies and Toddlers, 2:543

Teens Speak Out: A Report from Today's Teens on Their Most Intimate Thoughts, Feelings, and Hopes for the Future, 2:543

Telecommunications and the Computer, 1:558

The Telematic Society: A Challenge for Tomorrow, 1:554

Telephone Poles and Other Poems, 1:292

The Telescope, 2:435

Television: The Critical View, 1:465

Television Access and Political Power: The Networks, the Presidency, and the "Loyal Opposition," 1:442

Television and Aggression: Results of a Panel Study, 2:98

Television and Antisocial Behavior: Field Experiments, 2:98, 2:104

Television in America, 1:465

Television in the Lives of Our Children, 2:130

Television Today: A Close-Up View, 1:465

The Television Writer's Handbook, 1:485

Tell Me a Story: A New Look at Real and Artificial Memory, 1:582

Tell Me How Long the Train's Been Gone, 1:195

Tell Me If the Lovers Are Losers, 1:294

Telling Lives: The Biographer's Art, 1:483

Telling Writing, 1:477

Tempest Tost, 1:137, 1:138

The Temple, 1:10

Temple of Gold, 1:227

The Temple of My Familiar, 1:296, 1:297

Ten Best Plays of John Galsworthy, 1:88

Ten Heavy Facts about Sex, 2:542

Ten Little Indians, 1:74

Ten Poems and Lyrics by Mao Tse-tung, 2:402

The Tenacity of Prejudice: Anti-Semitism in Contemporary America, 2:136

The Tenants, 1:262

Tender Is the Night, 1:222

Tennessee Williams, 1:304

Tennyson, 1:60

A Tennyson Companion: Life and Works, 1:60

Tennyson's Camelot: The Idylls of the King and Its Medieval Sources, 1:60

The Tenth Muse, Lately Sprung Up in America, 1:151

Tepoztlán, a Mexican Village: A Study of Folk Life, 2:54

Terence, 1:324

Terence: The Comedies, 1:323

The Terminal Beach, 1:67

Ternura, 1:405

Terra Nostra, 1:403

Territorial Rights, 1:121

Terrorism: Past, Present, Future, 2:258

Terrorism: What Should Be Our Response?, 2:255

Tess of the D'Urbervilles, 1:52

Test Your Word Power, 1:439

The Testament, 1:302

The Testament of Adolf Hitler, 2:376

Test-Tube Babies, 2:451

Test-Tube Mysteries, 2:432

Tevye the Dairyman and the Railroad Stories, 1:383

Tex, 1:240

Texas, 1:264

Textbook of Fungi, Bacteria, and Viruses, 2:443, 2:446
Thaddeus Stevens, 2:15
Thaddeus Stevens, Commoner, 2:15
Thaïs, 1:335
The Thames and Hudson Encyclopedia of Twentieth Century Music, 2:154
"Thanatopsis," 1:156
That Hideous Strength, 1:104
That Was Then, This Is Now, 1:240
That Woman: Indira Gandhi's Seven Years in Power, 2:401
The Thatcher Effect: A Decade of Change, 2:408
Thatcherism and British Politics: The End of Consensus, 2:408
That's Not What I Meant! How Conversational Style Makes or Breaks Your Relations with Others, 1:445
The Theater of the Absurd, 1:187
The Theater of the Bauhaus, 2:268
The Theatre of Jean Anouilh, 1:328
Théâtre, Tome I (Sartre), 1:340
Theatres for Literature, 1:449
Their Eyes Were Watching God, 1:242
Their Father's God, 1:379
Thematic Maps: Their Design and Production, 2:92
Themes and Conclusions (Stravinsky), 2:426
Then Again, Maybe I Won't, 1:201
Theodicy, 1:527
Theodore Dreiser, 1:217
Theodore Dreiser, An American Journey 1908–1945, 1:217
Theodore Dreiser, At the Gates of the City 1871–1907, 1:217
Theodore Roosevelt, 2:222
Theodore Roosevelt: Twenty-Sixth President of the United States, 2:222
Theodore Roosevelt, the Citizen, 2:212, 2:222
Theogony, 1:312
Theophilus North, 1:303
The Theoretic Arithmetic of the Pythagoreans, 1:502
Theories of Learning, 2:112
Theories of Mass Communication, 2:130
Theories of Nationalism, 2:341
The Theory and Practice of Compiler Writing, 1:586
The Theory of Business Enterprise, 2:64
Theory of Chemical Reaction Dynamics, 2:504
The Theory of Committees and Elections, 2:39
Theory of Culture Change, 2:43
The Theory of Economic Development: An Inquiry into Profits, Capital, Credit,

Interest and the Business Cycle, 2:57, 2:63
The Theory of Gambling and Statistical Logic, 1:535
Theory of Heat, 2:527
The Theory of Inequality Among Men and the Collision of the Cultures, 2:11
The Theory of Legislation, 2:8
The Theory of Moral Sentiments, 2:61
Theory of Personality: The Psychology of Personal Constructs, 2:114
The Theory of Public Choice, II, 2:71
Theory of Relativity, 2:503
The Theory of Social and Economic Organization, 2:56, 2:140, 2:143
Theory of Solutions and Stereo Chemistry, 2:507
Theory of Sound, 2:522
Theory of the Earth, 2:489, 2:490
Theory of the Earth's Gravity Field, 2:513
The Theory of the Leisure Class, 2:62, 2:64, 2:69, 2:145, 2:146
Thereby Hangs a Tale: Stories of Curious Word Origins, 1:433
There's a Country in My Collar: The Best of Russell Baker, 1:481
There's a Monster in Your Closet! Understanding Phobias, 2:536
Therese Raquin, 1:344, 1:345
Thermodynamics and the Kinetic Theory of Gases, 2:503
The Thesaurus of Slang, 1:433
These Were the Romans, 2:291
They All Played Ragtime, 2:261
They and We: Racial and Ethnic Relations in the United States, 2:136
They Called Him Stonewall: A Life of Lt. General T. J. Jackson, 2:192
They Sought A New World, 2:207
They Stooped to Folly, 1:226
A Thief, 1:200
The Thin Man, 1:231
Things Fall Apart, 1:411
Thinking and Deciding, 2:110
The Thinking Computer: Mind Inside Matter, 1:581
Thinking Economically: How Economic Principles Can Contribute to Clear Thinking, 2:56
Thinking Machines: The Evolution of Artificial Intelligence, 1:581
Thinking Machines: The Search for Artificial Intelligence, 1:580
The Third Apple: Personal Computers and the Cultural Revolution, 1:540
The Third Experiment: Is There Life on Mars?, 2:475
The Third International after Lenin, 2:381

The Third Life of Grange Copeland, 1:296, 1:297
The Third Life of Per Smevik, 1:379
The Third Man, 1:91
The Third Wave, 1:453
The Third World: Exploring U. S. Interests, 2:258
The Third World: Opposing Viewpoints, 2:37
The Third World City, 2:85, 2:273
The Thirteen Books of Euclid's Elements, 1:514
Thirteen Days: A Memoir of the Cuban Missile Crisis, 2:248, 2:388
Thirteen Detectives, 1:72
Thirteen O'Clock, Stories of Several Worlds, 1:200
Thirty Seconds, 1:440
Thirty Years That Shook Physics: The Story of Quantum Mechanics, 2:518
This Chancy, Chancy, Chancy World, 1:529
This Constitution: From Ratification to the Bill of Rights, 2:16
This Constitution: Our Enduring Legacy, 2:16
This Fabulous Century, 2:207, 2:224, 2:226, 2:229, 2:235, 2:238, 2:241
This Family of Women, 1:275
This I Remember, 2:233
This Is London, 1:467
This Is My Century: New and Collected Poems, 1:297, 1:298
This Realm of England: 1399 to 1688, 2:311
This School Is Driving Me Crazy, 1:238
This Side of Paradise, 1:222; 2:226
This Strange New Feeling, 1:255
Thomas Alva Edison, 2:524
Thomas Alva Edison: Bringer of Light, 2:524
Thomas Cole, 2:187
Thomas Gainsborough, 2:335
Thomas Gray, 1:26
Thomas Hardy, 1:52
Thomas Hardy: A Biography, 1:52
Thomas Hardy: Selected Stories, 1:52
Thomas Hobbes and Political Theory, 2:10
Thomas Hunt Morgan: Pioneer of Genetics, 2:454
Thomas Jefferson, 2:175
Thomas Jefferson: Man on a Mountain, 2:175
Thomas Mann, 1:370
Thomas More, 1:14
Thomas More: A Biography, 1:14
Thomas Muskerry, 1:76
Thomas Nast: His Period and His Pictures, 1:460
Thomas Paine (Conway), 2:165

Thomas Paine (Vail), 2:166
Thomas Paine: American Revolutionary Writer, 2:165
Thomas Wolfe, 1:306
Thor Heyerdahl: Viking Scientist, 2:411
The Thorn in the Starfish: How the Human Immune System Works, 2:545
Thornton Wilder, 1:303
Thorstein Veblen, 2:146
Thorstein Veblen: A Critical Interpretation, 2:146
Thorstein Veblen and His America, 2:146
Those Other People, 1:212
Those Summer Girls I Never Met, 1:276
Those Who Knock at Our Gates, 2:209
Those Who Ride the Night Winds, 1:226
The Thoughts of Blaise Pascal, 1:533
Thoughts on the Cause of the Present Discontents, 2:8
Thoughts on the Present Discontents, 2:328
Thousand Days: John F. Kennedy in the White House, 2:248
Three: An Unfinished Woman, Pentimento, Scoundrel Time, 1:235
Three Comedies by Pedro Calderón de la Barca, 1:355
Three Essays on the Theory of Sexuality, 2:118
Three Faces of Eve, 2:122
Three Famous Short Novels: Spotted Horses, Old Man, and The Bear, 1:219
Three Films of Woody Allen: Broadway Danny Rose, Zelig, The Purple Rose of Cairo, 1:189, 1:471
The Three Greatest Prayers: Commentaries on the Lord's Prayer, the Hail Mary, and the Apostles' Creed, 2:307
Three Hundred Years of Gravitation, 2:516
Three Loves, 1:78
Three Mile Island, 2:255
The Three Musketeers, 1:333, 1:334
Three Novels (Capek), 1:385
Three Phases of Matter, 2:498
Three Plays (Coward), 1:78
Three Plays (O'Neill), 1:274
Three Plays (Pirandello), 1:351
Three Plays (Wilder), 1:303
Three Plays (A Collier's Friday Night, The Daughter-in-Law, The Widowing of Mrs. Holroyd), 1:101
Three Plays: Juno and the Paycock; The Shadow of a Gunman; The Plough and the Stars, 1:108
Three Portraits: Hitler, Mussolini, Stalin, 2:376
The Three Sisters, 1:390
The Three Theban Plays: Antigone, Oedipus the King, Oedipus at Colonus, 1:316

Three Thousand Years in Africa: Man and His Environment in the Lake Chad Region of Nigeria, 2:299
Three Thousand Years of Hebrew Literature: From the Earliest Times Through the Twentieth Century, 1:420
Three Victorian Women Who Changed Their World, 2:570
Three Who Made a Revolution, 2:382
Three Winters, 1:386
Three Years in Europe, 1:170
The Threepenny Opera, 1:364, 1:365
Through a Brief Darkness, 1:276
Through a Window: My Thirty Years with the Chimpanzees of Gombe, 2:463
Through Chinese Eyes: Revolution and Transformation, 2:399
Through Japanese Eyes, 2:399
Through the Looking Glass, 1:45
Throwing Things Away, 2:82
Thucydides, 2:290
Thucydides on the Nature of Power, 2:290
Thumbs Up: The Jim Brady Story, 2:257
Thunderball, 1:84
Thunderstones and Shooting Stars: The Meaning of Meteorites, 2:475
The Thurber Carnival, 1:290
Thursday's Children, 1:88
Thyestes, 1:323
Tickets for a Prayer Wheel, 1:482, 1:483
Tidal Energy, 2:486
The Tiger and the Horse, 1:68
Tiger Eyes, 1:201
The Tigris Expedition, 2:411
Tik-Tok of Oz, 1:199
Till the Day I Die, 1:272
Time Cat, 1:187, 1:188
A Time for Choosing: The Speeches of Ronald Reagan, 2:260
Time for the Stars, 1:234
Time Frames: The Rethinking of Darwinian Evolution and the Theory of Punctuated Equilibrium, 2:456
Time in Dynamic Geometry, 1:516
Time-Life Books History of World War II, 2:384
The Time Machine, 1:128, 1:129
Time of Change: An Inside View of Russia's Transformation, 2:15
Time of Desecration, 1:350
Time of Indifference, 1:350
The Time of Stalin: Portrait of a Tyranny, 2:380
Time on the Cross, 2:189
Time Remembered, 1:328
A Time to Be Born: An Almanac of Animal Courtship and Parenting, 2:462
A Time to Dance, No Time to Weep: A Memoir, 1:89

A Time to Listen: Preventing Youth Suicide, 2:537
Time Travel and Other Mathematical Bewilderments, 1:536
Timebends, 1:266
The Times Atlas of the Second World War, 2:235
The Times Atlas of World History, 2:272
Time's Power, 1:281
Timescale: An Atlas of the Fourth Dimension, 2:469
The Timing of Biological Clocks, 2:462
The Tin Can Tree, 1:291
The Tin Drum, 1:367
The Tin Woodman of Oz, 1:199
Tinker, Tailor, Soldier, Spy, 1:102
The Tinker's Wedding, 1:123
Tinsel, 1:227
Tintern Abbey, 1:38
Tiny Alice, 1:186
The Titan, 1:216, 1:217
To a God Unknown, 1:288
"To a Mouse," 1:32
"To Autumn," 1:35
To Be a Pilgrim, 1:72
To Be a Slave, 1:255; 2:189
To Be Young, Gifted, and Black, 1:232
To Build a Fire and Other Stories, 1:257
To Dwell Among Friends: Personal Networks in Town and City, 2:138
To Have and Have Not, 1:236
"To His Coy Mistress," 1:13
To Kill a Mockingbird, 1:253
To My Mother, on the Anniversary of Her Birth, 1:56
To Purge This Land with Blood: A Biography of John Brown, 2:189
To Space and Back, 2:481
To the Is-Land, 1:139
To the Lighthouse, 1:132
To the North, 1:69
"To Virginia, To Make Much of Time," 1:11
Today's Isms: Communism, Fascism, Capitalism, and Socialism, 2:5, 2:15, 2:58, 2:274
Tolkien, Four Volumes, 1:125
Tolkien: The Authorized Biography, 1:126
Toltec Heritage: From the Fall of Tula to the Rise of Tenochtitlan, 2:299
Toltecs: Until the Fall of Tula, 2:299
Tom and Viv, 1:82
Tom Jones, 1:24
Tom O'Bedlam, 1:286
Tom Sawyer, 1:141
Tom Stoppard, 1:123
Tom Stoppard: A Casebook, 1:123
Tom, the Bootblack, 1:169
Tomas Masaryk: President of Czechoslovakia, 2:406

The Tombs of Atuan, 1:254
Tomorrow Is Today, 2:561
Toni Morrison, 1:269
Tonio Kröger, 1:370
Too Far to Go, 1:292
Too Late the Phalarope, 1:416
Topaz, 1:293
Topics for Mathematics Clubs, 1:496
Topological Picturebook, 1:516
Topology, 1:516
Topology: A First Course, 1:516
Torch, 1:126
Torquato Tasso, 1:366
Tortilla Flat, 1:288, 1:289
Tossing and Turning, 1:292
Total Eclipses of the Sun, 2:476
A Touch of the Poet, 1:273
Touch, Taste and Smell, 2:553
Toward a Functioning Federalism, 2:36
Toward a Metric of Science: The Advent
    of Science Indicators, 2:141
Toward a Psychology of Being, 2:114
Toward a Systems Theory of
    Organization, 1:558
Toward an Urban Vision: Ideas and
    Institutions in Nineteenth Century
    America, 2:206
Toward Colonial Freedom, 2:396
Toward the Radical Center: A Karel
    Capek Reader, 1:385
Toward the Year 2000, 2:149
Towards a New Architecture, 2:419
Towards the Mountain: An
    Autobiography, 1:416
The Towers of Silence, 1:118; 2:363
Town and Country in Brazil, 2:47
The Town and the City, 1:246
The Town Beyond the Wall, 1:302
A Town like Alice, 1:147
The Town That Started the Civil War,
    2:189
Toxic Waste: Cleanup or Coverup, 2:467
Toxic Waste and Recycling, 2:81
Toxicology of Halogenated Hydrocarbons:
    Health and Ecological Effects, 2:510
The Toynbee Convector, 1:202
Toys and Reasons: Stages in the
    Ritualization of Experience, 2:108
Toys in the Attic, 1:235
Tracks, 2:465
Trade and Market in the Early Empires:
    Economies in History and Theory, 2:47
The Trade Threat and U.S. Trade Policy,
    2:71, 2:257
The Tragedy of American Diplomacy,
    2:242
Trail Maker, 2:367
Trails West, 2:185
Traité de radioactivité, 2:510

Transatlantic Industrial Revolution: The
    Diffusion of Textile Technologies
    Between Britain and America,
    1790–1830, 2:339
The Transformation of Turkish Culture,
    2:89
Transformations, 2:106
The Transitive Vampire: A Handbook of
    Grammar for the Innocent, the Eager,
    and the Doomed, 1:478
Translations from the Poetry of Rainer
    Maria Rilke, 1:371
Translations of Eastern Poetry and Prose,
    1:420
Transmutation: Natural and Artificial,
    2:509
Transportation in America, 2:84
Travel and Writing for Profit and
    Pleasure, 1:488
Travel Light, 1:107
Travelers of a Hundred Ages: The
    Japanese as Revealed Through 1,000
    Years of Diaries, 2:275
Traveling the Trans-Canada from
    Newfoundland to British Columbia,
    2:90
Travels in Asia and Africa, 1325–1354,
    2:301
Travels in Mexico and California, 2:200
Travels in the Interior Districts of Africa,
    2:368
The Travels of Ibn Batuta, 2:300, 2:301
The Travels of Marco Polo, 2:308, 2:309
Travels with a Donkey in the Cevennes,
    1:58
Travels with Charley in Search of
    America, 1:288, 1:289; 2:242
Travels with My Aunt, 1:91
Travesties, 1:122
Treason in Tudor England: Politics and
    Paranoia, 2:327
The Treason of Isengard, 1:125
Treasure Island, 1:58
The Treasure of Sierra Madre, 1:472
Treasures of Taliesin: Seventy-Six Unbuilt
    Designs of Frank Lloyd Wright, 2:270
A Treasury of Russian Literature, 1:389
A Treasury of Writings of Kahlil Gibran,
    1:420
A Treasury of Yiddish Poetry, 1:383
A Treasury of Yiddish Stories, 1:383
Treaties on the Panama Canal Signed
    Between the United States of America
    and the Republic of Panama, 2:255
A Treatise on Money, 2:67
Treatise on Painting, 2:315
A Treatise on the Family, 2:136
Treatises of Benvenuto Cellini on
    Goldsmithing and Sculpture, 2:312

Tree and Leaf, 1:482
Tree By Leaf, 1:294
The Tree of Man, 1:147, 1:148
The Trembling Earth: Probing and
   Predicting Quakes, 2:83, 2:494
Trends in American Electoral Behavior,
   2:39
The Trenton Pickle Ordinance and
   Other Bonehead Legislation,
   2:41
The Trespasser, 1:100, 1:101
The Trial, 1:369
The Trial of Dedan Kimathi, 1:415
The Trial of God: A Play in Three Acts,
   1:302
The Trial of Socrates, 2:285
Trials of Jawaharlal Nehru, 2:404
The Trials of Persiles and Sigismunda,
   1:356
Triggers: A New Approach to
   Self-Motivation, 2:112
Trigonometry, 1:524
Trigonometry: A Functions Approach,
   1:524
Trigonometry for the Practical Worker,
   1:524
The Trinity (St. Augustine), 2:304
Trinity (Uris), 1:293
A Trip Through Time: Principles of
   Historical Geology, 2:495
Tristes Tropiques, 2:53
Triumfo de la fee en los reynos del Japon,
   1:358
Triumph! Conquering Your Physical
   Disability, 2:563
The Triumph of Conservatism: A
   Reinterpretation of American History,
   1900–1916, 2:207
The Triumph of Life, 1:38
Triumphant Democracy, 2:206
Troilus and Criseyde, 1:310
The Troll Garden, 1:209
Tropical Rainforests: Endangered
   Environments, 2:467
Trotsky: A Study in the Dynamic of His
   Thought, 2:382
Trotsky for Beginners, 2:382
Trotsky Papers, 1917–1922, 2:381
Trotsky's Diary in Exile, 2:381
Trouble in Mind, 1:211
Trouble Is My Business, 1:210
The Troubled Encounter: The United
   States and Japan, 2:235
Troubled Sleep, 1:340
Trout Fishing in America, 1:203
Troylus and Criseyde, 1:6
The True Gen: An Intimate Portrait of
   Hemingway by Those Who Knew Him,
   1:237

The Truly Disadvantaged: The Inner City,
   the Underclass, and Public Policy,
   2:136
The Truman Administration, Its Principles
   and Practice, 2:237
The Truman Doctrine and the Origins of
   McCarthyism: Foreign Policy, Domestic
   Policy, and Internal Security, 2:235
Truman Speaks: On the Presidency, the
   Constitution, and Statecraft, 2:237
The Trumpet of Conscience, 2:250
The Trumpet Soundeth: William Jennings
   Bryan and His Democracy, 1896–1912,
   2:205
Trust Me, 1:292
The Truth About AIDS: Evolution of an
   Epidemic, 2:560
The Truth About Reparations and War
   Debts, 2:373
Truth on Trial: The Story of Galileo
   Galilei, 2:473
Tsunami!, 2:486
Tube of Plenty: The Evolution of
   American Television, 1:464
Tudor England, 2:326
Tunc, 1:81
The Tuning of the World, 2:522
Tunnel in the Sky, 1:234
Turbulent Years: A History of the
   American Worker 1933–1941, 2:69,
   2:229
The Turing Omnibus: Excursions in
   Computer Science, 1:537
Turing's Man: Western Culture in the
   Computer Age, 1:554
Turn Homeward, Hannalee, 2:192
Turn of the Screw, 1:179
Turner, 2:358
Turner: Paintings, Watercolors, Prints, and
   Drawings, 2:358
Turner's Sketches and Drawings, 2:358
Turtle Geometry: The Computer as a
   Medium for Exploring Mathematics,
   1:511, 1:569
Tutankhamun and the Mysteries of
   Ancient Egypt, 2:280
Tutu: Voice of the Voiceless, 2:398
TV Action Book, 1:468
TV Facts, 1:465
'Twas the Night Before Christmas: A Visit
   from St. Nicholas, 1:460
The Tweed Ring, 1:460
The Twelve-Minute Total-Body Workout,
   2:552
Twelve Steps for Overeaters: An
   Interpretation of the Twelve Steps of
   Overeaters Anonymous, 2:551
The Twelve-Stringed Guitar as Played by
   Leadbelly, 1:255

Twelve to Sixteen: Early Adolescence, 2:106

Twenties: Fords, Flappers, and Fanatics, 2:226

Twenties in America, 2:226

The Twentieth Century: An American History, 2:155

Twentieth-Century Africa, 2:393

Twentieth Century African and Latin American Verse, 1:399, 1:411

Twentieth Century Chinese Drama: An Anthology, 1:423

Twentieth Century Chinese Poetry: An Anthology, 1:423

Twentieth-Century Russia, 2:92, 2:406

The Twentieth-Century Scientists: Studies in the Biography of Ideas, 2:439, 2:440

Twentieth-Century Sociology, 2:125

Twenty Letters to a Friend: A Memoir, 2:380

Twenty Poems of Love and a Song of Despair, 1:407

Twenty Thousand Leagues Under the Sea, 1:342, 1:343

Twenty Years After, 1:333

Twenty Years at Hull-House, 2:208

Twenty Years Later: Kibbutz Children Grown Up, 2:138

A Twenty-fifth Anniversary Picture Album of NASA, 2:482

Twenty-Seven Wagons Full of Cotton, 1:303, 1:304

Twice-Told Tales, 1:177

Twilight, 1:302

Twilight of Empire, 2:168

Twilight of Federalism: The Disintegration of the Federalist Party, 1815–1830, 2:169

The Twilight Zone, 1:486

The Twilight Zone Omnibus, 1:486

Twisted Tales from Shakespeare, 1:193

Two Gentle Men: The Lives of George Herbert and Robert Herrick, 1:11

Two Hundred and Fifty Years of Afro-American Art: An Annotated Bibliography, 2:261

Two Plays (Weiss), 1:373

Two Stories (Mann), 1:370

2001: A Space Odyssey, 1:74, 1:75

Two Tickets to Freedom: The True Story of Ellen and William Croft, Fugitive Slaves, 2:189

The Two Tocquevilles, Father and Son: Hervé and Alexis de Tocqueville on the Coming of the French Revolution, 2:330

Two Treatises on Civil Government, 2:17, 2:18

Two Trips to Gorilla Land and The Cataracts of the Congo, 2:364

Two Women, 1:350

The Twyborn Affair, 1:148

Tycho Brahe: A Picture of Scientific Life and Work in the Sixteenth Century, 2:471

Type, Graphics, and Macintosh: A Hands-On Instructional Manual Designed to Teach the Finer Points of Macintosh-Based Type and Graphics, 1:575

Typee: A Peep at Polynesian Life, 1:162, 1:163

Tyrannus Nix?, 1:221

The Tyranny of Change: America in the Progressive Era, 1900–1917, 2:218

The Tyranny of Words, 1:437

U

U. S. Grant and the American Military Tradition, 2:200

U-Boat Offensive, Nineteen Fourteen to Nineteen Forty-Five, 2:372

UCSMP-University of Chicago School Mathematics Project Advanced Algebra, 1:506

UCSMP-University of Chicago School Mathematics Project Algebra, 1:506

UCSMP-University of Chicago School Mathematics Project Geometry, 1:512

UCSMP-University of Chicago School Mathematics Project Transition Mathematics, 1:505

UFO's: A Scientific Debate, 2:480

Uganda, 2:85

Ujmaa: Essays on Socialism, 2:397

The Ultimate Entrepreneur: The Story of Ken Olsen and Digital Equipment Corporation, 1:538

Ultimate Sports Nutrition: A Scientific Approach to Peak Athletic Performance, 2:551

The Ultra Rich: How Much Is Too Much, 2:61, 2:258

Ulysses, 1:98, 1:99

Ulysses S. Grant: Eighteenth President of the United States, 2:200

Un métier de Seigneur, 1:332

The Unanswered Question: Six Talks at Harvard, 2:265

The Unbearable Lightness of Being, 1:385

Unbought and Unbossed: An Autobiography, 2:34

Uncle Sam at Home: Civilian Mobilization, Wartime Federalism, and the Council of National Defense, 1917–1919, 2:223

Uncle Tom's Cabin, 2:135, 2:189

Uncle Tom's Children, 1:307

Uncle Vanya, 1:390

Uncle's Dream and Other Stories, 1:392
An Uncommon Man: The Triumph of
    Herbert Hoover, 2:231
Und Sagte Kein Einziges Wort, 1:364
The Undecidable: Basic Papers on
    Undecidable Propositions, Unsolvable
    Problems and Computable Functions,
    1:500
Under Milk Wood, 1:124
Under the Cape of Heaven: Religion,
    Society, and Politics in Colonial
    America, 2:161
Under the Greenwood Tree, 1:51, 1:52
Under the High Seas: New Frontiers in
    Oceanography, 2:486
Under the Net, 1:107
Under the North Star, 1:95
Under the Sea Wind, 2:243
Under Western Eyes, 1:77
The Underground Shopper's Guide to
    Health and Fitness, 2:566
Understanding Abnormal Behavior, 2:121
Understanding American Government, 2:6
Understanding America's Drinking
    Problem: How to Combat the Hazards
    of Alcohol, 2:555
Understanding and Using Paradox 3.5,
    1:572
Understanding and Writing Compilers: A
    Do It Yourself Guide, 1:586
Understanding Artificial Intelligence, 1:581
Understanding Computers (Cassel), 1:556
Understanding Computers (Hopper), 1:545,
    1:557
Understanding Computers and Cognition:
    A New Foundation for Design, 1:583
Understanding Gabriel García Márquez,
    1:404
Understanding Günter Grass, 1:368
Understanding Human Behavior in Health
    and Disease, 2:531
Understanding Hypertext: Concepts and
    Applications, 1:580
Understanding Intergovernmental
    Relations, 2:41
Understanding Language, 1:434
Understanding Lasers, 2:519
Understanding LOGO, 1:565
Understanding Magnetism: Magnets,
    Electromagnets, and Superconducting
    Magnets, 2:522
Understanding Maps, 2:92
Understanding Mass Communication,
    2:130
Understanding Media: The Extensions of
    Man, 1:453, 1:454; 2:130
Understanding Movement, 2:513
Understanding Movies, 1:469
Understanding News, 1:457
Understanding Nutrition, 1:569

Understanding Piaget: An Introduction to
    Children's Cognitive Development,
    2:112
Understanding Radioactivity, 2:509
Understanding RBASE 5000, 1:572
Understanding Soviet Politics: The
    Perspective of Russian History, 2:404
Understanding Television: Essays on
    Television as a Cultural and Social
    Force, 1:465
Understanding the Alcoholic's Mind: The
    Nature of Craving and How to Control
    It, 2:555
Understanding Your Immune System,
    2:545
Understanding Your Parents, 2:539
The Undertaker's Gone Bananas, 1:308
Unelected Representatives: Congressional
    Staff and the Future of Representative
    Governments, 2:33
Unemployment Versus Inflation, 2:66
The Unfinished Revolution: Marxism and
    Communism in the Modern World,
    2:375
Unfinished Tales, 1:125
The Unfolding Universe, 2:470
Unfolding Westward in Treaty and Law:
    Land Documents in United States
    History from the Appalachians to the
    Pacific, 1783–1934, 2:154
The Unguarded House, 1:363
The Unicorn, 1:108
The Unification of Italy, Eighteen
    Fifty-Nine to Eighteen Sixty-One,
    2:340
The United States and Iran: A
    Documentary History, 2:255
U.S. and Soviet Space Programs: A
    Comparison, 2:481
The United States and the Origins of the
    Cold War, 1941–1947, 2:238
The U.S. and World Trade, 2:72, 2:257
U.S. Constitutional History: A Selected
    Bibliography of Books, 2:5
The United States Congress: A
    Bibliography, 2:6, 2:33
The United States Constitution for
    Everyone: A Guide to the Most
    Important Document Written by and
    for the People of the United States,
    2:166
U.S.–Cuban Relations in the 1990s, 2:408
United States Government Manual,
    1989–1990, 2:6
The United States in 1800, 2:214
The United States in the 1980s, 2:257
The United States in the
    Spanish-American War, 2:218
The United States in the Vietnam War,
    2:242

U.S. Interests and Policies in the
Caribbean and Central America, 2:408
Unity of the Senses, 2:113
The Universal Machine: Confessions of a
Technological Optimist, 1:581
The Universal Turing Machine: A
Half-Century Survey, 1:581
Universals of Human Language, 2:50
Universe (Asimov), 2:478
Universe (Kaufman), 2:470
Universe Guide to Stars and Planets, 2:470
UNIX for Beginners, 1:562
UNIX for Beginners: A Step-by-Step
Introduction, 1:562
UNIX Made Easy, 1:562
UNIX Primer Plus, 1:562
UNIX Quick Reference Guide, 1:562
UNIX System V Release 4: The Complete
Reference, 1:561
UNIX Text Processing, 1:561
Unleaving, 1:126
The Unlimited Dream Company, 1:67
Unnatural Causes, 1:98
Unnatural Causes: The Three Leading
Killer Diseases in America, 2:537
Unnatural Death, 1:117
The Unpleasantness at the Bellona Club,
1:117
Unplugging the Plug-In Drug, 1:468
Unpopular Essays, 1:503
The Unreality Industry, 1:465
Unsafe at Any Speed, 2:61, 2:252
The Unseen Hand and Other Plays,
1:285
The Unseen World, 2:444, 2:445
Unspeakable Practices, Unnatural Acts,
1:198
Unstable Ideas: Temperament, Cognition,
and Self, 2:103
An Unsuitable Job for a Woman, 1:98
The Unsuspected Revolution: The Birth
and Rise of Castroism, 2:410
Until the Sun Dies, 2:456
Unusual Algebra, 1:506
Up from Slavery, 2:213
Uplift the Race: The Construction of
School Daze, 1:486
Uprooted Children: The Early Life of
Migrant Farm Workers, 2:106, 2:241
The Ups and Downs of Carl Davis III,
1:229
Upton Sinclair, 1:288
Urban Decline and the Future of
American Cities, 2:147
The Urban Experience, 2:147
The Urban Predicament, 2:147
The Urban Villagers, 2:147
Urbanization in the World Economy, 2:94,
2:147

An Urchin in the Storm: Essays About
Books and Ideas, 2:458
Ursula K. Le Guin, 1:254
Ursule Mirouet, 1:329
The Uses of Enchantment: The Meaning
and Importance of Fairy Tales, 2:97
Using C++, 1:564
Using Computer Bulletin Boards, 1:573
Using Computer Color Effectively: An
Illustrated Reference to Computer Color
Interface, 1:578
Using Computers, 1:557
Using Computers in Religious Education,
1:570
Using Computers in the Teaching of
Reading, 1:571
Using Computers to Create Art, 1:578
Using Macromind Director, 1:579
Using Microcomputers in Physical
Education and Sport Sciences, 1:569
Using Minitab for Introductory Statistical
Analysis, 1:574
Using Minitab with Basic Statistics, 1:574
Using MultiMate, 1:576
Using Norton Utilities, 1:574
Using Novell Netware, 1:558
Using P.C. Tools Deluxe Version 6, 1:574
Using Quick C, 1:564
Using Quicken on the Mac: Tips and
Techniques to Enhance Your Business
Productivity, 1:572
Using QuickPascal, 1:565
Using SideKick Plus, 1:574
Using SQL, 1:572
Using Statistics, 1:530
Using Turbo Pascal 5, 1:565
Using WordPerfect: Windows Version,
1:576
Using WordPerfect 5.1: Special Edition,
1:576
Using WordPerfect Library: Featuring WP
Office, 1:576
Utopia and Other Essential Writings, 1:14

V

V. S. Naipaul, 1:406
V. S. Naipaul and the West Indies,
1:406
V Was for Victory: Politics and American
Culture During World War II, 2:234
Valentine Pontifex, 1:285, 1:286
The Valley of Horses, 2:277
The Value of Honesty: The Story of
Confucius, 2:283
Van Gogh (Bonafoux), 2:359
Van Gogh (Schapiro), 2:360

Van Gogh: A Documentary Biography, 2:360

Van Gogh: His Life and Art, 2:360

Van Gogh: Twenty-Five Masterworks, 2:360

Van Gogh Drawings: Forty Three Plates, 2:359

Van Gogh in Arles, 2:360

Van Gogh in Saint-Remy and Auvers, 2:360

Van Nostrand's Scientific Encyclopedia, 1:498

Vanishing Habitats, 2:497

Vanity Fair, 1:61

The Vantage Point: Perspectives on the Presidency, 1963–1969, 2:246

Varieties of American English: Essays by Raven I. McDavid, Jr, 1:432

The Varieties of Religious Experience, 2:96

Vega and Other Poems, 1:81

Vein of Iron, 1:226, 1:227

Veinte poemas de amor y una canción desesperada, 1:407

Ventura: The Complete Reference, 1:575

Ventura Publisher for Beginners, 1:575

Venus: An Errant Twin, 2:475

Venus, Near Neighbor of the Sun, 2:475

Venus Observed, 1:87

Verdi, 2:361

Verdi: A Documentary Study, 2:361

Verdi: The Man in His Letters, 2:361

The Verdi Companion, 2:361

Verdi in the Age of Italian Romanticism, 2:361

Verdict on Schweitzer: The Man Behind the Legend of Lambaréné, 2:535

Verdi's Aida: The History of an Opera in Letters and Documents, 2:361

Vermilion Sands, 1:67

Vers une architecture (Towards a New Architecture), 2:419

Verses (C. Rosetti), 1:56

Versos libres, 2:370

Very Far Away from Anywhere Else, 1:254

The Vicar of Wakefield, 1:25

The Vicomte de Bragelonne, 1:333

The Victim, 1:200

Victor Hugo, 1:337

Victoria: An Intimate Biography, 2:369

Victorian England: Aspects of English and Imperial History 1837–1901, 2:363

Victory, 1:77

Victory in Europe, 2:384

Victory over Europe: D-Day to VE Day, 2:235, 2:384

Victory over Japan, 1:225

Vida de Don Quijote y Sancho, 1:360

The Video Primer: Equipment, Production, and Concepts, 1:470

Vietnam: A History, 2:399

Vietnam Literature Anthology, 1:426

The Vietnam War: The Illustrated History of the Conflict in Southeast Asia, 2:242

Vietnam, Why We Fought: An Illustrated History, 2:241

The View from Afar, 2:53

A View from the Bridge, 1:266

Viga-Glum's Saga, 1:374

The Viking Book of Folk Ballads of the English Speaking World, 1:8

Viking Raiders, 2:320

Vile Bodies, 1:127

"The Village Blacksmith," 1:160

Village India: Studies in the Little Community, 2:131

Ville Cruelle, 1:412

Villette, 1:42

Vincent Van Gogh (Bitossi), 2:359

Vincent Van Gogh (Hagen), 2:360

Vincent Van Gogh: A Psychological Study, 2:360

Vincent Van Gogh: Genius and Disaster, 2:360

Vindication of the Rights of Women, 1:37

Vingt ans après, 1:334

Vingt mille lieues sous la mer, 1:343

Vintage Mencken, 1:436

Violence and the Family, 2:539

The Violent Bear It Away, 1:270

Virgil, 1:325; 2:298

Virgil's Aeneid, 2:298

Virginia, 1:226, 1:227

The Virginia Report of 1799–1800, Touching the Alien and Sedition Laws, 2:177

Virginia Woolf, 1:133

Virginia Woolf: A Biography, 1:133

The Virginians, 1:61

A Virus of Love and Other Tales of Medical Detection, 2:557

Virus! The Secret World of Computer Invaders That Breed and Destroy, 1:554

The Virus That Ate Cannibals: Six Great Medical Detective Stories, 2:557

Viruses, 2:443

Viruses: Life's Smallest Enemies, 2:443

Vision and Nightmares: America After Reagan, 2:65

A Vision for America, 2:253

A Vision of Battlements, 1:71

The Vision of Sir Launfel, 1:161

The Vision of the Void: Theological Reflections on the Works of Elie Wiesel, 1:302

Visions of Gerard, 1:247

Visions of War: Hollywood Combat Films of World War Two, 1:468
The Visual Arts: A History, 2:154
Visual Illusions: Their Causes, Characteristics, and Applications, 1:515
Visual Languages, 1:563
Visual Thinking, 2:113
Vital Involvement in Old Age, 2:108
Vital Lies, Simple Truths: The Psychology of Self-Deception, 2:536
Vital Statistics on American Politics, 2:6
Vitamin C, the Common Cold, and the Flu, 2:506
Viva Villa: A Recovery of the Real Pancho Villa: Peon, Bandit, Soldier, Patriot, 2:369
Vivat! Vivat! Regina, 1:69
Vivian Grey, 2:342
The Vivisector, 1:148
The Vocabulary of Physics, 2:512
Voice and Diction: A Program for Improvement, 1:451
Voice and Diction Fitness: A Comprehensive Approach, 1:451
The Voice of the People, 1:226, 1:227
The Voice of the Poor: Essays in Economic and Political Persuasion, 2:66
Voice Technology, 1:579
Voices After Midnight, 1:276
"Voices of Freedom," 1:166
Voices of Freedom. An Oral History of the Civil Rights Movement from the 1950s Through the 1980s, 2:154
Voices of Protest: Huey Long, Father Coughlin, and the Great Depression, 2:229
Voices of the Night, 1:160
Voices of the Past: Key Documents in the History of American Journalism, 1:457
Volcano, 2:83, 2:494
Volcano: The Eruption of Mount St. Helens, 2:494
Volcano. The Eruption and Healing of Mount St. Helens, 2:494
Volcano Weather: The Story of 1816, the Year Without a Summer, 2:485
Volcanoes (Carson), 2:493
Volcanoes (Decker and Decker), 2:83
Volcanoes, Earthquakes, and the Formation of Continents, 2:494
Volcanoes in Our Solar System, 2:476
Volga, 2:84
Voltaire, 1:344
Voltaire's Politics: The Poet as Realist, 2:326
Voss, 1:147, 1:148
Voting: A Study of Opinion Formation in a Presidential Campaign, 2:39
Voyage au centre de la terre, 1:343
Voyage de Humboldt et Bonplaud, 2:77

The Voyage of the Beagle, 2:457
The Voyage Out, 1:132
A Voyage to Pagany, 1:305
Voyager: The Story of a Space Mission, 2:481
Voyagers to the West: A Passage in the Peopling of America on the Eve of the Revolution, 2:327
Voyages and Discoveries, 2:324
The Voyages of Captain Cook, 2:320, 2:322
The Voyages of Columbia: The First True Spaceship, 2:481
Voyages of Discovery (Cook), 2:321
Voyages of Discovery: 1400–1500, 2:320
Voyages to Paradise, 2:91
Voyages to the Virginia Colonies, 2:324

W

W. E. B. Du Bois: A Biography, 1:230; 2:211
W. E. B. Du Bois on Sociology and the Black Community, 2:135
W. H. Auden, 1:66
W. H. Auden: A Biography, 1:66
W. L. Garrison and His Times, 2:191
W. S. Gilbert: His Life and Letters, 1:50
W. Somerset Maugham, 1:106
Wagner, 2:362
Wagner: A Biography, 1813–1833, 2:362
Waite Group's Inside the AMIGA with C, 1:564
Waiting for Godot, 1:330, 1:331
Waiting for Lefty, 1:272
Waiting for the Barbarians, 1:413
The Wake of the Gods: Melville's Mythology, 1:163
Waking Up: Overcoming the Obstacles to Human Potential, 2:537
Walden, 1:165; 2:13
Walden and Civil Disobedience, 1:165
Walden Two, 2:101
Waldo Emerson, 1:157
A Walk to Amager, 1:375
Wall: The Berlin Story, 2:388
Wall Street: How It Works, 2:70
Walt Disney: A Biography, 1:475
Walt Disney and Assorted Other Characters: An Unauthorized Account of the Early Years at Disney's, 1:475
Walt Whitman: The Making of the Poet, 1:185
Walter Gropius: Selected Journal Articles Published 1970–1986, 2:268
Walter Reuther: Modern Leader of the United Automobile Workers Union, 2:238

Walter Scott: The Making of the Novelist, 1:36

Walter Winchell, 1:464

Waltzing with a Dictator: The Marcoses and the Making of American Policy, 2:398

Wampeters, Foma and Granfallons, 1:296

Wanderings: Chaim Potok's History of the Jews, 1:280

Wanderings in West Africa from Liverpool to Fernando Po, 2:364

The Waning of Humaneness, 2:464

The Wanting Seed, 1:71

The Wapshot Chronicle, 1:210, 1:211

The Wapshot Scandal, 1:210, 1:211

The War Against the Jews, 1933–1945, 2:235

War Against Want: America's Food for Peace Program, 2:251

War and Peace, 1:396, 1:397

War and Peace in the Nuclear Age, 2:252

War and Society in Renaissance Europe, 1450–1620, 2:310

War at Sea: Pearl Harbor to Midway, 2:235

The War Chief, 1:208

The War In the Desert, 2:384

War in the Outposts, 2:384

War Is Kind, 1:173

War Memoirs of David Lloyd George, 2:373

War Nurses, 2:153

The War of Eighteen Twelve: A Forgotten Conflict, 2:169

The War of the Two Emperors: The Confrontation Between Napoleon and Tzar Alexander, 2:329

The War of the Worlds, 1:129

War, Peace, and International Politics, 2:37

The War Poems of Siegfried Sassoon, 1:116

War Under the Pacific, 2:384

The War with Hannibal, 2:295

The War with Spain in Eighteen Ninety-Eight, 2:219

The War with the Newts, 1:385

The War Years, 1939–1945, 2:385

Ward Number Six and Other Stories, 1:391

Warlord of Mars, 1:208

Warren Court: Constitutional Decision as an Instrument of Reform, 2:26

Warren Report, 2:32

The Warrior and the Priest: Woodrow Wilson and Theodore Roosevelt, 2:218

The War's Long Shadow: How World War II Shaped the Dynamics of Global Power in the Post-War Era, 2:385

The Wars of the Roses: From Richard II to the Fall of Richard III at Bosworth Field Seen Through the Eyes of Their Contemporaries, 2:305

Wars of the Third Kind: Conflict in Underdeveloped Countries, 2:276

The Wartime Papers of Robert E. Lee, 2:196

Was It Murder?, 1:94

Was Pythagoras Chinese? An Examination of Right Triangle Theory in Ancient China, 1:498

Washington: The Indispensable Man, 2:179

Washington Bedtime Stories: The Politics of Money and Jobs, 2:65

Washington Information Directory, 1989–1990, 2:5

Washington Irving, 1:159

Washington Is Leaking, 1:488

The Washington Merry-Go-Round, 1:458

Washington Square, 1:179

The Waste Land, 1:63, 1:82

Watch It Come Down, 1:112

Watch on the Rhine, 1:235

Watching TV, 1:468

Watchmen in the Night: Presidential Accountability After Watergate, 2:21

Water: The Life-Sustaining Resource, 2:493

Water: The Next Great Resource Battle, 2:83, 2:467

Water: The Web of Life, 2:83

Water: Too Much, Too Little, Too Polluted, 2:81, 2:467, 2:486

Water Ecology, 2:467

Water for the World, 2:492

Water World, 2:486

The Waterfall, 1:80

The Watershed: A Biography of Johannes Kepler, 2:474

Watt, 1:331

Wave Mechanics, 2:503

Waverly, 1:36

The Waves, 1:132

Waves and Beaches: The Dynamics of the Ocean Surface, 2:486

A Way of Being, 2:114

The Way of Life: Tao Te Ching, 1:423; 2:283

The Way of the World, 1:21

The Way the Future Was: A Memoir, 1:279

The Way to Write for Children, 1:484

The Way We Lived: A Photographic Record of Work in a Vanished America, 2:156

The Ways of White Folks, 1:241

The Wayward Bus, 1:288, 1:289

We Are Not Alone, 1:94

We Have Always Lived in the Castle, 1:243

We Hold These Truths: Understanding the Ideas and Ideals of the Constitution, 2:16

We the People: The Way We Were, 1783–1793, 2:169

We Were There: The Story of Working Women in America, 2:156

The Weaker Vessel: Woman's Lot in Seventeenth Century England, 2:327

The Weald of Youth, 1:116

Weather, 2:485

Weather and Climate, 2:80, 2:485

Weather and Forecasting, 2:485

Weather and Its Work, 2:485

Weather Atlas of the United States, 2:91

The Weather Book, 2:485

The Weather Factor, 2:485

Weather Forecasting, 2:484

The Web and the Rock, 1:306

The Web of Victory: Grant at Vicksburg, 2:200

Weber, Irrationality, and Social Order, 2:143

Webster: Three Plays, 1:18

Webster and Hayne's Speeches in the United States Senate, 2:183

The Webster Bible, 1:430

Webster's New Geographical Dictionary, 2:75

Webster's New World Dictionary of Computer Terms, 1:539

Webster's Spelling Book, 1:430

Wee Willie Winkie, 1:55

A Week on the Concord and Merrimack Rivers, 1:165

Weep Not, Child, 1:415

Weimar Culture: The Outsider As Insider, 2:374

Weimar Republic and Nazi Germany, 2:375

Weir of Hermiston and Other Stories, 1:58

Welcome to the Monkey House, 1:296

Welfare: The Political Economy of Welfare Reform in the United States, 2:68

Welfare, Planning, and Employment: Selected Essays in Economic Theory, 2:68

The Well of Days, 1:390

The Well-Tempered Sentence: A Punctuation Handbook for the Innocent, the Eager, and the Doomed, 1:478

The Wellsprings of Music, 2:262

Wernher von Braun, 2:483

Wessex Tales, 1:52

West Africa, 2:272

The West at Bay, 2:74

The West in Russia and China, 2:277

West of Eden: The End of Innocence at Apple Computer, 1:540

Western Europe, 2:405

Western Europe: Geographical Perspectives, 2:87

Western Star, 1:200

Westmark, 1:188

The Westmark Trilogy, 1:187

Westward Expansion, 2:184

Westward the Tide, 1:252

Wetlands, 2:466

A Whale for the Killing, 1:144

Whales, Dolphins, and Porpoises, 2:449

Whales, Dolphins, and Porpoises of the World, 2:449

What Are the Chances? Risks, Odds, and Likelihoods in Everyday Life, 1:530

What Computers Can't Do: A Critique of Artificial Reason, 1:554

What Do I Do Now? Talking About Teenage Pregnancy, 2:543

What Do Unions Do, 2:70

What Does a Meteorologist Do?, 2:484

What Every Engineer Should Know About Artificial Intelligence, 1:581

What Happens in Therapy, 2:536

What I Really Think of You, 1:248

What Is a Masterpiece?, 2:261

What is Calculus About?, 1:523

What Is Intelligence, 2:110

What is Mathematics? An Elementary Approach to Ideas and Methods, 1:496

What Is Science?, 2:434

What Is to Be Done? Burning Questions of Our Movement, 2:378

What Mad Pursuit: A Personal View of Scientific Discovery, 2:439

What Neural Networks Can Do, 1:583

What Shall We Do with the Land? Choices for America, 2:497

What Teenagers Want to Know About Sex, 2:543

What to Do About AIDS: Physicians and Mental Health Professionals Discuss the Issues, 2:560

What to Do About the Flu, 2:557

What to Do After You Turn Off the TV, 1:468

What to Say When You Don't Know What to Say, 1:445

What's Bred in the Bone, 1:138

What's Happened Since Seventeen Seventy-Six, 2:155

What's Happening to My Body? Book for Boys: A Growing Up Guide for Parents and Sons, 2:542

What's Happening to My Body? Book for Girls: A Growing Up Guide for Parents and Daughters, 2:542

What's the Good Word, 1:442

Wheels, Life, and Other Mathematical Amusements, 1:536

When Elephants Last in the Dooryard
   Bloomed, 1:203
When Harlem Was in Vogue, 2:226
"When Lilacs Last in the Dooryard
   Bloom'd," 1:184
When Prophecy Fails: A Social and
   Psychological Study of a Modern Group
   That Predicted the Destruction of the
   World, 2:140
When Rock Was Young: A Nostalgic
   Review of the Top Forty Era, 2:262
When the Bough Breaks and Other
   Stories, 1:107
When the Going Was Good: American
   Life in the Fifties, 2:238
When We Dead Awaken, 1:378
When You Look Like Your Passport
   Photo, It's Time to Go Home, 1:447
Where Angels Fear to Tread, 1:85
Where Do We Go From Here? Chaos or
   Community, 2:250
Where Is Science Going?, 2:521
Where the Air Is Clear, 1:402, 1:403
Where the Bald Eagles Gather, 2:462
Where the Queens All Strayed, 1:140
Which Word When? The Indispensable
   Dictionary of 1,500 Commonly
   Confused Words, 1:439
While England Slept: A Survey of World
   Affairs, 1932–1938, 2:386
While Reagan Slept, 1:488
The Whilomville Stories, 1:173
Whiskey Rebels: The Story of a Frontier
   Uprising, 2:168
White African: An Early Autobiography,
   2:49
White Attitudes Toward Black People,
   2:135
White Collar Crime, 2:133
The White Devil, 1:18
The White Goddess, 1:90
A White Heron, 1:180
The White House Years, 2:38
White-Jacket, or The World in a
   Man-of-War, 1:163
White Man, Listen!, 1:307
White Man's Burden: Historical Origins of
   Racism in the United States, 2:154
White Mule, 1:305
White Over Black: American Attitudes
   Toward the Negro, 1550–1812, 2:154
The White Peacock, 1:100, 1:101
The White Plague, 1:238
A White Romance, 1:230
White Stones and Fir Trees: An
   Anthology of Contemporary Slavic
   Literature, 1:383
The Whitsun Weddings, 1:100
Who Gets Sick: Thinking and Health,
   2:531

Who Governs: Democracy and Power in
   an American City, 2:40, 2:130
Who Paid the Taxes, 1966–1985?, 2:71
Who Put the Butter in Butterfly and
   Other Fearless Investigations into Our
   Illogical Language, 1:432
Who Was St. Patrick, 2:306
Who Was Who in the Greek World, 2:284
Who Was Who in the Roman World,
   2:290
The Whole Birth Catalog: A Sourcebook
   for Choices in Childbirth, 2:543
Whole Body Healing, 2:531
Whole Earth Software Catalog for 1986,
   1:566
The Whole Film Sourcebook, 1:468
Whom the Gods Love: The Story of
   Evariste Galois, 1:509
Who's Afraid of Big Blue? How
   Companies are Challenging IBM—and
   Winning, 1:540
Who's Afraid of Virginia Woolf?, 1:186,
   1:187
Who's Who in AI—A Guide to People,
   Products, Companies, Resources,
   Schools, 1:581
Who's Who in American Art, 1991–92,
   2:263
Who's Who in American Politics, 2:6
Who's Who in the People's Republic of
   China, 2:398
Who's Who of Jazz, 2:261
Whose Body?, 1:116
Whose Rose Garden Is It Anyway, 1:488
Why Am I So Miserable If These Are the
   Best Years of My Life, 2:97
Why Americans Don't Vote, 2:40, 2:258
Why Are They Starving Themselves?
   Understanding Anorexia Nervosa and
   Bulimia, 2:551
Why Can't They Be Like Us? Facts and
   Fallacies About Ethnic Differences and
   Group Conflicts in America, 2:135
Why Do I Write?, 1:69
Why England Slept, 2:247
Why Not Victory? A Fresh Look at
   American Foreign Policy, 2:244
Why Nothing Works: The Anthropology
   of Daily Life, 2:48
Why Study Sociology?, 2:125
Why We Can't Wait, 2:12, 2:250
Why You Feel Down and What You Can
   Do About It, 2:537
Wieland, or The Transformation, 1:150,
   1:152
The Wife of His Youth, 1:172
The Wild Abyss: The Story of the Men
   Who Made Modern Astronomy, 2:469
The Wild Ass's Skin, 1:329
The Wild Duck, 1:377, 1:378

A Wild Patience Has Taken Me This Far,
1:281
Wilderness Empire Seventeen Fifty-Five,
2:163
The Wilderness War, 2:163
Wildland Fire Fighting, 2:496
Wilfred Owen, 1:113
Wilhelm Meister, 1:366
Wilhelm Tell, 1:372
Wilhelm Wundt and the Making of a
Scientific Psychology, 2:114
Wilkie Collins: A Critical and Biographical
Study, 1:46
Will Rogers (Musso), 1:462
Will Rogers (Rogers), 1:462; 2:229
Will Rogers: America's Cowboy
Philosopher, 1:462
Will Rogers' Daily Telegrams: 1926–1935,
1:462
Will Rogers Treasury: Reflections and
Observations, 1:462; 2:230
The Will to Believe, 2:96
Willa Cather, 1:209
Willa Cather: A Literary Life, 1:209
Willa Cather's Collected Short Fiction,
1:209
William Blake, 1:32
William Carlos Williams, 1:305
The William Carlos Williams Reader,
1:305
William Congreve: The Man, 1:22
William Cowper: A Biography, 1:22
William Cowper: A Critical Life, 1:22
William Cullen Bryant, 1:156
William Faulkner, 1:220
William Faulkner: The Yoknapatawpha
Country, 1:220
William Gladstone, 2:345
William Golding, 1:90
William Golding: The Man and His
Books, 1:90
William Harvey: His Life and Times, His
Discoveries, His Methods, 2:547
William Harvey and His Age: The
Professional and Social Context of the
Discovery of the Circulation, 2:547
William Harvey, Englishman, 2:548
William Howard Taft, 2:223
William Howard Taft: Chief Justice, 2:223
William Howard Taft: In the Public
Service, 2:223
William James, 2:97
William James: His Life and Thought, 2:97
William James: The Center of His Vision,
2:97
William James and Phenomenology, 2:97
William Jennings Bryan: Champion of
Democracy, 2:205
William Lloyd Garrison, 2:191
William Lloyd Garrison, 1805–1879, 2:191

William Lloyd Garrison on
Non-Resistance, 2:191
William Lloyd's Life of Pythagoras, with a
New Thesis on the Origin of the New
Testament, 1:501
William Makepeace Thackeray, 1:61
William Marshall: The Flower of Chivalry,
2:305
William Tell, 1:372
William Wells Brown: Author and
Reformer, 1:170
William Wells Brown and Clotel: A
Portrait of the Artist in the First Negro
Novel, 1:170
William Wordsworth, 1:39
Wilson and His Peacemakers: The Paris
Peace Conference, 1919, 2:372
Wilson Harris and the Modern Tradition:
A New Architecture of the World, 1:405
Wind Energy Systems, 2:484
Wind from the Sun: Stories of the Space
Age, 1:75
The Winding Passage: Essays and
Sociological Journeys, 1960–1980, 2:149
"The Windhover," 1:53
Windows in Space, 2:481
Windows Programming: An Introduction,
1:562
Windows 3 Made Easy, 1:562
Windsor Forest, 1:27
Windy McPherson's Son, 1:189
Winesburg, Ohio, 1:189, 1:190
The Wings of the Dove, 1:179
The Winn Rosch Hardware Bible, 1:560
Winner Take Nothing, 1:236
The Winning of the West, 2:222
Winslow Homer, 2:216
Winslow Homer Illustrations: Forty-Four
Wood Engravings After Drawings by
the Artist, 2:216
Winslow Homer's Images of Blacks: The
Civil War and Reconstruction Years,
2:216
Winsome Winnie and Other New
Nonsense Novels, 1:141
Winston Churchill, 2:386
Winston S. Churchill: Philosopher and
Statesman, 2:386
The Winter at Valley Forge, Survival and
Victory, 2:164
The Winter of Our Discontent, 1:288,
1:289
Winter's Tales, 1:376
Wires and Watts: Understanding and
Using Electricity, 2:522
Wisdom and Wit, 2:198
The Wisdom of Confucius, 2:283
Wise Blood, 1:270
The Wit and Humor of Oscar Wilde, 1:62
The Witch in the Wood, 1:130

The Witch of Blackbird Pond, 2:162
Witchcraft and Magic in Sixteenth and
    Seventeenth Century Europe, 2:310
Witchcraft in Salem Village, 1:243
The Witches of Eastwick, 1:292
With a Daughter's Eye: A Memoir of
    Margaret Mead and Gregory Bateson,
    2:47
With Fire and Sword, 1:387
With Lawrence in Arabia, 1:463
With No Apologies, 2:244
With Walker in Nicaragua and Other
    Early Poems, 1:400
Without Feathers, 1:189
Without Precedent: The Life and Career
    of Eleanor Roosevelt, 2:233
Witness at the Creation: Hamilton,
    Madison, Jay, and the Constitution,
    2:167
Witness for the Prosecution, 1:73
Witnesses at the Creation: Hamilton,
    Madison, Jay and the Constitution, 2:17
A Wizard of Earthsea, 1:254
The Wizard of Oz: The Screenplay, 1:473
Wolves and Other Love Stories, 1:390
Woman as Force in History: A Study in
    Tradition and Realities, 2:272
The Woman at Point Sur, 1:244
The Woman at the Washington Zoo,
    1:243
A Woman Called Golda, 2:413
Woman in the Mists: The Story of Diane
    Fossey and the Mountain Gorillas of
    Africa, 1:144
The Woman in White, 1:45
The Woman of Andros, 1:302
A Woman of Egypt, 2:412
A Woman of No Importance, 1:62
A Woman on Paper, 2:268
The Woman Who Was Changed and
    Other Stories, 1:207
A Woman's Kingdom and Other Stories,
    1:391
Woman's Life, 1:337
Woman's Proper Place: A History of
    Changing Ideals and Practices, 1870 to
    the Present, 2:148
Women: A Feminist Perspective, 2:148
Women and Change in Latin America:
    New Directions in Sex and Class,
    2:409
Women and Family in the Middle East:
    New Voices of Change, 2:89, 2:411
Women and Film, Both Sides of the
    Camera, 1:468
Women and Indians on the Frontier,
    1825–1915, 2:201
Women and Men: An Anthropologist's
    View, 2:52
Women and Sex Roles, 2:148

Women and the Family: Two Decades of
    Change, 2:148
The Women and the Men, 1:226
Women as Healers: A History of Women
    and Medicine, 2:530
Women Astronauts: Aboard the Shuttle,
    2:481
Women, Culture, and Society, 2:148
Women Directors: The Emergence of a
    New Cinema, 1:470
Women for Human Rights, 2:12, 2:241
Women in Ancient Greece and Rome,
    2:284
Women in Divorce, 2:148
Women in Love, 1:101
Women in Mathematics, 1:498, 1:510
Women in Power, 2:155
Women in Science: Antiquity Through the
    Nineteenth Century—A Biographical
    Dictionary with Annotated Biography,
    2:433
Women in Science: 100 Journeys into the
    Territory, 2:432
Women in Space: Reaching the Last
    Frontier, 2:257, 2:480
Women in the First Capitalist Society:
    Experiences in Seventeenth-Century
    England, 2:310
Women in the Middle Ages, 2:305
Women in the Twentieth Century: A
    Study of Their Political, Social, and
    Economic Activities, 2:152
Women in the World: An International
    Atlas, 2:75
Women of America: A History, 2:152
Women of Crises, 2:148
Women of the West, 2:201
Women Physicians: Careers, Status, and
    Power, 2:148
Women Pioneers of Science, 2:432
Women, War, and Work: The Impact of
    World War I on Women Workers in the
    United States, 2:224
Women, Work, and Family, 2:340
Women, Work and Wages, 2:69, 2:147,
    2:228, 2:241
Women's Atlas of the United States, 2:91
The Women's Computer Literacy
    Handbook, 1:556
Women's Life in Greece and Rome, 2:285
Women's Work and Family Values,
    1920–1940, 2:156
A Wonder Book for Girls and Boys, 1:177
The Wonder of Being Human: Our Brain
    and Our Mind, 2:110
The Wonder of Birds, 2:450
The Wonderful Wizard of Oz, 1:198
The Wonderful World of Maps, 2:92
Wonders of Sponges, 2:449
Won't Know Till I Get There, 1:270

The Woodlanders, 1:52

Woodrow Wilson, 2:225

Woodrow Wilson's Case for the League of Nations, 2:225

Woody Allen, 1:189, 1:470, 1:471

Woody Allen: His Films and Career, 1:189, 1:471

The Wooing of Earth, 2:496

Word 5.0 Know-How, 1:576

Word for Windows Know-How, 1:575

Word for Word, 1:480

Word Games, 1:439

Word Processing Glossary, 1:575

Word Processing Secrets for Writers, 1:577

WordPerfect 5.1: The Complete Reference, 1:575

WordPerfect 5.1: The Pocket Reference, 1:576

WordPerfect Office: The Complete Reference, 1:575

Words: A Book About the Origins of Everyday Words and Phrases, 1:433

Words and What They Do to You: Beginning Lessons in General Semantics for Junior and Senior High School, 1:437

Words by Heart, 2:198

Words from the Myths, 1:318

Words in the Blood: Contemporary Indian Writers of North and South America, 2:154

Words in the Mourning Time, 1:233

Words into Type, 1:478

The Words of Desmond Tutu, 2:397

The Words of Gandhi, 2:366

The Words of Martin Luther King, Jr, 2:250

Words of Wisdom: More Good Advice, 1:442

Words to Rhyme With: A Rhyming Dictionary, 1:439

WordStar 6.0 Made Easy, 1:575

Wordstruck, 1:443

Work and Personality: An Inquiry into the Impact of Social Stratification, 2:145

Work and Retirement: A Longitudinal Study of Men, 2:70

The Work of the Wind, 2:485

Work, Retirement, and Social Policy, 2:148

A Workbook for Software Entrepreneurs, 1:563

Worker Cooperatives in America, 2:148

Worker Participation and Ownership: Cooperative Strategies for Strengthening Local Economies, 2:150

Workers at Risk: Voices from the Workplace, 2:149

Working, 2:70, 2:252

Working: People Talk About What They Do All Day and How They Feel About What They Do, 1:489; 2:149

Working Days: The Journals of The Grapes of Wrath, 1:289

Working It Through, 2:107

Working Papers in the Theory of Action, 2:128

Working with Computers: Computer Orientation for Foreign Students, 1:556

Working with Word for Windows, 1:575

Works (Stalin), 2:380

Works and Correspondence of David Ricardo, 2:73

The Works of Abigail (Smith) Adams, 1744–1818, 2:170

The Works of Alexander Hamilton, 2:174

The Works of Anne Bradstreet, 1:151

The Works of Archimedes with the Method of Archimedes, 1:521

The Works of Benjamin Disraeli, Earl of Beaconsfield, 2:343

The Works of Horace, 2:294

Works of James Abram Garfield, 2:195

The Works of John Adams, 1704–1740, 2:171

Works of John C. Calhoun, 2:181

The Works of John Locke, 2:18

The Works of John Philip Sousa, 2:216

The Works of the Honourable Robert Boyle, 2:499

The Workshop of Democracy: The American Experiment from the Emancipation Proclamation to the Eve of the New Deal, 2:152

The World and Africa: An Inquiry into the Part Which Africa Has Played in World History, 2:211

World Armies, 2:275

The World as a Total System, 2:71

World Atlas of Archaeology, 2:279

The World Beneath Our Feet: The Story of Soil, 2:492

The World Beneath Us, 2:489

World Book Encyclopedia of Science: The Planet Earth, 2:84

A World Destroyed: Hiroshima and the Origins of the Arms Race, 2:236

World Development Report, 1989, 2:56

World Economics Data, 1989: A Compendium of Current Economic Information for All Countries of the World. World Facts and Figures Ser, 2:56

World Encompassed by Sir Francis Drake, 2:323

World Factbook, 2:75

World Facts and Maps, 1991, 2:75

World Handbook of Political and Social Indicators, 2:37
World History Dates, 2:273
World History Factfinder, 2:275
World History for Children and Young Adults, 2:277
World Hunger and Social Justice, 2:85
The World in Arms 1900–1925, 2:371
The World is Built on Probability, 1:530
The World of Birds, 2:449
The World of Count Basie, 2:226
The World of Duke Ellington, 2:267
The World of GEM, 1:561
A World of Ideas: Conversations with Thoughtful Men and Women About American Life Today and the Ideas Shaping Our Future, 1:466
The World of Jeeves, 1:131
World of Leonardo da Vinci, 2:316
A World of Love, 1:69
The World of M. C. Escher, 1:515
The World of Mathematics, 1:498
World of Mathew Brady, 2:193
The World of Mr. Mulliner, 1:131
The World of Odysseus, 2:284
World of Rodin, 2:356
The World of Sholem Aleichem, 1:384
A World of Strangers: Order and Action in Urban Public Space, 2:147
The World of Swing, 2:226
World of the Brain, 2:545
World of the Buddha: An Introduction to Buddhist Literature, 1:427
The World of the Cell, 2:437
World of the French Revolution, 2:330
The World of the Shining Prince: Court Life in Ancient Japan, 1:425
A World of Women: Anthropological Studies of Women in the Societies of the World, 2:51
World of Wonders, 1:137, 1:138
The World of Young Andrew Jackson, 2:182
The World of Young George Washington, 2:179
The World of Young Herbert Hoover, 2:231
World Politics and Personal Insecurity, 2:10
World Politics Since Nineteen Forty-Five, 2:36, 2:387
World Powers in the Twentieth Century, 2:277
World Religions: From Ancient History to the Present, 2:276
World Revolution and Family Patterns, 2:138
The World the Slaveholders Made: Two Essays in Interpretation, 2:189

The World Theater of Wagner: A Celebration of 150 Years of Wagner Productions, 2:362
A World to Care for: The Autobiography of Howard A. Rusk, M.D, 2:565
World War, 1939-1943: The Cartoonist's Vision, 2:385
World War I, 2:371
World War I and the Origin of Civil Liberties in the United States, 2:12
World War One in the Air, 2:371
World War I Tommy, 2:372
World War II (Snyder), 2:385
World War II (Time-Life), 2:274
World War II: A Concise History, 2:235
World War II Resistance Stories, 2:384
World War Two Through German Eyes, 2:384
The Worldly Philosophers: The Lives, Times, and Ideas of the Great Economic Thinkers, 2:56, 2:59, 2:60, 2:61, 2:67, 2:339
Worlds Beyond Dune: The Best of Frank Herbert, 1:238
The World's Great Dailies: Profiles of 50 Newspapers, 1:458
Worlds Imagined, 1:286
World's Most Famous Court Trial: State of Tennessee vs. John T. Scopes, 2:226
The World's Wild Shores, 2:83
The Would-Be Gentleman, 1:338
The Wounded Generation: America After Vietnam, 2:252
Wrapped for Eternity: The Story of the Egyptian Mummies, 2:281
"The Wreck of the Hesperus," 1:160
The Writer as Social Historian, 1:384
The Writer on Her Work, 1:196, 1:481
A Writer Teaches Writing, 1:482
Writers at Work, 1:481
A Writer's Diary, 1:132
Writer's Guide and Index to English, 1:478
The Writer's Home Companion: Anecdotes, Comforts, Recollections, and Other Amusements for Every Writer, Editor, and Reader, 1:481
The Writer's Hotline Handbook, 1:478
A Writer's Notebook, 1:106
Writin' Is Fightin': Thirty-Seven Years of Boxing on Paper, 1:482
Writing a Thriller, 1:490
Writing About Food and Families, Fashion and Furnishings, 1:487
Writing and Editing School News, 1:487
Writing and Logic, 1:477
Writing and Researching Term Papers and Reports, 1:483
Writing Books for Children, 1:484

Writing Broadcast News: Shorter, Sharper, Stronger, 1:487
Writing Crime Fiction, 1:490
Writing Essays About Literature: A Guide and Style Sheet, 1:483
Writing for Children, 1:484
Writing for Many Roles, 1:478
Writing for Story: Craft Secrets of Dramatic Nonfiction, 1:488
Writing for the Fun of It: An Experience-Based Approach to Composition, 1:477
Writing for the Twenty-First Century: Computers and Research Writing, 1:483
Writing Historical Fiction, 1:490
Writing in General and the Short Story in Particular, 1:490
Writing Interactive Compilers and Interpreters, 1:586
The Writing Life, 1:482, 1:483
Writing Logically, 1:477
The Writing on the Wall: An Anthology of Czechoslovak Literature Today, 1:383
Writing Poetry: Where Poems Come from and How to Write Them, 1:489
Writing Research Papers Across the Curriculum, 1984 MLA Version, 1:483
Writing Science Fiction, 1:490
The Writing Space: The Computer and the History of Writing, 1:579
Writing the Natural Way: Using Right-Brain Techniques to Release Your Expressive Powers, 1:478
Writing the Script: A Practical Guide for Films and Television, 1:485
Writing to Be Read, 1:477
Writing to Learn, 1:478
Writing with a Computer: Using Your Word Processor for a New Freedom and Creativity in Writing, 1:575
Writing with a Voice: A Rhetoric and Handbook, 1:477
Writing with Power: Techniques for Mastering the Writing Process, 1:477
Writing Without Teachers, 1:477
Writing Your Way, 1:478
Writings (Monroe), 2:178
The Writings and Speeches of Daniel Webster, 2:183
The Writings and Speeches of Edmund Burke: Party, Parliament, and the American Crisis, 1766–1774, 2:9, 2:329
Writings from the Original Manuscript Sources, 1754–1799 (Washington), 2:179
Writings Nineteen Two to Nineteen Ten (James), 2:96
The Writings of Hippocrates on the Human Body, Its Diseases and Their Cure, 2:533

The Writings of John Quincy Adams, 2:173
Writings of Leon Trotsky, 2:381
The Writings of Sam Houston, 1813–1836, 2:186
The Writings of Thomas Paine: The Standard Edition, 2:165
Writings on Writing, 1:482
Wuthering Heights, 1:42
Wyeth People: A Portrait of Andrew Wyeth as Seen by His Friends and Neighbors, 2:271

X

X-Ray Information Book: A Consumer's Guide to Avoiding Unnecessary Medical and Dental X-Rays, 2:566
XX Poems, 1:100
XYWrite Made Easier, 1:576

Y

Yangtze: Nature, History, and the River, 2:87
Yankee Stepfather: General O. O. Howard and the Freedmen, 2:198
A Yard of Sun, 1:87
A Year of PC Hardware and Software Reviews, 1:558
The Years, 1:132
The Years of Apprenticeship, 1:366
The Years of Challenge: Selected Speeches of Indira Gandhi, 1966–1969, 2:401
The Years of Endeavour, 2:401
The Years of Lyndon Johnson, 2:246
Years of Poverty, Years of Plenty: The Changing Economic Fortunes of American Workers and Families, 2:68, 2:153
The Years of Travel, 1:366
Years with Frank Lloyd Wright: Apprentice to Genius, 2:270
The Years with Ross, 1:291
Yeats, 1:134
Yeats: A Collection of Critical Essays, 1:134
Yemen: Country Studies, 2:89
Yerma: A Tragic Poem in Three Acts and Six Scenes, 1:357, 1:358
Yesterdays: Popular Song in America, 2:154
Yesterday's Tomorrows: Favorite Stories from Forty Years as a Science Fiction Writer, 1:279
Yiddish Stories Old and New, 1:383

Yiddish Tales, 1:383
Yonadab, 1:119
Yondering, 1:253
The Yosemite, 2:221
You All Spoken Here, 1:431
You and Your Hearing: How to Protect It, Preserve It, and Restore It, 2:552
You Are Somebody Special, 2:537
You Can Fool All of the People All of the Time, 1:488
You Can Say No to a Drink or a Drug: What Every Kid Should Know, 2:554
You Can Stop: The Smokenders Guide on How to Give Up Cigarettes, 2:556
You Can't Go Home Again, 1:306
You Can't Keep A Good Woman Down, 1:296, 1:297
You Could Look It Up: More on Language, 1:442
You Learn by Living, 2:233
You Must Relax, 2:536
You Only Live Twice, 1:84
You'll Be Old Someday, Too, 2:129, 2:544
The Young Astronomer, 2:471
The Young Duke, 2:342
The Young Landlords, 1:270
Young Learners and the Microcomputer, 1:556
Young Man Luther, 2:108, 2:317
The Young United States, 1783–1830, 2:169
The Young Victoria, 2:369
Young Writer's Handbook: A Practical Guide for the Beginner Who Is Serious About Writing, 1:478
Your Attitude: Key to Success, 2:97
Your Body Is Trying to Tell You Something, 2:531
Your Child's Teeth. A Parent's Guide to Making and Keeping Them Perfect, 2:552
Your Future in Space: The U.S. Space Camp Training Program, 2:481
Your Good Health: How to Stay Well and What to Do When You're Not, 2:530

Your Immune System, 2:451, 2:545
Your Parents and Your Self: Alike-Unlike, Agreeing-Disagreeing, 2:539
Your Skin: Its Problems and Care, 2:553
Your Son, Calvin Coolidge, 2:228
Your Weight, 2:549
You're a Knockout, Charlie Brown, 1:459
Youth, 1:77
Youth Suicide: Depression and Loneliness, 2:537

Z

Zalmen, or the Madness of God, 1:302
The Zambesi Expedition, 1858–1863, 2:367
Zanuck: The Rise and Fall of Hollywood's Last Tycoon, 1:470
Zanzibar: City, Island, and Coast, 2:364
Zapata: A Biography, 2:369
Zapotecs: The Princes, Priests, and Peasants, 2:300
Zeely, 1:229, 1:230
Zelda, 1:223
Zenobia; or, the Fall of Palmyra, 2:291
Zero Hour and Other Documentary Poems, 1:400
The Zero-Sum Solution, 2:144
Zhenia's Childhood, 1:394
Zhou Enlai, 2:398
Zhou Enlai and Deng Xiaping in the Chinese Leadership Succession Crisis, 2:398
Zia, 1:272
Zimbabwe, 2:393
Zimmermann Telegram, 2:224
The Zoo Story, 1:186
Zoological Philosophy: An Exposition with Regard to the Natural History of Animals, 2:459
Zora Neale Hurston, 1:242
Zora Neale Hurston: A Literary Biography, 1:242
Zuni Mythology, 2:44